BASIC ECONOMETRICS

BASIC ECONOMETRICS

Third Edition

Damodar N. Gujarati

United States Military Academy, West Point

McGraw-Hill, Inc.

New York St. Louis San Francisco Auckland Bogotá Caracas
Lisbon London Madrid Mexico City Milan Montreal New Delhi
San Juan Singapore Sydney Tokyo Toronto

This book was set in New Aster by Publication Services, Inc.
The editors were Scott D. Stratford and Lucille H. Sutton;
the production supervisor was Friederich W. Schulte.
The cover was designed by Tana Kamine.
Project supervision was done by Publication Services, Inc.
R. R. Donnelley & Sons Company was printer and binder.

BASIC ECONOMETRICS

This book is printed on acid-free paper.

6 7 8 9 0 DOC DOC 9 0 9 8 7

ISBN 0-07-025214-9

Library of Congress Cataloging-in-Publication Data

Gujarati, Damodar N.
  Basic econometrics / Damodar N. Gujarati. —3rd ed.
    p.   cm.
  Includes bibliographical references (p.   ) and index.
  ISBN 0-07-025214-9
  1. Econometrics.   I. Title.
  HB139.G84   1995
  330'.01'5118—dc20
                                        94-35295

ABOUT THE AUTHOR

After teaching for more than 28 years at the City University of New York, Damodar N. Gujarati is currently a professor of economics in the Department of Social Sciences at the U.S. Military Academy at West Point, New York. Dr. Gujarati received his M.Com. degree from the University of Bombay in 1960, his M.B.A. degree from the University of Chicago in 1963, and his Ph.D. degree from the University of Chicago in 1965. Dr. Gujarati has published extensively in recognized national and international journals, such as the *Review of Economics and Statistics,* the *Economic Journal,* the *Journal of Financial and Quantitative Analysis,* the *Journal of Business,* the *American Statistician,* and the *Journal of Industrial and Labor Relations.* Dr. Gujarati is an editorial referee to several journals and book publishers and is a member of the Board of Editors of the *Journal of Quantitative Economics,* the official journal of the Indian Econometric Society. Dr. Gujarati is also the author of *Pensions and the New York City Fiscal Crisis* (the American Enterprise Institute, 1978), *Government and Business* (McGraw-Hill, 1984), and *Essentials of Econometrics* (McGraw-Hill, 1992). Dr. Gujarati's books on econometrics have been translated into several languages.

Dr. Gujarati was a Visiting Professor at the University of Sheffield, U.K. (1970–1971), a Visiting Fulbright Professor to India (1981–1982), a Visiting Professor in the School of Management of the National University of Singapore (1985–1986), and a Visiting Professor of Econometrics, University of New South Wales, Australia (summer of 1988). As a regular participant in USIA's lectureship program abroad, Dr. Gujarati has lectured extensively on micro- and macroeconomic topics in countries such as Australia, Bangladesh, Germany, India, Israel, Mauritius, and the Republic of South Korea. Dr. Gujarati has also given seminars and lectures in Canada and Mexico.

To the Memory of
"Akka" (Shalini)
and
"Suru" (Suryakant)

CONTENTS

8 Multiple Regression Analysis: The Problem of Inference

Part 2 Relaxing the Assumptions of the Classical Model

Part 4   Simultaneous-Equation Models

Part 5   Time Series Econometrics

21   Time Series Econometrics I: Stationarity, Unit Roots, and Cointegration

PREFACE

As in the previous two editions, the primary objective of the third edition of *Basic Econometrics* is to provide an elementary but comprehensive introduction to econometrics without resorting to matrix algebra, calculus, or statistics beyond the elementary level.

In this edition I have attempted to incorporate some of the developments in the theory and practice of econometrics that have taken place since the publication of the second edition in 1988. In addition, this revision has given me the opportunity to simplify the discussion of some topics included in the previous editions and to add some new material on these topics. The major changes in this edition are as follows:

1. In Chapter 1, I have expanded the discussion of the nature and sources of data available for econometric analysis. In view of the increasing use of time series data in economic analysis, I have introduced very early the concept of a **stationary time series,** a concept that is crucial for analyzing data involving economic time series.

2. In Chapter 3, I present a more extended discussion of the assumptions of the classical linear regression model (CLRM). The CLRM is the foundation of econometrics. In this chapter I also discuss the **Monte Carlo** simulation experiments.

3. In Chapter 5, on hypothesis testing, I have introduced the concept of the *p* **value,** or the exact level of significance, of a test statistic. In this chapter, I also discuss the **Jarque-Bera test of normality.**

4. In Chapter 8, on hypothesis testing in the context of multiple regression models, I have streamlined the discussion. This chapter also includes a discussion of the choice between linear and log-linear regression models. In the appendix to this chapter, I discuss, at an elementary level, the **likelihood ratio (LR) test of hypothesis.**

5. In Chapter 10, on multicollinearity, I now give equal billing to **micronumerosity** (smallness of sample size), a concept due to Arthur Gold-

berger. I also introduce **tolerance** and **inflation-variance** tools for detecting multicollinearity.

6. In Chapter 11, on heteroscedasticity, I have now included the **Breusch-Pagan-Godfrey test** and **White's test** of heteroscedasticity. I also discuss White's heteroscedasticity-consistent variances and standard errors of OLS estimators.

7. In Chapter 12, on autocorrelation, I have included these tests: asymptotic test of autocorrelation, Breusch-Godfrey test of higher-order autocorrelation, and Berenblut-Webb test. Included in this chapter is also the **ARCH model,** which has been increasingly used in financial economics.

8. Chapter 13, on model building, discusses nominal versus true level of significance in the presence of data mining, and the **Lagrange multiplier (LM) test** for adding variables to a regression model.

9. In Chapter 14, which is new, I discuss alternatives to the traditional econometric methodology. In particular, I discuss Leamer's and Hendry's approaches to econometrics. Also included in this chapter are tests of non-nested hypotheses, in particular the **Davidson-MacKinnon *J* test.**

10. Chapter 15, on dummy variables, now includes a discussion of dummies in combining time series and cross-sectional data. I also show how the dummies can be used in the presence of autocorrelation and heteroscedasticity. An exercise in this chapter discusses Zellner's **seemingly unrelated regression (SURE)** technique.

11. Chapter 16, on dummy dependent variable regression models, now includes a discussion of the **Tobit model.**

12. Chapter 17, on dynamic regression models, now includes a discussion of both the **Granger test** and **Sims's test** of causality.

13. Chapters 18, 19, and 20, on simultaneous-equation models, now contain tests of simultaneity and exogeneity. These chapters also discuss the relationship between causality and exogeneity.

14. In recognition of the growing importance of time series data in economic analysis, I have included two new chapters on time series econometrics. In Chapter 21, I introduce the key concepts of time series analysis, such as **stationarity, random walk, unit root, Dickey-Fuller** and **augmented Dickey-Fuller tests of stationarity, deterministic** and **stochastic trends, trend-stationary** and **difference-stationary stochastic processes, cointegration, Engle-Granger tests of cointegration, error correction mechanism,** and **spurious regression.** In Chapter 22 I discuss the **Box-Jenkins,** or **ARIMA,** and **vector autoregression (VAR)** approaches to economic forecasting. These are alternatives to the traditional single- and simultaneous-equation approaches to forecasting.

I have added several new exercises. The exercises given at the end of chapters are now divided into two groups: questions and problems. The latter are data-based exercises (I am a firm believer in learning by doing).

All these changes have considerably expanded the scope of this book. I hope this gives the instructor substantial flexibility in choosing topics that are appropriate to the intended audience. Here are some suggestions about how this book may be used: **One-semester course for the nonspecialist:** Appendix A; Chaps. 1 through 8; an overview of Chaps. 10, 11, and 12 (omitting all the proofs); and Chap. 15. The theoretical exercises can be omitted. **One-semester course for economics majors:** Appendix A; Chaps. 1 through 8; and Chaps. 10 through 15. If matrix algebra is used, include Appendix B and Chap. 9. Some of the theoretical exercises can be omitted. **Two-semester course for economics majors:** Appendices A and B, and Chaps. 1 through 22. Mathematical proofs given in the various appendices can be covered on a selective basis. Additionally, the instructor may want to cover the topic of nonlinear (in parameters) regression models.

This revision would not have been possible without the constructive comments, suggestions, and encouragement that I have received from several people who have read the various drafts. In particular, I would like to acknowledge my debt to the following professors, without, of course, holding them responsible for any deficiencies that remain in the book: Ted Amato, University of North Carolina; Dale Belman, University of Wisconsin–Milwaukee; Tom Daula, U.S. Military Academy; Mary Deily, Lehigh University; Frank Diebold, University of Pennsylvania; David Garman, Tufts University; Sushila Gidwani-Bushchi, Manhattan College; William Greene, New York University; Dennis Jansen, Texas A&M University; Jane Lillydahl, University of Colorado; Dagmar Rajagopal, Ryerson Polytechnic University; Bo Ruck, U.S. Military Academy; John Spitzer, State University of New York, Brockport; and H. D. Vinod, Fordham University.

I owe a great debt of gratitude to Professor Kenneth J. White and Steven A. Theobald for checking numerical calculations and for preparing the handbook: *Basic Econometrics: A Computer Handbook Using SHAZAM,* 3d ed., McGraw-Hill, New York, 1995. My wife Pushpa and my daughters Joan and Diane have been a constant source of inspiration and encouragement. Beyond a simple thank-you, I want them to know that I love them all very dearly.

On a personal note, after some 28 years of teaching at the City University of New York (CUNY), I have now joined the Department of Social Sciences at the U.S. Military Academy at West Point, New York. I am grateful to CUNY for providing me with my first job and to the Academy for offering me new challenges and opportunities.

Damodar N. Gujarati

BASIC ECONOMETRICS

INTRODUCTION

1 WHAT IS ECONOMETRICS?

Literally interpreted, *econometrics* means "economic measurement." Although measurement is an important part of econometrics, the scope of econometrics is much broader, as can be seen from the following quotations:

> Econometrics, the result of a certain outlook on the role of economics, consists of the application of mathematical statistics to economic data to lend empirical support to the models constructed by mathematical economics and to obtain numerical results.[1]

> ...econometrics may be defined as the quantitative analysis of actual economic phenomena based on the concurrent development of theory and observation, related by appropriate methods of inference.[2]

> Econometrics may be defined as the social science in which the tools of economic theory, mathematics, and statistical inference are applied to the analysis of economic phenomena.[3]

> Econometrics is concerned with the empirical determination of economic laws.[4]

> The art of the econometrician consists in finding the set of assumptions that are both sufficiently specific and sufficiently realistic to allow him to take the best possible advantage of the data available to him.[5]

> Econometricians...are a positive help in trying to dispel the poor public image of economics (quantitative or otherwise) as a subject in which empty boxes

---

[1] Gerhard Tintner, *Methodology of Mathematical Economics and Econometrics,* The University of Chicago Press, Chicago, 1968, p. 74.

[2] P. A. Samuelson, T. C. Koopmans, and J. R. N. Stone, "Report of the Evaluative Committee for *Econometrica,*" *Econometrica,* vol. 22, no. 2, April 1954, pp. 141–146.

[3] Arthur S. Goldberger, *Econometric Theory,* John Wiley & Sons, New York, 1964, p. 1.

[4] H. Theil, *Principles of Econometrics,* John Wiley & Sons, New York, 1971, p. 1.

[5] E. Malinvaud, *Statistical Methods of Econometrics,* Rand McNally, Chicago, 1966, p. 514.

are opened by assuming the existence of can-openers to reveal contents which any ten economists will interpret in 11 ways.[6]

The method of econometric research aims, essentially, at a conjunction of economic theory and actual measurements, using the theory and technique of statistical inference as a bridge pier.[7]

2 WHY A SEPARATE DISCIPLINE?

As the preceding definitions suggest, econometrics is an amalgam of economic theory, mathematical economics, economic statistics, and mathematical statistics. Yet the subject deserves to be studied in its own right for the following reasons.

Economic theory makes statements or hypotheses that are mostly qualitative in nature. For example, microeconomic theory states that, other things remaining the same, a reduction in the price of a commodity is expected to increase the quantity demanded of that commodity. Thus, economic theory postulates a negative or inverse relationship between the price and quantity demanded of a commodity. But the theory itself does not provide any numerical measure of the relationship between the two; that is, it does not tell by how much the quantity will go up or down as a result of a certain change in the price of the commodity. It is the job of the econometrician to provide such numerical estimates. Stated differently, econometrics gives empirical content to most economic theory.

The main concern of mathematical economics is to express economic theory in mathematical form (equations) without regard to measurability or empirical verification of the theory. Econometrics, as noted previously, is mainly interested in the empirical verification of economic theory. As we shall see, the econometrician often uses the mathematical equations proposed by the mathematical economist but puts these equations in such a form that they lend themselves to empirical testing. And this conversion of mathematical into econometric equations requires a great deal of ingenuity and practical skill.

Economic statistics is mainly concerned with collecting, processing, and presenting economic data in the form of charts and tables. These are the jobs of the economic statistician. It is he or she who is primarily responsible for collecting data on GNP, employment, unemployment, prices, etc. The data thus collected constitute the raw data for econometric work. But the economic statistician does not go any further, not being concerned with using the collected data to test economic theories. Of course, one who does that becomes an econometrician.

Although mathematical statistics provides many of the tools used in the trade, the econometrician often needs special methods in view of the unique

---

[6]Adrian C. Darnell and J. Lynne Evans, *The Limits of Econometrics*, Edward Elgar Publishing, Hants, England, 1990, p. 54.

[7]T. Haavelmo, "The Probability Approach in Econometrics," Supplement to *Econometrica*, vol. 12, 1944, preface p. iii.

nature of most economic data, namely, that the data are not generated as the result of a controlled experiment. The econometrician, like the meteorologist, generally depends on data that cannot be controlled directly. Thus, data on consumption, income, investment, savings, prices, etc., which are collected by public and private agencies, are nonexperimental data. The econometrician takes these data as given. This action creates special problems not normally dealt with in mathematical statistics. Moreover, such data are likely to contain errors of measurement, and the econometrician may be called upon to develop special methods of analysis to deal with such errors of measurement.

3 METHODOLOGY OF ECONOMETRICS

How do econometricians proceed in their analysis of an economic problem? That is, what is their methodology? Although there are several schools of thought on econometric methodology, we present here the **traditional** or **classical methodology,** which still dominates empirical research in economics and related fields. In Chapters 13 and 14 we discuss the question of econometric methodology in general in greater detail.

Broadly speaking, traditional econometric methodology proceeds along the following lines:

1. Statement of theory or hypothesis
2. Specification of the mathematical model of the theory
3. Specification of the econometric model of the theory
4. Obtaining the data
5. Estimation of the parameters of the econometric model
6. Hypothesis testing
7. Forecasting or prediction
8. Using the model for control or policy purposes

To illustrate the preceding steps, let us consider the well-known Keynesian theory of consumption.

1. Statement of Theory or Hypothesis

Keynes stated:

> The fundamental psychological law ... is that men [women] are disposed, as a rule and on average, to increase their consumption as their income increases, but not as much as the increase in their income.[8]

---

[8]John Maynard Keynes, *The General Theory of Employment, Interest and Money,* Harcourt Brace Jovanovich, New York, 1936, p. 96.

In short, Keynes postulated that the **marginal propensity to consume (MPC)**, the rate of change of consumption for a unit (say, a dollar) change in income, is greater than zero but less than 1.

2. Specification of the Mathematical Model of Consumption

Although Keynes postulated a positive relationship between consumption and income, he did not specify the precise form of the functional relationship between the two. For simplicity, a mathematical economist might suggest the following form of the Keynesian consumption function:

$$Y = \beta_1 + \beta_2 X \qquad 0 < \beta_2 < 1 \qquad\qquad (I.3.1)$$

where Y = consumption expenditure and X = income, and where β_1 and β_2, known as the **parameters** of the model are, respectively, the **intercept** and **slope** coefficients.

The slope coefficient β_2 measures the MPC. Geometrically, Eq.(I.3.1) is as shown in Fig. I.1. This equation, which states that consumption is linearly related to income, is an example of a mathematical model of the relationship between consumption and income that is called the **consumption function** in economics. A model is simply a set of mathematical equations. If the model has only one equation, as in the preceding example, it is called a **single equation model**, whereas if it has more than one equation, it is known as a **multiple equation model** (the latter will be considered later in the book).

In Eq. (I.3.1) the variable appearing on the left side of the equality sign is called the **dependent variable** and the variable(s) on the right side are called

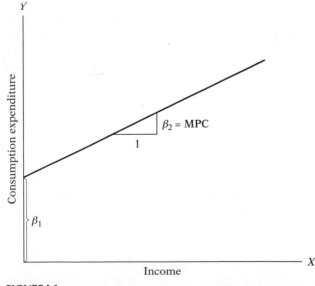

FIGURE I.1
Keynesian consumption function.

the **independent**, or **explanatory**, variable(s). Thus, in the Keynesian consumption function, Eq. (I.3.1), consumption (expenditure) is the dependent variable and income is the explanatory variable.

3. Specification of the Econometric Model of Consumption

The purely mathematical model of the consumption function given in Eq. (I.3.1) is of limited interest to the econometrician, for it assumes that there is an *exact* or *deterministic* relationship between consumption and income. But relationships between economic variables are generally inexact. Thus, if we were to obtain data on consumption expenditure and disposable (i.e., after-tax) income of a sample of, say, 500 American families and plot these data on a graph paper with consumption expenditure on the vertical axis and disposable income on the horizontal axis, we would not expect all 500 observations to lie exactly on the straight line of Eq. (I.3.1) because, in addition to income, other variables affect consumption expenditure. For example, size of family, ages of the members in the family, family religion, etc., are likely to exert some influence on consumption.

To allow for the inexact relationships between economic variables, the econometrician would modify the deterministic consumption function (I.3.1) as follows:

$$Y = \beta_1 + \beta_2 X + u \qquad (I.3.2)$$

where u, known as the **disturbance**, or **error, term**, is a **random (stochastic) variable** that has well-defined probabilistic properties. The disturbance term u may well represent all those factors that affect consumption but are not taken into account explicitly.

Equation (I.3.2) is an example of an **econometric model**. More technically, it is an example of a **linear regression model**, which is the major concern of this book. The econometric consumption function hypothesizes that the dependent variable Y (consumption) is linearly related to the explanatory variable X (income) but that the relationship between the two is not exact; it is subject to individual variation.

The econometric model of the consumption function can be depicted as shown in Fig. I.2.

4. Obtaining Data

To estimate the econometric model given in (I.3.2), that is, to obtain the numerical values of β_1 and β_2, we need data. Although we will have more to say about the crucial importance of data for economic analysis in the next chapter, for now let us look at the data pertaining to the U.S. economy given in Table I.1. The Y variable in this table is the *aggregate* (for the economy as a whole) personal consumption expenditure and the X variable is Gross Domestic Product (GDP), a measure of aggregate income, both measured in billions of 1987

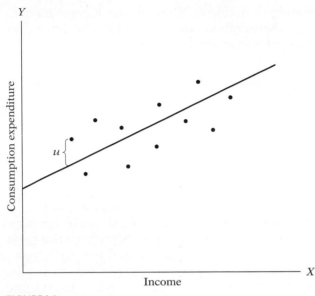

FIGURE I.2
Econometric model of the Keynesian consumption function.

dollars. Therefore, the data are in "real" terms, that is, they are measured in constant (1987) prices. These data are plotted in Fig. I.3 (cf. Fig. I.2).

5. Estimation of the Econometric Model

Now that we have the data, our next task is to estimate the parameters of the consumption function. The numerical estimates of the parameters give empir-

TABLE I.1
Data on Y (personal consumption expenditure) and X (Gross Domestic Product), 1980–1991, all in 1987 billions of dollars

Year	Y	X
1980	2,447.1	3,776.3
1981	2,476.9	3,843.1
1982	2,503.7	3,760.3
1983	2,619.4	3,906.6
1984	2,746.1	4,148.5
1985	2,865.8	4,279.8
1986	2,969.1	4,404.5
1987	3,052.2	4,539.9
1988	3,162.4	4,718.6
1989	3,223.3	4,838.0
1990	3,260.4	4,877.5
1991	3,240.8	4,821.0

Source: Economic Report of the President, 1993, Table B-2, p. 350.

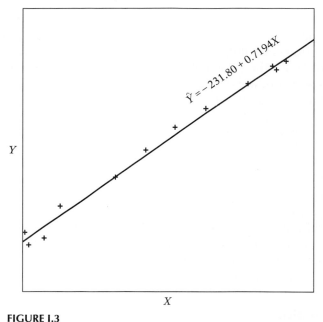

FIGURE I.3
Personal consumption expenditure (*Y*) in relation to GDP (*X*), 1980–1991 (regression line not drawn to scale).

ical content to the consumption function. The actual mechanics of estimating the parameters will be illustrated in Chapter 3. For now, note that the statistical technique of **regression analysis** is the main tool used to obtain the estimates. Using this technique and the data given in Table I.1, we obtained the following estimates of β_1 and β_2, namely, -231.8 and 0.7194. Thus, the estimated consumption function is

$$\hat{Y} = -231.8 + 0.7194X \qquad (I.3.3)$$

The hat on Y indicates that it is an estimate.[9]

From this equation we find that for the period 1980 to 1991 the slope coefficient (i.e., the MPC) was about 0.72, suggesting that for the sample period an increase in real income of one dollar led, on *average*, to increases of about 72 cents in real consumption expenditure.[10] We say on average because the relationship between consumption and income is inexact, as is clear from Fig. I.3, which shows the regression line obtained in (I.3.3).

---

[9]As a matter of convention, a hat over a variable or parameter indicates that it is an estimated value.

[10]Do not worry here about how these values were obtained; as we show in Chap. 3, the statistical method of least squares has produced these estimates. Also, for now, do not worry about the negative value of the intercept.

6.   Hypothesis Testing

Assuming that the fitted model is a reasonably good approximation of reality, we have to develop suitable criteria to find out whether the estimates obtained in, say, Eq.(I.3.3) are in accord with the expectations of the theory that is being tested. According to "positive" economists like Milton Friedman, a theory or hypothesis that is not verifiable by appeal to empirical evidence may not be admissible as a part of scientific enquiry.[11]

As noted earlier, Keynes expected the MPC to be positive but less than 1. In our example we found the MPC to be about 0.72. But before we accept this finding as confirmation of Keynesian consumption theory, we must enquire whether this estimate is sufficiently below unity to convince us that this is not a chance occurrence or peculiarity of the particular data we have used. In other words, is 0.72 *statistically less than 1?* If it is, it may support Keynes' theory.

Such confirmation or refutation of economic theories on the basis of sample evidence is based on a branch of statistical theory known as **statistical inference (hypothesis testing)**. Throughout this book we shall see how this inference process is actually conducted.

7.   Forecasting or Prediction

If the chosen model confirms the hypothesis or theory under consideration, we may use it to predict the future value(s) of the dependent, or **forecast**, **variable** Y, on the basis of known or expected future value(s) of the explanatory, or **predictor**, **variable** X.

To illustrate, suppose the real GDP is expected to be $6000 (billions) in 1994. What is the forecast consumption expenditure in 1994? If we believe that the consumption function (I.3.3) will continue to hold in 1994, we can answer this question simply as

$$\hat{Y} = -231.8 + 0.7196(6000)$$
$$= 4084.6 \tag{I.3.4}$$

or about 4085 billions of dollars.

There is another use of the estimated model (I.3.3). Soon after taking office in 1993, President Clinton announced his economic plan, which included a tax increase for people with incomes beyond a threshold level of about $140,000. He also proposed energy and other taxes to cut the federal budget deficit; the gasoline tax was in fact raised 5 cents a gallon. What will be the effect of these policies on income and thereby on consumption expenditure and ultimately on employment?

Suppose as a result of these policy changes investment expenditure declines. What will be the effect on the economy? As macroeconomic theory

---

[11] See Milton Friedman, "The Methodology of Positive Economics," *Essays in Positive Economics*, University of Chicago Press, Chicago, 1953.

shows, the change in income following, say, a dollar's worth of change in investment expenditure is given by the **income multiplier (M)**, which is defined as

$$M = \frac{1}{1 - \text{MPC}} \tag{I.3.5}$$

If we use the MPC of 0.72 obtained from (I.3.3), this multiplier becomes $M = 1/(1 - 0.72) = 3.57$. That is, a decrease (increase) of a dollar in investment will *eventually* lead to about a fourfold decrease (increase) in income; note that it takes time for the multiplier to work.

The critical value in this computation is MPC, for M depends on it. And this estimate of the MPC is obtained from regression models such as (I.3.3). Thus, a quantitative estimate of MPC provides valuable information for policy purposes. Knowing MPC, one can predict the future course of income and consumption expenditure following a change in the government's fiscal policies.

8. Use of the Model for Control or Policy Purposes

Suppose we have the estimated Keynesian consumption function given in (I.3.3). Suppose further the government believes that an expenditure level of 4000 (billions of 1987 dollars) will keep the unemployment rate at its current level of about 6.5 percent (April 1994 estimate made by the Bureau of Labor Statistics). What level of income will guarantee the target amount of consumption expenditure?

If the consumption function given in (I.3.3) is acceptable, simple arithmetic will show that

$$4000 = -231.8 + 0.7194X$$
$$X = 5882 \text{ (approx.)} \tag{I.3.6}$$

That is, an income level of \$5882 (billions), given an MPC of about 0.72, will produce an expenditure of \$4000 billions.

As these calculations suggest, an estimated model may be used for control, or policy, purposes. By appropriate fiscal and monetary policy mix, the government can manipulate the **control variable X** to produce the desired level of the **target variable Y**.

Figure I.4 summarizes the anatomy of classical econometric modeling.

4. TYPES OF ECONOMETRICS

As the classificatory scheme in Figure I.5 suggests, econometrics may be divided into two broad categories: **theoretical econometrics** and **applied econometrics**. In each category, one can approach the subject in the **classical** or **Bayesian** tradition. In this book the emphasis is on the classical approach. For the Bayesian approach, the reader may consult the references given at the end of the chapter.

Economic Theory
Mathematical Model of Theory
Econometric Model of Theory
Data
Estimation of Econometric Model
Hypothesis Testing
Forecasting or Prediction
Using the Model for Control or Policy Purposes

FIGURE I.4
Anatomy of econometric modeling.

Theoretical econometrics is concerned with the development of appropriate methods for measuring economic relationships specified by econometric models. In this aspect, econometrics leans heavily on mathematical statistics. For example, one of the methods used extensively in this book is **least squares**. Theoretical econometrics must spell out the assumptions of this method, its properties, and what happens to these properties when one or more of the assumptions of the method are not fulfilled.

In applied econometrics we use the tools of theoretical econometrics to study some special field(s) of economics and business, such as the production function, investment function, demand and supply functions, portfolio theory, etc.

This book is concerned largely with the development of econometric methods, their assumptions, their uses, their limitations. These methods are illustrated with examples from various areas of economics and business. But this is *not* a book of applied econometrics in the sense that it delves deeply into any particular field of economic application. That job is best left to books written specifically for this purpose. References to some of these books are provided at the end of this book.

5.   MATHEMATICAL AND STATISTICAL PREREQUISITES

Although this book is written at an elementary level, the author assumes that the reader is familiar with the basic concepts of statistical estimation and hypothesis testing. However, a broad but nontechnical overview of the basic

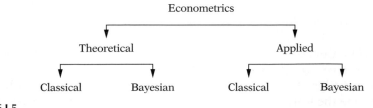

FIGURE I.5
Categories of econometrics.

statistical concepts used in this book is provided in Appendix A for the benefit of those who want to refresh their knowledge. Insofar as mathematics is concerned, a nodding acquaintance with the notions of differential calculus is desirable, although not essential. Although most graduate level books in econometrics make heavy use of matrix algebra, I want to make it clear that it is not needed to study this book. It is my strong belief that the fundamental ideas of econometrics can be conveyed without the use of matrix algebra. However, for the benefit of the mathematically inclined student Chapter 9, an *optional chapter*, gives the summary of basic regression theory in matrix notation. For these students, Appendix B provides a succinct summary of the main results from matrix algebra.

6. THE ROLE OF THE COMPUTER

Regression analysis, the bread-and-butter tool of econometrics, these days is unthinkable without the computer and some access to statistical software. (Believe me, I grew up in the generation of the slide rule!) Fortunately, several excellent regression packages are commercially available, both for the mainframe and the microcomputers, and the list is growing by the day. Regression software packages, such as **ET**, **LIMDEP**, **SHAZAM**, **MICRO TSP**, **MINITAB**, **SAS**, **SPSS**, and **BMD** have most of the econometric techniques and tests discussed in this book. A detailed list of several computer packages and their vendors is given in Appendix C. Some of these packages are available in student version at comparatively inexpensive prices.

In this book, from time to time, the reader will be asked to conduct **Monte Carlo** experiments using one or more of the statistical packages. Monte Carlo experiments are "fun" exercises that will enable the reader to appreciate the properties of several statistical methods discussed in this book. The details of the Monte Carlo experiments will be discussed at appropriate places.

7. SUGGESTIONS FOR FURTHER READING

The topic of econometric methodology is vast and controversial. For those interested in this topic, I suggest the following books:

Neil de Marchi and Christopher Gilbert, eds., *History and Methodology of Econometrics*, Oxford University Press, New York, 1989. This collection of readings discusses some early work on econometric methodology and has an extended discussion of the British approach to econometrics relating to time series data, that is, data collected over a period of time.

Wojciech W. Charemza and Derek F. Deadman, *New Directions in Econometric Practice: General to Specific Modelling, Cointegration and Vector Autogression*, Edward Elgar Publishing Ltd., Hants, England, 1992. The authors of this book critique the traditional approach to econometrics and give a detailed exposition of new approaches to econometric methodology.

Adrian C. Darnell and J. Lynne Evans, *The Limits of Econometrics*, Edward Elgar Publishing Ltd., Hants, England, 1990. This book presents a somewhat balanced discussion of the various methodological approaches to econometrics, with renewed allegiance to traditional econometric methodology.

Mary S. Morgan, *The History of Econometric Ideas*, Cambridge University Press, New York, 1990. The author provides an excellent historical perspective on the theory and practice of econometrics, with an in-depth discussion of the early contributions of Haavelmo (1990 Nobel Laureate in Economics) to econometrics.

David Colander and Reuven Brenner, eds., *Educating Economists*, University of Michigan Press, Ann Arbor, Michigan, 1992. Text presents a critical, at times agnostic, view of economic teaching and practice.

For Bayesian statistics and econometrics, an accessible source is John H. Dey, *Data in Doubt*, Basil Blackwell Ltd., Oxford, England, 1985. An advanced reference is Arnold Zellner, *An Introduction to Bayesian Inference in Econometrics*, John Wiley & Sons, New York, 1971.

PART

I

SINGLE-EQUATION REGRESSION MODELS

Part I of this text introduces single-equation regression models. In these models, one variable, called the *dependent variable*, is expressed as a linear function of one or more other variables, called the *explanatory variables*. In such models it is assumed implicitly that causal relationships, if any, between the dependent and explanatory variables flow in one direction only, namely, from the explanatory variables to the dependent variable.

In Chapter 1, we discuss the historical as well as the modern interpretation of the term *regression* and illustrate the difference between the two interpretations with several examples drawn from economics and other fields.

In Chapter 2, we introduce some fundamental concepts of regression analysis with the aid of the two-variable linear regression model, a model in which the dependent variable is expressed as a linear function of only a single explanatory variable.

In Chapter 3, we continue to deal with the two-variable model and introduce what is known as the *classical linear regression model*, a model that makes several simplifying assumptions. With these assumptions, we introduce the method of *ordinary least squares* (OLS) to estimate the parameters of the two-variable regression model. The method of OLS is simple to apply, yet it has some very desirable statistical properties.

In Chapter 4, we introduce the (two-variable) classical *normal* linear regression model, a model that assumes that the random dependent variable follows the normal probability distribution. With this assumption, the OLS estimators obtained in Chapter 3 possess some stronger statistical properties than the nonnormal classical linear regression model—properties that enable us to engage in statistical inference, namely, hypothesis testing.

Chapter 5 is devoted to the topic of hypothesis testing. In this chapter, we try to find out whether the estimated regression coefficients are compatible with the hypothesized values of such coefficients, the hypothesized values being suggested by theory and/or prior empirical work.

Chapter 6 considers some extensions of the two-variable regression model. In particular, it discusses topics such as (1) regression through the origin, (2) scaling and units of measurement, and (3) functional forms of regression models such as double-log, semilog, and reciprocal models.

In Chapter 7, we consider the multiple regression model, a model in which there is more than one explanatory variable, and show how the method of OLS can be extended to estimate the parameters of such models.

In Chapter 8, we extend the concepts introduced in Chapter 5 to the multiple regression model and point out some of the complications arising from the introduction of several explanatory variables.

Chapter 9, an optional chapter, summarizes the developments of the first eight chapters in terms of matrix algebra. Although matrix notation does not introduce any new concepts, it provides a very compact method of presenting regression theory involving any number of explanatory variables.

CHAPTER

1

THE NATURE
OF REGRESSION
ANALYSIS

As mentioned in the Introduction, regression is a main tool of econometrics, and in this chapter we consider very briefly the nature of this tool.

1.1 HISTORICAL ORIGIN OF THE TERM "REGRESSION"

The term *regression* was introduced by Francis Galton. In a famous paper, Galton found that, although there was a tendency for tall parents to have tall children and for short parents to have short children, the average height of children born of parents of a given height tended to move or "regress" toward the average height in the population as a whole.[1] In other words, the height of the children of unusually tall or unusually short parents tends to move toward the average height of the population. Galton's *law of universal regression* was confirmed by his friend Karl Pearson, who collected more than a thousand records of heights of members of family groups.[2] He found that the average height of sons of a group of tall fathers was less than their fathers' height and the average height of sons of a group of short fathers was greater than their fathers' height, thus "regressing" tall and short sons alike toward the average height of all men. In the words of Galton, this was "regression to mediocrity."

---

[1]Francis Galton, "Family Likeness in Stature," *Proceedings of Royal Society, London*, vol. 40, 1886, pp. 42–72.

[2]K. Pearson and A. Lee, "On the Laws of Inheritance," *Biometrika*, vol. 2, Nov. 1903, pp. 357–462.

1.2 THE MODERN INTERPRETATION OF REGRESSION

The modern interpretation of regression is, however, quite different. Broadly speaking, we may say

> Regression analysis is concerned with the study of the dependence of one variable, the *dependent variable*, on one or more other variables, the *explanatory variables*, with a view to estimating and/or predicting the (population) mean or average value of the former in terms of the known or fixed (in repeated sampling) values of the latter.

The full import of this view of regression analysis will become clearer as we progress, but a few simple examples will make the basic concept quite clear.

Examples

1. Reconsider Galton's law of universal regression. Galton was interested in finding out why there was a stability in the distribution of heights in a population. But in the modern view our concern is not with this explanation but rather with finding out how the *average* height of sons changes, given the fathers' height. In other words, our concern is with predicting the average height of sons knowing the height of their fathers. To see how this can be done, consider Fig. 1.1, which is a **scatter diagram**, or **scattergram**.

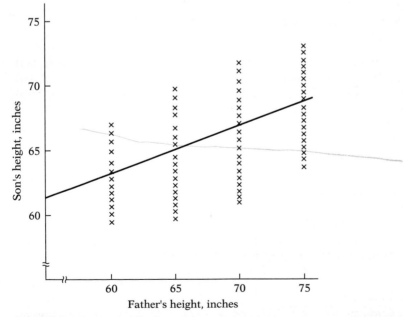

FIGURE 1.1
Hypothetical distribution of sons' heights corresponding to given heights of fathers.

The figure shows the distribution of heights of sons in a hypothetical population corresponding to the given or fixed values of the father's height. Notice that corresponding to any given height of a father is a range (distribution) of the heights of the sons. However, notice that the average height of sons increases as the height of the fathers increases. To see this clearly, we have sketched through the scatter points a straight line that shows how the average height of the sons increases with the fathers' height. This line, as we shall see, is known as the **regression line**.[3]

2. Consider the scattergram in Fig. 1.2, which gives the distribution in a hypothetical population of heights of boys measured at fixed ages. Notice that corresponding to any given age we have a range of heights. Obviously not all boys of a given age are likely to have identical heights. But height on the average increases with age (of course, up to a certain age). Thus, knowing the age, we may be able to predict the average height corresponding to that age.

3. Turning to economic examples, an economist may be interested in studying the dependence of personal consumption expenditure on after-tax or dis-

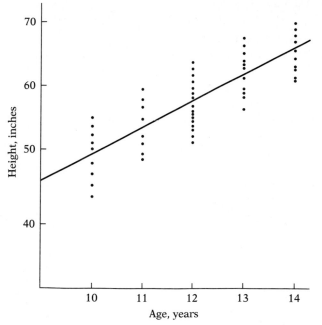

FIGURE 1.2
Hypothetical distribution of heights corresponding to selected ages.

---

[3]At this stage of the development of the subject matter we shall call this regression line simply the *line of average relationship between the dependent variable (son's height) and the explanatory variable (father's height)*. Note that this line has a positive slope; but the slope is less than 1, which is in conformity with Galton's regression to mediocrity. (Why?)

posable real personal income. Such an analysis may be helpful in estimating the marginal propensity to consume (MPC), that is, average change in consumption expenditure for, say, a dollar's worth of change in real income.

4. A monopolist who can fix the price or output (but not both) may want to find out the response of the demand for a product to changes in price. Such an experiment may enable the estimation of the **price elasticity** (i.e., price responsiveness) of the demand for the product and may help determine the most profitable price.

5. A labor economist may want to study the rate of change of money wages in relation to the unemployment rate. The historical data are shown in the scattergram given in Fig. 1.3. The curve in Fig. 1.3 is an example of the celebrated *Phillips curve* relating changes in the money wages to the unemployment rate. Such a scattergram may enable the labor economist to predict the average change in money wages given a certain unemployment rate. Such knowledge may be helpful in stating something about the inflationary process in an economy, for increases in money wages are likely to be reflected in increased prices.

6. From monetary economics it is known that, other things remaining remaining the same, the higher the rate of inflation π, the lower the proportion k of their income that people would want to hold in the form of money, as depicted in Fig. 1.4. A quantitative analysis of this relationship will enable the monetary economist to predict the amount of money, as a proportion of their income, that people would want to hold at various rates of inflation.

7. The marketing director of a company may want to know how the demand for the company's product is related to, say, advertising expenditure. Such a study will be of considerable help in finding out the **elasticity of demand**

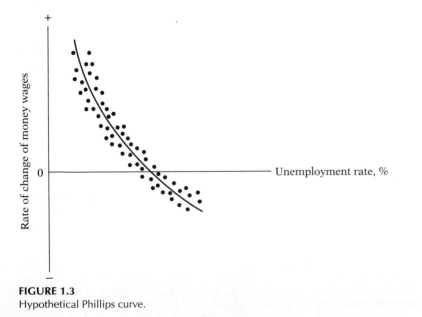

FIGURE 1.3
Hypothetical Phillips curve.

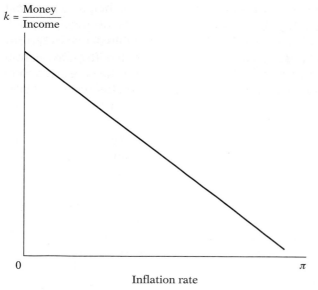

Inflation rate

FIGURE 1.4
Money holding in relation to the inflation rate π.

with respect to advertising expenditure, that is, the percent change in demand in response to, say, a 1 percent change in the advertising budget. This knowledge may be helpful in determining the "optimum" advertising budget.

8. Finally, an agronomist may be interested in studying the dependence of crop yield, say, of wheat, on temperature, rainfall, amount of sunshine, and fertilizer. Such a dependence analysis may enable the prediction or forecasting of the average crop yield, given information about the explanatory variables.

The reader can supply scores of such examples of the dependence of one variable on one or more other variables. The techniques of regression analysis discussed in this text are specially designed to study such dependence among variables.

1.3 STATISTICAL VS. DETERMINISTIC RELATIONSHIPS

From the examples cited in Section 1.2 the reader will notice that in regression analysis we are concerned with what is known as the *statistical*, not *functional* or *deterministic*, dependence among variables, such as those of classical physics. In statistical relationships among variables we essentially deal with **random** or **stochastic**[4] variables, that is, variables that have probability distri-

---

[4]The word *stochastic* comes from the Greek word *stokhos* meaning "a bull's eye." The outcome of throwing darts on a dart board is a stochastic process, that is, a process fraught with misses.

butions. In functional or deterministic dependency, on the other hand, we also deal with variables, but these variables are not random or stochastic.

The dependence of crop yield on temperature, rainfall, sunshine, and fertilizer, for example, is statistical in nature in the sense that the explanatory variables, although certainly important, will not enable the agronomist to predict crop yield exactly because of errors involved in measuring these variables as well as a host of other factors (variables) that collectively affect the yield but may be difficult to identify individually. Thus, there is bound to be some "intrinsic" or random variability in the dependent-variable crop yield that cannot be fully explained no matter how many explanatory variables we consider.

In deterministic phenomena, on the other hand, we deal with relationships of the type, say, exhibited by Newton's law of gravity, which states: Every particle in the universe attracts every other particle with a force directly proportional to the product of their masses and inversely proportional to the square of the distance between them. Symbolically, $F = k(m_1 m_2/r^2)$, where F = force, m_1 and m_2 are the masses of the two particles, r = distance, and k = constant of proportionality. Another example is Ohm's law, which states: For metallic conductors over a limited range of temperature the current C is proportional to the voltage V; that is, $C = (\frac{1}{k})V$ where $\frac{1}{k}$ is the constant of proportionality. Other examples of such deterministic relationships are Boyle's gas law, Kirchhoff's law of electricity, and Newton's law of motion.

In this text we are not concerned with such deterministic relationships. Of course, if there are errors of measurement, say, in the k of Newton's law of gravity, the otherwise deterministic relationship becomes a statistical relationship. In this situation force can be predicted only approximately from the given value of k (and m_1, m_2, and r), which contains errors. The variable F in this case becomes a random variable.

1.4 REGRESSION VS. CAUSATION

Although regression analysis deals with the dependence of one variable on other variables, it does not necessarily imply causation. In the words of Kendall and Stuart, "A statistical relationship, however strong and however suggestive, can never establish causal connection: our ideas of causation must come from outside statistics, ultimately from some theory or other."[5]

In the crop-yield example cited previously, there is no *statistical reason* to assume that rainfall does not depend on crop yield. The fact that we treat crop yield as dependent on rainfall (among other things) is due to nonstatistical considerations: Common sense suggests that the relationship cannot be reversed, for we cannot control rainfall by varying crop yield.

In all the examples cited in Section 1.2 the point to note is that **a statistical relationship per se cannot logically imply causation.** To ascribe causal-

---

[5]M. G. Kendall and A. Stuart, *The Advanced Theory of Statistics*, Charles Griffin Publishers, New York, 1961, vol. 2, chap. 26, p. 279.

ity, one must appeal to a priori or theoretical considerations. Thus, in the third example cited, one can invoke economic theory in saying that consumption expenditure depends on real income.[6]

1.5 REGRESSION VS. CORRELATION

Closely related to but conceptually very much different from regression analysis is **correlation analysis**, where the primary objective is to measure the *strength* or *degree* of *linear association* between two variables. The **correlation coefficient**, which we shall study in detail in Chapter 3, measures this strength of (linear) association. For example, we may be interested in finding the correlation (coefficient) between smoking and lung cancer, between scores on statistics and mathematics examinations, between high school grades and college grades, and so on. In regression analysis, as already noted, we are not primarily interested in such a measure. Instead, we try to estimate or predict the average value of one variable on the basis of the fixed values of other variables. Thus, we may want to know whether we can predict the average score on a statistics examination by knowing a student's score on a mathematics examination.

Regression and correlation have some fundamental differences that are worth mentioning. In regression analysis there is an asymmetry in the way the dependent and explanatory variables are treated. The dependent variable is assumed to be statistical, random, or stochastic, that is, to have a probability distribution. The explanatory variables, on the other hand, are assumed to have fixed values (in repeated sampling),[7] which was made explicit in the definition of regression given in Section 1.2. Thus, in Fig. 1.2 we assumed that the variable age was fixed at given levels and height measurements were obtained at these levels. In correlation analysis, on the other hand, we treat any (two) variables symmetrically; there is no distinction between the dependent and explanatory variables. After all, the correlation between scores on mathematics and statistics examinations is the same as that between scores on statistics and mathematics examinations. Moreover, both variables are assumed to be random. As we shall see, most of the correlation theory is based on the assumption of randomness of variables, whereas most of the regression theory to be expounded in this book is conditional upon the assumption that the dependent variable is stochastic but the explanatory variables are fixed or nonstochastic.[8]

---

[6]But as we shall see in Chap. 3, classical regression analysis is based on the assumption that the model used in the analysis is the correct model. Therefore, the direction of causality may be implicit in the model postulated.

[7]It is crucial to note that the explanatory variables may be intrinsically stochastic, but for the purpose of regression analysis we assume that their values are fixed in repeated sampling (that is, X assumes the same values in various samples), thus rendering them in effect nonrandom or nonstochastic. But more on this in Chap. 3, Sec. 3.2.

[8]In advanced treatment of econometrics one can relax the assumption that the explanatory variables are nonstochastic (see introduction to Part II).

1.6   TERMINOLOGY AND NOTATION

Before we proceed to a formal analysis of regression theory, let us dwell briefly on the matter of terminology and notation. In the literature the terms *dependent variable* and *explanatory variable* are described variously. A representative list is as follows:

Dependent variable	Explanatory variable
↓↑	↓↑
Explained variable	Independent variable
↓↑	↓↑
Predictand	Predictor
↓↑	↓↑
Regressand	Regressor
↓↑	↓↑
Response	Stimulus or control variable
↓↑	↓↑
Endogenous	Exogenous

Although it is a matter of personal taste and tradition, in this text we use the dependent-variable–explanatory-variable terminology.

If we are studying the dependence of a variable on only a single explanatory variable, such as that of consumption expenditure on real income, such a study is known as the *simple*, or **two-variable, regression analysis**. However, if we are studying the dependence of one variable on more than one explanatory variable, such as the crop-yield, rainfall, temperature, sunshine, and fertilizer example, it is known as **multiple regression analysis**. In other words, in two-variable regression there is only one explanatory variable, whereas in multiple regression there is more than one explanatory variable.

The term **random** is a synonym for the term **stochastic**. As noted earlier, a random or stochastic variable is a variable that can take on any set of values, positive or negative, with a given probability.[9]

Unless stated otherwise, the letter Y will denote the dependent variable and the X's $(X_1, X_2, \ldots, X_k)$ will denote the explanatory variables, X_k being the kth explanatory variable. The subscript i or t will denote the ith or the tth observation or value. X_{ki} (or X_{kt}) will denote the ith (or tth) observation on variable X_k. N (or T) will denote the total number of observations or values in the population, and n (or t) the total number of observations in a sample. As a matter of convention, the observation subscript i will be used for **cross-sectional data** (i.e., data collected at one point in time) and the subscript t will be used for **time series data** (i.e., data collected over a period of time). The nature of cross-sectional and time series data, as well as the important topic of the nature and sources of data for empirical analysis, is discussed in the following section.

---

[9]See App. A for formal definition and further details.

1.7 THE NATURE AND SOURCES OF DATA FOR ECONOMETRIC ANALYSIS[10]

The success of any econometric analysis ultimately depends on the availability of the appropriate data. It is therefore essential that we spend some time discussing the nature, sources, and limitations of the data that one may encounter in empirical analysis.

Types of Data

Three types of data may be available for empirical analysis: **Time series**, **cross-sectional**, and **pooled** (combination of time series and cross-sectional) data.

TIME SERIES DATA. The data shown in Table I.1 of the Introduction are an example of time series data. A time series is a set of observations on the values that a variable takes at different times. Such data may be collected at regular time intervals, such as *daily* (e.g., stock prices), *weekly* (e.g., money supply figures provided by the Federal Reserve Board), *monthly* (e.g., the unemployment rate, the Consumer Price Index), *quarterly* (e.g., GNP), *annually* (e.g., government budgets), *quinquennially*, i.e., every 5 years (e.g., the Census of Manufactures), or *decennially* (e.g., the census of population). Sometimes data are available both quarterly and annually, as in the case of the data on GDP and consumer expenditure (e.g., the annual data on GDP and consumer expenditure given in Table I.1 of the Introduction is also available quarterly).

The data thus collected may be *quantitative* (e.g., income, prices, money supply) or *qualitative* (e.g., male or female, working or not working, married or unmarried, college graduate or not). As we will show later, qualitative variables, also called **dummy variables** or **categorical variables**, can be every bit as important as the quantitative variables.

Although time series data are used in many econometric studies, they present some special problems for econometricians. As we will show in chapters on **Time Series Econometrics**, most of the empirical work based on time series data assumes that the underlying time series are **stationary**. Although it is too early to introduce the precise technical meaning of stationarity, loosely speaking a time series, such as that of GDP given in Table I.1 of the Introduction, is stationary if its mean value and its variance do not vary systematically over time.[11] Just keep in mind that whenever you deal with time series data, its stationarity has to be looked into.

---

[10]For an informative account, see Michael D. Intriligator, *Econometric Models, Techniques, and Applications*, Prentice Hall, Englewood Cliffs, N.J., 1978, chap. 3.

[11]Another intuitive way to look at the concept of stationarity is to consider the data on real personal consumption expenditure (PCE) and real GDP given in Table I.1 of the Introduction. These data pertain to the period 1980–1991. Suppose we had data on the same variables for the period 1968 to 1979. Consider, for instance, the data on PCE. If the 12 observations on PCE in the period 1968 to 1979 and the 12 observations on PCE in the period 1980 to 1991 have the same mean, variance, and covariance, then we say that the PCE time series is stationary. We will expound on this concept in the chapters on Time Series Econometrics discussed in Part V of the book, although this material is optional.

CROSS-SECTIONAL DATA.   Cross-sectional data are data on one or more variables collected *at the same point in time*, such as the census of population conducted by the Census Bureau every 10 years, the surveys of consumer expenditures conducted by the University of Michigan, and, of course, the opinion polls such as those conducted by Gallup and umpteen other organizations. A concrete example of cross-sectional data is given in Table 1.1 This table gives data on U.S. egg production and egg prices for the 50 states in the Union for 1990 and 1991. For each year the data on the 50 states are cross-sectional data. Thus, in Table 1.1 we have two cross-sectional samples.

Just as time series data create their own special problems because of the stationarity issue, the cross-sectional data too have their own problems, specifically of *heterogeneity*. We have some states that produce huge amounts of eggs (e.g., Pennsylvania) and some that produce very little (e.g., Alaska). When we include heterogeneous units in a statistical analysis, the **size** or **scale effect** must be taken into account so as not to mix apples with oranges. If you plot prices of eggs and number of eggs produced for the year, say, 1990 from the data in Table 1.1 (see exercise 1.3) you will see how widely scattered the observations are. In Chapter 11 we will see how the scale effect can be an important factor in assessing relationships among economic variables.

POOLED DATA.   In the pooled data are elements of both time series and cross-sectional data. The data in Table 1.1 are an example of pooled data. For each year we have 50 cross-sectional observations and for each state we have two time series observations on prices and output of eggs, a total of 100 pooled observations. Likewise, the data given in exercise 1.1 are pooled data in that the inflation rate for each country for 1960–1980 is time series data, whereas the data on the inflation rate given for the five countries for a single year are cross-sectional. In the pooled data we have 105 observations—21 annual observations for each of the five countries.

There is a special type of pooled data, the **panel** or **longitudinal data**, also called micropanel data, in which the same cross-sectional unit (say, a family or a firm) is surveyed over time. For example, the U.S. Department of Commerce carries out a census of housing at periodic intervals. At each periodic survey the same household (or the people living at the same address) is interviewed to find out if there has been any change in the housing and financial conditions of that household since the last survey. By interviewing the same household periodically, the panel data provide very useful information on the dynamics of household behavior.

The Sources of Data[12]

The data used in empirical analysis may be collected by a governmental agency (e.g., the Department of Commerce), an international agency (e.g., the IMF or

---

[12] For an illuminating account, see Albert T. Somers, *The U.S. Economy Demystified: What the Major Economic Statistics Mean and Their Significance for Business*, D.C. Heath, Lexington, Mass., 1985.

TABLE 1.1
U.S. egg production

State	Y_1	Y_2	X_1	X_2
AL	2,206	2,186	92.7	91.4
AK	0.7	0.7	151.0	149.0
AZ	73	74	61.0	56.0
AR	3,620	3,737	86.3	91.8
CA	7,472	7,444	63.4	58.4
CO	788	873	77.8	73.0
CT	1,029	948	106.0	104.0
DE	168	164	117.0	113.0
FL	2,586	2,537	62.0	57.2
GA	4,302	4,301	80.6	80.8
HI	227.5	224.5	85.0	85.5
ID	187	203	79.1	72.9
IL	793	809	65.0	70.5
IN	5,445	5,290	62.7	60.1
IA	2,151	2,247	56.5	53.0
KS	404	389	54.5	47.8
KY	412	483	67.7	73.5
LA	273	254	115.0	115.0
ME	1,069	1,070	101.0	97.0
MD	885	898	76.6	75.4
MA	235	237	105.0	102.0
MI	1,406	1,396	58.0	53.8
MN	2,499	2,697	57.7	54.0
MS	1,434	1,468	87.8	86.7
MO	1,580	1,622	55.4	51.5
MT	172	164	68.0	66.0
NE	1,202	1,400	50.3	48.9
NV	2.2	1.8	53.9	52.7
NH	43	49	109.0	104.0
NJ	442	491	85.0	83.0
NM	283	302	74.0	70.0
NY	975	987	68.1	64.0
NC	3,033	3,045	82.8	78.7
ND	51	45	55.2	48.0
OH	4,667	4,637	59.1	54.7
OK	869	830	101.0	100.0
OR	652	686	77.0	74.6
PA	4,976	5,130	61.0	52.0
RI	53	50	102.0	99.0
SC	1,422	1,420	70.1	65.9
SD	435	602	48.0	45.8
TN	277	279	71.0	80.7
TX	3,317	3,356	76.7	72.6
UT	456	486	64.0	59.0
VT	31	30	106.0	102.0
VA	943	988	86.3	81.2
WA	1,287	1,313	74.1	71.5
WV	136	174	104.0	109.0
WI	910	873	60.1	54.0
WY	1.7	1.7	83.0	83.0

Note: Y_1 = eggs produced in 1990 (millions)
Y_2 = eggs produced in 1991 (millions)
X_1 = price per dozen (cents) in 1990
X_2 = price per dozen (cents) in 1991

Source: World Almanac, 1993, p.119. The data are from the Economic Research Service, U.S. Department of Agriculture.

the World Bank), a private organization (e.g., the Standard & Poor's Corporation), or an individual. Literally, there are thousands of such agencies collecting data for one purpose or another.

The data collected by these agencies may be *experimental* or *nonexperimental* in nature. In experimental data, often collected in the natural sciences, the investigator may want to collect data holding certain factors constant in order to assess the impact of some other factors on a given phenomenon. For example, in assessing the impact of obesity on blood pressure, the researcher would want to collect data holding constant the eating, smoking, and drinking habits of the people in order to minimize the influence of these variables on blood pressure.

In the social sciences the data that one generally obtains are nonexperimental in nature, that is, not subject to the control of the researcher. For example, the data on GNP, unemployment, stock prices, etc. are not directly under the control of the investigator. As we shall see, this lack of control often creates special problems for the researcher in pinning down the exact cause or causes affecting a particular situation. For example, is it the money supply that determines the (nominal) GNP or is it the other way around?

A practical problem facing the researcher is to obtain the data. In the appendix to this chapter, we list some of the sources of economic and financial data. This list is by no means exhaustive.

The Accuracy of Data[13]

Although plenty of data are available for economic research, the quality of the data is often not that good. There are several reasons for that. First, as noted, most social science data are nonexperimental in nature. Therefore, there is the possibility of observational errors, either of omission or commission. Second, even in experimentally collected data errors of measurement arise from approximations and roundoffs. Third, in questionnaire-type surveys, the problem of nonreponse can be serious; a researcher is lucky to get a 40 percent response to a questionnaire. Analysis based on such partial response may not truly reflect the behavior of the 60 percent who did not respond, thereby leading to what is known as (sample) **selectivity bias**. Then there is the further problem that those who respond to the questionnaire may not answer all the questions, especially questions of financially sensitive nature, thus leading to additional selectivity bias. Fourth, the sampling methods used in obtaining the data may vary so widely that it is often difficult to compare the results obtained from the various samples. Fifth, economic data are generally available at a highly aggregate level. For example, most macrodata (e.g., GNP, employment, inflation, unemployment) are available for the economy as a whole or at the most for

---

[13]For a critical view, see O. Morgenstern, *The Accuracy of Economic Observations*, 2d ed., Princeton University Press, Princeton, N.J., 1963.

some broad geographical regions. Such highly aggregated data may not tell us much about the individual or micro units that may be the ultimate object of study. Sixth, because of confidentiality, certain data can be published only in highly aggregate form. The IRS, for example, is not allowed by law to disclose data on individual tax returns; it can only release some broad summary data. Therefore, if one wants to find out how much individuals with a certain level of income spent on health care, one cannot do that analysis except at a very highly aggregate level. But such macroanalysis often fails to reveal the dynamics of the behavior of the microunits. Similarly, the Department of Commerce, which conducts the Census of Business every five years, is not allowed to disclose information on production, employment, energy consumption, research and development expenditure, etc. at the firm level. It is therefore difficult to study the interfirm differences on these items.

Because of all these and many other problems, **the researcher should always keep in mind that the results of research are only as good as the quality of the data**. Therefore, if in given situations researchers find that the results of the research are "unsatisfactory," the cause may be not that they used the wrong model but that the quality of the data was poor. Unfortunately, because of the nonexperimental nature of the data used in most social science studies, researchers very often have no choice but to depend on the available data. But they should always keep in mind that the data used may not be the best and should try not to be too dogmatic about the results obtained from a given study, especially when the quality of the data is suspect.

1.8 SUMMARY AND CONCLUSIONS

1. The key idea behind regression analysis is the statistical dependence of one variable, the dependent variable, on one or more other variables, the explanatory variables.

2. The objective of such analysis is to estimate and/or predict the mean or average value of the dependent variable on the basis of the known or fixed values of the explanatory variables.

3. In practice the success of regression analysis depends on the availability of the appropriate data. This chapter discussed the nature, sources, and limitations of the data that are generally available for research, especially in the social sciences.

4. In any research, the researcher should clearly state the sources of the data used in the analysis, their definitions, their methods of collection, and any gaps or omissions in the data as well as any revisions in the data. Keep in mind that the macroeconomic data published by the government are often revised.

5. Since the reader may not have the time, energy, or resources to track down the data, the reader has the right to presume that the data used by the researcher are properly gathered and that the computations and analysis are correct.

EXERCISES

1.1. The following table gives the inflation rates for five industrial countries for the period 1960–1980.

Rates of inflation in five industrialized countries, 1960–1980 (% per annum)

Year	U.S.A.	U.K.	Japan	Germany	France
1960	1.5	1.0	3.6	1.5	3.6
1961	1.1	3.4	5.4	2.3	3.4
1962	1.1	4.5	6.7	4.5	4.7
1963	1.2	2.5	7.7	3.0	4.8
1964	1.4	3.9	3.9	2.3	3.4
1965	1.6	4.6	6.5	3.4	2.6
1966	2.8	3.7	6.0	3.5	2.7
1967	2.8	2.4	4.0	1.5	2.7
1968	4.2	4.8	5.5	1.8	4.5
1969	5.0	5.2	5.1	2.6	6.4
1970	5.9	6.5	7.6	3.7	5.5
1971	4.3	9.5	6.3	5.3	5.5
1972	3.6	6.8	4.9	5.4	5.9
1973	6.2	8.4	12.0	7.0	7.5
1974	10.9	16.0	24.6	7.0	14.0
1975	9.2	24.2	11.7	5.9	11.7
1976	5.8	16.5	9.3	4.5	9.6
1977	6.4	15.9	8.1	3.7	9.4
1978	7.6	8.3	3.8	2.7	9.1
1979	11.4	13.4	3.6	4.1	10.7
1980	13.6	18.0	8.0	5.5	13.3

Source: Richard Jackman. Charles Mulvey. and James Trevithick, *The Economics of Inflation.* 2d ed., Martin Roberston, 1981. Table 1.1. p. 5.

(*a*) Plot the inflation rate for each country against time. (Use the horizontal axis for time and the vertical axis for the inflation rate.)

(*b*) What broad conclusions can you draw about the inflation experience in the five countries?

(*c*) Which country's inflation rate seems to be more variable? Can you offer any explanation?

1.2. Use the data given for Exercise 1.1.

(*a*) Plot the inflation rate for the U.K., Japan, Germany, and France against the U.S. inflation rate. (Use the horizontal axis for the U.S. inflation rate and the vertical axis for the inflation rates of the other four countries. If you prefer, you may draw four separate diagrams.)

(*b*) Comment generally about the behavior of the inflation rate in the four countries vis-à-vis the U.S. inflation rate.

(*c*) Do you observe any noticeable change in the inflationary behavior of each country over time and of the four countries in relation to the United States?

(*d*) Do you think the oil embargoes of 1974 and 1979 have had a significant effect on the inflation rate in the various countries. If so, why?

(e) Obtain information on the inflation rate in the five countries since 1980 and comment on the behavior of inflation since then in these countries. Do you think the world oil situation prevailing since 1980 has had any effect on the inflation rate since then?

1.3 Use the data given in Table 1.1.

(a) Plot the quantity of eggs on the vertical axis and the price of eggs per dozen produced on the horizontal axis for each year separately.

(b) Sketch the regression line. Is there a discernible relationship between the two variables, price and quantity of eggs produced?

(c) If you observe a positive relationship between the two variables, can you say that the observed regression line suggests a supply function?

(d) On the other hand, if you observe a negative relationship between the two variables, can you say that the sketched regression line suggests a demand function?

(e) From the scatter plot of price and output data, how can you tell whether the regression line represents a demand function or a supply function? This question is the famous **Identification Problem** in econometrics, which we will study in detail in Part IV of the book. Roughly speaking, the identification problem occurs when it is impossible to tell from the data which function is being estimated, e.g., the demand or supply function in the present case.

(f) Since the scale of egg production varies from state to state, do you think that the scatter plot in (a) is meaningful? How would you plot the scattergram, taking into account the heterogeneity (i.e., the scale effect) of the data?

APPENDIX 1A
SOURCES OF ECONOMIC AND FINANCIAL DATA

1A.1 SOURCES OF ECONOMIC DATA

Several sources of economic data are as follows:

1. *Business Statistics*, published by the Bureau of Economic Analysis (BEA) of the Department of Commerce, presents historical data and methodological notes for approximately 2100 series that appear in the BEA's monthly journal, the *Survey of Current Business*. As of the time of writing, the latest edition of *Business Statistics* covers annual data for 1963–1991 and monthly data from 1988–1991 for approximately 1900 series. Appendix I presents monthly data for 1963–1987 for about 260 series and Appendix II presents quarterly and annual data for 1960–1991 for several selected time series.

The BEA also publishes *Statistical Abstract of the United States* each year. It gives data for the states, the United States, and foreign countries in areas such as population, vital statistics, health and nutrition, education, law enforcement, courts and prisons, geography and environment, parks, recreation and travel, elections, state and local government finances and employment, federal government finances and employment, national defense and veterans affairs, social insurance and human services, labor force, employment and earnings, income, expenditure and wealth, prices, banking and insurance, business enterprise, communications, energy, science, transportation (land, air, and water), agriculture, forests and fisheries, mining and mineral products, construction and housing, manufactures, domestic trade and services, foreign commerce, and foreign aid.

The vast amount of statistical data collected by the BEA is now electronically stored in the **Economic Bulletin Board (EBB)**, which can be easily accessed 24 hours a day by anyone with a personal computer. The easiest way to access EBB is to open an account with the U.S. Department of Commerce's National Technical Information Service (NTIS). The registration fee of $35 gives two hours of free connect time. You will be provided with an ID and a password that will enable you to access all the files collected by EBB. Currently, the BEA charges 20 cents per minute from 8 A.M. to 12 P.M., 15 cents from 12 P.M. to 6 P.M., and 5 cents per minute from 6 P.M. to 8 A.M (EST). These amounts will be charged to your account and you will be billed monthly. Details can be be obtained from NTIS by calling (703) 487-4064.

2. Detailed data on national income and product accounts can be found in *National Income and Product Accounts of the United States: Vol. 1, 1929–1958* and *National Income and Product Accounts of the United States: Vol. 2, 1958–1988*, both published by the Department of Commerce.

3. A handy and most popular source of economic data is the *Economic Report of the President*, usually published in February of each year.

4. The Federal Reserve Bank of St. Louis, among its various statistical publications, publishes *National Economic Trend* (monthly) and *International Economic Conditions* (annually), the former giving data on key U.S. economic variables and the latter on comparative economic data on key economic variables for United States, Canada, France, Germany, Italy, Japan, the United Kingdom, Australia, Mexico, The Netherlands, New Zealand, Singapore, Republic of Korea, Spain, Switzerland, and Venezuela.

5. CITIBASE is a data bank of over 5600 economic time series, maintained and published by Citicorp Database Services. The database can be purchased on a subscription basis. Most universities subscribe to CITIBASE. Users of **Micro Tsp** statistical package can also get access to that data.

6. Several private agencies collect data for a variety of purposes. For example, the Conference Board in New York City collects data on several economic variables. The Institute for Social Research at the University of Michigan collects data on consumer expenditure and consumer sentiment.

7. Various branches of the U.S. government publish data pertaining to their jurisdictions. For example, the Labor Department publishes extensive data on employment, unemployment, and earnings. The *Monthly Labor Review* gives information on the data the Department collects. Similarly, the U.S. Department of Agriculture publishes every year *Agricultural Statistics*, which gives voluminous data on all kinds of agricultural statistics.

8. At the international level, the following sources provide a mass of statistical information. *International Financial Statistics*, published monthly by the International Monetary Fund (IMF), gives comparative economic and financial data on member countries. The Organization of Economic Cooperation and Development (OECD) publishes *Basic Statistics of the Community*, which gives key statistics on several macroeconomic variables. It also publishes voluminous statistical data for 24 of its members. These member countries are Australia, Austria, Belgium, Canada, Denmark, Finland, France, Germany, Greece, Iceland, Ireland, Italy, Japan, Luxembourg, The Netherlands, New Zealand, Norway, Portugal, Spain, Sweden, Switzerland, Turkey, United Kingdom, and United States. For its various statistical publications, contact OECD, Publications and Information Center, 2001 L Street, N.W., Washington, D.C. 20036-4910.

The United Nations (U.N.) publishes *World Statistics*, which contains massive amounts of data for member countries. The U.N. also publishes *Yearbook of National Accounts Statistics*. The Food and Agricultural Organization (FAO) publishes the *FAO Trade Year Book*.

To learn about other sources of economic data, the reader may consult the following:

Albert T. Somers, *The U.S. Economy Demystified: What the Major Economic Statistics Mean and Their Significance for Business*, D.C. Heath, Lexington, Mass., 1985

Norman Frumkin, *Tracking America's Economy*, 2d ed., M.E. Sharpe, Armonk, N.Y., 1992

Gary E. Clayton and Martin Gerhard Giesbrecht, *A Guide to Every Day Economic Statistics*, 2d ed., McGraw-Hill, New York, 1992

L. M. Daniels, *Business Information Sources*, University of California Press, Berkeley, 1976.

1A.2 SOURCES OF FINANCIAL DATA

Sources of financial data are legion. Some important data files for computers follow:

1. The CRSP File: The Center for Research in Security Prices (CRSP) maintains in a magnetic tape form data on market prices and quarterly dividends for every company listed on the New York Stock Exchange (NYSE) since 1926. The tape is available on a subscription basis from the Graduate School of Business, University of Chicago, 1101 E. 58 St., Chicago, Ill. 60607.

2. ISL Tape: The ISL tape, produced by Interactive Data Corporation (IDC), is a magnetic tape that contains daily stock-trading volume, prices, quarterly dividends, and earnings for all NYSE and AMEX (American Stock Exchange) securities, and some OTC (over-the-counter) securities. For information, write to IDC, 122 E. 42nd St., New York, N.Y. 10017.

3. Compustat Tapes: These tapes, produced by Investors Management Sciences, Inc. (IMSI), contain over 20 years of annual data for more than 3500 stocks. Quarterly data on 2700 stocks from 1962 are also available. For information, write IMSI, 7400 S. Alton Court, Englewood, Colo. 80110.

CHAPTER
2

TWO-VARIABLE REGRESSION ANALYSIS: SOME BASIC IDEAS

In Chapter 1 we discussed the concept of regression in broad terms. In this chapter we approach the subject matter somewhat formally. Specifically, this and the following three chapters introduce the reader to the theory underlying the simplest possible regression analysis, namely, the two-variable case. This case is considered first, not necessarily because of its practical adequacy, but because it presents the fundamental ideas of regression analysis as simply as possible and some of these ideas can be illustrated with the aid of two-dimensional diagrams. Moreover, as we shall see, the more general multiple regression analysis is in many ways a logical extension of the two-variable case.

2.1 A HYPOTHETICAL EXAMPLE

As pointed out in Section 1.2, regression analysis is largely concerned with estimating and/or predicting the (population) mean or average value of the dependent variable on the basis of the known or fixed values of the explanatory variable(s). To understand how this is done, consider the following example.

Imagine a hypothetical country with a total **population**[1] of 60 families. Suppose we are interested in studying the relationship between weekly family consumption expenditure Y and weekly after-tax or disposable family income X. More specifically, assume that we want to predict the (population) mean level of weekly consumption expenditure knowing the family's weekly income. To this end, suppose we divide these 60 families into 10 groups of approximately the same income and examine the consumption expenditures of families in each of these income groups. The hypothetical data are given in Table 2.1. (For the purpose of discussion, assume that only the income levels given in Table 2.1 were actually observed.)

Table 2.1 is to be interpreted as follows: Corresponding to a weekly income of $80, for example, there are five families whose weekly consumption expenditures range between $55 and $75. Similarly, given $X = \$240$, there are six families whose weekly consumption expenditures fall between $137 and $189. In other words, each column (vertical array) of Table 2.1 gives the distribution of consumption expenditure Y corresponding to a fixed level of income X; that is, it gives the **conditional distribution** of Y conditional upon the given values of X.

Noting that the data of Table 2.1 represent the population, we can easily compute the **conditional probabilities** of Y, $p(Y \mid X)$, probability of Y given X, as follows.[2] For $X = \$80$, for instance, there are five Y values: $55, $60, $65, $70, and $75. Therefore, given $X = 80$, the probability of obtaining any one of these consumption expenditures is $\frac{1}{5}$. Symbolically, $p(Y = 55 \mid X = 80) = \frac{1}{5}$. Similarly, $p(Y = 150 \mid X = 260) = \frac{1}{7}$, and so on. The conditional probabilities for the data of Table 2.1 are given in Table 2.2.

Now for each of the conditional probability distributions of Y we can compute its mean or average value, known as the **conditional mean** or **conditional expectation**, denoted by $E(Y \mid X = X_i)$ and read as "the expected value of Y given that X takes the specific value X_i," which for notational simplicity will be written as $E(Y \mid X_i)$. (*Note:* An expected value is simply a population mean or average value.) For our hypothetical data, these conditional expectations can be easily computed by multiplying the relevant Y values given in Table 2.1 by their conditional probabilities given in Table 2.2 and summing up these products. As an illustration, the conditional mean or expectation of Y given $X = 80$

---

[1]The statistical meaning of the term populaton is explained in App. A. Informally, it means the set of all possible outcomes of an experiment or measurement, e.g., tossing a coin repeatedly or recording the prices of all the securities listed on the New York Stock Exchange at the end of a business day.

[2]*A word about notation:* The expression $p(Y \mid X)$ or $p(Y \mid X_i)$ is a shorthand for $p(Y = Y_i \mid X = X_i)$, that is, the probability that the (discrete) random variable Y takes the numerical value of Y_i given that the (discrete) random variable X has taken the numerical value of X_i. However, to avoid cluttering up the notation, we will use the subscript i (the index of observation) on both the variables. Thus, $p(Y \mid X)$ or $p(Y \mid X_i)$ will stand for $p(Y = Y_i \mid X = X_i)$, that is, the probability that Y takes the value Y_i given that X has assumed the value X_i, the problem at hand making clear the range of the values taken by Y and X. In Table 2.1, when $X = \$220$, Y takes seven different values, but when $X = \$120$, Y takes only five different values.

TABLE 2.1
Weekly family income X, $

Y ↓ \ X →	80	100	120	140	160	180	200	220	240	260
Weekly family	55	65	79	80	102	110	120	135	137	150
consumption	60	70	84	93	107	115	136	137	145	152
expenditure Y, $	65	74	90	95	110	120	140	140	155	175
	70	80	94	103	116	130	144	152	165	178
	75	85	98	108	118	135	145	157	175	180
	–	88	–	113	125	140	–	160	189	185
	–	–	–	115	–	–	–	162	–	191
Total	325	462	445	707	678	750	685	1043	966	1211

is $55(\frac{1}{5}) + 60(\frac{1}{5}) + 65(\frac{1}{5}) + 70(\frac{1}{5}) + 75(\frac{1}{5}) = 65$. The conditional means thus computed are given in the last row of Table 2.2.

Before proceeding further, it is instructive to see the data of Table 2.1 on a scattergram, as shown in Fig. 2.1. The scattergram shows the conditional distribution of Y corresponding to various X values. Although there are variations in individual family consumption expenditures, Fig. 2.1 shows very clearly that consumption expenditure *on the average* increases as income increases. Stated differently, the scattergram reveals that the (conditional) mean values of Y increase as X increases. This observation can be seen more vividly if we concentrate on the oversized points representing various conditional means of Y. The scattergram shows that these conditional means lie on a straight line with a positive slope.[3] This line is known as the **population regression line**, or, more

TABLE 2.2
Conditional probabilities $p(Y \mid X_i)$ for the data of Table 2.1

$p(Y \mid X_i)$ ↓ \ X →	80	100	120	140	160	180	200	220	240	260
Conditional	$\frac{1}{5}$	$\frac{1}{6}$	$\frac{1}{5}$	$\frac{1}{7}$	$\frac{1}{6}$	$\frac{1}{6}$	$\frac{1}{5}$	$\frac{1}{7}$	$\frac{1}{6}$	$\frac{1}{7}$
probabilities	$\frac{1}{5}$	$\frac{1}{6}$	$\frac{1}{5}$	$\frac{1}{7}$	$\frac{1}{6}$	$\frac{1}{6}$	$\frac{1}{5}$	$\frac{1}{7}$	$\frac{1}{6}$	$\frac{1}{7}$
$p(Y \mid X_i)$	$\frac{1}{5}$	$\frac{1}{6}$	$\frac{1}{5}$	$\frac{1}{7}$	$\frac{1}{6}$	$\frac{1}{6}$	$\frac{1}{5}$	$\frac{1}{7}$	$\frac{1}{6}$	$\frac{1}{7}$
	$\frac{1}{5}$	$\frac{1}{6}$	$\frac{1}{5}$	$\frac{1}{7}$	$\frac{1}{6}$	$\frac{1}{6}$	$\frac{1}{5}$	$\frac{1}{7}$	$\frac{1}{6}$	$\frac{1}{7}$
	$\frac{1}{5}$	$\frac{1}{6}$	$\frac{1}{5}$	$\frac{1}{7}$	$\frac{1}{6}$	$\frac{1}{6}$	$\frac{1}{5}$	$\frac{1}{7}$	$\frac{1}{6}$	$\frac{1}{7}$
	–	$\frac{1}{6}$	–	$\frac{1}{7}$	$\frac{1}{6}$	$\frac{1}{6}$	–	$\frac{1}{7}$	$\frac{1}{6}$	$\frac{1}{7}$
	–	–	–	$\frac{1}{7}$	–	–	–	$\frac{1}{7}$	–	$\frac{1}{7}$
Conditional means of Y	65	77	89	101	113	125	137	149	161	173

---

[3]The reader should keep in mind the hypothetical nature of our data. It is not suggested here that the conditional means will always lie on a straight line; they may lie on a curve.

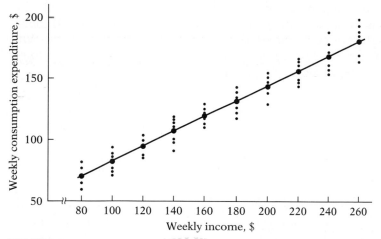

FIGURE 2.1
Conditional distribution of expenditure for various levels of income (data of Table 2.1).

generally, the **population regression curve**. More simply, **it is the regression of Y on X**.

Geometrically, then, a population regression curve is simply the locus of the conditional means or expectations of the dependent variable for the fixed values of the explanatory variable(s). It can be depicted as in Fig. 2.2, which shows

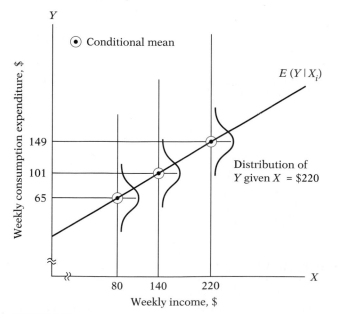

FIGURE 2.2
Population regression line (data of Table 2.1).

that for each X_i there is a population of Y values (assumed to be normally distributed for reasons explained later) and a corresponding (conditional) mean. And the regression line or curve passes through these conditional means. With this interpretation of regression curve the reader may find it instructive to re-read the definition of regression given in Section 1.2.

2.2 THE CONCEPT OF POPULATION REGRESSION FUNCTION (PRF)

From the preceding discussion and especially Figs. 2.1 and 2.2, it is clear that each conditional mean $E(Y \mid X_i)$ is a function of X_i. Symbolically,

$$E(Y \mid X_i) = f(X_i) \qquad (2.2.1)$$

where $f(X_i)$ denotes some function of the explanatory variable X_i. [In our hypothetical example, $E(Y \mid X_i)$ is a linear function of X_i.] Equation (2.2.1) is known as the (two-variable) **population regression function** (PRF), or **population regression** (PR) for short. It states merely that the (*population*) mean of the distribution of Y given X_i is functionally related to X_i. In other words, it tells how the mean or average response of Y varies with X.

What form does the function $f(X_i)$ assume? This question is important because in real situations we do not have the entire population available for examination. The functional form of the PRF is therefore an empirical question, although in specific cases theory may have something to say. For example, an economist might posit that consumption expenditure is linearly related to income. Therefore, as a first approximation or a working hypothesis, we may assume that the PRF $E(Y \mid X_i)$ is a linear function of X_i, say, of the type

$$E(Y \mid X_i) = \beta_1 + \beta_2 X_i \qquad (2.2.2)$$

where β_1 and β_2 are unknown but fixed parameters known as the **regression coefficients**; β_1 and β_2 are also known as the **intercept** and **slope coefficient**, respectively. Equation (2.2.2) itself is known as the **linear population regression function**, or simply the **linear population regression**. Some alternative expressions used in the literature are linear population regression model or linear population regression equation. In the sequel, the terms **regression, regression equation**, and **regression model** will be used synonymously.

In regression analysis our interest is in estimating the PRFs like (2.2.2), that is, estimating the values of the unknowns β_1 and β_2 on the basis of observations on Y and X. This topic will be studied in detail in Chapter 3.

2.3 THE MEANING OF THE TERM "LINEAR"

Since this text is concerned primarily with linear models like (2.2.2), it is essential to know what the term *linear* really means, for it can be interpreted in two different ways.

Linearity in the Variables

The first and perhaps more "natural" meaning of linearity is that the conditional expectation of Y is a linear function of X_i, such as, for example, (2.2.2).[4] Geometrically, the regression curve in this case is a straight line. In this interpretation, a regression function such as $E(Y \mid X_i) = \beta_1 + \beta_2 X_i^2$ is not a linear function because the variable X appears with a power or index of 2.

Linearity in the Parameters

The second interpretation of linearity is that the conditional expectation of Y, $E(Y \mid X_i)$, is a linear function of the parameters, the β's; it may or may not be linear in the variable X.[5] In this interpretation, $E(Y \mid X_i) = \beta_1 + \beta_2 X_i^2$ is a linear regression model but $E(Y \mid X_i) = \beta_1 + \sqrt{\beta_2} X_i$ is not. The latter is an example of a nonlinear (in the parameters) regression model; we shall not deal with such models in this text.

Of the two interpretations of linearity, linearity in the parameters is relevant for the development of the regression theory to be presented shortly. Therefore, *from now on the term "linear" regression will always mean a regression that is linear in the parameters, the β's (that is, the parameters are raised to the first power only); it may or may not be linear in the explanatory variables, the X's.* Schematically, we have Table 2.3. Thus, $E(Y \mid X_i) = \beta_1 + \beta_2 X_i$, which is linear both in the parameters and variable, is a LRM, and so is $E(Y \mid X_i) = \beta_1 + \beta_2 X_i^2$, which is linear in the parameters but nonlinear in variable X.

TABLE 2.3
Linear regression models

Model linear in parameters?	Model linear in variables?	
	Yes	No
Yes	LRM	LRM
No	NLRM	NLRM

Note: LRM = linear regression model
     NLRM = nonlinear regression model

---

[4] A function $Y = f(X)$ is said to be linear in X if X appears with a power or index of 1 only (that is, terms such as X^2, $\sqrt{X}$, and so on, are excluded) and is not multiplied or divided by any other variable (for example, $X \cdot Z$ or X/Z, where Z is another variable). If Y depends on X alone, another way to state that Y is linearly related to X is that the rate of change of Y with respect to X (i.e., the slope, or derivative, of Y with respect to X, dY/dX) is independent of the value of X. Thus, if $Y = 4X$, $dY/dX = 4$, which is independent of the value of X. But if $Y = 4X^2$, $dY/dX = 8X$, which is not independent of the value taken by X. Hence this function is not linear in X.

[5] A function is said to be linear in the parameter, say, β_1, if β_1 appears with a power of 1 only and is not multiplied or divided by any other parameter (for example, $\beta_1\beta_2$, β_2/β_1, and so on).

2.4 STOCHASTIC SPECIFICATION OF PRF

It is clear from Fig. 2.1 that as family income increases, family consumption expenditure on the average increases, too. But what about the consumption expenditure of an individual family in relation to its (fixed) level of income? It is obvious from Table 2.1 and Fig. 2.1 that an individual family's consumption expenditure does not necessarily increase as the income level increases. For example, from Table 2.1 we observe that corresponding to the income level of $100 there is one family whose consumption expenditure of $65 is less than the consumption expenditures of two families whose weekly income is only $80. But notice that the *average* consumption expenditure of families with a weekly income of $100 is greater than the average consumption expenditure of families with a weekly income of $80 ($77 vs. $65).

What, then, can we say about the relationship between an individual family's consumption expenditure and a given level of income? We see from Fig. 2.1 that, given the income level of X_i, an individual family's consumption expenditure is clustered around the average consumption of all families at that X_i, that is, around its conditional expectation. Therefore, we can express the *deviation* of an individual Y_i around its expected value as follows:

$$u_i = Y_i - E(Y \mid X_i)$$

or

$$Y_i = E(Y \mid X_i) + u_i \tag{2.4.1}$$

where the deviation u_i is an unobservable random variable taking positive or negative values. Technically, u_i is known as the **stochastic disturbance** or **stochastic error term.**

How do we interpret (2.4.1)? We can say that the expenditure of an individual family, given its income level, can be expressed as the sum of two components: (1) $E(Y \mid X_i)$, which is simply the mean consumption expenditure of all the families with the same level of income. This component is known as the **systematic**, or **deterministic**, component, and (2) u_i, which is the random, or **nonsystematic**, component. We shall examine shortly the nature of the stochastic disturbance term, but for the moment assume that it is a *surrogate or proxy* for all the omitted or neglected variables that may affect Y but are not (or cannot) be included in the regression model.

If $E(Y \mid X_i)$ is assumed to be linear in X_i, as in (2.2.2), Eq. (2.4.1) may be written as

$$
\begin{aligned}
Y_i &= E(Y \mid X_i) + u_i \\
&= \beta_1 + \beta_2 X_i + u_i
\end{aligned}
\tag{2.4.2}
$$

Equation (2.4.2) posits that the consumption expenditure of a family is linearly related to its income plus the disturbance term. Thus, the individual consumption expenditures, given $X = \$80$ (see Table 2.1), can be expressed as

$$Y_1 = 55 = \beta_1 + \beta_2(80) + u_1$$
$$Y_2 = 60 = \beta_1 + \beta_2(80) + u_2$$

$$Y_3 = 65 = \beta_1 + \beta_2(80) + u_3$$

$$Y_4 = 70 = \beta_1 + \beta_2(80) + u_4 \qquad (2.4.3)$$

$$Y_5 = 75 = \beta_1 + \beta_2(80) + u_5$$

Now if we take the expected value of (2.4.1) on both sides, we obtain

$$E(Y_i \mid X_i) = E[E(Y \mid X_i)] + E(u_i \mid X_i)$$

$$= E(Y \mid X_i) + E(u_i \mid X_i) \qquad (2.4.4)$$

where use is made of the fact that the expected value of a constant is that constant itself.[6] Notice carefully that in (2.4.4) we have taken the conditional expectation, conditional upon the given X's.

Since $E(Y_i \mid X_i)$ is the same thing as $E(Y \mid X_i)$, Eq. (2.4.4) implies that

$$E(u_i \mid X_i) = 0 \qquad (2.4.5)$$

Thus, the assumption that the regression line passes through the conditional means of Y (see Fig. 2.2) implies that the conditional mean values of u_i (conditional upon the given X's) are zero.

From the previous discussion it is clear (2.2.2) and (2.4.2) are equivalent forms if $E(u_i \mid X_i) = 0$.[7] But the stochastic specification (2.4.2) has the advantage that it clearly shows that there are other variables besides income that affect consumption expenditure and that an individual family's consumption expenditure cannot be fully explained only by the variable(s) included in the regression model.

2.5 THE SIGNIFICANCE OF THE STOCHASTIC DISTURBANCE TERM

As noted in Section 2.4, the disturbance term u_i is a surrogate for all those variables that are omitted from the model but that collectively affect Y. The obvious question is: Why not introduce these variables into the model explicitly? Stated otherwise, why not develop a multiple regression model with as many variables as possible? The reasons are many.

1. *Vagueness of theory*: The theory, if any, determining the behavior of Y may be, and often is, incomplete. We might know for certain that weekly income X influences weekly consumption expenditure Y, but we might be ignorant or unsure about the other variables affecting Y. Therefore, u_i may be used as a substitute for all the excluded or omitted variables from the model.

---

[6] See App. A for a brief discussion of the properties of the expectation operator E. Note that $E(Y \mid X_i)$, once the value of X_i is fixed, is a constant.

[7] As a matter of fact, in the method of least squares to be developed in Chap. 3 it is assumed explicitly that $E(u_i \mid X_i) = 0$. See Sec. 3.2.

2. *Unavailability of data*: Even if we know what some of the excluded variables are and therefore consider a multiple regression rather than a simple regression, we may not have quantitative information about these variables. It is a common experience in empirical analysis that the data we would ideally like to have often are not available. For example, in principle we could introduce family wealth as an explanatory variable in addition to the income variable to explain family consumption expenditure. But unfortunately, information on family wealth generally is not available. Therefore, we may be forced to omit the wealth variable from our model despite its great theoretical relevance in explaining consumption expenditure.

3. *Core variables vs. peripheral variables*: Assume in our consumption-income example that besides income X_1, the number of children per family X_2, sex X_3, religion X_4, education X_5, and geographical region X_6 also affect consumption expenditure. But it is quite possible that the joint influence of all or some of these variables may be so small and at best nonsystematic or random that as a practical matter and for cost considerations it does not pay to introduce them into the model explicitly. One hopes that their combined effect can be treated as a random variable u_i.[8]

4. *Intrinsic randomness in human behavior*: Even if we succeed in introducing all the relevant variables into the model, there is bound to be some "intrinsic" randomness in individual Y that cannot be explained no matter how hard we try. The disturbances, the u's, may very well reflect this intrinsic randomness.

5. *Poor proxy variables*: Although the classical regression model (to be developed in Chapter 3) assumes that the variables Y and X are measured accurately, in practice the data may be plagued by errors of measurement. Consider, for example, Milton Friedman's well-known theory of the consumption function.[9] He regards *permanent consumption* (Y^p) as a function of *permanent income* (X^p). But since data on these variables are not directly observable, in practice we use proxy variables, such as current consumption (Y) and current income (X), which can be observable. Since the observed Y and X may not equal Y^p and X^p, there is the problem of errors of measurement. The disturbance term u may in this case then also represent the errors of measurement. As we will see in a later chapter, if there are such errors of measurement, they can have serious implications for estimating the regression coefficients, the β's.

6. *Principle of parsimony*: Following Occam's razor,[10] we would like to keep our regression model as simple as possible. If we can explain the behavior of Y

---

[8]A further difficulty is that variables such as sex, education, religion, etc. are difficult to quantify.

[9]Milton Friedman, *A Theory of the Consumption Function*, Princeton University Press, Princeton, N.J., 1957.

[10]"That descriptions be kept as simple as possible until proved inadequate," *The World of Mathematics*, vol. 2, J. R. Newman (ed), Simon & Schuster, New York, 1956, p. 1247, or, "Entities should not be multiplied beyond necessity," Donald F. Morrison, *Applied Linear Statistical Methods*, Prentice Hall, Englewood Cliffs, N.J., 1983, p. 58.

"substantially" with two or three explanatory variables and if our theory is not strong enough to suggest what other variables might be included, why introduce more variables? Let u_i represent all other variables. Of course, we should not exclude relevant and important variables just to keep the regression model simple.

7. *Wrong functional form*: Even if we have theoretically correct variables explaining a phenomenon and even if we can obtain data on these variables, very often we do not know the form of the functional relationship between the regressand and the regressors. Is consumption expenditure a linear (in-variable) function of income or a nonlinear (in-variable) function? If it is the former, $Y_i = \beta_1 + \beta_2 X_i + u_i$ is the proper functional relationship between Y and X, but if it is the latter, $Y_i = \beta_1 + \beta_2 X_i + \beta_3 X_i^2 + u_i$ may be the correct functional form. In two-variable models the functional form of the relationship can often be judged from the scattergram. But in a multiple regression model, it is not easy to determine the appropriate functional form, for graphically we cannot visualize scattergrams in multiple dimensions.

For all these reasons, the stochastic disturbances u_i assume an extremely critical role in regression analysis, which we will see as we progress.

2.6 THE SAMPLE REGRESSION FUNCTION (SRF)

By confining our discussion so far to the population of Y values corresponding to the fixed X's, we have deliberately avoided sampling considerations (note that the data of Table 2.1 represent the population, not a sample). But it is about time to face up to the sampling problems, for in most practical situations what we have is but a sample of Y values corresponding to some fixed X's. Therefore, our task now is to estimate the PRF on the basis of the sample information.

As an illustration, pretend that the population of Table 2.1 was not known to us and the only information we had was a randomly selected sample of Y values for the fixed X's as given in Table 2.4. Unlike Table 2.1, we now have only one Y value corresponding to the given X's; each Y (given X_i) in Table 2.4 is chosen randomly from similar Y's corresponding to the same X_i from the population of Table 2.1.

The question is: From the sample of Table 2.4 can we predict the average weekly consumption expenditure Y in the population as a whole corresponding to the chosen X's? In other words, can we estimate the PRF from the sample data? As the reader surely suspects, we may not be able to estimate the PRF "accurately" because of sampling fluctuations. To see this, suppose we draw another random sample from the population of Table 2.1, as presented in Table 2.5.

Plotting the data of Tables 2.4 and 2.5, we obtain the scattergram given in Fig. 2.3. In the scattergram two sample regression lines are drawn so as to "fit" the scatters reasonably well: SRF_1 is based on the first sample, and SRF_2 is based on the second sample. Which of the two regression lines represents the "true" population regression line? If we avoid the temptation of looking at

TABLE 2.4
A random sample from the population of Table 2.1

Y	X
70	80
65	100
90	120
95	140
110	160
115	180
120	200
140	220
155	240
150	260

Fig. 2.1, which purportedly represents the PR, there is no way we can be absolutely sure that either of the regression lines shown in Fig. 2.3 represents the true population regression line (or curve). The regression lines in Fig. 2.3 are known as the **sample regression lines.** Supposedly they represent the population regression line, but because of sampling fluctuations they are at best an approximation of the true PR. In general, we would get N different SRFs for N different samples, and these SRFs are not likely to be the same.

Now, analogous to the PRF that underlies the population regression line, we can develop the concept of the **sample regression function** (SRF) to represent the sample regression line. The sample counterpart of (2.2.2) may be written as

$$\hat{Y}_i = \hat{\beta}_1 + \hat{\beta}_2 X_i \tag{2.6.1}$$

where $\hat{Y}$ is read as "Y-hat" or "Y-cap"
$\hat{Y}_i$ = estimator of $E(Y \mid X_i)$

TABLE 2.5
Another random sample from the population of Table 2.1

Y	X
55	80
88	100
90	120
80	140
118	160
120	180
145	200
135	220
145	240
175	260

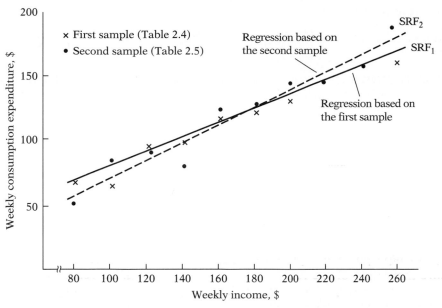

FIGURE 2.3
Regression lines based on two different samples.

where $\hat{\beta}_1$ = estimator of β_1

$\hat{\beta}_2$ = estimator of β_2

Note that an **estimator**, also known as a (sample) **statistic**, is simply a rule or formula or method that tells how to estimate the population parameter from the information provided by the sample at hand. A particular numerical value obtained by the estimator in an application is known as an **estimate**.[11]

Now just as we expressed the PRF in two equivalent forms, (2.2.2) and (2.4.2), we can express the SRF (2.6.1) in its stochastic form as follows:

$$Y_i = \hat{\beta}_1 + \hat{\beta}_2 X_i + \hat{u}_i \qquad (2.6.2)$$

where, in addition to the symbols already defined, $\hat{u}_i$ denotes the (sample) **residual** term. Conceptually $\hat{u}_i$ is analogous to u_i and can be regarded as an *estimate* of u_i. It is introduced in the SRF for the same reasons as u_i was introduced in the PRF.

To sum up, then, we find our primary objective in regression analysis is to estimate the PRF

$$Y_i = \beta_1 + \beta_2 X_i + u_i \qquad (2.4.2)$$

---

[11]As noted in the Introduction, a hat above a variable will signify an estimator of the relevant population value.

on the basis of the SRF

$$Y_i = \hat{\beta}_1 + \hat{\beta}_2 X_i + \hat{u}_i \qquad (2.6.2)$$

because more often than not our analysis is based upon a single sample from some population. But because of sampling fluctuations our estimate of the PRF based on the SRF is at best an approximate one. This approximation is shown diagrammatically in Fig. 2.4.

For $X = X_i$, we have one (sample) observation $Y = Y_i$. In terms of the SRF, the observed Y_i can be expressed as

$$Y_i = \hat{Y}_i + \hat{u}_i \qquad (2.6.3)$$

and in terms of the PRF, it can be expressed as

$$Y_i = E(Y \mid X_i) + u_i \qquad (2.6.4)$$

Now obviously in Fig. 2.4 $\hat{Y}_i$ *overestimates* the true $E(Y \mid X_i)$ for the X_i shown therein. By the same token, for any X_i to the left of the point A, the SRF will *underestimate* the true PRF. But the reader can readily see that such over- and underestimation is inevitable because of sampling fluctuations.

The critical question now is: Granted that the SRF is but an approximation of the PRF, can we devise a rule or a method that will make this approximation as "close" as possible? In other words, how should the SRF be constructed so that $\hat{\beta}_1$ is as "close" as possible to the true β_1 and $\hat{\beta}_2$ is as "close" as possible to the true β_2 even though we will never know the true β_1 and β_2?

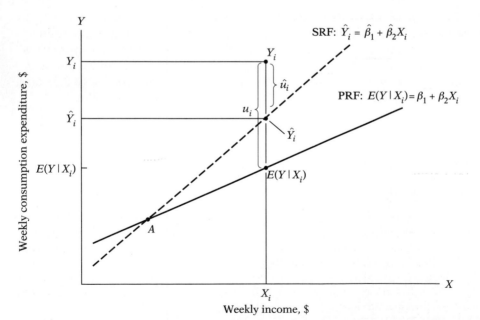

FIGURE 2.4
Sample and population regression lines.

The answer to this question will occupy much of our attention in Chapter 3. We note here that we can develop procedures that tell us how to construct the SRF to mirror the PRF as faithfully as possible. It is fascinating to consider that this can be done even though we never actually determine the PRF itself.

2.7 SUMMARY AND CONCLUSIONS

1. The key concept underlying regression analysis is the concept of the **population regression function** (PRF).

2. This book deals with linear PRFs, that is, regressions that are linear in the unknown parameters. They may or may not be linear in the dependent variable or regressand Y and the independent variable(s) or regressor(s) X.

3. For empirical purposes, it is the stochastic PRF that matters. The stochastic disturbance term u_i plays a critical role in estimating the PRF.

4. The PRF is an idealized concept, since in practice one rarely has access to the entire population of interest. Generally, one has a sample of observations from the population. Therefore, one uses the stochastic sample regression function (SRF) to estimate the PRF. How this is accomplished is considered in Chapter 3.

EXERCISES

2.1. The following table gives the anticipated one-year rates of return from a certain investment and their associated probabilities.

Rate of return X, %	Probability, p_i
−20	0.10
−10	0.15
10	0.45
25	0.25
30	0.05

Using the definitions given in Appendix A, do the following:
(a) Calculate the expected rate of return, $E(X)$.
(b) Calculate the variance (σ^2) and standard deviation (σ) of the returns.
(c) Calculate the coefficient of variation, V, defined as $V = \sigma/E(X)$. *Note:* V is often multiplied by 100 to express it in the percentage form.
(d) Using the definition of skewness, estimate the skewness of the distribution of rates of return given in the table. Is the distribution of returns in the present example positively skewed or negatively skewed?
(e) Using the definition of kurtosis, estimate the kurtosis in the present example. Is the distribution of rates of return given in the table **leptokurtic** (narrow-tailed) or **platykurtic** (longer-tailed)?

2.2 The following table gives the joint probability distribution, $p(X, Y)$, of variables X and Y.

X Y	1	2	3
1	0.03	0.06	0.06
2	0.02	0.04	0.04
3	0.09	0.18	0.18
4	0.06	0.12	0.12

Using the definitions given in Appendix A, determine the following:
(a) Marginal or unconditional probability distributions of X and Y.
(b) Conditional probability distributions $p(X \mid Y_i)$ and $p(Y \mid X_i)$.
(c) Conditional expectations $E(X \mid Y_i)$ and $E(Y \mid X_i)$.

2.3 The following table gives the joint probability distribution $p(X, Y)$ of random variables X and Y where X = the first-year rate of return (%) expected from project A and Y = the first-year rate of return (%) expected from project B.

X Y	−10	0	20	30
20	0.27	0.08	0.16	0.00
50	0.00	0.04	0.10	0.35

(a) Calculate the expected rate of return from project A, $E(X)$.
(b) Calculate the expected rate of return from project B, $E(Y)$.
(c) Are the rates of return of the two projects independent? (*Hint* : Is $E(XY) = E(X)E(Y)$?) Note that

$$E(X\,Y) = \sum_{i=1}^{4}\sum_{j=1}^{2} X_i Y_j p(X_i Y_j)$$

2.4 For 50 married couples the ages (in years) of wife X and husband Y are grouped in the following table with class intervals of 10 years for each, the frequencies for the different classes being shown in the body of the table. The values of X and Y shown are the midvalues in the classes.

X Y	20	30	40	50	60	70	Total
20	1						1
30	2	11	1				14
40		4	10	1			15
50			3	6	1		10
60				2	3	2	7
70					1	2	3
Total	3	15	14	9	5	4	50

Thus, for the class in which the age of the husband is between 35 and 45 and the age of the wife is between 25 and 35, the values of Y and X are taken (as centered on) 40 and 30, respectively, and the frequency is 4.
(a) Determine the mean of each array, that is, of each row and each column.
(b) Using the abscissa for the X variable and the ordinate for the Y variable, plot

the array (or conditional) means obtained previously. You may use a + symbol for the column means and $\oplus$ for the row means.

(c) What can you say about the relationship between X and Y?

(d) Do the conditional row and column means lie on approximately straight lines? Sketch the regression lines.

2.5 The following table gives the rating (X) and the yield to maturity $Y(\%)$ of 50 bonds, where the rating is measured at three levels: $X = 1$ (Bbb), $X = 2$ (Bb), and $X = 3$ (B). Per Standard & Poor's bond rating, Bbb, Bb, and B are all medium-quality bonds, Bb being slightly higher-rated than B and Bbb slightly higher-rated than Bb.

Y \ X	1 Bbb	2 Bb	3 B	Total
8.5	13	5	0	18
11.5	2	14	2	18
17.5	0	1	13	14
Total	15	20	15	50

(a) Convert the preceding table into a table giving the joint probability distribution, $p(X, Y)$, e.g., $p(X = 1, Y = 8.5) = 13/50 = .26$.

(b) Compute $p(Y \mid X = 1), p(Y \mid X = 2)$, and $p(Y \mid X = 3)$.

(c) Compute $E(Y \mid X = 1), E(Y \mid X = 2)$, and $E(Y \mid X = 3)$.

(d) Are the computed rates of return in (c) in accord with a priori expectations about the relationship between bond rating and the yield to maturity?

*2.6 The joint density function of two continuous random variables X and Y is as follows

$$f(X, Y) = 4 - X - Y \qquad 0 \le X \le 1; \qquad 0 \le Y \le 1$$
$$= 0 \qquad\qquad \text{otherwise}$$

(a) Find the marginal density functions, $f(X)$ and $f(Y)$.

(b) Find the conditional density functions, $f(X \mid Y)$ and $f(Y \mid X)$.

(c) Find $E(X)$ and $E(Y)$.

(d) Find $E(X \mid Y = 0.4)$.

2.7 Consider the data at the top of the next page.

(a) What do the preceding data suggest?

(b) Is age or experience more closely related to salary level? How do you know?

(c) Draw two separate figures, one showing median salary in relation to age and another showing median salary in relation to professional experience (in years).

2.8 Examine the data at the bottom of the next page.

(a) Using the Y axis for mean money earnings and the X axis to represent these levels of education—8 years or less, 1–3 years of high school, 4 years of high school, 1–3 years of college, 4 years of college, and 5 or more years of college— plot the data for males and females separately for each age group.

(b) What general conclusions can you draw?

---

* Optional.

Median salaries of economists in selected age and experience groups, national register, 1966 (thousands of dollars)

| Age | \multicolumn{10}{c}{Years of professional experience} |
	0–2	2–4	5–9	10–14	15–19	20–24	25–29	30–34	35–39	40–44*
20–24	7.5									
25–29	9.0	9.1	10.0							
30–34	9.0	9.5	11.0	12.6						
35–39		10.0	11.7	13.2	15.0					
40–44		9.6	11.0	13.0	15.5	17.0				
45–49				12.0	15.0	17.0	20.0			
50–54				11.3	13.3	15.0	18.2	20.0		
55–59						13.8	16.0	18.0	19.0	
60–64							13.1	16.0	17.2	18.8
65–69									13.8	17.0
70–74†										12.5

Note: Selected groups comprise all those represented by 25 or more respondents who reported the indicated combinations of age and experience.

*The actual category is 40 or more.

†The actual category is 70 and over.

Source: N. Arnold Tolles and Emanuel Melichar, "Studies of the Structure of Economists' Salaries and Income," *American Economic Review*, vol. 57, no. 5, pt. 2, Suppl., December 1968, table H, p. 119.

Mean money earnings of persons, by educational attainment, sex, and age: 1990 (In dollars. For year-round full-time workers 25 years old and over. As of March 1991)

| Age and sex | Total | Ele-men-tary, 8 years or less | High school | | | College | | | |
			Total	1–3 years	4 years	Total	1–3 years	4 years	5 or more years
Male, total	34,886	19,188	27,131	22,564	28,043	43,217	34,188	44,554	55,831
25 to 34 years old	27,743	15,887	23,255	19,453	24,038	33,003	28,298	35,534	39,833
35 to 44 years old	37,958	18,379	28,205	23,621	28,927	45,819	36,180	47,401	58,542
45 to 54 years old	40,231	19,686	31,235	24,133	32,862	50,545	39,953	50,718	62,902
55 to 64 years old	37,469	22,379	29,460	25,280	30,779	50,585	36,954	55,518	61,647
65 years old and over	33,145	17,028	24,003	19,530	25,516	44,424	34,323	43,092	52,149
Female, total	22,768	13,322	18,469	15,381	18,954	27,493	22,654	28,911	35,827
25 to 34 years old	21,337	11,832	16,673	13,385	17,076	25,194	20,872	27,210	32,563
35 to 44 years old	24,453	13,714	19,344	15,695	19,886	29,287	23,307	31,631	37,599
45 to 54 years old	23,429	13,490	19,500	16,651	19,986	29,334	24,608	29,242	38,307
55 to 64 years old	21,388	13,941	18,607	15,202	19,382	26,930	23,364	27,975	33,383
65 years old and over	19,194	*	18,281	*	18,285	23,277	*	*	*

*Base figure too small to meet statistical standards for reliability of derived figure.

Source: Statistical Abstract of the United States, 1992, U.S. Department of Commerce, Table 713, p. 454.

2.9 Examine the following table:

Median salaries of economists (thousands of dollars) by academic degrees, 1966

Years of experience	Ph.D.	Masters	Bachelors
Under 2	9.8	8.0	9.0
2–4	10.0	8.8	8.9
5–9	11.5	10.5	10.6
10–14	13.0	12.3	13.0
15–19	15.0	15.0	15.6
20–24	16.2	15.6	17.0
25–29	18.0	17.0	20.0
30–34	17.9	17.7	20.0
35–39	16.9	16.2	20.5
40–44*	17.5	14.2	22.0

*The actual category is 40 or more.

Source: N. Arnold Tolles and Emanuel Melichar, "Studies of the Structure of Economists' Salaries and Income," *American Economic Review*, vol. 57, no. 5, pt. 2, Suppl., December 1968, table III-B-3, p. 92.

(a) Plot the median salaries for the three groups against the midvalues of the various years of experience intervals and sketch the regression lines.
(b) What factors account for the differences in the salaries of the three groups of economists? Especially, why is it that economists with a bachelor's degree earn more than their Ph.D. counterparts for 15 or more years of experience? Does this observation imply that it does not pay to hold a Ph.D. degree?

2.10 Consider the following table:

Number of economists by years of experience and age (full-time professionally employed economists only)

Age group (years)	Years of experience						Total
	0–2	2–4	5–9	10–14	15–19	20–24*	
20–24	24	13	1	–	–	–	38
25–29	121	405	184	–	–	–	710
30–34	77	497	825	197	3	–	1599
35–39	18	125	535	780	194	1	1653
40–44	6	36	161	652	761	235	1851
45–49	1	15	48	183	433	751	1431
50–54	1	5	19	52	119	784	980
55–59	1	2	10	18	27	612	670
60–64	1	–	3	6	8	382	400
65–69	–	1	1	2	4	206	214
70–74†	–	–	–	–	1	27	28
Total	250	1099	1787	1890	1550	2998	9574

*The actual category is 20 or more.

†The actual category is 70 and over.

Source: Adapted from "The Structure of Economists' Employment and Salaries, 1964," *American Economic Review*, vol. 55, no. 4, December 1965, table VII, p. 40.

The preceding table gives the joint absolute frequencies of the variables age and years of experience. Using relative frequencies (absolute frequencies divided by the total number) as measures of probabilities, do the following:

(a) Obtain the joint probability distribution of age and years of experience.

(b) Obtain the conditional probability distributions of age for various years of experience.

(c) Obtain the conditional probability distribution of years of experience for various ages.

(d) Using the midpoints of the various age and years of experience intervals, obtain the conditional means from the distributions derived in (b) and (c).

(e) Draw appropriate scattergrams showing the various conditional means.

(f) If you connect the conditional means shown in (e), what do you obtain?

(g) What can you say about the relationship between years of experience and age?

2.11 Determine whether the following models are linear in the parameters, or the variables, or both. Which of these models are linear regression models?

Model	**Descriptive Title**
$(a)\ Y_i = \beta_1 + \beta_2 \left(\dfrac{1}{X_i}\right) + u_i$	Reciprocal
$(b)\ Y_i = \beta_1 + \beta_2 \ln X_i + u_i$	Semilogarithmic
$(c)\ \ln Y_i = \beta_1 + \beta_2 X_i + u_i$	Inverse semilogarithmic
$(d)\ \ln Y_i = \ln \beta_1 + \beta_2 \ln X_i + u_i$	Logarithmic or double logarithmic
$(e)\ \ln Y_i = \beta_1 - \beta_2 \left(\dfrac{1}{X_i}\right) + u_i$	Logarithmic reciprocal

Note: ln = natural log (i.e., log to the base e); u_i is the stochastic disturbance term. We will study these models in Chapter 6.

2.12 Are the following models linear regression models? Why or why not?

(a) $Y_i = e^{\beta_1 + \beta_2 X_i + u_i}$

(b) $Y_i = \dfrac{1}{1 + e^{\beta_1 + \beta_2 X_i + u_i}}$

(c) $\ln Y_i = \beta_1 + \beta_2 \left(\dfrac{1}{X_i}\right) + u_i$

(d) $Y_i = \beta_1 + (0.75 - \beta_1)e^{-\beta_2(X_i - 2)} + u_i$

(e) $Y_i = \beta_1 + \beta_2^3 X_i + u_i$

2.13 If $\beta_2 = 0.8$ in (d) of problem 2.12, would the model become a linear regression model? Why?

*2.14 Consider the following nonstochastic models. Are they linear models, that is, models linear in the parameters? If not, is it not possible, by suitable algebraic manipulations, to convert them into linear models?

(a) $Y_i = \dfrac{1}{\beta_1 + \beta_2 X_i}$

(b) $Y_i = \dfrac{X_i}{\beta_1 + \beta_2 X_i}$

(c) $Y_i = \dfrac{1}{1 + \exp(-\beta_1 - \beta_2 X_i)}$

*2.15 A discrete random variable X has a (discrete) **rectangular** or **uniform distribution** if its PDF is of the following form:

---

* Optional.

$$f(X) = 1/k \quad \text{for } X = X_1, X_2, \ldots, X_k \qquad [X_i \neq X_j \text{ when } i \neq j]$$

(a) Show that for this distribution $E(X) = \sum X_i(1/k)$ and the variance $\sigma_X^2 = \sum [X_i - E(X_i)]^2 \cdot (1/k)$, where $E(X)$ is as just shown.

(b) What are the values of $E(X)$ and σ_X^2 if $X = 1, 2, \ldots, k$?

2.16 The following table gives data on mean Scholastic Aptitude Test (SAT) scores for college-bound seniors for 1967–1990.

(a) Use the horizontal axis for years and the vertical axis for SAT scores to plot the verbal and math scores for males and females separately.

(b) What general conclusions can you draw?

Mean Scholastic Aptitude Test scores for college-bound seniors, 1967–1990*

Year	Verbal			Math		
	Males	**Females**	**Total**	**Males**	**Females**	**Total**
1967	463	468	466	514	467	492
1968	464	466	466	512	470	492
1969	459	466	463	513	470	493
1970	459	461	460	509	465	488
1971	454	457	455	507	466	488
1972	454	452	453	505	461	484
1973	446	443	445	502	460	481
1974	447	442	444	501	459	480
1975	437	431	434	495	449	472
1976	433	430	431	497	446	472
1977	431	427	429	497	445	470
1978	433	425	429	494	444	468
1979	431	423	427	493	443	467
1980	428	420	424	491	443	466
1981	430	418	424	492	443	466
1982	431	421	426	493	443	467
1983	430	420	425	493	445	468
1984	433	420	426	495	449	471
1985	437	425	431	499	452	475
1986	437	426	431	501	451	475
1987	435	425	430	500	453	476
1988	435	422	428	498	455	476
1989	434	421	427	500	454	476
1990	429	419	424	499	455	476

*Data for 1967–1971 are estimates.

Source: The College Board. The *New York Times*, Aug. 28, 1990, p. B-5.

(c) Knowing the verbal scores of males and females, how would you go about predicting their math scores?

(d) Plot the female total SAT score against the male total SAT score. Sketch a regression line through the scatter points. What do you observe?

2.17 Is the regression line shown in Fig. I.3 of the Introduction the PRF or the SRF? Why? How would you interpret the scatter points around the regression line? Besides GDP, what other factors, or variables, might determine personal consumption expenditure?

CHAPTER
3

TWO-VARIABLE REGRESSION MODEL: THE PROBLEM OF ESTIMATION

As noted in Chapter 2, our first task is to estimate the population regression function (PRF) on the basis of the sample regression function (SRF) as accurately as possible. There are several methods of constructing the SRF, but insofar as regression analysis is concerned, the method that is used most extensively is the **method of ordinary least squares (OLS)**.[1] In this chapter we shall discuss this method in terms of the two-variable regression model. The generalization of the method to multiple regression models is given in Chapter 7.

3.1 THE METHOD OF ORDINARY LEAST SQUARES

The method of ordinary least squares is attributed to Carl Friedrich Gauss, a German mathematician. Under certain assumptions (discussed in Section 3.2), the method of least squares has some very attractive statistical properties that have made it one of the most powerful and popular methods of regression analysis. To understand this method, we first explain the least-squares principle.

Recall the two-variable PRF:

$$Y_i = \beta_1 + \beta_2 X_i + u_i \qquad (2.4.2)$$

---

[1]Another method, known as the *method of maximum likelihood,* will be considered very briefly in Chap. 4.

However, as we noted in Chapter 2, the PRF is not directly observable. We estimate it from the SRF:

$$Y_i = \hat{\beta}_1 + \hat{\beta}_2 X_i + \hat{u}_i \qquad (2.6.2)$$

$$= \hat{Y}_i + \hat{u}_i \qquad (2.6.3)$$

where $\hat{Y}_i$ is the estimated (conditional mean) value of Y_i.

But how is the SRF itself determined? To see this, let us proceed as follows. First, express (2.6.3) as

$$\hat{u}_i = Y_i - \hat{Y}_i$$

$$= Y_i - \hat{\beta}_1 - \hat{\beta}_2 X_i \qquad (3.1.1)$$

which shows that the $\hat{u}_i$ (the residuals) are simply the differences between the actual and estimated Y values.

Now given n pairs of observations on Y and X, we would like to determine the SRF in such a manner that it is as close as possible to the actual Y. To this end, we may adopt the following criterion: Choose the SRF in such a way that the sum of the residuals $\sum \hat{u}_i = \sum (Y_i - \hat{Y}_i)$ is as small as possible. Although intuitively appealing, this is not a very good criterion, as can be seen in the hypothetical scattergram shown in Fig. 3.1.

If we adopt the criterion of minimizing $\sum \hat{u}_i$, Fig. 3.1 shows that the residuals $\hat{u}_2$ and $\hat{u}_3$ as well as the residuals $\hat{u}_1$ and $\hat{u}_4$ receive the same weight in the sum $(\hat{u}_1 + \hat{u}_2 + \hat{u}_3 + \hat{u}_4)$, although the first two residuals are much closer to the SRF than the latter two. In other words, all the residuals receive equal importance no matter how close or how widely scattered the individual observations

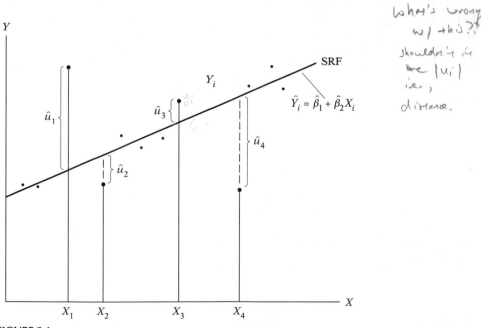

FIGURE 3.1
Least-squares criterion.

are from the SRF. A consequence of this is that it is quite possible that the algebraic sum of the $\hat{u}_i$ is small (even zero) although the $\hat{u}_i$ are widely scattered about the SRF. To see this, let $\hat{u}_1$, $\hat{u}_2$, $\hat{u}_3$, and $\hat{u}_4$ in Fig. 3.1 assume the values of 10, -2, $+2$, and -10, respectively. The algebraic sum of these residuals is zero although $\hat{u}_1$ and $\hat{u}_4$ are scattered more widely around the SRF than $\hat{u}_2$ and $\hat{u}_3$. We can avoid this problem if we adopt the _least-squares criterion,_ which states that the SRF can be fixed in such way that

$$\sum \hat{u}_i^2 = \sum (Y_i - \hat{Y}_i)^2$$
$$= \sum (Y_i - \hat{\beta}_1 - \hat{\beta}_2 X_i)^2 \tag{3.1.2}$$

is as small as possible, where $\hat{u}_i^2$ are the squared residuals. By squaring $\hat{u}_i$, this method gives more weight to residuals such as $\hat{u}_1$ and $\hat{u}_4$ in Fig. 3.1 than the residuals $\hat{u}_2$ and $\hat{u}_3$. As noted previously, under the minimum $\sum \hat{u}_i$ criterion, the sum can be small even though the $\hat{u}_i$ are widely spread about the SRF. But this is not possible under the least-squares procedure, for the larger the $\hat{u}_i$ (in absolute value), the larger the $\sum \hat{u}_i^2$. A further justification for the least-squares method lies in the fact that the estimators obtained by it have some very desirable statistical properties, as we shall see shortly.

It is obvious from (3.1.2) that

$$\sum \hat{u}_i^2 = f(\hat{\beta}_1, \hat{\beta}_2) \tag{3.1.3}$$

that is, the sum of the squared residuals is some function of the estimators $\hat{\beta}_1$ and $\hat{\beta}_2$. For any given set of data, choosing different values for $\hat{\beta}_1$ and $\hat{\beta}_2$ will give different $\hat{u}$'s and hence different values of $\sum \hat{u}_i^2$. To see this clearly, consider the hypothetical data on Y and X given in the first two columns of Table 3.1. Let us now conduct two experiments. In experiment 1, let $\hat{\beta}_1 = 1.572$ and $\hat{\beta}_2 = 1.357$ (let us not worry right now about how we got these values; say, it is just a guess).[2] Using these $\hat{\beta}$ values and the X values given in column

TABLE 3.1
Experimental determination of the SRF

Y_i (1)	X_t (2)	$\hat{Y}_{1i}$ (3)	$\hat{u}_{1i}$ (4)	$\hat{u}_{1i}^2$ (5)	$\hat{Y}_{2i}$ (6)	$\hat{u}_{2i}$ (7)	$\hat{u}_{2i}^2$ (8)
4	1	2.929	1.071	1.147	4	0	0
5	4	7.000	-2.000	4.000	7	-2	4
7	5	8.357	-1.357	1.841	8	-1	1
12	6	9.714	2.286	5.226	9	3	9
Sum: 28	16		0.0	12.214		0	14

Notes: $\hat{Y}_{1i} = 1.572 + 1.357 X_i$ (i.e., $\hat{\beta}_1 = 1.572$ and $\hat{\beta}_2 = 1.357$)
$\hat{Y}_{2i} = 3.0 + 1.0 X_i$ (i.e., $\hat{\beta}_1 = 3$ and $\hat{\beta}_2 = 1.0$)
$\hat{u}_{1i} = (Y_i - \hat{Y}_{1i})$
$\hat{u}_{2i} = (Y_i - \hat{Y}_{2i})$

---

[2]For the curious, these values are obtained by the method of least squares, discussed shortly. See Eqs. (3.1.6) and (3.1.7).

(2) of Table 3.1, we can easily compute the estimated Y_i given in column (3) of the table as $\hat{Y}_{1i}$ (the subscript 1 is to denote the first experiment). Now let us conduct another experiment, but this time using the values of $\hat{\beta}_1 = 3$ and $\hat{\beta}_2 = 1$. The estimated values of Y_i from this experiment are given as $\hat{Y}_{2i}$ in column (6) of Table 3.1. Since the $\hat{\beta}$ values in the two experiments are different, we get different values for the estimated residuals, as shown in the table; $\hat{u}_{1i}$ are the residuals from the first experiment and $\hat{u}_{2i}$ from the second experiment. The squares of these residuals are given in columns (5) and (8). Obviously, as expected from (3.1.3), these residual sums of squares are different since they are based on different sets of $\hat{\beta}$ values.

Now which sets of $\hat{\beta}$ values should we choose? Since the $\hat{\beta}$ values of the first experiment give us a lower $\sum \hat{u}_i^2 (= 12.214)$ than that obtained from the $\hat{\beta}$ values of the second experiment $(= 14)$, we might say that the $\hat{\beta}$'s of the first experiment are the "best" values. But how do we know? For, if we had infinite time and infinite patience, we could have conducted many more such experiments, choosing different sets of $\hat{\beta}$s each time and comparing the resulting $\sum \hat{u}_i^2$ and then choosing that set of $\hat{\beta}$ values that gives us the least possible value of $\sum \hat{u}_i^2$ assuming of course that we have considered all the conceivable values of β_1 and β_2. But since time, and certainly patience, are generally in short supply, we need to consider some shortcuts to this trial-and-error process. Fortunately, the method of least squares provides us such a shortcut. The principle or the method of least squares chooses $\hat{\beta}_1$ and $\hat{\beta}_2$ in such a manner that for a given sample or set of data $\sum \hat{u}_i^2$ is as small as possible. In other words, for a given sample, the method of least squares provides us with unique estimates of β_1 and β_2 that give the smallest possible value of $\sum \hat{u}_i^2$. How is this accomplished? This is a straight-forward exercise in differential calculus. As shown in Appendix 3A, Section 3A.1, the process of differentiation yields the following equations for estimating β_1 and β_2:

$$\sum Y_i = n\hat{\beta}_1 + \hat{\beta}_2 \sum X_i \tag{3.1.4}$$

$$\sum Y_i X_i = \hat{\beta}_1 \sum X_i + \hat{\beta}_2 \sum X_i^2 \tag{3.1.5}$$

where n is the sample size. These simultaneous equations are known as the **normal equations.**

Solving the normal equations simultaneously, we obtain

$$\hat{\beta}_2 = \frac{n \sum X_i Y_i - \sum X_i \sum Y_i}{n \sum X_i^2 - (\sum X_i)^2}$$

$$= \frac{\sum (X_i - \bar{X})(Y_i - \bar{Y})}{\sum (X_i - \bar{X})^2}$$

$$= \frac{\sum x_i y_i}{\sum x_i^2} \tag{3.1.6}$$

where $\bar{X}$ and $\bar{Y}$ are the sample means of X and Y and where we define $x_i = (X_i - \bar{X})$ and $y_i = (Y_i - \bar{Y})$. *Henceforth we adopt the convention of letting the lowercase letters denote deviations from mean values.*

$$\hat{\beta}_1 = \frac{\sum X_i^2 \sum Y_i - \sum X_i \sum X_i Y_i}{n \sum X_i^2 - (\sum X_i)^2}$$

$$= \bar{Y} - \hat{\beta}_2 \bar{X} \tag{3.1.7}$$

The last step in (3.1.7) can be obtained directly from (3.1.4) by simple algebraic manipulations.

Incidentally, note that, by making use of simple algebraic identities, formula (3.1.6) for estimating β_2 can be alternatively expressed as

$$\hat{\beta}_2 = \frac{\sum x_i y_i}{\sum x_i^2}$$

$$= \frac{\sum x_i Y_i}{\sum X_i^2 - n\bar{X}^2} \tag{3.1.8}[3]$$

$$= \frac{\sum X_i y_i}{\sum X_i^2 - n\bar{X}^2}$$

which may reduce the computational burden if one uses a hand calculator to solve a regression problem involving a small set of data.

The estimators obtained previously are known as the **least-squares estimators,** for they are derived from the least-squares principle. Note the following **numerical properties** of estimators obtained by the method of OLS: "Numerical properties are those that hold as a consequence of the use of ordinary least squares, regardless of how the data were generated."[4] Shortly, we will also consider the **statistical properties** of OLS estimators, that is, properties "that hold only under certain assumptions about the way the data were generated."[5] (See the classical linear regression model in Section 3.2.)

I. The OLS estimators are expressed solely in terms of the observable (i.e., sample) quantities (i.e., X and Y). Therefore, they can be easily computed.

II. They are **point estimators,** that is, given the sample, each estimator will provide only a single (point) value of the relevant population parameter. (In Chapter 5 we will consider the so-called **interval estimators,** which

---

[3]*Note 1:* $\sum x_i^2 = \sum (X_i - \bar{X})^2 = \sum X_i^2 - 2\sum X_i \bar{X} + \sum \bar{X}^2 = \sum X_i^2 - 2\bar{X}\sum X_i + \sum \bar{X}^2$, since $\bar{X}$ is a constant. Further noting that $\sum X_i = n\bar{X}$ and $\sum \bar{X}^2 = n\bar{X}^2$ since $\bar{X}$ is a constant, we finally get $\sum x_i^2 = \sum X_i^2 - n\bar{X}^2$.

Note 2: $\sum x_i y_i = \sum x_i (Y_i - \bar{Y}) = \sum x_i Y_i - \bar{Y}\sum x_i = \sum x_i Y_i - \bar{Y}\sum (X_i - \bar{X}) = \sum x_i Y_i$, since $\bar{Y}$ is a constant and since the sum of deviations of a variable from its mean value [e.g., $\sum (X_i - \bar{X})$] is always zero. Likewise, $\sum y_i = \sum (Y_i - \bar{Y}) = 0$.

[4]Russell Davidson and James G. MacKinnon, *Estimation and Inference in Econometrics*, Oxford University Press, New York, 1993, p. 3.

[5]*Ibid.*

provide a range of possible values for the unknown population parameters.)

III. Once the OLS estimates are obtained from the sample data, the sample regression line (Fig. 3.1) can be easily obtained. The regression line thus obtained has the following properties:

1. It passes through the sample means of Y and X. This fact is obvious from (3.1.7), for the latter can be written as $\bar{Y} = \hat{\beta}_1 + \hat{\beta}_2\bar{X}$, which is shown diagrammatically in Fig. 3.2.

2. The mean value of the estimated $Y = \hat{Y}_i$ is equal to the mean value of the actual Y for

$$\hat{Y}_i = \hat{\beta}_1 + \hat{\beta}_2 X_i$$

$$= (\bar{Y} - \hat{\beta}_2\bar{X}) + \hat{\beta}_2 X_i$$

$$= \bar{Y} + \hat{\beta}_2(X_i - \bar{X}) \qquad (3.1.9)$$

Summing both sides of this last equality over the sample values and dividing through by the sample size n gives

$$\bar{\hat{Y}} = \bar{Y} \qquad (3.1.10)^6$$

where use is made of the fact that $\sum(X_i - \bar{X}) = 0$. (Why?)

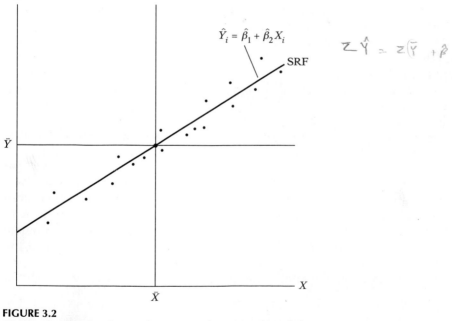

FIGURE 3.2
Diagram showing that the sample regression line passes through the sample mean values of Y and X.

---

[6]Note that this result is true only when the regression model has the intercept term β_1 in it. As App. 6A, Sec. 6A.1 shows, this result need not hold when β_1 is absent from the model.

3. The mean value of the residuals $\hat{u}_i$ is zero. From Appendix 3A, Section 3A.1, the first equation is

$$-2\sum(Y_i - \hat{\beta}_1 - \hat{\beta}_2 X_i) = 0$$

But since $\hat{u}_i = Y_i - \hat{\beta}_1 - \hat{\beta}_2 X_i$, the preceding equation reduces to $-2\sum \hat{u}_i = 0$, whence $\hat{u} = 0$.[7]

As a result of the proceeding property, the sample regression

$$Y_i = \hat{\beta}_1 + \hat{\beta}_2 X_i + \hat{u}_i \qquad (2.6.2)$$

can be expressed in an alternative form where both Y and X are expressed as deviations from their mean values. To see this, sum (2.6.2) on both sides to give

$$\sum Y_i = n\hat{\beta}_1 + \hat{\beta}_2 \sum X_i + \sum \hat{u}_i \qquad (3.1.11)$$

$$= n\hat{\beta}_1 + \hat{\beta}_2 \sum X_i \qquad \text{since } \sum \hat{u}_i = 0$$

Dividing Equation (3.1.11) through by n, we obtain

$$\bar{Y} = \hat{\beta}_1 + \hat{\beta}_2 \bar{X} \qquad (3.1.12)$$

which is the same as (3.1.7). Subtracting Equation (3.1.12) from (2.6.2), we obtain

$$Y_i - \bar{Y} = \hat{\beta}_2(X_i - \bar{X}) + \hat{u}_i$$

or

$$y_i = \hat{\beta}_2 x_i + \hat{u}_i \qquad (3.1.13)$$

where y_i and x_i, following our convention, are deviations from their respective (sample) mean values.

Equation (3.1.13) is known as the **deviation form.** Notice that the intercept term $\hat{\beta}_1$ is no longer present in it. But the intercept term can always be estimated by (3.1.7), that is, from the fact that the sample regression line passes through the sample means of Y and X. An advantage of the deviation form is that it often simplifies arithmetical calculations while working on a desk calculator. But in this age of the computer, this advantage may be rather minor.

In passing, note that in the deviation form, the SRF can be written as

$$\hat{y}_i = \hat{\beta}_2 x_i \qquad (3.1.14)$$

---

[7] This result also requires that the intercept term β_1 be present in the model (see App. 6A, Sec. 6A.1).

whereas in the original units of measurement it was $\hat{Y}_i = \hat{\beta}_1 + \hat{\beta}_2 X_i$, as shown in (2.6.1).

4. The residuals $\hat{u}_i$ are uncorrelated with the predicted Y_i. This statement can be verified as follows: using the deviation form, we can write

$$
\begin{aligned}
\sum \hat{y}_i \hat{u}_i &= \hat{\beta}_2 \sum x_i \hat{u}_i \\
&= \hat{\beta}_2 \sum x_i (y_i - \hat{\beta}_2 x_i) \\
&= \hat{\beta}_2 \sum x_i y_i - \hat{\beta}_2^2 \sum x_i^2 \\
&= \hat{\beta}_2^2 \sum x_i^2 - \hat{\beta}_2^2 \sum x_i^2 \\
&= 0
\end{aligned}
\tag{3.1.15}
$$

where use is made of the fact that $\hat{\beta}_2 = \sum x_i y_i / \sum x_i^2$.

5. The residuals $\hat{u}_i$ are uncorrelated with X_i; that is, $\sum \hat{u}_i X_i = 0$. This fact follows from Eq. (2) in Appendix 3A, Section 3A.1.

3.2 THE CLASSICAL LINEAR REGRESSION MODEL: THE ASSUMPTIONS UNDERLYING THE METHOD OF LEAST SQUARES

If our objective is to estimate β_1 and β_2 only, the method of OLS discussed in the preceding section will suffice. But recall from Chapter 2 that in regression analysis our objective is not only to obtain $\hat{\beta}_1$ and $\hat{\beta}_2$ but also to draw inferences about the true β_1 and β_2. For example, we would like to know how close $\hat{\beta}_1$ and $\hat{\beta}_2$ are to their counterparts in the population or how close is $\hat{Y}_i$ to the true $E(Y \mid X_i)$. To that end, we must not only specify the functional form of the model, as in (2.4.2), but also make certain assumptions about the manner in which Y_i are generated. To see why this requirement is needed, look at the PRF: $Y_i = \beta_1 + \beta_2 X_i + u_i$. It shows that Y_i depends on both X_i and u_i. Therefore, unless we are specific about how X_i and u_i are created or generated, there is no way we can make any statistical inference about the Y_i and also, as we shall see, about β_1 and β_2. Thus, the assumptions made about the X_i variable(s) and the error term are extremely critical to the valid interpretation of the regression estimates.

The Gaussian, standard, or classical linear regression model (CLRM), which is the cornerstone of most econometric theory, makes 10 assumptions.[8] We first discuss these assumptions in the context of the two-variable regression model; and in Chapter 7 we extend them to multiple regression models, that is, models in which there is more than one regressor.

---

[8]It is classical in the sense that it was developed first by Gauss in 1821 and since then has served as a norm or a standard against which may be compared the regression models that do not satisfy the Gaussian assumptions.

> **Assumption 1: Linear regression model.** The regression model is **linear in the parameters,** as shown in (2.4.2)
>
> $$Y_i = \beta_1 + \beta_2 X_i + u_i \qquad (2.4.2)$$

We already discussed model (2.4.2) in Chapter 2. Since linear-in-parameter regression models are the starting point of the CLRM, we will maintain this assumption throughout this book. Keep in mind that the regressand Y and the regressor X themselves may be nonlinear, as discussed in Chapter 2.[9]

> **Assumption 2: X values are fixed in repeated sampling.** Values taken by the regressor X are considered fixed in repeated samples. More technically, X is assumed to be *nonstochastic.*

This assumption is implicit in our discussion of the PRF in Chapter 2. But it is very important to understand the concept of "fixed values in repeated sampling," which can be explained in terms of our example given in Table 2.1. Consider the various Y populations corresponding to the levels of income shown in that table. Keeping the value of income X fixed, say, at level \$80, we draw at random a family and observe its weekly family consumption expenditure Y as, say, \$60. Still keeping X at \$80, we draw at random another family and observe its Y value as \$75. In each of these drawings (i.e., repeated sampling), the value of X is fixed at \$80. We can repeat this process for all the X values shown in Table 2.1. As a matter of fact, the sample data shown in Tables 2.4 and 2.5 were drawn in this fashion.

What all this means is that our regression analysis is **conditional regression analysis,** that is, conditional on the given values of the regressor(s) X.

> **Assumption 3: Zero mean value of disturbance u_i.** Given the value of X, the mean, or expected, value of the random disturbance term u_i is zero. Technically, the conditional mean value of u_i is zero. Symbolically, we have
>
> $$E(u_i \mid X_i) = 0 \qquad (3.2.1)$$

Assumption 3 states that the mean value of u_i, conditional upon the given X_i, is zero. Geometrically, this assumption can be pictured as in Fig. 3.3, which shows a few values of the variable X and the Y populations associated with each of them. As shown, each Y population corresponding to a given X is distributed around its mean value (shown by the circled points on the PRF) with some Y values above the mean and some below it. The distances above and below

---

[9]This is not to suggest that nonlinear-in-parameter regression models are unimportant or rarely used. However, the level of mathematical and statistical knowledge required to deal with such models is beyond the scope of this introductory text. For an excellent discussion of nonlinear-in-parameter regression models, see Russell Davidson and James MacKinnon, *Estimation and Inference in Econometrics*, Oxford University Press, New York, 1993. This text is not for the beginner.

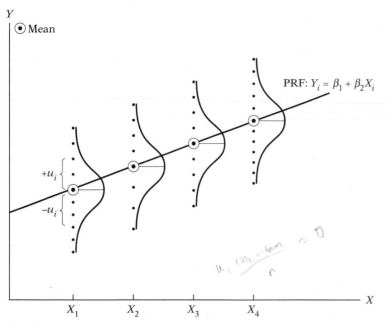

FIGURE 3.3
Conditional distribution of the disturbances u_i.

the mean values are nothing but the u_i, and what (3.2.1) requires is that the average or mean value of these deviations corresponding to any given X should be zero.[10]

This assumption should not be difficult to comprehend in view of the discussion in Section 2.4 (see Eq. 2.4.5). All that this assumption says is that the factors not explicitly included in the model, and therefore subsumed in u_i, do not systematically affect the mean value of Y; so to speak, the positive u_i values cancel out the negative u_i values so that their average or mean effect on Y is zero.[11]

In passing, note that the assumption $E(u_i \mid X_i) = 0$ implies that $E(Y_i \mid X_i) = \beta_i + \beta_2 X_i$. (Why?) Therefore, the two assumptions are equivalent.

> **Assumption 4: Homoscedasticity or equal variance of u_i.** Given the value of X, the variance of u_i is the same for all observations. That is, the conditional variances of u_i are identical. Symbolically, we have
>
> $$\mathbf{var}\,(u_i \mid X_i) = E\,[u_i - E\,(u_i)\mid X_i]^2$$
> $$= E(u_i^2 \mid X_i) \text{ because of Assumption 3}$$
> $$= \sigma^2 \qquad\qquad (3.2.2)$$
>
> where **var** stands for variance.

---

[10]For illustration, we are assuming merely that the u's are distributed symmetrically as shown in Fig. 3.3. But in Chap. 4 we shall assume that the u's are distributed normally.

[11]For a more technical reason why Assumption 3 is necessary see E. Malinvaud, *Statistical Methods of Econometrics*, Rand McNally, Chicago, 1966, p. 75. See also exercise 3.3.

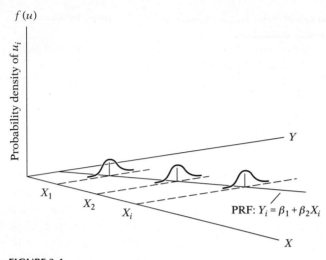

FIGURE 3.4
Homoscedasticity.

Equation (3.2.2) states that the variance of u_i for each X_i (that is, the conditional variance of u_i) is some positive constant number equal to σ^2. Technically, (3.2.2) represents the assumption of **homoscedasticity,** or *equal* (homo) *spread* (scedasticity), or *equal variance.* Stated differently, (3.2.2) means that the Y populations corresponding to various X values have the same variance. Diagrammatically, the situation is shown in Fig. 3.4.

In contrast, consider Fig. 3.5, where the conditional variance of the Y population varies with X. This situation is known appropriately as **heteroscedasticity,** or *unequal spread,* or *variance.* Symbolically, in this situation (3.2.2) can be written as

$$\operatorname{var}\,(u_i \mid X_i) = \sigma_i^2 \tag{3.2.3}$$

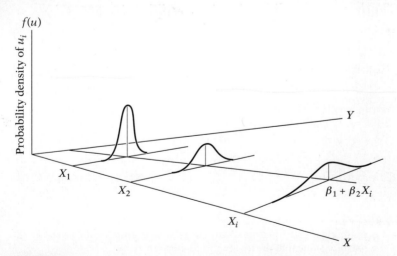

FIGURE 3.5
Heteroscedasticity.

Notice the subscript on σ^2 in Equation (3.2.3), which indicates that the variance of the Y population is no longer constant.

To make the difference between the two situations clear, let Y represent weekly consumption expenditure and X weekly income. Figures 3.4 and 3.5 show that as income increases the average consumption expenditure also increases. But in Fig. 3.4 the variance of consumption expenditure remains the same at all levels of income whereas in Fig. 3.5 it increases with increase in income. In other words richer families on the average consume more than poorer families, but there is also more variability in the consumption expenditure of the former.

To understand the rationale behind this assumption, refer to Fig. 3.5. As this figure shows, $\text{var}(u \mid X_1) < \text{var}(u \mid X_2), \ldots, < \text{var}(u \mid X_i)$. Therefore, the likelihood is that the Y observations coming from the population with $X = X_1$ would be closer to the PRF than those coming from populations corresponding to $X = X_2, X = X_3$, and so on. In short, not all Y values corresponding to the various X's will be equally reliable, reliability being judged by how closely or distantly the Y values are distributed around their means, that is, the points on the PRF. If this is in fact the case, would we not prefer to sample from those Y populations that are closer to their mean than those that are widely spread? But doing so might restrict the variation we obtain across X values.

By invoking Assumption 4, we are saying that at this stage all Y values corresponding to the various X's are equally important. In Chapter 11 we shall see what happens if this is not the case, that is, where there is heteroscedasticity.

In passing, note that Assumption 4 implies that the conditional variances of Y_i are also homoscedastic. That is,

$$\text{var}\,(Y_i \mid X_i) = \sigma^2 \tag{3.2.4}$$

Of course, the *unconditional variance* of Y is σ_Y^2. Later we will see the importance of distinguishing between conditional and unconditional variances of Y (see Appendix A for details of conditional and unconditional variances).

Assumption 5: No autocorrelation between the disturbances. Given any two X values, X_i and $X_j(i \neq j)$, the correlation between any two u_i and $u_j(i \neq j)$ is zero. Symbolically,

$$\mathbf{cov}(u_i, u_j \mid X_i, X_j) = E[u_i - E(u_i \mid X_i)][u_j - E(u_j \mid X_j)]$$

$$= E(u_i \mid X_i)(u_j \mid X_j) \quad \text{(why?)}$$

$$= 0 \tag{3.2.5}$$

where i and j are two different observations and where **cov** means **covariance.**

In words, (3.2.5) postulates that the disturbances u_i and u_j are uncorrelated. Technically, this is the assumption of **no serial correlation,** or **no autocorrelation.** This means that, given X_i, the deviations of any two Y values from their mean value do not exhibit patterns such as those shown in Fig. 3.6a and

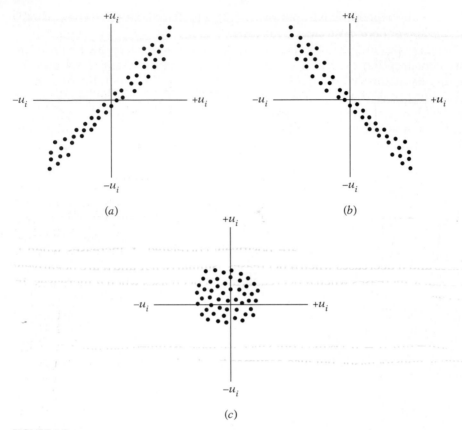

FIGURE 3.6
Patterns of correlation among the disturbances. (a) positive serial correlation; (b) negative serial correlation; (c) zero correlation.

b. In Fig. 3.6a we see that the u's are **positively correlated,** a positive u followed by a positive u or a negative u followed by a negative u. In Fig. 3.6b the u's are **negatively correlated,** a positive u followed by a negative u and vice versa.

If the disturbances (deviations) follow systematic patterns, such as those shown in Figs. 3.6a and b, there is auto- or serial correlation, and what Assumption 5 requires is that such correlations be absent. Figure 3.6c shows that there is no systematic pattern to the u's, thus indicating zero correlation.

The full import of this assumption will be explained thoroughly in Chapter 12. But intuitively one can explain this assumption as follows. Suppose in our PRF ($Y_t = \beta_1 + \beta_2 X_t + u_t$) that u_t and u_{t-1} are positively correlated. Then Y_t depends not only on X_t but also on u_{t-1} for u_{t-1} to some extent determines u_t. At this stage of the development of the subject matter, by invoking Assumption 5, we are saying that we will consider the systematic effect, if any, of X_t on Y_t and not worry about the other influences that might act on Y as a result of the possible intercorrelations among the u's. But, as noted in Chapter 12, we will see how intercorrelations among the disturbances can be brought into the analysis and with what consequences.

Assumption 6: Zero covariance between u_i and X_i, or $E(u_i X_i) = 0$. Formally,

$$
\begin{aligned}
\text{cov}(u_i, X_i) &= E[u_i - E(u_i)][X_i - E(X_i)] \\
&= E[u_i(X_i - E(X_i))], \qquad \text{since } E(u_i) = 0 \\
&= E(u_i X_i) - E(X_i)E(u_i), \qquad \text{since } E(X_i) \text{ is nonstochastic} \\
&= E(u_i X_i), \qquad \text{since } E(u_i) = 0 \\
&= 0, \qquad \text{by assumption} \tag{3.2.6}
\end{aligned}
$$

Assumption 6 states that the disturbance u and explanatory variable X are uncorrelated. The rationale for this assumption is as follows: When we expressed the PRF as in (2.4.2), we assumed that X and u (which may represent the influence of all the omitted variables) have separate (and additive) influence on Y. But if X and u are correlated, it is not possible to assess their individual effects on Y. Thus, if X and u are positively correlated, X increases when u increases and it decreases when u decreases. Similarly, if X and u are negatively correlated, X increases when u decreases and it decreases when u increases. In either case, it is difficult to isolate the influence of X and u on Y.

Assumption 6 is automatically fulfilled if X variable is nonrandom or nonstochastic and Assumption 3 holds, for in that case, $\text{cov}(u_i, X_i) = [X_i - E(X_i)]E[u_i - E(u_i)] = 0$. (Why?) But since we have assumed that our X variable not only is nonstochastic but also assumes fixed values in repeated samples,[12] Assumption 6 is not very critical for us; it is stated here merely to point out that the regression theory presented in the sequel holds true even if the X's are stochastic or random, provided they are independent or at least uncorrelated with the disturbances u_i.[13] (We shall examine the consequences of relaxing Assumption 6 in Part II.)

Assumption 7: The number of observations n must be greater than the number of parameters to be estimated. Alternatively, the number of observations n must be greater than the number of explanatory variables.

This assumption is not so innocuous as it seems. In the hypothetical example of Table 3.1, imagine that we had only the first pair of observations on Y and X (4 and 1). From this single observation there is no way to estimate the two unknowns, β_1 and β_2. We need at least two pairs of observations to estimate the two unknowns. In a later chapter we will see the critical importance of this assumption.

---

[12] Recall that in obtaining the samples shown in Tables 2.4 and 2.5, we kept the same X values.

[13] As we will discuss in Part II, if the X's are stochastic but distributed independently of u_i, the properties of least estimators discussed shortly continue to hold, but if the stochastic X's are merely uncorrelated with u_i, the properties of OLS estimators hold true only if the sample size is very large. At this stage, however, there is no need to get bogged down with this theoretical point.

I don't know

> **Assumption 8: Variability in X values.** The X values in a given sample must not all be the same. Technically, **var(X)** must be a finite positive number.[14]

This assumption too is not so innocuous as it looks. Look at Eq. (3.1.6). If all the X values are identical, then $X_i = \bar{X}$ (Why?) and the denominator of that equation will be zero, making it impossible to estimate β_2 and therefore β_1. Intuitively, we readily see why this assumption is important. Looking at our family consumption expenditure example in Chapter 2, if there is very little variation in family income, we will not be able to explain much of the variation in the consumption expenditure. The reader should keep in mind that variation in both Y and X is essential to use regression analysis as a research tool. In short, the variables must vary!

> **Assumption 9: The regression model is correctly specified.** Alternatively, there is no **specification bias or error** in the model used in empirical analysis.

As we discussed in the Introduction, the classical econometric methodology assumes implicitly, if not explicitly, that the model used to test an economic theory is "correctly specified." This assumption can be explained informally as follows. An econometric investigation begins with the specification of the econometric model underlying the phenomenon of interest. Some important questions that arise in the specification of the model include the following: (1) What variables should be included in the model? (2) What is the functional form of the model? Is it linear in the parameters, the variables, or both? (3) What are the probabilistic assumptions made about the Y_i, the X_i, and the u_i entering the model?

These are extremely important questions, for, as we will show in Chapter 13, by omitting important variables from the model, or by choosing the wrong functional form, or by making wrong stochastic assumptions about the variables of the model, the validity of interpreting the estimated regression will be highly questionable. To get an intuitive feeling about this, refer to the Phillips curve shown in Fig. 1.3. Suppose we choose the following two models to depict the underlying relationship between the rate of change of money wages and the unemployment rate:

$$Y_i = \alpha_1 + \alpha_2 X_i + u_i \qquad (3.2.7)$$

---

[14]The sample variance of X is

$$\text{var}(X) = \frac{\sum (X_i - \bar{X})^2}{n - 1}$$

where n is sample size.

$$Y_i = \beta_1 + \beta_2\left(\frac{1}{X_i}\right) + u_i \tag{3.2.8}$$

where Y_i = the rate of change of money wages, and X_i = the unemployment rate.

The regression model (3.2.7) is linear both in the parameters and the variables, whereas (3.2.8) is linear in the parameters (hence a linear regression model by our definition) but nonlinear in the variable X. Now consider Figure 3.7 at the bottom of the page.

If model (3.2.8) is the "correct" or the "true" model, fitting the model (3.2.7) to the scatterpoints shown in Fig. 3.7 will give us wrong predictions: Between points A and B, for any given X_i the model (3.2.7) is going to overestimate the true mean value of Y, whereas to the left of A (or to the right of B) it is going to underestimate (or overestimate, in absolute terms) the true mean value of Y.

The preceding example is an instance of what is called a **specification bias** or a **specification error;** here the bias consists in choosing the wrong functional form. We will see other types of specification errors in Chapter 13.

Unfortunately, in practice one rarely knows the correct variables to include in the model or the correct functional form of the model or the correct probabilistic assumptions about the variables entering the model for the theory underlying the particular investigation (e.g., the Phillips-type money wage change–unemployment rate tradeoff) may not be strong or robust enough to answer all these questions. Therefore, in practice, the econometrician has to use some judgment in choosing the number of variables entering the model and the functional form of the model and has to make some assumptions about the stochastic nature of the variables included in the model. To some extent, there

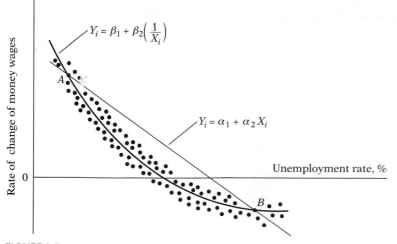

FIGURE 3.7
Linear and nonlinear Phillips curves.

is some trial and error involved in choosing the "right" model for empirical analysis.[15]

If judgment is required in selecting a model, what is the need for Assumption 9? Without going into details here (see Chapter 13), this assumption is there to remind us that our regression analysis and therefore the results based on that analysis are conditional upon the chosen model and to warn us that we should give very careful thought in formulating econometric models, especially when there may be several competing theories trying to explain an economic phenomenon, such as the inflation rate, or the demand for money, or the determination of the appropriate or equilibrium value of a stock or a bond. Thus, econometric model-building, as we shall discover, is more often an art rather than a science.

Our discussion of the assumptions underlying the classical linear regression model is now completed. It is important to note that all these assumptions pertain to the PRF only and not the SRF. But it is interesting to observe that the method of least squares discussed previously has some properties that are similar to the assumptions we have made about the PRF. For example, the finding that $\sum \hat{u}_i = 0$, and, therefore, $\bar{\hat{u}} = 0$, is akin to the assumption that $E(u_i \mid X_i) = 0$. Likewise, the finding that $\sum \hat{u}_i X_i = 0$ is similar to the assumption that $cov(u_i, X_i) = 0$. It is comforting to note that the method of least squares thus tries to "duplicate" some of the assumptions we have imposed on the PRF.

Of course, the SRF does not duplicate all the assumptions of the CLRM. As we will show later, although $cov(u_i, u_j) = 0(i \neq j)$ by assumption, it is *not* true that the *sample* $cov(\hat{u}_i, \hat{u}_j) = 0(i \neq j)$. As a matter of fact, we will show later that the residuals not only are autocorrelated but also are heteroscedastic (see Chapter 12).

When we go beyond the two-variable model and consider multiple regression models, that is, models containing several regressors, we add the following assumptions.

> **Assumption 10: There is no perfect multicollinearity.** That is, there are *no perfect linear relationships among the explanatory variables.*

We will discuss this assumption in Chapter 7, where we discuss multiple regression models.

How Realistic Are These Assumptions?

The million-dollar question is: How realistic are all these assumptions? The "reality of assumptions" is an age-old question in the philosophy of science. Some argue that it does not matter whether the assumptions are realistic. What

---

[15]But one should avoid what is known as "**data mining,**" that is, trying every possible model with the hope that at least one will fit the data well. That is why it is essential that there be some economic reasoning underlying the chosen model and that any modifications in the model should have some economic justification. A purely ad hoc model may be difficult to justify on theoretical or a priori grounds. In short, theory should be the basis of estimation.

matters are the predictions based on those assumptions. Notable among the "irrelevance-of-assumptions thesis" is Milton Friedman. To him, unreality of assumptions is a positive advantage: "to be important . . . a hypothesis must be descriptively false in its assumptions."[16]

One may not subscribe to this viewpoint fully, but recall that in any scientific study we make certain assumptions because they facilitate the development of the subject matter in gradual steps, not because they are necessarily realistic in the sense that they replicate reality exactly. As one author notes, " . . . if simplicity is a desirable criterion of good theory, all good theories idealize and oversimplify outrageously."[17]

An analogy might help here. Students of economics are generally introduced to the model of perfect competition before they are introduced to models of imperfect competition such as monopoly and oligopoly, because the implications derived from this model enable us to appreciate better the models of imperfect competition, not because the model of perfect competition is necessarily realistic. The CLRM in econometrics is the equivalent of the model of perfect competition in price theory!

What we plan to do is first study the properties of the CLRM thoroughly, and then in later chapters examine in depth what happens if one or more of the assumptions of CLRM are not fulfilled. At the end of this chapter, we provide in Table 3.5 a guide to where one can find out what happens to the CLRM if a particular assumption is not satisfied.

As a colleague pointed out to me, when we review research done by others, we need to consider whether the assumptions made by the researcher are appropriate to the data and problem. All too often, published research is based on implicit assumptions about problem and data that are likely not correct and that produce estimates based on these assumptions. Clearly, the knowledgeable reader should, realizing these problems, adopt a skeptical attitude toward the research. The assumptions listed in Table 3.5 therefore provide a checklist for guiding our research and for evaluating the research of others.

With this backdrop, we are now ready to study the CLRM. In particular, we want to find out the **statistical properties** of OLS compared with the purely **numerical properties** discussed earlier. The statistical properties of OLS are based on the assumptions of CLRM already discussed and are enshrined in the famous **Gauss–Markov theorem.** But before we turn to this theorem, which provides the theoretical justification for the popularity of OLS, we first need to consider the **precision** or **standard errors** of the least-squares estimates.

3.3 PRECISION OR STANDARD ERRORS OF LEAST-SQUARES ESTIMATES

From Eqs. (3.1.6) and (3.1.7) it is evident that least-squares estimates are a function of the sample data. But since the data are likely to change from

---

[16] Milton Friedman, *Essays in Positive Economics*, University of Chicago Press, Chicago, 1953, p. 14.

[17] Mark Blaug, *The Methodology of Economics: Or How Economists Explain*, 2d ed., Cambridge University Press, New York, 1992, p. 92.

sample to sample, the estimates will change ipso facto. Therefore, what is needed is some measure of "reliability" or **precision** of the estimators $\hat{\beta}_1$ and $\hat{\beta}_2$. In statistics the precision of an estimate is measured by its standard error (se).[18] Given the Gaussian assumptions, it is shown in Appendix 3A, Section 3A.3 that the standard errors of the OLS estimates can be obtained as follows:

$$\operatorname{var}(\hat{\beta}_2) = \frac{\sigma^2}{\sum x_i^2} \tag{3.3.1}$$

$$\operatorname{se}(\hat{\beta}_2) = \frac{\sigma}{\sqrt{\sum x_i^2}} \tag{3.3.2}$$

$$\operatorname{var}(\hat{\beta}_1) = \frac{\sum X_i^2}{n \sum x_i^2} \sigma^2 \tag{3.3.3}$$

$$\operatorname{se}(\hat{\beta}_1) = \sqrt{\frac{\sum X_i^2}{n \sum x_i^2}} \sigma \tag{3.3.4}$$

where var = variance and se = standard error and where σ^2 is the constant or homoscedastic variance of u_i of Assumption 4.

All the quantities entering into the preceding equations except σ^2 can be estimated from the data. As shown in Appendix 3A, Section 3A.5, σ^2 itself is estimated by the following formula:

$$\hat{\sigma}^2 = \frac{\sum \hat{u}_i^2}{n-2} \tag{3.3.5}$$

where $\hat{\sigma}^2$ is the OLS estimator of the true but unknown σ^2 and where the expression $n - 2$ is known as the **number of degrees of freedom (df),** $\sum \hat{u}_i^2$ being the sum of the residual squared or the **residual sum of squares (RSS).**[19]

Once $\sum \hat{u}_i^2$ is known, $\hat{\sigma}^2$ can be easily computed. $\sum \hat{u}_i^2$ itself can be computed either from (3.1.2) or from the following expression (see Section 3.5 for the proof):

$$\sum \hat{u}_i^2 = \sum y_i^2 - \hat{\beta}_2^2 \sum x_i^2 \tag{3.3.6}$$

---

[18]The **standard error** is nothing but the standard deviation of the sampling distribution of the estimator, and the sampling distribution of an estimator is simply a probability or frequency distribution of the estimator, that is, a distribution of the set of values of the estimator obtained from all possible samples of the same size from a given population. Sampling distributions are used to draw inferences about the values of the population parameters on the basis of the values of the estimators calculated from one or more samples. (For details, see App. A).

[19]The term **number of degrees of freedom** means the total number of observations in the sample (= n) less the number of independent (linear) constraints or restrictions put on them. In other words, it is the number of independent observations out of a total of n observations. For example, before the RSS (3.1.2) can be computed, $\hat{\beta}_1$ and $\hat{\beta}_2$ must first be obtained. These two estimates therefore put two restrictions on the RSS. Therefore, there are $n - 2$, not n, independent observations to compute the RSS. Following this logic, in the three-variable regression RSS will have $n - 3$ df, and for the k variable model it will have $n - k$ df. The general rule is this: df = $n - $ number of parameters estimated.

Compared with Eq. (3.1.2), Eq. (3.3.6) is easy to use, for it does not require computing $\hat{u}_i$ for each observation although such a computation will be useful in its own right (as we shall see in Chapters 11 and 12).

Since

$$\hat{\beta}_2 = \frac{\sum x_i y_i}{\sum x_i^2}$$

an alternative expression for computing $\sum \hat{u}_i^2$ is

$$\sum \hat{u}_i^2 = \sum y_i^2 - \frac{(\sum x_i y_i)^2}{\sum x_i^2} \tag{3.3.7}$$

In passing, note that the positive square root of $\hat{\sigma}^2$

$$\hat{\sigma} = \sqrt{\frac{\sum \hat{u}_i^2}{n-2}} \tag{3.3.8}$$

is known as the **standard error of the estimate.** It is simply the standard deviation of the Y values about the estimated regression line and is often used as a summary measure of the "goodness of fit" of the estimated regression line, a topic discussed in Section 3.5.

Earlier we noted that, given X_i, σ^2 represents the (conditional) variance of both u_i and Y_i. Therefore, the standard error of the estimate can also be called the (conditional) standard deviation of u_i and Y_i. Of course, as usual, σ_Y^2 and σ_Y represent, respectively, the unconditional variance and unconditional standard deviation of Y.

Note the following features of the variances (and therefore the standard errors) of $\hat{\beta}_1$ and $\hat{\beta}_2$.

1. The variance of $\hat{\beta}_2$ is directly proportional to σ^2 but inversely proportional to $\sum x_i^2$. That is, given σ^2, the larger the variation in the X values, the smaller the variance of $\hat{\beta}_2$ and hence the greater the precision with which β_2 can be estimated. In short, given σ^2, if there is substantial variation in the X values (recall Assumption 8), β_2 can be measured more accurately than when the X_i do not vary substantially. Also, given $\sum x_i^2$, the larger the variance of σ^2, the larger the variance of $\hat{\beta}_2$. Note that as the sample size n increases, the number of terms in the sum, $\sum x_i^2$, will increase. As n increases the precision with which β_2 can be estimated also increases. (Why?)

2. The variance of $\hat{\beta}_1$ is directly proportional to σ^2 and $\sum X_i^2$ but inversely proportional to $\sum x_i^2$ and the sample size n.

3. Since $\hat{\beta}_1$ and $\hat{\beta}_2$ are estimators, they will not only vary from sample to sample but in a given sample they are likely to be dependent on each other, this dependence being measured by the covariance between them. It is shown

in Appendix 3A, Section 3A.4 that

$$\text{cov}(\hat{\beta}_1, \hat{\beta}_2) = -\bar{X} \text{ var}(\hat{\beta}_2)$$
$$= -\bar{X} \left(\frac{\sigma^2}{\sum x_i^2} \right)$$

(3.3.9)

Since $\text{var}(\hat{\beta}_2)$ is always positive, as is the variance of any variable, the nature of the covariance between $\hat{\beta}_1$ and $\hat{\beta}_2$ depends on the sign of $\bar{X}$. If $\bar{X}$ is positive, then as the formula shows, the covariance will be negative. Thus, if the slope coefficient β_2 is *overestimated* (i.e., the slope is too steep), the intercept coefficient β_1 will be *underestimated* (i.e., the intercept will be too small). Later on (especially in the chapter on multicollinearity, Chapter 10), we will see the utility of studying the covariances between the estimated regression coefficients.

How do the variances and standard errors of the estimated regression coefficients enable one to judge the reliability of these estimates? This is a problem in statistical inference, and it will be pursued in Chapters 4 and 5.

3.4   PROPERTIES OF LEAST-SQUARES ESTIMATORS: THE GAUSS-MARKOV THEOREM[20]

As noted earlier, given the assumptions of the classical linear regression model, the least-squares estimates possess some ideal or optimum properties. These properties are contained in the well-known **Gauss-Markov theorem.** To understand this theorem, we need to consider the **best linear unbiasedness property** of an estimator.[21] As explained in Appendix A, an estimator, say the OLS estimator $\hat{\beta}_2$, is said to be a best linear unbiased estimator (BLUE) of β_2 if the following hold:

1. It is **linear,** that is, a linear function of a random variable, such as the dependent variable Y in the regression model.
2. It is **unbiased,** that is, its average or expected value, $E(\hat{\beta}_2)$, is equal to the true value, β_2.
3. It has minimum variance in the class of all such linear unbiased estimators; an unbiased estimator with the least variance is known as an **efficient estimator.**

---

[20]Although known as the *Gauss-Markov Theorem*, the least-squares approach of Gauss antedates (1821) the minimum-variance approach of Markov (1900).

[21]The reader should refer to App. A for the importance of linear estimators as well as for a general discussion of the desirable properties of statistical estimators.

In the regression context it can be proved that the OLS estimators are BLUE. This is the gist of the famous Gauss-Markov theorem, which can be stated as follows:

> **Gauss-Markov Theorem:** Given the assumptions of the classical linear regression model, the least-squares estimators, in the class of unbiased linear estimators, have minimum variance, that is, they are BLUE.

The proof of this theorem is sketched in Appendix 3A, Section 3A.6. The full import of the Gauss-Markov theorem will become clearer as we move along. It is sufficient to note here that the theorem has theoretical as well as practical importance.[22]

What all this means can be explained with the aid of Fig. 3.8.

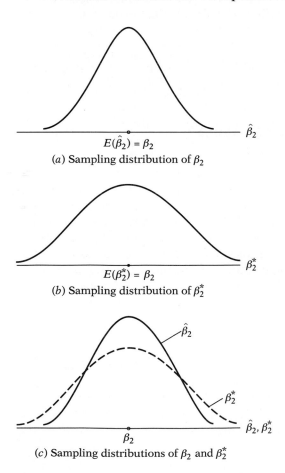

$E(\hat{\beta}_2) = \beta_2$

(a) Sampling distribution of β_2

$E(\beta_2^*) = \beta_2$

(b) Sampling distribution of β_2^*

$\hat{\beta}_2$

β_2^*

$\hat{\beta}_2, \beta_2^*$

β_2

(c) Sampling distributions of β_2 and β_2^*

FIGURE 3.8
Sampling distribution of OLS estimator $\hat{\beta}_2$ and alternative estimator β_2^*.

---

[22]For example, it can be proved that any linear combination of the β's, such as $(\beta_1 - 2\beta_2)$, can be estimated by $(\hat{\beta}_1 - 2\hat{\beta}_2)$, and this estimator is BLUE. For details, see Henri Theil, *Introduction to Econometrics*, Prentice-Hall, Englewood Cliffs, N.J., 1978, pp. 401–402.

In Fig. 3.8(*a*) we have shown the **sampling distribution** of the OLS estimator $\hat{\beta}_2$, that is, the distribution of the values taken by $\hat{\beta}_2$ in repeated sampling experiments (recall Table 3.1). For convenience we have assumed $\hat{\beta}_2$ to be distributed symmetrically (but more on this in Chapter 4). As the figure shows, the mean of the $\hat{\beta}_2$ values, $E(\hat{\beta}_2)$, is equal to the true β_2. In this situation we say that $\hat{\beta}_2$ is an *unbiased estimator* of β_2. In Fig. 3.8(*b*) we have shown the sampling distribution of β_2^*, an alternative estimator of β_2 obtained by using another (i.e., other than OLS) method. For convenience, assume that β_2^*, like $\hat{\beta}_2$, is unbiased, that is, its average or expected value is equal to β_2. Assume further that both $\hat{\beta}_2$ and β_2^* are linear estimators, that is, they are linear functions of *Y*. Which estimator, $\hat{\beta}_2$ or β_2^*, would you choose?

To answer this question, superimpose the two figures, as in Fig. 3.8(*c*). It is obvious that although both $\hat{\beta}_2$ and β_2^* are unbiased the distribution of β_2^* is more diffused or widespread around the mean value than the distribution of $\hat{\beta}_2$. In other words, the variance of β_2^* is larger than the variance of $\hat{\beta}_2$. Now given two estimators that are both linear and unbiased, one would choose the estimator with the smaller variance because it is more likely to be close to β_2 than the alternative estimator. In short, one would choose the BLUE estimator.

The statistical properties that we have just discussed are known as **finite sample properties:** These properties hold regardless of the sample size on which the estimators are based. Later we will have occasions to consider the **asymptotic properties,** that is, properties that hold only if the sample size is very large (technically, infinite). A general discussion of finite-sample and large-sample properties of estimators is given in Appendix A.

3.5   THE COEFFICIENT OF DETERMINATION r^2: A MEASURE OF "GOODNESS OF FIT"

Thus far we were concerned with the problem of estimating regression coefficients, their standard errors, and some of their properties. We now consider the **goodness of fit** of the fitted regression line to a set of data; that is, we shall find out how "well" the sample regression line fits the data. From Fig. 3.1 it is clear that if all the observations were to lie on the regression line, we would obtain a "perfect" fit, but this is rarely the case. Generally, there will be some positive $\hat{u}_i$ and some negative $\hat{u}_i$. What we hope for is that these residuals around the regression line are as small as possible. The **coefficient of determination** r^2 (two-variable case) or R^2 (multiple regression) is a summary measure that tells how well the sample regression line fits the data.

Before we show how r^2 is computed, let us consider a heuristic explanation of r^2 in terms of a graphical device, known as the **Venn diagram,** or the **Ballentine,** as shown in Fig. 3.9.[23]

---

[23]See Peter Kennedy, "Ballentine: A Graphical Aid for Econometrics," *Austrialian Economics Papers,* vol. 20, 1981, pp. 414–416. The name Ballentine is derived from the emblem of the well-known Ballentine beer with its circles.

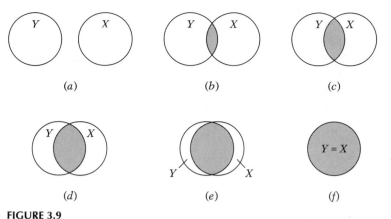

FIGURE 3.9
The Ballentine view of r^2: (a) $r^2 = 0$; (f) $r^2 = 1$.

In this figure the circle Y represents variation in the dependent variable Y and the circle X represents variation in the explanatory variable X.[24] The overlap of the two circles (the shaded area) indicates the extent to which the variation in Y is explained by the variation in X (say, via an OLS regression). The greater the extent of the overlap, the greater the variation in Y is explained by X. The r^2 is simply a numerical measure of this overlap. In the figure, as we move from left to right, the area of the overlap increases, that is, successively a greater proportion of the variation in Y is explained by X. In short, r^2 increases. When there is no overlap, r^2 is obviously zero, but when the overlap is complete, r^2 is 1, since 100 percent of the variation in Y is explained by X. As we shall show shortly, r^2 lies between 0 and 1.

To compute this r^2, we proceed as follows: Recall that

$$Y_i = \hat{Y}_i + \hat{u}_i \qquad (2.6.3)$$

or in the deviation form

$$y_i = \hat{y}_i + \hat{u}_i \qquad (3.5.1)$$

where use is made of (3.1.13) and (3.1.14). Squaring (3.5.1) on both sides and summing over the sample, we obtain

$$\begin{aligned}
\sum y_i^2 &= \sum \hat{y}_i^2 + \sum \hat{u}_i^2 + 2\sum \hat{y}_i \hat{u}_i \\
&= \sum \hat{y}_i^2 + \sum \hat{u}_i^2 \\
&= \hat{\beta}_2^2 \sum x_i^2 + \sum \hat{u}_i^2
\end{aligned} \qquad (3.5.2)$$

since $\sum \hat{y}_i \hat{u}_i = 0$ (why?) and $\hat{y}_i = \hat{\beta}_2 x_i$.

---

[24]The term *variation* and *variance* are different. Variation means the sum of squares of the deviations of a variable from its mean value. Variance is this sum of squares divided by the appropriate degrees of freedom. In short, variance = variation/df.

The various sums of squares appearing in (3.5.2) can be described as follows: $\sum y_i^2 = \sum(Y_i - \bar{Y})^2 =$ total variation of the actual Y values about their sample mean, which may be called the **total sum of squares (TSS).** $\sum \hat{y}_i^2 = \sum(\hat{Y}_i - \hat{Y})^2 = \sum(\hat{Y}_i - \bar{Y})^2 = \hat{\beta}_2^2 \sum x_i^2 =$ variation of the estimated Y values about their mean ($\hat{Y} = \bar{Y}$), which appropriately may be called the sum of squares due to regression [i.e., due to the explanatory variable(s)], or explained by regression, or simply the **explained sum of squares (ESS).** $\sum \hat{u}_i^2 =$ residual or **unexplained** variation of the Y values about the regression line, or simply the **residual sum of squares (RSS)**. Thus, (3.5.2) is

$$TSS = ESS + RSS \tag{3.5.3}$$

and shows that the total variation in the observed Y values about their mean value can be partitioned into two parts, one attributable to the regression line and the other to random forces because not all actual Y observations lie on the fitted line. Geometrically, we have Fig. 3.10.

Now dividing (3.5.3) by TSS on both sides, we obtain

$$1 = \frac{ESS}{TSS} + \frac{RSS}{TSS}$$
$$= \frac{\sum(\hat{Y}_i - \bar{Y})^2}{\sum(Y_i - \bar{Y})^2} + \frac{\sum \hat{u}_i^2}{\sum(Y_i - \bar{Y})^2} \tag{3.5.4}$$

We now define r^2 as

$$r^2 = \frac{\sum(\hat{Y}_i - \bar{Y})^2}{\sum(Y_i - \bar{Y})^2} = \frac{\boxed{ESS}}{\boxed{TSS}} \tag{3.5.5}$$

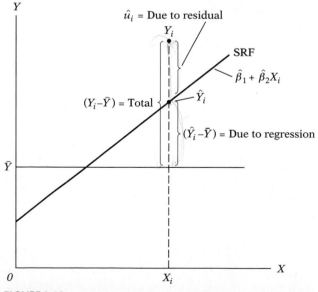

FIGURE 3.10
Breakdown of the variation of Y_i into two components.

or, alternatively, as

$$r^2 = 1 - \frac{\sum \hat{u}_i^2}{\sum (Y_i - \bar{Y})^2}$$

$$= 1 - \frac{\text{RSS}}{\text{TSS}}$$

(3.5.5a)

The quantity r^2 thus defined is known as the (sample) **coefficient of determination** and is the most commonly used measure of the goodness of fit of a regression line. Verbally, r^2 *measures the proportion or percentage of the total variation in Y explained by the regression model.*

Two properties of r^2 may be noted:

1. It is a nonnegative quantity. (Why?)
2. Its limits are $0 \le r^2 \le 1$. An r^2 of 1 means a perfect fit, that is, $\hat{Y}_i = Y_i$ for each i. On the other hand, an r^2 of zero means that there is no relationship between the regressand and the regressor whatsoever (i.e., $\beta_2 = 0$). In this case, as (3.1.9) shows, $\hat{Y}_i = \hat{\beta}_1 = \bar{Y}$, that is, the best prediction of any Y value is simply its mean value. In this situation therefore the regression line will be horizontal to the X axis.

Although r^2 can be computed directly from its definition given in (3.5.5), it can be obtained more quickly from the following formula:

$$r^2 = \frac{\text{ESS}}{\text{TSS}}$$

$$= \frac{\sum \hat{y}_i^2}{\sum y_i^2}$$

$$= \frac{\hat{\beta}_2^2 \sum x_i^2}{\sum y_i^2}$$

$$= \hat{\beta}_2^2 \left(\frac{\sum x_i^2}{\sum y_i^2} \right)$$

(3.5.6)

If we divide the numerator and the denominator of (3.5.6) by the sample size n (or $n - 1$ if the sample size is small), we obtain

$$r^2 = \hat{\beta}_2^2 \left(\frac{S_x^2}{S_y^2} \right)$$

(3.5.7)

where S_y^2 and S_x^2 are the sample variances of Y and X, respectively.

Since $\hat{\beta}_2 = \sum x_i y_i / \sum x_i^2$, Eq. (3.5.6) can also be expressed as

$$r^2 = \frac{(\sum x_i y_i)^2}{\sum x_i^2 \sum y_i^2} \tag{3.5.8}$$

an expression that may be computationally easy to obtain.

Given the definition of r^2, we can express ESS and RSS discussed earlier as follows:

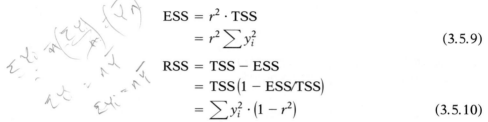

$$
\begin{aligned}
\text{ESS} &= r^2 \cdot \text{TSS} \\
&= r^2 \sum y_i^2
\end{aligned}
\tag{3.5.9}
$$

$$
\begin{aligned}
\text{RSS} &= \text{TSS} - \text{ESS} \\
&= \text{TSS}(1 - \text{ESS/TSS}) \\
&= \sum y_i^2 \cdot (1 - r^2)
\end{aligned}
\tag{3.5.10}
$$

Therefore, we can write

$$
\begin{aligned}
\text{TSS} &= \text{ESS} + \text{RSS} \\
\sum y_i^2 &= r^2 \sum y_i^2 + (1 - r^2) \sum y_i^2
\end{aligned}
\tag{3.5.11}
$$

an expression that we will find very useful later.

A quantity closely related to but conceptually very much different from r^2 is the **coefficient of correlation,** which, as noted in Chapter 1, is a measure of the degree of association between two variables. It can be computed either from

$$r = \pm \sqrt{r^2} \tag{3.5.12}$$

or from its definition

$$
\begin{aligned}
r &= \frac{\sum x_i y_i}{\sqrt{(\sum x_i^2)(\sum y_i^2)}} \\
&= \frac{n \sum X_i Y_i - (\sum X_i)(\sum Y_i)}{\sqrt{[n \sum X_i^2 - (\sum X_i)^2][n \sum Y_i^2 - (\sum Y_i)^2]}}
\end{aligned}
\tag{3.5.13}
$$

which is known as the **sample correlation coefficient.**[25]

Some of the properties of r are as follows (see Fig. 3.11):

1. It can be positive or negative, the sign depending on the sign of the term in the numerator of (3.5.13), which measures the sample *covariation* of two variables.

---

[25]The population correlation coefficient, denoted by ρ, is defined in App. A.

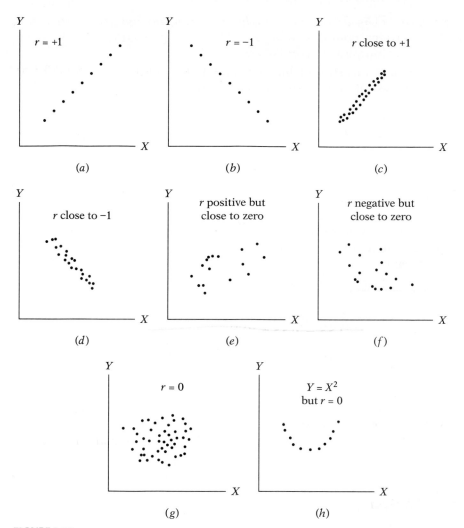

FIGURE 3.11
Correlation patterns (adapted from Henri Theil, *Introduction to Econometrics*, Prentice-Hall, Englewood Cliffs, N.J., 1978, p. 86).

2. It lies between the limits of -1 and $+1$; that is, $-1 \leq r \leq 1$.

3. It is symmetrical in nature; that is, the coefficient of correlation between X and $Y(r_{XY})$ is the same as that between Y and $X(r_{YX})$.

4. It is independent of the origin and scale; that is, if we define $X_i^* = aX_i + c$ and $Y_i^* = bY_i + d$, where $a > 0$, $b > 0$, and c and d are constants, then r between X^* and Y^* is the same as that between the original variables X and Y.

5. If X and Y are statistically independent (see Appendix A for the definition), the correlation coefficient between them is zero; but if $r = 0$, it does not mean that two variables are independent. In other words, **zero correlation does not necessarily imply independence.** [See Fig. 3.11(h).]

6. It is a measure of *linear association* or *linear dependence* only; it has no meaning for describing nonlinear relations. Thus in Fig. 3.11(h), $Y = X^2$ is an exact relationship yet r is zero. (Why?)

7. Although it is a measure of linear association between two variables, it does not necessarily imply any cause-and-effect relationship, as noted in Chapter 1.

In the regression context, r^2 is a more meaningful measure than r, for the former tells us the proportion of variation in the dependent variable explained by the explanatory variable(s) and therefore provides an overall measure of the extent to which the variation in one variable determines the variation in the other. The latter does not have such value.[26] Moreover, as we shall see, the interpretation of $r(= R)$ in a multiple regression model is of dubious value. However, we will have more to say about r^2 in Chapter 7.

In passing, note that the r^2 defined previously *can also be computed as the squared coefficient of correlation between actual Y_i and the estimated Y_i*, namely, $\hat{Y}_i$. That is, using (3.5.13), we can write

$$r^2 = \frac{[\sum(Y_i - \bar{Y})(\hat{Y}_i - \bar{Y})]^2}{\sum(Y_i - \bar{Y})^2 \sum(\hat{Y}_i - \bar{Y})^2}$$

That is,

$$r^2 = \frac{(\sum y_i \hat{y}_i)^2}{(\sum y_i^2)(\sum \hat{y}_i^2)} \tag{3.5.14}$$

where Y_i = actual Y, $\hat{Y}_i$ = estimated Y, and $\bar{Y} = \bar{\hat{Y}}$ = the mean of Y. For proof, see exercise 3.15. Expression (3.5.14) justifies the description of r^2 as a measure of goodness of fit, for it tells how close the estimated Y values are to their actual values.

3.6   A NUMERICAL EXAMPLE

We illustrate the econometric theory developed so far by considering the Keynesian consumption function discussed in the Introduction. Recall that Keynes stated that "The fundamental psychological law ... is that men [women] are disposed, as a rule and on average, to increase their consumption as their income increases, but not by as much as the increase in their income," that is, the marginal propensity to consume (MPC) is greater than zero but less than one. Although Keynes did not specify the exact functional form of the relationship between consumption

---

[26]In regression modeling the underlying theory will indicate the direction of causality between Y and X, which, in the context of single-equation models, is generally from X to Y.

TABLE 3.2
Hypothetical data on weekly family consumption expenditure Y and weekly family income X

Y($)	X($)
70	80
65	100
90	120
95	140
110	160
115	180
120	200
140	220
155	240
150	260

and income, for simplicity assume that the relationship is linear as in (2.4.2). As a test of the Keynesian consumption function, we use the sample data of Table 2.4, which for convenience is reproduced as Table 3.2. The raw data required to obtain the estimates of the regression coefficients, their standard errors, etc., are given in Table 3.3. Based on these raw data, the following calculations are obtained, and the reader is advised to check them.

TABLE 3.3
Raw data based on Table 3.2

Y_i (1)	X_i (2)	Y_iX_i (3)	X_i^2 (4)	$x_i =$ $X_i - \bar{X}$ (5)	$y_i =$ $Y_i - \bar{Y}$ (6)	x_i^2 (7)	x_iy_i (8)	$\hat{Y}_i$ (9)	$\hat{u}_i =$ $Y_i - \hat{Y}_i$ (10)	$\hat{Y}_i\hat{u}_i$ (11)
70	80	5600	6400	−90	−41	8100	3690	65.1818	4.8181	314.0524
65	100	6500	10000	−70	−46	4900	3220	75.3636	−10.3636	−781.0382
90	120	10800	14400	−50	−21	2500	1050	85.5454	4.4545	381.0620
95	140	13300	19600	−30	−16	900	480	95.7272	−0.7272	−69.6128
110	160	17600	25600	−10	−1	100	10	105.9090	4.0909	433.2631
115	180	20700	32400	10	4	100	40	116.0909	−1.0909	−126.6434
120	200	24000	40000	30	9	900	270	125.2727	−6.2727	−792.0708
140	220	30800	48400	50	29	2500	1450	136.4545	3.5454	483.7858
155	240	37200	57600	70	44	4900	3080	145.6363	8.3636	1226.4073
150	260	39000	67600	90	39	8100	3510	156.8181	−6.8181	−1069.2014
Sum 1110	1700	205500	322000	0	0	33000	16800	1109.9995 ÷ 1110.0	0	0.0040 ÷ 0.0
Mean 111	170	nc	nc	0	0	nc	nc	110	0	0

$$\hat{\beta}_2 = \frac{\sum x_iy_i}{\sum x_i^2} \qquad \hat{\beta}_1 = \bar{Y} - \hat{\beta}_2\bar{X}$$

$$= 16,800/33,000 \qquad = 111 - 0.5091(170)$$

$$= 0.5091 \qquad = 24.4545$$

Notes: ÷ symbolizes "approximately equal to"; nc means "not computed."

$$\hat{\beta}_1 = 24.4545 \qquad \text{var}(\hat{\beta}_1) = 41.1370 \qquad \text{and} \qquad \text{se}(\hat{\beta}_1) = 6.4138$$
$$\hat{\beta}_2 = 0.5091 \qquad \text{var}(\hat{\beta}_2) = 0.0013 \qquad \text{and} \qquad \text{se}(\hat{\beta}_2) = 0.0357$$
$$(3.6.1)$$

$$\text{cov}(\hat{\beta}_1, \hat{\beta}_2) = -0.2172 \quad \hat{\sigma}^2 = 42.1591$$
$$r^2 = 0.9621 \qquad r = 0.9809 \qquad \text{df} = 8$$

The estimated regression line therefore is

$$\hat{Y}_i = 24.4545 + 0.5091X_i \tag{3.6.2}$$

which is shown geometrically as Fig. 3.12.

Following Chapter 2, the SRF [Eq. (3.6.2)] and the associated regression line are interpreted as follows: Each point on the regression line gives an *estimate* of the expected or mean value of Y corresponding to the chosen X value; that is, $\hat{Y}_i$ is an estimate of $E(Y \mid X_i)$. The value of $\hat{\beta}_2 = 0.5091$, which measures the slope of the line, shows that, within the sample range of X between \$80 and \$260 per week, as X increases, say, by \$1, the estimated increase in the mean or average weekly consumption expenditure amounts to about 51 cents. The value of $\hat{\beta}_1 = 24.4545$, which is the intercept of the line, indicates the average level of weekly consumption expenditure when weekly income is zero. However, this is a mechanical interpretation of the intercept term. In regression analysis such literal interpretation of the intercept term may not be always meaningful, although in

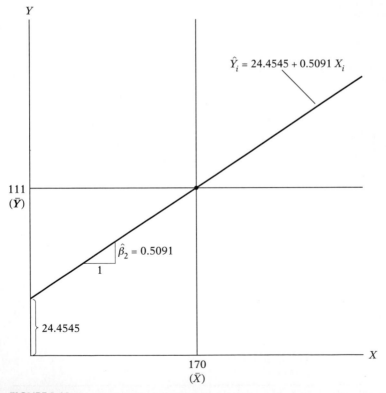

FIGURE 3.12
Sample regression line based on the data of Table 3.2.

the present example it can be argued that a family without any income (because of unemployment, layoff, etc.) might maintain some minimum level of consumption expenditure either by borrowing or dissaving. But in general one has to use common sense in interpreting the intercept term for very often the sample range of X values may not include zero as one of the observed values.

Perhaps it is best to interpret the intercept term as the mean or average effect on Y of all the variables omitted from the regression model. The value of r^2 of 0.9621 means that about 96 percent of the variation in the weekly consumption expenditure is explained by income. Since r^2 can at most be 1, the observed r^2 suggests that the sample regression line fits the data very well.[27] The coefficient of correlation of 0.9809 shows that the two variables, consumption expenditure and income, are highly positively correlated. The estimated standard errors of the regression coefficients will be interpreted in Chapter 5.

3.7 ILLUSTRATIVE EXAMPLES

Coffee Consumption in the United States, 1970–1980

Consider the data given in Table 3.4.[28]

From microeconomics it is known that the demand for a commodity generally depends on the price of that commodity, prices of other goods competing

TABLE 3.4
U.S. coffee consumption (Y) in relation to average real retail price (X),* 1970–1980

Year	Y (cups per person per day)	X ($ per lb)
1970	2.57	0.77
1971	2.50	0.74
1972	2.35	0.72
1973	2.30	0.73
1974	2.25	0.76
1975	2.20	0.75
1976	2.11	1.08
1977	1.94	1.81
1978	1.97	1.39
1979	2.06	1.20
1980	2.02	1.17

Note: The nominal price was divided by the Consumer Price Index (CPI) for food and beverages, 1967 = 100.

Source: The data for Y are from *Summary of National Coffee Drinking Study*, Data Group, Elkins Park, Penn., 1981; and the data on nominal X (i.e., X in current prices) are from *Nielsen Food Index*, A. C. Nielsen, New York, 1981.

[27] A formal test of the significance of r^2 will be presented in Chap. 8.
[28] I am indebted to Scott E. Sandberg for collecting the data.

with or complementary to the commodity, and the income of the consumer. To incorporate all these variables into the demand function, assuming the data are available, would require us to go into a multiple regression model. We are not yet ready for that. Therefore, what we will do is to assume a *partial* or *ceteris paribus* (other things remaining the same) demand function, relating the quantity demanded to its price only—for now we assume that the other variables entering the demand function remain constant. Then, if we fit the two-variable linear model (2.4.2) to the data given in Table 3.4, we obtain the following results (the SAS computer printout is given in Appendix 3A, Section 3A.7):

$$\hat{Y}_t = 2.6911 - 0.4795X_t$$

$$\text{var}(\hat{\beta}_1) = 0.0148; \ \text{se}(\hat{\beta}_1) = 0.1216$$

$$\text{var}(\hat{\beta}_2) = 0.0129; \ \text{se}(\hat{\beta}_2) = 0.1140; \qquad \hat{\sigma}^2 = 0.01656$$

$$r^2 = 0.6628$$

(3.7.1)

The interpretation of the estimated regression is as follows: If the average real retail price of coffee per pound goes up, say, by a dollar, the average consumption of coffee per day is expected to decrease by about half a cup. If the price of coffee were to be zero, the average per person consumption of coffee is expected to be about 2.69 cups a day. Of course, as stated earlier, very often we cannot attach any physical meaning to the intercept. However, keep in mind that even if the price of coffee were zero, people would not consume inordinate amounts of coffee because of the purported ill effects of caffeine on health. The r^2 value means that about 66 percent of the variation in per capita daily coffee consumption is explained by variation in the retail price of coffee.

How realistic is the model we have fitted to the data? Noticing that it does not include all the relevant variables, we cannot say that it is a complete demand function for coffee. The simple model chosen for this example was of course for pedagogical purposes at this stage of our study. In Chapter 7 we will present a more complete demand function. (See exercise 7.23, which gives a demand function for chicken consumption in the United States.)

Keynesian Consumption Function for the United States, 1980–1991

Return to the data given in Table I.1 of the Introduction. On the basis of these data, the following OLS regression was estimated, where Y represents personal consumption expenditure (PCE) in billions of 1987 dollars and X represents Gross Domestic Product (GDP), a measure of income, in billions of 1987 dollars (the results were obtained using **SHAZAM**™ 7.0 version):

$$\hat{Y}_t = -231.80 + 0.71943\, X_t$$

$$\text{se}(\hat{\beta}_1) = 94 - 5275; \ \text{se}(\hat{\beta}_2) = 0.02175$$

$$r^2 = 0.9909$$

(3.7.2)

As these results suggest, over the period 1980–1991 the mean consumption expenditure increased by about 72 cents for a dollar's increase in GDP; that is, the marginal propensity to consume (MPC) was about 72 cents. Literally interpreted, the intercept value of about -232 suggests that if the GDP were zero, the mean consumption expenditure would have been -232 billions of dollars. Again such a mechanical interpretation of the intercept does not make economic sense in the present case because it is out of the range of values we are working with and so does not really represent a likely outcome. The r^2 value of about 0.99 means that GDP explains about 99 percent of the variation in mean consumption expenditure, indeed a high value.

Despite its high r^2 value, one may question whether such a simple Keynesian consumption function is the appropriate model to explain the aggregate U.S. consumption expenditure. Sometimes very simple (i.e., bivariate) regression models can provide useful information. Estimates of the MPC for the United States based on complicated models also show that the MPC is around 0.7. But we will have more to say about model adequacy in later chapters.

3.8 COMPUTER OUTPUT FOR THE COFFEE DEMAND FUNCTION

As noted in the Introduction, throughout this book we will be making heavy use of the computer to obtain answers to illustrative examples so as to familiarize the reader with some packaged regression programs. In Appendix C we discuss in detail some of these programs. The illustrative examples in this book use one or more of these programs. For our coffee demand function, the SAS computer output is as shown in Appendix 3A, Section 3A.7.

3.9 A NOTE ON MONTE CARLO EXPERIMENTS

In this chapter we showed that under the assumptions of CLRM the least-squares estimators have certain desirable statistical features summarized in the BLUE property. In the appendix to this chapter we prove this property more formally. But in practice how does one know that the BLUE property holds? For example, how does one find out if the OLS estimators are unbiased? The answer is accomplished by the so-called **Monte Carlo** experiments, which are essentially computer simulation, or sampling, experiments.

To introduce the basic ideas, consider our two-variable PRF:

$$Y_i = \beta_1 + \beta_2 X_i + u_i \qquad (3.9.1)$$

A Monte Carlo experiment proceeds as follows:

1. Suppose the true values of the parameters are as follows: $\beta_1 = 20$ and $\beta_2 = 0.6$.
2. You choose the sample size, say $n = 25$.
3. You fix the values of X for each observation. In all you will have 25 X values.
4. Suppose you go to a random number table, choose 25 values, and call them u_i (these days most statistical packages have built-in random number generators).[29]

---

[29] In practice it is assumed that u_i follows a certain probability distribution, say, normal, with certain parameters (e.g., the mean and variance). Once the values of the parameters are specified, one can easily generate the u_i using statistical packages.

5. Since you *know* β_1, β_2, X_i, and u_i, using (3.9.1) you obtain 25 Y_i values.
6. Now using the 25 Y_i values thus generated, you regress these on the 25 X values chosen in step 3, obtaining $\hat{\beta}_1$ and $\hat{\beta}_2$, the least-squares estimators.
7. Suppose you repeat this experiment 99 times, each time using the same β_1, β_2, and X values. Of course, the u_i values will vary from experiment to experiment. Therefore, in all you have 100 experiments, thus generating 100 values each of β_1 and β_2. (In practice, many such experiments are conducted, sometimes 1000 to 2000).
8. You take the averages of these 100 estimates and call them $\bar{\hat{\beta}}_1$ and $\bar{\hat{\beta}}_2$.
9. If these average values are about the same as the true values of β_1 and β_2 assumed in step 1, this Monte Carlo experiment "establishes" that the least-squares estimators are indeed unbiased. Recall that under CLRM $E(\hat{\beta}_1) = \beta_1$ and $E(\hat{\beta}_2) = \beta_2$.

These steps characterize the general nature of the Monte Carlo experiments. Such experiments are often used to study the statistical properties of various methods of estimating population parameters. They are particularly useful to study the behavior of estimators in small, or finite, samples. These experiments are also an excellent means of driving home the concept of **repeated sampling** that is the basis of most of classical statistical inference, as we shall see in Chapter 5. We shall provide several examples of Monte Carlo experiments by way of exercises for classroom assignment. (See exercise 3.26.)

3.10 SUMMARY AND CONCLUSIONS

The important topics and concepts developed in this chapter can be summarized as follows.

1. The basic framework of regression analysis is the **CLRM.**
2. The CLRM is based on a set of assumptions.
3. Based on these assumptions, the least-squares estimators take on certain properties summarized in the Gauss-Markov theorem, which states that in the class of linear unbiased estimators, the least-squares estimators have minimum variance. In short, they are BLUE.
4. The *precision* of OLS estimators is measured by their **standard errors.** In Chapters 4 and 5 we shall see how the standard errors enable one to draw inferences on the population parameters, the β coefficients.
5. The overall goodness of fit of the regression model is measured by the **coefficient of determination,** r^2. It tells what proportion of the variation in the dependent variable, or regressand, is explained by the explanatory variable, or regressor. This r^2 lies between 0 and 1; the closer it is to 1, the better is the fit.
6. A concept related to the coefficient of determination is the **coefficient of correlation,** r. It is a measure of *linear association* between two variables and it lies between -1 and $+1$.

TABLE 3.5
What happens if the assumptions of CLRM are violated?

Assumption number	Type of violation	Where to study?
1	Nonlinearity in parameters	Not covered in this book
2	Stochastic regressor(s)	Introduction to Part II
3	Nonzero mean of u_i	Introduction to Part II
4	Heteroscedasticity	Chapter 11
5	Autocorrelated disturbances	Chapter 12
6	Nonzero covariance between disturbances and regressor	Introduction to Part II and Part IV
7	Sample observations less than the number of regressors	Chapter 10
8	Insufficient variability in regressors	Chapter 10
9	Specification bias	Chapters 13, 14
10	Multicollinearity	Chapter 10
11*	Nonnormality of disturbances	Introduction to Part II

* *Note:* The assumption that the disturbances u_i are normally distributed is not a part of the CLRM. But more on this in Chapter 4.

7. The CLRM is a theoretical construct or abstraction because it is based on a set of assumptions that may be stringent or "unrealistic." But such abstraction is often necessary in the initial stages of studying any field of knowledge. Once the CLRM is mastered, one can find out what happens if one or more of its assumptions are not satisfied. The first part of this book is devoted to studying the CLRM. The other parts of the book consider the refinements of the CLRM. Table 3.5 gives the road map ahead.

EXERCISES

Questions

3.1. Given the assumptions in column 1 of the following table, show that the assumptions in column 2 are equivalent to them.

Assumptions of the classical model

(1)	(2)
$E(u_i \mid X_i) = 0$	$E(Y_i \mid X_i) = \beta_2 + \beta_2 X$
$\text{cov}(u_i, u_j) = 0 \ i \neq j$	$\text{cov}(Y_i, Y_j) = 0 \ i \neq j$
$\text{var}(u_i \mid X_i) = \sigma^2$	$\text{var}(Y_i \mid X_i) = \sigma^2$

3.2. Show that the estimates $\hat{\beta}_1 = 1.572$ and $\hat{\beta}_2 = 1.357$ used in the first experiment of Table 3.1 are in fact the OLS estimators.

3.3. According to Malinvaud (see footnote 11), the assumptions that $E(u_i \mid X_i) = 0$ are quite important. To see this, consider the PRF: $Y = \beta_1 + \beta_2 X_i + u_i$. Now consider two situations: (i) $\beta_1 = 0$, $\beta_2 = 1$, and $E(u_i) = 0$; and (ii) $\beta_1 = 1$, $\beta_2 = 0$, and $E(u_i) = (X_i - 1)$. Now take the expectation of the PRF conditional upon X in the two preceding cases and see if you agree with Malinvaud about the significance of the assumption $E(u_i \mid X_i) = 0$.

3.4. Consider the sample regression

$$Y_i = \hat{\beta}_1 + \hat{\beta}_2 X_i + \hat{u}_i$$

Imposing the restrictions (i) $\sum \hat{u}_i = 0$ and (ii) $\sum \hat{u}_i X_i = 0$, obtain the estimators $\hat{\beta}_1$ and $\hat{\beta}_2$ and show that they are identical with the least-squares estimators given in (3.1.6) and (3.1.7). This method of obtaining estimators is called the **analogy principle.** Give an intuitive justification for imposing restrictions (i) and (ii). (*Hint:* Recall the CLRM assumptions about u_i.) In passing, note that the analogy principle of estimating unknown parameters is also known as the **method of moments** in which sample moments (e.g., sample mean) are used to estimate population moments (e.g., the population mean). As noted in Appendix A, a moment is a summary statistic of a probability distribution, such as the expected value and variance.

3.5. Show that r^2 defined in (3.5.5) ranges between 0 and 1. You may use the Cauchy-Schwarz inequality, which states that for any random variables X and Y the following relationship holds true:

$$[E(XY)]^2 \leq E(X^2)E(Y^2)$$

3.6. Let $\hat{\beta}_{YX}$ and $\hat{\beta}_{XY}$ represent the slopes in the regression of Y on X and X on Y, respectively. Show that

$$\hat{\beta}_{YX}\hat{\beta}_{XY} = r^2$$

where r is the coefficient of correlation between X and Y.

3.7. Suppose in question 3.6 that $\hat{\beta}_{YX}\hat{\beta}_{XY} = 1$. Does it matter then if we regress Y on X or X on Y? Explain carefully.

3.8. Spearman's rank correlation coefficient r_s is defined as follows:

$$r_s = 1 - \frac{6 \sum d^2}{n(n^2 - 1)}$$

where d = difference in the ranks assigned to the same individual or phenomenon

n = number of individuals or phenomena ranked

Derive r_s from r defined in (3.5.13). *Hint:* Rank the X and Y values from 1 to n. Note that the sum of X and Y ranks is $n(n + 1)/2$ each and therefore their means are $(n + 1)/2$.

3.9. Consider the following formulations of the two-variable PRF:

Model I: $Y_i = \beta_1 + \beta_2 X_i + u_i$

Model II: $Y_i = \alpha_1 + \alpha_2(X_i - \bar{X}) + u_i$

(a) Find the estimators of β_1 and α_1. Are they identical? Are their variances identical?

(b) Find the estimators of β_2 and α_2. Are they identical? Are their variances identical?

(c) What is the advantage, if any, of model II over model I?

3.10. Suppose you run the following regression:

$$y_i = \hat{\beta}_1 + \hat{\beta}_2 x_i + \hat{u}_i$$

where, as usual, y_i and x_i are deviations from their respective mean values. What will be the value of $\hat{\beta}_1$? Why? Will $\hat{\beta}_2$ be the same as that obtained from Eq. (3.1.6)? Why?

3.11. Let r_1 = coefficient of correlation between n pairs of values (Y_i, X_i) and r_2 = coefficient of correlation between n pairs of values $(aX_i + b, cY_i + d)$, where a, b, c, and d are constants. Show that $r_1 = r_2$ and hence *establish the principle that the coefficient of correlation is invariant with respect to the change of scale and the change of origin.*

Hint: Apply the definition of r given in (3.5.13).

Note: The operations, aX_i, $X_i + b$, and $aX_i + b$ are known, respectively, as the *change of scale, change of origin,* and *change of both scale and origin.*

3.12. If r, the coefficient of correlation between n pairs of values (X_i, Y_i), is positive, then determine whether each of the following statements is true or false:

(a) r between $(-X_i, -Y_i)$ is also positive.

(b) r between $(-X_i, Y_i)$ and that between $(X_i, -Y_i)$ can be either positive or negative.

(c) Both the slope coefficients β_{yx} and β_{xy} are positive, where β_{yx} = slope coefficient in the regression of Y on X and β_{xy} = slope coefficient in the regression of X on Y.

3.13. If X_1, X_2, and X_3 are uncorrelated variables each having the same standard deviation, show that the coefficient of correlation between $X_1 + X_2$ and $X_2 + X_3$ is equal to $\frac{1}{2}$. Why is the correlation coefficient not zero?

3.14. In the regression $Y_i = \beta_1 + \beta_2 X_i + u_i$ suppose we *multiply* each X value by a constant, say, 2. Will it change the residuals and fitted values of Y? Explain. What if we *add* a constant value, say, 2, to each X value?

3.15. Show that (3.5.14) in fact measures the coefficient of determination. *Hint:* Apply the definition of r given in (3.5.13) and recall that $\sum y_i \hat{y}_i = \sum (\hat{y}_i + \hat{u}_i) \hat{y}_i = \sum \hat{y}_i^2$, and remember (3.5.6).

Problems

3.16. You are given the ranks of 10 students in midterm and final examinations in statistics. Compute Spearman's coefficient of rank correlation and interpret it:

					Student					
Rank	**A**	**B**	**C**	**D**	**E**	**F**	**G**	**H**	**I**	**J**
Midterm	1	3	7	10	9	5	4	8	2	6
Final	3	2	8	7	9	6	5	10	1	4

3.17. The following table gives data on quit rate per 100 employees in manufacturing and the unemployment rate in manufacturing in the United States for the period 1960–1972.

> *Note:* The term *quit* refers to people leaving their jobs voluntarily.

Quit and unemployment rates in U.S. manufacturing, 1960–1972

Year	Quit rate per 100 employees, Y	Unemployment rate (%), X
1960	1.3	6.2
1961	1.2	7.8
1962	1.4	5.8
1963	1.4	5.7
1964	1.5	5.0
1965	1.9	4.0
1966	2.6	3.2
1967	2.3	3.6
1968	2.5	3.3
1969	2.7	3.3
1970	2.1	5.6
1971	1.8	6.8
1972	2.2	5.6

Source: Manpower Report of the President, 1973, Tables C-10 and A-18.

(*a*) Plot the data in a scattergram.
(*b*) Assume that quit rate Y is linearly related to the unemployment rate X as $Y_i = \beta_1 + \beta_2 X_i + u_i$. Estimate β_1, β_2, and their standard errors.
(*c*) Compute r^2 and r.
(*d*) Interpret your results.
(*e*) Plot the residuals $\hat{u}_i$. What can you learn from these residuals?
(*f*) By using the annual data for the period 1966–1978 and by using the same model as in (*b*) above, the following results were obtained:

$$\hat{Y}_i = 3.1237 - 0.1714X_i$$

$$\text{se}(\hat{\beta}_2) = 0.0210 \quad \text{and} \quad r^2 = 0.8575$$

If these results are different from the ones you have obtained in (*b*), how do you rationalize the difference?

3.18. Based on a sample of 10 observations, the following results were obtained:

$$\sum Y_i = 1110 \qquad \sum X_i = 1700 \qquad \sum X_i Y_i = 205{,}500$$

$$\sum X_i^2 = 322{,}000 \qquad \sum Y_i^2 = 132{,}100$$

with coefficient of correlation $r = 0.9758$. But on rechecking these calculations it was found that two pairs of observations were recorded:

Y	X		Y	X
90	120	instead of	80	110
140	220		150	210

What will be the effect of this error on r? Obtain the correct r.

3.19. The following table gives data on gold prices, the Consumer Price Index (CPI), and the New York Stock Exchange (NYSE) Index for the United States for the period 1977–1991. The NYSE Index includes most of the stocks listed on the NYSE, some 1500 plus.

Year	Price of gold at New York, $ per troy ounce	Consumer Price Index (CPI), 1982–84 = 100	New York Stock Exchange Index (NYSE), Dec. 31, 1965 = 100
1977	147.98	60.6	53.69
1978	193.44	65.2	53.70
1979	307.62	72.6	58.32
1980	612.51	82.4	68.10
1981	459.61	90.9	74.02
1982	376.01	96.5	68.93
1983	423.83	99.6	92.63
1984	360.29	103.9	92.46
1985	317.30	107.6	108.90
1986	367.87	109.6	136.00
1987	446.50	113.6	161.70
1988	436.93	118.3	149.91
1989	381.28	124.0	180.02
1990	384.08	130.7	183.46
1991	362.04	136.2	206.33

Source: Data on CPI and NYSE Index are from the *Economic Report of the President*, January 1993, Tables B-59 and B-91, respectively. Data on gold prices are from U.S. Department of Commerce, Bureau of Economic Analysis, *Business Statistics, 1963–1991*, p. 68.

(a) Plot in the same scattergram gold prices, CPI, and the NYSE Index.
(b) An investment is supposed to be a hedge against inflation if its price and or rate of return at least keeps pace with inflation. To test this hypothesis, suppose you decide to fit the following model, assuming the scatterplot in (a) suggests that this is appropriate:

$$\text{Gold price}_t = \beta_1 + \beta_2\, \text{CPI}_t + u_t$$
$$\text{NYSE Index}_t = \beta_1 + \beta_2\, \text{CPI}_t + u_t$$

If the hypothesis is correct, what value of β_2 would you expect?
(c) Which is a better hedge against inflation, gold or the stock market?

3.20. Fit a suitable linear model to the following data, which relate to consumer price index and money supply in Japan for the period 1988-1 to 1992-3, and comment on your results.

Consumer prices and money supply in Japan, 1988-1 to 1992-3

Year and quarter	CPI (1985 = 100)	Money stock (M_1) (billions of yen)
1988-1	101.0	101,587
1988-2	101.1	102,258
1988-3	101.6	104,653
1988-4	102.1	107,561
1989-1	102.1	109,525
1989-2	103.7	108,442
1989-3	104.4	109,176
1989-4	104.7	107,660
1990-1	105.7	111,600
1990-2	106.3	111,929
1990-3	107.1	112,753
1990-4	108.5	112,155
1991-1	109.7	113,150
1991-2	109.9	115,827
1991-3	110.5	120,718
1991-4	111.5	125,891
1992-1	111.7	123,589
1992-2	112.4	125,583
1992-3	112.5	126,816

Source: Federal Reserve Bank of St. Louis, *International Economic Conditions*, February 1993, pp. 26, 28.

3.21. The following table gives data on the number of telephones per 1000 persons (Y) and the per capita Gross Domestic Product (GDP), at factor cost (X) (in 1968 Singapore dollars) for Singapore for the period 1960 to 1981. Is there any relationship between the two variables? How do you know?

Telephone ownership and per capita GDP in Singapore, 1960–1981

Year	Y	X	Year	Y	X
1960	36	1299	1971	90	2723
1961	37	1365	1972	102	3033
1962	38	1409	1973	114	3317
1963	41	1549	1974	126	3487
1964	42	1416	1975	141	3575
1965	45	1473	1976	163	3784
1966	48	1589	1977	196	4025
1967	54	1757	1978	223	4286
1968	59	1974	1979	262	4628
1969	67	2204	1980	291	5038
1970	78	2462	1981	317	5472

Source: Lim Chong-Yah, *Economic Restructuring in Singapore*, Federal Publications, Pvt. Ltd., Singapore, 1984, pp. 110–113.

3.22. The following table gives data on Gross Domestic Product (GDP) for the United States for the years 1972–1991.

Gross Domestic Product (GDP) in current and 1987 dollars, 1972–1991

Year	GDP (current dollars, billions)	GDP (1987 dollars, billions)
1972	1207.0	3107.1
1973	1349.6	3268.6
1974	1458.6	3248.1
1975	1585.9	3221.7
1976	1768.4	3380.8
1977	1974.1	3533.3
1978	2232.7	3703.5
1979	2488.6	3796.8
1980	2708.0	3776.3
1981	3030.6	3843.1
1982	3149.6	3760.3
1983	3405.0	3906.6
1984	3777.2	4148.5
1985	4038.7	4279.8
1986	4268.6	4404.5
1987	4539.9	4539.9
1988	4900.4	4718.6
1989	5250.8	4838.0
1990	5522.2	4877.5
1991	5677.5	4821.0

Source: Economic Report of the President, January 1993, Tables B-1 and B-2, pp. 348-349.

(a) Plot the GDP data in current and constant (i.e., 1987) dollars against time.

(b) Letting Y denote GDP and X time (measured chronologically starting with 1 for 1972, 2 for 1973, through 20 for 1991), see if the following model fits the GDP data:

$$Y_t = \beta_1 + \beta_2 X_t + u_t$$

Estimate this model for both current and constant-dollar GDP.

(c) How would you interpret β_2?

(d) If there is a difference between β_2 estimated for current-dollar GDP and that estimated for constant-dollar GDP, what explains the difference?

(e) From your results what can you say about the nature of inflation in the United States over the sample period?

3.23. Using the data given in Table I.1 of the Introduction, verify Eq. (3.7.2).

3.24. For the S.A.T. example given in exercise 2.16 do the following:

(a) Plot the female verbal score against the male verbal score.

(b) If the scatterplot suggests that a linear relationship between the two seems appropriate, obtain the regression of female verbal score on male verbal score.

(c) If there is a relationship between the two verbal scores, is the relationship causal?

3.25. Repeat the exercise in problem 3.24 replacing math scores for verbal scores.

3.26. Monte Carlo study *classroom assignment:*

Refer to the 10 X values given in Table 3.2. Let $\beta_1 = 25$ and $\beta_2 = 0.5$. Assume $u_i \sim N(0, 9)$, that is, u_i are normally distributed with mean 0 and variance 9. Generate 100 samples using these values, obtaining 100 estimates of β_1 and β_2. Graph these estimates. What conclusions can you draw from the Monte Carlo study? *Note:* Most statistical packages now can generate random variables from most well-known probability distributions. Ask your instructor for help, in case you have difficulty generating such variables.

APPENDIX 3A

3A.1   DERIVATION OF LEAST-SQUARES ESTIMATES

Differentiating (3.1.2) partially with respect to $\hat{\beta}_1$ and $\hat{\beta}_2$, we obtain

$$\frac{\partial(\sum \hat{u}_i^2)}{\partial \hat{\beta}_1} = -2\sum(Y_i - \hat{\beta}_1 - \hat{\beta}_2 X_i) = -2\sum \hat{u}_i \tag{1}$$

$$\frac{\partial(\sum \hat{u}_i^2)}{\partial \hat{\beta}_2} = -2\sum(Y_i - \hat{\beta}_1 - \hat{\beta}_2 X_i)X_i = -2\sum \hat{u}_i X_i \tag{2}$$

Setting these equations to zero, after algebraic simplification and manipulation, gives the estimators given in Eqs. (3.1.6) and (3.1.7).

3A.2   LINEARITY AND UNBIASEDNESS PROPERTIES OF LEAST-SQUARES ESTIMATORS

From (3.1.8) we have

$$\hat{\beta}_2 = \frac{\sum x_i Y_i}{\sum x_i^2} = \sum k_i Y_i \tag{3}$$

where

$$k_i = \frac{x_i}{(\sum x_i^2)}$$

which shows that $\hat{\beta}_2$ is a **linear estimator** because it is a linear function of Y; actually it is a weighted average of Y_i with k_i serving as the weights. It can similarly be shown that $\hat{\beta}_1$ too is a linear estimator.

Incidentally, note these properties of the weights k_i:

1. Since the X_i are assumed to be nonstochastic, the k_i are nonstochastic too.
2. $\sum k_i = 0$.
3. $\sum k_i^2 = 1/\sum x_i^2$.
4. $\sum k_i x_i = \sum k_i X_i = 1$. These properties can be directly verified from the definition of k_i.

For example,

$$\sum k_i = \sum \left(\frac{x_i}{\sum x_i^2}\right) = \frac{1}{\sum x_i^2} \sum x_i, \qquad \text{since for a given sample } \sum x_i^2 \text{ is known}$$

$$= 0, \qquad \begin{array}{l}\text{since } \sum x_i, \text{ the sum of deviations} \\ \text{from the mean value, is always zero}\end{array}$$

Now substitute the PRF $Y_i = \beta_1 + \beta_2 X_i + u_i$ into (3) to obtain

$$\hat{\beta}_2 = \sum k_i(\beta_1 + \beta_2 X_i + u_i)$$

$$= \beta_1 \sum k_i + \beta_2 \sum k_i X_i + \sum k_i u_i$$

$$= \beta_2 + \sum k_i u_i \tag{4}$$

where use is made of the properties of k_i noted earlier.

Now taking expectation of (4) on both sides and noting that k_i, being nonstochastic, can be treated as constants, we obtain

$$E(\hat{\beta}_2) = \beta_2 + \sum k_i E(u_i)$$

$$= \beta_2 \tag{5}$$

since $E(u_i) = 0$ by assumption. Therefore, $\hat{\beta}_2$ is an unbiased estimator of β_2. Likewise, it can be proved that $\hat{\beta}_1$ is also an unbiased estimator of β_1.

3A.3 VARIANCES AND STANDARD ERRORS OF LEAST-SQUARES ESTIMATORS

Now by the definition of variance, we can write

$$\text{var}(\hat{\beta}_2) = E[\hat{\beta}_2 - E(\hat{\beta}_2)]^2$$

$$= E(\hat{\beta}_2 - \beta_2)^2, \qquad \text{since } E(\hat{\beta}_2) = \beta_2$$

$$= E\left(\sum k_i u_i\right)^2, \qquad \text{using Eq. (4) above}$$

$$= E(k_1^2 u_1^2 + k_2^2 u_2^2 + \cdots + k_n^2 u_n^2 + 2k_1 k_2 u_1 u_2 + \cdots + 2k_{n-1} k_n u_{n-1} u_n) \tag{6}$$

Since by assumption, $E(u_i^2) = \sigma^2$ for each i and $E(u_i u_j) = 0$, $i \neq j$, it follows that

$$
\begin{aligned}
\operatorname{var}\left(\hat{\beta}_2\right) &= \sigma^2 \sum k_i^2 \\
&= \frac{\sigma^2}{\sum x_i^2}, \qquad \text{(using the definition of } k_i^2) \\
&= \text{Eq. (3.3.1)}
\end{aligned}
\tag{7}
$$

The variance of $\hat{\beta}_1$ can be obtained following the same line of reasoning already given. Once the variances of $\hat{\beta}_1$ and $\hat{\beta}_2$ are obtained, their positive square roots give the corresponding standard errors.

3A.4 COVARIANCE BETWEEN $\hat{\beta}_1$ AND $\hat{\beta}_2$

By definition,

$$
\begin{aligned}
\operatorname{cov}(\hat{\beta}_1, \hat{\beta}_2) &= E\{[\hat{\beta}_1 - E(\hat{\beta}_1)][\hat{\beta}_2 - E(\hat{\beta}_2)]\} \\
&= E(\hat{\beta}_1 - \beta_1)(\hat{\beta}_2 - \beta_2) \qquad \text{(Why?)} \\
&= -\bar{X} E(\hat{\beta}_2 - \beta_2)^2 \\
&= -\bar{X} \operatorname{var}(\hat{\beta}_2) \\
&= \text{Eq. (3.3.9)}
\end{aligned}
\tag{8}
$$

where use is made of the fact that $\hat{\beta}_1 = \bar{Y} - \hat{\beta}_2 \bar{X}$ and $E(\hat{\beta}_1) = \bar{Y} - \beta_2 \bar{X}$, giving $\hat{\beta}_1 - E(\hat{\beta}_1) = -\bar{X}(\hat{\beta}_2 - \beta_2)$. *Note:* $\operatorname{var}(\hat{\beta}_2)$ is given in (3.3.1).

3A.5 THE LEAST-SQUARES ESTIMATOR OF σ^2

Recall that

$$
Y_i = \beta_1 + \beta_2 X_i + u_i
\tag{9}
$$

Therefore,

$$
\bar{Y} = \beta_1 + \beta_2 \bar{X} + \bar{u}
\tag{10}
$$

Subtracting (10) from (9) gives

$$
y_i = \beta_2 x_i + (u_i - \bar{u})
\tag{11}
$$

Also recall that

$$
\hat{u}_i = y_i - \hat{\beta}_2 x_i
\tag{12}
$$

Therefore, substituting (11) into (12) yields

$$
\hat{u}_i = \beta_2 x_i + (u_i - \bar{u}) - \hat{\beta}_2 x_i
\tag{13}
$$

Collecting terms, squaring, and summing on both sides, we obtain

$$\sum \hat{u}_i^2 = (\hat{\beta}_2 - \beta_2)^2 \sum x_i^2 + \sum (u_i - \bar{u})^2 - 2(\hat{\beta}_2 - \beta_2) \sum x_i (u_i - \bar{u}) \quad (14)$$

Taking expectations on both sides gives

$$E(\sum \hat{u}_i^2) = \sum x_i^2 E(\hat{\beta}_2 - \beta_2)^2 + E[\sum (u_i - \bar{u})^2] - 2E[(\hat{\beta}_2 - \beta_2) \sum x_i (u_i - \bar{u})]$$

$$= \quad\quad A \quad\quad + \quad\quad B \quad\quad + \quad\quad C$$

$$(15)$$

Now by the assumptions of the classical linear regression model as well as some of the results just established, it can be verified that

$$A = \sigma^2$$
$$B = (n-1)\sigma^2$$
$$C = -2\sigma^2$$

Therefore, substituting these values into (15), we obtain

$$E\left(\sum \hat{u}_i^2\right) = (n-2)\sigma^2 \quad (16)$$

Therefore, if we define

$$\hat{\sigma}^2 = \frac{\sum \hat{u}_i^2}{n-2} \quad (17)$$

its expected value is

$$E(\hat{\sigma}^2) = \frac{1}{n-2} E\left(\sum \hat{u}_i^2\right) = \sigma^2 \quad \text{using (16)} \quad (18)$$

which shows that $\hat{\sigma}^2$ is an unbiased estimator of true σ^2.

3A.6 MINIMUM-VARIANCE PROPERTY OF LEAST-SQUARES ESTIMATORS

It was shown in Appendix 3A, Section 3A.2 that the least-squares estimator $\hat{\beta}_2$ is linear as well as unbiased (this holds true of $\hat{\beta}_1$ too). To show that these estimators are also minimum variance in the class of all linear unbiased estimators, consider the least-squares estimator $\hat{\beta}_2$:

$$\hat{\beta}_2 = \sum k_i Y_i$$

where

$$k_i = \frac{X_i - \bar{X}}{\sum (X_i - \bar{X})^2} = \frac{x_i}{\sum x_i^2} \quad \text{(see Appendix 3A.2)} \quad (19)$$

which shows that $\hat{\beta}_2$ is a weighted average of the Y's, with k_i serving as the weights.

Let us define an alternative linear estimator of β_2 as follows:

$$\beta_2^* = \sum w_i Y_i \tag{20}$$

where w_i are also weights, not necessarily equal to k_i. Now

$$E(\beta_2^*) = \sum w_i E(Y_i)$$

$$= \sum w_i(\beta_1 + \beta_2 X_i)$$

$$= \beta_1 \sum w_i + \beta_2 \sum w_i X_i \tag{21}$$

Therefore, for β_2^* to be unbiased, we must have

$$\sum w_i = 0 \tag{22}$$

and

$$\sum w_i X_i = 1 \tag{23}$$

Also, we may write

$$\text{var}(\beta_2^*) = \text{var} \sum w_i Y_i$$

$$= \sum w_i^2 \, \text{var}\, Y_i \qquad [\textit{Note: } \text{var}\, Y_i = \text{var}\, u_i = \sigma^2]$$

$$= \sigma^2 \sum w_i^2 \qquad [\textit{Note: } \text{cov}(Y_i, Y_j) = 0(i \neq j)]$$

$$= \sigma^2 \sum \left(w_i - \frac{x_i}{\sum x_i^2} + \frac{x_i}{\sum x_i^2} \right)^2 \qquad \text{(Note the mathematical trick)}$$

$$= \sigma^2 \sum \left(w_i - \frac{x_i}{\sum x_i^2} \right)^2 + \sigma^2 \frac{\sum x_i^2}{\left(\sum x_i^2 \right)^2} + 2\sigma^2 \sum \left(w_i - \frac{x_i}{\sum x_i^2} \right)\left(\frac{x_i}{\sum x_i^2} \right)$$

$$= \sigma^2 \sum \left(w_i - \frac{x_i}{\sum x_i^2} \right)^2 + \sigma^2 \left(\frac{1}{\sum x_i^2} \right) \tag{24}$$

because the last term in the next to the last step drops out. (Why?)

Since the last term in (24) is constant, the variance of (β_2^*) can be minimized only by manipulating the first term. If we let

$$w_i = \frac{x_i}{\sum x_i^2}$$

Eq. (24) reduces to

$$\text{var}(\beta_2^*) = \frac{\sigma^2}{\sum x_i^2}$$

$$= \text{var}(\hat{\beta}_2) \tag{25}$$

In words, with weights $w_i = k_i$, which are the least-squares weights, the variance of the linear estimator β_2^* is equal to the variance of the least-squares estimator $\hat{\beta}_2$; otherwise $\text{var}(\beta_2^*) > \text{var}(\hat{\beta}_2)$. To put it differently, if there is a minimum-variance linear unbiased estimator of β_2, it must be the least-squares estimator. Similarly it can be shown that $\hat{\beta}_1$ is a minimum-variance linear unbiased estimator of β_1.

3A.7 SAS OUTPUT OF THE COFFEE DEMAND FUNCTION (3.7.1)

Since this is the first time that we are presenting the SAS output, it may be helpful to comment on the output briefly. The results are obtained from the REGRESSION procedure of SAS. The dependent variable is Y (cups per person per day) and the regressor is X_2 [average real retail price, $ per lb. Note this is variable X in (3.7.1)]. For expositional purposes, the output given on the next page is divided into six parts. Notice that a great many decimal places are shown in the output, although in practice we need not go beyond four or five.

Part I: This gives the Analysis of Variance (ANOVA) table, which is discussed in Chapter 5.

Part II: *Root MSE* means the square root of the mean square error ($= \hat{\sigma}^2$), that is, it gives the standard error of the estimate, $\hat{\sigma}$.
     Dep Mean means the mean value of the dependent variable Y ($= \bar{Y}$).
     C.V. is the coefficient of variation defined as $(\hat{\sigma}/\bar{Y}) \times 100$, and it expresses the unexplained variability remaining in the data (i.e., Y variable) relative to the mean value, $\bar{Y}$.
     R^2 = coefficient of determination.
     $\bar{R}^2$ = adjusted R^2 (see Chapter 7).

Part III: This part gives the estimated values of the parameters, their standard errors, their t-ratios, and the significance level of the t-ratios. These latter two will be taken up fully in Chapter 5.

Part IV: This section gives what is known as the variance-covariance matrix of the estimated parameters. The elements on the diagonal running from the upper left corner to the lower right corner give the variances (i.e., squares of the standard errors given in Part III)[30] and the off-diagonal elements give the covariances between the estimated parameters, here $\text{cov}(\hat{\beta}_1, \hat{\beta}_2)$, as defined in (3.3.9).

Part V: This gives the actual Y_i and X_i values, the estimated Y values ($= \hat{Y}_i$), and the residuals $\hat{u}_i = (Y_i - \hat{Y}_i)$.

Part VI: This part gives the Durbin-Watson d statistic and the first-order autocorrelation coefficient, topics discussed in Chapter 12.

---

[30]Thus, 0.01479 is the variance of $\hat{\beta}_1$, and 0.0130 is the variance of $\hat{\beta}_2$; taking the square roots of these numbers, we obtain 0.1216 and 0.1140, which are, respectively, the standard errors of the two coefficients, as shown in Part III, except for the roundoff errors.

DEP VARIABLE: Y

I	SOURCE	DF	SUM OF SQUARES	MEAN SQUARE	F VALUE	PROB > F
	MODEL	1	0.292975	0.292975	17.687	0.0023
	ERROR	9	0.149080	0.016564		
	C TOTAL	10	0.442055			

II					
	ROOT MSE	0.128703	R-SQUARE	0.6628	
	DEP MEAN	2.206364	ADJ R-SC	0.6253	
	C.V.	5.833255			

III	VARIABLE	DF	PARAMETER ESTIMATE	STANDARD ERROR	T FOR HO: PARAMETER = 0	PROB > |T|
	INTERCEP	1	2.691124	0.121622	22.127	0.0001
	X	1	−0.479529	0.114022	−4.206	0.0023

IV	COVARIANCE OF ESTIMATES		
	COVB	INTERCEP	X
	INTERCEP	0.01479203	−0.0131428
	X	−0.0131428	0.01300097

V	OBS	Y	X	YHAT	YRESID = $\hat{u}_i$
	1	2.57	0.77	2.32189	0.24811
	2	2.50	0.74	2.33627	0.16373
	3	2.35	0.72	2.34586	0.00414
	4	2.25	0.73	2.34107	−0.04107
	5	2.20	0.76	2.32668	−0.07668
	6	2.20	0.75	2.33148	−0.13148
	7	2.11	1.08	2.17323	−0.06323
	8	1.94	1.81	1.82318	0.11682
	9	1.97	1.39	2.02458	−0.05458
	10	2.06	1.20	2.11569	−0.05569
	11	2.02	1.17	2.13007	−0.11007

VI		
	DURBIN-WATSON d	0.727
	1ST ORDER AUTOCORRELATION	0.390

4

THE NORMALITY ASSUMPTION: CLASSICAL NORMAL LINEAR REGRESSION MODEL (CNLRM)

In this chapter we continue to deal with the two-variable classical linear regression model but assume that the population disturbances u_i are normally distributed. Such a model is called a two-variable **classical normal linear regression model** (CNLRM). In what follows, we offer justification for the normality assumption for u_i and point out the consequences of this assumption.

4.1 THE PROBABILITY DISTRIBUTION OF DISTURBANCES u_i

Recall that for the application of the method of ordinary least squares (OLS) to the classical linear regression model we did not make any assumptions about the probability distribution of the disturbances u_i. The only assumptions made about u_i were that they had zero expectations, were uncorrelated, and had a constant variance. With these assumptions, we saw (in Chapter 3) that the OLS

₂ learn this.

estimators $\hat{\beta}_1$, $\hat{\beta}_2$, and $\hat{\sigma}^2$ satisfy several desirable statistical properties, such as unbiasedness and minimum variance. If our objective is point estimation only, the OLS method will therefore suffice. But point estimation is only one aspect of statistical inference, the other being hypothesis testing.[1]

Thus, our interest in not only in obtaining say, $\hat{\beta}_2$, but also in using it to make statements or inferences about true β_2. More generally, our goal is not merely to obtain the sample regression function (SRF) but to use it to draw inferences about the population regression function (PRF), as emphasized in Chapter 2.

Since our objective is estimation as well as hypothesis testing, we need to specify the probability distribution of the disturbances u_i. Why? The answer is not difficult. It was shown in Appendix 3A, Section 3A.2, that the OLS estimators $\hat{\beta}_1$ and $\hat{\beta}_2$ are both linear functions of u_i, which is random by assumption.[2] Therefore, the sampling or probability distributions of the OLS estimators will depend upon the assumptions made about the probability distribution of u_i. And since the probability distributions of these estimators are necessary to draw inferences about their population values, the nature of the probability distribution of u_i assumes an extremely important role in hypothesis testing.

Since the method of OLS does not make any assumption about the probabilistic nature of u_i, it is of little help for the purpose of drawing inferences about the PRF from SRF, the Gauss-Markov theorem notwithstanding. This void can be filled if we are willing to assume that the u's follow some probability distribution. For reasons to be explained shortly, in the regression context it is usually assumed that the u's follow the normal distribution.

4.2 THE NORMALITY ASSUMPTION

The classical *normal* linear regression assumes that each u_i is distributed *normally* with

$$\text{Mean:} \qquad E(u_i) = 0 \qquad\qquad (4.2.1)$$

$$\text{Variance:} \qquad E(u_i^2) = \sigma^2 \qquad\qquad (4.2.2)$$

$$\text{cov}(u_i, u_j): \qquad E(u_i, u_j) = 0 \qquad i \neq j \qquad\qquad (4.2.3)$$

---

[1] What is known as the **classical theory of statistical inference** consists of two branches, namely, estimation (point as well as interval) and hypothesis testing. Point estimation was considered in Chap. 3. The topics of interval estimation and hypothesis testing, which are intimately connected, will be discussed fully in Chap. 5. Here it suffices to note that in hypothesis testing we are generally concerned with the relationship between the population quantities (parameters) and their sample counterparts (estimators).

[2] Note that these estimators are actually linear functions of the dependent variable Y. But Y is itself a linear function of u, as postulated in (2.4.2). Hence, the estimators are ultimately linear functions of u, which is random by assumption. [See Eq. (4) in App. 3A, Sec. 3A.2.]

These assumptions may be more compactly stated as

$$u_i \sim N(0, \sigma^2) \tag{4.2.4}$$

where $\sim$ means "distributed as" and where N stands for the "normal distribution," the terms in the parentheses representing the two parameters of the normal distribution, namely, the mean and the variance.

In passing note that for **two normally distributed variables zero covariance or correlation means independence of the two variables**. Therefore, with the normality assumption, (4.2.3) means that u_i and u_j are not only uncorrelated but also independently distributed. (See exercise 4.1 in Appendix 4A.)

Therefore, we can write (4.2.4) as

$$u_i \sim \text{NID}(0, \sigma^2) \tag{4.2.5}$$

where **NID** stands for *normally and independently distributed*.

Why the normality assumption? There are several reasons.

1. As pointed out in Section 2.5, u_i represents the combined influence (on the dependent variable) of a large number of independent variables that are not explicitly introduced in the regression model. As noted, we hope that the influence of these omitted or neglected variables is small and at best random. Now by the celebrated **central limit theorem** of statistics it can be shown that if there are a large number of independent and identically distributed random variables, then, with a few exceptions, the distribution of their sum tends to a normal distribution as the number of such variables increases indefinitely.[3] It is this central limit theorem that provides a theoretical justification for the assumption of normality of u_i.

2. A variant of the central limit theorem states that even if the number of variables is not very large or if these variables are not strictly independent, their sum may still be normally distributed.[4]

3. With the normality assumption, the probability distributions of the OLS estimators can be easily derived because **one property of the normal distribution is that any linear function of normally distributed variables is itself normally distributed**. It is shown later that, under the normality assumption for u_i, the OLS estimators $\hat{\beta}_1$ and $\hat{\beta}_2$ are also normally distributed.

4. Finally, the normal distribution is a comparatively simple distribution involving only two parameters (mean and variance); it is very well-known,

---

[3]For a relatively simple discussion of the theorem, see Harald Cramer, *The Elements of Probability Theory and Some of Its Applications*, John Wiley & Sons, New York, 1955, pp. 114–116. One exception to the theorem is the Cauchy distribution; see M. G. Kendall and A. Stuart, *The Advanced Theory of Statistics*, Charles Griffin & Company, London, 1960, vol. 1, pp. 248–249.

[4]For the various forms of the central limit theorem, see Harald Cramer, *Mathematical Methods of Statistics*, Princeton University Press, Princeton, N.J., 1946, Chap. 17.

and its theoretical properties have been extensively studied in mathematical statistics. The properties of the normal distribution are discussed in Appendix A.

4.3 PROPERTIES OF OLS ESTIMATORS UNDER THE NORMALITY ASSUMPTION

With the assumption of normality, the OLS estimators $\hat{\beta}_1$, $\hat{\beta}_2$, and $\hat{\sigma}^2$ have the following statistical properties:[5]

Are we studying under assumptions of normality.

1. They are unbiased.
2. They have minimum variance. Combined with 1, this means they are **minimum-variance unbiased**, or **efficient estimators**.
3. **Consistency**; that is, as the sample size increases indefinitely, the estimators converge to their true population values.
4. $\hat{\beta}_1$ is *normally* distributed with

$$\text{Mean:} \quad E(\hat{\beta}_1) = \beta_1 \tag{4.3.1}$$

$$\text{var}(\hat{\beta}_1): \quad \sigma^2_{\hat{\beta}_1} = \frac{\sum X_i^2}{n \sum x_i^2}\sigma^2 \tag{4.3.2}$$

or, more compactly,

$$\hat{\beta}_1 \sim N(\beta_1, \sigma^2_{\hat{\beta}_1})$$

Then by the properties of the normal distribution the variable Z, which is defined as

$$Z = \frac{\hat{\beta}_1 - \beta_1}{\sigma_{\hat{\beta}_1}} \tag{4.3.3}$$

follows the **standardized normal distribution,** that is, normal distribution with zero mean and unit (= 1) variance, or

$$Z \sim N(0, 1)$$

Geometrically, the probability distribution of $\hat{\beta}_1$ can be depicted as shown in Fig. 4.1.

5. $\hat{\beta}_2$ is *normally* distributed with

$$\text{Mean:} \quad E(\hat{\beta}_2) = \beta_2$$

$$\text{var}(\hat{\beta}_2): \quad \sigma^2_{\hat{\beta}_2} = \frac{\sigma^2}{\sum x_i^2} \tag{4.3.4}$$

or, more compactly,

$$\hat{\beta}_2 \sim N(\beta_2, \sigma^2_{\hat{\beta}_2})$$

---

[5]The statistical properties of estimators are discussed fully in App. A.

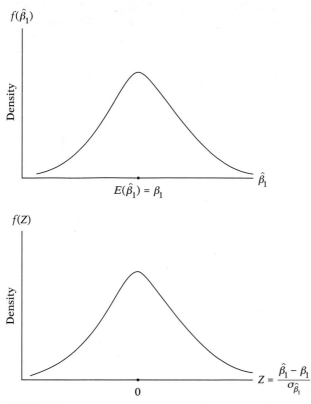

FIGURE 4.1
The probability distribution of $\hat{\beta}_1$.

Then, as in (4.3.3),

$$Z = \frac{\hat{\beta}_2 - \beta_2}{\sigma_{\hat{\beta}_2}} \tag{4.3.5}$$

which also follows the standardized normal distribution.

Geometrically, the probability distribution of $\hat{\beta}_2$ is as shown in Fig. 4.2.

6. $(n - 2)\hat{\sigma}^2/\sigma^2$ is distributed as the χ^2 (chi-square) distribution with $n - 2$ df. The chi-square distribution is discussed in App. A, and an application is given in Chapter 5.

7. $(\hat{\beta}_1, \hat{\beta}_2)$ are distributed independently of $\hat{\sigma}^2$.

8. $\hat{\beta}_1$ and $\hat{\beta}_2$ *have minimum variance in the entire class of unbiased estimators, whether linear or not.* This result, which is due to Rao, is very powerful because unlike the Gauss-Markov theorem it is not restricted to the class of linear estimators only.[6] Therefore, we can say that the least-squares estimators are **best unbiased estimators (BUE).**

---

[6]C. R. Rao, *Linear Statistical Inference and Its Applications*, John Wiley & Sons, New York, 1965, p. 258.

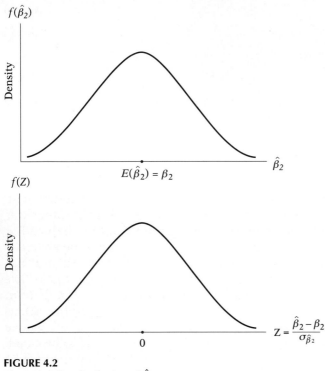

FIGURE 4.2
The probability distribution of $\hat{\beta}_2$.

The unbiasedness and minimum-variance properties of the OLS estimators have been proved in Appendix 3A, Sections 3A.2 and 3A.6. To show that $\hat{\beta}_1$ and $\hat{\beta}_2$ follow the normal distribution is easy. As noted in Chapter 3, $\hat{\beta}_1$ and $\hat{\beta}_2$ are linear functions of the stochastic disturbance term u_i (see footnote 2). Since the u_i are assumed to be normally distributed, then, following the rule that any linear function of normally distributed variables is itself normally distributed, it follows that $\hat{\beta}_1$ and $\hat{\beta}_2$ are themselves normally distributed with the means and variances given previously. The proof of the statement that $(n-2)\hat{\sigma}^2/\sigma^2$ follows the χ^2 distribution with $n-2$ df is slightly involved and may be found in the references.[7]

The important point to note is that the normality assumption enables us to derive the probability, or sampling, distributions of $\hat{\beta}_1$ (normal), $\hat{\beta}_2$ (normal), and $\hat{\sigma}^2$ (chi-square). As we shall see in Chapter 5, this simplifies the task of establishing confidence intervals and testing (statistical) hypotheses.

In passing, note that if we assume that u_i is distributed normally with mean 0 and variance σ^2, then Y_i itself is normally distributed with mean and variance given by

---

[7]See, for example, Robert V. Hogg and Allen T. Craig, *Introduction to Mathematical Statistics*, 2d ed., Macmillan, New York, 1965, p. 144.

$$E(Y_i) = \beta_1 + \beta_2 X_i \qquad (4.3.6)$$

$$\text{var}(Y_i) = \sigma^2 \qquad (4.3.7)$$

More compactly, we can write

$$Y_i \sim N(\beta_1 + \beta_2 X_i, \sigma^2) \qquad (4.3.8)$$

The proof of (4.3.8) follows from the fact that any linear function of normally distributed variables is itself normally distributed.

4.4 THE METHOD OF MAXIMUM LIKELIHOOD (ML)

A method of point estimation with some stronger theoretical properties than the method of OLS is the method of **maximum likelihood** (**ML**). Since this method is slightly involved, it is discussed in the appendix to this chapter. For the general reader, it will suffice to note that if u_i are assumed to be normally distributed, as we have done for reasons already discussed, the ML and OLS estimators of the regression coefficients, the β's, are identical, and this is true of simple as well as multiple regressions. The ML estimator of σ^2 is $\sum \hat{u}_i^2/n$. This estimator is biased, whereas the OLS estimator of $\sigma^2 = \sum \hat{u}_i^2/(n-2)$, as we have seen, is unbiased. But comparing these two estimators of σ^2, we see that as the sample size n gets larger the two estimators of σ^2 tend to be equal. Thus, asymptotically (i.e., as n increases indefinitely), the ML estimator of σ^2 is also unbiased.

Since the method of least squares with the added assumption of normality of u_i provides us with all the tools necessary for both estimation and hypothesis testing of the linear regression models, there is no loss for readers who may not want to pursue the maximum likelihood method because of its slight mathematical complexity.

4.5 PROBABILITY DISTRIBUTIONS RELATED TO THE NORMAL DISTRIBUTION: THE t, CHI-SQUARE (χ^2), AND F DISTRIBUTIONS

The t, the **chi-square** and the F probability distributions, whose salient features are discussed in Appendix A, are intimately related to the normal distribution. Since we will make heavy use of these probability distributions in the following chapters, we summarize their relationship with the normal distribution in the following theorems; the proofs, which are beyond the scope of this book, can be found in the references.[8]

---

[8]See App. A for a brief discussion of various probability distributions and their properties. For proofs of the theorems, refer to Alexander M. Mood, Franklin A. Graybill, and Duane C. Boes, *Introduction to the Theory of Statistics*, 3d ed., McGraw-Hill, New York, 1974, pp. 239–249.

Theorem 4.1. If $Z_1, Z_2, \ldots, Z_n$ are normally and independently distributed random variables such that $Z_i \sim N(\mu_i, \sigma_i^2)$, then the sum $Z = \sum k_i Z_i$, where k_i are constants not all zero, is also distributed normally with mean $\sum k_i \mu_i$ and variance $\sum k_i^2 \sigma_i^2$; that is, $Z \sim N(\sum k_i \mu_i, \sum k_i^2 \sigma_i^2)$. *Note:* μ denotes the mean value.

In short, linear combinations of normal variables are themselves normally distributed. For example, if Z_1 and Z_2 are normally and independently distributed as $Z_1 \sim N(10, 2)$ and $Z_2 \sim N(8, 1.5)$, then the linear combination $Z = 0.8Z_1 + 0.2Z_2$ is also normally distributed with mean $= 0.8(10) + 0.2(8) = 9.6$ and variance $= 0.64(2) + 0.04(1.5) = 1.34$, that is, $Z \sim (9.6, 1.34)$.

Theorem 4.2. If $Z_1, Z_2, \ldots, Z_n$ are normally distributed but are not independent, the sum $Z = \sum k_i Z_i$, where k_i are constants not all zero, is also normally distributed with mean $\sum k_i \mu_i$ and variance $[\sum k_i^2 \sigma_i^2 + 2 \sum k_i k_j \operatorname{cov}(Z_i, Z_j), \ i \neq j]$.

Thus, if $Z_1 \sim N(6, 2)$ and $Z_2 \sim N(7, 3)$ and $\operatorname{cov}(Z_1, Z_2) = 0.8$, then the linear combination $0.6Z_1 + 0.4Z_2$ is also normally distributed with mean $= 0.6(6) + 0.4(7) = 6.4$ and variance $= [0.36(2) + 0.16(3) + 2(0.6)(0.4)(0.8)] = 1.584$.

Theorem 4.3. If $Z_1, Z_2, \ldots, Z_n$ are normally and independently distributed random variables such that each $Z_i \sim N(0, 1)$, that is, a standardized normal variable, then $\sum Z_i^2 = Z_1^2 + Z_2^2 + \cdots + Z_n^2$ follows the chi-square distribution with n df. Symbolically, $\sum Z_i^2 \sim \chi_n^2$, where n denotes the degrees of freedom, df.

In short, "the sum of the squares of independent standard normal variables has a chi-square distribution with degrees of freedom equal to the number of terms in the sum."[9]

Theorem 4.4. If $Z_1, Z_2, \ldots, Z_n$ are independently distributed random variables each following chi-square distribution with k_i df, then the sum $\sum Z_i = Z_1 + Z_2 + \cdots + Z_n$ also follows a chi-square distribution with $k = \sum k_i$ df.

Thus, if Z_1 and Z_2 are independent χ^2 variables with df of k_1 and k_2, respectively, then $Z = Z_1 + Z_2$ is also a χ^2 variable with $(k_1 + k_2)$ degrees of freedom. This is called the **reproductive property** of the χ^2 distribution.

Theorem 4.5. If Z_1 is a standardized normal variable $[Z_1 \sim N(0, 1)]$ and another variable Z_2 follows the chi-square distribution with k df and is independent of Z_1, then the variable defined as

$$t = \frac{Z_1}{\sqrt{Z_2} / \sqrt{k}} = \frac{Z_1 \sqrt{k}}{\sqrt{Z_2}} = \frac{\text{standard normal variable}}{\sqrt{\text{independent chi-square variable} / \text{df}}} \sim t_k \qquad (4.5.1)$$

follows Student's t distribution with k df. *Note:* This distribution is discussed in Appendix A and is illustrated in Chapter 5.

---

[9]Ibid., p. 243.

Incidentally, note that as k, the df in (4.5.1), increases indefinitely (i.e., as $k \to \infty$), the Student's t distribution approaches the standardized normal distribution.[10] As a matter of convention, the notation t_k means Student's t distribution or variable with k df.

Theorem 4.6. If Z_1 and Z_2 are independently distributed chi-square variables with k_1 and k_2 df, respectively, then the variable

$$F = \frac{Z_1/k_1}{Z_2/k_2} \sim F_{k_1,k_2} \tag{4.5.2}$$

has the F distribution with k_1 and k_2 degrees of freedom, where k_1 is known as the **numerator degrees of freedom** and k_2 the **denominator degrees of freedom**.

Again as a matter of convention, the notation F_{k_1,k_2} means an F variable with k_1 and k_2 degrees of freedom, the df in the numerator being quoted first.

In other words, (4.5.2) states that the F variable is simply the ratio of two independently distributed chi-square variables divided by their respective degrees of freedom.

Theorem 4.7. The square of (Student's) t variable with k df has an F distribution with $k_1 = 1$ df in the numerator and $k_2 = k$ df in the denominator.[11] That is,

$$F_{1,k} = t_k^2 \tag{4.5.3}$$

Note that for this equality to hold, the numerator df of the F variable must be 1. Thus, $F_{1,4} = t_4^2$ or $F_{1,23} = t_{23}^2$ and so on.

As noted, we will see the practical utility of the preceding theorems as we progress.

4.6 SUMMARY AND CONCLUSIONS

1. This chapter discussed the classical *normal* linear regression model (CNLRM).
2. This model differs from the classical linear regression model (CLRM) in that it specifically assumes that the disturbance term u_i entering the regression model is normally distributed. The CLRM does not require any assumption about the probability distribution of u_i; it only requires that the mean value of u_i is zero and its variance is a finite constant.
3. The theoretical justification for the normality assumption is the **Central Limit Theorem**.
4. Without the normality assumption, under the other assumptions discussed in Chapter 3, the Gauss-Markov theorem showed that the OLS estimators are BLUE.

---

[10] For proof, see Henri Theil, *Introduction to Econometrics*, Prentice-Hall, Englewood Cliffs, N.J., 1978, pp. 237–245.

[11] For proof, see Eqs. (5.3.2) and (5.9.1) in Chap. 5. For an application, see Sec. 5.9.

5. With the additional assumption of normality, the OLS estimators are not only **best unbiased estimators (BUE)** but also follow well-known probability distributions. The OLS estimators of the intercept and slope are themselves normally distributed and the OLS estimator of the variance of $u_i (= \hat{\sigma}^2)$ is related to the chi-square distribution.

6. In Chapters 5 and 8 we show how this knowledge is useful in drawing inferences about the values of the population parameters.

7. An alternative to the least-squares method is the method of **maximum likelihood (ML)**. To use this method, however, one must make an assumption about the probability distribution of the disturbance term u_i. In the regression context, the assumption most popularly made is that u_i follows the normal distribution.

8. Under the normality assumption, the ML and OLS estimators of the intercept and slope parameters of the regression model are identical. However, the OLS and ML estimators of the variance of u_i are different. In large samples, however, these two estimators converge.

9. Thus the ML method is generally called a large-sample method. The ML method is of broader application in that it can also be applied to regression models that are nonlinear in the parameters. In the latter case, OLS is generally not used.

10. In this text, we will largely rely on the OLS method for practical reasons: (a) Compared to ML, the OLS is easy to apply; (b) the ML and OLS estimators of β_1 and β_2 are identical (which is true of multiple regressions too); and (c) even in moderately large samples the OLS and ML estimators of σ^2 do not differ vastly.

However, for the benefit of the mathematically inclined reader, a brief introduction to ML is given in the appendix to this chapter.

APPENDIX 4A

MAXIMUM LIKELIHOOD ESTIMATION OF TWO-VARIABLE REGRESSION MODEL

Assume that in the two-variable model $Y_i = \beta_1 + \beta_2 X_i + u_i$ the Y_i are normally and independently distributed with mean $= \beta_1 + \beta_2 X_i$ and variance $= \sigma^2$. [See Eq. (4.3.8).] As a result, the joint probability density function of $Y_1, Y_2, \ldots, Y_n$, given the preceding mean and variance, can be written as

$$f(Y_1, Y_2, \ldots, Y_n \mid \beta_1 + \beta_2 X_i, \sigma^2)$$

But in view of the independence of the Y's, this joint probability density function can be written as a product of n individual density functions as

$$f(Y_1, Y_2, \ldots, Y_n \mid \beta_1 + \beta_2 X_i, \sigma^2)$$
$$= f(Y_1 \mid \beta_1 + \beta_2 X_i, \sigma^2) f(Y_2 \mid \beta_1 + \beta_2 X_i, \sigma^2) \cdots f(Y_n \mid \beta_1 + \beta_2 X_i, \sigma^2) \quad (1)$$

where

$$f(Y_i) = \frac{1}{\sigma\sqrt{2\pi}} \exp\left\{ -\frac{1}{2} \frac{(Y_i - \beta_1 - \beta_2 X_i)^2}{\sigma^2} \right\} \tag{2}$$

which is the density function of a normally distributed variable with the given mean and variance.

(*Note*: exp means e to the power of the expression indicated by { }.)

Substituting (2) for each Y_i into (1) gives

$$f(Y_1, Y_2, \ldots, Y_n \mid \beta_1 + \beta_2 X_i, \sigma^2) = \frac{1}{\sigma^n \left(\sqrt{2\pi}\right)^n} \exp\left\{ -\frac{1}{2} \sum \frac{(Y_i - \beta_1 - \beta_2 X_i)^2}{\sigma^2} \right\} \tag{3}$$

If $Y_1, Y_2, \ldots, Y_n$ are known or given, but β_1, β_2, are σ^2 are not known, the function in (3) is called a **likelihood function**, denoted by LF($\beta_1, \beta_2, \sigma^2$), and written as[1]

$$\text{LF}(\beta_1, \beta_2, \sigma^2) = \frac{1}{\sigma^n \left(\sqrt{2\pi}\right)^n} \exp\left\{ -\frac{1}{2} \sum \frac{(Y_i - \beta_1 - \beta_2 X_i)^2}{\sigma^2} \right\} \tag{4}$$

The **method of maximum likelihood**, as the name indicates, consists in estimating the unknown parameters in such a manner that the probability of observing the given Y's is as high (or maximum) as possible. Therefore, we have to find the maximum of the function (4). This is a straightforward exercise in differential calculus. For differentiation it is easier to express (4) in the log term as follows.[2] (*Note*: ln = natural log.)

$$\ln \text{LF} = -n \ln \sigma - \frac{n}{2} \ln (2\pi) - \frac{1}{2} \sum \frac{(Y_i - \beta_1 - \beta_2 X_i)^2}{\sigma^2}$$

$$= -\frac{n}{2} \ln \sigma^2 - \frac{n}{2} \ln (2\pi) - \frac{1}{2} \sum \frac{(Y_i - \beta_1 - \beta_2 X_i)^2}{\sigma^2} \tag{5}$$

Differentiating (5) partially with respect to β_1, β_2 and σ^2, we obtain

$$\frac{\partial \ln \text{LF}}{\partial \beta_1} = -\frac{1}{\sigma^2} \sum (Y_i - \beta_1 - \beta_2 X_i)(-1) \tag{6}$$

$$\frac{\partial \ln \text{LF}}{\partial \beta_2} = -\frac{1}{\sigma^2} \sum (Y_i - \beta_1 - \beta_2 X_i)(-X_i) \tag{7}$$

$$\frac{\partial \ln \text{LF}}{\partial \sigma^2} = -\frac{n}{2\sigma^2} + \frac{1}{2\sigma^4} \sum (Y_i - \beta_1 - \beta_2 X_i)^2 \tag{8}$$

---

[1]Of course, if β_1, β_2, and σ^2 are known but the Y_i are not known, (4) represents the joint probability density function—the probability of jointly observing the Y_i.

[2]Since a log function is a monotonic function, ln LF will attain its maximum value at the same point as LF.

Setting these equations equal to zero (the first-order condition for optimization) and letting $\tilde{\beta}_1$, $\tilde{\beta}_2$, and $\tilde{\sigma}^2$ denote the ML estimators, we obtain[3]

$$\frac{1}{\tilde{\sigma}^2} \sum (Y_i - \tilde{\beta}_1 - \tilde{\beta}_2 X_i) = 0 \tag{9}$$

$$\frac{1}{\tilde{\sigma}^2} \sum (Y_i - \tilde{\beta}_1 - \tilde{\beta}_2 X_i) X_i = 0 \tag{10}$$

$$-\frac{n}{2\tilde{\sigma}^2} + \frac{1}{2\tilde{\sigma}^4} \sum (Y_i - \tilde{\beta}_1 - \tilde{\beta}_2 X_i)^2 = 0 \tag{11}$$

After simplifying, Eqs. (9) and (10) yield

$$\sum Y_i = n\tilde{\beta}_1 + \tilde{\beta}_2 \sum X_i \tag{12}$$

$$\sum Y_i X_i = \tilde{\beta}_1 \sum X_i + \tilde{\beta}_2 \sum X_i^2 \tag{13}$$

which are precisely the *normal equations* of the least squares theory obtained in (3.1.4) and (3.1.5). Therefore, the ML estimators, the $\tilde{\beta}$'s, are the same as the OLS estimators, the $\hat{\beta}$'s, given in (3.1.6) and (3.1.7). This equality is not accidental. Examining the likelihood (5), we see that the last term enters with a negative sign. Therefore, maximizing (5) amounts to minimizing this term, which is precisely the least squares approach, as can be seen from (3.1.2).

Substituting the ML (= OLS) estimators into (11) and simplifying, we obtain the ML estimator of $\tilde{\sigma}^2$ as

$$\tilde{\sigma}^2 = \frac{1}{n} \sum (Y_i - \tilde{\beta}_1 - \tilde{\beta}_2 X_i)^2$$

$$= \frac{1}{n} \sum (Y_i - \hat{\beta}_1 - \hat{\beta}_2 X_i)^2$$

$$= \frac{1}{n} \sum \hat{u}_i^2 \tag{14}$$

From (14) it is obvious that the ML estimator $\tilde{\sigma}^2$ differs from the OLS estimator $\hat{\sigma}^2 = [1/(n-2)] \sum \hat{u}_i^2$, which was shown to be an unbiased estimator of σ^2 in Appendix 3A, Section 3A.5. Thus, the ML estimator of σ^2 is biased. The magnitude of this bias can be easily determined as follows.

Taking the mathematical expectation of (14) on both sides, we obtain

$$E(\tilde{\sigma}^2) = \frac{1}{n} E\left(\sum \hat{u}_i^2\right)$$

$$= \left(\frac{n-2}{n}\right)\sigma^2 \qquad \text{using Eq. (16) of Appendix 3A, Section 3A.5}$$

$$= \sigma^2 - \frac{2}{n}\sigma^2 \tag{15}$$

---

[3]We use ˜ (tilde) for ML estimators and ˆ (cap or hat) for OLS estimators.

which shows that $\tilde{\sigma}^2$ is biased downward (i.e., it underestimates the true σ^2) in small samples. But notice that as n, the sample size, increases indefinitely, the second term in (15), the bias factor, tends to be zero. Therefore, *asymptotically* (i.e., in a very large sample), $\tilde{\sigma}^2$ is *unbiased* too, that is, $\lim E(\tilde{\sigma}^2) = \sigma^2$ as $n \to \infty$. It can further be proved that $\tilde{\sigma}^2$ is also a **consistent** estimator,[4] that is, as n increases indefinitely $\tilde{\sigma}^2$ converges to its true value σ^2.

MAXIMUM LIKELIHOOD ESTIMATION OF THE CONSUMPTION-INCOME EXAMPLE

Returning to the Keynesian consumption function example discussed in Section 3.6, we see that the ML estimators $\tilde{\beta}_1$ and $\tilde{\beta}_2$ are the same as the OLS estimators $\hat{\beta}_1$ and $\hat{\beta}_2$, namely, 24.4545 and 0.5091, respectively, but the ML estimator $\tilde{\sigma}^2 = 33.7272$ is smaller than the OLS estimator $\hat{\sigma}^2$ of 42.1591. As noted, in small samples the ML estimator is downward-biased, that is, on average, it underestimates the true variance, σ^2.

Putting the ML values of β_1, β_2, and σ^2 into the log-likelihood function given in Eq. (5), one can show that the maximum value of the log-likelihood function in the present example is -31.7809 (most regression packages routinely print out such values). If you want the maximum value of the likelihood function, just take the antilog of -31.7809. No other values of the parameters will give you a higher probability of obtaining the sample that you have used in the analysis.

It is left as an exercise for the reader to show that for the coffee example given in Table 3.4 the ML values of the intercept and slope coefficients are exactly the same as the OLS values. However, ML value of σ^2 is 0.01355, whereas that obtained by OLS is 0.01656, once again showing that in small samples the ML estimate is lower than the OLS estimate. Incidentally, for this example the maximum of the log-likelihood value is 8.04811.

APPENDIX 4A EXERCISES

4.1 "If two random variables are statistically independent, the coefficient of correlation between the two is zero. But the converse is not necessarily true; that is, zero correlation does not imply statistical independence. However, if two variables are normally distributed, zero correlation necessarily implies statistical independence." Verify this statement for the following joint probability density function of two normally distributed variables Y_1 and Y_2 (this joint probability density function is known as the **bivariate normal probability density function**):

---

[4]See App. A for a general discussion of the properties of the maximum likelihood estimators as well as for the distinction between asymptotic unbiasedness and consistency. Roughly speaking, in asymptotic unbiasedness we try to find out the $\lim E(\tilde{\sigma}_n^2)$ as n tends to infinity, where n is the sample size on which the estimator is based, whereas in consistency we try to find out how $\tilde{\sigma}_n^2$ behaves as n increases indefinitely. Notice that the unbiasedness property is a repeated sampling property of an estimator based on a sample of given size, whereas in consistency we are concerned with the behavior of an estimator as the sample size increases indefinitely.

$$f(Y_1, Y_2) =$$

$$\frac{1}{2\pi\sigma_1\sigma_2\sqrt{1-\rho^2}} \exp\left\{ -\frac{1}{2(1-\rho^2)} \left[\left(\frac{Y_1 - \mu_1}{\sigma_1}\right)^2 - 2\rho\frac{(Y_1 - \mu_1)(Y_2 - \mu_2)}{\sigma_1\sigma_2} + \left(\frac{Y_2 - \mu_2}{\sigma^2}\right)^2 \right] \right\}$$

where μ_1 = mean of Y_1

$\quad\quad \mu_2$ = mean of Y_2

$\quad\quad \sigma_1$ = standard deviation of Y_1

$\quad\quad \sigma_2$ = standard deviation of Y_2

$\quad\quad \rho$ = coefficient of correlation between Y_1 and Y_2

4.2 By applying the second-order conditions for optimization (i.e., second-derivative test), show that the ML estimators of β_1, β_2, and σ^2 obtained by solving Eqs. (9), (10), and (11) do in fact maximize the likelihood function (4).

4.3 A random variable X follows the **exponential distribution** if it has the following probability density function (PDF):

$$f(X) = (1/\theta)e^{-X/\theta} \quad\quad \text{for} \quad\quad X > 0$$

$$= 0 \quad\quad \text{elsewhere}$$

where $\theta > 0$ is the parameter of the distribution. Using the ML method, show that the ML estimator of θ is $\hat{\theta} = \sum X_i/n$, where n is the sample size. That is, show that the ML estimator of θ is the sample mean $\bar{X}$.

CHAPTER
5

TWO-VARIABLE REGRESSION: INTERVAL ESTIMATION AND HYPOTHESIS TESTING

Beware of testing too many hypotheses; the more you torture the data, the more likely they are to confess, but confession obtained under duress may not be admissible in the court of scientific opinion.[1]

As pointed out in Chapter 4, estimation and hypothesis testing constitute the two major branches of classical statistics. The theory of estimation consists of two parts: point estimation and interval estimation. We have discussed point estimation thoroughly in the previous two chapters where we introduced the OLS and ML methods of point estimation. In this chapter we first consider interval estimation and then take up the topic of hypothesis testing, a topic intimately related to interval estimation.

5.1 STATISTICAL PREREQUISITES

Before we demonstrate the actual mechanics of establishing confidence intervals and testing statistical hypotheses, it is assumed that the reader is familiar with the fundamental concepts of probability and statistics. Although not a substitute for a basic course in statistics, Appendix A provides the essentials of

---

[1]Stephen M. Stigler, "Testing Hypothesis or Fitting Models? Another Look at Mass Extinctions," in Matthew H. Nitecki and Antoni Hoffman, eds., *Neutral Models in Biology,* Oxford University Press, Oxford, 1987, p. 148.

statistics with which the reader should be totally familiar. Key concepts such as **probability, probability distributions, Type I and Type II errors, level of significance, power of a statistical test,** and **confidence interval** are crucial for understanding the material covered in this and the following chapters.

5.2   INTERVAL ESTIMATION: SOME BASIC IDEAS

To fix the ideas, consider the hypothetical consumption-income example of Chapter 3. Equation (3.6.2) shows that the estimated marginal propensity to consume (MPC) β_2 is 0.5091, which is a single (point) estimate of the unknown population MPC β_2. How reliable is this estimate? As noted in Chapter 3, because of sampling fluctuations, a single estimate is likely to differ from the true value, although in repeated sampling its mean value is expected to be equal to the true value. (*Note*: $E(\hat{\beta}_2) = \beta_2$.) Now in statistics the reliability of a point estimator is measured by its standard error. Therefore, instead of relying on the point estimate alone, we may construct an interval around the point estimator, say within two or three standard errors on either side of the point estimator, such that this interval has, say, 95 percent probability of including the true parameter value. This is roughly the idea behind **interval estimation**.

To be more specific, assume that we want to find out how "close" is, say, $\hat{\beta}_2$ to β_2. For this purpose we try to find out two positive numbers δ and α, the latter lying between 0 and 1, such that the probability that the **random interval** $(\hat{\beta}_2 - \delta, \hat{\beta}_2 + \delta)$ contains the true β_2 is $1 - \alpha$. Symbolically,

$$\Pr(\hat{\beta}_2 - \delta \le \beta_2 \le \hat{\beta}_2 + \delta) = 1 - \alpha \qquad (5.2.1)$$

Such an interval, if it exists, is known as a **confidence interval**; $1 - \alpha$ is known as the **confidence coefficient**; and $\alpha(0 < \alpha < 1)$ is known as the **level of significance**.[2] The endpoints of the confidence interval are known as the **confidence limits** (also known as *critical* values), $\hat{\beta}_2 - \delta$ being the **lower confidence** *limit* and $\hat{\beta}_2 + \delta$ the **upper confidence** *limit*. In passing, note that in practice α and $1 - \alpha$ are often expressed in percentage forms as 100α and $100(1 - \alpha)$ percent.

Equation (5.2.1) shows that an **interval estimator,** in contrast to a point estimator, is an interval constructed in such a manner that it has a specified probability $1 - \alpha$ of including within its limits the true value of the parameter. For example, if $\alpha = 0.05$, or 5 percent, (5.2.1) would read: The probability that the (random) interval shown there includes the true β_2 is 0.95, or 95 percent. The interval estimator thus gives a range of values within which the true β_2 may lie.

It is very important to know the following aspects of interval estimation:

1. Equation (5.2.1) does not say that the probability of β_2 lying between the given limits is $1 - \alpha$. Since β_2, although an unknown, is assumed to be some fixed number, either it lies in the interval or it does not. What (5.2.1) states

---

[2]Also known as the **probability of committing a Type I error.** A Type I error consists in rejecting a true hypothesis, whereas a Type II error consists in accepting a false hypothesis. (This topic is discussed more fully in App. A.) The symbol α is also known as the **size of the (statistical) test.**

is that, using the method described in this chapter, the probability of constructing an interval that contains β_2 is $1 - \alpha$.

2. The interval (5.2.1) is a **random interval;** that is, it will vary from one sample to the next because it is based on $\hat{\beta}_2$, which is random. (Why?)

3. Since the confidence interval is random, the probability statements attached to it should be understood in the long-run sense, that is, repeated sampling. More specifically, (5.2.1) means: If in repeated sampling confidence intervals like it are constructed a great many times on the $1 - \alpha$ probability basis, then, in the long run, on the average, such intervals will enclose in $1 - \alpha$ of the cases the true value of the parameter.

4. As noted in 2, the interval (5.2.1) is random so long as $\hat{\beta}_2$ is not known. But once we have a specific sample and once we obtain a specific numerical value of $\hat{\beta}_2$, the interval (5.2.1) is no longer random; it is fixed. In this case, we **cannot** make the probabilistic statement (5.2.1); that is, we cannot say that the probability is $1 - \alpha$ that a given *fixed* interval includes the true β_2. In this situation β_2 is either in the fixed interval or outside it. Therefore, the probability is either 1 or 0. Thus, for our hypothetical consumption-income example, if the 95% confidence interval were obtained as $(0.4268 \leq \beta_2 \leq 0.5914)$, as we do shortly in (5.3.9), we **cannot** say the probability is 95% that this interval includes the true β_2. That probability is either 1 or 0.

How are the confidence intervals constructed? From the preceding discussion one may expect that if the **sampling or probability distributions** of the estimators are known, one can make confidence interval statements such as (5.2.1). In Chapter 4 we saw that under the assumption of normality of the disturbances u_i the OLS estimators $\hat{\beta}_1$ and $\hat{\beta}_2$ are themselves normally distributed and that the OLS estimator $\hat{\sigma}^2$ is related to the χ^2 (chi-square) distribution. It would then seem that the task of constructing confidence intervals is a simple one. And it is!

5.3 CONFIDENCE INTERVALS FOR REGRESSION COEFFICIENTS β_1 AND β_2

Confidence Interval for β_2

It was shown in Chapter 4, Section 4.3 that, with the normality assumption for u_i, the OLS estimators $\hat{\beta}_1$ and $\hat{\beta}_2$ are themselves normally distributed with means and variances given therein. Therefore, for example, the variable

$$Z = \frac{\hat{\beta}_2 - \beta_2}{\text{se}(\hat{\beta}_2)}$$

$$= \frac{(\hat{\beta}_2 - \beta_2) \sqrt{\sum x_i^2}}{\sigma} \tag{5.3.1}$$

as noted in (4.3.5), is a standardized normal variable. It therefore seems that we can use the normal distribution to make probabilistic statments about β_2 provided the true population variance σ^2 is known. If σ^2 is known, an important property of a normally distributed variable with mean μ and variance σ^2 is that the area under the normal curve between $\mu \pm \sigma$ is about 68 percent, that between the limits $\mu \pm 2\sigma$ is about 95 percent, and that between $\mu \pm 3\sigma$ is about 99.7 percent.

But σ^2 is rarely known, and in practice it is determined by the unbiased estimator $\hat{\sigma}^2$. If we replace σ by $\hat{\sigma}$, (5.3.1) may be written as

$$t = \frac{\hat{\beta}_2 - \beta_2}{se(\hat{\beta}_2)} = \frac{\text{estimator} - \text{parameter}}{\text{estimated standard error of estimator}}$$

$$= \frac{(\hat{\beta}_2 - \beta_2)\sqrt{\sum x_i^2}}{\hat{\sigma}} \qquad (5.3.2)$$

where the se $(\hat{\beta}_2)$ now refers to the estimated standard error. It can be shown (see Appendix 5A, Section 5A.1) that the t variable thus defined follows the t distribution with $n - 2$ df. [Note the difference between (5.3.1) and (5.3.2).] Therefore, instead of using the normal distribution, we can use the t distribution to establish a confidence interval for β_2 as follows:

$$\Pr(-t_{\alpha/2} \leq t \leq t_{\alpha/2}) = 1 - \alpha \qquad (5.3.3)$$

where the t value in the middle of this double inequality is the t value given by (5.3.2) and where $t_{\alpha/2}$ is the value of the t variable obtained from the t distribution for $\alpha/2$ level of significance and $n - 2$ df; it is often called the **critical** t value at $\alpha/2$ level of significance. Substitution of (5.3.2) into (5.3.3) yields

$$\Pr\left[-t_{\alpha/2} \leq \frac{\hat{\beta}_2 - \beta_2}{se(\hat{\beta}_2)} \leq t_{\alpha/2}\right] = 1 - \alpha \qquad (5.3.4)$$

Rearranging (5.3.4), we obtain

$$\Pr[\hat{\beta}_2 - t_{\alpha/2}\,se(\hat{\beta}_2) \leq \beta_2 \leq \hat{\beta}_2 + t_{\alpha/2}\,se(\hat{\beta}_2)] = 1 - \alpha \qquad (5.3.5)^{[3]}$$

Equation (5.3.5) provides a $100(1 - \alpha)$ percent **confidence interval** for β_2, which can be written more compactly as

$$100(1 - \alpha)\% \text{ confidence interval for } \beta_2 :$$

$$\hat{\beta}_2 \pm t_{\alpha/2}\,se(\hat{\beta}_2) \qquad (5.3.6)$$

Arguing analogously, and using (4.3.1) and (4.3.2), we can then write:

$$\Pr[\hat{\beta}_1 - t_{\alpha/2}\,se(\hat{\beta}_1) \leq \beta_1 \leq \hat{\beta}_1 + t_{\alpha/2}\,se(\hat{\beta}_1)] = 1 - \alpha \qquad (5.3.7)$$

---

[3]Some authors prefer to write (5.3.5) with the df explicitly indicated. Thus, they would write

$$\Pr[\hat{\beta}_2 - t_{(n-2),\alpha/2}\,se(\hat{\beta}_2) \leq \beta_1 \leq \hat{\beta}_2 + t_{(n-2)\alpha/2}\,se(\hat{\beta}_2)] = 1 - \alpha$$

But for simplicity we will stick to our notation; the context clarifies the appropriate df involved.

or, more compactly,

$$100(1 - \alpha)\% \text{ confidence interval for } \beta_1 :$$

$$\hat{\beta}_1 \pm t_{\alpha/2} \text{ se}(\hat{\beta}_1) \tag{5.3.8}$$

Notice an important feature of the confidence intervals given in (5.3.6) and (5.3.8): In both cases *the width of the confidence interval is proportional to the standard error of the estimator.* That is, the larger is the standard error, the larger is the width of the confidence interval. Put differently, the larger is the standard error of the estimator, the greater is the uncertainty of estimating the true value of the unknown parameter. Thus, the standard error of an estimator is often described as a measure of the **precision** of the estimator, i.e., how precisely the estimator measures the true population value.

Returning to our illustrative consumption-income example, in Chapter 3 (Section 3.6) we found that $\hat{\beta}_2 = 0.5091$, se($\hat{\beta}_2$) = 0.0357, and df = 8. If we assume $\alpha = 5\%$, that is, 95% confidence coefficient, then the t table shows that for 8 df the **critical** $t_{\alpha/2} = t_{0.025} = 2.306$. Substituting these values in (5.3.5), the reader should verify that the 95% confidence interval for β_2 is as follows:

$$0.4268 \le \beta_2 \le 0.5914 \tag{5.3.9}$$

Or, using (5.3.6), it is

$$0.5091 \pm 2.306(0.0357)$$

that is,

$$0.5091 \pm 0.0823 \tag{5.3.10}$$

The interpretation of this confidence interval is: Given the confidence coefficient of 95 percent, in the long run, in 95 out of 100 cases intervals like (0.4268, 0.5914) will contain the true β_2. But, as warned earlier, note that we cannot say that the probability is 95 percent that the specific interval (0.4268 to 0.5914) contains the true β_2 because this interval is now fixed and no longer random; therefore, β_2 either lies in it or does not: The probability that the specified fixed interval includes the true β_2 is therefore 1 or 0.

Confidence Interval for β_1

Following (5.3.7), the reader can easily verify that the 95% confidence interval for β_1 of our consumption-income example is

$$9.6643 \le \beta_1 \le 39.2448 \tag{5.3.11}$$

Or, using (5.3.8), we find it is

$$24.4545 \pm 2.306(6.4138)$$

that is,

$$24.4545 \pm 14.7902 \tag{5.3.12}$$

Again you should be careful in interpreting this confidence interval. In the long run, in 95 out of 100 cases intervals like (5.3.11) will contain the true β_1; the probability that this particular fixed interval includes the true β_1 is either 1 or 0.

Confidence Interval for β_1 and β_2 Simultaneously

There are occasions when one needs to construct a joint confidence interval for β_1 and β_2 such that with a confidence coefficient $(1 - \alpha)$, say, 95%, both β_1 and β_2 lie simultaneously in that interval. Since this topic is involved, the reader may want to consult the references.[4] (See also Section 8.4 and Chapter 10).

5.4 CONFIDENCE INTERVAL FOR σ^2

As pointed out in Chapter 4, Section 4.3, under the normality assumption, the variable

$$\chi^2 = (n - 2)\frac{\hat{\sigma}^2}{\sigma^2} \tag{5.4.1}$$

follows the χ^2 distribution with $n - 2$ df.[5] Therefore, we can use the χ^2 distribution to establish confidence interval for σ^2

$$\Pr(\chi^2_{1-\alpha/2} \le \chi^2 \le \chi^2_{\alpha/2}) = 1 - \alpha \tag{5.4.2}$$

where the χ^2 value in the middle of this double inequality is as given by (5.4.1) and where $\chi^2_{1-\alpha/2}$ and $\chi^2_{\alpha/2}$ are two values of χ^2 (the **critical** χ^2 values) obtained from the chi-square table for $n - 2$ df in such a manner that they cut off $100(\alpha/2)$ percent tail areas of the χ^2 distribution, as shown in Fig. 5.1.

Substituting χ^2 from (5.4.1) into (5.4.2) and rearranging the terms, we obtain

$$\Pr\left[(n - 2)\frac{\hat{\sigma}^2}{\chi^2_{\alpha/2}} \le \sigma^2 \le (n - 2)\frac{\hat{\sigma}^2}{\chi^2_{1-\alpha/2}}\right] = 1 - \alpha \tag{5.4.3}$$

which gives the $100(1 - \alpha)\%$ confidence interval for σ^2.

To illustrate, consider this example. From Chapter 3, Section 3.6, we obtain $\hat{\sigma}^2 = 42.1591$ and df $= 8$. If α is chosen at 5 percent, the chi-square table for 8 df gives the following critical values: $\chi^2_{0.025} = 17.5346$, and $\chi^2_{0.975} = 2.1797$. These values show that the probability of a chi-square value exceeding 17.5346 is 2.5 percent and that of 2.1797 is 97.5 percent. Therefore,

---

[4]For an accessible discussion, see John Neter, William Wasserman, and Michael H. Kutner, *Applied Linear Regression Models*, Richard D. Irwin, Homewood, Ill., 1983, Chap. 5.

[5]For proof, see Robert V. Hogg and Allen T. Craig, *Introduction to Mathematical Statistics*, 2d ed., Macmillan, New York, 1965, p. 144.

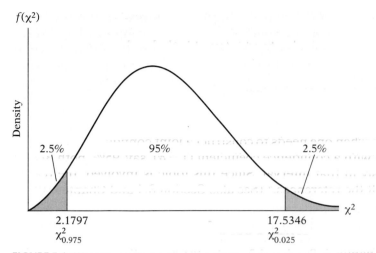

$f(\chi^2)$

Density

2.5%   95%   2.5%

2.1797   17.5346

$\chi^2_{0.975}$ $\chi^2_{0.025}$

χ^2

FIGURE 5.1
The 95 % confidence interval for χ^2 (8 df).

the interval between these two values is the 95% confidence interval for χ^2, as shown diagrammatically in Fig. 5.1. (Note the skewed characteristic of the chi-square distribution.)

Substituting the data of our example into (5.4.3), the reader should verify that the 95% confidence interval for σ^2 is as follows:

$$19.2347 \leq \sigma^2 \leq 154.7336 \tag{5.4.4}$$

The interpretation of this interval is: If we establish 95% confidence limits on σ^2 and if we maintain a priori that these limits will include true σ^2, we shall be right in the long run 95 percent of the time.

5.5 HYPOTHESIS TESTING: GENERAL COMMENTS

Having discussed the problem of point and interval estimation, we shall now consider the topic of hypothesis testing. In this section we discuss briefly some general aspects of this topic; Appendix A gives some additional details.

The problem of statistical hypothesis testing may be stated simply as follows: *Is a given observation or finding compatible with some stated hypothesis or not?* The word "compatible," as used here, means "sufficiently" close to the hypothesized value so that we do not reject the stated hypothesis. Thus, if some theory or prior experience leads us to believe that the true slope coefficient β_2 of the consumption-income example is unity, is the observed $\hat{\beta}_2 = 0.5091$ obtained from the sample of Table 3.2 consistent with the stated hypothesis? If it is, we do not reject the hypothesis; otherwise, we may reject it.

In the language of statistics, the stated hypothesis is known as the **null hypothesis** and is denoted by the symbol H_0. The null hypothesis is usually tested against an **alternative hypothesis** (also known as **maintained hypothesis**) denoted by H_1, which may state, for example, that true β_2 is different from unity. The alternative hypothesis may be **simple** or **composite**.[6] For example, $H_1: \beta_2 = 1.5$ is a simple hypothesis, but $H_1: \beta_2 \neq 1.5$ is a composite hypothesis.

The theory of hypothesis testing is concerned with developing rules or procedures for deciding whether to reject or not reject the null hypothesis. There are two *mutually complementary* approaches for devising such rules, namely, **confidence interval** and **test of significance.** Both these approaches predicate that the variable (statistic or estimator) under consideration has some probability distribution and that hypothesis testing involves making statements or assertions about the value(s) of the parameter(s) of such distribution. For example, we know that with the normality assumption $\hat{\beta}_2$ is normally distributed with mean equal to β_2 and variance given by (4.3.4). If we hypothesize that $\beta_2 = 1$, we are making an assertion about one of the parameters of the normal distribution, namely, the mean. Most of the statistical hypotheses encountered in this text will be of this type—making assertions about one or more values of the parameters of some assumed probability distribution such as the normal, F, t, or χ^2. How this is accomplished is discussed in the following two sections.

5.6 HYPOTHESIS TESTING: THE CONFIDENCE-INTERVAL APPROACH

Two-Sided or Two-Tail Test

To illustrate the confidence-interval approach, once again we revert to the consumption-income example. As we know, the estimated marginal propensity to consume (MPC), $\hat{\beta}_2$, is 0.5091. Suppose we postulate that

$$H_0: \beta_2 = 0.3$$

$$H_1: \beta_2 \neq 0.3$$

that is, the true MPC is 0.3 under the null hypothesis but it is less than or greater than 0.3 under the alternative hypothesis. The null hypothesis is a simple hypothesis, whereas the alternative hypothesis is composite; actually it is what is known as a **two-sided hypothesis.** Very often such a two-sided alternative hypothesis reflects the fact that we do not have a strong a priori or theoretical expectation about the direction in which the alternative hypothesis should move from the null hypothesis.

Is the observed $\hat{\beta}_2$ compatible with H_0? To answer this question, let us refer to the confidence interval (5.3.9). We know that in the long run intervals like (0.4268, 0.5914) will contain the true β_2 with 95 percent probability.

---

[6] A statistical hypothesis is called a **simple hypothesis** if it specifies the precise value(s) of the parameter(s) of a probability density function; otherwise, it is called a **composite hypothesis.** For example, in the normal pdf $(1/\sigma \sqrt{2\pi}) \exp\{-\frac{1}{2}[(X - \mu)/\sigma]^2\}$, if we assert that $H_1: \mu = 15$ and $\sigma = 2$, it is a simple hypothesis; but if $H_1: \mu = 15$ and $\sigma > 15$, it is a composite hypothesis, because the standard deviation does not have a specific value.

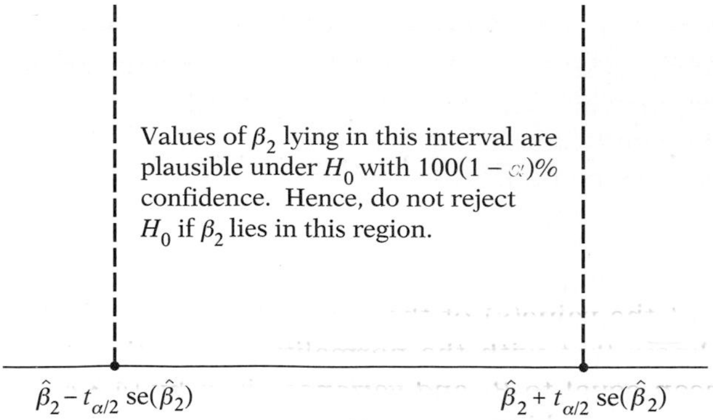

Values of β_2 lying in this interval are plausible under H_0 with $100(1 - \alpha)\%$ confidence. Hence, do not reject H_0 if β_2 lies in this region.

$$\hat{\beta}_2 - t_{\alpha/2}\ \text{se}(\hat{\beta}_2) \qquad\qquad\qquad \hat{\beta}_2 + t_{\alpha/2}\ \text{se}(\hat{\beta}_2)$$

FIGURE 5.2
A $100(1 - \alpha)\%$ confidence interval for β_2.

Consequently, in the long run (i.e., repeated sampling) such intervals provide a range or limits within which the true β_2 may lie with a confidence coefficient of, say, 95 percent. Thus, the confidence interval provides a set of plausible null hypotheses. Therefore, if β_2 under H_0 falls within the $100(1 - \alpha)\%$ confidence interval, we do not reject the null hypothesis; if it lies outside the interval, we may reject it.[7] This range is illustrated schematically in Fig. 5.2.

> **Decision Rule:** Construct a $100(1 - \alpha)\%$ confidence interval for β_2. If the β_2 under H_0 falls within this confidence interval, do not reject H_0, but if it falls outside this interval, reject H_0.

Following this rule, for our hypothetical example, H_0: $\beta_2 = 0.3$ clearly lies outside the 95% confidence interval given in (5.3.9). Therefore, we can reject the hypothesis that the true MPC is 0.3, with 95% confidence. If the null hypothesis were true, the probability of our obtaining a value of MPC of as much as 0.5091 by sheer chance is at the most about 5 percent, a small probability.

In statistics, when we reject the null hypothesis, we say that our finding is **statistically significant.** On the other hand, when we do not reject the null hypothesis, we say that our finding is **not statistically significant.**

Some authors use a phrase such as "highly statistically significant." By this they usually mean that when they reject the null hypothesis, the probability of committing a Type I error (i.e., α) is a small number, usually 1 percent. But as our discussion of the **p value** in Section 5.8 will show, it is better to leave it to the researcher to decide whether a statistical finding is "significant," "moderately significant," or "highly significant."

---

[7]Always bear in mind that there is a 100α percent chance that the confidence interval does not contain β_2 under H_0 even though the hypothesis is correct. In short, there is 100α percent chance of committing a **Type I error.** Thus, if $\alpha = 0.05$, there is a 5 percent chance that we could reject the null hypothesis even though it is true.

One-Sided or One-Tail Test

Sometimes we have a strong a priori or theoretical expectation (or expectations based on some previous empirical work) that the alternative hypothesis is one-sided or unidirectional rather than two-sided, as just discussed. Thus, for our consumption-income example, one could postulate that

$$H_0: \beta_2 \leq 0.3 \quad \text{and} \quad H_1: \beta_2 > 0.3$$

Perhaps economic theory or prior empirical work suggests that the marginal propensity to consume is greater than 0.3. Although the procedure to test this hypothesis can be easily derived from (5.3.5), the actual mechanics are better explained in terms of the test-of-significance approach discussed next.[8]

5.7   HYPOTHESIS TESTING: THE TEST-OF-SIGNIFICANCE APPROACH

Testing the Significance of Regression Coefficients: The *t*-test

An *alternative but complementary approach* to the confidence-interval method of testing statistical hypotheses is the **test-of-significance approach** developed along independent lines by R. A. Fisher and jointly by Neyman and Pearson.[9] **Broadly speaking, a test of significance is a procedure by which sample results are used to verify the truth or falsity of a null hypothesis.** The key idea behind tests of significance is that of a **test statistic** (estimator) and the sampling distribution of such a statistic under the null hypothesis. The decision to accept or reject H_0 is made on the basis of the value of the test statistic obtained from the data at hand.

As an illustration, recall that under the normality assumption the variable

$$t = \frac{\hat{\beta}_2 - \beta_2}{\text{se}(\hat{\beta}_2)}$$

$$= \frac{(\hat{\beta}_2 - \beta_2)\sqrt{\sum x_i^2}}{\hat{\sigma}} \tag{5.3.2}$$

follows the t distribution with $n - 2$ df. If the value of true β_2 is specified under the null hypothesis, the t value of (5.3.2) can readily be computed from the available sample, and therefore it can serve as a test statistic. And since this test statistic follows the t distribution, confidence-interval statements such as the following can be made:

$$\Pr\left[-t_{\alpha/2} \leq \frac{\hat{\beta}_2 - \beta_2^*}{\text{se}(\hat{\beta}_2)} \leq t_{\alpha/2}\right] = 1 - \alpha \tag{5.7.1}$$

---

[8]If you want to use the confidence interval approach, construct a $(100 - \alpha)\%$ *one-sided* or *one-tail* confidence interval for β_2. Why?

[9]Details may be found in E. L. Lehman, *Testing Statistical Hypotheses*, John Wiley & Sons, New York, 1959.

where β_2^* is the value of β_2 under H_0 and where $-t_{\alpha/2}$ and $t_{\alpha/2}$ are th t (the **critical** t values) obtained from the t table for $(\alpha/2)$ level of s and $n - 2$ df [cf. (5.3.4)]. The t table is given in Appendix D.

Rearranging (5.7.1), we obtain

$$\Pr[\beta_2^* - t_{\alpha/2}\,se(\hat{\beta}_2) \le \hat{\beta}_2 \le \beta_2^* + t_{\alpha/2}\,se(\hat{\beta}_2)] = 1 - \alpha \qquad (5.7.2)$$

which gives the interval in which $\hat{\beta}_2$ will fall with $1 - \alpha$ probability, given $\beta_2 = \beta_2^*$. In the language of hypothesis testing, the $100(1 - \alpha)\%$ confidence interval established in (5.7.2) is known as the **region of acceptance** (of the null hypothesis) and the *region(s)* outside the confidence interval is (are) called the **region(s) of rejection** (of H_0) or the **critical region(s).** As noted previously, the confidence limits, the endpoints of the confidence interval, are also called **critical values.**

The intimate connection between the confidence-interval and test-of-significance approaches to hypothesis testing can now be seen by comparing (5.3.5) with (5.7.2). In the confidence-interval procedure we try to establish a range or an interval that has a certain probability of including the true but unknown β_2, whereas in the test-of-significance approach we hypothesize some value for β_2 and try to see whether the computed $\hat{\beta}_2$ lies within reasonable (confidence) limits around the hypothesized value.

Once again let us revert to our consumption-income example. We know that $\hat{\beta}_2 = 0.5091$, se $(\hat{\beta}_2) = 0.0357$, and df $= 8$. If we assume $\alpha = 5$ percent, $t_{\alpha/2} = 2.306$. If we let $H_0: \beta_2 = \beta_2^* = 0.3$ and $H_1: \beta_2 \neq 0.3$, (5.7.2) becomes

$$\Pr(0.2177 \le \hat{\beta}_2 \le 0.3823) = 0.95 \qquad (5.7.3)^{[10]}$$

as shown diagrammatically in Fig. 5.3. Since the observed $\hat{\beta}_2$ lies in the critical region, we reject the null hypothesis that true $\beta_2 = 0.3$.

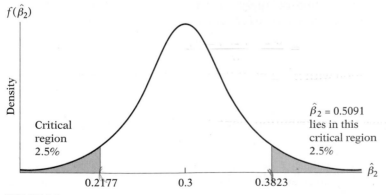

$f(\hat{\beta}_2)$

Density

Critical region 2.5%

$\hat{\beta}_2 = 0.5091$ lies in this critical region 2.5%

$\hat{\beta}_2$

0.2177   0.3   0.3823

FIGURE 5.3
The 95 percent confidence interval for $\hat{\beta}_2$ under the hypothesis that $\beta_2 = 0.3$.

---

[10]In Section 5.2, point 4, it was stated that we *cannot* say that the probability is 95 percent that the fixed interval (0.4268, 0.5914) includes the true β_2. But we can make the probabilistic statement given in (5.7.3) because $\hat{\beta}_2$, being an estimator, is a random variable.

In practice, there is no need to estimate (5.7.2) explicitly. One can compute the t value in the middle of the double inequality given by (5.7.1) and see whether it lies between the critical t values or outside them. For our example,

$$t = \frac{0.5091 - 0.3}{0.0357} = 5.86 \qquad (5.7.4)$$

which clearly lies in the critical region of Fig. 5.4. The conclusion remains the same; namely, we reject H_0.

Notice that if the estimated $\beta_2 (= \hat{\beta}_2)$ is the equal to the hypothesized β_2, the t value in (5.7.4) will be zero. However, as the estimated β_2 value departs from the hypothesized β_2 value, $|t|$ (that is, the absolute t value; *note: t can be positive as well as negative*) will be increasingly large. *Therefore, a "large" $|t|$ value will be evidence against the null hypothesis.* Of course, we can always use the t table to determine whether a particular t value is large or small; the answer, as we know, depends on the degrees of freedom as well as on the probability of Type I error that we are willing to accept. If you take a look at the t table given in Appendix D, you will observe that for any given value of df the probability of obtaining an increasingly large $|t|$ value becomes progressively smaller. Thus, for 20 df the probability of obtaining a $|t|$ value of 1.725 or greater is 0.10 or 10 percent, but for the same df the probability of obtaining a $|t|$ value of 3.552 or greater is only 0.002 or 0.2 percent.

Since we use the t distribution, the preceding testing procedure is called appropriately the **t test. In the language of significance tests, a statistic is said to be statistically significant if the value of the test statistic lies in the critical region. In this case the null hypothesis is rejected. By the same token, a test is said to be statistically insignificant if the value of the test statistic lies in the acceptance region.** In this situation, the null hypothesis is not rejected. In our example, the t test is significant and hence we reject the null hypothesis.

Before concluding our discussion of hypothesis testing, note that the testing procedure just outlined is known as a **two-sided, or two-tail,** test-of-significance procedure in that we consider the two extreme tails of the relevant

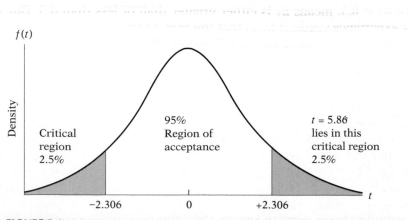

FIGURE 5.4
The 95 percent confidence interval for $t(8\ df)$.

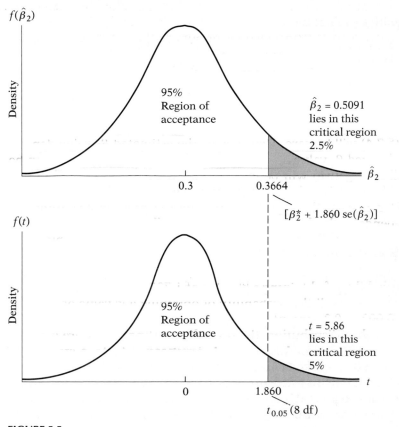

FIGURE 5.5
One-tail test of significance.

probability distribution, the rejection regions, and reject the null hypothesis if it lies in either tail. But this happens because our H_1 was a two-sided composite hypothesis; $\beta_2 \neq 0.3$. means β_2 is either greater than or less than 0.3. But suppose prior experience suggests to us that the MPC is expected to be greater than 0.3. In this case we have: $H_0: \beta_2 \leq 0.3$ and $H_1: \beta_2 > 0.3$. Although H_1 is still a composite hypothesis, it is now one-sided. To test this hypothesis, we use the **one-tail test** (the right tail), as shown in Fig. 5.5. (See also the discussion in Section 5.6.)

The test procedure is the same as before except that the upper confidence limit or critical value now corresponds to $t_\alpha = t_{.05}$, that is, the 5 percent level. As Fig. 5.5 shows, we need not consider the lower tail of the t distribution in this case. Whether one uses a two- or one-tail test of significance will depend upon how the alternative hypothesis is formulated, which, in turn, may depend upon some a priori considerations or prior empirical experience. (But more on this in Section 5.8.)

We can summarize the t-test of significance approach to hypothesis testing as shown in Table 5.1.

TABLE 5.1
The *t*-test of significance: Decision rules

Type of hypothesis	H_0: The null hypothesis	H_1: The alternative hypothesis	Decision rule: Reject H_0 if
Two-tail	$\beta_2 = \beta_2^*$	$\beta_2 \neq \beta_2^*$	$|t| > t_{\alpha/2, df}$
Right-tail	$\beta_2 \leq \beta_2^*$	$\beta_2 > \beta_2^*$	$t > t_{\alpha, df}$
Left-tail	$\beta_2 \geq \beta_2^*$	$\beta_2 < \beta_2^*$	$t < -t_{\alpha, df}$

Notes: β_2^* is the hypothesized numerical value of β_2.
$|t|$ means the absolute value of t.
t_α or $t_{\alpha/2}$ means the critical t value at the α or $\alpha/2$ level of significance.
df: degrees of freedom, $(n-2)$ for the two-variable model, $(n-3)$ for the three-variable model, and so on.
The same procedure holds to test hypotheses about β_1.

Testing the Significance of σ^2: The χ^2 Test

As another illustration of the test-of-significance methodology, consider the following variable:

$$\chi^2 = (n-2)\frac{\hat{\sigma}^2}{\sigma^2} \tag{5.4.1}$$

which, as noted previously, follows the χ^2 distribution with $n - 2$ df. For the hypothetical example, $\hat{\sigma}^2 = 42.1591$ and df $= 8$. If we postulate that $H_0: \sigma^2 = 85$ vs. $H_1: \sigma^2 \neq 85$, Eq. (5.4.1) provides the test statistic for H_0. Substituting the appropriate values in (5.4.1), it can be found that under H_0, $\chi^2 = 3.97$. If we assume $\alpha = 5\%$, the critical χ^2 values are 2.1797 and 17.5346. Since the computed χ^2 lies between these limits, the data support the null hypothesis and we do not reject it. (See Fig. 5.1.) This test procedure is called the **chi-square test of significance.** The χ^2-test of significance approach to hypothesis testing is summarized in Table 5.2.

TABLE 5.2
A summary of the χ^2 test

H_0: The null hypothesis	H_1: The alternative hypothesis	Critical region: Reject H_0 if
$\sigma^2 = \sigma_0^2$	$\sigma^2 > \sigma_0^2$	$\dfrac{df(\hat{\sigma}^2)}{\sigma_0^2} > \chi^2_{\alpha, df}$
$\sigma^2 = \sigma_0^2$	$\sigma^2 < \sigma_0^2$	$\dfrac{df(\hat{\sigma}^2)}{\sigma_0^2} < \chi^2_{(1-\alpha), df}$
$\sigma^2 = \sigma_0^2$	$\sigma^2 \neq \sigma_0^2$	$\dfrac{df(\hat{\sigma}^2)}{\sigma_0^2} > \chi^2_{\alpha/2, df}$ or $< \chi^2_{(1-\alpha/2), df}$

Note: σ_0^2 is the value of σ^2 under the null hypothesis. The first subscript on χ^2 in the last column is the level of significance, and the second subscript is the degrees of freedom. These are critical chi-square values. Note that df is $(n-2)$ for the two-variable regression model, $(n-3)$ for the three-variable regression model, and so on.

5.8 HYPOTHESIS TESTING: SOME PRACTICAL ASPECTS

The Meaning of "Accepting" or "Rejecting" a Hypothesis

If on the basis of a test of significance, say, the t-test, we decide to "accept" the null hypothesis, all we are saying is that on the basis of the sample evidence we have no reason to reject it; we are not saying that the null hypothesis is true beyond any doubt. Why? To answer this, let us revert to our consumption-income example and assume that $H_0: \beta_2$ (MPC) $= 0.50$. Now the estimated value of the MPC is $\hat{\beta}_2 = 0.5091$ with a se $(\hat{\beta}_2) = 0.0357$. Then on the basis of the t test we find that $t = (0.5091 - 0.50)/0.0357 = 0.25$, which is insignificant, say, at $\alpha = 5\%$. Therefore, we say "accept" H_0. But now let us assume $H_0: \beta_2 = 0.48$. Applying the t test, we obtain $t = (0.5091 - 0.48)/0.0357 = 0.82$, which too is statistically insignificant. So now we say "accept" this H_0. Which of these two null hypotheses is the "truth"? We do not know. Therefore, in "accepting" a null hypothesis we should always be aware that another null hypothesis may be equally compatible with the data. It is therefore preferable to say that we *may* accept the null hypothesis rather than we (do) accept it. Better still,

> ... just as a court pronounces a verdict as "not guilty" rather than "innocent," so the conclusion of a statistical test is "do not reject" rather than "accept."[11]

The "Zero" Null Hypothesis and the "2-t" Rule of Thumb

A null hypothesis that is commonly tested in empirical work is $H_0: \beta_2 = 0$, that is, the slope coefficient is zero. This "zero" null hypothesis is a kind of straw man, the objective being to find out whether Y is related at all to X, the explanatory variable. If there is no relationship between Y and X to begin with, then testing a hypothesis such as $\beta_2 = 0.3$ or any other value is meaningless.

This null hypothesis can be easily tested by the confidence interval or the t-test approach discussed in the preceding sections. But very often such formal testing can be shortcut by adopting the "2-t" rule of significance, which may be stated as

> **"2-t" Rule of Thumb.** If the number of degrees of freedom is 20 or more and if α, the level of significance, is set at 0.05, then the null hypothesis $\beta_2 = 0$ can be rejected if the t value $[= \hat{\beta}_2/\text{se}(\hat{\beta}_2)]$ computed from (5.3.2) exceeds 2 in absolute value.

The rationale for this rule is not too difficult to grasp. From (5.7.1) we know that we will reject $H_0: \beta_2 = 0$ if

$$t = \hat{\beta}_2/\text{se}(\hat{\beta}_2) > t_{\alpha/2} \qquad \text{when } \hat{\beta}_2 > 0$$

---

[11]Jan Kmenta, *Elements of Econometrics*, Macmillan, New York, 1971, p. 114.

or

$$t = \hat{\beta}_2/\operatorname{se}(\hat{\beta}_2) < -t_{\alpha/2} \qquad \text{when } \hat{\beta}_2 < 0$$

or when

$$|t| = \left|\frac{\hat{\beta}_2}{\operatorname{se}(\hat{\beta}_2)}\right| > t_{\alpha/2} \tag{5.8.1}$$

for the appropriate degrees of freedom.

Now if we examine the t table given in Appendix D, we see that for df of about 20 or more a computed t value in excess of 2 (in absolute terms), say, 2.1, is statistically significant at the 5 percent level, implying rejection of the null hypothesis. Therefore, if we find that for 20 or more df the computed t value is, say, 2.5 or 3, we do not even have to refer to the t table to assess the significance of the estimated slope coefficient. Of course, one can always refer to the t table to obtain the precise level of significance, and one should always do so when the df are fewer than, say, 20.

In passing, note that if we are testing the one-sided hypothesis $\beta_2 = 0$ vs. $\beta_2 > 0$ or $\beta_2 < 0$, then we should reject the null hypothesis if

$$|t| = \left|\frac{\hat{\beta}_2}{\operatorname{se}(\hat{\beta}_2)}\right| > t_\alpha \tag{5.8.2}$$

If we fix α at 0.05, then from the t table we observe that for 20 or more df a t value in excess of 1.73 is statistically significant at the 5% level of significance (one-tail). Hence, whenever a t value exceeds, say, 1.8 (in absolute terms) and the df are 20 or more, one need not consult the t table for the statistical significance of the observed coefficient. Of course, if we choose α at 0.01 or any other level, we will have to decide on the appropriate t value as the benchmark value. But by now the reader should be able to do that.

Forming the Null and Alternative Hypotheses[12]

Given the null and the alternative hypotheses, testing them for statistical significance should no longer be a mystery. But how does one formulate these hypotheses? There are no hard-and-fast rules. Very often the phenomenon under study will suggest the nature of the null and alternative hypotheses. For example, in Exercise 5.16 you are asked to estimate the capital market line (CML) of portfolio theory, which postulates that $E_i = \beta_1 + \beta_2\sigma_i$, where $E =$ expected return on portfolio and $\sigma =$ the standard deviation of return, a measure of risk. Since return and risk are expected to be positively related—the higher the risk, the higher the return—the natural alternative hypothesis to the null hypothesis that $\beta_2 = 0$ would be $\beta_2 > 0$. That is, one would not choose to consider values of β_2 less than zero.

---

[12]For an interesting discussion about formulating hypotheses, see J. Bradford De Long and Kevin Lang, "Are All Economic Hypotheses False?" *Journal of Political Economy*, vol. 100, no. 6, 1992, pp. 1257–1272.

But consider the case of the demand for money. As we shall show later, one of the important determinants of the demand for money is income. Prior studies of the money demand fuctions have shown that the income elasticity of demand for money (the percent change in the demand for money for a 1 percent change in income) has typically ranged between 0.7 and 1.3. Therefore, in a new study of demand for money if one postulates that the income-elasticity coefficient β_2 is 1, the alternative hypothesis could be that $\beta_2 \neq 1$, a two-sided alternative hypothesis.

Thus, theoretical expectations or prior empirical work or both can be relied upon to formulate hypotheses. But no matter how the hypotheses are formed, *it is extremely important that the researcher establish these hypotheses before carrying out the empirical investigation*. Otherwise, he or she will be guilty of circular reasoning or self-fulfilling prophesies. That is, if one were to formulate hypotheses after examining the empirical results, there may be the temptation to form hypotheses that justify one's results. Such a practice should be avoided at all costs, at least for the sake of scientific objectivity. Keep in mind the Stigler quotation given at the beginning of this chapter!

Choosing α, the Level of Significance

It should be clear from the discussion so far that whether we reject or do not reject the null hypothesis depends critically on α, the level of significance or the *probability of committing a* **Type I** *error*—the probability of rejecting the true hypothesis. In Appendix A we discuss fully the nature of a Type I error, its relationship to a **Type II** *error* (the probability of accepting the false hypothesis) and why classical statistics generally concentrates on a Type I error. But even then, why is α commonly fixed at the 1%, 5%, or at the most 10% levels? As a matter of fact, there is nothing sacrosanct about these values; any other values will do just as well.

In an introductory book like this it is not possible to discuss in depth why one chooses the 1, 5, or 10% levels of significance, for that will take us into the field of statistical decision making, a discipline unto itself. A brief summary, however, can be offered. As we discuss in Appendix A, for a given sample size, if we try to reduce a *Type I error*, a *Type II error* increases, and vice versa. That is, given the sample size, if we try to reduce the probability of rejecting the true hypothesis, we at the same time increase the probability of accepting the false hypothesis. So there is a trade-off involved between these two types of errors, given the sample size. Now the only way we can decide about the trade-off is to find out the relative costs of the two types of errors. Then,

> If the error of rejecting the null hypothesis which is in fact true (Error Type I) is costly relative to the error of not rejecting the null hypothesis which is in fact false (Error Type II), it will be rational to set the probability of the first kind of error low. If, on the other hand, the cost of making Error Type I is low relative to the cost of making Error Type II, it will pay to make the probability of the first kind of error high (thus making the probability of the second type of error low).[13]

---

[13] Jan Kmenta, *Elements of Econometrics,* Macmillan, New York, 1971, pp. 126–127.

Of course, the rub is that we rarely know the costs of making the two types of errors. Thus, applied econometricians generally follow the practice of setting the value of α at a 1 or a 5 or at most a 10% level and choose a test statistic that would make the probability of committing a Type II error as small as possible. Since one minus the probability of committing a Type II error is known as the **power of the test**, this procedure amounts to maximizing the power of the test. (See Appendix A for a discussion of the power of a test.)

But all this problem with choosing the appropriate value of α can be avoided if we use what is known as the **p value** of the test statistic, which is discussed next.

The Exact Level of Significance: The p Value

As just noted, the Achilles heel of the classical approach to the hypothesis testing is its arbitrariness in selecting α. Once a test statistic (e.g., the t statistic) is obtained in a given example, why not simply go to the appropriate statistical table and find out the actual probability of obtaining a value of the test statistic as much as or greater than that obtained in the example? This probability is called the **p value** (i.e., **probability value**), also known as the **observed or exact level of significance** or the **exact probability of committing a Type I error**. More technically, the p value is defined as **the lowest significance level at which a null hypothesis can be rejected**.

To illustrate, let us return to our consumption-income example. Given the null hypothesis that the true MPC is 0.3, we obtained a t value of 5.86 in (5.7.4). What is the p value of obtaining a t value of as much as or greater than 5.86? Looking up the t table given in Appendix D, we observe that for 8 df the probability of obtaining such a t value must be much smaller than 0.001 (one-tail) or 0.002 (two-tail). By using the computer, it can be shown that the probability of obtaining a t value of 5.86 or greater (for 8 df) is about 0.000189.[14] This is the p value of the observed t statistic. This observed, or exact, level of significance of the t statistic is much smaller than the conventionally, and arbitrarily, fixed level of significance, such as 1, 5, or 10 percent. As a matter of fact, if we were to use the p value just computed, and reject the null hypothesis that the true MPC is 0.3, the probability of our committing a Type I error is only about 0.02 percent, that is, only about 2 in 10,000!

As we noted earlier, if the data do not support the null hypothesis, $|t|$ obtained under the null hypothesis will be "large" and therefore the p value of obtaining such a $|t|$ value will be "small." In other words, for a given sample size, as $|t|$ increases, the p value decreases, and one can therefore reject the null hypothesis with increasing confidence.

---

[14]One can obtain the p value using electronic statistical tables to several decimal places. Unfortunately, the conventional statistical tables, for lack of space, cannot be that refined. Micro TSP, SHAZAM, ET, and several other statistical packages now routinely print out the p values.

What is the relationship of the p value to the level of significance α? If we make the habit of fixing α equal to the p value of a test statistic (e.g., the t statistic), then there is no conflict between the two values. To put it differently, **it is better to give up fixing α arbitrarily at some level and simply choose the p value of the test statistic.** It is preferable to leave it to the reader to decide whether to reject the null hypothesis at the given p value. If in an application the p value of a test statistic happens to be, say, 0.145, or 14.5 percent, and if the reader want to reject the null hypothesis at this (exact) level of significance, so be it. Nothing is wrong with taking a chance of being wrong 14.5 percent of the time if you reject the true null hypothesis. Similarly, as in our consumption-income example, there is nothing wrong if the researcher wants to choose a p value of about 0.02 percent and not take a chance of being wrong more than 2 out of 10,000 times. After all, some investigators may be risk-lovers and some risk-averters!

In the rest of this text, we will generally quote the p value of a given test statistic. Some readers may want to fix α at some level and reject the null hypothesis if the p value is less than α. That is their choice.

Statistical Significance versus Practical Significance

Let us revert to our consumption-income example and now hypothesize that the true MPC is 0.61 ($H_0: \beta_2 = 0.61$). Based on our sample result of $\hat{\beta}_2 = 0.5091$, we obtained the interval (0.4268, 0.5914) with 95 percent confidence. Since this interval does not include 0.61, we can, with 95 percent confidence, say that our estimate is statistically significant, that is, significantly different from 0.61.

But what is the practical or substantive significance of our finding? That is, what difference does it make if we take the MPC to be 0.61 rather than 0.5091? Is the 0.1009 difference between the two MPCs that important practically?

The answer to this question depends on what we really do with these estimates. For example, from macroeconomics we know that the income multiplier is $1/(1 - \text{MPC})$. Thus, if MPC is 0.5091, the multiplier is 2.04, but it is 2.56 if MPC is equal to 0.61. That is, if the government were to increase its expenditure by \$1 to lift the economy out of a recession, income will eventually increase by \$2.04 if the MPC is 0.5091 but by \$2.56 if the MPC is 0.61. And that difference could very well be crucial to resuscitating the economy.

The point of all this discussion is that one should not confuse statistical significance with practical, or economic, significance. As Goldberger notes:

> When a null, say, $\beta_j = 1$, is specified, the likely intent is that β_j is *close* to 1, so close that for all practical purposes it may be treated *as if it were* 1. But whether 1.1 is "practically the same as" 1.0 is a matter of economics, not of statistics. One cannot resolve the matter by relying on a hypothesis test, because the test statistic $[t =](b_j - 1)/\hat{\sigma}_{bj}$ measures the estimated coefficient in standard error units, which are not meaningful units in which to measure the economic parameter $\beta_j - 1$. It

may be a good idea to reserve the term "significance" for the statistical concept, adopting "substantial" for the economic concept.[15]

The point made by Goldberger is important. As sample size becomes very large, issues of statistical significance become much less important but issues of economic significance become critical. Indeed, since with very large samples almost any null hypothesis will be rejected, there may be studies in which the magnitude of the point estimates may be the only issue.

The Choice between Confidence-Interval and Test-of-Significance Approaches to Hypothesis Testing

In most applied economic analyses, the null hypothesis is set up as a straw man and the objective of the empirical work is to knock it down, that is, reject the null hypothesis. Thus, in our consumption/income example, the null hypothesis that the MPC, β_2, $= 0$ is patently absurd, but we often use it to dramatize the empirical results. Apparently editors of reputed journals do not find it exciting to publish an empirical piece that does not reject the null hypothesis. Somehow the finding that the MPC is statistically different from zero is more newsworthy than the finding that it is equal to, say, 0.7!

Thus, J. Bradford De Long and Kevin Lang argue that it is better for economists

> ... to concentrate on the magnitudes of coefficients and to report confidence levels and not significance tests. If all or almost all null hypotheses are false, there is little point in concentrating on whether or not an estimate is indistinguishable from its predicted value under the null. Instead, we wish to cast light on what models are good approximations, which requires that we know ranges of parameter values that are excluded by empirical estimates.[16]

In short, these authors prefer the confidence-interval approach to the test-of-significance approach. The reader may want to keep this advice in mind.

5.9 REGRESSION ANALYSIS AND ANALYSIS OF VARIANCE

In this section we study regression analysis from the point of view of the analysis of variance and introduce the reader to an illuminating and complementary way of looking at the statistical inference problem.

In Chapter 3, Section 3.5, we developed the following identity:

$$\sum y_i^2 = \sum \hat{y}_i^2 + \sum \hat{u}_i^2 = \hat{\beta}_2^2 \sum x_i^2 + \sum \hat{u}_i^2 \qquad (3.5.2)$$

---

[15]Arthur S. Goldberger, *A Course in Econometrics*, Harvard University Press, Cambridge, Massachusetts, 1991, p. 240. Note b_j is the OLS estimator of β_j and $\hat{\sigma}_{bj}$ is its standard error. For corroborating view, see D. N. McCloskey, "The Loss Function Has Been Mislaid: The Rhetoric of Significance Tests," *American Economic Review*, vol. 75, 1985, pp. 201–205.

[16]See their article cited in footnote 12, p. 1271.

that is, TSS = ESS + RSS, which decomposed the total sum of squares (TSS) into two components: explained sum of squares (ESS) and residual sum of squares (RSS). A study of these components of TSS is known as the **analysis of variance** (ANOVA) from the regression viewpoint.

Associated with any sum of squares is its df, the number of independent observations on which it is based. TSS has $n - 1$ df because we lose 1 df in computing the sample mean $\bar{Y}$. RSS has $n - 2$ df. (Why?) (*Note:* This is true only for the two-variable regression model with the intercept β_1 present.) ESS has 1 df (again true of the two-variable case only), which follows from the fact that ESS $= \hat{\beta}_2^2 \sum x_i^2$ is a function of $\hat{\beta}_2$ only since $\sum x_i^2$ is known.

Let us arrange the various sums of squares and their associated df in Table 5.3, which is the standard form of the AOV table, sometimes called the **ANOVA table**. Given the entries of Table 5.3, we now consider the following variable:

$$
F = \frac{\text{MSS of ESS}}{\text{MSS of RSS}}
$$

$$
= \frac{\hat{\beta}_2^2 \sum x_i^2}{\sum \hat{u}_i^2/(n - 2)}
$$

$$
= \frac{\hat{\beta}_2^2 \sum x_i^2}{\hat{\sigma}^2} \tag{5.9.1}
$$

If we assume that the disturbances u_i are normally distributed and $H_0: \beta_2 = 0$, it can be shown that the F of (5.9.1) satisfies the conditions of Theorem 4.6 (Section 4.5) and therefore follows the F distribution with 1 and $n - 2$ df. (See Appendix 5A, Section 5A.2.)

What use can be made of the preceding F ratio? It can be shown[17] that

$$
E\left(\hat{\beta}_2^2 \sum x_i^2\right) = \sigma^2 + \beta_2^2 \sum x_i^2 \tag{5.9.2}
$$

and

$$
E\frac{\sum \hat{u}_i^2}{n - 2} = E(\hat{\sigma}^2) = \sigma^2 \tag{5.9.3}
$$

TABLE 5.3
ANOVA table for the two-variable regression model

Source of variation	SS*	df	MSS†
Due to regression (ESS)	$\sum \hat{y}_i^2 = \hat{\beta}_2^2 \sum x_i^2$	1	$\hat{\beta}_2^2 \sum x_i^2$
Due to residuals (RSS)	$\sum \hat{u}_i^2$	$n - 2$	$\dfrac{\sum \hat{u}_i^2}{n - 2} = \hat{\sigma}^2$
TSS	$\sum y_i^2$	$n - 1$	

* SS means sum of squares.

† Mean sum of squares, which is obtained by dividing SS by their df.

[17] For proof, see K. A. Brownlee, *Statistical Theory and Methodology in Science and Engineering*, John Wiley & Sons, New York, 1960, pp. 278–280.

(Note that β_2 and σ^2 appearing on the right sides of these equations are the true parameters.) Therefore, if β_2 is in fact zero, Eqs. (5.9.2) and (5.9.3) both provide us with identical estimates of true σ^2. In this situation, the explanatory variable X has no linear influence on Y whatsoever and the entire variation in Y is explained by the random disturbances u_i. If, on the other hand, β_2 is not zero, (5.9.2) and (5.9.3) will be different and part of the variation in Y will be ascribable to X. Therefore, the F ratio of (5.9.1) provides a test of the null hypothesis $H_0: \beta_2 = 0$. Since all the quantities entering into this equation can be obtained from the available sample, this F ratio provides a test statistic to test the null hypothesis that true β_2 is zero. All that needs to be done is to compute the F ratio and compare it with the critical F value obtained from the F tables at the chosen level of significance, or obtain the **p value** of the computed F statistic.

To illustrate, let us continue with our consumption-income example. The ANOVA table for this example is as shown in Table 5.4. The computed F value is seen to be 202.87. The p value of this F statistic corresponding to 1 and 8 df cannot be obtained from the F table given in Appendix D, but by using electronic statistical tables it can be shown that the p value is 0.0000001, an extremely small probability indeed. If you decide to choose the level-of-significance approach to hypothesis testing and fix α at 0.01, or a 1% level, you can see that the computed F of 202.87 is obviously significant at this level. Therefore, if we reject the null hypothesis that $\beta_2 = 0$, the probability of committing a Type I error is very small. For all practical purposes, our sample could not have come from a population with zero β_2 value and we can conclude with great confidence that X, income, does affect Y, consumption expenditure.

Recall Theorem 4.7 of Section 4.5, which states that the square of the t value with k df is an F value with 1 df in the numerator and k df in the denominator. For our comsumption-income example, if we assume $H_0: \beta_2 = 0$, then from (5.3.2) it can be easily verified that the estimated t value is 14.24. This t value has 8 df. Under the same null hypothesis, the F value was 202.87 with 1 and 8 df. Hence $(14.24)^2 = F$ value, except for the rounding errors.

Thus, the t and the F tests provide us with two alternative but complementary ways of testing the null hypothesis that $\beta_2 = 0$. If this is the case, why not just rely on the t test and not worry about the F test and the accompanying analysis of variance? For the two-variable model there really is no need to resort to the F test. But when we consider the topic of multiple regression we will see that the F test has several interesting applications that make it a very useful and powerful method of testing statistical hypotheses.

TABLE 5.4
ANOVA table for the consumption-income example

Source of variation	SS	df	MSS	
Due to regression (ESS)	8552.73	1	8552.73	$F = \dfrac{8552.73}{42.159}$
Due to residuals (RSS)	337.27	8	42.159	$= 202.87$
TSS	8890.00	9		

5.10 APPLICATION OF REGRESSION ANALYSIS: THE PROBLEM OF PREDICTION

On the basis of the sample data of Table 3.2 we obtained the following sample regression:

$$\hat{Y}_i = 24.4545 + 0.5091X_i \qquad (3.6.2)$$

where $\hat{Y}_t$ is the estimator of true $E(Y_i)$ corresponding to given X. What use can be made of this **historical regression?** One use is to "predict" or "forecast" the future consumption expenditure Y corresponding to some given level of income X. Now there are two kinds of predictions: (1) prediction of the conditional mean value of Y corresponding to a chosen X, say, X_0, that is the point on the population regression line itself (see Fig. 2.2), and (2) prediction of an individual Y value corresponding to X_0. We shall call these two predictions the **mean prediction** and **individual prediction.**

Mean Prediction[18]

To fix the ideas, assume that $X_0 = 100$ and we want to predict $E(Y \mid X_0 = 100)$. Now it can be shown that the historical regression (3.6.2) provides the point estimate of this mean prediction as follows:

$$\begin{aligned} \hat{Y}_0 &= \hat{\beta}_1 + \hat{\beta}_2 X_0 \\ &= 24.4545 + 0.5091(100) \\ &= 75.3645 \end{aligned} \qquad (5.10.1)$$

where $\hat{Y}_0 = $ estimator of $E(Y \mid X_0)$. It can be proved that this point predictor is a best linear unbiased estimator (BLUE).

Since $\hat{Y}_0$ is an estimator, it is likely to be different from its true value. The difference between the two values will give some idea about the prediction or forecast error. To assess this error, we need to find out the sampling distribution of $\hat{Y}_0$. It is shown in Appendix 5A, Section 5A.3 that $\hat{Y}_0$ in Eq. (5.10.1) is normally distributed with mean $(\beta_1 + \beta_2 X_0)$ and the variance given by the following formula:

$$\text{var}(\hat{Y}_0) = \sigma^2 \left[\frac{1}{n} + \frac{(X_0 - \bar{X})^2}{\sum x_i^2} \right] \qquad (5.10.2)$$

By replacing the unknown σ^2 by its unbiased estimator $\hat{\sigma}^2$, it follows that the variable

$$t = \frac{\hat{Y}_0 - (\beta_1 + \beta_2 X_0)}{\text{se}(\hat{Y}_0)} \qquad (5.10.3)$$

---

[18]For the proofs of the various statements made, see App. 5A, Section 5A.3.

follows the t distribution with $n - 2$ df. The t distribution can therefore be used to derive confidence intervals for the true $E(Y_0 \mid X_0)$ and test hypotheses about it in the usual manner, namely,

$$\Pr[\hat{\beta}_1 + \hat{\beta}_2 X_0 - t_{\alpha/2} \operatorname{se}(\hat{Y}_0) \leq \beta_1 + \beta_2 X_0 \leq \hat{\beta}_1 + \hat{\beta}_2 X_0 + t_{\alpha/2} \operatorname{se}(\hat{Y}_0)] = 1 - \alpha$$

(5.10.4)

where $\operatorname{se}(\hat{Y}_0)$ is obtained from (5.10.2).

For our data (see Table 3.3),

$$\operatorname{var}(\hat{Y}_0) = 42.159 \left[\frac{1}{10} + \frac{(100 - 170)^2}{33,000} \right]$$
$$= 10.4759$$

and

$$\operatorname{se}(\hat{Y}_0) = 3.2366$$

Therefore, the 95% confidence interval for true $E(Y \mid X_0) = \beta_1 + \beta_2 X_0$ is given by

$$75.3645 - 2.306(3.2366) \leq E(Y_0 \mid X = 100) \leq 75.3645 + 2.306(3.2366)$$

that is,

$$67.9010 \leq E(Y \mid X = 100) \leq 82.8381 \qquad (5.10.5)$$

Thus, given $X_0 = 100$, in repeated sampling, 95 out of 100 intervals like (5.10.5) will include the true mean value; the single best estimate of the true mean value is of course the point estimate 75.3645.

If we obtain 95% confidence intervals like (5.10.5) for each of the X values given in Table 3.2, we obtain what is known as the **confidence interval**, or **confidence band**, for the population regression function, which is shown in Fig. 5.6.

Individual Prediction

If our interest lies in predicting an individual Y value, Y_0, corresponding to a given X value, say, X_0, then, as shown in Appendix 5, Section 5A.3, a best linear unbiased estimator of Y_0 is also given by (5.10.1), but its variance is as follows:

$$\operatorname{var}(Y_0 - \hat{Y}_0) = E[Y_0 - \hat{Y}_0]^2 = \sigma^2 \left[1 + \frac{1}{n} + \frac{(X_0 - \bar{X})^2}{\sum x_i^2} \right] \qquad (5.10.6)$$

It can be shown further that Y_0 also follows the normal distribution with mean and variance given by (5.10.1) and (5.10.6), respectively. Substituting $\hat{\sigma}^2$ for the unknown σ^2, it follows that

$$t = \frac{Y_0 - \hat{Y}_0}{\operatorname{se}(Y_0 - \hat{Y}_0)}$$

also follows the t distribution. Therefore, the t distribution can be used to draw inferences about the true Y_0. Continuing with our consumption-income example, we see that the point prediction of Y_0 is 75.3645, the same as that of $\hat{Y}_0$, and its variance is 52.6349 (the reader should verify this calculation). Therefore, the 95% confidence interval for Y_0 corresponding to $X_0 = 100$ is seen to be

$$(58.6345 \le Y_0 \mid X_0 = 100 \le 92.0945) \qquad (5.10.7)$$

Comparing this interval with (5.10.5), we see that the confidence interval for individual Y_0 is wider than that for the mean value of Y_0. (Why?) Computing confidence intervals like (5.10.7) conditional upon the X values given in Table 3.2, we obtain the 95% confidence band for the individual Y values corresponding to these X values. This confidence band along with the confidence band for $\hat{Y}_0$ associated with the same X's is shown in Fig. 5.6.

Notice an important feature of the confidence bands shown in Fig. 5.6. The width of these bands is smallest when $X_0 = \bar{X}$. (Why?) However, the width widens sharply as X_0 moves away from $\bar{X}$. (Why?) This change would suggest that the predictive ability of the *historical* sample regression line falls markedly as X_0 departs progressively from $\bar{X}$. **Therefore, one should exercise great caution in "extrapolating" the historical regression line to predict $E(Y \mid X_0)$ or Y_0 associated with a given X_0 that is far removed from the sample mean $\bar{X}$.**

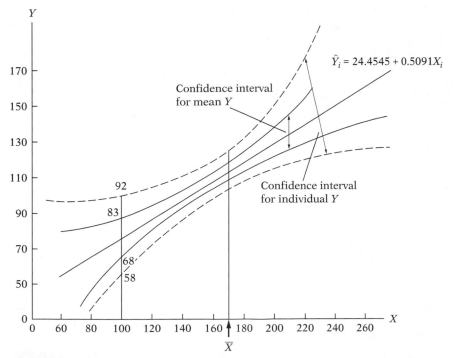

FIGURE 5.6
Confidence intervals (bands) for mean Y and individual Y values.

5.11 REPORTING THE RESULTS OF REGRESSION ANALYSIS

There are various ways of reporting the results of regression analysis, but in this text we shall use the following format, employing the consumption-income example of Chapter 3 as an illustration:

$$\hat{Y}_i = 24.4545 \quad + \quad 0.5091X_i$$

$$\begin{aligned}
se &= (6.4138) & (0.0357) & \qquad r^2 = 0.9621 \\
t &= (3.8128) & (14.2405) & \qquad df = 8 \\
p &= (0.002571) & (0.000000289) & \qquad F_{1,2} = 202.87
\end{aligned} \tag{5.11.1}$$

In Eq. (5.11.1) the figures in the first set of parentheses are the estimated standard errors of the regression coefficients, the figures in the second set are estimated t values computed from (5.3.2) under the null hypothesis that the true population value of each regression coefficient individually is zero (e.g., $3.8128 = 24.4545 \div 6.4138$), and the figures in the third set are the estimated p values. Thus, for 8 df the probability of obtaining a t value of 3.8128 or greater is 0.0026 and the probability of obtaining a t value of 14.2405 or larger is about 0.0000003.

By presenting the p values of the estimated t coefficients, we can see at once the exact level of significance of each estimated t value. Thus, under the null hypothesis that the true population intercept value is zero, the exact probability (i.e., the p value) of obtaining a t value of 3.8128 or greater is only about 0.0026. Therefore, if we reject this null hypothesis, the probability of our committing a Type I error is about 26 in 10,000, a very small probability indeed. For all practical purposes we can say that the true population intercept is different from zero. Likewise, the p value of the estimated slope coefficient is zero for all practical purposes. If the true MPC were in fact zero, our chances of obtaining an MPC of 0.5091 would be practically zero. Hence we can reject the null hypothesis that the true MPC is zero.

In Theorem 4.7 we showed the intimate connection between the F and t statistics, namely, $F_{1,k} = t_k^2$. Under the null hypothesis that the true $\beta_2 = 0$, (5.11.1) shows that the F value is 202.87 (for 1 numerator and 8 denominator df) and the t value is about 14.24 (8 df); as expected, the former value is the square of the latter value, except for the roundoff errors. The ANOVA table for this problem has already been discussed.

5.12 EVALUATING THE RESULTS OF REGRESSION ANALYSIS

In Fig. I.4 of the Introduction we sketched the anatomy of econometric modeling. Now that we have presented the results of regression analysis of our consumption-income example in (5.11.1), we would like to question the adequacy of the fitted model. How "good" is the fitted model? We need some criteria with which to answer this question.

First, are the signs of the estimated coefficients in accordance with theoretical or prior expectations? A priori, β_2, the marginal propensity to consume

(MPC) in the consumption function, should be positive. In the present example it is. Second, if theory says that the relationship should be not only positive but also statistically significant, is this the case in the present application? As we discussed in Section 5.11, the MPC is not only positive but also statistically significantly different from zero; the p value of the estimated t value is extremely small. The same comments apply about the intercept coefficient. Third, how well does the regression model explain variation in the consumption expenditure? One can use r^2 to answer this question. In the present example r^2 is about 0.96, which is a very high value considering that r^2 can be at most 1.

Thus, the model we have chosen for explaining consumption expenditure behavior seems quite good. But before we sign off, we would like to find out whether our model satisfies the assumptions of CNLRM. We will not look at the various assumptions now because the model is patently so simple. But there is one assumption that we would like to check, namely, the normality of the disturbance term, u_i. Recall that the t and F tests used before require that the error term follow the normal distribution. Otherwise, the testing procedure will not be valid in small, or finite, samples.

Normality Test

Although several tests of normality are discussed in the literature, we will consider just two: (1) the **chi-square goodness of fit test** and (2) the **Jarque-Bera test**. Both these tests use the residuals $\hat{u}_i$ and the chi-square probability distribution.

THE CHI-SQUARE (χ^2) GOODNESS OF FIT TEST.[19]   This test proceeds as follows: First we run the regression, obtain the residuals, $\hat{u}_i$, and compute the sample standard deviation of $\hat{u}_i$ [Note: var $(\hat{u}_i) = \sum(\hat{u}_i - \bar{\hat{u}})^2/(n-1) = \sum \hat{u}_i^2/(n-1)$, since $\bar{\hat{u}} = 0$]. Then we rank the residuals and put them into several groups (in our example, we have put them into six groups) corresponding to the number of standard deviations from zero. (*Note*: the mean value of the residuals is zero. Why?) For our example, we obtain the following data, which are then discussed.

Observed residuals (O_i)	0.0	2.0	3.0	4.0	1.0	0.0	
Expected residuals (E_i)	0.2	1.4	3.4	3.4	1.4	0.2	
$(O_i - E_i)^2/E_i$	0.2	0.26	0.05	0.10	0.11	0.2	Sum = 0.92

Note: $O_i = \hat{u}_i$, where $\hat{u}_i$ are OLS residuals.

---

[19]The following discussion is based on Kenneth J. White and Linda T. M. Bui, *Basic Econometrics: A Computer Handbook Using SHAZAM* for use with Gujarati, *Basic Econometrics*, McGraw-Hill, New York, 1988, p. 34. The TSP computer package also follows a similar procedure.

The row marked observed residuals give the *frequency distribution* of the residuals for specified standard deviations below and above zero. In our example there are no residuals 2 standard deviations below zero, 2 residuals between 1 and 2 standard deviations below zero, 3 residuals between 0 and 1 standard deviation below zero, 4 residuals between 0 and 1 standard deviation above zero, 1 residual between 1 and 2 standard deviations above zero and no residuals beyond 2 standard deviations above zero.

The entries in the expected residuals row give the *frequency distribution* of the residuals on the basis of a hypothesized probability distribution, normal in the present case.[20] In the third row we compute the difference between observed and expected frequencies, square the difference, divide it by the expected frequencies, and sum them. Algebraically, we have

$$X^2 = \sum_{i=1}^{k} \frac{(O_i - E_i)^2}{E_i} \tag{5.12.1}$$

where O_i = observed frequency in class or interval i and E_i = the frequency expected in class i on the basis of the hypothesized distribution, say, the normal. Now if the difference between the observed and expected frequencies is "small," it suggests that the disturbances u_i probably came from the hypothesized probability distribution. On the other hand, if the discrepancy between the observed and expected frequencies is "large," we could reject the null hypothesis that the disturbances came from the hypothesized probability distribution. For this reason the statistic given in (5.12.1) is called a **goodness of fit** measure, for it tells how well the hypothesized probability distribution fits the actual data (i.e., is the fit good?).

How "large" or "small" must the value of X^2 given in (5.12.1) be before we decide to reject or not reject the null hypothesis? It can be shown that if the sample size is reasonably large, the X^2 statistic given in (5.12.1) *approximately follows the chi-square (χ^2) distribution with ($N - 1$) df, where N is the number of classes or groups.*[21] One degree of freedom is lost because of the constraint that the total number of observed and expected frequencies must be the same.

Returning to our consumption income example, as shown in the preceding table, we see the value of X^2 is about 0.92. Although the sample size is rather small, just to illustrate the mechanics we will apply the chi-square test. We have six classes in the present example. It would seem that the degrees of freedom are $(6 - 1) = 5$. But as noted in footnote 21, we lose 3 more df—2

---

[20]SHAZAM, TSP, ET,™ and several statistical packages can fit a normal distribution to a set of data. These packages also provide the chi-square test that is discussed shortly.

[21]The general rule of finding the degrees of freedom is as follows: df = $(N - 1 - k)$, where N is the number of groups and k is the number of parameters estimated. In our case remember we are dealing with the residuals $\hat{u}_i$. But to obtain these residuals we first have to estimate the two unknowns, β_1 and β_2. So we lose 2 df. Now to fit the normal distribution to the u_i, we have to estimate the parameters of the normal distribution, namely, the mean and the variance. But since the mean value of $\hat{u}_i$ is zero (why?), we only have to estimate the variance. Hence we lose 1 df. Therefore, we lose $k = 3$ df. Given that we have $N = 6$, the df therefore are $(6 - 1 - 3) = 2$. On the use of the chi-square test in measuring the goodness of fit, see any introductory textbook in statistics.

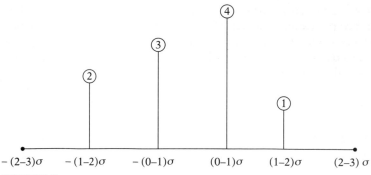

FIGURE 5.7
Distribution of residuals from consumption-income example, number of standard deviations (σ) below and above zero.

because we had to estimate β_1 and β_2 before we could compute the residuals $\hat{u}_i$ and 1 because we used the data to estimate the standard deviation of the residuals. Now for 2 df the **p value** of obtaining a chi-square value as much as or greater than 0.92 is about 0.63. Since this probability is quite high, the difference between the observed and expected values of the residuals is not serious enough to reject the normality assumption.

Incidentally, before one applies the chi-square test as just described, one can simply plot the observed residuals given in the preceding table in the form of the **histogram** as shown in Fig. 5.7. As this figure shows, the observed residuals (measured in terms of standard deviation units from zero) seem to be approximately normally distributed. *Very often such a visual picture is a good way of learning informally about the likely shape of the probability distribution of a random variable.*

THE JARQUE-BERA (JB) TEST OF NORMALITY.[22]   The JB test of normality is an asymptotic, or large-sample, test. It is also based on the OLS residuals. This test first computes the **skewness** and **kurtosis** (described in Appendix A) measures of the OLS residuals and uses the following test statistic:

$$\text{JB} = n\left[\frac{S^2}{6} + \frac{(K-3)^2}{24}\right] \qquad (5.12.2)$$

where S represents **skewness** and K represents **kurtosis**.

Since for a normal distribution the value of skewness is zero and the value of kurtosis is 3, in (5.12.2) $(K-3)$ represents excess kurtosis. Under the null hypothesis that the residuals are normally distributed, Jarque and Bera showed that **asymptotically (i.e., in large samples) the JB statistic given in (5.12.2) follows the chi-square distribution with 2 df.** If the p value of the computed chi-square statistic in an application is sufficiently low, one can reject the hypothesis that the residuals are normally distributed. But if the p value is reasonably high, one does not reject the normality assumption.

---

[22] See C. M. Jarque and A. K. Bera, "A Test for Normality of Observations and Regression Residuals," *International Statistical Review*, vol. 55, 1987, pp. 163–172.

Turning to our consumption-income example, we find (using the **SHAZAM, TSP,** or **ET** packages) the JB value of 0.7769. If the sample were reasonably large, the p value of obtaining such a chi-square value for 2 df is about 0.6781, which is quite a large probability. Therefore, asymptotically, we do not reject the normality assumption.

Other Tests of Model Adequacy

Remember that the CNLRM makes many more assumptions than the normality of the error term. As we develop our econometric theory further, we will consider several other tests of model adequacy. Until then, keep in mind that our regression modeling is based on several simplifying assumptions that may not hold in each and every case.

5.13   SUMMARY AND CONCLUSIONS

1. Estimation and hypothesis testing constitute the two main branches of classical statistics. Having discussed the problem of estimation in Chapters 3 and 4, we have taken up the problem of hypothesis testing in this chapter.
2. Hypothesis testing answers this question: Is a given finding compatible with a stated hypothesis or not?
3. There are two mutually complementary approaches to answering the preceding question: **confidence interval** and **test of significance**.
4. Underlying the confidence-interval approach is the concept of **interval estimation**. An interval estimator is an interval or range constructed in such a manner that it has a specified probability of including within its limits the true value of the unknown parameter. The interval thus constructed is known as a **confidence interval**, which is often stated in percent form, such as 90 or 95 percent. The confidence interval provides a set of plausible hypotheses about the value of the unknown parameter. If the null-hypothesized value lies in the confidence interval, the hypothesis is not rejected, whereas if it lies outside this interval, the null hypothesis can be rejected.
5. In the **significance test** procedure, one develops a **test statistic** and examines its sampling distribution under the null hypothesis. The test statistic usually follows a well-defined probability distribution such as the normal, t, F, or chi-square. Once a test statistic (e.g., the t statistic) is computed from the data at hand, its p value can be easily obtained. The p value gives the exact probability of obtaining the estimated test statistic under the null hypothesis. If this p value is small, one can reject the null hypothesis, but if it is large one may not reject it. What constitutes a small or large p value is up to the investigator. In choosing the p value the investigator has to bear in mind the probabilities of committing **Type I** and **Type II errors**.
6. In practice, one should be careful in fixing α, the probability of committing a **Type I error**, at arbitrary values such as 1, 5, or 10 percent. It is better to quote the ***p* value** of the test statistic. Also, the statistical significance of an estimate should not be confused with its practical significance.

7. Of course, hypothesis testing presumes that the model chosen for empirical analysis is adequate in the sense that it does not violate one or more assumptions underlying the classical normal linear regression model. Therefore, tests of model adequacy should precede tests of hypothesis. This chapter introduced one such test, the **normality test**, to find out whether the error term follows the normal distribution. Since in small, or finite, samples, the t, F, and chi-square tests require the normality assumption, it is important that this assumption be checked formally.

8. If the model is deemed practically adequate, it may be used for forecasting purposes. But in forecasting the future values of the regressand, one should not go too far out of the sample range of the regressor values. Otherwise, forecasting errors can increase dramatically.

EXERCISES

Questions

5.1. State with reason whether the following statements are true, false, or uncertain. Be precise.
(a) The t test of significance discussed in this chapter requires that the sampling distributions of estimators $\hat{\beta}_1$ and $\hat{\beta}_2$ follow the normal distribution.
(b) Even though the disturbance term in the CLRM is not normally distributed, the OLS estimators are still unbiased.
(c) If there is no intercept in the regression model, the estimated $u_i (= \hat{u}_i)$ will not sum to zero.
(d) The p value and the size of a test statistic mean the same thing.
(e) In a regression model that contains the intercept, the sum of the residuals is always zero.
(f) If a null hypothesis is not rejected, it is true.
(g) The higher is the value of σ^2, the larger is the variance of $\hat{\beta}_2$ given in (3.3.1).
(h) The conditional and unconditional means of a random variable are the same things.
(i) In the two-variable PRF, if the slope coefficient β_2 is zero, the intercept β_1 is estimated by the sample mean $\bar{Y}$.
(j) The conditional variance, $\text{var}(Y_i \mid X_i) = \sigma^2$, and the unconditional variance of Y, $\text{var}(Y) = \sigma_Y^2$, will be the same if X had no influence on Y.

5.2. Set up the ANOVA table in the manner of Table 5.4 for the regression model given in (3.7.2) and test the hypothesis that personal consumption expenditure and Gross Domestic Product in the U.S. economy for 1980–1991 were not related.

5.3. Consider the following regression results for the U.S. economy for 1968–1987 ($\hat{Y} =$ U.S. expenditure on imported goods and $X =$ personal disposable income, both measured in billions of 1982 dollars):

$$\hat{Y}_t = -261.09 + 0.2453\, X_t$$
$$\text{se} = \quad (31.327) \quad (\qquad) \qquad r^2 = 0.9388$$
$$t = \quad (\qquad) \quad (16.616) \qquad n = 20$$

(a) Fill in the missing numbers.
(b) How do you interpret the coefficient 0.2453? And the coefficient -261.09?
(c) Would you reject the hypothesis that the true slope coefficient is zero? Which test do you use? And why? What is the p value of your test statistic?

(d) Set up the ANOVA table for this example and test the hypothesis that the true slope coefficient is zero. Which test do you use and why?

(e) Are the answers you obtained in (a) and (d) in conflict? If they are not, what explains the harmony between the answers?

(f) Suppose in the regression just given the r^2 value was not given to you. Could you obtain it from the other results in the regression?

5.4. Let ρ^2 represent the true population coefficient of correlation. Suppose you want to test the hypothesis that $\rho^2 = 0$. Verbally explain how you would test this hypothesis. *Hint:* Use Eq. (3.5.11). See also exercise 5.7.

5.5. What is known as the **characteristic line** of modern investment analysis is simply the regression line obtained from the following model:

$$r_{it} = \alpha_i + \beta_i r_{mt} + u_t$$

where r_{it} = the rate of return on the ith security in time t

r_{mt} = the rate of return on the market portfolio in time t

u_t = stochastic disturbance term

In this model β_i is known as the **Beta coefficient** of the ith security, a measure of market (or systematic) risk of a security.[*]

Based on 240 monthly rates of return for the period 1956–1976, Fogler and Ganapathy obtained the following characteristic line for IBM stock in relation to the market portfolio index developed at the University of Chicago:[†]

$$r_{it} = 0.7264 + 1.0598 r_{mt} \qquad r^2 = 0.4710$$

$$\text{se} = (0.3001) \quad (0.0728) \qquad \text{df} = 238$$

$$F_{1,238} = 211.896$$

(a) A security whose Beta coefficient is greater than one is said to be a volatile or aggressive security. Was IBM a volatile security in the time period under study?

(b) Is the intercept coefficient significantly different from zero? If it is, what is its practical meaning?

5.6. Equation (5.3.5) can also be written as

$$\Pr\left[\hat{\beta}_2 - t_{\alpha/2}\text{se}(\hat{\beta}_2) < \beta_2 < \hat{\beta}_2 + t_{\alpha/2}\text{se}(\hat{\beta}_2)\right] = 1 - \alpha$$

That is, the weak inequality ($\leq$) can be replaced by the strong inequality ($<$). Why?

5.7. R. A. Fisher has derived the sampling distribution of the correlation coefficient defined in (3.5.13). If it is assumed that the variables X and Y are jointly normally distributed, that is, if they come from a bivariate normal distribution (see Appendix 4A, exercise 4.1), then under the assumption that the population correlation coefficient ρ is zero, it can be shown that $t = r\sqrt{n-2}/\sqrt{1-r^2}$ follows Student's t distribution with $n-2$ df.[**] Show that this t value is identical with the

---

[*]See Haim Levy and Marshall Sarnat, *Portfolio and Investment Selection: Theory and Practice*, Prentice-Hall International, Englewood Cliffs, N.J., 1984, Chap. 12.

[†]H. Russell Fogler and Sundaram Ganapathy, *Financial Econometrics*, Prentice-Hall, Englewood Cliffs, N.J., 1982, p. 13.

[**]If ρ is in fact zero, Fisher has shown that r follows the same t distribution provided either X or Y is normally distributed. But if ρ is not equal to zero, both variables must be normally distributed. See R. L. Anderson and T. A. Bancroft, *Statistical Theory in Research*, McGraw-Hill, New York, 1952, pp. 87–88.

t value given in (5.3.2) under the null hypothesis that $\beta_2 = 0$. Hence establish that under the same null hypothesis $F = t^2$. (See Section 5.9.)

Problems

5.8. Refer to the demand function for coffee estimated in Eq. (3.7.1).

(a) Establish *individual* 95% confidence intervals for β_1, β_2, and σ^2.

(b) Using the confidence-interval approach, test the hypothesis that the price of coffee has no effect whatsoever on the consumption of coffee.

(c) Repeat (b), using the test-of-significance approach. Which test do you use and why? Use $\alpha = 5\%$.

(d) What is the p value of the test statistic that you obtained in (c)? If this p value is smaller than α, what conclusion do you draw?

(e) Set up the ANOVA table for this problem and test the hypothesis that $\beta_2 = 0$. Is there a conflict between the answer you obtain here and that in (b)?

(f) Instead of testing the null hypothesis that $\beta_2 = 0$, could you have tested the hypothesis that the *true* coefficient of determination is zero? What is the relationship between these two hypotheses?

(g) Suppose you reject the null hypothesis that $\beta_2 = 0$. Could you also reject the null hypothesis that $\beta_2 = 1$? Which test do you use to test the latter hypothesis?

(h) Can you test the hypothesis that $\beta_2 = 1$ using the F test of ANOVA? Why or why not?

5.9. Refer to exercise 3.19.

(a) Estimate the two regressions given there, obtaining the usual output, such as standard errors, etc.

(b) Test the hypothesis that the disturbances in the two regression models are normally distributed.

(c) In the gold price regression, test the hypothesis that $\beta_2 = 1$, that is, there is one-to-one relationship between gold prices and CPI (i.e., gold is a perfect hedge). What is the p value of the estimated test statistic?

(d) Repeat step (c) for the NYSE Index regression. Is investment in the stock market a perfect hedge against inflation? What is the null hypothesis you are testing? What is its p value?

(e) Between gold and stock, which investment would you choose? What is the basis of your decision?

5.10. Refer to Exercise 3.20. Set up the ANOVA table to test the hypothesis that changes in money supply had no effect on consumer prices in Japan for the stated time period.

5.11. Refer to Exercise 3.21.

(a) Is there a relationship between telephone ownership and per capita GDP in Singapore for the period 1960–1981? How do you know?

(b) Suppose the per capita real GDP in 1982 was $5752. What is the estimated mean value of Y, the number of telephones per 1000 population, for that year? Establish a 95% confidence interval for this estimate.

5.12. Refer to Exercise 1.1. For each country shown there, fit the following model:

$$Y_t = \beta_1 + \beta_2 X_t + u_t$$

where Y_t = rate of inflation at time t
$\quad X_t$ = time, taking values of $1, 2, \ldots, 21$
$\quad u_t$ = the stochastic disturbance term

(*a*) What general conclusions can you draw about the behavior of inflation in each country?

(*b*) For each country regression, test the hypothesis that β_2, the trend coefficient, is greater than zero. (Use a 5% level of significance.)

5.13. Continue with the data of Exercise 1.1 and estimate the following regression:

$$Y_{it} = \beta_1 + \beta_2 X_t + u_t$$

where Y_{it} = the rate of inflation in country i, i being the United Kingdom, Japan, Germany, or France

X_t = the inflation rate for the United States.

(*a*) For each of the four regressions, is there any relationship between that country's inflation rate and the U.S. inflation rate?

(*b*) How would you go about testing that relationship formally?

(*c*) Can you use the model to predict the inflation rate in the four countries beyond 1980? Why or why not?

5.14. The following table gives data on GNP and four definitions of the money stock for the United States for 1970–1983.

GNP and four measures of money stock

Year	GNP, $ billion	M₁	M₂	M₃	L
		\multicolumn{4}{c}{Money stock measure, $ billion}			
1970	992.70	216.6	628.2	677.5	816.3
1971	1,077.6	230.8	712.8	776.2	903.1
1972	1,185.9	252.0	805.2	886.0	1,023.0
1973	1,326.4	265.9	861.0	985.0	1,141.7
1974	1,434.2	277.6	908.5	1,070.5	1,249.3
1975	1,549.2	291.2	1,023.3	1,174.2	1,367.9
1976	1,718.0	310.4	1,163.6	1,311.9	1,516.6
1977	1,918.3	335.4	1,286.7	1,472.9	1,704.7
1978	2,163.9	363.1	1,389.1	1,647.1	1,910.6
1979	2,417.8	389.1	1,498.5	1,804.8	2,117.1
1980	2,631.7	414.9	1,632.6	1,990.0	2,326.2
1981	2,957.8	441.9	1,796.6	2,238.2	2,599.8
1982	3,069.3	480.5	1,965.4	2,462.5	2,870.8
1983	3,304.8	525.4	2,196.3	2,710.4	3,183.1

Definitions:

M_1 = currency + demand deposits + travelers checks and other checkable deposits (OCDs)

$M_2 = M_1$ + overnight RPs and Eurodollars + MMMF (money market mutual fund) balances + MMDAs (money market deposit accounts) + savings and small deposits

$M_3 = M_2$ + large time deposits + term RPs + Institutional MMMF

$L = M_3$ + other liquid assets

Source: Economic Report of the President, 1985, GNP data from Table B-1, p. 232; Money Stock data from Table B-61, p. 303.

Regressing GNP on the various definitions of money, we obtain the results shown in the following table:

GNP-money stock regressions, 1970–1983

1) $\text{GNP}_t = -787.4723 + 8.0863\, M_{1t} \qquad r^2 = 0.9912$
$\phantom{1) \text{GNP}_t = } (77.9664)\quad (0.2197)$

2) $\text{GNP}_t = -44.0626 + 1.5875\, M_{2t} \qquad r^2 = 0.9905$
$\phantom{2) \text{GNP}_t = } (61.0134)\quad (0.0448)$

3) $\text{GNP}_t = 159.1366 + 1.2034\, M_{3t} \qquad r^2 = 0.9943$
$\phantom{3) \text{GNP}_t = } (42.9882)\quad (0.0262)$

4) $\text{GNP}_t = 164.2071 + 1.0290\, L_t \qquad r^2 = 0.9938$
$\phantom{4) \text{GNP}_t = } (44.7658)\quad (0.0234)$

Note: The figures in parentheses are the estimated standard errors.

The monetarists or quantity theorists maintain that nominal income (i.e., nominal GNP) is largely determined by changes in the quantity or the stock of money, although there is no consensus as to the "right" definition of money. Given the results in the preceding table, consider these questions:

(*a*) Which definition of money seems to be closely related to nominal GNP?

(*b*) Since the r^2 terms are uniformly high, does this fact mean that our choice for definition of money does not matter?

(*c*) If the Fed wants to control the money supply, which one of these money measures is a better target for that purpose? Can you tell from the regression results?

5.15. Suppose the equation of an **indifference curve** between two goods is

$$X_i Y_i = \beta_1 + \beta_2 X_i$$

How would you estimate the parameters of this model? Apply the preceding model to the following data and comment on your results:

Consumption of good X:	1	2	3	4	5
Consumption of good Y:	4	3.5	2.8	1.9	0.8

5.16. The capital market line (CML) of portfolio theory* postulates a linear relationship between expected return and risk (measured by the standard deviation) for efficient portfolios as follows:

$$E_i = \beta_1 + \beta_2 \sigma_i$$

where E_i = expected return on portfolio i and σ_i = standard deviation of return. You are given the following data on expected return and standard deviation of return of the portfolios of 34 mutual funds in the United States for the period 1954–1963. Check whether the data support the theory.

---

*See William F. Sharpe, *Portfolio Theory and Capital Markets*, McGraw-Hill, New York, 1970, p. 83.

Performance of 34 mutual funds, 1954–1963

	Average annual return, %	Standard deviation of annual return, %
Affiliated Fund	14.6	15.3
American Business Shares	10.0	9.2
Axe-Houghton, Fund A	10.5	13.5
Axe-Houghton, Fund B	12.0	16.3
Axe-Houghton, Stock Fund	11.9	15.6
Bosten Fund	12.4	12.1
Board Street Investing	14.8	16.8
Bullock Fund	15.7	19.3
Commonwealth Investment Company	10.9	13.7
Delaware Fund	14.4	21.4
Dividend Shares	14.4	15.9
Eaton and Howard Balanced Fund	11.0	11.9
Eaton and Howard Stock Fund	15.2	19.2
Equity Fund	14.6	18.7
Fidelity Fund	16.4	23.5
Financial Industrial Fund	14.5	23.0
Fundamental Investors	16.0	21.7
Group Securities. Common Stock Fund	15.1	19.1
Group Securities. Fully Administered Fund	11.4	14.1
Incorporated Investors	14.0	25.5
Investment Company of America	17.4	21.8
Investors Mutual	11.3	12.5
Loomis-Sales Mutual Fund	10.0	10.4
Massachusetts Investors Trust	16.2	20.8
Massachusetts Investors—Growth Stock	18.6	22.7
National Investors Corporation	18.3	19.9
National Securities—Income Series	12.4	17.8
New England Fund	10.4	10.2
Putnam Fund of Boston	13.1	16.0
Scudder, Stevens & Clark Balanced Fund	10.7	13.3
Selected American Shares	14.4	19.4
United Funds—Income Fund	16.1	20.9
Wellington Fund	11.3	12.0
Wisconsin Fund	13.8	16.9

Source: William F. Sharpe, "Mutual Fund Performance," *Journal of Business*, January 1966 suppl., p. 125.

5.17. Refer to exercise 3.22. Using the data given there, estimate the model suggested there for current dollar GDP for the period 1972 to 1986. Using the estimated model, obtain the forecast values of current dollar GDP for 1987, 1988, 1989, 1990, and 1991 and compare them with the actual values.

5.18. Since 1986 the *Economist* has been publishing the Big Mac Index as a crude, and hilarious, measure of whether international currencies are at their "correct" exchange rate, as judged by the theory of **purchasing power parity (PPP)**. The PPP holds that a unit of currency should be able to buy the same bundle of goods in all countries. The proponents of PPP argue that, in the long run, currencies tend to move toward their PPP. The *Economist* uses McDonald's Big Mac as a representative bundle and gives the following information.

The hamburger standard

	Big Mac prices		Actual $ exchange rate 4/5/94	Implied PPP† of the dollar	Local currency under (−)/over (+) valuation**, %
	In local currency*	In dollars			
UNITED STATES‡	$2.30	2.30	—	—	—
Argentina	Peso3.60	3.60	1.00	1.57	+57
Australia	A$2.45	1.72	1.42	1.07	−25
Austria	Sch34.00	2.84	12.0	14.8	+23
Belgium	BFr109	3.10	35.2	47.39	−35
Brazil	Cr1,500	1.58	949	652	−31
Britain	£1.81	2.65	1.46‡‡	1.27‡‡	+15
Canada	C$2.86	2.06	1.39	1.24	−10
Chile	Peso948	2.28	414	412	−1
China	Yuan9.00	1.03	8.70	3.91	−55
Czech Rep	CKr50	1.71	29.7	21.7	−27
Denmark	DKr25.75	3.85	6.69	11.2	+67
France	FFr18.5	3.17	5.83	8.04	+38
Germany	DM4.60	2.69	1.71	2.00	+17
Greece	Dr620	2.47	251	270	+8
Holland	Fl5.45	2.85	1.91	2.37	+24
Hong Kong	HK$9.20	1.19	7.73	4.00	−48
Hungary	Forint169	1.66	103	73.48	−29
Italy	Lire4,550	2.77	1,641	1,978	+21
Japan	¥391	3.77	104	170	+64
Malaysia	M$3.77	1.40	2.69	1.64	−39
Mexico	Peso8.10	2.41	3.36	3.52	+5
Poland	Zloty31,000	1.40	22,433	13,478	−40
Portugal	Esc440	2.53	174	191	+10
Russia	Rouble2,900	1.66	1,775	1,261	−29
Singapore	$2.98	1.90	1.57	1.30	−17
S Korea	Won2,300	2.84	810	1,000	+24
Spain	Ptas345	2.50	138	150	+9
Sweden	Skr25.5	3.20	7.97	11.1	+39
Switzerland	SFr5.70	3.96	1.44	2.48	+72
Taiwan	NT$62	2.35	26.4	26.96	+2
Thailand	Baht48	1.90	25.3	20.87	−17

*Prices vary locally.
†Purchasing-power parity: local price divided by price in United States.
**Against dollar.
‡Average of New York, Chicago, San Francisco, and Atlanta.
‡‡Dollars per pound.
Source: McDonald's and *The Economist*, April 9, 1994, p. 88.

Consider the following regression model:

$$Y_i = \beta_1 + \beta_2 X_i + u_i$$

where Y = actual exchange rate and X = implied PPP of the dollar.
(a) If the PPP holds, what values of β_1 and β_2 would you expect a priori?
(b) Do the regression results support your expectation? What formal test do you use to test your hypothesis?
(c) Should the *Economist* continue to publish the Big Mac Index? Why or why not?

5.19. Refer to the S.A.T. data given in exercise 2.16. Suppose you want to predict the male math (Y) scores on the basis of the female math scores (X) by running the following regression:

$$Y_t = \beta_1 + \beta_2 X_t + u_t$$

(a) Estimate the preceding model.
(b) From the estimated residuals, find out if the normality assumption can be sustained.
(c) Now test the hypothesis that $\beta_2 = 1$, that is, there is a one-to-one correspondence between male and female math scores.
(d) Set up the ANOVA table for this problem.

5.20. Repeat the exercise in the preceding problem but let Y and X denote the male and female verbal scores, respectively.

APPENDIX 5A

5A.1   DERIVATION OF EQUATION (5.3.2)

Let

$$Z_1 = \frac{\hat{\beta}_2 - \beta_2}{\text{se}(\hat{\beta}_2)} = \frac{(\hat{\beta}_2 - \beta_2)\sqrt{x_i^2}}{\sigma} \tag{1}$$

and

$$Z_2 = (n - 2)\frac{\hat{\sigma}^2}{\sigma^2} \tag{2}$$

Provided σ is known, Z_1 follows the standardized normal distribution; that is, $Z_1 \sim N(0, 1)$. (Why?) Z_2, follows the χ^2 distribution with $(n - 2)$ df. (For proof, see footnote 5.) Furthermore, it can be shown that Z_2 is distributed independently of Z_1.* Therefore, by virtue of Theorem 4.5, the variable

$$t = \frac{Z_1 \sqrt{n - 2}}{\sqrt{Z_2}} \tag{3}$$

follows the t distribution with $n - 2$ df. Substitution of (1) and (2) into (3) gives equation (5.3.2).

5A.2   DERIVATION OF EQUATION (5.9.1)

Equation (1) shows that $Z_1 \sim N(0, 1)$. Therefore, by Theorem 4.3, the preceding quantity

$$Z_1^2 = \frac{(\hat{\beta}_2 - \beta_2)^2 \sum x_i^2}{\sigma^2}$$

---

*For proof, see J. Johnston, *Econometric Methods*, McGraw-Hill, 3d. ed., New York, 1984, pp. 181–182. (Knowledge of matrix algebra is required to follow the proof.)

follows the χ^2 distribution with 1 df. As noted in Section 5A.1,

$$Z_2 = (n-2)\frac{\hat{\sigma}^2}{\sigma^2} = \frac{\sum \hat{u}_i^2}{\sigma^2}$$

also follows the χ^2 distribution with $n-2$ df. Moreover, as noted in Section 4.3., Z_2 is distributed independently of Z_1. Then applying Theorem 4.6, it follows that

$$F = \frac{Z_1^2/1}{Z_2/(n-2)} = \frac{(\hat{\beta}_2 - \beta_2)^2 (\sum x_i^2)}{\sum \hat{u}_i^2/(n-2)}$$

follows the F distribution with 1 and $n-2$ df, respectively. Under the null hypothesis $H_0: \beta_2 = 0$, the preceding F ratio reduces to Eq. (5.9.1).

5.A.3 DERIVATIONS OF EQUATIONS (5.10.2) AND (5.10.6)

Variance of Mean Prediction

Given $X_i = X_0$, the true mean prediction $E(Y_0 \mid X_0)$ is given by

$$E(Y_0 \mid X_0) = \beta_1 + \beta_2 X_0 \tag{1}$$

We estimate (1) from

$$\hat{Y}_0 = \hat{\beta}_1 + \hat{\beta}_2 X_0 \tag{2}$$

Taking the expectation of (2), given X_0, we get

$$E(\hat{Y}_0) = E(\hat{\beta}_1) + E(\hat{\beta}_2)X_0$$
$$= \beta_1 + \beta_2 X_0$$

because $\hat{\beta}_1$ and $\hat{\beta}_2$ are unbiased estimators. Therefore,

$$E(\hat{Y}_0) = E(Y_0 \mid X_0) = \beta_1 + \beta_2 X_0 \tag{3}$$

That is, $\hat{Y}_0$ is an unbiased predictor of $E(Y_0 \mid X_0)$.

Now using the property that var $(a + b) = \text{var}(a) + \text{var}(b) + 2\,\text{cov}(a, b)$, we obtain

$$\text{var}\,(\hat{Y}_0) = \text{var}(\hat{\beta}_1) + \text{var}(\hat{\beta}_2)X_0^2 + 2\,\text{cov}(\hat{\beta}_1\hat{\beta}_2)X_0 \tag{4}$$

Using the formulas for variances and covariance of $\hat{\beta}_1$ and $\hat{\beta}_2$ given in (3.3.1), (3.3.3), and (3.3.9) and manipulating terms, we obtain

$$\text{var}(\hat{Y}_0) = \sigma^2 \left[\frac{1}{n} + \frac{(X_0 - \bar{X})^2}{\sum x_i^2} \right] \qquad = (5.10.2)$$

Variance of Individual Prediction

We want to predict an individual Y corresponding to $X = X_0$, that is, we want to obtain

$$Y_0 = \beta_1 + \beta_2 X_0 + u_0 \tag{5}$$

We predict this as

$$\hat{Y}_0 = \hat{\beta}_1 + \hat{\beta}_2 X_0 \tag{6}$$

The prediction error, $Y_0 - \hat{Y}_0$, is

$$Y_0 - \hat{Y}_0 = \beta_1 + \beta_2 X_0 + u_0 - (\hat{\beta}_1 + \hat{\beta}_2 X_0)$$
$$= (\beta_1 - \hat{\beta}_1) + (\beta_2 - \hat{\beta}_2)X_0 + u_0 \tag{7}$$

Therefore,

$$E(Y_0 - \hat{Y}_0) = E(\beta_1 - \hat{\beta}_1) + E(\beta_2 - \hat{\beta}_2)X_0 - E(u_0)$$
$$= 0$$

because $\hat{\beta}_1$, $\hat{\beta}_2$ are unbiased, X_0 is a fixed number, and $E(u_o)$ is zero by assumption.

Squaring (7) on both sides and taking expectations, we get $\text{var}(Y_0 - \hat{Y}_0) = \text{var}(\hat{\beta}_1) + X_0^2 \text{var}(\hat{\beta}_2) + 2X_0 \text{cov}(\beta_1, \beta_2) + \text{var}(u_0)$. Using the variance and covariance formulas for $\hat{\beta}_1$ and $\hat{\beta}_2$ given earlier, and noting that $\text{var}(u_0) = \sigma^2$, we obtain

$$\text{var}(Y_0 - \hat{Y}_0) = \sigma^2 \left[1 + \frac{1}{n} + \frac{(X_0 - \bar{X})^2}{\sum x_i^2} \right] \qquad = (5.10.6)$$

EXTENSIONS OF THE TWO-VARIABLE LINEAR REGRESSION MODEL

Some aspects of linear regression analysis can be easily introduced within the framework of the two-variable linear regression model that we have been discussing so far. First we consider the case of **regression through the origin**, that is, a situation where the intercept term, β_1, is absent from the model. Then we consider the question of the **units of measurement**, that is, how the Y and X variables are measured and whether a change in the units of measurement affects the regression results. Finally, we consider the question of the **functional form** of the linear regression model. So far we have considered models that are linear in the parameters as well as in the variables. But recall that the regression theory developed in the previous chapters only requires that the parameters be linear; the variables may or may not enter linearly in the model. By considering models that are linear in the parameters but not necessarily in the variables, we show in this chapter how the two-variable models can deal with some interesting practical problems.

Once the ideas introduced in this chapter are grasped, their extension to multiple regression models is quite straightforward, as we shall show in Chapters 7 and 8.

6.1 REGRESSION THROUGH THE ORIGIN

There are occasions when the two-variable PRF assumes the following form:

$$Y_i = \beta_2 X_i + u_i \tag{6.1.1}$$

155

In this model the intercept term is absent or zero, hence the name **regression through the origin**.

As an illustration, consider the Capital Asset Pricing Model (CAPM) of modern portfolio theory, which, in its risk-premium form, may be expressed as[1]

$$(ER_i - r_f) = \beta_i(ER_m - r_f) \tag{6.1.2}$$

where ER_i = expected rate of return on security i

ER_m = expected rate of return on the market portfolio as represented by, say, the S&P 500 composite stock index

r_f = risk-free rate of return, say, the return on 90-day Treasury bills

β_i = the Beta coefficient, a measure of systematic risk, i.e., risk that cannot be eliminated through diversification. Also, a measure of the extent to which the ith security's rate of return moves with the market. A $\beta_i > 1$ implies a volatile or aggressive security, whereas a $\beta_i < 1$ a defensive security. (*Note:* Do not confuse this β_i with the slope coefficient of the two-variable regression, β_2.)

If capital markets work efficiently, then CAPM postulates that security i's expected risk premium ($= ER_i - r_f$) is equal to that security's β coefficient times the expected market risk premium ($= ER_m - r_f$). If the CAPM holds, we have the situation depicted in Fig. 6.1. The line shown in the figure is known as the **security market line** (SML).

For empirical purposes, (6.1.2) is often expressed as

$$R_i - r_f = \beta_i(R_m - r_f) + u_i \tag{6.1.3}$$

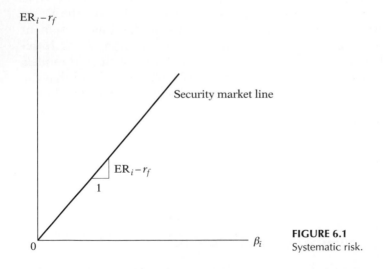

FIGURE 6.1
Systematic risk.

[1]See Haim Levy and Marshall Sarnat, *Portfolio and Investment Selection: Theory and Practice*, Prentice-Hall International, Englewood Cliffs, N.J., 1984, Chap. 14.

or

$$R_i - r_f = \alpha_i + \beta_i(R_m - r_f) + u_i \qquad (6.1.4)$$

The latter model is known as the **Market Model**.[2] If CAPM holds, α_i is expected to be zero. (See Fig. 6.2.)

In passing, note that in (6.1.4) the dependent variable, Y, is $(R_i - r_f)$ and the explanatory variable, X, is β_i, the volatility coefficient, and *not* $(R_m - r_f)$. Therefore, to run regression (6.1.4), one must first estimate β_i, which is usually derived from the **characteristic line**, as described in exercise 5.5. (For further details, see exercise 8.34.)

As this example shows, sometimes the underlying theory dictates that the intercept term be absent from the model. Other instances where the zero-intercept model may be appropriate are Milton Friedman's permanent income hypothesis, which states that permanent consumption is proportional to permanent income; cost analysis theory, where it is postulated that the variable cost of production is proportional to output; and some versions of monetarist theory that state that the rate of change of prices (i.e., the rate of inflation) is proportional to the rate of change of the money supply.

How do we estimate models like (6.1.1), and what special problems do they pose? To answer these questions, let us first write the SRF of (6.1.1), namely,

$$Y_i = \hat{\beta}_2 X_i + \hat{u}_i \qquad (6.1.5)$$

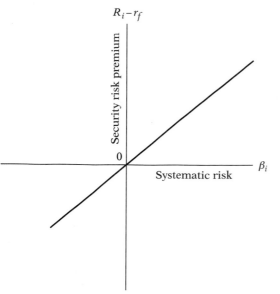

FIGURE 6.2
The Market Model of Portfolio Theory
(assuming $\alpha_i = 0$).

[2]See, for instance, Diana R. Harrington, *Modern Portfolio Theory and the Capital Asset Pricing Model: A User's Guide*, Prentice-Hall, Englewood Cliffs, N.J., 1983, p. 71.

Now applying the OLS method to (6.1.1), we obtain the following formulas for $\hat{\beta}_2$ and its variance (proofs are given in Appendix 6A, Section 6A.1):

$$\hat{\beta}_2 = \frac{\sum X_i Y_i}{\sum X_i^2} \tag{6.1.6}$$

$$\text{var}(\hat{\beta}_2) = \frac{\sigma^2}{\sum X_i^2} \tag{6.1.7}$$

where σ^2 is estimated by

$$\hat{\sigma}^2 = \frac{\sum \hat{u}_i^2}{n-1} \tag{6.1.8}$$

It is interesting to compare these formulas with those obtained when the intercept term is included in the model:

$$\hat{\beta}_2 = \frac{\sum x_i y_i}{\sum x_i^2} \tag{3.1.6}$$

$$\text{var}(\hat{\beta}_2) = \frac{\sigma^2}{\sum x_i^2} \tag{3.3.1}$$

$$\hat{\sigma}^2 = \frac{\sum \hat{u}_i^2}{n-2} \tag{3.3.5}$$

The differences between the two sets of formulas should be obvious: In the model with the intercept term absent, we use **raw** sums of squares and cross products but in the intercept-present model, we use adjusted (from mean) sums of squares and cross products. Second, the df for computing $\hat{\sigma}^2$ is $(n-1)$ in the first case and $(n-2)$ in the second case. (Why?)

Although the interceptless or zero intercept model may be appropriate on occasions, there are some features of this model that need to be noted. First, $\sum \hat{u}_i$, which is always zero for the model with the intercept term (the conventional model), need not be zero when that term is absent. In short, $\sum \hat{u}_i$ need not be zero for the regression through the origin. Second, r^2, the coefficient of determination introduced in Chapter 3, which is always nonnegative for the conventional model, can on occasions turn out to be *negative* for the interceptless model! This anomalous result arises because the r^2 introduced in Chapter 3 explicitly assumes that the intercept is included in the model. Therefore, the conventionally computed r^2 may not be appropriate for regression-through-the-origin models.[3]

---

[3]For additional discussion, see Dennis J. Aigner, *Basic Econometrics*, Prentice-Hall, Englewood Cliffs, N.J., 1971, pp. 85–88.

r^2 for Regression-through-Origin Model

As just noted, and as further discussed in Appendix 6A, Section 6A.1, the conventional r^2 given in Chapter 3 is not appropriate for regressions that do not contain the intercept. But one can compute what is known as the **raw r^2** for such models, which is defined as

$$\text{raw } r^2 = \frac{\sum (X_i Y_i)^2}{\sum X_i^2 \sum Y_i^2} \tag{6.1.9}$$

Note: These are raw (i.e., not mean-corrected) sums of squares and cross products.

Although this raw r^2 satisfies the relation $0 < r^2 < 1$, it is not directly comparable to the conventional r^2 value. For this reason some authors do not report the r^2 value for zero intercept regression models.

Because of these special features of this model, one needs to exercise great caution in using the zero intercept regression model. *Unless there is very strong a priori expectation*, one would be well advised to stick to the conventional, intercept-present model. This has a dual advantage. First, if the intercept term is included in the model but it turns out to be statistically insignificant (i.e., statistically equal to zero), for all practical purposes we have a regression through the origin.[4] Second, and more important, if in fact there is an intercept in the model but we insist on fitting a regression through the origin, we would be committing a **specification error**, thus violating Assumption 9 of the classical linear regression model.

An Illustrative Example: The Characteristic Line of Portfolio Theory

Table 6.1 gives data on the annual rates of return (%) on Afuture Fund, a mutual fund whose primary investment objective is maximum capital gain, and on the market portfolio, as measured by the Fisher Index, for the period 1971–1980.

In exercise 5.5 we introduced the *characteristic line* of investment analysis, which can be written as

$$Y_i = \alpha_i + \beta_i X_i + u_i \tag{6.1.10}$$

where Y_i = annual rate of return (%) on Afuture Fund
$\quad X_i$ = annual rate of return (%) on the market portfolio
$\quad \beta_i$ = slope coefficient, also known as the **Beta** coefficient in portfolio theory, and
$\quad \alpha_i$ = the intercept

In the literature there is no consensus about the prior value of α_i. Some empirical results have shown it to be positive and statistically significant and some

---

[4]Henri Theil points out that if the intercept is in fact absent, the slope coefficient may be estimated with far greater precision than with the intercept term left in. See his *Introduction to Econometrics*, Prentice-Hall, Englewood Cliffs, N.J., 1978, p. 76. See also the numerical example given next.

TABLE 6.1
Annual rates of return on Afuture Fund and on the Fisher Index (market portfolio), 1971–1980

Year	Return on Afuture Fund, % Y	Return on Fisher Index, % X
1971	67.5	19.5
1972	19.2	8.5
1973	−35.2	−29.3
1974	−42.0	−26.5
1975	63.7	61.9
1976	19.3	45.5
1977	3.6	9.5
1978	20.0	14.0
1979	40.3	35.3
1980	37.5	31.0

Source: Haim Levy and Marshall Sarnat, *Portfolio and Investment Selection: Theory and Practice*, Prentice-Hall International, Englewood Cliffs, N.J., 1984, pp. 730 and 738. These data were obtained by the authors from Weisenberg Investment Service, *Investment Companies*, 1981 edition.

have shown it to be not statistically significantly different from zero; in the latter case we could write the model as

$$Y_i = \beta_i X_i + u_i \qquad (6.1.11)$$

that is, a regression through the origin.

If we decide to use model (6.1.11), we obtain the following regression results (see the SAS printout in Appendix 6A, Section 6A.2):

$$\hat{Y}_i = 1.0899 X_i$$
$$(0.1916) \qquad \text{raw } r^2 = 0.7825 \qquad (6.1.12)$$
$$t = (5.6884)$$

which shows that β_i is significantly greater than zero. The interpretation is that a 1 percent increase in the market rate of return leads on the average to about 1.09 percent increase in the rate of return on Afuture Fund.

How can we be sure that model (6.1.11), not (6.1.10), is appropriate, especially in view of the fact that there is no strong a priori belief in the hypothesis that α_i is in fact zero? This can be checked by running the regression (6.1.10). Using the data given in Table 6.1, we obtained the following results:

$$\hat{Y}_i = 1.2797 + 1.0691 X_i$$
$$(7.6886) \quad (0.2383) \qquad (6.1.13)$$
$$t = (0.1664) \quad (4.4860) \qquad r^2 = 0.7155$$

Note: The r^2 values of (6.1.12) and (6.1.13) are *not* directly comparable. From these results one cannot reject the hypothesis that the true intercept is equal to zero, thereby justifying the use of (6.1.1), that is, regression through the origin.

In passing, note that there is not a great deal of difference in the results of (6.1.12) and (6.1.13), although the estimated standard error of $\hat{\beta}$ is slightly lower for the regression-through-the-origin model, thus supporting Theil's argument given in footnote 4 that if α_i is in fact zero, the slope coefficient may be measured with greater precision: using the data given in Table 6.1 and the regression results, the reader can easily verify that the 95% confidence interval for the slope coefficient of the regression-through-the-origin model is (0.6566, 1.5232) whereas for the model (6.1.13) it is (0.5195, 1.6186); that is, the former confidence interval is narrower that the latter.

6.2 SCALING AND UNITS OF MEASUREMENT

To grasp the ideas developed in this section, consider the data given in Table 6.2. The data in this table refer to U.S. gross private domestic investment (GPDI) and Gross National Product (GNP) in 1972 dollars for the period 1974–1983. Column (1) gives data on GPDI in billions of dollars whereas column (2) gives it in millions of dollars. Columns (3) and (4) give, respectively, data on GNP in billions and millions of dollars.

Suppose in the regression of GPDI on GNP one researcher uses data measured in billions of dollars but another uses data on these variables measured in millions of dollars. Will the regression results be the same in both cases? If not, which results should one use? In short, do the units in which the Y and X variables are measured make any difference in regression results? If so, what is the sensible course to follow in choosing units of measurement for regression analysis?

To answer these questions, let us proceed systematically. Let

$$Y_i = \hat{\beta}_1 + \hat{\beta}_2 X_i + \hat{u}_i \tag{6.2.1}$$

TABLE 6.2
Gross private domestic investment (GPDI) and Gross National Product (GNP) in 1972 dollars, United States, 1974–1983

Year	GPDI (billions of 1972 dollars) (1)	GPDI (millions of 1972 dollars) (2)	GNP (billions of 1972 dollars) (3)	GNP (millions of 1972 dollars) (4)
1974	195.5	195,500	1246.3	1,246,300
1975	154.8	154,800	1231.6	1,231,600
1976	184.5	184,500	1298.2	1,298,200
1977	214.2	214,200	1369.7	1,369,700
1978	236.7	236,700	1438.6	1,438,600
1979	236.3	236,300	1479.4	1,479,400
1980	208.5	208,500	1475.0	1,475,000
1981	230.9	230,900	1512.2	1,512,200
1982	194.3	194,300	1480.0	1,480,000
1983	221.0	221,000	1534.7	1,534,700

Source: Economic Report of the President, 1985, p. 234 (for data expressed in billions of dollars).

where Y = GPDI and X = GNP. Define

$$Y_i^* = w_1 Y_i \tag{6.2.2}$$

$$X_i^* = w_2 X_i \tag{6.2.3}$$

where w_1 and w_2 are constants, called the **scale factors**; w_1 may equal w_2 or be different.

From (6.2.2) and (6.2.3) it is clear that Y_i^* and X_i^* are *rescaled* Y_i and X_i. Thus, if Y_i and X_i are measured in billions of dollars and one wants to express them in millions of dollars, we will have $Y_i^* = 1000\, Y_i$ and $X_i^* = 1000\, X_i$; here $w_1 = w_2 = 1000$.

Now consider the regression using Y_i^* and X_i^* variables:

$$Y_i^* = \hat{\beta}_1^* + \hat{\beta}_2^* X_i + \hat{u}_i^* \tag{6.2.4}$$

where $Y_i^* = w_1 Y_i$, $X_i^* = w_2 X_i$, and $\hat{u}_i^* = w_1 \hat{u}_i$. (Why?)

We want to find out the relationships between the following pairs:

1. $\hat{\beta}_1$ and $\hat{\beta}_1^*$
2. $\hat{\beta}_2$ and $\hat{\beta}_2^*$
3. $\text{var}(\hat{\beta}_1)$ and $\text{var}(\hat{\beta}_1^*)$
4. $\text{var}(\hat{\beta}_2)$ and $\text{var}(\hat{\beta}_2^*)$
5. $\hat{\sigma}^2$ and $\hat{\sigma}^{*2}$
6. r_{xy}^2 and $r_{x^*y^*}^2$

From least-squares theory we know (see Chapter 3) that

$$\hat{\beta}_1 = \bar{Y} - \hat{\beta}_2 \bar{X} \tag{6.2.5}$$

$$\hat{\beta}_2 = \frac{\sum x_i y_i}{\sum x_i^2} \tag{6.2.6}$$

$$\text{var}(\hat{\beta}_1) = \frac{\sum X_i^2}{n \sum x_i^2} \cdot \sigma^2 \tag{6.2.7}$$

$$\text{var}(\hat{\beta}_2) = \frac{\sigma^2}{\sum x_i^2} \tag{6.2.8}$$

$$\hat{\sigma}^2 = \frac{\sum u_i^2}{n-2} \tag{6.2.9}$$

Applying the OLS method to (6.2.4), we obtain similarly

$$\hat{\beta}_1^* = \bar{Y}^* - \hat{\beta}_2^* \bar{X}^* \tag{6.2.10}$$

$$\hat{\beta}_2^* = \frac{\sum x_i^* y_i^*}{\sum x_i^{*2}} \tag{6.2.11}$$

$$\text{var}(\hat{\beta}_1^*) = \frac{\sum X_i^{*2}}{n \sum x_i^{*2}} \cdot \sigma^{*2} \tag{6.2.12}$$

$$\text{var}(\hat{\beta}_2^*) = \frac{\sigma^{*2}}{\sum x_i^{*2}} \tag{6.2.13}$$

$$\hat{\sigma}^{*2} = \frac{\sum \hat{u}_i^{*2}}{(n - 2)} \tag{6.2.14}$$

From these results it is easy to establish relationships between the two sets of parameter estimates. All that one has to do is recall these definitional relationships: $Y_i^* = w_1 Y_i$ (or $y_i^* = w_1 y_i$); $X_i^* = w_2 X_i$ (or $x_i^* = w_2 x_i$); $\hat{u}_i^* = w_1 \hat{u}_i$; $\bar{Y}^* = w_1 \bar{Y}$ and $\bar{X}^* = w_2 \bar{X}$. Making use of these definitions, the reader can easily verify that

$$\hat{\beta}_2^* = \left(\frac{w_1}{w_2}\right)\hat{\beta}_2 \tag{6.2.15}$$

$$\hat{\beta}_1^* = w_1 \hat{\beta}_1 \tag{6.2.16}$$

$$\hat{\sigma}^{*2} = w_1^2 \hat{\sigma}^2 \tag{6.2.17}$$

$$\text{var}(\hat{\beta}_1^*) = w_1^2 \, \text{var}(\hat{\beta}_1) \tag{6.2.18}$$

$$\text{var}(\hat{\beta}_2^*) = \left(\frac{w_1}{w_2}\right)^2 \text{var}(\hat{\beta}_2) \tag{6.2.19}$$

$$r_{xy}^2 = r_{x^*y^*}^2 \tag{6.2.20}$$

From the preceding results it should be clear that, given the regression results based on one scale of measurement, one can derive the results based on another scale of measurement once the scaling factors, the w's, are known. In practice, though, one should choose the units of measurement sensibly; there is little point in carrying all those zeros in expressing numbers in millions or billions of dollars.

From the results given in (6.2.15) through (6.2.20) one can easily derive some special cases. For instance, if $w_1 = w_2$, that is, the scaling factors are identical, the slope coefficient and its standard error remain unaffected in going from the (Y_i, X_i) to the (Y_i^*, W_i^*) scale, which should be intuitively clear. However, the intercept and its standard error are both multiplied by w_1. But if the X scale is not changed (i.e., $w_2 = 1$) and the Y scale is changed by the factor w_1, the slope as well as the intercept coefficients and their respective standard errors are all multiplied by the same w_1 factor. Finally, if the Y scale remains unchanged (i.e., $w_1 = 1$) but the X scale is changed by the factor w_2, the slope coefficient and its standard error are multiplied by the factor $(1/w_2)$ but the intercept coefficient and its standard error remain unaffected.

It should, however, be noted that the transformation from the (Y, X) to the (Y^*, X^*) scale does not affect the properties of the OLS estimators discussed in the preceding chapters.

A Numerical Example: The Relationship between GPDI and GNP, United States, 1974–1983

To substantiate the preceding theoretical results, let us revert to the example of Table 6.2 and examine the following regression results. (Figures in parentheses are the estimated standard errors.)

Both GPDI and GNP in billions of dollars:

$$\widehat{GPDI}_t = -37.0015205 + 0.17395\ GNP_t$$
$$(76.2611278)\quad (0.05406) \qquad\qquad (6.2.21)$$
$$r^2 = 0.5641$$

Both GPDI and GNP in millions of dollars:

$$\widehat{GPDI}_t = -37001.5205 + 0.17395\ GNP_t$$
$$(76261.1278)\quad (0.05406) \qquad\qquad (6.2.22)$$
$$r^2 = 0.5641$$

Notice that the intercept as well as its standard error is 1000 (i.e., $w_1 = 1000$ in going from billions to millions of dollars) times the corresponding values in the regression (6.2.21), but the slope coefficient as well as its standard error is unchanged, as per the theory.

GPDI in billions of dollars and GNP in millions of dollars:

$$\widehat{GPDI}_t = -37.0015205 + 0.00017395\ GNP_t$$
$$(76.2611278)\quad (0.00005406) \qquad\qquad (6.2.23)$$
$$r^2 = 0.5641$$

As expected, the slope coefficient as well as its standard error is (1/1000) its value in (6.2.21) since only the X or GNP scale is changed.

GPDI in millions of dollars and GNP in billions of dollars:

$$\widehat{GPDI}_t = -37001.5205 + 173.95\ GNP_t$$
$$(76261.1278)\quad (54.06) \qquad\qquad (6.2.24)$$
$$r^2 = 0.5641$$

Again notice that both the intercept and the slope coefficients as well as their respective standard errors are 1000 times their values in (6.2.21), as per our theoretical results.

A Word About Interpretation

Since the slope coefficient, β_2, is simply the rate of change, it is measured in units of the ratio[5]

$$\frac{\text{Units of the dependent variable, } Y}{\text{Units of the explanatory variable, } X}$$

Thus in regression (6.2.21) the interpretation of the slope coefficient 0.17395 is that if GNP changes by a unit, which is a billion dollars, GPDI on the average changes by 0.17395 billions of dollars. In regression (6.2.23) a unit change in GNP, which is one million dollars, leads on the average to a 0.00017395 billions of dollars change in the GPDI. The two results are of course identical in

---

[5]For further discussion and extension to multiple regression, see Donald F. Morrison, *Applied Linear Statistical Methods*, Prentice-Hall, Englewood Cliffs, N.J., 1983, p. 72.

their effects of GNP on GPDI; they are simply expressed in different units of measurement.

6.3 FUNCTIONAL FORMS OF REGRESSION MODELS

As noted in Chapter 2, this text is concerned primarily with models that are linear in the parameters; they may or may not be linear in the variables. In the sections that follow we consider some commonly used regression models that may be nonlinear in the variables but are linear in the parameters or that can be made so by suitable transformations of the variables. In particular, we discuss the following regression models:

1. The log-linear model
2. Semilog models
3. Reciprocal models

We discuss the special features of each model, where they are appropriate, and how they are estimated. Each model is illustrated with suitable examples.

6.4 HOW TO MEASURE ELASTICITY: THE LOG-LINEAR MODEL

Consider the following model, known as the **exponential regression model**:

$$Y_i = \beta_1 X_i^{\beta_2} e^{u_i} \tag{6.4.1}$$

which may be expressed alternatively as[6]

$$\ln Y_i = \ln \beta_1 + \beta_2 \ln X_i + u_i \tag{6.4.2}$$

where $\ln$ = natural log (i.e., log to the base e, and where e = 2.718).[7]
    If we write (6.4.2) as

$$\ln Y_i = \alpha + \beta_2 \ln X_i + u_i \tag{6.4.3}$$

where $\alpha = \ln \beta_1$, this model is linear in the parameters α and β_2, linear in the logarithms of the variables Y and X, and can be estimated by OLS regression. Because of this linearity, such models are called **log-log**, **double-log**, or **log-linear** models.

---

[6]Note these properties of the logarithms: (1) $\ln(AB) = \ln A + \ln B$, (2) $\ln(A/B) = \ln A - \ln B$, and (3) $\ln(A^k) = k \ln A$, assuming that A and B are positive, and where k is some constant.

[7]In practice one may use common logarithms, that is, log to the base 10. The relationship between the natural log and common log is: $\ln_e X = 2.3026 \log_{10} X$. By convention, ln means natural logarithm, and log means logarithm to the base 10; hence there is no need to write the subscripts e and 10 explicitly.

If the assumptions of the classical linear regression model are fulfilled, the parameters of (6.4.3) can be estimated by the OLS method by letting

$$Y_i^* = \alpha + \beta_2 X_i^* + u_i \qquad (6.4.4)$$

where $Y_i^* = \ln Y_i$ and $X_i^* = \ln X_i$. The OLS estimators $\hat{\alpha}$ and $\hat{\beta}_2$ obtained will be best linear unbiased estimators of α and β_2, respectively.

One attractive feature of the log-log model, which has made it popular in applied work, is that the slope coefficient β_2 measures the **elasticity** of Y with respect to X, that is, the percentage change in Y for a given (small) percentage change in X.[8] Thus, if Y represents the quantity of a commodity demanded and X its unit price, β_2 measures the price elasticity of demand, a parameter of considerable economic interest. If the relationship between quantity demanded and price is as shown in Fig. 6.3a, the double-log transformation as shown in Fig. 6.3b will then give the estimate of the price elasticity $(-\beta_2)$.

Two special features of the log-linear model may be noted: The model assumes that the elasticity coefficient between Y and X, β_2, remains constant throughout (why?), hence the alternative name **constant elasticity model**.[9] In other words, as Fig. 6.3b shows, the change in $\ln Y$ per unit change in $\ln X$ (i.e., the elasticity, β_2) remains the same no matter at which $\ln X$ we measure the elasticity. Another feature of the model is that although $\hat{\alpha}$ and $\hat{\beta}_2$ are unbiased estimates of α and β_2, β_1 (the parameter entering the original model) when estimated as $\hat{\beta}_1 = $ antilog $(\hat{\alpha})$ is itself a biased estimator. In most practical problems, however, the intercept term is of secondary importance, and one need not worry about obtaining its unbiased estimate.[10]

In the two-variable model, the simplest way to decide whether the log-linear model fits the data is to plot the scattergram of $\ln Y_i$ against $\ln X_i$ and see if the scatter points lie approximately on a straight line, as in Fig. 6.3b.

---

[8]The elasticity coefficient, in calculus notation, is defined as $(dY/Y)/(dX/X) = [(dY/dX)(X/Y)]$. Readers familiar with differential calculus will readily see that β_2 is in fact the elasticity coefficient.

A technical note: The calculus-minded reader will note that $d(\ln X)/dX = 1/X$ or $d(\ln X) = dX/X$, that is, for infinitesimally small changes (note the differential operator d) change in $\ln X$ is equal to the relative or proportional change in X. In practice, though, if the change in X is small, this relationship can be written as: change in $\ln X \doteq$ relative change in X, where $\doteq$ means approximately. Thus, for small changes,

$$(\ln X_t - \ln X_{t-1}) \doteq (X_t - X_{t-1})/X_{t-1} = \text{relative change in } X$$

Incidentally, the reader should note these terms, which will occur frequently: (1) **absolute change**, (2) **relative** or **proportional change**, and (3) **percentage change**, or **percent growth rate**. Thus, $(X_t - X_{t-1})$ represents absolute change, $(X_t - X_{t-1})/X_{t-1} = (X_t/X_{t-1} - 1)$ is relative or proportional change and $[(X_t - X_{t-1})/X_{t-1}]100$ is the percentage change, or the growth rate. X_t and X_{t-1} are, respectively, the current and previous values of the variable X.

[9]A constant elasticity model will give a constant total revenue change for a given percentage change in price regardless of the absolute level of price. Readers should contrast this result with the elasticity conditions implied by a simple linear demand function, $Y_i = \beta_1 + \beta_2 X_i + u_i$. However, a simple linear function gives a constant quantity change per unit change in price. Contrast this with what the log-linear model implies for a given dollar change in price.

[10]Concerning the nature of the bias and what can be done about it, see Arthur S. Goldberger, *Topics in Regression Analysis*, Macmillan, New York, 1978, p. 120.

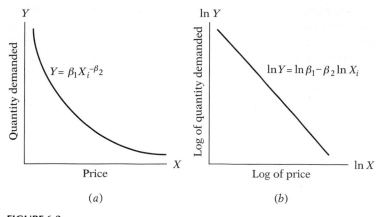

FIGURE 6.3
Constant-elasticity model.

An Illustrative Example: The Coffee Demand Function Revisited

Refer to the coffee demand function of Section 3.7. My research assistant had informed me that when the data were plotted using the $\ln Y$ and $\ln X$ scale, the scattergram seemed to indicate that the log-log model might give just as good a fit as the linear model (3.7.1).[11] Carrying out the calculations, the assistant obtained the following results:

$$\widehat{\ln Y}_t = \quad 0.7774 - 0.2530 \ \ln X_t \qquad r^2 = 0.7448$$
$$(0.0152) \quad (0.0494) \qquad F_{1,9} = 26.27 \qquad (6.4.5)$$
$$t = (51.1447)(-5.1214)$$
$$\textbf{\textit{P} value} = \quad (0.000) \quad (0.0003)$$

where Y_t = coffee consumption, cups per person per day, and X_t = real price of coffee, dollars per pound.

From these results we see that the price elasticity coefficient is -0.25, implying that for a 1 percent increase in the real price of coffee per pound, the demand for coffee (as measured by cups of coffee consumed per day) on the average decreases by about 0.25 percent. Since the price elasticity value of 0.25 is less than 1 in absolute terms, we can say that the demand for coffee is price-inelastic.

An interesting question: Comparing the results of the log-linear demand function vs. the linear demand function of (3.7.1), how do we decide which is a better model? Can we say that (6.4.5) is better than (3.7.1) because its r^2 value is higher (0.7448 vs. 0.6628)? Unfortunately, we cannot say that, for as will be shown in Chapter 7, when the dependent variable of two models is not the same (here, $\ln Y$ vs. Y), the two r^2 values are not directly comparable. We cannot directly compare the two slope coefficients either, for in (3.7.1) the

---

[11]Of course, (3.7.1) was introduced purely for pedagogical purposes.

slope coefficient gives the effect of a unit change in the price of coffee, say $1 per pound, on the constant absolute (i.e., not relative) amount of decrease in coffee consumption, which is 0.4795 cups per day. On the other hand, the coefficient of −0.2530 obtained from (6.4.5) gives the constant percentage decrease in coffee consumption as a result of a 1 percent increase in the price of coffee per pound (i.e., it gives the price elasticity).[12]

How then can we compare the results of the two models? This question is part of the much larger one of **specification analysis**, a topic discussed in Chapter 13. For now, one way we can compare the two models is to compute an approximate measure of the price elasticity for the model (3.7.1). This can be done as follows:

The elasticity E of a variable Y (e.g., quantity demanded) with respect to another variable X (e.g., price) is defined as

$$
\begin{aligned}
E &= \frac{\% \text{ change in } Y}{\% \text{ change in } X} \\[2mm]
&= \frac{(\Delta Y/Y) \cdot 100}{(\Delta X/X) \cdot 100} \\[2mm]
&= \frac{\Delta Y}{\Delta X} \cdot \frac{X}{Y} \\[2mm]
&= (\text{slope})(X/Y)
\end{aligned}
\tag{6.4.6}
$$

where Δ denotes a (small) change. If Δ is sufficiently small, we can replace $\Delta Y/\Delta X$ by the calculus derivative notation, dY/dX (see footnote 8).

Now for the linear model (3.7.1), an estimate of the slope is given by the estimated β_2 coefficient, which for the coffee demand function is −0.4795. As (6.4.6) shows, to obtain elasticity, we have to multiply this slope coefficient by the ratio (X/Y), that is, price over quantity. But which X and Y values do we choose? As Table 3.4 shows, there are 11 pairs of price (X) and quantity demanded (Y) values. If we use all these values, we will have 11 estimates of price elasticity.

In practice, however, elasticity is computed at the mean, or average, values of Y and X. That is, we obtain an estimate of the *average* elasticity. For our example, $\bar{Y} = 2.43$ cups and $\bar{X} = \$1.11$. Using these values and the slope estimate of −0.4795, we obtain from (6.4.6) an average price elasticity coefficient of $(-0.4795)(1.11/2.43) = -0.219$, or about −0.22. This result is in contrast to the elasticity coefficient of about −0.25 obtained from the log-linear model. Notice that the latter elasticity remains the same regardless of the price at which it is measured (why?), whereas the former depends on the particular mean values.

---

[12]There is a difference between the slope coefficient and the elasticity measure. As footnote 8 shows, elasticity is equal to slope $(= dY/dX)$ times the ratio (X/Y). The slope coefficient of model (3.7.1) only gives (dY/dX), whereas the slope coefficient of (6.4.5) gives the elasticity measure, $(dY/dX)(X/Y)$. In short, **for the log-linear model the slope and elasticity coefficients are the same, but not so for the linear model.**

6.5 SEMILOG MODELS: LOG-LIN AND LIN-LOG MODELS

How to Measure the Growth Rate: The Log-Lin Model

Economists, businesspeople, and governments are often interested in finding out the rate of growth of certain economic variables, such as population, GNP, money supply, employment, productivity, trade deficit, etc.

In exercise 3.22 we presented data on U.S. real GDP for the period 1972–1991. Suppose we want to find out the rate of growth of real GDP in this period. Let Y_t = real GDP (RGDP) at time t and Y_O = the initial (i.e., 1972) value of real GDP. Now recall the following well-known compound interest formula from your introductory courses in money, banking, and finance.

$$Y_t = Y_O(1 + r)^t \tag{6.5.1}$$

where r is the compound (i.e., over time) rate of growth of Y. Taking the natural logarithm of (6.5.1), we can write

$$\ln Y_t = \ln Y_O + t \ln(1 + r) \tag{6.5.2}$$

Now letting

$$\beta_1 = \ln Y_O \tag{6.5.3}$$

$$\beta_2 = \ln(1 + r) \tag{6.5.4}$$

we can write (6.5.2) as

$$\ln Y_t = \beta_1 + \beta_2 t \tag{6.5.5}$$

Adding the disturbance term to (6.5.5), we obtain[13]

$$\ln Y_t = \beta_1 + \beta_2 t + u_t \tag{6.5.6}$$

This model is like any other linear regression model in that the parameters β_1 and β_2 are linear. The only difference is that the regressand is the logarithm of Y and the regressor is "time," which will take values of 1, 2, 3, etc.

Models like (6.5.6) are called **semilog models** because only one variable (in this case the regressand) appears in the logarithmic form. For descriptive purposes a model in which the regressand is logarithmic will be called a **log-lin model**. Later we will consider a model in which the regressand is linear but the regressor(s) are logarithmic and call it a **lin-log model**.

Before we present the regression results, let us examine the properties of model (6.5.5). In this model *the slope coefficient measures the constant proportional or relative change in Y for a given absolute change in the value of the regressor* (in this case the variable t), that is,[14]

---

[13]We add the error term because the compound interest formula will not hold exactly. Why we add the error after the logarithmic transformation is explained in Sec. 6.8.

[14]Using differential calculus one can show that $\beta_2 = d(\ln Y)/dX = (1/Y)(dY/dX) = (dY/Y)/dX$, which is nothing but (6.5.7). For small changes in Y and X this relation may be approximated by

$$\frac{(Y_t - Y_{t-1})/Y_{t-1}}{(X_t - X_{t-1})}$$

$$\beta_2 = \frac{\text{Relative change in regressand}}{\text{Absolute change in regressor}} \qquad (6.5.7)$$

If we multiply the relative change in Y by 100, (6.5.7) will then give the percentage change, or the *growth rate*, in Y for an absolute change in X, the regressor.

A log-lin model like (6.5.5) is particularly useful in situations where the X variable is time, as in our GNP example, since in that case the model describes the constant relative ($= \beta_2$) or constant percentage ($100 \cdot \beta_2$) *rate of growth* (if $\beta_2 > 0$) or *rate of decay* ($\beta_2 < 0$) in the variable Y. That is why models like (6.5.5) are called **(constant) growth models**.

Returning to the real GDP example, we may write the regression results based on (6.5.6) as follows:

$$
\begin{aligned}
\widehat{\ln \text{RGDP}_t} &= & 8.0139 &+ 0.02469t \\
\text{se} &= & (0.0114) &(0.00956) \qquad r^2 = 0.9738 \qquad (6.5.8) \\
t &= & (700.54) &(25.8643) \\
p \text{ value} &= & (0.0000)* &(0.0000)*
\end{aligned}
$$

* Denotes a very small value.

The interpretation of this regression is as follows: Over the period 1972–1991, the real GDP in the United States grew at the rate of 2.469 percent per year. Since $8.0139 = \widehat{\ln Y_o}$ (why?), if we take the antilog of 8.0139, we find that $\hat{Y}_o = 3022.7$ (approx.), that is, at the beginning of 1972 the estimated real GDP was about 3023 billions of dollars. The regression line obtained from (6.5.8) is sketched in Fig. 6.4.

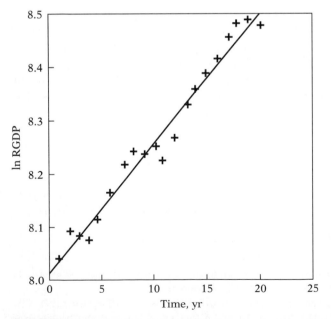

FIGURE 6.4
Growth of real GDP, United States, 1972–1991; semilog model.

Instantaneous versus compound rate of growth. The slope coefficient of 0.02469 obtained in (6.5.8) or, more generally, the coefficient of β_2 of the growth model (6.5.5) gives the **instantaneous** (at a point in time) rate of growth and not the **compound** (over a period of time) rate of growth. But the latter can be easily found from (6.5.4): Simply take the antilog of 0.02469, subtract 1 from it, and multiply the difference by 100. Thus, in the present case antilog(0.02469) − 1 = 0.024997 or about 2.499 percent. That is, over the study period, the *compound rate of growth of real GDP was about 2.499 percent per year*. This growth rate is slightly higher than the instantaneous rate of growth of about 2.469 percent.

The linear trend model. Instead of estimating model (6.5.6), researchers sometimes estimate the following model:

$$Y_t = \beta_1 + \beta_2 t + u_t \tag{6.5.9}$$

That is, instead of regressing the log of Y on time, they regress Y on time. Such a model is called a **linear trend model** and the time variable t is known as the **trend variable**. By *trend* we mean a sustained upward or downward movement in the behavior of a variable. If the slope coefficient in (6.5.9) is positive, there is an *upward trend* in Y, whereas if it is negative, there is a *downward trend* in Y.

For our real GDP data the results based on (6.5.9) are as follows:

$$
\begin{aligned}
\widehat{\text{RGDP}_1} &= 2933.0538 \;+\; 97.6806\,t \\
\text{se} &= \quad (50.5913) \qquad (4.2233) \qquad r^2 = 0.9674 \qquad (6.5.10) \\
t &= \quad (57.9754) \qquad (23.1291) \\
p \text{ value} &= \quad (0.0000)* \qquad (0.0000)*
\end{aligned}
$$

* Denotes very small value.

In contrast to (6.5.8), the interpretation of this regression is as follows. Over the period 1972 to 1991, on average, the real GDP increased at the absolute (*Note:* not relative) rate of about 97.68 billions of dollars. Thus, over that period there was an upward trend in real GDP.

The choice between the growth model (6.5.8) and the linear trend model (6.5.10) will depend upon whether one is interested in the relative or absolute change of real GDP, although for many purposes it is the relative change that is more important. In passing, note that *we cannot compare the r^2 values of models (6.5.8) and (6.5.10) because the regressands in the two models are different*.

A caution on log-lin and linear trend models. Although these models are used quite frequently to estimate relative or absolute change in the dependent variable over time, their routine use for this purpose has been questioned by time series analysts. Their main argument is that such models may be appropriate only if a time series is stationary in the sense defined in Section 1.7. For the advanced reader this topic is discussed in considerable detail in Chapter 21 on Time Series Econometrics (*note:* This is an optional chapter).

The Lin-Log Model

Suppose you have the data given in Table 6.3, where Y is GNP and X is money supply (M_2 definition). Next suppose you are interested in finding out by how much (the absolute value of) GNP increases if the money supply increases by, say, a percent.

Unlike the growth model just discussed, in which we were interested in finding the percent growth in Y for an absolute unit change in X, we are now interested in finding the absolute change in Y for a percent change in X. A model that can accomplish this purpose can be written as

$$Y_i = \beta_1 + \beta_2 \ln X_i + u_i \qquad (6.5.11)$$

For descriptive purposes we call such a model a **lin-log model**.

Let us interpret the slope coefficient β_2.[15] As usual,

$$\beta_2 = \frac{\text{Change in } Y}{\text{Change in } \ln X}$$

$$= \frac{\text{Change in } Y}{\text{Relative change in } X}$$

The second step follows from the fact that *a change in the log of a number is a relative change.*

Symbolically, we have

$$\beta_2 = \frac{\Delta Y}{\Delta X/X} \qquad (6.5.12)$$

where, as usual, Δ denotes a small change. Equation (6.5.12) can be written, equivalently, as

$$\Delta Y = \beta_2(\Delta X/X) \qquad (6.5.13)$$

This equation states that the absolute change in Y ($= \Delta Y$) is equal to β_2 times the relative change in X. If the latter is multiplied by 100, then (6.5.13) gives the absolute change in Y for a percentage change in X. Thus, if $\Delta X/X$ changes by 0.01 unit (or 1 percent), the absolute change in Y is $0.01(\beta_2)$. Thus, if in an application one finds that $\beta_2 = 500$, the absolute change in Y is $(0.01)(500)$, or 5.0. Therefore, *when regressions like (6.5.11) are estimated by OLS, multiply the value of the estimated slope coefficient, β_2, by 0.01, or, what amounts to the same thing, divide it by 100.*

Reverting to the data given in Table 6.3, we may write our regression results as follows:

$$\hat{Y}_t = -16329.0 + 2584.8X_t$$
$$t = \quad (-23.494) \ (27.549) \qquad r^2 = 0.9832 \qquad (6.5.14)$$
$$p \text{ value} = \qquad (0.0000)*(0.0000)*$$

* Denotes very small value.

---

[15] Again using differential calculus, we have $dY/dX = \beta_2(1/X)$. Therefore, $\beta_2 = dY/(dX/X) = $ (6.5.12).

TABLE 6.3
GNP and money supply, United States, 1973–1987

Year	GNP Dollars, in billions	M_2
1973	1,359.3	861.0
1974	1,472.8	908.5
1975	1,598.4	1023.2
1976	1,782.8	1163.7
1977	1,990.5	1286.7
1978	2,249.7	1389.0
1979	2,508.2	1500.2
1980	2,723.0	1633.1
1981	3,052.6	1795.5
1982	3,166.0	1954.0
1983	3,405.7	2185.2
1984	3,772.2	2363.6
1985	4,014.9	2562.6
1986	4,240.3	2807.7
1987	4,526.7	2901.0

Notes: The GNP figures are quarterly in terms of seasonally adjusted annual rates.

M_2 = currency + demand deposits + travelers checks

+ other checkable deposits + overnight RPs and Eurodollars

+ MMMF (money market mutual funds) balances

+ MMDAs (money market deposit accounts) + savings and small deposits

These are average daily figures, seasonally adjusted.

Source: *Economic Report of the President*, 1989, GNP data from Table B-1, p. 308, and M_2 data from Table B-67, p. 385.

Note that we have not given the standard errors (can you find them?).

Interpreted in the manner just described, the slope coefficient of about 2585 means that in the sample period an increase in the money supply of 1 percent was, on the average, followed by an increase in the GNP of about $25.85 billions (*note:* Divide the estimated slope coefficient by 100).

Before proceeding further, note that if you want to compute the elasticity coefficient for the log-lin or lin-log models, it can be done from the definition of the elasticity coefficient given before, namely, $(dY/dX)(X/Y)$. As a matter of fact, once the functional form of a model is known, one can compute elasticities by applying the preceding definition. Table 6.5, given later, summarizes the elasticity coefficients for the various models we have considered in this chapter.

6.6   RECIPROCAL MODELS

Models of the following type are known as **reciprocal** models.

$$Y_i = \beta_1 + \beta_2\left(\frac{1}{X_i}\right) + u_i \tag{6.6.1}$$

Although this model is nonlinear in the variable X because it enters inversely or reciprocally, the model is linear in β_1 and β_2 and is therefore a linear regression model.[16]

This model has these features: As X increases indefinitely, the term $\beta_2(1/X)$ approaches zero (*note:* β_2 is a constant) and Y approaches the limiting or *asymptotic* value β_1. Therefore, models like (6.6.1) have built in them an **asymptote** or limit value that the dependent variable will take when the value of the X variable increases indefinitely.[17]

Some likely shapes of the curve corresponding to (6.6.1) are shown in Fig. 6.5. An example of Fig. 6.5a is given in Fig. 6.6, which relates the average fixed cost (AFC) of production to the level of output. As this figure shows, the AFC declines continuously as output increases (because the fixed cost is spread over a large number of units) and eventually becomes asymptotic with the output axis at level β_1.

One of the important applications of Fig. 6.5b is the celebrated Phillips curve of macroeconomics. Based on the data on percent rate of change of money wages (Y) and the unemployment rate in percent (X) for the United Kingdom for the period 1861 to 1957, Phillips obtained a curve whose general shape resembles Fig. 6.5b and is reproduced in Fig. 6.7.[18]

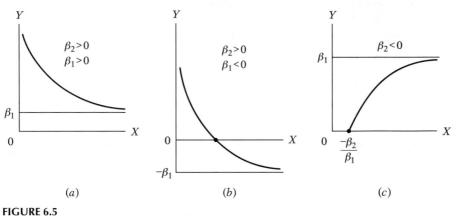

FIGURE 6.5

The reciprocal model: $Y = \beta_1 + \beta_2 \left(\dfrac{1}{X} \right)$.

---

[16]If we let $X_i^* = (1/X_i)$, then (6.6.1) is linear in the parameters as well as the variables Y_i and X_i^*.

[17]The slope of (6.6.1) is: $dY/dX = -\beta_2(1/X^2)$, implying that if β_2 is positive, the slope is negative throughout, and if β_2 is negative, the slope is positive throughout. See Figs. 6.5a and 6.5c, respectively.

[18]A. W. Phillips, "The Relation between Unemployment and the Rate of Change of Money Wages in the United Kingdom, 1861–1957," *Economica*, November 1958, vol. 25, pp. 283–299. Note that the original curve was fitted to the data for the period 1861 to 1913 and did not cross the unemployment axis, but Fig. 6.7 represents the modern picture of the Phillips version.

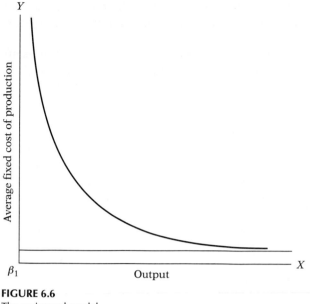

FIGURE 6.6
The reciprocal model.

As Fig. 6.7 shows, there is an asymmetry in the response of wage changes to the level of unemployment: Wages rise faster for a unit change in unemployment if the unemployment rate is below U^N, which is called the *natural rate of unemployment* by economists, than they fall for an equivalent change when the unemployment rate is above the natural level, β_1 indicating the asymptotic floor for wage change. This particular feature of the Phillips curve may be due to institutional factors, such as union bargaining power, minimum wages, unemployment compensation, etc.

An important application of Fig. 6.5c is the Engel expenditure curve (named after the German statistician Ernst Engel, 1821–1896), which relates a consumer's expenditure on a commodity to his or her total expenditure or income. If we let Y stand for expenditure on a commodity and X the income, then certain commodities have these features: (a) There is some critical or *threshold level* of income below which the commodity is not purchased; in Fig. 6.5c this threshold level of income is at the level $-(\beta_2/\beta_1)$. (b) There is a satiety level of consumption beyond which the consumer will not go no matter how high the income. This level is nothing but the asymptote β_1 shown in this figure. For such commodities the reciprocal model represented in Fig. 6.5c is the most appropriate.[19]

---

[19]For concrete examples, see S. J. Prais and H. S. Houthakker, *The Analysis of Family Budgets*, Cambridge University Press, London, 1971, chap. 7.

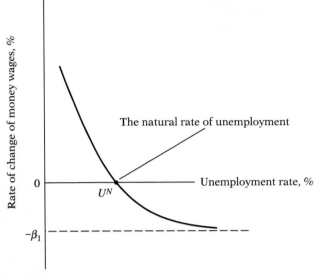

FIGURE 6.7
The Phillips curve.

An Illustrative Example: The Phillips Curve for the United Kingdom, 1950–1966

Table 6.4 gives data on annual percentage change in wage rates, Y and the unemployment rate, X for the United Kingdom for the period 1950–1966.

An attempt to fit the reciprocal model (6.6.1) gave the following results (see the SAS printout in Appendix 6A, Section 6A.3):

$$\hat{Y}_t = -1.4282 + 8.7243\frac{1}{X_t} \qquad r^2 = 0.3849 \qquad (6.6.2)$$

$$(2.0675) \ (2.8478) \qquad F_{1,15} = 9.39$$

where the figures in parentheses are the estimated standard errors.

The estimated regression line is depicted in Fig. 6.8. From this figure it is clear that the wage floor is -1.43 percent, that is, as X increases indefinitely, the percentage decrease in wages will not be more than 1.43 percent per year.

Incidentally, notice that the estimated r^2 value is rather low yet the slope coefficient is statistically significantly different from zero, and it has the right sign. This observation, as we will argue in Chapter 7, is one reason why one should not unduly emphasize the r^2 value.

6.7 SUMMARY OF FUNCTIONAL FORMS

In Table 6.5 we summarize the salient features of the various functional forms considered thus far.

TABLE 6.4
Year to year increase in wage rates and the unemployment rate, United Kingdom, 1950–1966

Year	Year to year increase in wage rates, % Y	Unemployment, % X
1950	1.8	1.4
1951	8.5	1.1
1952	8.4	1.5
1953	4.5	1.5
1954	4.3	1.2
1955	6.9	1.0
1956	8.0	1.1
1957	5.0	1.3
1958	3.6	1.8
1959	2.6	1.9
1960	2.6	1.5
1961	4.2	1.4
1962	3.6	1.8
1963	3.7	2.1
1964	4.8	1.5
1965	4.3	1.3
1966	4.6	1.4

Source: Cliff Pratten, *Applied Macroeconomics*, Oxford University Press, Oxford, 1985, p. 85.

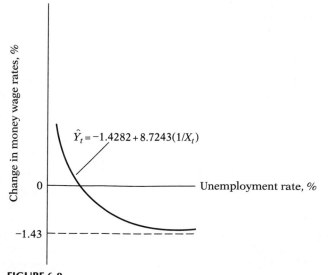

$$\hat{Y}_t = -1.4282 + 8.7243(1/X_t)$$

FIGURE 6.8
The Phillips curve for the United Kingdom, 1950–1966.

TABLE 6.5

Model	Equation	Slope $\left(= \dfrac{dY}{dX}\right)$	Elasticity $\left(= \dfrac{dY}{dX} \cdot \dfrac{X}{Y}\right)$
Linear	$Y = \beta_1 + \beta_2 X$	β_2	$\beta_2\left(\dfrac{X}{Y}\right)$*
Log-linear or log-log	$\ln Y = \beta_1 + \beta_2 \ln X$	$\beta_2\left(\dfrac{Y}{X}\right)$	β_2
Log-lin	$\ln Y = \beta_1 + \beta_2 X$	$\beta_2(Y)$	$\beta_2(X)$*
Lin-log	$Y = \beta_1 + \beta_2 \ln X$	$\beta_2\left(\dfrac{1}{X}\right)$	$\beta_2\left(\dfrac{1}{Y}\right)$*
Reciprocal	$Y = \beta_1 + \beta_2\left(\dfrac{1}{X}\right)$	$-\beta_2\left(\dfrac{1}{X^2}\right)$	$-\beta_2\left(\dfrac{1}{XY}\right)$*

Note: * indicates that the elasticity coefficient is variable, depending on the value taken by X or Y or both. When no X and Y values are specified, in practice, very often these elasticities are measured at the mean values, $\bar{X}$ and $\bar{Y}$.

*6.8   A NOTE ON THE NATURE OF THE STOCHASTIC ERROR TERM: ADDITIVE VERSUS MULTIPLICATIVE STOCHASTIC ERROR TERM

Consider the following regression model, which is the same as (6.4.1) but without the error term:

$$Y_i = \beta_1 X^{\beta_2} \tag{6.8.1}$$

For estimation purposes, we can express this model in three different forms:

$$Y_i = \beta_1 X_i^{\beta_2} u_i \tag{6.8.2}$$

$$Y_i = \beta_1 X_i^{\beta_2} e^{u_i} \tag{6.8.3}$$

$$Y_i = \beta_1 X_i^{\beta_2} + u_i \tag{6.8.4}$$

Taking the logarithms on both sides of these equations, we obtain

$$\ln Y_i = \alpha + \beta_2 \ln X_i + \ln u_i \tag{6.8.2a}$$

$$\ln Y_i = \alpha + \beta_2 \ln X_i + u_i \tag{6.8.3a}$$

$$\ln Y_i = \ln(\beta_1 X_i^{\beta_2} + u_i) \tag{6.8.4a}$$

where $\alpha = \ln \beta_1$.

Models like (6.8.2) are *intrinsically linear (in-parameter)* regression models in the sense that by suitable (log) transformation the models can be made linear in the parameters α and β_2. (*Note:* These models are nonlinear in β_1.) But model

---

*Optional

(6.8.4) is *intrinsically nonlinear-in-parameter*. There is no simple way to take the log of (6.8.4) because $\ln(A + B) \neq \ln A + \ln B$.

Although (6.8.2) and (6.8.3) are linear regression models and can be estimated by OLS or ML, we have to be careful about the properties of the stochastic error term that enters these models. Remember that the BLUE property of OLS requires that u_i has zero mean value, constant variance, and zero autocorrelation. For hypothesis testing, we further assume that u_i follows the normal distribution with mean and variance values just discussed. In short, we have assumed that $u_i \sim N(0, \sigma^2)$.

Now consider model (6.8.2). Its statistical counterpart is given in (6.8.2a). To use the classical normal linear regression model (CNLRM), we have to assume that

$$\ln u_i \sim N(0, \sigma^2) \tag{6.8.5}$$

Therefore, when we run the regression (6.8.2a), we will have to apply the normality tests discussed in Chapter 5 to the residuals obtained from this regression. Incidentally, note that if $\ln u_i$ follows the normal distribution with zero mean and constant variance, then statistical theory shows that u_i in (6.8.2) must follow the **log-normal distribution** with mean $e^{\sigma^2/2}$ and variance $e^{\sigma^2}(e^{\sigma^2} - 1)$.

As the preceding analysis shows, one has to pay very careful attention to the error term in transforming a model for regression analysis. As for (6.8.4), this model is a *nonlinear-in-parameter* regression model and will have to be solved by some iterative computer routine. Model (6.8.3) should not pose any problems for estimation.

To sum up, pay very careful attention to the disturbance term when you transform a model for regression analysis. Otherwise, a blind application of OLS to the transformed model will not produce a model with desirable statistical properties.

6.9 SUMMARY AND CONCLUSIONS

This chapter introduced several of the finer points of the classical linear regression model (CLRM).

1. Sometimes a regression model may not contain an explicit intercept term. Such models are known as **regression through the origin**. Although the algebra of estimating such models is simple, one should use such models with caution. In such models the sum of the residuals $\sum \hat{u}_i$ is nonzero; additionally, the conventionally computed r^2 may not be meaningful. Unless there is strong theoretical reason, it is better to introduce the intercept in the model explicitly.

2. The units and scale in which the regressand and the regressor(s) are expressed are very important because the interpretation of regression coefficients critically depends on them. In empirical research the researcher should not only quote the sources of data but also state explicitly how the variables are measured.

3. Just as important is the functional form of the relationship between the regressand and the regressor(s). Some of the important functional forms discussed in this chapter are (*a*) the log-linear or constant elasticity model, (*b*) semilog regression models, and (*c*) reciprocal models.

4. In the log-linear model both the regressand and the regressor(s) are expressed in the logarithmic form. The regression coefficient attached to the log of a regressor is interpreted as the elasticity of the regressand with respect to the regressor.

5. In the semilog model either the regressand or the regressor(s) are in the log form. In the semilog model where the regressand is logarithmic and the regressor X is time, the estimated slope coefficient (multiplied by 100) measures the (instantaneous) rate of growth of the regressand. Such models are often used to measure the growth rate of many economic phenomena. In the semilog model if the regressor is logarithmic, its coefficient measures the absolute rate of change in the regressand for a given percent change in the value of the regressor.

6. In the reciprocal models, either the regressand or the regressor is expressed in reciprocal, or inverse, form to capture nonlinear relationships between economic variables, as in the celebrated Phillips curve.

7. In choosing the various functional forms, great attention should be paid to the stochastic disturbance term u_i. As noted in Chapter 5, the CLRM explicitly assumes that the disturbance term has zero mean value and constant (homoscedastic) variance and that it is uncorrelated with the regressor(s). It is under these assumptions that the OLS estimators are BLUE. Further, under the CNLRM, the OLS estimators are also normally distributed. One should therefore find out if these assumptions hold in the functional form chosen for empirical analysis. After the regression is run, the researcher should apply diagnostic tests, such as the normality test, discussed in Chapter 5. This point cannot be overemphasized, for the classical tests of hypothesis, such as the t, F, and χ^2, rest on the assumption that the disturbances are normally distributed. This is especially critical if the sample size is small.

8. Although the discussion so far has been confined to two-variable regression models, the subsequent chapters will show that in many cases the extension to multiple regression models simply involves more algebra without necessarily introducing more fundamental concepts. That is why it is so very important that the reader have a firm grasp of the two-variable regression model.

EXERCISES

Questions

6.1. Consider the regression model

$$y_i = \beta_1 + \beta_2 x_i + u_i$$

where $y_i = (Y_i - \bar{Y})$ and $x_i = (X_i - \bar{X})$. In this case, the regression line must pass through the origin. True or false? Show your calculations.

6.2. Based on monthly data over the period January 1978 to December 1987, the following regression results were obtained:

$$\hat{Y}_t = \quad 0.00681 \quad + \quad 0.75815X_t$$
$$\text{se} = \quad (0.02596) \quad\quad (0.27009)$$
$$t = \quad (0.26229) \quad\quad (2.80700)$$
$$p\ \text{value} = \quad (0.7984) \quad\quad (0.0186) \quad\quad r^2 = 0.4406$$

$$\hat{Y}_t = \quad 0.76214X_t$$
$$\text{se} = \quad (0.265799)$$
$$t = \quad (2.95408)$$
$$p\ \text{value} = \quad (0.0131) \quad\quad\quad\quad r^2 = 0.43684$$

where Y = monthly rate of return on Texaco common stock, %

X = monthly market rate of return, %*

(a) What is the difference between the two regression models?
(b) Given the preceding results, would you retain the intercept term in the first model? Why or why not?
(c) How would you interpret the slope coefficients in the two models?
(d) What is the theory underlying the two models?
(e) Can you compare the r^2 terms of the two models? Why or why not?
(f) The Jarque-Bera normality statistic for the first model in this problem is 1.1167 and for the second model it is 1.1170. What conclusions can you draw from these statistics?
(g) The t value of the slope coefficient in the zero intercept model is about 2.95, whereas that with the intercept present is about 2.81. Can you rationalize this result?

6.3. Consider the following regression model:

$$\frac{1}{Y_i} = \beta_1 + \beta_2\left(\frac{1}{X_i}\right) + u_i$$

Note: Neither Y nor X assumes zero value.
(a) Is this a linear regression model?
(b) How would you estimate this model?
(c) What is the behavior of Y as X tends to infinity?
(d) Can you give an example where such a model may be appropriate?

6.4. Consider the log-linear model:

$$\ln Y_i = \beta_1 + \beta_2 \ln X_i + u_i$$

Plot Y on the vertical axis and X on the horizontal axis. Draw the curves showing the relationship between Y and X when $\beta_2 = 1$, and when $\beta_2 > 1$, and when $\beta_2 < 1$.

6.5. Log hyperbola or logarithmic reciprocal model. In exercise 2.11e we introduced the following model, called the logarithmic reciprocal model:

$$\ln Y_i = \beta_1 - \beta_2\left(\frac{1}{X_i}\right) + u_i$$

---

* The underlying data were obtained from the data diskette included in Ernst R. Berndt, *The Practice of Econometrics: Classic and Contemporary*, Addison-Wesley, Reading, Massachusetts, 1991.

(*a*) What are the properties of this model? (*Hint:* Consider the slope coefficient, the asymptote, etc.)

(*b*) Let X = time. What kind of growth curve is traced by this model?

(*c*) In what situations would you consider using such a model?

6.6. Refer to the coffee demand function given in Section 3.7. Suppose coffee prices were given in cents instead of dollars per pound.

(*a*) How will this affect the estimated intercept and slope given in (3.7.1)? Show the necessary calculations.

(*b*) What is the change, if any, in the estimated standard errors?

(*c*) Will the r^2 be affected? Why or why not?

6.7. Regression on standardized variables. Let $X_i^* = (X_i - \bar{X})/S_x$ and $Y_i^* = (Y_i - \bar{Y})/S_y$, where S_x and S_y are standard deviations of X and Y, respectively, in the sample. Show that in the model

$$Y_i^* = \alpha_1 + \alpha_2 X_i^* + u_i$$

$\hat{\alpha}_1 = 0$ and $\hat{\alpha}_2 = r$, the coefficient of correlation between X and Y. Can you think of a reason why one would want to use a regression model using standardized variables?

Note: Y_i^* and X_i^* defined above are known as **standardized variables**. A variable is said to be standardized or in standard (deviation) units if it is expressed in terms of deviation from its mean (i.e., a change of the origin) and divided by its sample standard deviation (i.e., a change of scale). Thus, standardization involves both a change of the origin and change of scale.

Such standardized variables have these properties: They each have a zero mean value and variance of 1. As a result, a unit change in, say, X^* becomes a 1 standard deviation change. Therefore, the slope coefficient in the present model can be interpreted as giving the number of standard deviations that the dependent variable on the average changes when the explanatory variable changes by 1 standard deviation. Incidentally, the slope coefficient in this model is known as the beta coefficient, not to be confused with the beta coefficient of portfolio theory.

6.8. Consider the following models:

$$\text{Model I:} \quad Y_i = \beta_1 + \beta_2 X_i + u_i$$
$$\text{Model II:} \quad Y_i^* = \alpha_1 + \alpha_2 X_i^* + u_i$$

where Y^* and X^* are standardized variables as defined in exercise 6.7. Show that $\hat{\alpha}_2 = \hat{\beta}_2(S_x/S_y)$ and hence *establish that although the regression slope coefficients are independent of the change of origin they are not independent of the change of scale.*

6.9. Consider the following models:

$$\ln Y_i^* = \alpha_1 + \alpha_2 \ln X_i^* + u_i^*$$
$$\ln Y_i = \beta_1 + \beta_2 \ln X_i + u_i$$

where $Y_i^* = w_1 Y_i$ and $X_i^* = w_2 X_i$, the w's being constants.

(*a*) Establish the relationships between the two sets of regression coefficients and their standard errors.

(*b*) Is the r^2 different between the two models?

6.10. Between regressions (6.5.8) and (6.5.10), which model do you prefer? Why?

6.11. Given the estimated coffee demand function (6.4.5), would you accept the hypothesis that the price elasticity of demand for coffee is not significantly different from zero? Use the one-tail test at the 5% level of significance. Consider why a one-tail test is appropriate.

6.12. For the regression (6.5.8) test the hypothesis that the slope coefficient is not significantly different from 0.03.

6.13. From the estimated Phillips curve given in (6.6.2), is it possible to estimate the natural rate of unemployment? How?

6.14. For the log-log model (6.4.3) if Y is the quantity of a commodity consumed and X the consumer's income, how would you compute the income elasticity: $(dY/dX)(X/Y)$? And for the lin-log model (6.5.11)?

6.15. The Engel expenditure curve relates a consumer's expenditure on a commodity to his or her total income. Letting Y = consumption expenditure on a commodity and X = consumer income, consider the following models:

$$Y_i = \beta_1 + \beta_2 X_i + u_i$$
$$Y_i = \beta_1 + \beta_2 (1/X_i) + u_i$$
$$\ln Y_i = \ln \beta_1 + \beta_2 \ln X_i + u_i$$
$$\ln Y_i = \ln \beta_1 + \beta_2 (1/X_i) + u_i$$
$$Y_i = \beta_1 + \beta_2 \ln X_i + u_i$$

Which of these model(s) would you choose for the Engel expenditure curve and why? (*Hint:* Interpret the various slope coefficients, find out the expressions for elasticity of expenditure with respect to income, etc.)

Problems

6.16. The following table gives data on the GDP (gross domestic product) deflator for domestic goods and the GDP deflator for imports for Singapore for the period 1968–1982. The GDP deflator is often used as an indicator of inflation in place of the CPI. Singapore is a small, open economy, heavily dependent on foreign trade for its survival.

Year	GDP deflator for domestic goods, Y	GDP deflator for imports, X
1968	1000	1000
1969	1023	1042
1970	1040	1092
1971	1087	1105
1972	1146	1110
1973	1285	1257
1974	1485	1749
1975	1521	1770
1976	1543	1889
1977	1567	1974
1978	1592	2015
1979	1714	2260
1980	1841	2621
1981	1959	2777
1982	2033	2735

Source: Colin Simkin, "Does Money Matter in Singapore?" *The Singapore Economic Review*, vol. XXIX, no. 1, April 1984, Table 6, p.8.

To study the relationship between domestic and world prices, you are given the following models:

$$\text{1. } Y_t = \alpha_1 + \alpha_2 X_t + u_t$$
$$\text{2. } Y_t = \beta_2 X_t + u_t$$

where Y = GDP deflator for domestic goods
$\quad\quad\quad X$ = GDP deflator for imports

(a) How would you choose between the two models a priori?
(b) Fit both models to the data and decide which gives a better fit.
(c) What other model(s) might be appropriate for the data?

6.17. Refer to the data given in exercise 6.16. The means of Y and X are 1456 and 1760, respectively, and the corresponding standard deviations are 346 and 641. Estimate the following regression:

$$Y_t^* = \alpha_1 + \alpha_2 X_t^* + u_t$$

where the starred variables are standardized variables, and interpret the results.

6.18. Refer to the data of exercise 1.1. For each country estimate the growth rate of inflation obtained from the model:

$$\ln Y_t = \beta_1 + \beta_2 \text{Time} + u_t$$

where Y is the inflation rate. How do these results differ from the ones you obtained in exercise 5.12?

6.19. Refer to the data of exercise 3.22. Compute the rate of growth of the U.S. GDP in nominal terms for the period 1972–1991 and compare your results with those given in Eq. (6.5.8). Would the two regression results help you to estimate the rate of inflation in the United States for the said time period? How?

6.20. Suppose you fit the following version of the Phillips curve to the data given in Table 6.4:

$$Y_t = \alpha_1 + \alpha_2 X_t + u_t$$

where Y = % annual change in the money wage rates
$\quad\quad\quad X$ = the unemployment rate

(a) A priori, what is the expected sign of α_2?
(b) Estimate this regression, obtaining the usual statistics.
(c) How do these results compare with those of regression (6.6.2)? Is there any conflict in the results?
(d) Can you compare the two r^2 values?
(e) Which model do you prefer? Why?

6.21. The following table gives data on GNP and money supply (M_1) in millions of dollars for Canada for the period 1970–1984.

Year	GNP	Money supply, M_1
1970	85,685	9,077
1971	94,450	10,178
1972	105,234	11,626
1973	123,560	13,320
1974	147,528	14,555
1975	165,343	16,566

Year	GNP	Money supply, M_1
1976	191,857	17,889
1977	210,189	19,381
1978	232,211	21,328
1979	264,279	22,823
1980	297,556	24,254
1981	339,797	25,379
1982	358,302	25,541
1983	390,340	28,137
1984	420,819	28,798

Source: The Federal Reserve Bank of St. Louis, *International Economic Conditions*, Annual Edition, June 1985, p. 14 (M_1 data) and p. 17 (GNP data).

Use these data to fit the following model and comment on the results.

$$\text{GNP}_t = \beta_1 + \beta_2 \ln \text{Money}_t + u_t$$

6.22. You are given the following data:

Y_i	X_i	Y_i	X_i
86	3	62	35
79	7	52	45
76	12	51	55
69	17	51	70
65	25	48	120

Source: Adapted from J. Johnston, *Econometric Methods*, 3d ed., McGraw-Hill, New York, 1984, p. 87. Actually, this is taken from an econometric examination of Oxford University, 1975.

Fit the following model to these data and obtain the usual regression statistics:

$$\left(\frac{100}{100 - Y_i}\right) = \beta_1 + \beta_2 \left(\frac{1}{X_i}\right)$$

6.23. To measure the elasticity of substitution between capital and labor inputs, Arrow, Chenery, Minhas, and Solow, the authors of the now famous CES (constant elasticity of substitution) production function, used the following model:[*]

$$\log\left(\frac{V}{L}\right) = \log \beta_1 + \beta_2 \log W + u$$

where (V/L) = value added per unit of labor

L = labor input

W = real wage rate

---

[*]"Capital-Labor Substitution and Economic Efficiency," *Review of Economics and Statistics*, August 1961, vol. 43, no. 5, pp. 225–254.

The coefficient β_2 measures the elasticity of substitution between labor and capital (i.e., proportionate change in factor proportions/proportionate change in relative factor prices). From the data given in the following table verify that the estimated elasticity is 1.3338 and that it is not statistically significantly different from 1.

Industry	$\log(V/L)$	$\log W$
Wheat flour	3.6973	2.9617
Sugar	3.4795	2.8532
Paints and varnishes	4.0004	3.1158
Cement	3.6609	3.0371
Glass and glassware	3.2321	2.8727
Ceramics	3.3418	2.9745
Plywood	3.4308	2.8287
Cotton textiles	3.3158	3.0888
Woolen textiles	3.5062	3.0086
Jute textiles	3.2352	2.9680
Chemicals	3.8823	3.0909
Aluminum	3.7309	3.0881
Iron and steel	3.7716	3.2256
Bicycles	3.6601	3.1025
Sewing machines	3.7554	3.1354

Source: Damodar Gujarati, "A Test of ACMS Production Function: Indian Industries, 1958," *Indian Journal of Industrial Relations*, vol. 2, no. 1, July 1966, pp. 95–97.

APPENDIX 6.A

6A.1 DERIVATION OF LEAST-SQUARES ESTIMATORS FOR REGRESSION THROUGH THE ORIGIN

We want to minimize

$$\sum \hat{u}_i^2 = \sum (Y_i - \hat{\beta}_2 X_i)^2 \tag{1}$$

with respect to $\hat{\beta}_2$.

Differentiating (1) with respect to $\hat{\beta}_2$, we obtain

$$\frac{d\sum \hat{u}_i^2}{d\hat{\beta}_2} = 2\sum (Y_i - \hat{\beta}_2 X_i)(-X_i) \tag{2}$$

Setting (2) equal to zero and simplifying, we get

$$\hat{\beta}_2 = \frac{\sum X_i Y_i}{\sum X_i^2} \tag{6.1.6} = (3)$$

Now substituting the PRF: $Y_i = \beta_2 X_i + u_i$ into this equation, we obtain

$$\hat{\beta}_2 = \frac{\sum X_i(\beta_2 X_i + u_i)}{\sum X_i^2} \tag{4}$$

$$= \beta_2 + \frac{\sum X_i u_i}{\sum X_i^2}$$

(*Note:* $E(\hat{\beta}_2) = \beta_2$.) Therefore,

$$E(\hat{\beta}_2 - \beta_2)^2 = E\left[\frac{\sum X_i u_i}{\sum X_i^2}\right]^2 \tag{5}$$

Expanding the right-hand side of (5) and noting that the X_i are nonstochastic and the u_i are homoscedastic and uncorrelated, we obtain

$$\text{var}(\hat{\beta}_2) = E(\hat{\beta}_2 - \beta_2)^2 = \frac{\sigma^2}{\sum X_i^2} \qquad (6.1.7) = (6)$$

Incidentally, note that from (2) we get, after equating it to zero

$$\sum \hat{u}_i X_i = 0 \tag{7}$$

From Appendix 3A, Section 3A.1 we see that when the intercept term is present in the model, we get in addition to (7) the condition $\sum \hat{u}_i = 0$. From the mathematics just given it should be clear why the regression through the origin model may not have the error sum, $\sum \hat{u}_i$, equal to zero.

Suppose we want to impose the condition that $\sum \hat{u}_i = 0$. In that case we have

$$\sum Y_i = \hat{\beta}_2 \sum X_i + \sum \hat{u}_i \tag{8}$$

$$= \hat{\beta}_2 \sum X_i, \qquad \text{since } \sum \hat{u}_i = 0 \text{ by construction}$$

This expression then gives

$$\hat{\beta}_2 = \frac{\sum Y_i}{\sum X_i} \tag{9}$$

$$= \frac{\bar{Y}}{\bar{X}} = \frac{\text{mean value of } Y}{\text{mean value of } X}$$

But this estimator is not the same as (3) above or (6.1.6). And since the $\hat{\beta}_2$ of (3) is unbiased (why?), the $\hat{\beta}_2$ of (9) cannot be unbiased.

The upshot is that, in regression through the origin, we cannot have both $\sum \hat{u}_i X_i$ and $\sum \hat{u}_i$ equal to zero, as in the conventional model. The only condition that is satisfied is that $\sum \hat{u}_i X_i$ is zero.

Recall that

$$Y_i = \hat{Y}_i + \hat{u} \tag{2.6.3}$$

Summing this equation on both sides and dividing by N, the sample size, we obtain

$$\bar{Y} = \bar{\hat{Y}} + \bar{\hat{u}} \tag{10}$$

Since for the zero intercept model $\sum \hat{u}_i$ and, therefore $\bar{\hat{u}}$, need not be zero, it then follows that

$$\bar{Y} \neq \bar{\hat{Y}} \tag{11}$$

that is, the mean of actual Y values need not be equal to the mean of the estimated Y values; the two mean values are identical for the intercept-present model, as can be seen from (3.1.10).

It was noted that for the zero-intercept model r^2 can be negative, whereas for the conventional model it can never be negative. This condition can be shown as follows.

Using (3.5.5a), we can write

$$r^2 = 1 - \frac{\text{RSS}}{\text{TSS}} = 1 - \frac{\sum \hat{u}_i^2}{\sum y_i^2} \tag{12}$$

Now for the conventional, or intercept-present, model, Eq. (3.3.6) shows that

$$\text{RSS} = \sum \hat{u}_i^2 = \sum y_i^2 - \hat{\beta}_2^2 \sum x_i^2 \leq \sum y_i^2 \tag{13}$$

unless $\hat{\beta}_2$ is zero (i.e., X has no influence on Y whatsoever). That is, for the conventional model, RSS $\leq$ TSS, or, r^2 can never be negative.

For the zero-intercept model it can be shown analogously that

$$\text{RSS} = \sum \hat{u}_i^2 = \sum Y_i^2 - \hat{\beta}_2^2 \sum X_i^2 \tag{14}$$

(*Note:* The sums of squares of Y and X are not mean-adjusted.) Now there is no guarantee that this RSS will always be less than $\sum y_i^2 = \sum Y_i^2 - N\bar{Y}^2$ (the TSS), which suggests that RSS can be greater than TSS, implying that r^2, as conventionally defined, can be negative. Incidentally, notice that in this case RSS will be greater than TSS if $\hat{\beta}_2^2 \sum X_i^2 < N\bar{Y}^2$.

APPENDIX 6A.2 SAS OUTPUT OF THE CHARACTERISTIC LINE (6.1.12)

DEP VARIABLE: Y

SOURCE	DF	SUM OF SQUARES	MEAN SQUARE	F VALUE	PROB > F
MODEL	1	12364.263	12364.263	32.375	0.0008
ERROR	9	3437.147	381.905		
TOTAL	10	15801.410			

ROOT MSE	19.542396	R-SQUARE		0.7825
DEP MEAN	19.390000	ADJ R-SQ		0.7825
C.V.	100.786			

NOTE: NO INTERCEPT TERM IS USED. R-SQUARE IS REDEFINED.

VARIABLE	DF	PARAMETER ESTIMATE	STANDARD ERROR	T FOR HO: PARAMETER = 0	PROB > |T|
X	1	1.089912	0.191551	5.690	0.0008

OBS	Y	X	YHAT	YRESID
1	67.5	19.5	21.253	46.247
2	19.2	8.5	9.264	9.936
3	−35.2	−29.3	−31.394	−3.266
4	−42.0	−26.5	−28.883	−13.117
5	63.7	61.9	67.466	−3.766
6	19.3	45.5	49.591	−30.291
7	3.6	9.5	10.354	−6.754
8	20.0	14.0	15.259	4.741
9	40.3	35.3	38.474	1.826
10	37.5	31.0	33.787	3.713

DURBIN-WATSON d	0.896
1ST ORDER AUTOCORRELATION	0.239

Note: The value **PROB** > |T| = 0.0008 represents the *p* value.

APPENDIX 6A.3   SAS OUTPUT OF THE UNITED KINGDOM PHILLIPS REGRESSION (6.6.2)

DEP VARIABLE: Y

SOURCE	DF	SUM OF SQUARES	MEAN SQUARE	F VALUE	PROB > F
MODEL	1	25.054647	25.054647	9.385	0.0079
ERROR	15	40.043000	2.669533		
TOTAL	16	65.097647			

ROOT MSE		1.633871	R-SQUARE		0.3849
DEP MEAN		4.788235	ADJ R-SQ		0.3439
C.V.		34.12261			

VARIABLE	DF	PARAMETER ESTIMATE	STANDARD ERROR	T FOR HO: PARAMETER = 0	PROB > |T|
INTERCEP	1	−1.4282	2.067478	−0.691	0.5003
X_1	1	8.724344	2.847779	3.064	0.0079

OBS	Y	X	$X_1 = 1/X$	YHAT	YRESID
1	1.8	1.4	0.71429	4.80350	−3.0035
2	8.5	1.1	0.90909	6.50304	1.9970
3	8.4	1.5	0.66667	4.38805	4.0119
4	4.5	1.5	0.66667	4.38805	0.1119
5	4.8	1.2	0.83333	5.84211	−1.5421
6	6.9	1.0	1.00000	7.29617	−0.3962
7	8.0	1.1	0.90909	6.50304	1.4970
8	5.0	1.3	0.76923	5.28286	−0.2829
9	3.6	1.8	.055556	3.41868	0.1813
10	2.6	1.9	0.52632	3.16358	−0.5636
11	2.6	1.5	0.66667	4.38805	−1.7881
12	4.2	1.4	0.71429	4.80350	−0.6035
13	3.6	1.8	0.55556	3.41868	0.1813
14	3.7	2.1	0.47619	2.72627	0.9737
15	4.8	1.5	0.66667	4.38805	0.4119
16	4.3	1.3	0.76923	5.28286	−0.9829
17	4.6	1.4	0.71429	4.80350	−0.2035

Note: The numbers under the heading PROB > |T| represent *p* values.

CHAPTER
7

MULTIPLE REGRESSION ANALYSIS: THE PROBLEM OF ESTIMATION

The two-variable model studied extensively in the previous chapters is often inadequate in practice. In our consumption-income example, for instance, it was assumed implicitly that only income X affects consumption Y. But economic theory is seldom so simple for, besides income, a number of other variables are also likely to affect consumption expenditure. An obvious example is wealth of the consumer. As another example, the demand for a commodity is likely to depend not only on its own price but also on the prices of other competing or complementary goods, income of the consumer, social status, etc. Therefore, we need to extend our simple two-variable regression model to cover models involving more than two variables. Adding more variables leads us to the discussion of multiple regression models, that is, models in which the dependent variable, or regressand, Y depends on two or more explanatory variables, or regressors.

The simplest possible multiple regression model is three-variable regression, with one dependent variable and two explanatory variables. In this and the next chapter we shall study this model, and in Chapter 9 we shall generalize it to more than three variables. Throughout, we are concerned with multiple linear regression models, that is, models linear in the parameters; they may or may not be linear in the variables.

7.1 THE THREE-VARIABLE MODEL: NOTATION AND ASSUMPTIONS

Generalizing the two-variable population regression function (PRF) (2.4.2), we may write the three-variable PRF as

$$Y_i = \beta_1 + \beta_2 X_{2i} + \beta_3 X_{3i} + u_i \qquad (7.1.1)$$

where Y is the dependent variable, X_2 and X_3 the explanatory variables (or regressors), u the stochastic disturbance term, and i the ith observation; in case the data are time series, the subscript t will denote the tth observation.[1]

In Eq. (7.1.1) β_1 is the intercept term. As usual, it gives the mean or average effect on Y of all the variables excluded from the model, although its mechanical interpretation is the average value of Y when X_2 and X_3 are set equal to zero. The coefficients β_2 and β_3 are called the **partial regression coefficients**, and their meaning will be explained shortly.

We continue to operate within the framework of the classical linear regression model (CLRM) first introduced in Chapter 3. Specifically, we assume the following:

Zero mean value of u_i, or

$$E(u_i \mid X_{2i}, X_{3i}) = 0 \qquad \text{for each } i \qquad (7.1.2)$$

No serial correlation, or

$$\text{cov}(u_i, u_j) = 0 \quad i \neq j \qquad (7.1.3)$$

Homoscedasticity, or

$$\text{var}(u_i) = \sigma^2 \qquad (7.1.4)$$

Zero covariance between u_i and each X variable, or

$$\text{cov}(u_i, X_{2i}) = \text{cov}(u_i, X_{3i}) = 0 \qquad (7.1.5)[2]$$

No specification bias, or

$$\text{The model is correctly specified} \qquad (7.1.6)$$

No exact collinearity between the X variables, or

$$\text{No } \textbf{exact linear relationship} \text{ between } X_2 \text{ and } X_3 \qquad (7.1.7)$$

In addition, as in Chapter 3, we assume that the multiple regression model is *linear in the parameters*, that the values of the regressors are fixed in repeat-

---

[1] For notational symmetry, Eq. (7.1.1) can also be written as

$$Y_i = \beta_1 X_{1i} + \beta_2 X_{2i} + \beta_3 X_{3i} + u_i$$

with the provision that $X_{1i} = 1$ for all i.

[2] This assumption is automatically fulfilled if X_2 and X_3 are nonstochastic and (7.1.2) holds.

ed sampling, and that there is sufficient variability in the values of the regressors.

The rationale for assumptions (7.1.2) through (7.1.6) is the same as discussed in Section 3.2. Assumption (7.1.7), that there be no exact linear relationship between X_2 and X_3, technically known as the assumption of *no collinearity*, or **no multicollinearity** if more than one exact linear relationship is involved, is new and needs some explanation.[3]

Informally, no collinearity means none of the explanatory variables can be written as linear combinations of the remaining explanatory variables. What this means can be seen from the Venn diagram, or the Ballentine, first introduced in Chapter 3. In this figure, the circle Y represents variation in the dependent variable Y and the circles X_2 and X_3 represent, respectively, variations in the regressors X_2 and X_3. In Fig. 7.1a area 1 represents the variation in Y explained by X_2 (via an OLS regression) and area 2 represents the variation in Y explained by X_3. In Fig. 7.1b, areas 3 and 4 represent the variation in Y explained by X_2 and areas 4 and 5 represent the variation in Y explained by X_3. But since area 4 is common to both X_2 and X_3, a priori we do not know what part of 4 belongs to X_2 and what to X_3. The common area 4 represents the situation of collinearity. What the assumption of no collinearity requires is that there should not be any overlap between X_2 and X_3, that is, the common area 4 should be zero. In other words, what we want is something like the situation depicted in Fig. 7.1a.

Formally no collinearity means that there exists no set of numbers λ_2 and λ_3, not both zero, such that

$$\lambda_2 X_{2i} + \lambda_3 X_{3i} = 0 \qquad (7.1.8)$$

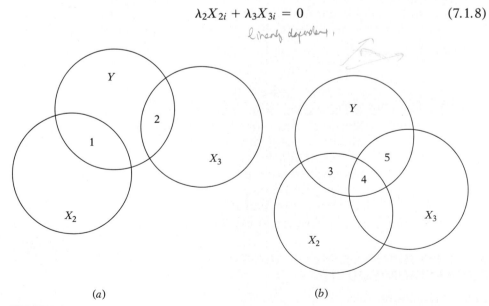

(a)   (b)

FIGURE 7.1
The Ballentine, showing no collinearity (a) and collinearity (b).

---

[3]In the two-variable model we did not need this assumption. Why?

If such a linear relationship exists, then X_2 and X_3 are said to be **collinear** or **linearly dependent**. On the other hand, if (7.1.8) holds true only when $\lambda_2 = \lambda_3 = 0$, then X_2 and X_3 are said to be *linearly independent*.

Thus, if

$$X_{2i} = -4X_{3i} \qquad \text{or} \qquad X_{2i} + 4X_{3i} = 0 \qquad (7.1.9)$$

the two variables are linearly dependent, and if both are included in a regression model we will have perfect collinearity or an exact linear relationship between the two regressors.

But suppose $X_{3i} = X_{2i}^2$. Would this violate the assumption of no collinearity? No, because the relationship between the two variables here is *nonlinear* and does not violate the requirement that there be *no exact linear relationships* between the regressors. However, it should be noted that in this case the conventionally computed r^2 and r will be high, particularly in samples of X_2 and X_3 with few values at the extreme. But more on this in Chapter 10.

Although we shall consider the problem of multicollinearity in depth in Chapter 10, intuitively the logic behind the assumption of no multicollinearity is not too difficult to grasp. Suppose that in (7.1.1) Y, X_2, and X_3 represent consumption expenditure, income, and wealth of the consumer, respectively. In postulating that consumption expenditure is linearly related to income and wealth, economic theory presumes that wealth and income may have some independent influence on consumption. If not, there is no sense in including both income and wealth variables in the model. In the extreme, if there is an exact linear relationship between income and wealth, we have only one independent variable, not two, and there is no way to assess the *separate* influence of income and wealth on consumption. To see this clearly, let $X_{3i} = 2X_{2i}$ in the consumption-income-wealth regression. Then the regression (7.1.1) becomes

$$
\begin{aligned}
Y_i &= \beta_1 + \beta_2 X_{2i} + \beta_3 (2X_{2i}) + u_i \\
&= \beta_1 + (\beta_2 + 2\beta_3) X_{2i} + u_i \\
&= \beta_1 + \alpha X_{2i} + u_i
\end{aligned}
\qquad (7.1.10)
$$

where $\alpha = (\beta_2 + 2\beta_3)$. That is, we in fact have a two-variable and not a three-variable regression. Moreover, if we run the regression (7.1.10) and obtain α, there is no way to estimate the separate influence of $X_2(=\beta_2)$ and $X_3(=\beta_3)$ on Y, for α gives the *combined influence* of X_2 and X_3 on Y.[4]

In short, the assumption of no multicollinearity requires that in the PRF we include only those variables that are not linear functions of some of the variables in the model. Whether this can always be accomplished in practice is another matter and we shall explore it extensively in Chapter 10.

7.2 INTERPRETATION OF MULTIPLE REGRESSION EQUATION

Given the assumptions of the classical regression model, it follows that, on taking the conditional expectation of Y on both sides of (7.1.1), we obtain

---

[4]Mathematically speaking, $\alpha = (\beta_2 + 2\beta_3)$ is one equation in two unknowns and there is no *unique* way of estimating β_2 and β_3 from the estimated α.

[handwritten: what exactly is this and why can we do it.]

$$E(Y_i \mid X_{2i}, X_{3i}) = \beta_1 + \beta_2 X_{2i} + \beta_3 X_{3i} \qquad (7.2.1)$$

In words, (7.2.1) gives the **conditional mean or expected value of** Y **conditional upon the given or fixed values of the variables** X_2 **and** X_3. Therefore, as in the two-variable case, multiple regression analysis is regression analysis conditional upon the fixed values of the explanatory variables, and what we obtain is the average or mean value of Y or mean response of Y for the fixed values of the X variables.

7.3 THE MEANING OF PARTIAL REGRESSION COEFFICIENTS

The meaning of **partial regression coefficient** is as follows: β_2 measures the change in the mean value of Y, $E(Y \mid X_2, X_3)$, per unit change in X_2, *holding* X_3 *constant*. In others words, it gives the slope of $E(Y \mid X_2, X_3)$ with respect to X_2, holding X_3 constant.[5] Put differently, it gives the "direct" or the "net" effect of a unit change in X_2 on the mean value of Y, net of X_3. Likewise, β_3 measures the change in the mean value of Y per unit change in X_3, *holding* X_2 *constant*. That is, it gives the "direct" or "net" effect of a unit change in X_3 on the mean value of Y, net of X_2.

What precisely is the meaning of the term *holding constant*?[6] To understand this, assume that Y represents output and X_2 and X_3 represent labor and capital inputs, respectively. Assume further that both X_2 and X_3 are required in the production of Y and the proportions in which they can be employed in the production of Y can be varied. Now suppose we increase the labor input by a unit, which results in some increase in the output (the gross marginal product of labor). Can we ascribe the resulting change in output exclusively to the labor input X_2?[7] If we were to do so, we would be *inflating* the contribution of X_2 to Y; X_2 gets "credit" for that portion of the change in Y that is due to the concomitant increase in the capital input. Therefore, to assess the "true" contribution of X_2 to the change in Y (the net marginal product of labor), we must somehow "control" the influence of X_3. Similarly, to assess the true contribution of X_3, we must also control the influence of X_2. *[handwritten: why control the influence if it has one ??]*

How do we go about this control procedure? For concreteness, assume that we want to control the linear influence of the capital input X_3 in measuring the impact of a unit change in the labor input X_2 on the output. To this end, we may proceed as follows:

Stage I: Regress Y on X_3 only as follows:

$$Y_i = b_1 + b_{13} X_{3i} + \hat{u}_{1i} \qquad (7.3.1)$$

---

[5]The calculus-minded reader will notice at once that β_2 and β_3 are partial derivatives of $E(Y \mid X_2, X_3)$ with respect to X_2 and X_3.

[6]The terms *controlling, holding constant, allowing or accounting for the influence of*, and *correcting the influence of* are all synonymous and will be used interchangeably in this text.

[7]Since both labor and capital are required in production, this increase may lead to some increase in capital; the amount of change in the latter will depend on the technology of production.

Equation (7.3.1) is nothing but a two-variable regression, save the new but self-explanatory notation, where $\hat{u}_{1i}$ is the (sample) residual term. (*Note:* In b_{13} the subscript 1 refers to variable Y.)

Stage II: Regress X_2 on X_3 only as follows:

$$X_{2i} = b_2 + b_{23}X_{3i} + \hat{u}_{2i} \qquad (7.3.2)$$

where $\hat{u}_{2i}$ is also the residual term. Now

$$\hat{u}_{1i} = Y_i - b_1 - b_{13}X_{3i}$$
$$= Y_i - \hat{Y}_i \qquad (7.3.3)$$

and

$$\hat{u}_{2i} = X_{2i} - b_2 - b_{23}X_{3i}$$
$$= X_{2i} - \hat{X}_{2i} \qquad (7.3.4)$$

where $\hat{Y}_i$ and $\hat{X}_{2i}$ are the estimated values from the regression (7.3.1) and (7.3.2), respectively.

What do the residuals $\hat{u}_{1i}$ and $\hat{u}_{2i}$ imply? The term $\hat{u}_{1i}$ represents the value of Y_i after removing the (linear) influence on it of X_3, and similarly $\hat{u}_{2i}$ represents the value of X_{2i} after removing the (linear) influence on it of X_3. So to speak, $\hat{u}_{1i}$ and $\hat{u}_{2i}$ are "purified" Y_i and X_{2i}, that is, purified of the influence (contamination?) of X_3.

Stage III: Therefore, if we now proceed to regress $\hat{u}_{1i}$ on $\hat{u}_{2i}$ as follows,

$$\hat{u}_{1i} = a_0 + a_1\hat{u}_{2i} + \hat{u}_{3i} \qquad (7.3.5)$$

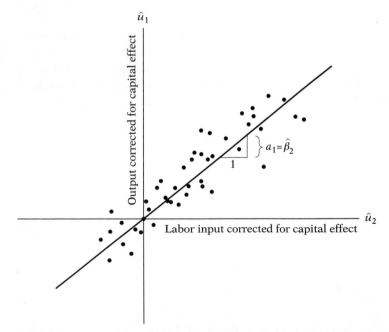

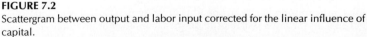

FIGURE 7.2
Scattergram between output and labor input corrected for the linear influence of capital.

where $\hat{u}_{3i}$ is also the sample residual term. Then a_1 should give us an estimate of the "true" or net effect of a unit change in X_2 on Y (i.e., net marginal product of labor) or the true slope of Y with respect to X_2, that is, an estimate of β_2. As a matter of fact it does, as we show in Appendix 7A, Section 7A.2. (See also exercise 7.5.)

Geometrically, we have Fig. 7.2. In practice, though, there is no need to go through this cumbersome and time-consuming procedure, as a_1 can be estimated directly from the formulas given in Section 7.4 [see Eq. (7.4.7)]. The three-stage procedure just outlined is merely a pedagogic device to drive home the meaning of "partial" regression coefficient.

7.4 OLS AND ML ESTIMATION OF THE PARTIAL REGRESSION COEFFICIENTS

To estimate the parameters of the three-variable regression model (7.1.1), we first consider the method of ordinary least squares (OLS) introduced in Chapter 3 and then consider briefly the method of maximum likelihood (ML) discussed in Chapter 4.

OLS Estimators

To find the OLS estimators, let us first write the sample regression function (SRF) corresponding to the PRF of (7.1.1) as follows:

$$Y_i = \hat{\beta}_1 + \hat{\beta}_2 X_{2i} + \hat{\beta}_3 X_{3i} + \hat{u}_i \tag{7.4.1}$$

where $\hat{u}_i$ is the residual term, the sample counterpart of the stochastic disturbance term u_i.

As noted in Chapter 3, the OLS procedure consists in so choosing the values of the unknown parameters that the residual sum of squares (RSS) $\sum \hat{u}_i^2$ is as small as possible. Symbolically,

$$\min \sum \hat{u}_i^2 = \sum (Y_i - \hat{\beta}_1 - \hat{\beta}_2 X_{2i} - \hat{\beta}_3 X_{3i})^2 \tag{7.4.2}$$

where the expression for the RSS is obtained by simple algebraic manipulations of (7.4.1).

The most straightforward procedure to obtain the estimators that will minimize (7.4.2) is to differentiate it with respect to the unknowns, set the resulting expressions to zero, and solve them simultaneously. As shown in Appendix 7A, Section 7A.1, this procedure gives the following *normal equations* [cf. Eqs. (3.1.4) and (3.1.5):

$$\bar{Y} = \hat{\beta}_1 + \hat{\beta}_2 \bar{X}_2 + \hat{\beta}_3 \bar{X}_3 \tag{7.4.3}$$

$$\sum Y_i X_{2i} = \hat{\beta}_1 \sum X_{2i} + \hat{\beta}_2 \sum X_{2i}^2 + \hat{\beta}_3 \sum X_{2i} X_{3i} \tag{7.4.4}$$

$$\sum Y_i X_{3i} = \hat{\beta}_1 \sum X_{3i} + \hat{\beta}_2 \sum X_{2i} X_{3i} + \hat{\beta}_3 \sum X_{3i}^2 \tag{7.4.5}$$

From Eq. (7.4.3) we see at once that

$$\hat{\beta}_1 = \bar{Y} - \hat{\beta}_2 \bar{X}_2 - \hat{\beta}_3 \bar{X}_3 \qquad (7.4.6)$$

which is the OLS estimator of the population intercept β_1.

Following the convention of letting the lowercase letters denote deviations from sample mean values, one can derive the following formulas from the normal equations (7.4.3) to (7.4.5):

$$\hat{\beta}_2 = \frac{(\sum y_i x_{2i})(\sum x_{3i}^2) - (\sum y_i x_{3i})(\sum x_{2i} x_{3i})}{(\sum x_{2i}^2)(\sum x_{3i}^2) - (\sum x_{2i} x_{3i})^2} \qquad (7.4.7)[8]$$

$$\hat{\beta}_3 = \frac{(\sum y_i x_{3i})(\sum x_{2i}^2) - (\sum y_i x_{2i})(\sum x_{2i} x_{3i})}{(\sum x_{2i}^2)(\sum x_{3i}^2) - (\sum x_{2i} x_{3i})^2} \qquad (7.4.8)$$

which give the OLS estimators of the population partial regression coefficients β_2 and β_3, respectively.

In passing note the following: (1) Equations (7.4.7) and (7.4.8) are symmetrical in nature because one can be obtained from the other by interchanging the roles of X_2 and X_3; (2) the denominators of these two equations are identical; and (3) the three-variable case is a natural extension of the two-variable case.

Variances and Standard Errors of OLS Estimators

Having obtained the OLS estimators of the partial regression coefficients, we can derive the variances and standard errors of these estimators in the manner indicated in Appendix 3A.3. As in the two-variable case, we need the standard errors for two main purposes: to establish confidence intervals and to test statistical hypotheses. The relevant formulas are as follows:[9]

$$\text{var}(\hat{\beta}_1) = \left[\frac{1}{n} + \frac{\bar{X}_2^2 \sum x_{3i}^2 + \bar{X}_3^2 \sum x_{2i}^2 - 2\bar{X}_2 \bar{X}_3 \sum x_{2i} x_{3i}}{\sum x_{2i}^2 \sum x_{3i}^2 - (\sum x_{2i} x_{3i})^2} \right] \cdot \sigma^2 \qquad (7.4.9)$$

$$\text{se}(\hat{\beta}_1) = +\sqrt{\text{var}(\hat{\beta}_1)} \qquad (7.4.10)$$

$$\text{var}(\hat{\beta}_2) = \frac{\sum x_{3i}^2}{(\sum x_{2i}^2)(\sum x_{3i}^2) - (\sum x_{2i} x_{3i})^2} \sigma^2 \qquad (7.4.11)$$

or, equivalently,

$$\text{var}(\hat{\beta}_2) = \frac{\sigma^2}{\sum x_{2i}^2 (1 - r_{23}^2)} \qquad (7.4.12)$$

---

[8]This estimator is equal to a_1 of (7.3.5), as shown in App. 7A, Sec. 7A.2.

[9]The derivations of these formulas are easier using matrix notation. Hence the proofs are deferred until Chap. 9.

where r_{23} is the sample coefficient of correlation between X_2 and X_3 as defined in Chapter 3.[10]

$$se(\hat{\beta}_2) = +\sqrt{\text{var}(\hat{\beta}_2)} \qquad (7.4.13)$$

$$\text{var}(\hat{\beta}_3) = \frac{\sum x_{2i}^2}{(\sum x_{2i}^2)(\sum x_{3i}^2) - (\sum x_{2i}x_{3i})^2}\sigma^2 \qquad (7.4.14)$$

or, equivalently,

$$\text{var}(\hat{\beta}_3) = \frac{\sigma^2}{\sum x_{3i}^2(1 - r_{23}^2)} \qquad (7.4.15)$$

$$se(\hat{\beta}_3) = +\sqrt{\text{var}(\hat{\beta}_3)} \qquad (7.4.16)$$

$$\text{cov}(\hat{\beta}_2, \hat{\beta}_3) = \frac{-r_{23}\sigma^2}{(1 - r_{23}^2)\sqrt{x_{2i}^2}\sqrt{x_{3i}^2}} \qquad (7.4.17)$$

In all these formulas σ^2 is the (homoscedastic) variance of the population disturbances u_i.

Following the argument of Appendix 3A, Section 3A.5, the reader can verify that an unbiased estimator of σ^2 is given by

$$\hat{\sigma}^2 = \frac{\sum \hat{u}_i^2}{n - 3} \qquad (7.4.18)$$

Note the similarity between this estimator of σ^2 and its two-variable counterpart [$\hat{\sigma}^2 = (\sum \hat{u}_i^2)/(n - 2)$]. The degrees of freedom are now $(n - 3)$ because in estimating $\sum \hat{u}_i^2$ we must first estimate β_1, β_2, and β_3, which consume 3 df. (The argument is quite general. Thus, in the four-variable case the df will be $n - 4$.)

The estimator $\hat{\sigma}^2$ can be computed from (7.4.18) once the residuals are available, but it can also be obtained more readily by using the following relation (for proof, see Appendix 7A, Section 7A.3):

$$\sum \hat{u}_i^2 = \sum y_i^2 - \hat{\beta}_2 \sum y_i x_{2i} - \hat{\beta}_3 \sum y_i x_{3i} \qquad (7.4.19)$$

which is the three-variable counterpart of the relation given in (3.3.6).

Properties of OLS Estimators

The properties of OLS estimators of the multiple regression model parallel those of the two-variable model. Specifically:

1. The three-variable regression line (surface) passes through the means $\bar{Y}$, $\bar{X}_2$, and $\bar{X}_3$, which is evident from (7.4.3) [cf. Eq. (3.1.7) of the two-variable

---

[10]Using the definition of r given in Chap. 3, we have

$$r_{23}^2 = \frac{(\sum x_{2i}x_{3i})^2}{\sum x_{2i}^2 \sum x_{3i}^2}$$

model]. This property holds generally. Thus in the k-variable linear regression model [a regressand and $(k-1)$ regressors]

$$Y_i = \beta_1 + \beta_2 X_{2i} + \beta_3 X_{3i} + \cdots + \beta_k X_{ki} + u_i \tag{7.4.20}$$

we have

$$\hat{\beta}_1 = \bar{Y} - \beta_2 \bar{X}_2 - \beta_3 \bar{X}_3 - \cdots - \beta_k \bar{X}_k \tag{7.4.21}$$

2. The mean value of the estimated $Y_i (= \hat{Y}_i)$ is equal to the mean value of the actual Y_i, which is easy to prove:

$$
\begin{aligned}
\hat{Y}_i &= \hat{\beta}_1 + \hat{\beta}_2 X_{2i} + \hat{\beta}_3 X_{3i} \\
&= (\bar{Y} - \hat{\beta}_2 \bar{X}_2 - \hat{\beta}_3 \bar{X}_3) + \hat{\beta}_2 X_{2i} + \hat{\beta}_3 X_{3i} \quad \text{(Why?)} \\
&= \bar{Y} + \hat{\beta}_2 (X_{2i} - \bar{X}_2) + \hat{\beta}_3 (X_{3i} - \bar{X}_3) \\
&= \bar{Y} + \hat{\beta}_2 x_{2i} + \hat{\beta}_3 x_{3i}
\end{aligned} \tag{7.4.22}
$$

where as usual small letters indicate values of the variables as deviations from their respective means.

Summing both sides of (7.4.22) over the sample values and dividing through by the sample size n gives $\hat{Y} = \bar{Y}$. (*Note:* $\sum x_{2i} = \sum x_{3i} = 0$. Why?) Notice that by virtue of (7.4.22) we can write

$$\hat{y}_i = \hat{\beta}_2 x_{2i} + \hat{\beta}_3 x_{3i} \tag{7.4.23}$$

where $\hat{y}_i = (\hat{Y}_i - \bar{Y})$.

Therefore, the SRF (7.4.1) can be expressed in the *deviation form* as

$$y_i = \hat{y}_i + \hat{u}_i = \hat{\beta}_2 x_{2i} + \hat{\beta}_3 x_{3i} + \hat{u}_i \tag{7.4.24}$$

3. $\sum \hat{u}_i = \bar{\hat{u}} = 0$, which can be verified from (7.4.24). [*Hint:* Sum both sides of (7.4.24) over the sample values.]

4. The residuals $\hat{u}_i$ are uncorrelated with X_{2i} and X_{3i}, that is, $\sum \hat{u}_i X_{2i} = \sum \hat{u}_i X_{3i} = 0$ (see Appendix 7A.1) for proof).

5. The residuals $\hat{u}_i$ are uncorrelated with $\hat{Y}_i$, that is, $\sum \hat{u}_i \hat{Y}_i = 0$. Why? [*Hint:* Multiply (7.4.23) on both sides by $\hat{u}_i$ and sum over the sample values.]

6. From (7.4.12) and (7.4.15) it is evident that as r_{23}, the correlation coefficient between X_2 and X_3, increases toward 1, the variances of $\hat{\beta}_2$ and $\hat{\beta}_3$ increase for given values of σ^2 and $\sum x_{2i}^2$ or $\sum x_{3i}^2$. In the limit, when $r_{23} = 1$ (i.e., perfect collinearity), these variances become infinite. The implications of this will be explored fully in Chapter 10, but intuitively the reader can see that as r_{23} increases it is going to be increasingly difficult to know what the true values of β_2 and β_3 are. [More on this in the next chapter, but refer to Eq. (7.1.10).]

7. It is also clear from (7.4.12) and (7.4.15) that for given values of r_{23} and $\sum x_{2i}^2$ or $\sum x_{3i}^2$, the variances of the OLS estimators are directly proportional to σ^2, that is, they increase as σ^2 increases. Similarly, for given values of σ^2 and r_{23} the variance of $\hat{\beta}_2$ is inversely proportional to $\sum x_{2i}^2$, that is, the greater the variation in the sample values of X_2, the smaller the variance of $\hat{\beta}_2$ and therefore β_2 can be estimated more precisely. A similar statement can be made about the variance of $\hat{\beta}_3$.

8. Given the assumptions of the classical linear regression model, which are spelled out in Section 7.1, one can prove that the OLS estimators of the partial regression coefficients not only are linear and unbiased but also have minimum variance in the class of all linear unbiased estimators. In short, *they are BLUE*: Put differently, they satisfy the Gauss-Markov theorem. (The proof parallels the two-variable case proved in Appendix 3A, Section 3A.6 and will be presented more compactly using matrix notation in Chapter 9.)

Maximum Likelihood Estimators

We noted in Chapter 4 that under the assumption that u_i, the population disturbances, are normally distributed with zero mean and constant variance σ^2, the maximum likelihood (ML) estimators and the OLS estimators of the regression coefficients of the two-variable model are identical. This equality extends to models containing any number of variables. (For proof, see Appendix 7A, Section 7A.4.) However, this is not true of the estimator of σ^2. It can be shown that the ML estimator of σ^2 is $\sum \hat{u}_i^2/n$ regardless of the number of variables in the model, whereas the OLS estimator of σ^2 is $\sum \hat{u}_i^2/(n-2)$ in the two-variable case, $\sum \hat{u}_i^2/(n-3)$ in the three-variable case, and $\sum \hat{u}_i^2/(n-k)$ in the case of the k-variable model (7.4.20). In short, the OLS estimator of σ^2 takes into account the number of degrees of freedom, whereas the ML estimator does not. Of course, if n is very large, the ML and OLS estimators of σ^2 will tend to be close to each other. (Why?)

7.5 THE MULTIPLE COEFFICIENT OF DETERMINATION R^2 AND THE MULTIPLE COEFFICIENT OF CORRELATION R

In the two-variable case we saw that r^2 as defined in (3.5.5) measures the goodness of fit of the regression equation; that is, it gives the proportion or percentage of the total variation in the dependent variable Y explained by the (single) explanatory variable X. This notation of r^2 can be easily extended to regression models containing more than two variables. Thus, in the three-variable model we would like to know the proportion of the variation in Y explained by the variables X_2 and X_3 jointly. The quantity that gives this information is known as the **multiple coefficient of determination** and is denoted by R^2; conceptually it is akin to r^2.

To derive R^2, we may follow the derivation of r^2 given in Section 3.5. Recall that

$$Y_i = \hat{\beta}_1 + \hat{\beta}_2 X_{2i} + \hat{\beta}_3 X_{3i} + \hat{u}_i$$

$$= \hat{Y}_i + \hat{u}_i \tag{7.5.1}$$

where $\hat{Y}_i$ is the estimated value of Y_i from the fitted regression line and is an estimator of true $E(Y_i \mid X_{2i}, X_{3i})$. Upon shifting to lowercase letters to indicate deviations from the mean values, Eq. (7.5.1) may be written as

$$y_i = \hat{\beta}_2 x_{2i} + \hat{\beta}_3 x_{3i} + \hat{u}_i$$

$$= \hat{y}_i + \hat{u}_i \tag{7.5.2}$$

Squaring (7.5.2) on both sides and summing over the sample values, we obtain

$$\sum y_i^2 = \sum \hat{y}_i^2 + \sum \hat{u}_i^2 + 2\sum \hat{y}_i \hat{u}_i$$
$$= \sum \hat{y}_i^2 + \sum \hat{u}_i^2 \quad \text{(Why?)} \tag{7.5.3}$$

Verbally, Eq. (7.5.3) states that the total sum of squares (TSS) equals the explained sum of squares (ESS) + the residual sum of squares (RSS). Now substituting for $\sum \hat{u}_i^2$ from (7.4.19), we obtain

$$\sum y_i^2 = \sum \hat{y}_i^2 + \sum y_i^2 - \hat{\beta}_2 \sum y_i x_{2i} - \hat{\beta}_3 \sum y_i x_{3i}$$

which, on rearranging, gives

$$\text{ESS} = \sum \hat{y}_i^2 = \hat{\beta}_2 \sum y_i x_{2i} + \hat{\beta}_3 \sum y_i x_{3i} \tag{7.5.4}$$

Now, by definition

$$R^2 = \frac{\text{ESS}}{\text{TSS}}$$
$$= \frac{\hat{\beta}_2 \sum y_i x_{2i} + \hat{\beta}_3 \sum y_i x_{3i}}{\sum y_i^2} \tag{7.5.5}[11]$$

[Cf. (7.5.5) with (3.5.6).]

Since the quantities entering (7.5.5) are generally computed routinely, R^2 can be computed easily. Note that R^2, like r^2, lies between 0 and 1. If it is 1, the fitted regression line explains 100 percent of the variation in Y. On the other hand, if it is 0, the model does not explain any of the variation in Y. Typically, however, R^2 lies between these extreme values. The fit of the model is said to be "better" the closer is R^2 to 1.

Recall that in the two-variable case we defined the quantity r as the coefficient of correlation and indicated that it measures the degree of (linear) association between two variables. The three-or-more-variable analogue of r is the coefficient of **multiple correlation**, denoted by R, and it is a measure of the degree of association between Y and all the explanatory variables jointly. Although r can be positive or negative, R is always taken to be positive. In practice, however, R is of little importance. The more meaningful quantity is R^2.

Before proceeding further, let us establish the following relationship between R^2 and the variance of a partial regression coefficient in the k-variable multiple regression model given in (7.4.20):

$$\text{var}(\hat{\beta}_j) = \frac{\sigma^2}{\sum x_j^2} \left(\frac{1}{1 - R_j^2} \right) \tag{7.5.6}$$

where $\hat{\beta}_j$ is the partial regression coefficient of regressor X_j and R_j^2 is the R^2 in the regression of X_j on the remaining $(k - 2)$ regressors. [*Note:* There are $(k-1)$ regressors in the k-variable regression model.] Although the utility of Eq. (7.5.6) will become apparent in Chapter 10 on multicollinearity, observe that this equation is simply an extension of the formula given in (7.4.12) or (7.4.15) for the three-variable regression model, one regressand and two regressors.

---

[11]Note that R^2 can also be computed as follows: $R^2 = 1 - \sum \hat{u}_i^2 / \sum y_i^2$. Why?

7.6 EXAMPLE 7.1: THE EXPECTATIONS-AUGMENTED PHILLIPS CURVE FOR THE UNITED STATES, 1970–1982

By way of illustrating the ideas introduced thus far in the chapter, consider the following model:

$$Y_t = \beta_1 + \beta_2 X_{2t} + \beta_3 X_{3t} + u_t \qquad (7.6.1)$$

where Y_t = actual rate of inflation (%) at time t, X_{2t} = unemployment rate (%) at time t, and X_{3t} = expected or anticipated inflation rate (%) at time t. This model is known as the *expectations-augmented Phillips curve*.[12]

According to macroeconomic theory β_2 is expected to be negative (why?) and β_3 is expected to be positive (can you see the rationale?); as a matter of fact, theory would have us believe that $\beta_3 = 1$.

As a test of this model, we obtained the data shown in Table 7.1. Based on these data, the OLS method gave the following results.[13]

$$\hat{Y}_t = 7.1933 - 1.3925 X_{2t} + 1.4700 X_{3t}$$
$$\qquad (1.5948) \quad (0.3050) \qquad (0.1758) \qquad (7.6.2)$$
$$R^2 = 0.8766$$

TABLE 7.1
Actual inflation rate $Y(\%)$, unemployment rate $X_2(\%)$, and expected inflation rate $X_3(\%)$; United States, 1970–1982

Year	Y^*	X_2	X_3
1970	5.92	4.9	4.78
1971	4.30	5.9	3.84
1972	3.30	5.6	3.13
1973	6.23	4.9	3.44
1974	10.97	5.6	6.84
1975	9.14	8.5	9.47
1976	5.77	7.7	6.51
1977	6.45	7.1	5.92
1978	7.60	6.1	6.08
1979	11.47	5.8	8.09
1980	13.46	7.1	10.01
1981	10.24	7.6	10.81
1982	5.99	9.7	8.00

Source: Data on Y and X_2 are from various pages of *Business Statistics*, 1982, U.S. Department of Commerce, Bureau of Economic Analysis; data on X_3 are from *Economic Review*, Federal Reserve Bank of Richmond, various issues. I am indebted to Alan Gilbert for collecting the data.
*Percentage change in Consumer Price Index.

---

[12]For a comparatively accessible discussion, see Rudiger Dornbush and Stanley Fischer, *Macroeconomics*, McGraw-Hill, 3d ed., New York, 1984, p. 425.
[13]I am indebted to Alan Gilbert for collecting the data.

where figures in parentheses are the estimated standard errors. The interpretation of this regression is as follows: For the sample period, if both X_2 and X_3 were fixed at zero, the average rate of actual inflation would have been about 7.19 percent. But as noted on several occasions, this interpretation of the intercept is purely mechanical. Very often it has no physical or economic meaning. The partial regression coefficient of -1.3925 means that by holding X_3 (the expected inflation rate) constant the actual inflation rate on the average increased (decreased) by about 1.4 percent for every one unit (here one percentage point) decrease (increase) in the unemployment rate over the period 1970–1982. Likewise, by holding the unemployment rate constant, the coefficient value of 1.4700 implies that over the same time period the actual inflation rate on the average increased by about 1.47 percent for every one percentage point increase in the anticipated or expected rate of inflation. The R^2 value of 0.88 means that the two explanatory variables together account for about 88 percent of the variation in the actual inflation rate, a fairly high amount of explanatory power since the R^2 can at most be one.

In terms of prior expectations, both the explanatory variables have the expected signs. Is the coefficient of the expected inflation variable statistically equal to one? We will answer this question in Chapter 8.

7.7 SIMPLE REGRESSION IN THE CONTEXT OF MULTIPLE REGRESSION: INTRODUCTION TO SPECIFICATION BIAS[14]

Assumption (7.1.6) of the classical linear regression model states that the regression model used in the analysis is correctly specified, that is, there is no specification bias or error (see Chapter 3 for some introductory remarks). Although the topic of specification analysis will be discussed more thoroughly in Chapter 13, the illustrative example given in the preceding section provides an opportunity not only to drive home the importance of assumption (7.1.6) but also to shed additional light on the meaning of partial regression coefficient and provide a somewhat formal introduction to the topic of specification bias.

Assume that (7.6.1) is the "true" model explaining the behavior of the actual rate of inflation in terms of the unemployment rate and the expected rate of inflation. But suppose someone persists in fitting the following two-variable regression model (the original Phillips curve):

$$Y_t = b_1 + b_{12}X_{2t} + \hat{u}_{1t} \tag{7.7.1}$$

where Y_t = actual inflation (%) at time t, X_{2t} = unemployment rate (%) at time t, and $\hat{u}_{1t}$ = residuals. The slope coefficient, b_{12}, gives the effect of a unit change in the unemployment rate on the average rate of actual inflation.

Since (7.6.1) is the "true" model, (7.7.1) would constitute a specification error; here the error consists in *omitting* the variable X_3, the expected rate of inflation, from the model.

---

[14]This section is influenced by Ronald J. Wonnacott and Thomas H. Wonnacott, *Econometrics*, 2d ed., John Wiley, New York, 1979, pp. 95–98.

We know that $\hat{\beta}_2$ of the multiple regression (7.6.1) is an unbiased estimator of true β_2, that is, $E(\hat{\beta}_2) = \beta_2$. (Why?) Will b_{12}, the simple regression coefficient in the regression of Y on X_2 only, also provide an unbiased estimator of β_2? That is, will $E(b_{12}) = \beta_2$? (If this is the case, $b_{12} = \hat{\beta}_2$). In terms of our example, will the coefficient of the unemployment rate variable in (7.7.1) provide an unbiased estimate of its true impact on the actual rate of inflation, knowing that we have omitted X_3, the expected rate of inflation, from the analysis? The answer *in general* is that b_{12} will not be an unbiased estimator of β_2. Also, var(b_{12}) may be a biased estimator of var($\hat{\beta}_2$). As a matter of fact, it can be proved that (see Appendix 7A, Section 7A.5)

$$b_{12} = \beta_2 + \beta_3 b_{32} + \text{error term} \qquad (7.7.2)$$

where b_{32} is the slope coefficient in the regression of X_3 on X_2, namely,[15]

$$X_{3t} = b_2 + b_{32}X_{2t} + \hat{u}_{2t} \qquad (7.7.3)$$

where $\hat{u}_2$ is the residual term. Notice that (7.7.3) is simply the regression of the omitted variable X_3 on X_2.

From (7.7.2) it can be readily verified that

$$E(b_{12}) = \beta_2 + \beta_3 b_{32} \qquad (7.7.4)$$

(*Note:* For a given sample $[b_{32} = (\sum x_{3i}x_{2i}/\sum x_{2i}^2]$ is a known constant.)

As Eq. (7.7.4) shows, so long as $\beta_3 b_{32}$ is nonzero, b_{12} will be a biased estimator of β_2. If $\beta_3 b_{32}$ is positive, b_{12}, on average, will overestimate β_2 (why?), that is, b_{12} is biased upward and if it is negative, b_{12}, on average, will underestimate β_2 (why?), that is, it is biased downward.

What does this all really mean? As (7.7.2) shows, the simple regression coefficient b_{12} not only measures the "direct" or "net" influence of X_2 on Y (i.e., holding the influence of X_3 constant) but also measures the indirect or induced influence on Y via its effect on the omitted variable X_3. In short, b_{12} measures the "gross" effect (direct as well as indirect) of X_2 on Y, whereas $\hat{\beta}_2$ measures only the direct or net effect of X_2 on Y, since the influence of X_3 is held constant when we estimate the multiple regression (7.6.1), as we did in (7.6.2). Verbally, then we have

Gross effect of X_2 on $Y(= b_{12})$
   $= $ direct effect on X_2 on $Y(= \beta_2)$
   $+ $ indirect effect of X_2 on $Y(= \beta_3 b_{32})$ (7.7.5)

In terms of our example, the gross effect of a unit change in the unemployment rate on the actual rate of inflation is equal to its direct influence (i.e., holding the influence of the expected inflation rate constant) plus the indirect effect as a result of the effect it (i.e., the unemployment rate) has on the expected rate of inflation ($= b_{32}$), which itself has some direct effect ($= \beta_3$) on the actual rate of inflation. All this can be seen more clearly in Fig. 7.3; the numbers shown there are from the illustrative example explained shortly.

---

[15]Is this a violation of the "no multicollinearity" assumption? The answer is given in footnote 16.

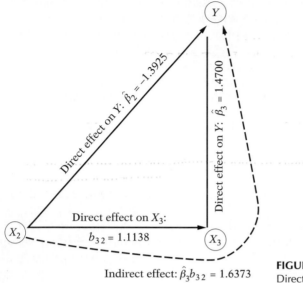

Indirect effect: $\hat{\beta}_3 b_{32} = 1.6373$

FIGURE 7.3
Direct and indirect effects on X_2 on Y.

So much for theory. Let us revert to the Phillips curve example for an illustration.

Using the data given in Table 7.1, we estimate (7.7.1) as follows:

$$\hat{Y}_t = \; 6.1272 \; + \; 0.2448 X_{2t}$$
$$\qquad (4.2853) \quad (0.6304) \qquad\qquad\qquad\qquad (7.7.6)$$
$$t = (1.4298) \quad (0.3885) \qquad\qquad r^2 = 0.0135$$

The striking feature of this equation is that $b_{12} = 0.2448$ not only is positive (a positively sloping Phillips curve?) but is statistically insignificantly different from zero. But from (7.6.2) we observe that $\hat{\beta}_2 = -1.3925$ not only has the correct a priori sign but, as we shall show in Chapter 8, is statistically significantly different from zero. How come? The answer lies in the indirect effect term, or the bias factor, $\beta_3 b_{32}$, given in (7.7.4). From (7.6.2) we know that $\hat{\beta}_3 = 1.4700$. To obtain b_{32}, we run the regression (7.7.3), obtaining the following results:

$$X_{3t} = \; 0.7252 \; + \; 1.1138 X_{2t}$$
$$\qquad (2.7267) \quad (0.4011) \qquad\qquad\qquad\qquad (7.7.7)$$
$$t = (-0.2659) \quad (2.7769) \qquad\qquad r^2 = 0.4120$$

As this equation shows, $b_{32} = 1.1138$ means as X_2 increases by a unit, X_3 on the average increases by about 1.11 units.[16] But if X_3 increases by these units, its effect on Y will be $(1.4700)(1.1138) = \hat{\beta}_3 b_{32} = 1.6373$. Therefore, from (7.7.2)

---

[16]But aren't we supposed, by the assumption of no multicollinearity, to preclude including correlated regressors in our model? The full answer will be given in Chap. 10. Suffice it to note here that the assumption of no multicollinearity pertains to the population regression function and not to the sample regression function; in a given sample we have no control about how the X variables are related, short of carrying out controlled experiments, a rather dim prospect in most social sciences.

we finally have

$$\hat{\beta}_2 + \hat{\beta}_3 b_{32} = -1.3925 + 1.6373$$
$$= 0.2448$$
$$= b_{12} \text{ [see Eq.(7.7.6)]}$$

The moral of the discussion in this section is simply this: If a three-variable regression is called for, do not run a simple or two-variable regression. Or, more generally, if you adopt a particular regression model as the "true" model, do not modify it by omitting one or more variables from it. If you neglect this principle, you are likely to get biased estimates of the parameters. Not only that, you are likely to underestimate the true variance (σ^2) and therefore the estimated standard errors of the regression coefficients. Although we will prove this formally in Chapter 13, you can get a glimpse of this by comparing the results of the regressions (7.6.2) and (7.7.6): The standard error of $\hat{\beta}_2$ is much smaller (in relation to its coefficient) in (7.6.2) than it is (in relation to its coefficient) in (7.7.6). Therefore, the confidence intervals and hypothesis testing based on the (correct) model (7.6.2) are likely to be much more reliable than those based on the mis-specified model (7.7.6).

7.8 R^2 AND THE ADJUSTED R^2

An important property of R^2 is that it is a nondecreasing function of the number of explanatory variables or regressors present in the model; as the number of regressors increases, R^2 almost invariably increases and never decreases. Stated differently, an additional X variable will not decrease R^2. To see this, recall the definition of the coefficient of determination:

$$R^2 = \frac{\text{ESS}}{\text{TSS}}$$

$$= 1 - \frac{\text{RSS}}{\text{TSS}}$$

$$= 1 - \frac{\sum \hat{u}_i^2}{\sum y_i^2} \qquad (7.8.1)$$

Now $\sum y_i^2$ is independent of the number of X variables in the model because it is simply $\sum (Y_i - \bar{Y})^2$. The RSS, $\sum \hat{u}_i^2$, however, depends on the number of regressors present in the model. Intuitively, it is clear that as the number X variables increases, $\sum \hat{u}_i^2$ is likely to decrease (at least it will not increase); hence R^2 as defined in (7.8.1) will increase. In view of this, in comparing two regression models with the *same dependent variable* but differing number of X variables, one should be very wary of choosing the model with the highest R^2.

To compare two R^2 terms, one must take into account the number of X variables present in the model. This can be done readily if we consider an alternative coefficient of determination, which is as follows:

$$\bar{R}^2 = 1 - \frac{\sum \hat{u}_i^2/(n-k)}{\sum y_i^2/(n-1)} \qquad (7.8.2)$$

where k = the number of parameters in the model *including the intercept term*. (In the three-variable regression, $k = 3$. Why?) The R^2 thus defined is known as the **adjusted R^2**, denoted by $\bar{R}^2$. The term *adjusted* means adjusted for the df associated with the sums of squares entering into (7.8.1): $\sum \hat{u}_i^2$ has $n - k$ df in a model involving k parameters, which include the intercept term, and $\sum y_i^2$ has $n - 1$ df. (Why?) For the three-variable case, we know that $\sum \hat{u}_i^2$ has $n - 3$ df.

Equation (7.8.2) can also be written as

$$\bar{R}^2 = 1 - \frac{\hat{\sigma}^2}{S_Y^2} \tag{7.8.3}$$

where $\hat{\sigma}^2$ is the residual variance, an unbiased estimator of true σ^2, and S_Y^2 is the sample variance of Y.

It is easy to see that $\bar{R}^2$ and R^2 are related because, substituting (7.8.1) into (7.8.2), we obtain

$$\bar{R}^2 = 1 - (1 - R^2)\frac{n - 1}{n - k} \tag{7.8.4}$$

It is immediately apparent from Eq. (7.8.4) that (1) for $k > 1$, $\bar{R}^2 < R^2$ which implies that as the number of X variables increases, the adjusted R^2 increases less than the unadjusted R^2; and (2) $\bar{R}^2$ can be negative, although R^2 is necessarily nonnegative.[17] In case $\bar{R}^2$ turns out to be negative in an application, its value is taken as zero. (The reader should verify that for the illustrative example given earlier the $\bar{R}^2$ is 0.8519, which is less than the R^2 value of 0.8766.)

Which R^2 should one use in practice? As Theil notes:

> ...it is good practice to use $\bar{R}^2$ rather than R^2 because R^2 tends to give an overly optimistic picture of the fit of the regression, particularly when the number of explanatory variables is not very small compared with the number of observations.[18]

But Theil's view is not uniformly shared, for he has offered no general theoretical justification for the "superiority" of $\bar{R}^2$. For example, Goldberger argues that the following R^2, call it **modified** R^2, will do just as well:[19]

$$\text{Modified } R^2 = (1 - k/n)R^2 \tag{7.8.5}$$

His advice is to report R^2, n, and k and let the reader decide how to adjust R^2 by allowing for n and k.

Despite this advice, it is the adjusted R^2, as given in (7.8.4), that is reported by most statistical packages along with the conventional R^2. The reader is well advised to treat $\bar{R}^2$ as just another summary statistic.

---

[17]Note, however, that if $R^2 = 1$, $\bar{R}^2 = R^2 = 1$. When $R^2 = 0$, $\bar{R}^2 = (1 - k)/(n - k)$, in which case $\bar{R}^2$ can be negative if $k > 1$.

[18]Henri Theil, *Introduction to Econometrics*, Prentice-Hall, Englewood Cliffs, N.J., 1978, p. 135.

[19]Arthur S. Goldberger, *A Course in Econometrics*, Harvard University Press, Cambridge, Massachusetts, 1991, p. 178. For a more critical view of R^2, see S. Cameron, "Why is the R Squared Adjusted Reported?", *Journal of Quantitative Economics*, vol. 9, no. 1, January 1993, pp. 183–186. He argues that "It [R^2] is NOT a test statistic and there seems to be no clear intuitive justification for its use as a descriptive statistic. Finally, we should be clear that it is not an effective tool for the prevention of data mining" (p. 186).

Besides R^2 and adjusted R^2 as goodness of fit measures, other criteria are often used to judge the adequacy of a regression model. Two of these are **Akaike's Information criterion** and **Amemiya's Prediction criteria**, which are used to select between competing models. We will discuss these criteria when we consider the problem of model selection in greater detail in a later chapter (see Chapter 14).

Comparing Two R^2 Values

It is crucial to note that in comparing two models on the basis of the coefficient of determination, whether adjusted or not, *the sample size n and the dependent variable must be the same*; the explanatory variables may take any form. Thus for the models

$$\ln Y_i = \beta_1 + \beta_2 X_{2i} + \beta_3 X_{3i} + u_i \qquad (7.8.6)$$

$$Y_i = \alpha_1 + \alpha_2 X_{2i} + \alpha_3 X_{3i} + u_i \qquad (7.8.7)$$

the computed R^2 terms cannot be compared. The reason is as follows: By definition, R^2 measures the proportion of the variation in the dependent variable accounted for by the explanatory variable(s). Therefore, in (7.8.6) R^2 measures the proportion of the *variation in* $\ln Y$ explained by X_2 and X_3, whereas in (7.8.7) it measures the proportion of the *variation in* Y, and the two are not the same thing: As noted in Chapter 6, a change in $\ln Y$ gives a relative or proportional change in Y, whereas a change in Y gives an absolute change. Therefore, var $\hat{Y}_i$/var Y_i is not equal to var$(\widehat{\ln Y_i})$/var$(\ln Y_i)$, that is, the two coefficients of determination are not the same.[20]

If we refer to the coffee demand function (3.7.1), which is the linear specification, and (6.4.5), which is the log-linear specification, the two r^2 terms of 0.6628 and 0.7448, respectively, are therefore not directly comparable.[21] How then do we compare the R^2 terms of models like (3.7.1) and (6.4.5)? We show this with our coffee demand example.

---

[20]From the definition of R^2, we know that

$$1 - R^2 = \frac{\text{RSS}}{\text{TSS}} = \frac{\sum \hat{u}_i^2}{\sum (Y_i - \overline{Y})^2}$$

for the linear model and

$$1 - R^2 = \frac{\sum \hat{u}_i^2}{\sum (\ln Y_i - \overline{\ln Y})^2}$$

for the log model. Since the denominators on the right-hand sides of these expressions are different, we cannot compare the two R^2 terms directly.

[21]For the linear specification, the RSS = 0.1491 (the residual sum of squares of coffee consumption), and for the log-linear specification, the RSS = 0.0226 (the residual sum of squares of log of coffee consumption). These residuals are of different orders of magnitude and hence are not directly comparable.

Example 7.2: Coffee Demand Function Revisited

To compare the R^2 values obtained from two models where the dependent variables are not the same, as in models (3.7.1) and (6.4.5), we proceed as follows:

1. Obtain $\widehat{\ln Y}_t$ from model (6.4.5), obtain their antilog values, and then compute R^2 between the antilog of $\widehat{\ln Y}_t$ and Y_t in the manner indicated by Eq. (3.5.14). This R^2 value is comparable with the R^2 value of model (3.7.1).

2. *Alternatively*, we obtain $\widehat{Y}_t$ from (3.7.1), convert them into $(\ln \widehat{Y}_t)$, and finally compute R^2 between $\ln(\widehat{Y}_t)$ and $\ln(Y_t)$ as per equation (3.5.14). This R^2 value is comparable with the R^2 value obtained from (6.4.5).

Suppose we first decide to compare the R^2 value of the linear model (3.7.1) with the R^2 value of the double-log model (6.4.5). From the estimated Y given by (3.7.1) we first obtain $\ln(\widehat{Y}_t)$, then obtain the log of actual Y_t, and then compute r^2 between these two sets of values as per Eq. (3.5.14). Using the data given in Table 7.2, the reader can verify that the R^2 value thus computed is 0.7318, which is directly comparable with the r^2 value of the log-linear model (6.4.5), namely, 0.7448, although the R^2 value obtained from the log-linear model is slightly higher.

On the other hand, if we want to compare the R^2 value of the log-linear model with that obtained from the linear model, we estimate $\widehat{\ln Y}_t$ from (6.4.5), obtain their antilog values, and finally compute R^2 between these antilog values and the actual Y values using formula (3.5.14). The reader can check from the data given in Table 7.2 that this R^2 value is 0.7187, which is higher than the R^2 value of 0.6628 obtained from the linear model (3.7.1).

Using either method, we see that the log-linear model gives a slightly better fit.

TABLE 7.2
Raw data for comparing two R^2 values

Year	Y_t	$\hat{Y}_t$	$\widehat{\ln Y}_t$	Antilog of $\widehat{\ln Y}_t$	$\ln Y_t$	$\ln(\hat{Y}_t)$
	(1)	(2)	(3)	(4)	(5)	(6)
1970	2.57	2.321887	0.843555	2.324616	0.943906	0.842380
1971	2.50	2.336272	0.853611	2.348111	0.916291	0.848557
1972	2.35	2.345863	0.860544	2.364447	0.854415	0.852653
1973	2.30	2.341068	0.857054	2.356209	0.832909	0.850607
1974	2.25	2.326682	0.846863	2.332318	0.810930	0.844443
1975	2.20	2.331477	0.850214	2.340149	0.788457	0.846502
1976	2.11	2.173233	0.757943	2.133882	0.746688	0.776216
1977	1.94	1.823176	0.627279	1.872508	0.662688	0.600580
1978	1.97	2.024579	0.694089	2.001884	0.678034	0.705362
1979	2.06	2.115689	0.731282	2.077742	0.722706	0.749381
1980	2.02	2.130075	0.737688	2.091096	0.703098	0.756157

Notes: Column (1): Actual Y values from Table 3.4
Column (2): Estimated Y values from the linear model (3.7.1)
Column (3): Estimated Y values from the double-log model (6.4.5)
Column (4): Antilog of values in column (3)
Column (5): Log values of Y in column (1)
Column (6): Log values of $\hat{Y}_t$ in column (2)

The "Game" of Maximizing $\bar{R}^2$

In concluding this section, a warning is in order: Sometimes researchers play the game of maximizing $\bar{R}^2$, that is, choosing the model that gives the highest $\bar{R}^2$. But this may be dangerous, for in regression analysis our objective is not to obtain a high $\bar{R}^2$ per se but rather to obtain dependable estimates of the true population regression coefficients and draw statistical inferences about them. In empirical analysis it is not unusual to obtain a very high $\bar{R}^2$ but find that some of the regression coefficients either are statistically insignificant or have signs that are contrary to a priori expectations. Therefore, the researcher should be more concerned about the logical or theoretical relevance of the explanatory variables to the dependent variable and their statistical significance. If in this process we obtain a high $\bar{R}^2$, well and good; on the other hand, if $\bar{R}^2$ is low, it does not mean the model is necessarily bad.[22]

As a matter of fact, Goldberger is very critical about the role of R^2. He has said:

> From our perspective, R^2 has a very modest role in regression analysis, being a measure of the goodness of fit of a sample LS [least-squares] linear regression in a body of data. Nothing in the CR [CLRM] model requires that R^2 be high. Hence a high R^2 is not evidence in favor of the model and a low R^2 is not evidence against it.
>
> In fact the most important thing about R^2 is that it is not important in the CR model. The CR model is concerned with parameters in a population, not with goodness of fit in the sample.... If one insists on a measure of predictive success (or rather failure), then σ^2 might suffice: after all, the parameter σ^2 is the expected squared forecast error that would result if the population CEF [PRF] were used as the predictor. Alternatively, the squared standard error of forecast...at relevant values of x [regressors] may be informative.[23]

7.9 PARTIAL CORRELATION COEFFICIENTS

Explanation of Simple and Partial Correlation Coefficients

In Chapter 3 we introduced the coefficient of correlation r as a measure of the degree of linear association between two variables. For the three-variable regression model we can compute three correlation coefficients: r_{12} (correlation

---

[22]Some authors would like to deemphasize the use of R^2 as a measure of goodness of fit as well as its use for comparing two or more R^2 values. See Christopher H. Achen, *Interpreting and Using Regression*, Sage Publications, Beverly Hills, Calif., 1982, pp. 58–67 and C. Granger and P. Newbold, "R^2 and the Transformation of Regression Variables," *Journal of Econometrics*, vol. 4, 1976, pp. 205–210. Incidentally, the practice of choosing a model on the basis of highest R^2, a kind of data mining, introduces what is known as **pretest bias**, which might destroy some of the properties of OLS estimators of the classical linear regression model. On this topic, the reader may want to consult George G. Judge, Carter R. Hill, William E. Griffiths, Helmut Lütkepohl and Tsoung-Chao Lee, *Introduction to the Theory and Practice of Econometrics*, John Wiley, New York, 1982, Chap. 21.

[23]Arther S. Goldberger, op. cit., pp. 177–178.

between Y and X_2), r_{13} (correlation coefficient between Y and X_3), and r_{23} (correlation coefficient between X_2 and X_3); notice that we are letting the subscript 1 represent Y for notational convenience. These correlation coefficients are called **gross** or **simple correlation coefficients**, or **correlation coefficients of zero order**. These coefficients can be computed by the definition of correlation coefficient given in (3.5.13).

But now consider this question: Does, say, r_{12} in fact measure the "true" degree of (linear) association between Y and X_2 when a third variable X_3 may be associated with both of them? This question is analogous to the following question: Suppose the true regression model is (7.1.1) but we omit from the model the variable X_3 and simply regress Y on X_2, obtaining the slope coefficient of, say, b_{12}. Will this coefficient be equal to the true coefficient β_2 if the model (7.1.1) were estimated to begin with? The answer should be apparent from our discussion in Section 7.7. In general, r_{12} is not likely to reflect the true degree of association between Y and X_2 in the presence of X_3. As a matter of fact, it is likely to give a false impression of the nature of association between Y and X_2, as will be shown shortly. Therefore, what we need is a correlation coefficient that is independent of the influence, if any, of X_3 on X_2 and Y. Such a correlation coefficient can be obtained and is known appropriately as the **partial correlation coefficient**. Conceptually, it is similar to the partial regression coefficient. We define

$r_{12.3}$ = partial correlation coefficient between Y and X_2, holding X_3 constant

$r_{13.2}$ = partial correlation coefficient between Y and X_3, holding X_2 constant

$r_{23.1}$ = partial correlation coefficient between X_2 and X_3, holding Y constant

One way of computing the preceding partial correlation coefficients is as follows: Recall the three-stage procedure discussed in Section 7.3. In the third stage we regressed $\hat{u}_{1i}$ on $\hat{u}_{2i}$, which were purified Y_i and X_{2i}, that is, purified of the linear influence of X_3. Therefore, if we now compute the simple coefficient of correlation between $\hat{u}_{1i}$ and $\hat{u}_{2i}$, we should obtain $r_{12.3}$ because the variable X_3 is now held constant. Symbolically,

$$r_{\hat{u}_1\hat{u}_2} = r_{12.3}$$

$$= \frac{\sum(\hat{u}_{1i} - \bar{\hat{u}}_1)(u_{2i} - \bar{\hat{u}}_2)}{\sqrt{\sum(\hat{u}_{1i} - \text{var}\,\hat{u}_1)^2(\hat{u}_{2i} - \bar{\hat{u}}_2)^2}}$$

$$= \frac{\sum \hat{u}_{1i}\hat{u}_{2i}}{\sqrt{\sum(\hat{u}_{1i}^2 \sum \hat{u}_{2i}^2)}} \tag{7.9.1}$$

where use is made of the fact that $\bar{\hat{u}}_1 = \bar{\hat{u}}_2 = 0$. (Why?)

From the preceding discussion it is clear that the partial correlation between Y and X_2 holding X_3 constant is nothing but the simple (or zero-order) correlation coefficient between residuals from the regression of Y on X_3 and of X_2 on X_3, respectively. The terms $r_{13.2}$ and $r_{23.1}$ are to be interpreted similarly.

In reality, one need not go through the three-stage procedure to compute the partial correlations because they can be easily obtained from the simple, or zero-order, correlation coefficients as follows (for proofs, see the exercises):[24]

$$r_{12.3} = \frac{r_{12} - r_{13}r_{23}}{\sqrt{(1 - r_{13}^2)(1 - r_{23}^2)}} \qquad (7.9.2)$$

$$r_{13.2} = \frac{r_{13} - r_{12}r_{23}}{\sqrt{(1 - r_{12}^2)(1 - r_{23}^2)}} \qquad (7.9.3)$$

$$r_{23.1} = \frac{r_{23} - r_{12}r_{13}}{\sqrt{(1 - r_{12}^2)(1 - r_{13}^2)}} \qquad (7.9.4)$$

The partial correlations given in Eqs. (7.9.2) to (7.9.4) are called **first-order correlation coefficients**. By *order* we mean the number of secondary subscripts. Thus $r_{12.34}$ would be the correlation coefficient of order two, $r_{12.345}$ would be the correlation coefficient of order three, and so on. As noted previously, r_{12}, r_{13}, and so on are called *simple* or *zero-order correlations*. The interpretation of, say, $r_{12.34}$ is that it gives the coefficient of correlation between Y and X_2, holding X_3 and X_4 constant.

Interpretation of Simple and Partial Correlation Coefficients

In the two-variable case, the simple r had a straightforward meaning: It measured the degree of (linear) association (and not causation) between the dependent variable Y and the single explanatory variable X. But once we go beyond the two-variable case, we need to pay careful attention to the interpretation of the simple correlation coefficient. From (7.9.2), for example, we observe the following:

1. Even if $r_{12} = 0, r_{12.3}$ will not be zero unless r_{13} or r_{23} or both are zero.
2. If $r_{12} = 0$ and r_{13} and r_{23} are nonzero and are of the same sign, $r_{12.3}$ will be negative, whereas if they are of the opposite signs, it will be positive. An example will make this point clear. Let $Y = $ crop yield, $X_2 = $ rainfall, and $X_3 = $ temperature. Assume $r_{12} = 0$, that is, no association between crop yield and rainfall. Assume further that r_{13} is positive and r_{23} is negative. Then, as (7.9.2) shows, $r_{12.3}$ will be positive; that is, holding temperature constant, there is a positive association between yield and rainfall. This seemingly paradoxical result, however, is not surprising. Since temperature X_3 affects both yield Y and rainfall X_2, in order to find out the net relationship between crop yield and rainfall, we need to remove the influence of the "nuisance" variable temperature. This example shows how one might be misled by the simple coefficient of correlation.
3. The terms $r_{12.3}$ and r_{12} (and similar comparisons) need not have the same sign.

---

[24]Most computer programs for multiple regression analysis routinely compute the simple correlation coefficients; hence the partial correlation coefficients can be readily computed.

4. In the two-variable case we have seen that r^2 lies between 0 and 1. The same property holds true of the squared partial correlation coefficients. Using this fact, the reader should verify that one can obtain the following expression from (7.9.2):

$$0 \leq r_{12}^2 + r_{13}^2 + r_{23}^2 - 2r_{12}r_{13}r_{23} \leq 1 \qquad (7.9.5)$$

which gives the interrelationships among the three zero-order correlation coefficients. Similar expressions can be derived from Eqs. (7.9.3) and (7.9.4).

5. Suppose that $r_{13} = r_{23} = 0$. Does this mean that r_{12} is also zero? The answer is obvious from (7.9.5). The fact that Y and X_3 and X_2 and X_3 are uncorrelated does not mean that Y and X_2 are uncorrelated.

In passing, note that the expression $r_{12.3}^2$ may be called the **coefficient of partial determination** and may be interpreted as the proportion of the variation in Y not explained by the variable X_3 that has been explained by the inclusion of X_2 into the model (see exercise 7.6). Conceptually it is similar to R^2.

Before moving on, note the following relationships between R^2, simple correlation coefficients, and partial correlation coefficients:

$$R^2 = \frac{r_{12}^2 + r_{13}^2 - 2r_{12}r_{13}r_{23}}{1 - r_{23}^2} \qquad (7.9.6)$$

$$R^2 = r_{12}^2 + (1 - r_{12}^2)r_{13.2}^2 \qquad (7.9.7)$$

$$R^2 = r_{13}^2 + (1 - r_{13}^2)r_{12.3}^2 \qquad (7.9.8)$$

In concluding this section, consider the following: It was stated previously that R^2 will not decrease if an additional explanatory variable is introduced into the model, which can be seen clearly from (7.9.7). This equation states that the proportion of the variation in Y explained by X_2 and X_3 jointly is the sum of two parts: the part explained by X_2 alone ($= r_{12}^2$) and the part not explained by $X_2 (= 1 - r_{12}^2)$ times the proportion that is explained by X_3 after holding the influence of X_2 constant. Now $R^2 > r_{12}^2$ so long as $r_{13.2}^2 > 0$. At worst, $r_{13.2}^2$ will be zero, in which case $R^2 = r_{12}^2$.

7.10   EXAMPLE 7.3: THE COBB-DOUGLAS PRODUCTION FUNCTION: MORE ON FUNCTIONAL FORM

In Section 6.4 we showed how with appropriate transformations we can convert nonlinear relationships into linear ones so that we can work within the framework of the classical linear regression model. The various transformations discussed there in the context of the two-variable case can be easily extended to multiple regression models. We demonstrate transformations in this section by taking up the multivariable extension of the two-variable log-linear model; others can be found in the exercises and in the illustrative examples discussed throughout the rest of this book. The specific example we discuss is the celebrated **Cobb-Douglas production function** of production theory.

The Cobb-Douglas production function, in its stochastic form, may be expressed as

$$Y_i = \beta_1 X_{2i}^{\beta_2} X_{3i}^{\beta_3} e^{u_i} \tag{7.10.1}$$

where Y = output
  X_2 = labor input
  X_3 = capital input
  u = stochastic disturbance term
  e = base of natural logarithm

From Eq. (7.10.1) it is clear that the relationship between output and the two inputs is nonlinear. However, if we log-transform this model, we obtain

$$\begin{aligned} \ln Y_i &= \ln \beta_1 + \beta_2 \ln X_{2i} + \beta_3 \ln X_{3i} + u_i \\ &= \beta_0 + \beta_2 \ln X_{2i} + \beta_3 \ln X_{3i} + u_i \end{aligned} \tag{7.10.2}$$

where $\beta_0 = \ln \beta_1$.

Thus written, the model is linear in the parameters β_0, β_2, and β_3 and is therefore a linear regression model. Notice, though, it is nonlinear in the variables Y and X but linear in the logs of these variables. In short, (7.10.2) is a *log-log, double-log*, or *log-linear model*, the multiple regression counterpart of the two-variable log-linear model (6.4.3).

The properties of the Cobb-Douglas production function are quite well known:

1. β_2 is the (partial) elasticity of output with respect to the labor input, that is, it measures the percentage change in output for, say, a 1 percent change in the labor input, holding the capital input constant (see exercise 7.10).

2. Likewise, β_3 is the (partial) elasticity of output with respect to the capital input, holding the labor input constant.

3. The sum $(\beta_2 + \beta_3)$ gives information about the *returns to scale*, that is, the response of output to a proportionate change in the inputs. If this sum is 1, then there are *constant returns to scale*, that is, doubling the inputs will double the output, tripling the inputs will triple the output, and so on. If the sum is less than 1, there are *decreasing returns to scale*—doubling the inputs will less than double the output. Finally, if the sum is greater than 1, there are *increasing returns to scale*—doubling the inputs will more than double the output.

Before proceeding further, note that whenever you have a log-linear regression model involving any number of variables the coefficient of each of the X variables measures the (partial) elasticity of the dependent variable Y with respect to that variable. Thus, if you have a k-variable log-linear model:

$$\ln Y_i = \beta_0 + \beta_2 \ln X_{2i} + \beta_3 \ln X_{3i} + \cdots + \beta_k \ln X_{ki} + u_i \tag{7.10.3}$$

each of the (partial) regression coefficients, β_2 through β_k, is the (partial) elasticity of Y with respect to variables X_2 through X_k.[25]

---

[25]To see this, differentiate (7.10.3) partially with respect to the log of each X variable. Therefore, $\partial \ln Y / \partial \ln X_2 = (\partial Y/\partial X_2)(X_2/Y) = \beta_2$, which, by definition, is the elasticity of Y with respect to X_2 and $\partial \ln Y / \partial \ln X_3 = (\partial Y/\partial X_3)(X_3/Y) = \beta_3$, which is the elasticity of Y with respect to X_3, and so on.

TABLE 7.3
Real gross product, labor days, and real capital input in the agricultural sector of Taiwan, 1958–1972

Year	Real gross product (millions of NT $)*, Y	Labor days (millions of days), X_2	Real capital input (millions of NT $), X_3
1958	16,607.7	275.5	17,803.7
1959	17,511.3	274.4	18,096.8
1960	20,171.2	269.7	18,271.8
1961	20,932.9	267.0	19,167.3
1962	20,406.0	267.8	19,647.6
1963	20,831.6	275.0	20,803.5
1964	24,806.3	283.0	22,076.6
1965	26,465.8	300.7	23,445.2
1966	27,403.0	307.5	24,939.0
1967	28,628.7	303.7	26,713.7
1968	29,904.5	304.7	29,957.8
1969	27,508.2	298.6	31,585.9
1970	29,035.5	295.5	33,474.5
1971	29,281.5	299.0	34,821.8
1972	31,535.8	288.1	41,794.3

Source: Thomas Pei-Fan Chen. "Economic Growth and Structural Change in Taiwan—1952–1972, A Production Function Approach,"unpublished Ph.D. thesis, Dept. of Economics, Graduate Center, City University of New York, June 1976, Table II.
*New Taiwan dollars.

To illustrate the Cobb-Douglas production function, we obtained the data shown in Table 7.3; these data are for the agricultural sector of Taiwan for 1958–1972.

Assuming that the model (7.10.2) satisfies the assumptions of the classical linear regression model,[26] we obtained the following regression by the OLS method (see Appendix 7A, Section 7A.7 for the computer printout):

$$\widehat{\ln Y_i} = -3.3384 + 1.4988 \ln X_{2i} + 0.4899 \ln X_{3i}$$
$$(2.4495) \quad (0.5398) \quad (0.1020)$$
$$t = (-1.3629) \quad (2.7765) \quad (4.8005)$$
$$R^2 = 0.8890 \qquad \text{df} = 12$$
$$\bar{R}^2 = 0.8705 \tag{7.10.4}$$

From Eq. (7.10.4) we see that in the Taiwanese agricultural sector for the period 1958–1972 the output elasticities of labor and capital were 1.4988 and 0.4899, respectively. In other words, over the period of study, holding the capital input constant, a 1 percent increase in the labor input led on the average to about a 1.5 percent increase in the output. Similarly, holding the labor input constant, a 1 percent increase in the capital input led on the average to about a 0.5 percent increase

---

[26]Notice that in the Cobb-Douglas production function (7.10.1) we have introduced the stochastic error term in a special way so that in the resulting logarithmic transformation it enters in the usual linear form. On this, see Sec. 6.8.

in the output. Adding the two output elasticities, we obtain 1.9887, which gives the value of the returns to scale parameter. As is evident, over the period of the study, the Taiwanese agricultural sector was characterized by increasing returns to scale.[27]

From a purely statistical viewpoint, the estimated regression line fits the data quite well. The R^2 value of 0.8890 means that about 89 percent of the variation in the (log of) output is explained by the (logs of) labor and capital. In Chapter 8, we shall see how the estimated standard errors can be used to test hypotheses about the "true" values of the parameters of the Cobb-Douglas production function for the Taiwanese economy (see exercise 8.15).

7.11 POLYNOMIAL REGRESSION MODELS

We conclude this chapter by considering a class of multiple regression models, the **polynomial regression models**, that have found extensive use in econometric research relating to cost and production functions. In introducing these models, we further extend the range of models to which the classical linear regression model can easily be applied.

To fix the ideas, consider Fig. 7.4, which relates the short-run marginal cost (MC) of production (Y) of a commodity to the level of its output (X). The visually-drawn MC curve in the figure, the textbook U-shaped curve, shows that the relationship between MC and output is nonlinear. If we were to quantify this relationship from the given scatterpoints, how would we go about it? In other words, what type of econometric model would capture first the declining and then the increasing nature of marginal cost?

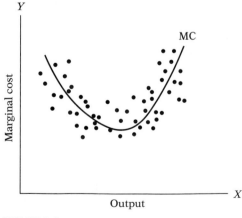

FIGURE 7.4
The U-shaped marginal cost curve.

---

[27]We abstain from the question of the appropriateness of the model from the theoretical viewpoint as well as the question of whether one can measure returns to scale from time series data.

Geometrically, the MC curve depicted in Fig. 7.4 represents a *parabola*. Mathematically, the parabola is represented by the following equation:

$$Y = \beta_0 + \beta_1 X + \beta_2 X^2 \qquad (7.11.1)$$

which is called a *quadratic function*, or more generally, a *second-degree polynomial* in the variable X—the highest power of X represents the degree of the polynomial (if X^3 were added to the preceding function, it would be a third-degree polynomial, and so on).

The stochastic version of (7.11.1) may be written as

$$Y_i = \beta_0 + \beta_1 X_i + \beta_2 X_i^2 + u_i \qquad (7.11.2)$$

which is called a *second-degree polynomial* regression.

The general *kth degree polynomial regression* may be written as

$$Y_i = \beta_0 + \beta_1 X_i + \beta_2 X_i^2 + \cdots + \beta_k X_i^k + u_i \qquad (7.11.3)$$

Notice that in these types of polynomial regressions there is only one explanatory variable on the right-hand side but it appears with various powers, thus making them multiple regression models. Incidentally, note that if X_i is assumed to be fixed or nonstochastic, the powered terms of X_i also become fixed or nonstochastic.

Do these models present any special estimation problems? Since the second-degree polynomial (7.11.2) or the kth degree polynomial (7.11.13) is linear in the parameters, the β's, they can be estimated by the usual OLS or ML methodology. But what about the collinearity problem? Aren't the various X's highly correlated since they are all powers of X? Yes, but remember that terms like X^2, X^3, X^4, etc. are all nonlinear functions of X and hence, strictly speaking, do not violate the no multicollinearity assumption.[28] In short, polynomial regression models can be estimated by the techniques presented in this chapter and present no new estimation problems.

Example 7.4: Estimating the Total Cost Function

As an example of the polynomial regression, consider the data on output and total cost of production of a commodity in the short run given in Table 7.4. What type of regression model will fit these data? For this purpose, let us first draw the scattergram, which is shown in Fig. 7.5.

From this figure it is clear that the relationship between total cost and output resembles the elongated S curve; notice how the total cost curve first increases gradually and then rapidly, as predicted by the celebrated law of *diminishing returns*. This S shape of the total cost curve can be captured by the following cubic or *third-degree polynomial*:

$$Y_i = \beta_0 + \beta_1 X_i + \beta_2 X_i^2 + \beta_3 X_i^3 + u_i \qquad (7.11.4)$$

where Y = total cost and X = output.

---

[28]We will consider this problem again in Chapter 10 where we discuss the whole question of multicollinearity thoroughly.

TABLE 7.4
Total cost (Y) and output (X)

Output	Total cost, $
1	193
2	226
3	240
4	244
5	257
6	260
7	274
8	297
9	350
10	420

Given the data of Table 7.4, we can apply the OLS method to estimate the parameters of (7.11.4). But before we do that, let us find out what economic theory has to say about the short-run cubic cost function (7.11.4). Elementary price theory shows that in the short run the marginal cost (MC) and average cost (AC) curves of production are typically U-shaped—initially, as output increases both MC and AC decline, but after a certain level of output they both turn upward, again the consequence of the law of diminishing return. This can be seen in Fig. 7.6 (see also Fig. 7.4). And since the MC and AC curves are derived from the total cost curve, the U-shaped nature of these curves puts some restrictions on the parameters of the total cost curve (7.11.4). As a matter of fact, it can be shown that the parameters

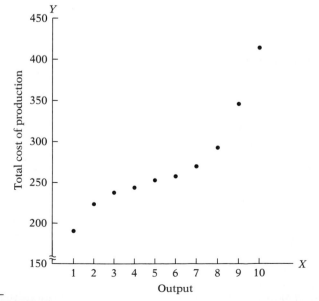

FIGURE 7.5
The total cost curve.

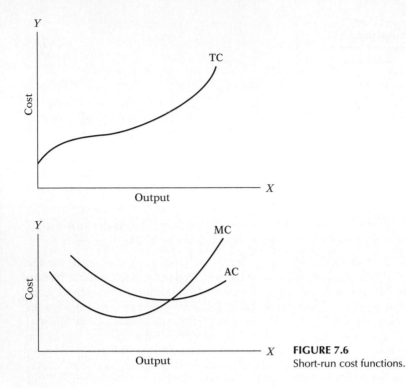

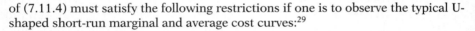

FIGURE 7.6
Short-run cost functions.

of (7.11.4) must satisfy the following restrictions if one is to observe the typical U-shaped short-run marginal and average cost curves:[29]

1. $\beta_0, \beta_1,$ and $\beta_3 > 0$

2. $\beta_2 < 0$ $\qquad\qquad\qquad\qquad$ (7.11.5)

3. $\beta_2^2 < 3\beta_1\beta_3$

All this theoretical discussion might seem a bit tedious. But this knowledge is extremely useful when we examine the empirical results, for if the empirical results do not agree with prior expectations, then, assuming we have not committed a specification error (i.e., chosen the wrong model), we will have to modify our theory or look for a new theory and start the empirical enquiry all over again. But as noted in the **Introduction**, this is the nature of any empirical investigation.

Empirical Results

When the third-degree polynomial regression was fitted to the data of Table 7.4, we obtained the following results:

---

[29]See Alpha C. Chiang, *Fundamental Methods of Mathematical Economics*, 3d ed., McGraw-Hill, New York, 1984, pp. 250–252.

$$\hat{Y}_i = 141.7667 + 63.4776X_i - 12.9615X_i^2 + 0.9396X_i^3$$
$$\qquad (6.3753) \qquad (4.7786) \qquad (0.9857) \qquad (0.0591) \qquad\qquad (7.11.6)$$
$$R^2 = 0.9983$$

(*Note:* The figures in parentheses are the estimated standard errors.) Although we will examine the statistical significance of these results in the next chapter, the reader can verify that they are in conformity with the theoretical expectations listed in (7.11.5). We leave it as an exercise for the reader to interpret the regression (7.11.6).

7.12 SUMMARY AND CONCLUSIONS

1. This chapter introduced the simplest possible multiple linear regression model, namely, the three-variable regression model. It is understood that the term *linear* refers to linearity in the parameters and not necessarily in the variables.

2. Although a three-variable regression model is in many ways an extension of the two-variable model, there are some new concepts involved, such as *partial regression coefficients, partial correlation coefficients, multiple correlation coefficient, adjusted and unadjusted (for degrees of freedom) R^2, multicollinearity*, and *specification bias*.

3. This chapter also considered the functional form of the multiple regression model, such as the *Cobb-Douglas production function* and the *polynomial regression model*.

4. Although R^2 and adjusted R^2 are overall measures of how the chosen model fits a given set of data, their importance should not be overplayed. What is critical is the underlying theoretical expectations about the model in terms of a priori signs of the coefficients of the variables entering the model and, as it is shown in the following chapter, their statistical significance.

5. The results presented in this chapter can be easily generalized to a multiple linear regression model involving any number of regressors. But the algebra becomes very tedious. This tedium can be avoided by resorting to matrix algebra. For the interested reader, the extension to the k-variable regression model using matrix algebra is presented in Chapter 9, which is optional. But the general reader can read the remainder of the text without knowing much of matrix algebra.

EXERCISES

Questions

7.1. Consider the following data:

Y	X_2	X_3
1	1	2
3	2	1
8	3	−3

Based on these data, estimate the following regressions:

$$Y_i = \alpha_1 + \alpha_2 X_{2i} + u_{1i} \tag{1}$$
$$Y_i = \lambda_1 + \lambda_3 X_{3i} + u_{2i} \tag{2}$$
$$Y_i = \beta_1 + \beta_2 X_{2i} + \beta_3 X_{3i} + u_i \tag{3}$$

Note: Estimate only the coefficients and not the standard errors.
(a) Is $\alpha_2 = \beta_2$? Why or why not?
(b) Is $\lambda_3 = \beta_3$? Why or why not?
What important conclusion do you draw from this exercise?

7.2. From the following data estimate the partial regression coefficients, their standard errors, and the adjusted and unadjusted R^2 values:

$$\bar{Y} = 367.693 \qquad \bar{X}_2 = 402.760 \qquad \bar{X}_3 = 8.0$$

$$\sum(Y_i - \bar{Y})^2 = 66042.269 \qquad \sum(X_{2i} - \bar{X}_2)^2 = 84855.096$$

$$\sum(X_{3i} - \bar{X}_3)^2 = 280.000 \qquad \sum(Y_i - \bar{Y})(X_{2i} - \bar{X}_2) = 74778.346$$

$$\sum(Y_i - \bar{Y})(X_{3i} - \bar{X}_3) = 4250.900 \qquad \sum(X_{2i} - \bar{X}_2)(X_{3i} - \bar{X}_3) = 4796.000$$

$$n = 15$$

7.3. Show that (7.9.1) and (7.9.2) are equivalent.

7.4. Prove that $a_0 = 0$ in Eq. (7.3.5). (*Hint:* Recall that the least-squares residuals sum to zero, assuming that the intercept is present in the model.)

7.5. Show that Eq. (7.4.7) can also be expressed as

$$\hat{\beta}_2 = \frac{\sum y_i(x_{2i} - b_{23}x_{3i})}{\sum(x_{2i} - b_{23}x_{3i})^2}$$

$$= \frac{\text{net (of } x_3) \text{ covariation between } y \text{ and } x_2}{\text{net (of } x_3) \text{ variation in } x_2}$$

where b_{23} is the slope coefficient in the regression of X_2 on X_3 as in (7.3.2). (*Hint:* Recall that $b_{23} = \sum x_{2i}x_{3i}/\sum x_{3i}^2$.)

7.6. Show that $r_{12.3}^2 = (R^2 - r_{13}^2)/(1 - r_{13}^2)$ and interpret the equation.

7.7. If the relation $\alpha_1 X_1 + \alpha_2 X_2 + \alpha_3 X_3 = 0$ holds true for all values of X_1, X_2, and X_3, find the values of the three partial correlation coefficients.

7.8. Is it possible to obtain the following from a set of data?
(a) $r_{23} = 0.9, r_{13} = -0.2, r_{12} = 0.8$
(b) $r_{12} = 0.6, r_{23} = -0.9, r_{31} = -0.5$
(c) $r_{21} = 0.01, r_{13} = 0.66, r_{23} = -0.7$

*7.9. If $Z = aX + bY$ and $W = cX - dY$, and if the correlation coefficient between X and Y is r but Z and W are uncorrelated, show that $\sigma_z \sigma_w = (a^2 + b^2)\sigma_x \sigma_y (1 - r^2)^{1/2}$, where $\sigma_z, \sigma_w, \sigma_x$, and σ_y are the standard deviations of the four variables and where a, b, c, and d are constants.

7.10. Show that β_2 and β_3 in (7.10.2) do, in fact, give output elasticities of labor and capital. (This question can be answered without using calculus; just recall the definition of the elasticity coefficient and remember that a change in the logarithm of a variable is a relative change, assuming the changes are rather small.)

---

*Optional

7.11. If $X_3 = a_1X_1 + a_2X_2$, where a_1 and a_2 are constants, show that the three partial correlations are numerically equal to 1, $r_{13.2}$ having the sign of a_1, $r_{23.1}$ the sign of a_2, and $r_{12.3}$ the opposite sign of a_1/a_2.

7.12. In general $R^2 \neq r_{12}^2 + r_{13}^2$, but it is so only if $r_{23} = 0$. Comment and point out the significance of this finding. [*Hint:* See Eq. (7.9.6).]

7.13. Under what condition is $\beta_2 = b_{12}$, where b_{12} is the slope coefficient in the regression of Y on X_2 only as shown in (7.7.1)?

7.14. Consider the following models.*

$$\text{Model A: } Y_t = \alpha_1 + \alpha_2 X_{2t} + \alpha_3 X_{3t} + u_{1t}$$
$$\text{Model B: } (Y_t - X_{2t}) = \beta_1 + \beta_2 X_{2t} + \beta_3 X_{3t} + u_{2t}$$

(a) Will OLS estimates of α_1 and β_1 be the same? Why?
(b) Will OLS estimates of α_3 and β_3 be the same? Why?
(c) What is the relationship between α_2 and β_2?
(d) Can you compare the R^2 terms of the two models? Why or why not?

7.15. Suppose you estimate the consumption function†

$$Y_i = \alpha_1 + \alpha_2 X_i + u_{1i}$$

and the savings function

$$Z_i = \beta_1 + \beta_2 X_i + u_{2i}$$

where Y = consumption, Z = savings, X = income, and $X = Y + Z$, that is, income is equal to consumption plus savings.

(a) What is the relationship, if any, between α_2 and β_2? Show your calculations.
(b) Will the residual sum of squares, RSS, be the same for the two models? Explain.
(c) Can you compare the R^2 terms of the two models? Why or why not?

7.16. Suppose you express the Cobb-Douglas model given in (7.10.1) as follows:

$$Y_i = \beta_1 X_{2i}^{\beta_2} X_{3i}^{\beta_3} u_i$$

If you take the log-transform of this model, you will have $\ln u_i$ as the disturbance term on the right-hand side.

(a) What probabilistic assumptions do you have to make about $\ln u_i$ to be able to apply the classical normal linear regression model (CNLRM)? How would you test this with the data given in Table 7.3?
(b) Do the same assumptions apply to u_i? Why or why not?

7.17. *Regression through the origin.* Consider the following regression through the origin:

$$Y_i = \hat{\beta}_2 X_{2i} + \hat{\beta}_3 X_{3i} + \hat{u}_i$$

(a) How would you go about estimating the unknowns?
(b) Will $\sum \hat{u}_i$ be zero for this model? Why or why not?
(c) Will $\sum \hat{u}_i X_{2i} = \sum \hat{u}_i X_{3i} = 0$ for this model?

---

*Adapted from Wojciech W. Charemza and Derek F. Deadman, *Econometric Practice: General to Specific Modelling, Cointegration and Vector Autogression*, Edward Elgar, Brookfield, Vermont, 1992, p. 18.

†Adapted from Peter Kennedy, *A Guide To Econometrics*, 3d ed., The MIT Press, Cambridge, Massachusetts, 1992, p. 308, Question #9.

(d) When would you use such a model?
(e) Can you generalize your results to the k-variable model?
(*Hint:* Follow the discussion for the two-variable case given in Chapter 6.)

Problems

7.18. The following table gives data on real gross product, labor input, and real capital input in the Taiwanese manufacturing sector.

Year	Real gross product (millions of NT $)*, Y	Labor input (per thousand persons), X_2	Real capital input (millions of NT $), X_3
1958	8911.4	281.5	120,753
1959	10,873.2	284.4	122,242
1960	11,132.5	289.0	125,263
1961	12,086.5	375.8	128,539
1962	12,767.5	375.2	131,427
1963	16,347.1	402.5	134,267
1964	19,542.7	478.0	139,038
1965	21,075.9	553.4	146,450
1966	23,052.0	616.7	153,714
1967	26,128.2	695.7	164,783
1968	29,563.7	790.3	176,864
1969	33,376.6	816.0	188,146
1970	38,354.3	848.4	205,841
1971	46,868.3	873.1	221,748
1972	54,308.0	999.2	239,715

*New Taiwan dollars.

Source: Thomas Pei-Fan Chen, "Economic Growth and Structural Change in Taiwan—1952–1972, A Production Function Approach," unpublished Ph.D. thesis, Dept. of Economics, Graduate Center, City University of New York, June 1976, Table II.

(a) Fit the following models to the preceding data:

$$Y_t = \beta_1 + \beta_2 X_{2t} + \beta_3 X_{3t} + u_t$$
$$\ln Y_t = \alpha_1 + \alpha_2 \ln X_{2t} + \alpha_3 \ln X_{3t} + u_t$$

(b) Which model gives a better fit and why?
(c) For the log-linear model α_2 and α_3 give, respectively, the output elasticities with respect to labor and capital. How would you compute similar elasticities for the linear model?
(d) How would you compare the R^2 values of the two models? (Show your calculations.)
(e) How do the results for the manufacturing sector differ from those for the agricultural sector given in Table 7.3?
(f) What assumptions are made about the disturbance term in the log-linear model? How do you test these assumptions?

7.19. Refer to the U.K. data on percent wage changes and the unemployment rate given in Table 6.4. Using these data, examine whether the following version of the Phillips curve provides a good fit to the U.K. data:

$$Y_i = \beta_1 + \beta_2 X_t + \beta_3 X_t^2 + u_t$$

where Y = annual percentage change in wage rates and X = unemployment rate.

(a) Interpret your results.
(b) What is the rationale for introducing the square of the unemployment rate in the model? A priori, would you expect β_3 to be positive or negative?
(c) Is this model really a multiple regression model since only one explanatory variable, the unemployment rate, enters the model?
(d) How do your results compare with those obtained in (6.6.2) and in exercise 6.20?
(e) Can you compare the R^2 terms of the various models? Why or why not?
(f) Which model would you choose: the quadratic model given here, the reciprocal model given in (6.6.2), or the linear model given in exercise 6.20? What criteria do you use?

7.20. *The demand for roses.** * The following table gives quarterly data on these variables:

Y = quantity of roses sold, dozens
X_2 = average wholesale price of roses, \$/dozen
X_3 = average wholesale price of carnations, \$/dozen
X_4 = average weekly family disposable income, \$/week
X_5 = the trend variable taking values of 1, 2, and so on, for the period 1971–III to 1975–II in the Detroit metropolitan area

Year and quarter	Y	X_2	X_3	X_4	X_5
1971–III	11,484	2.26	3.49	158.11	1
–IV	9,348	2.54	2.85	173.36	2
1972–I	8,429	3.07	4.06	165.26	3
–II	10,079	2.91	3.64	172.92	4
–III	9,240	2.73	3.21	178.46	5
–IV	8,862	2.77	3.66	198.62	6
1973–I	6,216	3.59	3.76	186.28	7
–II	8,253	3.23	3.49	188.98	8
–III	8,038	2.60	3.13	180.49	9
–IV	7,476	2.89	3.20	183.33	10
1974–I	5,911	3.77	3.65	181.87	11
–II	7,950	3.64	3.60	185.00	12
–III	6,134	2.82	2.94	184.00	13
–IV	5,868	2.96	3.12	188.20	14
1975–I	3,160	4.24	3.58	175.67	15
–II	5,872	3.69	3.53	188.00	16

You are asked to consider the following demand functions:

$$Y_t = \alpha_1 + \alpha_2 X_{2t} + \alpha_3 X_{3t} + \alpha_4 X_{4t} + \alpha_5 X_{5t} + u_t$$
$$\ln Y_t = \beta_1 + \beta_2 \ln X_{2t} + \beta_3 \ln X_{3t} + \beta_4 \ln X_{4t} + \beta_5 \ln X_{5t} + u_t$$

(a) Estimate the parameters of the linear model and interpret the results.
(b) Estimate the parameters of the log-linear model and interpret the results.
(c) β_2, β_3, and β_4 give, respectively, the *own-price, cross-price,* and *income elasticities* of demand. What are their a priori signs? Do the results concur with the a priori expectations?

---

*I am indebted to Joe Walsh for collecting these data from a major wholesaler in the Detroit metropolitan area and subsequently processing them.

(d) How would you compute the own-price, cross-price, and income elasticities for the linear model?

(e) Based on your analysis, which model, if either, would you choose and why?

7.21. *Wildcat activity.* Wildcats are wells drilled to find and produce oil and/or gas in an improved area or to find a new reservoir in a field previously found to be productive of oil or gas or to extend the limit of a known oil or gas reservoir. The following table gives data on these variables:*

Y = the number of wildcats drilled

X_2 = price at the wellhead in the previous period
(in constant dollars, 1972 = 100)

X_3 = domestic output

Thousands of wildcats, (Y)	Per barrel price, constant $, ($X_2$)	Domestic output (millions of barrels per day), (X_3)	GNP, constant $ Billions, (X_4)	Time, (X_5)
8.01	4.89	5.52	487.67	1948 = 1
9.06	4.83	5.05	490.59	1949 = 2
10.31	4.68	5.41	533.55	1950 = 3
11.76	4.42	6.16	576.57	1951 = 4
12.43	4.36	6.26	598.62	1952 = 5
13.31	4.55	6.34	621.77	1953 = 6
13.10	4.66	6.81	613.67	1954 = 7
14.94	4.54	7.15	654.80	1955 = 8
16.17	4.44	7.17	668.84	1956 = 9
14.71	4.75	6.71	681.02	1957 = 10
13.20	4.56	7.05	679.53	1958 = 11
13.19	4.29	7.04	720.53	1959 = 12
11.70	4.19	7.18	736.86	1960 = 13
10.99	4.17	7.33	755.34	1961 = 14
10.80	4.11	7.54	799.15	1962 = 15
10.66	4.04	7.61	830.70	1963 = 16
10.75	3.96	7.80	874.29	1964 = 17
9.47	3.85	8.30	925.86	1965 = 18
10.31	3.75	8.81	980.98	1966 = 19
8.88	3.69	8.66	1,007.72	1967 = 20
8.88	3.56	8.78	1,051.83	1968 = 21
9.70	3.56	9.18	1,078.76	1969 = 22
7.69	3.48	9.03	1,075.31	1970 = 23
6.92	3.53	9.00	1,107.48	1971 = 24
7.54	3.39	8.78	1,171.10	1972 = 25
7.47	3.68	8.38	1,234.97	1973 = 26
8.63	5.92	8.01	1,217.81	1974 = 27
9.21	6.03	7.78	1,202.36	1975 = 28
9.23	6.12	7.88	1,271.01	1976 = 29
9.96	6.05	7.88	1,332.67	1977 = 30
10.78	5.89	8.67	1,385.10	1978 = 31

Source: Energy Information Administration, 1978 Report to Congress.

*I am indebted to Raymond Savino for collecting and processing the data.

$$X_4 = \text{GNP constant dollars (1972 = 100)}$$
$$X_5 = \text{trend variable, } 1948 = 1, 1949 = 2, \ldots, 1978 = 31$$

See if the following model fits the data:

$$Y_t = \beta_1 + \beta_2 X_{2t} + \beta_3 \ln X_{3t} + \beta_4 X_{4t} + \beta_5 X_{5t} + u_t$$

(a) Can you offer an a priori rationale to this model?
(b) Assuming the model is acceptable, estimate the parameters of the model and their standard errors, and obtain R^2 and $\bar{R}^2$.
(c) Comment on your results in view of your prior expectations.
(d) What other specification would you suggest to explain wildcat activity? Why?

7.22. *U.S. defense budget outlays, 1962–1981.* In order to explain the U.S. defense budget, you are asked to consider the following model:

$$Y_t = \beta_1 + \beta_2 X_{2t} + \beta_3 X_{3t} + \beta_4 X_{4t} + \beta_5 X_{5t} + u_t$$

where Y_t = defense budget-outlay for year t, \$/billions
X_{2t} = GNP for year t, \$/billions
X_{3t} = U.S. military sales/assistance in year t, \$/billions
X_{4t} = aerospace industry sales, \$/billions
X_{5t} = military conflicts involving more than 100,000 troops. This variable takes a value of 1 when 100,000 or more troops are involved but is equal to zero when that number is under 100,000.

To test this model, you are given the following data:

Year	Defense budget outlays, Y	GNP, X_2	U.S. military sales/ assistance, X_3	Aerospace industry sales, X_4	Conflicts 100,000+, X_5
1962	51.1	560.3	0.6	16.0	0
1963	52.3	590.5	0.9	16.4	0
1964	53.6	632.4	1.1	16.7	0
1965	49.6	684.9	1.4	17.0	1
1966	56.8	749.9	1.6	20.2	1
1967	70.1	793.9	1.0	23.4	1
1968	80.5	865.0	0.8	25.6	1
1969	81.2	931.4	1.5	24.6	1
1970	80.3	992.7	1.0	24.8	1
1971	77.7	1,077.6	1.5	21.7	1
1972	78.3	1,185.9	2.95	21.5	1
1973	74.5	1,326.4	4.8	24.3	0
1974	77.8	1,434.2	10.3	26.8	0
1975	85.6	1,549.2	16.0	29.5	0
1976	89.4	1,718.0	14.7	30.4	0
1977	97.5	1,918.3	8.3	33.3	0
1978	105.2	2,163.9	11.0	38.0	0
1979	117.7	2,417.8	13.0	46.2	0
1980	135.9	2,633.1	15.3	57.6	0
1981	162.1	2,937.7	18.0	68.9	0

Source: The data were collected by Albert Lucchino from various government publications.

(a) Estimate the parameters of this model and their standard errors and obtain R^2, modified R^2, and $\bar{R}^2$.

(b) Comment on the results, taking into account any prior expectations you have about the relationship between Y and the various X variables.

(c) What other variable(s) might you want to include in the model and why?

7.23. *The demand for chicken in the United States, 1960–1982.* To study the per capita consumption of chicken in the United States, you are given the following data:

Year	Y	X₂	X₃	X₄	X₅	X₆
1960	27.8	397.5	42.2	50.7	78.3	65.8
1961	29.9	413.3	38.1	52.0	79.2	66.9
1962	29.8	439.2	40.3	54.0	79.2	67.8
1963	30.8	459.7	39.5	55.3	79.2	69.6
1964	31.2	492.9	37.3	54.7	77.4	68.7
1965	33.3	528.6	38.1	63.7	80.2	73.6
1966	35.6	560.3	39.3	69.8	80.4	76.3
1967	36.4	624.6	37.8	65.9	83.9	77.2
1968	36.7	666.4	38.4	64.5	85.5	78.1
1969	38.4	717.8	40.1	70.0	93.7	84.7
1970	40.4	768.2	38.6	73.2	106.1	93.3
1971	40.3	843.3	39.8	67.8	104.8	89.7
1972	41.8	911.6	39.7	79.1	114.0	100.7
1973	40.4	931.1	52.1	95.4	124.1	113.5
1974	40.7	1,021.5	48.9	94.2	127.6	115.3
1975	40.1	1,165.9	58.3	123.5	142.9	136.7
1976	42.7	1,349.6	57.9	129.9	143.6	139.2
1977	44.1	1,449.4	56.5	117.6	139.2	132.0
1978	46.7	1,575.5	63.7	130.9	165.5	132.1
1979	50.6	1,759.1	61.6	129.8	203.3	154.4
1980	50.1	1,994.2	58.9	128.0	219.6	174.9
1981	51.7	2,258.1	66.4	141.0	221.6	180.8
1982	52.9	2,478.7	70.4	168.2	232.6	189.4

Source: Data on Y are from *Citibase* and on X_2 through X_6 are from the U.S. Department of Agriculture. I am indebted to Robert J. Fisher for collecting the data and for the statistical analysis.

Note: The real prices were obtained by dividing the nominal prices by the Consumer Price Index for food.

where Y = per capita consumption of chickens, lbs

X_2 = real disposable income per capita, \$

X_3 = real retail price of chicken per lb, ¢

X_4 = real retail price of pork per lb, ¢

X_5 = real retail price of beef per lb, ¢

X_6 = composite real price of chicken substitutes per lb, ¢, which is a weighted average of the real retail prices per lb of pork and beef, the weights being the relative consumptions of beef and pork in total beef and pork consumption

Now consider the following demand functions:

$$\ln Y_t = \alpha_1 + \alpha_2 \ln X_{2t} + \alpha_3 \ln X_{3t} + u_t \tag{1}$$

$$\ln Y_t = \gamma_1 + \gamma_2 \ln X_{2t} + \gamma_3 \ln X_{3t} + \gamma_4 \ln X_{4t} + u_t \tag{2}$$

$$\ln Y_t = \lambda_1 + \lambda_2 \ln X_{2t} + \lambda_3 \ln X_{3t} + \lambda_4 \ln X_{5t} + u_t \tag{3}$$

$$\ln Y_t = \theta_1 + \theta_2 \ln X_{2t} + \theta_3 \ln X_{3t} + \theta_4 \ln X_{4t} + \theta_5 \ln X_{5t} + u_t \tag{4}$$

$$\ln Y_t = \beta_1 + \beta_2 \ln X_{2t} + \beta_3 \ln X_{3t} + \beta_4 \ln X_{6t} + u_t \tag{5}$$

From microeconomic theory it is known that the demand for a commodity generally depends on the real income of the consumer, the real price of the commodity, and the real prices of competing or complementary commodities. In view of these considerations, answer the following questions.

(a) Which demand function among the ones given here would you choose, and why?

(b) How would you interpret the coefficients of $\ln X_{2t}$ and $\ln X_{3t}$ in these models?

(c) What is the difference between specifications (2) and (4)?

(d) What problems do you foresee if you adopt specification (4)? (*Hint:* Prices of both pork and beef are included along with the price of chicken.)

(e) Since specification (5) includes the composite price of beef and pork, would you prefer the demand function (5) to the function (4)? Why?

(f) Are pork and/or beef competing or substitute products to chicken? How do you know?

(g) Assume function (5) is the "correct" demand function. Estimate the parameters of this model, obtain their standard errors, and R^2, $\bar{R}^2$, and modified R^2. Interpret your results.

(h) Now suppose you run the "incorrect" model (2). Assess the consequences of this mis-specification by considering the values of γ_2 and γ_3 in relation to β_2 and β_3, respectively. (*Hint:* Pay attention to the discussion in Section 7.7.)

7.24. In a study of turnover in the labor market, James F. Ragan, Jr., obtained the following results for the U.S. economy for the period of 1950–I to 1979–IV.* (Figures in the parentheses are the estimated t statistics.)

$$\widehat{\ln Y_t} = \begin{array}{cccc} 4.47 & - & 0.34 \ln X_{2t} + & 1.22 \ln X_{3t} + & 1.22 \ln X_{4t} \\ (4.28) & (-5.31) & (3.46) & (3.10) \end{array}$$

$$\begin{array}{cc} + & 0.80 \ln X_{5t} - 0.0054 X_{6t} \qquad \bar{R}^2 = 0.5370 \\ (1.10) & (-3.09) \end{array}$$

Note: We will discuss the t statistics in the next chapter.

where Y = quit rate in manufacturing, defined as number of people leaving jobs voluntarily per 100 employees

    X_2 = an instrumental or proxy variable for adult male unemployment rate

    X_3 = percentage of employees younger than 25

    X_4 = N_{t-1}/N_{t-4} = ratio of manufacturing employment in quarter $(t-1)$ to that in quarter $(t-4)$

    X_5 = percentage of women employees

    X_6 = time trend (1950–I = 1)

Source: See Ragan's article, "Turnover in the Labor Market: A Study of Quit and Layoff Rates," *Economic Review*, Federal Reserve Bank of Kansas City, May 1981, pp. 13–22.

(a) Interpret the foregoing results.

(b) Is the observed negative relationship between the logs of Y and X_2 justifiable a priori?

(c) Why is the coefficient of $\ln X_3$ positive?

(d) Since the trend coefficient is negative, there is a secular decline of what percent in the quit rate and why is there such a decline?

(e) Is the $\bar{R}^2$ "too" low?

(f) Can you estimate the standard errors of the regression coefficients from the given data? Why or why not?

7.25. Consider the following simple demand function for money:

$$M_t = \beta_0 Y_t^{\beta_1} r_t^{\beta_2} e^{u_t}$$

where M_t = aggregate real cash balances at time t

Y_t = aggregate real national income at time t

r_t = long-term interest rate

(a) Given the following data, estimate the elasticities of aggregate real cash balances with respect to aggregate real income and the long-term interest rate.

(b) If instead of fitting the preceding demand function you were to fit the model $(M/Y)_t = \alpha r_t^{\beta}$, how would you interpret the results? Show the necessary computations.

Note: To convert the nominal quantities into real quantities, divide the former by the implicit price deflator.

Data on money, national income, and implicit price deflator for India, 1948–1965

Year	Nominal money, crores of rupees	Nominal net income, per 100 crores of rupees	Implicit price deflator	Long-term interest rate,%
1948–1949	1,898.69	86.5	100.00	3.03
1949–1950	1,880.29	90.1	102.15	3.07
1950–1951	1,979.49	95.3	107.68	3.15
1951–1952	1,803.79	99.7	109.56	3.41
1952–1953	1,764.71	98.2	103.81	3.66
1953–1954	1,793.97	104.8	104.49	3.64
1954–1955	1,920.63	96.1	93.48	3.70
1955–1956	2,216.95	99.8	95.23	3.74
1956–1957	2,341.89	113.1	102.82	3.99
1957–1958	2,413.16	113.9	104.59	4.18
1958–1959	2,526.02	126.9	108.15	4.13
1959–1960	2,720.22	129.5	109.19	4.05
1960–1961	2,868.61	141.4	111.19	4.06
1961–1962	3,045.82	148.0	113.32	4.16
1962–1963	3,309.98	154.0	115.70	4.49
1963–1964	3,752.12	172.1	123.19	4.66
1964–1965	4,080.06	200.1	132.96	4.80

Source: Damodar Gujarati, "The Demand for Money in India," *The Journal of Development Studies*, vol. V, no. 1, 1968, pp. 59–64.

Note: One crore rupees is equal to ten million rupees. A rupee is approximately equal to about 3.4 cents at 1994 prices.

7A.1 DERIVATION OF OLS ESTIMATORS GIVEN IN EQUATIONS (7.4.3) TO (7.4.5)

Differentiating the equation

$$\sum \hat{u}_i^2 = \sum (Y_i - \hat{\beta}_1 - \hat{\beta}_2 X_{2i} - \hat{\beta}_3 X_{3i})^2 \qquad (7.4.2)$$

partially with respect to the three unknowns and setting the resulting equations to zero, we obtain

$$\frac{\partial \sum \hat{u}_i^2}{\partial \hat{\beta}_1} = 2 \sum (Y_i - \hat{\beta}_1 - \hat{\beta}_2 X_{2i} - \hat{\beta}_3 X_{3i})(-1) = 0$$

$$\frac{\partial \sum \hat{u}_i^2}{\partial \hat{\beta}_2} = 2 \sum (Y_i - \hat{\beta}_1 - \hat{\beta}_2 X_{2i} - \hat{\beta}_3 X_{3i})(-X_{2i}) = 0$$

$$\frac{\partial \sum \hat{u}_i^2}{\partial \hat{\beta}_3} = 2 \sum (Y_i - \hat{\beta}_1 - \hat{\beta}_2 X_{2i} - \hat{\beta}_3 X_{3i})(-X_{3i}) = 0$$

Simplifying these, we obtain Eqs. (7.4.3) to (7.4.5).

In passing note that the three preceding equations can also be written as

$$\sum \hat{u}_i = 0$$

$$\sum \hat{u}_i X_{2i} = 0 \qquad \text{(Why?)}$$

$$\sum \hat{u}_i X_{3i} = 0$$

which show the properties of the least-squares fit, namely, that the residuals sum to zero and that they are uncorrelated with the explanatory variables X_2 and X_3.

Incidentally, notice that to obtain the OLS estimators of the k-variable linear regression model (7.4.20) we proceed analogously. Thus, we first write

$$\sum \hat{u}_i^2 = \sum (Y_i - \hat{\beta}_1 - \hat{\beta}_2 X_{2i} - \cdots - \hat{\beta}_k X_{ki})^2$$

Differentiating this expression partially with respect to each of the k unknowns, setting the resulting equations equal to zero, and rearranging, we obtain the following k normal equations in the k unknowns:

$$\sum Y_i = n\hat{\beta}_1 + \hat{\beta}_2 \sum X_{2i} + \hat{\beta}_3 \sum X_{3i} + \cdots + \hat{\beta}_k \sum X_{ki}$$

$$\sum Y_i X_{2i} = \hat{\beta}_1 \sum X_{2i} + \hat{\beta}_2 \sum X_{2i}^2 + \hat{\beta}_3 \sum X_{2i} X_{3i} + \cdots + \hat{\beta}_k \sum X_{2i} X_{ki}$$

$$\sum Y_i X_{3i} = \hat{\beta}_1 \sum X_{3i} + \hat{\beta}_2 \sum X_{2i} X_{3i} + \hat{\beta}_3 \sum X_{3i}^2 + \cdots + \hat{\beta}_k \sum X_{3i} X_{ki}$$

$$\cdots\cdots\cdots\cdots\cdots\cdots\cdots\cdots\cdots\cdots\cdots\cdots\cdots\cdots\cdots\cdots$$

$$\sum Y_i X_{ki} = \hat{\beta}_1 \sum X_{ki} + \hat{\beta}_2 \sum X_{2i} X_{ki} + \hat{\beta}_3 \sum X_{3i} X_{ki} + \cdots + \hat{\beta}_k \sum X_{ki}^2$$

Or, switching to small letters, these equations can be expressed as

$$\sum y_i x_{2i} = \hat{\beta}_2 \sum x_{2i}^2 + \hat{\beta}_3 \sum x_{2i} x_{3i} + \cdots + \hat{\beta}_k \sum x_{2i} x_{ki}$$

$$\sum y_i x_{3i} = \hat{\beta}_2 \sum x_{2i} x_{3i} + \hat{\beta}_3 \sum x_{3i}^2 + \cdots + \hat{\beta}_k \sum x_{3i} x_{ki}$$

$$\cdots\cdots\cdots\cdots\cdots\cdots\cdots\cdots\cdots\cdots\cdots\cdots\cdots\cdots$$

$$\sum y_i x_{ki} = \hat{\beta}_2 \sum x_{2i} x_{ki} + \hat{\beta}_3 \sum x_{3i} x_{ki} + \cdots + \hat{\beta}_k \sum x_{ki}^2$$

It should further be noted that the k-variable model also satisfies these equations:

$$\sum \hat{u}_i = 0$$

$$\sum \hat{u}_i X_{2i} = \sum \hat{u}_i X_{3i} = \cdots = \sum \hat{u}_i X_{ki} = 0$$

7A.2   EQUALITY BETWEEN a_1 OF (7.3.5) AND β_2 OF (7.4.7)

The OLS estimators of a_1 is

$$a_1 = \frac{\sum (\hat{u}_{1i} - \bar{\hat{u}}_1)(\hat{u}_{2i} - \bar{\hat{u}}_2)}{\sum (\hat{u}_{2i} - \bar{\hat{u}}_2)^2}$$

$$= \frac{\sum \hat{u}_{1i}\hat{u}_{2i}}{\sum \hat{u}_{2i}^2} \qquad \text{since } \bar{\hat{u}}_1 = \bar{\hat{u}}_2 = 0 \qquad \text{(Why?)}$$

Since $\bar{\hat{u}}_1 = \bar{\hat{u}}_2 = 0$, Eqs. (7.3.1) and (7.3.2) can be written as

$$y_i = b_{13} x_{3i} + \hat{u}_{1i}$$

$$x_{2i} = b_{23} x_{3i} + \hat{u}_{2i}$$

where the small letters, as usual, denote deviations from mean values.

Substituting for $\hat{u}_{1i}$ and $\hat{u}_{2i}$ from the preceding equations into the equation for a_1, we obtain

$$a_i = \frac{\sum (y_i - b_{13} x_{3i})(x_{2i} - b_{23} x_{3i})}{\sum (x_{2i} - b_{23} x_{3i})^2}$$

$$= \frac{\sum y_i x_{2i} - b_{23} \sum y_i x_{3i} - b_{13} \sum x_{2i} x_{3i} + b_{13} b_{23} \sum x_{3i}^2}{\sum x_{2i}^2 + b_{23}^2 \sum x_{3i}^2 - 2 b_{23} \sum x_{2i} x_{3i}}$$

Noting that $b_{23} = \sum x_{2i} x_{3i} / \sum x_{3i}^2$ and $b_{13} = \sum y_i x_{3i} / \sum x_{3i}^2$, the reader can easily verify that a_1 above does, in fact, reduce to β_2 given in (7.4.7).

7A.3   DERIVATION OF EQUATION (7.4.19)

Recall that

$$\hat{u}_i = Y_i - \hat{\beta}_1 - \hat{\beta}_2 X_{2i} - \hat{\beta}_3 X_{3i}$$

which can also be written as

$$\hat{u}_i = y_i - \hat{\beta}_2 x_{2i} - \hat{\beta}_3 x_{3i}$$

where small letters, as usual, indicate deviations from mean values.

Now

$$\sum \hat{u}_i^2 = \sum (\hat{u}_i \hat{u}_i)$$
$$= \sum \hat{u}_i(y_i - \hat{\beta}_2 x_{2i} - \hat{\beta}_3 x_{3i})$$
$$= \sum \hat{u}_i y_i$$

where use is made of the fact that $\sum \hat{u}_i x_{2i} = \sum \hat{u}_i x_{3i} = 0$. (Why?) Also

$$\sum \hat{u}_i y_i = \sum y_i \hat{u}_i = \sum y_i(y_i - \hat{\beta}_2 x_{2i} - \hat{\beta}_3 x_{3i})$$

that is,

$$\sum \hat{u}_i^2 = \sum y_i^2 - \hat{\beta}_2 \sum y_i x_{2i} - \hat{\beta}_3 \sum y_i x_{3i}$$

which is the required result.

7A.4 MAXIMUM LIKELIHOOD ESTIMATION OF THE MULTIPLE REGRESSION MODEL

Extending the ideas introduced in Chapter 4, Appendix 4A, we can write the log-likelihood function for the k-variable linear regression model (7.4.20) as

$$\ln L = -\frac{n}{2} \ln \sigma^2 - \frac{n}{2} \ln(2\pi) - \frac{1}{2} \sum \frac{(Y_i - \beta_1 - \beta_2 X_{2i} - \cdots - \beta_k X_{ki})^2}{\sigma^2}$$

Differentiating this function partially with respect to $\beta_1, \beta_2, \ldots, \beta_k$ and σ^2, we obtain the following $(K + 1)$ equations:

$$\frac{\partial \ln L}{\partial \beta_1} = -\frac{1}{\sigma^2} \sum (Y_i - \beta_1 - \beta_2 X_{2i} - \cdots - \beta_k X_{ki})(-1) \tag{1}$$

$$\frac{\partial \ln L}{\partial \beta_2} = -\frac{1}{\sigma^2} \sum (Y_i - \beta_1 - \beta_2 X_{2i} - \cdots - \beta_k X_{ki})(-X_{2i}) \tag{2}$$

$$\cdots\cdots\cdots\cdots\cdots\cdots\cdots\cdots\cdots\cdots\cdots\cdots\cdots\cdots\cdots\cdots\cdots\cdots\cdots\cdots$$

$$\frac{\partial \ln L}{\partial \beta_k} = -\frac{1}{\sigma^2} \sum (Y_i - \beta_1 - \beta_2 X_{2i} - \cdots - \beta_k X_{ki})(-X_{ki}) \tag{K}$$

$$\frac{\partial \ln L}{\partial \sigma^2} = -\frac{n}{2\sigma^2} + \frac{1}{2\sigma^4} \sum (Y_i - \beta_1 - \beta_2 X_{2i} - \cdots - \beta_k X_{ki})^2 \tag{K+1}$$

Setting these equations equal to zero (the first-order condition for optimization) and letting $\tilde{\beta}_1, \tilde{\beta}_2, \ldots, \tilde{\beta}_k$ and $\tilde{\sigma}^2$ denote the ML estimators, we obtain, after simple algebraic manipulations,

$$\sum Y_i = n\tilde{\beta}_1 + \tilde{\beta}_2 \sum X_{2i} + \cdots + \tilde{\beta}_k \sum X_{ki}$$

$$\sum Y_i X_{2i} = \tilde{\beta}_1 \sum X_{2i} + \tilde{\beta}_2 \sum X_{2i}^2 + \cdots + \tilde{\beta}_k \sum X_{2i} X_{ki}$$

$$\cdots\cdots\cdots\cdots\cdots\cdots\cdots\cdots\cdots\cdots\cdots\cdots\cdots\cdots\cdots\cdots\cdots$$

$$\sum Y_i X_{ki} = \tilde{\beta}_1 \sum X_{ki} + \tilde{\beta}_2 \sum X_{2i} X_{ki} + \cdots + \tilde{\beta}_k \sum X_{ki}^2$$

which are precisely the normal equations of the least-squares theory, as can be seen from Appendix 7A, Section 7A.1. Therefore, the ML estimators, the $\tilde{\beta}$'s, are the same as the OLS estimators, the $\hat{\beta}$'s, given previously. But as noted in Chapter 4, Appendix 4A this equality is not accidental.

Substituting the ML (= OLS) estimators into the $(K + 1)$st equation just given, we obtain, after simplification, the ML estimator of σ^2 as

$$\tilde{\sigma}^2 = \frac{1}{n} \sum (Y_i - \tilde{\beta}_1 - \tilde{\beta}_2 X_{2i} - \cdots - \tilde{\beta}_k X_{ki})^2$$

$$= \frac{1}{n} \sum \hat{u}_i^2$$

As noted in the text, this estimator differs from the OLS estimator $\hat{\sigma}^2 = \sum \hat{u}_i^2/(n - k)$. And since the latter is an unbiased estimator of σ^2, this conclusion implies that the ML estimator $\tilde{\sigma}^2$ is a biased estimator. But, as can be readily verified, asymptotically, $\tilde{\sigma}^2$ is unbiased too.

7A.5   THE PROOF THAT $E(b_{12}) = \beta_2 + \beta_3 b_{32}$ (EQUATION 7.7.4)

In the deviation form the three-variable population regression model can be written as

$$y_i = \beta_2 x_{2i} + \beta_3 x_{3i} + (u_i - \bar{u}) \tag{1}$$

First multiplying by x_2 and then by x_3, the usual normal equations are

$$\sum y_i x_{2i} = \beta_2 \sum x_{2i}^2 + \beta_3 \sum x_{2i} x_{3i} + \sum x_{2i}(u_i - \bar{u}) \tag{2}$$

$$\sum y_i x_{3i} = \beta_2 \sum x_{2i} x_{3i} + \beta_3 \sum x_{3i}^2 + \sum x_{3i}(u_i - \bar{u}) \tag{3}$$

Dividing (2) by $\sum x_{2i}^2$ on both sides, we obtain

$$\frac{\sum y_i x_{2i}}{\sum x_{2i}^2} = \beta_2 + \beta_3 \frac{\sum x_{2i} x_{3i}}{\sum x_{2i}^2} + \frac{\sum x_{2i}(u_i - \bar{u})}{\sum x_{2i}^2} \tag{4}$$

Now recalling that

$$b_{12} = \frac{\sum y_i x_{2i}}{\sum x_{2i}^2}$$

$$b_{32} = \frac{\sum x_{2i} x_{3i}}{\sum x_{2i}^2}$$

Eq (4) can be written as

$$b_{12} = \beta_2 + \beta_3 b_{32} + \frac{\sum x_{2i}(u_i - \bar{u})}{\sum x_{2i}^2} \tag{5}$$

Taking the expected value of (5) on both sides, we finally obtain

$$E(b_{12}) = \beta_2 + \beta_3 b_{32} \tag{6}$$

where use is made of the facts that (a) for a given sample, b_{32} is a known fixed quantity, (b) β_2 and β_3 are constants, and (c) u_i is uncorrelated with X_{2i} (as well as X_{3i}).

Not only is b_{12} biased, but its variance is also likely to be biased. This fact can be proved as follows. By definition,

$$\text{var}(b_{12}) = E[b_{12} - E(b_{12})]^2 \tag{7}$$

Substituting (5) and (6) into (7) and simplifying, we can show that

$$\text{var}(b_{12}) = \frac{\sigma^2}{\sum x_{2i}^2} \tag{8}$$

whereas from (7.4.12) we know that

$$\text{var}(\hat{\beta}_2) = \frac{\sigma^2}{\sum x_{2i}^2(1 - r_{23}^2)} \tag{7.4.12}$$

Obviously, (8) and (7.4.12) are not the same. Note an interesting finding, though. Although b_{12} is a biased estimator, its variance could be smaller than the variance of $\hat{\beta}_2$ *if the estimated* σ^2 in the two models is not vastly different. In that case the variance of b_{12} could be much smaller than that of $\hat{\beta}_2$ if r_{23}^2 is high (why?). Of course, it is quite possible that the estimate of σ^2 in the mis-specified model could be larger than that obtained from the correctly specified model, in which case the variance of b_{12} may not necessarily be smaller than that of $\hat{\beta}_2$.

7A.6   SAS OUTPUT OF THE EXPECTATIONS-AUGMENTED PHILLIPS CURVE (7.6.2)

DEP VARIABLE: Y

SOURCE	DF	SUM OF SQUARES	MEAN SQUARE	F VALUE	PROB > F
MODEL	2	97.334119	48.667060	35.515	0.0001
ERROR	10	13.703158	1.370816		
C TOTAL	12	111.037			

ROOT MSE		1.170605	R-SQUARE	0.8766
DEP MEAN		7.756923	ADJ R-SQ	0.8519
C.V.		15.0911		

VARIABLE	DF	PARAMETER ESTIMATE	STANDARD ERROR	T FOR H0: PARAMETER = 0	PROB > |T|
INTERCEP	1	7.193357	1.594789	4.511	0.0011
X2	1	−1.392472	0.305018	−4.565	0.0010
X3	1	1.470032	0.175736	8.363	0.0001

COVARIANCE OF ESTIMATES

COVB	INTERCEP	X2	X3
INTERCEP	2.543353	−0.388917	0.02241163
X2	−0.388917	0.09303593	−0.0344189
X3	0.02241163	−0.0344189	0.03090064

CBS	Y	X2	X3	YHAT	YRESID
1	5.92	4.9	4.78	7.3970	−1.4770
2	4.30	5.9	3.84	4.6227	−0.3227
3	3.30	5.6	3.13	3.9967	−0.6967
4	6.23	4.9	3.44	5.4272	0.8028
5	10.97	5.6	6.84	9.4505	1.5195
6	9.14	8.5	9.47	9.2785	−0.1385
7	5.77	7.7	6.51	6.0412	−0.2712
8	6.45	7.1	5.92	6.0094	0.4406
9	7.60	6.1	6.08	7.6371	−0.0371
10	11.47	5.8	8.09	11.0096	0.4604
11	13.46	7.1	10.01	12.0218	1.4382
12	10.24	7.6	10.81	12.5016	−2.2616
13	5.99	9.7	8.00	5.4466	0.5434

DURBIN-WATSON d	2.225
1ST ORDER AUTOCORRELATION	−0.203

Notes: The numbers under the heading **PROB**> |T| represent p values.
See Chapter 12 for a discussion of the Durbin-Watson d statistic and of first order autocorrelation.

7A.7   SAS OUTPUT OF THE COBB-DOUGLAS PRODUCTION FUNCTION (7.10.4)

DEP VARIABLE: Y1

SOURCE	DF	SUM OF SQUARES	MEAN SQUARE	F VALUE	PROB > F
MODEL	2	0.538038	0.269019	48.069	0.0001
ERROR	12	0.067153	0.005596531		
C TOTAL	14	0.605196			

ROOT MSE	0.074810	R-SQUARE	0.8890	
DEP MEAN	10.096535	ADJ R-SQ	0.8705	
C.V.	0.7409469			

VARIABLE	DF	PARAMETER ESTIMATE	STANDARD ERROR	T FOR H0: PARAMETER = 0	PROB > |T|
INTERCEP	1	−3.338455	2.449508	−1.363	0.1979
Y2	1	1.498767	0.539803	2.777	0.0168
Y3	1	0.489858	0.102043	4.800	0.0004

COVARIANCE OF ESTIMATES

COVB	INTERCEP	Y2	Y3
INTERCEP	6.000091	−1.26056	0.1121951
Y2	−1.26056	0.2913868	−0.0384272
Y3	0.01121951	−0.0384272	0.01041288

Y	X2	X3	Y1	Y2	Y3	Y1HAT	Y1RESID
16607.7	275.5	17803.7	9.7176	5.61859	9.7872	9.8768	−0.15920
17511.3	274.4	18096.8	9.7706	5.61459	9.8035	9.8788	−0.10822
20171.2	269.7	18271.8	9.9120	5.59731	9.8131	9.8576	0.05437
20932.9	267.0	19167.3	9.9491	5.58725	9.8610	9.8660	0.08307
20406.0	267.8	19647.6	9.9236	5.59024	9.8857	9.8826	0.04097
20831.6	275.0	20803.5	9.9442	5.61677	9.9429	9.9504	−0.00615
24806.3	283.0	22076.6	10.1189	5.64545	10.0023	10.0225	0.09640
26465.8	300.7	23445.2	10.1836	5.70611	10.0624	10.1428	0.04077
27403.0	307.5	24939.0	10.2184	5.72848	10.1242	10.2066	0.01180
28628.7	303.7	26713.7	10.2622	5.71604	10.1929	10.2217	0.04051
29904.5	304.7	29957.8	10.3058	5.71933	10.3075	10.2827	0.02304
27508.2	298.6	31585.9	10.2222	5.69910	10.3605	10.2783	−0.05610
29035.5	295.5	33474.5	10.2763	5.68867	10.4185	10.2911	−0.01487
29281.5	299.0	34821.8	10.2847	5.70044	10.4580	10.3281	−0.04341
31535.8	288.1	41794.3	10.3589	5.66331	10.6405	10.3619	−0.00299

COLLINEARITY DIAGNOSTICS   VARIANCE PROPORTIONS

NUMBER	CONDITION EIGENVALUE	PORTION INDEX	PORTION INTERCEP	PORTION Y2	Y3
1	3.000	1.000	0.0000	0.0000	0.0000
2	.000375451	89.383	0.0491	0.0069	0.5959
3	.000024219	351.925	0.9509	0.0031	0.4040

DURBIN-WATSON *d*		0.891
1ST ORDER AUTOCORRELATION		0.366

Notes: Y1 = ln Y; Y2 = ln X2; Y3 = ln X3. The numbers under the heading **PROB**> \|T\| represent *p* values. See Chapter 10 for a discussion of collinearity diagnostics.

CHAPTER
8

MULTIPLE REGRESSION ANALYSIS: THE PROBLEM OF INFERENCE

This chapter, a continuation of Chapter 5, extends the ideas of interval estimation and hypothesis testing developed there to models involving three or more variables. Although in many ways the concepts developed in Chapter 5 can be applied straightforwardly to the multiple regression model, a few additional features are unique to such models, and it is these features that will receive more attention in this chapter.

8.1 THE NORMALITY ASSUMPTION ONCE AGAIN

We know by now that if our sole objective is point estimation of the parameters of the regression models, the method of ordinary least squares (OLS), which does not make any assumption about the probability distribution of the disturbances u_i, will suffice. But if our objective is estimation as well as inference, then, as argued in Chapters 4 and 5, we need to assume that the u_i follow some probability distribution.

For reasons already clearly spelled out, we assumed that the u_i follow the normal distribution with zero mean and constant variance σ^2. We continue to make the same assumption for multiple regression models. With the normality assumption and following the discussion of Chapters 4 and 7, we find that the OLS estimators of the partial regression coefficients, which are identical with the maximum likelihood (ML) estimators, are best linear unbiased estimators (BLUE).[1] Moreover, the estimators $\hat{\beta}_2$, $\hat{\beta}_3$, and $\hat{\beta}_1$ are themselves normally distributed with means equal to true β_2, β_3, and β_1 and the variances given in Chapter 7. Furthermore, $(n - 3)\hat{\sigma}^2/\sigma^2$ follows the χ^2 distribution with $n - 3$ df, and the three OLS estimators are distributed independently of $\hat{\sigma}^2$. The proofs follow the two-variable case discussed in Appendix 3. As a result and following Chapter 5, one can show that, upon replacing σ^2 by its unbiased estimator $\hat{\sigma}^2$ in the computation of the standard errors, each of the variables then

$$t = \frac{\hat{\beta}_1 - \beta_1}{\text{se}(\hat{\beta}_1)} \tag{8.1.1}$$

$$t = \frac{\hat{\beta}_2 - \beta_2}{\text{se}(\hat{\beta}_2)} \tag{8.1.2}$$

$$t = \frac{\hat{\beta}_3 - \beta_3}{\text{se}(\hat{\beta}_3)} \tag{8.1.3}$$

follows the t distribution with $n - 3$ df.

Note that the df are now $n - 3$ because in computing $\sum \hat{u}_i^2$ and hence $\hat{\sigma}^2$ we first need to estimate the three partial regression coefficients, which therefore put three restrictions on the residual sum of squares (RSS) (following this logic in the four-variable case there will be $n - 4$ df, and so on). Therefore, the t distribution can be used to establish confidence intervals as well as test statistical hypotheses about the true population partial regression coefficients. Similarly, the χ^2 distribution can be used to test hypotheses about the true σ^2. To demonstrate the actual mechanics, we use the following illustrative example.

8.2 EXAMPLE 8.1: U.S. PERSONAL CONSUMPTION AND PERSONAL DISPOSAL INCOME RELATION, 1956–1970

Suppose that we want to study the behavior of personal consumption expenditure in the United States over the past several years. To this end, we use the following simple model:

$$E(Y \mid X_2, X_3) = \beta_1 + \beta_2 X_{2i} + \beta_3 X_{3i} \tag{8.2.1}$$

where Y = personal consumption expenditure (PCE)
X_2 = personal disposable (after-tax) income (PDI)
X_3 = time measured in years

---

[1] With the normality assumption, the OLS estimators $\hat{\beta}_2$, $\hat{\beta}_3$, and $\hat{\beta}_1$ are minimum-variance estimators in the entire class of unbiased estimators, whether linear or not. In short, they are BUE (best unbiased estimator). See C. R. Rao, *Linear Statistical Inference and Its Applications*, John Wiley & Sons, New York, 1965, p. 258.

Equation (8.2.1) postulates that PCE is linearly related to PDI and time or the **trend variable.** In most multiple regression analyses involving time-series data it is a common practice to introduce the time or trend variable in addition to several other explanatory variables for the following reasons.

1. Our interest may be simply to find out how the dependent variable behaves over time. For example, charts are often drawn showing, say, the behavior of GNP, employment, unemployment, stock prices, etc. over several time periods. A look at such charts can reveal whether the general movement of the time series under consideration is upward (upward trend), downward (downward trend), or trendless (i.e., no discernible pattern). In such an analysis we may not be interested in the causes behind the upward or downward trend; our objective may be simply to describe the data over time.

2. Many a time the trend variable is a surrogate for a basic variable affecting Y. But this basic variable may not be directly observable or, if observable, data on it may not be available or may be difficult to obtain. For instance, in production theory technology is one such variable. We may feel the impact of technology, but we may not know how to measure it. Therefore, it may be "convenient" to assume that technology is some function of the time measured chronologically. In some situations it may be believed that a measurable variable affecting Y is so closely related to time that it is easier (costwise, at least) to introduce the time variable itself rather than the basic variable. For example, in (8.2.1), time X_3 may very well represent population. The aggregate PCE increases as population increases, and population may very well have some (linear) relationship with time.

3. Another reason for introducing the trend variable is to avoid the problem of **spurious correlation**. Data involving economic time series, such as PCE and PDI in regression (8.2.1), often tend to move in the same direction, reflecting an upward or downward trend. Therefore, if one were to regress PCE on PDI and obtain a high R^2 value, this high value may not reflect the true association between PCE and PDI; it may simply reflect the common trend present in them. To avoid such a spurious association between economic time series, one may proceed in either of two ways: Assuming that the time series exhibit a linear trend, one may introduce the time, or trend, variable explicitly into the model, as in Eq. (8.2.1).[2] As a result, β_2 in (8.2.1) now reflects the true association between PCE and PDI, that is, association net of the (linear) time effect (recall the definition of the partial regression coefficient).

   Alternatively, one can **detrend** Y (PCE) and X_2 (PDI) and run the regression on **detrended** Y and X_2. Assuming again a linear time trend, the detrending can be effected by the three-stage procedure discussed in Chapter 7. First we regress Y on X_3 (time) and obtain the residuals from this regression, say, $\hat{u}_{1t}$. Second, regress X_2 on X_3 and obtain the residuals from this regression, say $\hat{u}_{2t}$. Finally, regress $\hat{u}_{1t}$ on $\hat{u}_{2t}$, which are both free of the (linear) influence of time. The slope coefficient in this regression will reflect the true association between Y and X_2 and should therefore equal β_2 (see exercise 8.7). Computationally, the former method is more economical than the latter.

---

[2]The procedure is quite general. If a time series exhibits a quadratic trend, we introduce X_3^2 in (8.2.1), where X_3 is time.

4. *A cautionary note:* The procedure just described to detrend a time series, although common in applied work, has recently come under critical scrutiny by the theoreticians of time series analysis.[3] As we will discuss in the chapters on time series analysis, the detrending procedure just described in (3) may be appropriate if a time series exhibits a **deterministic trend** and not a **stochastic (or variable) trend**. In those chapters we will outline the methods used to determine whether a particular time series exhibits a deterministic or a stochastic trend.

As a test of model (8.2.1), we obtained the data in Table 8.1. The estimated regression line is as follows:

$$\hat{Y}_i = 53.1603 + 0.7266X_{2i} + 2.7363X_{3i}$$
$$(13.0261) \quad (0.0487) \quad (0.8486)$$

$$t = (4.0811) \quad (14.9060) \quad (3.2246)$$

$$p \text{ value} = (0.0008) \quad (0.000)^* \quad (0.0036) \tag{8.2.2}$$

$$\text{df} = 12 \quad \begin{matrix} R^2 = 0.9988 \\ \bar{R}^2 = 0.9986 \end{matrix} \quad F_{2,12} = 5128.88$$

* Denotes very small value.

TABLE 8.1
Personal consumption expenditure and personal disposable income in the United States, 1956–1970, billions of 1958 dollars

PCE, Y	PDI, X_2	Time, X_3
281.4	309.3	1956 = 1
288.1	316.1	1957 = 2
290.0	318.8	1958 = 3
307.3	333.0	1959 = 4
316.1	340.3	1960 = 5
322.5	350.5	1961 = 6
338.4	367.2	1962 = 7
353.3	381.2	1963 = 8
373.7	408.1	1964 = 9
397.7	434.8	1965 = 10
418.1	458.9	1966 = 11
430.1	477.5	1967 = 12
452.7	499.0	1968 = 13
469.1	513.5	1969 = 14
476.9	533.2	1970 = 15

Source: Survey of Current Business, U.S. Department of Commerce, various issues.

---

[3]As noted in Chapter 1, empirical analysis based on time series data implicitly assumes that the underlying time series is stationary. Detrending is one of the procedures used to make a time series stationary. As we will show in Chapter 21, the detrending procedure described previously can be recommended if the underlying time series has a **deterministic trend**.

where, following the format of equation (5.11.1), the figures in the first set of parentheses are the estimated standard errors, those in the second set are the t values under the null hypothesis that the relevant population coefficient has a value of zero, and those in the third are the estimated p values.

The interpretation of Eq. (8.2.2) is as follows: If X_2 and X_3 are both fixed at zero, the average or mean value of the personal consumption expenditure (perhaps reflecting the influence of all the omitted variables) is estimated at approximately 53.16 billions of 1958 dollars. As cautioned before, in most cases the intercept term has no economic meaning. The partial regression coefficient 0.7266 means that, holding all other variables constant (X_3 in the present case), as personal income increases, say, by \$1, the mean consumption expenditure increases by about 73 cents. By the same token, if X_2 is held constant, the mean personal consumption expenditure is estimated to increase at the rate of 2.7 billions of dollars per year. The R^2 value of 0.9988 shows that the two explanatory variables explain about 99.9 percent of the variation in personal consumption expenditure in the United States over the period 1956–1970. The adjusted R^2 shows that, after taking into account the df, X_2 and X_3 still explain about 99.8 percent of the variation in Y.

8.3   HYPOTHESIS TESTING IN MULTIPLE REGRESSION: GENERAL COMMENTS

Once we go beyond the simple world of the two-variable linear regression model, hypothesis testing assumes several interesting forms, such as the following:

1. Testing hypotheses about an individual partial regression coefficient (Section 8.4)
2. Testing the overall significance of the estimated multiple regression model, that is, finding out if all the partial slope coefficients are simultaneously equal to zero (Section 8.5)
3. Testing that two or more coefficients are equal to one another (Section 8.6)
4. Testing that the partial regression coefficients satisfy certain restrictions (Section 8.7)
5. Testing the stability of the estimated regression model over time or in different cross-sectional units (Section 8.8)
6. Testing the functional form of regression models (Section 8.9)

Since testing of one or more of these types occurs so commonly in empirical analysis, we devote a section to each type.

8.4   HYPOTHESIS TESTING ABOUT INDIVIDUAL PARTIAL REGRESSION COEFFICIENTS

If we invoke the assumption that $u_i \sim N(0, \sigma^2)$, then, as noted in Section 8.1, we can use the t test to test a hypothesis about any *individual* partial regression coefficient. To illustrate the mechanics, consider our numerical example. Let us postulate that

$$H_0: \beta_2 = 0 \quad \text{and} \quad H_1: \beta_2 \neq 0$$

The null hypothesis states that, holding X_3 constant, personal disposable income has no (linear) influence on personal consumption expenditure.[4] To test the null hypothesis, we use the t test given in (8.1.2). Following Chapter 5, if the computed t value exceeds the critical t value at the chosen level of significance, we may reject the hypothesis; otherwise, we may not reject it. For our example, using (8.1.2) and noting that $\beta_2 = 0$ under the null hypothesis, we obtain

$$t = \frac{0.7266}{0.0487} = 14.9060 \tag{8.4.1}$$

If we assume $\alpha = 0.05$, $t_{\alpha/2} = 2.179$ for 12 df. [*Note:* We are using the two-tail t test. (Why?)] Since the computed t value of 14.9060 far exceeds the critical t value of 2.179, we may reject the null hypothesis and say that $\hat{\beta}_2$ is statistically significant, that is, significantly different from zero. As a matter of fact, as (8.2.2) shows, the p value of obtaining a t value of as much as or greater than 14.9060 is extremely small. Graphically, the situation is shown in Fig. 8.1.

In Chapter 5 we saw the intimate connection between hypothesis testing and confidence-interval estimation. For our example, the 95 percent confidence interval for β_2 is

$$\hat{\beta}_2 - t_{\alpha/2}\,\text{se}(\hat{\beta}_2) \leq \beta_2 \leq \hat{\beta}_2 + t_{\alpha/2}\,\text{se}(\hat{\beta}_2)$$

which in our case becomes

$$0.7266 - 2.179(0.0487) \leq \beta_2 \leq 0.7266 + 2.179(0.0487)$$

that is,

$$0.6205 \leq \beta_2 \leq 0.8327 \tag{8.4.2}$$

that is, β_2 lies between 0.6205 and 0.8327 with a 95 percent confidence coefficient. Thus, if 100 samples of size 15 are selected and 100 confidence intervals like $\hat{\beta}_2 \pm t_{\alpha/2}\,\text{se}(\hat{\beta}_2)$ are constructed, we expect 95 of them to contain the true

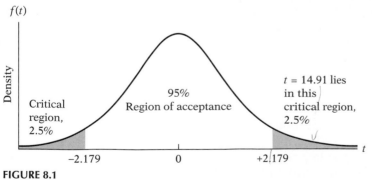

FIGURE 8.1
The 95 percent confidence interval for t(12 df).

---

[4]In most empirical investigations, the null hypothesis is stated in this form, that is, taking the extreme position (a kind of straw man) that there is no relationship between the dependent variable and the explanatory variable under consideration. The idea here is to find out whether the relationship between the two is a trivial one to begin with.

population parameter β_2. Since the null-hypothesized value of zero does not lie in the interval (8.4.2), we can reject the null hypothesis that $\beta_2 = 0$ with 95 percent confidence coefficient. Thus, whether we use the t test of significance as in (8.4.1) or the confidence-interval estimation as in (8.4.2), we reach the same conclusion. But this should not be surprising in view of the close connection between confidence-interval estimation and hypothesis testing.

Following the procedure just described, we can test hypotheses about other parameters of model (8.2.1) from the information presented in Eq. (8.2.2). If, for example, we assume that $\alpha = 0.05$ and hypothesize that each of the true partial regression coefficients is *individually* equal to zero, then, it is apparent from (8.2.2) that each estimated partial regression coefficient is statistically significant, that is, significantly different from zero, because the computed t value in each case exceeds the critical t value; *individually* we may reject the (individual) null hypothesis.

In passing, note that the p values of the various regression coefficients in (8.2.2) are extremely low, suggesting that each partial regression coefficient is statistically significant at a much lower level of significance than the conventional 5 or 1 percent levels.

8.5 TESTING THE OVERALL SIGNIFICANCE OF THE SAMPLE REGRESSION

Throughout the previous section we were concerned with testing the significance of the estimated partial regression coefficients individually, that is, under the separate hypothesis that each true population partial regression coefficient was zero. But now consider the following hypothesis:

$$H_0: \beta_2 = \beta_3 = 0 \tag{8.5.1}$$

This null hypothesis is a joint hypothesis that β_2 and β_3 are jointly or simultaneously equal to zero. A test of such a hypothesis is called a test of the **overall significance** of the observed or estimated regression line, that is, whether Y is linearly related to both X_2 and X_3.

Can the joint hypothesis in (8.5.1) be tested by testing the significance of $\hat{\beta}_2$ and $\hat{\beta}_3$ individually as in Section 8.4? The answer is no, and the reasoning is as follows.

In testing the individual significance of an observed partial regression coefficient in Section 8.4, we assumed implicitly that each test of significance was based on a different (i.e., independent) sample. Thus, in testing the significance of $\hat{\beta}_2$ under the hypothesis that $\beta_2 = 0$, it was assumed tacitly that the testing was based on a different sample from the one used in testing the significance of $\hat{\beta}_3$ under the null hypothesis that $\beta_3 = 0$. But to test the **joint** hypothesis of (8.5.1), if we use the same sample data (Table 8.1), we shall be violating the assumption underlying the test procedure.[5] The matter can

---

[5]In any given sample the cov $(\hat{\beta}_2, \hat{\beta}_3)$ may not be zero; that is, $\hat{\beta}_2$ and $\hat{\beta}_3$ may be correlated. See (7.4.17).

be put differently: In (8.4.2) we established a 95 percent confidence interval for β_2. But if we use the same sample data to establish a confidence interval for β_3, say, with a confidence coefficient of 95 percent, we cannot assert that both β_2 and β_3 lie in their respective confidence intervals with a probability of $(1 - \alpha)(1 - \alpha) = (0.95)(0.95)$.

In other words, although the statements

$$\Pr[\hat{\beta}_2 - t_{\alpha/2}\, se(\hat{\beta}_2) \le \beta_2 \le \hat{\beta}_2 + t_{\alpha/2}\, se(\hat{\beta}_2)] = 1 - \alpha$$

$$\Pr[\hat{\beta}_3 - t_{\alpha/2}\, se(\hat{\beta}_3) \le \beta_3 \le \hat{\beta}_3 + t_{\alpha/2}\, se(\hat{\beta}_3)] = 1 - \alpha$$

are individually true, *it is not true that* the probability that β_2 and β_3 simultaneously lie in the intervals $[\hat{\beta}_2 \pm t_{\alpha/2}\, se(\hat{\beta}_2), \hat{\beta}_3 \pm t_{\alpha/2}\, se(\hat{\beta}_3)]$ is $(1 - \alpha)^2$, because the intervals may not be independent when the same data are used to derive them. To state the matter differently,

> ...testing a series of single [individual] hypotheses is *not* equivalent to testing those same hypotheses jointly. The intuitive reason for this is that in a joint test of several hypotheses any single hypothesis is "affected" by the information in the other hypotheses.[6]

The upshot of the preceding argument is that for a given example (sample) only one confidence interval or only one test of significance can be obtained. How, then, does one test the simultaneous null hypothesis that $\beta_2 = \beta_3 = 0$? The answer follows.

The Analysis of Variance Approach to Testing the Overall Significance of an Observed Multiple Regression: The *F* Test

For reasons just explained, we cannot use the usual t test to test the joint hypothesis that the true partial slope coefficients are zero simultaneously. However, this joint hypothesis can be tested by the **analysis of variance** (ANOVA) technique first introduced in Section 5.9, which can be demonstrated as follows.

Recall the identity

$$\sum y_i^2 = \hat{\beta}_2 \sum y_i x_{2i} + \hat{\beta}_3 \sum y_i x_{3i} + \sum \hat{u}_i^2 \tag{8.5.2}$$

$$\text{TSS} = \qquad \text{ESS} \qquad + \text{RSS}$$

TSS has, as usual, $n - 1$ df and RSS has $n - 3$ df for reasons already discussed. ESS has 2 df since it is a function of $\hat{\beta}_2$ and $\hat{\beta}_3$. Therefore, following the ANOVA procedure discussed in Section 5.9, we can set up Table 8.2.

---

[6]Thomas B. Fomby, R. Carter Hill, and Stanley R. Johnson, *Advanced Econometric Methods*, Springer-Verlag, New York, 1984, p. 37.

TABLE 8.2
ANOVA table for the three-variable regression

Source of variation	SS	df	MSS
Due to regression (ESS)	$\hat{\beta}_2 \sum y_i x_{2i} + \hat{\beta}_3 \sum y_i x_{3i}$	2	$\dfrac{\hat{\beta}_2 \sum y_i x_{2i} + \hat{\beta}_3 \sum y_i x_{3i}}{2}$
Due to residual (RSS)	$\sum \hat{u}_i^2$	$n - 3$	$\hat{\sigma}^2 = \dfrac{\sum \hat{u}_i^2}{n - 3}$
Total	$\sum y_i^2$	$n - 1$	

Now it can be shown[7] that, under the assumption of normal distribution for u_i and the null hypothesis $\beta_2 = \beta_3 = 0$, the variable

$$F = \frac{(\hat{\beta}_2 \sum y_i x_{2i} + \hat{\beta}_3 \sum y_i x_{3i})/2}{\sum \hat{u}_i^2/(n-3)} \tag{8.5.3}$$

$$= \frac{\text{ESS}/\text{df}}{\text{RSS}/\text{df}}$$

is distributed as the F distribution with 2 and $n - 3$ df.

What use can be made of the preceding F ratio? It can be proved[8] that under the assumption that the $u_i \sim N(0, \sigma^2)$,

$$E \frac{\sum \hat{u}_i^2}{n-3} = E(\hat{\sigma}^2) = \sigma^2 \tag{8.5.4}$$

With the additional assumption that $\beta_2 = \beta_3 = 0$, it can be shown that

$$\frac{E(\hat{\beta}_2 \sum y_i x_{2i} + \hat{\beta}_3 \sum y_i x_{3i})}{2} = \sigma^2 \tag{8.5.5}$$

Therefore, if the null hypothesis is true, both (8.5.4) and (8.5.5) give identical estimates of true σ^2. This statement should not be surprising because if there is a trivial relationship between Y and X_2 and X_3, the sole source of variation in Y is due to the random forces represented by u_i. If, however, the null hypothesis is false, that is X_2 and X_3 definitely influence Y, the equality between (8.5.4) and (8.5.5) will not hold. In this case, the ESS will be relatively larger than the RSS, taking due account of their respective df. Therefore, the F value of (8.5.3) provides a test of the null hypothesis that the true slope coefficients are simultaneously zero. If the F value computed from (8.5.3) exceeds the critical F value from the F table at the α percent level of significance, we reject H_0; otherwise we do not reject it. Alternatively, if the p value of the observed F is sufficiently low, we can reject H_0.

[7] See K. A. Brownlee, *Statistical Theory and Methodology in Science and Engineering*, John Wiley & Sons, New York, 1960, pp. 278–280.

[8] Ibid.

TABLE 8.3
ANOVA table for the illustrative example

Source of variation	SS	df	MSS
Due to regression	65,965.1003	2	32,982.5502
Due to residuals	77.1690	12	6.4308
Total	66,042.2693	14	

Turning to our example, we obtain Table 8.3. Using (8.5.3), we obtain

$$F = \frac{32982.5502}{6.4308} = 5128.8781 \qquad (8.5.6)$$

If we use the 5 percent level of significance, the critical F value for 2 and 12 df, $F_{0.05}(2, 12)$, is 3.89. Obviously the computed F value is significant, and hence we can reject the null hypothesis. (If the null hypothesis were true, the probability of obtaining an F value of as much as 5129 is less than 5 in 100.) If the level of significance is assumed to be 1 percent, $F_{0.01}(2, 12) = 6.93$. The computed F still exceeds this critical value by a large margin. We still reject the null hypothesis; if the null hypothesis were true, the chance of obtaining an F value of 5129 is less than 1 in 100.[9] Incidentally, the p value of the observed F is extremely small.

We can generalize the preceding F-testing procedure as follows.

Testing the Overall Significance of a Multiple Regression: The F-Test

Decision Rule. Given the k-variable regression model:

$$Y_i = \beta_1 + \beta_2 X_{2i} + \beta_3 X_{3i} + \cdots + \beta_k X_{ki} + u_i$$

To test the hypothesis

$$H_0: \beta_2 = \beta_3 = \cdots = \beta_k = 0$$

(i.e., all slope coefficients are simultaneously zero) versus

H_1: Not all slope coefficients are simultaneously zero.

compute

$$F = \frac{\text{ESS}/\text{df}}{\text{RSS}/\text{df}} = \frac{\text{ESS}/(k-1)}{\text{RSS}/(n-k)} \qquad (8.5.7)$$

If $F > F_\alpha(k-1, n-k)$, reject H_0; otherwise you do not reject it, where $F_\alpha(k-1, n-k)$ is the *critical F* value at the α level of significance and $(k-1)$ numerator df and $(n-k)$ denominator df. Alternatively, if the p value of F obtained from (8.5.7) is sufficiently low, one can reject H_0.

---

[9]By convention, in this case we say that the computed F value is highly significant because the probability of committing the type 1 error (i.e., the level of significance) is very low—1 in 100.

Needless to say, in the three-variable case (Y and X_2, X_3) k is 3, in the four-variable case k is 4, and so on.

In passing, note that most regression packages routinely calculate the F value (given in the analysis of variance table) along with the usual regression output, such as the estimated coefficients, their standard errors, t values, etc. The null hypothesis for the t computation is usually assumed to be $\beta_i = 0$.

Individual versus Joint Testing of Hypotheses. In Section 8.4 we discussed the test of significance of a single regression coefficient and in Section 8.5 we have discussed the joint or overall test of significance of the estimated regression (i.e., all slope coefficients are simultaneously equal to zero). **We reiterate that these tests are different.** Thus, on the basis of the t test or confidence interval (of Section 8.4) it is possible to accept the hypothesis that a particular slope coefficient, β_k, is zero, and yet reject the joint hypothesis that all slope coefficients are zero.

> The lesson to be learned is that the joint "message" of individual confidence intervals is no substitute for a joint confidence region [implied by the F test] in performing joint tests of hypotheses and making joint confidence statements.[10]

An Important Relationship between R^2 and F

There is an intimate relationship between the coefficient of determination R^2 and the F test used in the analysis of variance. Assuming the normal distribution for the disturbances u_i and the null hypothesis that $\beta_2 = \beta_3 = 0$, we have seen that

$$F = \frac{\text{ESS}/2}{\text{RSS}/(n-3)} \tag{8.5.8}$$

is distributed as the F distribution with 2 and $n - 3$ df.

More generally, in the k-variable case (including intercept), if we assume that the disturbances are normally distributed and that the null hypothesis is

$$H_0: \beta_2 = \beta_3 = \cdots = \beta_k = 0 \tag{8.5.9}$$

then it follows that

$$F = \frac{\text{ESS}/(k-1)}{\text{RSS}/(n-k)} \tag{8.5.10}$$

follows the F distribution with $k - 1$ and $n - k$ df. (*Note:* The total number of parameters to be estimated is k, of which one is the intercept term.)

---

[10]Fomby et al., op. cit., p. 42.

Let us manipulate (8.5.10) as follows:

$$
\begin{aligned}
F &= \frac{n-k}{k-1} \frac{\text{ESS}}{\text{RSS}} \\[2mm]
&= \frac{n-k}{k-1} \frac{\text{ESS}}{\text{TSS}-\text{ESS}} \\[2mm]
&= \frac{n-k}{k-1} \frac{\text{ESS/TSS}}{1-(\text{ESS/TSS})} \\[2mm]
&= \frac{n-k}{k-1} \frac{R^2}{1-R^2} \\[2mm]
&= \frac{R^2/(k-1)}{(1-R^2)/(n-k)}
\end{aligned}
\tag{8.5.11}
$$

where use is made of the definition $R^2 = \text{ESS/TSS}$. Equation (8.5.11) shows how F and R^2 are related. These two vary directly. When $R^2 = 0$, F is zero ipso facto. The larger the R^2, the greater the F value. In the limit, when $R^2 = 1$, F is infinite. *Thus the F test, which is a measure of the overall significance of the estimated regression, is also a test of significance of R^2.* In other words, testing the null hypothesis (8.5.9) is equivalent to testing the null hypothesis that (the population) R^2 is zero.

For the three-variable case (8.5.11) becomes

$$
F = \frac{R^2/2}{(1-R^2)/(n-3)}
\tag{8.5.12}
$$

By virtue of the close connection between F and R^2, the ANOVA Table 8.2 can be recast as Table 8.4.

For our illustrative example, the reader should verify that the F of (8.5.12) is 4994, which is approximately equal to the F value of (8.5.6), the difference being due to the rounding errors. As before, the F value is highly significant, and we can reject the null hypothesis that Y is not linearly related to X_2 and X_3.

TABLE 8.4
ANOVA table in terms of R^2

Source of variation	SS	df	MSS*
Due to regression	$R^2(\sum y_i^2)$	2	$R^2(\sum y_i^2)/2$
Due to residuals	$(1-R^2)(\sum y_i^2)$	$n-3$	$(1-R^2)(\sum y_i^2)/(n-3)$
Total	$\sum y_i^2$	$n-1$	

*Note that in computing the F value there is no need to multiply R^2 and $(1-R^2)$ by $\sum y_i^2$ because it drops out, as shown in (8.5.12).

One advantage of the F test expressed in terms of R^2 is its ease of computation: All that one needs to know is the R^2 value. Therefore, the overall F test of significance given in (8.5.7) can be recast in terms of R^2 as shown in Table 8.4.

Testing the Overall Significance of a Multiple Regression in Terms of R^2

Decision Rule. Testing the overall significance of a regression in terms of R^2: Alternative but equivalent test to (8.5.7).
Given the k-variable regression model:

$$Y_i = \beta_i + \beta_2 X_{2i} + \beta_3 X_{3i} + \cdots + \beta_x X_{ki} + u_i$$

To test the hypothesis

$$H_0: \beta_2 = \beta_3 = \cdots = \beta_k = 0$$

versus

$$H_1: \text{Not all slope coefficients are simultaneously zero}$$

compute

$$F = \frac{R^2/(k-1)}{(1-R^2)/(n-k)} \qquad (8.5.13)$$

If $F > F_{\alpha(k-1,n-k)}$, reject H_0; otherwise you may accept H_0 where $F_{\alpha(k-1,n-k)}$ is the critical F value at the α level of significance and $(k-1)$ numerator df and $(n-k)$ denominator df. Alternatively, if the p value of F obtained from (8.5.13) is sufficiently low, reject H_0.

The "Incremental," or "Marginal," Contribution of an Explanatory Variable

Let us return to our illustrative example. We know from (8.2.2) that the coefficient of X_2 (income) and X_3 (trend) are statistically significantly different from zero on the basis of *separate t* tests. We have also seen that the regression line obtained is itself-significant on the basis of the F test given in (8.5.7) or (8.5.13). Now suppose that we introduce X_2 and X_3 *sequentially*; that is, we first regress Y on X_2 and assess its significance and then add X_3 to the model to find out whether it contributes anything (of course, the order in which X_2 and X_3 enter can be reversed). By contribution we mean whether the addition of the variable to the model increases the ESS (and thus R^2) "significantly" in relation to the RSS. This contribution may appropriately be called the **incremental**, or **marginal**, contribution of an explanatory variable.

The topic of incremental contribution is an important one in practice. In most empirical investigations the researcher may not be completely sure whether it is worth adding an X variable to the model knowing that several other X variables are already present in the model. One does not wish to include variable(s) that contribute very little toward ESS. By the same token, one does not want to exclude variable(s) that substantially increase ESS. But how does one decide whether an X variable significantly reduces RSS? The analysis of variance technique can be easily extended to answer this question.

Suppose we first regress Y (personal consumption expenditure) on X_2 (personal disposable income) and obtain the following regression:

$$\hat{Y}_i = \hat{\beta}_1 \quad + \hat{\beta}_{12}X_{2i}$$
$$= 12.762 \quad + \quad 0.8812X_{2i}$$
$$(4.6818) \quad (0.0114)$$
$$t = \quad (2.7259) \quad (77.2982) \qquad\qquad r^2 = 0.9978 \qquad (8.5.14)$$
$$\text{adj}\, r^2 = 0.9977$$

Under the null hypothesis $\beta_{12} = 0$, it can be seen that the estimated t value of 77.2982 ($= 0.8812/0.0114$) is obviously statistically significant either at the 5 or 1 percent level of significance. Thus, X_2 significantly affects Y. The ANOVA table for regression (8.5.14) is given as Table 8.5.

Assuming the disturbances u_i to be normally distributed and the null hypothesis $\beta_{12} = 0$, we know that

$$F = \frac{65898.235}{11.080} = 5947.494 \qquad (8.5.15)$$

follows the F distribution with 1 and 13 df. This F value is obviously significant at the usual levels of significance. Thus, as before, we can reject the hypothesis that $\beta_{12} = 0$. Incidentally, note that $t^2 = (77.2982)^2 = 5975.012$, which is equal to the F value of (8.5.15) save the rounding error. But this result should not be surprising because, as noted in Chapter 5, under the same null hypotheses and the same level of significance, the square of t value with $n - 2$ df is equal to the F value with 1 and $n - 2$ df.

Having run the regression (8.5.14), let us suppose we decide to add X_3 to the model and obtain the multiple regression (8.2.2). The questions we want to answer are these: (1) What is the marginal, or incremental, contribution of X_3 knowing that X_2 is already in the model and that it is significantly related to Y? (2) Is the incremental contribution statistically significant? (3) What is the criterion for adding variables into the model? These questions can be answered by the ANOVA technique. To see this, let us construct Table 8.6. For our numerical example, Table 8.6 becomes Table 8.7.

TABLE 8.5
ANOVA table for regression (8.5.14)

Source of variation	SS	df	MSS
ESS (due to X_2)	65898.2353	1	65898.2353
RSS	144.0340	13	11.0800
Total	66042.2693	14	

TABLE 8.6
ANOVA table to assess incremental contribution of a variable(s)

Source of variation	SS	df	MSS
ESS due to X_2 alone	$Q_1 = \hat{\beta}_{12}^2 \sum x_2^2$	1	$\dfrac{Q_1}{1}$
ESS due to the addition of X_3	$Q_2 = Q_3 - Q_1$	1	$\dfrac{Q_2}{1}$
ESS due to both X_2, X_3	$Q_3 = \hat{\beta}_2 \sum y_i x_{2i} + \hat{\beta}_3 \sum y_i x_{3i}$	2	$\dfrac{Q_3}{2}$
RSS	$Q_4 = Q_5 - Q_3$	$n - 3$	$\dfrac{Q_4}{n-3}$
Total	$Q_5 = \sum y_i^2$	$n - 1$	

To assess the *incremental* contribution of X_3 after allowing for the contribution of X_2, we form

$$
\begin{aligned}
F' &= \frac{Q_2/\mathrm{df}}{Q_4/\mathrm{df}} \\[2mm]
&= \frac{\mathrm{ESS}_{\mathrm{new}} - \mathrm{ESS}_{\mathrm{old}}/\text{number of new regressors}}{\mathrm{RSS}_{\mathrm{new}}/\mathrm{df}\ (= n - \text{number of parameters in the new model})} \\[2mm]
&= \frac{Q_2/1}{Q_4/12} \quad \text{for our example}
\end{aligned}
$$

(8.5.16)

where $\mathrm{ESS}_{\mathrm{new}} = $ ESS under the new model (i.e., after adding the new regressors $= Q_3$), $\mathrm{ESS}_{\mathrm{old}} = $ ESS under the old model $(= Q_1)$ and $\mathrm{RSS}_{\mathrm{new}} = $ RSS under the new model (i.e., after taking into account all the regressors $= Q_4$).

For our illustrative example, we obtain

$$
F = \frac{66.865/1}{77.1693/12}
$$

$$
= 10.3973 \tag{8.5.17}
$$

TABLE 8.7
ANOVA table for the illustrative example: Incremental analysis

Source of variation	SS	df	MSS
ESS due to X_2 alone	$Q_1 = 65898.2353$	1	65898.2353
ESS due to the addition of X_3	$Q_2 = 66.8647$	1	66.8647
Ess due to X_2 and X_3	$Q_3 = 65965.1000$	2	32982.5500
RSS	$Q_4 = 77.1693$	12	6.4302
Total	$Q_5 = 66042.2693$	14	

Now under the usual assumption of the normality of u_i and the null hypothesis that $\beta_3 = 0$, it can be shown that the F of (8.5.16) follows the F distribution with 1 and 12 df. From the F table it is obvious that the F value of 10.3973 is significant beyond the 1 percent level of significance, the p value being 0.0073.

Incidentally, the F ratio of (8.5.16) can be recast using the R^2 values only, as we did in (8.5.13). As exercise 8.2 shows, the F ratio of (8.5.16) is *equivalent* to the following F ratio:[11]

$$
\begin{aligned}
F &= \frac{(R_{\text{new}}^2 - R_{\text{old}}^2)/\text{df}}{(1 - R_{\text{new}}^2)/\text{df}} \\
&= \frac{(R_{\text{new}}^2 - R_{\text{old}}^2)/\text{ number of new regressors}}{(1 - R_{\text{new}}^2)/\text{df}\,(= n - \text{ number of parameters in the new model})}
\end{aligned}
$$

(8.5.18)

This F ratio also follows the F distribution with the appropriate numerator and denominator df, 1 and 12, respectively, in our example.

For our example, $R_{\text{new}}^2 = 0.9988$ [from (8.2.2)] and $R_{\text{old}}^2 = 0.9978$ [(from (8.5.14)]. Therefore,

$$
\begin{aligned}
F &= \frac{(0.9988 - 0.9978)/1}{(1 - 0.9988)/12} \\
&= 10.3978
\end{aligned}
$$

(8.5.19)

which is about the same as the F value of (8.5.17), except for the errors of approximations.

Thus, based on either F test, we can reject the null hypothesis and conclude that the addition of X_3 to the model significantly increases ESS and hence the R^2 value. Therefore, the trend variable X_3 should be added to the model.

Recall that in (8.2.2) we obtained the t value of 3.2246 for the coefficient of X_3 under $H_0 : \beta_3 = 0$. Now $t^2 = (3.2246)^2 = 10.3980 = F$ value given in (8.5.17) save for the rounding errors. But this result is expected in view of the close relationship between F and t^2, as noted previously.

When to Add a New Variable. The F-test procedure just outlined provides a formal method of deciding whether a variable should be added to a regression model. Often researchers are faced with the task of choosing from several competing models **involving the same dependent variable** but with different explanatory variables. As a matter of ad hoc choice (because very often the theoretical foundation of the analysis is weak), these researchers frequently choose the model that gives the highest adjusted R^2. Therefore, if the inclusion of a variable increases $\bar{R}^2$, it is retained in the model although it does not

---

[11]The following F test is a special case of the more general F test given in (8.7.9) or (8.7.10) in Section 8.7.

reduce RSS significantly in the statistical sense. The question then becomes: When does the adjusted R^2 increase? It can be shown that $\bar{R}^2$ *will increase if the t value of the coefficient of the newly added variable is larger than 1 in absolute value*, where the t value is computed under the hypothesis that the population value of the said coefficient is zero (i.e., the t value computed from (5.3.2) under the hypothesis that the true β value is zero).[12] The preceding criterion can also be stated differently: $\bar{R}^2$ *will increase with the addition of an extra explanatory variable only if the F $(= t^2)$ value of that variable exceeds 1.*

Applying either criterion, our trend variable X_3 with a t value of 3.2246 or an F value of 10.3973 should increase $\bar{R}^2$, which indeed it does—when X_3 is added to the model, $\bar{R}^2$ increases from 0.9977 to 0.9986. Of course, X_3 also happens to be statistically significant.

When to Add a Group of Variables.   Can we develop a similar rule for deciding whether it is worth adding (or dropping) a group of variables from a model? The answer should be apparent from (8.5.18): *If adding (dropping) a group of variables to the model gives an F value greater (less) than 1, R^2 will increase (decrease).* Of course, from (8.5.18) one can easily find out whether the addition (subtraction) of a group of variables significantly increases (decreases) the explanatory power of a regression model.

8.6   TESTING THE EQUALITY OF TWO REGRESSION COEFFICIENTS

Suppose in the multiple regression

$$Y_i = \beta_1 + \beta_2 X_{2i} + \beta_3 X_{3i} + \beta_4 X_{4i} + u_i \tag{8.6.1}$$

we want to test the hypotheses

$$
\begin{aligned}
H_0: \beta_3 &= \beta_4 &\quad \text{or} \quad& (\beta_3 - \beta_4) = 0 \\
H_1: \beta_3 &\neq \beta_4 &\quad \text{or} \quad& (\beta_3 - \beta_4) \neq 0
\end{aligned}
\tag{8.6.2}
$$

that is, the two slope coefficients β_3 and β_4 are equal.

Such a null hypothesis is of practical importance. For example, let (8.6.1) represent the demand function for a commodity where Y = amount of a commodity demanded, X_2 = the price of the commodity, X_3 = income of the consumer, and X_4 = wealth of the consumer. The null hypothesis in this case means that the income and wealth coefficients are the same. Or, if Y_i and the X's are expressed in logarithmic form, the null hypothesis in (8.6.2) implies that the income and wealth elasticities of consumption are the same. (Why?)

How do we test such a null hypothesis? Under the classical assumptions, it can be shown that

$$t = \frac{(\hat{\beta}_3 - \hat{\beta}_4) - (\beta_3 - \beta_4)}{se(\hat{\beta}_3 - \hat{\beta}_4)} \tag{8.6.3}$$

---

[12]For proof, see Dennis J. Aigner, *Basic Econometrics*, Prentice-Hall, Englewood Cliffs, New Jersey, 1971, pp. 91–92.

follows the t distribution with $(n-4)$ df because (8.6.1) is a four-variable model or, more generally, with $(n-k)$ df, where k is the total number of parameters estimated, including the constant term. The $se(\hat{\beta}_3 - \hat{\beta}_4)$ is obtained from the following well-known formula (see the statistical appendix for details):

$$se(\hat{\beta}_3 - \hat{\beta}_4) = \sqrt{var(\hat{\beta}_3) + var(\hat{\beta}_4) - 2 \, cov(\hat{\beta}_3, \hat{\beta}_4)} \qquad (8.6.4)$$

If we substitute the null hypothesis and the expression for the se $(\hat{\beta}_3 - \hat{\beta}_4)$ into (8.6.3), our test statistic becomes

$$t = \frac{\hat{\beta}_3 - \hat{\beta}_4}{\sqrt{var(\hat{\beta}_3) + var(\hat{\beta}_4) - 2 \, cov(\hat{\beta}_3, \hat{\beta}_4)}} \qquad (8.6.5)$$

Now the testing procedure involves the following steps:

1. Estimate $\hat{\beta}_3$ and $\hat{\beta}_4$. Any standard computer package such as SAS, SPSS, or SHAZAM can do that.
2. Most standard computer packages routinely compute the variances and covariances of the estimated parameters.[13] From these estimates the standard error in the denominator of (8.6.5) can be easily obtained.
3. Obtain the t ratio from (8.6.5). Note the null hypothesis in the present case is $(\beta_3 - \beta_4) = 0$.
4. If the t variable computed from (8.6.5) exceeds the critical t value at the designated level of significance for given df, then you can reject the null hypothesis; otherwise, you do not reject it. Alternatively, if the p value of the t statistic from (8.6.5) is reasonably low, one can reject the null hypotheses.

Example 8.2: The Cubic Cost Function Revisited

Recall the cubic total cost function estimated in Section 7.11, which for convenience is reproduced below:

$$\hat{Y}_i = \quad 141.7667 + 63.4777X_i - 12.9615X_i^2 + 0.9396X_i^3$$
$$se = \quad (6.3753) \quad\quad (4.7786) \quad\quad (0.9857) \quad\quad (0.0591) \qquad (7.11.6)$$
$$cov(\hat{\beta}_3, \hat{\beta}_4) = -0.0576; \quad\quad R^2 = 0.9983$$

where Y is total cost and X is output, and where the figures in parentheses are the estimated standard errors.

Suppose we want to test the hypothesis that the coefficients of the X^2 and X^3 terms in the cubic cost function are the same, that is, $\beta_3 = \beta_4$ or $(\beta_3 - \beta_4) = 0$. In the regression (7.11.6) we have all the necessary output to conduct the t test of

---

[13]The algebraic expression for the covariance formula is rather involved. Chapter 9 provides a compact expression for it, however, using matrix notation.

(8.6.5). The actual mechanics are as follows:

$$t = \frac{\hat{\beta}_3 - \hat{\beta}_4}{\sqrt{\text{var}(\hat{\beta}_3) + \text{var}(\hat{\beta}_4) - 2\,\text{cov}(\hat{\beta}_3, \hat{\beta}_4)}}$$

$$= \frac{-12.9615 - 0.9396}{\sqrt{(0.9867)^2 + (0.0591)^2 - 2(-0.0576)}}$$

$$= \frac{-13.9011}{1.0442}$$

$$= -13.3130 \qquad\qquad (8.6.6)$$

The reader can verify that for 6 df (why?) the observed t value exceeds the critical t value even at the 0.002 (or 0.2%) level of significance (two-tail test); the p value is extremely small, 0.000006. Hence we can reject the hypothesis that the coefficients of X^2 and X^3 in the cubic cost function are identical.

8.7 RESTRICTED LEAST SQUARES: TESTING LINEAR EQUALITY RESTRICTIONS

There are occasions where economic theory may suggest that the coefficients in a regression model satisfy some linear equality restrictions. For instance, consider the Cobb-Douglas production function:

$$Y_i = \beta_1 X_{2i}^{\beta_2} X_{3i}^{\beta_3} e^{u_i} \qquad\qquad (7.10.1) = (8.7.1)$$

where Y = output, X_2 = labor input, and X_3 = capital input. Written in log form, the equation becomes

$$\ln Y_i = \beta_0 + \beta_2 \ln X_{2i} + \beta_3 \ln X_{3i} + u_i \qquad\qquad (8.7.2)$$

where $\beta_0 = \ln \beta_1$.

Now if there are constant returns to scale (equiproportional change in output for an equiproportional change in the inputs), economic theory would suggest that

$$\beta_2 + \beta_3 = 1 \qquad\qquad (8.7.3)$$

which is an example of a linear equality restriction.[14]

How does one find out if there are constant returns to scale, that is, if the restriction (8.7.3) is valid? There are two approaches.

The t Test Approach

The simplest procedure is to estimate (8.7.2) in the usual manner without taking into account the restriction (8.7.3) explicitly. This is called the **unrestricted** or **unconstrained regression**. Having estimated β_2 and β_3 (say, by

---

[14]If we had $\beta_2 + \beta_3 < 1$, this relation would be an example of linear inequality restriction. To handle such restrictions, one needs to use mathematical programming techniques.

OLS method), a test of the hypothesis or restriction (8.7.3) can be conducted by the t test of (8.6.3), namely,

$$t = \frac{(\hat{\beta}_2 + \hat{\beta}_3) - (\beta_2 + \beta_3)}{se(\hat{\beta}_2 + \hat{\beta}_3)}$$

$$= \frac{(\hat{\beta}_2 + \hat{\beta}_3) - 1}{\sqrt{var(\hat{\beta}_2) + var(\hat{\beta}_3) + 2\,cov(\hat{\beta}_2\hat{\beta}_3)}} \tag{8.7.4}$$

where $(\beta_2 + \beta_3) = 1$ under the null hypothesis and where the denominator is the standard error of $(\hat{\beta}_2 + \hat{\beta}_3)$. Then following Section 8.6, if the t value computed from (8.7.4) exceeds the critical t value at the chosen level of significance, we reject the hypothesis of constant returns to scale; otherwise we do not reject it.

The *F* Test Approach: Restricted Least Squares

The preceding t test is a kind of postmortem examination because we try to find out whether the linear restriction is satisfied after estimating the "unrestricted" regression. A direct approach would be to incorporate the restriction (8.7.3) into the estimating procedure at the outset. In the present example, this procedure can be done easily. From (8.7.3) we see that

$$\beta_2 = 1 - \beta_3 \tag{8.7.5}$$

or

$$\beta_3 = 1 - \beta_2 \tag{8.7.6}$$

Therefore, using either of these equalities, we can eliminate one of the β coefficients in (8.7.2) and estimate the resulting equation. Thus, if we use (8.7.5), we can write the Cobb-Douglas production function as

$$\ln Y_i = \beta_0 + (1 - \beta_3)\ln X_{2i} + \beta_3 \ln X_{3i} + u_i$$
$$= \beta_0 + \ln X_{2i} + \beta_3(\ln X_{3i} - \ln X_{2i}) + u_i$$

or

$$(\ln Y_i - \ln X_{2i}) = \beta_0 + \beta_3(\ln X_{3i} - \ln X_{2i}) + u_i \tag{8.7.7}$$

or

$$\ln(Y_i / X_{2i}) = \beta_0 + \beta_3 \ln(X_{3i} / X_{2i}) + u_i \tag{8.7.8}$$

where (Y_i/X_{2i}) = output/labor ratio and (X_{3i}/X_{2i}) = capital labor ratio, quantities of great economic importance.

Notice how the original equation (8.7.2) is transformed. Once we estimate β_3 from (8.7.7) or (8.7.8), β_2 can be easily estimated from the relation (8.7.5). Needless to say, this procedure will guarantee that the sum of the estimated coefficients of the two inputs will equal 1. The procedure outlined in (8.7.7) or (8.7.8) is known as **restricted least squares (RLS)**. This procedure can be generalized to models containing any number of explanatory variables and more than one linear equality restriction. The generalization can be found in Theil.[15] (See also general F testing below.)

How do we compare the unrestricted and restricted least-squares regressions? In other words, how do we know that, say, the restriction (8.7.3) is valid? This question can be tested by applying the F test as follows. Let

$$\sum \hat{u}_{\text{UR}}^2 = \text{RSS of the unrestricted regression} \quad (8.7.2)$$

$$\sum \hat{u}_{\text{R}}^2 = \text{RSS of the restricted regression} \quad (8.7.7)$$

m = number of linear restrictions (1 in the present example)

k = number of parameters in the unrestricted regression

n = number of observations

Then,

$$F = \frac{(\text{RSS}_{\text{R}} - \text{RSS}_{\text{UR}})/m}{\text{RSS}_{\text{UR}}/(n-k)}$$

$$= \frac{\left(\sum \hat{u}_{\text{R}}^2 - \sum \hat{u}_{\text{UR}}^2\right)/m}{\sum \hat{u}_{\text{UR}}^2/(n-k)} \quad (8.7.9)$$

follows the F distribution with $m, (n-k)$ df. (*Note:* UR and R stand for unrestricted and restricted, respectively.)

The F test above can also be expressed in terms of R^2 as follows:

$$F = \frac{(R_{\text{UR}}^2 - R_{\text{R}}^2)/m}{(1 - R_{\text{UR}}^2)/(n-k)} \quad (8.7.10)$$

where R_{UR}^2 and R_{R}^2 are, respectively, the R^2 values obtained from the unrestricted and restricted regressions, that is, from the regressions (8.7.2) and (8.7.7). It should be noted that

$$R_{\text{UR}}^2 \geq R_{\text{R}}^2 \quad (8.7.11)$$

and

$$\sum \hat{u}_{\text{UR}}^2 \leq \sum \hat{u}_{\text{R}}^2 \quad (8.7.12)$$

In exercise 8.4 you are asked to justify these statements.

A Cautionary Note: In using (8.7.10) keep in mind that if the dependent variable in the restricted and unrestricted models is not the same, R_{UR}^2 and R_{R}^2 are not directly comparable. In that case, use the procedure described in Chapter 7 to render the two R^2 values comparable (see Example 8.3 below).

---

[15]Henri Theil, *Principles of Econometrics*, John Wiley & Sons, New York, 1971, pp. 43–45.

It should be added that we have warned against overemphasizing R^2; its use in (8.7.10) is for mere convenience in case the RSS values are not readily available.

Example 8.3: The Cobb-Douglas Production Function for Taiwanese Agricultural Sector, 1958–1972

By way of illustrating the preceding discussion let us refer to the data in Table 7.3 and the resulting Cobb-Douglas production function given in (7.10.4). This is the unrestricted regression since no restrictions are put on the parameters. Now suppose we want to impose the restriction that $(\beta_2 + \beta_3) = 1$, that is, there are constant returns to scale in the Taiwanese agricultural sector, for the said period. Imposing this restriction, we estimate the regression (8.7.8), which gives the following results:

$$\widehat{\ln(Y_i / X_{2i})} = \begin{array}{cc} 1.7086 & + & 0.61298 \ln(X_{3i} / X_{2i}) \\ (0.4159) & & (0.0933) \end{array}$$

$$R^2 = 0.7685$$

$$\bar{R}^2 = 0.7507$$

(8.7.13)

where figures in the parentheses are the estimated standard errors.

Note: The R^2 values of (7.10.4), the unrestricted regression, and (8.7.13), the restricted regression, are not directly comparable because the dependent variable in the two models is not the same. By using the method of comparing two R^2 values discussed in Section 7.8, we obtain an R^2 value of 0.8489 for model (8.7.13), which can now be compared with the R^2 value of 0.8890 of the unrestricted regression (7.10.4).

From the unrestricted regression (7.10.4) we obtain the unrestricted R^2_{UR} of 0.8890 whereas the restricted regression (8.7.13) gives the restricted R^2_R of 0.8489. Therefore, we can readily use the F test of (8.7.10) to test the validity of the constant returns to scale assumption imposed on the production function.

$$F = \frac{(R^2_{UR} - R^2_R)/m}{(1 - R^2_{UR})/(n - k)}$$

$$= \frac{(0.8890 - 0.8489)/1}{(1 - 0.8890)/12}$$

$$= \frac{0.0401}{0.0092}$$

$$= 4.3587$$

(8.7.14)

which has the F distribution with 1 and 12 df, respectively. From the F table we see that $F_{0.05}(1, 12) = 4.75$ but $F_{0.10}(1, 12) = 3.18$. That is, the observed F value of 4.3587 is not significant at the 5% level but is significant at the 10% level. If we decide to stick to the 5% level of significance, then the observed F value is not significant, implying that we can accept the hypothesis that there were constant returns to scale in the Taiwanese agricultural sector for the period 1958–1972; the observed return to scale value of 1.9887 seen in regression (7.10.4) is not *statistically* different from unity. This example illustrates why it is essential that one should consider formal testing of a hypothesis and not rely merely on the estimated coefficients. This example also reminds us that we should specify the significance level before we actually test a statistical hypothesis and not choose it after the regression is estimated. As noted on several occasions, it is better to quote the p value of the estimated statistic, which, in the present example, is 0.0588. Thus the observed F value of 4.3587 is significant at about the 0.06 level.

In passing, observe that the estimated slope coefficient of 0.61298 is $\hat{\beta}_3$ and therefore, from the Eq. (8.7.5), we can easily obtain the value of $\hat{\beta}_2$ as 0.38702. As noted, the sum of these coefficients is guaranteed to be 1.

General F Testing[16]

The F test given in (8.7.10) or its equivalent (8.7.9) provides a general method of testing hypotheses about one or more parameters of the k-variable regression model:

$$Y_i = \beta_1 + \beta_2 X_{2i} + \beta_3 X_{3i} + \cdots + \beta_k X_{ki} + u_i \qquad (8.7.15)$$

The F test of (8.5.16) or the t test of (8.6.3) is but a specific application of (8.7.10). Thus, hypotheses such as

$$H_0: \beta_2 = \beta_3 \qquad (8.7.16)$$
$$H_0: \beta_3 + \beta_4 + \beta_5 = 3 \qquad (8.7.17)$$

which involve some linear restrictions on the parameters of the k-variable model, or hypotheses such as

$$H_0: \beta_3 = \beta_4 = \beta_5 = \beta_6 = 0 \qquad (8.7.18)$$

which imply that some regressors are absent from the model, can all be tested by the F test of (8.7.10).

From the discussion in Section 8.5 and 8.7, the reader will have noticed that the general strategy of F testing is this: There is a larger model, the *unconstrained model* (8.7.15), and then there is a smaller model, the *constrained* or *restricted model*, which is obtained from the larger model by deleting some variables from it, e.g., (8.7.18), or by putting some linear restrictions on one or more coefficients of the larger model, e.g., (8.7.16) or (8.7.17).

We then fit the unconstrained and constrained models to the data and obtain the respective coefficients of determination, namely, R^2_{UR} and R^2_R. We note the df in the unconstrained model ($= n - k$) and also note the df in the constrained model ($= m$), m being the number of linear restriction [e.g., 1 in (8.7.16) or (8.7.18)] or the number of regressors omitted from the model [e.g., $m = 4$ if (8.7.18) holds, since four regressors are assumed to be absent from the model.] We then compute the F ratio as indicated in (8.7.10) and use this *Decision Rule: If the computed F exceeds $F_\alpha(m, n - k)$, where $F_\alpha(m, n - k)$ is the critical F at the α level of significance, we reject the null hypothesis: otherwise we do not reject it.*

---

[16]If one is using the maximum likelihood approach to estimation, then a test similar to the one discussed shortly is the **likelihood ratio test**, which is slightly involved and is therefore discussed in the appendix to the chapter. For further discussion, see Theil, op. cit., pp. 179–184.

Let us illustrate:

Example 8.4: The Demand for Chicken in the United States, 1960–1982.
In exercise 7.23, among other things, you were asked to consider the following demand function for chicken:

$$\ln Y_t = \beta_1 + \beta_2 \ln X_{2t} + \beta_3 \ln X_{3t} + \beta_4 \ln X_{4t} + \beta_5 \ln X_{5t} + u_i \qquad (8.7.19)$$

where Y = per capita consumption of chicken, lbs, X_2 = real disposable per capita income, $, X_3$ = real retail price of chicken per lb, ¢, X_4 = real retail price of pork per lb, ¢, and X_5 = real retail price of beer per lb, ¢.

In this model β_2, β_3, β_4, and β_5 are, respectively, the income, own-price, cross-price (pork), and cross- price (beef) elasticities. (Why?) According to economic theory,

$$\beta_2 > 0$$
$$\beta_3 < 0$$

$\beta_4 > 0$,	if chicken and pork are competing products
< 0,	if chicken and pork are complementary products (8.7.20)
$= 0$,	if chicken and pork are unrelated products
$\beta_5 > 0$,	if chicken and beef are competing products
< 0,	if they are complementary products
$= 0$,	if they are unrelated products

Suppose someone maintains that chicken and pork and beef are unrelated products in the sense that chicken consumption is not affected by the prices of pork and beef. In short,

$$H_0: \beta_4 = \beta_5 = 0 \qquad (8.7.21)$$

Therefore, the constrained regression becomes

$$\ln Y_t = \beta_1 + \beta_2 \ln X_{2t} + \beta_3 \ln X_{3t} + u_t \qquad (8.7.22)$$

Equation (8.7.19) is of course the unconstrained regression.

Using the data given in Exercise 7.23, we obtain the following:

Unconstrained regression

$$\widehat{\ln Y_t} = 2.1898 + 0.3425 \ln X_{2t} - 0.5046 \ln X_{3t} + 0.1485 \ln X_{4t} + 0.0911 \ln X_{5t}$$
$$\quad (0.1557) \quad (0.0833) \qquad (0.1109) \qquad (0.0997) \qquad (0.1007)$$
$$R_{\text{UR}}^2 = 0.9823 \qquad (8.7.23)$$

Constrained regression

$$\widehat{\ln Y_t} = 2.0328 + 0.4515 \ln X_{2t} - 0.3772 \ln X_{3t} \qquad (8.7.24)$$
$$\quad (0.1162) \quad (0.0247) \qquad (0.0635)$$
$$R_{\text{R}}^2 = 0.9801$$

where the figures in parentheses are the estimated standard errors. *Note:* The R^2 values of (8.7.23) and (8.7.24) are comparable since the dependent variable in the two models is the same.

Now the F ratio to test the hypothesis (8.7.21) is

$$F = \frac{(R_{UR}^2 - R_R^2)/m}{(1 - R_{UR}^2)/(n - k)} \tag{8.7.10}$$

The value of m in the present case is 2, since there are two restrictions involved: $\beta_4 = 0$ and $\beta_5 = 0$. The denominator df, $(n - k)$, is 18, since $n = 23$ and $k = 5$ (5 β coefficients).

Therefore, the F ratio is

$$F = \frac{(0.9823 - 0.9801)/2}{(1 - 0.9823)/18}$$

$$= 1.1224 \tag{8.7.25}$$

which has the F distribution with 2 and 18 df.

At 5%, clearly this F value is not statistically significant [$F_{0.5}(2, 18) = 3.55$]. The p value is 0.3472. Therefore, there is no reason to reject the null hypothesis—the demand for chicken does not depend on pork and beef prices. In short, we can accept the constrained regression (8.7.24) as representing the demand function for chicken.

Notice that the demand function satisfies a priori economic expectations in that the own-price elasticity is negative and that the income elasticity is positive. However, the estimated price elasticity, in absolute value, is statistically less than unity, implying that the demand for chicken is price inelastic. (Why?) Also, the income elasticity, although positive, is also statistically less than unity, suggesting that chicken is not a luxury item; by convention, an item is said to be a luxury item if its income elasticity is greater than one.

8.8 COMPARING TWO REGRESSIONS: TESTING FOR STRUCTURAL STABILITY OF REGRESSION MODELS

Table 8.8 gives data on personal savings and personal income in the United Kingdom for the period 1946–1963.

TABLE 8.8
Personal savings and income data, United Kingdom, 1946–1963 (millions of pounds)

Period I: 1946–1954	Savings	Income	Period II: 1955–1963	Savings	Income
1946	0.36	8.8	1955	0.59	15.5
1947	0.21	9.4	1956	0.90	16.7
1948	0.08	10.0	1957	0.95	17.7
1949	0.20	10.6	1958	0.82	18.6
1950	0.10	11.0	1959	1.04	19.7
1951	0.12	11.9	1960	1.53	21.1
1952	0.41	12.7	1961	1.94	22.8
1953	0.50	13.5	1962	1.75	23.9
1954	0.43	14.3	1963	1.99	25.2

Source: Central Statistical Office, U.K.

Suppose we want to find out how personal savings behave in relation to personal income, that is, we want to estimate a simple *savings function*. A glance at the data given in Table 8.8 shows that the behavior of savings in relation to income for the period 1946–1954, the immediate post–World War II period (call it the reconstruction period), seems to differ from the period 1955–1963 (call it the postreconstruction period). To put it another way, the savings function has undergone a *structural change* between the two periods, that is, the parameters of the savings function have changed.

To see if this change is real, let us suppose that the savings functions for the two periods are as follows:

$$\text{Reconstruction Period:} \qquad Y_t = \alpha_1 + \alpha_2 x_t + u_{1t} \qquad (8.8.1)$$

$$t = 1, 2, \ldots n_1$$

$$\text{Postreconstruction Period:} \qquad Y_t = \beta_1 + \beta_2 x_t + u_{2t} \qquad (8.8.2)$$

$$t = 1, 2, \ldots n_2$$

where Y is personal savings, X is personal income, the u's are the disturbance terms in the two equations, and n_1 and n_2 are the number of observations in the two periods. Notice that the number of observations in the two periods can be the same or different.

Now a structural change may mean that the two intercepts are different, or the two slopes are different, or both the intercept and the slopes are different, or any other suitable combination of the parameters. Of course, if there is no structural change (i.e., structural stability), we can combine all the n_1 and n_2 observations and just estimate one savings function as

$$Y_t = \lambda_1 + \lambda_2 X_t + u_t \qquad (8.8.3)$$

How do we find out whether there is a structural change in the savings-income relationship between the two periods? A popularly used test to answer this question is known as the **Chow test**, after Gregory Chow,[17] although it is simply the F test discussed earlier.

The assumptions underlying the Chow test are twofold:

$$(a) \quad u_{1t} \sim N(0, \sigma^2) \qquad \text{and} \qquad u_{2t} \sim N(0, \sigma^2)$$

that is, the two error terms are normally distributed with the same (homoscedastic) variance σ^2, and

$$(b) \quad u_{1t} \text{ and } u_{2t} \text{ are independently distributed.}[18]$$

---

[17]Gregory C. Chow, "Tests of Equality between Sets of Coefficients in Two Linear Regressions," *Econometrica*, vol. 28, no. 3, 1960, pp. 591–605.

[18]In Chapter 11 on homoscedasticity we will show how one finds out if two (or more) variances are the same. The Chow test has been modified to take into account heteroscedasticity. See W. A. Jayatissa, "Tests of Equality between Sets of Coefficients in Two Linear Regressions When Disturbance Variances Are Unequal," *Econometrica*, vol. 45, 1977, pp. 1291–1292.

With these assumptions, the Chow test proceeds as follows.

Step I: Combining all the n_1 and n_2 observations, we estimate (8.8.3) and obtain its residual sum of squares (RSS), say, S_1 with df $= (n_1 + n_2 - k)$, where k is the number of parameters estimated, 2 in the present case.

Step II: Estimate (8.8.1) and (8.8.2) individually and obtain their RSS, say, S_2 and S_3, with df $= (n_1 - k)$ and $(n_2 - k)$, respectively. Add these two RSS, say, $S_4 = S_2 + S_3$ with df $= (n_1 + n_2 - 2k)$.

Step III: Obtain $S_5 = S_1 - S_4$.

Step IV: Given the assumptions of the Chow test, it can be shown that

$$F = \frac{S_5/k}{S_4/(n_1 + n_2 - 2k)} \tag{8.8.4}$$

follows the F distribution with df $= (k, n_1 + n_2 - 2k)$. If the F computed from (8.8.4) exceeds the critical F value at the chosen level of α, reject the hypothesis that the regressions (8.8.1) and (8.8.2) are the same, that is, reject the hypothesis of structural stability. Alternatively, if the p value of the F obtained from (8.8.4) is low, reject the null hypothesis of structural stability.

Returning to our example, the results are as follows: Note that in our example $n_1 = n_2 = 9$.

Step I:

$$\hat{Y}_t = -1.0821 + 0.1178 X_t$$
$$(0.1452) \quad (0.0088)$$
$$t = (-7.4548) \quad (13.4316) \quad r^2 = 0.9185$$
$$S_1 = 0.5722; \quad df = 16 \tag{8.8.5}$$

Step II: Reconstruction period, 1946–1954

$$\hat{Y}_t = -0.2622 + 0.0470 X_t$$
$$(0.3054) \quad (0.0266)$$
$$t = (-0.8719) \quad (1.7700) \quad r^2 = 0.3092$$
$$S_2 = 0.1396; \quad df = 7 \tag{8.8.6}$$

Postreconstruction period, 1955–1963

$$\hat{Y}_t = -1.7502 + 0.1504 X_t$$
$$(0.3576) \quad (0.0175)$$
$$t = (-4.8948) \quad (8.5749) \quad r^2 = 0.9131$$
$$S_3 = 0.1931; \quad df = 7 \tag{8.8.7}$$

Step III:

$$S_4 = (S_2 + S_3) = 0.3327$$
$$S_5 = (S_1 - S_4) = 0.2395$$

Step IV:

$$F = \frac{0.2395/2}{0.3327/14}$$

$$= 5.04$$

If α is fixed at the 5% level, the critical $F_{2,14} = 3.74$. And since the observed F value of 5.04 exceeds this critical value, one can reject the hypothesis that the savings function in the two time periods is the same. Incidentally, the **p value** of the observed F is 0.0224.

If we accept the conclusion that the savings functions in the two time periods are different, is this difference due to a difference in the intercept values, or the slope values, or both? Although the Chow test can be adapted to answer these questions, in the chapter on dummy variables (see Chapter 15) we will present an alternative to the Chow test that can answer these questions more readily.

*8.9 TESTING THE FUNCTIONAL FORM OF REGRESSION: CHOOSING BETWEEN LINEAR AND LOG-LINEAR REGRESSION MODELS

The choice between a linear regression model (the regressor is a linear function of the regressors) or a log-linear regression model (the log of the regressor is a function of the logs of the regressors) is a perennial question in empirical analysis. We can use a test proposed by MacKinnon, White, and Davidson, which for brevity we call the **MWD test** to choose between the two models.[19]

To illustrate this test, assume the following

H_0: *Linear Model:* Y is a linear function of regressors, the X's.

H_1: *Log-linear Model:* $\ln Y$ is a linear function of logs of regressors, the logs of X's.

where, as usual, H_0 and H_1 denote the null and alternative hypotheses.

The MWD test involves the following steps:[20]

Step I: Estimate the linear model and obtain the estimated Y values. Call them Yf (i.e., $\hat{Y}$).

Step II: Estimate the log-linear model and obtain the estimated $\ln Y$ values; call them $\ln f$ (i.e., $\widehat{\ln Y}$).

---

*Optional.

[19]J. Mackinnon, H. White, and R. Davidson, "Tests for Model Specification in the Presence of Alternative Hypothesis; Some Further Results," *Journal of Econometrics*, vol. 21, 1983, pp. 53–70. A similar test is proposed in A. K. Bera and C. M. Jarque, "Model Specification Tests: A Simultaneous Approach," *Journal of Econometrics*, vol. 20, 1982, pp. 59–82.

[20]This discussion is based on William H. Greene, *ET: The Econometrics Toolkit Version 3*, Econometric Software, Bellport, New York, 1992, pp. 245–246.

Step III: Obtain $Z_1 = (\ln Yf - \ln f)$.

Step IV: Regress Y on X's and Z_1 obtained in Step III. Reject H_0 if the coefficient of Z_1 is statistically significant by the usual t test.

Step V: Obtain $Z_2 = (\text{antilog of } \ln f - Yf)$.

Step VI: Regress log of Y on the logs of X's and Z_2. Reject H_1 if the coefficient of Z_2 is statistically significant by the usual t test.

Although the MWD test seems involved, the logic of the test is quite simple. If the linear model is in fact the correct model, the constructed variable Z_1 should not be statistically significant in Step IV, for in that case the estimated Y values from the linear model and those estimated from the log-linear model (after taking their antilog values for comparative purposes) should not be different. The same comment applies to the alternative hypothesis H_1.

Example 8.5: The Demand for Roses

Refer to exercise 7.20 where we have presented data on the demand for roses in the Detroit metropolitan area for the period 1971-II to 1975-II. For illustrative purposes we will consider the demand for roses as a function only of the prices of roses and carnations, leaving out the income variable for the time being. Now we consider the following models:

Linear Model: $\qquad Y_t = \alpha_1 + \alpha_2 X_{2t} + \alpha_3 X_{3t} + u_t \qquad$ (8.9.1)

Log-linear Model: $\qquad \ln Y_t = \beta_1 + \beta_2 \ln X_{2t} + \beta_3 \ln X_{3t} + u_t \qquad$ (8.9.2)

where Y is the quantity of roses in dozens, X_2 is the average wholesale price of roses (\$/dozen), and X_3 is the average wholesale price of carnations (\$/dozen). A priori, α_2 and β_2 are expected to be negative (why?), and α_3 and β_3 are expected to be positive (why?). As we know, the slope coefficients in the log-linear models are elasticity coefficients.

The regression results are as follows:

$$\widehat{Y_t} = \underset{t = (3.3705)}{0.9734.2176} - \underset{(-6.6069)}{3782.1956 X_{2t}} + \underset{(2.9712)}{2815.2515 X_{3t}}$$

$$F = 21.84; \quad R^2 = 0.77096 \qquad (8.9.3)$$

$$\widehat{\ln Y_t} = \underset{t = (16.2349)}{9.2278} - \underset{(-5.9044)}{1.7607 \ln X_{2t}} + \underset{(2.5407)}{1.3398 \ln X_{3t}}$$

$$F = 17.50; \quad R^2 = 0.7292 \qquad (8.9.4)$$

As these results show, both the linear and the log-linear models seem to fit the data reasonably well: The parameters have the expected signs and the t and R^2 values are statistically significant.

To decide between these models on the bass of the **MWD test,** we first test the hypothesis that the true model is linear. Then, following Step IV of the test, we obtain the following regression:

$$\widehat{Y_t} = \underset{t = (3.2178)}{9727.5685} - \underset{(-6.3337)}{3783.0623 X_{2t}} + \underset{(2.8366)}{2817.7157 X_{3t}} + \underset{(0.0207)}{85.2319 Z_{1t}}$$

$$F = 13.44; \quad R^2 = 0.7707 \qquad (8.9.5)$$

Since the coefficient of Z_1 is not statistically significant (the p value of the estimated t is 0.98), we do not reject the hypothesis that the true model is linear.

Suppose we switch gears and assume that the true model is log-linear. Following Step VI of the MWD test, we obtain the following regression results:

$$\widehat{\ln Y_t} = \quad 9.1486 \quad - \quad 1.9699 \ln X_t + \quad 1.5891 \ln X_{2t} - \quad 0.0013 Z_{2t}$$
$$t = (17.0825) \quad (-6.4189) \quad (3.0728) \quad (-1.6612) \tag{8.9.6}$$
$$F = 14.17; \quad R^2 = 0.7798$$

The coefficient of Z_2 is statistically significant at about the 12% level (p value is 0.1225). Therefore, we can reject the hypothesis that the true model is log-linear at this level of significance. Of course, if one sticks to the conventional 1 or 5% significance levels, then one cannot reject the hypothesis that the true model is log-linear. As this example shows, it is quite possible that in a given situation we cannot reject either of the specifications.

8.10 PREDICTION WITH MULTIPLE REGRESSION

In Section 5.10 we showed how the estimated two-variable regression model can be used for (a) mean prediction, i.e., predicting the point on the population regression function (PRF) as well as for (b) individual prediction, i.e., predicting an individual value of Y, given the value of the regressor $X = X_0$, where X_0 is the specified numerical value of X.

The estimated multiple regression too can be used for similar purposes and the procedure for doing that is a straightforward extension of the two-variable case, except the formulas for estimating the variance and standard error of the forecast values [comparable to (5.10.2) and (5.10.6) of the two-variable model] are rather involved and are better handled by the matrix methods discussed in Chapter 9. (See Section 9.9.)

To illustrate the mechanics of mean and individual predictions, let us recall the personal consumption regression estimated earlier for the United States for the period 1956–1970.

$$\hat{Y}_i = 53.1603 + 0.7266 X_{2i} + 2.7363 X_{3i}$$
$$(13.0261) \quad (0.0487) \quad (0.8486) \tag{8.10.1}$$
$$R^2 = 0.9988 \tag{= (8.2.2)}$$

where Y = personal consumption expenditure, X_2 = personal disposable income, and X_3 = time trend.

$\hat{Y}_i$, as we know, is an *estimator* of $E(Y \mid X_2, X_3)$, that is, the true mean of Y given X_2 and X_3.

Now suppose that the data for 1971 are as follows: X_2 = \$567 billion and X_3 = 16. Plugging these values into (8.10.1), we obtain

$$(\hat{Y}_{1971} \mid X_2 = 567, X_3 = 16)$$
$$= 53.1603 + 0.7266(567) + 2.7363(16) = 508.9297 \tag{8.10.2}$$

Thus, for 1971 the *mean* PCE is about \$509 billion. For the reasons noted in Section 5.10, \$509 billion is also the value of *individual* prediction for 1971, Y_{1971}.

However, the variances of $\hat{Y}_{1971}$ and Y_{1971} are different. From the formulas given in Chapter 9, it can be shown that:

$$\text{var}(\hat{Y}_{1971} \,|\, X_2, X_3) = 3.6580 \quad \text{and} \quad \text{se}(\hat{Y}_{1971} \,|\, X_2, X_3) = 1.9126 \qquad (8.10.3)$$

$$\text{var}(Y_{1971} \,|\, X_2, X_3) = 10.0887 \quad \text{and} \quad \text{se}(Y_{1971} \,|\, X_2, X_3) = 3.1763 \qquad (8.10.4)$$

where $\text{var}(Y_{1971} \,|\, X_2, X_3)$ stands for $E(Y_{1971} - \hat{Y}_{1971} \,|\, X_2, X_3)^2$. As to be expected, $\text{var}(Y_{1971}) > \text{var}(\hat{Y}_{1971})$. (Why?) *Note:* $\text{var}\, Y_{1971}$ is a short-hand for $\text{var}(Y_{1971} - \hat{Y}_{1971})$.

Under the assumptions of the classical model, and following the discussion in Section 5.10, we can establish the $100(1-\alpha)$ *confidence interval* for *mean prediction* as

$$[\hat{Y}_{1971} - t_{\alpha/2}\, \text{se}(\hat{Y}_{1971}) \le E(Y_{1971}) \le \hat{Y}_{1971} + t_{\alpha/2}\, \text{se}(\hat{Y}_{1971})] \qquad (8.10.5)$$

where $\text{se}(\hat{Y}_{1971})$ is obtained from (8.10.3) and where it is assumed that this prediction is based on the given values of X_2 and X_3 for 1971. Needless to say, the same procedure can be repeated for any other values of X_2 and X_3.

The equivalent $100(1-\alpha)$ confidence interval for *individual prediction*, Y_{1971} is

$$[\hat{Y}_{1971} - t_{\alpha/2}\, \text{se}(Y_{1971}) \le \hat{Y}_{1971} \le \hat{Y}_{1971} + t_{\alpha/2}\, \text{se}(Y_{1971})]$$

where $\text{se}(Y_{1971})$, a shorthand for $\text{se}(Y_{1971} - \hat{Y}_{1971})$, is now obtained from (8.10.4).

For our illustrative example the reader can verify that these confidence intervals are as follows:

Mean prediction:

$$508 \cdot 9297 - 2 \cdot 179(1 \cdot 9126) \le E(Y_{1971}) \le 508 \cdot 9297 + 2 \cdot 179(1 \cdot 9126)$$

that is,

$$504 \cdot 7518 \le E(Y_{1971}) \le 513 \cdot 0868 \qquad (8.10.6)$$

Individual prediction:

$$508 \cdot 9297 - 2 \cdot 179(3 \cdot 1763) \le Y_{1971} \le 508 \cdot 9297 + 2 \cdot 179(3 \cdot 1763)$$

$$501 \cdot 9988 \le Y_{1971} \le 515 \cdot 8412 \qquad (8.10.7)$$

Remember that the df for the t value is $(n-3)$ for the three-variable model, $(n-4)$ for the four-variable model, or $(n-k)$ for the k-variable model.

*8.11 THE TROIKA OF HYPOTHESIS TESTS: THE LIKELIHOOD RATIO (LR), WALD (W), AND LAGRANGE MULTIPLIER (LM) TESTS[21]

In this and the previous chapters we have, by and large, used the t, F, and chi-square tests to test a variety of hypotheses in the context of linear (in-

---

*Optional.

[21]For an accessible discussion, see A. Buse, "The Likelihood Ratio, Wald and Lagrange Multiplier Tests: An Expository Note," *American Statistician*, vol. 36, 1982, pp. 153–157.

parameter) regression models. But once we go beyond the somewhat comfortable world of linear regression models, we need method(s) to test hypotheses that can handle regression models, linear or not.

The well-known trinity of **likelihood, Wald, and Lagrange multiplier tests** can accomplish this purpose. The interesting thing to note is that *asymptotically* (i.e., in large samples) all three tests are equivalent in that the test statistic associated with each of these tests follows the chi-square distribution.

Although we will discuss the **likelihood Ratio Test** in the appendix to this chapter, in general we will not use these tests in this textbook for the pragmatic reason that in small, or finite, samples, which is unfortunately what most researchers deal with, the F test that we have used so far will suffice. As Davidson and MacKinnon note:

> For linear regression models, with or without normal errors, there is of course no need to look at LM, W and LR at all, since no information is gained from doing so over and above what is already contained in F.[22]

8.12 SUMMARY AND CONCLUSIONS

1. This chapter extended and refined the ideas of interval estimation and hypothesis testing first introduced in Chapter 5 in the context of the two-variable linear regression model.

2. In a multiple regression, testing the *individual significance* of a partial regression coefficient (using the t test) and testing the *overall significance* of the regression (i.e., H_0: all partial slope coefficients are zero or $R^2 = 0$) are not the same thing.

3. In particular, the finding that one or more partial regression coefficients are statistically insignificant on the basis of the *individual t* test does not mean that all partial regression coefficients are also (collectively) statistically insignificant. The latter hypothesis can be tested only by the F test.

4. The **F test** is given versatile in that it can test a variety of hypotheses, such as whether (1) an individual regression coefficient is statistically significant, (2) all partial slope coefficients are zero, (3) two or more coefficients are statistically equal, (4) the coefficients satisfy some linear restrictions, and (5) there is structural stability of the regression model.

5. As in the two-variable case, the multiple regression model can be used for the purpose of mean and or individual prediction.

THE ROAD AHEAD

With this chapter we conclude our discussion of the classical linear regression model, which began in Chapter 2. As we have pointed out from time to time, the classical model is based on some ideal or stringent assumptions. But it has provided us with a standard or norm against which we can judge other regression models that try to inject "realism" by relaxing one or more assumptions

---

[22]Russell Davidson and James G. MacKinnon, *Estimation and Inference in Econometrics*, Oxford University Press, New York, 1993, p. 456.

of the classical model. Our task in the rest of the text will be to find out what happens if one or more assumptions of the classical model are relaxed. We would like to know how "robust" the classical model is in case we adopt less stringent assumptions. We would like to know, for example, what happens if the normality assumption is relaxed, or if we allow for heteroscedasticity or serial correlation or specification errors.

But before we turn to that enquiry, we introduce in Chapter 9 the classical model in matrix notation. This chapter not only provides a convenient summary of Chapters 1 through 8 but also shows why matrix algebra is such a useful tool once we go beyond the two- or three-variable regression models; without it manipulating the k-variable regression model would be a terribly messy job.

It should be noted that Chapter 9 is not essential to understand the rest of the text. It is there primarily for the benefit of the more mathematically inclined students. Yet with the rudiments of matrix algebra given in Appendix B the reader without prior knowledge of matrix algebra will find it worthwhile to peruse the chapter. **But let me reiterate, this chapter is not critical to understanding the rest of the text;** it can be omitted without loss of continuity.

EXERCISES

Questions

8.1. Suppose you want to study the behavior of sales of a product, say, automobiles over a number of years and suppose someone suggests you try the following models:

$$Y_t = \beta_0 + \beta_1 t$$
$$Y_t = \alpha_0 + \alpha_1 t + \alpha_2 t^2$$

where Y_t = sales at time t and t = time, measured in years. The first model postulates that sales is a linear function of time, whereas the second model states that it is a quadratic function of time.
(a) Discuss the properties of these models.
(b) How would you decide between the two models?
(c) In what situations will the quadratic model be useful?
(d) Try to obtain data on automobile sales in the United States over the past 20 years and see which of the models fits the data better.

8.2. Show that the F ratio of (8.5.16) is equal to the F ratio of (8.5.18). (*Hint:* ESS/TSS = R^2.)

8.3. Show that F tests of (8.5.18) and (8.7.10) are equivalent.

8.4. Establish statements (8.7.11) and (8.7.12).

8.5. Consider the Cobb-Douglas production function

$$Y = \beta_1 L^{\beta_2} K^{\beta_3} \tag{1}$$

where Y = output, L = labor input, and K = capital input. Dividing (1) through by K, we get

$$(Y/K) = \beta_1 (L/K)^{\beta_2} K^{\beta_2 + \beta_3 - 1} \tag{2}$$

Taking the natural log of (2), we obtain

$$\ln (Y/K) = \beta_0 + \beta_2 \ln (L/K) + (\beta_2 + \beta_3 - 1)\ln K \tag{3}$$

where $\beta_0 = \ln \beta_1$.

(a) Suppose you had data to run the regression (3). How would you test the hypothesis that there are constant returns to scale, i.e., $(\beta_2 + \beta_3) = 1$?

(b) If there are constant returns to scale, how would you interpret regression (3)?

(c) Does it make any difference whether we divide (1) by L rather than by K?

8.6. Critical values of R^2 when true $R^2 = 0$. Equation (8.5.11) gave the relationship between F and R^2 under the hypothesis that all partial slope coefficients are simultaneously equal to zero (i.e., $R^2 = 0$). Just as we can find the critical F value at the α level of significance from the F table, we can find the critical R^2 value from the following relation:

$$R^2 = \frac{(k-1)F}{(k-1)F + (n-k)}$$

where k is the number of parameters in the regression model including the intercept and where F is the critical F value at the α level of significance. If the observed R^2 exceeds the critical R^2 obtained from the preceding formula, we can reject the hypothesis that the true R^2 is zero.

Establish the preceding formula and find out the critical R^2 value (at $\alpha = 5\%$) for the regression (8.2.2).

8.7. Following the procedure to detrend a time series discussed in Section 8.2, verify that for the data given in Table 8.1 the slope coefficient in the regression of detrended Y on detrended X_2 is indeed equal to β_2 given in (8.2.2).

8.8. Will the R^2 obtained in (8.2.2) be the same as that obtained from the regression of detrended Y on detrended X_2? Explain.

8.9. Following Section 8.2, consider the following regressions:

$$\hat{u}_{1i} = a_1 + a_2\hat{u}_{2i} + w_{1i} \tag{1}$$

where $\hat{u}_{1i} = $ (linear) detrended Y, $\hat{u}_{2i} = $ (linear) detrended X_2 and $w_{1i} = $ residual (all the w's in the following regressions are residuals).

$$Y_i = b_1 + b_2\hat{u}_{2i} + w_{2i} \tag{2}$$
$$\hat{u}_{1i} = c_1 + c_2X_{2i} + c_3X_{3i} + w_{3i} \qquad (X_3 \text{ is time}) \tag{3}$$
$$Y_i = d_1 + d_2\hat{u}_{2i} + d_3X_{3i} + w_{4i} \tag{4}$$

Show that $a_2 = b_2 = c_2 = d_2$. What general conclusions can you draw? (*Note:* $a_2 = \beta_2$.)

8.10. Based on annual data for the years 1968–1987, the following regression results were obtained:

$$\hat{Y}_t = -859.92 + 0.6470X_{2t} - 23.195X_{3t} \qquad R^2 = 0.9776 \tag{1}$$
$$\hat{Y}_t = -261.09 + 0.2452X_{2t} \qquad R^2 = 0.9388 \tag{2}$$

where $Y = $ U.S. expenditure on imported goods, billions of 1982 dollars, $X_2 = $ personal disposable income, billions of 1982 dollars, and $X_3 = $ trend variable. *True or false:* The standard error of X_3 in (1) is 4.2750. Show your calculations. (*Hint:* Use the relationship between R^2, F, and t.)

8.11. Suppose in the regression

$$\ln(Y_i/X_{2i}) = \alpha_1 + \alpha_2 \ln X_{2i} + \alpha_3 \ln X_{3i} + u_i$$

the values of the regression coefficients and their standard errors are known.* From this knowledge, how would you estimate the parameters and standard errors of the following regression model?

$$\ln Y_i = \beta_1 + \beta_2 \ln X_{2i} + \beta_3 \ln X_{3i} + u_i$$

8.12. Assume the following:

$$Y_i = \beta_1 + \beta_2 X_{2i} + \beta_3 X_{3i} + \beta_4 X_{2i} X_{3i} + u_i$$

where Y is personal consumption expenditure, X_2 is personal income, and X_3 is personal wealth.† The term $(X_{2i}X_{3i})$ is known as the **interaction term**. What is meant by this expression? How would you test the hypothesis that the marginal propensity to consume (MPC) (i.e., β_2) is independent of the wealth of the consumer?

8.13. You are given the following regression results:

$$\hat{Y}_t = 16899 \quad - \quad 2978.5 X_{2t} \qquad\qquad R^2 = 0.6149$$
$$t = \quad (8.5152) \quad\quad (-4.7280)$$
$$\hat{Y}_t = 9734.2 \quad - \quad 3782.2 X_{2t} \quad + \quad 2815 X_{3t} \qquad R^2 = 0.7706$$
$$t = \quad (3.3705) \quad\quad (-6.6070) \quad\quad (2.9712)$$

Can you find out the sample size underlying these results? (*Hint:* Recall the relationship between R^2, F, and t values.)

8.14. Based on our discussion of *individual* and *joint* tests of hypothesis based, respectively, on the t and F tests, which of the following situations are likely?

1. reject the joint null on the basis of the F statistic, but do not reject each separate null on the basis of the individual t-tests;
2. reject the joint null on the basis of the F statistic, reject one individual hypothesis on the basis of the t-test, and do not reject other individual hypothesis on the basis of the t-test;
3. reject the joint null hypothesis on the basis of the F-statistic, and reject each separate null hypothesis on the basis of the individual t-tests;
4. do not reject the joint null on the basis of the F-statistic, and do not reject each separate null on the basis of individual t-tests.
5. do not reject the joint null on the basis of the F-statistic, reject one individual hypothesis on the basis of a t-test, and do not reject other individual hypothesis on the basis of the t-test;
6. do not reject the joint null on the basis of the F-statistic, but reject each separate null on the basis of individual t-tests.**

---

*Adapted from Peter Kennedy, *A Guide to Econometrics*, the MIT Press, 3d ed., Cambridge, Massachusetts, 1992, p. 310.

†Ibid., p. 327.

**Quoted from Ernst R. Berndt, *The Practice of Econometrics: Classic and Contemporary*, Addison-Wesley, Reading, Massachusetts, 1991, p. 79.

Problems

8.15. Refer to exercise 7.18.

(a) Are $\hat{\beta}_2$ and $\hat{\beta}_3$ individually statistically significant?

(b) Are they statistically different from unity?

(c) Are $\hat{\alpha}_2$ and $\hat{\alpha}_3$ statistically significant individually?

(d) Do the data support the hypothesis that $\beta_2 = \beta_3 = 0$?

(e) Test the hypothesis that $\alpha_2 = \alpha_3 = 0$.

(f) How would you compute the output elasticities of labor and capital for the first model? For the second model?

(g) Which of the models do you prefer? Why?

(h) Compare the R^2 values of the two models. You may use the 5% level of significance.

8.16. Refer to exercise 7.19.

(a) Test the overall significance of the estimated regression.

(b) What is the incremental contribution of X_i^2?

(c) Would you keep X_i^2 in the model on the basis of the F test? On the basis of R^2?

8.17. Refer to exercise 7.25.

(a) What are the real income and interest rate elasticities of real cash balances?

(b) Are the preceding elasticities statistically significant individually?

(c) Test the overall significance of the estimated regression.

(d) Is the income elasticity of demand for real cash balances significantly different from unity?

(e) Should the interest rate variable be retained in the model? Why?

8.18. Continue with exercise 7.25. Suppose that we run the following regression:

$$M_t^n = \alpha_0 Y_t^{\alpha_1} r_t^{\alpha_2} P_t^{\alpha_3}$$

where M_t^n = aggregate *nominal* money cash balances at time t, Y_t = aggregate real income at time t, r_t = long-term interest rate at time t, and P_t = implicit price deflator at time t (as a measure of general price level).

(a) Run the preceding regression and interpret the results.

(b) Compare the results of this regression with those obtained from the regression of exercise 7.25.

(c) A priori, what would be the value of α_3? Why?

(d) What can you say about "money illusion" in the Indian economy for the period 1948–1965?

8.19. Continuing with exercise 8.18, consider the following demand for money function:

$$M_t^n = \lambda_0 (Y_t^n)^{\lambda_1} r_t^{\lambda_2} P_t^{\lambda_3}$$

where, in addition to the definitions given in exercise 8.18, Y_t^n stands for aggregate nominal net national income.

(a) Run the preceding regression and comment on your results.

(b) Compare the results of this regression with those obtained from Exercises 7.25 and 8.18.

(c) What is the relationship, if any, between α_1 and λ_1?

8.20. Assuming that Y and $X_2, X_3, \ldots, X_k$ are jointly normally distributed and assuming that the null hypothesis is that the population partial correlations are individually equal to zero, R. A. Fisher has shown that

$$t = \frac{r_{12.34...k} \sqrt{n-k-2}}{\sqrt{1-r^2_{12.34...k}}}$$

follows the t distribution with $n - k - 2$ df, where k is the kth-order partial correlation coefficient and where n is the total number of observations. (*Note:* $r_{12.3}$ is a first-order partial correlation coefficient, $r_{12.34}$ is a second-order partial correlation coefficient, and so on.) Refer to exercise 7.2. Assuming Y and X_2 and X_3 to be jointly normally distributed, compute the three partial correlations $r_{12.3}, r_{13.2}$ and $r_{23.1}$ and test their significance under the hypothesis that the corresponding population correlations are individually equal to zero.

8.21. In studying the demand for farm tractors in the United States for the periods 1921–1941 and 1948–1957, Griliches* obtained the following results:

$$\widehat{\log Y_t} = \text{constant} - 0.519 \ \log X_{2t} - 4.933 \ \log X_{3t} \qquad R^2 = 0.793$$
$$(0.231) \qquad\qquad (0.477)$$

where Y_t = value of stock of tractors on farms as of January 1, in 1935–1939 dollars, X_2 = index of prices paid for tractors divided by an index of prices received for all crops at time $t - 1$, X_3 = interest rate prevailing in year $t - 1$, and where the estimated standard errors are given in the parentheses.

(a) Interpret the preceding regression.

(b) Are the estimated slope coefficients individually statistically significant? Are they significantly different from unity?

(c) Use the analysis of variance technique to test the significance of the overall regression. *Hint:* Use the R^2 variant of the ANOVA technique.

(d) How would you compute the interest-rate elasticity of demand for farm tractors?

(e) How would you test the significance of estimated R^2?

8.22. Consider the following wage-determination equation for the British economy† for the period 1950–1969:

$$\hat{W}_t = 8.582 + 0.364(\text{PF})_t + 0.004(\text{PF})_{t-1} - 2.560U_t$$
$$(1.129) \quad (0.080) \qquad\quad (0.072) \qquad\qquad (0.658)$$

$$R^2 = 0.873; \quad \text{df} = 15$$

where W = wages and salaries per employee, PF = prices of final output at factor cost, U = unemployment in Great Britain as a percentage of the total number of employees of Great Britain, and t = time. (The figures in the parentheses are the estimated standard errors.)

(a) Interpret the preceding equation.

(b) Are the estimated coefficients individually significant?

(c) What is the rationale for the introduction of $(\text{PF})_{t-1}$?

(d) Should the variable $(\text{PF})_{t-1}$ be dropped from the model? Why?

---

*Z. Griliches, "The Demand for a Durable Input: Farm Tractors in the United States, 1921–1957," in *The Demand for Durable Goods*, Arnold C. Harberger (ed.), The University of Chicago Press, Chicago, 1960, Table 1, p. 192.

†Taken from *Prices and Earnings in 1951–1969: An Econometric Assessment*, Dept. of Employment, HMSO, 1971, Eq. (19), p. 35.

(e) How would you compute the elasticity of wages and salaries per employee with respect to the unemployment rate U?

8.23. A variation of the wage-determination equation given in exercise 8.22 is as follows:*

$$\hat{W}_t = \begin{array}{ccccc} 1.073 & + & 5.288V_t & - & 0.116X_t & + & 0.054M_t & + & 0.046M_{t-1} \\ (0.797) & & (0.812) & & (0.111) & & (0.022) & & (0.019) \end{array}$$

$$R^2 = 0.934; \quad \text{df} = 14$$

where W is as before, V = unfilled job vacancies in Great Britain as a percentage of the total number of employees in Great Britain, X = gross domestic product per person employed, M = import prices, and M_{t-1} = import prices in the previous (or lagged) year. (The estimated standard errors are given in the parentheses.)

(a) Interpret the preceding equation.

(b) Which of the estimated coefficients are individually statistically significant?

(c) What is the rationale for the introduction of the X variable? A priori, is the sign of X expected to be negative?

(d) What is the purpose of introducing both M_t and M_{t-1} in the model?

(e) Which of the variables may be dropped from the model? Why?

(f) Test the overall significance of the observed regression.

8.24. Refer to the expectations-augmented Phillips curve regression (7.6.2). Is the coefficient of X_3, the expected inflation rate, statistically equal to unity as per the theory? Show your calculations.

8.25. For the demand for chicken function estimated in (8.7.24), is the estimated income elasticity equal to 1? Is the price elasticity equal to -1?

8.26. For the demand function (8.7.24) how would you test the hypothesis that the income elasticity is equal in value but opposite in sign to the price elasticity of demand? Show the necessary calculations. (*Note:* $\text{cov}(\hat{\beta}_2, \hat{\beta}_3) = -0.00142$.)

8.27. Refer to the demand for roses function of Exercise 7.20. Confining your considerations to the logarithmic specification,

(a) What is the estimated own-price elasticity of demand (i.e., elasticity with respect to the price of roses)?

(b) Is it statistically significant?

(c) If so, is it significantly different from unity?

(d) A priori, what are the expected signs of X_3 (price of carnations) and X_4 (income)? Are the empirical results in accord with these expectations?

(e) If the coefficients of X_3 and X_4 are statistically insignificant, what may be the reasons?

8.28. Refer to exercise 7.21 relating to wildcat activity.

(a) Is each of the estimated slope coefficients individually statistically significant at the 5% level?

(b) Would you reject the hypothesis that $R^2 = 0$?

(c) What is the instantaneous rate of growth of wildcat activity over the period 1948–1978? The corresponding compound rate of growth?

8.29. Refer to the U.S. defense budget outlay regression estimated in exercise 7.22.

(a) Comment generally on the estimated regression results.

(b) Set up the ANOVA table and test the hypothesis that all the partial slope coefficients are zero.

---

*Ibid., Eq. (67), p. 37.

8.30. The following is known as the **transcendental production function** (TPF), a generalization of the well-known Cobb-Douglas production function:

$$Y_i = \beta_1 L^{\beta_2} k^{\beta_3} e^{\beta_4 L + \beta_5 K}$$

where Y = output, L = labor input, and K = capital input.

After taking logarithms and adding the stochastic disturbance term, we obtain the stochastic TPF as

$$\ln Y_i = \beta_0 + \beta_2 \ln L_i + \beta_3 \ln K_i + \beta_4 L_i + \beta_5 K_i + u_i$$

where $\beta_0 = \ln \beta_1$.

(a) What are the properties of this function?

(b) For the TPF to reduce to the Cobb-Douglas production function, what must be the values of β_4 and β_5?

(c) If you had the data, how would you go about finding out whether the TPF reduces to the Cobb-Douglas production function? What testing procedure would you use?

(d) See if the TPF fits the data given in Exercise 7.18. Show your calculations.

8.31. *Energy prices and capital formation: United States, 1948–1978.* To test the hypothesis that a rise in the price of energy relative to output leads to a decline in the productivity of *existing* capital and labor resources, John A. Tatom estimated the following production function for the United States for the quarterly period 1948–I to 1978–II:*

$$\ln(y/k) = \quad 1.5492 + \quad 0.7135 \ln(h/k) - \quad 0.1081 \ln(P_e/P)$$
$$\qquad\qquad (16.33) \qquad (21.69) \qquad\qquad (-6.42)$$
$$\qquad\qquad\qquad + \quad 0.0045t \qquad R^2 = 0.98$$
$$\qquad\qquad\qquad\quad (15.86)$$

where y = real output in the private business sector, k = a measure of the flow of capital services, h = person hours in the private business sector, P_e = producer price index for fuel and related products, P = private business sector price deflator, and t = time. The numbers in parentheses are t statistics.

(a) Do the results support the author's hypothesis?

(b) Between 1972 and 1977 the relative price of energy, (P_e/P), increased by 60 percent. From the estimated regression, what is the loss in productivity?

(c) After allowing for the changes in (h/k) and (P_e/P), what has been the trend rate of growth of productivity over the sample period?

(d) How would you interpret the coefficient value of 0.7135?

(e) Does the fact that each estimated partial slope coefficient is individually statistically significant (why?) mean we can reject the hypothesis that $R^2 = 0$? Why or why not?

8.32. *The demand for cable.* The table on the next page gives data used by a telephone cable manufacturer to predict sales to a major customer for the period 1968–1983.†

The variables in the table are defined as follows:

$$Y = \text{annual sales in MPF, million paired feet}$$
$$X_2 = \text{Gross National Product (GNP), \$, billions}$$

---

*See his "Energy Prices and Capital Formation: 1972–1977," *Review*, Federal Reserve Bank of St. Louis, vol. 61, no. 5, May 1979, p. 4.

†I am indebted to Daniel J. Reardon for collecting and processing the data.

X_3 = housing starts, thousands of units
X_4 = unemployment rate, %
X_5 = prime rate lagged 6 months
X_6 = Customer line gains, %

Regression variables

Year	X_2, GNP	X_3, Housing starts	X_4, Unemployment, %	X_5, Prime rate lag, 6 mos.	X_6, Customer line gains, %	Y, Total plastic purchases (MPF)
1968	1,051.8	1,503.6	3.6	5.8	5.9	5,873
1969	1,078.8	1,486.7	3.5	6.7	4.5	7,852
1970	1,075.3	1,434.8	5.0	8.4	4.2	8,189
1971	1,107.5	2,035.6	6.0	6.2	4.2	7,497
1972	1,171.1	2,360.8	5.6	5.4	4.9	8,534
1973	1,235.0	2,043.9	4.9	5.9	5.0	8,688
1974	1,217.8	1,331.9	5.6	9.4	4.1	7,270
1975	1,202.3	1,160.0	8.5	9.4	3.4	5,020
1976	1,271.0	1,535.0	7.7	7.2	4.2	6,035
1977	1,332.7	1,961.8	7.0	6.6	4.5	7,425
1978	1,399.2	2,009.3	6.0	7.6	3.9	9,400
1979	1,431.6	1,721.9	6.0	10.6	4.4	9,350
1980	1,480.7	1,298.0	7.2	14.9	3.9	6,540
1981	1,510.3	1,100.0	7.6	16.6	3.1	7,675
1982	1,492.2	1,039.0	9.2	17.5	0.6	7,419
1983	1,535.4	1,200.0	8.8	16.0	1.5	7,923

You are to consider the following model:

$$Y_i = \beta_1 + \beta_2 X_{2t} + \beta_3 X_{3t} + \beta_4 X_{4t} + \beta_5 X_{5t} + \beta_6 X_{6t} + u_t$$

(a) Estimate the preceding regression.
(b) What are the expected signs of the coefficients of this model?
(c) Are the empirical results in accordance with prior expectations?
(d) Are the estimated partial regression coefficients individually statistically significant at the 5% level of significance?
(e) Suppose you first regress Y on X_2, X_3, and X_4 only and then decide to add the variables X_5 and X_6. How would you find out if it is worth adding the variables X_5 and X_6? Which test do you use? Show the necessary calculations.

8.33. Marc Nerlove has estimated the following cost function for electricity generation:*

$$Y = A X^\beta P_1^{\alpha_1} P_2^{\alpha_2} P_3^{\alpha_3} u \tag{1}$$

where Y = total cost of production, X = output in kilowatt hours, P_1 = price of labor input, P_2 = price of capital input, P_3 = price of fuel, and u = disturbance term. Theoretically, the sum of the price elasticities is expected to be unity, i.e., $(\alpha_1 + \alpha_2 + \alpha_3) = 1$. By imposing this restriction, the preceding cost function can be written as

$$(Y/P_3) = A X^\beta (P_1/P_3)^{\alpha_1} (P_2/P_3)^{\alpha_2} u \tag{2}$$

In other words, (1) is an unrestricted and (2) is the restricted cost function.

---

*Marc Nerlove, "Returns to Scale in Electric Supply," in Carl Christ, ed., *Measurement in Economics*, Stanford University Press, Palo Alto, California, 1963. The notation has been changed.

On the basis of a sample of 29 medium-sized firms, and after logarithmic transformation, Nerlove obtained the following regression results

$$\widehat{\ln Y_i} = -4.93 \qquad + 0.94 \ln X_i + \qquad\qquad\qquad 0.31 \ln P_1 \qquad (3)$$
$$\text{se} = \quad (1.96) \qquad\quad (0.11) \qquad\qquad\qquad\qquad\qquad (0.23)$$

$$-0.26 \ln P_2 + 0.44 \ln P_3$$
$$(0.29) \qquad\quad (0.07) \qquad\qquad\quad \text{RSS} = 0.336$$

$$\widehat{\ln (Y/P_3)} = -6.55 + 0.91 \ln X + 0.51 \ln(P_1/P_3) + 0.09 \ln(P_2/P_3)$$
$$\text{se} = \quad (0.16) \quad (0.11) \qquad (0.19) \qquad\qquad\quad (0.16) \quad \text{RSS} = 0.364$$
$$(4)$$

(*a*) Interpret Eqs. (3) and (4).
(*b*) How would you find out if the restriction $(\alpha_1 + \alpha_2 + \alpha_3) = 1$ is valid? Show your calculations.

8.34. *Estimating the capital asset pricing model (CAPM).* In Section 6.1 we considered briefly the well-known capital asset pricing model of modern portfolio theory. In empirical analysis, the CAPM is estimated in two stages.

Stage I (Time-series regression). For each of the N securities included in the sample, we run the following regression over time:

$$R_{it} = \hat{\alpha}_i + \hat{\beta}_i R_{mt} + e_{it} \qquad (1)$$

where R_{it} and R_{mt} are the rates of return on the ith security and on the market portfolio (say, the S&P 500) in year t; β_i, as noted elsewhere, is the Beta or market volatility coefficient of the ith security, and e_{it} are the residuals. In all there are N such regressions, one for each security, giving therefore N estimates of β_i.

Stage II (Cross-section regression). In this stage we run the following regression over the N securities:

$$\bar{R}_i = \hat{\gamma}_1 + \hat{\gamma}_2 \hat{\beta}_i + u_i \qquad (2)$$

where $\bar{R}_i$ is the average or mean rate of return for security i computed over the sample period covered by Stage I, $\hat{\beta}_i$ is the estimated beta coefficient from the first-stage regression, and u_i is the residual term.

Comparing the second-stage regression (2) with the CAPM Eq. (6.1.2), written as

$$\text{ER}_i = r_f + \beta_i(\text{ER}_m - r_f) \qquad (3)$$

where r_f is the risk-free rate of return, we see that $\hat{\gamma}_1$ is an estimate of r_f and $\hat{\gamma}_2$ is an estimate of $(\text{ER}_m - r_f)$, the market risk premium.

Thus, in the empirical testing of CAPM, $\bar{R}_i$ and $\hat{\beta}_i$ are used as estimators of ER_i and β_i, respectively. Now if CAPM holds, statistically,

$$\hat{\gamma}_1 = r_f$$
$$\hat{\gamma}_2 = R_m - r_f, \text{ the estimator of } (\text{ER}_m - r_f)$$

Next consider an alternative model:

$$\bar{R}_i = \hat{\gamma}_1 + \hat{\gamma}_2 \hat{\beta}_i + \hat{\gamma}_3 s_{e_i}^2 + u_i \qquad (4)$$

where $s_{e_i}^2$ is the residual variance of the ith security from the first-stage regression. Then, if CAPM is valid, $\hat{\gamma}_3$ should not be significantly different from zero.

To test the CAPM, Levy ran regressions (2) and (4) on a sample of 101 stocks for the period 1948–1968 and obtained the following results:*

$$\bar{R}_i = \underset{(0.009)}{0.109} + \underset{(0.008)}{0.037\beta_i} \tag{2'}$$

$$t = (12.0) \qquad (5.1) \qquad R^2 = 0.21$$

$$\bar{R}_i = \underset{(0.008)}{0.106} + \underset{(0.007)}{0.0024\hat{\beta}_i} + \underset{(0.038)}{0.201s_{\epsilon i}^2} \tag{4'}$$

$$t = (13.2) \qquad (3.3) \qquad (5.3) \qquad R^2 = 0.39$$

(a) Are these results supportive of the CAPM?
(b) Is it worth adding the variable $s_{\epsilon_i}^2$ to the model? How do you know?
(c) If the CAPM holds, $\hat{\gamma}_1$ in (2)' should approximate the average value of the risk-free rate, r_f. The estimated value is 10.9 percent. Does this seem a reasonable estimate of the risk-free rate of return during the observation period, 1948–1968? (You may consider the rate of return on Treasury bills or a similar comparatively risk-free asset.)
(d) If the CAPM holds, the market risk premium $(\bar{R}_m - r_f)$ from (2)' is about 3.7 percent. If r_f is assumed to be 10.9 percent, this implies $\bar{R}_m$ for the sample period was about 14.6 percent. Does this sound a reasonable estimate?
(e) What can you say about the CAPM generally?

8.35. The accompanying table gives data on personal savings (Y) and personal income (X), both in billions of dollars for the years 1970–1991.

Personal savings (Y) and personal income (X), United States, 1970–1991; data in billions of dollars

Year	Savings, Y	Income, X
1970	57.5	831.0
1971	65.4	893.5
1972	59.7	980.5
1973	86.1	1,098.7
1974	93.4	1,205.7
1975	100.3	1,307.3
1976	93.0	1,446.3
1977	87.9	1,601.3
1978	107.8	1,807.9
1979	123.3	2.033.1
1980	153.8	2,265.4
1981	191.8	2,534.7
1982	199.5	2,690.9
1983	168.7	2,862.5
1984	222.0	3,154.6
1985	189.3	3,379.8
1986	187.5	3,590.4
1987	142.0	3,802.0
1988	155.7	4,075.9
1989	152.1	4,380.3
1990	175.6	4,664.2
1991	199.6	4,828.3

Source: Economic Report of the President, 1993, Table B-24, p. 376.

---

*H. Levy, "Equilibrium in an Imperfect Market: A Constraint on the Number of Securities in the Portfolio," *American Economic Review*, vol. 68, no. 4, September 1978, pp. 643–658.

To see if there has been a significant change in the savings-income relationship for the period 1970–1980 and 1981–1991 (Reagan-Bush presidency era), carry out the **Chow test**. You may use a linear or log-linear model relating savings to income. Show all your calculations clearly. What general conclusions do you draw from this analysis? Intuitively, how would you find out if the assumptions underlying the Chow test are fulfilled?

*APPENDIX 8A

LIKELIHOOD RATIO (LR) TEST

The **LR test** is based on the maximum likelihood (ML) principle discussed in Appendix 4A where we showed how one obtains the ML estimators of the two-variable regression model. That principle can be straightforwardly extended to the multiple regression model. Under the assumption that the disturbances u_i are normally distributed, we showed that for the two-variable regression model the OLS and ML estimators of the regression coefficients are identical, but the estimated error variances are different. The OLS estimator of σ^2 is $\sum \hat{u}_i^2/(n-2)$ but the ML estimator is $\sum \hat{u}_i^2/n$, the former being unbiased and the latter biased, although in large samples the bias disappears.

The same is true in the multiple regression case. To illustrate, consider the linear demand function for roses given in Eq. (8.9.1). Corresponding to Eq. (5) of Appendix 4A, the log-likelihood function for (8.91) can be written as:

$$\ln LF = -\frac{n}{2}\sigma^2 - \frac{n}{2}\ln(2\pi) - \frac{1}{2}\sum(Y_i - \alpha_1 - \alpha_2 X_{2i} - \alpha_3 X_{3i})^2 \tag{1}$$

As shown in Appendix 4A, differentiating this function with respect to $\alpha_1, \alpha_2, \alpha_3$, and σ^2, setting the resulting expressions to zero, and solving, we obtain the ML estimators of these parameters; the ML estimators of α_1, α_2, and α_3 will be identical to OLS estimators, which are already given in Eq. (8.9.3), but the error variance will be different in that the residual sum of squares (RSS) will be divided by n rather than by $(n-3)$ as in the case of OLS.

Now let us suppose that our null hypothesis H_0 is that α_3, the coefficient of the carnation price variable, X_3, is zero. In this case, our log-likelihood function given in (1) will become

$$\ln LF = -\frac{n}{2}\ln\sigma^2 - \frac{n}{2}\ln(2\pi) - \frac{1}{2}\sum(Y_i - \alpha_1 - \alpha_2 X_{2i})^2 \tag{2}$$

---

*Optional.

Equation (2) is known as the **restricted log-likelihood function (RLLF)** because it is estimated with the restriction that a priori α_3 is zero, whereas Eq. (1) is known as the **unrestricted log LF (ULLF)** because a priori there are no restrictions put on the parameters. To test the validity of the a priori restriction that α_3 is zero, the LR test obtains the following test statistic:

$$\lambda = 2(\text{ULLF} - \text{RLLF}) \tag{3}*$$

where ULLF and RLLF are, respectively, unrestricted log-likelihood function [Eq. (1)] and restricted log-likelihood function [Eq. (2)]. If the sample size is large, it can be shown that the test statistic λ given in (3) follows the chi-square (χ^2) distribution with df equal to the number of restrictions imposed by the null hypothesis, 1 in the present case.

The basis idea behind the LR test is simple: If the a priori restriction(s) are valid, the restricted and unrestricted (log) LF should not be different, in which case λ in (3) will be zero. But if that is not case, the two LFs will diverge. And since in a large sample we know that λ follows the chi-square distribution, we can find out if the divergence is statistically significant, say, at a 1 or 5% level of significance. Or else, we can find out the p value of the estimated λ.

To continue with our example, using **MICRO TSP 7.0** version, we obtain the following data:

$$\text{ULLF} = -132.3601 \quad \text{and} \quad \text{RLLF} = -136.5061$$

Therefore,

$$\lambda = 2[-132.3601 - (-136.50610)] = 8.2992$$

Asymptotically, this is distributed as the chi-square distribution with 1 df (because we have only one restriction imposed).† The p value of obtaining a chi-square value of 8.2992 or greater is about 0.004, which is a small probability. Hence one could reject the null hypothesis that the price of carnations has no effect on the demand for roses, that is, in Eq. (8.9.3) the variable X_3 should be retained. It is unsurprising then that the t value of the coefficient of X_3 is significant in this equation.

Because of the mathematical complexity of the Wald and LM tests, we will not discuss them here. But as noted in the text, asymptotically, the LR, Wald, and LM tests give identical answers, the choice of the test depending on computational convenience.

---

*This expression can also be expressed as $-2(\text{RLLF} - \text{ULLF})$ or as $-2\ln(\text{RLF/ULF})$.

†In the present example the sample size is rather small. Therefore, one should exercise caution in using asymptotic results. Our example is, of course, for pedagogy.

CHAPTER
9

THE MATRIX APPROACH TO LINEAR REGRESSION MODEL*

This chapter presents the classical linear regression model involving k variables (Y and $X_2, X_3, \ldots, X_k$) in matrix algebra notation. Conceptually, the k-variable model is a logical extension of the two- and three-variable models considered thus far in this text. Therefore, this chapter presents very few new concepts save for the matrix notation.[1]

A great advantage of matrix algebra over scalar algebra (elementary algebra dealing with scalars or real numbers) is that it provides a compact method of handling regression models involving any number of variables; once the k-variable model is formulated and solved in matrix notation, the solution applies to one, two, three, or any number of variables.

9.1 THE k-VARIABLE LINEAR REGRESSION MODEL

If we generalize the two- and three-variable linear regression models, the k-variable population regression model (PRF) involving the dependent variable Y and $k - 1$ explanatory variables $X_2, X_3, \ldots, X_k$ may be written as

$$\text{PRF: } Y_i = \beta_1 + \beta_2 X_{2i} + \beta_3 X_{3i} + \cdots + \beta_k X_{ki} + u_i \qquad i = 1, 2, 3, \ldots, n \qquad (9.1.1)$$

---

*This chapter is optional and can be skipped without loss of continuity.

[1] Readers not familiar with matrix algebra should review Appendix B before proceeding any further. Appendix B provides the essentials of matrix algebra needed to follow this chapter.

where β_1 = the intercept, β_2 to β_k = partial slope coefficients, u = stochastic disturbance term, and i = ith observation, n being the size of the population. The PRF (9.1.1) is to be interpreted in the usual manner: It gives the mean or expected value of Y conditional upon the fixed (in repeated sampling) values of $X_2, X_3, \ldots, X_k$, that is, $E(Y \mid X_{2i}, X_{3i}, \ldots, X_{ki})$.

Equation (9.1.1) is a shorthand expression for the following set of n simultaneous equations:

$$
\begin{aligned}
Y_1 &= \beta_1 + \beta_2 X_{21} + \beta_3 X_{31} + \cdots + \beta_k X_{k1} + u_1 \\
Y_2 &= \beta_1 + \beta_2 X_{22} + \beta_3 X_{32} + \cdots + \beta_k X_{k2} + u_2 \\
&\ \cdots\cdots\cdots\cdots\cdots\cdots\cdots\cdots\cdots\cdots\cdots\cdots\cdots\cdots \\
Y_n &= \beta_1 + \beta_2 X_{2n} + \beta_3 X_{3n} + \cdots + \beta_k X_{kn} + u_n
\end{aligned}
\tag{9.1.2}
$$

Let us write the system of equations (9.1.2) in an alternative but more illuminating way as follows:[2]

$$
\begin{bmatrix} Y_1 \\ Y_2 \\ \vdots \\ Y_n \end{bmatrix}
=
\begin{bmatrix}
1 & X_{21} & X_{31} & \cdots & X_{k1} \\
1 & X_{22} & X_{32} & \cdots & X_{k2} \\
\vdots & \vdots & \vdots & \ddots & \vdots \\
1 & X_{2n} & X_{3n} & \cdots & X_{kn}
\end{bmatrix}
\begin{bmatrix} \beta_1 \\ \beta_2 \\ \vdots \\ \beta_k \end{bmatrix}
+
\begin{bmatrix} u_1 \\ u_2 \\ \vdots \\ u_n \end{bmatrix}
\tag{9.1.3}
$$

$$
\begin{array}{cccc}
\mathbf{y} & = & \mathbf{X} & \quad \boldsymbol{\beta} & + & \mathbf{u} \\
n \times 1 & & n \times k & \quad k \times 1 & & n \times 1
\end{array}
$$

where $\mathbf{y}$ = $n \times 1$ column vector of observations on the dependent variable Y

$\mathbf{X}$ = $n \times k$ matrix giving n observations on $k - 1$ variables X_2 to X_k, the first column of 1's representing the intercept term. (This matrix is also known as the **data matrix**.)

$\boldsymbol{\beta}$ = $k \times 1$ column vector of the unknown parameters $\beta_1, \beta_2, \ldots, \beta_k$

$\mathbf{u}$ = $n \times 1$ column vector of n disturbances u_i

Using the rules of matrix multiplication and addition, the reader should verify that systems (9.1.2) and (9.1.3) are equivalent.

System (9.1.3) is known as the *matrix representation of the general (k-variable) linear regression model*. It can be written more compactly as

$$
\begin{array}{ccccc}
\mathbf{y} & = & \mathbf{X} & \boldsymbol{\beta} & + & \mathbf{u} \\
n \times 1 & & n \times k & k \times 1 & & n \times 1
\end{array}
\tag{9.1.4}
$$

Where there is no confusion about the dimensions or orders of the matrix $\mathbf{X}$ and the vectors $\mathbf{y}$, $\boldsymbol{\beta}$, and $\mathbf{u}$, Eq. (9.1.4) may be written simply as

$$
\mathbf{y} = \mathbf{X}\boldsymbol{\beta} + \mathbf{u}
\tag{9.1.5}
$$

---

[2]Following the notation introduced in Appendix B, we shall represent vectors by lowercase bold-faced letters and matrices by uppercase boldfaced letters.

As an illustration of the matrix representation, consider the two-variable consumption-income model considered in Chapter 3, namely, $Y_i = \beta_1 + \beta_2 X_i + u_i$, where Y is consumption expenditure and X is income. Using the data given in Table 3.2, we may write the matrix formulation as

$$
\begin{bmatrix} 70 \\ 65 \\ 90 \\ 95 \\ 110 \\ 115 \\ 120 \\ 140 \\ 155 \\ 150 \end{bmatrix} = \begin{bmatrix} 1 & 80 \\ 1 & 100 \\ 1 & 120 \\ 1 & 140 \\ 1 & 160 \\ 1 & 180 \\ 1 & 200 \\ 1 & 220 \\ 1 & 240 \\ 1 & 260 \end{bmatrix} \begin{bmatrix} \beta_1 \\ \beta_2 \end{bmatrix} + \begin{bmatrix} u_1 \\ u_2 \\ u_3 \\ u_4 \\ u_5 \\ u_6 \\ u_7 \\ u_8 \\ u_9 \\ u_{10} \end{bmatrix} \tag{9.1.6}
$$

$$
\begin{matrix} \mathbf{y} & = & \mathbf{X} & \boldsymbol{\beta} & + & \mathbf{u} \\ 10 \times 1 & & 10 \times 2 & 2 \times 1 & & 10 \times 1 \end{matrix}
$$

As in the two- and three-variable cases, our objective is to estimate the parameters of the multiple regression (9.1.1) and to draw inferences about them from the data at hand. In matrix notation this amounts to estimating $\boldsymbol{\beta}$ and drawing inferences about this $\boldsymbol{\beta}$. For the purpose of estimation, we may use the method of ordinary least squares (OLS) or the method of maximum likelihood (ML). But as noted before, these two methods yield identical estimates of the regression coefficients.[3] Therefore, we shall confine our attention to the method of OLS.

9.2 ASSUMPTIONS OF THE CLASSICAL LINEAR REGRESSION MODEL IN MATRIX NOTATION

The assumptions underlying the classical linear regression model are given in Table 9.1; they are presented both in scalar notation and in matrix notation. Assumption 1 given in (9.2.1) means that the expected value of the disturbance vector $\mathbf{u}$, that is, of each of its elements, is zero. More explicitly, $E(\mathbf{u}) = \mathbf{0}$ means

$$
E \begin{bmatrix} u_1 \\ u_2 \\ \vdots \\ u_n \end{bmatrix} = \begin{bmatrix} E(u_1) \\ E(u_2) \\ \vdots \\ E(u_n) \end{bmatrix} = \begin{bmatrix} 0 \\ 0 \\ \vdots \\ 0 \end{bmatrix} \tag{9.2.1}
$$

Assumption 2 [Eq. (9.2.2)] is a compact way of expressing the two assumptions given in (3.2.5) and (3.2.2) by the scalar notation. To see this, we can

---

[3]The proof that this is so in the k-variable case can be found in the footnote reference given in Chap. 4.

TABLE 9.1
Assumptions of the classical linear regression model

Scalar notation	Matrix notation
1. $E(u_i) = 0,$ for each i (3.2.1)	**1.** $E(\mathbf{u}) = \mathbf{0}$ where $\mathbf{u}$ and $\mathbf{0}$ are $n \times 1$ column vectors, $\mathbf{0}$ being a null vector
2. $E(u_i u_j) = 0$ $i \neq j$ (3.2.5) $= \sigma^2,$ $i = j$ (3.2.2)	**2.** $E(\mathbf{u}\mathbf{u}') = \sigma^2 \mathbf{I}$ where $\mathbf{I}$ is an $n \times n$ identity matrix
3. $X_2, X_3, \ldots, X_k$ are nonstochastic or fixed	**3.** The $n \times k$ matrix $\mathbf{X}$ is nonstochastic, that is, it consists of a set of fixed numbers
4. There is no exact linear (7.1.7) relationship among the X variables, that is, no multicollinearity	**4.** The rank of $\mathbf{X}$ is $\rho(\mathbf{X}) = k$, where k is the number of columns in $\mathbf{X}$ and k is less than the number of observations, n
5. For hypothesis testing, (4.2.4) $u_i \sim N(0, \sigma^2)$	**5.** The $\mathbf{u}$ vector has a multivariate normal distribution, i.e., $\mathbf{u} \sim N(\mathbf{0}, \sigma^2 \mathbf{I})$

write

$$E(\mathbf{u}\mathbf{u}') = E \begin{bmatrix} u_1 \\ u_2 \\ \vdots \\ u_n \end{bmatrix} \begin{bmatrix} u_1 & u_2 & \cdots & u_n \end{bmatrix}$$

where $\mathbf{u}'$ is the transpose of the column vector $\mathbf{u}$, or a row vector. Performing the multiplication, we obtain

$$E(\mathbf{u}\mathbf{u}') = E \begin{bmatrix} u_1^2 & u_1 u_2 & \cdots & u_1 u_n \\ u_2 u_1 & u_2^2 & \cdots & u_2 u_n \\ \cdots\cdots\cdots\cdots\cdots\cdots\cdots \\ u_n u_1 & u_n u_2 & \cdots & u_n^2 \end{bmatrix}$$

Applying the expectations operator E to each element of the preceding matrix, we obtain

$$E(\mathbf{u}\mathbf{u}') = \begin{bmatrix} E(u_1^2) & E(u_1 u_2) & \cdots & E(u_1 u_n) \\ E(u_2 u_1) & E(u_2^2) & \cdots & E(u_2 u_n) \\ \cdots\cdots\cdots\cdots\cdots\cdots\cdots\cdots \\ E(u_n u_1) & E(u_n u_2) & \cdots & E(u_n^2) \end{bmatrix} \tag{9.2.2}$$

Because of the assumptions of homoscedasticity and no serial correlation, matrix (9.2.2) reduces to

$$E(\mathbf{uu'}) = \begin{bmatrix} \sigma^2 & 0 & 0 & \cdots & 0 \\ 0 & \sigma^2 & 0 & \cdots & 0 \\ \multicolumn{5}{c}{\cdots\cdots\cdots\cdots\cdots\cdots} \\ 0 & 0 & 0 & \cdots & \sigma^2 \end{bmatrix}$$

$$= \sigma^2 \begin{bmatrix} 1 & 0 & 0 & \cdots & 0 \\ 0 & 1 & 0 & \cdots & 0 \\ \multicolumn{5}{c}{\cdots\cdots\cdots\cdots\cdots} \\ 0 & 0 & 0 & \cdots & 1 \end{bmatrix}$$

$$= \sigma^2 \mathbf{I} \tag{9.2.3}$$

where $\mathbf{I}$ is an $N \times N$ identity matrix.

Matrix (9.2.2) [and its representation given in (9.2.3)] is called the **variance-covariance matrix** of the disturbances u_i; the elements on the main diagonal of this matrix (running from the upper left corner to the lower right corner) give the variances, and the elements off the main diagonal give the covariances.[4] Note that the variance-covariance matrix is **symmetric**: The elements above and below the main diagonal are reflections of one another.

Assumption 3 states that the $n \times k$ matrix $\mathbf{X}$ is nonstochastic; that is, it consists of fixed numbers. As noted previously, our regression analysis is conditional regression analysis, conditional upon the fixed values of the X variables.

Assumption 4 states that the $\mathbf{X}$ matrix has full column rank equal to k, the number of columns in the matrix. This means that the columns of the X matrix are linearly independent; that is, there is no **exact linear relationship** among the X variables. In other words there is no multicollinearity. In scalar notation this is equivalent to saying that there exists no set of numbers $\lambda_1, \lambda_2, \ldots, \lambda_k$ not all zero such that [cf. (7.1.8)]

$$\lambda_1 X_{1i} + \lambda_2 X_{2i} + \cdots + \lambda_k X_{ki} = 0 \tag{9.2.4}$$

where $X_{1i} = 1$ for all i (to allow for the column of 1's in the $\mathbf{X}$ matrix). In matrix notation, (9.2.4) can be represented as

$$\boldsymbol{\lambda}'\mathbf{x} = 0 \tag{9.2.5}$$

where $\boldsymbol{\lambda}'$ is a $1 \times k$ row vector and $\mathbf{x}$ is a $k \times 1$ column vector.

If an exact linear relationship such as (9.2.4) exists, the variables are said to be collinear. If, on the other hand, (9.2.4) holds true only if $\lambda_1 = \lambda_2 = \lambda_3 = \cdots = 0$, then the X variables are said to be linearly independent. An intuitive reason for the *no multicollinearity* assumption was given in Chapter 7, and we shall explore this assumption further in Chapter 10.

---

[4]By definition, the variance of $u_i = E[u_i - E(u_i)]^2$ and the covariance between u_i and $u_j = E[u_i - E(u_i)][u_j - E(u_j)]$. But because of the assumption $E(u_i) = 0$ for each i, we have the variance-covariance matrix (9.2.3).

9.3 OLS ESTIMATION

To obtain the OLS estimate of $\boldsymbol{\beta}$, let us first write the k-variable sample regression (SRF):

$$Y_i = \hat{\beta}_1 + \hat{\beta}_2 X_{2i} + \hat{\beta}_3 X_{3i} + \cdots + \hat{\beta}_k X_{ki} + \hat{u}_i \tag{9.3.1}$$

which can be written more compactly in matrix notation as

$$\mathbf{y} = \mathbf{X}\hat{\boldsymbol{\beta}} + \hat{\mathbf{u}} \tag{9.3.2}$$

and in matrix form as

$$
\begin{bmatrix} Y_1 \\ Y_2 \\ \vdots \\ Y_n \end{bmatrix}
=
\begin{bmatrix} 1 & X_{21} & X_{31} & \cdots & X_{k1} \\ 1 & X_{22} & X_{32} & \cdots & X_{k2} \\ \cdots & \cdots & \cdots & \cdots & \cdots \\ 1 & X_{2n} & X_{3n} & \cdots & X_{kn} \end{bmatrix}
\begin{bmatrix} \hat{\beta}_1 \\ \hat{\beta}_2 \\ \vdots \\ \hat{\beta}_k \end{bmatrix}
+
\begin{bmatrix} \hat{u}_1 \\ \hat{u}_2 \\ \vdots \\ \hat{u}_n \end{bmatrix}
\tag{9.3.3}
$$

$$
\begin{matrix} \mathbf{y} & & \mathbf{X} & & \hat{\boldsymbol{\beta}} & + & \hat{\mathbf{u}} \\ n \times 1 & & n \times k & & k \times 1 & & n \times 1 \end{matrix}
$$

where $\hat{\boldsymbol{\beta}}$ is a k-element column vector of the OLS estimators of the regression coefficients and where $\hat{\mathbf{u}}$ is an $n \times 1$ column vector of n residuals.

As in the two- and three-variable models, in the k-variable case the OLS estimators are obtained by minimizing

$$\sum \hat{u}_i^2 = \sum (Y_i - \hat{\beta}_1 - \hat{\beta}_2 X_{2i} - \cdots - \hat{\beta}_k X_{ki})^2 \tag{9.3.4}$$

where $\sum \hat{u}_i^2$ is the residual sum of squares (RSS). In matrix notation, this amounts to minimizing $\hat{\mathbf{u}}'\hat{\mathbf{u}}$ since

$$
\hat{\mathbf{u}}'\hat{\mathbf{u}} = \begin{bmatrix} \hat{u}_1 & \hat{u}_2 & \cdots & \hat{u}_n \end{bmatrix}
\begin{bmatrix} \hat{u}_1 \\ \hat{u}_2 \\ \vdots \\ \hat{u}_n \end{bmatrix}
= \hat{u}_1^2 + \hat{u}_2^2 + \cdots + \hat{u}_n^2 = \sum \hat{u}_i^2 \tag{9.3.5}
$$

Now from (9.3.2) we obtain

$$\hat{\mathbf{u}} = \mathbf{y} - \mathbf{X}\hat{\boldsymbol{\beta}} \tag{9.3.6}$$

Therefore,

$$
\begin{aligned}
\hat{\mathbf{u}}'\hat{\mathbf{u}} &= (\mathbf{y} - \mathbf{X}\hat{\boldsymbol{\beta}})'(\mathbf{y} - \mathbf{X}\hat{\boldsymbol{\beta}}) \\
&= \mathbf{y}'\mathbf{y} - 2\hat{\boldsymbol{\beta}}'\mathbf{X}'\mathbf{y} + \hat{\boldsymbol{\beta}}'\mathbf{X}'\mathbf{X}\hat{\boldsymbol{\beta}}
\end{aligned} \tag{9.3.7}
$$

where use is made of the properties of the transpose of a matrix, namely, $(\mathbf{X}\hat{\boldsymbol{\beta}})' = \hat{\boldsymbol{\beta}}'\mathbf{X}'$; and since $\hat{\boldsymbol{\beta}}'\mathbf{X}'\mathbf{y}$ is a scalar (a real number), it is equal to its transpose $\mathbf{y}'\mathbf{X}\hat{\boldsymbol{\beta}}$.

Equation (9.3.7) is the matrix representation of (9.3.4). In scalar notation, the method of OLS consists in so estimating $\beta_1, \beta_2, \ldots, \beta_k$ that $\sum \hat{u}_i^2$ is as small as possible. This is done by differentiating (9.3.4) partially with respect to $\hat{\beta}_1, \hat{\beta}_2, \ldots, \hat{\beta}_k$ and setting the resulting expressions to zero. This process yields

k simultaneous equations in k unknowns, the normal equations of the least-squares theory. As shown in Appendix 9A, Section 9A.1, these equations are as follows:

$$n\hat{\beta}_1 + \hat{\beta}_2 \sum X_{2i} + \hat{\beta}_3 \sum X_{3i} + \cdots + \hat{\beta}_k \sum X_{ki} = \sum Y_i$$

$$\hat{\beta}_1 \sum X_{2i} + \hat{\beta}_2 \sum X_{2i}^2 + \hat{\beta}_3 \sum X_{2i}X_{3i} + \cdots + \hat{\beta}_k \sum X_{2i}X_{ki} = \sum X_{2i}Y_i$$

$$\hat{\beta}_1 \sum X_{3i} + \hat{\beta}_2 \sum X_{3i}X_{2i} + \hat{\beta}_3 \sum X_{3i}^2 + \cdots + \hat{\beta}_k \sum X_{3i}X_{ki} = \sum X_{3i}Y_i$$

$$\cdots\cdots\cdots\cdots\cdots\cdots\cdots\cdots\cdots\cdots\cdots\cdots\cdots\cdots\cdots\cdots\cdots\cdots\cdots\cdots\cdots\cdots \quad (9.3.8)^5$$

$$\hat{\beta}_1 \sum X_{ki} + \hat{\beta}_2 \sum X_{ki}X_{2i} + \hat{\beta}_3 \sum X_{ki}X_{3i} + \cdots + \hat{\beta}_k \sum X_{ki}^2 = \sum X_{ki}Y_i$$

In matrix form, Eq. (9.3.8) can be represented as

$$
\underbrace{\begin{bmatrix}
n & \sum X_{2i} & \sum X_{3i} & \cdots & \sum X_{ki} \\
\sum X_{2i} & \sum X_{2i}^2 & \sum X_{2i}X_{3i} & \cdots & \sum X_{2i}X_{ki} \\
\sum X_{3i} & \sum X_{3i}X_{2i} & \sum X_{3i}^2 & \cdots & \sum X_{3i}X_{ki} \\
\cdots & \cdots & \cdots & & \cdots \\
\sum X_{ki} & \sum X_{ki}X_{2i} & \sum X_{ki}X_{3i} & \cdots & \sum X_{ki}^2
\end{bmatrix}}_{(\mathbf{X'X})}
\underbrace{\begin{bmatrix}
\hat{\beta}_1 \\ \hat{\beta}_2 \\ \hat{\beta}_3 \\ \vdots \\ \hat{\beta}_k
\end{bmatrix}}_{\hat{\boldsymbol{\beta}}}
=
\underbrace{\begin{bmatrix}
1 & 1 & \cdots & 1 \\
X_{21} & X_{22} & \cdots & X_{2n} \\
X_{31} & X_{32} & \cdots & X_{3n} \\
\cdots & \cdots & & \cdots \\
X_{k1} & X_{k2} & \cdots & X_{kn}
\end{bmatrix}}_{\mathbf{X'}}
\underbrace{\begin{bmatrix}
Y_1 \\ Y_2 \\ Y_3 \\ \vdots \\ Y_n
\end{bmatrix}}_{\mathbf{y}}
$$

$$(9.3.9)$$

or, more compactly, as

$$(\mathbf{X'X})\hat{\boldsymbol{\beta}} = \mathbf{X'y} \qquad (9.3.10)$$

Note these features of the $(\mathbf{X'X})$ matrix: (1) It gives the raw sums of squares and cross products of the X variables, one of which is the intercept term taking the value of 1 for each observation. The elements on the main diagonal give the raw sums of squares, and those off the main diagonal give the raw sums of cross products (by *raw* we mean in original units of measurement). (2) It is symmetrical since the cross product between X_{2i} and X_{3i} is the same as that between X_{3i} and X_{2i}. (3) It is of order $(k \times k)$, that is, k rows and k columns.

In (9.3.10) the known quantities are $(\mathbf{X'X})$ and $(\mathbf{X'y})$ (the cross product between the X variables and y) and the unknown is $\hat{\boldsymbol{\beta}}$. Now using matrix algebra, if the inverse of $(\mathbf{X'X})$ exists, say, $(\mathbf{X'X})^{-1}$, then premultiplying both sides of (9.3.10) by this inverse, we obtain

$$(\mathbf{X'X})^{-1}(\mathbf{X'X})\hat{\boldsymbol{\beta}} = (\mathbf{X'X})^{-1}\mathbf{X'y}$$

But since $(\mathbf{X'X})^{-1}(\mathbf{X'X}) = \mathbf{I}$, an identity matrix of order $k \times k$, we get

$$\mathbf{I}\hat{\boldsymbol{\beta}} = (\mathbf{X'X})^{-1}\mathbf{X'y}$$

---

[5] These equations can be remembered easily. Start with the equation $Y_i = \hat{\beta}_1 + \hat{\beta}_2 X_{2i} + \hat{\beta}_3 X_{3i} + \cdots + \hat{\beta}_k X_{ki}$. Summing this equation over the n values gives the first equation in (9.3.8); multiplying it by X_2 on both sides and summing over n gives the second equation; multiplying it by X_3 on both sides and summing over n gives the third equation; and so on. In passing, note that the first equation in (9.3.8) gives at once $\hat{\beta}_1 = \bar{Y} - \hat{\beta}_2 \bar{X}_2 - \cdots - \hat{\beta}_k \bar{X}_k$ [cf. (7.4.6)].

or

$$\hat{\boldsymbol{\beta}} = (\mathbf{X'X})^{-1} \quad \mathbf{X'} \quad \mathbf{y}$$
$$k \times 1 \quad k \times k \quad (k \times n)(n \times 1)$$

(9.3.11)

Equation (9.3.11) is a fundamental result of the OLS theory in matrix notation. It shows how the $\hat{\boldsymbol{\beta}}$ vector can be estimated from the given data. Although (9.3.11) was obtained from (9.3.9), it can be obtained directly from (9.3.7) by differentiating $\hat{\mathbf{u}}'\hat{\mathbf{u}}$ with respect to $\hat{\boldsymbol{\beta}}$. The proof is given in Appendix 9A, Section 9A.2.

An Illustration

As an illustration of the matrix methods developed so far, let us rework the consumption-income example of Chapter 3, whose data are reproduced in (9.1.6). For the two-variable case we have

$$\hat{\boldsymbol{\beta}} = \begin{bmatrix} \hat{\beta}_1 \\ \hat{\beta}_2 \end{bmatrix}$$

$$(\mathbf{X'X}) = \begin{bmatrix} 1 & 1 & 1 & \cdots & 1 \\ X_1 & X_2 & X_3 & \cdots & X_n \end{bmatrix} \begin{bmatrix} 1 & X_1 \\ 1 & X_2 \\ 1 & X_3 \\ & \cdots \\ 1 & X_N \end{bmatrix} = \begin{bmatrix} n & \sum X_i \\ \sum X_i & \sum X_i^2 \end{bmatrix}$$

and

$$\mathbf{X'y} = \begin{bmatrix} 1 & 1 & 1 & \cdots & 1 \\ X_1 & X_2 & X_3 & \cdots & X_n \end{bmatrix} \begin{bmatrix} Y_1 \\ Y_2 \\ Y_3 \\ \vdots \\ Y_n \end{bmatrix} = \begin{bmatrix} \sum Y_i \\ \sum X_i Y_i \end{bmatrix}$$

Using the data given in (9.1.6), we obtain

$$\mathbf{X'X} = \begin{bmatrix} 10 & 1700 \\ 1700 & 322000 \end{bmatrix}$$

and

$$\mathbf{X'y} = \begin{bmatrix} 1110 \\ 205500 \end{bmatrix}$$

Using the rules of matrix inversion given in Appendix B, we can see that the inverse of the preceding $(\mathbf{X'X})$ matrix is

$$(\mathbf{X'X})^{-1} = \begin{bmatrix} 0.97576 & -0.005152 \\ -0.005152 & 0.0000303 \end{bmatrix}$$

Therefore,

$$\hat{\boldsymbol{\beta}} = \begin{bmatrix} \hat{\beta}_1 \\ \hat{\beta}_2 \end{bmatrix} = \begin{bmatrix} 0.97576 & -0.005152 \\ -0.005152 & 0.0000303 \end{bmatrix} \begin{bmatrix} 1110 \\ 205500 \end{bmatrix}$$

$$= \begin{bmatrix} 24.4545 \\ 0.5079 \end{bmatrix}$$

Previously we obtained $\hat{\beta}_1 = 24.4545$ and $\hat{\beta}_2 = 0.5091$ using the computer. The difference between the two estimates is due to the rounding errors. In passing, note that in working on a desk calculator it is essential to obtain results to several significant digits to minimize the rounding errors.

Variance-Covariance Matrix of $\hat{\boldsymbol{\beta}}$

Matrix methods enable us to develop formulas not only for the variance of $\hat{\beta}_i$, any given element of $\hat{\boldsymbol{\beta}}$, but also for the covariance between any two elements of $\hat{\boldsymbol{\beta}}$, say, $\hat{\beta}_i$ and $\hat{\beta}_j$. We need these variances and covariances for the purpose of statistical inference.

By definition, the variance-covariance matrix of $\hat{\boldsymbol{\beta}}$ is [cf. (9.2.2)]

$$\text{var-cov}(\hat{\boldsymbol{\beta}}) = E\{[\hat{\boldsymbol{\beta}} - E(\hat{\boldsymbol{\beta}})][\hat{\boldsymbol{\beta}} - E(\hat{\boldsymbol{\beta}})]'\}$$

which can be written explicitly as

$$\text{var-cov}(\hat{\boldsymbol{\beta}}) = \begin{bmatrix} \text{var}(\hat{\beta}_1) & \text{cov}(\hat{\beta}_1, \hat{\beta}_2) & \cdots & \text{cov}(\hat{\beta}_1, \hat{\beta}_k) \\ \text{cov}(\hat{\beta}_2, \hat{\beta}_1) & \text{var}(\hat{\beta}_2) & \cdots & \text{cov}(\hat{\beta}_2, \hat{\beta}_k) \\ \cdots & \cdots & \cdots & \cdots \\ \text{cov}(\hat{\beta}_k, \hat{\beta}_1) & \text{cov}(\hat{\beta}_k, \hat{\beta}_2) & \cdots & \text{var}(\hat{\beta}_k) \end{bmatrix} \quad (9.3.12)$$

It is shown in Appendix 9A, Section 9A.3, that the preceding variance-covariance matrix can be obtained from the following formula:

$$\text{var-cov}(\hat{\boldsymbol{\beta}}) = \sigma^2(\mathbf{X'X})^{-1} \quad (9.3.13)$$

where σ^2 is the homoscedastic variance of u_i and $(\mathbf{X'X})^{-1}$ is the inverse matrix appearing in Eq. (9.3.11), which gives the OLS estimator $\hat{\boldsymbol{\beta}}$.

In the two- and three-variable linear regression models an unbiased estimator of σ^2 was given by $\hat{\sigma}^2 = \sum \hat{u}_i^2/(n-2)$ and $\hat{\sigma}^2 = \sum \hat{u}_i^2/(n-3)$, respectively. In the k-variable case, the corresponding formula is

$$\hat{\sigma}^2 = \frac{\sum \hat{u}_i^2}{n-k}$$

$$= \frac{\hat{\mathbf{u}}'\hat{\mathbf{u}}}{n-k} \quad (9.3.14)$$

where there are now $n - k$ df. (Why?)

Although in principle $\hat{\mathbf{u}}'\hat{\mathbf{u}}$ can be computed from the estimated residuals, in practice it can be obtained directly as follows. Recalling that $\sum \hat{u}_i^2$ (= RSS) = TSS − ESS, in the two-variable case we may write

$$\sum \hat{u}_i^2 = \sum y_i^2 - \hat{\beta}_2^2 \sum x_i^2 \quad (3.3.6)$$

and in the three-variable case

$$\sum \hat{u}_i^2 = \sum y_i^2 - \hat{\beta}_2 \sum y_i x_{2i} - \hat{\beta}_3 \sum y_i x_{3i} \qquad (7.4.19)$$

By extending this principle, it can be seen that for the k- variable model

$$\sum \hat{u}_i^2 = \sum y_i^2 - \hat{\beta}_2 \sum y_i x_{2i} - \cdots - \hat{\beta}_k \sum y_i x_{ki} \qquad (9.3.15)$$

In matrix notation,

$$\text{TSS:} \sum y_i^2 = \mathbf{y'y} - n\bar{Y}^2 \qquad (9.3.16)$$

$$\text{ESS:} \hat{\beta}_2 \sum y_i x_{2i} + \cdots + \hat{\beta}_k \sum y_i x_{ki} = \hat{\boldsymbol{\beta}}' \mathbf{X'y} - n\bar{Y}^2 \qquad (9.3.17)$$

where the term $n\bar{Y}^2$ is known as the correction for mean.[6] Therefore,

$$\hat{\mathbf{u}}'\hat{\mathbf{u}} = \mathbf{y'y} - \hat{\boldsymbol{\beta}}' \mathbf{X'y} \qquad (9.3.18)$$

Once $\hat{\mathbf{u}}'\hat{\mathbf{u}}$ is obtained, $\hat{\sigma}^2$ can be easily computed from (9.3.14), which, in turn, will enable us to estimate the variance-covariance matrix (9.3.13).

For our illustrative example,

$$\hat{\mathbf{u}}'\hat{\mathbf{u}} = 132100 - [24.4545 \quad 0.5091] \begin{bmatrix} 1110 \\ 205500 \end{bmatrix}$$

$$= 337.373$$

Hence, $\hat{\sigma}^2 = (337.273/8) = 42.1591$, which is approximately the value obtained previously in Chapter 3.

Properties of OLS Vector $\hat{\boldsymbol{\beta}}$

In the two- and three-variable cases we know that the OLS estimators are linear and unbiased, and in the class of all linear unbiased estimators they have minimum variance (the Gauss-Markov property). In short, the OLS estimators are best linear unbiased estimators (BLUE). This property extends to the entire $\hat{\boldsymbol{\beta}}$ vector; that is, $\hat{\boldsymbol{\beta}}$ is linear (each of its elements is a linear function of Y, the dependent variable). $E(\hat{\boldsymbol{\beta}}) = \hat{\boldsymbol{\beta}}$, that is, the expected value of each element of $\hat{\boldsymbol{\beta}}$ is equal to the corresponding element of the true $\boldsymbol{\beta}$, and in the class of all linear unbiased estimators of $\boldsymbol{\beta}$, the OLS estimator $\hat{\boldsymbol{\beta}}$ has minimum variance.

The proof is given in Appendix 9A, Section 9A.4. As stated in the introduction, the k-variable case is in most cases a straight extension of the two- and three-variable cases.

---

[6]*Note:* $\sum y_i^2 = \sum(Y_i - \bar{Y})^2 = \sum Y_i^2 - n\bar{Y}^2 = \mathbf{y'y} - n\bar{Y}^2$. Therefore, without the correction term, $\mathbf{y'y}$ will give simply the raw sum of squares, not the sum of squared deviations.

9.4   THE COEFFICIENT OF DETERMINATION R^2 IN MATRIX NOTATION

The coefficient of determination R^2 has been defined as

$$R^2 = \frac{\text{ESS}}{\text{TSS}}$$

In the two-variable case,

$$R^2 = \frac{\hat{\beta}_2^2 \sum x_i^2}{\sum y_i^2} \tag{3.5.6}$$

and in the three-variable case

$$R^2 = \frac{\hat{\beta}_2 \sum y_i x_{2i} + \hat{\beta}_3 \sum y_i x_{3i}}{\sum y_i^2} \tag{7.5.5}$$

Generalizing we obtain for the k-variable case

$$R^2 = \frac{\hat{\beta}_2 \sum y_i x_{2i} + \hat{\beta}_3 \sum y_i x_{3i} + \cdots + \hat{\beta}_k \sum y_i x_{ki}}{\sum y_i^2} \tag{9.4.1}$$

By using (9.3.16) and (9.3.17), Eq. (9.4.1) can be written as

$$R^2 = \frac{\hat{\boldsymbol{\beta}}'\mathbf{X}'\mathbf{y} - n\bar{Y}^2}{\mathbf{y}'\mathbf{y} - n\bar{Y}^2} \tag{9.4.2}$$

which gives the matrix representation of R^2.

For our illustrative example,

$$\hat{\boldsymbol{\beta}}'\mathbf{X}'\mathbf{y} = [\,24.3571 \quad 0.5079\,] \begin{bmatrix} 1,110 \\ 205,500 \end{bmatrix}$$

$$= 131,409.831$$

$$\mathbf{y}'\mathbf{y} = 132,100$$

and

$$n\bar{Y}^2 = 123,210$$

Plugging these values into (9.4.2), we see that $R^2 = 0.9224$, which is about the same as obtained before, save for the rounding errors.

9.5   THE CORRELATION MATRIX

In the previous chapters we came across the zero-order, or simple, correlation coefficients r_{12}, r_{13}, r_{23}, and the partial, or first-order, correlations $r_{12.3}, r_{13.2}, r_{23.1}$, and their interrelationships. In the k-variable case, we shall have in all $k(k-1)/2$ zero-order correlation coefficients. (Why?) These $k(k-1)/2$ correlations can be put into a matrix, called the **correlation matrix R** as follows:

$$R = \begin{bmatrix} r_{11} & r_{12} & r_{13} & \cdots & r_{1k} \\ r_{21} & r_{22} & r_{23} & \cdots & r_{2k} \\ \cdots\cdots\cdots\cdots\cdots\cdots\cdots \\ r_{k1} & r_{k2} & r_{k3} & \cdots & r_{kk} \end{bmatrix}$$

$$= \begin{bmatrix} 1 & r_{12} & r_{13} & \cdots & r_{1k} \\ r_{21} & 1 & r_{23} & \cdots & r_{2k} \\ \cdots\cdots\cdots\cdots\cdots\cdots\cdots \\ r_{k1} & r_{k2} & r_{k3} & \cdots & 1 \end{bmatrix} \tag{9.5.1}$$

where the subscript 1, as before, denotes the dependent variable Y (r_{12} means correlation coefficient between Y and X_2, and so on) and where use is made of the fact the coefficient of correlation of a variable with respect to itself is always 1 ($r_{11} = r_{22} = \cdots = r_{kk} = 1$).

From the correlation matrix **R** one can obtain correlation coefficients of first order (see Chapter 7) and of higher order such as $r_{12.34\ldots k}$. (See exercise 9.4.) Many computer programs routinely compute the **R** matrix. We shall discuss the correlation matrix in our future work (see Chapter 10).

9.6 HYPOTHESIS TESTING ABOUT INDIVIDUAL REGRESSION COEFFICIENTS IN MATRIX NOTATION

For reasons spelled out in the previous chapters, if our objective is inference as well as estimation, we shall have to assume that the disturbances u_i follow some probability distribution. Also for reasons given previously, in regression analysis we usually assume that each u_i follows the normal distribution with zero mean and constant variance σ^2. In matrix notation, we have

$$\mathbf{u} \sim N(\mathbf{0}, \sigma^2 \mathbf{I}) \tag{9.6.1}$$

where **u** and **0** are $n \times 1$ column vectors and **I** is an $n \times n$ identity matrix, **0** being the **null vector**.

Given the normality assumption, we know that in two- and three-variable linear regression models (1) the OLS estimators $\hat{\beta}_i$ and the ML estimators $\tilde{\beta}_i$ are identical, but the ML estimator $\tilde{\sigma}^2$ is biased, although this bias can be removed by using the unbiased OLS estimator $\hat{\sigma}^2$; and (2) the OLS estimators $\hat{\beta}_i$ are also normally distributed. Generalizing, in the k-variable case we can show that

$$\hat{\boldsymbol{\beta}} \sim N[\boldsymbol{\beta}, \sigma^2 (\mathbf{X'X})^{-1}] \tag{9.6.2}$$

that is, each element of $\hat{\boldsymbol{\beta}}$ is normally distributed with mean equal to the corresponding element of true $\boldsymbol{\beta}$ and the variance given by σ^2 times the appropriate diagonal element of the inverse matrix $(\mathbf{X'X})^{-1}$.

Since in practice σ^2 is unknown, it is estimated by $\hat{\sigma}^2$. Then by the usual shift to the t distribution, it follows that each element of $\hat{\boldsymbol{\beta}}$ follows the t

distribution with $n - k$ df. Symbolically,

$$t = \frac{\hat{\beta}_i - \beta_i}{\text{se}(\hat{\beta}_i)} \qquad (9.6.3)$$

with $n - k$ df, where $\hat{\beta}_i$ is any element of $\hat{\boldsymbol{\beta}}$.

The t distribution can therefore be used to test hypotheses about the true β_i as well as to establish confidence intervals about it. The actual mechanics have already been illustrated in Chapters 5 and 8. For a fully worked example, see Section 9.10.

9.7 TESTING THE OVERALL SIGNIFICANCE OF REGRESSION: ANALYSIS OF VARIANCE IN MATRIX NOTATION

In Chapter 8 we developed the ANOVA technique (1) to test the overall significance of the estimated regression, that is, to test the null hypothesis that the true (partial) slope coefficients are simultaneously equal to zero, and (2) to assess the incremental contribution of an explanatory variable. The ANOVA technique can be easily extended to the k-variable case. Recall that the ANOVA technique consists of decomposing the TSS into two components: the ESS and the RSS. The matrix expressions for these three sums of squares are already given in (9.3.16), (9.3.17), and (9.3.18), respectively. The degrees of freedom associated with these sums of squares are $n - 1$, $k - 1$, and $n - k$, respectively. (Why?) Then, following Chapter 8, Table 8.2, we can set up Table 9.2.

Assuming that the disturbances u_i are normally distributed and the null hypothesis is $\beta_2 = \beta_3 = \cdots = \beta_k = 0$, and following Chapter 8, one can show that

$$F = \frac{(\hat{\boldsymbol{\beta}}'\mathbf{X}'\mathbf{y} - n\bar{Y}^2)/(k-1)}{(\mathbf{y}'\mathbf{y} - \hat{\boldsymbol{\beta}}'\mathbf{X}'\mathbf{y})/(n-k)} \qquad (9.7.1)$$

follows the F distribution with $k - 1$ and $n - k$ df.

TABLE 9.2
Matrix formulation of the ANOVA table for k-variable linear regression model

Source of variation	SS	df	MSS
Due to regression (that is, due to $X_2, X_3, \ldots, X_k$)	$\hat{\boldsymbol{\beta}}'\mathbf{X}'\mathbf{y} - n\bar{Y}^2$	$k - 1$	$\dfrac{\hat{\boldsymbol{\beta}}'\mathbf{X}'\mathbf{y} - n\bar{Y}^2}{k - 1}$
Due to residuals	$\mathbf{y}'\mathbf{y} - \hat{\boldsymbol{\beta}}'\mathbf{X}'\mathbf{y}$	$n - k$	$\dfrac{\mathbf{y}'\mathbf{y} - \hat{\boldsymbol{\beta}}'\mathbf{X}'\mathbf{y}}{n - k}$
Total	$\mathbf{y}'\mathbf{y} - n\bar{Y}^2$	$n - 1$	

TABLE 9.3
k-variable ANOVA table in matrix form in terms of R^2

Source of variation	SS	df	MSS
Due to regression (that is, due to $X_2, X_3, \ldots, X_k$)	$R^2(\mathbf{y'y} - n\bar{Y}^2)$	$k-1$	$\dfrac{R^2(\mathbf{y'y} - n\bar{Y}^2)}{k-1}$
Due to residuals	$(1 - R^2)(\mathbf{y'y} - n\bar{Y}^2)$	$n-k$	$\dfrac{(1 - R^2)(\mathbf{y'y} - n\bar{Y}^2)}{n-k}$
Total	$\mathbf{y'y} - n\bar{Y}^2$	$n-1$	

In Chapter 8 we saw that, under the assumptions stated previously, there is a close relationship between F and R^2, namely,

$$F = \frac{R^2/(k-1)}{(1 - R^2)/(n-k)} \tag{8.5.11}$$

Therefore, the ANOVA Table 9.2 can be expressed as Table 9.3. One advantage of Table 9.3 over Table 9.2 is that the entire analysis can be done in terms of R^2; one need not consider the term $(\mathbf{y'y} - n\bar{Y}^2)$, for it drops out in the F ratio.

9.8 TESTING LINEAR RESTRICTIONS: GENERAL F TESTING USING MATRIX NOTATION

In Section 8.7 we introduced the general F test to test the validity of linear restrictions imposed on one or more parameters of the k-variable linear regression model. The appropriate test was given in (8.7.9) [or its equivalent (8.7.10)]. The matrix counterpart of (8.7.9) can be easily derived.

Let

$\hat{\mathbf{u}}_R$ = the residual vector from the restricted least-squares regression

$\hat{\mathbf{u}}_{UR}$ = the residual vector from the unrestricted least-squares regression

Then

$\hat{\mathbf{u}}_R'\hat{\mathbf{u}}_R = \sum \hat{u}_R^2$ = RSS from the restricted regression

$\hat{\mathbf{u}}_{UR}'\hat{\mathbf{u}}_{UR} = \sum \hat{u}_{UR}^2$ = RSS from the unrestricted regression

m = number of linear restrictions

k = number of parameters (including the intercept) in the unrestricted regression

n = number of observations

The matrix counterpart of (8.7.9) is then

$$F = \frac{(\hat{\mathbf{u}}_R'\hat{\mathbf{u}}_R - \hat{\mathbf{u}}_{UR}'\hat{\mathbf{u}}_{UR})/m}{(\hat{\mathbf{u}}_{UR}'\hat{\mathbf{u}}_{UR})/(n-k)} \tag{9.8.1}$$

which follows the F distribution with $(m, n-k)$ df. As usual, if the computed F value from (9.8.1) exceeds the critical F value, we can reject the restricted regression; otherwise, we do not reject it.

9.9 PREDICTION USING MULTIPLE REGRESSION: MATRIX FORMULATION

In Section 8.10 we discussed, using scalar notation, how the estimated multiple regression can be used for predicting (1) the mean and (2) individual values of Y, given the values of the X regressors. In this section we show how to express these predictions in matrix form. We also present the formulas to estimate the variances and standard errors of the predicted values; in Chapter 8 we noted that these formulas are better handled in matrix notation, for the scalar or algebraic expressions of these formulas become rather unwieldy.

Mean Prediction

Let

$$\mathbf{x}_0 = \begin{bmatrix} 1 \\ X_{02} \\ X_{03} \\ \vdots \\ X_{0k} \end{bmatrix} \tag{9.9.1}$$

be the vector of values of the X variables for which we wish to predict $\hat{Y}_0$, the mean prediction of Y.

Now the estimated multiple regression, in scalar form, is

$$\hat{Y}_i = \hat{\beta}_1 + \hat{\beta}_2 X_{2i} + \hat{\beta}_3 X_{3i} + \cdots + \hat{\beta}_k X_{ki} \tag{9.9.2}$$

which in matrix notation can be written compactly as

$$\hat{Y}_i = \mathbf{x}_i' \hat{\boldsymbol{\beta}} \tag{9.9.3}$$

where $\mathbf{x}_i' = [1 \quad X_{2i} \quad X_{3i} \quad \cdots \quad X_{ki}]$ and

$$\hat{\boldsymbol{\beta}} = \begin{bmatrix} \hat{\beta}_1 \\ \hat{\beta}_2 \\ \vdots \\ \hat{\beta}_k \end{bmatrix}$$

Equation (9.9.2) or (9.9.3) is of course the mean prediction of Y_i corresponding to given $\mathbf{x}_i'$.

If $\mathbf{x}_i'$ is as given in (9.9.1), (9.9.3) becomes

$$(\hat{Y}_i \mid \mathbf{x}_0') = \mathbf{x}_0' \hat{\boldsymbol{\beta}} \tag{9.9.4}$$

where, of course, the values of $\mathbf{x}_0$ are specified. Note that (9.9.4) gives an unbiased prediction of $E(Y_i \mid \mathbf{x}_0')$, since $E(\mathbf{x}_0' \hat{\beta}) = \mathbf{x}_0' \boldsymbol{\beta}$. (Why?)

Individual Prediction

As we know from Chapters 5 and 8, the individual prediction of Y, Y_0, is given generally by (9.9.3) too, or by (9.9.4) specifically. That is,

$$(Y_0 \mid \mathbf{x}_0') = \mathbf{x}_0' \hat{\boldsymbol{\beta}} \tag{9.9.5}$$

Thus, for the illustrative example of Section 8.10, the matrix formulation of mean and individual predictions is

$$\mathbf{x}_0 = \mathbf{x}_{1971} = \begin{bmatrix} 1 \\ 567 \\ 16 \end{bmatrix}$$

and

$$\hat{\boldsymbol{\beta}} = \begin{bmatrix} 53.1603 \\ 0.7266 \\ 2.7363 \end{bmatrix}$$

Therefore,

$$(\hat{Y}_{1971} \mid \mathbf{x}'_{1971}) = \begin{bmatrix} 1 & 567 & 16 \end{bmatrix} \begin{bmatrix} 53.1603 \\ 0.7266 \\ 2.7363 \end{bmatrix}$$

$$= 508.9297 \tag{9.9.6}$$

$$= (8.10.2)$$

and

$$(Y_{1971} \mid \mathbf{x}'_{1971}) = 508.9297 \qquad \text{(Why?)} \tag{9.9.7}$$

Variance of Mean Prediction

The formula to estimate the variance of $(\hat{Y}_0 \mid \mathbf{x}'_0)$ is as follows:[7]

$$\text{var}(\hat{Y}_0 \mid \mathbf{x}'_0) = \sigma^2 \mathbf{x}'_0 (\mathbf{X}'\mathbf{X})^{-1} \mathbf{x}_0 \tag{9.9.8}$$

where σ^2 is the variance of u_i, $\mathbf{x}'_0$ are the given values of the X variables at which we wish to predict, and $(\mathbf{X}'\mathbf{X})$ is the matrix given in (9.3.9), that is, the matrix used to estimate the multiple regression. Replacing σ^2 by its unbiased estimator $\hat{\sigma}^2$, we can write formula (9.9.8) as

$$\text{var}(\hat{Y}_0 \mid \mathbf{x}'_0) = \hat{\sigma}^2 \mathbf{x}'_0 (\mathbf{X}'\mathbf{X})^{-1} \mathbf{x}_0 \tag{9.9.9}$$

For the illustrative example of Section 8.10, we have the following values:

$$\hat{\sigma}^2 = 6.4308 \qquad \mathbf{X}'\mathbf{X}^{-1} = \begin{bmatrix} 26.3858 & -0.0982 & 1.6532 \\ -0.0982 & 0.0004 & -0.0063 \\ 1.6532 & -0.0063 & 0.1120 \end{bmatrix}$$

Using these data, we get from (9.9.9)

$$(\text{var}\,\hat{Y}_{1971} \mid \mathbf{x}'_{1971}) = 6.4308 \begin{bmatrix} 1 & 567 & 16 \end{bmatrix} (\mathbf{X}'\mathbf{X})^{-1} \begin{bmatrix} 1 \\ 567 \\ 16 \end{bmatrix}$$

$$= 6.4308 \quad (0.5688)$$

$$= 3.6580 \tag{9.9.10}$$

$$= (8.10.3)$$

---

[7]For derivation, see J. Johnston, *Econometric Methods*, McGraw-Hill, 3d ed., New York, 1984, pp. 195–196.

and

$$se\,(\hat{Y}_{1971} \mid x_{1971}) = \sqrt{3.6580} = 1.9126 \qquad (9.9.11)$$
$$= (8.10.3)$$

Then following our discussion in Chapters 5 and 8, we find that the $100(1-\alpha)\,\%$ confidence interval on the mean response, given $\mathbf{x}_0$, is

$$\hat{Y}_0 - t_{\alpha/2}\,\sqrt{\hat{\sigma}^2 \mathbf{x}_0(\mathbf{X}'\mathbf{X})^{-1}\mathbf{x}_0} \le E(Y \mid \mathbf{x}_0) \le \hat{Y}_0 + t_{\alpha/2}\,\sqrt{\hat{\sigma}^2 \mathbf{x}_0(\mathbf{X}'\mathbf{X})^{-1}\mathbf{x}_0} \quad (9.9.12)$$

For our example, the 95% confidence interval for mean response is as shown in (8.10.6): $504 \cdot 7518 \le E(Y_{1971}) \ge 513 \cdot 0868$.

Variance of Individual Prediction

The formula for the variance of an individual prediction is as follows:[8]

$$\text{var}\,(Y_0 \mid \mathbf{x_0}) = \hat{\sigma}^2[1 + \mathbf{x}_0'(\mathbf{X}'\mathbf{X})^{-1}\mathbf{x}_0] \qquad (9.9.13)$$

where $\text{var}\,(Y_0 \mid \mathbf{x_0})$ stands for $E[Y_0 - \hat{Y}_0 \mid X]^2$. [See also (5.10.6).] Again using our data, we obtain

$$\text{var}\,(Y_{1971} \mid \mathbf{x}_{1971}) = 6.4308(1 + 0.5688)$$
$$= 10.0887 \qquad (9.9.14)$$
$$= (8.10.4)$$

and

$$se\,(Y_{1971} \mid \mathbf{x}_{1971}) = \sqrt{10.0887} = 3.1763 \qquad (9.9.15)$$
$$= (8.10.4)$$

If we want to establish a $100(1 - \alpha)\%$ confidence interval for individual prediction we proceed as in (9.9.12) except that the standard error of prediction is now obtained from (9.9.13). Needless to say, the standard error of prediction for individual prediction is expected to be larger than that of mean prediction. [See (8.10.7).]

9.10   SUMMARY OF THE MATRIX APPROACH: AN ILLUSTRATIVE EXAMPLE

By way of summarizing the matrix approach to regression analysis, we shall present a numerical example involving three variables. Recall the illustrative example of Chapter 8, which involved the regression of aggregate personal consumption expenditure on aggregate personal disposable income and time for the period 1956–1970. It was stated there that the trend variable t may represent, among other things, aggregate or total population: Aggregate consumption expenditure is expected to increase as population increases. One way of isolating the influence of population is to convert the aggregate consumption expenditure and aggregate income figures to per capita or per head basis by dividing them by total population. A regression of per capital consumption expenditure on per capita income will then give the relationship between consumption expenditure and income net of population changes (or the scale effect). The trend variable may still be retained in the model as a catch-all for all other influences affecting consumption expenditure (e.g., technology). For

[8]Ibid.

empirical purposes therefore the regression model is

$$Y_i = \hat{\beta}_1 + \hat{\beta}_2 X_{2i} + \hat{\beta}_3 X_{3i} + \hat{u}_i \qquad (9.10.1)$$

where Y = per capita consumption expenditure, X_2 = per capita disposable income, and X_3 = time. The data required to run the regression (9.10.1) are given in Table 9.4.

In matrix notation, our problem may be shown as follows:

$$
\begin{bmatrix}
1673 \\
1688 \\
1666 \\
1735 \\
1749 \\
1756 \\
1815 \\
1867 \\
1948 \\
2048 \\
2128 \\
2165 \\
2257 \\
2316 \\
2324
\end{bmatrix}
=
\begin{bmatrix}
1 & 1839 & 1 \\
1 & 1844 & 2 \\
1 & 1831 & 3 \\
1 & 1881 & 4 \\
1 & 1883 & 5 \\
1 & 1910 & 6 \\
1 & 1969 & 7 \\
1 & 2016 & 8 \\
1 & 2126 & 9 \\
1 & 2239 & 10 \\
1 & 2336 & 11 \\
1 & 2404 & 12 \\
1 & 2487 & 13 \\
1 & 2535 & 14 \\
1 & 2595 & 15
\end{bmatrix}
\begin{bmatrix}
\hat{\beta}_1 \\
\hat{\beta}_2 \\
\hat{\beta}_3
\end{bmatrix}
+
\begin{bmatrix}
\hat{u}_1 \\
\hat{u}_2 \\
\hat{u}_3 \\
\hat{u}_4 \\
\hat{u}_5 \\
\hat{u}_6 \\
\hat{u}_7 \\
\hat{u}_8 \\
\hat{u}_9 \\
\hat{u}_{10} \\
\hat{u}_{11} \\
\hat{u}_{12} \\
\hat{u}_{13} \\
\hat{u}_{14} \\
\hat{u}_{15}
\end{bmatrix}
\qquad (9.10.2)
$$

$$
\begin{array}{cccc}
\mathbf{y} & = & \mathbf{X} & \hat{\mathbf{\beta}} & + & \hat{\mathbf{u}} \\
15 \times 1 & & 15 \times 3 & 3 \times 1 & & 15 \times 1
\end{array}
$$

TABLE 9.4
Per capita personal consumption expenditure (PPCE) and per capita personal disposable income (PPDI) in the United States, 1956–1970, in 1958 dollars

PPCE, Y	PPDI, X_2	Time, X_3
1673	1839	1 (= 1956)
1688	1844	2
1666	1831	3
1735	1881	4
1749	1883	5
1756	1910	6
1815	1969	7
1867	2016	8
1948	2126	9
2048	2239	10
2128	2336	11
2165	2404	12
2257	2487	13
2316	2535	14
2324	2595	15 (= 1970)

Source: Economic Report of the President, January 1972, Table B-16.

From the preceding data we obtain the following quantities:

$$\bar{Y} = 1942.333 \qquad \bar{X}_2 = 2126.333 \qquad \bar{X}_3 = 8.0$$

$$\sum (Y_i - \bar{Y})^2 = 830{,}121.333$$

$$\sum (X_{2i} - \bar{X}_2)^2 = 1{,}103{,}111.333 \qquad \sum (X_{3i} - \bar{X}_3)^2 = 280.0$$

$$\mathbf{X'X} = \begin{bmatrix} 1 & 1 & 1 & \cdots & 1 \\ X_{21} & X_{22} & X_{23} & \cdots & X_{2n} \\ X_{31} & X_{32} & X_{33} & \cdots & X_{3n} \end{bmatrix} \begin{bmatrix} 1 & X_{21} & X_{31} \\ 1 & X_{22} & X_{32} \\ 1 & X_{23} & X_{33} \\ \vdots & \vdots & \vdots \\ 1 & X_{2n} & X_{3n} \end{bmatrix}$$

$$= \begin{bmatrix} n & \sum X_{2i} & \sum X_{3i} \\ \sum X_{2i} & \sum X_{2i}^2 & \sum X_{2i}X_{3i} \\ \sum X_{3i} & \sum X_{2i}X_{3i} & \sum X_{3i}^2 \end{bmatrix}$$

$$= \begin{bmatrix} 15 & 31{,}895 & 120 \\ 31{,}895 & 68{,}922.513 & 272{,}144 \\ 120 & 272{,}144 & 1240 \end{bmatrix} \tag{9.10.3}$$

$$\mathbf{X'y} = \begin{bmatrix} 29{,}135 \\ 62{,}905{,}821 \\ 247{,}934 \end{bmatrix} \tag{9.10.4}$$

Using the rules of matrix inversion given in Appendix B, one can see that

$$(\mathbf{X'X})^{-1} = \begin{bmatrix} 37.232491 & -0.0225082 & 1.336707 \\ -0.0225082 & 0.0000137 & -0.0008319 \\ 1.336707 & -0.0008319 & 0.054034 \end{bmatrix} \tag{9.10.5}$$

Therefore,

$$\hat{\boldsymbol{\beta}} = (\mathbf{X'X})^{-1}\mathbf{X'y} = \begin{bmatrix} 300.28625 \\ 0.74198 \\ 8.04356 \end{bmatrix} \tag{9.10.6}$$

The residual sum of squares can now be computed as

$$\sum \hat{u}_i^2 = \hat{\mathbf{u}}'\hat{\mathbf{u}}$$

$$= \mathbf{y'y} - \hat{\boldsymbol{\beta}}'\mathbf{X'y}$$

$$= 57{,}420{,}003 - [\, 300.28625 \quad 0.74198 \quad 8.04356\,] \begin{bmatrix} 29{,}135 \\ 62{,}905{,}821 \\ 247{,}934 \end{bmatrix}$$

$$= 1976.85574 \tag{9.10.7}$$

whence we obtain

$$\hat{\sigma}^2 = \frac{\hat{\mathbf{u}}'\hat{\mathbf{u}}}{12} = 164.73797 \tag{9.10.8}$$

The variance-covariance matrix for $\hat{\boldsymbol{\beta}}$ can therefore be shown as

$$\text{var-cov}(\hat{\boldsymbol{\beta}}) = \hat{\sigma}^2(\mathbf{X'X})^{-1} = \begin{bmatrix} 6133.650 & -3.70794 & 220.20634 \\ -3.70794 & 0.00226 & -0.13705 \\ 220.20634 & -0.13705 & 8.90155 \end{bmatrix} \tag{9.10.9}$$

The diagonal elements of this matrix give the variances of $\hat{\beta}_1$, $\hat{\beta}_2$, and $\hat{\beta}_3$, respectively, and their positive square roots give the corresponding standard errors.

From the previous data, it can be readily verified that

$$\text{ESS: } \hat{\boldsymbol{\beta}}'\mathbf{X}'\mathbf{y} - n\bar{Y}^2 = 828,144.47786 \tag{9.10.10}$$

$$\text{TSS: } \mathbf{y}'\mathbf{y} - n\bar{Y}^2 = 830,121.333 \tag{9.10.11}$$

Therefore,

$$
\begin{aligned}
R^2 &= \frac{\hat{\boldsymbol{\beta}}'\mathbf{X}'\mathbf{y} - n\bar{Y}^2}{\mathbf{y}'\mathbf{y} - n\bar{Y}^2} \\
&= \frac{828,144.47786}{830,121.333} \\
&= 0.99761
\end{aligned}
\tag{9.10.12}
$$

Applying (7.8.4) the **adjusted coefficient of determination** can be seen to be

$$\bar{R}^2 = 0.99722 \tag{9.10.13}$$

Collecting our results thus far, we have

$$
\begin{aligned}
\hat{Y}_i = {} & 300.28625 + 0.74198X_{2i} + 8.04356X_{3i} \\
& (78.31763) \quad (0.04753) \quad (2.98354) \\
t = {} & (3.83421) \quad (15.60956) \quad (2.69598) \\
& R^2 = 0.99761 \quad \bar{R}^2 = 0.99722 \quad \text{df} = 12
\end{aligned}
\tag{9.10.14}
$$

The interpretation of (9.10.14) is this: If both X_2 and X_3 are fixed at zero value, the average value of per capita personal consumption expenditure is estimated at about $300. As usual, this mechanical interpretation of the intercept should be taken with a grain of salt. The partial regression coefficient of 0.74198 means that, holding all other variables constant, an increase in per capita income of, say, a dollar is accompanied by an increase in the mean per capita personal consumption expenditure of about 74 cents. In short, the marginal propensity to consume is estimated to be about 0.74, or 74 percent. Similarly, holding all other variables constant, the mean per capita personal consumption expenditure increased at the rate of about $8 per year during the period of the study, 1956–1970. The R^2 value of 0.9976 shows that the two explanatory variables accounted for over 99 percent of the variation in per capita consumption expenditure in the United States over the period 1956–1970. Although $\bar{R}^2$ dips slightly, it is still very high.

Turning to the statistical significance of the estimated coefficients, we see from (9.10.14) that each of the estimated coefficients is *individually* statistically significant at, say, the 5% level of significance: The ratios of the estimated coefficients to their standard errors (that is, t ratios) are 3.83421, 15.61077, and 2.69598, respectively. Using a two-tail t test at the 5% level of significance, we see that the critical t value for 12 df is 2.179. Each of the computed t values exceeds this critical value. Hence, individually we may reject the null hypothesis that the true population value of the relevant coefficient is zero.

As noted previously, we cannot apply the usual t test to test the hypothesis that $\beta_2 = \beta_3 = 0$ simultaneously because the t-test procedure assumes that an independent sample is drawn every time the t test is applied. If the same sample is used to test hypotheses about β_2 and β_3 simultaneously, it is likely that the estimators $\hat{\beta}_2$ and $\hat{\beta}_3$ are correlated, thus violating the assumption underlying the t-test procedure.[9] As a matter of fact, a look at the variance-covariance matrix of $\hat{\boldsymbol{\beta}}$ given

---

[9]See Sec. 8.5 for details.

in (9.10.9) shows that the estimators $\hat{\beta}_2$ and $\hat{\beta}_3$ are negatively correlated (the covariance between the two is -0.13705). Hence we cannot use the t test to test the null hypothesis that $\beta_2 = \beta_3 = 0$.

But recall that a null hypothesis like $\beta_2 = \beta_3 = 0$, simultaneously, can be tested by the analysis of variance technique and the attendant F test, which were introduced in Chapter 8. For our problem, the analysis of variance table is Table 9.5. Under the usual assumptions, we obtain

$$F = \frac{414{,}072.3893}{164.73797} = 2513.52 \tag{9.10.15}$$

which is distributed as the F distribution with 2 and 12 df. The computed F value is obviously highly significant; we can reject the null hypothesis that $\beta_2 = \beta_3 = 0$, that is, that per capita personal consumption expenditure is not linearly related to per capita disposable income and trend.

In Section 9.9 we discussed the mechanics of forecasting, mean as well as individual. Assume that for 1971 the PPDI figure is $2610 and we wish to forecast the PPCE corresponding to this figure. Then, the mean as well as individual forecast of PPCE for 1971 is the same and is given as

$$(\text{PPCE}_{1971} \mid \text{PPDI}_{1971}, X_3 = 16) = \mathbf{x}'_{1971}\hat{\boldsymbol{\beta}}$$

$$= [1 \quad 2610 \quad 16] \begin{bmatrix} 300.28625 \\ 0.74198 \\ 8.04356 \end{bmatrix}$$

$$= 2365.55 \tag{9.10.16}$$

where use is made of (9.9.3).

The variances of $\hat{Y}_{1971}$ and Y_{1971}, as we know from Section 9.9, are different and are as follows:

$$\text{var}(\hat{Y}_{1971} \mid \mathbf{x}'_{1971}) = \hat{\sigma}^2[\mathbf{x}'_{1971}(\mathbf{X}'\mathbf{X})^{-1}\mathbf{x}_{1971}]$$

$$= 164.73797[1 \quad 2610 \quad 16](\mathbf{X}'\mathbf{X})^{-1}\begin{bmatrix} 1 \\ 2610 \\ 16 \end{bmatrix} \tag{9.10.17}$$

where $(\mathbf{X}'\mathbf{X})^{-1}$ is as shown in (9.10.5). Substituting this into (9.10.17), the reader should verify that

$$\text{var}(\hat{Y}_{1971} \mid \mathbf{x}'_{1971}) = 48.6426 \tag{9.10.18}$$

and therefore

$$\text{se}(\hat{Y}_{1971} \mid \mathbf{x}'_{1971}) = 6.9744$$

We leave it to the reader to verify, using (9.9.13), that

$$\text{var}(Y_{1971} \mid \mathbf{x}'_{1971}) = 213.3806 \tag{9.10.19}$$

TABLE 9.5
The ANOVA table for the data of Table 9.4

Source of variation	SS	df	MSS
Due to X_2, X_3	828,144.47786	2	414,072.3893
Due to residuals	1,976.85574	12	164.73797
Total	830,121.33360	14	

and

$$se(Y_{1971} \mid \mathbf{x}'_{1971}) = 14.6076$$

Note: $\text{var}(Y_{1971} \mid \mathbf{x}'_{1971}) = E[Y_{1971} - \hat{Y}_{1971} \mid \mathbf{x}'_{1971}]^2$.

In Section 9.5 we introduced the correlation matrix **R**. For our data, the correlation matrix is as follows:

$$R = \begin{array}{c} \\ Y \\ X_2 \\ X_3 \end{array} \begin{array}{ccc} Y & X_2 & X_3 \end{array} \\ \begin{bmatrix} 1 & 0.9980 & 0.9743 \\ 0.9980 & 1 & 0.9664 \\ 0.9743 & 0.9664 & 1 \end{bmatrix} \qquad (9.10.20)$$

Note that in (9.10.20) we have bordered the correlation matrix by the variables of the model so that we can readily identify which variables are involved in the computation of the correlation coefficient. Thus, the coefficient 0.9980 in the first row of matrix (9.10.20) tells us that it is the correlation coefficient between Y and X_2 (that is, r_{12}). From the zero-order correlations given in the correlation matrix (9.10.20) one can easily derive the first-order correlation coefficients. (See exercise 9.7.)

9.11 SUMMARY AND CONCLUSIONS

The primary purpose of this chapter was to introduce the matrix approach to classical linear regression model. Although very few new concepts of regression analysis were introduced, the matrix notation provides a compact method of dealing with linear regression models involving any number of variables.

In concluding this chapter note that if the Y and X variables are measured in the deviation form, that is, as deviations from their sample means, there are a few changes in the formulas presented previously. These changes are listed in Table 9.6.[10] As this table shows, in the deviation form the correction for mean

TABLE 9.6
k*-variable regression model in original units and in the deviation form

Original units		Deviation form	
$\mathbf{y} = \mathbf{X}\hat{\boldsymbol{\beta}} + \hat{\mathbf{u}}$	(9.3.2)	$\mathbf{y} = \mathbf{X}\hat{\boldsymbol{\beta}} + \hat{\mathbf{u}}$ The column of 1's in the **X** matrix drops out. (Why?)	
$\hat{\boldsymbol{\beta}} = (\mathbf{X}'\mathbf{X})^{-1}\mathbf{X}'\mathbf{y}$	(9.3.11)	Same	
$\text{var-cov}(\hat{\boldsymbol{\beta}}) = \sigma^2(\mathbf{X}'\mathbf{X})^{-1}$	(9.3.13)	Same	
$\hat{\mathbf{u}}'\hat{\mathbf{u}} = \mathbf{y}'\mathbf{y} - \hat{\boldsymbol{\beta}}'\mathbf{X}'\mathbf{y}$	(9.3.18)	Same	
$\sum y_i^2 = \mathbf{y}'\mathbf{y} - n\bar{Y}^2$	(9.3.16)	$\sum y_i^2 = \mathbf{y}'\mathbf{y}$	(9.11.1)
$\text{ESS} = \hat{\boldsymbol{\beta}}'\mathbf{X}'\mathbf{y} - n\bar{Y}^2$	(9.3.17)	$\text{ESS} = \hat{\boldsymbol{\beta}}'\mathbf{X}'\mathbf{y}$	(9.11.2)
$R^2 = \dfrac{\hat{\boldsymbol{\beta}}'\mathbf{X}'\mathbf{y} - n\bar{Y}^2}{\mathbf{y}'\mathbf{y} - n\bar{Y}^2}$	(9.4.2)	$R^2 = \dfrac{\hat{\boldsymbol{\beta}}'\mathbf{X}'\mathbf{y}}{\mathbf{y}'\mathbf{y}}$	(9.11.3)

*Note that although in both cases the symbols for the matrices and vectors are the same, in the deviation form the elements of the matrices and vectors are assumed to be deviations rather than the raw data. Note also that in the deviation form $\hat{\boldsymbol{\beta}}$ is of order $k - 1$ and the var-cov $(\hat{\boldsymbol{\beta}})$ is of order $(k - 1)(k - 1)$.

[10]In these days of high-speed computers there may not be need for the deviation form. But it simplifies formulas and therefore calculations if one is working with a desk calculator and dealing with large numbers.

$n\bar{Y}^2$ drops out from the TSS and ESS. (Why?) This loss results in a change for the formula for R^2. Otherwise, most of the formulas developed in the original units of measurement hold true for the deviation form.

EXERCISES

9.1. For the illustrative example discussed in Section 9.10 the $\mathbf{X'X}$ and $\mathbf{X'y}$ using the data in the deviation form are as follows:

$$\mathbf{X'X} = \begin{bmatrix} 1,103,111.333 & 16,984 \\ 16,984 & 280 \end{bmatrix}$$

$$\mathbf{X'y} = \begin{bmatrix} 955,099.333 \\ 14,854.000 \end{bmatrix}$$

(a) Estimate β_2 and β_3.
(b) How would you estimate β_1?
(c) Estimate the variance of $\hat{\beta}_2$ and $\hat{\beta}_3$ and their covariances.
(d) Obtain R^2 and $\bar{R}^2$.
(e) Comparing your results with those given in Section 9.10, what do you find are the advantages of the deviation form?

9.2. For Example 8.1 of Chapter 8, you have been given the following data, where all the variables are measured in the deviation form, that is, as deviations from their sample means:

$$\mathbf{X'X} = \begin{bmatrix} 84,855.096 & 4796.00 \\ 4796.00 & 280.000 \end{bmatrix}$$

$$\mathbf{X'y} = \begin{bmatrix} 74,778.346 \\ 4250.900 \end{bmatrix}$$

Furthermore, $\bar{Y} = 367.693$, $\bar{X}_2 = 402.760$, and $\bar{X}_3 = 8.0$.
(a) Obtain $\hat{\beta}_2$ and $\hat{\beta}_3$ and their variances and covariances.
(b) Estimate the intercept term β_1.
(c) Calculate R^2.
(d) Using the calculated R^2, test the hypothesis that $\beta_2 = \beta_3 = 0$.

9.3. Testing the equality of two regression coefficients. Suppose that you are given the following regression model:

$$Y_i = \beta_1 + \beta_2 X_{2i} + \beta_3 X_{3i} + u_i$$

and you want to test the hypothesis that $\beta_2 = \beta_3$. If we assume that the u_i are normally distributed, it can be shown that

$$t = \frac{\hat{\beta}_2 - \hat{\beta}_3}{\sqrt{\text{var}(\hat{\beta}_2) + \text{var}(\hat{\beta}_3) - 2\,\text{cov}(\hat{\beta}_2, \hat{\beta}_3)}}$$

follows the t distribution with $n - 3$ df (see Section 8.6). (In general, for the k-variable case the df are $n - k$.) Therefore, the preceding t test can be used to test the null hypothesis $\beta_2 = \beta_3$.

Apply the preceding t test to test the hypothesis that the true values of β_2 and β_3 in the regression (9.10.14) are identical.
Hint: Use the var-cov matrix of $\boldsymbol{\beta}$ given in (9.10.9).

9.4. Expressing higher-order correlations in terms of lower-order correlations. Correlation coefficients of order p can be expressed in terms of correlation coefficients of order $p - 1$ by the following **reduction formula**:

$$r_{12.345...p} = \frac{r_{12.345...(p-1)} - [r_{1p.345...(p-1)}r_{2p.345...(p-1)}]}{\sqrt{[1 - r^2_{1p.345...(p-1)}]}\sqrt{[1 - r^2_{2p.345...(p-1)}]}}$$

Thus,

$$r_{12.3} = \frac{r_{12} - r_{13}r_{23}}{\sqrt{1 - r^2_{13}}\sqrt{1 - r^2_{23}}}$$

as found in Chapter 7.

You are given the following correlation matrix:

$$\mathbf{R} = \begin{array}{c} \\ Y \\ X_2 \\ X_3 \\ X_4 \\ X_5 \end{array} \begin{array}{ccccc} Y & X_2 & X_3 & X_4 & X_5 \\ \left[\begin{array}{ccccc} 1 & 0.44 & -0.34 & -0.31 & -0.14 \\ & 1 & 0.25 & -0.19 & -0.35 \\ & & 1 & 0.44 & 0.33 \\ & & & 1 & 0.85 \\ & & & & 1 \end{array}\right] \end{array}$$

Find the following:

(a) $r_{12.345}$ (b) $r_{12.34}$ (c) $r_{12.3}$

(d) $r_{13.245}$ (e) $r_{13.24}$ (f) $r_{13.2}$

9.5. Expressing higher-order regression coefficients in terms of lower-order regression coefficients. A regression coefficient of order p can be expressed in terms of a regression coefficient of order $p - 1$ by the following reduction formula:

$$\hat{\beta}_{12.345...p} = \frac{\hat{\beta}_{12.345...(p-1)} - [\hat{\beta}_{1p.345...(p-1)}\hat{\beta}_{p2.345...(p-1)}]}{1 - \hat{\beta}_{2p.345...(p-1)}\hat{\beta}_{p2.345...(p-1)}}$$

Thus,

$$\hat{\beta}_{12.3} = \frac{\hat{\beta}_{12} - \hat{\beta}_{13}\hat{\beta}_{32}}{1 - \hat{\beta}_{23}\hat{\beta}_{32}}$$

where $\beta_{12.3}$ is the slope coefficient in the regression of y on X_2 holding X_3 constant. Similarly, $\beta_{12.34}$ is the slope coefficient in the regression of Y on X_2 holding X_3 and X_4 constant, and so on.

   Using the preceding formula, find expressions for the following regression coefficients in terms of lower-order regression coefficients: $\hat{\beta}_{12.3456}$, $\hat{\beta}_{12.345}$, and $\hat{\beta}_{12.34}$.

9.6. Establish the following identity:

$$\hat{\beta}_{12.3}\hat{\beta}_{23.1}\hat{\beta}_{31.2} = r_{12.3}r_{23.1}r_{31.2}$$

9.7. For the correlation matrix **R** given in (9.10.20) find all the first-order partial correlation coefficients.

9.8. In studying the variation in crime rates in certain large cities in the United States, Ogburn obtained the following data:[*]

$$\begin{array}{lll} \bar{Y} = 19.9 & S_1 = 7.9 \\ \bar{X}_2 = 49.2 & S_2 = 1.3 \\ \bar{X}_3 = 10.2 & S_3 = 4.6 \\ \bar{X}_4 = 481.4 & S_4 = 74.4 \\ \bar{X}_5 = 41.6 & S_5 = 10.8 \end{array}$$

$$\mathbf{R} = \begin{array}{c} \\ Y \\ X_2 \\ X_3 \\ X_4 \\ X_5 \end{array} \begin{array}{ccccc} Y & X_2 & X_3 & X_4 & X_5 \\ \left[\begin{array}{ccccc} 1 & 0.44 & -0.34 & -0.31 & -0.14 \\ & 1 & 0.25 & -0.19 & -0.35 \\ & & 1 & 0.44 & 0.33 \\ & & & 1 & 0.85 \\ & & & & 1 \end{array}\right] \end{array}$$

[*]W. F. Ogburn, "Factors in the Variation of Crime among Cities," *Journal of American Statistical Association*, vol. 30, 1935, p. 12.

where Y = crime rate, number of known offenses per thousand of population

   X_2 = percentage of male inhabitants

   X_3 = percentage of total inhabitants who are foreign-born males

   X_4 = number of children under 5 years of age per thousand married women between ages 15 and 44 years

   X_5 = church membership, number of church members 13 years of age and over per 100 of total population 13 years of age and over; S_1 to S_5 are the sample standard deviations of variables Y through X_5 and $\mathbf{R}$ is the correlation matrix

(a) Treating Y as the dependent variable, obtain the regression of Y on the four X variables and interpret the estimated regression.

(b) Obtain $r_{12.3}$, $r_{14.35}$, and $r_{15.34}$.

(c) Obtain R^2 and test the hypothesis that all partial slope coefficients are simultaneously equal to zero.

9.9. The following table gives data on output and total cost of production of a commodity in the short run. (See Example 7.4.)

Output	Total cost, $
1	193
2	226
3	240
4	244
5	257
6	260
7	274
8	297
9	350
10	420

To test whether the preceding data suggest the U-shaped average and marginal cost curves typically encountered in the short run, one can use the following model:

$$Y_i = \beta_1 + \beta_2 X_i + \beta_3 X_i^2 + \beta_4 X_i^3 + u_i$$

where Y = total cost and X = output. The additional explanatory variables X_i^2 and X_i^3 are derived from X.

(a) Express the data in the deviation form and obtain $(\mathbf{X'X})$, $(\mathbf{X'y})$, and $(\mathbf{X'X})^{-1}$.

(b) Estimate β_2, β_3, and β_4.

(c) Estimate the var-cov matrix of $\hat{\boldsymbol{\beta}}$.

(d) Estimate β_1. Interpret $\hat{\beta}_1$ in the context of the problem.

(e) Obtain R^2 and $\bar{R}^2$.

(f) A priori, what are the signs of β_2, β_3, and β_4? Why?

(g) From the total cost function given previously obtain expressions for the marginal and average cost functions.

(h) Fit the average and marginal cost functions to the data and comment on the fit.

(i) If $\beta_3 = \beta_4 = 0$, what is the nature of the marginal cost function? How would you test the hypothesis that $\beta_3 = \beta_4 = 0$?

(j) How would you derive the total variable cost and average variable cost functions from the given data?

9.10. In order to study the labor force participation of urban poor families (families earning less than \$3943 in 1969), the accompanying data were obtained from the 1970 Census of Population.

(a) Using the regression model $Y_i = \beta_1 + \beta_2 X_{2i} + \beta_3 X_{3i} + \beta_4 X_{4i} + u_i$, obtain the estimates of the regression coefficients and interpret your results.

(b) A priori, what are the expected signs of the regression coefficients in the preceding model and why?

(c) How would you test the hypothesis that the overall unemployment rate has no effect on the labor force participation of the urban poor in the census tracts given in the accompanying table?

(d) Should any variables be dropped from the preceding model? Why?

(e) What other variables would you consider for inclusion in the model?

Labor force participation experience of the urban poor: census tracts, New York City, 1970

Tract no.	% in labor force, Y^*	Mean family income, X_2†	Mean family size, X_3	Unemployment rate, X_4**
137	64.3	1,998	2.95	4.4
139	45.4	1,114	3.40	3.4
141	26.6	1,942	3.72	1.1
142	87.5	1,998	4.43	3.1
143	71.3	2,026	3.82	7.7
145	82.4	1,853	3.90	5.0
147	26.3	1,666	3.32	6.2
149	61.6	1,434	3.80	5.4
151	52.9	1,513	3.49	12.2
153	64.7	2,008	3.85	4.8
155	64.9	1,704	4.69	2.9
157	70.5	1,525	3.89	4.8
159	87.2	1,842	3.53	3.9
161	81.2	1,735	4.96	7.2
163	67.9	1,639	3.68	3.6

$^*Y$ = family heads under 65 years old

†X_2 = dollars

$^{**}X_4$ = percent of civilian labor force unemployed

Source: Census Tracts: New York, Bureau of the Census, U.S. Department of Commerce, 1970.

9.11. In an application of the Cobb-Douglas production function the following results were obtained:

$$\widehat{\ln Y_i} = 2.3542 + 0.9576 \ln X_{2i} + 0.8242 \ln X_{3i}$$
$$\qquad\qquad (0.3022) \qquad\quad (0.3571)$$

$$R^2 = 0.8432 \qquad df = 12$$

where Y = output, X_2 = labor input, and X_3 = capital input, and where the figures in parentheses are the estimated standard errors.

(a) As noted in Chapter 7, the coefficients of the labor and capital inputs in the preceding equation give the elasticities of output with respect to labor and capital. Test the hypothesis that these elasticities are *individually* equal to unity.

(b) Test the hypothesis that the labor and capital elasticities are equal, assuming (i) the covariance between the estimated labor and capital coefficients is zero, and (ii) it is -0.0972.

(c) How would you test the overall significance of the preceding regression equation?

*9.12. Express the likelihood function for the k-variable regression model in matrix notation and show that $\tilde{\beta}$, the vector of maximum likelihood estimators, is identical to $\hat{\beta}$, the vector of OLS estimators of the k-variable regression model.

9.13. **Regression using standardized variables.** Consider the following sample regression functions (SRFs):

$$Y_i = \hat{\beta}_1 + \hat{\beta}_2 X_{2i} + \hat{\beta}_3 X_{3i} + \hat{u}_i \tag{1}$$

$$Y_i* = b_1 + b_2 X_{2i}* + b_3 X_{3i}* + \hat{u}_i* \tag{2}$$

where

$$Y_i* = \frac{Y_i - \bar{Y}}{s_Y}$$

$$X_{2i}* = \frac{X_{2i} - \bar{X}_2}{s_2}$$

$$X_{3i}* = \frac{X_{3i} - \bar{X}_3}{s_3}$$

where the s's denote the sample standard deviations. As noted in Chapter 6, exercise 6.7, the starred variables above are known as the *standardized variables*. These variables have zero means and unit ($=1$) standard deviations. Expressing all the variables in the deviation form, show the following for model (2):

(a) $\mathbf{X'X} = \begin{bmatrix} 1 & r_{23} \\ r_{23} & 1 \end{bmatrix} n$

(b) $\mathbf{X'y} = \begin{bmatrix} r_{12} \\ r_{13} \end{bmatrix} n$

(c) $(\mathbf{X'X})^{-1} = \dfrac{1}{n(1 - r_{23}^2)} \begin{bmatrix} 1 & -r_{23} \\ -r_{23} & 1 \end{bmatrix}$

(d) $\hat{\beta} = \begin{bmatrix} b_2 \\ b_3 \end{bmatrix} = \dfrac{1}{1 - r_{23}^2} \begin{bmatrix} r_{12} - r_{23}r_{13} \\ r_{13} - r_{23}r_{12} \end{bmatrix}$

(e) $b_1 = 0$

Also establish the relationship between the b's and the $\hat{\beta}$'s.

(Note that in the preceding relations n denotes the sample size; r_{12}, r_{13}, and r_{23} denote the correlations between Y and X_2, between Y and X_3, and between X_2 and X_3, respectively.)

9.14. Verify the Eqs. (9.10.18) and (9.10.19).

*9.15. **Constrained least-squares.** Assume

$$\mathbf{y} = \mathbf{X\beta} + \mathbf{u} \tag{1}$$

---

*Optional

which we want to estimate subject to a set of equality restrictions or constraints:

$$\mathbf{R}\boldsymbol{\beta} = \mathbf{r} \tag{2}$$

where $\mathbf{R} =$ is a *known* matrix of order qxk ($q \le k$) and $\mathbf{r}$ is a *known* vector of q elements. To illustrate, suppose our model is

$$Y_i = \beta_1 + \beta_2 X_{2i} + \beta_3 X_{3i} + \beta_4 X_{4i} + \beta_5 X_{5i} + u_i \tag{3}$$

and suppose we want to estimate this model subject to these restrictions:

$$\begin{aligned} \beta_2 - \beta_3 &= 0 \\ \beta_4 + \beta_5 &= 1 \end{aligned} \tag{4}$$

We can use some of the techniques discussed in Chapter 8 to incorporate these restrictions (e.g., $\beta_2 = \beta_3$ and $\beta_4 = 1 - \beta_5$, thus removing β_2 and β_4 from the model) and test for the validity of these restrictions by the F test discussed there. But a more direct way of estimating (3) incorporating the restrictions (4) directly in the estimating procedure is first to express the restrictions in the form of Eq. (2), which in the present case becomes

$$\mathbf{R} = \begin{bmatrix} 0 & 1 & -1 & 0 & 0 \\ 0 & 0 & 0 & 1 & 1 \end{bmatrix} \qquad \mathbf{r} = \begin{bmatrix} 0 \\ 1 \end{bmatrix} \tag{5}$$

Letting $\boldsymbol{\beta}^*$ denote the restricted least-squares or constrained least-squares estimator, one can show that $\boldsymbol{\beta}^*$ can be estimated by the following formula:*

$$\hat{\boldsymbol{\beta}}^* = \hat{\boldsymbol{\beta}} + (\mathbf{X'X})^{-1}\mathbf{R'}[\mathbf{R}(\mathbf{X'X})^{-1}\mathbf{R'}]^{-1}(\mathbf{r} - \mathbf{R}\hat{\boldsymbol{\beta}}) \tag{6}$$

where $\hat{\boldsymbol{\beta}}$ is the usual (unconstrained) estimator estimated from the usual formula $(\mathbf{X'X})^{-1}\mathbf{X'y}$.

(*a*) What is the β vector in (3)?

(*b*) Given this β vector, verify that the $\mathbf{R}$ matrix and $\mathbf{r}$ vector given in (5) do in fact incorporate the restrictions in (4).

(*c*) Write down the $\mathbf{R}$ and $\mathbf{r}$ in the following cases:

    (*i*) $\beta_2 = \beta_3 = \beta_4 = 2$

    (*ii*) $\beta_2 = \beta_3$ and $\beta_4 = \beta_5$

    (*iii*) $\beta_2 - 3\beta_3 = 5\beta_4$

    (*iv*) $\beta_2 + 3\beta_3 = 0$

(*d*) When will $\hat{\boldsymbol{\beta}}^* = \hat{\boldsymbol{\beta}}$?

APPENDIX 9A

9A.1 DERIVATION OF k NORMAL OR SIMULTANEOUS EQUATIONS

Differentiating

$$\sum \hat{u}_i^2 = \sum (Y_i - \hat{\beta}_1 - \hat{\beta}_2 X_{2i} - \cdots - \hat{\beta}_k X_{ki})^2$$

partially with respect to $\hat{\beta}_1, \hat{\beta}_2, \ldots, \hat{\beta}_k$, we obtain

---

*See J. Johnston, op. cit., p. 205.

$$\frac{\partial \sum \hat{u}_i^2}{\partial \hat{\beta}_1} = 2 \sum (Y_i - \hat{\beta}_1 - \hat{\beta}_2 X_{2i} - \cdots - \hat{\beta}_k X_{ki})(-1)$$

$$\frac{\partial \sum \hat{u}_i^2}{\partial \hat{\beta}_2} = 2 \sum (Y_i - \hat{\beta}_1 - \hat{\beta}_2 X_{2i} - \cdots - \hat{\beta}_k X_{ki})(-X_{2i})$$

$$\cdots\cdots\cdots\cdots\cdots\cdots\cdots\cdots\cdots\cdots\cdots\cdots\cdots\cdots\cdots\cdots\cdots\cdots$$

$$\frac{\partial \sum \hat{u}_i^2}{\partial \hat{\beta}_k} = 2 \sum (Y_i - \hat{\beta}_1 - \hat{\beta}_2 X_{ki} - \cdots - \hat{\beta}_k X_{ki})(-X_{ki})$$

Setting the preceding partial derivatives equal to zero and rearranging the terms, we obtain the k normal equations given in (9.3.8).

9A.2   MATRIX DERIVATION OF NORMAL EQUATIONS

From (9.3.7) we obtain

$$\hat{\mathbf{u}}'\hat{\mathbf{u}} = \mathbf{y}'\mathbf{y} - 2\hat{\boldsymbol{\beta}}'\mathbf{X}'\mathbf{y} + \hat{\boldsymbol{\beta}}'\mathbf{X}'\mathbf{X}\hat{\boldsymbol{\beta}}$$

Using rules of matrix differentiation given in Appendix B, we obtain

$$\frac{\partial(\hat{\mathbf{u}}'\hat{\mathbf{u}})}{\partial \hat{\boldsymbol{\beta}}} = -2\mathbf{X}'\mathbf{y} + 2\mathbf{X}'\mathbf{X}\hat{\boldsymbol{\beta}}$$

Setting the preceding equation to zero gives

$$(\mathbf{X}'\mathbf{X})\hat{\boldsymbol{\beta}} = \mathbf{X}'\mathbf{y}$$

whence $\hat{\boldsymbol{\beta}} = (\mathbf{X}'\mathbf{X})^{-1}\mathbf{X}'\mathbf{y}$, provided the inverse exists.

9A.3   VARIANCE-COVARIANCE MATRIX OF $\hat{\boldsymbol{\beta}}$

From (9.3.11) we obtain

$$\hat{\boldsymbol{\beta}} = (\mathbf{X}'\mathbf{X})^{-1}\mathbf{X}'\mathbf{y}$$

Substituting $\mathbf{y} = \mathbf{X}\boldsymbol{\beta} + \mathbf{u}$ into the preceding expression gives

$$\begin{aligned}
\hat{\boldsymbol{\beta}} &= (\mathbf{X}'\mathbf{X})^{-1}\mathbf{X}'(\mathbf{X}\boldsymbol{\beta} + \mathbf{u}) \\
&= (\mathbf{X}'\mathbf{X})^{-1}\mathbf{X}'\mathbf{X}\boldsymbol{\beta} + (\mathbf{X}'\mathbf{X})^{-1}\mathbf{X}'\mathbf{u} \\
&= \boldsymbol{\beta} + (\mathbf{X}'\mathbf{X})^{-1}\mathbf{X}'\mathbf{u}
\end{aligned} \tag{1}$$

Therefore,

$$\hat{\boldsymbol{\beta}} - \boldsymbol{\beta} = (\mathbf{X}'\mathbf{X})^{-1}\mathbf{X}'\mathbf{u} \tag{2}$$

By definition

$$\begin{aligned}
\text{var-cov}\,(\hat{\boldsymbol{\beta}}) &= E[(\hat{\boldsymbol{\beta}} - \boldsymbol{\beta})(\hat{\boldsymbol{\beta}} - \boldsymbol{\beta})'] \\
&= E\{[\mathbf{X}'\mathbf{X})^{-1}\mathbf{X}'\mathbf{u}][(\mathbf{X}'\mathbf{X})^{-1}\mathbf{X}'\mathbf{u}]'\} \\
&= E[(\mathbf{X}'\mathbf{X})^{-1}\mathbf{X}'\mathbf{u}\mathbf{u}'\mathbf{X}(\mathbf{X}'\mathbf{X})^{-1}]
\end{aligned} \tag{3}$$

where in the last step use is made of the fact that $(\mathbf{AB})' = \mathbf{B}'\mathbf{A}'$.

Noting that the X's are nonstochastic, on taking expectation of (3) we obtain

$$\text{var-cov } (\hat{\boldsymbol{\beta}}) = (\mathbf{X'X})^{-1}\mathbf{X'}E(\mathbf{uu'})\mathbf{X}(\mathbf{X'X})^{-1}$$
$$= (\mathbf{X'X})^{-1}\mathbf{X'}\sigma^2\mathbf{IX}(\mathbf{X'X})^{-1}$$
$$= \sigma^2(\mathbf{X'X})^{-1}$$

which is the result given in (9.3.13). Note that in deriving the preceding result use is made of the assumption that $E(\mathbf{uu'}) = \sigma^2\mathbf{I}$.

9A.4 BLUE PROPERTY OF OLS ESTIMATORS

From (9.3.11) we have

$$\hat{\boldsymbol{\beta}} = (\mathbf{X'X})^{-1}\mathbf{X'y} \tag{1}$$

Since $(\mathbf{X'X})^{-1}\mathbf{X'}$ is a matrix of fixed numbers, $\hat{\boldsymbol{\beta}}$ is a linear function of Y. Hence, by definition it is a linear estimator.

Recall that the PRF is

$$\mathbf{y} = \mathbf{X\boldsymbol{\beta}} + \mathbf{u} \tag{2}$$

Substituting this into (1), we obtain

$$\hat{\boldsymbol{\beta}} = (\mathbf{X'X})^{-1}\mathbf{X'}(\mathbf{X\boldsymbol{\beta}} + \mathbf{u}) \tag{3}$$
$$= \boldsymbol{\beta} + (\mathbf{X'X})^{-1}\mathbf{X'u} \tag{4}$$

since $(\mathbf{X'X})^{-1}\mathbf{X'X} = \mathbf{I}$.

Taking expectation of (4) gives

$$E(\hat{\boldsymbol{\beta}}) = E(\boldsymbol{\beta}) + (\mathbf{X'X})^{-1}\mathbf{X'}E(\mathbf{u})$$
$$= \boldsymbol{\beta} \tag{5}$$

since $E(\boldsymbol{\beta}) = \boldsymbol{\beta}$ (why?) and $E(\mathbf{u}) = \mathbf{0}$ by assumption, which shows that $\hat{\boldsymbol{\beta}}$ is an unbiased estimator of $\boldsymbol{\beta}$.

Let $\hat{\boldsymbol{\beta}}^*$ be any other linear estimator of $\boldsymbol{\beta}$, which can be written as

$$\boldsymbol{\beta}^* = [(\mathbf{X'X})^{-1}\mathbf{X'} + \mathbf{C}]\mathbf{y} \tag{6}$$

where $\mathbf{C}$ is a matrix of constants.

Substituting for $\mathbf{y}$ from (2) into (6), we get

$$\hat{\boldsymbol{\beta}}^* = [(\mathbf{X'X})^{-1}\mathbf{X'} + \mathbf{C}](\mathbf{X\boldsymbol{\beta}} + \mathbf{u})$$
$$= \boldsymbol{\beta} + \mathbf{CX\boldsymbol{\beta}} + (\mathbf{X'X})^{-1}\mathbf{X'u} + \mathbf{Cu} \tag{7}$$

Now if $\hat{\boldsymbol{\beta}}^*$ is to be an unbiased estimator of $\boldsymbol{\beta}$, we must have

$$\mathbf{CX} = \mathbf{0} \qquad \text{(Why?)} \tag{8}$$

Using (8), (7) can be written as

$$\hat{\boldsymbol{\beta}}^* - \boldsymbol{\beta} = (\mathbf{X'X})^{-1}\mathbf{X'u} + \mathbf{Cu} \tag{9}$$

By definition, the var-cov($\hat{\boldsymbol{\beta}}^*$) is

$$E(\hat{\boldsymbol{\beta}}^* - \boldsymbol{\beta})(\hat{\boldsymbol{\beta}}^* - \boldsymbol{\beta})' = E[(\mathbf{X'X})^{-1}\mathbf{X'u} + \mathbf{Cu}][(\mathbf{X'X})^{-1}\mathbf{X'u} + \mathbf{Cu}]' \quad (10)$$

Making use of the properties of matrix inversion and transposition and after algebraic simplification, we obtain

$$\text{var-cov}(\hat{\boldsymbol{\beta}}^*) = \sigma^2(\mathbf{X'X})^{-1} + \sigma^2\mathbf{CC'}$$
$$= \text{var-cov}(\hat{\boldsymbol{\beta}}) + \sigma^2\mathbf{CC'} \quad (11)$$

which shows that the variance-covariance matrix of the alternative unbiased linear estimator $\hat{\boldsymbol{\beta}}^*$ is equal to the variance-covariance matrix of the OLS estimator $\hat{\boldsymbol{\beta}}$ plus σ^2 times $\mathbf{CC'}$, which is a positive semidefinite* matrix. Hence the variances of a given element of $\hat{\boldsymbol{\beta}}^*$ must necessarily be equal to or greater than the corresponding element of $\hat{\boldsymbol{\beta}}$, which shows that $\hat{\boldsymbol{\beta}}$ is BLUE. Of course, if $\mathbf{C}$ is a null matrix, i.e., $\mathbf{C} = \mathbf{0}$, then $\hat{\boldsymbol{\beta}}^* = \hat{\boldsymbol{\beta}}$, which is another way of saying that if we have found a BLUE estimator, it must be the least-squares estimator $\hat{\boldsymbol{\beta}}$.

---

*See references in Appendix B.

PART

II

RELAXING THE ASSUMPTIONS OF THE CLASSICAL MODEL

In Part I we considered at length the classical normal linear regression model and showed how it can be used to handle the twin problems of statistical inference, namely, estimation and hypothesis testing, as well as the problem of prediction. But recall that this model is based on several simplifying assumptions, which are as follows.

Assumption 1. The regression model is linear in the parameters.

Assumption 2. The values of the regressors, the X's, are fixed in repeated sampling.

Assumption 3. For given X's, the mean value of the disturbance u_i is zero.

Assumption 4. For given X's, the variance of u_i is constant or homoscedastic.

Assumption 5. For given X's, there is no autocorrelation in the disturbances.

Assumption 6. If the X's are stochastic, the disturbance term and the (stochastic) X's are independent or at least uncorrelated.

Assumption 7. The number of observations must be greater than the number of regressors.

Assumption 8. There must be sufficient variability in the values taken by the regressors.

Assumption 9. The regression model is correctly specified.

Assumption 10. There is no exact linear relationship (i.e., multicollinearity) in the regressors.

Assumption 11. The stochastic (disturbance) term u_i is normally distributed.

Before proceeding further, let us note that most textbooks list fewer than 11 assumptions. For example, assumptions 7 and 8 are taken for granted rather than spelled out explicitly. We decided to state them explicitly because distinguishing between the assumptions required for OLS to have desirable statistical properties (such as BLUE) and the conditions required for OLS to be useful seems sensible. For example, OLS estimators are BLUE even if assumption 8 is not satisfied. But in that case the standard errors of the OLS estimators will be large relative to their coefficients (i.e., the t ratios will be small), thereby making it difficult to assess the contribution of one or more regressors to the explained sum of squares.

As Wetherill notes, in practice two major types of problems arise in applying the classical linear regression model: (1) those due to assumptions about the specification of the model and about the disturbances u_i and (2) those due to assumptions about the data.[1] In the first category are Assumptions 1, 2, 3, 4, 5, 9, and 11. Those in the second category include Assumptions 6, 7, 8, and 10. In addition, data problems, such as outliers (unusual or untypical observations) and errors of measurement in the data, also fall in the second category.

With respect to problems arising from the assumptions about disturbances and model specifications, three major questions arise: (1) How severe must the departure be from a particular assumption before it really matters? For example, if u_i are not exactly normally distributed, what level of departure from this assumption can one accept before the BLUE property of the OLS estimators is destroyed? (2) How do we find out whether a particular assumption is in fact violated in a concrete case? Thus, how does one find out if the disturbances are normally distributed in a given application? We have already discussed the **chi-square** and **Jarque-Bera** tests of normality. (3) What remedial measures can we take if one or more of the assumptions are false? For example, if the assumption of homoscedasticity is found to be false in an application, what do we do then?

With regard to problems attributable to assumptions about the data, we also face similar questions. (1) How serious is a particular problem? For exam-

---

[1]G. Barrie Wetherill, *Regression Analysis with Applications*, Chapman and Hall, New York, 1986, pp. 14–15.

ple, is multicollinearity so severe that it makes estimation and inference very difficult? (2) How do we find out the severity of the data problem? For example, how do we decide whether the inclusion or exclusion of an observation or observations that may represent outliers will make a tremendous difference in the analysis? (3) Can some of the data problems be easily remedied? For example, can one have access to the original data to find out the sources of errors of measurement in the data?

Unfortunately, satisfactory answers cannot be given to all these questions. What we will do in the rest of Part II is to look at some of the assumptions more critically, but not all will receive full scrutiny. In particular, we will not discuss in depth the following: Assumptions 1, 2, 3, 6, and 11. The reasons are as follows:

Assumption 1: Linear-in-parameters regression model. In Section 6.8 we briefly touched upon nonlinear-in-parameter regression models. Such models are usually estimated by some iterative, or trial and error, procedure. We do not discuss such models in this book because some of the mathematics required to do justice to such models is beyond the scope of this introductory book. There is also the more pragmatic reason that linear-in-parameters regression models have proved quite successful in many an empirical phenomenon. Sometimes, such models are first-degree approximations to the more complicated nonlinear regression models.

Assumptions 2 and 6: Fixed vs. stochastic regressors. Remember that our regression analysis is based on the assumption that the regressors are nonstochastic and assume fixed values in repeated sampling. There is a good reason for this strategy. Unlike scientists in the physical sciences, as noted in Chapter 1, economists generally have no control over the data they use. More often than not, economists depend on secondary data, that is, data collected by someone else, such as the government and private organizations. Therefore, the practical strategy to follow is to assume that for the problem at hand the values of the explanatory variables are given even though the variables themselves may be intrinsically stochastic or random. Hence, the results of the regression analysis are conditional upon these given values.

But suppose that we cannot regard the X's as truly nonstochastic or fixed. This is the case of **random** or **stochastic regressors**. Now the situation is rather involved. The u_i, by assumption, are stochastic. If the X's too are stochastic, then we must specify how the X's and u_i are distributed. If we are willing to make Assumption 6 (i.e., the X's, although random, are distributed independently of, or at least uncorrelated with, u_i), then for all practical purposes we can continue to operate as if the X's were nonstochastic. As Kmenta notes:

> Thus, *relaxing the assumption that X is nonstochastic and replacing it by the assumption that X is stochastic but independent of [u] does not change the desirable properties and feasibility of least squares estimation.*[2]

---

[2]Jan Kmenta, *Elements of Econometrics*, 2d ed., Macmillan, New York, 1986, p. 338. (Emphasis in the original.)

Therefore, we will retain Assumption 2 or Assumption 6 until we come to deal with simultaneous equations models in Part IV.[3]

Assumption 3: Zero mean value of u_i. Recall the k-variable linear regression model:

$$Y_i = \beta_1 + \beta_2 X_{2i} + \beta_3 X_{3i} + \cdots + \beta_k X_{ki} + u_i \tag{1}$$

Let us now assume that

$$E(u_i \mid X_{2i}, X_{3i}, \ldots, X_{ki}) = w \tag{2}$$

where w is a constant; note in the standard model $w = 0$, but now we let it be any constant.

Taking the conditional expectation of (1), we obtain

$$
\begin{aligned}
E(Y_i \mid X_{2i}, X_{3i}, \ldots, X_{ki}) &= \beta_1 + \beta_2 X_{2i} + \beta_3 X_{3i} + \cdots + \beta_k X_{ki} + w \\
&= (\beta_1 + w) + \beta_2 X_{2i} + \beta_3 X_{3i} + \cdots + \beta_k X_{ki} \\
&= \alpha + \beta_2 X_{2i} + \beta_3 X_{3i} + \cdots + \beta_k X_{ki}
\end{aligned}
\tag{3}
$$

where $\alpha = (\beta_1 + w)$ and where in taking the expectations one should note that the X's are treated as constants. (Why?)

Therefore, if Assumption 3 is not fulfilled, we see that we cannot estimate the original intercept β_1; what we obtain is α, which contains β_1 and $E(u_i) = w$. In short, we obtain a *biased* estimate of β_1.

But as we have noted on many occasions, in many practical situations the intercept term, β_1, is of little importance; the more meaningful quantities are the slope coefficients, which remain unaffected even if Assumption 3 is violated.[4] Besides, in many applications the intercept term has no physical interpretation.

Assumption 11: Normality of u. This assumption is not essential if our objective is estimation only. As noted in Chapter 3, the OLS estimators are BLUE regardless of whether the u_i are normally distributed or not. With the normality assumption, however, we were able to establish that the OLS estimators of the regression coefficients follow the normal distribution, that $(n - k)\hat{\sigma}^2/\sigma^2$ has the χ^2 distribution, and that one could use the t and F tests to test various statistical hypotheses regardless of the sample size.

---

[3]A technical point may be noted here. Instead of the strong assumption that the X's and u are independent, we may use the weaker assumption that the values of X variables and u are uncorrelated contemporaneously (i.e., at the same point in time). In this case OLS estimators may be biased but they are **consistent**, that is, as the sample size increases indefinitely, the estimators converge on their true values. If, however, the X's and u are contemporaneously correlated, the OLS estimators are biased as well as inconsistent. In Chap. 17 we will show how the method of **instrumental variables** can sometimes be used to obtain consistent estimators in this situation.

[4]It is very important to note that this statement is true only if $E(u_i) = w$ for each i. However, if $E(u_i) = w_i$, that is, a different constant for each i, the partial slope coefficients may be biased as well as inconsistent. In this case violation of Assumption 3 will be critical. For proof and further details, see Peter Schmidt, *Econometrics*, Marcel Dekker, New York, 1976, pp. 36–39.

But what happens if the u_i are not normally distributed? We then rely on the following extension of the central limit theorem; recall that it was the central limit theorem we invoked to justify the normality assumption in the first place:

If the disturbances [u_i] are independently and identically distributed with zero mean and [constant] variance σ^2 and if the explanatory variables are constant in repeated samples, the [O]LS coefficient estimators are asymptotically normally distributed with means equal to the corresponding β's.[5]

Therefore, the usual test procedures—the t and F tests—are still valid *asymptotically*, that is, in the large sample, but not in the finite or small samples.

The fact that if the disturbances are not normally distributed the OLS estimators are still normally distributed asymptotically (under the assumption of homoscedastic variance and fixed X's) is of little comfort to practicing economists, who often do not have the luxury of large-sample data. Therefore, the normality assumption becomes extremely important for the purposes of hypothesis testing and prediction. Hence, with the twin problems of estimation and hypothesis testing in mind, and given the fact that small samples are the rule rather than the exception in most economic analyses, we shall continue to use the normality assumption.[6]

Of course, this means that when we deal with a finite sample, we must explicitly test for the normality assumption. We have already considered the **chi-square goodness of fit** and the **Jarque-Bera tests** of normality. The reader is strongly urged to apply these or other tests of normality to regression residuals. Keep in mind that in finite samples without the normality assumption the usual t and F statistics may not follow the t and F distributions.

We are left with Assumptions 4, 5, 7, 8, 9, and 10. Assumptions 7, 8, and 10 are closely interrelated and are discussed in the chapter on multicollinearity (Chapter 10). Assumption 4 is discussed in the chapter on heteroscedasticity (Chapter 11). Assumption 5 is discussed in the chapter on autocorrelation (Chapter 12). Finally, Assumption 9 is discussed in the chapter on model specification (Chapter 13) and further elaborated in Chapter 14.

For pedagogical reasons, in each of these chapters we follow a common format, namely, (1) identify the nature of the problem, (2) examine its consequences, (3) suggest methods of detecting it, and (4) consider remedial measures so that they may lead to estimators that possess the desirable statistical properties discussed in Part I.

A cautionary note is in order: As noted earlier, satisfactory answers to all the problems arising out of the violation of the assumptions of the CLRM do not exist. Moreover, there may be more than one solution to a particular

---

[5]Henri Theil, *Introduction to Econometrics*, Prentice-Hall, Englewood Cliffs, N.J., 1978, p. 240. It must be noted the assumptions of fixed X's and constant σ^2 are crucial for this result.

[6]In passing, note that the effects of departure from normality and related topics are often discussed under the topic of **robust estimation** in the literature, a topic beyond the scope of this book.

problem, and often it is not clear which method is best. Besides, in a particular application more than one violation of the CLRM may be involved. Thus, specification bias, multicollinearity, and heteroscedasticity may coexist in an application, and there is no single omnipotent test that will solve all the problems simultaneously.[7] Furthermore, a particular test that was popular at one time may not be in vogue later because somebody found a flaw in the earlier test. But this is how science progresses. Econometrics is no exception.

---

[7]This is not for lack of trying. See A. K. Bera and C. M. Jarque, "Efficient Tests for Normality, Homoscedasticity and Serial Independence of Regression Residuals: Monte Carlo Evidence," *Economic Letters*, vol. 7, 1981, pp. 313–318.

CHAPTER
10

MULTICOLLINEARITY
AND MICRONUMEROSITY[1]

There is no pair of words that is more misused both in econometrics texts and in the applied literature than the pair "multi-collinearity problem." That many of our explanatory variables are highly collinear is a fact of life. And it is completely clear that there are experimental designs $\mathbf{X'X}$ [i.e., data matrix] which would be much preferred to the designs the natural experiment has provided us [i.e., the sample at hand]. But a complaint about the apparent malevolence of nature is not at all constructive, and the *ad hoc* cures for a bad design, such as stepwise regression or ridge regression, can be disastrously inappropriate. Better that we should rightly accept the fact that our non-experiments [i.e., data not collected by designed experiments] are sometimes not very informative about parameters of interest.[2]

Assumption 10 of the *classical linear regression model (CLRM)* is that there is no multicollinearity among the regressors included in the regression model. Assumption 7, that the number of observations must be greater than the number of regressors (the question of micronumerosity), and Assumption 8, that there must be sufficient variability in the values of the regressors, are complementary to the multicollinearity assumption. In this chapter we take a critical

---

[1] This term is due to Arthur S. Goldberger and means "small sample size." See his *A Course in Econometrics*, Harvard University Press, Cambridge, Mass., 1991, p. 249.

[2] Edward E. Leamer, "Model Choice and Specification Analysis," in Zvi Griliches and Michael D. Intriligator, eds., *Handbook of Econometrics*, vol. I, North Holland Publishing Company, Amsterdam, 1983, pp. 300–301.

look at the assumption of no multicollinearity by seeking answers to the following questions:

1. What is the nature of multicollinearity?
2. Is multicollinearity really a problem?
3. What are its practical consequences?
4. How does one detect it?
5. What remedial measures can be taken to alleviate the problem of multicollinearity?

We will also show how Assumptions 7 and 8 fit in with the assumption of no multicollinearity.

10.1 THE NATURE OF MULTICOLLINEARITY

The term *multicollinearity* is due to Ragnar Frisch.[3] Originally it meant the existence of a "perfect," or exact, linear relationship among some or all explanatory variables of a regression model.[4] For the k-variable regression involving explanatory variable $X_1, X_2, \ldots, X_k$ (where $X_1 = 1$ for all observations to allow for the intercept term), an exact linear relationship is said to exist if the following condition is satisfied:

$$\lambda_1 X_1 + \lambda_2 X_2 + \cdots + \lambda_k X_k = 0 \qquad (10.1.1)$$

where $\lambda_1, \lambda_2, \ldots, \lambda_k$ are constants such that not all of them are zero simultaneously.[5]

Today, however, the term multicollinearity is used in a broader sense to include the case of perfect multicollinearity, as shown by (10.1.1), as well as the case where the X variables are intercorrelated but not perfectly so, as follows:[6]

$$\lambda_1 X_1 + \lambda_2 X_2 + \cdots + \lambda_2 X_k + v_i = 0 \qquad (10.1.2)$$

where v_i is a stochastic error term.

---

[3]Ragnar Frisch, *Statistical Confluence Analysis by Means of Complete Regression Systems*, Institute of Economics, Oslo University, publ. no. 5, 1934.

[4]Strictly speaking, *multicollinearity* refers to the existence of more than one exact linear relationship, and *collinearity* refers to the existence of a single linear relationship. But this distinction is rarely maintained in practice, and multicollinearity refers to both cases.

[5]The chances of one's obtaining a sample of values where the regressors are related in this fashion are indeed very small in practice except by design when, for example, the number of observations is smaller than the number of regressors or if one falls into the "dummy variable trap" as discussed later in Chap. 15. See exercise 10.2.

[6]If there are only two explanatory variables, *intercorrelation* can be measured by the zero-order or simple correlation coefficient. But if there are more than two X variables, intercorrelation can be measured by the partial correlation coefficients or by the multiple correlation coefficient R of one X variable with all other X variables taken together.

To see the difference between *perfect* and *less than perfect* multicollinearity, assume, for example, that $\lambda_2 \neq 0$. Then, (10.1.1) can be written as

$$X_{2i} = -\frac{\lambda_1}{\lambda_2}X_{1i} - \frac{\lambda_3}{\lambda_2}X_{3i} - \cdots - \frac{\lambda_k}{\lambda_2}X_{ki} \qquad (10.1.3)$$

which shows how X_2 is exactly linearly related to other variables or how it can be derived from a linear combination of other X variables. In this situation, the coefficient of correlation between the variable X_2 and the linear combination on the right side of (10.1.3) is bound to be unity.

Similarly, if $\lambda_2 \neq 0$, Eq. (10.1.2) can be written as

$$X_{2i} = -\frac{\lambda_1}{\lambda_2}X_{1i} - \frac{\lambda_3}{\lambda_2}X_{3i} - \cdots - \frac{\lambda_k}{\lambda_2}X_{ki} - \frac{1}{\lambda_2}v_i \qquad (10.1.4)$$

which shows that X_2 is not an exact linear combination of other X's because it is also determined by the stochastic error term v_i.

As a numerical example, consider the following hypothetical data:

X_2	X_3	X_3^*
10	50	52
15	75	75
18	90	97
24	120	129
30	150	152

It is apparent that $X_{3i} = 5X_{2i}$. Therefore, there is perfect collinearity between X_2 and X_3 since the coefficient of correlation r_{23} is unity. The variable X_3^* was created from X_3 by simply adding to it the following numbers, which were taken from a table of random numbers: 2, 0, 7, 9, 2. Now there is no longer perfect collinearity between X_2 and X_3^*. However, the two variables are highly correlated because calculations will show that the coefficient of correlation between them is 0.9959.

The preceding algebraic approach to multicollinearity can be portrayed succinctly by the Ballentine (recall Fig. 7.1). In this figure the circles Y, X_2, and X_3 represent, respectively, the variations in Y (the dependent variable) and X_2 and X_3 (the explanatory variables). The degree of collinearity can be measured by the extent of the overlap (shaded area) of the X_2 and X_3 circles. In Fig. 10.1a there is no overlap between X_2 and X_3, and hence no collinearity. In Figs. 10.1b through 10.1e there is a "low" to "high" degree of collinearity—the greater the overlap between X_2 and X_3 (i.e., the larger the shaded area), the higher the degree of collinearity. In the extreme, if X_2 and X_3 were to overlap completely (or if X_2 were completely inside X_3, or vice versa), collinearity would be perfect.

In passing, note that multicollinearity, as we have defined it, refers only to linear relationships among the X variables. It does not rule out nonlinear relationships among them. For example, consider the following regression model:

$$Y_i = \beta_0 + \beta_1 X_i + \beta_2 X_i^2 + \beta_3 X_i^3 + u_i \qquad (10.1.5)$$

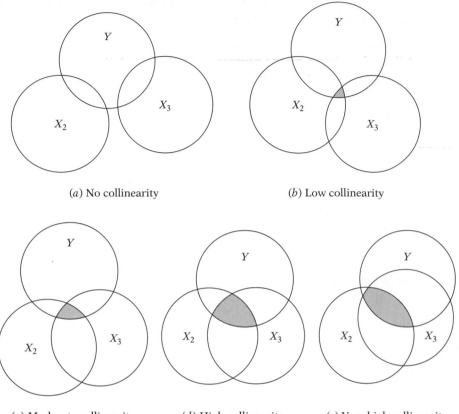

(a) No collinearity   (b) Low collinearity

(c) Moderate collinearity   (d) High collinearity   (e) Very high collinearity

FIGURE 10.1
The Ballentine view of multicollinearity.

where, say, Y = total cost of production and X = output. The variables X_i^2 (output squared) and X_i^3 (output cubed) are obviously functionally related to X_i, but the relationship is nonlinear. Strictly, therefore, models such as (10.1.5) do not violate the assumption of no multicollinearity. However, in concrete applications, the conventionally measured correlation coefficient will show X_i, X_i^2, and X_i^3 to be highly correlated, which, as we shall show, will make it difficult to estimate the parameters of (10.1.5) with greater precision (i.e., with smaller standard errors).

Why does the classical linear regression model assume that there is no multicollinearity among the X's? The reasoning is this: **If multicollinearity is perfect in the sense of (10.1.1), the regression coefficients of the X variables are indeterminate and their standard errors are infinite. If multicollinearity is less than perfect, as in (10.1.2), the regression coefficients, although determinate, possess large standard errors (in relation to the coefficients themselves), which means the coefficients cannot be estimated with great precision or accuracy.** The proofs of these statements are given in the following sections.

There are several sources of multicollinearity. As Montgomery and Peck note, multicollinearity may be due to the following factors:[7]

1. *The data collection method employed*, for example, sampling over a limited range of the values taken by the regressors in the population.
2. *Constraints on the model or in the population being sampled.* For example, in the regression of electricity consumption on income (X_2) and house size (X_3) there is a physical constraint in the population in that families with higher incomes generally have larger homes than families with lower incomes.
3. *Model specification*, for example, adding polynomial terms to a regression model, especially when the range of the X variable is small.
4. *An overdetermined model.* This happens when the model has more explanatory variables than the number of observations. This could happen in medical research where there may be a small number of patients about whom information is collected on a large number of variables.

10.2 ESTIMATION IN THE PRESENCE OF PERFECT MULTICOLLINEARITY

It was stated previously that in the case of perfect multicollinearity the regression coefficients remain indeterminate and their standard errors are infinite. This fact can be demonstrated readily in terms of the three-variable regression model. Using the deviation form, where all the variables are expressed as deviations from their sample means, we can write the three-variable regression model as

$$y_i = \hat{\beta}_2 x_{2i} + \hat{\beta}_3 x_{3i} + \hat{u}_i \tag{10.2.1}$$

Now from Chapter 7 we obtain

$$\hat{\beta}_2 = \frac{(\sum y_i x_{2i})(\sum x_{3i}^2) - (\sum y_i x_{3i})(\sum x_{2i} x_{3i})}{(\sum x_{2i}^2)(\sum x_{3i}^2) - (\sum x_{2i} x_{3i})^2} \tag{7.4.7}$$

$$\hat{\beta}_3 = \frac{(\sum y_i x_{3i})(\sum x_{2i}^2) - (\sum y_i x_{2i})(\sum x_{2i} x_{3i})}{(\sum x_{2i}^2)(\sum x_{3i}^2) - (\sum x_{2i} x_{3i})^2} \tag{7.4.8}$$

Assume that $X_{3i} = \lambda X_{2i}$, where λ is a nonzero constant (e.g., 2, 4, 1.8, etc.). Substituting this into (7.4.7), we obtain

$$\hat{\beta} = \frac{(\sum y_i x_{2i})(\lambda^2 \sum x_{2i}^2) - (\lambda \sum y_i x_{2i})(\lambda \sum x_{2i}^2)}{(\sum x_{2i}^2)(\lambda^2 \sum x_{2i}^2) - \lambda^2 (\sum x_{2i}^2)^2}$$

$$= \frac{0}{0} \tag{10.2.2}$$

---

[7]Douglas Montgomery and Elizabeth Peck, *Introduction to Linear Regression Analysis*, John Wiley & Sons, New York, 1982, pp. 289–290. See also R. L. Mason, R. F. Gunst, and J. T. Webster, "Regression Analysis and Problems of Multicollinearity," *Communications in Statistics A*, vol. 4, no. 3, 1975, pp. 277–292; R. F. Gunst, and R. L. Mason, "Advantages of Examining Multicollinearities in Regression Analysis," *Biometrics*, vol. 33, 1977, pp. 249–260.

which is an indeterminate expression. The reader can verify that $\hat{\beta}_3$ is also indeterminate.[8]

Why do we obtain the result shown in (10.2.2)? Recall the meaning of $\hat{\beta}_2$: It gives the rate of change in the average value of Y as X_2 changes by a unit, holding X_3 constant. But if X_3 and X_2 are perfectly collinear, there is no way X_3 can be kept constant: As X_2 changes, so does X_3 by the factor λ. What it means, then, is that there is no way of disentangling the separate influences of X_2 and X_3 from the given sample: For practical purposes X_2 and X_3 are indistinguishable. In applied econometrics this problem is most damaging since the entire intent is to separate the partial effects of each X upon the dependent variable.

To see this differently, let us substitute $X_{3i} = \lambda X_{2i}$ into (10.2.1) and obtain the following [see also (7.1.10)]:

$$y_i = \hat{\beta}_2 x_{2i} + \hat{\beta}_3(\lambda x_{2i}) + \hat{u}_i$$
$$= (\hat{\beta}_2 + \lambda\hat{\beta}_3)x_{2i} + \hat{u}_i$$
$$= \hat{\alpha}x_{2i} + \hat{u}_i \qquad (10.2.3)$$

where

$$\hat{\alpha} = (\hat{\beta}_2 + \lambda\hat{\beta}_3) \qquad (10.2.4)$$

Applying the usual OLS formula to (10.2.3), we get

$$\hat{\alpha} = (\hat{\beta}_2 + \lambda\hat{\beta}_3) = \frac{\sum x_{2i}y_i}{\sum x_{2i}^2} \qquad (10.2.5)$$

Therefore, although we can estimate α uniquely, there is no way to estimate β_2 and β_3 uniquely; mathematically

$$\hat{\alpha} = \hat{\beta}_2 + \lambda\hat{\beta}_3 \qquad (10.2.6)$$

gives us only one equation in two unknowns (note λ is given) and there is an infinity of solutions to (10.2.6) for given values of $\hat{\alpha}$ and λ. To put this idea in concrete terms, let $\hat{\alpha} = 0.8$ and $\lambda = 2$. Then we have

$$0.8 = \hat{\beta}_2 + 2\hat{\beta}_3 \qquad (10.2.7)$$

or

$$\hat{\beta}_2 = 0.8 - 2\hat{\beta}_3 \qquad (10.2.8)$$

Now choose a value of $\hat{\beta}_3$ arbitrarily, and we will have a solution for $\hat{\beta}_2$. Choose another value for $\hat{\beta}_3$, and we will have another solution for $\hat{\beta}_2$. No matter how hard we try, there is no unique value for $\hat{\beta}_2$.

The upshot of the preceding discussion is that in the case of perfect multicollinearity one cannot get a unique solution for the individual regression coefficients. But notice that one can get a unique solution for linear combinations of these coefficients. The linear combination $(\beta_2 + \lambda\beta_3)$ is uniquely estimated by α, given the value of λ.[9]

---

[8]Another way of seeing this is as follows: By definition, the coefficient of correlation between X_2 and X_3, r_{23}, is $\sum x_{2i}x_{3i}/\sqrt{\sum x_{2i}^2 \sum x_{3i}^2}$. If $r_{23}^2 = 1$, i.e., perfect collinearity between X_2 and X_3, the denominator of (7.4.7) will be zero, making estimation of β_2 (or of β_3) impossible.

[9]In econometric literature, a function such as $(\beta_2 + \lambda\beta_3)$ is known as an **estimable function**.

In passing, note that in the case of perfect multicollinearity the variances and standard errors of $\hat{\beta}_2$ and $\hat{\beta}_3$ individually are infinite. (See exercise 10.21.)

10.3   ESTIMATION IN THE PRESENCE OF "HIGH" BUT "IMPERFECT" MULTICOLLINEARITY

The perfect multicollinearity situation is a pathological extreme. Generally, there is no exact linear relationship among the X variables, especially in data involving economic time series. Thus, turning to the three-variable model in the deviation form given in (10.2.1), instead of exact multicollinearity, we may have

$$x_{3i} = \lambda x_{2i} + v_i \tag{10.3.1}$$

where $\lambda \neq 0$ and where v_i is a stochastic error term such that $\sum x_{2i}v_i = 0$. (Why?)

Incidentally, the Ballentines shown in Fig. 10.1b to 10.1e represent cases of imperfect collinearity.

In this case, estimation of regression coefficients β_2 and β_3 may be possible. For example, substituting (10.3.1) into (7.4.7), we obtain

$$\hat{\beta}_2 = \frac{\sum(y_i x_{2i})(\lambda^2 \sum x_{2i}^2 + \sum v_i^2) - (\lambda \sum y_i x_{2i} + \sum y_i v_i)(\lambda \sum x_{2i}^2)}{\sum x_{2i}^2(\lambda^2 \sum x_{2i}^2 + \sum v_i^2) - (\lambda \sum x_{2i}^2)^2} \tag{10.3.2}$$

where use is made of $\sum x_{2i}v_i = 0$. A similar expression can be derived for $\hat{\beta}_3$.

Now, unlike (10.2.2), there is no reason to believe a priori that (10.3.2) cannot be estimated. Of course, if v_i is sufficiently small, say, very close to zero, (10.3.1) will indicate almost perfect collinearity and we shall be back to the indeterminate case of (10.2.2).

10.4   MULTICOLLINEARITY: MUCH ADO ABOUT NOTHING? THEORETICAL CONSEQUENCES OF MULTICOLLINEARITY

Recall that if the assumptions of the classical model are satisfied, the OLS estimators of the regression estimators are BLUE (or BUE, if the normality assumption is added). Now it can be shown that even if multicollinearity is very high, as in the case of *near multicollinearity*, the OLS estimators still retain the property of BLUE.[10] Then what is the multicollinearity fuss all about? As Christopher Achen remarks (note also the Leamer quote at the beginning of this chapter):

> Beginning students of methodology occasionally worry that their independent variables are correlated—the so-called multicollinearity problem. But multicollinearity violates no regression assumptions. Unbiased, consistent estimates

---

[10]Since near multicollinearity per se does not violate the other assumptions listed in Chap. 7, the OLS estimators are BLUE as indicated there.

will occur, and their standard errors will be correctly estimated. The only effect of multicollinearity is to make it hard to get coefficient estimates with small standard error. But having a small number of observations also has that effect, as does having independent variables with small variances. (In fact, at a theoretical level, multicollinearity, few observations and small variances on the independent variables are essentially all the same problem.) Thus "What should I do about multicollinearity?" is a question like "What should I do if I don't have many observations?" No statistical answer can be given.[11]

To drive home the importance of sample size, Goldberger coined the term **micronumerosity**, to counter the exotic polysyllabic name *multicollinearity*. According to Goldberger, **exact micronumerosity** (the counterpart of exact multicollinearity) arises when n, the sample size, is zero, in which case any kind of estimation is impossible. *Near micronumerosity*, like near perfect multicollinearity, arises when the number of observations barely exceeds the number of parameters to be estimated.

Leamer, Achen, and Goldberger are right in bemoaning the lack of attention given to the sample size problem and the undue attention to the multicollinearity problem. Unfortunately, in applied work involving secondary data (i.e., data collected by some agency, such as the GNP data collected by the government), an individual researcher may not be able to do much about the size of the sample data and may have to face "estimating problems important enough to warrant our treating it [i.e., multicollinearity] as a violation of the CLR [classical linear regression] model."[12]

First, it is true that even in the case of near multicollinearity the OLS estimators are unbiased. But unbiasedness is a multisample or repeated sampling property. What it means is that, keeping the values of the X variables fixed, if one obtains repeated samples and computes the OLS estimators for each of these samples, the average of the sample values will converge to the true population values of the estimators as the number of samples increases. But this says nothing about the properties of estimators in any given sample.

Second, it is also true that collinearity does not destroy the property of minimum variance: In the class of all linear unbiased estimators, the OLS estimators have minimum variance; that is, they are efficient. But this does not mean that the variance of an OLS estimator will necessarily be small (in relation to the value of the estimator) in any given sample, as we shall demonstrate shortly.

Third, *multicollinearity is essentially a sample (regression) phenomenon* in the sense that even if the X variables are not linearly related in the population, they may be so related in the particular sample at hand: When we postulate the theoretical or population regression function (PRF), we believe that all the X variables included in the model have a separate or independent influence on the dependent variable Y. But it may happen that in any given sample that is used

---

[11]Christopher H. Achen, *Interpreting and Using Regression*, Sage Publications, Beverly Hills, Calif., 1982, pp. 82–83.

[12]Peter Kennedy, *A Guide to Econometrics*, 3d ed., The MIT Press, Cambridge, Mass., 1992, p. 177.

to test the PRF some or all of the X variables are so highly collinear that we cannot isolate their individual influence on Y. So to speak, our sample lets us down, although the theory says that all the X's are important. In short, our sample may not be "rich" enough to accommodate all X variables in the analysis.

As an illustration, reconsider the consumption-income example of Chapter 3. Economists theorize that, besides income, the wealth of the consumer is also an important determinant of consumption expenditure. Thus, we may write

$$\text{Consumption}_i = \beta_1 + \beta_2 \text{ Income}_i + \beta_3 \text{ Wealth}_i + u_i$$

Now it may happen that when we obtain data on income and wealth, the two variables may be highly, if not perfectly, correlated: Wealthier people generally tend to have higher incomes. Thus, although in theory income and wealth are logical candidates to explain the behavior of consumption expenditure, in practice (i.e., in the sample) it may be difficult to disentangle the separate influences of income and wealth on consumption expenditure.

Ideally, to assess the individual effects of wealth and income on consumption expenditure we need a sufficient number of sample observations of wealthy individuals with low income, and high-income individuals with low wealth (recall Assumption 8). Although this may be possible in cross-sectional studies (by increasing the sample size), it is very difficult to achieve in aggregate time series work.

For all these reasons, the fact that the OLS estimators are BLUE despite multicollinearity is of little consolation in practice. We must see what happens or is likely to happen in any given sample, a topic discussed in the following section.

10.5 PRACTICAL CONSEQUENCES OF MULTICOLLINEARITY

In cases of near or high multicollinearity, one is likely to encounter the following consequences:

1. Although BLUE, the OLS estimators have large variances and covariances, making precise estimation difficult.
2. Because of consequence 1, the confidence intervals tend to be much wider, leading to the acceptance of the "zero null hypothesis" (i.e., the true population coefficient is zero) more readily.
3. Also because of consequence 1, the t ratio of one or more coefficients tends to be statistically insignificant.
4. Although the t ratio of one or more coefficients is statistically insignificant, R^2, the overall measure of goodness of fit, can be very high.
5. The OLS estimators and their standard errors can be sensitive to small changes in the data.

The preceding consequences can be demonstrated as follows.

Large Variances and Covariances of OLS Estimators

To see large variances and covariances, recall that for the model (10.2.1) the variances and covariances of $\hat{\beta}_2$ and $\hat{\beta}_3$ are given by

$$\text{var}(\hat{\beta}_2) = \frac{\sigma^2}{\sum x_{2i}^2(1 - r_{23}^2)} \qquad (7.4.12)$$

$$\text{var}(\hat{\beta}_3) = \frac{\sigma^2}{\sum x_{3i}^2(1 - r_{23}^2)} \qquad (7.4.15)$$

$$\text{cov}(\hat{\beta}_2, \hat{\beta}_3) = \frac{-r_{23}\sigma^2}{(1 - r_{23}^2)\sqrt{\sum x_{2i}^2 \sum x_{3i}^2}} \qquad (7.4.17)$$

where r_{23} is the coefficient of correlation between X_2 and X_3.

It is apparent from (7.4.12) and (7.4.15) that as r_{23} tends toward 1, that is, as collinearity increases, the variances of the two estimators increase and in the limit when $r_{23} = 1$, they are infinite. It is equally clear from (7.4.17) that as r_{23} increases toward 1, the covariance of the two estimators also increases in absolute value. [*Note:* $\text{cov}(\hat{\beta}_2, \hat{\beta}_3) \equiv \text{cov}(\hat{\beta}_3, \hat{\beta}_2)$.]

The speed with which variances and covariances increase can be seen with the **variance-inflating factor (VIF)**, which is defined as

$$\text{VIF} = \frac{1}{(1 - r_{23}^2)} \qquad (10.5.1)$$

VIF shows how the variance of an estimator is *inflated* by the presence of multicollinearity. As r_{23}^2 approaches 1, the VIF approaches infinity. That is, as the extent of collinearity increases, the variance of an estimator increases, and in the limit it can become infinite. As can be readily seen, if there is no collinearity between X_2 and X_3, VIF will be 1.

Using this definition, we can express (7.4.12) and (7.4.15) as

$$\text{var}(\hat{\beta}_2) = \frac{\sigma^2}{\sum x_{2i}^2}\text{VIF} \qquad (10.5.2)$$

$$\text{var}(\hat{\beta}_3) = \frac{\sigma^2}{\sum x_{3i}^2}\text{VIF} \qquad (10.5.3)$$

which show that the variances of $\hat{\beta}_2$ and $\hat{\beta}_3$ are directly proportional to the VIF.

To give some idea about how fast the variances and covariances increase as r_{23} increases, consider Table 10.1, which gives these variances and covariances for selected values of r_{23}. As this table shows, increases in r_{23} have dramatic effect on the estimated variances and covariances of the OLS estimators. When $r_{23} = 0.50$, the $\text{var}(\hat{\beta}_2)$ is 1.33 times the variance when r_{23} is zero, but by the time r_{23} reaches 0.95 it is about 10 times as high as when there is no collinearity. And lo and behold, an increase of r_{23} from 0.95 to 0.995 makes the estimated variance 100 times that when collinearity is zero. The same dramatic effect is seen on the estimated covariance. All this can be seen in Fig. 10.2.

Incidentally, the results just discussed can be easily extended to the k-variable model (see exercises 10.15 and 10.16).

TABLE 10.1
The effect of increasing r_{23} on var($\hat{\beta}_2$) and cov($\hat{\beta}_2, \hat{\beta}_3$)

Value of r_{23} (1)	VIF (2)	var($\hat{\beta}_2$) (3)*	$\dfrac{\text{var}(\hat{\beta}_2)\ (r_{23} \neq 0)}{\text{var}(\hat{\beta}_2)\ (r_{23} = 0)}$ (4)	cov($\hat{\beta}_2, \hat{\beta}_3$) (5)
0.00	1.00	$\dfrac{\sigma^2}{\sum x_{2i}^2} = A$	—	0
0.50	1.33	$1.33 \times A$	1.33	$0.67 \times B$
0.70	1.96	$1.96 \times A$	1.96	$1.37 \times B$
0.80	2.78	$2.78 \times A$	2.78	$2.22 \times B$
0.90	5.76	$5.26 \times A$	5.26	$4.73 \times B$
0.95	10.26	$10.26 \times A$	10.26	$9.74 \times B$
0.97	16.92	$16.92 \times A$	16.92	$16.41 \times B$
0.99	50.25	$50.25 \times A$	50.25	$49.75 \times B$
0.995	100.00	$100.00 \times A$	100.00	$99.50 \times B$
0.999	500.00	$500.00 \times A$	500.00	$499.50 \times B$

Note: $A = \dfrac{\sigma^2}{\sum x_{2i}^2}$

$B = \dfrac{-\sigma^2}{\sqrt{\sum x_{2i}^2 \sum x_{3i}^2}}$

$\times$ = times

*To find out the effect of increasing r_{23} on var($\hat{\beta}_3$), note that $A = \sigma^2/\sum x_{3i}^2$ when $r_{23} = 0$, but the variance and covariance magnifying factors remain the same.

Wider Confidence Intervals

Because of the large standard errors, the confidence intervals for the relevant population parameters tend to be larger, as can be seem from Table 10.2. For example, when $r_{23} = 0.95$, the confidence interval for β_2 is larger than when $r_{23} = 0$ by a factor of $\sqrt{10.26}$, or about 3.

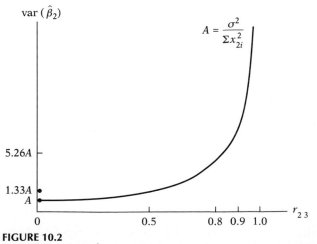

FIGURE 10.2
The behavior of var($\hat{\beta}_2$) as a function of r_{23}.

TABLE 10.2
The effect of increasing collinearity on the 95 percent confidence interval for $\beta_2 : \hat{\beta}_2 \pm 1.96\,\mathrm{se}(\hat{\beta}_2)$

Value of r_{23}	95% confidence interval for β_2
0.00	$\hat{\beta}_2 \pm 1.96\sqrt{\dfrac{\sigma^2}{\sum x_{2i}^2}}$
0.50	$\hat{\beta}_2 \pm 1.96\sqrt{(1.33)}\sqrt{\dfrac{\sigma^2}{\sum x_{2i}^2}}$
0.95	$\hat{\beta}_2 \pm 1.96\sqrt{(10.26)}\sqrt{\dfrac{\sigma^2}{\sum x_{2i}^2}}$
0.99	$\hat{\beta}_2 \pm 1.96\sqrt{(100)}\sqrt{\dfrac{\sigma^2}{\sum x_{2i}^2}}$
0.999	$\hat{\beta}_2 \pm 1.96\sqrt{(500)}\sqrt{\dfrac{\sigma^2}{\sum x_{2i}^2}}$

Note: We are using the normal distribution because σ^2 is assumed for convenience to be known. Hence the use of 1.96, the 95% confidence factor for the normal distribution.

The standard errors corresponding to the various r_{23} values are obtained from Table 10.1.

Therefore, in cases of high multicollinearity, the sample data may be compatible with a diverse set of hypotheses. Hence, the probability of accepting a false hypothesis (i.e., type II error) increases.

"Insignificant" t Ratios

Recall that to test the null hypothesis that, say, $\beta_2 = 0$, we use the t ratio, that is, $\hat{\beta}_2/\mathrm{se}(\hat{\beta}_2)$, and compare the estimated t value with the critical t value from the t table. But as we have seen, in cases of high collinearity the estimated standard errors increase dramatically, thereby making the t values smaller. Therefore, in such cases, one will increasingly accept the null hypothesis that the relevant true population value is zero.[13]

A High R^2 but Few Significant t Ratios

Consider the k-variable linear regression model:

$$Y_i = \beta_1 + \beta_2 X_{2i} + \beta_3 X_{3i} + \cdots + \beta_k X_{ki} + u_i$$

In cases of high collinearity, it is possible to find, as we have just noted, that one or more of the partial slope coefficients are individually statistically insignifi-

---

[13]In terms of the confidence intervals, $\beta_2 = 0$ value will lie increasingly in the acceptance region as the degree of collinearity increases.

cant on the basis of the t test. Yet the $\bar{R}^2$ in such situations may be so high, say, in excess of 0.9, that on the basis of the F test one can convincingly reject the hypothesis that $\beta_2 = \beta_3 = \cdots = \beta_k = 0$. Indeed, this is one of the signals of multicollinearity—insignificant t values but a high overall R^2 (and a significant F value)!

We shall demonstrate this signal in the next section, but this outcome should not be surprising in view of our discussion on individual vs. joint testing in Chapter 8. As you may recall, the real problem here is the covariances between the estimators, which, as formula (7.4.17) indicates, are related to the correlations between the regressors.

Sensitivity of OLS Estimators and Their Standard Errors to Small Changes in Data

As long as multicollinearity is not perfect, estimation of the regression coefficients is possible but the estimates and their standard errors become very sensitive to even the slightest change in the data.

To see this, consider Table 10.3. Based on these data, we obtain the following multiple regression:

$$\hat{Y}_i = \begin{array}{ccc} 1.1939 & + \ 0.4463X_{2i} & + \ 0.0030X_{3i} \\ (0.7737) & (0.1848) & (0.0851) \\ t = (1.5431) & (2.4151) & (0.0358) \end{array} \tag{10.5.4}$$
$$R^2 = 0.8101 \qquad r_{23} = 0.5523$$
$$\mathrm{cov}(\hat{\beta}_2, \hat{\beta}_3) = -0.00868 \qquad df = 2$$

Regression (10.5.4) shows that none of the regression coefficients is individually significant at the conventional 1 or 5% levels of significance, although $\hat{\beta}_2$ is significant at the 10% level on the basis of a one-tail t test.

Now consider Table 10.4. The only difference between Tables 10.3 and 10.4 is that the third and fourth values of X_3 are interchanged. Using the data of Table 10.4, we now obtain

$$\hat{Y}_i = \begin{array}{ccc} 1.2108 & + \ 0.4014X_{2i} & + \ 0.0270X_{3i} \\ (0.7480) & (0.2721) & (0.1252) \\ t = (1.6187) & (1.4752) & (0.2158) \end{array} \tag{10.5.5}$$
$$R^2 = 0.8143 \qquad r_{23} = 0.8285$$
$$\mathrm{cov}(\hat{\beta}_2, \hat{\beta}_3) = -0.0282 \qquad df = 2$$

TABLE 10.3			TABLE 10.4		
Hypothetical data on Y, X_2, and X_3			Hypothetical data on Y, X_2, and X_3		
Y	X_2	X_3	Y	X_2	X_3
1	2	4	1	2	4
2	0	2	2	0	2
3	4	12	3	4	0
4	6	0	4	6	12
5	8	16	5	8	16

As a result of a slight change in the data, we see that $\hat{\beta}_2$, which was statistically significant before at the 10% level of significance, is no longer significant even at that level. Also note that in (10.5.4) $\text{cov}(\hat{\beta}_2, \hat{\beta}_3) = -0.00868$ whereas in (10.5.5) it is -0.0282, a more than threefold increase. All these changes may be attributable to increased multicollinearity: In (10.5.4) $r_{23} = 0.5523$, whereas in (10.5.5) it is 0.8285. Similarly, the standard errors of $\hat{\beta}_2$ and $\hat{\beta}_3$ increase between the two regressions, a usual symptom of collinearity.

We noted earlier that in the presence of high collinearity one cannot estimate the individual regression coefficients precisely but that linear combinations of these coefficients may be estimated more precisely. This fact can be substantiated from the regressions (10.5.4) and (10.5.5). In the first regression the sum of the two partial slope coefficients is 0.4493 and in the second it is 0.4284, practically the same. Not only that, their standard errors are practically the same, 0.1550 vs 0.1823.[14] Note, however, the coefficient of X_3 has changed dramatically, from 0.003 to 0.027.

Consequences of Micronumerosity

In a parody of the consequences of multicollinearity, and in a tongue-in-cheek manner, Goldberger cites exactly similar consequences of micronumerosity, that is, analysis based on small sample size.[15] The reader is advised to read Goldberger's analysis to see why he regards micronumerosity as being as important (or unimportant) as multicollinearity.

10.6   AN ILLUSTRATIVE EXAMPLE: CONSUMPTION EXPENDITURE IN RELATION TO INCOME AND WEALTH

To illustrate the various points made thus far, let us reconsider the consumption-income example of Chapter 3. In Table 10.5 we reproduce the data of Table 3.2 and add to it data on wealth of the consumer. If we assume that consumption expenditure is linearly related to income and wealth, then, based on Table 10.5 we obtain the following regression:

$$\hat{Y}_i = 24.7747 + 0.9415X_{2i} - 0.0424X_{3i}$$
$$\quad\quad (6.7525) \quad (0.8229) \quad\quad (0.0807)$$
$$t = (3.6690) \quad (1.1442) \quad (-0.5261) \tag{10.6.1}$$
$$R^2 = 0.9635 \quad\quad \bar{R}^2 = 0.9531 \quad\quad df = 7$$

Regression (10.6.1) shows that income and wealth together explain about 96 percent of the variation in consumption expenditure, and yet neither of the slope

---

[14]These standard errors are obtained from the formula

$$\text{se}(\hat{\beta}_2 + \hat{\beta}_3) = \sqrt{\text{var}(\hat{\beta}_2) + \text{var}(\hat{\beta}_3) + 2\,\text{cov}(\hat{\beta}_2, \hat{\beta}_3)}$$

Note that increasing collinearity increases the variances of $\hat{\beta}_2$ and $\hat{\beta}_3$, but these variances may be offset if there is high negative covariance between the two, as our results clearly point out.

[15]Goldberger, op. cit., pp. 248–250.

TABLE 10.5
Hypothetical data on consumption expenditure Y, income X_2, and wealth X_3

Y, \$	X_2, \$	X_3, \$
70	80	810
65	100	1009
90	120	1273
95	140	1425
110	160	1633
115	180	1876
120	200	2052
140	220	2201
155	240	2435
150	260	2686

coefficients is individually statistically significant. Moreover, not only is the wealth variable statistically insignificant but also it has a wrong sign. A priori, one would expect a positive relationship between consumption and wealth. Although $\hat{\beta}_2$ and $\hat{\beta}_3$ are individually statistically insignificant, if we test the hypothesis that $\beta_2 = \beta_3 = 0$ simultaneously, this hypothesis can be rejected, as Table 10.6 shows. Under the usual assumption we obtain

$$F = \frac{4282.7770}{46.3494}$$

$$= 92.4019 \qquad (10.6.2)$$

This F value is obviously highly significant.

It is interesting to look at this result geometrically. (See Fig. 10.3.) Based on the regression (10.6.1), we have established the individual 95% confidence intervals for β_2 and β_3 following the usual procedure discussed in Chapter 8. As these intervals show, individually each of them includes the value of zero. Therefore, *individually* we can accept the hypothesis that the two partial slopes are zero. But, when we establish the joint confidence interval to test the hypothesis that $\beta_2 = \beta_3 = 0$, that hypothesis cannot be accepted since the joint confidence interval, actually an ellipse, does not include the origin.[16] As already

TABLE 10.6
ANOVA table for the consumption-income-wealth example

Source of variation	SS	df	MSS
Due to regression	8,565.5541	2	4,282.7770
Due to residual	324.4459	7	46.3494

---

[16] As noted in Sec. 5.3, the topic of joint confidence interval is rather involved. The interested reader may consult the reference cited there.

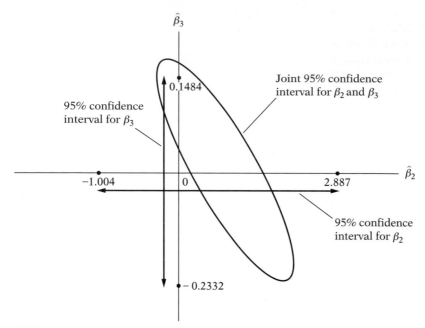

FIGURE 10.3
Individual confidence intervals for β_2 and β_3 and joint confidence interval (ellipse) for β_2 and β_3.

pointed out, when collinearity is high, tests on individual regressors are not reliable; in such cases it is the overall F test that will show if Y is related to the various regressors.

Our example shows dramatically what multicollinearity does. The fact that the F test is significant but the t values of X_2 and X_3 are individually insignificant means that the two variables are so highly correlated that it is impossible to isolate the individual impact of either income or wealth on consumption. As a matter of fact, if we regress X_3 on X_2, we obtain

$$\hat{X}_{3i} = \begin{array}{cc} 7.5454 & + \quad 10.1909X_{2i} \end{array}$$
$$\begin{array}{cc} (29.4758) & (0.1643) \end{array} \qquad\qquad (10.6.3)$$
$$t = \begin{array}{ccc} (0.2560) & (62.0405) & R^2 = 0.9979 \end{array}$$

which shows that there is almost perfect collinearity between X_3 and X_2.

Now let us see what happens if we regress Y on X_2 only:

$$\hat{Y}_i = \begin{array}{cc} 24.4545 & + \quad 0.5091X_{2i} \end{array}$$
$$\begin{array}{cc} (6.4138) & (0.0357) \end{array} \qquad\qquad (10.6.4)$$
$$t = \begin{array}{ccc} (3.8128) & (14.2432) & R^2 = 0.9621 \end{array}$$

In (10.6.1) the income variable was statistically insignificant, whereas now it is highly significant. If instead of regressing Y on X_2, we regress it on X_3, we obtain

$$\hat{Y}_i = \begin{array}{cc} 24.411 & + \quad 0.0498X_{3i} \end{array}$$
$$\begin{array}{cc} (6.874) & (0.0037) \end{array} \qquad\qquad (10.6.5)$$
$$t = \begin{array}{ccc} (3.551) & (13.29) & R^2 = 0.9567 \end{array}$$

We see that wealth has now a significant impact on consumption expenditure, whereas in (10.6.1) it had no effect on consumption expenditure.

Regressions (10.6.4) and (10.6.5) show very clearly that in situations of extreme multicollinearity dropping the highly collinear variable will often make the other X variable statistically significant. This result would suggest that a way out of extreme collinearity is to drop the collinear variable, but we shall have more to say about it in Section 10.8.

10.7 DETECTION OF MULTICOLLINEARITY

Having studied the nature and consequences of multicollinearity, the natural question is: How does one know that collinearity is present in any given situation, especially in models involving more than two explanatory variables? Here it is useful to bear in mind Kmenta's warning:

1. Multicollinearity is a question of degree and not of kind. The meaningful distinction is not between the presence and the absence of multicollinearity, but between its various degrees.

2. Since multicollinearity refers to the condition of the explanatory variables that are assumed to be nonstochastic, it is a feature of the sample and not of the population.

   Therefore, we do not "test for multicollinearity" but can, if we wish, measure its degree in any particular sample.[17]

Since multicollinearity is essentially a sample phenomenon, arising out of the largely nonexperimental data collected in most social sciences, we do not have one unique method of detecting it or measuring its strength. What we have are some rules of thumb, some informal and some formal, but rules of thumb all the same. We now consider some of these rules.

1. **High R^2 but few significant t ratios.** As noted, this is the "classic" symptom of multicollinearity. If R^2 is high, say, in excess of 0.8, the F test in most cases will reject the hypothesis that the partial slope coefficients are simultaneously equal to zero, but the individual t tests will show that none or very few of the partial slope coefficients are statistically different from zero. This fact was clearly demonstrated by our consumption-income-wealth example.

   Although this diagnostic is sensible, its disadvantage is that "it is too strong in the sense that multicollinearity is considered as harmful only when all of the influences of the explanatory variables on Y cannot be disentangled."[18]

2. **High pair-wise correlations among regressors.** Another suggested rule of thumb is that if the pair-wise or zero-order correlation coefficient between two regressors is high, say, in excess of 0.8, then multicollinearity is a serious problem. The problem with this criterion is that, although high zero-order correlations may suggest collinearity, it is not necessary that they be high to

[17]Jan Kmenta, *Elements of Econometrics*, 2d. ed., Macmillan, New York, 1986, p. 431.
[18]Ibid., p. 439.

have collinearity in any specific case. To put the matter somewhat technically, *high zero-order correlations are a sufficient but not a necessary condition for the existence of multicollinearity because it can exist even though the zero-order or simple correlations are comparatively low* (say, less than 0.50). To see this relationship, suppose we have a four-variable model:

$$Y_i = \beta_1 + \beta_2 X_{2i} + \beta_3 X_{3i} + \beta_4 X_{4i} + u_i$$

and suppose that

$$X_{4i} = \lambda_2 X_{2i} + \lambda_3 X_{3i}$$

where λ_2 and λ_3 are constants, not both zero. Obviously, X_4 is an exact linear combination of X_2 and X_3, giving $R^2_{4.23} = 1$, the coefficient of determination in the regression of X_4 on X_2 and X_3.

Now recalling the formula (7.9.6) from Chapter 7, we can write

$$R^2_{4.23} = \frac{r^2_{42} + r^2_{43} - 2r_{42}r_{43}r_{23}}{1 - r^2_{23}} \qquad (10.7.1)$$

But since $R^2_{4.23} = 1$ because of perfect collinearity, we obtain

$$1 = \frac{r^2_{42} + r^2_{43} - 2r_{42}r_{43}r_{23}}{1 - r^2_{23}} \qquad (10.7.2)$$

It is not difficult to see that (10.7.2) is satisfied by $r_{42} = 0.5, r_{43} = 0.5$, and $r_{23} = -0.5$, which are not very high values.

Therefore, in models involving more than two explanatory variables, the simple or zero-order correlation will not provide an infallible guide to the presence of multicollinearity. Of course, if there are only two explanatory variables, the zero-order correlations will suffice.

3. **Examination of partial correlations.** Because of the problem just mentioned in relying on zero-order correlations, Farrar and Glauber have suggested that one should look at the partial correlation coefficients.[19] Thus, in the regression of Y on X_2, X_3 and X_4, a finding that $R^2_{1.234}$ is very high but $r^2_{12.34}, r^2_{13.24}$, and $r^2_{14.23}$ are comparatively low may suggest that the variables X_2, X_3, and X_4 are highly intercorrelated and that at least one of these variables is superfluous.

Although a study of the partial correlations may be useful, there is no guarantee that they will provide an infallible guide to multicollinearity, for it may happen that both R^2 and all the partial correlations are sufficiently high. But more importantly, C. Robert Wichers has shown[20] that the Farrar-Glauber partial correlation test is ineffective in that a given partial correlation may be compatible with different multicollinearity patterns. The

[19]D. E. Farrar and R. R. Glauber, "Multicollinearity in Regression Analysis: The Problem Revisited," *Review of Economics and Statistics*, vol. 49, 1967, pp. 92–107.

[20]"The Detection of Multicollinearity: A Comment," *Review of Economics and Statistics*, vol. 57, 1975, pp. 365–366.

Farrar-Glauber test has also been severely criticized by T. Krishna Kumar,[21] John O'Hagan and Brendan McCabe.[22]

4. **Auxiliary regressions.** Since multicollinearity arises because one or more of the regressors are exact or approximately linear combinations of the other regressors, one way of finding out which X variable is related to other X variables is to regress each X_i on the remaining X variables and compute the corresponding R^2, which we designate as R_i^2; each one of these regressions is called an **auxiliary regression**, auxiliary to the main regression of Y on the X's. Then, following the relationship between F and R^2 established in (8.5.11), the variable

$$R_i = \frac{R_{x_1 \cdot x_2 x_3 \cdots x_k}^2 / (k - 2)}{(1 - R_{x_1 \cdot x_2 x_3 \cdots x_k}^2) / (n - k + 1)} \tag{10.7.3}$$

follows the F distribution with $k - 2$ and $n - k + 1$ df. In Eq. (10.7.3) n stands for the sample size, k stands for the number of explanatory variables including the intercept term, and $R_{x_i \cdot x_2 x_3 \cdots x_k}^2$ is the coefficient of determination in the regression of variable X_i on the remaining X variables.[23]

If the computed F exceeds the critical F_i at the chosen level of significance, it is taken to mean that the particular X_i is collinear with other X's; if it does not exceed the critical F_i, we say that it is not collinear with other X's, in which case we may retain that variable in the model. If F_i is statistically significant, we will still have to decide whether the particular X_i should be dropped from the model. This question will be taken up in Section 10.8.

But this method is not without its drawbacks, for

> ... if the multicollinearity involves only a few variables so that the auxiliary regressions do not suffer from extensive multicollinearity, the estimated coefficients may reveal the nature of the linear dependence among the regressors. Unfortunately, if there are several complex linear associations, this curve fitting exercise may not prove to be of much value as it will be difficult to identify the separate interrelationships.[24]

Instead of formally testing all auxiliary R^2 values, one may adopt **Klien's rule of thumb**, which suggests that multicollinearity may be a troublesome problem only if the R^2 obtained from an auxiliary regression is

[21] "Multicollinearity in Regression Analysis," *Review of Economics and Statistics*, vol. 57, 1975, pp. 366–368.

[22] "Tests for the Severity of Multicollinearity in Regression Analysis: A Comment," *Review of Economics and Statistics*, vol. 57, 1975, pp. 368–370.

[23] For example, $R_{x_2}^2$ can be obtained by regressing X_{2i} as follows: $X_{2i} = a_1 + a_3 X_{3i} + a_4 X_{4i} + \cdots + a_k X_{ki} + \hat{u}_i$.

[24] George G. Judge, R. Carter Hill, William E. Griffiths, Helmut Lütkepohl, and Tsoung-Chao Lee, *Introduction to the Theory and Practice of Econometrics*, John Wiley & Sons, New York, 1982, p. 621.

greater than the overall R^2, that is, that obtained from the regression of Y on all the regressors.[25] Of course, like all other rules of thumb, this one should be used judiciously.

5. **Eigenvalues and condition index.** If you examine the SAS output of the Cobb-Douglas production function given in Appendix 7A.7 you will see that SAS uses *eigenvalues* and the *condition index* to diagnose multicollinearity. We will not discuss eigenvalues here, for that would take us into topics in matrix algebra that are beyond the scope of this book. From these eigenvalues, however, we can derive what is known as the **condition number k** defined as

$$k = \frac{\text{Maximum eigenvalue}}{\text{Minimum eigenvalue}}$$

and the **condition index (CI)** defined as

$$\text{CI} = \sqrt{\frac{\text{Maximum eigenvalue}}{\text{Minimum eigenvalue}}} = \sqrt{k}$$

Then we have this rule of thumb. If k is between 100 and 1000 there is moderate to strong multicollinearity and if it exceeds 1000 there is severe multicollinearity. Alternatively, if the CI ($= \sqrt{k}$) is between 10 and 30, there is moderate to strong multicollinearity and if it exceeds 30 there is severe multicollinearity.

For the illustrative example, $k = 3.0/0.00002422$ or about 123,864, and $\text{CI} = \sqrt{123864} =$ about 352; both k and the CI therefore suggest severe multicollinearity. Of course, k and CI can be calculated between the maximum eigenvalue and any other eigenvalue, as is done in the printout. (*Note:* The printout does not explicitly compute k, but that is simply the square of CI.) Incidentally, note that a low eigenvalue (in relation to the maximum eigenvalue) is generally an indication of near-linear dependencies in the data.

Some authors believe that the condition index is the best available multicollinearity diagnostic. But this opinion is not shared widely. For us, then, the CI is just a rule of thumb, a bit more sophisticated perhaps. But for further details, the reader may consult the references.[26]

6. **Tolerance and variance inflation factor.** For the k-variable regression model [Y, intercept, and $(k - 1)$ regressors], as we have seen in (7.5.6), the variance of a partial regression coefficient can be expressed as

$$\text{var}(\hat{\beta}_j) = \frac{\sigma^2}{\sum x_j^2} \cdot \left(\frac{1}{1 - R_j^2}\right) \tag{7.5.6}$$

$$= \frac{\sigma^2}{\sum x_j^2} \cdot \text{VIF}_j \tag{10.7.4}$$

---

[25]Lawrence R. Klien, *An Introduction to Econometrics,* Prentice-Hall, Englewood Cliffs, N.J., 1962, p. 101.

[26]See especially D. A. Belsley, E. Kuh, and R. E. Welsch, *Regression Diagnostics: Identifying Influential Data and Sources of Collinearity,* John Wiley & Sons, New York, 1980, Chap. 3. However, this book is not for the beginner.

where β_j is the (partial) regression coefficient of the regressor X_j, R_j^2 is the R^2 in the (auxiliary) regression of X_j on the remaining $(k - 2)$ regressors and VIF_j is the variance-inflation factor first introduced in Section 10.5. As R_j^2 increases toward unity, that is, as the collinearity of X_j with the other regressors increases, the VIF also increases and in the limit it can be infinite.

Some authors therefore use the VIF as an indicator of multicollinearity: The larger is the value of VIF_j, the more "troublesome" or collinear is the variable X_j. But how high should VIF be before a regressor becomes troublesome? **As a rule of thumb**, if the VIF of a variable exceeds 10 (this will happen if R_j^2 exceeds 0.90), that variable is said to be highly collinear.[27]

Other authors use the measure of **tolerance** to detect multicollinearity. It is defined as

$$\text{TOL}_j = (1 - R_j^2)$$
$$= (1/\text{VIF}_j) \tag{10.7.5}$$

Clearly, $\text{TOL}_j = 1$ if X_j is not correlated with the other regressors, whereas it is zero if it is perfectly related to the other regressors.

VIF (or tolerance) as a measure of collinearity is not free of criticism. As (10.7.4) shows, $\text{var}(\hat{\beta}_j)$ depends on three factors: σ^2, $\sum x_j^2$ and VIF_j. A high VIF can be counterbalanced by a low σ^2 or a high $\sum x_j^2$. To put it differently, a high VIF is neither necessary nor sufficient to get high variances and high standard errors. Therefore, high multicollinearity, as measured by a high VIF, may not necessarily cause high standard errors. In all this discussion, the terms *high* and *low* are used in a relative sense.

To conclude our discussion of detecting multicollinearity, we stress that the various methods we have discussed are essentially in the nature of "fishing expeditions," for we cannot tell which of these methods will work in any particular application. Alas, not much can be done about it, for multicollinearity is specific to a given sample over which the researcher may not have much control, especially if the data are nonexperimental in nature—the usual fate of researchers in the social sciences.

Again as a parody of multicollinearity, Goldberger cites numerous ways of detecting micronumerosity, such as developing critical values of the sample size, n^*, such that micronumerosity is a problem only if the actual sample size, n, is smaller than n^*. The point of Goldberger's parody is to emphasize that small sample size and lack of variability in the explanatory variables may cause problems that are at least as serious as those due to multicollinearity.

10.8 REMEDIAL MEASURES

What can be done if multicollinearity is serious? As in the case of detection, there are no infallible guides because multicollinearity is essentially a sample problem. However, one can try the following rules of thumb, the success depending on the severity of the collinearity problem.

---

[27] See David G. Kleinbaum, Lawrence L. Kupper, and Keith E. Muller, *Applied Regression Analysis and Other Multivariate Methods*, 2d. ed., PWS-Kent, Boston, Mass., 1988, p. 210.

1. **A priori information.** Suppose we consider the model

$$Y_i = \beta_1 + \beta_2 X_{2i} + \beta_3 X_{3i} + u_i$$

where Y = consumption, X_2 = income, and X_3 = wealth. As noted before, income and wealth variables tend to be highly collinear. But suppose a priori we believe that $\beta_3 = 0.10\beta_2$; that is, the rate of change of consumption with respect to wealth is one-tenth the corresponding rate with respect to income. We can then run the following regression:

$$Y_i = \beta_1 + \beta_2 X_{2i} + 0.10\beta_2 X_{3i} + u_i$$
$$= \beta_1 + \beta_2 X_i + u_i$$

where $X_i = X_{2i} + 0.1X_{3i}$. Once we obtain $\hat{\beta}_2$, we can estimate $\hat{\beta}_3$ from the postulated relationship between β_2 and β_3.

How does one obtain a priori information? It could come from previous empirical work in which the collinearity problem happens to be less serious or from the relevant theory underlying the field of study. For example, in the Cobb-Douglas–type production function (7.10.1), if one expects constant returns to scale to prevail, then $(\beta_2 + \beta_3) = 1$ in which case we could run the regression (8.7.13), regressing the output-labor ratio on the capital-labor ratio. If there is collinearity between labor and capital, as generally is the case in most sample data, such a transformation may reduce or eliminate the collinearity problem. But a warning is in order here regarding imposing such a priori restrictions, "...since in general we will want to test economic theory's a priori predictions rather than simply impose them on data for which they may not be true."[28] However, we know from Section 8.7 how to test for the validity of such restrictions explicitly.

2. **Combining cross-sectional and time-series data.** A variant of the extraneous or a priori information technique is the combination of cross-sectional and time-series data, known as *pooling the data*. Suppose we want to study the demand for automobiles in the United States and assume we have time-series data on the number of cars sold, average price of the car, and consumer income. Suppose also that

$$\ln Y_t = \beta_1 + \beta_2 \ln P_t + \beta_3 \ln I_t + u_t$$

where Y = number of cars sold, P = average price, I = income, and t = time. Out objective is to estimate the price elasticity β_2 and income elasticity β_3.

In time-series data the price and income variables generally tend to be highly collinear. Therefore, if we run the preceding regression, we shall be faced with the usual multicollinearity problem. A way out of this has been suggested by Tobin.[29] He says that if we have cross-sectional data (for example, data generated by consumer panels, or budget studies conducted

---

[28] Mark B. Stewart and Kenneth F. Wallis, *Introductory Econometrics*, 2d ed., John Wiley & Sons, A Halstead Press Book, New York, 1981, p. 154.

[29] J. Tobin, "A Statistical Demand Function for Food in the U.S.A.," *Journal of the Royal Statistical Society*, Ser. A, 1950, pp. 113–141.

by various private and governmental agencies), we can obtain a fairly reliable estimate of the income elasticity β_3 because in such data, which are at a point in time, the prices do not vary much. Let the cross-sectionally estimated income elasticity be $\hat{\beta}_3$. Using this estimate, we may write the preceding time-series regression as

$$Y_t^* = \beta_1 + \beta_2 \ln P_t + u_t$$

where $Y^* = \ln Y - \hat{\beta}_3 \ln I$, that is, Y^* represents that value of Y after removing from it the effect of income. We can now obtain an estimate of the price elasticity β_2 from the preceding regression.

Although it is an appealing technique, pooling the time-series and cross-sectional data in the manner just suggested may create problems of interpretation, because we are assuming implicitly that the cross-sectionally estimated income elasticity is the same thing as that which would be obtained from a pure time-series analysis.[30] Nonetheless, the technique has been used in many applications and is worthy of consideration in situations where the cross-sectional estimates do not vary substantially from one cross section to another. An example of this technique is provided in exercise 10.25.

3. **Dropping a variable(s) and specification bias.** When faced with severe multicollinearity, one of the "simplest" things to do is to drop one of the collinear variables. Thus, in our consumption-income-wealth illustration, when we drop the wealth variable, we obtain regression (10.6.4), which shows that, whereas in the original model the income variable was statistically insignificant, it is now "highly" significant.

But in dropping a variable from the model we may be committing a **specification bias** or **specification error.** Specification bias arises from incorrect specification of the model used in the analysis. Thus, if economic theory says that income and wealth should both be included in the model explaining the consumption expenditure, dropping the wealth variable would constitute specification bias.

Although we will discuss the topic of specification bias in Chapter 13, we caught a glimpse of it in Section 7.7 where we saw that if the true model is

$$Y_i = \beta_1 + \beta_2 X_{2i} + \beta_3 X_{3i} + u_i$$

but we mistakenly fit the model

$$Y_i = b_1 + b_{12} X_{2i} + \hat{u}_i \tag{7.7.1}$$

then

$$E(b_{12}) = \beta_2 + \beta_3 b_{32} \tag{7.7.4}$$

where b_{32} = slope coefficient in the regression of X_3 on X_2. Therefore, it is obvious from (7.7.4) that b_{12} will be a biased estimate of β_2 as long as b_{32}

---

[30]For a thorough discussion and application of the pooling technique, see Edwin Kuh, *Capital Stock Growth: A Micro-Econometric Approach*, North-Holland Publishing Company, Amsterdam, 1963, Chaps. 5 and 6.

is different from zero (it is assumed that β_3 is different from zero; otherwise there is no sense in including X_3 in the original model).[31] Of course, if b_{32} is zero, we have no multicollinearity problem to begin with. It is also clear from (7.7.4) that if both b_{32} and β_3 are positive, $E(b_{12})$ will be greater than β_2; hence, on the average b_{12} will overestimate β_2, leading to a positive bias. Similarly, if the product $b_{32}\beta_3$ is negative, on the average b_{12} will underestimate β_2, leading to a negative bias.

From the preceding discussion it is clear that dropping a variable from the model to alleviate the problem of multicollinearity may lead to the specification bias. Hence the remedy may be worse than the disease in some situations because, whereas multicollinearity may prevent precise estimation of the parameters of the model, omitting a variable may seriously mislead us as to the true values of the parameters. Recall that OLS estimators are BLUE despite near collinearity.

4. **Transformation of variables.** Suppose we have time-series data on consumption expenditure, income, and wealth. One reason for high multicollinearity between income and wealth in such data is that over time both the variables tend to move in the same direction. One way of minimizing this dependence is to proceed as follows.

If the relation

$$Y_t = \beta_1 + \beta_2 X_{2t} + \beta_3 X_{3t} + u_t \qquad (10.8.1)$$

holds at time t, it must also hold at time $t - 1$ because the origin of time is arbitrary anyway. Therefore, we have

$$Y_{t-1} = \beta_1 + \beta_2 X_{2,t-1} + \beta_3 X_{3,t-1} + u_{t-1} \qquad (10.8.2)$$

If we subtract (10.8.2) from (10.8.1), we obtain

$$Y_t - Y_{t-1} = \beta_2(X_{2t} - X_{2,t-1}) + \beta_3(X_{3t} - X_{3,t-1}) + v_t \qquad (10.8.3)$$

where $v_t = u_t - u_{t-1}$. Equation (10.8.3) is known as the **first difference form** because we run the regression, not on the original variables, but on the differences of successive values of the variables.

The first difference regression model often reduces the severity of multicollinearity because, although the levels of X_2 and X_3 may be highly correlated, there is no a priori reason to believe that their differences will also be highly correlated.

The first difference transformation, however, creates some additional problems. The error term v_t appearing in (10.8.3) may not satisfy one of the assumptions of the classical linear regression model, namely, that the disturbances are not serially correlated. As we shall see in Chapter 12, if the original u_t is serially independent or uncorrelated, the error term v_t obtained previously will in most cases be serially correlated. Again the remedy may be worse than the disease! Moreover, there is a loss of one observation due to the differencing procedure, and therefore the degrees of freedom are

---

[31]Note further that if b_{32} does not approach zero as the sample size is increased indefinitely, then b_{12} will be not only biased but also inconsistent.

reduced by one. In a small sample this could be a factor one would wish at least to take into consideration. Furthermore, the first differencing procedure may not be appropriate in cross-sectional data where there is no logical ordering of the observations.

5. **Additional or new data.** Since multicollinearity is a sample feature, it is possible that in another sample involving the same variables collinearity may not be so serious as in the first sample. Sometimes simply increasing the size of the sample (if possible) may attenuate the collinearity problem. For example, in the three-variable model we saw that

$$\text{var}(\hat{\beta}_2) = \frac{\sigma^2}{\sum x_{2i}^2 (1 - r_{23}^2)}$$

Now as the sample size increases, $\sum x_{2i}^2$ will generally increase. (Why?) Therefore, for any given r_{23}, the variance of $\hat{\beta}_2$ will decrease, thus decreasing the standard error, which will enable us to estimate β_2 more precisely.

As an illustration, consider the following regression of consumption expenditure Y on income X_2 and wealth X_3 based on 10 observations:[32]

$$\hat{Y}_i = 24.377 + 0.8716X_{2i} - 0.0349X_{3i}$$
$$t = (3.875) \quad (2.7726) \quad (-1.1595) \quad R^2 = 0.9682 \tag{10.8.4}$$

The wealth coefficient in this regression not only has the wrong sign but is also statistically insignificant at the 5% level. But when the sample size was increased to 40 observations (micronumerosity?), the following results were obtained:

$$\hat{Y}_i = 2.0907 + 0.7299X_{2i} + 0.0605X_{3i}$$
$$t = (0.8713) \quad (6.0014) \quad (2.0014) \quad R^2 = 0.9672 \tag{10.8.5}$$

Now the wealth coefficient not only has the correct sign but also is statistically significant at the 5% level.

Obtaining additional or "better" data is not always that easy, for as Judge et al. note:

> Unfortunately, economists seldom can obtain additional data without bearing large costs, much less choose the values of the explanatory variables they desire. In addition, when adding new variables in situations that are not controlled, we must be aware of adding observations that were generated by a process other than that associated with the original data set; that is, we must be sure that the economic structure associated with the new observations is the same as the original structure.[33]

6. **Reducing collinearity in polynomial regressions.** In Section 7.11 we discussed polynomial regression models. A special feature of these models is that the explanatory variable(s) appear with various powers. Thus, in the total cubic cost function involving the regression of total cost on output,

---

[32] I am indebted to Albert Zucker for providing the results given in the following regressions.

[33] Judge et al., op. cit., p. 625. See also Sec. 10.9.

(output)^2, and (output)^3, as in (7.11.4), the various output terms are going to be correlated, making it difficult to estimate the various slope coefficients precisely.[34] In practice though, it has been found that if the explanatory variable(s) are expressed in the deviation form (i.e., deviation from the mean value), multicollinearity is substantially reduced. But even then the problem may persist,[35] in which case one may want to consider techniques such as **orthogonal polynomials.**[36]

7. **Other methods of remedying multicollinearity.** Multivariate statistical techniques such as **factor analysis** and **principal components** or techniques such as **ridge regression** are often employed to "solve" the problem of multicollinearity. Unfortunately, these techniques are beyond the scope of this book, for they cannot be discussed competently without resorting to matrix algebra.[37]

10.9 IS MULTICOLLINEARITY NECESSARILY BAD? MAYBE NOT IF THE OBJECTIVE IS PREDICTION ONLY

It has been said that if the sole purpose of regression analysis is prediction or forecasting, then multicollinearity is not a serious problem because the higher the R^2, the better the prediction.[38] But this may be so "...as long as the values of the explanatory variables for which predictions are desired obey the same near-exact linear dependencies as the original design [data] matrix X."[39] Thus, if in an estimated regression it was found that $X_2 = 2X_3$ approximately, then in a future sample used to forecast Y, X_2 should also be approximately equal to $2X_3$, a condition difficult to meet in practice (see footnote 33), in which case prediction will become increasingly uncertain.[40] Moreover, if the objective of the analysis is not only prediction but also reliable estimation of the parame-

---

[34]As noted, since the relationship between X, X^2, and X^3 is nonlinear, polynomial regressions do not violate the assumption of no multicollinearity of the classical model, strictly speaking.

[35]See R. A. Bradley and S. S. Srivastava, "Correlation and Polynomial Regression," *American Statistician*, vol. 33, 1979, pp. 11–14.

[36]See Norman Draper and Harry Smith, *Applied Regression Analysis*, 2d ed., John Wiley & Sons, New York, 1981, pp. 266–274.

[37]A readable account of these techniques from an applied viewpoint can be found in Samprit Chatterjee and Bertram Price, *Regression Analysis by Example*, John Wiley & Sons, New York, 1977, Chaps. 7 and 8. See also H.D. Vinod, "A Survey of Ridge Regression and Related Techniques for Improvements over Ordinary Least Squares," *Review of Economics and Statistics*, vol. 60, February 1978, pp. 121–131.

[38]See R. C. Geary, "Some Results about Relations between Stochastic Variables: A Discussion Document," *Review of International Statistical Institute*, vol. 31, 1963, pp. 163–181.

[39]Judge et al., op. cit., p. 619. You will also find on this page proof of why, despite collinearity, one can obtain better mean predictions if the existing collinearity structure also continues in the future samples.

[40]For an excellent discussion, see E. Malinvaud, *Statistical Methods of Econometrics*, 2d ed., North-Holland Publishing Company, Amsterdam, 1970, pp. 220–221.

ters, serious multicollinearity will be a problem because we have seen that it leads to large standard errors of the estimators.

In one situation, however, multicollinearity may not pose a serious problem. This is the case when R^2 is high and the regression coefficients are individually significant as revealed by the higher t values. Yet, multicollinearity diagnostics, say, the condition index, indicate that there is serious collinearity in the data. When can such a situation arise? As Johnston notes:

> This can arise if individual coefficients happen to be numerically well in excess of the true value, so that the effect still shows up in spite of the inflated standard error and/or because the true value itself is so large that even an estimate on the downside still shows up as significant.[41]

10.10 SUMMARY AND CONCLUSIONS

1. One of the assumptions of the classical linear regression model is that there is no multicollinearity among the explanatory variables, the X's. Broadly interpreted, multicollinearity refers to the situation where there is either an exact or approximately exact linear relationship among the X variables.

2. The consequences of multicollinearity are as follows: If there is perfect collinearity among the X's, their regression coefficients are indeterminate and their standard errors are not defined. If collinearity is high but not perfect, estimation of regression coefficients is possible but their standard errors tend to be large. As a result, the population values of the coefficients cannot be estimated precisely. However, if the objective is to estimate linear combinations of these coefficients, *the estimable functions*, this can be done even in the presence of perfect multicollinearity.

3. Although there are no sure methods of detecting collinearity, there are several indicators of it, which are as follows:

   (*a*) The clearest sign of multicollinearity is when R^2 is very high but none of the regression coefficients is statistically significant on the basis of the conventional t test. This case is, of course, extreme.

   (*b*) In models involving just two explanatory variables, a fairly good idea of collinearity can be obtained by examining the zero-order, or simple, correlation coefficient between the two variables. If this correlation is high, multicollinearity is generally the culprit.

   (*c*) However, the zero-order correlation coefficients can be misleading in models involving more than two X variables since it is possible to have low zero-order correlations and yet find high multicollinearity. In situations like these, one may need to examine the partial correlation coefficients.

   (*d*) If R^2 is high but the partial correlations are low, multicollinearity is a possibility. Here one or more variables may be superfluous. But if R^2 is high and the partial correlations are also high, multicollinearity may not be readily detectable. Also, as pointed out by C. Robert, Krishna

---

[41] J. Johnston, *Econometric Methods*, 3d ed., McGraw-Hill, New York, 1984, p. 249.

Kumar, John O'Hagan, and Brendan McCabe, there are some statistical problems with the partial correlation test suggested by Farrar and Glauber.

(e) Therefore, one may regress each of the X_i variables on the remaining X variables in the model and find out the corresponding coefficients of determination R_i^2. A high R_i^2 would suggest that X_i is highly correlated with the rest of the X's. Thus, one may drop that X_i from the model, provided it does not lead to serious specification bias.

4. Detection of multicollinearity is half the battle. The other half is concerned with how to get rid of the problem. Again there are no sure methods, only a few rules of thumb. Some of these rules are as follows: (1) using extraneous or prior information, (2) combining cross-sectional and time-series data, (3) omitting a highly collinear variable, (4) transforming data, and (5) obtaining additional or new data. Of course, which of these rules will work in practice will depend on the nature of the data and severity of the collinearity problem.

5. We noted the role of multicollinearity in prediction and pointed out that unless the collinearity structure continues in the future sample it is hazardous to use the estimated regression that has been plagued by multicollinearity for the purpose of forecasting.

6. Although multicollinearity has received extensive (some would say excessive) attention in the literature, an equally important problem encountered in empirical research is that of micronumerosity, smallness of sample size. According to Goldberger, "When a research article complains about multicollinearity, readers ought to see whether the complaints would be convincing if "micronumerosity" were substituted for "multicollinearity."[42] He suggests that the reader ought to decide how small n, the number of observations, is before deciding that one has a small-sample problem, just as one decides how high an R^2 value is in an auxiliary regression before declaring that the collinearity problem is very severe.

EXERCISES

Questions

10.1. In the k-variable linear regression model there are k normal equations to estimate the k unknowns. These normal equations are given in (9.3.8). Assume that X_k is a perfect linear combination of the remaining X variables. How would you show that in this case it is impossible to estimate the k regression coefficients?

10.2. Consider the set of hypothetical data on the following page. Suppose you want to fit the model

$$Y_i = \beta_1 + \beta_2 X_{2i} + \beta_3 X_{3i} + u_i$$

to the data.

(a) Can you estimate the three unknowns? Why or why not?

---

[42] Goldberger, op. cit., p. 250.

(b) If not, what linear functions of these parameters, the estimable functions, can you estimate? Show the necessary calculations.

Y	X_2	X_3
−10	1	1
−8	2	3
−6	3	5
−4	4	7
−2	5	9
0	6	11
2	7	13
4	8	15
6	9	17
8	10	19
10	11	21

10.3. Recall Chapter 8, Section 5, where we considered the marginal or incremental contribution of an explanatory variable. The example discussed there involved the regression of personal consumption expenditure Y on personal disposable income X_2, and the trend X_3. When we introduced variable X_2 into the model first and then variable X_3, we obtained Table 8.7. But suppose we introduce X_3 first and then X_2. The ANOVA table corresponding to this change is as follows:

ANOVA table when X_3 enters first

Source of variation	SS	df	MSS
ESS due to X_3 alone	$Q_1 = $ 64,536.2529	1	64,536.2529
ESS due to addition of X_2	$Q_2 = $ 1,428.8471	1	1,428.8471
ESS due to X_2 and X_3	$Q_3 = $ 65,965.1000	2	32,982.5500
Due to residual	$Q_4 = $ 77.1693	12	6.4310
Total	$Q_5 = $ 66,042.2693		

Although the ESS due to X_2 and X_3 together is the same in both the tables, its allocation between the two X's is different. In Table 8.7, where X_2 enters first, its contribution to ESS is 65,898.2353, but when it enters marginally as in the preceding table, its contribution is only 1428.8471. The same thing is true of X_3. How do you explain this phenomenon?

10.4. If the relation $\lambda_1 X_{1i} + \lambda_2 X_{2i} + \lambda_3 X_{3i} = 0$ holds true for all values of λ_1, λ_2, and λ_3, estimate $r_{12.3}$, $r_{13.2}$, and $r_{23.1}$. Also find $R^2_{1.23}$, $R^2_{2.13}$, and $R^2_{3.12}$. What is the degree of multicollinearity in this situation? *Note:* $R^2_{1.23}$ is the coefficient of determination in the regression of Y on X_2 and X_3. Other R^2 values are to be interpreted similarly.

10.5. Consider the following model:

$$Y_t = \beta_1 + \beta_2 X_t + \beta_3 X_{t-1} + \beta_4 X_{t-2} + \beta_5 X_{t-3} + \beta_6 X_{t-4} + u_t$$

where $Y = $ consumption, $X = $ income, and $t = $ time. The preceding model postulates that consumption expenditure at time t is a function not only of income at time t but also of income through previous periods. Thus, consumption expenditure in the first quarter of 1976 is a function of income in that quarter and the four quarters of 1975. Such models are called **distributed lag models**, and we shall discuss them in a later chapter.

(a) Would you expect multicollinearity in such models and why?

(b) If collinearity is expected, how would you resolve the problem?

10.6. Consider the illustrative example of Section 10.6. How would you reconcile the difference in the marginal propensity to consume obtained from (10.6.1) and (10.6.4)?

10.7. In data involving economic time series such as GNP, money supply, prices, income, unemployment, etc. multicollinearity is usually suspected. Why?

10.8. Suppose in the model

$$Y_i = \beta_1 + \beta_2 X_{2i} + \beta_3 X_{3i} + u_i$$

that r_{23}, the coefficient of correlation between X_2 and X_3, is zero. Therefore, someone suggests that you run the following regressions:

$$Y_i = \alpha_1 + \alpha_2 X_{2i} + u_{1i}$$
$$Y_i = \gamma_1 + \gamma_3 X_{3i} + u_{2i}$$

(a) Will $\hat{\alpha}_2 = \hat{\beta}_2$ and $\hat{\gamma}_3 = \hat{\beta}_3$? Why?

(b) Will $\hat{\beta}_1$ equal $\hat{\alpha}_1$ or $\hat{\gamma}_1$ or some combination thereof?

(c) Will $\text{var}(\hat{\beta}_2) = \text{var}(\hat{\alpha}_2)$ and $\text{var}(\hat{\beta}_3) = \text{var}(\hat{\gamma}_3)$?

10.9. Refer to the illustrative example of Chapter 7 where we fitted the Cobb-Douglas production function to the Taiwanese agricultural sector. The results of the regression given in (7.10.4) show that both the labor and capital coefficients are individually statistically significant.

(a) Find out whether the variables labor and capital are highly correlated.

(b) If your answer to (a) is affirmative, would you drop, say, the labor variable from the model and regress the output variable on capital input only?

(c) If you do so, what kind of specification bias is committed? Find out the nature of this bias.

10.10. Refer to Example 7.4. For this problem the correlation matrix is as follows:

	X_i	X_i^2	X_i^3
X_i	1	0.9742	0.9284
X_i^2		1.0	0.9872
X_i^3			1.0

(a) "Since the zero-order correlations are very high, there must be serious multicollinearity." Comment.

(b) Would you drop variables X_i^2 and X_i^3 from the model?

(c) If you drop them, what will happen to the value of the coefficient of X_i?

10.11. Stepwise regression. In deciding on the "best" set of explanatory variables for a regression model, researchers often follow the method of stepwise regression. In this method one proceeds either by introducing the X variables one at a time (**stepwise forward regression**) or by including all the possible X variables in one multiple regression and rejecting them one at a time (**stepwise backward regression**). The decision to add or drop a variable is usually made on the basis of the contribution of that variable to the ESS, as judged by the F test. Knowing

what you do now about multicollinearity, would you recommend either procedure? Why or why not?*

10.12. State *with reason* whether the following statements are true, false or uncertain:
   (*a*) Despite perfect multicollinearity, OLS estimators are BLUE.
   (*b*) In cases of high multicollinearity, it is not possible to assess the individual
significance of one or more partial regression coefficients.
   (*c*) If an auxiliary regression shows that a particular R_i^2 is high, there is definite
evidence of high collinearity.
   (*d*) High pair-wise correlations do not suggest that there is high multicollinearity.
   (*e*) Multicollinearity is harmless if the objective of the analysis is prediction
only.
   (*f*) Ceteris paribus, the higher the VIF is, the larger the variances of OLS estimators.
   (*g*) The tolerance (TOL) is a better measure of multicollinearity than the VIF.
   (*h*) You will not obtain a high R^2 value in a multiple regression if all the partial
slope coefficients are *individually* statistically insignificant on the basis of
the usual t test.
   (*i*) In the regression of Y on X_2 and X_3, suppose there is little variability in
the values of X_3. This would increase var($\hat{\beta}_3$). In the extreme, if all X_3 are
identical, var($\hat{\beta}_3$) is infinite.

10.13. (*a*) Show that if $r_{1i} = 0$ for $i = 2, 3, \ldots, k$ then

$$R_{1.23\ldots k} = 0$$

   (*b*) What is the importance of this finding for the regression of variable $X_1 (= Y)$
on $X_2, X_3, \ldots, X_k$?

10.14. Suppose all the zero-order correlation coefficients of $X_1 (= Y), X_2, \ldots, X_k$ are
equal to r.
   (*a*) What is the value of $R_{1.23\ldots k}^2$?
   (*b*) What are the values of the first-order correlation coefficients?

**10.15. In matrix notation we saw in Chapter 9 that

$$\hat{\boldsymbol{\beta}} = (\mathbf{X'X})^{-1}\mathbf{X'y}$$

   (*a*) What happens to $\hat{\boldsymbol{\beta}}$ when there is perfect collinearity among the X's?
   (*b*) How would you know if perfect collinearity exists?

**10.16. Using matrix notation, we obtained in (9.3.13)

$$\text{var-cov}(\hat{\boldsymbol{\beta}}) = \sigma^2(\mathbf{X'X})^{-1}$$

What happens to this var-cov matrix (*a*) when there is perfect multicollinearity
and (*b*) when collinearity is high but not perfect.

10.17. Consider the following **correlation matrix:

$$\mathbf{R} = \begin{matrix} & \begin{matrix} X_2 & X_3 & \cdots X_k \end{matrix} \\ \begin{matrix} X_2 \\ X_3 \\ \\ X_k \end{matrix} & \begin{bmatrix} 1 & r_{23} & \cdots & r_{2k} \\ r_{32} & 1 & \cdots & r_{3k} \\ \cdots & \cdots & \cdots & \\ r_{k2} & r_{k3} & \cdots & 1 \end{bmatrix} \end{matrix}$$

---

*See if your reasoning agrees with that of Arthur S. Goldberg and D. B. Jochems, "Note on Stepwise
Least-Squares," *Journal of the American Statistical Association*, vol. 56, March 1961, pp. 105–110.
**Optional.

How would you find out from the correlation matrix whether (a) there is perfect collinearity, (b) there is less than perfect collinearity, and (c) the X's are uncorrelated.

Hint: You may use $|\mathbf{R}|$ to answer these questions, where $|\mathbf{R}|$ denotes the determinant of $\mathbf{R}$.

**10.18. Orthogonal explanatory variables. Suppose in the model

$$Y_i = \beta_1 + \beta_2 X_{2i} + \beta_3 X_{3i} + \cdots + \beta_k X_{ki} + u_i$$

X_2 to X_k are all uncorrelated. Such variables are called **orthogonal variables**. If this is the case:

(a) What will be the structure of the $(\mathbf{X'X})$ matrix?

(b) How would you obtain $\hat{\boldsymbol{\beta}} = (\mathbf{X'X})^{-1}\mathbf{X'y}$?

(c) What will be the nature of the var-cov matrix of $\hat{\boldsymbol{\beta}}$?

(d) Suppose you have run the regression and afterward you want to introduce another orthogonal variable, say, X_{k+1} into the model. Do you have to recompute all the previous coefficients $\hat{\beta}_1$ to $\hat{\beta}_k$? Why or why not?

10.19. Consider the following model:

$$\text{GNP}_t = \beta_1 + \beta_2 M_t + \beta_3 M_{t-1} + \beta_4 (M_t - M_{t-1}) + u_t$$

where $\text{GNP}_t = $ GNP at time t, $M_t = $ money supply at time t, $M_{t-1} = $ money supply at time $(t-1)$ and $(M_t - M_{t-1}) = $ change in the money supply between time t and time $(t-1)$. This model thus postulates that the level of GNP at time t is a function of the money supply at time t and time $(t-1)$ as well as the change in the money supply between these time periods.

(a) Assuming you have the data to estimate the preceding model, would you succeed in estimating all the coefficients of this model? Why or why not?

(b) If not, what coefficients can be estimated?

(c) Suppose that the $\beta_3 M_{t-1}$ term were absent from the model. Would your answer to (a) be the same?

(d) Repeat (c), assuming that the term $\beta_2 M_t$ were absent from the model.

10.20. Show that (7.4.7) and (7.4.8) can also be expressed as

$$\hat{\beta}_2 = \frac{(\sum y_i x_{2i})(\sum x_{3i}^2) - (\sum y_i x_{3i})(\sum x_{2i}x_{3i})}{(\sum x_{2i}^2)(\sum x_{3i}^2)(1 - r_{23}^2)}$$

$$\hat{\beta}_3 = \frac{(\sum y_i x_{3i})(\sum x_{2i}^2) - (\sum y_i x_{2i})(\sum x_{2i}x_{3i})}{(\sum x_{2i}^2)(\sum x_{3i}^2)(1 - r_{23}^2)}$$

where r_{23} is the coefficient of correlation between X_2 and X_3.

10.21. Using (7.4.12) and (7.4.15), show that when there is perfect collinearity, the variances of $\hat{\beta}_2$ and $\hat{\beta}_3$ are infinite.

10.22. Verify that the standard errors of the sums of the slope coefficients estimated from (10.5.4) and (10.5.5) are, respectively, 0.1549 and 0.1825. (See Section 10.5.)

10.23. For the k-variable regression model (9.1.1) it can be shown that the variance of the kth ($k = 2, 3, \ldots, K$) partial regression coefficient can be expressed as*

---

*This formula is given by R. Stone, "The Analysis of Market Demand," *Journal of the Royal Statistical Society*, vol. B7, 1945, p. 297. Also recall (7.5.6). For further discussion, see Peter Kennedy, *A Guide to Econometrics*, 2d ed., The MIT Press, Cambridge, Mass., 1985, p. 156.
**Optional.

$$\text{var}(\hat{\beta}_k) = \frac{1}{n-k}\frac{\sigma_y^2}{\sigma_k^2}\left(\frac{1-R^2}{1-R_k^2}\right)$$

where σ_y^2 = variance of Y, σ_k^2 = variance of the kth explanatory variable, $R_k^2 = R^2$ from the regression of X_k on the remaining X variables, and R^2 = coefficient of determination from the multiple regression (9.1.1), that is, regression of Y on all the X variables.

(a) Other things the same, if σ_k^2 increases, what happens to $\text{var}(\hat{\beta}_k)$? What are the implications for the multicollinearity problem?

(b) What happens to the preceding formula when collinearity is perfect?

(c) True or false: "The variance of $\hat{\beta}_k$ decreases as R^2 rises, so that the effect of a high R_k^2 can be offset by a high R^2."

10.24. Based on the annual data for the U.S. manufacturing sector for 1899–1922, Dougherty obtained the following regression results:*

$$\widehat{\log Y} = 2.81 - 0.53\log K + 0.91\log L + 0.047t \tag{1}$$
$$\text{se} = (1.38) \quad (0.34) \quad\quad (0.14) \quad\quad (0.021) \quad\quad R^2 = 0.97$$
$$F = 189.8$$

where Y = index of real output, K = index of real capital input, L = index of real labor input, t = time or trend.

Using the same data, he also obtained the following regression:

$$\widehat{\log(Y/L)} = -0.11 + 0.11\log(K/L) + 0.006t \tag{2}$$
$$\text{se} = (0.03) \quad (0.15) \quad\quad\quad (0.006) \quad\quad R^2 = 0.65$$
$$F = 19.5$$

(a) Is there multicollinearity in regression (1)? How do you know?

(b) In regression (1), what is the a priori sign of $\log K$? Do the results conform to this expectation? Why or why not?

(c) How would you justify the functional form of regression (1): (*Hint:* Cobb-Douglas production function.)

(d) Interpret regression (1). What is the role of the trend variable in this regression?

(e) What is the logic behind estimating regression (2)?

(f) If there was multicollinearity in regression (1), has that been reduced by regression (2)? How do you know?

(g) If regression (2) is a restricted version of regression (1), what restriction is imposed by the author? (*Hint:* returns to scale.) How do you know if this restriction is valid? Which test do you use? Show all your calculations.

(h) Are the R^2 values of the two regressions comparable? Why or why not? How would you make them comparable, if they are not comparable in the present form?

Problems

10.25. Klein and Goldberger attempted to fit the following regression model to the U.S. economy:

$$Y_i = \beta_1 + \beta_2 X_{2i} + \beta_3 X_{3i} + \beta_4 X_{4i} + u_i$$

---

*Christopher Dougherty, *Introduction to Econometrics*, Oxford University Press, New York, 1992, pp. 159–160.

where Y = consumption, X_2 = wage income, X_3 = nonwage, nonfarm income, and X_4 = farm income. But since $X_2, X_3,$ and X_4 are expected to be highly collinear, they obtained estimates of β_3 and β_4 from cross-sectional analysis as follows: $\beta_3 = 0.75\beta_2$ and $\beta_4 = 0.625\beta_2$. Using these estimates, they reformulated their consumption function as follows:

$$Y_i = \beta_1 + \beta_2(X_{2i} + 0.75X_{3i} + 0.625X_{4i}) + u_i = \beta_1 + \beta_2 Z_i + u_i$$

where $Z_i = X_{2i} + 0.75X_{3i} + 0.625X_{4i}$.
(a) Fit the modified model to the accompanying data and obtain estimates of β_1 to β_4.
(b) How would you interpret the variable Z?

Year	Y	X_2	X_3	X_4	Year	Y	X_2	X_3	X_4
1936	62.8	43.41	17.10	3.96	1946	95.7	76.73	28.26	9.76
1937	65.0	46.44	18.65	5.48	1947	98.3	75.91	27.91	9.31
1938	63.9	44.35	17.09	4.37	1948	100.3	77.62	32.30	9.85
1939	67.5	47.82	19.28	4.51	1949	103.2	78.01	31.39	7.21
1940	71.3	51.02	23.24	4.88	1950	108.9	83.57	35.61	7.39
1941	76.6	58.71	28.11	6.37	1951	108.5	90.59	37.58	7.98
1945*	86.3	87.69	30.29	8.96	1952	111.4	95.47	35.17	7.42

*The data for the war years 1942–1944 are missing. The data for other years are billions of 1939 dollars.

Source: L. R. Klein and A. S. Goldberger, *An Economic Model of the United States, 1929–1952,* North Holland Publishing Company, Amsterdam, 1964, p. 131.

10.26. The following table gives data on imports, GNP, and the consumer price index (CPI) for the United States over the period 1970–1983.

Merchandise imports, GNP, and CPI, United States, 1970–1983

Year	Merchandise imports ($, million)	GNP ($, billion)	CPI, all items (1967 = 100)
1970	39,866	992.7	116.3
1971	45,579	1,077.6	121.3
1972	55,797	1,185.9	125.3
1973	70,499	1,326.4	133.1
1974	103,811	1,434.2	147.7
1975	98,185	1,549.2	161.2
1976	124,228	1,718.0	170.5
1977	151,907	1,918.3	181.5
1978	176,020	2,163.9	195.4
1979	212,028	2,417.8	217.4
1980	249,781	2,631.7	246.8
1981	265,086	2,957.8	272.4
1982	247,667	3,069.3	289.1
1983	261,312	3,304.8	298.4

Source: *Economic Report of the President, 1985.* Data on imports from Table B-98 (p. 344), GNP from Table B-1 (p. 232) and CPI from Table B-52 (p. 291).

You are asked to consider the following model:

$$\ln \text{Imports}_t = \beta_1 + \beta_2 \ln \text{GNP}_t + \beta_3 \ln \text{CPI}_t + u_t$$

(a) Estimate the parameters of this model using the data given in the table.
(b) Do you suspect that there is multicollinearity in the data?
(c) Examine the nature of collinearity using the condition index.
(d) Regress: (1) $\ln \text{Imports}_t = A_1 + A_2 \ln \text{GNP}_t$
    (2) $\ln \text{Imports}_t = B_1 + B_2 \ln \text{CPI}_t$
    (3) $\ln \text{GNP}_t = C_1 + C_2 \ln \text{CPI}_t$
  Based on these regressions, what can you say about the nature of multicollinearity in the data?
(e) Suppose there is multicollinearity in the data but $\hat{\beta}_2$ and $\hat{\beta}_3$ are individually significant at the 5% level and the overall F test is also significant. In this case should we worry about the collinearity problem?

10.27. Refer to Exercise 7.23 about the demand function for chicken in the United States.
(a) Using the log-linear, or double-log, model, estimate the various auxiliary regressions. How many are there?
(b) From these auxiliary regressions, how do you decide which of the regressor(s) are highly collinear? Which test do you use? Show the details of your calculations.
(c) If there is significant collinearity in the data, which variable(s) would you drop to reduce the severity of the collinearity problem? If you do that, what econometric problems do you face?
(d) Do you have any suggestions, other than dropping variables, to ameliorate the collinearity problem? Explain.

10.28. The accompanying table gives data on new passenger cars sold in the United States as a function of several variables.
(a) Develop a suitable linear or log-linear model to estimate a demand function for automobiles in the United States.
(b) If you decide to include all the regressors given in the table as explanatory variables, do you expect to face the multicollinearity problem? Why?
(c) If you do, how would you go about resolving the problem? State your assumptions clearly and show all the calculations explicitly.

Year	Y	X_2	X_3	X_4	X_5	X_6
1971	10,227	112.0	121.3	776.8	4.89	79,367
1972	10,872	111.0	125.3	839.6	4.55	82,153
1973	11,350	111.1	133.1	949.8	7.38	85,064
1974	8,775	117.5	147.7	1,038.4	8.61	86,794
1975	8,539	127.6	161.2	1,142.8	6.16	85,846
1976	9,994	135.7	170.5	1,252.6	5.22	88,752
1977	11,046	142.9	181.5	1,379.3	5.50	92,017
1978	11,164	153.8	195.3	1,551.2	7.78	96,048
1979	10,559	166.0	217.7	1,729.3	10.25	98,824
1980	8,979	179.3	247.0	1,918.0	11.28	99,303
1981	8,535	190.2	272.3	2,127.6	13.73	100,397
1982	7,980	197.6	286.6	2,261.4	11.20	99,526
1983	9,179	202.6	297.4	2,428.1	8.69	100,834
1984	10,394	208.5	307.6	2,670.6	9.65	105,005
1985	11,039	215.2	318.5	2,841.1	7.75	107,150
1986	11,450	224.4	323.4	3,022.1	6.31	109,597

Y = new passenger cars sold (thousands), seasonally unadjusted

X_2 = new cars, Consumer Price Index, 1967 = 100, seasonally unadjusted

X_3 = Consumer Price Index, all items, all urban consumers, 1967 = 100, seasonally unadjusted

X_4 = the personal disposable income (PDI), billions of dollars, unadjusted for seasonal variation

X_5 = the interest rate, percent, finance company paper placed directly

X_6 = the employed civilian labor force (thousands), unadjusted for seasonal variation

Source: Business Statistics, 1986, A Supplement to the *Current Survey of Business,* U.S. Department of Commerce.

CHAPTER 11

HETEROSCEDASTICITY

Heteroscedasticity has never been a reason to throw out an otherwise good model.*

But it should not be ignored either!
                    Author

An important assumption of the classical linear regression model (Assumption 4) is that the disturbances u_i appearing in the population regression function are homoscedastic; that is, they all have the same variance. In this chapter we examine the validity of this assumption and find out what happens if this assumption is not fulfilled. As in Chapter 10, we seek answers to the following questions:

1. What is the nature of heteroscedasticity?
2. What are its consequences?
3. How does one detect it?
4. What are the remedial measures?

11.1 THE NATURE OF HETEROSCEDASTICITY

As noted in Chapter 3, one of the important assumptions of the classical linear regression model is that the variance of each disturbance term u_i, conditional on the chosen values of the explanatory variables, is some constant number

---

*N. Gregory Mankiw, "A Quick Refresher Course in Macroeconomics," *Journal of Economic Literature*, vol. XXVIII, December 1990, p. 1648.

equal to σ^2. This is the assumption of **homoscedasticity**, or *equal* (homo) *spread* (scedasticity), that is, *equal variance*. Symbolically,

$$E(u_i^2) = \sigma^2 \qquad i = 1, 2, \ldots, n \tag{11.1.1}$$

Diagrammatically, in the two-variable regression model homoscedasticity can be shown as in Fig. 3.4, which, for convenience, is reproduced as Fig. 11.1. As Fig. 11.1 shows, the conditional variance of Y_i (which is equal to that of u_i), conditional upon the given X_i, remains the same regardless of the values taken by the variable X.

In contrast, consider Fig. 11.2, which shows that the conditional variance of Y_i increases as X increases. Here, the variances of Y_i are not the same. Hence, there is heteroscedasticity. Symbolically,

$$E(u_i^2) = \sigma_i^2 \tag{11.1.2}$$

Notice the subscript of σ^2, which reminds us that the conditional variances of u_i (= conditional variances of Y_i) are no longer constant.

To make the difference between homoscedasticity and heteroscedasticity clear, assume that in the two-variable model $Y_i = \beta_1 + \beta_2 X_i + u_i$, Y represents savings and X represents income. Figures 11.1 and 11.2 show that as income increases, savings on the average also increase. But in Fig. 11.1 the variance of savings remains the same at all levels of income, whereas in Fig. 11.2 it increases with income. It seems that in Fig. 11.2 the higher-income families on the average save more than the lower-income families, but there is also more variability in their savings.

There are several reasons why the variances of u_i may be variable, some of which are as follows.[1]

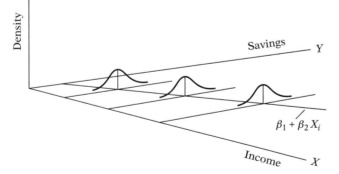

FIGURE 11.1
Homoscedastic disturbances.

---

[1] See Stefan Valavanis, *Econometrics*, McGraw-Hill, New York, 1959, p. 48.

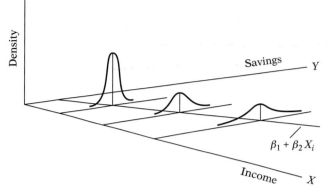

FIGURE 11.2
Heteroscedastic disturbances.

1. Following the *error-learning models*, as people learn, their errors of behavior become smaller over time. In this case, σ_i^2 is expected to decrease. As an example, consider Fig. 11.3, which relates the number of typing errors made in a given time period on a test to the hours put in typing practice. As Fig. 11.3 shows, as the number of hours of typing practice increases, the average number of typing errors as well as their variances decreases.

2. As incomes grow, people have more *discretionary income*[2] and hence more scope for choice about the disposition of their income. Hence, σ_i^2 is likely to increase with income. Thus in the regression of savings on income one is likely to find σ_i^2 increasing with income (as in Fig. 11.2) because people have more choices about their savings behavior. Similarly, companies with larger

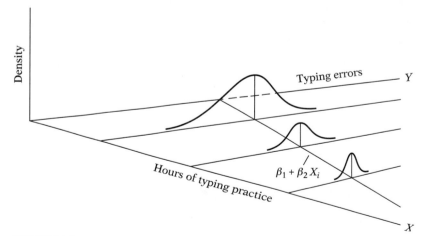

FIGURE 11.3
Illustration of heteroscedasticity.

[2] As Valavanis puts it, "Income grows, and people now barely discern dollars whereas previously they discerned dimes," ibid., p. 48.

profits are generally expected to show greater variability in their dividend policies than companies with lower profits. Also, *growth-oriented* companies are likely to show more variability in their dividend payout ratio than established companies.

3. As data collecting techniques improve, σ_i^2 is likely to decrease. Thus, banks that have sophisticated data processing equipment are likely to commit fewer errors in the monthly or quarterly statements of their customers than banks without such facilities.

4. Heteroscedasticity can also arise as a result of the presence of **outliers**. An outlying observation, or outlier, is an observation that is much different (either very small or very large) in relation to the other observations in the sample. The inclusion or exclusion of such an observation, especially if the sample size is small, can substantially alter the results of regression analysis. As an example, consider the scattergram given in Fig. 11.4. Based on the data given in exercise 11.20, this figure plots percent rate of change of stock prices (Y) and consumer prices (X) for the post–World War II period through 1969 for 20 countries. In this figure the observation on Y and X for Chile can be regarded as an outlier because the given Y and X values are much larger than for the rest of the countries. In situations such as this, it would be hard to maintain the assumption of homoscedasticity. In exercise 11.20 you are asked to find out what happens to the regression results if the observations for Chile are dropped from the analysis.

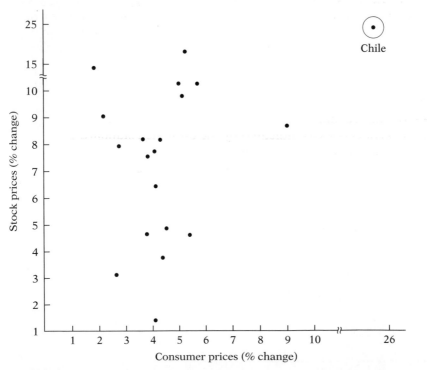

FIGURE 11.4
The relationship between stock prices and consumer prices.

5. Another source of heteroscedasticity arises from violating Assumption 9 of CLRM, namely, that the regression model is correctly specified. Although we will discuss the topic of specification errors more fully in Chapter 13, very often what looks like heteroscedasticity may be due to the fact that some important variables are omitted from the model. Thus, in the demand function for a commodity, if we do not include the prices of commodities complementary to or competing with the commodity in question (the omitted variable bias), the residuals obtained from the regression may give the distinct impression that the error variance may not be constant. But if the omitted variables are included in the model, that impression may disappear.

Note that the problem of heteroscedasticity is likely to be more common in cross-sectional than in time series data. In cross-sectional data, one usually deals with members of a population at a given point in time, such as individual consumers or their families, firms, industries, or geographical subdivisions such as state, country, city, etc. Moreover, these members may be of different sizes, such as small, medium, or large firms or low, medium, or high income. In time series data, on the other hand, the variables tend to be of similar orders of magnitude because one generally collects the data for the same entity over a period of time. Examples are GNP, consumption expenditure, savings, or employment in the United States, say, for the period 1950 to 1994.

As an illustration of heteroscedasticity likely to be encountered in cross-sectional analysis, consider Table 11.1. This table gives data on compensation per employee in 10 nondurable goods manufacturing industries, classified by the employment size of the firm or the establishment for the year 1958. Also given in the table are average productivity figures for nine employment classes.

Although the industries differ in their output composition, Table 11.1 shows clearly that on the average large firms pay more than the small firms. As an example, firms employing one to four employees paid on the average about \$3396, whereas those employing 1000 to 2499 employees on the average paid about \$4843. But notice that there is considerable variability in earning among various employment classes as indicated by the estimated standard deviations of earnings. This can be seen also from the accompanying figure, which shows the range of earnings within each employment class. As Fig. 11.5 shows, the range (highest value − lowest value), a crude measure of variability, differs from class to class, indicating heteroscedasticity in earnings in the various employment classes.

11.2 OLS ESTIMATION IN THE PRESENCE OF HETEROSCEDASTICITY

What happens to OLS estimators and their variances if we introduce heteroscedasticity by letting $E(u_i^2) = \sigma_i^2$ but retain all other assumptions of the classical model? To answer this question, let us revert to the two-variable model:

$$Y_i = \beta_1 + \beta_2 X_i + u_i$$

TABLE 11.1
Compensation per employee ($) in nondurable manufacturing industries according to employment size of establishment, 1958

Industry	Employment size (average number of employees)								
	1–4	5–9	10–19	20–49	50–99	100–249	250–499	500–999	1000–2499
Food and kindred products	2,994	3,295	3,565	3,907	4,189	4,486	4,676	4,968	5,342
Tobacco products	1,721	2,057	3,336	3,320	2,980	2,848	3,072	2,969	3,822
Textile mill products	3,600	3,657	3,674	3,437	3,340	3,334	3,225	3,163	3,168
Apparel and related products	3,494	3,787	3,533	3,215	3,030	2,834	2,750	2,967	3,453
Paper and allied products	3,498	3,847	3,913	4,135	4,445	4,885	5,132	5,342	5,326
Printing and publishing	3,611	4,206	4,695	5,083	5,301	5,269	5,182	5,395	5,552
Chemicals and allied products	3,875	4,660	4,930	5,005	5,114	5,248	5,630	5,870	5,876
Petroleum and coal products	4,616	5,181	5,317	5,337	5,421	5,710	6,316	6,455	6,347
Rubber and plastic products	3,538	3,984	4,014	4,287	4,221	4,539	4,721	4,905	5,481
Leather and leather products	3,016	3,196	3,149	3,317	3,414	3,254	3,177	3,346	4,067
Average compensation	3,396	3,787	4,013	4,014	4,146	4,241	4,387	4,538	4,843
Standard deviation	743.7	851.4	727.8	805.06	929.9	1080.6	1243.2	1307.7	1112.5
Average productivity	9,355	8,584	7,962	8,275	8,389	9,418	9,795	10,281	11,750

Source: The Census of Manufacturers, U.S. Department of Commerce, 1958 (computed by author).

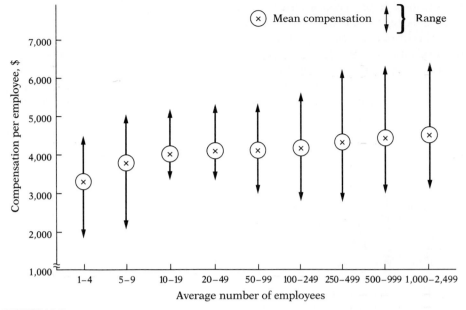

FIGURE 11.5
Per employee compensation in relation to employment size.

Applying the usual formula, the OLS estimator of β_2 is

$$\hat{\beta}_2 = \frac{\sum x_i y_i}{\sum x_i^2}$$

$$= \frac{n \sum X_i Y_i - \sum X_i \sum Y_i}{n \sum X_i^2 - (\sum X_i)^2} \qquad (11.2.1)$$

but its variance is now given by the following expression (see Appendix 11A, Section 11A.1):

$$\text{var}(\hat{\beta}_2) = \frac{\sum x_i^2 \sigma_i^2}{(\sum x_i^2)^2} \qquad (11.2.2)$$

which is obviously different from the usual variance formula obtained under the assumption of homoscedasticity, namely,

$$\text{var}(\hat{\beta}_2) = \frac{\sigma^2}{\sum x_i^2} \qquad (11.2.3)$$

Of course, if $\sigma_i^2 = \sigma^2$ for each i, the two formulas will be identical. (Why?)

Recall that $\hat{\beta}_2$ is best linear unbiased estimator (BLUE) if the assumptions of the classical model, including homoscedasticity, hold. Is it still BLUE when we drop only the homoscedasticity assumption and replace it with the assumption of heteroscedasticity? It is easy to prove that $\hat{\beta}_2$ is still linear and unbiased. As a matter of fact, as shown in Appendix 3A, Section 3A.2, to establish the unbiasedness of $\hat{\beta}_2$ it is not necessary that the disturbances (u_i) be homoscedastic. In fact, the variance of u_i, homoscedastic or heteroscedastic, plays no part in the determination of the unbiasedness property.

Granted that $\hat{\beta}_2$ is still linear unbiased, is it "efficient" or "best," that is, does it have minimum variance in the class of linear unbiased estimators? And is that minimum variance given by Eq. (11.2.2)? The answer is *no* to both the questions: $\hat{\beta}_2$ is no longer best and the minimum variance is not given by (11.2.2). Then what is BLUE in the presence of heteroscedasticity? The answer is given in the following section.

11.3 THE METHOD OF GENERALIZED LEAST SQUARES (GLS)

Why is the usual OLS estimator of β_2 given in (11.2.1) not best, although it is still unbiased? Intuitively, we can see the reason from Fig. 11.5. As this figure shows, there is considerable variability in the earnings between employment classes. If we were to regress per-employee compensation on the size of employment, we would like to make use of the knowledge that there is considerable interclass variability in earnings. Ideally, we would like to devise the estimating scheme in such a manner that observations coming from populations with greater variability are given less weight than those coming from populations with smaller variability. Examining Fig. 11.5, we would like to weight observations coming from employment classes 10–19 and 20–49 more heavily than those coming from employment classes like 5–9 and 250–499, for the former are more closely clustered around their mean values than the latter, thereby enabling us to estimate the PRF more accurately.

Unfortunately, the usual OLS method does not follow this strategy and therefore does not make use of the "information" contained in the unequal variability of the dependent variable Y, say, employee compensation of Fig. 11.5: It assigns equal weight or importance to each observation. But a method of estimation, known as **generalized least squares (GLS)**, takes such information into account explicitly and is therefore capable of producing estimators that are BLUE. To see how this is accomplished, let us continue with the now-familiar two-variable model:

$$Y_i = \beta_1 + \beta_2 X_i + u_i \tag{11.3.1}$$

which for ease of algebraic manipulation we write as

$$Y_i = \beta_1 X_{0i} + \beta_2 X_i + u_i \tag{11.3.2}$$

where $X_{0i} = 1$ for each i. The reader can see that these two formulations are identical.

Now assume that the heteroscedastic variances σ_i^2 are *known*. Divide (11.3.2) through by σ_i to obtain

$$\frac{Y_i}{\sigma_i} = \beta_1 \left(\frac{X_{0i}}{\sigma_i}\right) + \beta_2 \left(\frac{X_i}{\sigma_i}\right) + \left(\frac{u_i}{\sigma_i}\right) \tag{11.3.3}$$

which for ease of exposition we write as

$$Y_i^* = \beta_1^* X_{0i}^* + \beta_2^* X_i^* + u_i^* \tag{11.3.4}$$

where the starred or transformed variables are the original variables divided by (the known) σ_i. We use the notation β_1^* and β_2^*, the parameters of the transformed model, to distinguish them from the usual OLS parameters β_1 and β_2.

What is the purpose of transforming the original model? To see this, notice the following feature of the transformed error term u_i^*:

$$\mathrm{var}(u_i^*) = E(u_i^*)^2 = E\left(\frac{u_i}{\sigma_i}\right)^2$$

$$= \frac{1}{\sigma_i^2} E(u_i^2) \qquad \text{since } \sigma_i^2 \text{ is known}$$

$$= \frac{1}{\sigma_i^2} (\sigma_i^2) \qquad \text{since } E(u_i^2) = \sigma_i^2$$

$$= 1 \tag{11.3.5}$$

which is a constant. That is, the variance of the transformed disturbance term u_i^* is now homoscedastic. Since we are still retaining the other assumptions of the classical model, the finding that it is u^* that is homoscedastic suggests that if we apply OLS to the transformed model (11.3.3) it will produce estimators that are BLUE. In short, the estimated β_1^* and β_2^* are now BLUE and not the OLS estimators $\hat{\beta}_1$ and $\hat{\beta}_2$.

This procedure of transforming the original variables in such a way that the transformed variables satisfy the assumptions of the classical model and then applying OLS to them is known as the method of generalized least squares (GLS). *In short, GLS is OLS on the transformed variables that satisfy the standard least-squares assumptions.* The estimators thus obtained are known as **GLS estimators**, and it is these estimators that are BLUE.

The actual mechanics of estimating β_1^* and β_2^* are as follows. First, we write down the SRF of (11.3.3)

$$\frac{Y_i}{\sigma_i} = \hat{\beta}_1^* \left(\frac{X_{0i}}{\sigma_i}\right) + \hat{\beta}_2^* \left(\frac{X_i}{\sigma_i}\right) + \left(\frac{\hat{u}_i}{\sigma_i}\right)$$

or

$$Y_i^* = \hat{\beta}_1^* X_{0i}^* + \hat{\beta}_2^* X_i^* + \hat{u}_i^* \tag{11.3.6}$$

Now, to obtain the GLS estimators, we minimize

$$\sum \hat{u}_i^{*2} = \sum (Y_i^* - \hat{\beta}_1^* X_{0i}^* - \hat{\beta}_2^* X_i^*)^2$$

that is,

$$\sum \left(\frac{\hat{u}_i}{\sigma_i}\right)^2 = \sum \left[\left(\frac{Y_i}{\sigma_i}\right) - \hat{\beta}_1^* \left(\frac{X_{0i}}{\sigma_i}\right) - \hat{\beta}_2^* \left(\frac{X_i}{\sigma_i}\right)\right]^2 \tag{11.3.7}$$

The actual mechanics of minimizing (11.3.7) follow the standard calculus techniques and are given in Appendix 11A, Section 11A.2. As shown there, the GLS estimator of β_2^* is

$$\hat{\beta}_2^* = \frac{(\sum w_i)(\sum w_i X_i Y_i) - (\sum w_i X_i)(\sum w_i Y_i)}{(\sum w_i)(\sum w_i X_i^2) - (\sum w_i X_i)^2} \tag{11.3.8}$$

and its variance is given by

$$\text{var}(\hat{\beta}_2^*) = \frac{\sum w_i}{(\sum w_i)(\sum w_i X_i^2) - (\sum w_i X_i)^2} \tag{11.3.9}$$

where $w_i = 1/\sigma_i^2$.

Difference between OLS and GLS

Recall from Chapter 3 that in OLS we minimize

$$\sum \hat{u}_i^2 = \sum (Y_i - \hat{\beta}_1 - \hat{\beta}_2 X_i)^2 \tag{11.3.10}$$

but in GLS we minimize the expression (11.3.7), which can also be written as

$$\sum w_i \hat{u}_i^2 = \sum w_i (Y_i - \hat{\beta}_1^* - \hat{\beta}_2^* X_i)^2 \tag{11.3.11}$$

where $w_i = 1/\sigma_i^2$ [verify that (11.3.11) and (11.3.7) are identical].

Thus, in GLS we minimize a *weighted sum of residual squares* with $w_i = 1/\sigma_i^2$ acting as the weights, but in OLS we minimize an unweighted or (what amounts to the same thing) equally weighted RSS. As (11.3.7) shows, in GLS the weight assigned to each observation is inversely proportional to its σ_i, that is, observations coming from a population with larger σ_i will get relatively smaller weight and those from a population with smaller σ_i will get proportionately larger weight in minimizing the RSS (11.3.11). To see the difference between OLS and GLS clearly, consider the hypothetical scattergram given in Fig. 11.6.

In the (unweighted) OLS, each $\hat{u}_i^2$ associated with points A, B, and C will receive the same weight in minimizing the RSS. Obviously, in this case the $\hat{u}_i^2$ associated with point C will dominate the RSS. But in GLS the extreme observation C will get relatively smaller weight than the other two observations. As noted earlier, this is the right strategy, for in estimating the population regression function (PRF) more reliably we would like to give more weight to observations that are closely clustered around their (population) mean than to those that are widely scattered about.

Since (11.3.11) minimizes a weighted RSS, it is appropriately known as **weighted least squares (WLS),** and the estimators thus obtained and given in (11.3.8) and (11.3.9) are known as **WLS estimators**. But WLS is just a special case of the more general estimating technique, GLS. In the context of

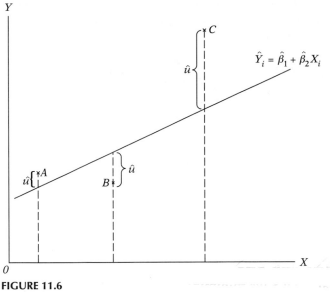

FIGURE 11.6
Hypothetical scattergram.

heteroscedasticity, one can treat the two terms WLS and GLS interchangeably. In later chapters we will come across other special cases of GLS.

In passing, note that if $w_i = w$, a constant for all i, $\hat{\beta}_2^*$ is identical with $\hat{\beta}_2$ and var($\hat{\beta}_2^*$) is identical with the usual (i.e., homoscedastic) var($\hat{\beta}_2$) given in (11.2.3), which should not be surprising. (Why?) (See exercise 11.8.)

11.4 CONSEQUENCES OF USING OLS IN THE PRESENCE OF HETEROSCEDASTICITY

As we have seen, both $\hat{\beta}_2^*$ and $\hat{\beta}_2$ are (linear) unbiased estimators: In repeated sampling, on the average, $\hat{\beta}_2^*$ and $\hat{\beta}_2$ will equal the true β_2,[3] that is, they are both unbiased estimators. But we know that it is $\hat{\beta}_2^*$ that is efficient, that is, has the smallest variance. What happens to our confidence interval, hypotheses testing, and other procedures if we continue to use the OLS estimator $\hat{\beta}_2$? We distinguish two cases.

OLS Estimation Allowing for Heteroscedasticity

Suppose we use $\hat{\beta}_2$ and use the variance formula given in (11.2.2), which takes into account heteroscedasticity explicitly. Using this variance, and assuming σ_i^2 are known, can we establish confidence intervals and test hypotheses with

---

[3]It can also be shown that both $\hat{\beta}_2^*$ and $\hat{\beta}_2$ are **consistent estimators**, that is, they converge to true β_2 as the sample size n increases indefinitely.

the usual t and F tests? The answer generally is no because it can be shown that $\text{var}(\hat{\beta}_2^*) \leq \text{var}(\hat{\beta}_2)$,[4] which means that confidence intervals based on the latter will be unnecessarily larger. As a result, the t and F tests are likely to give us inaccurate results in that $\text{var}(\hat{\beta}_2)$ is overly large and what appears to be a statistically insignificant coefficient (because the t value is smaller than what is appropriate) may in fact be significant if the correct confidence intervals were established on the basis of the GLS procedure.

OLS Estimation Disregarding Heteroscedasticity

The situation becomes very serious if we not only use $\hat{\beta}_2$ but also continue to use the usual (homoscedastic) variance formula given in (11.2.3) even if heteroscedasticity is present or suspected: Note that this is the more likely case of the two we discuss here, because running a standard OLS regression package and ignoring (or being ignorant of) heteroscedasticity will yield variance of $\hat{\beta}_2$ as given in (11.2.3). First of all, $\text{var}(\hat{\beta}_2)$ given in (11.2.3) is a *biased* estimator of $\text{var}(\hat{\beta}_2)$ given in (11.2.2), that is, on the average it overestimates or underestimates the latter, and *in general* we cannot tell whether the bias is positive (overestimation) or negative (underestimation) because it depends on the nature of the relationship between σ_i^2 and the values taken by the explanatory variable X, as can be seen clearly from (11.2.2) (see exercise 11.9). The bias arises from the fact that $\hat{\sigma}^2$, the conventional estimator of σ^2, namely, $\sum \hat{u}_i^2/(n-2)$ is no longer an unbiased estimator of the latter when heteroscedasticity is present. As a result, we can no longer rely on the conventionally computed confidence intervals and the conventionally employed t and F tests.[5] **In short, if we persist in using the usual testing procedures despite heteroscedasticity, whatever conclusions we draw or inferences we make may be very misleading.**

To throw more light on this topic, we refer to a **Monte Carlo** study conducted by Davidson and MacKinnon.[6] They consider the following simple model, which in our notation is

$$Y_i = \beta_1 + \beta_2 X_i + u_i \tag{11.4.1}$$

They assume that $\beta_1 = 1$, $\beta_2 = 1$, and $u_i \sim N(0, X_i^\alpha)$. As the last expression shows, they assume that the error variance is heteroscedastic and is related to the value of the regressor X with power α. If, for example, $\alpha = 1$, the error variance is proportional to the value of X; if $\alpha = 2$, the error variance is proportional to the square of the value of X, and so on. In Section 11.6 we will consider

---

[4]A formal proof can be found in Phoebus J. Dhrymes, *Introductory Econometrics*, Springer-Verlag, New York, 1978, pp. 110–111. In passing, note that the loss of efficiency of $\hat{\beta}_2$ [i.e., by how much $\text{var}(\hat{\beta}_2)$ exceeds $\text{var}(\hat{\beta}_2^*)$] depends on the sample values of the X variables and the value of σ_i^2.

[5]From (5.3.6) we know that the $100(1-\alpha)\%$ confidence interval for β_2 is $[\hat{\beta}_2 \pm t_{\alpha/2}\text{se}(\hat{\beta}_2)]$. But if $\text{se}(\hat{\beta}_2)$ cannot be estimated unbiasedly, what trust can we put in the conventionally computed confidence interval?

[6]Russell Davidson and James G. MacKinnon, *Estimation and Inference in Econometrics*, Oxford University Press, New York, 1993, pp. 549–550.

the logic behind such a procedure. Based on 20,000 replications and allowing for various values for α, they obtain the standard errors of the two regression coefficients using OLS [see Eq. (11.2.3)], OLS allowing for heteroscedasticity [see Eq. (11.2.2)], and GLS [see Eq. (11.3.9)]. We quote their results for selected values of α:

Value of α	Standard error of $\hat{\beta}_1$			Standard error of $\hat{\beta}_2$		
	OLS	**OLS**$_{\text{het.}}$	**GLS**	**OLS**	**OLS**$_{\text{het.}}$	**GLS**
0.5	0.164	0.134	0.110	0.285	0.277	0.243
1.0	0.142	0.101	0.048	0.246	0.247	0.173
2.0	0.116	0.074	0.0073	0.200	0.220	0.109
3.0	0.100	0.064	0.0013	0.173	0.206	0.056
4.0	0.089	0.059	0.0003	0.154	0.195	0.017

Note: OLS$_{\text{het.}}$ means OLS allowing for heteroscedasticity.

The most striking feature of these results is that OLS, with or without correction for heteroscedasticity, consistently overestimates the true standard error obtained by the (correct) GLS procedure, especially for large values of α, thus establishing the superiority of GLS. These results also show that if we do not use GLS and rely on OLS—allowing for or not allowing for heteroscedasticity—the picture is mixed. The usual OLS standard errors are either too large (for the intercept) or generally too small (for the slope coefficient) in relation to those obtained by OLS allowing for heteroscedasticity. The message is clear: In the presence of heteroscedasticity, use GLS. However, for reasons explained later in the chapter, in practice it is not always easy to apply GLS.

From the preceding discussion it is clear that heteroscedasticity is potentially a serious problem and the researcher needs to know whether it is present in a given situation. If its presence is detected, then one can take corrective action, such as using the weighted least-squares regression or some other technique. Before we turn to examining the various corrective procedures, however, we must first find out whether heteroscedasticity is present or likely to be present in a given case. This topic is discussed in the following section.

11.5 DETECTION OF HETEROSCEDASTICITY

As with multicollinearity, the important practical question is: How does one know that heteroscedasticity is present in a specific situation? Again, as in the case of multicollinearity, there are no hard-and-fast rules for detecting heteroscedasticity, only a few rules of thumb. But this situation is inevitable because σ_i^2 can be known only if we have the entire Y population corresponding to the chosen X's, such as the population shown in Table 2.1 or Table 11.1. But such data are an exception rather than the rule in most economic investigations. In this respect the econometrician differs from scientists in fields such as agriculture and biology, where researchers have a good deal of control over their subjects. More often than not, in economic studies there is only one sample Y value corresponding to a particular value of X. And there is no way one can know σ_i^2 from just one Y observation. Therefore, in most cases involving econometric investigations, heteroscedasticity may be a matter of intuition, educated guesswork, prior empirical experience, or sheer speculation.

With the preceding caveat in mind, let us examine some of the informal and formal methods of detecting heteroscedasticity. As the following discussion will reveal, most of these methods are based on the examination of the OLS residuals $\hat{u}_i$ since they are the ones we observe, and not the disturbances u_i. One hopes that they are good estimates of u_i, a hope that may be fulfilled if the sample size is fairly large.

Informal Methods

Nature of the problem. Very often the nature of the problem under consideration suggests whether heteroscedasticity is likely to be encountered. For example, following the pioneering work of Prais and Houthakker on family budget studies, where they found that the residual variance around the regression of consumption on income increased with income, one now generally assumes that in similar surveys one can expect unequal variances among the disturbances.[7] As a matter of fact, in cross-sectional data involving heterogeneous units, heteroscedasticity may be the rule rather than the exception. Thus, in a cross-sectional analysis involving the investment expenditure in relation to sales, rate of interest, etc., heteroscedasticity is generally expected if small-, medium-, and large-size firms are sampled together.

Graphical method. If there is no a priori or empirical information about the nature of heteroscedasticity, in practice one can do the regression analysis on the assumption that there is no heteroscedasticity and then do a postmortem examination of the residual squared $\hat{u}_i^2$ to see if they exhibit any systematic pattern. Although $\hat{u}_i^2$ are not the same thing as u_i^2, they can be used as proxies especially if the sample size is sufficiently large.[8] An examination of the $\hat{u}_i^2$ may reveal patterns such as those shown in Fig. 11.7.

In Fig. 11.7, $\hat{u}_i^2$ are plotted against $\hat{Y}_i$, the estimated Y_i from the regression line, the idea being to find out whether the estimated mean value of Y is systematically related to the squared residual. In Fig. 11.7a we see that there is no systematic pattern between the two variables, suggesting that perhaps no heteroscedasticity is present in the data. Figures 11.7b to e, however, exhibit definite patterns. For instance, Fig. 11.7c suggests a linear relationship, whereas Figs. 11.7d and e indicate a quadratic relationship between $\hat{u}_i^2$ and $\hat{Y}_i$. Using such knowledge, albeit informal, one may transform the data in such a manner that the transformed data do not exhibit heteroscedasticity. In Section 11.6 we shall examine several such transformations.

Instead of plotting $\hat{u}_i^2$ against $\hat{Y}_i$, one may plot them against one of the explanatory variables, especially if plotting $\hat{u}_i^2$ against $\hat{Y}_i$ results in the pattern

---

[7] S. J. Prais and H. S. Houthakker, *The Analysis of Family Budgets*, Cambridge University Press, New York, 1955.

[8] For the relationship between $\hat{u}_i$ and u_i, see E. Malinvaud, *Statistical Methods of Econometrics*, North Holland Publishing Company, Amsterdam, 1970, pp. 88–89.

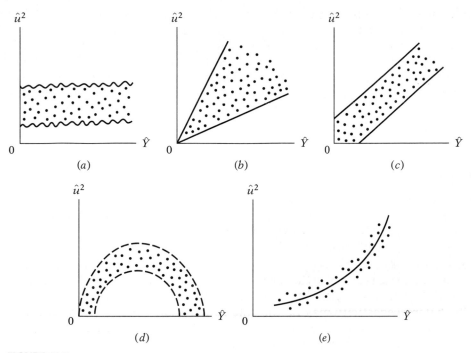

FIGURE 11.7
Hypothetical patterns of estimated squared residuals.

shown in Fig. 11.7a. Such a plot, which is shown in Fig. 11.8, may reveal patterns similar to those given in Fig. 11.7. (In the case of the two-variable model, plotting $\hat{u}_i^2$ against $\hat{Y}_i$ is equivalent to plotting it against X_i, and therefore Fig. 11.8 is similar to Fig. 11.7. But this is not the situation when we consider a model involving two or more X variables; in this instance, $\hat{u}_i^2$ may be plotted against any X variable included in the model.)

A pattern such as that shown in Fig. 11.8c, for instance, suggests that the variance of the disturbance term is linearly related to the X variable. Thus, if in the regression of savings on income one finds a pattern such as that shown in Fig. 11.8c, it suggests that the heteroscedastic variance may be *proportional* to the value of the income variable. This knowledge may help us in transforming our data in such a manner that in the regression on the transformed data the variance of the disturbance is homoscedastic. We shall return to this topic in the next section.

Formal Methods

Park test.[9]   Park formalizes the graphical method by suggesting that σ_i^2 is some function of the explanatory variable X_i. The functional form he suggested

[9]R. E. Park, "Estimation with Heteroscedastic Error Terms," *Econometrica*, vol. 34, no. 4, October 1966, p. 888. The Park test is a special case of the general test proposed by A. C. Harvey in "Estimating Regression Models with Multiplicative Heteroscedasticity," *Econometrica*, vol. 44, no. 3, 1976, pp. 461–465.

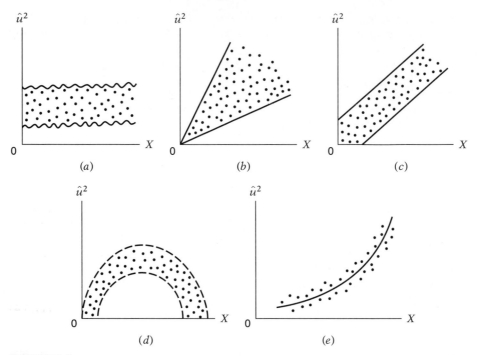

FIGURE 11.8
Scattergram of estimated squared residuals against X.

was

$$\sigma_i^2 = \sigma^2 X_i^\beta e^{v_i}$$

or

$$\ln \sigma_i^2 = \ln \sigma^2 + \beta \ln X_i + v_i \tag{11.5.1}$$

where v_i is the stochastic disturbance term.

Since σ_i^2 is generally not known, Park suggests using $\hat{u}_i^2$ as a proxy and running the following regression:

$$
\begin{aligned}
\ln \hat{u}_i^2 &= \ln \sigma^2 + \beta \ln X_i + v_i \\
&= \alpha + \beta \ln X_i + v_i
\end{aligned}
\tag{11.5.2}
$$

If β turns out to be statistically significant, it would suggest that heteroscedasticity is present in the data. If it turns out to be insignificant, we may accept the assumption of homoscedasticity. The Park test is thus a two-stage procedure. In the first stage we run the OLS regression disregarding the heteroscedasticity question. We obtain $\hat{u}_i$ from this regression, and then in the second stage we run the regression (11.5.2).

Although empirically appealing, the Park test has some problems. Goldfeld and Quandt have argued that the error term v_i entering into (11.5.2) may not satisfy the OLS assumptions and may itself be heteroscedastic.[10] Nonetheless, as a strictly exploratory method, one may use the Park test.

---

[10] Stephen M. Goldfeld and Richard E. Quandt, *Nonlinear Methods in Econometrics*, North Holland Publishing Company, Amsterdam, 1972, pp. 93–94.

Example 11.1. Relationship between compensation and productivity. To illustrate the Park approach, we use the data given in Table 11.1 to run the following regression:

$$Y_i = \beta_1 + \beta_2 X_i + u_i$$

where Y = average compensation in thousands of dollars, X = average productivity in thousands of dollars, and i = ith employment size of the establishment. The results of the regression were as follows:

$$\hat{Y}_i = 1992.3452 + 0.2329 X_i$$
$$\text{se} = (936.4791) \quad (0.0998) \tag{11.5.3}$$
$$t = (2.1275) \quad (2.333) \qquad R^2 = 0.4375$$

The results reveal that the estimated slope coefficient is significant at the 5% level on the basis of a one-tail t test. The equation shows that as labor productivity increases by, say, a dollar, labor compensation on the average increases by about 23 cents.

The residuals obtained from regression (11.5.3) were regressed on X_i as suggested in Eq. (11.5.2), giving the following results:

$$\ln \hat{u}_i^2 = 35.817 - 2.8099 \ln X_i$$
$$\text{se} = (38.319) \quad (4.216) \tag{11.5.4}$$
$$t = (0.934)(-0.667) \qquad R^2 = 0.0595$$

Obviously, there is no statistically significant relationship between the two variables. Following the Park test, one may conclude that there is no heteroscedasticity in the error variance.[11]

Glejser test.[12]   The Glejser test is similar in spirit to the Park test. After obtaining the residuals $\hat{u}_i$ from the OLS regression, Glejser suggests regressing the absolute values of $\hat{u}_i$ on the X variable that is thought to be closely associated with σ_i^2. In his experiments, Glejser used the following functional forms:

$$|\hat{u}_i| = \beta_1 + \beta_2 X_i + v_i$$
$$|\hat{u}_i| = \beta_1 + \beta_2 \sqrt{X_i} + v_i$$
$$|\hat{u}_i| = \beta_1 + \beta_2 \frac{1}{X_i} + v_i$$
$$|\hat{u}_i| = \beta_1 + \beta_2 \frac{1}{\sqrt{X_i}} + v_i$$
$$|\hat{u}_i| = \sqrt{\beta_1 + \beta_2 X_i} + v_i$$
$$|\hat{u}_i| = \sqrt{\beta_1 + \beta_2 X_i^2} + v_i$$

where v_i is the error term.

---

[11]The particular functional form chosen by Park is only suggestive. A different functional form may reveal significant relationships. For example, one may use $\hat{u}_i^2$ instead of $\ln \hat{u}_i^2$ as the dependent variable.

[12]H. Glejser, "A New Test for Heteroscedasticity," *Journal of the American Statistical Association*, vol. 64, 1969, pp. 316–323.

Again as an empirical or practical matter, one may use the Glejser approach. But Goldfeld and Quandt point out that the error term v_i has some problems in that its expected value is nonzero, it is serially correlated (see Chapter 12), and ironically it is heteroscedastic.[13] An additional difficulty with the Glejser method is that models such as

$$|\hat{u}_i| = \sqrt{\beta_1 + \beta_2 X_i} + v_i \quad \text{and} \quad |\hat{u}_i| = \sqrt{\beta_1 + \beta_2 X_i^2} + v_i$$

are nonlinear in the parameters and therefore cannot be estimated with the usual OLS procedure.

Glejser has found that for large samples the first four of the preceding models give generally satisfactory results in detecting heteroscedasticity. As a practical matter, therefore, the Glejser technique may be used for large samples and may be used in the small samples strictly as a qualitative device to learn something about heteroscedasticity. For an application of the Glejser method, see Section 11.7.

Spearman's rank correlation test.   In exercise 3.8 we defined the Spearman's rank correlation coefficient as

$$r_s = 1 - 6 \left[\frac{\sum d_i^2}{n(n^2 - 1)} \right] \tag{11.5.5}$$

where d_i = difference in the ranks assigned to two different characteristics of the ith individual or phenomenon and n = number of individuals or phenomena ranked. The preceding rank correlation coefficient can be used to detect heteroscedasticity as follows: Assume $Y_i = \beta_0 + \beta_1 X_i + u_i$.

Step 1.   Fit the regression to the data on Y and X and obtain the residuals $\hat{u}_i$.

Step 2.   Ignoring the sign of $\hat{u}_i$, that is, taking their absolute value $|\hat{u}_i|$, rank both $|\hat{u}_i|$ and X_i (or $\hat{Y}_i$) according to an ascending or descending order and compute the Spearman's rank correlation coefficient given previously.

Step 3.   Assuming that the population rank correlation coefficient ρ_s is zero and $n > 8$, the significance of the sample r_s can be tested by the t test as follows:[14]

$$t = \frac{r_s \sqrt{n - 2}}{\sqrt{1 - r_s^2}} \tag{11.5.6}$$

with df $= n - 2$.

---

[13] For details, see Goldfeld and Quandt, op. cit., Chap. 3.

[14] See G. Udny Yule and M. G. Kendall, *An Introduction to the Theory of Statistics*, Charles Griffin & Company, London, 1953, p. 455.

If the computed t value exceeds the critical t value, we may accept the hypothesis of heteroscedasticity; otherwise we may reject it. If the regression model involves more than one X variable, r_s can be computed between $|\hat{u}_i|$ and each of the X variables separately and can be tested for statistical significance by the t test given in Eq. (11.5.6).

Example 11.2. Illustration of the rank correlation test. To illustrate the rank correlation test, consider the data given in Table 11.2, which are a subsample from the data of the table pertaining to exercise 5.16, which asks you to estimate the capital market line of the portfolio theory, namely, $E_i = \beta_1 + \beta_2 \sigma_i$, where E is expected return on portfolio and σ is the standard deviation of return. Since the data relate to 10 mutual funds of differing sizes and investment goals, a priori one might expect heteroscedasticity. To test this hypothesis, we apply the rank correlation technique. The necessary calculations are also shown in Table 11.2.

Applying formula (11.5.5), we obtain

$$r_s = 1 - 6\frac{110}{10(100 - 1)}$$

$$= 0.3333 \tag{11.5.7}$$

Applying the t test given in (11.5.6), we obtain

$$t = \frac{(0.3333)(\sqrt{8})}{\sqrt{1 - 0.1110}}$$

$$= 0.9998 \tag{11.5.8}$$

TABLE 11.2
Rank correlation test of heteroscedasticity

Name of mutual fund	E_i, average annual return, %	σ_i, standard deviation of annual return, %	$\hat{E}_i$*	$\|\hat{u}_i\|$† residuals, $\|(E_i - \hat{E}_i)\|$	Rank of $\|\hat{u}_i\|$	Rank of σ_i	d, difference between two rankings	d^2
Boston Fund	12.4	12.1	11.37	1.03	9	4	5	25
Delaware Fund	14.4	21.4	15.64	1.24	10	9	1	1
Equity Fund	14.6	18.7	14.40	0.20	4	7	−3	9
Fundamental Investors	16.0	21.7	15.78	0.22	5	10	−5	25
Investors Mutual	11.3	12.5	11.56	0.26	6	5	1	1
Loomis-Sales Mutual Fund	10.0	10.4	10.59	0.59	7	2	5	25
Massachusetts Investors Trust	16.2	20.8	15.37	0.83	8	8	0	0
New England Fund	10.4	10.2	10.50	0.10	3	1	2	4
Putnam Fund of Boston	13.1	16.0	13.16	0.06	2	6	−4	16
Wellington Fund	11.3	12.0	11.33	0.03	1	3	−2	4
Total							0	110

*Obtained from the regression: $\hat{E}_i = 5.8194 + 0.4590\sigma_i$.

†Absolute value of the residuals.

Note: The ranking is in ascending order of values.

For 8 df this t value is not significant even at the 10% level of significance; the p **value** is 0.17. Thus, there is no evidence of a systematic relationship between the explanatory variable and the absolute values of the residuals, which might suggest that there is no heteroscedasticity.

Goldfeld-Quandt test.[15] This popular method is applicable if one assumes that the heteroscedastic variance, σ_i^2, is positively related to *one* of the explanatory variables in the regression model. For simplicity, consider the usual two-variable model:

$$Y_i = \beta_1 + \beta_2 X_i + u_i$$

Suppose σ_i^2 is positively related to X_i as

$$\sigma_i^2 = \sigma^2 X_i^2 \qquad (11.5.9)$$

where σ^2 is a constant.[16]

Assumption (11.5.9) postulates that σ_i^2 is proportional to the square of the X variable. Such an assumption has been found quite useful by Prais and Houthakker in their study of family budgets. (See Section 11.6.)

If (11.5.9) is appropriate, it would mean σ_i^2 would be larger, the larger the values of X_i. If that turns out to be the case, heteroscedasticity is most likely to be present in the model. To test this explicitly, Goldfeld and Quandt suggest the following steps:

Step 1. Order or rank the observations according to the values of X_i, beginning with the lowest X value.

Step 2. Omit c central observations, where c is specified a priori, and divide the remaining $(n - c)$ observations into two groups each of $(n - c)/2$ observations.

Step 3. Fit separate OLS regressions to the first $(n-c)/2$ observations and the last $(n - c)/2$ observations, and obtain the respective residual sums of squares RSS_1 and RSS_2, RSS_1 representing the RSS from the regression corresponding to the smaller X_i values (the small variance group) and RSS_2 that from the larger X_i values (the large variance group). These RSS each have

$$\frac{(n - c)}{2} - k \quad \text{or} \quad \left(\frac{n - c - 2k}{2}\right) \text{df}$$

where k is the number of parameters to be estimated, including the intercept. (Why?) For the two-variable case k is of course 2.

Step 4. Compute the ratio

$$\lambda = \frac{RSS_2/\text{df}}{RSS_1/\text{df}} \qquad (11.5.10)$$

---

[15] Goldfeld and Quandt, op. cit., Chap. 3.

[16] This is only one plausible assumption. Actually, what is required is that σ_i^2 be monotonically related to X_i.

If u_i are assumed to be normally distributed (which we usually do), and *if the assumption of homoscedasticity is valid*, then it can be shown that λ of (11.5.10) follows the F distribution with numerator and denominator df each of $(n - c - 2k)/2$.

If in an application the computed $\lambda(= F)$ is greater than the critical F at the chosen level of significance, we can reject the hypothesis of homoscedasticity, that is, we can say that heteroscedasticity is very likely.

Before illustrating the test, a word about omitting the c central observations is in order. These observations are omitted to sharpen or accentuate the difference between the small variance group (i.e., RSS_1) and the large variance group (i.e., RSS_2). But the ability of the Goldfeld-Quandt test to do this successfully depends on how c is chosen.[17] For the two-variable model the Monte Carlo experiments done by Goldfeld and Quandt suggest that c is about 8 if the sample size is about 30, and it is about 16 if the sample size is about 60. But Judge et al. note that $c = 4$ if $n = 30$ and $c = 10$ if n is about 60 have been found satisfactory in practice.[18]

Before moving on, it may be noted that in case there is more than one X variable in the model, the ranking of observations, the first step in the test, can be done according to any one of them. Thus in the model: $Y_i = \beta_1 + \beta_2 X_{2i} + \beta_3 X_{3i} + \beta_4 X_{4i} + u_i$, we can rank-order the data according to any one of these X's. If a priori we are not sure which X variable is appropriate, we can conduct the test on each of the X variables, or via a Park test, in turn, on each X.

Example 11.3. The Goldfeld-Quandt test. To illustrate the Goldfeld-Quandt test, we present in Table 11.3 data on consumption expenditure in relation to income for a cross section of 30 families. Suppose we postulate that consumption expenditure is linearly related to income but that heteroscedasticity is present in the data. We further postulate that the nature of heteroscedasticity is as given in (11.5.9). The necessary reordering of the data for the application of the test is also presented in Table 11.3.

Dropping the middle 4 observations, the OLS regressions based on the first 13 and the last 13 observations and their associated residual sums of squares are as shown next (standard errors in the parentheses).

Regression based on the first 13 observations:

$$\hat{Y}_i = 3.4094 + 0.6968X_i$$
$$(8.7049) \quad (0.0744) \qquad r^2 = 0.8887$$
$$RSS_1 = 377.17$$
$$df = 11$$

---

[17]Technically, the **power** of the test depends on how c is chosen. In statistics, the *power of a test* is measured by the probability of rejecting the null hypothesis when it is false [i.e., by $1 - \text{Prob}$ (type II error)]. Here the null hypothesis is that the variances of the two groups are the same, i.e., homoscedasticity. For further discussion, see M. M. Ali and C. Giaccotto, "A Study of Several New and Existing Tests for Heteroscedasticity in the General Linear Model," *Journal of Econometrics*, vol. 26, 1984, pp. 355–373.

[18]George G. Judge, R. Carter Hill, William E. Griffiths, Helmut Lütkepohl, and Tsoung-Chao Lee, *Introduction to the Theory and Practice of Econometrics*, John Wiley & Sons, New York, 1982, p. 422.

TABLE 11.3
Hypothetical data on consumption expenditure $Y(\$)$ and income $X(\$)$ to illustrate the Goldfeld-Quandt test

Y	X	Data ranked by X values Y	Data ranked by X values X	
55	80	55	80	
65	100	70	85	
70	85	75	90	
80	110	65	100	
79	120	74	105	
84	115	80	110	
98	130	84	115	
95	140	79	120	
90	125	90	125	
75	90	98	130	
74	105	95	140	
110	160	108	145	
113	150	113	150	
125	165	110	160	
108	145	125	165	Middle 4
115	180	115	180	observations
140	225	130	185	
120	200	135	190	
145	240	120	200	
130	185	140	205	
152	220	144	210	
144	210	152	220	
175	245	140	225	
180	260	137	230	
135	190	145	240	
140	205	175	245	
178	265	189	250	
191	270	180	260	
137	230	178	265	
189	250	191	270	

Regression based on the last 13 observations:

$$\hat{Y}_i = -28.0272 + 0.7941X_i$$
$$(30.6421) \quad (0.1319) \qquad\qquad r^2 = 0.7681$$
$$\text{RSS}_2 = 1536.8$$
$$\text{df} = 11$$

From these results we obtain

$$\lambda = \frac{\text{RSS}_2/\text{df}}{\text{RSS}_1/\text{df}} = \frac{1536.8/11}{377.17/11}$$
$$\lambda = 4.07$$

The critical F value for 11 numerator and 11 denominator df at the 5% level is 2.82. Since the estimated $F(= \lambda)$ value exceeds the critical value, we may conclude that there is heteroscedasticity in the error variance. However, if the level of significance is fixed at 1 percent, we may not reject the assumption of homoscedasticity. (Why?) Note that the p value of the observed λ is 0.014.

Breusch-Pagan-Godfrey test.[19] The success of the Goldfeld-Quandt test depends not only on the value of c (the number of central observations to be omitted) but also on identifying the correct X variable with which to order the observations. This limitation of this test can be avoided if we consider the **Breusch-Pagan-Godfrey (BPG) test**.

To illustrate this test, consider the k-variable linear regression model

$$Y_i = \beta_1 + \beta_2 X_{2i} + \cdots + \beta_k X_{ki} + u_i \tag{11.5.11}$$

Assume that the error variance σ_i^2 is described as

$$\sigma_i^2 = f(\alpha_1 + \alpha_2 Z_{2i} + \cdots + \alpha_m Z_{mi}) \tag{11.5.12}$$

that is, σ_i^2 is some function of the nonstochastic variables Z's; some or all of the X's can serve as Z's. Specifically, assume that

$$\sigma_i^2 = \alpha_1 + \alpha_2 Z_{2i} + \cdots + \alpha_m Z_{mi} \tag{11.5.13}$$

that is, σ_i^2 is a linear function of the Z's. If $\alpha_2 = \alpha_3 = \cdots = \alpha_m = 0$, $\sigma_i^2 = \alpha_1$, which is a constant. Therefore, to test whether σ_i^2 is homoscedastic, one can test the hypothesis that $\alpha_2 = \alpha_3 = \cdots = \alpha_m = 0$. This is the basic idea behind the Breusch-Pagan test. The actual test procedure is as follows.

Step 1. Estimate (11.5.11) by OLS and obtain the residuals $\hat{u}_1, \hat{u}_2, \ldots, \hat{u}_n$.

Step 2. Obtain $\tilde{\sigma}^2 = \sum \hat{u}_i^2/n$. Recall from Chapter 4 that this is the maximum likelihood (ML) estimator of σ^2. [*Note:* The OLS estimator is $\sum \hat{u}_i^2/(n - k)$.]

Step 3. Construct variables p_i defined as

$$p_i = \hat{u}_i^2/\tilde{\sigma}^2$$

which is simply each residual squared divided by $\tilde{\sigma}^2$.

Step 4. Regress p_i thus constructed on the Z's as

$$p_i = \alpha_1 + \alpha_2 Z_{2i} + \cdots + \alpha_m Z_{mi} + v_i \tag{11.5.14}$$

where v_i is the residual term of this regression.

Step 5. Obtain the ESS (explained sum of squares) from (11.5.14) and define

$$\Theta = \tfrac{1}{2}(\text{ESS}) \tag{11.5.15}$$

[19]T. Breusch and A. Pagan, "A Simple Test for Heteroscedasticity and Random Coefficient Variation," *Econometrica*, vol. 47, 1979, pp. 1287–1294. See also L. Godfrey, "Testing for Multiplicative Heteroscedasticity," *Journal of Econometrics*, vol. 8, 1978, pp. 227–236. Because of similarity, these tests are known as Breusch-Pagan-Godfrey tests of heteroscedasticity.

Assuming u_i are normally distributed, one can show that if there is homoscedasticity and if the sample size n increases indefinitely, then

$$\Theta \underset{\text{asy}}{\sim} \chi^2_{m-1} \qquad (11.5.16)$$

that is, Θ follows the chi-square distribution with $(m - 1)$ degrees of freedom. (*Note: asy* means asymptotically.)

Therefore, if in an application the computed $\Theta (= \chi^2)$ exceeds the critical χ^2 value at the chosen level of significance, one can reject the hypothesis of homoscedasticity; otherwise one does not reject it.

Example 11.4. The Breusch-Pagan-Godfrey test. As an example, let us revisit the data (Table 11.3) that were used to illustrate the Goldfeld-Quandt heteroscedasticity test. Regressing Y on X, we obtain the following:

Step 1.

$$\hat{Y}_i = 9.2903 + 0.6378X_i$$
$$\text{se} = (5.2314) \quad (0.0286) \qquad \text{RSS} = 2361.153 \qquad (11.5.17)$$
$$R^2 = 0.9466$$

Step 2.

$$\tilde{\sigma}^2 = \sum \hat{u}_i^2/30 = 2361.153/30 = 78.7051$$

Step 3. Divide the residuals $\hat{u}_i$ obtained from regression (11.5.17) by 78.7051 to construct the variable p_i.

Step 4. Assuming that p_i are linearly related to $X_i (= Z_i)$ as per (11.5.13), we obtain the regression

$$\hat{p}_i = -0.7426 + 0.0101X_i$$
$$\text{se} = (0.7529) \quad (0.0041) \qquad \text{ESS} = 10.4280 \qquad (11.5.18)$$
$$R^2 = 0.18$$

Step 5.

$$\Theta = \tfrac{1}{2}(\text{ESS}) = 5.2140 \qquad (11.5.19)$$

Under the assumptions of the BPG test Θ in (11.5.19) asymptotically follows the chi-square distribution with 1 df. [*Note:* There is only one regressor in (11.5.18).] Now from the chi-square table we find that for 1 df the 5% critical chi-square value is 3.8414 and the 1% critical F value is 6.6349. Thus, the observed chi-square value of 5.2140 is significant at the 5% but not the 1% level of significance. Therefore, we reach the same conclusion as the Goldfeld-Quandt test. But keep in mind that, strictly speaking, the BPG test is an asymptotic, or large-sample, test and in the present example 30 observations may not constitute a large sample. It should also be pointed out that in small samples the test is sensitive to the assumption that the disturbances u_i are normally distributed. Of course, we can test the normality assumption by the chi-square or **Bera-Jarque** tests discussed previously.[20]

---

[20] On this, see R. Koenker, "A Note on Studentizing a Test for Heteroscedasticity," *Journal of Econometrics*, vol. 17, 1981, pp. 1180–1200.

White's general heteroscedasticity test. Unlike the Goldfeld-Quandt test, which requires reordering the observations with respect to the X variable that supposedly caused heteroscedasticity, or the BGP test, which is sensitive to the normality assumption, the general test of heteroscedasticity proposed by White does not rely on the normality assumption and is easy to implement.[21] As an illustration of the basic idea, consider the following three-variable regression model (the generalization to the k-variable model is straightforward):

$$Y_i = \beta_1 + \beta_2 X_{2i} + \beta_3 X_{3i} + u_i \tag{11.5.20}$$

The White test proceeds as follows:

Step 1. Given the data, we estimate (11.5.20) and obtain the residuals, $\hat{u}_i$.

Step 2. We then run the following (*auxiliary*) regression:

$$\hat{u}_i^2 = \alpha_1 + \alpha_2 X_{2i} + \alpha_3 X_{3i} + \alpha_4 X_{2i}^2 + \alpha_5 X_{3i}^2$$
$$+ \alpha_6 X_{2i} X_{3i} + v_i \tag{11.5.21}^{22}$$

That is, the squared residuals from the original regression are regressed on the original X variables or regressors, their squared values, and the cross product(s) of the regressors. Higher powers of regressors can also be introduced. Note that there is a constant term in this equation even though the original regression may or may not contain it. Obtain the R^2 from this (auxiliary) regression.

Step 3. Under the null hypothesis that there is no heteroscedasticity, it can be shown that sample size (n) times the R^2 obtained from the auxiliary regression *asymptotically* follows the chi-square distribution with df equal to the number of regressors (excluding the constant term) in the auxiliary regression. That is,

$$n \cdot R^2 \underset{\text{asy}}{\sim} \chi_{\text{df}}^2 \tag{11.5.22}$$

where df is as defined previously. In our example, there are 5 df since there are 5 regressors in the auxiliary regression.

Step 4. If the chi-square value obtained in (11.5.22) exceeds the critical chi-square value at the chosen level of significance, the conclusion is that there is heteroscedasticity. If it does not exceed the critical chi-square value, there is no heteroscedasticity, which is to say that in the auxiliary regression (11.5.21), $\alpha_2 = \alpha_3 = \alpha_4 = \alpha_5 = \alpha_6 = 0$ (see footnote 22).

---

[21] H. White, "A Heteroscedasticity Consistent Covariance Matrix Estimator and a Direct Test of Heteroscedasticity," *Econometrica*, vol. 48, 1980, pp. 817–818.

[22] Implied in this procedure is the assumption that the error variance of u_i, σ_i^2, is functionally related to the regressors, their squares, and their cross products. If all the partial slope coefficients in this regression are simultaneously equal to zero, then the error variance is the homoscedastic constant equal to α_1.

Example 11.5. White's heteroscedasticity test. Based on cross-sectional data on 41 countries, Stephen Lewis estimated the following regression model:[23]

$$\ln Y_i = \beta_1 + \beta_2 \ln X_{2i} + \beta_3 \ln X_{3i} + u_i \qquad (11.5.23)$$

where Y = ratio of trade taxes (import and export taxes) to total government revenue, X_2 = ratio of the sum of exports plus imports to GNP, and X_3 = GNP per capita; and ln stands for natural log. His hypotheses were that Y and X_2 would be positively related (the higher the trade volume, the higher the trade tax revenue) and that Y and X_3 would be negatively related (as income increases, government finds it is easier to collect direct taxes—e.g., income tax—than rely on trade taxes).

The empirical results supported the hypotheses. For our purpose, the important point is whether there is heteroscedasticity in the data. Since the data are cross-sectional involving a heterogeneity of countries, a priori one would expect heteroscedasticity in the error variance. By applying **White's heteroscedasticity test** to the residuals obtained from regression (11.5.23), the following results were obtained:[24]

$$\hat{u}_i^2 = -5.8417 + 2.5629 \ln \text{Trade}_i + 0.6918 \ln \text{GNP}_i$$
$$-0.4081(\ln \text{Trade}_i)^2 - 0.0491(\ln \text{GNP}_i)^2 \qquad (11.5.24)$$
$$+0.0015(\ln \text{Trade}_i)(\ln \text{GNP}_i) \qquad\qquad R^2 = 0.1148$$

Note: The standard errors are not given, as they are not pertinent for our purpose here.

Now $n \cdot R^2 = 41(0.1148) = 4.7068$, which has, asymptotically, a chi-square distribution with 5 df (why?). The 5% critical chi-square value for 5 df is 11.0705, the 10% critical value is 9.2363, and the 25% critical value is 6.62568. For all practical purposes, one can conclude, on the basis of the White test, that there is no heteroscedasticity.

A comment is in order regarding the White test. If a model has several regressors, then introducing all the regressors, their squared (or higher powered) terms, and their cross products can quickly consume degrees of freedom. Therefore, one must exercise caution in using the test. Sometimes one can omit the cross product terms. In cases where the test statistic is significant, heteroscedasticity may not necessarily be the cause, but specification errors, about which more will be said in Chapter 13 (recall Point #5 of Sec. 11.1). In other words, **the White test can be a test of (pure) heteroscedasticity or specification error or both.**

Other tests of heteroscedasticity. There are several other tests of heteroscedasticity, each based on certain assumptions. The interested reader may want to consult the references.[25]

---

[23]Stephen R. Lewis, "Government Revenue from Foreign Trade," *Manchester School of Economics and Social Studies*, vol. 31, 1963, pp. 39–47.

[24]These results, with change in notation, are reproduced from William F. Lott and Subhash C. Ray, *Applied Econometrics: Problems with Data Sets*, Instructor's Manual, Chap. 22, pp. 137–140.

[25]See M. J. Harrison and B. P. McCabe, "A Test for Heteroscedasticity Based on Ordinary Least Squares Residuals," *Journal of the American Statistical Association*, vol. 74, 1979, pp. 494–499; J. Szroeter, "A Class of Parametric Tests for Heteroscedasticity in Linear Econometric Models," *Econometrica*, vol. 46, 1978, pp. 1311–1327; M. A. Evans and M. L. King, "A Further Class of Tests for Heteroscedasticity," *Journal of Econometrics*, vol. 37, 1988, pp. 265–276.

11.6 REMEDIAL MEASURES

As we have seen, heteroscedasticity does not destroy the unbiasedness and consistency properties of the OLS estimators, but they are no longer efficient, not even asymptotically (i.e., large sample size). This lack of efficiency makes the usual hypothesis-testing procedure of dubious value. Therefore, remedial measures are clearly called for. There are two approaches to remediation: when σ_i^2 is known and when σ_i^2 is not known.

When σ_i^2 Is Known: The Method of Weighted Least Squares

As we have seen in Section 11.3, if σ_i^2 is known, the most straightforward method of correcting heteroscedasticity is by means of weighted least squares, for the estimators thus obtained are BLUE.

> **Example 11.6. Illustration of the method of weighted least squares.** To illustrate the method, suppose we want to study the relationship between compensation and employment size for the data presented in Table 11.1. For simplicity, we measure employment size by 1 (1–4 employees), 2 (5–9 employees), ..., 9 (1000–2499 employees), although we could also measure it by the midpoint of the various employment classes given in the table (see exercise 11.21.)
>
> Now letting Y represent average compensation per employee (\$) and X the employment size, we run the following regression [see Eq. (11.3.6)]:
>
> $$Y_i/\sigma_i = \hat{\beta}_1^*(1/\sigma_i) + \hat{\beta}_2^*(X_i/\sigma_i) + (\hat{u}_i/\sigma_i) \qquad (11.6.1)$$
>
> where σ_i are the standard deviations of wages as reported in Table 11.1. The necessary raw data to run this regression are given in Table 11.4.
>
> Before going on to the regression results, note that (11.6.1) has no intercept term. (Why?) Therefore, one will have to use the regression-through-the-origin

TABLE 11.4
Illustration of weighted least-squares regression

Compensation, Y	Employment size, X	σ_i	Y_i/σ_i	X_i/σ_i
3396	1	743.7	4.5664	0.0013
3787	2	851.4	4.4480	0.0023
4013	3	727.8	5.5139	0.0041
4104	4	805.06	5.0978	0.0050
4146	5	929.9	4.4585	0.0054
4241	6	1080.6	3.9247	0.0055
4387	7	1243.2	3.5288	0.0056
4538	8	1307.7	3.4702	0.0061
4843	9	1112.5	4.3532	0.0081

Note: In regression (11.6.2), the dependent variable is (Y_i/σ_i) and the independent variables are $(1/\sigma_i)$ and (X_i/σ_i).

Source: Data on Y and σ_i (standard deviation of compensation) are from Table 11.1. Employment size: 1 = 1–4 employees, 2 = 5–9 employees, etc. The latter data are also from Table 11.1.

model to estimate β_1^* and β_2^*, a topic discussed in Chapter 6. But most computer packages these days have an option to suppress the intercept term (see SAS, for example). Also note another interesting feature of (11.6.1): It has two explanatory variables, $(1/\sigma_i)$ and (X_i/σ_i), whereas if we were to use OLS, regressing compensation on employment size, that regression would have a single explanatory variable, X_i. (Why?)

The regression results of WLS are as follows:

$$\widehat{(Y_i/\sigma_i)} = 3406.639(1/\sigma_i) + 154.153(X_i/\sigma_i)$$
$$(80.983) \qquad\qquad (16.959) \qquad\qquad\qquad (11.6.2)$$
$$t = \quad (42.066) \qquad\qquad (9.090)$$
$$R^2 = 0.9993^{26}$$

For comparison, we give the usual or unweighted OLS regression results:

$$\hat{Y_i} = 3417.833 + 148.767X_i$$
$$(81.136) \quad (14.418) \qquad\qquad\qquad (11.6.3)$$
$$t = \quad (42.125) \quad (10.318) \qquad R^2 = 0.9383$$

In exercise 11.7 you are asked to compare these two regressions.

When σ_i^2 Is Not Known

As noted earlier, if true σ_i^2 are known, we can use the WLS method to obtain BLUE estimators. Since the true σ_i^2 are rarely known, is there a way of obtaining *consistent* (in the statistical sense) estimates of the variances and covariances of OLS estimators even if there is heteroscedasticity? The answer is yes.

White's heteroscedasticity-consistent variances and standard errors. White has shown that this estimate can be performed so that asymptotically valid (i.e., large-sample) statistical inferences can be made about the true parameter values.[27] We will not present the mathematical details, for they are beyond the scope of this book. But several computer packages (e.g., TSP, ET, SHAZAM) now present White's heteroscedasticity-corrected variances and standard errors along with the usual OLS variances and standard errors.[28]

Example 11.7. Illustration of White's procedure. As an example, we quote the following results due to Greene:[29]

---

[26] As noted in footnote 3 of Chap. 6, the R^2 of the regression through the origin is not directly comparable with the R^2 of the intercept-present model. The reported R^2 of 0.9993 takes this difference into account. (See the SAS package for further details about how the R^2 is corrected to take into account the absence of the intercept term. See also App. 6A, Sec. 6A1.)

[27] See H. White, op. cit.

[28] More technically, they are known as **heteroscedasticity-consistent covariance matrix estimators, HCCME** for short.

[29] William H. Greene, *Econometric Analysis*, 2d ed., Macmillan, New York, 1993, p. 385.

$$\hat{Y}_i = 832.91 - 1834.2\,(\text{Income}) + 1587.04\,(\text{Income})^2$$

$$
\begin{aligned}
\text{OLS se} &= (327.3) \quad\quad (829.0) \quad\quad\quad (519.1) \\
t &= \quad (2.54) \quad\quad\; (2.21) \quad\quad\quad\; (3.06) \quad\quad\quad\quad (11.6.4) \\
\text{White se} &= (460.9) \quad\quad (1243.0) \quad\quad\quad (830.0) \\
t &= \quad (1.81) \quad\quad (-1.48) \quad\quad\quad\; (1.91)
\end{aligned}
$$

where Y = per capita expenditure on public schools by state in 1979 and Income = per capita income by state in 1979. The sample consisted of 50 states plus Washington, D.C.

. As the preceding results show, (White's) heteroscedasticity-corrected standard errors are considerably larger than the OLS standard errors and therefore the estimated t values are much smaller than those obtained by OLS. On the basis of the latter, both the regressors are statistically significant at the 5% level, whereas on the basis of White estimators they are not. However, it should be pointed out that White's heteroscedasticity-corrected standard errors can be larger or smaller than the uncorrected standard errors.

Since White's heteroscedasticity-consistent estimators of the variances are now available in established regression packages, it is recommended that the reader report them. As Wallace and Silver note:

> Generally speaking, it is probably a good idea to use the WHITE option [available in regression programs] routinely, perhaps comparing the output with regular OLS output as a check to see whether heteroscedasticity is a serious problem in a particular set of data.[30]

Plausible assumptions about heteroscedasticity pattern. Apart from being a large-sample procedure, one drawback of the White procedure is that the estimators thus obtained may not be so efficient as those obtained by methods that transform data to reflect specific types of heteroscedasticity. To illustrate this, let us revert to the two-variable regression model:

$$Y_i = \beta_1 + \beta_2 X_i + u_i$$

We now consider several assumptions about the pattern of heteroscedasticity.

Assumption 1: The error variance is proportional to X_i^2:

$$E(u_i^2) = \sigma^2 X_i^2 \qquad (11.6.5)^{31}$$

If, as a matter of "speculation," graphical methods, or Park and Glejser approaches, it is believed that the variance of u_i is proportional to the square

---

[30] T. Dudley Wallace and J. Lew Silver, *Econometrics: An Introduction*, Reading, Mass., 1988, p. 265.
[31] Recall that we have already encountered this assumption in our discussion of the Goldfeld-Quandt test.

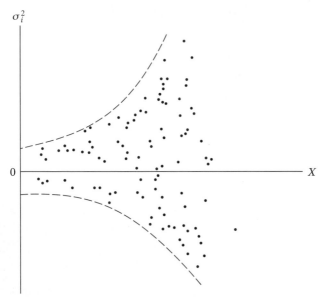

FIGURE 11.9
Error variance proportional to X^2.

of the explanatory variable X (see Fig. 11.9), one may transform the original model as follows. Divide the original model through by X_i:

$$\frac{Y_i}{X_i} = \frac{\beta_1}{X_i} + \beta_2 + \frac{u_i}{X_i}$$

$$= \beta_1 \frac{1}{X_i} + \beta_2 + v_i \tag{11.6.6}$$

where v_i is the transformed disturbance term, equal to u_i/X_i. Now it is easy to verify that

$$E\left(v_i^2\right) = E\left(\frac{u_i}{X_i}\right)^2 = \frac{1}{X_i^2} E\left(u_i^2\right)$$

$$= \sigma^2 \quad \text{using (11.6.5)}$$

Hence the variance of v_i is now homoscedastic, and one may proceed to apply OLS to the transformed equation (11.6.6), regressing Y_i/X_i on $1/X_i$.

Notice that in the transformed regression the intercept term β_2 is the slope coefficient in the original equation and the slope coefficient β_1 is the intercept term in the original model. Therefore, to get back to the original model we shall have to multiply the estimated (11.6.6) by X_i. An application of this transformation is given in exercise 11.17.

Assumption 2: The error variance is proportional to X_i. The **square root transformation**:

$$E(u_i^2) = \sigma^2 X_i \tag{11.6.7}$$

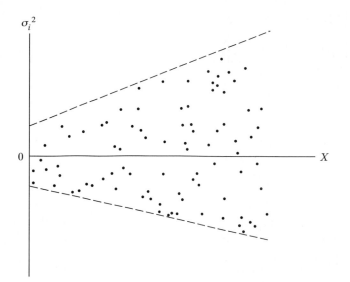

FIGURE 11.10
Error variance proportional to X.

If it is believed that the variance of u_i, instead of being proportional to the squared X_i, is proportional to X_i itself, then the original model can be transformed as follows (see Fig. 11.10):

$$\frac{Y_i}{\sqrt{X_i}} = \frac{\beta_1}{\sqrt{X_i}} + \beta_2 \sqrt{X_i} + \frac{u_i}{\sqrt{X_i}}$$

$$= \beta_1 \frac{1}{\sqrt{X_i}} + \beta_2 \sqrt{X_i} + v_i \tag{11.6.8}$$

where $v_i = u_i/\sqrt{X_i}$ and where $X_i > 0$.

Given assumption 2, one can readily verify that $E(v_i^2) = \sigma^2$, a homoscedastic situation. Therefore, one may proceed to apply OLS to (11.6.8), regressing $Y_i/\sqrt{X_i}$ on $1/\sqrt{X_i}$ and $\sqrt{X_i}$.

Note an important feature of the transformed model: It has no intercept term. Therefore, one will have to use the regression-through-the-origin model to estimate β_1 and β_2. Having run (11.6.8), one can get back to the original model simply by multiplying (11.6.8) by $\sqrt{X_i}$.

Assumption 3: The error variance is proportional to the square of the mean value of Y.

$$E(u_i^2) = \sigma^2 [E(Y_i)]^2 \tag{11.6.9}$$

Equation (11.6.9) postulates that the variance of u_i is proportional to the square of the expected value of Y (see Fig. 11.7e). Now

$$E(Y_i) = \beta_1 + \beta_2 X_i$$

Therefore, if we transform the original equation as follows,

$$\frac{Y_i}{E(Y_i)} = \frac{\beta_1}{E(Y_i)} + \beta_2 \frac{X_i}{E(Y_i)} + \frac{u_i}{E(Y_i)}$$

$$= \beta_1 \left(\frac{1}{E(Y_i)}\right) + \beta_2 \frac{X_i}{E(Y_i)} + v_i \qquad (11.6.10)$$

where $v_i = u_i/E(Y_i)$, it can be seen that $E(v_i^2) = \sigma^2$; that is, the disturbances v_i are homoscedastic. Hence, it is regression (11.6.10) that will satisfy the homoscedasticity assumption of the classical linear regression model.

The transformation (11.6.10) is, however, inoperational because $E(Y_i)$ depends on β_1 and β_2, which are unknown. Of course, we know $\hat{Y}_i = \hat{\beta}_1 + \hat{\beta}_2 X_i$, which is an estimator of $E(Y_i)$. Therefore, we may proceed in two steps: First, we run the usual OLS regression, disregarding the heteroscedasticity problem, and obtain $\hat{Y}_i$. Then, using the estimated $\hat{Y}_i$, we transform our model as follows:

$$\frac{Y_i}{\hat{Y}_i} = \beta_1 \left(\frac{1}{\hat{Y}_i}\right) + \beta_2 \left(\frac{X_i}{\hat{Y}_i}\right) + v_i \qquad (11.6.11)$$

where $v_i = (u_i/\hat{Y}_i)$. In Step 2, we run the regression (11.6.11). Although $\hat{Y}_i$ are not exactly $E(Y_i)$, they are consistent estimators; that is, as the sample size increases indefinitely, they converge to true $E(Y_i)$. Hence, the transformation (11.6.11) will perform satisfactorily in practice if the sample size is reasonably large.

Assumption 4: A log transformation such as

$$\ln Y_i = \beta_1 + \beta_2 \ln X_i + u_i \qquad (11.6.12)$$

very often reduces heteroscedasticity when compared with the regression $Y_i = \beta_1 + \beta_2 X_i + u_i$.

This result arises because log transformation compresses the scales in which the variables are measured, thereby reducing a tenfold difference between two values to a twofold difference. Thus, the number 80 is 10 times the number 8, but $\ln 80 (= 4.3280)$ is about twice as large as $\ln 8 (= 2.0794)$.

An additional advantage of the log transformation is that the slope coefficient β_2 measures the elasticity of Y with respect to X, that is, the percentage change in Y for a percentage change in X. For example, if Y is consumption and X is income, β_2 in (11.6.12) will measure income elasticity, whereas in the original model β_2 measures only the rate of change of mean consumption for a unit change in income. It is one reason why the log models are quite popular in empirical econometrics. (For some of the problems associated with log transformation, see exercise 11.4.)

To conclude our discussion of the remedial measures, we reemphasize that all the transformations discussed previously are ad hoc; we are essentially speculating about the nature of σ_i^2. Which of the transformations discussed previously will work will depend on the nature of the problem and the severity of heteroscedasticity. There are some additional problems with the transformations we have considered that should be borne in mind:

1. When we go beyond the two-variable model we may not know a priori which of the X variables should be chosen for transforming the data.[32]
2. Log transformation as discussed in Assumption 4 is not applicable if some of the Y and X values are zero or negative.[33]
3. Then there is the problem of **spurious correlation**. This term, due to Karl Pearson, refers to the situation where correlation is found to be present between the ratios of variables even though the original variables are uncorrelated or random.[34] Thus, in the model $Y_i = \beta_1 + \beta_2 X_i + u_i$, Y and X may not be correlated but in the transformed model $Y_i/X_i = \beta_1(1/X_i) + \beta_2$, Y_i/X_i and $1/X_i$ are often found to be correlated.
4. When σ_i^2 are not directly known and are estimated from one or more of the transformations that we have discussed earlier, all our testing procedures using the t tests, F tests, etc. are strictly speaking valid only in large samples. Therefore, one has to be careful in interpreting the results based on the various transformations in small or finite samples.[35]

11.7 A CONCLUDING EXAMPLE

In concluding our discussion of heteroscedasticity we present an example illustrating various methods of detecting it and some of the remedial measures.

> **Example 11.8: R&D Expenditure in the United States, 1988.** Data on research and development (R&D) expenditures for 18 industry groups in relation to sales and profits are reproduced in Table 11.5. Since the cross-sectional data presented in Table 11.5 are quite heterogeneous, in a regression of R&D on sales (or profits) heteroscedasticity is likely. The results of regressing R&D on sales were as follows:
>
> $$\widehat{R\&D}_i = 192.99 + 0.0319 \, \text{Sales}_i$$
> $$\text{se} = (990.99) \quad (0.0083) \tag{11.7.1}$$
> $$t = (0.1948) \quad (3.8434) \qquad r^2 = 0.4783$$
>
> As expected, R&D expenditure and sales are positively correlated. The computed t value "seems" to be statistically significant at the 0.002 level (two-tail

---

[32] However, as a practical matter, one may plot $\hat{u}_i^2$ against each variable and decide which X variable may be used for transforming the data. (See Fig. 11.8.)

[33] Sometimes we can use $\ln(Y_i + k)$ or $\ln(X_i + k)$, where k is a positive number chosen in such a way that all the values of Y and X become positive. See exercise 11.22.

[34] For example, if X_1, X_2, and X_3 are mutually uncorrelated $r_{12} = r_{13} = r_{23} = 0$ and we find that the (values of the) ratios X_1/X_3 and X_2/X_3 are correlated, then there is spurious correlation. "More generally, correlation may be described as spurious if it is induced by the method of handling the data and is not present in the original material." M. G. Kendall and W. R. Buckland, *A Dictionary of Statistical Terms*, Hafner Publishing, New York, 1972, p. 143.

[35] For further details, see George G. Judge et al., op. cit., Sec. 14.4, pp. 415–420.

TABLE 11.5
Innovation in America: Research and development (R&D) expenditure in the United States, 1988 (all figures in millions of dollars)

Industry grouping	Sales	R&D expenses	Profits
1. Containers and packaging	6,375.3	62.5	185.1
2. Nonbank financial	11,626.4	92.9	1,569.5
3. Service industries	14,655.1	178.3	276.8
4. Metals and mining	21,869.2	258.4	2,828.1
5. Housing and construction	26,408.3	494.7	225.9
6. General manufacturing	32,405.6	1,083.0	3,751.9
7. Leisure time industries	35,107.7	1,620.6	2,884.1
8. Paper and forest products	40,295.4	421.7	4,645.7
9. Food	70,761.6	509.2	5,036.4
10. Health care	80,552.8	6,620.1	13,869.9
11. Aerospace	95,294.0	3,918.6	4,487.8
12. Consumer products	101,314.1	1,595.3	10,278.9
13. Electrical and electronics	116,141.3	6,107.5	8,787.3
14. Chemicals	122,315.7	4,454.1	16,438.8
15. Conglomerates	141,649.9	3,163.8	9,761.4
16. Office equipment and computers	175,025.8	13,210.7	19,774.5
17. Fuel	230,614.5	1,703.8	22,626.6
18. Automotive	293,543.0	9,528.2	18,415.4

Note: The industries are listed in increasing order of sales volume.

Source: Business Week, Special 1989 Bonus Issue, R&D Scorecard, pp. 180–224.

test). Of course, if there is heteroscedasticity, we cannot trust the estimated standard errors or the estimated t values. Applying the Park test on the estimated residuals from (11.7.1), we obtain the following results:

$$\widehat{\ln \hat{u}_i^2} = 5.6877 + 0.7014 \ln \text{Sales}_i$$
$$se = (6.6877) \quad (0.6033) \tag{11.7.2}$$
$$t = (0.8572) \quad (1.1626) \qquad r^2 = 0.0779$$

On the basis of the Park test, we have no reason to reject the assumption of homoscedasticity.

On the basis of the Glejser test, we obtain the following results (to save space, we only present the t values):

$$|\hat{u}_i| = 578.57 + 0.0119 \text{ Sales}_i \tag{11.7.3}$$
$$t = (0.8525)(2.0931) \qquad r^2 = 0.2150$$
$$|\hat{u}_i| = -507.02 + 7.9270 \sqrt{\text{Sales}_i} \tag{11.7.4}$$
$$t = (-0.5032)(2.3704) \qquad r^2 = 0.2599$$
$$|\hat{u}_i| = 2{,}273.7 + 19{,}925{,}000(1/\text{Sales}_i) \tag{11.7.5}$$
$$t = (3.7601)(-1.6175) \qquad r^2 = 0.1405$$

As Eq. (11.7.3) and (11.7.4) suggest, the assumption of homoscedastic variances can be rejected. Therefore, the estimated standard errors and t values cannot be accepted at their face value. In exercise 11.23 the reader is asked to apply the Breusch-Pagan and White tests of heteroscedasticity to the data given in Table 11.5.

Since there seems to be doubt about the homoscedasticity assumption, let us see if we can transform the data so as to reduce the severity of heteroscedasticity, if not totally get rid of it. Plotting the residuals obtained from regression (11.7.1), we can see that the error variance is proportional to the sales variable (check this) and hence, following Assumption 2 discussed earlier, we can use the square root transformation, which gives the following results:

$$\frac{R\&D_i}{\sqrt{Sales_i}} = -246.68\frac{1}{\sqrt{Sales_i}} + 0.0368\sqrt{Sales_i}$$

$$se = \quad (341.13) \qquad\qquad (0.0071)$$

$$t = \quad (-0.6472) \qquad\qquad (5.1723) \qquad\qquad R^2 = 0.6258$$

(11.7.6)

If you multiply (11.7.6) by $\sqrt{Sales_i}$ on both sides, you will get results comparable to the original regression (11.7.1). There is very little difference in the two slope coefficients. But note that compared to (11.7.1) the standard error of the slope coefficient in (11.7.6) is smaller, suggesting that the (original) OLS regression actually overestimated the standard error. As noted before, in the presence of heteroscedasticity, OLS estimators of standard errors are biased and one cannot foretell which way the bias will go. In the present example the bias is upward, that is, it *overestimated* the standard error. Incidentally, note that (11.7.6) represents *weighted least squares* (why?).

In exercise 11.25 the reader is asked to obtain White's heteroscedasticity-corrected standard errors for the preceding example and compare the results with those given in (11.7.6).

11.8 SUMMARY AND CONCLUSIONS

1. A critical assumption of the classical linear regression model is that the disturbances u_i have all the same variance, σ^2. If this assumption is not satisfied, there is heteroscedasticity.
2. Heteroscedasticity does not destroy the unbiasedness and consistency properties of OLS estimators.
3. But these estimators are no longer minimum variance or efficient. That is, they are not BLUE.
4. The BLUE estimators are provided by the method of weighted least squares, provided the heteroscedastic error variances, σ_i^2, are known.
5. In the presence of heteroscedasticity, the variances of OLS estimators are not provided by the usual OLS formulas. But if we persist in using the usual OLS formulas, the t and F tests based on them can be highly misleading, resulting in erroneous conclusions.
6. Documenting the consequences of heteroscedasticity is easier than detecting it. There are several diagnostic tests available, but one cannot tell for sure which will work in a given situation.
7. Even if heteroscedasticity is suspected and detected, it is not easy to correct the problem. If the sample is large, one can obtain White's heteroscedasticity-corrected standard errors of OLS estimators and conduct statistical inference based on these standard errors.
8. Otherwise, based on OLS residuals, one can make educated guesses of the likely pattern of heteroscedasticity and transform the original data in such a way that in the transformed data there is no heteroscedasticity.

9. Finally, the OLS residuals disturbances not only may be heteroscedastic but also can be autocorrelated. A technique called **autoregressive conditional heteroscedasticity, ARCH** for short, can be employed to attack this problem. We will deal with it in Chapter 12, where we consider the topic of autocorrelation in depth.

EXERCISES

Questions

11.1. State *with brief reason* whether the following statements are true, false, or uncertain:

(a) In the presence of heteroscedasticity OLS estimators are biased as well as inefficient.

(b) If heteroscedasticity is present, the conventional t and F tests are invalid.

(c) In the presence of heteroscedasticity the usual OLS method always overestimates the standard errors of estimators.

(d) If residuals estimated from an OLS regression exhibit a systematic pattern, it means heteroscedasticity is present in the data.

(e) There is no general test of heteroscedasticity that is free of any assumption about which variable the error term is correlated with.

(f) If a regression model is mis-specified (e.g., an important variable is omitted), the OLS residuals will show a distinct pattern.

(g) If a regressor that has nonconstant variance is (incorrectly) omitted from a model, the (OLS) residuals will be heteroscedastic.

11.2. In a regression of average wages (W) on the number of employees (N) for a random sample of 30 firms, the following regression results were obtained:[*]

$$\widehat{W} = 7.5 + 0.009\,N$$
$$t = \text{n.a.} \quad (16.10) \qquad R^2 = 0.90 \tag{1}$$

$$\widehat{W}/N = 0.008 + 7.8(1/N)$$
$$t = (14.43) \quad (76.58) \qquad R^2 = 0.99 \tag{2}$$

(a) How do you interpret the two regressions?

(b) What is the author assuming in going from Eq. (1) to (2)? Was he worried about heteroscedasticity? How do you know?

(c) Can you relate the slopes and intercepts of the two models?

(d) Can you compare the R^2 values of the two models? Why or why not?

11.3. (a) Can you estimate the parameters of the models

$$|\hat{u}_i| = \sqrt{\beta_1 + \beta_2 X_i} + v_i$$

$$|\hat{u}_i| = \sqrt{\beta_1 + \beta_2 X_i^2} + v_i$$

by the method of ordinary least squares? Why or why not?

(b) If not, can you suggest a method, informal or formal, of estimating the parameters of such models?

---

[*]See Dominick Salvatore, *Managerial Economics*, McGraw-Hill, New York, 1989, p. 157.

11.4. Although log models as shown in Eq. (11.6.12) often reduce heteroscedasticity, one has to pay careful attention to the properties of the disturbance term of such models. For example, the model

$$Y_i = \beta_1 X_i^{\beta_2} u_i \tag{1}$$

can be written as

$$\ln Y_i = \ln \beta_1 + \beta_2 \ln X_i + \ln u_i \tag{2}$$

(a) If $\ln u_i$ is to have zero expectation, what must be the distribution of u_i?
(b) If $E(u_i) = 1$, will $E(\ln u_i) = 0$? Why or why not?
(c) If $E(\ln u_i)$ is not zero, what can be done to make it zero?

11.5. Show that β_2^* of (11.3.8) can also be expressed as

$$\beta_2^* = \frac{\sum w_i y_i^* x_i^*}{\sum w_i x_i^{2*}}$$

and var(β_2^*) given in (11.3.9) can also be expressed as

$$\text{var}(\beta_2^*) = \frac{1}{\sum w_i x_i^{2*}}$$

where $y_i^* = Y_i - \bar{Y}^*$ and $x_i^* = X_i - \bar{X}^*$ represent deviations from the weighted means $\bar{Y}^*$ and $\bar{X}^*$ defined as

$$\bar{Y}^* = \sum w_i Y_i \bigg/ \sum w_i$$

$$\bar{X}^* = \sum w_i X_i \bigg/ \sum w_i$$

11.6. For pedagogic purposes Hanushek and Jackson estimate the following model:

$$C_t = \beta_1 + \beta_2 \text{GNP}_t + \beta_3 D_t + u_i \tag{1}$$

where C_t = aggregate private consumption expenditure in year t, GNP_t = gross national product in year t, and D = national defense expenditures in year t, the objective of the analysis being to study the effect of defense expenditures on other expenditures in the economy.

Postulating that $\sigma_t^2 = \sigma^2(\text{GNP}_t)^2$, they transform (1) and estimate

$$C_t/\text{GNP}_t = \beta_1 (1/\text{GNP}_t) + \beta_2 + \beta_3 (D_t/\text{GNP}_t) + u_t/\text{GNP}_t \tag{2}$$

The empirical results based on the data for 1946–1975 were as follows (standard errors in the parentheses):[*]

$$\hat{C}_t = \quad 26.19 \qquad\quad + \ 0.6248 \,\text{GNP}_t - \ 0.4398 \,D_t$$
$$\qquad (2.73) \qquad\qquad\quad (0.0060) \qquad\quad (0.0736) \qquad\qquad R^2 = 0.999$$
$$\widehat{C_t/\text{GNP}_t} = \ 25.92(1/\text{GNP}_t) + \ 0.6246 \qquad\quad - \ 0.4315(D_t/\text{GNP}_t)$$
$$\qquad\quad (2.22) \qquad\qquad\qquad (0.0068) \qquad (0.0597) \qquad\qquad R^2 = 0.875$$

(a) What assumption is made by the authors about the nature of heteroscedasticity? Can you justify it?

---

[*]Eric A. Hanushek and John E. Jackson, *Statistical Methods for Social Scientists*, Academic, New York, 1977, p. 160.

(b) Compare the results of the two regressions. Has the transformation of the original model improved the results, that is, reduced the estimated standard errors? Why or why not?

(c) Can you compare the two R^2 values? Why or why not? (*Hint:* Examine the dependent variables.)

11.7. Refer to the estimated regressions (11.6.2) and (11.6.3). The regression results are quite similar. What could account for this outcome? (*Hint:* Refer to exercise 11.13.)

11.8. Prove that if $w_i = w$ a constant, for each i, β_2^*, and $\hat{\beta}_2$ as well as their variance are identical.

11.9. Refer to formulas (11.2.2) and (11.2.3). Assume

$$\sigma_i^2 = \sigma^2 k_i$$

where σ^2 is a constant and where k_i are *known* weights, not necessarily all equal.
    Using this assumption, show that the variance given in (11.2.2) can be expressed as

$$\text{var}(\hat{\beta}_2) = \frac{\sigma^2}{\sum x_i^2} \cdot \frac{\sum x_i^2 k_i}{\sum x_i^2}$$

The first term on the right side is the variance formula given in (11.2.3), that is, $\text{var}(\hat{\beta}_2)$ under homoscedasticity. What can you say about the nature of the relationship between $\text{var}(\hat{\beta}_2)$ under heteroscedasticity and under homoscedasticity? (*Hint:* Examine the second term on the right side of the preceding formula.) Can you draw any general conclusions about the relationships between (11.2.2) and (11.2.3)?

11.10. In the model

$$Y_i = \beta_2 X_i + u_i \quad \text{(Note: there is no intercept)}$$

you are told that $\text{var}(u_i) = \sigma^2 X_i^2$. Show that

$$\text{var}(\hat{\beta}_2) = \left(\sigma^2 \sum X_i^4\right) \Big/ \left(\sum X_i^2\right)^2$$

Problems

11.11. For the data given in Table 11.1, regress average compensation Y on average productivity X, treating employment size as the unit of observation. Interpret your results, and see if your results agree with those given in (11.5.3).

(a) From the preceding regression obtain the residuals $\hat{u}_i$.

(b) Following the Park test, regress $\ln \hat{u}_i^2$ on $\ln X_i$ and verify the regression (11.5.4).

(c) Following the Glejser approach, regress $|\hat{u}_i|$ on X_i and then regress $|\hat{u}_i|$ on $\sqrt{X_i}$ and comment on your results.

(d) Find the rank correlation between $|\hat{u}_i|$ and X_i and comment on the nature of heteroscedasticity, if any, present in the data.

11.12. The accompanying table gives data on sales/cash ratio in U.S. manufacturing industries classified by the asset size of the establishment for the period 1971–I to 1973–IV. (The data are on a quarterly basis.) The sales/cash ratio may be regarded as a measure of income velocity in the corporate sector, that is, the number of times a dollar turns over.

(a) For each asset size compute the mean and standard deviation of the sales/cash ratio.

(b) Plot the mean value against the standard deviation as computed in (a), using asset size as the unit of observation.
(c) By means of a suitable regression model decide whether standard deviation of the ratio increases with the mean value. If not, how would you rationalize the result?
(d) If there is a statistically significant relationship between the two, how would you transform the data so that there is no heteroscedasticity?

Asset size (millions of dollars)

Year and quarter	1–10	10–25	25–50	50–100	100–250	250–1,000	1,000 +
1971–I	6.696	6.929	6.858	6.966	7.819	7.557	7.860
–II	6.826	7.311	7.299	7.081	7.907	7.685	7.351
–III	6.338	7.035	7.082	7.145	7.691	7.309	7.088
–IV	6.272	6.265	6.874	6.485	6.778	7.120	6.765
1972–I	6.692	6.236	7.101	7.060	7.104	7.584	6.717
–II	6.818	7.010	7.719	7.009	8.064	7.457	7.280
–III	6.783	6.934	7.182	6.923	7.784	7.142	6.619
–IV	6.779	6.988	6.531	7.146	7.279	6.928	6.919
1973–I	7.291	7.428	7.272	7.571	7.583	7.053	6.630
–II	7.766	9.071	7.818	8.692	8.608	7.571	6.805
–III	7.733	8.357	8.090	8.357	7.680	7.654	6.772
–IV	8.316	7.621	7.766	7.867	7.666	7.380	7.072

Source: Quarterly Financial Report for Manufacturing Corporations, Federal Trade Commission and the Securities and Exchange Commission, U.S. government, various issues (computed).

11.13. Bartlett's homogeneity-of-variance test.[*] Suppose there are k independent sample variances $s_1^2, s_2^2, \ldots, s_k^2$ with $f_1, f_2, \ldots, f_k$ df, each from populations which are normally distributed with mean μ and variance σ_i^2. Suppose further that we want to test the null hypothesis $H_0 : \sigma_1^2 = \sigma_2^2 = \cdots = \sigma_k^2 = \sigma^2$; that is, each sample variance is an estimate of the same population variance σ^2.

If the null hypothesis is true, then

$$s^2 = \frac{\sum_{i=1}^{k} f_i s_i^2}{\sum f_i} = \frac{\sum f_i s_i^2}{f}$$

provides an estimate of the common (pooled) estimate of the population variance σ^2, where $f_i = (n_i - 1)$, n_i being the number of observations in the ith group and where $f = \sum_{i=1}^{k} f_i$.

Bartlett has shown that the null hypothesis can be tested by the ratio A/B, which is approximately distributed as the χ^2 distribution with $k - 1$ df, where

$$A = f \ln s^2 - \sum \left(f_i \ln s_i^2 \right)$$

and

$$B = 1 + \frac{1}{3(k-1)} \left[\sum \left(\frac{1}{f_i} \right) - \frac{1}{f} \right]$$

---

[*]See "Properties of Sufficiency and Statistical Tests," *Proceedings of the Royal Society of London,* A, vol. 160, 1937, p. 268.

Apply Bartlett's test to the data of Table 11.1 and verify that the hypothesis that population variances of employee compensation are the same in each employment size of the establishment cannot be rejected at the 5% level of significance.

Note: f_i, the df for each sample variance, is 9, since n_i for each sample (i.e., employment class) is 10.

11.14. The data in the accompanying table refer to median salaries of female and male economists by field of specialization for the year 1964.

    (*a*) Find the average salary and the standard deviation of salary of the two groups of economists.

    (*b*) Is there a significant difference between the two standard deviations? (You may use the Bartlett test.)

    (*c*) Suppose you want to predict male economists' median salary from female economists' median salary. Develop a suitable linear regression model for this purpose. If you expect heteroscedasticity in such a model, how will you deal with it?

	Median salaries (thousands of dollars)	
Field of specialization	**Women**	**Men**
Business, finance, etc.	9.3	13.0
Labor economics	10.3	12.0
Monetary-fiscal	8.0	11.6
General economic theory	8.7	10.8
Population, welfare programs, etc.	12.0	11.5
Economic systems and development	9.0	12.2

Source: "The Structure of Economists' Employment and Salaries," Committee on the National Science Foundation Report on the Economic Profession, *American Economic Review,* vol. 55, no. 4, December 1965, p. 62.

11.15. The following data give economists' median salaries classified by degree attained and age:

	Median salaries (thousands of dollars)	
Age, years	**M.A.**	**Ph.D.**
25–29	8.0	8.8
30–34	9.2	9.6
35–39	11.0	11.0
40–44	12.8	12.5
45–49	14.2	13.6
50–54	14.7	14.3
55–59	14.5	15.0
60–64	13.5	15.0
65–69	12.0	15.0

Source: "The Structure of Economists' Employment and Salaries," Committee on National Science Foundation Report on the Economics Profession, *American Economic Review,* vol. 55, no. 4, December 1965, p. 37.

    (*a*) Are the variances of median salaries of economists with M.A. and Ph.D. degrees equal?

(b) If they are, how would you test the hypothesis that the average median salaries for the two groups are the same?

(c) Economists with an M.A. degree earned more than their Ph.D. counterparts between the ages 35 and 54. How would you explain this finding if you believe that a Ph.D. economist should earn more than an M.A. economist?

11.16. Refer to the data on average productivity and standard deviation of productivity given in the accompanying table. Assume that

$$Y_i = \beta_1 + \beta_2 X_i + u_i$$

where Y_i = average productivity in the ith employment class, X_i = employment size measured by $1 = 1$–4 employees, $2 = 5$–9 employees, $\ldots$, $9 = 1000$–2499.

Using these data, estimate the weighted and unweighted least-squares regressions in the manner of Eqs. (11.6.2) and (11.6.3) and comment on your results.

Employment size (no. of employees)	Average productivity, $	Standard deviation of productivity, $
1–4	9,355	2,487
5–9	8,584	2,642
10–19	7,962	3,055
20–49	8,275	2,706
50–99	8,389	3,119
100–249	9,418	4,493
250–499	9,795	4,910
500–999	10,281	5,893
1,000–2,499	11,750	5,550

Source: The Census of Manufactures, U.S. Department of Commerce, 1958 (computed).

11.17. In a survey of some 9966 economists in 1964 the following data were obtained:

Age, years	Median salary, $
20–24	7,800
25–29	8,400
30–34	9,700
35–39	11,500
40–44	13,000
45–49	14,800
50–54	15,000
55–59	15,000
60–64	15,000
65–69	14,500
70+	12,000

Source: "The Structure of Economists' Employment and Salaries," Committee on the National Science Foundation Report on the Economics Profession, *American Economic Review,* vol. 55, no. 4, December 1965, p. 36.

(a) Develop a suitable regression model explaining median salary in relation to age.

> *Note:* For the purpose of regression assume that the median salaries refer to the midpoint of the age interval. Thus, $7800 refers to age 22.5 years, and so on. For the last age interval, assume that the maximum age is 75 years.

(b) Assuming that the variance of the disturbance term is proportional to the square of age, transform the data so as to make the resulting disturbance term homoscedastic.

(c) Repeat (b) assuming that the variance is proportional to age. Which of the transformations seems to be plausible?

(d) If none of the preceding transformations seems plausible, assume that the variance term is proportional to the conditional expectation of median salary, conditional upon the given age. How would you transform the data so that the resulting variance is homoscedastic?

11.18. The accompanying table gives data on special drawing rights (SDRs), also known as *paper gold*, and balance of payments for 10 countries for the year 1974.

Country	SDRs, millions of dollars	Balance of payments, millions of dollars
Belgium	715	346
Canada	574	26
France	248	−83*
Germany	1,763	−466
Italy	221	−4,633
Japan	529	1,241
Netherlands	595	985
Sweden	131	−802
United Kingdom	843	−4,355
United States	2,370	−8,374

*Negative sign denotes balance of payment deficit.

Source: International Financial Statistics, International Monetary Fund, December 1975.

Since the SDRs are used as an international currency, SDR size is expected to be related to the balance of payments position of a country.

(a) From the data given, is there a discernible relationship between the SDRs and the balance of payments? Answer by regressing the former on the latter.

(b) Using your results in (a), test separately the following hypothesis: the disturbance variance is proportional to the
  (i) square of the balance of payment value
  (ii) conditional expected value of the SDRs conditional upon the value of the balance of payments

(c) Can you use the log transformation discussed in the text to transform the data? Why or why not?

(d) Apply the rank correlation test to $\hat{u}_i$ obtained from the regression in (a) and the balance of payments figures. Can you say anything about heteroscedasticity based on this test?

11.19. You are given the following data:

$$\text{RSS}_1 \text{ based on the first 30 observations } = 55, \text{ df } = 25$$
$$\text{RSS}_2 \text{ based on the first 30 observations } = 140, \text{ df } = 25$$

Carry out the Goldfeld-Quandt test of heteroscedasticity at the 5% level of significance.

11.20. The accompanying table gives data on percent change per year for stock prices (Y) and consumer prices (X) for a cross section of 20 countries.

Stock and consumer prices, post–World War II period (through 1969)

	Rate of change, % per year	
Country	Stock prices, Y	Consumer prices, X
1. Australia	5.0	4.3
2. Austria	11.1	4.6
3. Belgium	3.2	2.4
4. Canada	7.9	2.4
5. Chile	25.5	26.4
6. Denmark	3.8	4.2
7. Finland	11.1	5.5
8. France	9.9	4.7
9. Germany	13.3	2.2
10. India	1.5	4.0
11. Ireland	6.4	4.0
12. Israel	8.9	8.4
13. Italy	8.1	3.3
14. Japan	13.5	4.7
15. Mexico	4.7	5.2
16. Netherlands	7.5	3.6
17. New Zealand	4.7	3.6
18. Sweden	8.0	4.0
19. United Kingdom	7.5	3.9
20. United States	9.0	2.1

Source: Phillip Cagan, *Common Stock Values and Inflation: The Historical Record of Many Countries,* National Bureau of Economic Research, Suppl., March 1974, Table 1, p. 4.

(a) Plot the data in a scattergram.
(b) Regress Y on X and examine the residuals from this regression. What do you observe?
(c) Since the data for Chile seem atypical (outlier?), repeat the regression in (b), dropping the data on Chile. Now examine the residuals from this regression. What do you observe?
(d) If on the basis of the results in (b) you conclude that there was heteroscedasticity in error variance but on the basis of the results in (c) you reverse your conclusion, what general conclusions do you draw?

11.21. Obtain regressions similar to (11.6.2) and (11.6.3) by measuring employment size by the class-mark (i.e., midpoint) of the various employment classes (e.g., 2.5, 7.0, etc.) and compare your results with those given in (11.6.2) and (11.6.3).

Which method of measuring employment size do you prefer and why? What would be a potential problem if you had an open-ended employment class, for instance, 2500 or more employees?

11.22. Refer to the table accompanying exercise 11.18. Add the number 8500 to all the balance of payments figures shown in the table, and
   (a) regress SDRs on the new balance of payments figures using the linear model.
   (b) regress SDRs on the new balance of payments figures using the log-linear or double-log model.
   (c) compare the two regression results and comment on your results.
   (d) Why was the number 8500 added to the balance of payments figures? Will any other number do?

11.23. Refer to the data given in Table 11.5. Regress R&D expenditure on sales and find out on the basis of Breusch-Pagan and White tests whether the error variance in this regression is homoscedastic.

11.24. Repeat Exercise 11.23, this time regressing R&D expenditure on profits.

11.25. For Example 11.8 discussed in Section 11.7, obtain White's heteroscedasticity-corrected standard errors in the regression of R&D expenditure on sales and compare your results with regression (11.7.1). What important conclusion do you draw from this example?

APPENDIX 11A

11A.1   PROOF OF EQUATION (11.2.2)

From Appendix 3A, Section 3A.3, we have

$$\text{var}(\hat{\beta}_2) = E(k_1^2 u_1^2 + k_2^2 u_2^2 + \cdots + k_n^2 u_n^2 + 2 \text{ cross products terms})$$

$$= E(k_1^2 u_1^2 + k_2^2 u_2^2 + \cdots + k_n^2 u_n^2)$$

since the expectations of the cross products terms are zero because of the assumption of no serial correlation,

$$\text{var}(\hat{\beta}_2) = k_1^2 E(u_1^2) + k_2^2 E(u_2^2) + \cdots + k_n^2 E(u_n^2)$$

since the k_i are known. (Why?)

$$\text{var}(\hat{\beta}_2) = k_1^2 \sigma_1^2 + k_2^2 \sigma_2^2 + \cdots + k_n^2 \sigma_n^2$$

since $E(u_i^2) = \sigma_i^2$.

$$\text{var}(\hat{\beta}_2) = \sum k_i^2 \sigma_i^2$$

$$= \sum \left[\left(\frac{x_i}{\sum x_i^2} \right)^2 \sigma_i^2 \right] \quad \text{since } k_i = \frac{x_i}{\sum x_i^2}$$

$$= \frac{\sum x_i^2 \sigma_i^2}{(\sum x_i^2)^2} \tag{11.2.2}$$

11A.2 THE METHOD OF WEIGHTED LEAST SQUARES

To illustrate the method, we use the two-variable model $Y_i = \beta_1 + \beta_2 X_i + u_i$. The unweighted least-squares method minimizes

$$\sum \hat{u}_i^2 = \sum (Y_i - \hat{\beta}_1 - \hat{\beta}_2 X_i)^2 \tag{1}$$

to obtain the estimates, whereas the weighted least-squares method minimizes the weighted residual sum of squares:

$$\sum w_i \hat{u}_i^2 = \sum w_i (Y_i - \hat{\beta}_1^* - \hat{\beta}_2^* X_i)^2 \tag{2}$$

where β_1^* and β_2^* are the weighted least-squares estimators and where the weights w_i are such that

$$w_i = \frac{1}{\sigma_i^2} \tag{3}$$

that is, the weights are inversely proportional to the variance of u_i or Y_i conditional upon the given X_i, it being understood that $\text{var}(u_i \mid X_i) = \text{var}(Y_i \mid X_i) = \sigma_i^2$.

Differentiating (2) with respect to $\hat{\beta}_1^*$ and $\hat{\beta}_2^*$, we obtain

$$\frac{\partial \sum w_i \hat{u}_i^2}{\partial \beta_1^*} = 2 \sum w_i (Y_i - \hat{\beta}_1^* - \hat{\beta}_2^* X_i)(-1)$$

$$\frac{\partial \sum w_i \hat{u}_i^2}{\partial \beta_2^*} = 2 \sum w_i (Y_i - \hat{\beta}_1^* - \hat{\beta}_2^* X_i)(-X_i)$$

Setting the preceding expressions equal to zero, we obtain the following two normal equations:

$$\sum w_i Y_i = \hat{\beta}_1^* \sum w_i + \hat{\beta}_2^* \sum w_i X_i \tag{4}$$

$$\sum w_i X_i Y_i = \hat{\beta}_1^* \sum w_i X_i + \hat{\beta}_2^* \sum w_i X_i^2 \tag{5}$$

Notice the similarity between these normal equations and the normal equations of the unweighted least squares.

Solving these equations simultaneously, we obtain

$$\hat{\beta}_1^* = \bar{Y}^* - \hat{\beta}_2^* \bar{X}^* \tag{6}$$

and

$$\hat{\beta}_2^* = \frac{(\sum w_i)(\sum w_i X_i Y_i) - (\sum w_i X_i)(\sum w_i Y_i)}{(\sum w_i)(\sum w_i X_i^2) - (\sum w_i X_i)^2} \tag{7} = \text{(11.3.8)}$$

The variance of $\hat{\beta}_2^*$ shown in (11.3.9) can be obtained in the manner of the variance of $\hat{\beta}_2$ shown in Appendix 3A, Section 3A.3.

Note: $\bar{Y}^* = \sum w_i Y_i / \sum w_i$ and $\bar{X}^* = \sum w_i X_i / \sum w_i$. As can be readily verified, these weighted means coincide with the usual or unweighted means $\bar{Y}$ and $\bar{X}$ when $w_i = w$, a constant, for all i.

CHAPTER
12

AUTOCORRELATION

There is no universally effective way of avoiding misinterpreting misspecification of the regression function as the presence of serially correlated errors.*

An important assumption of the classical linear model presented in Part I is that there is no autocorrelation or serial correlation among the disturbances u_i entering into the population regression function. In this chapter, we take a critical look at this assumption with a view to seeking answers to the following questions:

1. What is the nature of autocorrelation?
2. What are the theoretical and practical consequences of autocorrelation?
3. Since the assumption of nonautocorrelation relates to the unobservable disturbances u_i, how does one know that there is autocorrelation in any given situation?
4. How does one remedy the problem of autocorrelation?

The reader will find this chapter in many ways similar to the preceding chapter on heteroscedasticity in that **under both autocorrelation and heteroscedasticity the usual OLS estimators, although unbiased, are no longer minimum variance among all linear unbiased estimators. In short, they are no longer BLUE.**

12.1 THE NATURE OF THE PROBLEM

The term **autocorrelation** may be defined as "correlation between members of series of observations ordered in time [as in time series data] or space [as in

---

*Russell Davidson and James G. MacKinnon, *Estimation and Inference in Econometrics*, Oxford University Press, New York 1993, p. 364.

400

cross-sectional data]."[1] In the regression context, the classical linear regression model assumes that such autocorrelation does not exist in the disturbances u_i. Symbolically,

$$E(u_i u_j) = 0 \qquad i \neq j \qquad (3.2.5)$$

Put simply, the classical model assumes that the disturbance term relating to any observation is not influenced by the disturbance term relating to any other observation. For example, if we are dealing with quarterly time series data involving the regression of output on labor and capital inputs and if, say, there is a labor strike affecting output in one quarter, there is no reason to believe that this disruption will be carried over to the next quarter. That is, if output is lower this quarter, there is no reason to expect it to be lower next quarter. Similarly, if we are dealing with cross-sectional data involving the regression of family consumption expenditure on family income, the effect of an increase of one family's income on its consumption expenditure is not expected to affect the consumption expenditure of another family.

However, if there is such a dependence, we have autocorrelation. Symbolically,

$$E(u_i u_j) \neq 0 \qquad i \neq j \qquad (12.1.1)$$

In this situation, the disruption caused by a strike this quarter may very well affect output next quarter, or the increases in the consumption expenditure of one family may very well prompt another family to increase its consumption expenditure if it wants to keep up with the Joneses.

Before we find out why autocorrelation exists, it is essential to clear up some terminological questions. Although it is now a common practice to treat the terms **autocorrelation** and **serial correlation** synonymously, some authors prefer to distinguish the two terms. For example, Tintner defines autocorrelation as "lag correlation of a given series with itself, lagged by a number of time units," whereas he reserves the term serial correlation to "lag correlation between two different series."[2] Thus, correlation between two time series such as $u_1, u_2, \ldots, u_{10}$ and $u_2, u_3, \ldots, u_{11}$, where the former is the latter series lagged by one time period, is *autocorrelation*, whereas correlation between time series such as $u_1, u_2, \ldots, u_{10}$ and $v_2, v_3, \ldots, v_{11}$, where u and v are two different time series, is called *serial correlation*. Although the distinction between the two terms may be useful, in this book we shall treat them synonymously.

Let us visualize some of the plausible patterns of auto- and nonautocorrelation, which are given in Fig. 12.1. Figure 12.1a to d shows that there is a discernible pattern among the u's. Figure 12.1a shows a cyclical pattern; Fig. 12.1b and c suggest an upward or downward linear trend in the disturbances; whereas Fig. 12.1d indicates that both linear and quadratic trend terms are present in the disturbances. Only Fig. 12.1e indicates no systematic pattern, supporting the nonautocorrelation assumption of the classical linear regression model.

---

[1] Maurice G. Kendall and William R. Buckland, *A Dictionary of Statistical Terms*, Hafner Publishing Company, New York, 1971, p. 8.

[2] Gerhard Tintner, *Econometrics*, science ed., John Wiley & Sons, New York, 1965, p. 187.

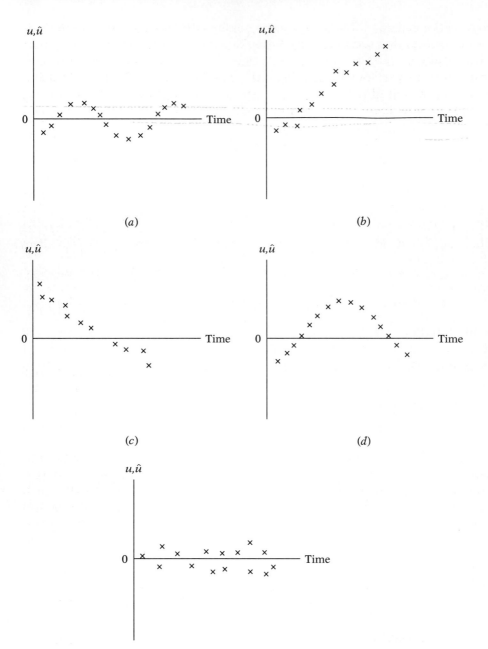

FIGURE 12.1
Patterns of autocorrelation.

The natural question is: Why does serial correlation occur? There are several reasons, some of which are as follows:

Inertia. A salient feature of most economic time series is inertia, or sluggishness. As is well known, time series such as GNP, price indexes, production, employment, and unemployment exhibit (business) cycles. Starting at the bottom of the recession, when economic recovery starts, most of these series start moving upward. In this upswing, the value of a series at one point in time is greater than its previous value. Thus there is a "momentum" built into them, and it continues until something happens (e.g., increase in interest rate or taxes or both) to slow them down. Therefore, in regressions involving time series data, successive observations are likely to be interdependent.

Specification bias: excluded variables case. In empirical analysis the researcher often starts with a plausible regression model that may not be the most "perfect" one. After the regression analysis, the researcher does the postmortem to find out whether the results accord with a priori expectations. If not, surgery is begun. For example, the researcher may plot the residuals $\hat{u}_i$ obtained from the fitted regression and may observe patterns such as those shown in Fig. 12.1a to d. These residuals (which are proxies for u_i) may suggest that some variables that were originally candidates but were not included in the model for a variety of reasons should be included. This is the case of **excluded variable** specification bias. Often the inclusion of such variables removes the correlation pattern observed among the residuals. For example, suppose we have the following demand model:

$$Y_t = \beta_1 + \beta_2 X_{2t} + \beta_3 X_{3t} + \beta_4 X_{4t} + u_t \qquad (12.1.2)$$

where Y = quantity of beef demanded, X_2 = price of beef, X_3 = consumer income, X_4 = price of pork, and t = time.[3] However, for some reason we run the following regression:

$$Y_t = \beta_1 + \beta_2 X_{2t} + \beta_3 X_{3t} + v_t \qquad (12.1.3)$$

Now if (12.1.2) is the "correct" model or the "truth" or true relation, running (12.1.3) is tantamount to letting $v_t = \beta_4 X_{4t} + u_t$. And to the extent the price of pork affects the consumption of beef, the error or disturbance term v will reflect a systematic pattern, thus creating (false) autocorrelation. A simple test of this would be to run both (12.1.2) and (12.1.3) and see whether autocorrelation, if any, observed in model (12.1.3) disappears when (12.1.2) is run.[4] The actual mechanics of detecting autocorrelation will be discussed in Section 12.5 where we will show that a plot of the residuals from regressions (12.1.2) and (12.1.3) will often shed considerable light on serial correlation.

Specification bias: incorrect functional form. Suppose the "true" or correct model in a cost-output study is as follows:

$$\text{Marginal cost}_i = \beta_1 + \beta_2 \text{ output}_i + \beta_3 \text{ output}_i^2 + u_i \qquad (12.1.4)$$

---

[3]As a matter of convention, we shall use the subscript t to denote time series data and the usual subscript i for cross-sectional data.

[4]If it is found that the real problem is one of specification bias, not autocorrelation, then as shown in Sec. 7.7, the OLS estimators of the parameters (12.1.3) may be biased as well as inconsistent. For further details, see Davidson and MacKinnon, op. cit., pp. 327–328. See also their quote given at the beginning of this chapter.

but we fit the following model:

$$\text{Marginal cost}_i = \alpha_1 + \alpha_2 \text{ output}_i + v_i \qquad (12.1.5)$$

The marginal cost curve corresponding to the "true" model is shown in Fig. 12.2 along with the "incorrect" linear cost curve.

As Fig. 12.2 shows, between points A and B the linear marginal cost curve will consistently overestimate the true marginal cost, whereas beyond these points it will consistently underestimate the true marginal cost. This result is to be expected, because the disturbance term v_i is, in fact, equal to $\text{output}^2 + u_i$, and hence will catch the systematic effect of the output^2 term on marginal cost. In this case, v_i will reflect autocorrelation because of the use of an incorrect functional form. In Chapter 13 we will consider several methods of detecting specification bias.

Cobweb phenomenon. The supply of many agricultural commodities reflects the so-called Cobweb phenomenon, where supply reacts to price with a lag of one time period because supply decisions take time to implement (the gestation period). Thus, at the beginning of this year's planting of crops, farmers are influenced by the price prevailing last year, so that their supply function is

$$\text{Supply}_t = \beta_1 + \beta_2 P_{t-1} + u_t \qquad (12.1.6)$$

Suppose at the end of period t, price P_t turns out to be lower than P_{t-1}. Therefore, in period $t + 1$ farmers may very well decide to produce less than they did in period t. Obviously, in this situation the disturbances u_t are not expected to be random because if the farmers overproduce in year t, they are likely to reduce their production in $t + 1$, and so on, leading to a Cobweb pattern.

Lags. In a time series regression of consumption expenditure on income, it is not uncommon to find that the consumption expenditure in the current period depends, among other things, on the consumption expenditure of the previous period. That is,

$$\text{Consumption}_t = \beta_1 + \beta_2 \text{ income}_t + \beta_3 \text{ consumption}_{t-1} + u_t \qquad (12.1.7)$$

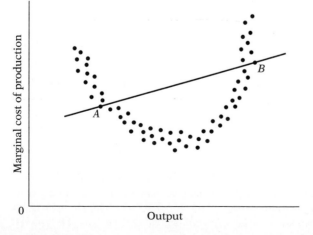

FIGURE 12.2
Specification bias: incorrect functional form.

A regression such as (12.1.7) is known as **autoregression** because one of the explanatory variables is the lagged value of the dependent variable. (We shall study such models in Chapter 17.) The rationale for a model such as (12.1.7) is simple. Consumers do not change their consumption habits readily for psychological, technological, or institutional reasons. Now if we neglect the lagged term in (12.1.7), the resulting error term will reflect a systematic pattern due to the influence of lagged consumption on current consumption.

"Manipulation" of data. In empirical analysis, the raw data are often "manipulated." For example, in time series regressions involving quarterly data, such data are usually derived from the monthly data by simply adding three monthly observations and dividing the sum by 3. This averaging introduces smoothness into the data by dampening the fluctuations in the monthly data. Therefore, the graph plotting the quarterly data looks much smoother than the monthly data, and this smoothness may itself lend to a systematic pattern in the disturbances, thereby introducing autocorrelation. Another source of manipulation is **interpolation** or **extrapolation** of data. For example, the Census of Population is conducted every 10 years in this country, the last being in 1990 and the one before that in 1980. Now if there is a need to obtain data for some year within the intercensus period 1980–1990, the common practice is to interpolate on the basis of some ad hoc assumptions. All such data "massaging" techniques might impose upon the data a systematic pattern that might not exist in the original data.[5]

Before concluding this section, note that the problem of autocorrelation is usually more common in time series data, although it can and does occur in cross-sectional data. In time series data, the observations are ordered in chronological order. Therefore, there are likely to be intercorrelations among successive observations especially if the time interval between successive observations is short, such as a day, a week, or a month rather than a year. There is generally no such chronological order in the cross-sectional data, although in some cases a similar order may exist. Hence in a cross-sectional regression of consumption expenditure on income where the units of observations are the 50 states of the United States, it is possible that the data are so arranged that they fall into groups such as the South, Southwest, North, etc. Since the consumption pattern is likely to differ from one geographical region to another, although substantially similar within any given region, the estimated residuals from the regression may exhibit a systematic pattern associated with the regional differences. The point to note is that, although the incidence of autocorrelation is predominantly associated with time series data, it can occur in cross-sectional data. Some authors call autocorrelation in cross-sectional data **spatial autocorrelation**, that is, correlation in space rather than over time. However, it is important to remember that in cross-sectional analysis the ordering of the data must have some logic, or economic interest, to make sense of any determination of whether autocorrelation is present or not.

It should be noted also that autocorrelation can be positive as well as negative, although most economic time series generally exhibit positive autocor-

---

[5]On this, see William H. Greene, *Econometric Analysis*, Macmillan, 2d ed., New York, 1993, p. 413.

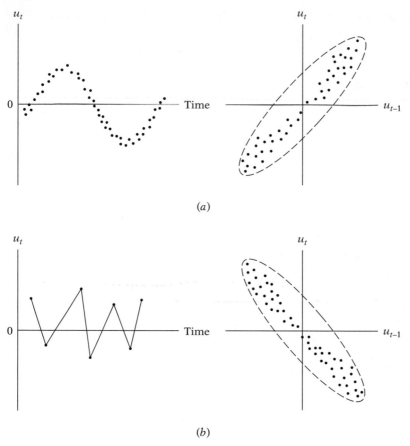

FIGURE 12.3
(a) Positive and (b) negative autocorrelation.

relation because most of them ether move upward or downward over extended time periods and do not exhibit a constant up-and-down movement such as that shown in Fig. 12.3b.

12.2   OLS ESTIMATION IN THE PRESENCE OF AUTOCORRELATION

What happens to OLS estimators and their variances if we introduce auto-correlation in the disturbances by assuming that $E(u_iu_j) \neq 0$ $(i \neq j)$ but retain all the other assumptions of the classical model? We revert once again to the two-variable regression model to explain the basic ideas involved, namely, $Y_t = \beta_1 + \beta_2X_t + u_t$, where t denotes data or observation at time t; note that we are now dealing with time series data.

To make any headway, we must assume the mechanism that generates u_t, for $E(u_t \cdot u_{t+s}) \neq 0$ $(s \neq 0)$ is too general an assumption to be of any practical use. As a starting point, or first approximation, one can assume that the disturbances are generated as follows:

$$u_t = \rho u_{t-1} + \varepsilon_t \qquad -1 < \rho < 1 \qquad (12.2.1)$$

where ρ is known as the **coefficient of autocovariance** and where ε_t is the stochastic disturbance such that it satisfies the standard OLS assumptions, namely,

$$
\begin{aligned}
E(\varepsilon_t) &= 0 \\
\mathrm{var}(\varepsilon_t) &= \sigma^2 \\
\mathrm{cov}(\varepsilon_t, \varepsilon_{t+s}) &= 0 \qquad s \neq 0
\end{aligned}
\qquad (12.2.2)
$$

The scheme (12.2.1) is known as a **Markov first-order autoregressive scheme** or simply a **first-order autoregressive scheme**, usually denoted as AR(1). The name *autoregressive* is appropriate because (12.2.1) can be interpreted as the regression of u_t on itself lagged one period. It is first-order because only u_t and its immediate past value are involved, that is, the maximum lag is 1. If the model were $u_t = \rho_1 u_{t-1} + \rho_2 u_{t-2} + \varepsilon_t$, it would be an AR(2) or a second-order autoregressive scheme, and so on. In passing, note that ρ, the coefficient of autocovariance, can also be interpreted as the *first-order coefficient of autocorrelation* or, more accurately, *the coefficient of autocorrelation of lag 1*. [6]

What (12.2.1) postulates is that the movement or shift in u_t consists of two parts: a part ρu_{t-1}, which accounts for a systematic shift, and the other ε_t, which is purely random.

Before proceeding further, note that a priori there is no reason why we could not adopt an AR(2) or AR(3) or any higher-order autoregressive scheme than the one in (12.2.1). As a matter of fact, one could have assumed that u_t is generated by the following mechanism:

$$u_t = v_t + \lambda v_{t-1} \qquad (12.2.3)$$

where v is a random disturbance term with zero mean and constant variance and λ is a constant such that $|\lambda| < 1$. The error-generating scheme (12.2.3) is known as a **first-order moving average** or **MA(1) scheme** because it involves taking the average of two adjacent random variables. One could also consider higher-order MA schemes.

---

[6] This name can be easily justified. By definition, the (population) coefficient of correlation between u_t and u_{t-1} is

$$
\begin{aligned}
\rho &= \frac{E\{[u_t - E(u_t)][u_{t-1} - E(u_{t-1})]\}}{\sqrt{\mathrm{var}(u_t)}\,\sqrt{\mathrm{var}(u_{t-1})}} \\
&= \frac{E(u_t u_{t-1})}{\mathrm{var}(u_{t-1})}
\end{aligned}
$$

since $E(u_t) = 0$ for each t and $\mathrm{var}(u_t) = \mathrm{var}(u_{t-1})$ because we are retaining the assumption of homoscedasticity. The reader can see that ρ is also the slope coefficient in the regression of u_t on u_{t-1}.

Not only that, one could assume that the u_t is generated by a mixture of autoregressive and moving average processes. For example, one can consider

$$u_t = \rho u_{t-1} + v_t + \lambda v_{t-1} \tag{12.2.4}$$

which is called, appropriately, an **ARMA(1,1) scheme** since it is a combination of first-order autoregressive and first-order moving average schemes. Of course, higher-order ARMA schemes can also be considered. In the chapter on time series econometrics (Chapter 22) we will return to this topic.[7]

For now, we use the AR(1) scheme given in (12.2.1) not only for its simplicity but also because in many applications it has proved to be quite useful. Additionally, a considerable amount of theoretical and empirical work has been done on the AR(1) scheme.

Now the OLS estimator of β_2, as usual, is

$$\hat{\beta}_2 = \frac{\sum x_t y_t}{\sum x_t^2} \tag{12.2.5}$$

but its variance, given the AR(1) scheme, is now

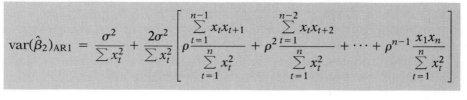

$$ \tag{12.2.6}$$

where $\text{var}(\hat{\beta}_2)_{AR1}$ means the variance of $\hat{\beta}_2$ under first-order autoregressive scheme. Contrast this formula with the usual formula in the absence of autocorrelation:

$$\text{var}(\hat{\beta}_2) = \frac{\sigma^2}{\sum x_t^2} \tag{12.2.7}$$

A comparison of (12.2.6) with (12.2.7) shows that the former is equal to the latter plus a term that depends on ρ as well as the sample covariances between the values taken by X. And in general we cannot tell whether $\text{var}(\hat{\beta}_2)$ is less than or greater than $\text{var}(\hat{\beta}_2)_{AR1}$ [but see Eq. (12.4.1) below]. Of course, if ρ is zero, the two formulas will coincide, as they should. (Why?)

Suppose we continue to use the OLS estimator $\hat{\beta}_2$ and adjust the usual variance formula by taking into account the AR(1) scheme. That is, we use $\hat{\beta}_2$ given by (12.2.5) but use the variance formula given by (12.2.6). What now are the properties of $\hat{\beta}_2$? It is easy to prove that $\hat{\beta}_2$ is still linear and unbiased. As a matter of fact, as shown in Appendix 3A, Section 3A.2, the assumption of no serial correlation, like the assumption of no heteroscedasticity, is not required to prove that $\hat{\beta}_2$ is unbiased. Is $\hat{\beta}_2$ still BLUE? Unfortunately, it is not; in the class of linear unbiased estimators, it does not have minimum variance.

---

[7]What is known as the Box-Jenkins approach to time series modeling is based on the AR, MA, and ARMA error-generating mechanisms.

In short, $\hat{\beta}_2$, although linear-unbiased, is not efficient (relatively speaking, of course). The reader will notice that this finding is quite similar to the finding that $\hat{\beta}_2$ is less efficient in the presence of heteroscedasticity. There we saw that it was the weighted least-square estimator $\hat{\beta}_2^*$ given in (11.3.8), a special case of the generalized least-squares (GLS) estimator, that was efficient. In the case of autocorrelation can we find an estimator that is BLUE? The answer is yes, as can be seen from the discussion in the following section.

$$\frac{\Sigma\, x k y}{\Sigma x^2} = \Sigma x\, (\beta x + \rho \xi_{t-1} + v)$$

12.3 THE BLUE ESTIMATOR IN THE PRESENCE OF AUTOCORRELATION

Continuing with the two-variable model and assuming the AR(1) process, we can show that the BLUE estimator of β_2 is given by the following expression:[8]

$$\hat{\beta}_2^{GLS} = \frac{\sum\limits_{t=2}^{n} (x_t - \rho x_{t-1})(y_t - \rho y_{t-1})}{\sum\limits_{t=2}^{n} (x_t - \rho x_{t-1})^2} + C \qquad (12.3.1)$$

where C is a correction factor that may be disregarded in practice. Note that the subscript t now runs from $t = 2$ to $t = n$. And its variance is given by

$$\text{var } \hat{\beta}_2^{GLS} = \frac{\sigma^2}{\sum\limits_{t=2}^{n} (x_t - \rho x_{t-1})^2} + D \qquad (12.3.2)$$

where D too is a correction factor that may also be disregarded in practice. (See exercise 12.18.)

The estimator $\hat{\beta}_2^{GLS}$, as the superscript suggests, is obtained by the method of GLS. As noted in Chapter 11, in GLS we incorporate any additional information we have (e.g., the nature of the heteroscedasticity or of the autocorrelation) directly into the estimating procedure by transforming the variables, whereas in OLS such side information is not directly taken into consideration. As the reader can see, the GLS estimator of β_2 given in (12.3.1) incorporates the autocorrelation parameter ρ in the estimating formula, whereas the OLS formula given in (12.2.5) simply neglects it. Intuitively, this is the reason why the GLS estimator is BLUE and not the OLS estimator—the GLS estimator makes the most use of the available information.[9] It hardly needs to be added that if $\rho = 0$, there is no additional information to be considered and hence both the GLS and OLS estimators are identical.

---

[8]For proofs, see Jan Kmenta, *Elements of Econometrics*, Macmillan, New York, 1971, pp. 274–275. The correction factor C pertains to the first observation, (Y_1, X_1). On this point see exercise 12.18.
[9]The formal proof that $\hat{\beta}_2^{GLS}$ is BLUE can be found in Kmenta, ibid. But the tedious algebraic proof can be simplified considerably using matrix notation. See J. Johnston, *Econometric Methods*, 3d ed., McGraw-Hill, New York, 1984, pp. 291–293.

In short, under autocorrelation, it is the GLS estimator given in (12.3.1) that is BLUE, and the minimum variance is now given by (12.3.2) and not by (12.2.6) and obviously not by (12.2.7).

What happens if we blithely continue to work with the usual OLS procedure despite autocorrelation? The answer is provided in the following section.

12.4 CONSEQUENCES OF USING OLS IN THE PRESENCE OF AUTOCORRELATION

As in the case of heteroscedasticity, in the presence of autocorrelation the OLS estimators are still linear-unbiased as well as consistent, but they are no longer efficient (i.e., minimum variance). What then happens to our usual hypothesis testing procedures if we continue to use the OLS estimators? Again, as in the case of heteroscedasticity, we distinguish two cases. For pedagogical purposes we still continue to work with the two-variable model, although the following discussion can be extended to multiple regressions without much trouble.[10]

OLS Estimation Allowing for Autocorrelation

As noted, $\hat{\beta}_2$ is not BLUE, and even if we use var($\hat{\beta}_2$)$_{AR1}$, the confidence intervals derived from there are likely to be wider than those based on the GLS procedure. As Kmenta shows, this result is likely to be the case even if the sample size increases indefinitely.[11] That is, $\hat{\beta}_2$ is not asymptotically efficient. The implication of this finding for hypothesis testing is clear: We are likely to declare a coefficient statistically insignificant (i.e., not different from zero) even though in fact (i.e., based on the correct GLS procedure) it may be. This difference can be seen clearly from Fig. 12.4. In this figure we show the 95% OLS [AR(1)] and GLS confidence intervals assuming that true $\beta_2 = 0$. Consider a particular estimate of β_2, say, b_2. Since b_2 lies in the OLS confidence interval, we could accept the hypothesis that true β_2 is zero with 95% confidence. But if we were to use the (correct) GLS confidence interval, we could reject the null hypothesis that true β_2 is zero, for b_2 lies in the region of rejection.

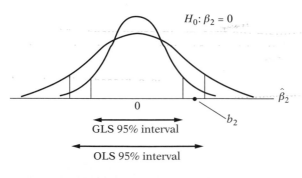

FIGURE 12.4
GLS and OLS 95% confidence intervals.

---

[10]But matrix algebra becomes almost a necessity to avoid tedious algebraic manipulations.
[11]See Kmenta, op. cit., pp. 277–278.

makes use of information !!

The message is: To establish confidence intervals and to test hypotheses, one should use GLS and not OLS even though the estimators derived from the latter are unbiased and consistent.

OLS Estimation Disregarding Autocorrelation

The situation is potentially very serious if we not only use $\hat{\beta}_2$ but also continue to use $\text{var}(\hat{\beta}_2) = \sigma^2/\sum x_t^2$, which completely disregards the problem of autocorrelation, that is, we mistakenly believe that the usual assumptions of the classical model hold true. Errors will arise for the following reasons:

1. The residual variance $\hat{\sigma}^2 = \sum \hat{u}_t^2/(n-2)$ is likely to underestimate the true σ^2.

2. As a result, we are likely to overestimate R^2.

3. Even if σ^2 is not underestimated, $\text{var}(\hat{\beta}_2)$ may underestimate $\text{var}(\hat{\beta}_2)_{\text{AR1}}$ [Eq. 12.2.6], its variance under (first-order) autocorrelation, even though the latter is inefficient compared to $\text{var}(\hat{\beta}_2)^{\text{GLS}}$.

4. Therefore, the usual t and F tests of significance are no longer valid, and if applied, are likely to give seriously misleading conclusions about the statistical significance of the estimated regression coefficients.

To establish some of these propositions, let us revert to the two-variable model. We know from Chapter 3 that under the classical assumption

$$\hat{\sigma}^2 = \frac{\sum \hat{u}_i^2}{(n-2)}$$

provides an unbiased estimator of σ^2, that is, $E(\hat{\sigma}^2) = \sigma^2$. But if there is autocorrelation, given by AR(1), it can be shown that

$$E(\hat{\sigma}^2) = \frac{\sigma^2\{n - [2/(1-\rho)] - 2\rho r\}}{n-2} \tag{12.4.1}$$

where $r = \sum_{t=1}^{n-1} x_t x_{t-1}/\sum_{t=1}^{n} x_t^2$, which can be interpreted as the (sample) correlation coefficient between successive values of the X's.[12] If ρ and r are both positive (not an unlikely assumption for most economic time series), it is apparent from (12.4.1) that $E(\hat{\sigma}^2) < \sigma^2$; that is, the usual residual variance formula, on average, will underestimate the true σ^2. In other words, $\hat{\sigma}^2$ will be biased downward. Needless to say, this bias in $\hat{\sigma}^2$ will be transmitted to $\text{var}(\hat{\beta}_2)$ because in practice we estimate the latter by the formula $\hat{\sigma}^2/\sum x_t^2$.

But even if σ^2 is not underestimated, $\text{var}(\hat{\beta}_2)$ is a *biased* estimator of $\text{var}(\hat{\beta}_2)_{\text{AR1}}$, which can be readily seen by comparing (12.2.6) with (12.2.7),[13] for the two formulas are not the same. As a matter of fact, if ρ is positive (which

---

[12] See S. M. Goldfield and R. E. Quandt, *Nonlinear Methods in Econometrics*, North Holland Publishing Company, Amsterdam, 1972, p. 183. In passing, note that if the errors are positively autocorrelated, the R^2 value tends to have an upward bias, that is, it tends to be larger than the R^2 in the absence of such correlation.

[13] For a formal proof, see Kmenta, op. cit., p. 281.

is true of most economic time series) and the X's are positively correlated (also true of most economic time series), then it is clear that

$$\text{var}(\hat{\beta}_2) < \text{var}(\hat{\beta}_2)_{AR1} \qquad (12.4.2)$$

that is, the usual OLS variance of $\hat{\beta}_2$ underestimates its variance under AR(1). Therefore, if we use $\text{var}(\hat{\beta}_2)$, we shall inflate the precision or accuracy (i.e., underestimate the standard error) of the estimator $\hat{\beta}_2$. As a result, in computing the t ratio as $t = \hat{\beta}_2/\text{se}(\hat{\beta}_2)$ (under the hypothesis that $\beta_2 = 0$), we shall be overestimating the t value and hence the statistical significance of the estimated β_2. The situation is likely to get worse if additionally σ^2 is underestimated, as noted previously.

To see how OLS is likely to underestimate σ^2 and the variance of $\hat{\beta}_2$, let us conduct the following **Monte Carlo experiment.** Suppose in the two-variable model we "know" that the true $\beta_1 = 1$ and $\beta_2 = 0.8$. Therefore, the stochastic PRF is

$$Y_t = 1.0 + 0.8X_t + u_t \qquad (12.4.3)$$

Hence,

$$E(Y_t \mid X_t) = 1.0 + 0.8X_t \qquad (12.4.4)$$

which gives the true population regression line. Let us assume that u_t are generated by the first-order autoregressive scheme as follows:

$$u_t = 0.7u_{t-1} + \varepsilon_t \qquad (12.4.5)$$

where ε_t satisfy all the OLS assumptions. We assume further for convenience that the ε_t are normally distributed with zero mean and unit $(= 1)$ variance. Equation (12.4.5) postulates that the successive disturbances are positively correlated, with a coefficient of autocorrelation of $+0.7$, a rather high degree of dependence.

Now, using a table of random normal numbers with zero mean and unit variance, we generated 10 random numbers shown in Table 12.1 by the scheme

TABLE 12.1
A hypothetical example of positively autocorrelated error terms

	ε_t^*	$u_t = 0.7u_{t-1} + \varepsilon_t$
0	0	$u_0 = 5$ (assumed)
1	0.464	$u_1 = 0.7(5) + 0.464 = 3.964$
2	2.026	$u_2 = 0.7(3.964) + 2.0262 = 4.8008$
3	2.455	$u_3 = 0.7(4.8010) + 2.455 = 5.8157$
4	−0.323	$u_4 = 0.7(5.8157) - 0.323 = 3.7480$
5	−0.068	$u_5 = 0.7(3.7480) - 0.068 = 2.5556$
6	0.296	$u_6 = 0.7(2.5556) + 0.296 = 2.0849$
7	−0.288	$u_7 = 0.7(2.0849) - 0.288 = 1.1714$
8	1.298	$u_8 = 0.7(1.1714) + 1.298 = 2.1180$
9	0.241	$u_9 = 0.7(2.1180) + 0.241 = 1.7236$
10	−0.957	$u_{10} = 0.7(1.7236) - 0.957 = 0.2495$

*Obtained from *A Million Random Digits and One Hundred Thousand Deviates*, Rand Corporation, Santa Monica, Calif., 1950.

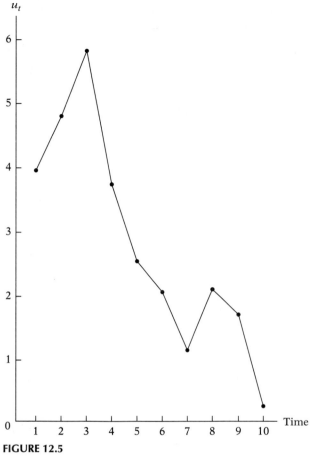

FIGURE 12.5
Correlation generated by the scheme $u_t = 0.7u_{t-1} + \varepsilon_t$ (Table 12.1).

(12.4.5). To start off the scheme, we need to specify the initial value of u, say, $u_0 = 5$.

Plotting the u_t generated in Table 12.1, we obtain Fig. 12.5, which shows that initially each successive u_t is higher than its previous value and subsequently it is generally smaller than its previous value showing, in general, a positive autocorrelation.

Now suppose the values of X are fixed at 1, 2, 3, ..., 10. Then, given these X's, we can generate a sample of 10 Y values from (12.4.3) and the values of u_t given in Table 12.1. The details are given in Table 12.2. Using the data of Table 12.2, if we regress Y on X, we obtain the following (sample) regression:

$$\hat{Y}_t = \quad 6.5452 + \ 0.3051X_t$$
$$\quad (0.6153) \quad (0.0992) \tag{12.4.6}$$
$$t = (10.6366) \quad (3.0763)$$
$$r^2 = 0.5419 \qquad \hat{\sigma}^2 = 0.8114$$

TABLE 12.2
Generation of Y sample values

X_t	u_t^*	$Y_t = 1.0 + 0.8X_t + u_t$
1	3.9640	$Y_1 = 1.0 + 0.8(1) + 3.9640 = 5.7640$
2	4.8010	$Y_2 = 1.0 + 0.8(2) + 4.8008 = 7.4008$
3	5.8157	$Y_3 = 1.0 + 0.8(3) + 5.8157 = 9.2157$
4	3.7480	$Y_4 = 1.0 + 0.8(4) + 3.7480 = 7.9480$
5	2.5556	$Y_5 = 1.0 + 0.8(5) + 2.5556 = 7.5556$
6	2.0849	$Y_6 = 1.0 + 0.8(6) + 2.0849 = 7.8849$
7	1.1714	$Y_7 = 1.0 + 0.8(7) + 1.1714 = 7.7714$
8	2.1180	$Y_8 = 1.0 + 0.8(8) + 2.1180 = 9.5180$
9	1.7236	$Y_9 = 1.0 + 0.8(9) + 1.7236 = 9.9236$
10	0.2495	$Y_{10} = 1.0 + 0.8(10) + 0.2495 = 9.2495$

*Obtained from Table 12.1.

whereas the true regression line is as given by (12.4.4). Both the regression lines are given in Fig. 12.6, which shows clearly how much the fitted regression line distorts the true regression line; it seriously underestimates the true slope coefficient but overestimates the true intercept. (But note that the OLS estimators are still unbiased.)

Figure 12.6 also shows why the true variance of u_i is likely to be underestimated by the estimator $\hat{\sigma}^2$, which is computed from the $\hat{u}_i$. The $\hat{u}_i$ are generally close to the fitted line (which is due to the OLS procedure) but deviate substantially from the true PRF. Hence, they do not give a correct picture of u_i.

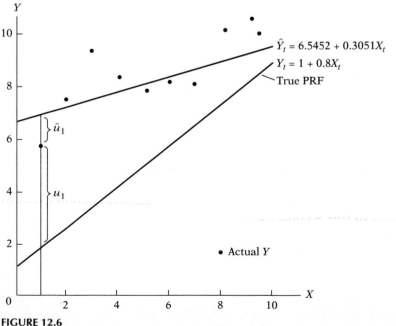

FIGURE 12.6
True PRF and the estimated regression line for the data of Table 12.2.

TABLE 12.3
Sample of Y values with zero serial correlation

X_t	$\varepsilon_t = u_t^*$	$Y_t = 1.0 + 0.8X_t + \varepsilon_t$
1	0.464	2.264
2	2.026	4.626
3	2.455	5.855
4	−0.323	3.877
5	−0.068	4.932
6	0.296	6.096
7	−0.288	6.312
8	1.298	8.698
9	0.241	8.441
10	−0.957	8.043

*Since there is no autocorrelation, the u_t and ε_t are identical. The ε_t are from Table 12.1.

To gain some insight into the extent of underestimation of true σ^2, suppose we conduct another sampling experiment. Keeping the X_t and ε_t given in Tables 12.1 and 12.2, let us assume $\rho = 0$, that is, no autocorrelation. The new sample of Y values thus generated is given in Table 12.3.

The regression based on Table 12.3 is as follows:

$$\hat{Y}_t = 2.5345 + 0.6145X_t$$
$$(0.6796) \quad (0.1087)$$
$$t = (3.7910) \quad (5.6541)$$
$$r^2 = 0.7997 \qquad \hat{\sigma}^2 = 0.9752$$

(12.4.7)

This regression is much closer to the "truth" because the Y's are now essentially random. Notice that $\hat{\sigma}^2$ has increased from 0.8114 ($\rho = 0.7$) to 0.9752 ($\rho = 0$). Also notice that the standard errors of $\hat{\beta}_1$ and $\hat{\beta}_2$ have increased. This result is in accord with the theoretical results considered previously.

12.5 DETECTING AUTOCORRELATION

As demonstrated in Section 12.4, autocorrelation is potentially a serious problem. Remedial measures are therefore surely appropriate. Of course, before one does anything, it is essential to find out whether autocorrelation exists in a given situation. In this section we will consider a few commonly used tests of serial correlation.

Graphical Method

Recall that the assumption of nonautocorrelation of the classical model relates to the population disturbances u_t, which cannot be observed directly. What we have instead are their proxies, the residuals $\hat{u}_t$ which can be obtained from the usual OLS procedure. Although the $\hat{u}_t$ are not the same thing as u_t,[14] very often a visual examination of the $\hat{u}$'s gives us some clues about the likely presence of autocorrelation in the u's. Actually, a visual examination of $\hat{u}_t$ (or $\hat{u}_t^2$) can provide useful information not only about autocorrelation but also about heteroscedasticity (as we saw in the preceding chapter), model inadequacy, or specification bias, as we shall see in the next chapter. As one author notes:

> The importance of producing and analyzing plots [of residuals] as a standard part of statistical analysis cannot be overemphasized. Besides occasionally providing an easy to understand summary of a complex problem, they allow the simultaneous examination of the data as an aggregate while clearly displaying the behavior of individual cases.[15]

There are various ways of examining the residuals. We can simply plot them against time, the **time sequence plot**, as we have done in Fig. 12.7, which shows the residuals obtained from the regression of wages on pro-

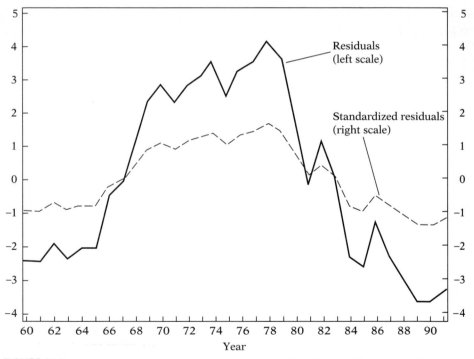

FIGURE 12.7
Residuals and standardized residuals from the regression of wages on productivity: see Appendix 12A.

[14]Even if the disturbances u_t are homoscedastic and uncorrelated, their estimators, $\hat{u}_t$, are heteroscedastic and autocorrelated. On this, see G. S. Maddala, *Introduction to Econometrics*, Macmillan, 2d ed., New York, 1992, pp. 480–481.

[15]Stanford Weisberg, *Applied Linear Regression*, John Wiley & Sons, New York, 1980, p. 120.

TABLE 12.4
**Residuals ($\hat{u}_t$) and standardized
residuals ($\hat{u}_t/\hat{\sigma}$) from the wages-
productivity regression, United States,
1960–1991**

Year	$\hat{u}_t$	$\hat{u}_t/\hat{\sigma}$	$\hat{u}_{t-1}$
1960	−2.409993	−0.922624	NA
1961	−2.433600	−0.931661	−2.409993
1962	−1.876264	−0.718295	−2.433600
1963	−2.342697	−0.896860	−1.876264
1964	−2.032917	−0.778266	−2.342697
1965	−2.032748	−0.778202	−2.032917
1966	−0.513517	−0.196591	−2.032748
1967	−0.132402	−0.050688	−0.513517
1968	1.063037	0.406965	−0.132402
1969	2.239265	0.857263	1.063037
1970	2.767930	1.059653	2.239265
1971	2.220547	0.850098	2.767930
1972	2.754114	1.054364	2.220547
1973	3.011447	1.152880	2.754114
1974	3.468447	1.327834	3.011447
1975	2.387666	0.914076	3.468447
1976	3.221236	1.233194	2.387666
1977	3.426122	1.311631	3.221236
1978	4.040456	1.546818	3.426122
1979	3.530841	1.351720	4.040456
1980	1.597454	0.611557	3.530841
1981	−0.254827	−0.097556	1.597454
1982	0.964233	0.369140	−0.254827
1983	−0.154652	−0.059206	0.964233
1984	−2.359201	−0.903179	−0.154652
1985	−2.673363	−1.023450	−2.359201
1986	−1.354143	−0.518410	−2.673363
1987	−2.344527	−0.897561	−1.354143
1988	−3.053972	−1.169159	−2.344527
1989	−3.725473	−1.426232	−3.053972
1990	−3.687362	−1.411642	−3.725473
1991	−3.311136	−1.267610	−3.687362

Source: $\hat{u}_t$ obtained from the regression of wages on
productivity; see App. 12A, Sec. 12A.1. The value of
$\hat{\sigma} = 2.6121$.

ductivity in the United States over the period 1960–1991 from the data shown
in Appendix 12A. The values of these residuals are given in Table 12.4. (See
also Appendix 12A, Section 12A.1.) Alternatively, we can plot the **standardized
residuals** against time, which are are also shown in Fig. 12.7 and Table 12.4.
The standardized residuals are simply u_t divided by $\hat{\sigma}$, the standard error of
the estimate $(= \sqrt{\hat{\sigma}^2})$. Notice that $\hat{u}_t$ as well as $\hat{\sigma}$ are measured in the units in
which the regressand Y is measured. The values for $\hat{u}_t/\hat{\sigma}$ will be pure numbers
(devoid of units of measurement) and can therefore be compared with the
standardized residuals of other regressions. Moreover, the standardized resid-

uals, like $\hat{u}_t$, have zero mean (why?) and *approximately* unit variance.[16] In large samples $(\hat{u}_t/\hat{\sigma})$ is approximately normally distributed with zero mean and unit variance.

Examining the time sequence plot given in Fig. 12.7, we observe that both $\hat{u}_t$ and the standardized $\hat{u}_t$ exhibit a pattern similar to that in Fig. 12.1d, suggesting that perhaps u_t are not random.

To see this differently, we can plot $\hat{u}_t$ against $\hat{u}_{t-1}$, that is, the residual at time t against its value at time $(t-1)$, a kind of empirical test of the AR(1) scheme. If the residuals are nonrandom, we should obtain pictures similar to those shown in Fig. 12.3. When we plot $\hat{u}_t$ against $\hat{u}_{t-1}$ for our wages-productivity regression, we obtain the picture shown in Fig. 12.8; the underlying data are given in Table 12.4. As this figure reveals, most of the residuals are bunched in the first (northeast) and the third (southwest) quadrants, suggesting very strongly that there is positive correlation in the residuals. Later on, we will see how we can utilize this knowledge to get rid of the autocorrelation problem. (See Section 12.6.)

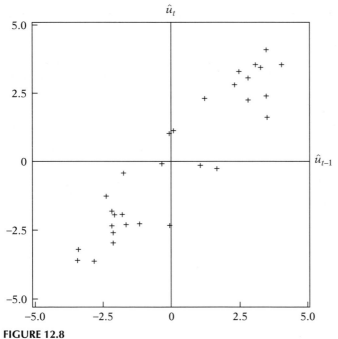

FIGURE 12.8
Residuals $\hat{u}_t$ vs. $\hat{u}_{t-1}$ from wages-productivity regression.

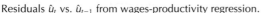

[16]Actually, it is the so-called **Studentized residuals** that have a unit variance. But in practice, the standardized residuals will generally give the same picture as the Studentized residuals and hence we may rely on them. On all this, see Normal Draper and Harry Smith, *Applied Regression Analysis*, 2d ed., John Wiley & Sons, New York, 1981, p. 144.

The graphical method we have just discussed is essentially subjective or qualitative in nature. But there are several quantitative tests that can be used to supplement the purely qualitative approach. We now consider some of these tests.

The Runs Test

If we reexamine Fig. 12.7, we notice a peculiar feature: Initially, we have several residuals that are negative, then there is a series of positive residuals, and finally there are several residuals that are again negative. If the residuals were purely random, could we observe such a pattern? Intuitively, it seems unlikely. This intuition can be checked by the so-called **runs test**, sometimes also known as the **Geary test**, a nonparametric test.[17] To explain this test, let us simply note down the signs ($+$ or $-$) of the residuals from the wages-productivity regression given in Table 12.4, Column 1.

$$(- - - - - - - -)(+ + + + + + + + + + + + +)(-)(+)(- - - - - - - - -)$$

$$(12.5.1)$$

Thus there are 8 negative residuals, followed by 13 positive residuals, followed by 1 negative and 1 positive residual, followed by 9 negative residuals. We now define a run as an uninterrupted sequence of one symbol or attribute, such as $+$ or $-$. We further define the **length of a run** as the number of elements in it. In the sequence shown in (12.5.1), there are 5 runs: a run of 8 minuses (i.e., of length 8), a run of 13 pluses (i.e., of length 13), a run of 1 minus (i.e., of length 1), a run of 1 plus (i.e., of length 1), and a run of 9 minuses (i.e., of length 9). For better visual effect, we have presented the various runs in parentheses.

By examining how runs behave in a strictly random sequence of observations one can derive a test of randomness of runs. We ask this question: Are the 5 runs observed in our illustrative example consisting of 32 observations too many or too few as compared with the number of runs expected in a strictly random sequence of 32 observations? If there are too many runs, it would mean that in our example the $\hat{u}$'s change sign frequently, thus indicating negative serial correlation (cf. Fig. 12.3b). Similarly, if there are too few runs, they may suggest positive autocorrelation, as in Fig. 12.3a. A priori, then, Fig. 12.7 would indicate positive correlation in the residuals.

Now let

$$n = \text{total number of observations} = n_1 + n_2$$
$$n_1 = \text{number of } + \text{ symbols (i.e., } + \text{ residuals)}$$
$$n_2 = \text{number of } - \text{ symbols (i.e., } - \text{ residuals)}$$
$$k = \text{number of runs}$$

---

[17]In **nonparametric tests** we make no assumptions about the distribution from which the observations were drawn. On the Geary test, see R. C. Geary, "Relative Efficiency of Count of Sign Changes for Assessing Residual Autoregression in Least Squares Regression," *Biometrika*, vol. 57, 1970, pp. 123–127.

Then under the null hypothesis that successive outcomes (here, residuals) are independent, and assuming that $n_1 > 10$ and $n_2 > 10$, the number of runs is distributed (asymptotically) *normally* with

$$\text{mean: } E(k) = \frac{2n_1 n_2}{n_1 + n_2} + 1$$

$$\text{variance: } \sigma_k^2 = \frac{2n_1 n_2 (2n_1 n_2 - n_1 - n_2)}{(n_1 + n_2)^2 (n_1 + n_2 - 1)}$$

(12.5.2)

If the hypothesis of randomness is sustainable, we should expect k, the number of runs obtained in a problem, to lie between $[E(k) \pm 1.96\sigma_k]$ with 95% confidence. (Why?) Therefore, we have this rule:

Decision Rule. Do not reject the null hypothesis of randomness with 95% confidence if $[E(k) - 1.96\sigma_k \le k \le E(k) + 1.96\sigma_k]$; reject the null hypothesis if the estimated k lies outside these limits.

In our example, $n_1 = 14$ and $n_2 = 18$. Therefore, we obtain

$$E(k) = 16.75$$
$$\sigma_k^2 = 7.49395$$
$$\sigma_k = 2.7375$$

(12.5.3)

Hence the 95% confidence interval[18] is

$$[16.75 \pm 1.96\,(2.7375)] = (11.3845, 22.1155)$$

Since the number of runs is 5, it clearly falls outside this interval. Therefore, we can reject the hypothesis that the observed sequence of residuals shown in Fig. 12.7 is random with 95% confidence.

Since the number of observations may be small for the preceding normal test, the reader is urged to verify that on the basis of the critical runs values given in Appendix D, Table D.6, we reach the same conclusion, namely, that the observed sequence is not random.[19]

If n_1 or n_2 is smaller than 20, Swed and Eisenhart have developed special tables that give critical values of the runs expected in a random sequence of n observations. These tables are given in Appendix D, Table D.6.

Durbin-Watson d Test[20]

The most celebrated test for detecting serial correlation is that developed by statisticians Durbin and Watson. It is popularly known as the **Durbin-Watson**

---

[18]The reader is advised to check the preceding calculations.
[19]Using the critical values of the runs given in this table, the reader should verify that for $n_1 = 14$ and $n_2 = 18$ the lower and upper critical values of the runs are 10 and 23, respectively.
[20]J. Durbin and G. S. Watson, "Testing for Serial Correlation in Least-Squares Regression," *Biometrika*, vol. 38, 1951, pp. 159–171.

***d* statistic,** which is defined as

$$d = \frac{\sum_{t=2}^{t=n} (\hat{u}_t - \hat{u}_{t-1})^2}{\sum_{t=1}^{t=n} \hat{u}_t^2} \qquad (12.5.4)$$

which is simply the ratio of the sum of squared differences in successive residuals to the RSS. Note that in the numerator of the d statistic the number of observations is $n - 1$ because one observation is lost in taking successive differences.

A great advantage of the d statistic is that it is based on the estimated residuals, which are routinely computed in regression analysis. Because of this advantage, it is now a common practice to report the Durbin-Watson d along with summary statistics such as R^2, adjusted R^2, t ratios, etc. Although it is now used routinely, **it is important to note the assumptions underlying the d statistic:**

1. The regression model includes an intercept term. If such term is not present, as in the case of the regression through the origin, it is essential to rerun the regression including the intercept term to obtain the RSS.[21]
2. The explanatory variables, the X's, are nonstochastic, or fixed in repeated sampling.
3. The disturbances u_t are generated by the first-order autoregressive scheme: $u_t = \rho u_{t-1} + \varepsilon_t$.
4. The regression model does not include lagged value(s) of the dependent variable as one of the explanatory variables. Thus, the test is *inapplicable* to models of the following type:

$$Y_t = \beta_1 + \beta_2 X_{2t} + \beta_3 X_{3t} + \cdots + \beta_k X_{kt} + \gamma Y_{t-1} + u_t \qquad (12.5.5)$$

   where Y_{t-1} is the one-period lagged value of Y. Such models are known as **autoregressive models**. We shall examine them fully in Chapter 17.
5. There are no missing observations in the data. Thus, in our wages-productivity regression for the period 1960–1991 if observations for, say, 1963 and 1972 were missing for some reason, the d statistic makes no allowance for such missing observations.

The exact sampling or probability distribution of the d statistic given in (12.5.4) is difficult to derive because, as Durbin and Watson have shown, it depends in a complicated way on the X values present in a given sample.[22] This difficulty should be understandable because d is computed from $\hat{u}_t$, which are, of course, dependent on the given X's. Therefore, unlike the t, F, or χ^2 tests, there is no unique critical value that will lead to the rejection or the acceptance of the null hypothesis that there is no first-order serial correlation in the dis-

---

[21] However, R. W. Farebrother has calculated d values when the intercept term is absent from the model. See his "The Durbin-Watson Test for Serial Correlation When There Is No Intercept in the Regression," *Econometrica*, vol.. 48, 1980, pp. 1553–1563.

[22] But see the discussion on the "exact" Durbin-Watson test given later in the section.

turbances u_i. However, Durbin and Watson were successful in deriving a lower bound d_L and an upper bound d_U such that if the computed d from (12.5.4) lies outside these critical values, a decision can be made regarding the presence of positive or negative serial correlation. Moreover, these limits depend only on the number of observations n and the number of explanatory variables and do not depend on the values taken by these explanatory variables. These limits, for n going from 6 to 200 and up to 20 explanatory variables, have been tabulated by Durbin and Watson and are reproduced in Appendix D, Table D.5 (up to 20 explanatory variables).

The actual test procedure can be explained better with the aid of Fig. 12.9 which shows that the limits of d are 0 and 4. These can be established as follows. Expand (12.5.4) to obtain

$$d = \frac{\sum \hat{u}_t^2 + \sum \hat{u}_{t-1}^2 - 2\sum \hat{u}_t\hat{u}_{t-1}}{\sum \hat{u}_t^2} \tag{12.5.6}$$

Since $\sum \hat{u}_t^2$ and $\sum \hat{u}_{t-1}^2$ differ in only one observation, they are approximately equal. Therefore, setting $\sum \hat{u}_{t-1}^2 = \sum \hat{u}_t^2$, (12.5.6) may be written as

$$d \doteq 2\left(1 - \frac{\sum \hat{u}_t\hat{u}_{t-1}}{\sum \hat{u}_t^2}\right) \tag{12.5.7}$$

where $\doteq$ means approximately.

Now let us define

$$\hat{\rho} = \frac{\sum \hat{u}_t\hat{u}_{t-1}}{\sum \hat{u}_t^2} \tag{12.5.8}$$

as the sample first-order coefficient of autocorrelation, an estimator of ρ. (See footnote 6.) Using (12.5.8), we can express (12.5.7) as

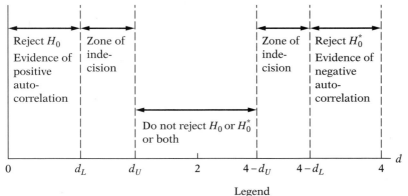

Legend
H_0: No positive autocorrelation
H_0^*: No negative autocorrelation

FIGURE 12.9
Durbin-Watson d statistic.

$$d \doteq 2 (1 - \hat{\rho}) \qquad (12.5.9)$$

But since $-1 \leq \rho \leq 1$, (12.5.9) implies that

$$0 \leq d \leq 4 \qquad (12.5.10)$$

These are the bounds of d; any estimated d value must lie within these limits.

It is apparent from Eq. (12.5.9) that if $\hat{\rho} = 0, d = 2$; that is, if there is no serial correlation (of the first-order), d is expected to be about 2. *Therefore, as a rule of thumb, if d is found to be 2 in an application, one may assume that there is no first-order autocorrelation, either positive or negative.* If $\hat{\rho} = +1$, indicating perfect positive correlation in the residuals, $d \doteq 0$. Therefore, the closer d is to 0, the greater the evidence of positive serial correlation. This relationship should be evident from (12.5.4) because if there is positive autocorrelation, the $\hat{u}_t$'s will be bunched together and their differences will therefore tend to be small. As a result, the numerator sum of squares will be smaller in comparison with the denominator sum of squares, which remains a unique value for any given regression.

If $\hat{\rho} = -1$, that is, there is perfect negative correlation among successive residuals, $d \doteq 4$. Hence, the closer d is to 4, the greater the evidence of negative serial correlation. Again, looking at (12.5.4), this is understandable. For if there is negative autocorrelation, a positive $\hat{u}_t$ will tend to be followed by a negative $\hat{u}_t$ and vice versa so that $|\hat{u}_t - \hat{u}_{t-1}|$ will usually be greater than $|\hat{u}_t|$. Therefore, the numerator of d will be comparatively larger than the denominator.

The mechanics of the Durbin-Watson test are as follows, assuming that the assumptions underlying the test are fulfilled:

1. Run the OLS regression and obtain the residuals.
2. Compute d from (12.5.4). (Most computer programs now do this routinely.)
3. For the given sample size and given number of explanatory variables, find out the critical d_L and d_U values.
4. Now follow the decision rules given in Table 12.5. For ease of reference, these decision rules are also depicted in Fig. 12.9.

To illustrate the mechanics, let us return to our wages-productivity regression. From the data given in Table 12.4 the estimated d value can be shown to be 0.1380, suggesting that there is positive serial correlation in the residuals.

TABLE 12.5
Durbin-Watson d test: Decision rules

Null hypothesis	Decision	If
No positive autocorrelation	Reject	$0 < d < d_L$
No positive autocorrelation	No decision	$d_L \leq d \leq d_U$
No negative correlation	Reject	$4 - d_L < d < 4$
No negative correlation	No decision	$4 - d_U \leq d \leq 4 - d_L$
No autocorrelation, positive or negative	Do not reject	$d_U < d < 4 - d_U$

(Why?) From the Durbin-Watson tables we find that for 32 observations and one explanatory variable (excluding the intercept), $d_L = 1.37$ and $d_U = 1.50$ at the 5% level. Since the estimated value of 0.1380 lies below 1.37, we cannot reject the hypothesis that there is positive serial correlation in the residuals.

Although extremely popular, the d test has one great drawback in that if it falls in the *indecisive zone*, or *region of ignorance*, one cannot conclude whether autocorrelation does or does not exist. To solve this problem, several authors have proposed modifications of the Durbin-Watson d test but they are rather involved and are beyond the scope of this text.[23] The computer program SHAZAM performs an **exact d test** (it gives the p value, the exact probability, of the computed d value), and those with access to this program may want to use that test in case the usual d statistic lies in the indecisive zone. In many situations, however, it has been found that the upper limit d_U is approximately the true significance limit[24] and therefore in case the estimated d value lies in the indecisive zone, one can use the following **modified d test** procedure. Given the level of significance α,

1. $H_0: \rho = 0$ vs. $H_1: \rho > 0$: If the estimated $d < d_U$, reject H_0 at level α, that is, there is statistically significant positive correlation.
2. $H_0: \rho = 0$ vs. $H_1: \rho < 0$: If the estimated $(4 - d) < d_U$, reject H_0 at level α; statistically there is significant evidence of negative autocorrelation.
3. $H_0: \rho = 0$ vs. $H_1: \rho \neq 0$: If the estimated $d < d_U$ or $(4 - d) < d_U$, reject H_0 at level 2α; statistically there is significant evidence of autocorrelation, positive or negative.

An Example. Suppose in a regression involving 50 observations and 4 regressors the estimated d was 1.43. From the Durbin-Watson tables we find that at the 5% level the critical d values are $d_L = 1.38$ and $d_U = 1.72$. On the basis of the usual d test we cannot say whether there is positive correlation or not because the estimated d value lies in the indecisive range. But on the basis of the modified d test we can reject the hypothesis of no (first-order) positive correlation since $d < d_U$.[25]

If one is not willing to use the modified d test, one can fall back on the nonparametric runs test discussed earlier.

In using the Durbin-Watson test, it is essential to note that it cannot be applied in violation of its assumptions. In particular, it should not be used to test for serial correlation in autoregressive models, that is, models containing

---

[23] For details, see Thomas B. Fomby, R. Carter Hill, and Stanley R. Johnson, *Advanced Econometric Methods*, Springer-Verlag, New York, 1984, pp. 225–228.

[24] For example, Theil and Nagar have shown that the upper limit d_U "is approximately equal to the true significance limit in all those cases in which the behavior of the explanatory variables is smooth in the sense that their first and second differences are small compared with the range of the corresponding variable itself." See Henri Theil, *Principles of Econometrics*, John Wiley & Sons, New York, 1971, p. 201. See also E. J. Hannon and R. D. Terrell, "Testing for Serial Correlation after Least-Squares Regression," *Econometrica*, vol. 34, 1961, pp. 646–660.

[25] On some practical advice about how to use the Durbin-Watson statistic, see Draper and Smith, op. cit., pp. 162–169. Also, see G. S. Maddala, op. cit., Chap. 6, on some of the uses and abuses of the Durbin-Watson statistic.

lagged value(s) of the dependent variable as explanatory variable(s). If applied mistakenly, the d value in such cases will often be around 2, which is the value of d expected in the absence of first-order autocorrelation [see (12.5.9)]. Hence, there is built-in bias against discovering serial correlation in such models. This result does not mean that autoregressive models do not suffer from the auto-correlation problem. As we shall see in a later chapter, Durbin has developed the so-called **h statistic** to test serial correlation in such models.

Additional Tests of Autocorrelation

An asymptotic, or large-sample, test. Under the null hypothesis that $\rho = 0$, and assuming that the sample size n is large (technically, infinite), it can be shown that $\sqrt{n} \cdot \hat{\rho}$ follows the normal distribution with mean 0 and variance $= 1$. That is, asymptotically,

$$\sqrt{n} \cdot \hat{\rho} \sim N(0, 1) \qquad (12.5.11)^{26}$$

As an illustration of the test, for our wages-productivity example the esti-mate of ρ can be found to be 0.8844. Given the sample size of 32, we find $\sqrt{32} \cdot (0.8844) = 5.003$. Asymptotically, if the null hypothesis that $\rho = 0$ were true, the probability of obtaining a value of about 5.00 or greater is extremely small. Recall that for a standard normal distribution, the (two-tail) 5% critical Z (i.e., standard normal variable) is 1.96 and the 1% critical Z value is about 2.58. Hence, we reject H_0 that $\rho = 0$.

The Breusch-Godfrey (BG) test of higher-order autocorrelation. Suppose that the disturbance term u_t is generated by the following pth-order autore-gressive scheme:

$$u_t = \rho_1 u_{t-1} + \rho_2 u_{t-2} + \cdots + \rho_p u_{t-p} + \varepsilon_t \qquad (12.5.12)$$

where ε_t is a purely random disturbance term with zero mean and constant variance.

Our null hypotheses H_0 is: $\rho_1 = \rho_2 = \cdots = \rho_p = 0$, that all autoregressive coefficients are simultaneously equal to zero, that is, there is no autocorrelation of any order. Breusch and Godfrey have shown that the null hypothesis can be tested as follows:[27]

1. Estimate the regression model by the usual OLS procedure and obtain the residuals $\hat{u}_t$.
2. Regress $\hat{u}_t$ against all the regressors in the model plus these additional regressors, $\hat{u}_{t-1}, \hat{u}_{t-2}, \ldots, \hat{u}_{t-p}$, where the latter are the lagged values of the

---

[26]See George G. Judge, R. Carter Hill, William E. Griffith, Helmut Lütkepohl, and Tsoung-Chao Lee, *Introduction to the Theory and Practice of Econometrics*, 2d ed., John Wiley & Sons, New York, 1988, p. 394.

[27]L. G. Godfrey "Testing against General Autoregressive and Moving Average Error Models When the Regressors Include Lagged Dependent Variables," *Econometrica*, vol. 46, 1978, pp. 1293–1302; and T. S. Breusch, "Testing for Autocorrelation in Dynamic Linear Models," *Australian Economic Papers*, vol. 17, 1978, pp. 334–355.

estimated residuals in Step 1. Thus, if $p = 4$, we will introduce four lagged values of the residuals as additional regressors in the model. Note that to run this regression we will have only $(n - p)$ observations (why?). Obtain the R^2 value from this regression, the auxiliary regression.

3. If the sample size is large, Breusch and Godfrey have shown that

$$(n - p) \cdot R^2 \sim \chi_p^2 \tag{12.5.13}$$

That is, asymptotically, $(n - p)$ times the R^2 just obtained in Step 2 follows the chi-square test with p df. If in an application $(n - p) \cdot R^2$ exceeds the critical chi-square value at the chosen level of significance, we can reject the null hypothesis, in which case at least one ρ is significantly different from zero.

The following *practical points* about the BG test may be noted:

1. The regressors included in the regression model may contain lagged values of the regressand Y, that is, Y_{t-1}, Y_{t-2}, etc. may appear as explanatory variables. Contrast this model with the Durbin-Watson test restriction that there be no lagged values of the regressand among the explanatory variables.

2. The BG test is applicable even if the disturbance term follows a pth order **MA process,** that is, the u_t are generated as

$$u_t = \varepsilon_t + \lambda_1 \varepsilon_{t-1} + \lambda_2 \varepsilon_{t-2} + \cdots + \lambda_p \varepsilon_{t-p} \tag{12.5.14}$$

where ε is a random disturbance term with zero mean and constant variance.

3. If in (12.5.12) $p = 1$, meaning first-order autoregression, then the BG test is known as **Durbin's m test**.

4. A drawback of the BG test is that the value of p, the length of the lag, cannot be specified a priori. Some experimentation with the value of p is inevitable. We will return to this topic when we discuss time series econometrics later in the text.

An illustrative example. Returning to the wages-productivity regression considered earlier, we followed the BG procedure, introducing five lag values of the OLS residuals in the auxiliary regression (i.e., regression of wages on productivity and five lagged values of the residuals obtained from the regression of wages on productivity alone). The R^2 value from this (auxiliary) regression was 0.8660. In all there are 32 observations in the original regression, but because of the five lags used, we have only 27 observations for the auxiliary regression. Therefore, (27) (0.8660) = 23.382; the *p value*, or the exact probability, of obtaining such a chi-square value is about 0.0003, which is quite low. So we can reject the hypothesis that all five lagged coefficients of the $\hat{u}$'s are equal to zero. At least one lagged coefficient must be nonzero. This fact is not surprising in view of our earlier finding that there is AR(1) autocorrelation in the residuals.

12.6   REMEDIAL MEASURES

Since in the presence of serial correlation the OLS estimators are inefficient, it is essential to seek remedial measures. The remedy, however, depends on what knowledge one has about the nature of interdependence among the disturbances. We distinguish two situations: when the structure of autocorrelation is known and when it is not known.

When the Structure of Autocorrelation Is Known

Since the disturbances u_t are unobservable, the nature of serial correlation is often a matter of speculation or practical exigencies. In practice, it is usually assumed that the u_t follow the first-order autoregressive scheme, namely,

$$u_t = \rho u_{t-1} + \varepsilon_t \tag{12.6.1}$$

where $|\rho| < 1$ and where the ε_t follow the OLS assumptions of zero expected value, constant variance, and nonautocorrelation, as shown in (12.2.2).

If we assume the validity of (12.6.1), the serial correlation problem can be satisfactorily resolved if ρ, the coefficient of autocorrelation, is known. To see this, let us revert to the two-variable model.[28]

$$Y_t = \beta_1 + \beta_2 X_t + u_t \tag{12.6.2}$$

If (12.6.2) holds true at time t, it also holds true at time $t - 1$. Hence,

$$Y_{t-1} = \beta_1 + \beta_2 X_{t-1} + u_{t-1} \tag{12.6.3}$$

Multiplying (12.6.3) by ρ on both sides, we obtain

$$\rho Y_{t-1} = \rho \beta_1 + \rho \beta_2 X_{t-1} + \rho u_{t-1} \tag{12.6.4}$$

Subtracting (12.6.4) from (12.6.2) gives

$$
\begin{aligned}
(Y_t - \rho Y_{t-1}) &= \beta_1 (1 - \rho) + \beta_2 X_t - \rho \beta_2 X_{t-1} + (u_t - \rho u_{t-1}) \\
&= \beta_1 (1 - \rho) + \beta_2 (X_t - \rho X_{t-1}) + \varepsilon_t
\end{aligned} \tag{12.6.5}
$$

where in the last step use is made of (12.6.1).
We can express (12.6.5) as

$$Y_t^* = \beta_1^* + \beta_2^* X_t^* + \varepsilon_t \tag{12.6.6}$$

where $\beta_1^* = \beta_1(1 - \rho)$, $Y_t^* = (Y_t - \rho Y_{t-1})$ and $X_t^* = (X_t - \rho X_{t-1})$.

Since ε_t satisfy all the OLS assumptions, one can proceed to apply OLS to the transformed variables Y^* and X^* and obtain estimators with all the optimum properties, namely, BLUE. In effect, running (12.6.6) is tantamount to using generalized least-squares (GLS) discussed in Section 12.3. (See exercise 12.19.) But note that the first observation (Y_1, X_1) is excluded. (Why?)

Regression (12.6.5) is known as the **generalized,** or **quasi-, difference equation**. It involves regressing Y on X, not in the original form, but in the difference form, which is obtained by subtracting a proportion ($= \rho$) of the

---

[28]It does not matter whether the model has more than one explanatory variable because autocorrelation is a property of the u_t's.

value of a variable in the previous time period from its value in the current time period. In this differencing procedure we lose one observation because the first observation has no antecedent. To avoid this loss of one observation, the first observation on Y and X is transformed as follows:[29] $Y_1 \sqrt{1 - \rho^2}$ and $X_1 \sqrt{1 - \rho^2}$. This transformation is known as the **Prais-Winsten transformation.**

When ρ Is Not Known

Although straightforward to apply, the generalized difference regression is generally difficult to run because ρ is rarely known in practice. Therefore, alternative methods need to be devised. Some of these methods are as follows.

The first-difference method. Since ρ lies between 0 and ± 1, one could start from two extreme positions. At one extreme we could assume that $\rho = 0$, that is, no serial correlation, and at the other extreme we could let $\rho = \pm 1$, that is, perfect positive or negative autocorrelation. As a matter of fact, when a regression is run, one generally assumes that there is no autocorrelation and then lets the Durbin-Watson or other tests show whether this assumption is justified. If, however, $\rho = +1$, the generalized difference equation (12.6.5) reduces to the **first-difference equation** as

$$Y_t - Y_{t-1} = \beta_2 (X_t - X_{t-1}) + (u_t - u_{t-1})$$
$$= \beta_2 (X_t - X_{t-1}) + \varepsilon_t$$

or

$$\Delta Y_t = \beta_2 \Delta X_t + \varepsilon_t \qquad (12.6.7)$$

where Δ, called *delta*, is the first-difference operator and is a symbol or operator (like the expected-value operator E) for successive differences of two values. (*Note:* Generally an operator is a symbol for expressing a mathematical operation.) In running (12.6.7) all one has to do is to form the first differences of both the dependent and explanatory variables and use them as inputs in the regression analysis.

Note an important feature of the first-difference model: **There is no intercept term in it.** Hence, to run (12.6.7), the regression through the origin model will have to be used. But suppose that the original model were

$$Y_t = \beta_1 + \beta_2 X_t + \beta_3 t + u_t \qquad (12.6.8)$$

where t is the trend variable and where u_t follows the first-order autoregressive scheme. The reader can verify that the first-difference transformation of (12.6.8) is as follows:

$$\Delta Y_t = \beta_2 \Delta X_t + \beta_3 + \varepsilon_t \qquad (12.6.9)$$

where $\Delta Y_t = Y_t - Y_{t-1}$ and $\Delta X_t = X_t - X_{t-1}$. Equation (12.6.9) shows that there is an intercept term in the first-difference form, which is in contrast to (12.6.7).

---

[29]The loss of one observation may not be very serious in a large sample but can make a substantial difference in the results in a small sample. On this, see J. Johnston, op. cit., Chap. 8, pp. 321–323, and also Sec. 12.7. For some Monte Carlo results on the importance of the first observation, see Davidson and MacKinnon, op. cit., Table 10.1, p. 349.

But of course, β_3 is the coefficient of the trend variable in the original model. Hence, *the presence of an intercept term in the first-difference form signifies that there was a linear trend term in the original model and the intercept term is, in fact, the coefficient of the trend variable.* If β_3, for instance, is positive in (12.6.9), it means that there is an upward trend in Y after allowing for the influence of all other variables.

Instead of assuming $\rho = +1$, if we assume that $\rho = -1$, that is, perfect negative serial correlation (which is not typical of economic time series), the generalized difference equation (12.6.5) now becomes

$$Y_t + Y_{t-1} = 2\beta_1 + \beta_2 (X_t + X_{t-1}) + \varepsilon_t$$

or

$$\frac{Y_t + Y_{t-1}}{2} = \beta_1 + \beta_2 \frac{X_t + X_{t-1}}{2} + \frac{\varepsilon_t}{2} \qquad (12.6.10)$$

The preceding model is known as the (two-period) **moving average regression** model because we are regressing the value of one moving average on another.[30]

The first-difference transformation presented previously is quite popular in applied econometrics since it is easy to perform. But note that this transformation rests on the assumption that $\rho = +1$; that is, the disturbances are perfectly positively correlated. If this is not the case, the remedy may be worse than the disease. But how does one find out whether the assumption of $\rho = +1$ is justifiable in a given situation? This can be tested by the **Berenblutt-Webb test**.

Berenblutt-Webb test of the hypothesis that $\rho = 1$. To test the hypothesis that $\rho = 1$ (i.e., perfect positive serial correlation of first order), Berenblutt and Webb have developed the following **g (test) statistic:**[31]

$$g = \frac{\sum\limits_{t=2}^{n} \hat{e}_t^2}{\sum\limits_{t=1}^{n} \hat{u}_t^2} \qquad (12.6.11)$$

where $\hat{u}_t$ are the OLS residuals from the original model and $\hat{e}_t$ are the OLS residuals from the regression on the first difference of Y, ΔY (i.e., $Y_t - Y_{t-1}$) on the first difference of the regressors, ΔX's {i.e., $[X_{2t} - X_{2(t-1)}]$, $[X_{3t} - X_{3(t-1)}]$, etc.}. But note that in the first-difference form, there is no intercept (why?).

If the original model contains a constant term, we can use the Durbin-Watson tables to test the g statistic, except that the null hypothesis now is that $\rho = 1$ rather than the Durbin-Watson hypothesis that $\rho = 0$.

To illustrate the Berenblutt-Webb test, let us return to our wages-productivity example and assume that $H_0: \rho = 1$. Regressing Y (wages) on X (pro-

---

[30]Since $(Y_t + Y_{t-1})/2$ and $(X_t + X_{t-1})/2$ are averages of two adjacent values they are called *two-period averages*. They are moving because in computing these averages in successive periods we drop one observation and add another. Hence, $(Y_{t+1} + Y_t)/2$ would be the next two-period average, etc.

[31]I. I. Berenblutt and G. I. Webb, "A New Test for Autocorrelated Errors in the Linear Regression Model," *Journal of the Royal Statistical Society, Series B*, vol. 35, No. 1, 1973, pp. 33–50.

ductivity), we obtain RSS = 204.6934. And regressing ΔY on ΔX (*Note:* no intercept in this regression), we obtain RSS = 28.1938. Therefore,

$$g = \frac{28.1938}{294.6934} = 0.1377$$

Consulting the Durbin-Watson table for 31 observations and 1 explanatory variable, we find that $d_L = 1.363$ and $d_U = 1.496$ (5% level of significance) and $d_L = 1.147$ and $d_U = 1.273$ (1% level of significance). Since the observed g value lies below the lower limit, we do not reject the null hypothesis that true $\rho = 1$. *Keep in mind that although we use the same Durbin-Watson tables, now the null hypothesis is that $\rho = 1$ and not that $\rho = 0$.* In view of this finding, the first-difference transformation discussed earlier, under the assumption that $\rho = 1$, may be appropriate.

ρ based on Durbin-Watson d statistic. Recall that earlier we established the following relation:

$$d \doteq 2(1 - \hat{\rho}) \qquad (12.5.9)$$

or

$$\hat{\rho} \doteq 1 - \frac{d}{2} \qquad (12.6.12)$$

which suggests a simple way of obtaining an estimate of ρ from the estimated d statistic. It is clear from (12.6.12) that the first-difference assumption that $\hat{\rho} = +1$ is valid only if $d = 0$ or approximately so. It is also clear that when $d = 2$, $\hat{\rho} = 0$ and when $d = 4$, $\hat{\rho} = -1$. Therefore, the d statistic provides us with a ready-made method of obtaining an estimate of ρ. But note that the relation (12.6.12) is only an approximate one and may not hold true for small samples. For small samples one may use the **Theil-Nagar modified d statistic.**[32]

For our wages-productivity example, $d = 0.1380$. Hence, $\hat{\rho} = 1 - (0.1382)/2 = 0.931$.

Once ρ is estimated from (12.6.12), one can transform the data as shown in (12.6.6) and proceed to the usual OLS estimation. We will illustrate this technique shortly. But before that we raise an important question: Will the estimated regression coefficients have the usual optimum properties of the classical model? Note that in the generalized difference equation ρ and not $\hat{\rho}$ appears, but in carrying out the OLS regression we use the latter. Without going into complex technicalities, it may be stated *as a general principal, whenever we use an estimator in place of the true value, the estimated OLS coefficients have the usual optimum properties only asymptotically, that is, in the large samples. Also, the conventional hypothesis testing procedures are, strictly speaking, valid asymptotically. In small samples, therefore, one has to be careful in interpreting the estimated results.*

---

[32]This modification is given in exercise 12.6. See the article, "Testing the Independence of Regression Disturbances," *Journal of the American Statistical Association*, vol. 56, 1961, pp. 793–806.

The Cochrane-Orcutt iterative procedure to estimate ρ.[33] An alternative to estimating ρ from the Durbin-Watson d is the frequently used Cochranc-Orcutt method that uses the estimated residuals $\hat{u}_t$ to obtain information about the unknown ρ.

To explain the method, consider the two-variable model:

$$Y_t = \beta_1 + \beta_2 X_t + u_t \tag{12.6.13}$$

and assume that u_t is generated by the AR(1) scheme, namely,

$$u_t = \rho u_{t-1} + \varepsilon_t \tag{12.2.1}$$

Cochrane and Orcutt then recommend the following steps to estimate ρ:

1. Estimate the two-variable model by the standard OLS routine and obtain the residuals, $\hat{u}_t$.
2. Using the estimated residuals, run the following regression:

$$\hat{u}_t = \hat{\rho}\hat{u}_{t-1} + v_t \tag{12.6.14}$$

which is the empirical counterpart of the AR(1) scheme given previously.[34]
3. Using $\hat{\rho}$ obtained from (12.6.14), run the generalized difference equation (12.6.5), namely,

$$(Y_t - \hat{\rho}Y_{t-1}) = \beta_1(1 - \hat{\rho}) + \beta_2(X_t - \hat{\rho}X_{t-1}) + (u_t - \hat{\rho}u_{t-1})$$

or

$$Y_t^* = \beta_1^* + \beta_2^* X_t^* + e_t^* \tag{12.6.15}$$

(*Note:* We can run this regression since $\hat{\rho}$ is known. Also note that $\beta_1^* = \beta_1(1 - \hat{\rho})$.)
4. Since a priori it is not known that the $\hat{\rho}$ obtained from (12.6.14) is the "best" estimate of ρ, substitute the values of $\hat{\beta}_1^* = \hat{\beta}_1(1 - \hat{\rho})$ and $\hat{\beta}_2^*$ obtained from (12.6.15) into the *original* regression (12.6.13) and obtain the new residuals, say $\hat{u}_t^{**}$, as

$$\hat{u}_t^{**} = Y_t - \hat{\beta}_1^* - \hat{\beta}_2^* X_t \tag{12.6.16}$$

which can be easily computed since Y_t, X_t, β_1^* and β_2^* are all known.
5. Now estimate this regression

$$\hat{u}_t^{**} = \hat{\rho}\hat{u}_{t-1}^{**} + w_t \tag{12.6.17}$$

which is similar to (12.6.14). Thus, $\hat{\hat{\rho}}$ is the second-round estimate of ρ.

---

[33]D. Cochrane and G. H. Orcutt, "Application of Least Squares Regressions to Relationships Containing Autocorrelated Error Terms," *Journal of the American Statistical Association*, vol. 44, 1949, pp. 32–61.

[34]*Note:* $\hat{\rho} = \sum_{t=2}^{n} \hat{u}_t \hat{u}_{t-1} / \sum_{t=2}^{n} \hat{u}_{t-1}^2$ (Why?) (cf. footnote 6). In passing note that although biased, this is a consistent estimator of ρ, that is, as sample size increases indefinitely, $\hat{\rho}$ converges to the true ρ.

Since we do not know whether this second-round estimate of ρ is the best estimate of ρ, we can go into the third-round estimate, and so on. As the preceding steps suggest, the Cochrane-Orcutt method is iterative. But how long should we go on? The general procedure is to stop carrying out iterations when the successive estimates of ρ differ by a very small amount, say, by less than 0.01 or 0.005. As an illustrative example will show later on, in practice very often three or four iterations will suffice.

The Cochrane-Orcutt two-step procedure. This is a shortened version of the iterative process. In step one we estimate ρ from the first iteration, that is, from regression (12.6.14), and in step two we use that estimate of ρ to run the generalized difference equation. Sometimes in practice this two-step method gives results quite similar to those obtained from the more elaborate iterative procedure discussed above.

For our wages-productivity example, ρ estimated from (12.6.14) can be found to be 0.9404. Using this estimate and the generalized difference equation (12.6.15), we obtain

$$\hat{Y}_t^* = 1.7152 + 0.7152X_t^*$$

$$\text{se} = (1.1069) \quad (0.1569) \qquad R^2 = 0.4174 \qquad (12.6.18)$$

$$d = 1.5886$$

where $Y_t^* = (Y_t - 0.9404Y_{t-1})$, $X_t^* = (X_t - 0.9404X_{t-1})$, and $1.7152 = \hat{\beta}_1(1 - 0.9404)$, from which β_1 can be estimated as 28.7785. Compare these results with the original regression given in Appendix 12A, Section 12A.1.

Durbin's two-step method of estimating ρ.[35] To illustrate this method, let us write the generalized difference equation (12.6.5) equivalently as

$$Y_t = \beta_1 (1 - \rho) + \beta_2 X_t - \rho\beta_2 X_{t-1} + \rho Y_{t-1} + \varepsilon_t \qquad (12.6.19)$$

Durbin suggests the following two-step procedure to estimate ρ:

1. Treat (12.6.19) as a multiple regression model, regressing Y_t on X_t, X_{t-1}, and Y_{t-1}, and treat the estimated value of the regression coefficient of $Y_{t-1}(= \hat{\rho})$ as an estimate of ρ. Although biased, it provides a consistent estimate of ρ.
2. Having obtained $\hat{\rho}$, transform the variables as $Y_t^* = (Y_t - \hat{\rho}Y_{t-1})$ and $X_t^* = (X_t - \hat{\rho}X_{t-1})$ and run the OLS regression on the transformed variables as in (12.6.6).

From the preceding discussion it is clear that the first step in the Durbin two-stage procedure is to get an estimate of ρ and the second step involves obtaining estimates of the parameters. Later we will comment on this method vis-à-vis the others.

For the wages-productivity example, we obtain the estimate of (12.6.19) as follows:

---

[35]J. Durbin, "Estimation of Parameters in Time-Series Regression Models," *Journal of the Royal Statistical Society*, ser. B, vol. 22, 1960, pp. 139–153,

$$\hat{Y}_t = 3.4879 + 0.7335X_t - 0.7122X_{t-1} + 0.9422Y_{t-1} \qquad (12.6.20)$$

se = (2.0889) (0.1578) (0.1681) (0.0699) $R^2 = 0.9922$

$$d = 1.7664$$

From the coefficient of Y_{t-1} we see that the estimate of ρ is 0.9422, which is not substantially different from that obtained from the d value in the original regression or that obtained from the Cochrane-Orcutt two-step procedure.

Other methods of estimating ρ. We have just discussed some of the commonly used methods of estimating ρ, but this list is by no means exhaustive. For instance, one could use the method of maximum likelihood to estimate the parameters of, say, (12.6.19) directly without resorting to some of the iterative routines discussed earlier. But the ML method involves nonlinear (in the parameters) estimation procedures and is beyond the scope of this text.[36] Then there is the Hildreth-Lu scanning or search procedure (see exercise 12.7). But this method is quite time-consuming and has been found to be grossly inefficient compared to ML estimation and is therefore not used much these days.

We conclude this section with these observations. The various methods just discussed are basically two-step methods: In Step 1 we obtain an estimate of the unknown ρ and in Step 2 we use that estimate to transform the variables to estimate the generalized difference equation, which is basically GLS. But since we use $\hat{\rho}$ instead of the true ρ, all these methods of estimation are known in the literature as **feasible** or **estimated generalized least-squares (EGLS)** methods.

12.7 AN ILLUSTRATIVE EXAMPLE: THE RELATIONSHIP BETWEEN HELP-WANTED INDEX AND THE UNEMPLOYMENT RATE, UNITED STATES: COMPARISON OF THE METHODS

As an illustration of the various methods just discussed, consider the following example. (See Table 12.7.)

The regression model chosen for empirical investigation was

$$\ln \text{HWI}_t = \beta_1 + \beta_2 \ln U_t + u_t$$

where HWI is the help-wanted index and U the unemployment rate.[37] A priori, β_2 is expected to be negative. (Why?) Assuming that all the OLS assumptions are fulfilled, we may write the estimated regression as

$$\widehat{\ln \text{HWI}}_t = 7.3084 - 1.5375 \ln U_t$$

(0.1110) (0.0711) $N = 24$

$t = (65.825)$ (-21.612) $r^2 = 0.9550$ $(12.7.1)$

$$d - 0.9108$$

From the estimated regression we observe that the Durbin-Watson d indicates the presence of positive serial correlation: For 24 observations and 1 explanatory

---

[36] See J. Johnston, op. cit., pp. 325–326.

[37] For now let us not worry about the simultaneity problem, that is, whether U causes the HWI or vice versa.

TABLE 12.6
Relationship between help-wanted index (HWI) and the unemployment rate (U)

Year and quarter	HWI, 1957–1959 = 100	U, %
1962–1	104.66	5.63
–2	103.53	5.46
–3	97.30	5.63
–4	95.96	5.60
1963–1	98.83	5.83
–2	97.23	5.76
–3	99.06	5.56
–4	113.66	5.63
1964–1	117.00	5.46
–2	119.66	5.26
–3	124.33	5.06
–4	133.00	5.06
1965–1	143.33	4.83
–2	144.66	4.73
–3	152.33	4.46
–4	178.33	4.20
1966–1	192.00	3.83
–2	186.00	3.90
–3	188.00	3.86
–4	193.33	3.70
1967–1	187.66	3.66
–2	175.33	3.83
–3	178.00	3.93
–4	187.66	3.96

Source: Damodar Gujarati, "The Relation between Help-Wanted Index and the Unemployment Rate: A Statistical Analysis, 1962–1967," *The Quarterly Review of Economics and Business,* vol. 8, 1968, pp. 67–73.

variable the 5% Durbin-Watson table shows that $d_L = 1.27$ and $d_U = 1.45$, and the estimated d of 0.9108 is below the lower critical limit.

Since the regression (12.7.1) is plagued by serial correlation, we cannot trust the estimated standard errors and t ratios for reasons already noted. Therefore, remedial measures are necessary. The remedy, of course, depends on ρ, which can be estimated by one or more of the methods discussed previously. For our illustrative example the ρ estimated from the various methods is as follows:

Method used	ρ	Comment
Durbin-Watson d	0.5446	See (12.6.12)
Theil-Nagar d	0.5554	See exercise 12.6
Step I of Cochrane-Orcutt procedure	0.5457	
Cochrane-Orcutt iterative procedure		
Iteration I	0.54571	
Iteration II	0.57223	
Iteration III	0.57836	
Iteration IV	0.57999	
Iteration V	0.58040	
Durbin two-step	0.79517	

As the reader can see, the Durbin-Watson d, the Theil-Nagar modified d, Step I of the Cochrane-Orcutt two-step procedure, and the Cochrane-Orcutt iterative procedure all yield estimates of ρ that are quite similar; but the one obtained from the Durbin two-step is quite different.[38]

The practical question then is: Which method of estimating ρ should one choose in practice? We will answer this question shortly. For now, we will continue with our example and illustrate how to estimate the generalized difference equation (or feasible GLS estimation) using one of these $\hat{\rho}$.

We use the Theil-Nagar small-sample approximation of d. Using the formula given in exercise 12.6, we obtain $\hat{\rho} = 0.5554$. With this estimate, we transform our data as follows:

$$\ln \text{HWI}_t^* = \ln \text{HWI}_t - 0.5554 \ln \text{HWI}_{t-1}$$
$$\ln U_t^* = \ln U_t - 0.5554 \ln U_{t-1}$$

That is, subtract 0.5554 times the previous value of the variable from its current value. Since the first observation does not have an antecedent, we have two options: (1) drop it from the analysis, or (2) include it via the Prais-Winsten transformation, which in the present case becomes $[\sqrt{1 - (0.5554)^2} \cdot \ln \text{HWI}_1]$ and $[\sqrt{1 - (0.5554)^2} \cdot \ln U_1]$. We present our results both ways.

Omitting the first observation

$$\widehat{\ln \text{HWI}_t^*} = \quad 3.1284 - \quad 1.4672 \ln U_t^* \quad N = 23$$
$$\text{se} = \quad (0.0886) \quad (0.1328) \quad r^2 = 0.9685 \qquad (12.7.2)$$
$$t = \quad (35.326) \quad (-11.045) \quad d = 1.77$$

where the starred variables are the transformed variables as indicated earlier. Note that $3.1284 = \hat{\beta}_1(1 - \hat{\rho}) = \hat{\beta}_1(1 - 0.5554)$ from which we obtain $\hat{\beta}_1 = 7.0364$, which is comparable with the $\hat{\beta}_1$ of the original regression (12.7.1).

Including the first observation (Prais-Winsten transformation)[39]

$$\ln \text{HWI}_t^* = \quad 3.1361 - \quad 1.4800 \ln U_t^* \qquad (12.7.3)$$
$$\text{se} = \quad (0.0813) \quad (0.1198) \quad N = 24$$
$$t = \quad (38.583) \quad (-12.351) \quad r^2 = 0.9684$$
$$d = 1.83$$

Comparing the original (autocorrelation-plagued) regression (12.7.1) with the transformed regression (12.7.2) and the Prais-Winsten regression (12.7.3), we

---

[38]There may be a technical reason for this difference. If you examine (12.6.19) carefully, you will see that there are two estimates of ρ, one obtained directly from the lagged value of Y and one obtained from dividing the coefficient of the lagged value of X by the coefficient of X. There is no guarantee that the two estimates will be identical. The real problem here is that (12.6.19) is *intrinsically* a nonlinear (in-parameter) regression model and should be estimated by nonlinear regression-estimating procedures, which are beyond the scope of this book.

[39]A technical point: The intercept term in the Prais-Winsten regression is somewhat complicated. As a result, one has to run this regression through the origin. The intercept reported in (12.7.3) has been unscrambled. For details, see Kenneth J. White and Linda T. M. Bui, *Computer Handbook Using SHAZAM*, McGraw-Hill, New York, 1985, p. 86. For theoretical details, see Jan Kmenta, *Elements of Econometrics*, 2d ed., Macmillan, New York, 1986, pp. 303–305.

see that the results are generally comparable.[40] The practical question is: Have we solved the autocorrelation problem? If we take the estimated Durbin-Watson values reported in (12.7.2) and (12.7.3) at their face values, it would seem that there is no longer (first-order) autocorrelation. (Why?) However, as noted by Kenneth White in his *SHAZAM* (p. 86), the Durbin-Watson tables may not be appropriate to test for serial correlation in the data that have already been adjusted for autocorrelation. Therefore, we may use one of the nonparametric tests discussed previously. For the regression (12.7.2), it can be shown that on the basis of the runs test one cannot reject the hypothesis that there is no serial correlation in the residuals from that regression. (See exercise 12.20). For the Prais-Winsten regression (12.7.3) also it can be shown that the estimated residuals from that regression are free from the serial correlation problem. (Check this explicitly. For your information, there are 11 positive residuals, 13 negative residuals, and the number of runs is 12.)

If we want to test hypotheses about the parameters, we can now proceed in the usual fashion. But note that since we are estimating ρ, the usual tests of significance will be strictly valid only in large samples. In small samples, the results of the tests will only be approximate. For example, from (12.7.2) we can conclude that the true slope coefficient is statistically different from zero. But we should be rather cautious here because our sample of 23 observations is not overly large.

Comparison of the methods. We revert to the question raised earlier: Which method of estimating ρ should one use in practice to run the generalized difference, or feasible GLS, regression? If we are dealing with large samples (say, in excess of 60–70 observations), it does not make much difference which method is chosen, for they all yield more or less similar results. But this is generally not the case in finite, or small, samples, for the results can depend on which method is chosen. In small samples, then, which method is preferable? Unfortunately, there is no definitive answer to this question because the small-sample studies done on the various methods, via the Monte Carlo simulations, do not favor any one method consistently.[41] In practice, however, the method that is often used is the Cochrane-Orcutt iterative method that is now incorporated in several computer programs, such as ET, SHAZAM, TSP, and SAS. As computer software becomes more sophisticated, we can use methods of estimating ρ specifically geared to deal with small samples. Already, packages like SAS have ML and some nonlinear procedures of estimating ρ. (See the AUTOREG routine of SAS.)

12.8 AUTOREGRESSIVE CONDITIONAL HETEROSCEDASTICITY (ARCH) MODEL

Conventional wisdom has it that the problem of autocorrelation is a feature of time series data and heteroscedasticity is a feature of cross-sectional data. Can heteroscedasticity arise in time series data? And how?

---

[40] But bear in mind that in small samples the results might be sensitive to the inclusion or exclusion of the first observation.

[41] For a review of these studies, see J. Johnston, op. cit., pp. 326–327. A rather advanced treatment may be found in A. C. Harvey, *The Econometric Analysis of Time Series*, John Wiley & Sons, New York, 1981, pp. 196–199.

Researchers engaged in forecasting financial time series, such as stock prices, inflation rates, foreign exchange rates, etc. have observed that their ability to forecast such variables varies considerably from one time period to another:[42] For some time periods the forecast errors are relatively small, for some time periods they are relatively large, and then they are small again for another time period. This variability could very well be due to volatility in financial markets, sensitive as they are to rumors, political upheavals, changes in government monetary and fiscal policies, and the like. This would suggest that the variance of forecast errors is not constant but varies from period to period, that is, there is some kind of autocorrelation in the variance of forecast errors.

Since the behavior of forecast errors can be assumed to depend on the behavior of the (regression) disturbances u_t, one can make a case for autocorrelation in the variance of u_t. To capture this correlation, Engle developed the **autoregressive conditional heteroscedasticity (ARCH) model**.[43] The key idea of ARCH is that the variance of u at time $t(= \sigma_t^2)$ depends on the size of the squared error term at time $(t - 1)$, that is, on u_{t-1}^2.

To be more specific, let us revert to the k-variable regression model:

$$Y_t = \beta_1 + \beta_2 X_{2t} + \cdots + \beta_k X_{kt} + u_t \qquad (12.8.1)$$

and assume that *conditional* on the information available at time $(t - 1)$, the disturbance term is distributed as

$$u_t \sim N[0, (\alpha_0 + \alpha_1 u_{t-1}^2)] \qquad (12.8.2)$$

that is, u_t is normally distributed with mean zero and variance of $(\alpha_0 + \alpha_1 u_{t-1}^2)$.

The normality of u_t is not new to us (why?). What is new is that the variance of u at time t is dependent on the squared disturbance at time $(t - 1)$, thus giving the appearance of serial correlation.

Since in (12.8.2) the variance of u_t depends on the squared disturbance term in the previous time period, it is called an **ARCH (1)** process. But we can generalize it easily. Thus, an **ARCH (p)** process can be written as

$$\text{var}(u_t) = \sigma_t^2 = \alpha_0 + \alpha_1 u_{t-1}^2 + \alpha_2 u_{t-2}^2 + \cdots + \alpha_p u_{t-p}^2 \qquad (12.8.3)$$

If there is no autocorrelation in the error variance, we have $H_0: \alpha_1 = \alpha_2 = \cdots = \alpha_p = 0$, in which case var($u_t$) = α_0, and we have the case of homoscedastic error variance.

As Engle has shown, a test of the preceding null hypothesis can be easily made by running the following regression:

$$\hat{u}_t^2 = \hat{\alpha}_0 + \hat{\alpha}_1 \hat{u}_{t-1}^2 + \hat{\alpha}_2 \hat{u}_{t-2}^2 + \cdots + \hat{\alpha}_p \hat{u}_{t-p}^2 \qquad (12.8.4)$$

---

[42] See, for example, M. Mandelbrot, "The Variation of Certain Speculative Prices," *Journal of Business*, vol. 36, 1963, pp. 394–419.

[43] R. Engle, "Autoregressive Conditional Heteroscedasticity with Estimates of the Variance of United Kingdom Inflation," *Econometrica*, vol. 50, no. 1, 1982, pp. 987–1007. See also A. Bera and M. Higgins, "A Review of ARCH Models: Motivation, Theory and Applications," *Journal of Economic Surveys*, Forthcoming.

where $\hat{u}$, as usual, denote the OLS residuals estimated from the original regression model, (12.8.1).

One can test the null hypothesis H_0 by the usual F test discussed in Chapter 8 or, alternatively, by computing nR^2, where R^2 is the coefficient of determination from the auxiliary regression (12.8.4). It can be shown that

$$nR^2 \sim \chi_p^2 \tag{12.8.5}$$

that is, nR^2 follows the chi-square distribution with df equal to the number of autoregressive terms in the auxiliary regression.

> **Illustrative example.** Let us continue with our overworked wages-productivity example. Using the residuals obtained from this regression, we estimated ARCH(1), ARCH(2), ARCH(3), ARCH(4), and ARCH(5) models. But only the ARCH(1) model proved to be significant. The results of this model were as follows:
>
> $$\hat{u}_t^2 = 2.0746 + 0.6946\hat{u}_{t-1}^2$$
> $$t = (1.0583) \quad (5.0364)$$
> $$R^2 = 0.4665 \tag{12.8.6}$$
> $$d = 1.67$$

Applying (12.8.5), we see that $nR^2 = (31)(0.4665) \doteq 14.46$, which is approximately χ^2 with 1 df. From the chi-square table it is clear that the probability of obtaining such a chi-square value is much less than 0.005 (the p value is about 0.000143). This suggests that in our example the error variance is serially correlated.

What to Do If ARCH Is Present?

Recall that we have discussed several methods of correcting heteroscedasticity, which basically involve applying OLS to transformed data. Remember that OLS applied to transformed data is generalized least-squares (GLS). If the ARCH effect is found, we will have to use GLS. To save space, the details of the theory and mechanics of this are left to the references.[44]

Incidentally, a generalization of the ARCH model is the so-called **GARCH,** in which the conditional variance of u at time t is dependent not only on past squared disturbances but also on past conditional variances. The details can be found in the references.[45]

A Word on the Durbin-Watson d Statistic and the ARCH Effect

Recall that when we regressed wages on productivity we obtained a d value of 0.1380, strongly suggesting that there was positive first-order serial correlation

---

[44]See Davidson and MacKinnon, op. cit., Sec. 16.4. See also William H. Greene, op. cit., Sec. 15.9, and also his *ET: The Econometrics Toolkit*, Version 3.0, Econometric Software, Inc., Bellport, New York, 1992, Chap. 29. MICRO TSP 7.0 and SHAZAM 7.0 have ARCH testing procedures.

[45]T. Bollerslev, "Generalized Autoregressive Conditional Heteroscedasticity," *Journal of Econometrics*, vol. 31, 1986, pp. 307–326.

in the error term. But this conclusion now seems premature because of the ARCH effect. In other words, the observed serial correlation in u_t may be due to the ARCH effect and not to serial correlation per se. Therefore, in time series analyses, especially those involving financial data, one should test for the ARCH effect before accepting the routinely printed d statistic at its face value.

12.9 SUMMARY AND CONCLUSIONS

1. If the assumption of the classical linear regression model that the errors or disturbances u_t entering into the population regression model are random or uncorrelated is violated, the problem of serial or autocorrelation arises.

2. Autocorrelation can arise for several reasons, such as inertia or sluggishness of economic time series, specification bias resulting from excluding important variables from the model or using the incorrect functional form, the Cobweb phenomenon, data manipulation, etc.

3. Although OLS estimators remain unbiased as well as consistent in the presence of autocorrelation, they are no longer efficient. As a result, the usual t and F tests of significance cannot be legitimately applied. Hence, remedial measures are needed.

3. The remedy depends on the nature of the interdependence among the disturbances u_t. But since u_t are unobservable, the common practice is to assume that they are generated by some mechanism.

4. The mechanism that is commonly assumed is the Markov first-order autoregressive scheme, which assumes that the disturbance in the current time period is linearly related to the disturbance term in the previous time period, the coefficient of autocorrelation providing the extent of the interdependence. This mechanism is known as the AR(1) scheme.

5. If the AR(1) scheme is valid and the coefficient of autocorrelation is known, the serial correlation problem can be easily attacked by transforming the data following the generalized difference procedure. The AR(1) scheme can be easily generalized to an AR(p) scheme. One can also assume a moving average (MA) mechanism or a mixture of AR and MA schemes, known as ARMA.

6. Even if we use an AR(1) scheme, the coefficient of autocorrelation ρ is not known a priori. We considered several methods of estimating ρ, such as Durbin-Watson d, Theil-Nagar modified d, Cochrane-Orcutt (C-O) two-step procedure, C-O iterative procedure, and the Durbin two-step method. In large samples, these methods generally yield similar estimates, although in small samples they perform differently. In practice, the C-O iterative method has become quite popular.

7. Of course, before remediation comes detection of autocorrelation. There are several methods of detection, of which the most celebrated is the Durbin-Watson d statistic. Although popularly used and routinely printed out by most computer software packages, the d statistic has several limitations. Very often, the d statistic is indication not of pure autocorrelation but of specification bias or the ARCH effect.

8. A special model that we discussed in this chapter is the ARCH model in which the conditional variance of the error term is serially correlated with the past squared values of the error term. This model has proved quite useful in modeling and forecasting many financial variables, such as exchange rates, inflation rates, etc.

EXERCISES

Questions

12.1. State whether the following statements are true or false. Briefly justify your answer.

(a) When autocorrelation is present, OLS estimators are biased as well as inefficient.

(b) The Durbin-Watson d test assumes that the variance of the error term u_t is homoscedastic.

(c) The first-difference transformation to eliminate autocorrelation assumes that the coefficient of autocorrelation ρ is -1.

(d) The R^2 values of two models, one involving regression in the first-difference form and another in the level form, are not directly comparable.

(e) A significant Durbin-Watson d does not necessarily mean there is autocorrelation of the first order.

(f) In the presence of autocorrelation, the conventionally computed variances and standard errors of forecast values are inefficient.

(g) The exclusion of an important variable(s) from a regression model may give a significant d value.

(h) In the AR(1) scheme, a test of the hypothesis that $\rho = 1$ can be made by the Berenblutt-Webb g statistic as well as the Durbin-Watson d statistic.

(i) In the regression of the first difference of Y on the first differences of X, if there is a constant term and a linear trend term, it means in the original model there is a linear as well as a quadratic trend term.

12.2. Given a sample of 50 observations and 4 explanatory variables, what can you say about autocorrelation if (a) $d = 1.05$? (b) $d = 1.40$? (c) $d = 2.50$? (d) $d = 3.97$?

12.3. In studying the movement in the production workers' share in the value added (i.e., labor's share), the following models were considered by Gujarati:*

$$\text{Model A:} \quad Y_t = \beta_0 + \beta_1 t + u_t$$
$$\text{Model B:} \quad Y_t = \alpha_0 + \alpha_1 t + \alpha_2 t^2 + u_t$$

where $Y =$ labor's share and $t =$ time. Based on annual data for 1949–1964, the following results were obtained for the primary metal industry:

$$\text{Model A:} \quad \hat{Y}_t = 0.4529 - 0.0041t \quad R^2 = 0.5284 \quad d = 0.8252$$
$$(-3.9608)$$

$$\text{Model B:} \quad \hat{Y}_t = 0.4786 - 0.0127t + 0.0005t^2$$
$$(-3.2724) \quad (2.7777)$$
$$R^2 = 0.6629 \quad d = 1.82$$

where the figures in the parentheses are t ratios.

---

*Damodar Gujarati, "Labor's Share in Manufacturing Industries," *Industrial and Labor Relations Review*, vol. 23, no. 1, October 1969, pp. 65–75.

(*a*) Is there serial correlation in model *A*? In model *B*?

(*b*) What accounts for the serial correlation?

(*c*) How would you distinguish between "pure" autocorrelation and specification bias?

12.4. *Detecting autocorrelation:* **von Neumann ratio test**.* Assuming that the residual $\hat{u}_t$ are random drawings from normal distribution, von Neumann has shown that for *large n*, the ratio

$$\frac{\delta^2}{s^2} = \frac{\sum (\hat{u}_i - \hat{u}_{i-1})^2 / (n-1)}{\sum (\hat{u}_i - \bar{\hat{u}})^2 / n} \quad Note: \bar{\hat{u}} = 0 \text{ in OLS}$$

called the *von Neumann ratio*, is approximately normally distributed with mean

$$E\frac{\delta^2}{s^2} = \frac{2n}{n-1}$$

and variance

$$\text{var}\,\frac{\delta^2}{s^2} = 4n^2 \frac{n-2}{(n+1)(n-1)^3}$$

(*a*) If *n* is sufficiently large, how would you use the von Neumann ratio to test for autocorrelation?

(*b*) What is the relationship between the Durbin- Watson *d* and the ratio?

(*c*) The *d* statistic lies between 0 and 4. What are the corresponding limits for the von Neumann ratio?

(*d*) Since the ratio depends on the assumption that the $\hat{u}$'s are random drawings from normal distribution, how valid is this assumption for the OLS residuals?

(*e*) Suppose in an application the ratio was found to be 2.88 with 100 observations. Test the hypothesis that there is no serial correlation in the data.

Note: B. I. Hart has tabulated the critical values of the von Neumann ratio for sample sizes of up to 60 observations.†

12.5. In a sequence of 17 residuals, 11 positive and 6 negative, the number of runs was 3. Is there evidence of autocorrelation? Would the answer change if there were 14 runs?

12.6. **Theil-Nagar ρ estimate based on d statistic.** Theil and Nagar have suggested that in small samples instead of estimating ρ as $(1 - d/2)$, it be estimated as

$$\hat{\rho} = \frac{n^2 (1 - d/2) + k^2}{n^2 - k^2}$$

where n = total number of observations, d = Durbin-Watson d, and k = number of coefficients (including the intercept) to be estimated.

Show that for large n, this estimate of ρ is equal to the one obtained by the simpler formula $(1 - d/2)$.

12.7. *Estimating ρ:* **The Hildreth-Lu scanning or search procedure.**** Since in the first-order autoregressive scheme

$$u_t = \rho u_{t-1} + \varepsilon_t$$

*J. von Neumann, "Distribution of the Ratio of the Mean Square Successive Difference to the Variance," *Annals of Mathematical Statistics*, vol. 12, 1941, pp. 367–395.

†The table may be found in Johnston, op. cit., 3d ed., p. 559.

**G. Hildreth and J. Y. Lu, "Demand Relations with Autocorrelated Disturbances," Michigan State University, *Agricultural Experiment Station*, Tech. Bull. 276, November 1960.

ρ is expected to lie between -1 and $+1$, Hildreth and Lu suggest a systematic "scanning" or search procedure to locate it. They recommend selecting ρ between -1 and $+1$ using, say, 0.1 unit intervals and transforming the data by the generalized difference equation (12.6.5). Thus, one may choose ρ from $-0.9, -0.8, \ldots,$ 0.8, 0.9. For each chosen ρ we run the generalized difference equation and obtain the associated RSS: $\sum \hat{u}_t^2$. Hildreth and Lu suggest choosing that ρ which minimizes the RSS (hence maximizing the R^2). If further refinement is needed, they suggest using smaller unit intervals, say, 0.01 unit such as $-0.99, -0.98, \ldots,$ 0.90, 0.91, and so on.

(a) What are the advantages of the Hildreth-Lu procedure?

(b) How does one know that the ρ value ultimately chosen to transform the data will, in fact, guarantee minimum $\sum \hat{u}_t^2$?

12.8. In measuring returns to scale in electricity supply, Nerlove used cross-sectional data of 145 privately owned utilities in the United States for the period 1955 and regressed the log of total cost on the logs of output, wage rate, price of capital, and price of fuel. He found that the residuals estimated from this regression exhibited "serial" correlation, as judged by the Durbin-Watson d. To seek a remedy, he plotted the estimated residuals on the log of output and obtained Fig. 12.10.

(a) What does Fig. 12.10 show?

(b) How can you get rid of "serial" correlation in the preceding situation?

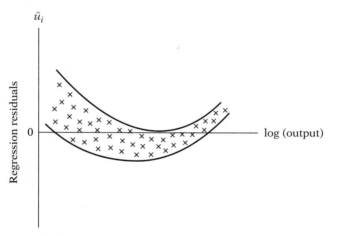

FIGURE 12.10
Regression residuals from the Nerlove study. (Adapted from Marc Nerlove, "Return to Scale in Electric Supply," in Carl F. Christ et al., *Measurement in Economics,* Stanford University Press, Stanford, Calif., 1963.)

12.9. The residuals from a regression when plotted against time gave the scattergram in Fig. 12.11. The encircled "extreme" residual is called an *outlier*. An outlier is an observation whose value exceeds the values of other observations in the sample by a large amount, perhaps three or four standard deviations away from the mean value of all the observations.

(a) What are the reasons for the existence of the outlier(s)?

(b) If there is an outlier(s), should that observation(s) be discarded and the regression run on the remaining observations?

(c) Is the Durbin-Watson d applicable in the presence of the outlier(s)?

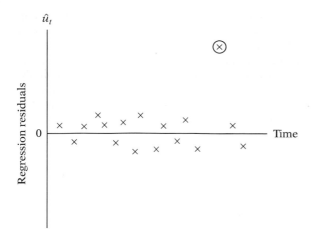

FIGURE 12.11
Hypothetical regression residuals plotted against time.

12.10. Verify Eq. (12.6.9).

*12.11. Assume the first-order autoregressive scheme $u_t = \rho u_{t-1} + \varepsilon_t$ where ε_t satisfies the assumptions of the classical linear regression model.
(a) Show that $\text{var}(u_t) = \sigma^2/(1 - \rho^2)$, where $\sigma^2 = \text{var}(\varepsilon_t)$.
(b) What is the covariance between u_t and u_{t-1}? Between u_t and u_{t-2}? Generalize your results.
(c) Write the variance-covariance matrix of the u's.
(d) If $\rho = 1$, what happens to the variance of u_t? What implications does it have for the first-difference transformation?

12.12. Refer to Eq. (12.4.1). Assume $r = 0$ but $\rho \neq 0$. what is the effect on $E(\hat{\sigma}^2)$ if (a) $0 < \rho < 1$ and (b) $-1 < \rho < 0$? When will the bias in $\hat{\sigma}^2$ be reasonably small?

12.13. Based on the Durbin-Watson d statistic, how would you distinguish "pure" autocorrelation from specification bias?

12.14. Suppose in the model

$$Y_t = \beta_1 + \beta_2 X_t + u_t$$

the u's are in fact serially independent. What would happen in this situation if, assuming that $u_t = \rho u_{t-1} + \varepsilon_t$, we use the generalized difference regression

$$Y_t - \rho Y_{t-1} = \beta_1 (1 - \rho) + \beta_2 X_t - \rho \beta_2 X_{t-1} + \varepsilon_t$$

Discuss in particular the properties of the disturbance term ε_t.

12.15. In a study of the determination of prices of final output at factor cost in the United Kingdom, the following results were obtained on the basis of annual data for the period 1951–1969:

$$\widehat{PF}_t = 2.033 + 0.273W_t - 0.521X_t + 0.256M_t + 0.028M_{t-1} + 0.121PF_{t-1}$$
$$se = (0.992)\ (0.127)\quad (0.099)\quad (0.024)\quad (0.039)\quad (0.119)$$
$$R^2 = 0.984 \quad d = 2.54$$

where PF = prices of final output at factor cost, W = wages and salaries per employee, X = gross domestic product per person employed, M = import prices, M_{t-1} = import prices lagged 1 year, and PF_{t-1} = prices of final output at factor cost in the previous year.†

---

*Optional

†*Source: Prices and Earnings in 1951–1969: An Econometric Assessment*, Department of Employment, Her Majesty's Stationery Office, 1971, Table no. C. p. 37, Eq. 63.

"Since for 18 observations and 5 explanatory variables, the 5% lower and upper d values are 0.71 and 2.06, the estimated d value of 2.54 indicates that there is no positive autocorrelation." Comment.

12.16. Give circumstances under which each of the following methods of estimating the first-order coefficient of autocorrelation ρ may be appropriate:

(a) First-difference regression
(b) Moving average regression
(c) Theil-Nagar transform
(d) Cochrane and Orcutt iterative procedure
(e) Hildreth-Lu scanning procedure
(f) Durbin two-step procedure

12.17. Will $\hat{\beta}_1 = 7.0364$ obtained from the regression (12.7.2) provide an unbiased estimate of the true β_1? Why or why not?

12.18. Including the correction factor C, the formula for $\hat{\beta}_2^{GLS}$ given in (12.3.1) is

$$\hat{\beta}_2^{GLS} = \frac{(1 - \rho^2)x_1 y_1 + \sum_{t=2}^{n} (x_t - \rho x_{t-1})(y_t - \rho y_{t-1})}{(1 - \rho^2)x_1^2 + \sum_{t=2}^{n} (x_t - \rho x_{t-1})^2}$$

Given this formula and (12.3.1), find the expression for the correction factor C.

12.19. Show that estimating (12.6.6) is equivalent to estimating the GLS discussed in Section 12.3, excluding the first observation on Y and X.

12.20. For the regression (12.7.2), the estimated residuals had the following signs:

$$- - - + - - + + - - + + + - + - + + - - - + +$$

On the basis of the runs test show that one can accept the hypothesis that there is no autocorrelation in these residuals.

*12.21. Testing for higher-order serial correlation. Suppose we have time series data on a quarterly basis. In regression models involving quarterly data, instead of using the AR(1) scheme given in (12.2.1), it may be more appropriate to assume an AR(4) scheme as follows:

$$u_t = \rho_4 u_{t-4} + \varepsilon_t$$

that is, to assume that the current disturbance term is correlated with that of the same quarter in the previous year rather than that of the preceding quarter.

To test the hypothesis that $\rho_4 = 0$, Wallis† suggests the following modified Durbin-Watson d test:

$$d_4 = \frac{\sum_{t=5}^{n}(\hat{u}_t - \hat{u}_{t-4})^2}{\sum_{t=1}^{n} \hat{u}_t^2}$$

The testing procedure follows the usual d test routine discussed in the text.

Wallis has prepared d_4 tables, which may be found in his original article.

Suppose now we have monthly data. Could the Durbin-Watson test be generalized to take into account such data? If so, write down the appropriate d_{12} formula.

12.22. Suppose you estimate the following regression:

$$\Delta \ln \text{output}_t = \beta_1 + \beta_2 \Delta \ln L_t + \beta_3 \Delta \ln K_t + u_t$$

---

*Optional.

†Kenneth Wallis, "Testing for Fourth Order Autocorrelation in Quarterly Regression Equations," *Econometrica*, vol. 40, 1972, pp. 617–636. Tables of d_4 can also be found in J. Johnston, op. cit., 3d ed., p. 558.

Determinants of U.S. domestic price of copper, 1951–1980

Year	C	G	I	L	H	A
1951	21.89	330.2	45.1	220.4	1,491.0	19.00
52	22.29	347.2	50.9	259.5	1,504.0	19.41
53	19.63	366.1	53.3	256.3	1,438.0	20.93
54	22.85	366.3	53.6	249.3	1,551.0	21.78
55	33.77	399.3	54.6	352.3	1,646.0	23.68
56	39.18	420.7	61.1	329.1	1,349.0	26.01
57	30.58	442.0	61.9	219.6	1,224.0	27.52
58	26.30	447.0	57.9	234.8	1,382.0	26.89
59	30.70	483.0	64.8	237.4	1,553.7	26.85
60	32.10	506.0	66.2	245.8	1,296.1	27.23
61	30.00	523.3	66.7	229.2	1,365.0	25.46
62	30.80	563.8	72.2	233.9	1,492.5	23.88
63	30.80	594.7	76.5	234.2	1,634.9	22.62
64	32.60	635.7	81.7	347.0	1,561.0	23.72
65	35.40	688.1	89.8	468.1	1,509.7	24.50
66	36.60	753.0	97.8	555.0	1,195.8	24.50
67	38.60	796.3	100.0	418.0	1,321.9	24.98
68	42.20	868.5	106.3	525.2	1,545.4	25.58
69	47.90	935.5	111.1	620.7	1,499.5	27.18
70	58.20	982.4	107.8	588.6	1,469.0	28.72
71	52.00	1,063.4	109.6	444.4	2,084.5	29.00
72	51.20	1,171.1	119.7	427.8	2,378.5	26.67
73	59.50	1,306.6	129.8	727.1	2,057.5	25.33
74	77.30	1,412.9	129.3	877.6	1,352.5	34.06
75	64.20	1,528.8	117.8	556.6	1,171.4	39.79
76	69.60	1,700.1	129.8	780.6	1,547.6	44.49
77	66.80	1,887.2	137.1	750.7	1,989.8	51.23
78	66.50	2,127.6	145.2	709.8	2,023.3	54.42
79	98.30	2,628.8	152.5	935.7	1,749.2	61.01
80	101.40	2,633.1	147.1	940.9	1,298.5	70.87

Note: The data were collected by Gary R. Smith from sources such as *American Metal Market, Metals Week,* and U.S. Department of Commerce publications.

C = twelve-month average U.S. domestic price of copper (cents per pound

G = annual Gross National Product ($, billions)

I = twelve-month average index of industrial production

L = twelve-month average London Metal Exchange price of copper (pounds sterling)

H = number of housing starts per year (thousands of units)

A = twelve-month average price of aluminum (cents per pound)

where Y is output, L is labor input, and K is capital input, and Δ is the first-difference operator. How would you interpret β_1 in this model? Could it be regarded as an estimate of technological change? Justify your answer.

12.23. Maddala suggests that if the Durbin-Watson d is smaller than R^2, one should run the regression in the first-difference form. What is the logic behind this suggestion?*

---

*G. S. Maddala, op. cit., p. 232.

Problems

12.24. Refer to the data on the copper industry in the table on page 445.

(a) Based on these data estimate the following regression model:

$$\ln C_t = \beta_1 + \beta_2 \ln I_t + \beta_3 \ln L_t + \beta_4 \ln H_t + \beta_5 \ln A_t + u_t$$

Interpret the results.

(b) Obtain the residuals and standardized residuals from the preceding regression and plot them. What can you surmise about the presence of autocorrelation in these residuals?

(c) Estimate the Durbin-Watson d statistic and comment on the nature of autocorrelation present in the data.

(d) Carry out the runs test and see if your answer differs from that just given in (c).

(e) Test the residuals for the ARCH effect.

(f) How would you find out if an AR(p) process better describes autocorrelation than an AR(1) process?

Note: Save the data for further analysis. (See exercise 12.26.)

12.25. You are given the accompanying data:

Y, Personal consumption expenditure (billions of 1958 dollars)	X, time	$\hat{Y}$, estimated Y*	$\hat{u}$, residuals
281.4	1 (= 1956)	261.4208	19.9791
288.1	2	276.6026	11.4973
290.0	3	291.7844	-1.7844
307.3	4	306.9661	0.3338
316.1	5	322.1479	-6.0479
322.5	6	337.3297	-14.8297
338.4	7	352.5115	-14.1115
353.3	8	367.6933	-14.3933
373.7	9	382.8751	-9.1751
397.7	10	398.0569	-0.3569
418.1	11	413.2386	4.8613
430.1	12	428.4206	1.6795
452.7	13	443.6022	9.0977
469.1	14	458.7840	10.3159
476.9	15 (= 1970)	473.9658	2.9341

*Obtained from the regression $Y_t = \beta_0 + \beta_1 X_t + u_t$.

(a) Verify that Durbin-Watson $d = 0.4148$.

(b) Is there positive serial correlation in the disturbances?

(c) If so, estimate ρ by the

   (i) Theil-Nagar method

   (ii) Durbin two-step procedure

   (iii) Cochrane-Orcutt method

(d) Use the Theil-Nagar method to transform the data and run the regression on the transformed data.

(e) Does the regression estimated in (d) exhibit autocorrelation? If so, how would you get rid of it?

12.26. Refer to exercise 12.24 and the data given in the table with 12.24. If the results of this exercise show serial correlation,

 (a) Use the Cochrane-Orcutt two-stage procedure and obtain the estimates of the feasible GLS or the generalized difference regression and compare your results.

 (b) If the ρ estimated from the Cochrane-Orcutt method in (a) differs substantially from that estimated from the d statistic, which method of estimating ρ would you choose and why?

12.27. Refer to Example 7.4. Omitting the variables X^2 and X^3, run the regression and examine the residuals for "serial" correlation. If serial correlation is found, how would you rationalize it? What remedial measures would you suggest?

12.28. Refer to exercise 7.25. A priori autocorrelation is expected in such data. Therefore, it is suggested that you regress the log of real money supply on the logs of real national income and long-term interest rate in the first-difference form. Run this regression, and then rerun the regression in the original form. Is the assumption underlying the first-difference transformation satisfied? If not, what kinds of biases are likely to result from such a transformation? Illustrate with the data at hand.

12.29. The use of Durbin-Watson d for testing nonlinearity. Continue with exercise 12.27. Arrange the residuals obtained in that regression according to increasing values of X. Using the formula given in (12.5.4), estimate d from the rearranged residuals. If the computed d value indicates autocorrelation, this would imply that the linear model was incorrect and that the full model should include X_i^2 and X_i^3 terms. Can you give an intuitive justification for such a procedure? See if your answer agrees with that given by Henri Theil.[*]

12.30. Refer to exercise 11.20. Obtain the residuals and find out if there is autocorrelation in the residuals. How would you transform the data in case serial correlation is detected? What is the meaning of serial correlation in the present instance?

12.31. Monte Carlo experiment. Refer to Tables 12.1 and 12.2. Using ε_t and X_t data given there, generate a sample of 10 Y values from the model

$$Y_t = 3.0 + 0.5X_t + u_t$$

where $u_t = 0.9u_{t-1} + \varepsilon_t$. Assume $u_0 = 10$.

 (a) Estimate the equation and comment on your results.

 (b) Now assume $\mu_0 = 17$. Repeat this exercise 10 times and comment on the results.

 (c) Keep the preceding setup intact except now let $\rho = 0.3$ instead of $\rho = 0.9$ and compare your results with those given in (b).

12.32. Using the data given in the accompanying table, estimate the model

$$Y_t = \beta_1 + \beta_2 X_t + u_t$$

where $Y =$ inventories and $X =$ sales, both measured in billions of dollars.

 (a) Estimate the preceding regression.

 (b) From the estimated residuals find out if there is positive autocorrelation using (i) the Durbin-Watson test and (ii) the the large-sample normality test given in (12.5.11).

---

[*]Henri Theil, *Introduction to Econometrics*, Prentice-Hall, Englewood Cliffs, N.J., 1978, pp. 307–308.

Inventories and sales in U.S. manufacturing, 1950–1991 (millions of dollars)

Year	Sales*	Inventories†	Year	Sales*	Inventories†
1950	38,596	59,822	1970	108,352	178,594
1951	43,356	70,242	1971	117,023	188,991
1952	44,840	72.377	1972	131,227	203,227
1953	47,987	76,122	1973	153,881	234,406
1954	46,443	73,175	1974	178,201	287,144
1955	51,694	79,516	1975	182,412	288,992
1956	54,063	87,304	1976	204,386	318,345
1957	55,879	89,052	1977	229,786	350,706
1958	54,201	87,055	1978	260,755	400,929
1959	59,729	92,097	1979	298,328	452,636
1960	60,827	94,719	1980	328,112	510,124
1961	61,159	95,580	1981	356,909	547,169
1962	65,662	101,049	1982	348,771	575,486
1963	68,995	105,463	1983	370,501	591,858
1964	73,682	111,504	1984	411,427	651,527
1965	80,283	120,929	1985	423,940	665,837
1966	87,187	136,824	1986	431,786	664,654
1967	90,918	145,681	1987	459,107	711,745
1968	98,794	156,611	1988	496,334	767,387
1969	105,812	170,400	1989	522,344	813,018
			1990	540,788	835,985
			1991	533,838	828,184

Source: Economic Report of the President, 1993, Table B-53, p. 408.

*Annual data are averages of monthly, not seasonally adjusted, figures.

†Seasonally adjusted, end of period figures beginning 1982 are not comparable with earlier period.

(c) If ρ is positive, apply the Berenblutt-Webb test to test the hypothesis that $\rho = 1$.

(d) If you suspect that the autoregressive error structure is of order p, use the Breusch-Godfrey test to verify this. How would you choose the order of p?

(e) Based on the results of this test, how would you transform the data to remove autocorrelation? Show all your calculations.

(f) Test your model for the ARCH effect. If an ARCH effect is observed, would you modify your conclusions about autocorrelation reached previously?

(g) Repeat the preceding steps using the following model:

$$\ln Y_t = \beta_1 + \beta_2 \ln X_t + u_t$$

(h) How would you decide between the linear and log-linear specifications? Show explicitly the test(s) you use.

12A.1 TSP OUTPUT OF UNITED STATES WAGES (Y)-PRODUCTIVITY (X), 1960–1991*

Residual Plot	obs	RESIDUAL	ACTUAL	FITTED
	1960	−2.40999	68.700	71.1100
	1961	−2.43360	70.700	73.1336
	1962	−1.87626	73.200	75.0763
	1963	−2.34270	75.000	77.3427
	1964	−2.03292	77.900	79.9329
	1965	−2.03275	79.600	81.6327
	1966	−0.51352	82.900	83.4135
	1967	−0.13240	84.900	85.0324
	1968	1.06304	88.200	87.1370
	1969	2.23926	89.700	87.4607
	1970	2.76793	91.200	88.4321
	1971	2.22055	93.000	90.7795
	1972	2.75411	95.800	93.0459
	1973	3.01145	98.000	94.9886
	1974	3.46845	97.000	93.5316
	1975	2.38767	97.700	95.3123
	1976	3.22124	100.800	97.5788
	1977	3.42612	102.300	98.8739
	1978	4.04046	103.400	99.3595
	1979	3.53084	102.000	98.4692
	1980	1.59745	99.500	97.9025
	1981	−0.25483	98.700	98.9548
	1982	0.96423	100.000	99.0358
	1983	−0.15465	100.500	100.6550
	1984	−2.35920	100.400	102.7590
	1985	−2.67336	101.300	103.9730
	1986	−1.35414	104.400	105.7540
	1987	−2.34453	104.300	106.6450
	1988	−3.05397	104.400	107.4540
	1989	−3.72547	103.000	106.7250
	1990	−3.68736	103.200	106.8870
	1991	−3.31114	103.900	107.2110

*The actual data are shown in the accompanying table.

OLSQ // Dependent Variable is Y
SMPL range: 1960–1991
Number of observations: 32

VARIABLE	COEFFICIENT	STD. ERROR	t-STATISTIC	2-TAIL SIG.
C	18.091487	3.3106307	5.4646648	0.0000
X	0.8094428	0.0351369	23.036851	0.0000

R-squared	0.946495	Mean of dependent var	93.61250
Adjusted R-squared	0.944712	S.D. of dependent var	11.10898
S.E. of regression	2.612109	Sum of squared resid	204.69340
Log likelihood	−75.098470	F-statistic	530.69650
Durbin-Watson stat	0.138039	Prob(F-statistic)	0.00000

SMPL range: 1960–1991
Number of observations: 32

VARIABLE	MEAN	STANDARD DEVIATION	MAXIMUM	MINIMUM
RESID	−1.537E−08	2.5696328	4.0404560	−3.7254730

INTERVAL	COUNT	HISTOGRAM
−4.0 ≥ RESID < −3.5	2	* * * * * * * * * * *
−3.5 ≥ RESID < −3.0	2	* * * * * * * * * * *
−3.0 ≥ RESID < −2.5	1	* * * * * *
−2.5 ≥ RESID < −2.0	7	* *
−2.0 ≥ RESID < −1.5	1	* * * * * *
−1.5 ≥ RESID < −1.0	1	* * * * * *
−1.0 ≥ RESID < −0.5	1	* * * * * *
−0.5 ≥ RESID < 0.0	3	* * * * * * * * * * * * * * * * * *
0.0 ≥ RESID < 0.5	0	
0.5 ≥ RESID < 1.0	1	* * * * * *
1.0 ≥ RESID < 1.5	1	* * * * * *
1.5 ≥ RESID < 2.0	1	* * * * * *
2.0 ≥ RESID < 2.5	3	* * * * * * * * * * * * * * * * * *
2.5 ≥ RESID < 3.0	2	* * * * * * * * * * * *
3.0 ≥ RESID < 3.5	4	* *
3.5 ≥ RESID < 4.0	1	* * * * * *
4.0 ≥ RESID < 4.5	1	* * * * * *

Skewness   0.109606

Jarque-Bera normality test statistic   3.306464

Kurtosis   1.440579

Probability   0.191430

Index of real compensation per hour (Y) and index of output per hour (X), business sector, U.S., 1960–1991, 1982 = 100

obs	Y	X
1960	68.7000	65.5000
1961	70.7000	68.0000
1962	73.2000	70.4000
1963	75.0000	73.2000
1964	77.9000	76.4000
1965	79.6000	78.5000
1966	82.9000	80.7000
1967	84.9000	82.7000
1968	88.2000	85.3000
1969	89.7000	85.7000
1970	91.2000	86.9000
1971	93.0000	89.8000
1972	95.8000	92.6000
1973	98.0000	95.0000
1974	97.0000	93.2000
1975	97.7000	95.4000
1976	100.8000	98.2000
1977	102.3000	99.8000
1978	103.4000	100.4000
1979	102.0000	99.3000
1980	99.5000	98.6000
1981	98.7000	99.9000
1982	100.0000	100.0000
1983	100.5000	102.0000
1984	100.4000	104.6000
1985	101.3000	106.1000
1986	104.4000	108.3000
1987	104.3000	109.4000
1988	104.4000	110.4000
1989	103.0000	109.5000
1990	103.2000	109.7000
1991	103.9000	110.1000

Source: Economic Report of the President, 1993, table B-44, p. 398.

CHAPTER
13

ECONOMETRIC MODELING I: TRADITIONAL ECONOMETRIC METHODOLOGY

> Economists' search for "truth" has over the years given rise to the view that economists are people searching in a dark room for a non-existent black cat; econometricians are regularly accused of finding one.[*]

Because of its theoretical and practical importance, in this and the following chapter we discuss in some depth the traditional and alternative approaches to building an econometric model.

13.1 THE TRADITIONAL VIEW OF ECONOMETRIC MODELING: AVERAGE ECONOMIC REGRESSION (AER)

Assumption 9 of the classical linear regression model (CLRM) is that the regression model chosen for empirical analysis is "correctly" specified. With this assumption, our main preoccupation thus far has been on estimating the parameters of the chosen model and testing hypotheses about them. If the diagnostic statistics, such as R^2, t, F, and Durbin-Watson d, are deemed satisfactory, the chosen model gets a pat on the back.

If, on the other hand, one or more of the test statistics are unsatisfactory, the researcher looks for more sophisticated methods of estimation, e.g., the

---

[*]Peter Kennedy, *A Guide to Econometrics*, 3d ed., The MIT Press, Cambridge, Mass., 1992, p. 82.

Durbin two-stage estimation procedure, to solve the autocorrelation problem. If the diagnostic tests are still unsatisfactory, the researcher begins to worry about specification errors or bias in the chosen model: Are some important variables omitted from the model? Or are some superfluous variables included in the model? Or is the functional form of the chosen model correct? Or is the specification of the stochastic error correct? Or is there more than one specification error?

If, for example, the bias results from omission of variables, the researcher starts adding "new" variables to the model and tries to "build up" the model. This traditional approach to econometric modeling is called the **bottom-up approach** because we start our model with a given number of regressors and, based on diagnostics, go on adding more variables to the model. This approach is also known as **Average Economic Regression (AER)**, a term due to Gilbert,[1] because this is how most economic research is done in practice.

In recent years this traditional AER methodology has come under heavy criticism. But before we get involved in alternative methodologies (see Chapter 14), let us look more closely at the AER methodology, because for many researchers it is still the standard methodology. Besides, econometricians like Darnell and Evans strongly argue that, with some modification of the traditional econometric methodology (given in Fig. I.4), the AER methodology may still be the preferred strategy.[2]

In this chapter we find out how the AER methodology handles the various kinds of specification errors or biases mentioned earlier. More specifically, we discuss the following topics:

1. The nature of specification errors
2. The consequences of specification errors
3. How to detect specification errors
4. Having detected specification errors, what remedies one can adopt and with what benefits

Before we proceed to discuss the various specification errors, the important question is: How does the classical, or AER, methodology choose a model in the first place? Criteria such as the following are often employed.[3]

Parsimony. A model can never be a completely accurate description of reality; to describe reality one may have to develop such a complex model that it will be of little practical use. Some amount of abstraction or simplification is

[1]C. L. Gilbert, "Professor Hendry's Econometric Methodology," *Oxford Bulletin of Economics and Statistics*, vol. 48, 1986, pp. 283–307.

[2]Adrian C. Darnell and J. Lynne Evans, *The Limits of Econometrics*, Edward Elgar Publishing, Hants, England, 1990, pp. 68–70. The modification they suggest is that before proceeding to test a hypothesis, one should apply several diagnostic tests to make sure that the chosen model is reasonably robust.

[3]The following discussion is from A. C. Harvey, *The Economic Analysis of Time Series*, John Wiley & Sons, New York, 1981, pp. 5–7.

inevitable in any model building. The Occam's razor (see Chapter 3), or the *principle of parsimony*, states that a model be kept as simple as possible or, as Milton Friedman would say, "A hypothesis [model] is important if it 'explains' much by little. . . ."[4] What this means is that one should introduce in the model a few key variables that capture the essence of the phenomenon under study and relegate all minor and random influences to the error term u_t.

Identifiability. For a given set of data this means that the estimated parameters must have unique values or, what amounts to the same thing, there is only one estimate for a given parameter. To see this concretely, recall the Durbin two-step procedure to solve the autocorrelation problem discussed in the preceding chapter. In the first step we run the following regression:

$$Y_t = \beta_1(1 - \rho) + \beta_2 X_t - \rho\beta_2 X_{t-1} + \rho Y_{t-1} + \varepsilon_t \qquad (12.6.19)$$

As the reader can easily note, there are two estimates of the first-order autocorrelation parameter ρ—one given by the coefficient of Y_{t-1} and the other obtained by dividing the coefficient of X_{t-1} by that of X_t and changing the sign. And there is no guarantee that the two estimates will be the same.

Goodness of fit. Since the basic thrust of regression modeling is to explain as much of the variation in the dependent variable as possible by the explanatory variables included in the model, a model is judged good if this explanation, as measured by $\bar{R}^2$, is as high as possible. Of course, as noted previously, the high $\bar{R}^2$ criterion per se should not be overplayed, but along with other criteria (e.g., a priori expected signs or values of the coefficients), a high $\bar{R}^2$ is always welcome.

Theoretical consistency. A model may not be good, despite a high R^2, if one or more of the estimated coefficients have the wrong signs. In the demand function considered in Eq. (8.7.23), if one were to obtain a positive sign for the coefficient of the price of chicken (positively sloped demand curve!) one should look at that result with great suspicion.

Predictive power. To quote Friedman again, "the only relevant test of the validity of a hypothesis [model] is comparison of its predictions with experience."[5] But does not a high R^2 attest to the predictive power of a model? Yes, but that is its predictive power *within* the given sample. What we want is its predictive power *outside* the sample period. As an example, refer to Eq. (8.7.23), which gives the estimated demand function for chickens in the United States for the period 1960–1982. The R^2 value was 0.9823, which is quite high. But if we were to predict the demand for chickens beyond the sample period (as long as we do not go too far out), would we obtain the same high explanatory power?

---

[4]Milton Friedman, "The Methodology of Positive Economics," in *Essays in Positive Economics*, University of Chicago Press, Chicago, 1953, p. 14.

[5]Ibid., p. 7.

13.2 TYPES OF SPECIFICATION ERRORS

Assume that on the basis of the criteria just listed we arrive at a model that we accept as a good model. To be concrete, let this model be

$$Y_i = \beta_1 + \beta_2 X_i + \beta_3 X_i^2 + \beta_4 X_i^3 + u_{1i} \qquad (13.2.1)$$

where Y = total cost of production and X = output. Equation (13.2.1) is the familiar textbook example of the cubic total cost function.

But suppose for some reason (say, laziness in plotting the scattergram) a researcher decides to use the following model:

$$Y_i = \alpha_1 + \alpha_2 X_i + \alpha_3 X_i^2 + u_{2i} \qquad (13.2.2)$$

Note that we have changed the notation to distinguish this model from the true model.

Since (13.2.1) is assumed true, adopting (13.2.2) would constitute a specification error, the error consisting in **omitting a relevant variable** (X_i^3). Therefore, the error term u_{2i} in (13.2.2) is in fact

$$u_{2i} = u_{1i} + \beta_4 X_i^3 \qquad (13.2.3)$$

We shall see shortly the importance of this relationship.

Now suppose that another researcher uses the following model:

$$Y_i = \lambda_1 + \lambda_2 X_i + \lambda_3 X_i^2 + \lambda_4 X_i^3 + \lambda_5 X_i^4 + u_{3i} \qquad (13.2.4)$$

If (13.2.1) is the "truth," (13.2.4) also constitutes a specification error, the error here consisting in **including an unnecessary or irrelevant variable** in the sense that the true model assumes λ_5 to be zero. The new error term is in fact

$$
\begin{aligned}
u_{3i} &= u_{1i} - \lambda_5 X_i^4 \\
&= u_{1i} \qquad \text{since } \lambda_5 = 0 \text{ in the true model} \qquad \text{(Why?)} \qquad (13.2.5)
\end{aligned}
$$

Now assume that yet another researcher postulates the following model:

$$\ln Y_i = \gamma_1 + \gamma_2 X_i + \gamma_3 X_i^2 + \gamma_4 X_i^3 + u_{4i} \qquad (13.2.6)$$

In relation to the true model, (13.2.6) would also constitute a specification bias, the bias here being the use of the **wrong functional form**: In (13.2.1) Y appears linearly, whereas in (13.2.6) it appears log-linearly.

Finally, consider the researcher who uses the following model:

$$Y_i^* = \beta_1^* + \beta_2^* X_i^* + \beta_3^* X_i^{*2} + \beta_4^* X_i^{*3} + u_i^* \qquad (13.2.7)$$

where $Y_i^* = Y_i + \varepsilon_i$ and $X_i^* = X_i + w_i$, ε_i and w_i being the errors of measurement. What (13.2.7) states is that instead of using the true Y_i and X_i we use their proxies, Y_i^* and X_i^*, which may contain errors of measurement. Therefore, in (13.2.7) we commit the **errors of measurement bias**. In applied work data are plagued by errors of approximations or errors of incomplete coverage or simply errors of omitting some observations. In the social sciences we often depend on secondary data and usually have no way of knowing the types of errors, if any, made by the primary data-collecting agency.

To sum up, having once specified a model as the correct model, one is likely to commit one or more of these specification errors:

1. Omission of a relevant variable, cf. (13.2.2)
2. Inclusion of an unnecessary variable, cf. (13.2.4)
3. Adopting the wrong functional form, cf. (13.2.6)
4. Errors of measurement,[6] cf. (13.2.7)

Before proceeding any further, we would like to know why anyone would commit such errors to begin with. In some cases we know what the correct model is but cannot implement it because the necessary data are not available. Thus, in consumption function analysis some have argued that besides income, wealth of the consumer should be included as an explanatory variable. But data on wealth are notoriously difficult to obtain. Therefore, that variable is often excluded from the analysis. Another reason is that one may know what variables to include in the model but he or she may not know the exact functional form in which the variables appear in the model: More often than not, the underlying theory will not tell us the precise functional form of the model; it will not tell us whether the model is linear in the variables or linear in the logs of the variables, some mixture thereof, or some other form. Finally, and more important, often a specification error is really a **model mis-specification error** because we do not know what the true model is in the first place. We will take up this point later in Chapter 14.

13.3 CONSEQUENCES OF SPECIFICATION ERRORS

Whatever the sources of specification errors, what are the consequences? To keep the discussion simple, we will answer this question in the context of the three-variable model and consider in detail two types of specification errors, namely, omitting a relevant variable and adding a superfluous or unnecessary variable. Of course, the results can be generalized to the k-variable case, but with tedious algebraic manipulations (matrix algebra becomes a necessity once we go beyond the three-variable case).

Omitting a Relevant Variable (Underfitting a Model)

Suppose that the true model is

$$Y_i = \beta_1 + \beta_2 X_{2i} + \beta_3 X_{3i} + u_i \qquad (13.3.1)$$

but for some reason we fit the following model:

$$Y_i = \alpha_1 + \alpha_2 X_{2i} + v_i \qquad (13.3.2)$$

---

[6]For completeness, we should mention another specification error, the incorrect specification of the disturbance term u_i. See exercise 13.5.

The consequences of omitting X_3 are as follows:

1. If the left-out variable X_3 is correlated with the included variable X_2, that is, r_{23} is nonzero, $\hat{\alpha}_1$ and $\hat{\alpha}_2$ are *biased as well as inconsistent*. That is, $E(\hat{\alpha}_1)$ is not equal to β_1 and $E(\hat{\alpha}_2)$ is not equal to β_2, and the bias does not disappear no matter how large the sample.
2. Even if X_2 and X_3 are uncorrelated ($r_{23} = 0$), $\hat{\alpha}_1$ is still biased, although $\hat{\alpha}_2$ is now unbiased.
3. The disturbance variance σ^2 is incorrectly estimated.
4. The conventionally measured variance of $\hat{\alpha}_2 (= \sigma^2/\sum x_{2i}^2)$ is a biased estimator of the variance of the true estimator $\hat{\beta}_2$.
5. In consequence, the usual confidence interval and hypothesis-testing procedures are likely to give misleading conclusions about the statistical significance of the estimated parameters.

Although formal proofs of each of these statements will take us far afield,[7] we have already provided some insight into the nature of the problem in Appendix 7A, Section 7A.5. It was shown there that (use $\hat{\alpha}_2$ in place of b_{12})

$$E(\hat{\alpha}_2) = \beta_2 + \beta_3 b_{32} \tag{13.3.3}$$

where b_{32} is the slope in the regression of the excluded variable X_3 on the included variable X_2 ($b_{32} = \sum x_{3i}x_{2i}/\sum x_{2i}^2$). As this expression shows, $\hat{\alpha}_2$ is biased, the bias depending on $\beta_3 b_{32}$. If, for instance, β_3 is positive (i.e., X_3 has positive effect on Y) and b_{32} is positive (i.e., X_2 and X_3 are positively correlated), $\hat{\alpha}_2$, on average, will overestimate the true β_2 (i.e., a positive bias), that is, it will exaggerate the importance of X_2. But this result should not be surprising, for X_2 represents not only its direct effect on Y but also its indirect effect (via X_3) on Y. In short, X_2 gets credit for the influence that is rightly attributable to X_3, the latter being prevented from showing its effect explicitly because it is not "allowed" to enter the model. We have shown this all with a numerical example in Section 7.7. (See also Fig. 7.3.)

Now let us examine the variances of $\hat{\alpha}_2$ and $\hat{\beta}_2$.

$$\text{var}(\hat{\alpha}_2) = \frac{\sigma^2}{\sum x_{2i}^2} \tag{13.3.4}$$

$$\text{var}(\hat{\beta}_2) = \frac{\sigma^2}{\sum x_{2i}^2(1 - r_{23}^2)} \tag{13.3.5}$$

$$= (7.4.12)$$

Since these two formulas are not the same, in general, $\text{var}(\hat{\alpha}_2)$ will be different from $\text{var}(\hat{\beta}_2)$. But we know that $\text{var}(\hat{\beta}_2)$ is unbiased (why?). Therefore, $\text{var}(\hat{\alpha}_2)$ is biased, thus substantiating the statement made earlier. In the present case

---

[7]For an algebraic treatment, see Jan Kmenta, *Elements of Econometrics*, Macmillan, New York, 1971, pp. 391–399. Those familiar with matrix algebra may want to consult J. Johnston, *Econometric Methods*, 3d ed., McGraw-Hill, New York, 1984, pp. 259–264.

var($\hat{\alpha}_2$) seems smaller than var($\hat{\beta}_2$) as long as r_{23} is nonzero (do you see this?). But one has to be careful here, for the σ^2 estimated from model (13.3.2) and that estimated from the true model (13.3.1) are not the same because the RSS of the two models as well as their df are different. Thus, it is quite possible that the standard error of the estimators from the mis-specified model could be larger than that for the correctly specified model.

Now let us consider a special case where $r_{23} = 0$, that is, X_2 and X_3 are uncorrelated. In this case b_{32} will be zero. (Why?) Therefore, it can be seen from (13.3.3) that $\hat{\alpha}_2$ is now unbiased.[8] Also, it seems from (13.3.4) and (13.3.5) that the variances of $\hat{\alpha}_2$ and $\hat{\beta}_2$ are the same. Is there no harm then in dropping the variable X_3 from the model even though it may be relevant theoretically? The answer generally is no, for in this case var($\hat{\alpha}_2$) estimated from (13.3.4) is still biased and therefore our hypothesis-testing procedures are likely to remain suspect.[9] Besides, in most economic research X_2 and X_3 will likely be correlated, thus creating the problems mentioned earlier. **The point is very clear: Once a model is formulated on the basis of the relevant theory, one is ill-advised to drop a variable from such a model.**

Inclusion of an Irrelevant Variable (Overfitting a Model)

Now let us assume that

$$Y_i = \beta_1 + \beta_2 X_{2i} + u_i \qquad (13.3.6)$$

is the truth, but we fit the following model:

$$Y_i = \alpha_1 + \alpha_2 X_{2i} + \alpha_3 X_{3i} + v_i \qquad (13.3.7)$$

and thus commit the specification error of including an unnecessary variable in the model.

The consequences of this specification error are as follows:

1. The OLS estimators of the parameters of the "incorrect" model are all *unbiased and consistent*, that is, $E(\alpha_1) = \beta_1$, $E(\hat{\alpha}_2) = \beta_2$, and $E(\hat{\alpha}_3) = \beta_3 = 0$.
2. The error variance σ^2 is correctly estimated.
3. The usual confidence interval and hypothesis-testing procedures remain valid.
4. However, the estimated α's will be generally inefficient, that is, their variances will be generally larger than those of the $\hat{\beta}$'s of the true model. The proofs of some of these statements can be found in Appendix 13A, Section 13A.1. The point of interest here is the relative inefficiency of the $\hat{\alpha}$'s. This can be shown easily.

---

[8]Note, though, $\hat{\alpha}_1$ is still biased, which can be seen intuitively as follows. We know that $\hat{\beta}_1 = \bar{Y} - \beta_2 \bar{X}_2 - \beta_3 \bar{X}_3$ whereas $\hat{\alpha}_1 = \bar{Y} - \hat{\alpha}_2 \bar{X}_2$ and even if $\hat{\alpha}_2 = \hat{\beta}_2$ the two estimators will not be the same.

[9]See Kmenta, op. cit., p. 394. See also exercise 10.8.

From the usual OLS formula we know that

$$\text{var}(\hat{\beta}_2) = \frac{\sigma^2}{\sum x_{2i}^2} \tag{13.3.8}$$

and

$$\text{var}(\hat{\alpha}_2) = \frac{\sigma^2}{\sum x_{2i}^2 (1 - r_{23}^2)} \tag{13.3.9}$$

Therefore,

$$\frac{\text{var}(\hat{\alpha}_2)}{\text{var}(\hat{\beta}_2)} = \frac{1}{1 - r_{23}^2} \tag{13.3.10}$$

Since $0 \leq r_{23}^2 \leq 1$, it follows that $\text{var}(\hat{\alpha}_2) \geq \text{var}(\hat{\beta}_2)$, that is, the variance of $\hat{\alpha}_2$ is generally greater than the variance of $\hat{\beta}_2$ even though, on average, $\hat{\alpha}_2 = \beta_2$ [i.e., $E(\hat{\alpha}_2) = \beta_2$].

The implication of this finding is that the inclusion of the unnecessary variable X_3 makes the variance of $\hat{\alpha}_2$ larger than necessary, thereby making $\hat{\alpha}_2$ less precise. This is also true of $\hat{\alpha}_1$.

Notice the **asymmetry** in the two types of specification biases we have considered. If we exclude a relevant variable, the coefficients of the variables retained in the model are generally biased as well as inconsistent, the error variance is incorrectly estimated, and the usual hypothesis-testing procedures become invalid. On the other hand, including an irrelevant variable in the model still gives us unbiased and consistent estimates of the coefficients in the true model, the error variance is correctly estimated, and the conventional hypothesis-testing methods are still valid; the only penalty we pay for the inclusion of the superfluous variable is that the estimated variances of the coefficients are larger, and as a result our probability inferences about the parameters are less precise. An unwanted conclusion here would be that it is better to include irrelevant variables than to omit the relevant ones. But this philosophy is not to be espoused because addition of unnecessary variables will lead to loss in efficiency of the estimators and may also lead to the problem of multicollinearity (why?), not to mention the loss of degrees of freedom. Therefore,

> In general, the best approach is to include only explanatory variables that, on theoretical grounds, *directly* influence the dependent variable and that are not accounted for by other included variables.[10]

13.4 TESTS OF SPECIFICATION ERRORS

Knowing the consequences of specification errors is one thing but finding out whether one has committed such errors is quite another, for we do not deliberately set out to commit such errors. Very often specification biases arise

---

[10]Michael D. Intriligator, *Econometric Models, Techniques and Applications*, Prentice-Hall, Englewood Cliffs, N.J., 1978, p. 189. Recall the Occam's razor principle.

inadvertently, perhaps from our inability to formulate the model as precisely as possible because the underlying theory is weak or because we do not have the right kind of data to test the model. The practical question is not how such errors are made, for they generally are, but how to detect them. Once it is found that specification errors have been made, the remedies often suggest themselves. If, for example, it can be shown that a variable is inappropriately omitted from a model, the obvious remedy is to include that variable in the analysis, assuming of course that data on that variable are available. In this section we discuss some tests that one may use to detect specification errors.

Detecting the Presence of Unnecessary Variables

Suppose we develop a k-variable model to explain a phenomenon:

$$Y_i = \beta_1 + \beta_2 X_{2i} + \beta_3 X_{3i} + \cdots + \beta_k X_{ki} + u_i \tag{13.4.1}$$

However, we are not totally sure that, say, the variable X_k really belongs there. One simple way to find this out is to test the significance of the estimated β_k with the usual t test: $t = \hat{\beta}_k/\text{se}(\hat{\beta}_k)$. But suppose that we are not sure whether, say, X_3 and X_4 legitimately belong in the model. In this case we would like to test whether $\beta_3 = \beta_4 = 0$. But this can be easily accomplished by the F test discussed in Chapter 8. Thus, detecting the presence of an irrelevant variable(s) is not a difficult task. But it is very important to remember that in carrying out these tests of significance we have a specific model in mind. We accept that model as the *maintained hypothesis* or the "truth," however tentative it may be. Given that model, then, we can find out whether one or more regressors are really relevant by the usual t and F tests. But note carefully that we cannot use the t and F tests to build a model *iteratively*, that is, we cannot say that initially Y is related to X_2 only because $\hat{\beta}_2$ is statistically significant and then expand the model to include X_3 and decide to keep that variable in the model if $\hat{\beta}_3$ turns out to be statistically significant, and so on.[11] This **data-mining** strategy, or **regression fishing, grubbing,** or **number-crunching,** is not to be recommended, for if X_3 legitimately belonged in the model it should have been introduced to begin with. Excluding X_3 in the initial regression would then lead to the omission-of-relevant-variable bias with the consequences that we have already seen. This point cannot be overemphasized: **Theory must be the guide to any model building.**

Nominal vs. true level of significance in the presence of data mining. A danger of data mining that the unwary researcher faces is that the conventional levels of significance (α) such as 1, 5, or 10% are not the true levels of signifi-

---

[11]This procedure is known as **stepwise regression**. For a critical review of this subject and the types of stepwise regressions, see Norman Draper and Harry Smith, *Applied Regression Analysis*, 2d ed., John Wiley & Sons, 1981, Chap. 6. See also Wojciech W. Charemza and Derek F. Deadman, *New Directions in Econometric Practice*, Edward Elgar Publishing, England, 1992, Chap. 2, Data Mining.

cance. Lovell has suggested that if there are c candidate regressors out of which k are finally selected ($k \leq c$) on the basis of data mining, then the true level of significance (α^*) is related to the nominal level of significance (α) as follows:[12]

$$\alpha^* = 1 - (1 - \alpha)^{c/k} \qquad (13.4.2)$$

or approximately as

$$\alpha^* = (c/k)\alpha \qquad (13.4.3)$$

For example, if $c = 15, k = 5$, and $\alpha = 5\%$, using (13.4.3), the true level of significance is $(15/5)(5) = 15\%$. Therefore, if a researcher data-mines and selects 5 out of 15 regressors and only reports the results at the nominal 5% level of significance and declares that these results are statistically significant, one should take this conclusion with a big grain of salt.

Of course, in practice researchers only report the final results without telling that they arrived at the results after considerable data mining. Perhaps such declaration might cost the researcher a publication and possibly a promotion and/or tenure at his or her university!

Tests for Omitted Variables and Incorrect Functional Form

In practice we are never sure that the model adopted for empirical testing is "the truth, the whole truth and nothing but the truth." On the basis of theory or introspection and prior empirical work, we develop a model that we believe captures the essence of the subject under study. We then subject the model to empirical testing. After we obtain the results, we begin the postmortem, keeping in mind the criteria of a good model discussed earlier. It is at this stage that we come to know if the chosen model is adequate. In determining model adequacy, we look at some broad features of the results, such as the $\bar{R}^2$ value, the estimated t ratios, the signs of the estimated coefficients in relation to their prior expectations, the Durbin-Watson statistic, and the like. If these diagnostics are reasonably good, we proclaim that the chosen model is a fair representation of reality. By the same token, if the results do not look encouraging because the $\bar{R}^2$ value is too low or because very few coefficients are statistically significant or have the correct signs or because the Durbin-Watson d is too low, then we begin to worry about model adequacy and look for remedies: Maybe we have omitted an important variable, or have used the wrong functional form, or have not first-differenced the time series (to remove serial correlation), and so on. To aid us in determining whether model inadequacy is on account of one or more of these problems, we can use some of the following methods.

Examination of residuals. As noted in Chapter 12, examination of the residuals is a good visual diagnostic to detect autocorrelation or heteroscedasticity.

---

[12]M. Lovell, "Data Mining," *Review of Economics and Statistics*, vol. 65, 1983, pp. 1–12.

But these residuals can also be examined, especially in cross-sectional data, for model specification errors, such as omission of an important variable or incorrect functional form. If in fact there are such errors, a plot of the residuals will exhibit distinct patterns.

To illustrate, let us reconsider the cubic total cost of production function first considered in Chapter 7. Assume that the true total cost function is described as follows, where Y = total cost and X = output:

$$Y_i = \beta_1 + \beta_2 X_i + \beta_3 X_i^2 + \beta_4 X_i^3 + u_i \tag{13.4.4}$$

but a researcher fits the following quadratic function:

$$Y_i = \alpha_1 + \alpha_2 X_i + \alpha_3 X_i^2 + u_{2i} \tag{13.4.5}$$

and another researcher fits the following linear function:

$$Y_i = \lambda_1 + \lambda_2 X_i + u_{3i} \tag{13.4.6}$$

Although we know that both researchers have made specification errors, for pedagogical purposes let us see how the estimated residuals look in the three models. (The cost-output data are given in Table 7.4.) Figure 13.1 speaks for itself: As we move from left to right, that is, as we approach the truth, not only are the residuals smaller (in absolute value) but also they do not exhibit the pronounced cyclical swings associated with the misfitted models.

The utility of examining the residual plot is thus clear: If there are specification errors, the residuals will exhibit noticeable patterns.

The Durbin-Watson d statistic once again. If we examine the routinely calculated Durbin-Watson d in Table 13.1, we see that for the linear cost function the estimated d is 0.716, suggesting that there is positive "correlation" in the

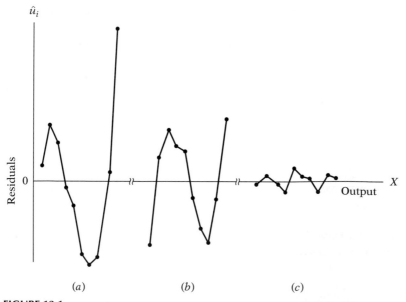

FIGURE 13.1
Residuals $\hat{u}_i$ from (a) linear, (b) quadratic, and (c) cubic total cost functions.

TABLE 13.1
**Estimated residuals from the linear, quadratic, and cubic
total cost functions**

Observation number	$\hat{u}_i,$ linear model*	$\hat{u}_i,$ quadratic model†	$\hat{u}_i,$ cubic model**
1	6.600	−23.900	−0.222
2	19.667	9.500	1.607
3	13.733	18.817	−0.915
4	−2.200	13.050	−4.426
5	−9.133	11.200	4.435
6	−26.067	−5.733	1.032
7	−32.000	−16.750	0.726
8	−28.933	−23.850	−4.119
9	4.133	−6.033	1.859
10	54.200	23.700	0.022

$$*\hat{Y}_i = 166.467 + 19.933\,X_i$$
$$\quad\;(19.021)\quad(3.066)$$
$$\quad\;(8.752)\quad(6.502)$$
$R^2 = 0.8409$
$\bar{R}^2 = 0.8210$
$d = 0.716$

$$^\dagger\hat{Y}_i = 222.383 - 8.0250\,X_i + 2.542\,X_i^2$$
$$\quad\;(23.488)\quad(9.809)\quad\;\;(0.869)$$
$$\quad\;(9.468)\;(-0.818)\quad\;(2.925)$$
$R^2 = 0.9284$
$\bar{R}^2 = 0.9079$
$d = 1.038$

$$**\hat{Y}_i = 141.767 + 63.478\,X_i - 12.962\,X_i^2 + 0.939\,X_i^3$$
$$\quad\;(6.375)\quad(4.778)\quad\;\;(0.9856)\quad\;(0.0592)$$
$$\quad(22.238)\;(13.285)\;(-13.151)\quad(15.861)$$
$R^2 = 0.9983$
$\bar{R}^2 = 0.9975$
$d = 2.70$

estimated residuals: for $n = 10$ and $k' = 1$, the 5% critical d values are $d_L = 0.879$ and $d_U = 1.320$. Likewise, the computed d value for the quadratic cost function is 1.038, whereas the 5% critical values are $d_L = 0.697$ and $d_U = 1.641$, indicating indecision. But if we use the modified d test (see Chapter 12), we can say that there is positive "correlation" in the residuals, for the computed d is less than d_U. For the cubic cost function, the true specification, the estimated d value does not indicate any positive "correlation" in the residuals.[13]

The observed positive "correlation" in the residuals when we fit the linear or quadratic model is not a measure of (first-order) serial correlation but of (model) specification error(s). The observed correlation simply reflects the fact that some variable(s) that belong in the model are included in the error term and need to be culled out from it and introduced in their own right as explanatory variables: If we exclude the X_i^3 from the cost function, then as (13.2.3) shows, the error term in the mis-specified model (13.2.2) is in fact $(u_{1i} + \beta_4 X_i^3)$ and it will exhibit a systematic pattern (e.g., positive autocorrelation) if X_i^3 in fact affects Y significantly.

To use the Durbin-Watson test for detecting model specification error(s), we proceed as follows:

1. From the assumed model, obtain the OLS residuals.
2. If it is believed that the assumed model is mis-specified because it excludes a relevant explanatory variable, say, Z from the model, order the residuals

---

[13]In the present context, a value of $d = 2$ will mean no specification error. (Why?)

obtained in Step 1 according to increasing values of Z. *Note:* The Z variable could be one of the X variables included in the assumed model or it could be some function of that variable, such as X^2 or X^3.

3. Compute the d statistic from the residuals thus ordered by the usual d formula, namely,

$$d = \frac{\sum_{t=2}^{n} (\hat{u}_t - \hat{u}_{t-1})^2}{\sum_{t=1}^{n} \hat{u}_t^2}$$

Note: The subscript t is the index of observation here and does not necessarily mean that the data are time series.

4. Based on the Durbin-Watson tables, if the estimated d value is significant, then one can accept the hypothesis of model mis-specification. If that turns out to be the case, the remedial measures will naturally suggest themselves.

In our cost example, the $Z(=X)$ variable (output) was already ordered.[14] Therefore, we do not have to compute the d statistic afresh. As we have seen, the d statistic for both the linear and quadratic cost functions suggests specification errors. The remedies are clear: Introduce the quadratic and cubic terms in the linear cost function and the cubic term in the quadratic cost function. In short, run the cubic cost model.

Ramsey's RESET test. Ramsey has proposed a general test of specification error called RESET (regression specification error test).[15] Here we will illustrate only the simplest version of the test. To fix ideas, let us continue with our cost-output example and assume that the cost function is linear in output as

$$Y_i = \lambda_1 + \lambda_2 X_i + u_{3i} \tag{13.4.6}$$

where Y = total cost and X = output. Now if we plot the residuals $\hat{u}_i$ obtained from this regression against $\hat{Y}_i$, the estimated Y_i from this model, we get the picture shown in Fig. 13.2. Although $\sum \hat{u}_i$ and $\sum \hat{u}_i \hat{Y}_i$ are necessarily zero (why? see Chapter 3), the residuals in this figure show a pattern in which their mean changes systematically with $\hat{Y}_i$. This would suggest that if we introduce $\hat{Y}_i$ in some form as a regressor(s) in (13.4.6), it should increase R^2. And if the increase in R^2 is statistically significant (on the basis of the F test discussed in Chapter 8), it would suggest that the linear cost function (13.4.6) was mis-specified. This is essentially the idea behind RESET. **The steps involved in RESET are as follows:**

---

[14]It does not matter if we order $\hat{u}_i$ according to X_i^2 or X_i^3 since these are functions of X_i, which is already ordered.

[15]J. B. Ramsey, "Tests for Specification Errors in Classical Linear Least Squares Regression Analysis," *Journal of the Royal Statistical Society*, series B, vol. 31, 1969, pp. 350–371.

1. From the chosen model, e.g., (13.4.6), obtain the estimated Y_i, that is, $\hat{Y}_i$.
2. Rerun (13.4.6) introducing $\hat{Y}_i$ in some form as an additional regressor(s). From Fig. 13.2, we observe that there is a curvilinear relationship between $\hat{u}_i$ and $\hat{Y}_i$, suggesting that one can introduce $\hat{Y}_i^2$ and $\hat{Y}_i^3$ as additional regressors. Thus, we run

$$Y_i = \beta_1 + \beta_2 X_i + \beta_3 \hat{Y}_i^2 + \beta_4 \hat{Y}_i^3 + u_i \tag{13.4.7}$$

3. Let the R^2 obtained from (13.4.7) be R_{new}^2 and that obtained from (13.4.6) be R_{old}^2. Then we can use the F test first introduced in (8.5.18), namely,

$$F = \frac{(R_{new}^2 - R_{old}^2)/\text{number of new regressors}}{(1 - R_{new}^2)/(n - \text{number of parameters in the new model})} \tag{8.5.18}$$

to find out if the increase in R^2 from using (13.4.7) is statistically significant.
4. If the computed F value is significant, say, at the 5% level, one can accept the hypothesis that the model (13.4.6) is misspecified.

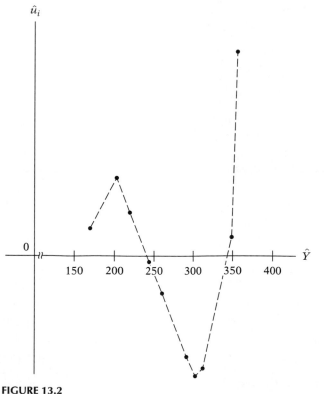

FIGURE 13.2
Residuals $\hat{u}_i$ and estimated Y from the linear cost function: $Y_i = \lambda_1 + \lambda_2 X_i + u_i$.

Returning to our illustrative example, we have the following results (standard errors in parentheses):

$$\hat{Y}_i = 166.467 + 19.933X_i \tag{13.4.8}$$
$$(19.021) \qquad (3.066) \qquad R^2 = 0.8409$$

$$\hat{Y}_i = 2140.7223 + 476.6557X_i - 0.09187\hat{Y}_i^2 + 0.000119\hat{Y}_i^3 \tag{13.4.9}$$
$$(132.0044) \qquad (33.3951) \qquad (0.00620) \qquad (0.0000074)$$
$$R^2 = 0.9983$$

Note: $\hat{Y}_i^2$ and $\hat{Y}_i^3$ in (13.4.9) are obtained from (13.4.8).

Now applying the F test we find

$$F = \frac{(0.9983 - 0.8409)/2}{(1 - 0.9983)/(10 - 4)}$$
$$= 284.4035 \tag{13.4.10}$$

The reader can easily verify that this F value is highly significant, indicating that the model (13.4.8) is mis-specified. Of course, we have reached the same conclusion on the basis of the visual examination of the residuals as well as the Durbin-Watson d value.

One advantage of RESET is that it is easy to apply, for it does not require one to specify what the alternative model is. But that is also its disadvantage because knowing that a model is mis-specified does not help us necessarily in choosing a better alternative.

Lagrange multiplier (LM) test for adding variables. This is an alternative to Ramsey's RESET test. To illustrate this test, we will continue with the preceding illustrative example.

If we compare the linear cost function (13.4.6) with the cubic cost function (13.4.4), the former is a *restricted version* of the latter (recall our discussion of **restricted least-squares** from Chapter 8). The restricted regression (13.4.6) assumes that the coefficients of the squared and cubed output terms are equal to zero. To test this, the LM test proceeds as follows:

1. Estimate the restricted regression (13.4.6) by OLS and obtain the residuals, $\hat{u}_i$.
2. If in fact the unrestricted regression (13.4.4) is the true regression, the residuals obtained in (13.4.6) should be related to the squared and cubed output terms, that is, X_i^2 and X_i^3.
3. This suggests that we regress the $\hat{u}_i$ obtained in Step 1 on all the regressors (including those in the restricted regression), which in the present case means

$$\hat{u}_i = \alpha_1 + \alpha_2 X_i + \alpha_3 X_i^2 + \alpha_4 X_i^3 + v_i \tag{13.4.11}$$

where v is an error term with the usual properties.
4. For large-sample size, Engle has shown that n (the sample size) times the R^2 estimated from the (auxiliary) regression (13.4.11) follows the chi-square

distribution with df equal to the number of restrictions imposed by the restricted regression, two in the present example since the terms X_i^2 and X_i^3 are dropped from the model.[16] Symbolically, we write

$$nR^2 \underset{\text{asy}}{\sim} \chi^2_{(\text{number of restrictions})} \qquad (13.4.12)$$

where *asy* means asymptotically, that is, in large samples.

5. If the chi-square value obtained from (13.4.12) exceeds the critical chi-square value at the chosen level of significance, we reject the restricted regression. Otherwise, we do not reject it.

For our example, the regression results are as follows:

$$\hat{Y}_i = 166.467 + 19.333X_i \qquad (13.4.13)$$

where Y is total cost and X is output. The standard errors for this regression are already given in Table 13.1.

When the residuals from (13.4.13) are regressed as just suggested in Step 3, we obtain the following results:

$$
\begin{aligned}
\hat{u}_i &= -24.7 + 43.5443X_i - 12.9615X_i^2 + 0.9396X_i^3 \qquad (13.4.14) \\
\text{se} &= \quad (6.375)\ (4.779) \qquad (0.986) \qquad (0.059) \\
& \qquad\qquad\qquad R^2 = 0.9896
\end{aligned}
$$

Although our sample size of 10 is by no means large, just to illustrate the LM mechanism, we obtain $nR^2 = (10)(0.9896) = 9.896$. From the chi-square table we observe that for 2 df the 1% critical chi-square value is about 9.21. Therefore, the observed value of 9.896 is significant at the 1% level, and our conclusion would be to reject the restricted regression (i.e., the linear cost function). We reached the similar conclusion on the basis of Ramsey's RESET test.

13.5 ERRORS OF MEASUREMENT

All along we have assumed implicitly that the dependent variable Y and the explanatory variables, the X's, are measured without any errors. Thus, in the regression of consumption expenditure on income and wealth of households, we assume that the data on these variables are "accurate"; they are not *guess estimates*, extrapolated, interpolated, or rounded off in any systematic manner, such as to the nearest hundredth dollar, and so on. Unfortunately, this ideal is not met in practice for a variety of reasons, such as nonresponse errors, reporting errors, and computing errors. Whatever the reasons, error of measurement is a potentially troublesome problem, for it constitutes yet another example of specification bias with the consequences noted below.

---

[16]R. F. Engle, "A General Approach to Lagrangian Multiplier Model Diagnostics," *Journal of Econometrics*, vol. 20, 1982, pp. 83–104.

Errors of Measurement in the Dependent Variable Y

Consider the following model:

$$Y_i^* = \alpha + \beta X_i + u_i \tag{13.5.1}$$

where Y_i^* = permanent consumption expenditure[17]

X_i = current income

u_i = stochastic disturbance term

Since Y_i^* is not directly measurable, we may use an observable expenditure variable Y_i such that

$$Y_i = Y_i^* + \varepsilon_i \tag{13.5.2}$$

where ε_i denote errors of measurement in Y_i^*. Therefore, instead of estimating (13.5.1), we estimate

$$\begin{aligned} Y_i &= (\alpha + \beta X_i + u_i) + \varepsilon_i \\ &= \alpha + \beta X_i + (u_i + \varepsilon_i) \\ &= \alpha + \beta X_i + v_i \end{aligned} \tag{13.5.3}$$

where $v_i = u_i + \varepsilon_i$ is a composite error term, containing the population disturbance term (which may be called the *equation error term*) and the measurement error term.

For simplicity assume that $E(u_i) = E(\varepsilon_i) = 0$, $\text{cov}(X_i, u_i) = 0$ (which is the assumption of the classical linear regression), and $\text{cov}(X_i, \varepsilon_i) = 0$; that is, the errors of measurement in Y_i^* are uncorrelated with X_i, and $\text{cov}(u_i, \varepsilon_i) = 0$; that is, the equation error and the measurement error are uncorrelated. With these assumptions, it can be seen that β estimated from either (13.5.1) or (13.5.3) will be an unbiased estimator of the true β (see exercise 13.8); that is, the errors of measurement in the dependent variable Y do not destroy the unbiasedness property of the OLS estimators. However, the variances and standard errors of β estimated from (13.5.1) and (13.5.3) will be different because, employing the usual formulas (see Chapter 3), we obtain

Model (13.5.1): $\qquad \text{var}(\hat{\beta}) = \dfrac{\sigma_u^2}{\sum x_i^2} \qquad\qquad (13.5.4)$

Model (13.5.3): $\qquad \text{var}(\hat{\beta}) = \dfrac{\sigma_v^2}{\sum x_i^2}$

$$= \frac{\sigma_u^2 + \sigma_\varepsilon^2}{\sum x_i^2} \tag{13.5.5}$$

Obviously, the latter variance is larger than the former.[18] Therefore, **although the errors of measurement in the dependent variable still give unbiased**

---

[17]This phrase is due to Milton Friedman. See also exercise 13.9.

[18]But note that this variance is still unbiased because under the stated conditions the composite error term $v_i = u_i + \varepsilon_i$ still satisfies the assumptions underlying the method of least squares.

estimates of the parameters and their variances, the estimated variances are now larger than in the case where there are no such errors of measurement.

Errors of Measurement in the Explanatory Variable X

Now assume that instead of (13.5.1), we have the following model:

$$Y_i = \alpha + \beta X_i^* + u_i \tag{13.5.6}$$

where Y_i = current consumption expenditure
X_i^* = permanent income
u_i = disturbance term (equation error)

Suppose instead of observing X_i^*, we observe

$$X_i = X_i^* + w_i \tag{13.5.7}$$

where w_i represents errors of measurement in X_i^*. Therefore, instead of estimating (13.5.6), we estimate

$$
\begin{aligned}
Y_i &= \alpha + \beta(X_i - w_i) + u_i \\
&= \alpha + \beta X_i + (u_i - \beta w_i) \\
&= \alpha + \beta X_i + z_i
\end{aligned}
\tag{13.5.8}
$$

where $z_i = u_i - \beta w_i$, a compound of equation and measurement errors.

Now even if we assume that w_i has zero mean, is serially independent, and is uncorrelated with u_i, we can no longer assume that the composite error term z_i is independent of the explanatory variable X_i because [assuming $E(z_i) = 0$]

$$
\begin{aligned}
\text{cov}(z_i, X_i) &= E\,[z_i - E(z_i)][X_i - E(X_i)] \\
&= E(u_i - \beta w_i)(w_i) \quad \text{using (13.5.7)} \\
&= E(-\beta w_i^2) \\
&= -\beta \sigma_w^2
\end{aligned}
\tag{13.5.9}
$$

Thus, the explanatory variable and the error term in (13.5.8) are correlated, which violates the crucial assumption of the classical linear regression model that the explanatory variable is uncorrelated with the stochastic disturbance term. If this assumption is violated, it can be shown that the *OLS estimators are not only biased but also inconsistent, that is, they remain biased even if the sample size n increases indefinitely.*[19]

---

[19]As shown in App. A, $\hat{\beta}$ is a consistent estimator of β if, as n increases indefinitely, the sampling distribution of $\hat{\beta}$ will ultimately collapse to the true β. Technically, this is stated as $\text{plim}_{n \to \infty}\hat{\beta} = \beta$. As noted in App. A, consistency is a large-sample property and is often used to study the behavior of an estimator when its finite or small-sample properties (e.g., unbiasedness) cannot be determined.

For the model (13.5.8), it is shown in Appendix 13A, Section 13A.2 that

$$\text{plim } \hat{\beta} = \beta \left[\frac{1}{1 + \sigma_w^2 / \sigma_{X^*}^2} \right] \tag{13.5.10}$$

where σ_w^2 and $\sigma_{X^*}^2$ are variances of w_i and X^*, respectively, and where plim $\hat{\beta}$ means the probability limit of β.

Since the term inside the brackets is expected to be less than 1 (why?), (13.5.10) shows that even if the sample size increases indefinitely, $\hat{\beta}$ will not converge to β. Actually, if β is assumed positive, $\hat{\beta}$ will underestimate β, that is, it is biased toward zero. Of course, if there are no measurement errors in X (i.e., $\sigma_w^2 = 0$), $\hat{\beta}$ will provide a consistent estimator of β.

Therefore, measurement errors pose a serious problem when they are present in the explanatory variable(s) because they make consistent estimation of the parameters impossible. Of course, as we saw, if they are present only in the dependent variable, the estimators remain unbiased and hence they are consistent too. If errors of measurement are present in the explanatory variable(s), what is the solution? The answer is not easy. At one extreme, we can assume that if σ_w^2 is small compared to $\sigma_{X^*}^2$, for all practical purposes we can "assume away" the problem and proceed with the usual OLS estimation. Of course, the rub here is that we cannot readily observe or measure σ_w^2 and $\sigma_{X^*}^2$ and therefore there is no way to judge their relative magnitudes.

One other suggested remedy is the use of **instrumental** or **proxy variables** that, although highly correlated with the original X variables, are uncorrelated with the equation and measurement error terms (i.e., u_i and w_i). If such proxy variables can be found, then one can obtain a consistent estimate of β. But this task is much easier said than done. In practice it is not easy to find good proxies; we are often in the situation of complaining about the bad weather without being able to do much about it. Besides, it is not easy to find out if the selected instrumental variable is in fact independent of the error terms u_i and w_i.

In the literature there are other suggestions to solve the problem.[20] But most of them are specific to the given situation and are based on restrictive assumptions. There is really no satisfactory answer to the measurement errors problem. That is why it is so crucial to measure the data as accurately as possible.

An Example

We conclude this section with an example constructed to highlight the preceding points.

---

[20]See Thomas B. Fomby, R. Carter Hill, and Stanley R. Johnson, *Advanced Econometric Methods*, Springer-Verlag, New York, 1984, pp. 273–277. See also Kennedy, op. cit., pp. 138–140, for a discussion of weighted regression as well as instrumental variables.

TABLE 13.2
Hypothetical data on Y^* (true consumption expenditure), X^* (true income), Y (measured consumption expenditure), and X (measured income). All data in dollars

Y^*	X^*	Y	X	ε	w	u
75.4666	80.00	67.6011	80.0940	−7.8655	0.0940	2.4666
74.9801	100.00	75.4438	91.5721	0.4636	−8.4279	−10.0199
102.8242	120.00	109.6956	112.1406	6.8714	2.1406	5.8242
125.7651	140.00	129.4159	145.5969	3.6509	5.5969	16.7651
106.5035	160.00	104.2388	168.5579	−2.2647	8.5579	−14.4965
131.4318	180.00	125.8319	171.4793	−5.5999	−8.5207	−1.5682
149.3693	200.00	153.9926	203.5366	4.6233	3.5366	4.3693
143.8628	220.00	152.9208	222.8533	9.0579	2.8533	−13.1372
177.5218	240.00	176.3344	232.9879	−1.1874	−7.0120	8.5218
182.2748	260.00	174.5252	261.1813	−7.7496	1.1813	1.2748

Note: The data on X^* are assumed to be given. In deriving the other variables the assumptions made were as follows: (1) $E(u_i) = E(\varepsilon_i) = E(w_i) = 0$; (2) $\text{cov}(X, u) = \text{cov}(X, \varepsilon) = \text{cov}(u, \varepsilon) = \text{cov}(w, u) = \text{cov}(\varepsilon, w) = 0$; (3) $\sigma_u^2 = 100$, $\sigma_\varepsilon^2 = 36$, and $\sigma_w^2 = 36$; and (4) $Y_i^* = 25 + 0.6X_i^* + u_i$; $Y_i = Y_i^* + \varepsilon_i$, and $X_i = X_i^* + w_i$.

Table 13.2 gives hypothetical data on true consumption expenditure Y^*, true income X^*, measured consumption Y, and measured income X. The table also explains how these variables were measured.[21]

Measurement Errors in the Dependent Variable Y Only

Based on the given data, the true consumption function is

$$\hat{Y}_i^* = \underset{(10.477)}{25.00} + \underset{(0.0584)}{0.6000X_i^*} \qquad (13.5.11)$$
$$t = \underset{(2.3861)}{} \quad \underset{(10.276)}{}$$
$$R^2 = 0.9296$$

whereas, if we use Y_i instead of Y_i^*, we obtain

$$\hat{Y}_i = \underset{(12.218)}{25.00} + \underset{(0.0681)}{0.6000X_i^*} \qquad (13.5.12)$$
$$t = \underset{(2.0461)}{} \quad \underset{(8.8118)}{}$$
$$R^2 = 0.9066$$

As these results show, and per the theory, the estimated coefficients remain the same. The only effect of errors of measurement in the dependent variable is that the estimated standard errors of the coefficients tend to be larger [see (13.5.5)], which is clearly seen in (13.5.12). In passing, note that the regression coefficients in (13.5.11) and (13.5.12) are the same because the sample was generated to match the assumptions of the measurement error model.

---

[21]I am indebted to Kenneth J. White for constructing this example. See his *Computer Handbook Using SHAZAM*, for use with Damodar Gujarati, *Basic Econometrics*, September 1985, pp. 117–121.

Errors of Measurement in X

We know that the true regression is (13.5.11). Suppose now that instead of using X_i^*, we use X_i. (*Note:* In reality X_i^* is rarely observable.) The regression results are as follows:

$$\hat{Y}_i^* = 25.992 + 0.5942X_i$$
$$(11.0810)\ (0.0617) \qquad\qquad (13.5.13)$$
$$t = (2.3457)\ (9.6270)$$
$$R^2 = 0.9205$$

These results are in accord with the theory—when there are measurement errors in the explanatory variable(s), the estimated coefficients are biased. Fortunately, in this example the bias is rather small—from (13.5.10) it is evident that the bias depends on $\sigma_w^2/\sigma_{X^*}^2$, and in generating the data it was assumed that $\sigma_w^2 = 36$ and $\sigma_{X^*}^2 = 3667$, thus making the bias factor rather small, about 0.98 percent ($= 36/3667$).

We leave it to the reader to find out what happens when there are errors of measurement in both Y and X, that is, if we regress Y_i on X_i rather than Y_i^* on X_i^* (see exercise 13.16).

13.6 SUMMARY AND CONCLUSIONS

1. The assumption of the CLRM that the econometric model used in analysis is correctly specified has two meanings. One, there are no **equation specification errors**, and two, there are no **model specification errors**. In this chapter the major focus was on equation specification errors; the latter are discussed in Chapter 14.

2. The equation specification errors discussed in this chapter were (1) omission of important variable(s), (2) inclusion of superfluous variable(s), (3) adoption of the wrong function form, (4) incorrect specification of the error term u_i, and (5) errors of measurement in the regressand and regressors.

3. When legitimate variables are omitted from a model, the consequences can be very serious: The OLS estimators of the variables retained in the model not only are biased but are inconsistent as well. Additionally, the variances and standard errors of these coefficients are incorrectly estimated, thereby vitiating the usual hypothesis-testing procedures.

4. The consequences of including irrelevant variables in the model are fortunately less serious: The estimators of the coefficients of the relevant as well as "irrelevant" variables remain unbiased as well as consistent, and the error variance σ^2 remains correctly estimated. The only problem is that the estimated variances tend to be larger than necessary, thereby making for less precise estimation of the parameters. That is, the confidence intervals tend to be larger than necessary.

5. To detect equation specification errors, we considered several tests, such as (1) examination of residuals, (2) Durbin-Watson d statistic, (3) Ramsey's RESET test, and (4) the Lagrange multiplier test.

6. A special kind of specification error is errors of measurement in the values of the regressand and regressors. If there are errors of measurement in the regressand only, the OLS estimators are unbiased as well as consistent but they are less efficient. If there are errors of measurement in the regressors, the OLS estimators are biased as well as inconsistent.

7. Even if errors of measurement are detected or suspected, the remedies are often not easy. The use of instrumental or proxy variables is theoretically attractive but not always practical. Thus it is very important in practice that the researcher be careful in stating the sources of his/her data, how they were collected, what definitions were used, etc. Data collected by official agencies often come with several footnotes and the researcher should bring those to the attention of the reader.

EXERCISES

Questions

13.1. Refer to the demand function for chicken estimated in Eq. (8.7.23). Considering the attributes of a good model discussed in Section 13.1, could you say that this demand function is "correctly" specified?

13.2. Suppose that the true model is

$$Y_i = \beta_1 X_i + u_i \tag{1}$$

but instead of fitting this regression through the origin you routinely fit the usual intercept-present model:

$$Y_i = \alpha_0 + \alpha_1 X_i + v_i \tag{2}$$

Assess the consequences of this specification error.

13.3. Continue with exercise 13.2 but assume that it is model (2) that is the truth. Discuss the consequences of fitting the mis-specified model (1).

13.4. Suppose that the "true" model is

$$Y_i = \beta_1 + \beta_2 X_{2i} + u_t \tag{1}$$

but we add an "irrelevant" variable X_3 to the model (irrelevant in the sense that the true β_3 coefficient attached to the variable X_3 is zero) and estimate

$$Y_i = \beta_1 + \beta_2 X_{2i} + \beta_3 X_{3i} + v_i \tag{2}$$

(a) Would the R^2 and the adjusted R^2 for model (2) be larger than that for model (1)?

(b) Are the estimates of β_1 and β_2 obtained from (2) unbiased?

(c) Does the inclusion of the "irrelevant" variable X_3 affect the variances of $\hat{\beta}_1$ and $\hat{\beta}_2$?

*13.5. Suppose the "true" model is

$$Y_i = \beta X_i u_i \tag{1}$$

where the error term u_i is such that $\ln u_i$ satisfies the assumptions of the classical normal linear model; namely, it has zero mean and constant variance. But suppose we fit the following model:

$$Y_i = \beta X_i + v_i \tag{2}$$

(a) Would the β estimated from (2) be an unbiased estimator of true β?

(b) If β estimated previously is biased, is it consistent, that is, does the bias disappear as the sample size increases?

---

*Optional

13.6. Consider the following "true" (Cobb-Douglas) production function:

$$\ln Y_i = \alpha_0 + \alpha_1 \ln L_{1i} + \alpha_2 \ln L_{2i} + \alpha_3 \ln K_i + u_i$$

where Y = output
  L_1 = production labor
  L_2 = nonproduction labor
  K = capital

But suppose the regression actually used in empirical investigation is

$$\ln Y_i = \beta_0 + \beta_1 \ln L_{1i} + \beta_2 \ln K_i + u_i$$

On the assumption that you have cross-sectional data on the relevant variables,
  (a) Will $E(\hat{\beta}_1) = \alpha_1$ and $E(\hat{\beta}_2) = \alpha_3$?
  (b) Will the answer in (a) hold if it is known that L_2 is an *irrelevant* input in the production function? Show the necessary derivations.

13.7. Refer to Eq. (13.3.4) and (13.3.5). As you can see, $\hat{\alpha}_2$, although biased, has a smaller variance than $\hat{\beta}_2$, which is unbiased. How would you decide on the trade-off between bias and smaller variance? *Hint:* The MSE (mean-square error) for the two estimators is expressed as

$$\text{MSE}(\hat{\alpha}_2) = \left(\sigma^2 / \sum x_{2i}^2\right) + \beta_3^2 b_{32}^2$$

$$= \text{sampling variance} + \text{square of bias}$$

$$\text{MSE}(\hat{\beta}_2) = \sigma^2 / \sum x_2^2(1 - r_{23}^2)$$

On MSE, see Appendix A.

13.8. Show that β estimated from either (13.5.1) or (13.5.3) provides an unbiased estimate of true β.

13.9. Following Friedman's permanent income hypothesis, we may write

$$Y_i^* = \alpha + \beta X_i^* \tag{1}$$

where Y_i^* = "permanent" consumption expenditure
  X_i^* = "permanent" income

Instead of observing the "permanent" variables, we observe

$$Y_i = Y_i^* + u_i$$
$$X_i = X_i^* + v_i$$

where Y_i and X_i are the quantities that can be observed or measured and where u_i and v_i are measurement errors in Y^* and X^*, respectively.
    Using the observable quantities, we can write the consumption function as

$$Y_i = \alpha + \beta(X_i - v_i) + u_i$$
$$= \alpha + \beta X_i + (u_i - \beta v_i) \tag{2}$$

Assuming that (1) $E(u_i) = E(v_i) = 0$, (2) $\text{var}(u_i) = \sigma_u^2$ and $\text{var}(v_i) = \sigma_v^2$, (3) $\text{cov}(Y_i^*, u_i) = 0$, $\text{cov}(X_i^*, v_i) = 0$, and (4) $\text{cov}(u_i, X_i^*) = \text{cov}(v_i, Y_i^*) = \text{cov}(u_i, v_i) = 0$, show that in large samples β estimated from (2) can be expressed as

$$\text{plim}(\hat{\beta}) = \frac{\beta}{1 + (\sigma_v^2/\sigma_{X^*}^2)}$$

(*a*) What can you say about the nature of the bias in $\hat{\beta}$?

(*b*) If the sample size increases indefinitely, will the estimated β tend to equality with the true β?

13.10. Capital asset pricing model. The capital asset pricing model (CAPM) of modern investment theory postulates the following relationship between the average rate of return of a security (common stock), measured over a certain period, and the volatility of the security, called the *Beta coefficient* (volatility is measure of risk):

$$\bar{R}_i = \alpha_1 + \alpha_2(\beta_i) + u_i \tag{1}$$

where $\bar{R}_i$ = average rate of return of security i

β_i = true Beta coefficient of security i

u_i = stochastic disturbance term

The true β_i is not directly observable but is measured as follows:

$$r_{it} = \alpha_1 + \beta^* r_{m_t} + e_t \tag{2}$$

where r_{it} = rate of return of security i for time t

r_{m_t} = market rate of return for time t (this rate is the rate of return on some broad market index, such as the **S&P** index of industrial securities)

e_t = residual term

and where β^* is an estimate of the "true" Beta coefficient. In practice, therefore, instead of estimating (1), one estimates

$$\bar{R}_i = \alpha_1 + \alpha_2(\beta_i^*) + u_i \tag{3}$$

where β_i^* are obtained from the regression (2). But since β_i^* are estimated, the relationship between true β and β^* can be written as

$$\beta_i^* = \beta_i + v_i \tag{4}$$

where v_i can be called the *error of measurement*.

(*a*) What will be the effect of this error of measurement on the estimate of α_2?

(*b*) Will the α_2 estimated from (3) provide an unbiased estimate of true α_2? If not, is it a consistent estimate of α_2? If not, what remedial measures do you suggest?

13.11. Consider the model

$$Y_i = \beta_1 + \beta_2 X_{2i} + u_i \tag{1}$$

To find out whether this model is mis-specified because it omits the variable X_3 from the model, you decide to regress the residuals obtained from model (1) on the variable X_3 only (*Note:* There is an intercept in this regression). The Lagrange multiplier (LM) test, however, requires you to regress the residuals from (1) on both X_2 and X_3 and a constant. Why is your procedure likely to be inappropriate?*

13.12. Consider the model

$$Y_i = \beta_1 + \beta_2 X_i^* + u_i$$

---

*See Maddala, op. cit., p. 477.

In practice we measure X_i^* by X_i such that

(a) $X_i = X_i^* + 5$

(b) $X_i = 3X_i^*$

(c) $X_i = (X_i^* + \varepsilon_i)$, where ε_i is a purely random term with the usual properties.

What will be the effect of these measurement errors on estimates of true β_1 and β_2?

13.13. Refer to the regression Eqs. (13.3.1) and (13.3.2). In manner similar to (13.3.3) show that

$$E(\hat{\alpha}_1) = \beta_1 + \beta_3(\bar{X}_3 - b_{32}\bar{X}_2)$$

where b_{32} is the slope coefficient in the regression of the omitted variable X_3 on the included variable X_2.

Problems

13.14. Use the data for the demand for chicken given in exercise 7.23. Suppose you are told that the true demand function is

$$\ln Y_t = \beta_1 + \beta_2 \ln X_{2t} + \beta_3 \ln X_{3t} + \beta_6 \ln X_{6t} + u_t \tag{1}$$

but you think differently and estimate the following demand function:

$$\ln Y_t = \alpha_1 + \alpha_2 \ln X_{2t} + \alpha_3 \ln X_{3t} + v_t \tag{2}$$

where Y = per capita consumption of chickens (lb)

$\quad X_2$ = real disposable per capita income

$\quad X_3$ = real retail price of chickens

$\quad X_6$ = composite real price of chicken substitutes

(a) Carry out RESET and LM tests of specification errors, assuming the demand function (1) just given is the truth.

(b) Suppose $\hat{\beta}_6$ in (1) turns out to be statistically insignificant. Does that mean there is no specification error if we fit (2) to the data?

(c) If $\hat{\beta}_6$ turns out to be insignificant, does that mean one should not introduce the price of a substitute product(s) as an argument in the demand function?

13.15. Continue with exercise 13.14. Strictly for pedagogical purposes, assume that model (2) is the true demand function.

(a) If we now estimate model (1), what type of specification error is committed in this instance?

(b) What are the theoretical consequences of this specification error? Illustrate with the data at hand.

13.16. The true model is

$$Y_i^* = \beta_1 + \beta_2 X_i^* + u_i \tag{1}$$

but because of errors of measurement you estimate

$$Y_i = \alpha_1 + \alpha_2 X_i + v_i \tag{2}$$

where $Y_i = Y_i^* + \varepsilon_i$ and $X_i = X_i^* + w_i$, where ε_i and w_i are measurement errors.

Using the data given in Table 13.2, document the consequences of estimating (2) instead of the true model (1).

13.17. In exercise 6.23 you were asked to estimate the elasticity of substitution between labor and capital using the CES (constant elasticity of substitution) production function. But the function shown there is based on the assumption that there is perfect competition in the labor market. If competition is imperfect, the correct formulation of the model is

$$\log\left(\frac{V}{L}\right) = \log\beta_1 + \beta_2 \log W + \beta_3 \log\left(1 + \frac{1}{E}\right)$$

where (V/L) = value added per unit of labor, L = labor input, W = real wage rate, and E = elasticity of supply of labor.

(a) What kind of specification error is involved in the original CES estimation of the elasticity of substitution if in fact the labor market is imperfect?

(b) What are the theoretical consequences of this error for β_2, the elasticity of substitution parameter?

(c) Assume that the labor supply elasticities in the industries shown in exercise 6.23 were as follows: 2.0, 1.8, 2.5, 2.3, 1.9, 2.1, 1.7, 2.7, 2.2, 2.1, 2.9, 2.8, 3.2, 2.9, and 3.1. Using these data along with those given in exercise 6.23, estimate the foregoing model and comment on your results in light of the theory of specification errors.

13.18. Monte Carlo experiment:[*] Ten individuals had weekly permanent income as follows: \$200, 220, 240, 260, 280, 300, 320, 340, 380, and 400. Permanent consumption (Y_i^*) was related to permanent income X_i^* as

$$Y_i^* = 0.8X_i^* \tag{1}$$

Each of these individuals had transitory income equal to 100 times a random number u_i drawn from a normal population with mean $= 0$ and $\sigma^2 = 1$ (i.e., standard normal variable). Assume that there is no transitory component in consumption. Thus, measured consumption and permanent consumption are the same.

(a) Draw 10 random numbers from a normal population with zero mean and unit variance and obtain 10 numbers for measured income X_i ($= X_i^* + 100u_i$).

(b) Regress permanent ($=$ measured) consumption on measured income using the data obtained in (a) and compare your results with those shown in (1). A priori, the intercept should be zero (why?). Is that the case? Why or why not?

(c) Repeat (a) 100 times and obtain 100 regressions as shown in (b) and compare your results with the true regression (1). What general conclusions do you draw?

13A.1 THE CONSEQUENCES OF INCLUDING AN IRRELEVANT VARIABLE: THE UNBIASEDNESS PROPERTY

For the true model (13.3.6), we have

$$\hat{\beta}_2 = \frac{\sum yx_2}{\sum x_2^2} \tag{1}$$

---

[*]Adapted from Christopher Dougherty, *Introduction to Econometrics*, Oxford University Press, New York, 1992, pp. 253–256.

and we know that it is unbiased.

For the model (13.3.7), we obtain

$$\hat{\alpha}_2 = \frac{(\sum yx_2)(\sum x_3^2) - (\sum yx_3)(\sum x_2x_3)}{\sum x_2^2 \sum x_3^2 - (\sum x_2x_3)^2} \tag{2}$$

Now the true model in deviation form is

$$y_i = \beta_2 x_2 + (u_i - \bar{u}) \tag{3}$$

Substituting for y_i from (3) into (2) and simplifying, we obtain

$$E(\hat{\alpha}_2) = \beta_2 \frac{\sum x_2^2 \sum x_3^2 - (\sum x_2x_3)^2}{\sum x_2^2 \sum x_3^2 - (\sum x_2x_3)^2}$$

$$= \beta_2 \tag{4}$$

that is, $\hat{\alpha}_2$ remains unbiased.

We also obtain

$$\hat{\alpha}_3 = \frac{(\sum yx_3)(\sum x_2^2) - (\sum yx_2)(\sum x_2x_3)}{\sum x_2^2 \sum x_3^2 - (\sum x_2x_3)^2} \tag{5}$$

Substituting for y_i from (3) into (5) and simplifying, we obtain

$$E(\hat{\alpha}_3) = \beta_2 \frac{[(\sum x_2x_3)(\sum x_2^2) - (\sum x_2x_3)(\sum x_2^2)]}{\sum x_2^2 \sum x_3^2 - (\sum x_2x_3)^2}$$

$$= 0 \tag{6}$$

which is its value in the true model since X_3 is absent from the true model.

13A.2   PROOF OF (13.5.10)

We have

$$Y = \alpha + \beta X_i^* + u_i \tag{1}$$
$$X_i = X_i^* + w_i \tag{2}$$

Therefore, in deviation form we obtain

$$y_i = \beta x_i^* + (u_i - \bar{u}) \tag{3}$$
$$x_i = x_i^* + (w_i - \bar{w}) \tag{4}$$

Now when we use

$$Y_i = \alpha + \beta X_i + u_i \tag{5}$$

$$= (13.5.8)$$

we obtain

$$\hat{\beta} = \frac{\sum yx}{\sum x^2}$$

$$= \frac{\sum [\beta x^* + (u - \bar{u})][x^* + (w - \bar{w})]}{\sum [x^* + (w - \bar{w})]^2}, \quad \text{using (3) and (4)}$$

$$= \frac{\beta \sum x^{*2} + \beta \sum x^*(w - \bar{w}) + \sum x^*(u - \bar{u}) + \sum (u - \bar{u})(w - \bar{w})}{\sum x^{*2} + 2\sum x^*(w - \bar{w}) + \sum (w - \bar{w})^2}$$

Since we cannot take expectation of this expression because the expectation of the ratio of two variables is not equal to the ratio of their expectations (*Note:* The expectations operator E is a linear operator), first we divide each term of the numerator and the denominator by n and take the probability limit, plim (see Appendix A for details of plim), of

$$\hat{\beta} = \frac{(1/n)\left[\beta\sum x^{*2} + \beta\sum x^*(w - \bar{w}) + \sum x^*(u - \bar{u}) + \sum (u - \bar{u})(w - \bar{w})\right]}{(1/n)\left[\sum x^{*2} + 2\sum x^*(w - \bar{w}) + \sum (w - \bar{w})^2\right]}$$

Now the probability limit of the ratio of two variables is the ratio of their probability limits. Applying this rule and taking plim of each term, we obtain

$$\text{plim}\,\hat{\beta} = \frac{\beta\sigma_{X^*}^2}{\sigma_{X^*}^2 + \sigma_w^2}$$

where $\sigma_{X^*}^2$ and σ_w^2 are variances of X^* and w as sample size increases indefinitely and where we have used the fact that as the sample size increases indefinitely there is no correlation between the errors u and w as well as between them and the true X^*. From the preceding expression, we finally obtain

$$\text{plim}\,\hat{\beta} = \beta\left[\frac{1}{1 + (\sigma_w^2 / \sigma_{X^*}^2)}\right]$$

which is the required result.

CHAPTER
14

ECONOMETRIC MODELING II: ALTERNATIVE ECONOMETRIC METHODOLOGIES

Three golden rules of econometrics are test, test, and test.[1]

It is a sin not to know why you are sinning. Pointless sin must be avoided.[2]

As noted in the previous chapter, the traditional econometric methodology assumes a particular econometric model and tries to see if it fits a given body of data. Thus, if the model is the Keynesian consumption function (where observed consumption is a function of observed income) or Friedman's consumption function (where permanent consumption is a function of permanent income), the researcher will take one of these consumption functions as given and try to find out if the data at hand support it. The decision to reject or not reject the particular consumption function is based on the usual regression diagnostics, such as R^2, t, F, and Durbin-Watson d statistic.

The critics of this **AER** (average economic regression) tradition maintain that in nonexperimentally collected data, which represents most practical economic research, this strategy surely is questionable. To them, once a model is given, estimating its parameters and engaging in hypothesis testing is trivial. But the task of determining what the appropriate model is to begin with is

---

[1] D. F. Hendry, "Econometrics—Alchemy or Science?" *Economica*, vol. 47, 1980, p. 403.

[2] Edward E. Leamer, *Specification Searches: Ad Hoc Inference with Nonexperimental Data*, John Wiley & Sons, New York, 1978, p. vi. See also his "Let's Take the Con Out of Econometrics," *American Economic Review*, vol. 73, 1983, pp. 31–43.

very demanding. The latter task is the subject of **specimetrics**. According to Leamer,

> Specimetrics describes the process by which a researcher is led to choose one specification of the model rather than another; furthermore, it attempts to identify the inferences that may be properly drawn from a data set when the data-generating mechanism is ambiguous.[3]

There are many adherents of this view.[4] As one practitioner of this subject notes, "The idea that a model must be tested before it can be taken to be an adequate basis for studying economic behaviour has become widely accepted."[5]

Notice that the advocates of the alternative methodologies are essentially saying that before one resorts to the AER methodology, one must pay very careful attention to specimetrics, that is, choice of the appropriate model. Once that is done, one can follow the AER technique. This point was essentially the one made by Darnell and Evans (see Chapter 13).

Let us now delve into the topic of specimetrics. Because of space constraints, we will discuss in this chapter only some aspects of the Leamer and Hendry approaches to specimetrics. For details, the reader may refer to the references.

14.1 LEAMER'S APPROACH TO MODEL SELECTION

Although Leamer has contributed extensively to econometrics, for our purpose we will note two of his contributions. First, he has discussed how the AER methodology conducts specification (i.e., model selection) searches and how, by using **Bayesian statistics**, one can improve this search process. Second, he has suggested how the reporting of regression results can be strengthened by undertaking an **extreme bound analysis (EBA)**. We will discuss these points briefly.

According to Leamer, there are six different reasons for model specification searches:[6]

Type of search	Purpose
1. Hypothesis-testing	To choose a "true" model
2. Interpretive	To interpret data involving several correlated variables

---

[3] Leamer, *Specification Searches*, op. cit., p. v.

[4] The enterprising student may want to consult the following references: E. E. Leamer, *Specification Searches: Ad Hoc Inference with Nonexperimental Data*, John Wiley & Sons, New York, 1978; G. E. Mizon, "Model Selection Procedures," in M. J. Artis and A. R. Nobay, eds., *Studies in Current Economic Analysis*, Basil Blackwell, Oxford, 1977, Chap. 4; and G. S. Maddala, ed., "Model Selection," *Journal of Econometrics*, vol. 16, 1981.

[5] L. G. Godfrey, *Misspecification Tests in Econometrics: The Lagrange Multiplier Principle and Other Approaches*, Cambridge University Press, New York, 1988, p. xi.

[6] Adapted from Leamer, op. cit., Table 1.1, p. 6.

3. Simplification   To construct a "fruitful" model
4. Proxy   To choose between measures that purport to
                                  measure the same variable
5. Data selection   To select the appropriate data for estimation and
                                  prediction
6. Post data model   To improve an existing model
   construction

To see what all these searches mean, we will present Leamer's empirical exploration of the theory of demand for a commodity or product. In its simplest form, the theory of demand states that, ceteris paribus, the quantity of a commodity (say, oranges) demanded depends on the consumer's income and the price of the commodity.

To implement this theory, suppose, based on the data for 150 households, that the researcher initially chooses a log-linear model and obtains the following results:[7]

$$\widehat{\log Y_i} = \ 6.2 + 0.85 \log I_i - 0.67 \log P_i \tag{14.1.1}$$
$$\text{se} = (1.1) \quad (0.21) \qquad (0.13)$$
$$R^2 = 0.15$$

where Y = quantity of oranges purchased
      I = monetary income
      P = price of oranges

Without subscribing to this log-linear model, Leamer next describes how a typical search program begins.

As an example of the **hypothesis-testing search**, suppose the researcher wants to test the hypothesis that the coefficient of price elasticity is -1. Imposing this restriction, the researcher estimates the following *restricted regression*:

$$\widehat{\log Y_i} + \log P_i = \ 7.2 + 0.96 \log I_i \tag{14.1.2}$$
$$\text{se} = (1.0) \quad (0.20) \qquad R^2 = 0.14$$

Using the F test (see Chapter 8), the researcher rejects the hypothesis that the price elasticity coefficient is -1.

Since the nutritional importance of oranges may be greatest in areas with limited sunlight, the researcher estimates two separate regressions, one for northerners and another for southerners, with the following results:

$$\widehat{\log Y_i^N} = 7.3 + 0.89 \log I_i^N - 0.60 \log P_i^N \tag{14.1.3}$$
$$\text{se} = (1.9) \quad (0.41) \qquad (0.25) \qquad R^2 = 0.18$$

$$\widehat{\log I_i^S} = 7.0 + 0.82 \log I_i^S - 1.10 \log P_i^S \tag{14.1.4}$$
$$\text{se} = (2.2) \quad (0.31) \qquad (0.26) \qquad R^2 = 0.19$$

---

[7] This and the other regression results given herein (with change of notation) are from Leamer, op. cit., pp. 6–8.

where the superscripts N and S stand for north and south. The hypothesis that the coefficients of the income and price variables are different is not rejected at the 5% level of significance. This is an example of a **data selection search**. Notice that the same model, i.e., (14.1.1) is used, except that the sample of 150 observations is divided into two data sets, south and north.

Believing that total expenditure E may be a better measure of income than I, or monetary income, the researcher substitutes E for I and obtains the following results:

$$\widehat{\log Y_i} = 5.2 + 1.1 \log E_i - 0.45 \log P_i \qquad (14.1.5)$$
$$se = (1.0) \quad (0.18) \qquad (0.16) \qquad R^2 = 0.18$$

As a result of this **proxy variable search** the coefficient of E, the income variable, has become more significant and R^2 has increased.

Noting that the R^2 values in (14.1.3) to (14.1.5) are low, the researcher thinks that the price of a substitute product, say, grapefruit, must be added to the demand function. So the investigator reestimates the demand function and obtains the following results:

$$\widehat{\log Y_i} = 3.1 + 0.83 \log E_i + 0.01 \log P_i - 0.56 \log GP_i \qquad (14.1.6)$$
$$se = (1.0) \quad (0.83) \qquad (0.15) \qquad (0.60)$$
$$R^2 = 0.20$$

where GP is the price of grapefruit. This equation is an example of **post data model construction**, that is, revising the original model in light of the initial results. Although in regression (14.1.6) the R^2 value has increased, the two price coefficients not only are *individually* statistically insignificant but also have the wrong signs (why?).

The researcher then remembers the *homogeneity postulate* of demand theory that there is no money illusion (if income and prices all change in the same proportion, purchases will not change) and reestimates the demand function with this restriction:

$$\widehat{\log Y_i} = 4.2 + 0.52 \log E_i - 0.61 \log P_i + 0.09 \log GP_i \qquad (14.1.7)$$
$$se = (0.9) \quad (0.19) \qquad (0.14) \qquad (0.31)$$
$$R^2 = 0.19$$

This regression is a result of **interpretive search**; in comparison with (14.1.6), the imposition of the homogeneity hypothesis has "improved" the regression results in that the price variables have the correct sign and that both the income and own-price variables are individually statistically significant.

Having noted that the grapefruit price variable is statistically insignificant and the income and own-price coefficients are numerically not very different, the researcher finally estimates the following model:

$$\widehat{\log Y_i} = 3.7 + 0.58 \log(E_i/P_i) \qquad (14.1.8)$$
$$se = (0.8) \quad (0.18) \qquad R^2 = 0.18$$

Regression (14.1.8) is an example of **simplification search**, the objective of which is to obtain a simple (remember Occam's razor) or economical but useful model.

Leamer then goes on to show in some six chapters of his book how this somewhat ad hoc search procedure can be made stronger by use of Bayesian statistical techniques. Since discussion of Bayesian statistics is beyond the scope of this book, the interested reader may refer to his book.

To explain Leamer's **extreme bound analysis**, suppose in a regression model there are some regressors that the investigator regards as *free* (i.e., key) regressors and some as *doubtful* (i.e., of secondary importance); the terms *free* and *doubtful* are Leamer's. Suppose regressions are run on the key variables including or excluding all combinations of the doubtful variables. In this exercise the coefficients of the key variables will change from regression to regression. Therefore, for the coefficient of each key variable we will have several estimates; the lowest and highest values of the estimate will constitute a *bound* or a range.[8]

If this bound is fairly narrow, we can say that the data yield fairly *sturdy* information on the coefficient in question. If, on the other hand, the bound is very wide, we conclude that the data yield a *fragile* estimate of the coefficient in question. In that case further analysis is called for.

As an example, suppose we want to study the effects of education (E), age (A), IQ, parental education (PE), and parental IQ (PIQ) on earnings.[9] Suppose we treat E, A, and IQ as key variables and PE and PIQ as doubtful variables. We first regress earnings on E, A, and IQ; then we regress it on E, A, IQ, and PE; then on E, A, IQ, and PIQ; and then on E, A, IQ, PE, and PIQ. Thus, we will have four estimates each of the coefficients of E, A, and IQ. Suppose the four estimates of the coefficient of E are in a very narrow bound. This result would suggest that the coefficient of E is not very sensitive to the inclusion or exclusion of the doubtful variables and therefore our data give a *robust* or *sturdy* estimate of the coefficient of E.

Although deciding which regressors are key or focus variables and which are doubtful sometimes may not be easy, Leamer's EBA has a great value. As Darnell and Evans note about EBA:

> It urges researchers to recognize explicitly the uncertainty they have about equation specification; and to provide a more honest statement of their activities at the computer terminal.[10]

In reporting their regression results, the researcher may want to keep this advice in mind.

---

[8]We can regard this bound as a kind of confidence interval for the coefficient in question, a confidence interval reflecting model specification uncertainty. Of course, this is different from the conventional confidence interval, which represents sampling uncertainty within a given model specification. This point is due to Adrian C. Darnell and J. Lynne Evans, *The Limits of Econometrics*, Edward Elgar Publishing, Hants, England, 1990, p. 109.

[9]This example is discussed in E. Leamer and H. Lenord, "Reporting the Fragility of Regression Estimates," *Review of Economics and Statistics*, vol. 65, 1983, pp. 306–317.

[10]Darnell and Evans, op. cit., p. 109.

14.2 HENDRY'S APPROACH TO MODEL SELECTION

The Hendry or London School of Economics (LSE) approach to economic modeling is popularly known as the **top-down** or **general to specific** approach in the sense that one starts with a model with several regressors and then whittles it down to a model containing only the "important" variables.

The LSE starting point is that economic theory postulates a long-run equilibrium relationship between economic variables, say, Y (permanent consumption) and X (permanent income). This relationship is summarized as

$$Y_t = \alpha X_t \tag{14.2.1}$$

Hendry and his colleagues index the observations with the time subscript t because the LSE methodology was developed to deal mainly with time series economic data.

Of course, the long-term relationship postulated in (14.2.1) takes time to achieve. Therefore, the LSE methodology proposes the following type of dynamic procedure in order to reach (14.2.1):

$$Y_t = \beta_0 X_t + \beta_1 X_{t-1} + \cdots + \beta_m X_{t-m} + \delta_1 Y_{t-1} + \delta_2 Y_{t-2} + \cdots + \delta_m Y_{t-m} + u_t \tag{14.2.2}$$

That is, we regress Y at time t on the values of the regressors X at time t, $(t - 1), \ldots, (t - m)$ as well as on the lagged values of the regressand at time $(t - 1), (t - 2), \ldots, (t - m)$. As we will see in Chapter 17, (14.2.2) is an example of an **autoregressive** (because lagged values of regressand appear as regressors) **distributed lag (ADL) model**; the term *distributed* refers to the fact that the effect of X on Y is spread over a period of time.

Models such as (14.2.2) are known as **dynamic models** because we are explicitly considering the behavior of a variable over time.

Model (14.2.2) is an example of what Hendry calls a general model in that it contains several lag values (m) of the regressors. Such a model is too general because the value of m remains to be specified. If you have data on Y and X, say, for 100 quarters, how many lagged values can you include? Remember that as you go on adding more regressors to a model, you lose one degree of freedom for each additional regressor. And as the degrees of freedom dwindle, statistical inference becomes increasingly shaky.

Then how do you go from a very general to a more specific or simplified model (i.e., from the top down)? That is, how do you decide the size of the lag m? According to Hendry and Richard, a simplified model should satisfy the following six criteria:[11]

1. *Be data admissible.* That is, predictions made from the model must be logically possible.

---

[11]D. F. Hendry and J. F. Richard, "The Econometric Analysis of Economic Time Series," *International Statistical Review*, vol. 51, 1983, pp. 3–33.

2. *Be consistent with theory.* That is, it must make good economic sense. Thus, if the permanent income hypothesis holds, the intercept value in the regression of permanent consumption on permanent income must be zero.
3. *Have weakly exogenous regressors.* That is, the regressors be uncorrelated with the error term.
4. *Exhibit parameter constancy.* That is, the values of the parameters should be stable. Otherwise, forecasting will be difficult.
5. *Exhibit data coherency.* That is, the residuals estimated from the model must be purely random (technically, white noise). If that is not the case, there is some specification error in the model.
6. *Be encompassing.* That is, the model should *encompass* or include all rival models in the sense that it is capable of explaining their results. In other words, other models cannot be an improvement over the chosen model.

Obviously, in choosing such a model, we will have to try several specifications (i.e., choosing different values of *m*) before we finally settle down on the "final" model (search for the Holy Grail?). That is why the Hendry methodology is also known as the **TTT methodology**, that is, "test, test, and test."

Whether such a stringent test procedure is possible in practice is open to debate.[12] Practitioners may want to keep the preceding criteria in mind in claiming success for their model.

14.3 SELECTED DIAGNOSTIC TESTS: GENERAL COMMENTS

In the process of choosing among competing models, econometricians have developed a battery of diagnostic tests. Broadly speaking, these tests fall into two categories:

1. Tests of nested models (hypotheses)
2. Tests of nonnested models (hypotheses)

To illustrate the difference between the two, consider the following models:

$$Model\ A: \quad Y_i = \beta_1 + \beta_2 X_{2i} + \beta_3 X_{3i} + \beta_4 X_{4i} + u_i$$
$$Model\ B: \quad Y_i = \beta_1 + \beta_2 X_{2i} + \beta_3 X_{3i} \qquad\quad + u_i$$

---

[12]For a critical analysis of the Hendry methodology, see Darnell and Evans, op. cit., pp. 77–94. For a comparatively recent view on the Hendry methodology, see Milton Friedman and Anna Schwartz, "Alternative Approaches to Analyzing Economic Data," *American Economic Review*, vol. 81, 1991, pp. 39–49. The latter was written in response to D. F. Hendry and N. R. Ericsson, "An Econometric Analysis of UK Money Demand in 'Monetary Trends in the United States and the United Kingdom' by Milton Friedman and Anna J. Schwartz," *American Economic Review*, vol. 81, 1991, pp. 8–38.

We say model B is *nested* within model A because it is a special case of model A: If we estimate model A and test the hypothesis that $H_0: \beta_4 = 0$ and do not reject it, model A reduces to model B.

Thus, if in model A Y represents quantity of a commodity demanded, X_2 its unit price, X_3 the income of the consumer, and X_4 the price of another product, the hypothesis $\beta_4 = 0$ means that the price of the other product has no effect on the quantity demanded of this product. We can test this hypothesis with the individual t test or the F test discussed in Chapter 8.[13]

Without calling them as such, the equation specification error tests that we discussed in Chapter 13 and the restricted least-squares test discussed in Chapter 8 are essentially tests of nested hypothesis. Therefore, we will not spend more time discussing them here, except by way of exercises.

Now consider the following models:

$$Model\ C: \quad Y_i = \alpha_1 + \alpha_2 X_{2i} + u_i$$
$$Model\ D: \quad Y_i = \beta_1 + \beta_2 Z_{2i} + v_i$$

where the X's and Z's are different sets of variables. We say that models C and D are **nonnested** because one cannot be derived as a special case of another. In economics, as in other sciences, more than one competing theory may explain a phenomenon. Thus, the monetarists would emphasize the role of money in explaining changes in GNP, whereas the Keynesians may explain them by changes in government expenditure.

How do we test such nonnested or competing theories or hypotheses? The answer follows.

14.4 TESTS OF NONNESTED HYPOTHESES

According to Harvey,[14] broadly speaking there are two approaches to testing a nonnested hypothesis: (1) the **discrimination approach** where, given two or more competing models, one chooses a model based on some criteria of goodness of fit, and (2) the **discerning approach** (my terminology) where, in investigating one model, we take into account information provided by other models. We explain these approaches briefly.

The Discrimination Approach

Consider models C and D above. Suppose we estimate both models. Then we can choose between these two (or more) models based on some goodness of fit criteria. For example, we can obtain the adjusted $R^2 (= \bar{R}^2)$ values of the two models and choose the models with the higher R^2. Of course, in comparing the

---

[13]More generally, one can use the likelihood ratio test, or the Wald test or the Lagrange multiplier test, all of which were briefly discussed in Chap. 8.

[14]Andrew Harvey, *The Econometric Analysis of Time Series*, The MIT Press, 2d ed., Cambridge, Mass., 1990, Chap. 5.

two R^2 values the dependent variable must be in the same form (why?). In the literature there are other criteria besides R^2 to measure the goodness of fit, such as **Hocking's S_p measure, Mallow's C_p measure, Amemiya's PC measure**, and **Akaike's AIC measure** plus the **Schwarz criterion**, the **Hannan-Quinn criterion**, and the **Shibata criterion**. A discussion of these measures would take us far afield and is better left for the references.[15] Computer packages such as **SHAZAM, ET**, and **TSP** now publish one or more of these statistics.

Regardless of the measure used, one drawback of the discrimination approach is that it simply ranks models on the basis of one of these criteria and chooses the model that gives the highest value of the chosen goodness of fit measure. Apparently, the belief is that if one model stands out among others in terms of, say, the highest R^2 value, it must fit the data best and therefore must be the "true" model. Common sense suggests that this might not be the best strategy. Therefore, we need to develop a testing procedure that pays attention to alternative models in estimating the model under consideration. This idea is the basis of the discerning approach, discussed next.

The Discerning Approach

The nonnested F test. Consider models C and D in Section 14.3. How do we choose between the two models? Let us suppose we estimate the following nested or *hybrid* model:

$$Model\ E : \quad Y_i = \lambda_1 + \lambda_2 X_{2i} + \lambda_3 Z_{2i} + u_i$$

Notice that model E *nests* or *encompasses* models C and D. But note that C is not nested in D and D is not nested in C, so they are nonnested models.[16]

Now if model C is correct, $\lambda_3 = 0$, whereas if model D is correct, $\lambda_2 = 0$. Therefore, a simple test of the competing models is to run the nested model and test for the statistical significance of λ_2 and λ_3 by the t test, or more generally, by the F test if more than one regressor is omitted from the competing models—hence the name (nonnested) F tests.

However, there are problems with this testing procedure. (1) If X_2 and Z_2 are highly collinear, then, as noted in the chapter on multicollinearity, it is quite likely that neither λ_2 nor λ_3 is significantly different from zero, although one can reject the hypothesis that $\lambda_2 = \lambda_3 = 0$. In this case, we have no way of deciding whether model C or model D is the correct model. (2) There is another problem. Suppose we choose model C as the reference hypothesis or model

---

[15]See, for instance, G. S. Maddala, *Introduction to Econometrics*, Macmillan, 2d ed., New York, 1992, Chap. 12.

[16]We can allow models C and D to contain regressors that are common to both. Thus, in model C Y could be a linear function of X_2 and X_3 and in model D Y could be a linear function of X_3 and Z_2. Now model C is not nested in model D because it does not contain Z_2 and model D is not nested in model C because it does not contain X_2.

and find that all its coefficients are significant.[17] We add Z_2 to the model and find, using the F test, that its incremental contribution to the explained sum of squares (ESS) is insignificant. Therefore, we decide to choose model C. But suppose we had instead chosen model D as the reference hypothesis and found that all its coefficients were statistically significant. But when X_2 is added to this model, we find, again using the F test, that its incremental contribution to ESS is insignificant. Therefore, we would have chosen model D as the correct model. Hence, "the choice of the reference hypothesis could determine the outcome of the choice of model,"[18] especially when severe multicollinearity is present in the competing regressors. (3) Finally, the artificially nested model E may not have any economic meaning.

An illustrative example: The St. Louis model. To determine whether changes in nominal GNP can be explained by changes in the money supply (monetarism) or by changes in government expenditure (Keynesianism), we consider the following models:

$$\dot{Y}_t = \alpha + \beta_0 \dot{M}_t + \beta_1 \dot{M}_{t-1} + \beta_2 \dot{M}_{t-2} + \beta_3 \dot{M}_{t-3} + \beta_4 \dot{M}_{t-4} + u_{1t}$$

$$= \alpha + \sum_{i=0}^{4} \beta_i \dot{M}_{t-i} + u_{1t} \tag{14.4.1}$$

$$\dot{Y}_t = \gamma + \lambda_0 \dot{E}_t + \lambda_1 \dot{E}_{t-1} + \lambda_2 \dot{E}_{t-2} + \lambda_3 \dot{E}_{t-3} + \lambda_4 \dot{E}_{t-4} + u_{2t}$$

$$= \gamma + \sum_{i=0}^{4} \lambda_i \dot{E}_{t-i} + u_{2t} \tag{14.4.2}$$

where $\dot{Y}_t$ = rate of growth in nominal GNP at time t

$\dot{M}_t$ = rate of growth in the money supply (M_1 version) at time t

$\dot{E}_t$ = rate of growth in full, or high, employment government expenditure at time t

In passing, note that (14.4.1) and (14.4.2) are examples of **distributed lag models**, a topic thoroughly discussed in Chapter 17. For the time being, simply note that the effect of a unit change in the money supply or government expenditure on GNP is distributed over a period of time and is not instantaneous.

Since a priori it may be difficult to decide between the two competing models, let us enmesh the two models as shown below:

$$\dot{Y}_t = \text{constant} + \sum_{i=0}^{4} \beta_i \dot{M}_{t-i} + \sum_{i=0}^{4} \lambda_i \dot{E}_{t-i} + u_{3t} \tag{14.4.3}$$

This nested model is one form in which the famous (Federal Reserve Bank of) St. Louis model, a pro-monetary-school bank, has been expressed and estimated. The

---

[17]Thomas B. Fomby, R. Carter Hill, and Stanley R. Johnson, *Advanced Econometric Methods*, Springer-Verlag, New York, 1984, p. 416.

[18]Ibid.

results of this model for the period 1953–I to 1976–IV for the United States are as follows (t ratios in parentheses):[19]

Coefficient	Estimate	
β_0	0.40	(2.96)
β_1	0.41	(5.26)
β_2	0.25	(2.14)
β_3	0.06	(0.71)
β_4	-0.05	(-0.37)
$\sum_{i=0}^{4} \beta_i$	1.06	(5.59)
λ_0	0.08	(2.26)
λ_1	0.06	(2.52)
λ_2	0.00	(0.02)
λ_3	-0.06	(-2.20)
λ_4	-0.07	(-1.83)
$\sum_{i=0}^{4} \lambda_i$	0.03	(0.40)

$$(14.4.4)$$

$$R^2 = 0.40$$
$$d = 1.78$$

What do these results suggest about the superiority of one model over the other? If we consider the cumulative effect of a unit change in $\dot{M}$ and $\dot{E}$ on $\dot{Y}$, we obtain, respectively, $\sum_{i=0}^{4} \beta_i = 1.06$ and $\sum_{i=0}^{4} \lambda_i = 0.03$, the former being statistically significant and the latter not. This comparison would tend to support the monetarist claim that it is changes in the money supply that determine changes in the (nominal) GNP. It is left as an exercise for the reader to evaluate critically this claim.

Davidson-MacKinnon J test.[20] Because of the problems just listed in the nonnested F testing procedure, alternatives have been suggested. One is the Davidson-MacKinnon J test. To illustrate this test, suppose we want to compare hypothesis or model C with hypothesis or model D. The **J test** proceeds as follows:

1. We estimate model D and from it we obtain the estimated Y values, $\hat{Y}_i^D$.
2. We add the predicted Y value in Step 1 as an additional regressor to model C and estimate the following model:

$$Y_t = \alpha_1 + \alpha_2 X_{2i} + \alpha_3 \hat{Y}_i^D + u_i \qquad (14.4.5)$$

where the $\hat{Y}_i^D$ values are obtained from Step 1. This model is an example of the **encompassing principle**, à la the Hendry methodology.

---

[19]See Keith M. Carlson, "Does the St. Louis Equation Now Believe in Fiscal Policy?" *Review, Federal Reserve Bank of St. Louis*, vol. 60, no. 2, February 1978, p. 17, table IV.

[20]R. Davidson and J. G. MacKinnon, "Several Tests for Model Specification in the Presence of Alternative Hypotheses," *Econometrica*, vol. 49, 1981, pp. 781–793.

3. Using the t test, test the hypothesis that $\alpha_3 = 0$.
4. If the hypothesis that $\alpha_3 = 0$ is not rejected, we can accept (i.e., not reject) model C as the true model because $\hat{Y}_i^D$ included in (14.4.5), which represent the influence of variables not included in model C, have no additional explanatory power beyond that contributed by model C. In other words, model C *encompasses* model D in the sense that the latter model does not contain any additional information that will improve the performance of model C. By the same token, if the null hypothesis is rejected, model C cannot be the true model (why?).
5. Now we reverse the roles of hypotheses, or models C and D. We now estimate model C first, use the estimated Y values from this model as regressor in (14.4.5), repeat Step 4, and decide whether to accept model D over model C. More specifically, we estimate the following model:

$$Y_i = \beta_1 + \beta_2 Z_{2i} + \beta_3 \hat{Y}_i^C + u_i \qquad (14.4.6)$$

where $\hat{Y}_i^C$ are the estimated Y values from model C. We now test the hypothesis that $\beta_3 = 0$. If this hypothesis is not rejected, we choose model D over C. If the hypothesis that $\beta_3 = 0$ is rejected, choose C over D, as the latter does not improve over the performance of C.

Although it is intuitively appealing, the J test has some problems. Since the tests given in (14.4.5) and (14.4.6) are performed independently, we have the following likely outcomes:

	Hypothesis: $\alpha_3 = 0$	
Hypothesis: $\beta_3 = 0$	**Do not reject**	**Reject**
Do not reject	Accept both C and D	Accept D, reject C
Reject	Accept C, reject D	Reject both C and D

As this table shows, we will not be able to get a clear answer if the J testing procedure leads to the acceptance or rejection of both models. In case both models are rejected, neither model helps us to explain the behavior of Y. Similarly, if both models are accepted, as Kmenta notes, "the data are apparently not rich enough to discriminate between the two hypotheses [models]."[21]

Another problem with the J test is that when we use the t statistic to test the significance of the estimated Y variable in models (14.4.5) and (14.4.6), the t statistic has the standard normal distribution only asymptotically, that is, in large samples. Therefore, the J test may not be very powerful (in the statistical sense) in small samples because it tends to reject the true hypothesis or model more frequently than it ought to.

An illustrative example. To illustrate the J test, consider the data given in Table 14.1. This table gives data on per capita personal consumption expenditure

---

[21] Jan Kmenta, *Elements of Econometrics*, Macmillan, 2d ed., New York, 1986, p. 597.

TABLE 14.1
Per capita personal consumption expenditure (PPCE) and per capita personal disposable income (PDPI), 1987 dollars, U.S., 1970–1991

Year	PPCE	PDPI
1970	8,842	9,875
1971	9,022	10,111
1972	9,425	10,414
1973	9,752	11,013
1974	9,602	10,832
1975	9,711	10,906
1976	10,121	11,192
1977	10,425	11,406
1978	10,744	11,851
1979	10,876	12,039
1980	10,746	12,005
1981	10,770	12,156
1982	10,782	12,146
1983	11,179	12,349
1984	11,617	13,029
1985	12,015	13,258
1986	12,336	13,552
1987	12,568	13,545
1988	12,903	13,890
1989	13,029	14,005
1990	13,044	14,068
1991	12,824	13,886

Source: Economic Report of the President, 1993,
Table B-5, p.355.

(PPCE) and per capita disposable personal income (PDPI), both measured in 1987 dollars, for the United States for the period 1970–1991. Now consider the following rival models:

$$Model\ A: \quad PPCE_t = \alpha_1 + \alpha_2 PDPI_t + \alpha_3 PDPI_{t-1} + u_t \qquad (14.4.7)$$

$$Model\ B: \quad PPCE_t = \beta_1 + \beta_2 PDPI_t + \beta_3 PPCE_{t-1} + u_t \qquad (14.4.8)$$

Model A states that PPCE depends on PDPI in the current and previous time period; this model is an example of what is known as the **distributed lag model** (see Chapter 17). Model B postulates that PPCE depends on current PDPI as well as PPCE in the previous time period; this model represents what is known as the **autoregressive model** (see Chapter 17). The reason for introducing the lagged value of PPCE in this model is to reflect inertia or habit persistence.

The results of estimating these models separately were as follows:

$$Model\ A: \quad \widehat{PPCE}_t = -1,299.0536 + 0.9204\ PDPI_t + 0.0931\ PDPI_{t-1}$$

$$t = \quad (-4.0378)\quad (6.0178)\qquad (0.6308)$$

$$R^2 = 0.9888 \quad d = 0.8092 \qquad (14.4.9)$$

$$\textit{Model B:} \quad \widehat{PPCE}_t = -841.8568 + 0.7117 \text{ PDPI}_t + 0.2954 \text{ PPCE}_{t-1}$$
$$t = \quad (-2.4137) \quad (5.4634) \quad (2.3681)$$
$$R^2 = 0.9912 \quad d = 1.0144 \tag{14.4.10}$$

If one were to choose between these two models on the basis of the discrimination approach, using, say, the highest R^2 criterion, one would choose (14.4.10); besides, in (14.4.10) both variables seem to be individually statistically significant, whereas in (14.4.9) only the current PDPI is statistically significant (but beware of the collinearity problem!).

But choosing (14.4.10) over (14.4.9) may not be appropriate because for predictive purposes there is not much difference in the two estimated R^2 values.

To apply the J test, suppose we assume model A is the null hypothesis, that is, the maintained model, and model B is the alternative hypothesis. Now following the J test steps discussed earlier, we use the estimated PPCE values from model (14.4.10) as an additional regressor in model A, giving the following outcome:

$$\widehat{PPCE}_t = 1{,}322.7958 \ - 0.7061 \text{PDPI}_t - 0.4357 \text{PDPI}_{t-1} + 2.1335 \widehat{PPCE}_t^B$$
$$t = \quad (1.5896)(-1.3958) \quad (-2.1926) \quad (3.3141)$$
$$R^2 = 0.9932 \quad d = 1.7115 \tag{14.4.11}$$

where $\widehat{PPCE}_t^B$ on the right side of (14.4.11) are the estimated PPCE values from model B, (14.4.10). Since the coefficient of this variable is statistically significant (at the two-tail 0.004 level), following the J test procedure, we have to reject model A in favor of model B.

Now assuming model B as the maintained hypothesis and model A as the alternative hypothesis, and following exactly the same procedure as before, we obtain the following results:

$$\widehat{PPCE}_t = -6{,}549.8659 \ + 5.1176 \text{PDPI}_t + 0.6302 \text{PPCE}_{t-1} - 4.6776 \widehat{PPCE}_t^A$$
$$t = \quad (-2.4976) \quad (2.5424) \quad (3.4141) \quad (-2.1926)$$
$$R^2 = 0.9920 \quad d = 1.7115 \tag{14.4.12}$$

where $\widehat{PPCE}^A$ on the right side of (14.4.12) is obtained from the model A, (14.4.9). But in this regression, the coefficient of $\widehat{PPCE}_t^A$ on the right side is also statistically significant (at the two-tail 0.0425 level). This result would suggest that we should now reject model B in favor of model A!

All this tells us is that neither model is particularly useful in explaining the behavior of per capita personal consumption expenditure in the United States over the period 1970–1991.

Of course, we have considered only two competing models. In reality, there may be more than two models. The J test procedure can be extended to multiple model comparisons, although the analysis can become quickly complex.

This example shows very vividly why the CLRM assumes that the regression model used in the analysis is correctly specified. Obviously it is very crucial in developing a model to pay very careful attention to the phenomenon being modeled.

Other tests of model selection. The J test just discussed is only one of a group of tests of model selection. There is the **Cox test**, the **JA test**, the **P test**, **Mizon-Richard encompassing test**, and variants of these tests. Obviously, we cannot hope to discuss these specialized tests, for which the reader may want to consult the references cited in the various footnotes.

14.5 SUMMARY AND CONCLUSIONS

The major points discussed in this chapter are as follows.

1. The emphasis in econometric research has shifted from merely estimating a given model to choosing among competing models.
2. In this shift, several econometricians have made contributions, notable among them being Leamer and Hendry.
3. Leamer has systematically laid out the types of searches one undertakes to find the "true" model. He is an advocate of the extreme bound analysis (EBA) and its value in reporting the results of regression analysis.
4. After defining what constitutes a good model, Hendry and his associates developed the *top-down* or *general to specific* modeling strategy, which develops a comprehensive model and then, using several diagnostics, ultimately narrows the scope of the model used in the final analysis.
5. In choosing models, econometricians have developed a variety of tests. In this chapter we only discussed the nonnested F test and the David-MacKinnon J test.
6. The major message of this chapter is that one should pay extremely careful attention to the choice of the model before one rushes to estimate it. Once a model is finally chosen, the classical techniques of estimation and hypothesis testing can be legitimately applied. Perhaps one should take the dictum of the classical linear regression model that the regression model is "correctly" specified to mean that the model chosen in empirical analysis has gone through the rigors of specimetrics.

EXERCISES

Questions

*14.1. Critically evaluate the following view expressed by Leamer:

> My interest in metastatistics [i.e., theory of inference actually drawn from data] stems from my observations of economists at work. The opinion that econometric theory is irrelevant is held by an embarrassingly large share of the economic profession. The wide gap between econometric theory and econometric practice might be expected to cause professional tension. In fact, a calm equilibrium permeates our journals and our [professional] meetings. We comfortably divide ourselves into a celibate priesthood of statistical theorists, on the one hand, and a legion of inveterate sinner-data analysts, on the other. The priests are empowered to draw up lists of sins and are revered for the special talents they display. Sinners are not expected to avoid sins; they need only confess their errors openly.[†]

14.2. Keeping in mind the discussion of extreme bound analysis, evaluate the following statement made by Henry Theil:

---

*Optional.

[†]Leamer, op. cit., p. vi.

Given the present state of the art, the most sensible procedure is to interpret confidence coefficients and significance limits liberally when confidence intervals and test statistics are computed from the final regression of a regression strategy in the conventional way. That is, a 95 percent confidence coefficient may actually be an 80 percent confidence coefficient and a 1 percent significance level may actually be a 10 percent level.[*]

14.3. Would you criticize Hendry's "test, test, and test" general to specific modeling methodology as nothing but data-mining? If so, do you see any merit in the Hendry methodology?

14.4. Commenting on the econometric methodology practiced in the 1950's and early 1960's, Blaug stated:[†]

...much of it [i.e., empirical research] is like playing tennis with the net down: instead of attempting to refute testable predictions, modern economists all too frequently are satisfied to demonstrate that the real world conforms to their predictions, thus replacing falsification [à la Popper], which is difficult, with verification, which is easy.

Do you agree with this view? You may want to peruse Blaug's book to learn more about his views.

14.5. According to Blaug, "There is no logic of proof but there is logic of disproof."[**] What does he mean by this?

14.6. Refer to the St. Louis model discussed in the text. Keeping in mind the problems associated with the nested F test, critically evaluate the results presented in regression (14.4.4).

Problems

14.7. Refer to Problem 8.32. With the definitions of the variables given there, consider the following two models to explain Y:

$$Model\ A: \quad Y_t = \alpha_1 + \alpha_2 X_{3t} + \alpha_3 X_{4t} + \alpha_4 X_{6t} + u_t$$
$$Model\ B: \quad Y_t = \beta_1 + \beta_2 X_{2t} + \beta_3 X_{5t} + \beta_4 X_{6t} + u_t$$

Using the nested F test, how will you choose between the two models?

14.8. Continue with exercise 14.7. Using the J test, how would you decide between the two models?

14.9. Refer to exercise 7.23, which is concerned with the demand for chicken in the United States. There you were given five models.

(a) What is the difference between model 1 and model 2? If model 2 is correct and you estimate model 1, what kind of error is committed? Which test would you apply—equation specification error or model selection error? Show the necessary calculations.

---

[*]Henry Theil, *Principles of Econometrics*, John Wiley & Sons, New York, 1971, pp. 605–606.

[†]M. Blaug, *The Methodology of Economics. Or How Economists Explain*, Cambridge University Press, New York, 1980, p. 256.

[**]Ibid., p. 14.

(b) Between models 1 and 5, which would you choose? Which test(s) do you use and why?

14.10. Refer to Exercise 8.35, which gives data on personal savings (Y) and personal income (X) for the period 1970–1991. Now consider the following models:

$$Model\ A:\quad Y_t = \alpha_1 + \alpha_2 X_t + \alpha_3 X_{t-1} + u_t$$
$$Model\ B:\quad Y_t = \beta_1 + \beta_2 X_t + \beta_3 Y_{t-1} + u_t$$

How would you choose between these two models? State clearly the test(s) procedure you use and all the calculations. Suppose someone contends that the interest rate variable belongs in the savings function. How would you test this? Collect data on the three-month Treasury bill rate as a proxy for the interest rate and demonstrate your answer.

PART

III

TOPICS IN ECONOMETRICS

In Part I we introduced the classical linear regression model with all its assumptions. In Part II we examined in detail the consequences that ensue when one or more of the assumptions are not satisfied and what can be done about them. In Part III we turn to a study of some selected but commonly encountered econometric techniques.

In Chapter 15, we consider the role of *qualitative* explanatory variables in regression analysis. The qualitative variables, called **dummy variables**, are a device of incorporating into the regression model variables that cannot be readily quantified, such as sex, religion, and color, and yet influence the behavior of the dependent variable. We show with several examples how such variables enhance the scope of the linear regression model.

In Chapter 16, we allow the dependent variable in a regression model itself to be qualitative in nature. Such models are used in situations where the dependent variable is of the "yes" or "no" type, such as ownership of house, car, and household appliances or possession of an attribute, such as membership in a trade union or professional society. Models which include yes–no–type dependent variables are called **dichotomous**, or **dummy, dependent-variable regression models**. We consider three approaches to estimating such models:

(1) the linear probability model (**LPM**), (2) the **logit model**, and (3) the **probit model**. Of these, the LPM, although easy computationally, is the least satisfactory as it violates some of the assumptions of the OLS. Because of this, the logit and the probit are the models most frequently used when the dependent variable happens to be dichotomous. We illustrate these models with numerical and practical examples.

We also consider the **tobit model**, a model related to probit. In the probit model we try to find out the probability of, say, owning a house. In the tobit model we try to find out the amount of money a consumer spends in buying a house in relation to his or her income, etc. But of course, if a consumer does not buy a house, we have no data on housing expenditure for such consumers; such information is available only for consumers who actually buy houses. Thus, we have a **censored sample**, that is, a sample in which the information on the dependent variable is not available for some observations, although information on the regressors may be available. The tobit model shows how one can estimate regression models involving censored samples.

In Chapter 17, we consider regression models that include current as well as past, or lagged, values of the explanatory variables in addition to models that include lagged value(s) of the dependent variable as one of the explanatory variables. These models are called, respectively, the **distributed lag** and **autoregressive models**. Although such models are extremely useful in empirical econometrics, they pose some special estimating problems because they violate one or more assumptions of the classical regression model. We consider these special problems in the context of the Koyck, the adaptive-expectations (AE), and the partial-adjustment models. We also note the criticism leveled against the AE model by the advocates of the so-called rational expectations (RE) school.

With Chapter 17 we conclude our discussion of the single-equation regression model that we began in Chapter 1. These 17 chapters cover a lot of ground in single-equation econometric models but they by no means exhaust the field. In particular we have not gone into nonlinear (in the parameters) estimation techniques nor have we considered the Bayesian approach to single-equation, linear as well as nonlinear, econometric models. But in an introductory book like this, it would not be possible to do justice to these topics, for they demand mathematical and statistical background far beyond that assumed in this book.

REGRESSION ON DUMMY VARIABLES

The purpose of this chapter is to consider the role of qualitative explanatory variables in regression analysis. It will be shown that the introduction of qualitative variables, often called **dummy variables**, makes the linear regression model an extremely flexible tool that is capable of handling many interesting problems encountered in empirical studies.

15.1 THE NATURE OF DUMMY VARIABLES

In regression analysis the dependent variable is frequently influenced not only by variables that can be readily quantified on some well-defined scale (e.g., income, output, prices, costs, height, and temperature), but also by variables that are essentially qualitative in nature (e.g., sex, race, color, religion, nationality, wars, earthquakes, strikes, political upheavals, and changes in government economic policy). For example, holding all other factors constant, female college professors are found to earn less than their male counterparts, and nonwhites are found to earn less than whites. This pattern may result from sex or racial discrimination, but whatever the reason, qualitative variables such as sex and race do influence the dependent variable and clearly should be included among the explanatory variables.

Since such qualitative variables usually indicate the presence or absence of a "quality" or an attribute, such as male or female, black or white, or Catholic or non-Catholic, one method of "quantifying" such attributes is by constructing artificial variables that take on values of 1 or 0, 0 indicating the absence of an attribute and 1 indicating the presence (or possession) of that attribute. For example, 1 may indicate that a person is a male, and 0 may designate a female; or 1 may indicate that a person is a college graduate, and 0 that he is not, and so on. Variables that assume such 0 and 1 values are called **dummy**

variables.[1] Alternative names are *indicator variables, binary variables, categorical variables, qualitative variables,* and *dichotomous variables.*

Dummy variables can be used in regression models just as easily as quantitative variables. As a matter of fact, a regression model may contain explanatory variables that are exclusively dummy, or qualitative, in nature. Such models are called **analysis-of-variance (ANOVA) models**. As an example, consider the following model:

$$Y_i = \alpha + \beta D_i + u_i \qquad (15.1.1)$$

where Y = annual salary of a college professor
  $D_i = 1$ if male college professor
  $= 0$ otherwise (i.e., female professor)

Note that (15.1.1) is like the two-variable regression models encountered previously except that instead of a quantitative X variable we have a dummy variable D (hereafter, we shall designate all dummy variables by the letter D).

Model (15.1.1) may enable us to find out whether sex makes any difference in a college professor's salary, assuming, of course, that all other variables such as age, degree attained, and years of experience are held constant. Assuming that the disturbances satisfy the usual assumptions of the classical linear regression model, we obtain from (15.1.1)

Mean salary of female college professor: $E(Y_i \mid D_i = 0) = \alpha$ (15.1.2)
Mean salary of male college professor: $E(Y_i \mid D_i = 1) = \alpha + \beta$

that is, the intercept term α gives the mean salary of female college professors and the *slope* coefficient β tells by how much the mean salary of a male college professor differs from the mean salary of his female counterpart, $\alpha + \beta$ reflecting the mean salary of the male college professor.

A test of the null hypothesis that there is no sex discrimination (H_0: $\beta = 0$) can be easily made by running regression (15.1.1) in the usual manner and finding out whether on the basis of the t test the estimated β is statistically significant.

Example 15.1   Professor's Salary by Sex

Table 15.1 gives hypothetical data on starting salaries of 10 college professors by the sex of the professor. The results corresponding to regression (15.1.1) are as follows:

$$\hat{Y}_i = 18.00 + 3.28 D_i$$
$$(0.32)\ \ (0.44) \qquad\qquad\qquad (15.1.3)$$
$$t = (57.74)\ \ (7.439)\qquad R^2 = 0.8737$$

---

[1] It is not absolutely essential that dummy variables take the values of 0 and 1. The pair (0, 1) can be transformed into any other pair by a linear function such that $Z = a + bD$ ($b \neq 0$), where a and b are constants and where $D = 1$ or 0. When $D = 1$, we have $Z = a + b$; and when $D = 0$, we have $Z = a$. Thus, the pair (0, 1) becomes ($a, a + b$). For example, if $a = 1$ and $b = 2$, the dummy variables will be (1, 3). **This expression shows that qualitative variables do not have a natural scale of measurement.**

TABLE 15.1
Hypothetical data on starting salaries of college professors by sex

Starting salary, Y (thousands of dollars)	Sex (1 = male, 0 = female)
22.0	1
19.0	0
18.0	0
21.7	1
18.5	0
21.0	1
20.5	1
17.0	0
17.5	0
21.2	1

As these results show, the estimated mean salary of female college professors is $18,000 (= $\hat{\alpha}$) and that of male professors is $21,280 ($\hat{\alpha} + \hat{\beta}$); from the data in Table 15.1 it can readily be calculated that the average salaries of female and male college professors are, respectively, $18,000 and $21,280 which are precisely the same as the estimated ones.

Since $\hat{\beta}$ is statistically significant, the results indicate that the mean salaries of the two categories are different; actually the female professor's average salary is lower than her male counterpart's. If all other variables are held constant (a big if), it may very well be that there is sex discrimination in the salaries of the two sexes. Of course, the present model is too simple to answer this question definitively, especially in view of the hypothetical nature of the data used in the analysis.

Incidentally, it is interesting to see the regression (15.1.3) graphically, which is given in Fig. 15.1. In this figure the data have been ordered so as to group them

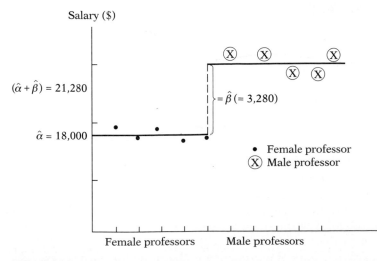

FIGURE 15.1
Female and male professor's salary functions.

into the two categories, female and male professors. As you can see from this figure, the resulting regression function is a *step function*—the average salary of female professors is \$18,000 and the average salary of male professors jumps by \$3,280 ($= \hat{\beta}_2$) to \$21,280; the salaries of the individual professors in the two groups hover around their respective mean salaries.

ANOVA models of type (15.1.1), although common in fields such as sociology, psychology, education, and market research, are not that common in economics. Typically, in most economic research a regression model contains some explanatory variables that are quantitative and some that are qualitative. Regression models containing an admixture of quantitative and qualitative variables are called **analysis-of-covariance (ANCOVA) models**, and in this chapter we shall be largely dealing with such models.

15.2 REGRESSION ON ONE QUANTITATIVE VARIABLE AND ONE QUALITATIVE VARIABLE WITH TWO CLASSES, OR CATEGORIES

As an example of the ANCOVA model, let us modify model (15.1.1) as follows:

$$Y_i = \alpha_1 + \alpha_2 D_i + \beta X_i + u_i \tag{15.2.1}$$

where Y_i = annual salary of a college professor
$\quad X_i$ = years of teaching experience
$\quad D_i = 1 \quad$ if male
$\quad\quad = 0 \quad$ otherwise

Model (15.2.1) contains one quantitative variable (years of teaching experience) and one qualitative variable (sex) that has two classes (or levels, classifications, or categories), namely, male and female.

What is the meaning of (15.2.1)? Assuming, as usual, that $E(u_i) = 0$, we see that

Mean salary of a female college professor:

$$E(Y_i \mid X_i, D_i = 0) = \alpha_1 + \beta X_i \tag{15.2.2}$$

Mean salary of a male college professor:

$$E(Y_i \mid X_i, D_i = 1) = (\alpha_1 + \alpha_2) + \beta X_i \tag{15.2.3}$$

Geometrically, we have the situation shown in Fig. 15.2 (for illustration, it is assumed that $\alpha_1 > 0$). In words, model (15.2.1) postulates that the male and female college professors' salary functions in relation to the years of teaching experience have the same slope (β) but different intercepts. In other words, it is assumed that the level of the male professor's mean salary is different from that of the female professor's mean salary (by α_2) but the rate of change in the mean annual salary by years of experience is the same for both sexes.

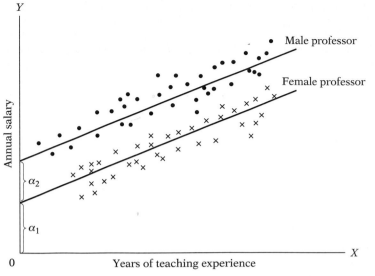

FIGURE 15.2
Hypothetical scattergram between annual salary and years of teaching experience
of college professors.

If the assumption of common slope is valid,[2] a test of the hypothesis that
the two regressions (15.2.2) and (15.2.3) have the same intercept (i.e., there is
no sex discrimination) can be made easily by running the regression (15.2.1)
and noting the statistical significance of the estimated α_2 on the basis of the
traditional t test. If the t test shows that $\hat{\alpha}_2$ is statistically significant, we reject
the null hypothesis that the male and female college professors' levels of mean
annual salary are the same.

Before proceeding further, note the following features of the dummy-
variable regression model considered previously.

1. To distinguish the two categories, male and female, we have introduced only
one dummy variable D_i. For if $D_i = 1$ always denotes a male, when $D_i = 0$
we know that it is a female since there are only two possible outcomes.
Hence, one dummy variable suffices to distinguish two categories. Let us
assume that the regression model contains an intercept term; if we were to
write model (15.2.1) as

$$Y_i = \alpha_1 + \alpha_2 D_{2i} + \alpha_3 D_{3i} + \beta X_i + u_i \qquad (15.2.4)$$

where Y_i and X_i are as defined before

$$D_{2i} = 1 \qquad \text{if male professor}$$
$$= 0 \qquad \text{otherwise}$$

---

[2]The validity of this assumption can be tested by the procedure outlined in Sec. 15.7.

$$D_{3i} = 1 \quad \text{if female professor}$$
$$= 0 \quad \text{otherwise}$$

then model (15.2.4), as it stands, cannot be estimated because of perfect collinearity between D_2 and D_3. To see this, suppose we have a sample of three male professors and two female professors. The data matrix will look something like that following:

		D_2	D_3	X
Male	Y_1	1	1	0	X_1
Male	Y_2	1	1	0	X_2
Female	Y_3	1	0	1	X_3
Male	Y_4	1	1	0	X_4
Female	Y_5	1	0	1	X_5

The first column on the right side of the preceding data matrix represents the common intercept term α_1. Now it can be seen readily that $D_2 = 1 - D_3$ or $D_3 = 1 - D_2$; that is, D_2 and D_3 are perfectly collinear. And as shown in Chapter 10, in cases of perfect multicollinearity the usual OLS estimation is not possible. There are various ways of resolving this problem, but the simplest one is to assign the dummies the way we did for model (15.2.1), namely, use only one dummy variable if there are two levels or classes of the qualitative variable. In this case, the preceding data matrix will not have the column labeled D_3, thus avoiding the perfect multicollinearity problem. The general rule is this: **If a qualitative variable has m categories, introduce only $m - 1$ dummy variables.** In our example, sex has two categories, and hence we introduced only a single dummy variable. If this rule is not followed, we shall fall into what might be called the **dummy variable trap**, that is, the situation of perfect multicollinearity. (For additional discussion, see Section 15.13.)

2. The assignment of 1 and 0 values to two categories, such as male and female, is arbitrary in the sense that in our example we could have assigned $D = 1$ for female and $D = 0$ for male. In this situation, the two regressions obtained from (15.2.1) will be

$$\text{Female professor:} \quad E(Y_i \mid X_i, D_i = 1) = (\alpha_1 + \alpha_2) + \beta X_i \quad (15.2.5)$$

$$\text{Male professor:} \quad E(Y_i \mid X_i, D_i = 0) = \alpha_1 + \beta X_i \quad (15.2.6)$$

In contrast with (15.2.2) and (15.2.3) in the preceding models, α_2 tells by how much the mean salary of a female college professor differs from the mean salary of a male college professor. In this case, if there is sex discrimination, α_2 is expected to be negative whereas before it was expected to be positive. **Therefore, in interpreting the results of the models that use the dummy variables it is critical to know how the 1 and 0 values are assigned.**

3. The group, category, or classification that is assigned the value of 0 is often referred to as the *base, benchmark, control, comparison, reference,* or *omitted* category. It is the base in the sense that comparisons are made with

that category. Thus in model (15.2.1) the female professor is the base category. Note that the (common) intercept term α_1 is the intercept term for the base category in the sense that if we run the regression with $D = 0$, that is, on females only, the intercept will be α_1. Also note that whichever category serves as the base category is a matter of choice sometimes dictated by a priori considerations.

4. The coefficient α_2 attached to the dummy variable D can be called the **differential intercept coefficient** because it tells by how much the value of the intercept term of the category that receives the value of 1 differs from the intercept coefficient of the base category.

Example 15.2 Are Inventories Sensitive to Interest Rates?

Dan M. Bechter and Stephen H. Pollock estimated the following model to explain inventory fluctuations in the wholesale trade sector of the U.S. economy for 1967–IV to 1979–IV (t ratios in the parentheses):[3]

$$I/S = 1.269 - 0.3615C + 0.0215S^e - 0.0227S$$
$$(19.6) \quad (-2.2) \qquad (5.7) \qquad (-2.4)$$
$$- 0.2552U + 0.0734\text{DUM}$$
$$(-2.4) \qquad (4.8) \qquad R^2 = 0.71 \qquad d = 1.91$$

where I/S = inventories in constant dollars divided by sales in constant dollars, C = 4- to 6-month rate on prime commercial paper minus the percent change from a year earlier in the producer price index for finished consumer goods, S^e = expected sales in the current period, where expected sales equal trend sales adjusted for deviations from trend in the previous period, all in constant dollars, U = uncertainty in sales measured by the volatility of sales around trend, and DUM = dummy variable, taking zero value for 1967–IV to 1974–I and 1 for 1974–II to 1979–IV.

Although all the coefficients are statistically significant and have the expected signs, for the present discussion we will concentrate on the dummy variable. The results show that the inventory sales ratio is higher ($= 1.2690 + 0.0734$) for the post-1974 recession period than in the earlier period. Thus the regression line, actually a plane, for the latter period is parallel but situated at a higher level than the one for the earlier period (cf. Fig. 15.2). The authors do not discuss the reasons for this but it probably reflects the severity of the 1974 recession.

15.3 REGRESSION ON ONE QUANTITATIVE VARIABLE AND ONE QUALITATIVE VARIABLE WITH MORE THAN TWO CLASSES

Suppose that, on the basis of the cross-sectional data, we want to regress the annual expenditure on health care by an individual on the income and education

---

[3]"Are Inventories Sensitive to Interest Rates?" *Economic Review*, Federal Reserve Bank of Kansas, April 1980, p. 24 (Table 2). *Note:* The results are corrected for second-order autocorrelation; the original d was 1.12.

of the individual. Since the variable *education* is qualitative in nature, suppose we consider three mutually exclusive levels of education: less than high school, high school, and college. Now, unlike the previous case, we have more than two categories of the qualitative variable education. Therefore, **following the rule that the number of dummies be one less than the number of categories of the variable**, we should introduce two dummies to take care of the three levels of education. Assuming that the three educational groups have a common slope but different intercepts in the regression of annual expenditure on health care on annual income, we can use the following model:

$$Y_i = \alpha_1 + \alpha_2 D_{2i} + \alpha_3 D_{3i} + \beta X_i + u_i \qquad (15.3.1)$$

where Y_i = annual expenditure on health care
$\quad\quad\ X_i$ = annual income
$\quad\quad D_2 = 1 \quad$ if high school education
$\quad\quad\quad\ = 0 \quad$ otherwise
$\quad\quad D_3 = 1 \quad$ if college education
$\quad\quad\quad\ = 0 \quad$ otherwise

Note that in the preceding assignment of the dummy variables we are arbitrarily treating the "less than high school education" category as the base category. Therefore, the intercept α_1 will reflect the intercept for this category. The differential intercepts α_2 and α_3 tell by how much the intercepts of the other two categories differ from the intercept of the base category, which can be readily checked as follows: Assuming $E(u_i) = 0$, we obtain from (15.3.1)

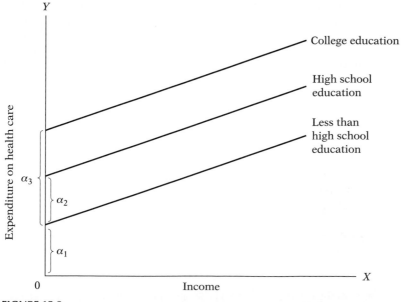

FIGURE 15.3
Expenditure on health care in relation to income for three levels of education.

$$E(Y_i \mid D_2 = 0, D_3 = 0, X_i) = \alpha_1 + \beta X_i \qquad (15.3.2)$$

$$E(Y_i \mid D_2 = 1, D_3 = 0, X_i) = (\alpha_1 + \alpha_2) + \beta X_i \qquad (15.3.3)$$

$$E(Y_i \mid D_2 = 0, D_3 = 1, X_i) = (\alpha_1 + \alpha_3) + \beta X_i \qquad (15.3.4)$$

which are, respectively, the mean health care expenditure functions for the three levels of education, namely, less than high school, high school, and college. Geometrically, the situation is shown in Fig. 15.3 (for illustrative purposes it is assumed that $\alpha_3 > \alpha_2$).

After running regression (15.3.1), one can easily find out whether the differential intercepts α_2 and α_3 are individually statistically significant, that is, different from the base group. A test of the hypothesis that $\alpha_2 = \alpha_3 = 0$ simultaneously can also be made by the ANOVA technique and the attendant F test, as shown in Chapter 8 [see Eq. (8.7.9)].

In passing, note that the interpretation of regression (15.3.1) would change if we were to adopt a different scheme of assigning the dummy variables. Thus, if we assign $D_2 = 1$ to "less than high school education" category and $D_3 = 1$ to "high school education category," the reference category will then be "college education" and all comparisons will be in relation to this category.

15.4 REGRESSION ON ONE QUANTITATIVE VARIABLE AND TWO QUALITATIVE VARIABLES

The technique of dummy variable can be easily extended to handle more than one qualitative variable. Let us revert to the college professors' salary regression (15.2.1), but now assume that in addition to years of teaching experience and sex the skin color of the teacher is also an important determinant of salary. For simplicity, assume that color has two categories: black and white. We can now write (15.2.1) as

$$Y_i = \alpha_1 + \alpha_2 D_{2i} + \alpha_3 D_{3i} + \beta X_i + u_i \qquad (15.4.1)$$

where Y_i = annual salary
      X_i = years of teaching experience
      $D_2 = 1$ if male
         $= 0$ otherwise
      $D_3 = 1$ if white
         $= 0$ otherwise

Notice that each of the two qualitative variables, sex and color, has two categories and hence needs one dummy variable for each. Note also that the omitted, or base, category now is "black female professor."

Assuming $E(u_i) = 0$, we can obtain the following regression from (15.4.1):

Mean salary for black female professor:

$$E(Y_i \mid D_2 = 0, D_3 = 0, X_i) = \alpha_1 + \beta X_i \qquad (15.4.2)$$

Mean salary for black male professor:

$$E(Y_i \mid D_2 = 1, D_3 = 0, X_i) = (\alpha_1 + \alpha_2) + \beta X_i \qquad (15.4.3)$$

Mean salary for white female professor:

$$E(Y_i \mid D_2 = 0, D_3 = 1, X_i) = (\alpha_1 + \alpha_3) + \beta X_i \qquad (15.4.4)$$

Mean salary for white male professor:

$$E(Y_i \mid D_2 = 1, D_3 = 1, X_i) = (\alpha_1 + \alpha_2 + \alpha_3) + \beta X_i \qquad (15.4.5)$$

Once again, it is assumed that the preceding regressions differ only in the intercept coefficient but not in the slope coefficient β.

An OLS estimation of (15.4.1) will enable us to test a variety of hypotheses. Thus, if α_3 is statistically significant, it will mean that color does affect a professor's salary. Similarly, if α_2 is statistically significant, it will mean that sex also affects a professor's salary. If both these differential intercepts are statistically significant, it would mean sex as well as color is an important determinant of professors' salaries.

From the preceding discussion it follows that we can extend our model to include more than one quantitative variable and more than two qualitative variables. **The only precaution to be taken is that the number of dummies for each qualitative variable should be one less than the number of categories of that variable.** An example is given in the following section.

15.5 EXAMPLE 15.3. THE ECONOMICS OF "MOONLIGHTING"

A person holding two or more jobs, one primary and one or more secondary, is known as a *moonlighter*. Shisko and Rostker were interested in finding out what factors determined the wages of moonlighters.[4] Based on a sample of 318 moonlighters, they obtained the following regression, which is given in the notation used by the authors (standard errors in the parentheses):

$$\hat{w}_m = 37.07 + 0.403w_0 - 90.06 \text{ race} + 75.51 \text{ urban}$$
$$(0.062) \quad (24.47) \qquad (21.60)$$
$$+ 47.33 \text{ hisch} + 113.64 \text{ reg} + 2.26 \text{ age} \qquad (15.5.1)$$
$$(23.42) \qquad (27.62) \quad (0.94)$$
$$R^2 = 0.34 \qquad df = 311$$

where w_m = moonlighting wage (cents/hour)
       w_0 = primary wage (cents/hours)
    race = 0   if white
          = 1   nonwhite
  urban = 0   nonurban
          = 1   urban

---

[4]Robert Shisko and Bernard Rostker, "The Economics of Multiple Job Holding," *The American Economic Review*, vol. 66, no. 3, June 1976, pp. 298–308.

reg = 0   nonwest
    = 1   west
hisch = 0   nongraduate
    = 1   high school graduate
age = age, years

In model (15.5.1) there are two quantitative explanatory variables, w_0 and age, and four qualitative variables. Note that the coefficients of all these variables are statistically significant at the 5% level. What is interesting to note is that all the qualitative variables affect moonlighting wages significantly. For instance, holding all other factors constant, the level of hourly wages is expected to be higher by about 47 cents for the high school graduate than for those with less than high school education.

From regression (15.5.1) one can derive several individual regressions, two of which are as follows: The mean hourly wage rate of white, nonurban, nonwest, nongraduate moonlighters (i.e., when all the dummies take a value of zero) is

$$\hat{w}_m = 37.07 + 0.403w_0 + 2.26 \text{ age} \qquad (15.5.2)$$

The mean hourly wage rate of a nonwhite, urban, west, high school graduate (i.e., when all the dummies are equal to 1) is

$$\hat{w}_m = 183.49 + 0.403w_0 + 2.26 \text{ age} \qquad (15.5.3)$$

15.6 TESTING FOR STRUCTURAL STABILITY OF REGRESSION MODELS

Until now, in the models considered in this chapter we assumed that the qualitative variables affect the intercept but not the slope coefficient of the various subgroup regressions. But what if the slopes are also different? If the slopes are in fact different, testing for differences in the intercepts may be of little practical significance. Therefore, we need to develop a general methodology to find out whether two (or more) regressions are different, where the difference may be in the intercepts or the slopes or both. To see how this can be done, let us consider the savings-income data for the United Kingdom given in Table 8.8, which for convenience is reproduced as Table 15.2.

Example 15.4 Savings and Income, United Kingdom, 1946–1963

As the table shows, the data are divided into two periods, 1946–1954 (immediate post–World War II period, call it the reconstruction period) and 1955–1963 (the postreconstruction period). Suppose we want to find out if the aggregate savings-income relationship has changed between the two periods. To be specific let

Reconstruction period: $Y_i = \lambda_1 + \lambda_2 X_i + u_{1i}$ $\qquad$ (15.6.1)
$$i = 1, 2, \ldots, n_1$$

Postreconstruction period: $Y_i = \gamma_1 + \gamma_2 X_i + u_{2i}$ $\qquad$ (15.6.2)
$$i = 1, 2, \ldots, n_2$$

TABLE 15.2
Personal savings and income data, United Kingdom 1946–1963 (millions of pounds)

Period I	Savings	Income	Period II	Savings	Income
1946	0.36	8.8	1955	0.59	15.5
1947	0.21	9.4	1956	0.90	16.7
1948	0.08	10.0	1957	0.95	17.7
1949	0.20	10.6	1958	0.82	18.6
1950	0.10	11.0	1959	1.04	19.7
1951	0.12	11.9	1960	1.53	21.1
1952	0.41	12.7	1961	1.94	22.8
1953	0.50	13.5	1962	1.75	23.9
1954	0.43	14.3	1963	1.99	25.2

Source: Central Statistical Office, U.K.

where Y = savings (millions of £)
   X = income (millions of £)
   u_{1i}, u_{2i} = disturbances in the two regressions

Note: The number of observations n_1 and n_2 in the two groups (periods) need not be the same.

Now regressions (15.6.1) and (15.6.2) present the following four possibilities:

1. $\lambda_1 = \gamma_1$ and $\lambda_2 = \gamma_2$; that is, the two regressions are identical. (**Coincident regressions.**)
2. $\lambda_1 \neq \gamma_1$ but $\lambda_2 = \gamma_2$; that is, the two regressions differ only in their locations (i.e., intercepts). (**Parallel regressions.**)
3. $\lambda_1 = \gamma_1$ but $\lambda_2 \neq \gamma_2$; that is, the two regressions have the same intercepts but different slopes. (**Concurrent regressions.**)
4. $\lambda_1 \neq \gamma_1$ and $\lambda_2 \neq \gamma_2$; that is, the two regressions are completely different. (**Dissimilar regressions.**) All these possibilities are depicted in Fig. 15.4.

From the data given in Table 15.2, we can run the two individual regressions (15.6.1) and (15.6.2) and then use some statistical technique(s) to test all the preceding possibilities, that is, to find out if the savings function has undergone a **structural change** between the two time periods. By structural change we mean that the parameters of the savings function have changed.

One such statistical technique is the **Chow test**,[5] which we discussed in Section 8.8. The Chow test showed that the parameters of the savings function between reconstruction and postreconstruction periods had indeed changed.

As an alternative to the Chow test, we show in the following section how the dummy variable technique handles the problem of structural change or break and what some of its advantages are over the Chow test.

---

[5] For details of the Chow test, see Sec. 8.8.

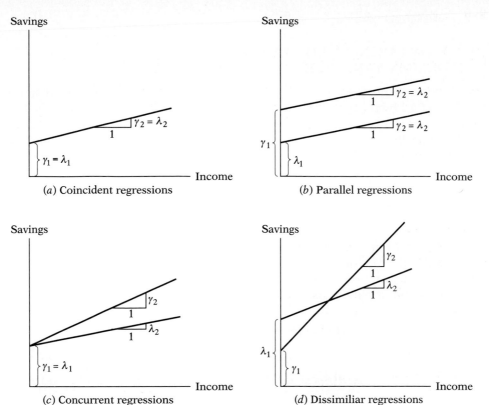

FIGURE 15.4
Plausible savings-income regressions.

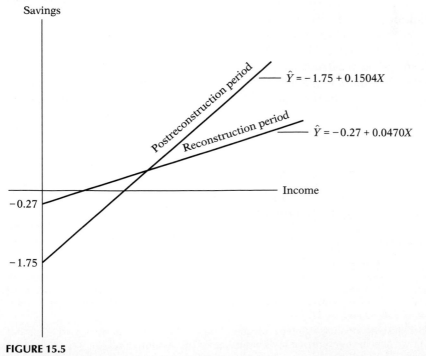

FIGURE 15.5
Savings-income regressions.

15.7   COMPARING TWO REGRESSIONS: THE DUMMY VARIABLE APPROACH

The multistep Chow test procedure discussed in Section 8.8 can be substantially abridged by the use of the dummy variables. Although the overall conclusions derived from the Chow and dummy variable tests in any given application are the same, there are some advantages to the dummy variable method that we shall explain after we first present the method using the same savings-income example.[6]

Let us pool all the n_1 and n_2 observations together and estimate the following regression.[7]

$$Y_i = \alpha_1 + \alpha_2 D_i + \beta_1 X_i + \beta_2(D_i X_i) + u_i \tag{15.7.1}$$

where Y_i and X_i are savings and income as before and where $D_i = 1$ for observations in the first or reconstruction period and zero for observations in the postreconstruction period.

To see the implications of model (15.7.1), and assuming that $E(u_i) = 0$, we obtain

$$E(Y_i \mid D_i = 0, X_i) = \alpha_1 + \beta_1 X_i \tag{15.7.2}$$

$$E(Y_i \mid D_i = 1, X_i) = (\alpha_1 + \alpha_2) + (\beta_1 + \beta_2)X_i \tag{15.7.3}$$

which are, respectively, the mean savings functions for the second (postreconstruction) and first (reconstruction) periods. They are the same as (15.6.2) and (15.6.1) with $\gamma_1 = \alpha_1, \gamma_2 = \beta_1, \lambda_1 = (\alpha_1 + \alpha_2)$, and $\lambda_2 = (\beta_1 + \beta_2)$. Therefore, estimating (15.7.1) is equivalent to estimating the two individual savings functions (15.6.1) and (15.6.2).

In (15.7.1), α_2 is the **differential intercept**, as previously, and β_2 is the **differential slope coefficient**, indicating by how much the slope coefficient of the first period's savings function differs from the slope coefficient of the second period's savings function. Note how the introduction of the dummy variable D in the *multiplicative* form (D multiplied by X) enables us to differentiate between slope coefficients of the two periods, just as the introduction of the dummy variable in the *additive form* enables us to distinguish between the intercepts of the two periods.

Turning to the savings-income data given in Table 15.2, we find the empirical counterpart of (15.7.1) is

$$\hat{Y}_t = -1.7502 + 1.4839 D_i + 0.1504 X_t - 0.1034 D_i X_t$$

$$(0.3319) \quad (0.4704) \quad (0.0163) \quad (0.0332) \tag{15.7.4}$$

$$t = (-5.2733) \quad (3.1545) \quad (9.2238) \quad (-3.1144)$$

$$\bar{R}^2 = 0.9425$$

---

[6]The material in this section draws heavily on the author's articles, "Use of Dummy Variables in Testing for Equality between Sets of Coefficients in Two Linear Regressions: A Note," and "Use of Dummy Variables . . . : A Generalization," both published in the *American Statistician*, vol. 24, nos. 1 and 5, 1970, pp. 50–52 and 18–21.

[7]As in the Chow test, the pooling technique assumes homoscedasticity, that is, $\sigma_1^2 = \sigma_2^2 = \sigma^2$. But from Chap. 11 we now have several methods of testing for this assumption.

As this regression shows, both the differential intercept and the differential slope coefficients are statistically significant, strongly indicating that the regressions for the two periods are different (cf. Fig. 15.4d). Then, following (15.7.2) and (15.7.3) we can derive the two regressions as follows (*Note: D* = 1 for the first period (see Fig. 15.5):

Reconstruction Period:

$$\hat{Y}_t = (-1.7502 + 1.4839) + (0.1504 - 0.1034)X_t$$
$$= -0.2663 + 0.0470X_t \qquad (15.7.5)$$

Postreconstruction period:

$$\hat{Y}_t = -1.7502 + 0.1504X_t \qquad (15.7.6)$$

As the reader can see, these regressions are the same as those obtained from the Chow multistep procedure, which can be seen from regressions given in Section 8.8.

The advantages of the dummy variable technique [i.e., estimating (15.7.1)] over the Chow test [i.e., estimating the three regressions (8.8.1), (8.8.2) and the "pooled" regression individually] can now be readily seen:

1. We need to run only a single regression because the individual regressions can easily be deduced from it in the manner indicated by equations (15.7.2) and (15.7.3).

2. The single regression can be used to test a variety of hypotheses. Thus, if the differential intercept coefficient α_2 is statistically insignificant, we may accept the hypothesis that the two regressions have the same intercept, that is, the two regressions are concurrent (see Fig. 15.4c). Similarly, if the differential slope coefficient β_2 is statistically insignificant but α_2 is significant, we may at least not reject the hypothesis that the two regressions have the same slope, that is, the two regression lines are parallel (cf. Fig. 15.4b). The test of the stability of the entire regression (i.e., $\alpha_2 = \beta_2 = 0$ simultaneously) can be made by the usual F test of the overall significance of the estimated regression discussed in Chapter 8. If this hypothesis is sustained, the regression lines will be coincident, as shown in Fig. 15.4a.

3. The Chow test does not explicitly tell us *which* coefficient, intercept, or slope is different, or whether (as in this example) both are different in the two periods, that is, one can get a significant Chow test because *slope only* is different or *intercept only* is different, or both are different. In other words, we cannot tell, via the Chow test, which one of the four possibilities depicted in Fig. 15.4 exists in a given instance. In this respect, the dummy variable approach has a distinct advantage, for it not only tells if two regressions are different but also pinpoints the source(s) of the difference—whether it is due to the intercept or the slope, or both. In practice the knowledge that two regressions differ in this or that coefficient is as important as, if not more than, the plain knowledge that they are different.

4. Finally, since pooling increases the degrees of freedom, it may improve the relative precision of the estimated parameters.[8]

15.8 COMPARING TWO REGRESSIONS: FURTHER ILLUSTRATION

Because of its practical importance, we consider another example of the use of the dummy variable technique in testing the equivalency of two (or more) regressions.

Example 15.5 The Behavior of Unemployment and Unfilled Vacancies: Great Britain, 1958–1971[9]

In studying the relationship between the unemployment rate and the unfilled job-vacancy rate in Great Britain for the period 1958–IV to 1971–II, the author obtained the scattergram shown in Fig. 15.6. As the figure shows, beginning with the fourth quarter of 1966, the unemployment-vacancy relationship seems to have changed; the curve relating the two seems to have shifted upward starting with that quarter. This upward shift implies that for a given job-vacancy rate there is more unemployment as of the fourth quarter of 1966 than before. In his study the author found that a plausible cause for the upward shift was that in October 1966 (that is, the fourth quarter) the then-Labor government liberalized the National Insurance Act by replacing the flat-rate system of short-term unemployment benefits by a mixed system of flat-rate and (previous) earnings-related benefits, which obviously increased the level of unemployment benefits. If unemployment benefits are increased, the unemployed are likely to take a longer time to look for a job, thus reflecting a higher amount of unemployment for any given job-vacancy rate.

To find out whether the observed drift in the unemployment–job-vacancy relationship beginning in the fourth quarter of 1966 was statistically significant, the author used the following model:

$$UN_t = \alpha_1 + \alpha_2 D_t + \beta_1 V_t + \beta_2 (D_t V_t) + u_t \qquad (15.8.1)$$

where UN = unemployment rate, %

$\quad V$ = job-vacancy rate, %

$\quad D = 1 \quad$ for period beginning in 1966–IV

$\quad\quad = 0 \quad$ for period before 1966–IV

$\quad t$ = time, measured in quarters

Based on 51 quarterly observations for the period 1958–IV to 1971–II, the following results were obtained (the actual data used are given in Appendix 15A, Section

---

[8]But note that every addition of a dummy variable will consume one degree of freedom.

[9]Damodar Gujarati, "The Behaviour of Unemployment and Unfilled Vacancies: Great Britain, 1958–1971," *The Economic Journal*, vol. 82, March 1972, pp. 195–202.

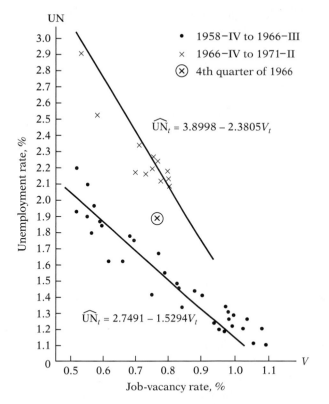

UN

$\widehat{UN}_t = 3.8998 - 2.3805V_t$

$\widehat{UN}_t = 2.7491 - 1.5294V_t$

• 1958–IV to 1966–III
× 1966–IV to 1971–II
⊗ 4th quarter of 1966

Unemployment rate, %

Job-vacancy rate, %

V

FIGURE 15.6
Scattergram of unemployment rate and job-vacancy rate, Great Britain, 1958–IV to 1971–II.

15A.1; the reader may want to examine these data, as they show how one introduces dummy variables):

$$\widehat{UN}_t = \quad 2.7491 + 1.1507D_t - 1.5294V_t - 0.8511(D_tV_t)$$

$$(0.1022)\ (0.3171) \quad (0.1218) \quad (0.4294) \qquad\qquad (15.8.2)$$

$$t = (26.896) \quad (3.6288)(-12.5552) \quad (-1.9819) \qquad R^2 = 0.9128$$

Judged by the usual criteria, the estimated regression gives an excellent fit. Note that both the differential intercept and slope coefficients are statistically significant at the 5% level (one-tail). Thus, one may accept the hypothesis that there definitely was a shift in the UN-V relationship beginning in the fourth quarter of 1966.[10]

From the preceding regression we can derive the following regressions:

1958–IV to 1966–III: $\quad \widehat{UN}_t = 2.7491 - 1.5294V_t \qquad\qquad (15.8.3)$

1966–IV to 1971–II: $\quad \widehat{UN}_t = (2.7491 + 1.15) - (1.5294 + 0.8511)V_t$

$$= 3.8998 - 2.3805V_t \qquad\qquad (15.8.4)$$

---

[10]The results were derived on the assumption that the error variances are the same in the two subperiods. But as noted in fn. 7, this assumption should be tested explicitly (see exercise 15.18).

which are shown in Fig. 15.6. These regressions show that in the period beginning in 1966–IV the UN-V curve has a much steeper slope and higher intercept than in the period beginning in 1958–IV.

15.9 INTERACTION EFFECTS

Consider the following model:

$$Y_i = \alpha_1 + \alpha_2 D_{2i} + \alpha_3 D_{3i} + \beta X_i + u_i \qquad (15.9.1)$$

where Y_i = annual expenditure on clothing

X_i = income

$D_2 = 1$ if female

     $= 0$ if male

$D_3 = 1$ if college graduate

     $= 0$ otherwise

Implicit in this model is the assumption that the differential effect of the sex dummy D_2 is constant across the two levels of education and the differential effect of the education dummy D_3 is also constant across the two sexes. That is, if, say, the mean expenditure on clothing is higher for females than males this is so whether they are college graduates or not. Likewise, if, say, college graduates on the average spend more on clothing than noncollege graduates, this is so whether they are female or males.

In many applications such an assumption may be untenable. A female college graduate may spend more on clothing than a male graduate. In other words, there may be *interaction* between the two qualitative variables D_2 and D_3 and therefore their effect on mean Y may not be simply *additive* as in (15.9.1) but *multiplicative* as well, as in the following model:

$$Y_i = \alpha_1 + \alpha_2 D_{2i} + \alpha_3 D_{3i} + \alpha_4 (D_{2i} D_{3i}) + \beta X_i + u_i \qquad (15.9.2)$$

From (15.9.2) we obtain

$$E(Y_i \mid D_2 = 1, D_3 = 1, X_i) = (\alpha_1 + \alpha_2 + \alpha_3 + \alpha_4) + \beta X_i \qquad (15.9.3)$$

which is the mean clothing expenditure of graduate females. Notice that

α_2 = differential effect of being a female

α_3 = differential effect of being a college graduate

α_4 = differential effect of being a female graduate

which shows that the mean clothing expenditure of graduate females is different (by α_4) from the mean clothing expenditure of females or college graduates. If α_2, α_3, and α_4 are all positive, the average clothing expenditure of females is higher (than the base category, which here is male nongraduate), but it is much more so if the females also happen to be graduates. Similarly, the average expenditure on clothing by a college graduate tends to be higher than the base category but much more so if the graduate happens to be a female. This shows how the **interaction dummy** modifies the effect of the two attributes considered individually.

Whether the coefficient of the interaction dummy is statistically significant can be tested by the usual t test. If it turns out to be significant, the simultaneous presence of the two attributes will attenuate or reinforce the individual effects of these attributes. Needless to say, omitting a significant interaction term incorrectly will lead to a specification bias.

15.10 THE USE OF DUMMY VARIABLES IN SEASONAL ANALYSIS

Many economic time series based on monthly or quarterly data exhibit seasonal patterns (regular oscillatory movement). Examples are sales of department stores at Christmas time, demand for money (cash balances) by households at holiday times, demand for ice cream and soft drinks during the summer, and prices of crops right after the harvesting season. Often it is desirable to remove the seasonal factor, or *component*, from a time series so that one may concentrate on the other components, such as the trend.[11] The process of removing the seasonal component from a time series is known as **deseasonalization**, or **seasonal adjustment**, and the time series thus obtained is called the **deseasonalized, or seasonally adjusted**, time series. Important economic time series, such as the consumer price index, the wholesale price index, the index of industrial production, are usually published in the seasonably adjusted form.

There are several methods of deseasonalizing a time series, but we shall consider only one of these methods, namely, the *method of dummy variables*.[12] To illustrate how the dummy variables can be used to deseasonalize economic time series, suppose that we want to regress profits of U.S. manufacturing corporations on their sales for the quarterly periods of 1965–1970. The relevant data without seasonal adjustment are given in Appendix 15A, Section 15A.2, which also shows how one prepares the *data matrix* to incorporate dummy variables. A look at these data reveals an interesting pattern. Both profits and sales are higher in the second quarter than in either the first quarter or the third quarter of each year. Perhaps the second quarter exhibits some seasonal effect. To investigate this, we proceed as follows:

Example 15.6 Profits-Sales Behavior in U.S. Manufacturing

$$\text{Profits}_t = \alpha_1 + \alpha_2 D_{2t} + \alpha_3 D_{3t} + \alpha_4 D_{4t} + \beta(\text{sales})_t + u_t \qquad (15.10.1)$$

where $D_2 = 1$ for second quarter
       $= 0$ otherwise

---

[11] A time series may contain four components: a seasonal, a cyclical, a trend, and one that is strictly random.

[12] Some other methods are the ratio-to-moving-average method, link-relative method, and percentage-of-annual-average method. For a nontechnical discussion of these methods, see Morris Hamburg, *Statistical Analysis for Decision Making*, Harcourt, Brace & World, New York, 1970, pp. 563–575.

$$D_3 = 1 \quad \text{for third quarter}$$
$$= 0 \quad \text{otherwise}$$
$$D_4 = 1 \quad \text{for fourth quarter}$$
$$= 0 \quad \text{otherwise}$$

Note that we are assuming that the variable "season" has four classes, the four quarters of a year, thereby requiring the use of three dummy variables. Thus, if there is a seasonal pattern present in various quarters, the estimated differential intercepts α_2, α_3, and α_4, if statistically significant, will reflect it. It is possible that only some of these differential intercepts are statistically significant so that only some quarters may reflect it. But model (15.10.1) is general enough to accommodate all these cases. (Note we treat the first quarter of the year as the base quarter.)

Using the data given in Appendix 15A, Section 15A.2, we obtain the following results (profit and sales figures are in millions of dollars):

$$\widehat{\text{Profits}}_t =$$

$$6688.3789 + 1322.8938 D_{2t} - 217.8037 D_{3t} + 183.8597 D_{4t} + 0.0383(\text{sales})_t$$
$$(1711.3707) \quad (638.4753) \quad (632.2561) \quad (654.2937) \quad (0.0115)$$
$$t = (3.9082) \quad (2.0720) \quad (-0.3445) \quad (0.2810) \quad (3.3313)$$
$$R^2 = 0.5255 \tag{15.10.2}$$

The results show that only the sales coefficient and differential intercept associated with the second quarter are statistically significant at the 5% level. Thus one may conclude that there is some seasonal factor operating in the second quarter of each year. The sales coefficient of 0.0383 tells us that, after taking into account the seasonal effect, if sales increase, say, by \$1, the average profits are expected to increase by about 4 cents. The average level of profits in the base or first quarter was \$6688 and in the second quarter it was higher by about \$1323 or was about \$8011. (See Fig. 15.7).[13]

Since the second quarter seems to be different from the rest, if one wishes one could rerun (15.10.2) using just one dummy to distinguish the second quarter from the rest as follows:

$$\hat{Y}_t = 6516.6 + 1311.4 D_2 + 0.0393(\text{sales})$$
$$(1623.1) \quad (493.02) \quad (0.0106)$$
$$t = (4.0143) \quad (2.7004)(3.7173) \tag{15.10.3}$$
$$R^2 = 0.5155$$

where $D_2 = 1$ for observation in the second quarter and zero otherwise.

The reader will realize that (15.10.3) is a restricted version of (15.10.2), the restrictions being that the intercept for the first, third, and fourth quarters are equal. To judge from the results (15.10.2) one would expect that these restrictions are valid but we know from Chapter 8 how to test for them explicitly. In exercise 15.21 you are asked to verify that these restrictions are indeed valid. Therefore, the conclusion remains as before—there is some seasonal pattern only in the second quarter.

In the formulation of model (15.10.1) it was assumed that only the intercept term differs between quarters, the slope coefficient of the sales variable being

---

[13]*Note:* Numerically the intercepts for the third and fourth quarters are different from that of the first quarter but statistically they are the same (Why?)

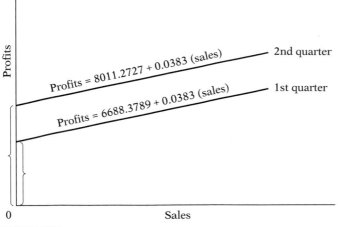

FIGURE 15.7
Relationship between profits and sales in U.S. manufacturing corporations,
1965–I to 1970–II.

the same in each quarter. But this assumption can be tested by the multiplicative
dummy technique discussed earlier. (See exercise 15.22.)

15.11 PIECEWISE LINEAR REGRESSION

To illustrate yet another use of dummy variables, consider Fig. 15.8, which
shows how a hypothetical company remunerates its sales representatives. It

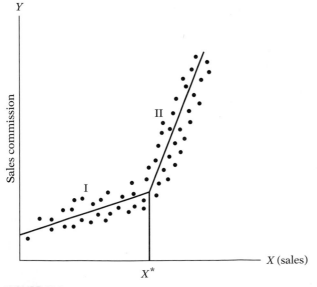

FIGURE 15.8
Hypothetical relationship between sales commission and sales volume. (*Note:* The intercept on the Y axis denotes minimum guaranteed
commission.)

pays commissions based on sales in such a manner that up to a certain level, the *target*, or *threshold*, level X^*, there is one (stochastic) commission structure and beyond that level another. (*Note:* Besides sales, other factors affect sales commission. Assume that these other factors are represented by the stochastic disturbance term.) More specifically, it is assumed that sales commission increases linearly with sales until the threshold level X^*, after which also it increases linearly with sales but at a much steeper rate. Thus, we have a **piecewise linear regression** consisting of two linear pieces or segments, which are labeled I and II in Fig. 15.8, and the commission function changes its slope at the threshold value. Given the data on commission, sales, and the value of the threshold level X^*, the technique of dummy variables can be used to estimate the (differing) slopes of the two segments of the piecewise linear regression shown in Fig. 15.8. We proceed as follows:

$$Y_i = \alpha_1 + \beta_1 X_i + \beta_2(X_i - X^*)D_i + u_i \qquad (15.11.1)$$

where Y_i = sales commission
  X_i = volume of sales generated by the sales person
  X^* = threshold value of sales also known as a **knot** (known in advance)[14]
  $D = 1$ if $X_i > X^*$
    $= 0$ if $X_i < X^*$

Assuming $E(u_i) = 0$, we see at once that

$$E(Y_i \mid D_i = 0, X_i, X^*) = \alpha_1 + \beta_1 X_i \qquad (15.11.2)$$

which gives the mean sales commission up to the target level X^* and

$$E(Y_i \mid D_i = 1, X_i, X^*) = \alpha_1 - \beta_2 X^* + (\beta_1 + \beta_2)X_i \qquad (15.11.3)$$

which gives the mean sales commission beyond the target level X^*.

Thus, β_1 gives the slope of the regression line in segment I, and $\beta_1 + \beta_2$ gives the slope of the regression line in segment II of the piecewise linear regression shown in Fig. 15.8. A test of the hypothesis that there is no break in the regression at the threshold value X^* can be conducted easily by noting the statistical significance of the estimated differential slope coefficient $\hat{\beta}_2$ (see Fig. 15.9).

Incidentally, the piecewise linear regression we have just discussed is an example of a more general class of functions known as **spline functions**.[15]

---

[14]The threshold value may not always be apparent, however. An ad hoc approach is to plot the dependent variable against the explanatory variable(s) and observe if there seems to be a sharp change in the relation after a given value of X (i.e., X^*). An analytical approach to finding the break point can be found in the so-called **switching regression models**. But this is an advanced topic and a textbook discussion may be found in Thomas Fomby, R. Carter Hill, and Stanley Johnson, *Advanced Econometric Methods*, Springer-Verlag, New York, 1984, Chap. 14.

[15]For an accessible discussion of splines (i.e., piecewise polynomials of order k), see Douglas C. Montgomery and Elizabeth A. Peck, *Introduction to Linear Regression Analysis*, John Wiley & Sons, 2d ed., New York, 1992, pp. 210–218.

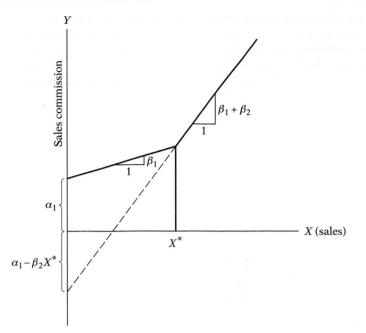

FIGURE 15.9
Parameters of the piecewise linear regression.

Example 15.7 Total Cost in Relation to Output

As an example of the application of the piecewise linear regression, consider the hypothetical total cost–total output data given in Table 15.3. We are told that the total cost may change its slope at the output level of 5500 units.

Letting Y in (15.11.1) represent total cost and X total output, we obtain the following results:

$$\hat{Y}_i = -145.72 + 0.2791X_i + 0.0945(X_i - X_i^*)D_i$$
$$t = \quad (-0.8245)(6.0669) \quad (1.1447) \qquad\qquad (15.11.4)$$
$$R^2 = 0.9737 \quad X^* = 5500$$

TABLE 15.3
Hypothetical data on output and total cost

Total cost, dollars	Output, units
256	1,000
414	2,000
634	3,000
778	4,000
1,003	5,000
1,839	6,000
2,081	7,000
2,423	8,000
2,734	9,000
2,914	10,000

As these results show, the marginal cost of production is about 28 cents per unit and although it is about 37 cents (28 + 9) for output over 5500 units, the difference between the two is not statistically significant because the dummy variable is not significant at, say, the 5% level. For all practical purposes, then, one can regress total cost on total output, dropping the dummy variable.

15.12 THE USE OF DUMMY VARIABLES IN COMBINING TIME SERIES AND CROSS-SECTIONAL DATA

To illustrate the versatility of the dummy variables, we consider in this section yet another application.

Pooled Regression: Pooling Time Series and Cross-Sectional Data

Consider the data given in Table 15.4, which are taken from a famous study of investment theory proposed by Y. Grunfeld.[16] Grunfeld was interested in finding out how gross investment (Y) depends on value of the firm (X_2) and on capital stock (X_3). In this table are data entries for each of these three variables for each year considered for G.M. and Westinghouse (For the moment, neglect the data for G.E., but see exercise 15.31). These are an example of **cross-sectional data**. Also, for each firm we have data on these variables for 20 years. These are an example of **time series data**. Now to study the response of Y to X_2 and X_3 we can proceed in one of three different ways.

First, we can run the following **time series regression** for each firm separately:

$$G.M.: \qquad Y_t = \alpha_1 + \alpha_2 X_{2t} + \alpha_3 X_{3t} + u_t \qquad (15.12.1)$$

$$Westinghouse: \qquad Y_t = \alpha_1' + \alpha_2' X_{2t} + \alpha_3' X_{3t} + u_t' \qquad (15.12.2)$$

Using the dummy variable technique or the Chow test, we can find out if the parameters of the two investment functions are the same.

Second, for each year we can estimate a **cross-sectional regression**. Unfortunately, in the present case we cannot do that because there are only two-cross sectional observations (the two firms) but there are three parameters to be estimated, which is impossible. If we had, say, data on at least four firms we could have estimated such cross-sectional regression for each of 20 years, giving a total of 20 cross-sectional regressions.

Third, why not pool all the 40 observations (20 times series observations for two firms) and estimate the following regression?

$$Y_{it} = \beta_1 + \beta_2 X_{2it} + \beta_3 X_{3it} + u_{it} \qquad (15.12.3)$$

---

[16]These data are reproduced in several books. We have taken them from H. D. Vinod and Aman Ullah, *Recent Advances in Regression Methods*, Marcel Dekker, New York, 1981, pp. 259–261. The original source is Y. Grunfeld, *The Determinants of Corporate Investment*, unpublished Ph. D. thesis, Department of Economics, University of Chicago, 1958.

TABLE 15.4
Investment data on G.M., Westinghouse, and G.E. companies

	G.M.			Westinghouse			G.E.		
	I	F_{-1}	C_{-1}	I	F_{-1}	C_{-1}	I	F_{-1}	C_{-1}
1935	317.6	3,078.5	2.8	12.93	191.5	1.8	33.1	1,170.6	97.8
36	391.8	4,661.7	52.6	25.90	516.0	.8	45.0	2,015.8	104.4
37	410.6	5,387.1	156.9	35.05	729.0	7.4	77.2	2,803.3	118.0
38	257.7	2,792.2	209.2	22.89	560.4	18.1	44.6	2,039.7	156.2
39	330.8	4,313.2	203.4	18.84	519.9	23.5	48.1	2,256.2	172.6
40	461.2	4,643.9	207.2	28.57	628.5	26.5	74.4	2,132.2	186.6
41	512.0	4,551.2	255.2	48.51	537.1	36.2	113.0	1,834.1	220.9
42	448.0	3,244.1	303.7	43.34	561.2	60.8	91.9	1,588.0	287.8
43	499.6	4,053.7	264.1	37.02	617.2	84.4	61.3	1,749.4	319.9
44	547.5	4,379.3	201.6	37.81	626.7	91.2	56.8	1,687.2	321.3
45	561.2	4,840.9	265.0	39.27	737.2	92.4	93.6	2,007.7	319.6
46	688.1	4,900.9	402.2	53.46	760.5	86.0	159.9	2,208.3	346.0
47	568.9	3,526.5	761.5	55.56	581.4	111.1	147.2	1,656.7	456.4
48	529.2	3,254.7	922.4	49.56	662.3	130.6	146.3	1,604.4	543.4
49	555.1	3,700.2	1,020.1	32.04	583.8	141.8	98.3	1,431.8	618.3
50	642.9	3,755.6	1,099.0	32.24	635.2	136.7	93.5	1,610.5	647.4
51	755.9	4,833.0	1,207.7	54.38	723.8	129.7	135.2	1,819.4	671.3
52	891.2	4,924.9	1,430.5	71.78	864.1	145.5	157.3	2,079.7	726.1
53	1,304.4	6,241.7	1,777.3	90.08	1,193.5	174.8	179.5	2,371.6	800.3
54	1,486.7	5,593.6	2,226.3	68.60	1,188.9	213.5	189.6	2,759.9	888.9

Notes: $Y = I$ = gross investment = additions to plant and equipment plus maintenance and repairs, in millions of dollars deflated by P_1

$X_2 = F$ = value of the firm = price of common and preferred shares at Dec. 31 (or average price of Dec. 31 and Jan. 31 of the following year) times number of common and preferred shares outstanding plus total book value of debt at Dec. 31, in millions of dollars deflated by P_2

$X_3 = C$ = stock of plant and equipment = accumulated sum of net additions to plant and equipment deflated by P_1 minus depreciation allowance deflated by P_3 in these definitions

P_1 = implicit price deflator of producers' durable equipment (1947 = 100)

P_2 = implicit price deflator of GNP (1947 = 100)

P_3 = depreciation expense deflator = 10-year moving average of wholesale price index of metals and metal products (1947 = 100)

Source: Reproduced from H. D. Vinod and Aman Ullah, *Recent Advances in Regression Methods*, Marcel Dekker, New York, 1981, pp. 259–261.

where i stands for the ith firm and t for the tth time period. In our example $i = 2$ and $t = 20$, thus giving us a total of 40 observations. Equation (15.12.3) is an example of a **pooled regression** where time series and cross-sectional observations are combined or pooled together. Such regressions are often estimated in situations where we have too few cross-sectional observations (as in the present case) and a fairly good number of time series observations. As Vinod and Ullah write:

> When dealing with cross-section and time series data, where each individual cross-section sample is small so that sharp inferences about the coefficients are not possible, it is a common practice in applied work to pool all data together, and estimate a common regression. The basic motivation for pooling time series

and cross-section data is that if the model is properly specified, pooling provides more efficient estimation, inference, and possibly prediction.[17]

Now let us consider the problems in estimating (15.12.3). Suppose we estimate it by the usual OLS procedure: We simply stack the G.M. and Westinghouse observations, the first 20 observations are for G.M. and the last 20 for Westinghouse. Is this procedure wrong?

Such a procedure implicitly assumes that the regression parameters do not change over time (temporal stability) and that they do not differ between various cross-sectional units (cross-sectional stability). Implicit also in such a procedure is the assumption that the error variance of the G.M. and Westinghouse investment functions are homoscedastic and the error in the G.M. investment function at time t is uncorrelated with the error term in the Westinghouse investment function at time t. These are obviously tall assumptions. There are various ways of relaxing these assumptions and incorporating them in the estimating procedure. Unfortunately, time, space and mathematical constraints prevent us from pursuing these further.[18] We will present only one case where we assume that the intercept values in the G.M. and Westinghouse investment functions are different (question of cross-sectional stability) but that the slope coefficients are the same. We also assume that the error term in the pooled regression has the usual OLS properties across time series and cross-section observations.

With these assumptions, we write (15.12.3) as

$$Y_{it} = \beta_1 + \beta_2 X_{2it} + \beta_3 X_{3it} + \beta_4 D_{it} + u_{it} \tag{15.12.4}$$

where $D_{1t} = 1$ for observations on G.M. and 0 otherwise. Thus, if β_4 in (15.12.4) is statistically significant, it would mean that the intercept value of the G.M. investment function is different from that of the Westinghouse investment function. In other words, β_4 is the *differential intercept* value. In exercise 15.32 the reader is asked to introduce the differential slope coefficients.

Example 15.8. Investment Functions for General Motors and Westinghouse Companies

Using the data given in Table 15.4, we obtain the following estimates of (15.12.4):[19]

$$\hat{Y}_{it} = -64.1679 + 0.1121 X_{2it} + 0.3716 X_{3it} - 54.7688 D_{it}$$
$$t = (-3.4026)(6.1205) \qquad (13.7927) \qquad (-0.8358)$$
$$R^2 = 0.9679 \qquad d = 0.8658 \tag{15.12.5}$$

---

[17]Ibid., p. 248.

[18]A best single source for the various estimating techniques is Terry E. Dielman, *Pooled Cross-Sectional and Time Series Data Analysis*, Marcel Dekker, New York, 1989.

[19]To estimate the regression, stack the observations for the two firms. That is, the first 20 observations belong to G.M. and the last 20 to Westinghouse. Create the dummy variable and give it a value of 1 for all G.M. observations and a value of 0 for all Westinghouse observations.

As these results show, since the differential intercept dummy is not statistically significant, we can conclude that the G.M. and Westinghouse investment functions have statistically the same intercepts. Of course, this conclusion should be taken with a dollop of salt, since we have only allowed the intercepts to differ and not the slopes. The fact that the Durbin-Watson statistic is low suggests that probably there are specification errors in (15.2.4). Admittedly, regression (15.2.4) was chosen only to demonstrate the use of dummy variables in pooled data.

*15.13   SOME TECHNICAL ASPECTS OF DUMMY VARIABLE TECHNIQUE

In this section we discuss some finer points about the use of dummy variables in regression analysis.

The Interpretation of Dummy Variables in Semilogarithmic Regressions

Recall our discussion regarding the log-lin regression models where the regressand is logarithmic and the regressors are linear. To be specific, consider the following model:

$$\ln Y_i = \beta_1 + \beta_2 X_i + \beta_3 D_i \qquad (15.13.1)$$

where Y = starting salary of college professors, X = years of teaching experience, and $D = 1$ for male and zero otherwise.

Following Chapter 6, we interpret the coefficient β_2 as giving the relative change (or percent change if the relative change is multiplied by 100) in the mean value of Y for a unit change in X. Thus, in the present example, if teaching experience increases by a year, the relative change in mean starting salary will be equal to β_2. Such an interpretation can be applied to a change in any regressor value, *provided the regressor is a continuous variable and not dichotomous as in the case of the dummy variable.* But one can obtain the relative change in mean Y even for the dummy variable by the device suggested by Halvorsen and Palmquist:[20] *Take the antilog (to base e) of the estimated dummy coefficient and subtract 1 from it.*

Example 15.9.   Semilogarithmic Regression with Dummy Variable

To illustrate, consider the data in Table 15.5 relating starting salary (Y) to years of teaching experience (X_2) and sex ($D = 1$ for male professors). Assuming model (15.13.1), we obtain the following results:

$$\widehat{\ln Y_i} = \quad 2.9298 + 0.0546 X_{2i} + 0.1341 D_i$$
$$t = (481.524) \quad (48.3356) \quad (27.2250) \qquad (15.13.2)$$
$$R^2 = 0.9958 \quad d = 2.51$$

---

*Optional.

[20]Robert Halvorsen and Raymond Palmquist, "The Interpretation of Dummy Variables in Semilogarithmic Equations," *American Economic Review*, vol. 70, no. 3, 1980, pp. 474–475.

TABLE 15.5
Hypothetical data on salaries of college professors in relation to years of teaching experience and sex

Starting salary, Y ($, in thousands)	Years of teaching experience, X_2	Sex (1 = male) (0 = female)
23.0	1	1
19.5	1	0
24.0	2	1
21.0	2	0
25.0	3	1
22.0	3	0
26.5	4	1
23.1	4	0
25.0	5	0
28.0	5	1
29.5	6	1
26.0	6	0
27.5	7	0
31.5	7	1
29.0	8	0

As these results show, holding other things the same (sex of the professor here), the average or mean salary increases by 5.46 percent per year. But *we cannot say that, holding teaching experience constant, the mean salary is higher by 13.41 percent for male professors.* Following Halvorsen and Palmquist, we find the antilog of $0.1341 \doteq 1.1435$. Subtracting 1 from this, we obtain 0.1435 or 14.35 percent; the mean salary of male professors is thus higher (than for female professors) by 14.35 percent. In exercise 15.33 you are asked to compare the regression results given in (15.13.2) with those obtained from the linear model.

Another Method of Avoiding the Dummy Variable Trap

There is another way of avoiding the dummy variable trap. To see this, continue with model (15.2.4) but write the model as

$$Y_i = \alpha_2 D_{2i} + \alpha_3 D_{3i} + \beta X_i + u_i \tag{15.13.3}$$

with the dummies as defined following Eq. (15.2.4). Notice that in (15.13.3) we have dropped the intercept term α_1. Now we will not fall into the dummy variable trap because we no longer have perfect collinearity, as can be seen from the data matrix given after Eq. (15.2.4) with the column of 1's eliminated.

Notice that as result of this change, we need to interpret α_2 and α_3 differently. They are no longer the differential intercept coefficients; they now give direct estimates of the intercepts in the various categories. Thus, in the present case, with α_1 dropped, α_2 will give the intercept value of male professors' salary regression and α_3 the intercept value of the female professors' salary regression. *But note that to estimate (15.13.3) we will have to use the regression-through-origin estimating procedure,* as discussed in Chapter 6. Of course, most software packages can do this routinely.

Returning to regression (15.1.3), we could have estimated that regression as

$$Y_i = \alpha_2 D_{2i} + \alpha_3 D_{3i} + u_i \qquad (15.13.4)$$

where $D_{2i} = 1$ for male professors and 0 otherwise, and $D_{3i} = 1$ for female professors and 0 otherwise. (*Note:* There is no common intercept in this regression.)

If you had followed this strategy, you would have obtained the following regression results:

$$
\begin{aligned}
\hat{Y}_i = \quad & 21.28 D_{2i} + 18.00 D_{3i} \\
\text{se} = \quad & (0.3118) \quad (0.3118) \\
t = \quad & (68.2556) \quad (57.7350) \quad R^2 = 0.8737
\end{aligned}
\qquad (15.13.5)
$$

which are the same as (15.1.3), but in a different garb.

The common practice is to assign the dummy variables in such a way that if a variable has m categories, we introduce only $(m - 1)$ dummies. The advantage of this scheme is that very often we want to compare our results in terms of a reference category. Besides, by keeping the common intercept, we obtain the usual R^2 value, whereas with the zero-intercept model the conventional R^2 is not usually meaningful. Therefore, we will follow the common practice.

Dummy Variables and Heteroscedasticity

Let us return to the U.K. savings-income example discussed in Section 15.6. In using the dummy variable technique to combine the two regressions (15.6.1) and (15.6.2) as in (15.7.1), we implicitly assumed that var(u_{1i}) = var(u_{2i}) = σ^2, that is, homoscedasticity. If this assumption is not valid, that is, if the two error variances are different, it is quite likely we will find that the two intercepts and the two slope coefficients are not statistically different yet find that the coefficient of the dummy variable in regression (15.7.1) is statistically significant.[21] Therefore, in applying the dummy variable technique (or the Chow test for that matter) we should verify that in a given case we do not face the problem of heteroscedasticity. But we know by now how to deal with that problem.

Dummy Variables and Autocorrelation

Consider the following model involving time series data:

$$Y_t = \beta_1 + \beta_2 D_t + \beta_3 X_t + \beta_4 (D_t X_t) + u_t \qquad (15.13.6)$$

where $D_t = 0$ for observations in the first time period and 1 for those in the second time period. Suppose there are n_1 observations in the first time period and n_2 in the second. Observe that (15.13.6), which allows for differential intercept and slope dummies, is precisely the model (15.7.1) that we used to study the U.K. savings-income relationship.

---

[21] On this see G. S. Maddala, *Introduction to Econometrics*, Macmillan, 2d ed., New York, 1992, pp. 320–322.

Assume further that the error term u_t in (15.13.6) is generated by the Markov first-order autoregressive scheme, the AR (1) scheme, namely,

$$u_t = \rho u_{t-1} + \varepsilon_t \qquad (15.13.7)$$

where ε satisfies the standard assumptions.

Now from Chapter 12 we know how to transform a regression model to get rid of (first-order) autocorrelation (recall the generalized difference method): Assuming ρ is known or estimated, we use $(Y_t - \rho Y_{t-1})$ as the regressand and $(X_t - \rho X_{t-1})$ as the regressor. But the presence of the dummy regressor D poses a special problem: Note that the dummy variable simply classifies an observation as belonging to the first or second period. How then do we transform it? Maddala suggests the following procedure:[22]

1. In (15.13.6) values of D are zero for all observations in the first period; in period 2 the value of D for the *first* observation is $1/(1 - \rho)$ instead of 1, and 1 for all other observations.
2. The variable X_t is transformed as $(X_t - \rho X_{t-1})$. Note that we lose one observation in this transformation, unless one resorts to the **Prais-Winsten transformation.**
3. The value of $D_t X_t$ is zero for all observations in the first period (*Note: D_t is zero in the first period*); in the second period the *first observation* takes the value of $D_t X_t = X_t$ and the remaining observations in the second period are set to $(D_t X_t - D_t X_{t-1}) = (X_t - \rho X_{t-1})$. (*Note:* Value of D_t in the second period is 1).

As the preceding discussion points out, the *critical observation* is the first observation in the second period. If this is taken care of in the manner suggested, there should be no problem in estimating regressions like (15.3.6) subject to autocorrelation as specified in (15.13.7).

15.14   TOPICS FOR FURTHER STUDY

Several topics related to dummy variables are discussed in the literature that are rather advanced, including (1) **random**, or **varying, parameters models**, (2) **switching regression models**, and (3) **disequilibrium models**.

In the regression models considered in this text it is assumed that the parameters, the β's, are unknown but fixed entities. The random coefficient models—and there are several versions of them—assume the β's can be random too. A major reference work in this area is by Swamy.[23]

In the dummy variable model using both the differential intercepts and differential slopes, it is implicitly assumed that we know the point of break. Thus, in our U.K. savings-income regression, we identified 1946–1954 as the re-

---

[22] Maddala, ibid., pp. 321–322.

[23] P. A. V. B. Swamy, *Statistical Inference in Random Coefficient Regression Models*, Springer-Verlag, Berlin, 1971.

construction period and 1955–1963 as the postreconstruction period. But what if we do not know whether the break took place in 1955 or 1954 or 1956? The technique of **switching regression models** handles this question by allowing the point of break to be itself random. The seminal work in this area is by Goldfeld and Quandt.[24]

Special estimation techniques are required to deal with what are known as **disequilibrium situations**, that is, situations where markets do not clear (i.e., demand is not equal to supply). The classic example is that of demand for and supply of a commodity. The demand for a commodity is a function of its price and other variables, and the supply of the commodity is a function of its price and other variables, some of which are different from those entering the demand function. Now the quantity actually bought and sold of the commodity may not necessarily be equal to the one obtained by equating the demand to supply, thus leading to disequilibrium. For a thorough discussion of **disequilibrium models**, the reader may refer to Quandt.[25]

15.15   SUMMARY AND CONCLUSIONS

1. Dummy variables taking values of 1 and 0 (or their linear transforms) are a means of introducing qualitative regressors in regression analysis.

2. Dummy variables are a data-classifying device in that they divide a sample into various subgroups based on qualities or attributes (sex, marital status, race, religion, etc.) and *implicitly* allow one to run individual regressions for each subgroup. If there are differences in the response of the regressand to the variation in the quantitative variables in the various subgroups, they will be reflected in the differences in the intercepts or slope coefficients, or both, of the various subgroup regressions.

3. Although a versatile tool, the dummy variable technique needs to be handled carefully. First, if the regression contains a constant term, the number of dummy variables must be less than the number of classifications of each qualitative variable. Second, the coefficient attached to the dummy variables must *always* be interpreted in relation to the base, or reference, group, that is, the group that gets the value of zero. Finally, if a model has several qualitative variables with several classes, introduction of dummy variables can consume a large number of degrees of freedom. Therefore, one should always weigh the number of dummy variables to be introduced against the total number of observations available for analysis.

4. Among its various applications, this chapter considered but a few. These included (1) comparing two (or more) regressions, (2) deseasonalizing time series data, (3) combining time series and cross-sectional data, and (4) piecewise linear regression models.

---

[24]S. Goldfeld and R. Quandt, *Nonlinear Methods in Econometrics*, North Holland, Amsterdam, 1972.

[25]Richard E. Quandt, *The Econometrics of Disequilibrium*, Basil Blackwell, New York, 1988.

5. Since the dummy variables are nonstochastic, they pose no special problems in the application of OLS. However, care must be exercised in transforming data involving dummy variables. In particular, the problems of autocorrelation and heteroscedasticity need to be handled very carefully.

EXERCISES

Questions

15.1. If you have monthly data over a number of years, how many dummy variables will you introduce to test the following hypotheses:
   (*a*) All the 12 months of the year exhibit seasonal patterns.
   (*b*) Only February, April, June, August, October, and December exhibit seasonal patterns.

15.2. Refer to regression (15.5.1), which explains the determination of moonlighters' hourly wages. From this equation derive the hourly wage equations for the following types of moonlighters:
   (*a*) White, nonurban, western resident, and high school graduate
   (*b*) Nonwhite, urban, nonwestern resident, and non–high school graduate
   (*c*) White, nonurban, nonwestern resident, and high school graduate

15.3. In studying the effect of a number of qualitative attributes on the prices charged for movie admissions in a large metropolitan area for the period 1961–1964, R. D. Lampson obtained the following regression for the year 1961:[*]

$$\hat{Y} = 4.13 + 5.77D_1 + 8.21D_2 - 7.68D_3 - 1.13D_4$$
$$\quad\quad (2.04) \quad (2.67) \quad (2.51) \quad (1.78)$$
$$\quad + 27.09D_5 + 31.46 \log X_1 + 0.81X_2 + 3 \text{ other dummy variables}$$
$$\quad\quad (3.58) \quad\quad (13.78) \quad\quad (0.17)$$
$$R^2 = 0.961$$

where D_1 = theater location: 1 if suburban, 0 if city center
$\quad\quad D_2$ = theater age: 1 if less than 10 years since construction or major renovation, 0 otherwise.
$\quad\quad D_3$ = type of theater: 1 if outdoor, 0 if indoor
$\quad\quad D_4$ = parking: 1 if provided, 0 otherwise
$\quad\quad D_5$ = screening policy: 1 if first run, 0 otherwise
$\quad\quad X_1$ = average percentage unused seating capacity per showing
$\quad\quad X_2$ = average film rental, cents per ticket charged by the distributor
$\quad\quad Y$ = adult evening admission price, cents

and where the figures in parentheses are standard errors.
   (*a*) Comment on the results.
   (*b*) How would you rationalize the introduction of the variable X_1?
   (*c*) How would you explain the negative value of the coefficient of D_4?

---

[*]R. D. Lampson, "Measured Productivity and Price Change: Some Empirical Evidence on Service Industry Bias, Motion Picture Theaters," *Journal of Political Economy*, vol. 78, March/April 1970, pp. 291–305.

15.4. Based on annual data for 1972–1979, William Nordhaus estimated the following model to explain the OPEC's oil price behavior (standard errors in parentheses):*

$$y_t = 0.3x_{1t} + 5.22x_{2t}$$

$$(0.03) \quad (0.50)$$

where y_t = difference between current and previous year's price ($ per barrel)

x_{1t} = difference between current year spot price and OPEC's price in the previous year

x_{2t} = 1 for 1974 and zero otherwise

(*Note:* 1973–1974 was the oil embargo year.) Interpret this result and show the result graphically for pre- and postembargo periods.

15.5. Suppose that we modify the college professors' salary regression (15.4.1) as follows:

$$Y_i = \alpha_1 + \alpha_2 D_{2i} + \alpha_3 D_{3i} + \alpha_4 (D_{2i}D_{3i}) + \beta X_i + u_i$$

where Y_i = annual salary of a college professor

X_i = years of teaching experience

D_2 = 1 if male and zero otherwise

D_3 = 1 if white and zero otherwise

(*a*) The term $D_{2i}D_{3i}$ represents the *interaction effect*. What is meant by this expression?

(*b*) What is the meaning of the coefficient α_4?

(*c*) Find $E(Y_i \,|\, D_2 = 1, D_3 = 1, X_i)$ and interpret it.

15.6. Dummy variables versus allocated codes. Refer to regression (15.2.1). Instead of adopting the dummy setup shown there, suppose we use the following *allocated codes*:

$$D_i = 1 \text{ if female}$$

$$= 2 \text{ if male}$$

(*a*) Interpret the regression using the allocated codes.

(*b*) What is the advantage, if any, of assigning the stated allocated codes versus using the zero-one dummy setup?

15.7. Continue with exercise 15.6 but now consider this allocation scheme:

$$D_i = 1 \text{ if female}$$

$$= -1 \text{ if male}$$

Interpret the regression using this scheme and compare the results with the usual zero-one dummy method.

15.8. Refer to regression (15.10.1). How would you test the hypothesis

(*a*) $\alpha_2 = \alpha_3$

(*b*) $\alpha_2 = \alpha_4$

*"Oil and Economic Performance in Industrial Countries," *Brookings Papers on Economic Activity*, 1980, pp. 341–388.

(c) If $\alpha_2 \neq \alpha_1$ and $\alpha_3 \neq \alpha_1$ statistically, does it mean that $\alpha_2 \neq \alpha_3$? *Hint:* $\text{var}(A + B) = \text{var}(A) + \text{var}(B) + 2\,\text{cov}(A, B)$, and $\text{var}(A - B) = \text{var}(A) + \text{var}(B) - 2\,\text{cov}(A, B)$.

15.9. (a) How would you obtain the standard errors of the regression coefficients in models (15.8.3) and (15.8.4), which were estimated from the "pooled" regression (15.8.2)?

(b) To obtain numerical answers, what additional information, if any, is required?

15.10. As stated in the text, the estimates of the regression coefficients obtained from (15.7.1) will be identical with those obtained from the individual estimation of two regressions (15.6.1) and (15.6.2). Will this also be true of $\hat{\sigma}^2$, the estimator of the true variance of σ^2; that is, will $\hat{\sigma}^2$ obtained from (15.7.1) be the same as that obtained from (15.6.1) or (15.6.2)? Why or why not?

15.11. Pooling cross-sectional and time series data. Suppose you have data on output, labor, and capital inputs for N firms in an industry for T time periods and suppose you want to fit a production function of the following type:

$$Y_{it} = \alpha + \beta_1 X_{1it} + \beta_2 X_{2it} + u_{it} \qquad \begin{matrix} i = 1, 2, 3, \ldots, N \\ t = 1, 2, 3, \ldots, T \end{matrix}$$

where Y = output

X_1 = capital input

X_2 = labor input

Assuming you have the relevant data, you are asked to develop models such that

(a) Firms differ in *managerial efficiency*, the differences affecting only the intercept α; this may be called the *firm effect*.

(b) All firms are of equal managerial efficiency, but the intercept α shifts from year to year; this may be called the *year effect*.

(c) The intercept of the preceding production function is affected by the firm as well as the year effect. In addition,

(d) What assumption do you make about the disturbance term u_{it}?

15.12. In his study on the labor hours spent by the FDIC (Federal Deposit Insurance Corporation) on 91 bank examinations, R. J. Miller estimated the following function:*

$$\widehat{\ln Y} = 2.41 + 0.3674\ln X_1 + 0.2217\ln X_2 + 0.0803\ln X_3$$
$$\qquad\qquad (0.0477) \qquad\quad (0.0628) \qquad\quad (0.0287)$$
$$\qquad\qquad\qquad - 0.1755 D_1 \qquad + 0.2799 D_2 + 0.5634 D_3 - 0.2572 D_4$$
$$\qquad\qquad\qquad (0.2905) \qquad\qquad (0.1044) \qquad (0.1657) \qquad (0.0787)$$
$$R^2 = 0.766$$

where Y = FDIC examiner labor hours

X_1 = total assets of bank

X_2 = total number of offices in bank

---

*"Examination of Man-Hour Cost for Independent, Joint, and Divided Examination Programs," *Journal of Bank Research*, vol. 11, 1980, pp. 28–35. *Note:* The notations have been altered to conform with our notations.

$$X_3 = \text{ratio of classified loans to total loans for bank}$$
$$D_1 = 1 \text{ if management rating was "good"}$$
$$D_2 = 1 \text{ if management rating was "fair"}$$
$$D_3 = 1 \text{ if management rating was "satisfactory"}$$
$$D_4 = 1 \text{ if examination was conducted jointly with the state}$$

The figures in parentheses are the estimated standard errors.
(a) Interpret these results.
(b) Is there any problem in interpreting the dummy variables in this model since Y is in the log form?
(c) How would you interpret the dummy coefficients?

15.13. To assess the effect of the Fed's policy of deregulating interest rates beginning in July 1979, Sidney Langer, a student of mine, estimated the following model for the quarterly period of 1975–III to 1983–II.*

$$\hat{Y}_t = 8.5871 - 0.1328 P_t - 0.7102 \text{Un}_t - 0.2389 M_t$$
$$\text{se}(1.9563) \quad (0.0992) \quad (0.1909) \quad (0.0727)$$
$$+ 0.6592 Y_{t-1} + 2.5831 \text{Dum}_t \qquad R^2 = 0.9156$$
$$(0.1036) \qquad (0.7549)$$

where Y = 3-month Treasury bill rate
$$P = \text{expected rate of inflation}$$
$$\text{Un} = \text{seasonally adjusted unemployment rate}$$
$$M = \text{changes in the monetary base}$$
$$\text{Dum} = \text{dummy, taking value of 1 for observations beginning July 1, 1979}$$

(a) Interpret these results.
(b) What has been the effect of rate deregulation? Do the results make economic sense?
(c) The coefficients of P_t, Un_t and M_t are negative. Can you offer an economic rationale?

15.14. Refer to the piecewise regression discussed in the text. Suppose there not only is a change in the slope coefficient at X^* but also the regression line jumps, as shown in Fig. 15.10. How would you modify (15.11.1) to take into account the jump in the regression line at X^*?

15.15. *Determinants of price per ounce of cola.* Cathy Schaefer, a student of mine, estimated the following regression based on cross-sectional data of 77 observations:†

$$P_i = \beta_0 + \beta_1 D_{1i} + \beta_2 D_{2i} + \beta_3 D_{3i} + \mu_i$$

where P_i = price per ounce of cola
$$D_{1i} = 001 \text{ if discount store}$$

---

*Sidney Langer, "Interest Rate Deregulation and Short-Term Interest Rates," unpublished term paper.
†Cathy Schaefer, "Price Per Ounce of Cola Beverage as a Function of Place of Purchase, Size of Container, and Branded or Unbranded Product," unpublished term project.

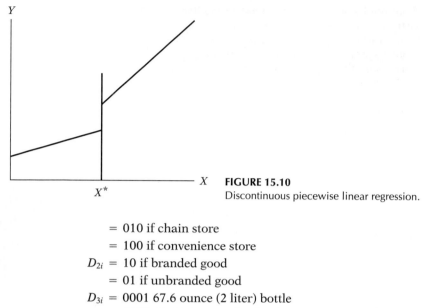

FIGURE 15.10
Discontinuous piecewise linear regression.

$$
\begin{aligned}
&= 010 \text{ if chain store}\\
&= 100 \text{ if convenience store}\\
D_{2i} &= 10 \text{ if branded good}\\
&= 01 \text{ if unbranded good}\\
D_{3i} &= 0001 \text{ 67.6 ounce (2 liter) bottle}\\
&= 0010 \text{ 28–33.8 ounce bottles } (\textit{Note:}\ 33.8\ \text{oz} = 1\ \text{liter})\\
&= 0100 \text{ 16-ounce bottle}\\
&= 1000 \text{ 12-ounce cans}
\end{aligned}
$$

The results were as follows:

$$
\hat{P}_i = 0.0143 - 0.000004 D_{1i} + 0.0090 D_{2i} + 0.00001 D_{3i}
$$
$$
\quad (0.00001) \qquad (0.00011) \quad (0.00000)
$$
$$
t = (-0.3837) \qquad (8.3927) \qquad (5.8125)
$$
$$
R^2 = 0.6033
$$

Note: The standard errors are shown only to five decimal places.

(*a*) Comment on the way the dummies have been introduced in the model.

(*b*) Assuming the dummy setup is acceptable, how would you interpret the results?

(*c*) The coefficient of D_3 is positive and statistically significant. How do you rationalize this result?

15.16. Based on data for 101 countries on per capita income in dollars (X) and life expectancy in years (Y) in the early 1970's, Sen and Srivastava obtained the following regression results:[*]

$$
\hat{Y}_i = -2.40 + 9.39 \ln X_i - 3.36[D_i (\ln X_i - 7)]
$$
$$
\text{se} = \quad (4.73) \quad (0.859) \qquad (2.42) \qquad\qquad R^2 = 0.752
$$

where $D_i = 1$ if $\ln X_i > 7$, and $D_i = 0$ otherwise. *Note:* When $\ln X_i = 7, X = \$1097$ (approximately).

---

[*]Ashish Sen and Muni Srivastava, *Regression Analysis: Theory, Methods, and Applications*, Springer-Verlag, New York, 1990, p. 92. Notation changed.

(a) What might be the reason(s) for introducing the income variable in the log form?

(b) How would you interpret the coefficient 9.39 of $\ln X_i$?

(c) What might be the reason for introducing the regressor $D_i(\ln X_i - 7)$? How do you explain this regressor verbally? And how do you interpret the coefficient -3.36 of this regressor (*Hint:* linear piecewise regression)?

(d) Assuming per capita income of \$1097 as the dividing line between poorer and richer countries, how would you derive the regression for countries whose per capita is less than \$1097 and the regression for countries whose per capita income is greater than \$1097?

(e) What general conclusions do you draw from the regression result presented in this problem?

15.17. Consider the following model:

$$Y_i = \beta_1 + \beta_2 D_i + u_i$$

where $D_i = 0$ for the first 20 observations and $D_i = 1$ for the remaining 30 observations. You are also told that var $(u_i^2) = 300$.

(a) How would you interpret β_1 and β_2?

(b) What are the mean values of the two groups?

(c) How would you compute the variance of $(\hat{\beta}_1 + \hat{\beta}_2)$? *Note:* You are given that the cov $(\hat{\beta}_1, \hat{\beta}_2) = -15$.

Problems

15.18. Using the data given in Appendix 15A, Section 15A.1, test the hypothesis that the error variances in the two subperiods 1958–IV to 1966–III and 1966–IV to 1971–II are the same. See Chapter 11 for the various methods of testing for homogeneity of variances.

15.19. Test the hypothesis that $\hat{\sigma}_2^2$ and $\hat{\sigma}_3^2$ estimated from (8.8.6) and (8.8.7) are equal. You may use Bartlett's homogeneity-of-variance test discussed in Chapter 11.

15.20. **Modified Chow test** (*when the observations are fewer than the number of parameters to be estimated*). Refer to the regressions (15.6.1) and (15.6.2). Assume that n_2, the number of observations in the second period, is less than or at the most equal to the number of parameters to be estimated. In this case, Chow suggests the following modification to his test: Let $S_1 =$ RSS from the pooled regression; $S_2 =$ RSS from the first period regression (it is assumed that $n_1 >$ number of parameters). Now use the following F test:

$$F = \frac{(S_1 - S_2)/n_2}{S_2/(n_1 - k)}$$

which has n_2 and $(n_1 - k)$ df.

If this F value turns out to be statistically significant, reject the hypothesis that the last n_2 observations came from the model that generated the first period's regression based on n_1 observations. If it is insignificant, you may not reject that hypothesis.

Use the data of Table 15.2 to test the hypothesis that the last two observations came from the same population that generated the first 16 observations.

15.21. Using the methodology discussed in Chapter 8, compare the unrestricted and restricted regressions (15.10.2) and (15.10.3), that is, test for the validity of the imposed restrictions.

15.22. Refer to the data given in Appendix 15A, Section 15A.2 and regression (15.10.2). Develop a regression model to test the hypothesis that the slope as well as the intercept term of the regression of profits on sales is different for the second quarter of the year as compared with the remaining quarters. Show the necessary calculations.

15.23. Deseasonalizing data. The illustrative example of Section 15.10 showed how the dummy variables can be used to take into account the seasonal effects. After estimating regression (15.10.2) we found that only the dummy associated with the second quarter of a year was statistically significant, indicating that only the second quarter exhibited some seasonal effect. Therefore, one method of deseasonalizing the data would be to subtract from the profits and sales figures of the second quarter of each year the value of 1,322.8938 (millions of dollars), the value of the dummy coefficient for the second quarter, and run the regression of profits on sales using the data thus transformed.

   (a) Transform the preceding data and run the regression. Do not introduce any dummy variables in this regression. (Why?)

   (b) Compare the coefficient of the sales variable in the estimated regression using the transformed data with that given in (15.10.2). Are these two coefficients expected to be identical statistically? Why?

   (c) Suppose in (a) you did introduce dummy variables. What should happen to the coefficients of the dummy variables?

15.24. In the savings-income regression (15.7.4), suppose that instead of using 1 and 0 values for the dummy D_i you were to use $Z_i = a + bD_i$, where $D_i = 1$ and 0 and where $a = 2$ and $b = 3$. Compare the two results.

15.25. Continuing with the savings-income regression (15.7.4), suppose you were to assign $D_i = 1$ to observations in the second period and $D_i = 0$ to observations in the first period. How would the results shown in (15.7.4) change?

15.26. How would you obtain the standard errors of the estimated coefficients for the regressions (15.7.5) and (15.7.6)? What additional information would you need, if any, to obtain the numerical results.

15.27. The following table gives quarterly data (not seasonally adjusted) on the sale of mutual fund shares by the mutual fund industry for the period 1968–1973.

Sale of mutual fund shares (millions of dollars)

	Quarter			
Year	I	II	III	IV
1968	1,564	1,654	1,607	1,994
1969	2,129	1,658	1,428	1,503
1970	1,381	1,039	975	1,230
1971	1,304	1,288	1,108	1,446
1972	1,398	1,176	1,099	1,219
1973	1,382	888	933	1,156

Source: 1974 Mutual Fund Fact Book, Investment Company Institute, Washington, D.C. (The figures are rounded to the nearest million dollars.)

Consider the following model:

$$\text{Sales}_t = \alpha_1 + \alpha_2 D_2 + \alpha_3 D_3 + \alpha_4 D_4 + u_t$$

where $D_2 = 1$ for the second quarter, 0 otherwise

$D_3 = 1$ for the third quarter, 0 otherwise

$D_4 = 1$ for the fourth quarter, 0 otherwise

(a) Estimate the preceding regression.

(b) How would you interpret the α's?

(c) How would you use the estimated α's to deseasonalize the sales data?

15.28. Use the data of exercise 15.27 but use the following model:

$$\text{Sales}_t = \alpha_1 D_1 + \alpha_2 D_2 + \alpha_3 D_3 + \alpha_4 D_4 + u_t$$

where the D's are the dummy variables taking values of 1 or 0 in quarters 1 to 4.

(a) How would you estimate the preceding equation?

(b) Does the preceding equation violate the rule that the number of dummies should be one less than the number of classifications (quarters)?

(c) Compare your results with those obtained in exercise 15.27.

*15.29. Seemingly unrelated regressions (SURE). Refer to the G.M. and Westinghouse investment functions given in (15.12.1) and (15.12.2). Although these functions can be estimated separately, it might be more efficient (in the statistical sense) if these functions are estimated jointly, because the two firms operate in the same capital markets and a shock (e.g., an increase in the interest rate) is likely to affect both the firms. Therefore, it is quite likely that the error term u for G.M. and the error term u' for Westinghouse at the same point in time may be correlated (this situation is called **contemporaneous correlation**). In this case Zellner has shown that estimating the two equations simultaneously, although they may be seemingly unrelated, can improve the efficiency of the estimators over that found if each is estimated separately.† Hence, the name SURE.

The actual procedure of estimating SURE is rather involved, but the standard econometric packages have the SURE routine.

(a) Using any econometric package, find the SURE estimates of the parameters of the two investment functions.

(b) Also obtain the OLS estimates of the two investment functions separately.

(c) Compare the standard errors of the various regression coefficients obtained by OLS and SURE methods. Which is a better method and why?

15.30. Refer to Example 15.5 given in Section 15.8. Apply the Chow test to the data given there and compare your results to those given in Example 15.5. Which method do you like? And why?

15.31. Using the investment data given in Table 15.4, run a pooled regression for Westinghouse and G.E. using model (15.12.3) and compare your results with the G.M. and Westinghouse pooled regression. If there is a difference in your results, what may be the reason for this difference?

How would you run a pooled regression for G.M., G.E., and Westinghouse using the dummy technique?

15.32. Using the data given in Table 15.4, estimate the G.M. and Westinghouse investment functions allowing for both differential intercept and slope dummies

---

*Optional.

†A. Zellner, "An Efficient Method of Estimating Seemingly Unrelated Regressions and Tests for Aggregation Bias," *Journal of the American Statistical Association*, vol. 57, 1962, pp. 348–368.

to distinguish the two companies and comment on your results vis-à-vis those given in (15.12.5).

15.33. Compare the results of regression (15.13.2) with those obtained from running the linear model, that is, where Y is a linear function of X_2 and D_i.

APPENDIX 15A

15A.1   DATA MATRIX FOR REGRESSION (15.8.2)

Year and quarter	Unem-ployment rate UN, %	Job vacancy rate V, %	D	DV	Year and quarter	Unem-ployment rate UN, %	Job vacancy rate V, %	D	DV
1958–IV	1.915	0.510	0	0	1965–I	1.201	0.997	0	0
1959–I	1.876	0.541	0	0	–II	1.192	1.035	0	0
–II	1.842	0.541	0	0	–III	1.259	1.040	0	0
–III	1.750	0.690	0	0	–IV	1.192	1.086	0	0
–IV	1.648	0.771	0	0	1966–I	1.089	1.101	0	0
1960–I	1.450	0.836	0	0	–II	1.101	1.058	0	0
–II	1.393	0.908	0	0	–III	1.243	0.987	0	0
–III	1.322	0.968	0	0	–IV	1.623	0.819	1	0.819
–IV	1.260	0.998	0	0	1967–I	1.821	0.740	1	0.740
1961–I	1.171	0.968	0	0	–II	1.990	0.661	1	0.661
–II	1.182	0.964	0	0	–III	2.114	0.660	1	0.660
–III	1.221	0.952	0	0	–IV	2.115	0.698	1	0.698
–IV	1.340	0.849	0	0	1968–I	2.150	0.695	1	0.695
1962–I	1.411	0.748	0	0	–II	2.141	0.732	1	0.732
–II	1.600	0.658	0	0	–III	2.167	0.749	1	0.749
–III	1.780	0.562	0	0	–IV	2.107	0.800	1	0.800
–IV	1.941	0.510	0	0	1969–I	2.104	0.783	1	0.783
1963–I	2.178	0.510	0	0	–II	2.056	0.800	1	0.800
–II	2.067	0.544	0	0	–III	2.170	0.794	1	0.794
–III	1.942	0.568	0	0	–IV	2.161	0.790	1	0.790
–IV	1.764	0.677	0	0	1970–I	2.225	0.757	1	0.757
1964–I	1.532	0.794	0	0	–II	2.241	0.746	1	0.746
–II	1.455	0.838	0	0	–III	2.366	0.739	1	0.739
–III	1.409	0.885	0	0	–IV	2.324	0.707	1	0.707
–IV	1.296	0.978	0	0	1971–I	2.516*	0.583*	1	0.583*
					–II	2.909*	0.524*	1	0.524*

* Preliminary estimates.

Source: Damodar Gujarati, "The Behaviour of Unemployment and Unfilled Vacancies: Great Britain, 1958–1971," *The Economic Journal*, vol. 82, March 1972, p. 202.

15A.2 DATA MATRIX FOR REGRESSION (15.10.2)

Year and quarter	Profits (millions of dollars)	Sales (millions of dollars)	D_2	D_3	D_4
1965–I	10,503	114,862	0	0	0
–II	12,092	123,968	1	0	0
–III	10,834	121,454	0	1	0
–IV	12,201	131,917	0	0	1
1966–I	12,245	129,911	0	0	0
–II	14,001	140,976	1	0	0
–III	12,213	137,828	0	1	0
–IV	12,820	145,465	0	0	1
1967–I	11,349	136,989	0	0	0
–II	12,615	145,126	1	0	0
–III	11,014	141,536	0	1	0
–IV	12,730	151,776	0	0	1
1968–I	12,539	148,862	0	0	0
–II	14,849	158,913	1	0	0
–III	13,203	155,727	0	1	0
–IV	14,947	168,409	0	0	1
1969–I	14,151	162,781	0	0	0
–II	15,949	176,057	1	0	0
–III	14,024	172,419	0	1	0
–IV	14,315	183,327	0	0	1
1970–I	12,381	170,415	0	0	0
–II	13,991	181,313	1	0	0
–III	12,174	176,712	0	1	0
–IV	10,985	180,370	0	0	1

Notes: D_2 = 1 for the second quarter, 0 otherwise

$\quad D_3$ = 1 for the third quarter, 0 otherwise

$\quad D_4$ = 1 for the fourth quarter, 0 otherwise

Source: Data on profits and sales pertain to the entire manufacturing center and are from *Quarterly Financial Report for Manufacturing Corporations*, U.S. Federal Trade Commission and the U.S. Securities and Exchange Commision.

REGRESSION ON DUMMY DEPENDENT VARIABLE: THE LPM, LOGIT, PROBIT, AND TOBIT MODELS

In the dummy variable regression models considered in Chapter 15, it was assumed implicitly that the dependent variable Y was quantitative whereas the explanatory variables were either quantitative or qualitative or a mixture thereof. In this chapter we consider regression models in which the dependent or response variable itself can be dichotomous in nature, taking a 1 or 0 value, and point out some of the interesting estimating problems associated with such models.

16.1 DUMMY DEPENDENT VARIABLE

Suppose we want to study the labor-force participation of adult males as a function of the unemployment rate, average wage rate, family income, education, etc. A person either is in the labor force or not. Hence, the dependent variable, labor-force participation, can take only two values: 1 if the person is in the labor force and 0 if he or she is not.

Consider another example. Suppose we want to study the union membership status of college professors as a function of several quantitative and qualitative variables. Now a college professor either belongs to a union or does not. Therefore, the dependent variable, union membership status, is a dummy variable taking on values of 0 or 1, 0 meaning no union membership and 1 mcaning union membership.

There are several such examples where the dependent variable is dichotomous. Thus, a family either owns a house or it does not, it has disability insurance or it does not, both husband and wife are in the labor force or only one person is. Similarly, a certain drug is effective in curing an illness or it is not. A firm decides to declare a stock dividend or not, a senator decides to vote for the Equal Rights Amendment or not, the President decides to veto a bill or accept it, etc.

A unique feature of all these examples is that the dependent variable is of the type that elicits a yes or no response; that is, it is dichotomous in nature.[1]

How do we handle models involving dichotomous response variables? That is, how do we estimate them? Are there special estimation and/or inference problems associated with such models? Or, can they be handled within the usual OLS setup? To answer these and related questions, we consider in this chapter the four most commonly used approaches to estimating such models:

1. The linear probability model (LPM)
2. The logit model
3. The probit model
4. The tobit (censored regression) model

16.2 THE LINEAR PROBABILITY MODEL (LPM)

To fix ideas, consider the following simple model:

$$Y_i = \beta_1 + \beta_2 X_i + u_i \tag{16.2.1}$$

where X = family income
$Y = 1$ if the family owns a house
$= 0$ if the family does not own a house

Models such as (16.2.1), which express the dichotomous Y_i as a linear function of the explanatory variable(s) X_i, are called **linear probability models** (LPM) since $E(Y_i \mid X_i)$, the conditional expectation of Y_i given X_i, can be interpreted as the *conditional probability* that the event will occur given X_i; that is, $\Pr(Y_i = 1 \mid X_i)$. Thus, in the preceding case, $E(Y_i \mid X_i)$ gives the probability of a family owing a house and whose income is the given amount X_i. The justification of the name LPM for models like (16.2.1) can be seen as follows.

---

[1] The dichotomous variable is a special case of the **polytomous** or multiple category dependent variable, e.g., party affiliation (Democrat, Republican, or Independent). The discussion in this chapter is, however, confined to dichotomous variables. For the polytomous models, see Moshe Ben-Akiva and Steven R. Lerman, *Discrete Choice Analysis*, The MIT Press, Cambridge, Mass., 1985, Chap. 5.

Assuming $E(u_i) = 0$, as usual (to obtain unbiased estimators), we obtain

$$E(Y_i \mid X_i) = \beta_1 + \beta_2 X_i \qquad (16.2.2)$$

Now, letting P_i = probability that $Y_i = 1$ (that is, that the event occurs) and $1 - P_i$ = probability that $Y_i = 0$ (that is, that the event does not occur), the variable Y_i has the following distribution:

Y_i	Probability
0	$1 - P_i$
1	P_i
Total	1

Therefore, by the definition of mathematical expectation, we obtain

$$\begin{aligned} E(Y_i) &= 0(1 - P_i) + 1(P_i) \\ &= P_i \end{aligned} \qquad (16.2.3)$$

Comparing (16.2.2) with (16.2.3), we can equate

$$E(Y_i \mid X_i) = \beta_1 + \beta_2 X_i = P_i \qquad (16.2.4)$$

that is, the conditional expectation of the model (16.2.1) can, in fact, be interpreted as the conditional probability of Y_i.

Since the probability P_i must lie between 0 and 1, we have the restriction

$$0 \le E(Y_i \mid X_i) \le 1 \qquad (16.2.5)$$

that is, the conditional expectation, or conditional probability, must lie between 0 and 1.

16.3 PROBLEMS IN ESTIMATION OF LPM

Since (16.2.1) "looks" like any other regression model, why not estimate it by the standard OLS method? As a mechanical routine, we can do this. But now we must face some special problems, which are as follows.

Nonnormality of the Disturbances u_i

Although OLS does not require the disturbances (u's) to be normally distributed, we assumed them to be so distributed for the purpose of statistical inference, that is, hypothesis testing, etc. But the assumption of normality for u_i is no longer tenable for the LPMs because like Y_i, u_i takes on only two values. To see this, we write (16.2.1) as

$$u_i = Y_i - \beta_1 - \beta_2 X_i \qquad (16.3.1)$$

Now when

$$Y_i = 1 \qquad u_i = 1 - \beta_1 - \beta_2 X_i$$

and when

$$Y_i = 0 \qquad u_i = -\beta_1 - \beta_2 X_i \qquad (16.3.2)$$

Obviously, u_i cannot be assumed to be normally distributed; actually it follows the binomial distribution. ok.

But the nonfulfillment of the normality assumption may not be so critical as it appears because we know that the OLS point estimates still remain unbiased (recall that if the objective is point estimation, the normality assumption is inconsequential). Furthermore, as sample size increases indefinitely, it can be shown that the OLS estimators tend to be normally distributed generally.[2] Therefore, in large samples the statistical inference of the LPM will follow the usual OLS procedure under the normality assumption.

Heteroscedastic Variances of the Disturbances

Even if $E(u_i) = 0$ and $E(u_i u_j) = 0$, for $i \neq j$ (that is, no serial correlation), it can no longer be maintained that the disturbances u_i are homoscedastic. To see this, the u's given in (16.3.2) have the following probability distribution:

u_i	Probability
$-\beta_1 - \beta_2 X_i$	$1 - P_i$
$1 - \beta_1 - \beta_2 X_i$	P_i
Total	1

The preceding probability distribution follows from the probability distribution for Y_i given previously.[3]

Now, by definition,

$$\text{var}(u_i) = E[u_i - E(u_i)]^2$$
$$= E(u_i^2) \qquad \text{for } E(u_i) = 0 \text{ by assumption}$$

Therefore, using the preceding probability distribution of u_i, we obtain

$$\text{var}(u_i) = E(u_i^2) = (-\beta_1 - \beta_2 X_i)^2 (1 - P_i) + (1 - \beta_1 - \beta_2 X_i)^2 (P_i)$$
$$= (-\beta_1 - \beta_2 X_i)^2 (1 - \beta_1 - \beta_2 X_i) + (1 - \beta_1 - \beta_2 X_i)^2 (\beta_1 + \beta_2 X_i)$$
$$= (\beta_1 + \beta_2 X_i)(1 - \beta_1 - \beta_2 X_i) \tag{16.3.3}$$

or

$$\text{var}(u_i) = E(Y_i \mid X_i)[1 - E(Y_i \mid X_i)]$$
$$= P_i(1 - P_i) \tag{16.3.4}$$

---

[2] The proof is based on the central limit theorem and may be found in E. Malinvaud, *Statistical Methods of Econometrics*, Rand McNally & Company, Chicago, 1966, pp. 195–197. If the regressors are deemed stochastic and are jointly normally distributed, the F and t tests can still be used even though the disturbances are nonnormal.

[3] This can also be seen as

Y_i	u_i	Probability
0	$-\beta_1 - \beta_2 X_i$	$1 - P_i$
1	$1 - \beta_1 - \beta_2 X_i$	P_i

where use is made of the fact that $E(Y_i \mid X_i) = \beta_1 + \beta_2 X_i = P_i$. Equation (16.3.4) shows that the variance of u_i is heteroscedastic because it depends on the conditional expectation of Y, which, of course, depends on the value taken by X. Thus, ultimately the variance of u_i depends on X and is thus not homoscedastic.

We already know that in the presence of heteroscedasticity the OLS estimators, although unbiased, are not efficient; that is, they do not have minimum variance. But again the problem of heteroscedasticity is not insurmountable. In Chapter 11 we discussed several methods of handling the heteroscedasticity problem. Since the variance of u_i depends on the expected value of Y conditional upon the X value, as shown in (16.3.3), one way of resolving the heteroscedasticity problem is to transform the data by dividing both sides of the model (16.2.1) by

$$\sqrt{E(Y_i \mid X_i)[1 - E(Y_i \mid X_i)]} = \sqrt{P_i(1 - P_i)} = \text{say,} \ \sqrt{w_i}$$

$$\frac{Y_i}{\sqrt{w_i}} = \frac{\beta_1}{\sqrt{w_i}} + \beta_2 \frac{X_i}{\sqrt{w_i}} + \frac{u_i}{\sqrt{w_i}} \qquad (16.3.5)$$

The disturbance term in (16.3.5) will now be homoscedastic. (Why?) Therefore, one may proceed to the OLS estimation of (16.3.5).

Of course, the true $E(Y_i \mid X_i)$ is not known; hence, w_i, the weights, are unknown. To estimate w_i, we may use the following two-step procedure:

Step 1. Run the OLS regression on (16.2.1) despite the heteroscedasticity problem and obtain $\hat{Y}_i$ = estimate of true $E(Y_i \mid X_i)$. Then obtain $\hat{w}_i = \hat{Y}_i(1 - \hat{Y}_i)$, the estimate of w_i.

Step 2. Use the estimated $\hat{w}_i$ to transform the data as in (16.3.5) and run the OLS regression on the data thus transformed.[4]

Nonfulfillment of $0 \leq E(Y_i \mid X) \leq 1$

Since $E(Y_i \mid X)$ in the linear probability models measures the conditional probability of the event Y occurring given X, it must necessarily lie between 0 and 1. Although this is true a priori, there is no guarantee that $\hat{Y}_i$, the estimators of $E(Y_i \mid X_i)$, will necessarily fulfill this restriction, *and this is the real problem with the OLS estimation of the LPM*. There are two ways of finding out whether the estimated $\hat{Y}_i$ lie between 0 and 1. One is to estimate the LPM by the usual OLS method and find out whether the estimated $\hat{Y}_i$ lie between 0 and 1. If some are less than 0 (that is, negative), $\hat{Y}_i$ is assumed to be zero for those cases; if they are greater than 1, they are assumed to be 1. The second procedure is to devise an estimating technique that will guarantee that the estimated conditional probabilities $\hat{Y}_i$ will lie between 0 and 1. The logit and probit models discussed later will guarantee that the estimated probabilities will indeed lie between the logical limits 0 and 1.

---

[4]For the justification of this procedure, see Arthur S. Goldberger, *Econometric Theory*, John Wiley & Sons, New York, 1964, pp. 249–250.

Questionable Value of R^2 as a Measure of Goodness of Fit

The conventionally computed R^2 is of limited value in the dichotomous response models. To see why, consider the following figure. Corresponding to a given X, Y is either 0 or 1. Therefore, all the Y values will either lie along the X axis or along the line corresponding to 1. Therefore, generally no LPM is expected to fit such a scatter well, whether it is the *unconstrained LPM* (Fig. 16.1a) or the *truncated* or *constrained LPM* (Fig. 16.1b), an LPM estimated in such a way that it will not fall outside the logical band 0–1. As a result, the conventionally computed R^2 is likely to be much lower than 1 for such models. In

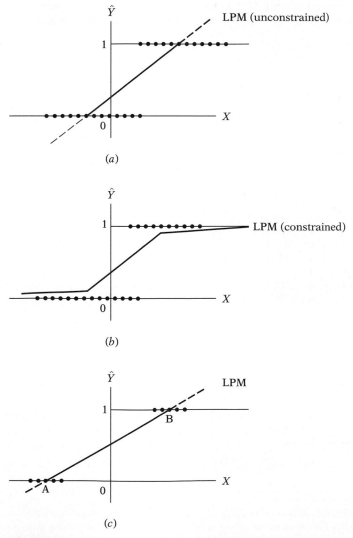

(a)

(b)

(c)

FIGURE 16.1
Linear probability models.

most practical applications the R^2 ranges between 0.2 to 0.6. R^2 in such models will be high, say, in excess of 0.8 only when the actual scatter is very closely clustered around points A and B (Fig. 16.1c), for in that case it is easy to fix the straight line by joining the two points A and B. In this case the predicted Y_i will be very close to either 0 or 1.

For these reasons John Aldrich and Forrest Nelson contend that "use of the coefficient of determination as a summary statistic should be avoided in models with qualitative dependent variable."[5]

16.4 LPM: A NUMERICAL EXAMPLE

To illustrate some of the points made about the LPM in the preceding section, we present a numerical example. Table 16.1 gives invented data on home ownership Y (1 = owns a house, 0 = does not own a house) and family income X (thousands

TABLE 16.1
Hypothetical data on home ownership ($Y = 1$ if owns home, 0 otherwise) and income X (thousands of dollars)

Family	Y	X	Family	Y	X
1	0	8	21	1	22
2	1	16	22	1	16
3	1	18	23	0	12
4	0	11	24	0	11
5	0	12	25	1	16
6	1	19	26	0	11
7	1	20	27	1	20
8	0	13	28	1	18
9	0	9	29	0	11
10	0	10	30	0	10
11	1	17	31	1	17
12	1	18	32	0	13
13	0	14	33	1	21
14	1	20	34	1	20
15	0	6	35	0	11
16	1	19	36	0	8
17	1	16	37	1	17
18	0	10	38	1	16
19	0	8	39	0	7
20	1	18	40	1	17

---

[5] See their very readable monograph, *Linear Probability, Logit, and Probit Models*, Sage Publications, Beverly Hills, Calif., 1984, p. 15. For other measures of goodness of fit in models involving dummy regressands, see T. Amemiya, "Qualitative Response Models," *Journal of Economic Literature*, vol. 19, 1981, pp. 331–354.

of dollars) for 40 families. Based on these data the LPM estimated by OLS was as follows:

$$\hat{Y}_i = -0.9457 + 0.1021X_i$$
$$(0.1228) \quad (0.0082)$$
$$t = (-7.6984) \quad (12.515)$$
$$R^2 = 0.8048$$

(16.4.1)

First, let us interpret this regression. The intercept of -0.9457 gives the "probability" that a family with zero income will own a house. Since this value is negative, and since probability cannot be negative, we treat this value as zero, which is sensible in the present instance.[6] The slope value of 0.1021 means that for a unit change in income (here \$1,000), on the average the probability of owning a house increases by 0.1021 or about 10 percent. Of course, given a particular level of income, we can estimate the actual probability of owning a house from (16.4.1). Thus, for $X = 12$ (\$12,000), the estimated probability of owning a house is

$$(\hat{Y}_i \mid X = 12) = -0.9457 + 12(0.1021)$$
$$= 0.2795$$

TABLE 16.2
Actual Y, estimated Y, and weights w_i for the home ownership example

Y_i	$\hat{Y}_i$	$\hat{w}_i$**	$\sqrt{\hat{w}_i}$	Y_i	$\hat{Y}_i$	$\hat{w}_i$**	$\sqrt{\hat{w}_i}$
0	−0.129*	—	—	1	1.301†	—	—
1	0.688	0.2146	0.4633	1	0.688	0.2147	0.4633
1	0.893	0.0956	0.3091	0	0.280	0.2016	0.4990
0	0.178	0.1463	0.3825	0	0.178	0.1463	0.3825
0	0.280	0.2016	0.4490	1	0.688	0.2147	0.4633
1	0.995	0.00498	0.0705	0	0.178	0.1463	0.3825
1	1.098†	—	—	1	1.097†	—	—
0	0.382	0.2361	0.4859	1	0.893	0.0956	0.3091
0	−0.0265*	—	—	0	0.178	0.1463	0.3825
0	0.076	0.0702	0.2650	0	0.076	0.0702	0.2650
1	0.791	0.1653	0.4066	1	0.791	0.1653	0.4055
1	0.893	0.0956	0.3091	0	0.382	0.2361	0.4859
0	0.484	0.2497	0.4997	1	1.199†	—	—
1	1.097†	—	—	1	1.097†	—	—
0	−0.333*	—	—	0	0.178	0.1463	0.3825
1	0.995	0.00498	0.0705	0	−0.129*	—	—
1	0.688	0.2147	0.4633	1	0.791	0.1653	0.4066
0	0.076	0.0702	0.2650	1	0.688	0.2147	0.4633
0	−0.129*	—	—	0	−0.231*	—	—
1	0.893	0.0956	0.3091	1	0.791	0.1653	0.4066

Note: *Treated as zero to avoid probabilities being negative.
†Treated as unity to avoid probabilities exceeding one.
**$\hat{Y}_i(1 - \hat{Y}_i)$

---

[6] One can loosely interpret the highly negative value as near improbability of owning a house when income is zero.

That is, the probability that a family with an income of $12,000 will own a house is about 28 percent. Table 16.2 shows the estimated probabilities, $\hat{Y}_i$, for the various income levels listed in the table. The most noticeable feature of this table is that six estimated values are negative and six values are in excess of one, demonstrating clearly the point made earlier that, although $E(Y_i \mid X)$ is positive and less than 1, their estimators, $\hat{Y}_i$, need not be necessarily positive or less than 1. This is one reason that the LPM is not the recommended model when the dependent variable is dichotomous.

Even if the estimated Y_i were all positive and less than 1, the LPM still suffers from the problem of heteroscedasticity, which can be seen readily from (16.3.4). As a consequence, we cannot trust the estimated standard errors reported in (16.4.1). (Why?) But we can use the weighted least-squares (WLS) procedure discussed earlier to obtain more efficient estimates of the standard errors. The necessary weights, $\hat{w}_i$, required for the application of WLS are also shown in Table 16.2. But note that since some Y_i are negative and some are in excess of one, the $\hat{w}_i$ corresponding to these values will be negative. Thus, we cannot use these observations in WLS (why?), thereby reducing the number of observations, from 40 to 28 in the present example.[7] Omitting these observations, the WLS regression is

$$\frac{Y_i}{\sqrt{w_i}} = -1.2456\frac{1}{\sqrt{w_i}} + 0.1196\frac{X_i}{\sqrt{w_i}}$$
$$\quad\quad (0.1206) \quad\quad (0.0069) \quad\quad\quad\quad\quad\quad\quad (16.4.2)$$
$$t = (-10.332) \quad\quad (17.454) \quad\quad\quad R^2 = 0.9214$$

These results show that, compared with (16.4.1), the estimated standard errors are smaller and, correspondingly, the estimated t ratios (in absolute value) larger. But one should take this result with a grain of salt since in estimating (16.4.2) we had to drop 12 observations. Also, since w_i are estimated, the usual statistical hypothesis-testing procedures are, strictly speaking, valid in the large samples (see Chapter 11).

16.5   APPLICATIONS OF LPM

Until the availability of readily accessible computer packages to estimate the logit and probit models (to be discussed shortly), the LPM was used quite extensively because of its simplicity. We now illustrate some of these applications.

Example 16.1   Cohen-Rea-Lerman study[8]

In a study prepared for the U.S. Department of Labor, Cohen, Rea, and Lerman were interested in examining the labor-force participation of various categories of labor as a function of several socioeconomic-demographic variables. In all their regressions, the dependent variable was a dummy, taking a value of 1 if a person is in the labor force, 0 if he or she is not. In Table 16.3 we reproduce one of their several dummy-dependent variable regressions.

Before interpreting the results, note these features: The preceding regression was estimated using the OLS. To correct for heteroscedasticity, the authors used

---

[7]To avoid the loss of the degrees of freedom, we could let $\hat{Y}_i = 0.01$ when the estimated Y_i are negative and $\hat{Y}_i = 0.99$ when they are in excess of or equal to 1. See exercise 16.1.

[8]Malcolm S. Cohen, Samuel A. Rea, Jr., and Robert I. Lerman, *A Micro Model of Labor Supply*, BLS Staff Paper 4, U.S. Department of Labor, 1970.

TABLE 16.3
Labor-force participation

Regression of women, age 22 and over, living in largest 96 standard metropolitan statistical areas (SMSA) (dependent variable: in or out of labor force during 1966)

Explanatory variable	Coefficient	t ratio
Constant	0.4368	15.4
Marital status		
Married, spouse present	. . .	. . .
Married, other	0.1523	13.8
Never married	0.2915	22.0
Age		
22–54	. . .	. . .
55–64	−0.0594	−5.7
65 and over	−0.2753	−9.0
Years of schooling		
0–4	. . .	. . .
5–8	0.1255	5.8
9–11	0.1704	7.9
12–15	0.2231	10.6
16 and over	0.3061	13.3
Unemployment rate (1966), %		
Under 2.5	. . .	. . .
2.5–3.4	−0.0213	−1.6
3.5–4.0	−0.0269	−2.0
4.1–5.0	−0.0291	−2.2
5.1 and over	−0.0311	−2.4
Employment change (1965–1966), %		
Under 3.5	. . .	. . .
3.5–6.49	0.0301	3.2
6.5 and over	0.0529	5.1
Relative employment opportunities, %		
Under 62	. . .	. . .
62–73.9	0.0381	3.2
74 and over	0.0571	3.2
FILOW, $		
Less than 1,500 and negative	. . .	. . .
1,500–7,499	−0.1451	−15.4
7,500 and over	−0.2455	−24.4
Interaction (marital status and age)		
Marital status Age		
Other 55–64	−0.0406	−2.1
Other 65 and over	−0.1391	−7.4
Never married 55–64	−0.1104	−3.3
Never married 65 and over	−0.2045	−6.4

TABLE 16.3 (continued)

Explanatory variable	Coefficient	t ratio
Interaction (age and years of schooling completed)		
Age Years of schooling		
65 and over 5–8	-0.0885	-2.8
65 and over 9–11	-0.0848	-2.4
65 and over 12–15	-0.1288	-4.0
65 and over 16 and over	-0.1628	-3.6

$$R^2 = 0.175$$

No. of observations = 25,153

Source: Malcolm S. Cohen, Samuel A. Rea, Jr., and Robert I. Lerman, *A Micro Model of Labor Supply*, BLS Staff Paper 4, U.S. Department of Labor, 1970, Table F-6, pp. 212–213.

Note: ⋯ indicates the base or omitted category.

FILOW: family income less own wage and salary income.

the two-step procedure outlined previously in some of their regressions but found that the standard errors of the estimates thus obtained did not differ materially from those obtained without correction for heteroscedasticity. Perhaps this result is due to the sheer size of the sample, namely, about 25,000. Because of this large sample size, the estimated t values may be tested for statistical significance by the usual OLS procedure even though the error term takes dichotomous values. The estimated R^2 of 0.175 may seem rather low, but in view of the large sample size, this R^2 is still significant on the basis of the F test given in Section 8.5. Finally, notice how the authors have blended quantitative and qualitative variables and how they have taken into account the interaction effects.

Turning to the interpretations of the findings, we see that each slope coefficient gives the rate of change in the conditional probability of the event occurring for a given unit change in the value of the explanatory variable. For instance, the coefficient of -0.2753 attached to the variable "age 65 and over" means, holding all other factors constant, the probability of participation in the labor force by women in this age group is smaller by about 27 percent (as compared with the base category of women aged 22 to 54). By the same token, the coefficient of 0.3061 attached to the variable "16 or more years of schooling" means, holding all other factors constant, the probability of women with this much education participating in the labor force is higher by about 31 percent (as compared with women with less than 5 years of schooling, the base category).

Now consider the **interaction term** marital status and age. The table shows that the labor-force participation probability is higher by some 29 percent for those women who were never married (as compared with the base category) and smaller by about 28 percent for those women who are 65 and over (again in relation to the base category). But the probability of participation of women who were never married and are 65 or over is smaller by about 20 percent as compared with the base category. This implies that women aged 65 and over but never married are likely to participate in the labor force more than those who are aged 65 and over and are married or fall into the "other" category.

Following this procedure, the reader can easily interpret the rest of the coefficients given in Table 16.3. From the given information, it is easy to obtain the estimates of the conditional probabilities of labor-force participation of the various categories. Thus, if we want to find the probability for married women (other), aged

22 to 54, with 12 to 15 years of schooling, with an unemployment rate of 2.5 to 3.4 percent, employment change of 3.5 to 6.49 percent, relative employment opportunities of 74 percent and over and with FILOW of $7500 and over, we obtain

$$0.4368 + 0.1523 + 0.2231 - 0.0213 + 0.0301 + 0.0571 - 0.2455 = 0.6326$$

In other words, the probability of labor-force participation by women with the preceding characteristics is estimated to be about 63 percent.

Example 16.2   Predicting a Bond Rating

Based on a pooled time series and cross-sectional data of 200 Aa (high-quality) and Baa (medium-quality) bonds over the period 1961–1966, Joseph Cappelleri estimated the following bond rating prediction model.[9]

$$Y_i = \beta_1 + \beta_2 X_{2i}^2 + \beta_3 X_{3i} + \beta_4 X_{4i} + \beta_5 X_{5i} + u_i$$

where $Y_i = 1$ if the bond rating is Aa (Moody's rating)

$\quad\quad\ = 0$ if the bond rating is Baa (Moody's rating)

$\quad X_2 =$ Debt capitalization ratio, a measure of leverage

$\quad\quad\ = \dfrac{\text{Dollar value of long-term debt}}{\text{Dollar value of total capitalization}} \cdot 100$

$\quad X_3 =$ Profit rate

$\quad\quad\ = \dfrac{\text{Dollar value of after-tax income}}{\text{Dollar value of net total assets}} \cdot 100$

$\quad X_4 =$ Standard deviation of the profit rate, a measure of profit rate variability.

$\quad X_5 =$ Net total assets (thousands of dollars), a measure of size

A priori, β_2 and β_4 are expected to be negative (why?) and β_3 and β_5 are expected to be positive.

After correcting for heteroscedasticity and first-order autocorrelation, Cappelleri obtained the following results:[10]

$$\hat{Y}_i = 0.6860 - 0.0179X_{2i}^2 + 0.0486X_{3i} + 0.0572X_{4i}$$
$$\quad\ (0.1775)\ (0.0024)\quad\quad (0.0486)\quad\quad (0.0178)$$
$$\quad + 0.378(E\text{-}7)X_5 \quad\quad\quad\quad\quad\quad\quad\quad (16.5.1)$$
$$\quad (0.039)(E\text{-}8)$$

$$R^2 = 0.6933$$

Note: 0.378 E-7 means 0.0000000378, etc.

All but the coefficient of X_4 have the correct signs. It is left to finance students to rationalize why the profit rate variability coefficient has a positive sign, for one

---

[9]Joseph Cappelleri, "Predicting a Bond Rating," unpublished term paper, C.U.N.Y.. The model used in the paper is a modification of the model used by Thomas F. Pogue and Robert M. Soldofsky, "What Is in a Bond Rating?" *Journal of Financial and Quantitative Analysis*, June 1969, pp. 201–228.

[10]Some of the estimated probabilities before correcting for heteroscedasticity were negative and some were in excess of 1; in these cases they were assumed to be 0.01 and 0.99, respectively, to facilitate the computation of the weights w_i.

would expect that the greater the variability in profits, the less likely it is Moody's would give an Aa rating, other things remaining the same.

The interpretation of the regression is straightforward. For example, 0.0486 attached to X_3 means that, other things being the same, a 1 percentage point increase in the profit rate will lead on average to about 0.05 increase in the probability of a bond getting the Aa rating. Similarly, the higher the squared leveraged ratio, the lower by 0.02 is the probability of a bond being classified as an Aa bond per unit increase in this ratio.

Example 16.3 Predicting Bond Defaults

To predict the probability of default on their bond obligations, Daniel Rubinfeld studied a sample of 35 municipalities in Massachusetts for the year 1930, several of which did in fact default. The LPM model he chose and estimated was as follows:[11]

$$\hat{P} = 1.96 - 0.029 \text{ TAX} - 4.86 \text{ INT} + 0.063 \text{ AV}$$
$$(0.29) \quad (0.009) \qquad (2.13) \qquad (0.028)$$
$$+ \ 0.007 \text{ DAV} \qquad - 0.48 \text{ WELF}$$
$$(0.003) \qquad\qquad (0.88) \qquad R^2 = 0.36 \tag{16.5.2}$$

Where $P = 0$ if the municipality defaulted and 1 otherwise, TAX = average of 1929, 1930, and 1931 tax rates: INT = percentage of current budget allocated to interest payments in 1930; AV = percentage growth in assessed property valuation from 1925 to 1930; DAV = ratio of total direct net debt to total assessed valuation in 1930; and WELF = percentage of 1930 budget allocated to charities, pensions, and soldiers' benefits.

The interpretation (16.5.2) is again fairly straightforward. Thus, other things being the same, an increase in the tax rate of $1 per thousand will raise the probability of default by about 0.03, or 3 percent. The R^2 value is rather low but, as noted previously, in LPMs the R^2 values generally tend to be lower and are of limited use in judging the goodness of fit of the model.

16.6 ALTERNATIVES TO LPM

As we have seen, the LPM is plagued by several problems, such as (1) non-normality of u_i, (2) heteroscedasticity of u_i, (3) possibility of $\hat{Y}_i$ lying outside the 0–1 range, and (4) the generally lower R^2 values. But these problems are surmountable. For example, we can use WLS to resolve the heteroscedasticity problem or increase the sample size to minimize the nonnormality problem. By resorting to restricted least-squares or mathematical programming techniques we can even make the estimated probabilities lie in the 0–1 interval.

But even then the fundamental problem with the LPM is that it is not logically a very attractive model because it assumes that $P_i = E(Y = 1 \mid X)$ increases linearly with X, that is, the marginal or incremental effect of X

---

[11]D. Rubinfeld, "An Econometric Analysis of the Market for General Municipal Bonds," unpublished doctoral dissertation, Massachusetts Institute of Technology, 1972. The results given in this example are reproduced from Robert S. Pindyck and Daniel L. Rubinfeld, *Econometric Models and Economic Forecasts*, 2d ed., McGraw-Hill, New York, 1981, p. 279.

remains constant throughout. Thus, in our home ownership example we found that as X increases by a unit ($1000), the probability of owning a house increases by the same constant amount of 0.10. This is so whether the income level is $8000, $10,000, $18,000, or $22,000. This seems patently unrealistic. In reality one would expect that P_i is nonlinearly related to X_i: At very low income a family will not own a house but at a sufficiently high level of income, say, X^*, it most likely will own a house. Any increase in income beyond X^* will have little effect on the probability of owning a house. Thus, at both ends of the income distribution, the probability of owning a house will be virtually unaffected by a small increase in X.

Therefore, what we need is a (probability) model that has these two features: (1) As X_i increases, $P_i = E(Y = 1 \mid X)$ increases but never steps outside the 0–1 interval, and (2) the relationship between P_i and X_i is nonlinear, that is, "one which approaches zero at slower and slower rates as X_i gets small and approaches one at slower and slower rates as X_i gets very large."[12]

Geometrically, the model we want would look something like Fig. 16.2. Notice in this model that the probability lies between 0 and 1 and that it varies nonlinearly with X.

The reader will realize that the sigmoid or S-shaped curve in the figure very much resembles the **cumulative distribution function** (CDF) of a random variable.[13] Therefore, one can easily use the CDF to model regressions where the response variable is dichotomous, taking 0–1 values. The practical question now is, which CDF? For although all CDFs are S-shaped, for each random variable there is a unique CDF. For historical as well as practical

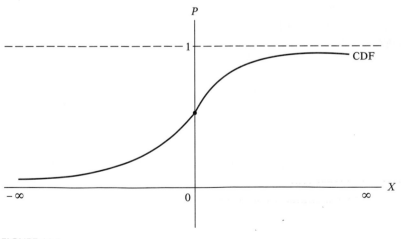

FIGURE 16.2
A cumulative distribution function (CDF).

---

[12] John Aldrich and Forrest Nelson, op. cit., p. 26.

[13] As discussed in Appendix A, the CDF of a random variable X is simply the probability that it takes a value less than or equal to x_0, where x_0 is some specified numerical value of X. In short, $F(X)$, the CDF of X, is $F(X = x_0) = P(X \leq x_0)$.

reasons, the CDFs commonly chosen to represent the 0–1 response models are (1) the logistic and (2) the normal, the former giving rise to the **logit** model and the latter to the **probit** (or **normit**) model.

Although a detailed discussion of the logit and probit models is beyond the scope of this book, we will indicate somewhat informally how one estimates such models and how one interprets them.

16.7   THE LOGIT MODEL

We will continue with our home ownership example to explain the basic ideas underlying the logit model. Recall that in explaining home ownership in relation to income, the LPM was

$$P_i = E(Y = 1 \mid X_i) = \beta_1 + \beta_2 X_i \qquad (16.7.1)$$

where X is income and $Y = 1$ means the family owns a house. But now consider the following representation of home ownership:

$$P_i = E(Y = 1 \mid X_i) = \frac{1}{1 + e^{-(\beta_1 + \beta_2 X_i)}} \qquad (16.7.2)$$

For ease of exposition, we write (16.7.2) as

$$P_i = \frac{1}{1 + e^{-Z_i}} \qquad (16.7.3)$$

where $Z_i = \beta_1 + \beta_2 X_i$.

Equation (16.7.3) represents what is known as the (cumulative) **logistic distribution function.**[14]

It is easy to verify that as Z_i ranges from $-\infty$ to $+\infty$, P_i ranges between 0 and 1 and that P_i is nonlinearly related to Z_i (i.e., X_i), thus satisfying the two requirements considered earlier.[15] But it seems that in satisfying these requirements, we have created an estimation problem because P_i is nonlinear not only in X but also in the β's as can be seen clearly from (16.7.2). This means that we cannot use the familiar OLS procedure to estimate the parameters.[16] But this problem is more apparent than real because (16.7.2) is intrinsically linear, which can be shown as follows.

---

[14]The logistic model has been used extensively in analyzing growth phenomena, such as population, GNP, money supply, etc. For theoretical and practical details of logit and probit models, see J. S. Kramer, *The Logit Model for Economists*, Edward Arnold Publishers, London, 1991; and G. S. Maddala, *Limited Dependent and Qualitative Variables in Econometrics*, Cambridge University Press, New York, 1983.

[15]Note that as $Z_i \to +\infty$, e^{-Z_i} tends to zero and as $Z_i \to -\infty$, e^{-Z_i} increases indefinitely. Recall that $e = 2.71828$.

[16]Of course, one could use nonlinear estimation techniques, but they are beyond the scope of this text.

If P_i, the probability of owning a house, is given by (16.7.3), then $(1 - P_i)$, the probability of not owning a house, is

$$1 - P_i = \frac{1}{1 + e^{Z_i}} \qquad (16.7.4)$$

Therefore, we can write

$$\frac{P_i}{1 - P_i} = \frac{1 + e^{Z_i}}{1 + e^{-Z_i}} = e^{Z_i} \qquad (16.7.5)$$

Now $P_i/(1 - P_i)$ is simply the **odds ratio** in favor of owning a house—the ratio of the probability that a family will own a house to the probability that it will not own a house. Thus, if $P_i = 0.8$, it means that odds are 4 to 1 in favor of the family owning a house.

Now if we take the natural log of (16.7.5), we obtain a very interesting result, namely,

$$L_i = \ln\left(\frac{P_i}{1 - P_i}\right) = Z_i \qquad (16.7.6)$$
$$= \beta_1 + \beta_2 X_i$$

that is, L, the log of the odds ratio, is not only linear in X, but also (from the estimation viewpoint) linear in the parameters.[17] L is called the **logit**, and hence the name **logit model** for models like (16.7.6).

Notice these features of the logit model.

1. As P goes from 0 to 1 (i.e., as Z varies from $-\infty$ to $+\infty$), the logit L goes from $-\infty$ to $+\infty$. That is, although the probabilities (of necessity) lie between 0 and 1, the logits are not so bounded.
2. Although L is linear in X, the probabilities themselves are not. This property is in contrast with the LPM model (16.7.1) where the probabilities increase linearly with X.[18]
3. The interpretation of the logit model is as follows: β_2, the slope, measures the change in L for a unit change in X, that is, it tells how the log-odds in favor of owning a house change as income changes by a unit, say, $1000. The intercept β_1 is the value of the log-odds in favor of owning a house if income is zero. Like most interpretations of intercepts, this interpretation may not have any physical meaning.
4. Given a certain income level, say, X^*, if we actually want to estimate not the odds in favor of owning a house but the probability of owning a house itself,

---

[17] Recall that the linearity assumption of OLS does not require that the X variable be necessarily linear. So we can have X^2, X^3, etc., as regressors in the model. For our purpose, it is linearity in the parameters that is crucial.

[18] Using calculus, it can be shown that $dP/dX = \beta_2 P(1 - P)$, which shows that the rate of change in probability with respect to X involves not only β_2 but also the level of probability from which the change is measured (but more on this in Section 16.9). In passing, note that the effect of a unit change in X_i on P is greatest when $P = 0.5$ and least when P is close to 0 or 1.

this can be done directly from (16.7.2) once the estimates of β_1 and β_2 are available. But this raises the most important question: How do we estimate β_1 and β_2 in the first place? The answer is given in the next section.

5. Whereas the LPM assumes that P_i is linearly related to X_i, the logit model assumes that the log of odds ratio is linearly related to X_i.

16.8   ESTIMATION OF THE LOGIT MODEL

For estimation purposes, we write (16.7.6) as follows:

$$L_i = \ln\left(\frac{P_i}{1 - P_i}\right) = \beta_1 + \beta_2 X_i + u_i \tag{16.8.1}$$

We will discuss the properties of the stochastic disturbance term shortly.

To estimate the model, we need, apart from X_i, the values of the logit L_i. But now we run into some difficulties. If we have data on individual families, as in Table 16.1, $P_i = 1$ if a family owns a house and $P_i = 0$ if it does not own a house. But if we put these values directly into the logit L_i, we obtain

$$L_i = \ln\left(\frac{1}{0}\right) \text{if a family owns a house}$$

$$L_i = \ln\left(\frac{0}{1}\right) \text{if a family does not own a house}$$

Obviously, these expressions are meaningless. Therefore, if we have data at the micro or individual level. we cannot estimate (16.8.1) by the standard OLS routine. In this situation one may have to resort to the maximum likelihood method to estimate the parameters. But because of its mathematical complexity, we will not pursue it here, although an example based on this method will be presented later.[19]

But suppose we have data, as shown in Table 16.4. Corresponding to each income level X_i in this table are N_i families, n_i among whom own a house $(n_i \leq N_i)$. Therefore, if we now compute

$$\hat{P}_i = \frac{n_i}{N_i} \tag{16.8.2}$$

that is, the *relative frequency*, we can use it as an estimate of the true P_i corresponding to each X_i. If N_i is fairly large, $\hat{P}_i$ will be a reasonably good estimate of P_i.[20] Using the estimated P_i, we can obtain the estimated logit as

$$\hat{L}_i = \ln\left(\frac{\hat{P}_i}{1 - \hat{P}_i}\right) = \hat{\beta}_1 + \hat{\beta}_2 X_i \tag{16.8.3}$$

---

[19]For a comparatively simple discussion of maximum likelihood in the context of the logit model, see John Aldrich and Forrest Nelson, op. cit., pp. 49–54. See also Alfred Demaris, *Logit Modeling: Practical Applications*, Sage Publications, Newbury Park, Calif., 1992.

[20]From elementary statistics recall that the probability of an event is the limit of the relative frequency as the sample size becomes infinitely large.

TABLE 16.4
Hypothetical data on X_i (Income), N_i (number of families at income X_i), and n_i (number of families owning a house)

X (thousands of dollars)	N_i	n_i
6	40	8
8	50	12
10	60	18
13	80	28
15	100	45
20	70	36
25	65	39
30	50	33
35	40	30
40	25	20

which will be a fairly good estimate of the true logit L_i if the number of observations N_i at each X_i is reasonably large.

In short, given the *grouped* or *replicated* (repeat observations) data, such as Table 16.4, one can obtain the data on the dependent variable, the logits, to estimate the model (16.8.1). Can we then apply OLS to (16.8.3) and estimate the parameters in the usual fashion? The answer is, not quite, since we have not yet said anything about the properties of the stochastic disturbance term. It can be shown that if N_i is fairly large and if each observation in a given income class X_i is distributed independently as a binomial variable, then

$$u_i \sim N\left[0, \frac{1}{N_i P_i(1 - P_i)}\right] \tag{16.8.4}$$

that is u_i follows the normal distribution with zero mean and variance equal to $1/[N_i P_i(1 - P_i)]$.[21]

Therefore, as in the case of the LPM, the disturbance term in the logit model is heteroscedastic. Thus, instead of using OLS we will have to use the weighted least squares (WLS). For empirical purposes, however, we will replace the unknown P_i by $\hat{P}_i$ and use

$$\hat{\sigma}^2 = \frac{1}{N_i \hat{P}_i(1 - \hat{P}_i)} \tag{16.8.5}$$

as estimator of σ^2.

---

[21] As shown in elementary probability theory, $\hat{P}_i$, the proportion of successes (here, owning a house), follows the binomial distribution with mean equal to true P_i and variance equal to $P_i(1 - P_i)/N_i$; and as N_i increases indefinitely the binomial distribution approximates the normal distribution. The distributional properties of u_i given in (16.8.4) follow from this basic theory. For details, see Henry Theil, "On the Relationships Involving Qualitative Variables," *American Journal of Sociology*, vol. 76, July 1970, pp. 103–154.

We now describe the various steps in estimating the logit regression (16.8.1):

1. For each income level X, compute the estimated probability of owning a house as $\hat{P}_i = n_i/N_i$.
2. For each X_i, obtain the logit as[22]

$$\hat{L}_i = \ln[\hat{P}_i/(1 - \hat{P}_i)]$$

3. To resolve the problem of heteroscedasticity, transform (16.8.1) as follows:[23]

$$\sqrt{w_i}L_i = \beta_1 \sqrt{w_i} + \beta_2 \sqrt{w_i}X_i + \sqrt{w_i}u_i \qquad (16.8.6)$$

which we write as

$$L_i^* = \beta_1 \sqrt{w_i} + \beta_2 X_i^* + v_i \qquad (16.8.7)$$

where the weights $w_i = N_i\hat{P}_i(1 - \hat{P}_i)$; $L_i^* =$ transformed or weighted L_i; $X_i^* =$ transformed or weighted X_i; and $v_i =$ transformed error term. It is easy to verify that the transformed error term v_i is homoscedastic, keeping in mind that the original error variance is $\sigma_u^2 = 1/[N_iP_i(1 - P_i)]$.

4. Estimate (16.8.6) by OLS—recall that WLS is OLS on the transformed data. Notice that in (16.8.6) there is no intercept term introduced explicitly (why?). Therefore, one will have to use the regression through the origin routine to estimate (16.8.6).

5. Establish confidence intervals and/or test hypotheses in the usual OLS framework, *but keep in mind that all the conclusions will be valid strictly speaking if the sample is reasonably large* (why?). Therefore, in small samples, the estimated results should be interpreted carefully.

16.9   THE LOGIT MODEL: A NUMERICAL EXAMPLE

Although packages such as SAS and SHAZAM now estimate logit models with comparative ease, one can more readily understand the underlying logic by working out a numerical problem. We will use the data given in Table 16.4. The necessary raw data and other relevant calculations are given in Table 16.5. The results of the weighted least-squares regression (16.8.6) based on the data given in Table 16.5 are as follows:

$$\hat{L}_i^* = \begin{array}{cc} -1.5932 \sqrt{w_i} & + 0.0787X_i^* \\ (0.1115) & (0.0054) \end{array} \qquad (16.9.1)$$

$$t = (-14.290) \qquad (14.4456)$$

$$R^2 = 0.9637 \qquad \hat{\sigma}^2 = 0.2921$$

---

[22]Since $\hat{P}_i = n_i/N_i$, L_i can be alternatively expressed as $\hat{L}_i = \ln n_i/(N_i - n_i)$. In passing it should be noted that to avoid $\hat{P}_i$ taking the value of 0 or 1, in practice $\hat{L}_i$ is measured as $\hat{L}_i = \ln(n_i + \frac{1}{2})/(N_i - n_i + \frac{1}{2}) = \ln(\hat{P}_i + 1/2N_i)/(1 - \hat{P}_i + 1/2N_i)$. It is recommended as a rule of thumb that N_i be at least 5 at each value of X_i. For additional details, see D. R. Cox, *Analysis of Binary Data*, Methuen, London, 1970, p. 33.

[23]If we estimate (16.8.1) disregarding heteroscedasticity, the estimators, although unbiased, will not be efficient, as we know from Chap. 11.

Note: $\hat{L}_i^*$ and X_i^* are weighted $\hat{L}_i$ and X_i as shown in (16.8.6) and the estimated intercept is $\beta_1 \sqrt{N_i \hat{P}_i (1 - \hat{P}_i)}$.

As this regression shows, the estimated slope coefficient suggests that for a unit ($1000) increase in weighted income the weighted log of the odds in favor of owning a house goes up by about 0.08. Taking the antilog of 0.0787 gives approximately 1.0818, which means that for a unit increase in X^* the weighted odds in favor of owning a house increase by 1.0818 or about 8.18 percent. *In general, if you take the antilog of the jth slope coefficient, subtract one from it, and multiply the result by 100, you will get the percent change in the odds for a unit increase in the jth regressor.*

Can we compute the probability of owning a house, given income, from the estimated odds ratio? This calculation can be done easily. Suppose we want to estimate the probability of owning a house at the income level of $20,000. Plugging $X = 20$ into (16.9.1), we obtain

$$\hat{L}_i^* \mid (X = 20) = -0.0944 \quad \text{and} \quad \hat{L}_i = \hat{L}_i^* / \sqrt{w_i} = -0.0199$$

Taking the antilog of $\hat{L}_i^* = \text{antilog}[\hat{P}_i/(1 - \hat{P}_i)] = \text{antilog}(-0.0199)$, we obtain $[P_i/(1 - \hat{P}_i)] = 0.9803$, from which we get $\hat{P}_i = 0.4950$, that is, the probability that a family with an income of $20,000 will own a house is about 0.49. Similar probabilities at other income levels can be easily estimated (see exercise 16.5).

As noted, the slope coefficient of 0.0787 gives the change in the weighted *log of the odds ratio* of owning a house per unit increase in weighted income. We have also seen that [the antilog of 0.0787 minus one] times 100 gives the percentage change in the weighted *odds* for a unit increase in weighted income. Can we compute the change in the probability of owning a house itself per unit change in income? As noted in footnote 18, that depends not only on the estimated β_2 but also on the level of the probability from which the change is measured; the latter of course depends on the income level at which the probability is computed. To illustrate, suppose we want to measure the change in the probability of owning a house starting at the income level of $20,000. Then from footnote 18 the change in probability for a unit increase in income from the level 20 (thousand) is $\hat{\beta}_2(1 - \hat{P})\hat{P} = 0.0787(0.5143)(0.4950) = 0.0197$. That is, measured at the income of $20,000, if income goes up by $1000, the probability of owning a home increases by about 0.02.[24] But at the income level 40 (thousand) the probability of owning a home goes up by only about 0.012 per $1000 increase in income. [*Note:* $\hat{\beta}_2(1 - \hat{P})\hat{P} = 0.0126$ at $X = 40$).] As the reader can see, this computation is very much different from the LPM where the change in the probability of owning a home remains constant throughout.[25] For our illustrative example, Fig. 16.3 shows the change in the probability of owning a home at various income levels.

Returning to the regression (16.9.1), we see that the estimated coefficients are individually statistically significant even at the 1% level. But as cautioned earlier, this statement is strictly correct in large samples, that is, when the number of observations N_i at each X_i is large—it is not necessary that the number of levels at which X_i is measured be necessarily large; in our example X_i has 10 different values.

---

[24]Since we are using the results derived from calculus, this calculation is strictly valid if the change in X is very small (infinitesimal in the calculus language).

[25]If we had more than one X variable in the model, the computed probability will depend on the values taken by all the X variables, which means the change in probability will take into consideration the values of all the X's simultaneously, thereby bringing into play the interaction effects of the other X's when a given X changes by a unit. (See example 16.5.)

TABLE 16.5
Data to estimate the logit model of ownership

X (thousands of dollars)	N_i	n_i	$\hat{P}_i$	$1 - \hat{P}_i$	$\dfrac{\hat{P}_i}{1 - \hat{P}_i}$	$\hat{L}_i = \ln\left(\dfrac{\hat{P}_i}{1 - \hat{P}_i}\right)$	$N_i\hat{P}_i(1 - \hat{P}_i) = w_i$	$\sqrt{w_i} = \sqrt{N_i\hat{P}_i(1 - \hat{P}_i)}$	$\hat{L}_i^* = \hat{L}_i\sqrt{w_i}$	$\hat{X}_i^* = X_i\sqrt{w_i}$
(1)	(2)	(3)	(4) = (3) ÷ (2)	(5)	(6)	(7)	(8)	(9) = $\sqrt{(8)}$	(10) = (7)(9)	(11) = (1)(9)
6	40	8	0.20	0.80	0.25	−1.3863	6.40	2.5298	−3.5071	15.1788
8	50	12	0.24	0.76	0.32	−1.1526	9.12	3.0199	−3.4807	24.1592
10	60	18	0.30	0.70	0.43	−0.8472	12.60	3.5496	−3.0072	35.4960
13	80	28	0.35	0.65	0.54	−0.6190	18.20	4.2661	−2.6407	55.4593
15	100	45	0.45	0.55	0.82	−0.2007	24.75	4.9749	−0.9985	74.6235
20	70	36	0.51	0.49	1.04	0.0400	17.49	4.1825	0.1673	83.6506
25	65	39	0.60	0.40	1.50	0.4054	15.60	3.9497	1.6012	98.7425
30	50	33	0.66	0.34	1.94	0.6633	11.20	3.3496	2.2218	100.4880
35	40	30	0.75	0.25	3.0	1.0986	7.50	2.7386	3.0086	95.8405
40	25	20	0.80	0.20	4.0	1.3863	4.00	2.000	2.7726	80.0000

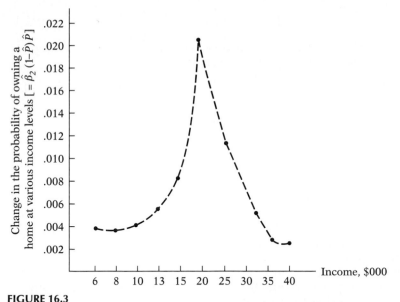

FIGURE 16.3
The *change* in the probability of owning a home at various income levels.

Examining Table 16.5, we observe that N_i, although not very large, are reasonably large, but keep in mind that the larger the N_i the better the testing procedures.

The estimated R^2 is quite "high," about 0.96. But we have pointed out that in dichotomous dependent variable models R^2 as a measure of goodness of fit is of questionable value.[26] There are several alternatives suggested in the literature, but we will not pursue them here. (But see exercise 16.11.)

To conclude our discussion of the logit models, we present next the regression results based on OLS, or unweighted regression, for the home ownership example:

$$\hat{L}_i = -1.6587 + 0.0792X_i$$
$$(0.0958) \quad (0.0041) \tag{16.9.2}$$
$$t = (-17.32) \quad (19.11) \quad R^2 = 0.9786$$

We leave it to the reader to comment on these results vis-à-vis those based on the WLS given in (16.9.1). (See Exercise 16.8.)

16.10 THE LOGIT MODEL: ILLUSTRATIVE EXAMPLES

Example 16.4 "An Application of Logit Analysis to Prediction of Merger Targets"

To predict the probability that a given firm will be a merger target, J. Kimball Dietrich and Eric Sorensen[27] estimated the following logit model:

---

[26] See Aldrich and Nelson, op. cit., pp. 55–58.

[27] *Journal of Business Research*, vol. 12, September 1984, pp. 393–402.

$$P(Y) = \frac{1}{1 + e^{-Y}}$$ (16.10.1)

where $Y = 1$ if the firm is a merger candidate and 0 if it is not. The authors assume that Y is linearly related to the variables shown below:

$$Y_i = \beta_1 + \beta_2 \text{ Payout} + \beta_3 \text{ Turnov} + \beta_4 \text{ Size} + \beta_5 \text{ Lev} + \beta_6 \text{ Vol} + \text{error}$$ (16.10.2)

where $Y_i = 1$ if a merger target, 0 otherwise; Payout = payout ratio (dividend/earnings); Turnov = asset turnover (sales/total asset); Size = market value of equity; Lev = leverage ratio (long-term debt/total assets); Vol = trading volume in the year of acquisition.

A priori, β_2, β_4, and β_5 are expected to be negative, β_6 positive, and β_3 to be positive or negative. Based on a sample of 24 merged ($Y = 1$) and 43 nonmerged ($Y = 0$) firms, the authors obtained the results shown in Table 16.6.[28] As expected, the estimated coefficients have the a priori expected signs and most are statistically significant at the 10 percent or better level (i.e., less than 10 percent). The results, for example, indicate that the higher the turnover and the larger the size, the lower the (log) odds of the firm being a takeover target. (Why?) On the other hand, the higher the trading volume the greater the odds of being a merger candidate, for high-volume firms may imply lower acquisition transaction costs due to marketability. Based on their analysis, the authors conclude:

> ... an important factor affecting the firm's attractiveness is the inability of incumbent management to generate sales per unit of assets. Moreover, low turnover must be accompanied by any one or a combination of low payout, low financial leverage, high trading volume, and smallness in aggregate market value in order to produce a high probability of merger.[29]

Example 16.5   Predicting a Bond Rating[30]

In Example 16.2 we considered Joseph Cappelleri's LPM estimates of the bond-rating model for a sample of 200 Aa and Baa bonds. For the same data Cappelleri estimated the following logit model using the method of maximum likelihood, but he did not adjust his results for heteroscedasticity (figures in parentheses are standard errors):

$$\ln\left(\frac{P_i}{1 - P_i}\right) = -1.6622 - 0.3185X_{2i}^2 + 0.6248X_3 - 0.9041X_4$$
$$\phantom{\ln\left(\frac{P_i}{1 - P_i}\right) = } (1.1968) \quad (0.0635) \qquad (0.1359) \qquad (0.2206)$$ (16.10.3)
$$+ \ 0.00000092X_5$$
$$(0.00000002)$$

where the variables are as defined in Example 16.2. All the estimated slope coefficients are significant at the 5% level and are in accordance with a priori expectations. Thus, the higher the profit rate variability (X_4) the lower the odds of being rated an Aa bond, or the larger the net total assets (X_5) the greater the odds

---

[28]The authors tried a few other variables but retained only those that were generally significant.
[29]Ibid., p. 402.
[30]Joseph Cappelleri, op. cit.

TABLE 16.6
Logit estimate results

Variable	Coefficient	Asymptotic error	t-value
Payout	-0.74	0.29	-2.51†
Turnov	-11.64	3.86	-3.01†
Size	-5.74	2.39	-2.40†
Lev	-1.33	0.97	-1.37
Vol	2.55	1.58	1.62*
Constant	-10.84	3.40	-3.20†

*Significance at 90%.
†Significance at 99%.
Source: J. Kimball Dietrich and Eric Sorenen, "An Application of Logit Analysis to Prediction of Merger Targets," *Journal of Business Research*, vol. 12, 1984, p. 401.

of being rated an Aa bond. Given $X_2^2 = 9.67\%, X_3 = 7.77\%, X_4 = 0.5933\%$, and $X_5 = 3429$ (000), the estimated log of the odds ratio from (16.10.3) is -0.4206, from which the estimated probability can be computed as 0.3964. Thus a bond with the stated X values has a probability of about 40 percent of being rated an Aa bond.

16.11 THE PROBIT MODEL

As we have noted, to explain the behavior of a dichotomous dependent variable we will have to use a suitably chosen CDF. The logit model uses the cumulative logistic function, as shown in (16.7.2). But this is not the only CDF that one can use. In some applications, the normal CDF has been found useful. The estimating model that emerges from the normal CDF[31] is popularly known as the **probit model**, although sometimes it is also known as the **normit model**. In principle one could substitute the normal CDF in place of the logistic CDF in (16.7.2) and proceed as in Section 16.7. But instead of following this route, we will present the probit model based on utility theory, or rational choice perspective on behavior, as developed by McFadden.[32]

To motivate the probit model, assume that in our home ownership example the decision of the ith family to own a house or not depends on an *unob-*

---

[31] See Appendix A for a discussion of the normal CDF. Briefly, if a variable Z follows the normal distribution with mean μ_z and variance σ^2, its PDF is

$$f(Z) = \frac{1}{\sqrt{2\pi}\sigma} e^{-(Z-\mu_z)^2/2\sigma^2}$$

and its CDF is

$$F(Z) = \int_{-\infty}^{Z_0} \frac{1}{\sqrt{2\pi}\sigma} e^{-(Z-\mu_z)^2/2\sigma^2}$$

where Z_0 is some specified value of Z.

[32] D. McFadden, "Conditional Logit Analysis of Qualitative Choice Behavior," in P. Zarembka (ed.), *Frontiers in Econometrics*, Academic Press, New York, 1973.

servable utility index I_i that is determined by an explanatory variable(s), say, income X_i, in such a way that the larger the value of the index I_i, the greater the probability of the family owning a home. We express the index I_i as

$$I_i = \beta_1 + \beta_2 X_i \tag{16.11.1}$$

where X_i is the income of the ith family.

How is the (unobservable) I_i related to the actual decision to own a house? As before, let $Y = 1$ if the family owns a house and $Y = 0$ if it does not. Now it is reasonable to assume that for each family there is a *critical or threshold level* of the index, call it I_i^*, such that if I_i exceeds I_i^* the family will own a house, otherwise it will not. The threshold I_i^*, like I_i, is not observable, but if we assume that it is normally distributed with the same mean and variance, it is possible not only to estimate the parameters of the index given in (16.11.1) but also to get some information about the unobservable index itself. This calculation is shown as follows.

Given the assumption of normality, the probability that I_i^* is less than or equal to I_i can be computed from the standardized normal CDF as[33]

$$P_i = \Pr(Y = 1) = \Pr(I_i^* \leq I_i) = F(I_i) = \frac{1}{\sqrt{2\pi}} \int_{-\infty}^{T_i} e^{-t^2/2} dt$$

$$= \frac{1}{\sqrt{2\pi}} \int_{-\infty}^{\beta_1 + \beta_2 X_i} e^{-t^2/2} dt \tag{16.11.2}$$

where t is a standardized normal variable, i.e., $t \sim N(0, 1)$.

Since P_i represents the probability that an event will occur, here the probability of owning a house, it is measured by the area of the standard normal curve from $-\infty$ to I_i, as shown in Fig. 16.4a.

Now to obtain information on I_i, the utility index, as well as β_1 and β_2, we take the inverse of (16.11.2) to obtain[34]

$$\begin{aligned} I_i &= F^{-1}(I_i) = F^{-1}(P_i) \\ &= \beta_1 + \beta_2 X_i \end{aligned} \tag{16.11.3}$$

where F^{-1} is the inverse of the normal CDF. What all this means can be made clear from Fig. 16.4. In panel a of this figure we obtain (from the ordinate) the (cumulative) probability of owning a house given $I_i^* \leq I_i$, whereas in panel b we obtain (from the abscissa) the value of I_i given the value of P_i, which is simply the reverse of the former.

---

[33]A normal distribution with zero mean and unit (= 1) variance is known as a standard or standardized normal variable. (See App. A.)

[34]Notice that (16.11.2) is highly nonlinear, but so was the cumulative logistic function (16.7.2). And just as taking the log of the odds ratio enabled us to linearize the logistic model, the inverse of the normal CDF also enables us to linearize the estimating (probit) model.

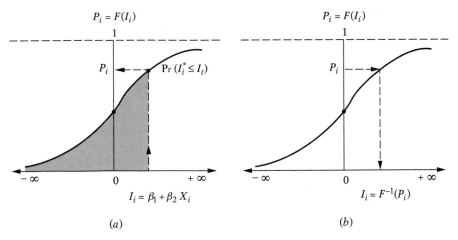

FIGURE 16.4
Probit model: (a) Given I_i, read P_i from the ordinate; (b) Given P_i, read I_i from the abscissa.

But how do we actually go about obtaining the index I_i as well as estimating β_1 and β_2, for the only data we have are on income X_i and $Y = 1$ or
0, depending on whether a family owns a house or not? Suppose we have the
grouped data as shown in Table 16.5 and we wish to fit the probit model to
these data as an alternative to the logit model. Since we already have $\hat{P}_i$, the relative frequency (the empirical measure of probability), we can use it to obtain
I_i from the normal CDF as shown in Table 16.7, or from Fig. 16.5. Once we have
the estimated I_i, estimating β_1 and β_2 is a relatively straightforward matter, as
we show shortly. In passing, note that in the language of probit analysis the unobservable utility index I_i is simply know as *normal equivalent deviate* (n.e.d.)
or simply **normit**. Since the n.e.d. or I_i will be negative whenever $P_i < 0.5$, in

TABLE 16.7
**Estimating the index I_i from the
standard normal CDF**

$\hat{P}_i$	$I_i = F^{-1}(\hat{P}_i)$
0.20	−0.84
0.24	−0.70
0.30	−0.52
0.35	−0.38
0.45	−0.12
0.51	0.03
0.60	0.25
0.66	0.40
0.75	0.67
0.80	0.84

Notes: (1) $\hat{P}_i$ are from Table 16.5; (2) I_i are
estimated from the standard normal CDF ta-
ble given in App. D. Note that the estimated
I_i are rather crude, but efficient computer
programs exist to estimate them more precisely.

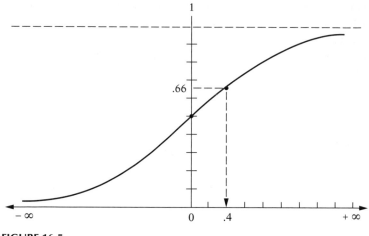

FIGURE 16.5
Normal CDF.

practice the number 5 is added to the n.e.d. and the result is called a probit.[35] In short,

$$\text{Probit} = \text{n.e.d.} + 5$$
$$= I_i + 5 \qquad (16.11.4)$$

Now to estimate β_1 and β_2, we write (16.11.1) as

$$I_i = \beta_1 + \beta_2 X_i + u_i \qquad (16.11.5)$$

where u is the stochastic disturbance term.

The steps involved in the estimation of the probit model are as follows:

1. From the grouped data, such as Table 16.5, estimate P_i as in the case of the logit model.[36]
2. Given $\hat{P}_i$, obtain n.e.d. ($= I_i$) from the standard normal CDF.
3. Use the estimated $I_i = \hat{I}_i$ obtained in Step 2 as the dependent variable in the regression (16.11.5).
4. If desired, add 5 to the estimated I_i to convert them into probits and use the probits thus obtained (see 16.11.4) as the dependent variables in the regression (16.11.5). Whether we use the n.e.d.'s or the probits, the regression results will be comparable in that the slope coefficient β_2 and R^2 will be identical in the two models (why?), although the intercepts will be different (why?).
5. The disturbance term in (16.11.5) is heteroscedastic. Therefore, to obtain efficient estimates of the parameters we will have to transform the data in such

---

[35] If you examine the standard normal CDF you will see that the addition of 5 will for all practical purposes make the n.e.d. positive (why?).

[36] If data are available at the individual level only, then we will have to use ML methods, which we do not pursue here. For details of this method, see Aldrich and Nelson, op. cit.

a way that the error term in the transformed model will be homoscedastic. The suggested transformation is given in exercise 16.10.

6. One can conduct hypothesis testings, etc. in the usual fashion, keeping in mind that the conclusions drawn will hold true asymptotically, that is, in the large samples.

7. For reasons already noted, R^2 obtained for such models is of questionable value as a measure of the goodness of fit (see exercise 16.11).

16.12   THE PROBIT MODEL: A NUMERICAL EXAMPLE

To illustrate the mechanics just discussed, we will use the data of Table 16.7, which are reproduced in Table 16.8 with some additions.

Based on the n.e.d.'s, we obtain the following results:[37]

$$\hat{I}_i = \quad -1.0088 + 0.0481X_i$$
$$(0.0582)\ (0.0025) \qquad R^2 = 0.9786 \qquad (16.12.1)$$
$$t = (-17.330)\ (19.105)$$

which shows that as X increases by a unit, on average, I increases by 0.05 units. As noted earlier, the higher the value of the index I_i, the greater the probability that a family will own a house. Thus if $X = 6$ (thousand), $\hat{I}_i$ from (16.12.1) is -0.7202 but if $X = 7$, $\hat{I}_i$ is -0.6721; the former corresponds to the probability of about 0.24 and the latter to about 0.25. All these can be obtained from the cumulative standardized normal CDF or, geometrically, from Fig. 16.4a.

The regression results based on the probits ($=$ n.e.d. $+$ 5) are as follows, where $Z_i = $ probit:

$$Z_i = \quad 3.9911 + 0.0481X_i$$
$$(0.0582)\ (0.0025) \qquad R^2 = 0.9786 \qquad (16.12.2)$$
$$t = (68.560)\ (19.105)$$

Except for the intercept term, these results are identical with those based on (16.12.1). But this should not be surprising. (Why?)

Logit versus Probit

Now that we have considered both the logit and probit models, which is preferable in practice? From a theoretical perspective, the difference between the two models is as shown in Fig. 16.6. As the reader can see, the logistic and probit formulations are quite comparable, the chief difference being that the logistic has slightly flatter tails, that is, the normal, or probit, curve approaches the axes more quickly than the logistic curve.[38] Therefore, the choice between the

---

[37] The following results are not corrected for heteroscedasticity (see exercise 16.10).

[38] As a matter of fact, Eric Hanushek and John Jackson state, "The logistic distribution is very similar to the t-distribution with seven degrees of freedom, while the normal distribution is a t-distribution with infinite degrees of freedom." See their *Statistical Methods for Social Scientists*, Academic Press, New York, 1977, p. 189.

TABLE 16.8
The probits for the home ownership example

$\hat{P}_i$	$I_i = F^{-1}(\hat{P}_i)$ (n.e.d.)	Probits (n.e.d. + 5)
0.20	−0.84	4.16
0.24	−0.70	4.30
0.30	−0.52	4.48
0.35	−0.38	4.62
0.45	−0.12	4.88
0.51	0.03	5.03
0.60	0.25	5.25
0.66	0.40	5.40
0.75	0.67	5.67
0.80	0.84	5.84

Source: See Table 16.7.

two is one of (mathematical) convenience and ready availability of computer programs. On this score, the logit model is generally used in preference to the probit.

Comparing Logit and Probit Estimates

Although logit and probit models qualitatively give similar results, the estimates of the parameters of the two models are not directly comparable.[39] Thus, for our home ownership example, the slope coefficient of the logit model of

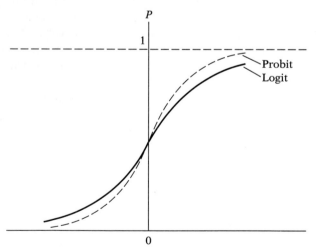

FIGURE 16.6
Logit and probit cumulative distributions.

---

[39]The reason for this is that the variance of the standard normal variable (the basis of probit) is one, whereas the variance of the logistic distribution (the basis of logit) is $\pi^2/\sqrt{3}$, where π equals approximately $\frac{22}{7}$.

0.0792 given in (16.9.2) and the corresponding estimate of the slope coefficient in the probit model of 0.0481 given in (16.12.1) are not directly comparable. But as Amemiya suggests, a logit estimate of a parameter multiplied by 0.625 gives a fairly good approximation of the probit estimate of the same parameter.[40] In our example, $(0.625)(0.0792) = 0.0495$, which is roughly equal to the corresponding probit estimate.

Incidentally, Amemiya has also shown that the coefficients of LPM and logit models are related as follows:

$$\beta_{LPM} \cong 0.25\beta_{Logit}, \text{ except for intercept}$$
$$\beta_{LPM} \cong 0.25\beta_{Logit} + 0.5 \text{ for intercept}$$

where $\cong$ means approximately.

All the preceding approximations work well when the average value of the probability (of the event happening) is not far from 0.5.

The Marginal Effect of a Unit Change in the Value of a Regressor

In a linear regression model the slope coefficient of a regressor measures the effect on the average value of the regressand for a unit change in the value of the regressor. But since LPM, logit and probit models deal with the probability of some event occurring, we have to be careful in interpreting the slope coefficient.

In the LPM, as noted before, the slope coefficient measures directly the change in the probability of an event occurring as the result of a unit change in the value of the regressor. Also, as noted in footnote 18, in logit the rate of change in the probability is given by $\beta_j P_i(1 - P_i)$, where β_j is the coefficient of the jth regressor. In probit the rate of change in the probability is somewhat complicated and is given by $\beta_j \phi(Z_i)$, where $\phi(.)$ is the density function of the standard normal variable and where $Z_i = \beta_1 + \beta_2 X_{2i} + \cdots + \beta_k X_{ji}$, that is, the regression model used in the analysis.

As the preceding discussion shows, in logit and probit models all the regressors are involved in computing the changes in probability, whereas in the LPM only the jth regressor is involved. This difference may be one reason for the early popularity of the LPM model.

16.13 THE PROBIT MODEL: EXAMPLE 16.5

To find out whether one-bank and multibank holding company subsidiaries in unit-banking states have different financial and market characteristics from other banks and whether differences in state banking laws about multibank holding companies per se make any difference in these characteristics, Ronald M. Brown estimated

---

[40]T. Amemiya, "Qualitative Response Model: A Survey," *Journal of Economic Literature*, vol. 19, 1981, pp. 481–536.

four probit regressions, which are shown in Table 16.9.[41] The definitions of the explanatory variables are given in Table 16.10. The following dependent variables are in the analysis:

Y_1 = 1, if a bank is owned by a multibank holding company

  = 0, otherwise

Y_2 = 1, if a bank is owned by a one-bank holding company

  = 0, otherwise

Y_3 = 1, if a bank is owned by either a one-bank or multibank holding company

  = 0, otherwise

In Table 16.9, a positive (negative) sign on an explanatory variable's coefficient indicates that higher values of the variable increase (decrease) the likelihood that a bank is owned by the specified type of bank holding company. For example, for the Y_1 regression, the positive coefficient on the variable TA (total assets/1,000,000), which is statistically significant, indicates that, other things being the same, as a bank's size increases, the likelihood that the bank is owned by a multibank holding company also increases. Similarly, the positive coefficient on SMSA suggests, ceteris paribus, that the bank is more likely to be owned by a multibank holding company.

The reader can make other comparisons very easily. But note that in all the regressions reported in Table 16.9 the likelihood ratios are high and statistically significant, indicating that holding companies' banks, as a group, can be distinguished from independent banks on the basis of the explanatory variables included in the table.[42] For other details of the analysis, the reader may refer to the original article.

16.14   THE TOBIT MODEL

An extension of the probit model is the **tobit model** developed by James Tobin, the Nobel Laureate economist. To explain this model, we continue with our home ownership example. But suppose we want to find out the amount of money the consumer spends in buying a house in relation to his or her income (and other economic variables). Now we have a problem: If a consumer does not purchase a house, obviously we have no data on housing expenditure for such consumers; we have such data only on consumers who actually purchase a house.

Thus consumers are divided into two groups, one consisting of, say, n_1 consumers about whom we have information on the regressors (say, income, mortgage interest rate, etc.) as well as the regressand (amount of expenditure

---

[41]"The Effect of State Banking Laws on Holding Company Banks," *Review*, Federal Reserve Bank of St. Louis, vol. 65, no. 7, August-September 1983, pp. 26–35.

Note: The data are individual observations and not grouped data. Therefore, the method of maximum likelihood has been used to estimate the parameters. For a discussion of maximum likelihood estimation in the present context, see John Aldrich and Forrest Nelson, op. cit.

[42]In this text we have not discussed the likelihood ratio approach to test statistical hypotheses in depth. In the present context a significant likelihood ratio means whether holding company banks exhibit characteristics different from independent banks. The results show that they do. For a clear discussion of the likelihood ratio test, consult Alexander M. Mood, Franklin A. Graybill, and Duane C. Boes, *Introduction to the Theory of Statistics*, 3d ed. McGraw-Hill, New York, 1974, Chap. IX.

TABLE 16.9
Coefficient estimate results of probit analysis (1978)
(t-statistics in parentheses)

Independent variables	MBHC subsample**		OBHC subsample‡	Full sample
	Y_1	Y_2	Y_2	Y_3
Financial variables				
RNI	−12.39	47.75†	30.57†	9.87*
	(−1.45)	(4.11)	(4.85)	(2.48)
ROE	−2.56	16.79†	−3.33	−1.22
	(−0.52)	(3.01)	(−1.50)	(−0.82)
REQ	0.24	−6.06†	−14.21†	−2.41†
	(0.23)	(−2.88)	(−7.28)	(−3.16)
RTL	2.01†	−0.44	1.82†	1.92†
	(4.30)	(−0.87)	(5.48)	(7.63)
RNFFS	−2.05*	1.62	−1.43*	−0.97*
	(−2.53)	(1.93)	(−2.26)	(−2.06)
TA	7.49†	−0.99	3.11†	6.49†
	(4.68)	(−1.02)	(3.17)	(6.14)
Market variables				
SMSA	0.44†	0.12	−0.26*	0.09
	(3.26)	(0.85)	(−2.49)	(1.18)
MBHC				0.46†
				(6.61)
CR	−1.17†	0.98†	0.16	0.16
	(−2.72)	(2.93)	(0.59)	(0.76)
MKGR	0.20	0.05	−1.38†	−0.31*
	(1.17)	(0.26)	(−5.64)	(−2.41)
DCRTA	7.18*	−2.77	−0.87	4.32*
	(2.22)	(−0.86)	(−0.52)	(2.10)
DCRSMSA	0.59	−0.36	0.13	0.29
	(1.40)	(−0.68)	(0.42)	(1.13)
DCRMBHC				−0.35†
				(3.55)
Constant	−1.60†	−2.09†	0.61	−1.26†
	(−3.58)	(−4.54)	(1.74)	(−5.75)
Likelihood ratio test	221.07†	45.77†	187.29†	348.92†
N‡‡	1,101	1,101	1,546	2,647
Y = 1§	369	181	529	1,100

*Significant at 5% confidence level.
†Significant at 1% confidence level.
**States that permit multibank holding companies (MBHC).
‡States that permit only one-bank holding companies (OBHC).
‡‡Number of observations.
§Number of observations on the dependent variables (Y_1, Y_2, or Y_3) at 1. Other observations at zero. The numbers do not add across because there are 21 subsidiary banks of multibank holding companies in the one-bank holding company subsample.
Source: Ronald M. Brown, "The Effect of State Banking Laws on Holding Company Banks," *Review,* Federal Reserve Bank of St. Louis, vol. 60, no. 7, August-September 1983, p. 32.

TABLE 16.10
Definitions of terms in Table 18.9 and summary statistics of independent variables

Variable	Definition	1978 Mean	1978 Standard deviation	1991 Mean	1991 Standard deviation
RNI	Net after-tax income/total assets	0.010	0.007	0.013	0.009
ROE	Operating expense/total assets	0.063	0.022	0.100	0.021
REQ	Equity capital plus reserves/total assets	0.092	0.037	0.092	0.038
RTL	Total loans, gross/total assets	0.551	0.116	0.518	0.122
RNFFS	Federal funds sold less federal funds purchased/total assets	0.038	0.065	0.061	0.082
TA	total assets/1,000,000	0.032	0.111	0.043	0.158
SMSA	= 1, if bank is located in an SMSA = 0, otherwise	0.293	0.455	0.303	0.460
MBHC	= 1, if state where bank is located allows MBHCs = 0, otherwise	0.416	0.493	0.427	0.495
CR*	Market Herfindahl index	0.257	0.155	0.254	0.150
MKGR	Five-year growth of total market assets	0.656	0.203	0.778	0.254
DCR†	= 1, if CR > 0.25 = 0, otherwise				
DCRTA	DCR × TA	0.009	0.022	0.011	0.029
DCRSMSA	DCR × SMSA	0.013	0.113	0.013	0.114
DCRMBHC	DCR × MBHC	0.178	0.383	0.187	0.390

*The index is calculated on the basis of shares of total assets:

$$CR = \sum_{t=1}^{n} \left(TA_i \Big/ \sum^{n} TA \right)$$

where TA_i is the total assets of the ith banking operation in the market. Note that $0 < CR \leq 1$.

†The variable DCR was not included in the probit models because it is highly correlated with CR. It does enter in the three interaction variables.

on housing) and another consisting of, say, n_2 consumers about whom we have information only on the regressors but not on the regressand. A sample in which information on regressand is available only for some observations is known as a **censored sample**.[43] Therefore, the tobit model is also known as a censored regression model. Some authors call such models **limited dependent variable models** because of the restriction put on the values taken by the regressand.

Mathematically, we can express the tobit model as

$$Y_i = \beta_1 + \beta_2 X_{2i} + u_{2i} \quad \text{if RHS} > 0$$
$$= 0, \quad \text{otherwise} \qquad (16.14.1)$$

---

[43]A censored sample should be distinguished from a **truncated sample** in which information on the regressors is available only if the regressand is observed. For the distinction and the estimating procedures for these two cases, the reader may consult William H. Greene, *Econometric Analysis*, Macmillan, 2d ed., New York, 1993, Chap. 22. For an intuitive discussion, see Peter Kennedy, *A Guide to Econometrics*, The MIT Press, Cambridge, Mass., 3d ed. 1992, Chap. 15.

where RHS = right-hand side. *Note:* Other X variables can be easily added to the model.

Can we estimate regression (16.14.1) using only n_1 observations and just not worry about the remaining n_2 observations? The answer is no, for the OLS estimates of the parameters obtained from the subset of n_1 observations will be *biased as well as inconsistent*.[44]

To see this, consider Fig. 16.7. As this figure shows, if Y is not observed, all such observations $(= n_2)$ will lie on the horizontal axis. If Y is observed, the observations $(= n_1)$ will lie in the Y-X plane. It is intuitively clear that if we estimate a regression based on the n_1 observations only, the resulting intercept and slope coefficients are bound to be different than if all the $n_1 + n_2$ observations were taken into account.

How then does one estimate tobit (or censored) regression models, such as (16.14.1)? We will not go into the mathematics of the calculation, but the method of maximum likelihood (see Chapter 4) can be used to estimate the parameters of such models. Most well-known computer packages, such as ET, SHAZAM, and RATS, now have routines to estimate the tobit models. We will now present an illustrative example.

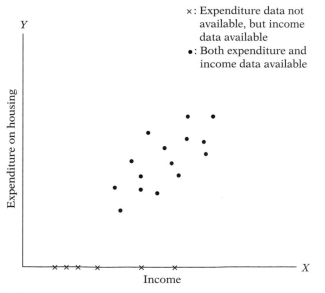

FIGURE 16.7
Plot of amount of money consumer spends in buying a house versus income.

---

[44]The bias arises from the fact that if we only consider the n_1 observations and omit the others, there is no guarantee that $E(u_i)$ will be necessarily zero. And without $E(u_i) = 0$ we cannot guarantee that the OLS estimators will be unbiased. This bias can be seen readily from the discussion in App. 3A, Eqs. (4) and (5).

Example 16.6. Sale of loans by commercial banks. Banks that give loans to commercial customers often resell them in secondary markets.[45] In their study, Pavel and Phillis use the logit as well as the tobit model to study the reselling activity of commercial banks.[46] They used the tobit model to determine the dollar amount of loans the banks sell annually. Their results based on a survey of data for 10,425 banks are given in Table 16.11; the regressand is SOLD, defined as total loans sold in 1985 divided by assets at year's end in 1984.

Direct interpretation of the various regression coefficients given in Table 16.11 is not easy. But from the estimated coefficients one can assess the impact of a change of one standard deviation (STD) unit in the value of the regressor on the regressand.[47] As Table 16.11 shows, a one standard deviation increase (decrease) in the value of NINTEXP (noninterest expense ratio), other things remaining constant, would decrease (increase) the proportion of loans a bank sells by about 1.74 percentage points. Likewise, holding other factors constant, a one standard deviation change in ASSETS would lead banks to increase their LOAN by about 0.19 percentage points.

TABLE 16.11
Multivariate tobit model

	Parameter estimates	t-statistics	Impact of a one STD change, %
Intercept	−0.060	−7.097	
RESERVES	0.962	3.488	0.25
PRMCAP	0.022	0.339	
BIND55	0.032	3.259	
BIND557	0.015	3.488	
PREMIUM	0.019	5.675	0.61
LNINDEX	0.059	23.194	1.80
LNGROW	0.005	3.700	0.25
NCHRGOFF	0.208	2.209	0.15
NINTEXP	−1.074	−16.847	−1.74
ASSETS	0.002	3.288	0.19
MULTI	0.044	13.226	
Sigma	0.150	123.770	

*Significant at the 5% level.
†Significant at the 1% level.

---

[45]This practice is very common in the housing mortgage market. A bank that gives a housing loan to an individual may later sell it to a third party instead of carrying it on its book for the length of the mortgage, typically 15, 25, or 30 years.

[46]Christine Pavel and David Phillis, "Why Commercial Banks Sell Loans: An Empirical Analysis," *Economic Perspectives*, Federal Reserve Bank of Chicago, May/June 1987, pp. 3–14.

[47]For a discussion of why the estimated probit coefficients cannot be used directly to assess the impact of a unit change in the value of the regressor on the regressand, the reader may consult the Maddala and Greene textbooks. See also our discussion in Sec. 16.12 about the marginal effect of a change in the regressor value.

	Expected sign
Regulatory taxes	
RESERVES = reserve requirements for the last reporting period in 1984 / total assets** at year-end 1984‡	Positive
PRMCAP = primary capital ratio for year-end 1984	Negative
BIND55 = 1 if prmcap is less than 5.5%; zero if prmcap is greater than 5.5%	Positive
BIND557 = 1 if prmcap is between 5.5% and 7%; zero if prmcap is less than 5.5%, greater than 7%	Positive
PREMIUM = total domestic deposits / total insured deposits at year-end 1984	Positive
Diversification	
LNINDEX = $(L_1^2 + \cdots + L_{10}^2)/1000$ where L_i is the loan-to-asset ratio for loan type i at year-end 1984	Positive
Funding/liquidity	
LNGROW = total loans at year-end 1984 / total loans at year-end 1983	Positive
Loan quality	
NCHRGOFF = loan charge-offs less recoveries / total loans at year-end 1984	?
Comparative advantage	
NINTEXP = noninterest expense during 1984 / total loans at year-end 1984 + loans sold during 1984	Negative
Control variables	
ASSETS = total assets at year-end 1984 in billions of dollars	Positive
MULTI = 1 if bank is a member of a multibank holding company; 0 otherwise	Positive
Dependent variable	
SOLD = total loans sold in 1985 / assets at year-end 1984 (for tobit)	

**Total assets include foreign and domestic assets.

‡Data on required reserves were unavailable for 3,338 banks. Therefore, an OLS regression model was estimated with required reserves as the dependent variable and total deposits as the independent variable, using data for the 10,425 banks in which data on required reserves were available. The model's R^2 was 97%.

Source: Christine Pavel and David Phillis, "Why Commercial Banks Sell Loans: An Empirical Analysis," Federal Reserve Bank of Chicago, May/June 1987, p. 6 and p. 11.

16.15 SUMMARY AND CONCLUSIONS

1. Regression models in which the regressand evokes a yes or no or present or absent response are known as dichotomous, or dummy, dependent variable regression models. They are applicable in a wide variety of fields and are used extensively in survey or census-type data.
2. Among the methods that are used to estimate such models, this chapter considered three—LPM, logit, and probit.

3. The LPM is the simplest of the three models to use but has several limitations, namely, (1) nonnormality of the error term, (2) heteroscedasticity, and (3) the possibility of the estimated probability lying outside the 0–1 bounds. Even if these problems are resolved, the LPM is logically not a very attractive model in that it assumes that the conditional probabilities increase linearly with the values of the explanatory variables. More likely, the probabilities will tend to taper off as the values of the explanatory variables increase or decrease indefinitely. Therefore, what is needed is a probability model that has the S-shaped feature of the cumulative distribution function (CDF).

4. Although the choice of the CDF is wide, in practice the logistic and normal CDFs are chosen, the former giving rise to the logit and latter to the probit model.

5. Both logit and probit models guarantee that the estimated probabilities lie in the 0–1 range and that they are nonlinearly related to the explanatory variables.

6. Of these two, the logit model is slightly less involved because by taking the logarithm of the odds ratio what appears to be a highly nonlinear model becomes a linear (in the parameter) model that can be estimated within the standard OLS framework. In the probit, one is required to invert the normal CDF, leading to errors of approximations unless one has a readily available computer routine.

7. In grouped data, logit and probit estimates are fairly straightforward. But if data are available only at the individual level, one has to use maximum likelihood estimation techniques. Fortunately, computer packages, such as ET, LIMPDEP, SHAZAM, TSP, RATS, and SAS can do this relatively easily.

8. A model related to the probit is the tobit. In tobit, which is an example of a general class of models known as censored regression models (also known as limited dependent variable models), values of the regressand are not available for some observations, although values of the regressors are available for all the observations. Such models are usually estimated by the maximum likelihood methods.

9. Various researchers have made extensions of the probit and logit models as well as the tobit model, including **bivariate probit**, **ordered probit**, **two-limit tobit**, etc. A detailed discussion of these and related topics can be found in the books of Maddala and Greene.[48]

EXERCISES

Questions

16.1. Refer to the data given in Table 16.2. If $\hat{Y}_i$ is negative, assume it to be equal to 0.01 and if it is greater than 1, assume it to be equal to 0.99. Recalculate the weights

---

[48]G. S. Maddala, op. cit., and William H. Greene, op. cit.

w_i and estimate the LPM using WLS. Compare your results with those given in (16.4.2) and comment.

16.2. For the home ownership data given in Table 16.1, the maximum likelihood estimates of the logit model are as follows:

$$\hat{L}_i = \ln\left(\frac{\hat{P}_i}{1 - \hat{P}_i}\right) = -493.54 + 32.96 \text{ income}$$
$$t(-0.000008)(0.000008)$$

Comment on these results, bearing in mind that all values of income above 16 (thousand dollars) correspond to $Y = 1$ and all values of income below 16 correspond to $Y = 0$. A priori, what would you expect in such a situation?

16.3. In studying the purchase of durable goods Y ($Y = 1$ if purchased, $Y = 0$ if no purchase) as a function of several variables for a total of 762 households, Janet A. Fisher* obtained the following LPM results:

Explanatory variable	Coefficient	Standard error
Constant	0.1411	...
1957 disposable income, X_1	0.0251	0.0118
(Disposable income $= X_1)^2$, X_2	−0.0004	0.0004
Checking accounts, X_3	−0.0051	0.0108
Savings accounts, X_4	0.0013	0.0047
U.S. Savings Bonds, X_5	−0.0079	0.0067
Housing status: rent, X_6	−0.0469	0.0937
Housing status: own, X_7	0.0136	0.0712
Monthly rent, X_8	−0.7540	1.0983
Monthly mortgage payments, X_9	−0.9809	0.5162
Personal noninstallment debt, X_{10}	−0.0367	0.0326
Age, X_{11}	0.0046	0.0084
Age squared , X_{12}	−0.0001	0.0001
Marital status, X_{13} (1 $=$ married)	0.1760	0.0501
Number of children, X_{14}	0.0398	0.0358
(Number of children $= X_{14})^2$, X_{15}	−0.0036	0.0072
Purchase plans, X_{16} (1 $=$ planned; 0 otherwise)	0.1760	0.0384
$R^2 = 0.1336$		

Notes: All financial variables are in thousands of dollars.

  Housing status: Rent (1 if rents; 0 otherwise)

  Housing status: Own (1 if owns; 0 otherwise)

Source: Janet A. Fisher, "An Analysis of Consumer Good Expenditure," *The Review of Economics and Statistics*, vol. 64, no. 1, Table 1, 1962, p. 67.

(a) Comment generally on the fit of the equation.

(b) How would you interpret the coefficient of −0.0051 attached to checking account variable? How would you rationalize the negative sign for this variable?

(c) What is the rationale behind introducing the age-squared and number of children-squared variables? Why is the sign negative in both cases?

(d) Assuming values of zero for all but the income variable, find out the conditional probability of a household whose income is $20,000 purchasing a durable good.

---

*"An Analysis of Consumer Good Expenditure," *The Review of Economics and Statistics*, vol. 64, no. 1, 1962, pp. 64–71.

(e) Estimate the conditional probability of owning durable good(s), given: $X_1 =$ $\$15,000, X_3 = \$3000, X_4 = \$5000, X_6 = 0, X_7 = 1, X_8 = \$500, X_9 = \$300,$ $X_{10} = 0, X_{11} = 35, X_{13} = 1, X_{14} = 2, X_{16} = 0.$

16.4. The R^2 value in the labor-force participation regression given in Table 16.3 is 0.175, which is rather low. Can you test this value for statistical significance? Which test do you use and why? Comment in general on the value of R^2 in such models.

16.5. Estimate the probabilities of owning a house at the various income levels underlying the regression (16.9.1). Plot them against income and comment on the resulting relationship.

*__16.6.__ In the probit regression (16.12.1) show that the intercept is equal to $-\mu_x/\sigma_x$ and the slope is equal to $1/\sigma_x$, where μ_x and σ_x are the mean and standard deviation of X.

16.7. Based on data for 54 standard metropolitan statistical areas (SMSA), Demaris estimated the following logit model to explain high murder rate vs. low murder rate:†

$$\ln \hat{O}_i = 1.1387 + 0.0014 P_i + 0.0561 C_i - 0.4050 R_i$$

$$\text{se} \quad = \quad\quad\quad\quad (0.0009) \quad (0.0227) \quad (0.1568)$$

where $O =$ the odds of a high murder rate, $P =$ 1980 population size in thousands, $C =$ population growth rate from 1970 to 1980, $R =$ reading quotient, and the se are the asymptotic standard errors.

(a) How would you interpret the various coefficients?

(b) Which of the coefficients are individually statistically significant?

(c) What is the effect of a unit increase in the reading quotient on the odds of having a higher murder rate?

(d) What is the effect of a percentage point increase in the population growth rate on the odds of having a higher murder rate?

16.8. Compare and comment on the OLS and WLS regressions (16.9.1) and (16.9.2).

Problems

16.9. To assess the effectiveness of a new method of teaching called PSI (personalized system of instruction) in an intermediate macroeconomics course, Spector and Mazzeo collected the data shown in the table on the facing page.**

In this example, the dependent variable is $Y = 1$ if the final grade is A and 0 if it is B or C. To predict the final grade, the researchers used the predictors GPA (the entering grade point average), TUCE (score on an examination given at the beginning of the term to test entering knowledge of macroeconomics), and PSI ($= 1$ if the new method is used, $= 0$ otherwise).

(a) Fit LPM to the data using both OLS and WLS and comment on the fit.

(b) Using a computer package, estimate the logit and probit models for the same data and compare your results.

(c) Which model would you choose and why?

---

*Optional.

†Demaris, op. cit., p. 46.

**L. Spector, and M. Mazzeo, "Probit Analysis and Economic Education," *Journal of Economic Education*, vol. 11, 1980, pp. 37–44.

Data on the effect of "Personalized System of Instruction" (PSI) on course grades

OBS	GPA Grade	TUCE Grade	PSI	Grade	Letter Grade	OBS	GPA Grade	TUCE Grade	PSI	Grade	Letter Grade
1	2.66	20	0	0	C	17	2.75	25	0	0	C
2	2.89	22	0	0	B	18	2.83	19	0	0	C
3	3.28	24	0	0	B	19	3.12	23	1	0	B
4	2.92	12	0	0	B	20	3.16	25	1	1	A
5	4.00	21	0	1	A	21	2.06	22	1	0	C
6	2.86	17	0	0	B	22	3.62	28	1	1	A
7	2.76	17	0	0	B	23	2.89	14	1	0	C
8	2.87	21	0	0	B	24	3.51	26	1	0	B
9	3.03	25	0	0	C	25	3.54	24	1	1	A
10	3.92	29	0	1	A	26	2.83	27	1	1	A
11	2.63	20	0	0	C	27	3.39	17	1	1	A
12	3.32	23	0	0	B	28	2.67	24	1	0	B
13	3.57	23	0	0	B	29	3.65	21	1	1	A
14	3.26	25	0	1	A	30	4.00	23	1	1	A
15	3.53	26	0	0	B	31	3.10	21	1	0	C
16	2.74	19	0	0	B	32	2.39	19	1	1	A

Source: Spector and Mazzeo, op. cit. This table is reproduced from Aldrich and Nelson, op. cit., p. 16.

16.10. In the probit model (16.11.5), the disturbance u_i has this variance:

$$\sigma_u^2 = \frac{P_i(1 - P_i)}{N_i f_i^2}$$

where f_i is the standard normal density function evaluated at $F^{-1}(P_i)$.

(a) Given the preceding variance of u_i, how would you transform (16.11.5) to make the resulting error term homoscedastic?

(b) Use the data of Table 16.7 to show the transformed data.

(c) Reestimate (16.12.1) using WLS and compare the results of the two regressions.

16.11. Since R^2 as a measure of goodness of fit is not particularly well-suited for the dichotomous dependent variable models, one suggested alternative is the χ^2 test described below:

$$\chi^2 = \sum_{i=1}^{G} \frac{N_i(\hat{P}_i - P_i^*)^2}{P_i^*(1 - P_i^*)}$$

where N_i = number of observations in the ith cell

P_i = actual probability of the event occurring ($= n_i/N_i$)

P_I^* = estimated probability

G = number of cells (i.e., the number of levels at which X_i is measured, e.g., 10 in Table 16.4)

It can be shown that for large samples χ^2 is distributed according to the χ^2 distribution with $(G - k)$ df, where k is the number of parameters in the estimating model ($k < G$).

Apply the preceding χ^2 test to regression (16.9.1) and comment on the resulting goodness of fit and compare it with the reported R^2 value.

16.12. The following table gives data on the results of spraying rotenone of different concentrations on the chrysanthemum aphis in batches of approximately fifty.

Toxicity study and rotenone on Chyrsanthemum Aphis

Concentration, milligrams per liter		Total,	Death,	
X	$\log(X)$	N_i	n_i	$\hat{P}_i = n_i/N_i$
2.6	0.4150	50	6	0.120
3.8	0.5797	48	16	0.333
5.1	0.7076	46	24	0.522
7.7	0.8865	49	42	0.857
10.2	1.0086	50	44	0.880

Source: D. J. Fennet, *Probit Analysis,* Cambridge University Press, London, 1964.

Develop a suitable model to express the probability of death as a function of the log of X, the log of dosage, and comment on the results. Also compute the χ^2 test of fit discussed in Exercise 16.11.

16.13. Fourteen applicants to a graduate program had the following quantitative and verbal scores on the GRE. Six students were admitted to the program.

	GRE aptitude test scores		Admitted to graduate program
Student number	Quantitative, Q	Verbal, V	(Yes = 1, No = 0)
1	760	550	1
2	600	350	0
3	720	320	0
4	710	630	1
5	530	430	0
6	650	570	0
7	800	500	1
8	650	680	1
9	520	660	0
10	800	250	0
11	670	480	0
12	670	520	1
13	780	710	1

Source: Donald F. Morrison, *Applied Linear Statistical Methods,* Prentice-Hall, Inc., Englewood Cliffs, N.J., 1983, p. 279 (adapted).

(*a*) Use the LPM model to predict the probability of admission to the program based on quantitative and verbal scores in the GRE.

(*b*) Is this a satisfactory model? If not, what alternative(s) do you suggest?

16.14. To study the effectiveness of a price discount coupon on a six-pack of a two-liter soft drink, Douglas Montgomery and Elizabeth Peck collected the data shown in the following table. A sample of 5500 consumers was randomly assigned to the eleven discount categories shown in the table, 500 per category. The response variable is whether or not consumers redeemed the coupon within one month.

(*a*) See if the logit model fits the data, treating the redemption rate as the dependent variable and price discount as the explanatory variable.

(*b*) See if the probit model does as well as the logit model.

(*c*) What is the predicted redemption rate if the price discount was 17 cents?

Price discount $X, ¢$	Sample size N_i	Number of coupons redeemed n_i
5	500	100
7	500	122
9	500	147
11	500	176
13	500	211
15	500	244
17	500	277
19	500	310
21	500	343
23	500	372
25	500	391

Source: Douglas C. Montgomery and Elizabeth A. Peck, *Introduction to Linear Regression Analysis,* John Wiley & Sons, New York, 1982, p. 243 (notation changed).

(d) Estimate the price discount for which 70 percent of the coupons will be redeemed.

16.15. To find out who has a bank account (checking, savings, etc.,) and who doesn't, John Caskey and Andrew Peterson estimated a probit model for the years 1977 and 1989, using data on U.S. households. The results are given in the accompanying table (p. 582). The values of the slope coefficients given in the table measure the implied effect of a unit change in a regressor on the probability that a household has a bank account, these marginal effects being calculated at the mean values of the regressors included in the model.
(a) For 1977, what is the effect of marital status on ownership of a bank account? And for 1989? Do these results make economic sense?
(b) Why is the coefficient for the *minority* variable negative for both 1977 and 1989?
(c) How can you rationalize the negative sign for the number of children variable?
(d) What does the chi-square statistic given in the table suggest? (*Hint:* exercise 16.11).

16.16. Monte Carlo Study: As an aid to understanding the probit model, William Becker and Donald Waldman assumed the following:[*]

$$E(Y \mid X) = -1 + 3X$$

Then, letting $Y_i = -1 + 3X + \varepsilon_i$, where ε_i is assumed standard normal (i.e., zero mean and unit variance), they generated a sample of 35 observations as shown in the table on page 583.
(a) From the data on Y and X given in this table, can you estimate an LPM? Remember that the true $E(Y \mid X) = -1 + 3X$.
(b) Given $X = 0.48$, estimate $E(Y \mid X = 0.48)$ and compare it with the true $E(Y \mid X = 0.48)$. Note $\bar{X} = 0.48$.

---

[*]William E. Becker and Donald M. Waldman, "A Graphical Interpretation of Probit Coefficients," *Journal of Economic Education*, vol. 20, no. 4, Fall 1989, pp. 371–378.

Probit regressions where dependent variable is ownership of a deposit account

	1977 data		1989 data	
	Coefficients	Implied slope	Coefficients	Implied slope
Constant	−1.06		−2.20	
	(3.3)*		(6.8)*	
Income (thousands 1991 $)	0.030	0.002	0.025	0.002
	(6.9)		(6.8)	
Married	0.127	0.008	0.235	0.023
	(0.8)		(1.7)	
Number of children	−0.131	−0.009	−0.084	−0.008
	(3.6)		(2.0)	
Age of head of household (HH)	0.006	0.0004	0.021	0.002
	(1.7)		(6.3)	
Education of HH	0.121	0.008	0.128	0.012
	(7.4)		(7.7)	
Male HH	−0.078	−0.005	−0.144	−0.011
	(0.5)		(0.9)	
Minority	−0.750	−0.050	−0.600	−0.058
	(6.8)		(6.5)	
Employed	0.186	0.012	0.402	0.039
	(1.6)		(3.6)	
Homeowner	0.520	0.035	0.522	0.051
	(4.7)		(5.3)	
Log-likelihood	−430.7		−526.0	
Chi squared statistic	408		602	
(H_0: All coefficients except constant equal zero)				
Number of observations	2,025		2,091	
Percentage in sample with correct predictions	91		90	

Source: John P. Caskey and Andrew Peterson, "Who Has a Bank Account and Who Doesn't: 1977 and 1989, Research Working Paper #93-10, Federal Reserve Bank of Kansas City, October 1993.

*Numbers in parenthesis are t statistics.

(c) Using the data on Y^* and X given in the table on the facing page, estimate a probit model. You may use any statistical package you want. The authors' estimated probit model is the following:

$$\hat{Y}_i^* = -0.969 + 2.764X_i$$

Find out the $P(Y^* = 1 \mid X = 0.48)$ that is, $P(Y_1 > 0 \mid X = 0.48)$. See if your answer agrees with the authors' answer of 0.64.

(d) The sample standard deviation of the X values given in the this table is 0.31. What is the predicted change in probability if X is one standard deviation above the mean value, that is, what is $P(Y^* = 1 \mid X = 0.79)$? The authors' answer is 0.25.

Hypothetical data set generated by the model $Y = -1 + 3X + \varepsilon$ and $Y^* = 1$ if $Y > 0$

Y	Y*	X
−0.3786	0	0.29
1.1974	1	0.59
−0.4648	0	0.14
1.1400	1	0.81
0.3188	1	0.35
2.2013	1	1.00
2.4473	1	0.80
0.1153	1	0.40
0.4110	1	0.07
2.6950	1	0.87
2.2009	1	0.98
0.6389	1	0.28
4.3192	1	0.99
−1.9906	0	0.04
−0.9021	0	0.37
0.9433	1	0.94
−3.2235	0	0.04
0.1690	1	0.07
−0.3753	0	0.56
1.9701	1	0.61
−0.4054	0	0.17
2.4416	1	0.89
0.8150	1	0.65
−0.1223	0	0.23
0.1428	1	0.26
−0.6681	0	0.64
1.8286	1	0.67
−0.6459	0	0.26
2.9784	1	0.63
−2.3326	0	0.09
0.8056	1	0.54
−0.8983	0	0.74
−0.2355	0	0.17
1.1429	1	0.57
−0.2965	0	0.18

Source: William E. Becker and Donald M. Waldman, "A Graphical Interpretation of Probit Coefficients," *Journal of Economic Education,* Fall 1989, Table 1, p. 373.

CHAPTER
17

DYNAMIC ECONOMETRIC MODELS: AUTOREGRESSIVE AND DISTRIBUTED-LAG MODELS

In regression analysis involving time series data, if the regression model includes not only the current but also the lagged (past) values of the explanatory variables (the X's), it is called a **distributed-lag model**. If the model includes one or more lagged values of the dependent variable among its explanatory variables, it is called an **autoregressive model**. Thus,

$$Y_t = \alpha + \beta_0 X_t + \beta_1 X_{t-1} + \beta_2 X_{t-2} + u_t$$

represents a distributed-lag model, whereas

$$Y_t = \alpha + \beta X_t + \gamma Y_{t-1} + u_t$$

is an example of an autoregressive model. The latter are also known as **dynamic models** since they portray the time path of the dependent variable in relation to its past value(s).

Autoregressive and distributed-lag models are used extensively in econometric analysis, and in this chapter we take a close look at such models with a view to finding out the following:

1. What is the role of lags in economics?
2. What are the reasons for the lags?
3. Is there any theoretical justification for the commonly used lagged models in empirical econometrics?

584

4. What is the relationship, if any, between autoregressive and distributed-lag models? Can one be derived from the other?

5. What are some of the statistical problems involved in estimating such models?

6. Does a lead-lag relationship between variables imply causality? If so, how does one measure it?

17.1 THE ROLE OF "TIME," OR "LAG," IN ECONOMICS

In economics the dependence of a variable Y (the dependent variable) on another variable(s) X (the explanatory variable) is rarely instantaneous. Very often, Y responds to X with a lapse of time. Such a lapse of time is called a *lag*. To illustrate the nature of the lag, we consider several examples.

> **Example 17.1 The consumption function.** Suppose a person receives a salary increase of \$2000 in annual pay, and suppose that this is a "permanent" increase in the sense that the increase in salary is maintained. What will be the effect of this increase in income on the person's annual consumption expenditure?
>
> Following such a gain in income, people usually do not rush to spend all the increase immediately. Thus, our recipient may decide to increase consumption expenditure by \$800 in the first year following the salary increase in income, by another \$600 in the next year, and by another \$400 in the following year, saving the remainder. By the end of the third year, the person's annual consumption expenditure will be increased by \$1800. We can thus write the consumption function as
>
> $$Y_t = \text{constant} + 0.4X_t + 0.3X_{t-1} + 0.2X_{t-2} + u_t \qquad (17.1.1)$$
>
> where Y is consumption expenditure and X is income.
>
> Equation (17.1.1) shows that the effect of an increase in income of \$2000 is spread, or distributed, over a period of three years. Models such as (17.1.1) are therefore called **distributed-lag models** because the effect of a given cause (income) is spread over a number of time periods. Geometrically, the distributed-lag model (17.1.1) is shown in Fig. 17.1, or alternatively, in Fig. 17.2.

More generally we may write

$$Y_t = \alpha + \beta_0 X_t + \beta_1 X_{t-1} + \beta_2 X_{t-2} + \cdots + \beta_k X_{t-k} + u_t \qquad (17.1.2)$$

which is a distributed-lag model with a finite lag of k time periods. The coefficient β_0 is known as the **short-run**, or **impact**, **multiplier** because it gives the change in the mean value of Y following a unit change in X in the same time period.[1] If the change in X is maintained at the same level thereafter, then, $(\beta_0 + \beta_1)$ gives the change in (the mean value of) Y in the next period, $(\beta_0 + \beta_1 + \beta_2)$ in the following period, and so on. These partial sums are called **interim**, or **intermediate, multipliers**. Finally, after k periods we obtain

---

[1] Technically, β_0 is the partial derivative of Y with respect to X_t, β_1 that with respect to X_{t-1}, β_2 that with respect to X_{t-2}, and so forth. Symbolically, $\partial Y_t / \partial X_{t-k} = \beta_k$.

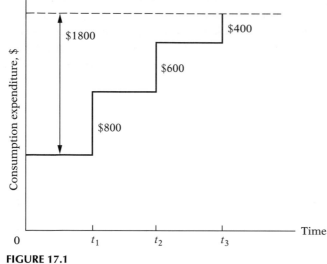

FIGURE 17.1
Example of distributed lags.

$$\sum_{i=0}^{k} \beta_i = \beta_0 + \beta_1 + \beta_2 + \cdots + \beta_k = \beta \qquad (17.1.3)$$

which is known as the **long-run**, or **total, distributed-lag multiplier**, provided the sum β exists (to be discussed elsewhere).

If we define

$$\beta_i^* = \frac{\beta_i}{\sum \beta_i} = \frac{\beta_i}{\beta} \qquad (17.1.4)$$

we obtain "standardized" β_i. Partial sums of the standardized β_i then give the proportion of the long-run, or total, impact felt by a certain time period.

Returning to the consumption regression (17.1.1), we see that the short-run multiplier, which is nothing but the short-run marginal propensity to consume (MPC), is 0.4, whereas the long-run multiplier, which is the long-run

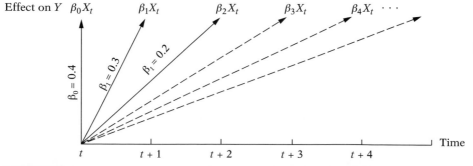

FIGURE 17.2
The effect of a unit change in X at time t on Y at time t and subsequent time periods.

marginal propensity to consume, is $0.4 + 0.3 + 0.2 = 0.9$. That is, following a $1 increase in income, the consumer will increase his or her level of consumption by about 40 cents in the year of increase, by another 30 cents in the next year, and by yet another 20 cents in the following year. The long-run impact of an increase of $1 in income is thus 90 cents. If we divide each β_i by 0.9, we obtain, respectively, 0.44, 0.33, and 0.23, which indicate that 44 percent of the total impact of a unit change in X on Y is felt immediately, 77 percent after one year, and 100 percent by the end of the second year.

Example 17.2. Creation of bank money (demand deposits). Suppose the Federal Reserve System pours $1000 of new money into the banking system by buying government securities. What will be the total amount of bank money, or demand deposits, that will be generated ultimately?

Following the fractional reserve system, if we assume that the law requires banks to keep a 20 percent reserve backing for the deposits they create, then by the well-known multiplier process the total amount of demand deposits that will be generated will be equal to $1000[1/(1 - 0.8)] = 5000. Of course, $5000 in demand deposits will be not created overnight. The process takes time, which can be shown schematically in Fig. 17.3.

Example 17.3. Link between money and prices. According to the monetarists, inflation is essentially a monetary phenomenon in the sense that a continuous increase in the general price level is due to the rate of expansion in money supply far in excess of the amount of money actually demanded by the economic units. Of course, this link between inflation and changes in money supply is not

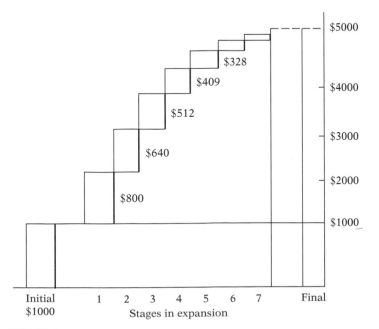

FIGURE 17.3
Cumulative expansion in bank deposits (initial reserve $1000 and 20 percent reserve requirement).

instantaneous. Studies have shown that the lag between the two is anywhere from 3 to about 20 quarters. The results of one such study are shown in Table 17.1,[2] where we see the effect of a 1 percent change in the M1B money supply (= currency + checkable deposits at financial institutions) is felt over a period of 20 quarters. The long-run impact of a 1 percent change in the money supply on inflation is about $1(=\sum m_i)$, which is statistically significant, whereas the short-run impact is about 0.04, which is not significant, although the intermediate multipliers seem to be generally significant. Incidentally, note that since P and M are both in percent forms, the m_i (β_i in our usual notation) give the elasticity of P with respect to M, that is, the percent response of prices to a 1 percent increase in the money supply. Thus, $m_0 = 0.041$ means that for a 1 percent increase in the money supply the short-run elasticity of prices is about 0.04 percent. The long-term elasticity is 1.03 percent, implying that in the long run a 1 percent increase in the money supply is reflected by just about the same percentage increase in the prices. In short, a 1 percent increase in the money supply is accompanied in the long run by a 1 percent increase in the inflation rate.

Example 17.4. Lag between R&D expenditure and productivity. The
decision to invest in research and development (R&D) expenditure and its ultimate payoff in terms of increased productivity involve considerable lag, actually several lags, such as, "... the lag between the investment of funds and the time inventions

TABLE 17.1
Estimate of money-price equation: Original specification

Sample period: 1955–I to 1969–IV: $m_{21} = 0$

$$\dot{P} = -.146 + \sum_{i=0}^{20} m_i \dot{M}_{-i}$$
$$(.395)$$

	Coeff.	$\|t\|$		Coeff.	$\|t\|$		Coeff.	$\|t\|$
m_0	0.041	1.276	m_8	0.048	3.249	m_{16}	0.069	3.943
m_1	0.034	1.538	m_9	0.054	3.783	m_{17}	0.062	3.712
m_2	0.030	1.903	m_{10}	0.059	4.305	m_{18}	0.053	3.511
m_3	0.029	2.171	m_{11}	0.065	4.673	m_{19}	0.039	3.338
m_4	0.030	2.235	m_{12}	0.069	4.795	m_{20}	0.022	3.191
m_5	0.033	2.294	m_{13}	0.072	4.694	$\sum m_i$	1.031	7.870
m_6	0.037	2.475	m_{14}	0.073	4.468	**Mean lag**	10.959	5.634
m_7	0.042	2.798	m_{15}	0.072	4.202			

$\bar{R}^2$	0.525
se	1.066
D.W.	2.00

Notation: $\dot{P}$ = compounded annual rate of change of GNP deflator
$\dot{M}$ = compounded annual rate of change of M1B

Source: Keith M. Carlson, "The Lag from Money to Prices," *Review,* Federal Reserve Bank of St. Louis, October 1980, Table 1, p. 4.

---

[2]Keith M. Carlson, "The Lag from Money to Prices," *Review*, Federal Reserve Bank of St. Louis, October, 1980, Table 1, p. 4.

actually begin to appear, the lag between the invention of an idea or device and its development up to a commercially applicable stage, and the lag which is introduced by the process of diffusion: it takes time before all the old machines are replaced by the better new ones."[3]

The preceding examples are only a sample of the use of lag in economics. Undoubtedly, the reader can produce several examples from his or her own experience.

17.2 THE REASONS FOR LAGS[4]

Although the examples cited in Section 17.1 point out the nature of lagged phenomena, they do not fully explain why lags occur. There are three main reasons:

1. **Psychological reasons.** As a result of the force of habit (inertia), people do not change their consumption habits immediately following a price decrease or an income increase perhaps because the process of change may involve some immediate disutility. Thus, those who become instant millionaires by winning lotteries may not change the lifestyles to which they were accustomed for a long time because they may not know how to react to such a windfall gain immediately. Of course, given reasonable time, they may learn to live with their newly acquired fortune. Also, people may not know whether a change is "permanent" or "transitory." Thus, my reaction to an increase in my income will depend on whether or not the increase is permanent. If it is only a nonrecurring increase and in succeeding periods my income returns to its previous level, I may save the entire increase, whereas someone else in my position might decide to "live it up."

2. **Technological reasons.** Suppose the price of capital relative to labor declines, making substitution of capital for labor economically feasible. Of course, addition of capital takes time (the gestation period). Moreover, if the drop in price is expected to be temporary, firms may not rush to substitute capital for labor, especially if they expect that after the temporary drop the price of capital may increase beyond its previous level. Sometimes, imperfect knowledge also accounts for lags. At present the market for personal computers is glutted with all kinds of computers with varying features and prices. Moreover, since their introduction in the late 1970s, the prices of most personal computers have dropped dramatically. As a result, prospective consumers for the personal computer may hesitate to buy until they have had time to look into the features and prices of all the competing brands. Moreover, they may hesitate to buy in the expectation of further decline in price or innovations.

---

[3]Zvi Griliches, "Distributed Lags: A Survey," *Econometrica*, vol. 36, no. 1, January 1967, pp. 16–49.

[4]This section leans heavily on Marc Nerlove, *Distributed Lags and Demand Analysis for Agricultural and Other Commodities*, Agricultural Handbook No. 141, U.S. Department of Agriculture, June 1958.

3. **Institutional reasons.** These reasons also contribute to lags. For example, contractual obligations may prevent firms from switching from one source of labor or raw material to another. As another example, those who have placed funds in long-term savings accounts for fixed durations such as one year, three years, or seven years, are essentially "locked in" even though money market conditions may be such that higher yields are available elsewhere. Similarly, employers often give their employees a choice among several health insurance plans, but once a choice is made, an employee may not switch to another plan for at least 1 year. Although this may be done for administrative convenience, the employee is locked in for 1 year.

For the reasons just discussed, lag occupies a central role in economics. This is clearly reflected in the short-run–long-run methodology of economics. It is for this reason we say that short-run price or income elasticities are generally smaller (in absolute value) than the corresponding long-run elasticities or that short-run marginal propensity to consume is generally smaller than long-run marginal propensity to consume.

17.3 ESTIMATION OF DISTRIBUTED-LAG MODELS

Granted that distributed-lag models play a highly useful role in economics, how does one estimate such models? Specifically, suppose we have the following distributed-lag model in one explanatory variable:[5]

$$Y_t = \alpha + \beta_0 X_t + \beta_1 X_{t-1} + \beta_2 X_{t-2} + \cdots + u_t \qquad (17.3.1)$$

where we have not defined the length of the lag, that is, how far back into the past we want to go. Such a model is called an **infinite (lag) model**, whereas a model of the type (17.1.2) is called a **finite (lag) distributed-lag model** because the length of the lag k is specified. We shall continue to use (17.3.1) because it is easy to handle mathematically, as we shall see.[6]

How do we estimate the α and β's of (17.3.1)? We may adopt two approaches: (1) ad hoc estimation and (2) a priori restrictions on the β's by assuming that the β's follow some systematic pattern. We shall consider ad hoc estimation in this section and the other approach in Section 17.4.

Ad Hoc Estimation of Distributed-Lag Models

Since the explanatory variable X_t is assumed to be nonstochastic (or at least uncorrelated with the disturbance term u_t), X_{t-1}, X_{t-2}, and so on, are non-

---

[5]If there is more than one explanatory variable in the model, each variable may have a lagged effect on Y. For simplicity only, we assume one explanatory variable.

[6]In practice, however, the coefficients of the distant X values are expected to have negligible effect on Y.

stochastic, too. Therefore, in principle, the ordinary least squares (OLS) can be applied to (17.3.1). This is the approach taken by Alt[7] and Tinbergen.[8] They suggest that to estimate (17.3.1) one may proceed *sequentially*; that is, first regress Y_t on X_t, then regress Y_t on X_t and X_{t-1}, then regress Y_t on X_t, X_{t-1}, and X_{t-2}, and so on. This sequential procedure stops when the regression coefficients of the lagged variables start becoming statistically insignificant and/or the coefficient of at least one of the variables changes signs from positive to negative or vice versa. Following this precept, Alt regressed fuel oil consumption Y on new orders X. Based on the quarterly data for the period 1930–1939, the results were as follows:

$$\hat{Y}_t = 8.37 + 0.171X_t$$
$$\hat{Y}_t = 8.27 + 0.111X_t + 0.064X_{t-1}$$
$$\hat{Y}_t = 8.27 + 0.109X_t + 0.071X_{t-1} - 0.055X_{t-2}$$
$$\hat{Y}_t = 8.32 + 0.108X_t + 0.063X_{t-1} + 0.022X_{t-2} - 0.020X_{t-3}$$

Alt chose the second regression as the "best" one because in the last two equations the sign of X_{t-2} was not stable and in the last equation the sign of X_{t-3} was negative, which may be difficult to interpret economically.

Although seemingly straightforward, ad hoc estimation suffers from many drawbacks, such as the following:

1. There is no a priori guide as to what is the maximum length of the lag.[9]
2. As one estimates successive lags, there are fewer degrees of freedom left, making statistical inference somewhat shaky. Economists are not usually that lucky to have a long series of data so that they can go on estimating numerous lags.
3. More importantly, in economic time series data, successive values (lags) tend to be highly correlated; hence multicollinearity rears its ugly head. As noted in Chapter 10, multicollinearity leads to imprecise estimation; that is, the standard errors tend to be large in relation to the estimated coefficients. As a result, based on the routinely computed t ratios, we may tend to declare (erroneously), that a lagged coefficient(s) is statistically insignificant.
4. The sequential search for the lag length opens the researcher to the charge of **data mining**. Also, as we noted in Section 13.4, the nominal and true level of significance to test statistical hypotheses becomes an important issue in such sequential searches [see Eq. (13.4.2)].

In view of the preceding problems, the ad hoc estimation procedure has very little to recommend it. Clearly, some prior or theoretical considerations

---

[7]F. F. Alt, "Distributed Lags," *Econometrica*, vol. 10, 1942, pp. 113–128.
[8]J. Tinbergen, "Long-Term Foreign Trade Elasticities," *Metroeconomica*, vol. 1, 1949, pp. 174–185.
[9]If the lag length, k, is incorrectly specified, we will have to contend with the problem of misspecification errors discussed in Chap. 13. Also keep in mind the warning about **data mining**.

must be brought to bear upon the various β's if we are to make headway with the estimation problem.

17.4 THE KOYCK APPROACH TO DISTRIBUTED-LAG MODELS

Koyck has proposed an ingenious method of estimating distributed-lag models. Suppose we start with the infinite lag distributed-lag model (17.3.1). *Assuming that the β's are all of the same sign*, Koyck assumes that they decline geometrically as follows.[10]

$$\beta_k = \beta_0 \lambda^k \qquad k = 0, 1, \dots \qquad (17.4.1)[11]$$

where λ, such that $0 < \lambda < 1$, is known as the *rate of decline*, or *decay*, of the distributed lag and where $1 - \lambda$ is known as the *speed of adjustment*.

What (17.4.1) postulates is that each successive β coefficient is numerically less than each preceding β (this statement follows since $\lambda < 1$), implying that as one goes back into the distant past, the effect of that lag on Y_t becomes progressively smaller, a quite plausible assumption. After all, current and recent past incomes are expected to affect current consumption expenditure more heavily than income in the distant past. Geometrically, the Koyck scheme is depicted in Fig. 17.4.

As this figure shows, the value of the lag coefficient β_k depends, apart from the common β_0, on the value of λ. The closer λ is to 1, the slower the rate of decline in β_k, whereas the closer it is to zero, the more rapid the decline in β_k. In the former case, distant past values of X will exert sizable impact on Y_t, whereas in the latter case their influence on Y_t will peter out quickly. This pattern can be seen clearly from the following illustration:

λ	β_0	β_1	β_2	β_3	β_4	β_5	$\cdots$	β_{10}
0.75	β_0	$0.75\beta_0$	$0.56\beta_0$	$0.42\beta_0$	$0.32\beta_0$	$0.24\beta_0$	$\cdots$	$0.06\beta_0$
0.25	β_0	$0.25\beta_0$	$0.06\beta_0$	$0.02\beta_0$	$0.004\beta_0$	$0.001\beta_0$	$\cdots$	0.0

Note these features of the Koyck scheme: (1) By assuming nonnegative values for λ, Koyck rules out the β's from changing sign; (2) by assuming $\lambda < 1$,

---

[10]L. M. Koyck, *Distributed Lags and Investment Analysis*, North Holland Publishing Company, Amsterdam, 1954.

[11]Sometimes this is also written as

$$\beta_k = \beta_0(1 - \lambda)\lambda^k \qquad k = 0, 1, \dots$$

for reasons given in footnote 12.

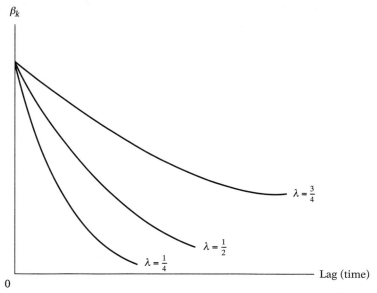

β_k

$\lambda = \frac{3}{4}$

$\lambda = \frac{1}{2}$

$\lambda = \frac{1}{4}$

Lag (time)

0

FIGURE 17.4
Koyck scheme (declining geometric distribution).

he gives lesser weight to the distant β's than the current ones; and (3) he ensures that the sum of the β's, which gives the long-run multiplier, is finite, namely,

$$\sum_{k=0}^{\infty} \beta_k = \beta_0 \left(\frac{1}{1-\lambda} \right) \qquad (17.4.2)^{12}$$

As a result of (17.4.1), the infinite lag model (17.3.1) may be written as

$$Y_t = \alpha + \beta_0 X_t + \beta_0 \lambda X_{t-1} + \beta_0 \lambda^2 X_{t-2} + \cdots + u_t \qquad (17.4.3)$$

As it stands, the model is still not amenable to easy estimation since a large (literally infinite) number of parameters remain to be estimated and the parameter λ enters in a highly nonlinear form: Strictly speaking, the method of linear (in the parameters) regression analysis cannot be applied to such a model. But now Koyck suggests an ingenious way out. He lags (17.4.3) by one period to obtain

$$Y_{t-1} = \alpha + \beta_0 X_{t-1} + \beta_0 \lambda X_{t-2} + \beta_0 \lambda^2 X_{t-3} + \cdots + u_{t-1} \qquad (17.4.4)$$

---

[12]This is because

$$\sum \beta_k = \beta_0 (1 + \lambda + \lambda^2 + \lambda^3 + \cdots) = \beta_0 \left(\frac{1}{1-\lambda} \right)$$

since the expression in the parentheses on the right side is an infinite geometric series whose sum is $1 / (1 - \lambda)$ provided $0 < \lambda < 1$. In passing, note that if β_k is as defined in footnote 11, $\sum \beta_k = \beta_0 (1 - \lambda) / (1 - \lambda) = \beta_0$ thus ensuring that the weights $(1 - \lambda)\lambda^k$ sum to one.

He then multiplies (17.4.4) by λ to obtain

$$\lambda Y_{t-1} = \lambda\alpha + \lambda\beta_0 X_{t-1} + \beta_0\lambda^2 X_{t-2} + \beta_0\lambda^3 X_{t-3} + \cdots + \lambda u_{t-1} \quad (17.4.5)$$

Subtracting (17.4.5) from (17.4.3), he gets

$$Y_t - \lambda Y_{t-1} = \alpha(1 - \lambda) + \beta_0 X_t + (u_t - \lambda u_{t-1}) \quad (17.4.6)$$

or, rearranging,

$$Y_t = \alpha(1 - \lambda) + \beta_0 X_t + \lambda Y_{t-1} + v_t \quad (17.4.7)$$

where $v_t = (u_t - \lambda u_{t-1})$, **a moving average of u_t and u_{t-1}**.

The procedure just described is known as the **Koyck transformation**. Comparing (17.4.7) with (17.3.1), we see the tremendous simplification accomplished by Koyck. Whereas before we had to estimate α and an infinite number of β's, we now have to estimate only three unknowns: α, β_0, and λ. Now there is no reason to expect multicollinearity. In a sense multicollinearity is resolved by replacing $X_{t-1}, X_{t-2}, \ldots$, by a single variable, namely, Y_{t-1}. But note the following features of the Koyck transformation:

1. We started with a distributed-lag model but ended up with an autoregressive model because Y_{t-1} appears as one of the explanatory variables. This transformation shows how one can "convert" a distributed-log model into an autoregressive model.

2. The appearance of Y_{t-1} is likely to create some statistical problems. Y_{t-1}, like Y_t, is stochastic, which means that we have a stochastic explanatory variable in the model. Recall that the classical least-squares theory is predicated on the assumption that the explanatory variables either are nonstochastic or, if stochastic, are distributed independently of the stochastic disturbance term. Hence, we must find out if Y_{t-1} satisfies this assumption. (We shall return to this point in Section 17.8.)

3. In the original model (17.3.1) the disturbance term was u_t, whereas in the transformed model it is $v_t = (u_t - \lambda u_{t-1})$. The statistical properties of v_t depend on what is assumed about the statistical properties of u_t, for, as shown later, if the original u_t's are serially uncorrelated, the v_t's are serially correlated. Therefore, we may have to face up to the serial correlation problem in addition to the stochastic explanatory variable Y_{t-1}. We shall do that in Section 17.8.

4. The presence of lagged Y violates one of the assumptions underlying the Durbin-Watson d test. Therefore, we will have to develop an alternative to test for serial correlation in the presence of lagged Y. One alternative is the **Durbin h test**, which is discussed in Section 17.10.

As we saw in (17.1.4), the partial sums of the standardized β_i tell us the proportion of the long-run, or total, impact felt by a certain time period. In practice, though, the **mean** or **median lag** is often used to characterize the nature of the lag structure of a distributed lag model.

The Median Lag

The median lag is the time required for the first half, or 50 percent, of the total change in Y following a unit sustained change in X. For the Koyck model, the median lag is as follows (see exercise 17.6):

$$\text{Koyck model: Median lag} = -\frac{\log 2}{\log \lambda} \qquad (17.4.8)$$

Thus, if $\lambda = 0.2$ the median lag is 0.4306, but if $\lambda = 0.8$ the median lag is 3.1067. Verbally, in the former case 50 percent of the total change in Y is accomplished in less than half a period, whereas in the latter case it takes more than 3 periods to accomplish the 50 percent change. But this contrast should not be surprising, for as we know, the higher the value of λ the lower the speed of adjustment, and the lower the value of λ the greater the speed of adjustment.

The Mean Lag

Provided all β_k are positive, the mean, or average, lag is defined as

$$\text{Mean lag} = \frac{\sum_0^\infty k\beta_k}{\sum_0^\infty \beta_k} \qquad (17.4.9)$$

which is simply the weighted average of all the lags involved, with the respective β coefficients serving as weights. In short, it is a **lag-weighted average** of time. For the Koyck model the mean lag is (see exercise 17.7)

$$\text{Koyck model: Mean lag} = \frac{\lambda}{1-\lambda} \qquad (17.4.10)$$

Thus, if $\lambda = \frac{1}{2}$, the mean lag is 1.

From the preceding discussion it is clear that the median and mean lags serve as a summary measure of the speed with which Y responds to X. In the example given in Table 17.1 the mean lag is about 11 quarters, showing that it takes quite some time, on the average, for the effect of changes in the money supply to be felt on price changes.

> **Example 17.5. Per capita personal consumption expenditure (PPCE) in relation to per capita disposable personal income (PDPI), United States.** Let us revisit the PPCE/PDPI example discussed in Chapter 14. For easy reference, we reproduce Eq. (14.4.10) here:
>
> $$\widehat{\text{PPCE}}_t = -841.8568 + 0.7117\,\text{PDPI}_t + 0.2954\,\text{PPCE}_{t-1}$$
> $$t = \quad (-2.4137) \quad (5.4634) \qquad (2.3681) \qquad\qquad (17.4.11)$$
> $$R^2 = 0.9912 \quad d = 1.0144$$

Note: The d statistic will be discussed under the heading of h statistic later in the text.

If we assume that this model resulted from a Koyck-type transformation, λ is 0.2954. The median lag is $-(\log 2 / \log \lambda) = -(\log 2 / \log 0.2954) = 0.5684$, and the mean lag is $(0.2954/0.7046) = 0.4192$. In other words, PPCE adjusts to PDPI within a relatively short time.

17.5 RATIONALIZATION OF THE KOYCK MODEL: THE ADAPTIVE EXPECTATIONS MODEL

Although very neat, the Koyck model (17.4.7) is ad hoc since it was obtained by a purely algebraic process; it is devoid of any theoretical underpinning. But this gap can be filled if we start from a different perspective. Suppose we postulate the following model:

$$Y_t = \beta_0 + \beta_1 X_t^* + u_t \qquad (17.5.1)$$

where Y = demand for money (real cash balances)

X^* = equilibrium, optimum, expected long-run or normal rate of interest

u = error term

Equation (17.5.1) postulates that the demand for money is a function of *expected* (in the sense of anticipation) rate of interest.

Since the expectational variable X^* is not directly observable, let us propose the following hypothesis about how expectations are formed:

$$X_t^* - X_{t-1}^* = \gamma(X_t - X_{t-1}^*) \qquad (17.5.2)[13]$$

where γ, such that $0 < \gamma \leq 1$, is known as the **coefficient of expectation**. Hypothesis (17.5.2) is known as the **adaptive expectation, progressive expectation**, or **error learning** hypothesis, popularized by Cagan[14] and Friedman.[15]

What (17.5.2) implies is that "economic agents will adapt their expectations in the light of past experience and that in particular they will learn from their mistakes."[16] More specifically, (17.5.2) states that expectations are revised

---

[13] Sometimes the model is expressed as

$$X_t^* - X_{t-1}^* = \gamma(X_{t-1} - X_{t-1}^*)$$

[14] P. Cagan, "The Monetary Dynamics of Hyperinflations," in M. Friedman (ed.), *Studies in the Quantity Theory of Money*, University of Chicago Press, Chicago, 1956.

[15] Milton Friedman, *A Theory of the Consumption Function*, National Bureau of Economic Research, Princeton University Press, Princeton, N.J., 1957.

[16] G. K. Shaw, *Rational Expectations: An Elementary Exposition*, St. Martin's Press, New York, 1984, p. 25.

each period by a fraction γ of the gap between the current value of the variable and its previous expected value. Thus, for our model this would mean that expectations about interest rates are revised each period by a fraction γ of the discrepancy between the rate of interest observed in the current period and what its anticipated value had been in the previous period. Another way of stating this would be to write (17.5.2) as

$$X_t^* = \gamma X_t + (1 - \gamma)X_{t-1}^* \tag{17.5.3}$$

which shows that the expected value of the rate of interest at time t is a weighted average of the actual value of the interest rate at time t and its value expected in the previous period, with weights of γ and $1 - \gamma$, respectively. If $\gamma = 1$, $X_t^* = X_t$, meaning that expectations are realized immediately and fully, that is, in the same time period. If, on the other hand, $\gamma = 0$, $X_t^* = X_{t-1}^*$, meaning that expectations are static, that is, "conditions prevailing today will be maintained in all subsequent periods. Expected future values then become identified with current values."[17]

Substituting (17.5.3) into (17.5.1), we obtain

$$\begin{aligned} Y_t &= \beta_0 + \beta_1[\gamma X_t + (1 - \gamma)X_{t-1}^*] + u_t \\ &= \beta_0 + \beta_1\gamma X_t + \beta_1(1 - \gamma)X_{t-1}^* + u_t \end{aligned} \tag{17.5.4}$$

Now lag (17.5.1) one period, multiply it by $1 - \gamma$, and subtract the product from (17.5.4). After simple algebraic manipulations, we obtain

$$\begin{aligned} Y_t &= \gamma\beta_0 + \gamma\beta_1 X_t + (1 - \gamma)Y_{t-1} + u_t - (1 - \gamma)u_{t-1} \\ &= \gamma\beta_0 + \gamma\beta_1 X_t + (1 - \gamma)Y_{t-1} + v_t \end{aligned} \tag{17.5.5}$$

where $v_t = u_t - (1 - \gamma)u_{t-1}$.

Before proceeding any further, let us note the difference between (17.5.1) and (17.5.5). In the former, β_1 measures the average response of Y to a unit change in X^*, the equilibrium or long-run value of X. In (17.5.5), on the other hand, $\gamma\beta_1$ measures the average response of Y to a unit change in the actual or observed value of X. These responses will not be the same unless, of course, $\gamma = 1$, that is, the current and long-run values of X are the same. In practice, we first estimate (17.5.5). Once an estimate of γ is obtained from the coefficient of lagged Y, we can easily compute β_1 by simply dividing the coefficient of $X_t(= \gamma\beta_1)$ by γ.

The similarity between the adaptive expectation model (17.5.5) and the Koyck model (17.4.7) should be readily apparent although the interpretations of the coefficients in the two models are different. Note that like the Koyck model, the adaptive expectations model is autoregressive and its error term is similar to the Koyck error term. We shall return to the estimation of the adaptive expectations model in Section 17.8 and to some examples in Section 17.12. Now that we have sketched the adaptive expectations (AE) model, how

---

[17]Ibid., pp. 19–20.

realistic is it? It is true that it is more appealing than the purely algebraic Koyck approach, but is the AE hypothesis reasonable? In favor of the AE hypothesis one can say the following:

> It provides a fairly simple means of modelling expectations in economic theory whilst postulating a mode of behaviour upon the part of economic agents which seems eminently sensible. The belief that people learn from experience is obviously a more sensible starting point than the implicit assumption that they are totally devoid of memory, characteristic of static expectations thesis. Moreover, the assertion that more distant experiences exert a lesser effect than more recent experience would accord with common sense and would appear to be amply confirmed by simple observation.[18]

Until the advent of the **rational expectations (RE) hypothesis**, initially put forward by J. Muth and later propagated by Robert Lucas and Thomas Sargent, the AE hypothesis was quite popular in empirical economics. The proponents of the RE hypothesis contend that the AE hypothesis is inadequate because it relies solely on the past values of a variable in formulating expectations,[19] whereas the RE hypothesis assumes, "that individual economic agents use *current available* and *relevant* information in forming their expectations and do not rely purely upon past experience."[20] In short, the RE hypothesis contends that "expectations are 'rational' in the sense that they efficiently incorporate *all* information available at the time the expectation is formulated"[21] and not just the past information.

The criticism directed by the RE proponents against the AE hypothesis is well-taken, although there are many critics of the RE hypothesis itself.[22] This is not the place to get bogged down with this rather heady material. Perhaps one could agree with Stephen McNees that, "At best, the adaptive expectations assumption can be defended only as a "working hypothesis" proxying for a more complex, perhaps changing expectations formulation mechanism."[23]

Example 17.6. Example 17.5 revisited. If we consider model (17.4.11) as generated by the adaptive expectations mechanism (i.e., PPCE a function of expected PDPI), then γ, the coefficient of expectations, can be obtained from (17.5.5) as $1 - 0.2954 = 0.7046$. Then following the preceding discussion about the AE model, we can say that about 70 percent of the discrepancy between actual and expected PDPI is eliminated within a year, a fairly rapid adjustment.

---

[18]Ibid., p. 27.

[19]Like the Koyck model, it can be shown that, under AE, expectations of a variable are an exponentially weighted average of past values of that variable.

[20]G. K. Shaw, op. cit., p. 47. For additional details of the RE hypothesis, see Steven M. Sheffrin, *Rational Expectations*, Cambridge University Press, New York, 1983.

[21]Stephen K. McNees, "The Phillips Curve: Forward- or Backward-Looking?" *New England Economic Review*, July-August 1979, p. 50.

[22]For a recent critical appraisal of the RE hypothesis, see Michael C. Lovell, "Test of the Rational Expectations Hypothesis," *American Economic Review*, March 1966, pp. 110–124.

[23]Stephen K. McNees, op. cit., p. 50.

17.6 ANOTHER RATIONALIZATION OF THE KOYCK MODEL: THE STOCK ADJUSTMENT, OR PARTIAL ADJUSTMENT, MODEL

The adaptive expectation model is one way of rationalizing the Koyck model. Another rationalization is provided by Marc Nerlove in the so-called **stock adjustment** or **partial adjustment model**.[24] To illustrate this model, consider the **flexible accelerator model** of economic theory, which assumes that there is an *equilibrium, optimal, desired,* or *long-run* amount of capital stock needed to produce a given output under the given state of technology, rate of interest, etc. For simplicity assume that this desired level of capital Y_t^* is a linear function of output X as follows:

$$Y_t^* = \beta_0 + \beta_1 X_t + u_t \qquad (17.6.1)$$

Since the desired level of capital is not directly observable, Nerlove postulates the following hypothesis, known as the **partial adjustment**, or **stock adjustment**, **hypothesis**:

$$Y_t - Y_{t-1} = \delta(Y_t^* - Y_{t-1}) \qquad (17.6.2)^{25}$$

where δ, such that $0 < \delta \le 1$, is known as the **coefficient of adjustment** and where $Y_t - Y_{t-1}$ = actual change and $(Y_t^* - Y_{t-1})$ = desired change.

Since $Y_t - Y_{t-1}$, the change in capital stock between two periods, is nothing but investment, (17.6.2) can alternatively be written as

$$I_t = \delta(Y_t^* - Y_{t-1}) \qquad (17.6.3)$$

where I_t = investment in time period t.

Equation (17.6.2) postulates that the actual change in capital stock (investment) in any given time period t is some fraction δ of the desired change for that period. If $\delta = 1$, it means that the actual stock of capital is equal to the desired stock; that is, actual stock adjusts to the desired stock instantaneously (in the same time period). However, if $\delta = 0$, it means that nothing changes since actual stock at time t is the same as that observed in the previous time period. Typically, δ is expected to lie between these extremes since adjustment to the desired stock of capital is likely to be incomplete because of rigidity, inertia, contractual obligations, etc.—hence the name **partial adjustment model**. Note that the adjustment mechanism (17.6.2) alternatively can be written as

---

[24] Marc Nerlove, *Distributed Lags and Demand Analysis for Agricultural and Other Commodities*, op. cit.

[25] Some authors do not add the stochastic disturbance term u_t to the relation (17.6.1) but add it to this relation, believing that if the former is truly an equilibrium relation, there is no scope for the error term, whereas the adjustment mechanism can be imperfect and may require the disturbance term. In passing, note that (17.6.2) is sometimes also written as

$$Y_t - Y_{t-1} = \delta(Y_{t-1}^* - Y_{t-1})$$

$$Y_t = \delta Y_t^* + (1 - \delta)Y_{t-1} \qquad (17.6.4)$$

showing that the observed capital stock at time t is a weighted average of the desired capital stock at that time and the capital stock existing in the previous time period, δ and $(1 - \delta)$ being the weights. Now substitution of (17.6.1) into (17.6.4) gives

$$\begin{aligned} Y_t &= \delta(\beta_0 + \beta_1 X_t + u_t) + (1 - \delta)Y_{t-1} \\ &= \delta\beta_0 + \delta\beta_1 X_t + (1 - \delta)Y_{t-1} + \delta u_t \end{aligned} \qquad (17.6.5)$$

This model is called the **partial adjustment model**.

Since (17.6.1) represents the long-run, or equilibrium, demand for capital stock, (17.6.5) can be called the *short-run* demand function for capital stock since in the short run the existing capital stock may not necessarily be equal to its long-run level. Once we estimate the short-run function (17.6.5) and obtain the estimate of the adjustment coefficient δ (from the coefficient of Y_{t-1}), we can easily derive the long-run function by simply dividing $\delta\beta_0$ and $\delta\beta_1$ by δ and omitting the lagged Y term, which will then give (17.6.1).

Geometrically, the partial adjustment model can be shown as in Fig. 17.5.[26] In this figure Y^* is the desired capital stock and Y_1 the current actual capital stock. For illustrative purposes assume that $\delta = 0.5$. This implies that the firm plans to close half the gap between the actual and the desired stock of capital each period. Thus, in the first period it moves to Y_2, with investment equal to $(Y_2 - Y_1)$, which in turn is equal to half of $(Y^* - Y_1)$. In each subsequent period it closes half the gap between the capital stock at the beginning of the period and the desired capital stock Y^*.

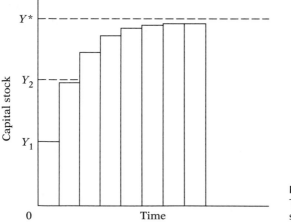

FIGURE 17.5
The gradual adjustment of the capital stock.

---

[26]This is adapted from Fig. 7.4 from Rudiger Dornbusch and Stanley Fischer, *Macroeconomics*, 3d ed., McGraw-Hill, New York, 1984, p 216.

The partial adjustment model resembles both the Koyck and adaptive expectation models in that it is autoregressive. But it has a much simpler disturbance term: the original disturbance term u_t multiplied by a constant δ. But bear in mind that although similar in appearance, the adaptive expectation and partial adjustment models are conceptually very different. The former is based on uncertainty (about the future course of prices, interest rates, etc.), whereas the latter is due to technical or institutional rigidities, inertia, cost of change, etc. However, both of these models are theoretically much sounder than the Koyck model.

Since in appearance the adaptive expectations and partial adjustment models are indistinguishable, the γ coefficient of 0.7046 of the adaptive expectations model can also be interpreted as the δ coefficient of the stock adjustment model if we assume that the latter model is operative in the present case (i.e., it is the desired or expected PPCE that is linearly related to the current PDPI).

The important point to keep in mind is that since Koyck, adaptive expectations, and stock adjustment models—apart from the difference in the appearance of the error term—yield the same final estimating model, one must be extremely careful in telling the reader which model the researcher is using and why. Thus, researchers must specify the theoretical underpinning of their model.

*17.7 COMBINATION OF ADAPTIVE EXPECTATIONS AND PARTIAL ADJUSTMENT MODELS

Consider the following model:

$$Y_t^* = \beta_0 + \beta_1 X_t^* + u_t \tag{17.7.1}$$

where Y_t^* = desired stock of capital and X_t^* = expected level of output.

Since both Y_t^* and X_t^* are not directly observable, one could use the partial adjustment mechanism for Y_t^* and the adaptive expectations model for X_t^* to arrive at the following estimating equation (see exercise 17.2):

$$
\begin{aligned}
Y_t &= \beta_0\,\delta\gamma + \beta_1\,\delta\gamma X_t + [(1-\gamma) + (1-\delta)]Y_{t-1} \\
&\quad - (1-\delta)(1-\gamma)Y_{t-2} + [\delta u_t - \delta(1-\gamma)u_{t-1}] \\
&= \alpha_0 + \alpha_1 X_t + \alpha_2 Y_{t-1} + \alpha_3 Y_{t-2} + v_t
\end{aligned}
\tag{17.7.2}
$$

where $v_t = \delta[u_t - (1-\gamma)u_{t-1}]$. This model too is autoregressive, the only difference from the purely adaptive expectations model being that Y_{t-2} appears along with Y_{t-1} as an explanatory variable. Like Koyck and the AE models, the error term in (17.7.2) follows a moving average process. Another feature of this model is that although the model is linear in the α's, it is nonlinear in the original parameters.

---

*Optional.

A celebrated application of (17.7.1) has been Friedman's permanent income hypothesis, which states that "permanent" or long-run consumption is a function of "permanent" or long-run income.[27]

The estimation of (17.7.2) presents the same estimation problems as the Koyck's or the AE model in that all these models are autoregressive with similar error structures. In addition, (17.7.2) involves some nonlinear estimation problems that we consider briefly in exercise 17.10, but do not delve into, in this book.

17.8 ESTIMATION OF AUTOREGRESSIVE MODELS

From our discussion thus far we have the following three models:

Koyck

$$Y_t = \alpha(1 - \lambda) + \beta_0 X_t + \lambda Y_{t-1} + (u_t - \lambda u_{t-1}) \tag{17.4.7}$$

Adaptive expectation

$$Y_t = \gamma\beta_0 + \gamma\beta_1 X_t + (1 - \gamma)Y_{t-1} + [u_t - (1 - \gamma)u_{t-1}] \tag{17.5.5}$$

Partial adjustment

$$Y_t = \delta\beta_0 + \delta\beta_1 X_t + (1 - \delta)Y_{t-1} + \delta u_t \tag{17.6.5}$$

All these models have the following common form:

$$Y_t = \alpha_0 + \alpha_1 X_t + \alpha_2 Y_{t-1} + v_t \tag{17.8.1}$$

that is, they are all autoregressive in nature. Therefore, we must now look at the estimation problem of such models, because the classical least-squares may not be directly applicable to them. **The reason is twofold: the presence of stochastic explanatory variables and the possibility of serial correlation.**

Now, as noted previously, for the application of the classical least-squares theory, it must be shown that the stochastic explanatory variable Y_{t-1} is distributed independently of the disturbance term v_t. To determine whether this is so, it is essential to know the properties of v_t. If we assume that the original disturbance term u_t satisfies all the classical assumptions, such as $E(u_t) = 0$, $\text{var}(u_t) = \sigma^2$ (the assumption of homoscedasticity), and $\text{cov}(u_t, u_{t+s}) = 0$ for $s \neq 0$ (the assumption of no autocorrelation), v_t may not inherit all these properties. Consider, for example, the error term in the Koyck model, which is $v_t = (u_t - \lambda u_{t-1})$. Given the assumptions about u_t, we can easily show that v_t is serially correlated because

---

[27] Milton Friedman, *A Theory of Consumption Function*, Princeton University Press, Princeton, N.J., 1957.

$$E(v_t v_{t-1}) = -\lambda\sigma^2 \tag{17.8.2}[28]$$

which is nonzero (unless λ happens to be zero). And since Y_{t-1} appears in the Koyck model as an explanatory variable, it is bound to be correlated with v_t (via the presence of u_{t-1} in it). As a matter of fact, it can be shown that

$$\text{cov}[Y_{t-1}, (u_t - \lambda u_{t-1})] = -\lambda\sigma^2 \tag{17.8.3}$$

which is the same as (17.8.2). The reader can verify that the same holds true of the adaptive expectations model.

What is the implication of the finding that in the Koyck model as well as the adaptive expectations model the stochastic explanatory variable Y_{t-1} is correlated with the error term v_t? As noted previously, **if an explanatory variable in a regression model is correlated with the stochastic disturbance term, the OLS estimators are not only biased but also not even consistent; that is, even if the sample size is increased indefinitely, the estimators do not approximate their true population values.[29] Therefore, estimation of the Koyck and adaptive expectation models by the usual OLS procedure may yield seriously misleading results.**

The partial adjustment model is different, however. In this model $v_t = \delta u_t$, where $0 < \delta \leq 1$. Therefore, if u_t satisfies the assumptions of the classical linear regression model given previously, so will δu_t. Thus, OLS estimation of the partial adjustment model will yield consistent estimates although the estimates tend to be biased (in finite or small samples).[30] Intuitively, the reason for consistency is this: Although Y_{t-1} depends on u_{t-1} and all the previous disturbance terms, it is not related to the current error term u_t. Therefore, as long as u_t is serially independent, Y_{t-1} will also be independent or at least uncorrelated with u_t, thereby satisfying an important assumption of OLS, namely, noncorrelation between the explanatory variable(s) and the stochastic disturbance term.

Although OLS estimation of the stock, or partial, adjustment model provides consistent estimation because of the simple structure of the error term in such a model, one should not assume that it applies rather than the Koyck or adaptive expectations model.[31] The reader is strongly advised against

---

[28] $E(v_t v_{t-1}) = E(u_t - \lambda u_{t-1})(u_{t-1} - \lambda u_{t-2})$

$\qquad = -\lambda E(u_{t-1})^2 \qquad$ since covariances between u's are zero by assumption

$\qquad = -\lambda\sigma^2$

[29] The proof is beyond the scope of this book and may be found in Griliches, op. cit., pp. 36–38. However, see Chap. 18 for an outline of the proof in another context.

[30] For proof, see J. Johnston, *Econometric Methods*, 3d ed., McGraw-Hill, New York, 1984, pp. 360–362. See also H. E. Doran and J. W. B. Guise, *Single Equation Methods in Econometrics: Applied Regression Analysis*, University of New England Teaching Monograph Series 3, Armidale, NSW, Australia, 1984, pp. 236–244.

[31] Also, as J. Johnston notes (op. cit., p. 350), "[the] pattern of adjustment [suggested by the partial adjustment model] . . . may sometimes be implausible."

doing so. A model should be chosen on the basis of strong theoretical consider-ations, not simply because it leads to easy statistical estimation. Every model should be considered on its own merit, paying due attention to the stochas-tic disturbances appearing therein. If in models such as the Koyck or adaptive expectations model OLS cannot be straightforwardly applied, methods need to be devised to resolve the estimation problem. Several alternative estimation methods are available although some of them may be computationally tedious. In the following section we consider one such method.

17.9 THE METHOD OF INSTRUMENTAL VARIABLES (IV)

The reason why OLS cannot be applied to the Koyck or adaptive expectations model is that the explanatory variable Y_{t-1} tends to be correlated with the er-ror term v_t. If somehow this correlation can be removed, one can apply OLS to obtain consistent estimates, as noted previously. (*Note:* There will be some small sample bias.) How can this be accomplished? Liviatan has proposed the following solution.[32]

Let us suppose that we find a *proxy* for Y_{t-1} that is highly correlated with Y_{t-1} but is uncorrelated with v_t, where v_t is the error term appearing in the Koyck or adaptive expectations model. Such a proxy is called an **instrumental variable** (IV).[33] Liviatan suggests X_{t-1} as the instrumental variable for Y_{t-1} and further suggests that the parameters of the regression (17.8.1) can be obtained by solving the following normal equations:

$$\sum Y_t = n\hat{\alpha}_0 + \hat{\alpha}_1 \sum X_t + \hat{\alpha}_2 \sum Y_{t-1}$$
$$\sum Y_t X_t = \hat{\alpha}_0 \sum X_t + \hat{\alpha}_1 \sum X_t^2 + \hat{\alpha}_2 \sum Y_{t-1}X_t \qquad (17.9.1)$$
$$\sum Y_t X_{t-1} = \hat{\alpha}_0 \sum X_{t-1} + \hat{\alpha}_1 \sum X_t X_{t-1} + \hat{\alpha}_2 \sum Y_{t-1}X_{t-1}$$

Notice that if we were to apply OLS directly to (17.8.1), the usual OLS normal equations would be (see Section 7.4)

$$\sum Y_t = n\hat{\alpha}_0 + \hat{\alpha}_1 \sum X_t + \hat{\alpha}_2 \sum Y_{t-1}$$
$$\sum Y_t X_t = \hat{\alpha}_0 \sum X_t + \hat{\alpha}_1 \sum X_t^2 + \hat{\alpha}_2 \sum Y_{t-1}X_t \qquad (17.9.2)$$
$$\sum Y_t Y_{t-1} = \hat{\alpha}_0 \sum Y_{t-1} + \hat{\alpha}_1 \sum X_t Y_{t-1} + \hat{\alpha}_2 \sum Y_{t-1}^2$$

The difference between the two sets of normal equations should be readily ap-parent. Liviatan has shown that the α's estimated from (17.9.1) are consistent, whereas those estimated from (17.9.2) may not be consistent because Y_{t-1} and

---

[32] N. Liviatan, "Consistent Estimation of Distributed Lags," *International Economic Review*, vol. 4, January 1963, pp. 44–52.

[33] Such instrumental variables are used frequently in simultaneous equation models (see Chap. 20).

$v_t[= u_t - \lambda u_{t-1}$ or $u_t - (1 - \gamma)u_{t-1}]$ may be correlated whereas X_t and X_{t-1} are uncorrelated with v_t. (Why?)

Although easy to apply in practice once a suitable proxy is found, the Liviatan technique is likely to suffer from the multicollinearity problem because X_t and X_{t-1}, which enter in the normal equations of (17.9.1), are likely to be highly correlated (as noted in Chapter 12, most economic time series typically exhibit a high degree of correlation between successive values). The implication, then, is that although the Liviatan procedure yields consistent estimates, the estimators are likely to be inefficient.[34]

Before we move on, the obvious question is: How does one find a "good" proxy for Y_{t-1} in such a way that, although highly correlated with Y_{t-1}, it is uncorrelated with v_t? There are some suggestions in the literature, which we take up by way of an exercise (see exercise 17.5). But it must be stated that finding good proxies is not always easy, in which case the IV method is of little practical use and one may have to resort to maximum likelihood estimation techniques, which are beyond the scope of this book.[35]

17.10 DETECTING AUTOCORRELATION IN AUTOREGRESSIVE MODELS: DURBIN h TEST

As we have seen, the likely serial correlation in the errors v_t make the estimation problem in the autoregressive model rather complex: In the stock adjustment model the error term v_t did not have (first-order) serial correlation if the error term u_t in the original model was serially uncorrelated, whereas in the Koyck and adaptive expectation models v_t was serially correlated even if u_t was serially independent. The question, then, is: How does one know if there is serial correlation in the error term appearing in the autoregressive models?

As noted in Chapter 12, the Durbin-Watson d statistic may not be used to detect (first-order) serial correlation in autoregressive models, because the computed d value in such models generally tends toward 2, which is the value of d expected in a truly random sequence. In other words, if we routinely compute the d statistic for such models, there is a built-in bias against discovering (first-order) serial correlation. Despite this, many researchers compute the d value for want of anything better. Recently, however, Durbin himself has proposed a *large-sample* test of first-order serial correlation in autoregressive models.[36] This test, called the **h statistic**, is as follows:

---

[34]To see how the efficiency of the estimators can be improved, consult Lawrence R. Klien, *A Textbook of Econometrics*, 2d ed., Prentice-Hall, Englewood Cliffs, N.J., 1974, p. 99. See also William H. Greene, *Econometric Analysis*, Macmillan, 2d ed., New York, 1993, pp. 535–538.

[35]For a condensed discussion of the ML methods, see J. Johnston, op. cit., pp. 366–371, as well as App. 4A.

[36]J. Durbin, "Testing for Serial Correlation in Least-Squares Regression When Some of the Regressors Are Lagged Dependent Variables," *Econometrica*, vol. 38, 1970, pp. 410–421.

$$h = \hat{\rho}\sqrt{\frac{n}{1 - n[\text{var}(\hat{\alpha}_2)]}} \qquad (17.10.1)$$

where n = sample size, $\text{var}(\hat{\alpha}_2)$ = variance of the coefficient of the lagged Y_{t-1}, and $\hat{\rho}$ = estimate of the first-order serial correlation ρ, which is given by the Eq. (12.5.8).

For large sample size, Durbin has shown that **if $\rho = 0$**, the h statistic follows the standardized normal distribution, that is, the normal distribution with zero mean and unit variance. Hence, the statistical significance of an observed h can easily be determined from the standardized normal distribution table (see Appendix D, Table D.1).

In practice there is no need to compute $\hat{\rho}$ because we have seen in Chapter 12 that it can be approximated from the estimated d as follows:

$$\hat{\rho} \doteq 1 - \tfrac{1}{2}d \qquad (12.6.12)$$

where d is the usual Durbin-Watson statistic.[37] Therefore, (17.10.1) can be written as

$$h \doteq (1 - \frac{1}{2}d)\sqrt{\frac{n}{1 - n[\text{var}(\hat{\alpha}_2)]}} \qquad (17.10.2)$$

The steps involved in the application of the h statistic are as follows:

1. Estimate (17.8.1) by OLS (don't worry about any estimation problems at this stage).
2. Note $\text{var}(\hat{\alpha}_2)$.
3. Compute $\hat{\rho}$ as indicated in (12.6.12).
4. Now compute h from (17.10.1), or (17.10.2).
5. Assuming n is large, we just saw that

$$h \sim \text{AN}(0, 1) \qquad (17.10.3)$$

that is, **h is asymptotically normally (AN) distributed with zero mean and unit variance**. Now from the normal distribution we know that

$$\Pr(-1.96 \le h \le 1.96) = 0.95 \qquad (17.10.4)$$

that is, the probability that h (i.e., any standardized normal variable) lying between -1.96 and $+1.96$ is about 95 percent. Therefore, the decision rule now is

(a) if $h > 1.96$ reject the null hypothesis that there is no positive first-order autocorrelation, and

---

[37] Note that this d value itself may not be used to test for serial correlation in the autoregressive models. It merely provides an *input* for the computation of the h statistic.

(b) if $h < -1.96$ reject the null hypothesis that there is no negative first-order autocorrelation, but

(c) if h lies between -1.96 and 1.96 do not reject the null hypothesis that there is no first-order (positive or negative) autocorrelation.

As an illustration, suppose in an application involving 100 observations it was found that $d = 1.9$ and $\text{var}(\hat{\alpha}_2) = 0.005$. Therefore

$$h = [1 - \frac{1}{2}(1.9)]\sqrt{\frac{100}{1 - 100(0.005)}}$$

$$= 0.7071$$

Since the computed h value lies in the bounds of (17.10.4), we cannot reject the hypothesis, at the 5 percent level, that there is no positive first-order autocorrelation.

Note these features of the h statistic:

1. It does not matter how many X variables or how many lagged values of Y are included in the regression model. To compute h, we need consider only the variance of the coefficient of lagged Y_{t-1}.

2. The test is not applicable if $[n \, \text{var}(\hat{\alpha}_2)]$ exceeds 1. (Why?) In practice, though, this does not usually happen.

3. Since the test is a large-sample test, its application in small samples is not strictly justified, as shown by Inder[38] and Kiviet.[39] It has been suggested that the Breusch-Godfrey (BG) test, also known as the Lagrange multiplier test, discussed in Chapter 12 is statistically more powerful not only in the large samples but also in finite, or small, samples and is therefore preferable to the h test.[40]

17.11 A NUMERICAL EXAMPLE: THE DEMAND FOR MONEY IN INDIA

Refer to exercise 7.25, which gives annual data on stock of money, national income, prices, and long-run interest rate in India for the period 1948–1949 to 1964–1965. Suppose we postulate the following demand for money relation.[41]

$$M_t^* = \beta_0 R_t^{\beta_1} Y_t^{\beta_2} e^{u_t} \tag{17.11.1}$$

[38] B. Inder, "An Approximation to the Null Distribution of the Durbin-Watson Statistic in Models Containing Lagged Dependent Variables," *Econometric Theory*, vol. 2, no. 3, 1986, pp. 413–428.

[39] J. F. Kiviet, "On the Vigour of Some Misspecification Tests for Modelling Dynamic Relationships," *Review of Economic Studies*, vol. 53, no. 173, 1986, pp. 241–262.

[40] Gabor Korosi, Laszlo Matyas, and Istvan P. Szekely, *Practical Econometrics*, Ashgate Publishing Company, Brookfield, Vermont, 1992, p. 92.

[41] For a similar model, see Gregory C. Chow, "On the Long-Run and Short-Run Demand for Money," *Journal of Political Economy*, vol. 74, no. 2, 1966, pp. 111–131. Note that one advantage of the multiplicative function is that the exponents of the variables give direct estimates of elasticities (see Chap. 6).

where M_t^* = desired, or long-run, demand for money (real cash balances)
$\quad\quad R_t$ = long-term interest rate, %
$\quad\quad Y_t$ = aggregate real national income

For statistical estimation, (17.11.1) may be expressed conveniently in log form as

$$\ln M_t^* = \ln \beta_0 + \beta_1 \ln R_t + \beta_2 \ln Y_t + u_t \tag{17.11.2}$$

Since the desired demand variable is not directly observable, let us assume the stock adjustment hypothesis, namely,

$$\frac{M_t}{M_{t-1}} = \left(\frac{M_t^*}{M_{t-1}}\right)^{\delta} \quad\quad 0 < \delta \le 1 \tag{17.11.3}$$

Equation (17.11.3) states that a constant percentage (why?) of the discrepancy between the actual and desired real cash balances is eliminated within a single period (year). In log form, Eq. (17.11.3) may be expressed as

$$\ln M_t - \ln M_{t-1} = \delta(\ln M_t^* - \ln M_{t-1}) \tag{17.11.4}$$

Substituting $\ln M_t^*$ from (17.11.2) into Eq. (17.11.4) and rearranging, we obtain

$$\ln M_t = \delta \ln \beta_0 + \beta_1 \delta \ln R_t + \beta_2 \delta \ln Y_t + (1 - \delta) \ln M_{t-1} + \delta u_t \tag{17.11.5}[42]$$

which may be called the *short-run demand function* for money. (Why?) If we assume that u_t and hence δu_t satisfy the usual OLS assumptions, the regression results based on the given data are as follows:

$$\widehat{\ln M_t} = \begin{matrix} 1.5484 & - & 0.1041 \ln R_t & + & 0.6859 \ln Y_t & + & 0.5297 \ln M_{t-1} \\ (0.8336) & & (0.3710) & & (0.3859) & & (0.2013) \\ t = (1.857) & & (-0.2807) & & (1.777) & & (2.631) \end{matrix} \tag{17.11.6}[43]$$
$$R^2 = 0.9379 \quad\quad d = 1.8801$$

The estimated short-run demand function shows that the short-run interest elasticity is statistically insignificant but the short-run income elasticity is statistically significant at the 5% level (one-tail test). The coefficient of adjustment is $\delta = 1 - 0.5297 = 0.4703$, implying that about 47 percent of the discrepancy between the desired and actual real cash balances is eliminated in a year. To get back to the long-run demand function (17.11.2), all that needs to be done is to divide the short-run demand function through by δ (why?) and drop the $\ln M_{t-1}$ term. The results are

---

[42] In passing, note that this model is essentially nonlinear in the parameters. Therefore, although OLS may give an unbiased estimate of, say, $\beta_1 \delta$ taken together, it may not give unbiased estimates of β_1 and δ individually, especially if the sample is small.

[43] Note this feature of the estimated standard errors. The standard error of, say, the coefficient of $\ln R_t$ refers to the standard error of $\widehat{\beta_1 \delta}$, an estimator of $\beta_1 \delta$. There is no simple way to obtain the standard errors of $\hat{\beta}_1$ and $\hat{\delta}$ individually from the standard error of $\widehat{\beta_1 \delta}$, especially if the sample is relatively small. For large samples, however, individual standard errors of $\hat{\beta}_1$ and $\hat{\delta}$ can be obtained approximately, but the computations are involved. See Jan Kmenta, *Elements of Econometrics*, Macmillan, New York, 1971, p. 444.

$$\ln M_t^* = 3.2923 - 0.2214 \ln R_t + 1.4584 \ln Y_t \qquad (17.11.7)^{44}$$

As can be seen, the long-run income elasticity of demand for money 1.4584 is substantially greater than the corresponding short-run elasticity 0.6859.

Note that the estimated Durbin-Watson d is 1.8801, which is close to 2. This substantiates our previous remark that in the autoregressive models the computed d is generally close to 2. Therefore, we cannot trust the computed d to find out whether there was serial correlation in our data. Although our sample size is rather small, rendering the h test strictly speaking inappropriate, we present it nonetheless to illustrate the mechanics behind its computation. Using the estimated d value and formula (17.10.2), we obtain

$$h = [1 - \frac{1}{2}(1.8801)]\sqrt{\frac{16}{1 - 16(0.0405)}}$$
$$= 0.1905$$

where the variance of the lagged dependent variable is obtained from the estimated standard error of that variable, namely, $(0.2013)^2$.

Although the estimated h is rather small, leading to the acceptance of the hypothesis that there is no serial correlation (of the first order), this conclusion should be taken with a grain of salt in view of the smallness of the sample.

17.12 ILLUSTRATIVE EXAMPLES

In this section we present a few examples of distributed lag models to show how researchers have used them in empirical studies.

Example 17.7. The Fed and the Real Rate of Interest

To assess the effect of M1 (currency + checkable deposits) growth on Aaa bond real interest rate measure, G. J. Santoni and Courtenay C. Stone[45] estimated, using monthly data, the following distributed lag model for the United States.

$$r_t = \text{constant} + \sum_{i=0}^{11} a_i \dot{M}_{t-i} + u_i \qquad (17.12.1)$$

where r_t = Moody's Index of Aaa bond yield minus the average annual rate of change in the seasonally adjusted consumer price index over the prior 36 months, which is used as the measure of real interest rate, and $\dot{M}_t$ = monthly M_1 growth.

According to the "neutrality of money doctrine," which states that real economic variables—such as output, employment, economic growth and the real rate of interest—are not influenced permanently by money growth and, therefore, are

---

[44]Note that we have not presented the standard errors of the estimated coefficients for reasons discussed in footnote 43.

[45]"The Fed and the Real Rate of Interest," *Review*, Federal Reserve Bank of St. Louis, December 1982, pp. 8–18.

TABLE 17.2
Influence of monthly M1 growth on an Aaa bond real interest rate measure: February 1951 to November 1982

$$r = \text{constant} + \sum_{i=0}^{11} a_i \dot{M}_{1_{t-1}}$$

	February 1951 to September 1979		October 1979 to November 1982	
	Coefficient	$\lvert t \rvert$*	Coefficient	$\lvert t \rvert$
Constant	1.4885†	2.068	1.0360	0.801
a_0	−0.00088	0.388	0.00840	1.014
a_1	0.00171	0.510	0.03960†	3.419
a_2	0.00170	0.423	0.03112	2.003
a_3	0.00233	0.542	0.02719	1.502
a_4	−0.00249	0.553	0.00901	0.423
a_5	−0.00160	0.348	0.01940	0.863
a_6	0.00292	0.631	0.02411	1.056
a_7	0.00253	0.556	0.01446	0.666
a_8	0.00000	0.001	−0.00036	0.019
a_9	0.00074	0.181	−0.00499	0.301
a_{10}	0.00016	0.045	−0.01126	0.888
a_{11}	0.00025	0.107	−0.00178	0.211
$\sum a_i$	0.00737	0.221	0.1549	0.926
$\bar{R}^2$	0.9826		0.8662	
D-W	2.07		2.04	
RH01	1.27†	24.536	1.40†	9.838
RH02	−0.28†	5.410	−0.48†	3.373
NOB	344.		38.	
SER (= RSS)	0.1548		0.3899	

*$\lvert t \rvert$ = absolute t value.

† Significantly different from zero at the 0.05 level.

Source: G. J. Santoni and Courtenay C. Stone, "The Fed and the Real Rate of Interest," *Review,* Federal Reserve Bank of St. Louis, December 1982, p. 16.

essentially unaffected by monetary policy.... Given this argument, the Federal Reserve has no permanent influence over the real rate of interest whatsoever.[46]

If this doctrine is valid, then one should expect the distributed lag coefficients a_i as well as their sum to be statistically indifferent from zero. To find out whether this is the case, the authors estimated (17.12.1) for two different time periods, February 1951 to September 1979 and October 1979 to November 1982, the latter to take into account the change in the Fed's monetary policy, which since October 1979 has paid more attention to the rate of growth of the money supply than to the rate of interest, which was the policy in the earlier period. Their regression results are presented in Table 17.2. The results seem to support the "neutrality of money doctrine," since for the period February 1951 to September 1979 the current as well as lagged money growth had no statistically significant effect on the

[46]Ibid., p. 15.

real interest rate measure. For the latter period, too, the neutrality doctrine seems to hold since $\sum a_i$ is not statistically different from zero; only the coefficient a_1 is significant, but it has the wrong sign. (Why?)

Example 17.8. The Short- and Long-Run Aggregate Consumption Functions for the United States, 1946–1972

Suppose consumption C is linearly related to permanent income X^*:

$$C_t = \beta_1 + \beta_2 X_t^* + u_t \tag{17.12.2}$$

Since X_t^* is not directly observable, we need to specify the mechanism that generates permanent income. Suppose we adopt the adaptive expectations hypothesis specified in (17.5.2). Using (17.5.2) and simplifying, we obtain the following estimating equation (cf. 17.5.5):

$$C_t = \alpha_1 + \alpha_2 X_t + \alpha_3 C_{t-1} + v_t \tag{17.12.3}$$

where $\alpha_1 = \gamma\beta_1$

$\quad\quad \alpha_2 = \gamma\beta_2$

$\quad\quad \alpha_3 = (1 - \gamma)$

$\quad\quad v_t = [u_t - (1 - \gamma)u_{t-1}]$

As we know, β_2 gives the mean response of consumption to, say, a \$1 increase in permanent income, whereas α_2 gives the mean response of consumption to a \$1 increase in current income.

Based on quarterly data for the United States for the period 1946–1972, Michael C. Lovell obtained the following results;[47] both aggregate consumption and aggregate disposable income figures were deflated by a price index to convert them into real quantities:

$$\hat{C}_t = 2.361 + 0.2959X_t + 0.6755C_{t-1}$$
$$(1.229) \quad (0.0582) \quad\quad (0.0666)$$
$$\bar{R}^2 = 0.999 \tag{17.12.4}$$
$$d = 1.77$$

This regression shows that the marginal propensity to consume (MPC) is 0.2959, or about 0.30. This would suggest that a \$1 increase in the current or observed disposable income would increase consumption on the average by about 30 cents. But if this increase in income is sustained, then eventually the MPC out of the permanent income will be $\beta_2 = \gamma\beta_2/\gamma = 0.2959/0.3245$, or about 91 cents. In other words, when consumers have had time to adjust to the \$1 change in income, they will increase their consumption by about 91 cents.

Now suppose that our consumption function were

$$C_t^* = \beta_1 + \beta_2 X_t + u_t \tag{17.12.5}$$

---

[47] *Macroeconomics: Measurement, Theory and Policy*, John Wiley & Sons, New York, 1975, p. 148. Note that Lovell does not specify the source of the data or the price index used to obtain the real quantities.

In this formulation permanent or long-run consumption C_t is a linear function of the current or observed income. Since C_t^* is not directly observable, let us invoke the partial adjustment model (17.6.2). Using this model, and after algebraic manipulations, we obtain

$$C_t = \delta\beta_1 + \delta\beta_2 X_t + (1 - \delta)C_{t-1} + \delta u_t$$
$$= \alpha_1 + \alpha_2 X_t + \alpha_3 C_{t-1} + v_t \qquad (17.12.6)$$

In appearance, this model is indistinguishable from the adaptive expectations model (17.12.3). Therefore, the regression results given in (17.12.4) are equally applicable here. However, there is a major difference in the interpretation of the two models, not to mention the estimation problem associated with the autoregressive and possibly serially correlated model (17.12.3).[48] The model (17.12.5) is the long-run, or equilibrium, consumption function, whereas (17.12.6) is the short-run consumption function. β_2 measures the long-run MPC, whereas $\alpha_2(= \delta\beta_2)$ gives the short-run MPC; the former can be obtained from the latter by dividing it by δ, the coefficient of adjustment.

Returning to (17.12.4), we can now interpret 0.2959 as the short-run MPC. Since $\delta = 0.3245$, the long-run MPC is 0.91, or about 91 cents. Note that the adjustment coefficient of about 0.33 suggests that in any given time period consumers only adjust their consumption one-third of the way toward its desired or long-run level.

This example brings out the crucial point that in appearance the adaptive expectations and the partial adjustment models, or the Koyck model for that matter, are so similar that by just looking at the estimated regression, such as (17.12.4), one cannot tell which is the correct specification. That is why it is so vital that one specify the theoretical underpinning of the model chosen for empirical analysis and then proceed appropriately. If habit or inertia characterizes consumption behavior, then the partial adjustment model is appropriate. On the other hand, if consumption behavior is forward-looking in the sense that it is based on expected future income, then the adaptive expectations model is appropriate. If it is the latter, then, one will have to pay close attention to the estimation problem to obtain consistent estimators. In the former case, the OLS will provide consistent estimators, provided the usual OLS assumptions are fulfilled.

17.13   THE ALMON APPROACH TO DISTRIBUTED-LAG MODELS: THE ALMON OR POLYNOMIAL DISTRIBUTED LAG (PDL)[49]

Although used extensively in practice, the Koyck distributed-lag model is based on the assumption that the β coefficients decline geometrically as the lag lengthens (see Fig. 17.4). This assumption may be too restrictive in some situations. Consider, for example, Fig. 17.6.

---

[48]From the regression results presented by Lovell it is not possible to know whether he has looked into this problem.

[49]Shirley Almon, "The Distributed Lag between Capital Appropriations and Expenditures," *Econometrica*, vol. 33, January 1965, pp. 178–196.

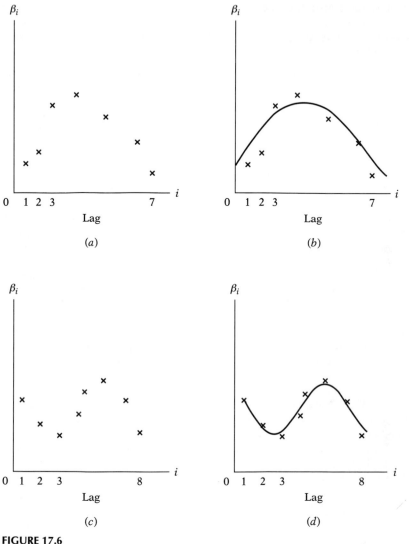

FIGURE 17.6
Almon polynomial-lag scheme.

In Fig. 17.6*a* it is assumed that the β's increase at first and then decrease, whereas in Fig. 17.6*c* it is assumed that they follow a cyclical pattern. Obviously, the Koyck scheme of distributed-lag models will not work in these cases. However, after looking at Fig. 17.6*a* and *c*, it seems that one can express β_i as a function of i, the length of the lag (time), and fit suitable curves to reflect the functional relationship between the two, as indicated in Fig. 17.6*b* and *d*. This approach is precisely the one suggested by Shirley Almon. To illustrate her technique, let us revert to the finite distributed-lag model considered previously, namely,

$$Y_t = \alpha + \beta_0 X_t + \beta_1 X_{t-1} + \beta_2 X_{t-2} + \cdots + \beta_k X_{t-k} + u_t \quad (17.1.2)$$

which may be written more compactly as

$$Y_t = \alpha + \sum_{i=0}^{k} \beta_i X_{t-i} + u_t \tag{17.13.1}$$

Following a theorem in mathematics known as **Weierstrass' theorem,** Almon assumes that β_i can be approximated by a suitable-degree polynomial in i, the length of the lag.[50] For instance, if the lag scheme shown in Fig. 17.6a applies, we can write

$$\beta_i = a_0 + a_1 i + a_2 i^2 \tag{17.13.2}$$

which is a quadratic, or second-degree, polynomial in i (see Fig. 17.6b). However, if the β's follow the pattern of Fig. 17.6c, we can write

$$\beta_i = a_0 + a_1 i + a_2 i^2 + a_3 i^3 \tag{17.13.3}$$

which is a third-degree polynomial in i (see Fig. 17.6d). More generally, we may write

$$\beta_i = a_0 + a_1 i + a_2 i^2 + \cdots + a_m i^m \tag{17.13.4}$$

which is an mth-degree polynomial in i. It is assumed that m (the degree of the polynomial) is less than k (the maximum length of the lag).

To explain how the Almon scheme works, let us assume that the β's follow the pattern shown in Fig. 17.6a and, therefore, the second-degree polynomial approximation is appropriate. Substituting (17.13.2) into (17.13.1), we obtain

$$Y_t = \alpha + \sum_{i=0}^{k} (a_0 + a_1 i + a_2 i^2) X_{t-i} + u_t$$

$$= \alpha + a_0 \sum_{i=0}^{k} X_{t-i} + a_1 \sum_{i=0}^{k} i X_{t-i} + a_2 \sum_{i=0}^{k} i^2 X_{t-i} + u_t \tag{17.13.5}$$

Defining

$$Z_{0t} = \sum_{i=0}^{k} X_{t-i}$$

$$Z_{1t} = \sum_{i=0}^{k} i X_{t-i} \tag{17.13.6}$$

$$Z_{2t} = \sum_{i=0}^{k} i^2 X_{t-i}$$

we may write (17.13.5) as

$$Y_t = \alpha + a_0 Z_{0t} + a_1 Z_{1t} + a_2 Z_{2t} + u_t \tag{17.13.7}$$

---

[50]Broadly speaking, the theorem states that on a finite closed interval any continuous function may be approximated uniformly by a polynomial of a suitable degree.

In the Almon scheme Y is regressed on the constructed variables Z, not the original X variables. Note that (17.13.7) can be estimated by the usual OLS procedure. The estimates of α and a_i thus obtained will have all the desirable statistical properties provided the stochastic disturbance term u satisfies the assumptions of the classical linear regression model. In this respect, the Almon technique has a distinct advantage over the Koyck method because, as we have seen, the latter has some serious estimation problems that result from the presence of the stochastic explanatory variable Y_{t-1} and its likely correlation with the disturbance term.

Once the a's are estimated from (17.13.7), the original β's can be estimated from (17.13.2) [or more generally from (17.13.4)] as follows:

$$
\begin{aligned}
\hat{\beta}_0 &= \hat{a}_0 \\
\hat{\beta}_1 &= \hat{a}_0 + \hat{a}_1 + \hat{a}_2 \\
\hat{\beta}_2 &= \hat{a}_0 + 2\hat{a}_1 + 4\hat{a}_2 \\
\hat{\beta}_3 &= \hat{a}_0 + 3\hat{a}_1 + 9\hat{a}_2 \\
&\dots\dots\dots\dots\dots\dots \\
\hat{\beta}_k &= \hat{a}_0 + k\hat{a}_1 + k^2\hat{a}_2
\end{aligned}
\qquad (17.13.8)
$$

Before we apply the Almon technique, we must resolve the following practical problems.

1. The maximum length of the lag k must be specified in advance. Here perhaps one can follow the advice of Davidson and MacKinnon:

> The best approach is probably to settle the question of lag length first, by starting with a very large value of q [the lag length] and then seeing whether the fit of the model deteriorates significantly when it is reduced without imposing any restrictions on the shape of the distributed lag.[51]

This advice is in the spirit of Hendry's top-down approach discussed in Chapter 14. Remember that if there is some "true" lag length, choosing fewer lags will lead to the "omission of relevant variable bias," whose consequences, as we saw in Chapter 13, can be very serious. On the other hand, choosing more lags than necessary will lead to the "inclusion of irrelevant variable bias," whose consequences are less serious; the coefficients can be consistently estimated by OLS, although their variances may be less efficient.

There is a formal test of lag length developed by Schwarz, and popularly known as the **Schwarz criterion**, which is discussed in exercise 17.28.

2. Having specified k, we must also specify the degree of the polynomial m. Generally, the degree of the polynomial should be at least one more than

---

[51]Russell Davidson and James G. MacKinnon, *Estimation and Inference in Econometrics*, Oxford University Press, New York, 1993, pp. 675–676.

the number of turning points in the curve relating β_i to i. Thus, in Fig. 17.6a there is only one turning point; hence a second-degree polynomial will be a good approximation. In Fig. 17.6c there are two turning points; hence a third-degree polynomial will provide a good approximation. A priori, however, one may not know the number of turning points, and therefore, the choice of m is largely subjective. However, theory may suggest a particular shape in some cases. In practice, one hopes that a fairly low-degree polynomial (say, $m = 2$ or 3) will give good results. Having chosen a particular value of m, if we want to find out whether a higher-degree polynomial will give a better fit, we can proceed as follows.

Suppose we must decide between the second- and third-degree polynomials. For the second-degree polynomial the estimating equation is as given by (17.13.7). For the third-degree polynomial the corresponding equation is

$$Y_t = \alpha + a_0 Z_{0t} + a_1 Z_{1t} + a_2 Z_{2t} + a_3 Z_{3t} + u_t \qquad (17.13.9)$$

where $Z_{3t} = \sum_{i=0}^{k} i^3 X_{t-i}$. After running regression (17.13.9), if we find that a_2 is statistically significant but a_3 is not, we may assume that the second-degree polynomial provides a reasonably good approximation.

Alternatively, as Davidson and MacKinnon suggest, "After q [the lag length] is determined, one can then attempt to determine d [the degree of the polynomial] once again starting with a large value and then reducing it."

However, we must beware of the problem of multicollinearity, which is likely to arise because of the way the Z's are constructed from the X's, as shown in (17.13.6) [see also (17.13.10)]. As shown in Chapter 10, in cases of serious multicollinearity, $\hat{a}_3$ may turn out to be statistically insignificant, not because the true a_3 is zero, but simply because the sample at hand does not allow us to assess the separate impact of Z_3 on Y. Therefore, in our illustration, before we accept the conclusion that the third-degree polynomial is not the correct choice, we must make sure that the multicollinearity problem is not serious enough, which can be done by applying the techniques discussed in Chapter 10.

3. Once m and k are specified, the Z's can be readily constructed. For instance, if $m = 2$ and $k = 5$, the Z's are

$$Z_{0t} = \sum_{i=0}^{5} X_{t-i} = (X_t + X_{t-1} + X_{t-2} + X_{t-3} + X_{t-4} + X_{t-5})$$

$$Z_{1t} = \sum_{i=0}^{5} iX_{t-i} = (X_{t-1} + 2X_{t-2} + 3X_{t-3} + 4X_{t-4} + 5X_{t-5}) \qquad (17.13.10)$$

$$Z_{2t} = \sum_{i=0}^{5} i^2 X_{t-i} = (X_{t-1} + 4X_{t-2} + 9X_{t-3} + 16X_{t-4} + 25X_{t-5})$$

Notice that the Z's are linear combinations of the original X's. Also notice why the Z's are likely to exhibit multicollinearity.

Before proceeding to a numerical example, note the advantages of the Almon method. First, it provides a flexible method of incorporating a variety of lag structures (see exercise 17.17). The Koyck technique, on the other hand, is quite rigid in that it assumes that the β's decline geometrically. Second, unlike the Koyck technique, in the Almon method we do not have to worry about the presence of the lagged dependent variable as an explanatory variable in the model and the problems it creates for estimation. Finally, if a sufficiently low-degree polynomial can be fitted, the number of coefficients to be estimated (the a's) is considerably smaller than the original number of coefficients (the β's).

But let us reemphasize the problems with the Almon technique. First, the degree of the polynomial as well as the maximum value of the lag is largely a subjective decision. Second, for reasons noted previously, the Z variables are likely to exhibit multicollinearity. Therefore, in models like (17.13.9) the estimated a's are likely to show large standard errors (relative to the values of these coefficients), thereby rendering one or more such coefficients statistically insignificant on the basis of the conventional t test. But this does not necessarily mean that one or more of the original $\hat{\beta}$ coefficients will also be statistically insignificant. (The proof of this statement is slightly involved but is suggested in exercise 17.18.) As a result, the multicollinearity problem may not be as serious as one might think. Besides, as we know, in cases of multicollinearity even if we cannot estimate an individual coefficient precisely, a linear combination of such coefficients (the **estimable function**) can be estimated more precisely.

A numerical example. To illustrate the Almon technique, Table 17.3 gives data on inventories Y and sales X in the United States manufacturing sector for the period 1955–1974. For illustrative purposes, assume that inventories depend on sales in the current year and in the three preceding years as follows:

$$Y_t = \alpha + \beta_0 X_t + \beta_1 X_{t-1} + \beta_2 X_{t-2} + \beta_3 X_{t-3} + u_t \qquad (17.13.11)$$

Furthermore, assume that β_i can be approximated by a second-degree polynomial as shown in (17.13.2). Then, following (17.13.5), we may write

$$Y_t = \alpha + a_0 Z_{0t} + a_1 Z_{1t} + a_2 Z_{2t} + u_t \qquad (17.13.12)$$

where

$$Z_{0t} = \sum_{i=0}^{3} X_{t-i} = (X_t + X_{t-1} + X_{t-2} + X_{t-3})$$

$$Z_{1t} = \sum_{i=0}^{3} i X_{t-i} = (X_{t-1} + 2X_{t-2} + 3X_{t-3}) \qquad (17.13.13)$$

$$Z_{2t} = \sum_{i=0}^{3} i^2 X_{t-i} = (X_{t-1} + 4X_{t-2} + 9X_{t-3})$$

The Z variables thus constructed are shown in Table 17.3. Using the data on Y and the Z's, we obtain the following regression:

$$\hat{Y}_t = -7140.7564 + 0.6612 Z_{0t} + 0.9020 Z_{1t} - 0.4322 Z_{2t}$$

$$(1992.9809) \quad (0.1655) \quad (0.4831) \quad (0.1665)$$

$$t = \quad (-4.0847) \quad (3.9960) \quad (1.8671) \quad (-2.5961)$$

$$\bar{R}^2 = 0.9961 \qquad df = 13$$

(17.13.14)

TABLE 17.3
**Inventories *Y* and sales *X* in U.S. manufacturing
industries, 1955–1974 (millions of dollars)**

Year	Y	X	Z_0	Z_1	Z_2
1955	45,069	26,480	...	...	...
1956	50,642	27,740	...	...	...
1957	51,871	28,736	...	...	...
1958	50,070	27,280	110,236	163,656	378,016
1959	52,707	30,219	113,975	167,972	391,884
1960	53,814	30,796	117,031	170,987	397,963
1961	54,939	30,896	119,191	173,074	397,192
1962	58,213	33,113	125,024	183,145	426,051
1963	60,043	35,032	129,837	187,293	433,861
1964	63,383	37,335	136,376	193,946	445,548
1965	68,221	41,003	146,483	206,738	475,480
1966	77,965	44,869	158,239	220,769	505,631
1967	84,655	46,449	169,656	238,880	544,896
1968	90,875	50,282	182,603	259,196	594,952
1969	97,074	53,555	195,155	277,787	639,899
1970	101,645	52,859	203,145	293,466	672,724
1971	102,445	55,917	212,613	310,815	719,617
1972	107,719	62,017	224,348	322,300	749,348
1973	120,870	71,398	242,191	332,428	761,416
1974	147,135	82,078	271,410	363,183	822,719

Source: Data on inventories and sales from *Economic Report of the President,* Table C-41, February 1975, p. 297.

(*Note:* Since we are assuming a 3-year lag, the total number of observations is reduced from 20 to 17.)

From the estimated *a* coefficients given in Eq. (17.13.14), we estimate the β coefficients from the relation (17.13.8) as follows:

$$\hat{\beta}_0 = \hat{a}_0 = 0.6612$$

$$\hat{\beta}_1 = (\hat{a}_0 + \hat{a}_1 + \hat{a}_2) = (0.6612 + 0.9020 - 0.4322) = 1.1310$$

$$\hat{\beta}_2 = (\hat{a}_0 + 2\hat{a}_1 + 4\hat{a}_2) = [0.6612 + 2(0.9020) - 4(0.4322)] = 0.7364$$

$$\hat{\beta}_3 = (\hat{a}_0 + 3\hat{a}_1 + 9\hat{a}_2) = [0.6612 + 3(0.9020) - 9(0.4322)] = -0.5226$$

Thus, the estimated distributed-lag model corresponding to (17.13.11) is

$$\hat{Y}_t = -7140.7564 + 0.6612X_t + 1.1311X_{t-1} + 0.7367X_{t-2} - 0.5220X_{t-3}$$

$$(1992.9803) \quad (0.1655) \quad (0.1799)^{52} \quad (0.1643)^{52} \quad (0.2348)^{52}$$

$$t = (-3.5829) \quad (3.9960) \quad (6.2844) \quad (4.4846) \quad (-2.2231)$$

$$(17.13.15)$$

Geometrically, the estimated β_i are shown in Fig. 17.7.

---

[52] These standard errors are computed from the formula given in exercise 17.18.

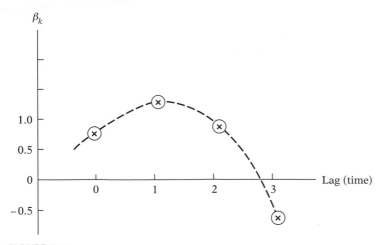

FIGURE 17.7
Lag structure of the illustrative example.

Our numerical example may be used to point out a few additional features of the Almon procedure:

1. The standard errors of the a coefficients are directly obtainable from the OLS regression (17.13.14), but the standard errors of some of the $\hat{\beta}$ coefficients, the objective of primary interest, cannot be so obtained. But these standard errors can be easily computed from the standard errors of the estimated a coefficients by using a well-known formula from statistics, which is given in exercise 17.18.[53]

2. The $\hat{\beta}$'s obtained in (17.13.15) are called *unrestricted estimates* in the sense that no a priori restrictions are placed on them. In some situations, however, one may want to impose the so-called **endpoint restrictions** on the β's by assuming that β_0 and β_k (the current and kth lagged coefficient) are zero. Because of psychological, institutional, or technological reasons, the value of the explanatory variable in the current period may not have any impact on the current value of the dependent variable, thereby justifying the zero value for β_0. By the same token, beyond a certain time period k the explanatory variable may not have any impact on the dependent variable, thus supporting the assumption that β_k is zero.[54] Sometimes the β's are estimated with the restriction that the sum of all the β coefficients is unity. (To see how such restrictions are taken into account, the reader is referred to the Almon article, footnote 49.) Computer packages such as ET, LIMDEP, SHAZAM, and TSP can now handle such endpoint restrictions routinely.

---

[53] Several computer programs on regression analysis with the Almon lag option now routinely compute these standard errors.

[54] In the current example one may note the negative value for $\hat{\beta}_3$. If such a negative value makes no sense in light of theory, one may wish to restrict $\beta_3 = 0$ and reestimate the lag structure. For a concrete application, see D. B. Batten and Daniel Thornton, "Polynomial Distributed Lags and the Estimation of St. Louis Equation," *Review*, Federal Bank of St. Louis, April 1983, pp. 13–25.

17.14 CAUSALITY IN ECONOMICS: THE GRANGER TEST

Back in Section 1.4 we noted that although regression analysis deals with the dependence of one variable on other variables, it does not necessarily imply causation. But consider this situation: Suppose two variables, say, GNP and money supply M affect each other with (distributed) lags. Is it then possible to say that money "causes" GNP ($M \rightarrow$ GNP) or GNP "causes" M(GNP $\rightarrow M$), or is there feedback between the two ($M \rightarrow$ GNP and GNP $\rightarrow M$)? In short, the question that we are raising is whether *statistically* one can detect the direction of causality (cause and effect relationship) when *temporally* there is a lead-lag relationship between two variables.

Without going too deeply into this question, for that will take us far afield,[55] we will only consider a relatively simple test of causality, that proposed by Granger.[56] We explain this test using the relationship between GNP and M as the example.

The Granger Test[57]

The Granger causality test assumes that the information relevant to the prediction of the respective variables, GNP and M, is contained solely in the time series data on these variables. The test involves estimating the following regressions:

$$\text{GNP}_t = \sum_{i=1}^{n} \alpha_i M_{t-i} + \sum_{j=1}^{n} \beta_j \text{GNP}_{t-j} + u_{1t} \qquad (17.14.1)$$

$$M_t = \sum_{i=1}^{m} \lambda_i M_{t-i} + \sum_{j=1}^{m} \delta_j \text{GNP}_{t-j} + u_{2t} \qquad (17.14.2)$$

where it is assumed that the disturbances u_{1t} and u_{2t} are uncorrelated.

Equation (17.14.1) postulates that current GNP is related to past values of GNP itself as well as of M, and (17.14.2) postulates a similar behavior for M_t. Note these regressions can be cast in growth forms, $\dot{\text{GNP}}$ and $\dot{M}$, where a dot over a variable indicates its growth rate. We now distinguish four cases:

---

[55]For an excellent discussion of this topic, see Arnold Zellner, "Causality and Econometrics," *Carnegie-Rochester Conference Series*, *10*, K. Brunner and A. H. Meltzer (eds.), North Holland Publishing Company, Amsterdam, 1979, pp. 9–50. Note that econometrician Edward Leamer prefers the term **precedence** over causality.

[56]C. W. J. Granger, "Investigating Causal Relations by Econometric Models and Cross-Spectral Methods," *Econometrica*, July 1969, pp. 424–438. Although popularly known as the Granger causality test, it is appropriate to call it the Wiener-Granger causality test, for it was earlier suggested by Wiener. See N. Wiener, "The Theory of Prediction," in E. F. Beckenback, ed., *Modern Mathematics for Engineers*, McGraw-Hill, New York, 1956, pp. 165–190.

[57]The discussion presented below leans heavily on R. W. Hafer, "The Role of Fiscal Policy in the St. Louis Equation," *Review*, Federal Reserve Bank of St. Louis, January 1982, pp. 17–22.

1. *Unidirectional causality from M to GNP* is indicated if the estimated coefficients on the lagged M in (17.14.1) are statistically different from zero as a group (i.e., $\sum \alpha_i \neq 0$) and the set of estimated coefficients on the lagged GNP in (17.14.2) is not statistically different from zero (i.e., $\sum \delta_j = 0$).

2. Conversely, *unidirectional causality from GNP to M* exists if the set of lagged M coefficients in (17.14.1) is not statistically different from zero (i.e., $\sum \alpha_i = 0$) and the set of the lagged GNP coefficients in (17.14.2) is statistically different from zero (i.e., $\sum \delta_j \neq 0$).

3. *Feedback*, or *bilateral causality*, is suggested when the sets of M and GNP coefficients are statistically significantly different from zero in both regressions.

4. Finally, *independence* is suggested when the sets of M and GNP coefficients are not statistically significant in both the regressions.

More generally, since the future cannot predict the past, if variable X (Granger) causes variable Y, then changes in X should *precede* changes in Y. Therefore, in a regression of Y on other variables (including its own past values) if we include past or lagged values of X and it significantly improves the prediction of Y, then we can say that X (Granger) causes Y. A similar definition applies if Y (Granger) causes X.

The steps involved in implementing the Granger causality test are as follows. We illustrate these steps with the GNP-money example given in Eq. (17.14.1).

1. Regress current GNP on all lagged GNP terms and other variables, if any, but *do not* include the lagged M variables in this regression. As per Chapter 8, this is the restricted regression. From this regression obtain the restricted residual sum of squares, RSS_R.

2. Now run the regression including the lagged M terms. In the language of Chapter 8, this is the unrestricted regression. From this regression obtain the unrestricted residual sum of squares, RSS_{UR}.

3. The null hypothesis is $H_0: \sum \alpha_i = 0$, that is, lagged M terms do not belong in the regression.

4. To test this hypothesis, we apply the F test given by (8.7.9), namely,

$$F = \frac{(RSS_R - RSS_{UR})/m}{RSS_{UR}/(n-k)} \tag{8.7.9}$$

which follows the F distribution with m and $(n-k)$ df. In the present case m is equal to the number of lagged M terms and k is the number of parameters estimated in the unrestricted regression.

5. If the computed F value exceeds the critical F value at the chosen level of significance, we reject the null hypothesis, in which case the lagged M terms belong in the regression. This is another way of saying that M causes GNP.

6. Steps 1 to 5 can be repeated to test the model (17.14.2), that is, whether GNP causes M.

Before proceeding to applications of the Granger test, keep in mind that the number of lagged terms to be included in regressions like (17.14.1) and (17.14.2) is an important practical question, similar to the one we encountered when we discussed distributed-lag models. As an illustrative example later shows, *the direction of causality may depend critically on the number of lagged terms included.*

Empirical Results

R. W. Hafer used the Granger test to find out the nature of causality between GNP and M for the United States for the period 1960–I to 1980–IV. He used four lagged values of the two variables in each of the two regressions in this section and obtained the following results:[58]

Direction of causality	F value	Decision
$\dot{M} \to \dot{Y}$	2.68	Do not reject
$\dot{Y} \to \dot{M}$	0.56	Reject

These results suggest that the direction of causality is from $\dot{M}$ to $\dot{Y}$ since the estimated F value is significant at the 5% level; the critical F value is 2.50 (for 4, 71 df). On the other hand, there is no "reverse causation" from $\dot{Y}$ to $\dot{M}$, since the computed F value is not statistically significant. (*Note:* The dots over the variables, as indicated earlier, indicate growth rates.)

Considerations of whether these results are specific to the particular sample, or whether the model used is the correct model, are questions better left to the references.[59] Our purpose in this section was merely to introduce the Granger method. For a critique of this method the reader is invited to read the Zellner article cited earlier. We conclude this section with another example.

Example 17.9. Causality between auto sales (AS) and Treasury Bill rate (TB), United States, 1960–I to 1978–4. By using four lags of each variable, regressions similar to (17.14.1) and (17.14.2) were estimated, giving the following results.[60]

Direction of causality	F value	P value of F	Decision
TB $\to$ AS	0.8693	0.4871	Reject
AS $\to$ TB	6.2412	0.0002	Do not reject

---

[58] See his article, especially his footnote 12, for the details of his estimation procedure.

[59] For an alternative test, known as **Sims' test**, see Christopher A. Sims, "Money, Income, and Causality," *American Economic Review*, vol. 62, September 1972, pp. 540–552.

[60] These results are reproduced from *MicroTsp: User's Manual*, Version 7.0, published by Quantitative Micro Software, Irvine, California, 1990, p. 16-15. The full sample consists of observations from 1958–Q1 to 1978–Q4.

Thus, TB does not "Granger-cause" AS, but AS Granger-causes TB! This result seems strange. But when we use 12 lags, we obtain the following results:

Direction of causality	F value	P value of F	Decision
TB → AS	2.3042	0.0209	Do not reject
AS → TB	1.3158	0.2418	Reject

Now TB seems to Granger-cause AS but AS does not Granger-cause TB, which seems a more sensible result.

But suppose we introduce eight lags. Now we have the following outcome:

Direction of causality	F value	P value of F	Decision
TB → AS	3.0784	0.0057	Do not reject
AS → TB	2.6217	0.0158	Do not reject

Now TB Granger-causes AS and AS Granger-causes TB, a case of bilateral causality.

Why are there such conflicting results? The reason is that the *Granger causality test is very sensitive to the number of lags used in the analysis*. That is why Davidson and MacKinnon suggest using more rather than fewer lags. From a practical viewpoint, if the Granger causality test is not very sensitive to the lag length, we will have more confidence in our conclusions than if the results are very sensitive to the lag length. That is, one has to be very careful in implementing the Granger causality test.[61]

17.15 SUMMARY AND CONCLUSIONS

1. For psychological, technological, and institutional reasons, a regressand may respond to a regressor(s) with a time lag. Regression models that take into account time lags are known as **dynamic** or **lagged regression models**.

2. There are two types of lagged models: **distributed-lag** and **autoregressive**. In the former, the current and lagged values of regressors are explanatory variables. In the latter, the lagged value(s) of the regressand appear as explanatory variables.

3. A purely distributed-lag model can be estimated by OLS, but in that case there is the problem of multicollinearity since successive lagged values of a regressor tend to be correlated.

4. As a result, some shortcut methods have been devised. These include the Koyck, the adaptive expectations, and partial adjustment mechanisms, the first being a purely algebraic approach and the other two being based on economic principles.

---

[61] For another causality test, known as **Sims' causality**, see Christopher Sims, op. cit., pp. 540–552. For details, see exercise 17.29.

5. But a unique feature of the **Koyck, adaptive expectations**, and **partial adjustment models** is that they all are autoregressive in nature in that the lagged value(s) of the regressand appear as one of the explanatory variables.

6. Autoregressiveness poses estimation challenges; if the lagged regressand is correlated with the error term, OLS estimators of such models are not only biased but also are inconsistent. Bias and inconsistency are the case with the Koyck and the adaptive expectations models; the partial adjustment model is different in that it can be consistently estimated by OLS despite the presence of the lagged regressand.

7. To estimate the Koyck and adaptive expectations models consistently, the most popular method is the **method of instrumental variable**. The instrumental variable is a proxy variable for the lagged regressand but with the property that it is uncorrelated with the error term.

8. An alternative to the lagged regression models just discussed is the **Almon polynomial distributed-lag model**, which avoids the estimation problems associated with the autoregressive models. The major problem with the Almon approach, however, is that one must *prespecify* both the lag length and the degree of the polynomial. There are both formal and informal methods of resolving the choice of the lag length and the degree of the polynomial.

9. Despite the estimation problems, which can be surmounted, the distributed and autoregressive models have proved extremely useful in empirical economics because they make the otherwise static economic theory a dynamic one by taking into account explicitly the role of time. Such models help us to distinguish between short- and long-run response of the dependent variable to a unit change in the value of the explanatory variable(s). Thus, for estimating short- and long-run price, income, substitution, and other elasticities these models have proved to be highly useful.[62]

10. Because of the lags involved, distributed and or autoregressive models raise the topic of causality in economic variables. In applied work, the **Granger causality** modeling has received considerable attention. But one has to exercise great caution in using the Granger methodology because it is very sensitive to the lag length used in the model.

EXERCISES

Questions

17.1. Explain with a brief reason whether the following statements are true, false, or uncertain:

(a) All econometric models are essentially dynamic.

---

[62]For applications of these models, see Arnold C. Harberger, ed., *The Demand for Durable Goods*, University of Chicago Press, Chicago, 1960.

(b) The Koyck model will not make much sense if some of the distributed-lag coefficients are positive and some negative.

(c) If the Koyck and adaptive expectations models are estimated by OLS, the estimators will be biased but consistent.

(d) In the partial adjustment model, OLS estimators are biased in finite samples.

(e) In the presence of a stochastic regressor(s) and an autocorrelated error term, the method of instrumental variables will produce unbiased as well as consistent estimates.

(f) In the presence of a lagged regressand as a regressor, the Durbin-Watson d statistic to detect autocorrelation is practically useless.

(g) The Durbin h test is valid in both large and small samples.

(h) The Granger test is a test of precedence rather than a test of causality.

17.2. Establish Eq. (17.7.2).

17.3. Prove Eq. (17.8.3).

17.4. Assume that prices are formed according to the following adaptive expectations hypothesis:

$$P_t^* = \gamma P_{t-1} + (1 - \gamma)P_{t-1}^*$$

where P^* is the expected price and P the actual price.

Complete the following table, assuming $\gamma = 0.5$:*

Period	P^*	P
$t - 3$	100	110
$t - 2$		125
$t - 1$		155
t		185
$t + 1$		—

17.5. Consider the model

$$Y_t = \alpha + \beta_1 X_{1t} + \beta_2 X_{2t} + \beta_3 Y_{t-1} + v_t$$

Suppose Y_{t-1} and v_t are correlated. To remove the correlation, suppose we use the following instrumental variable approach: First regress Y_t on X_{1t} and X_{2t} and obtain the estimated $\hat{Y}_t$ from this regression. Then regress

$$Y_t = \alpha + \beta_1 X_{1t} + \beta_2 X_{2t} + \beta_3 \hat{Y}_{t-1} + v_t$$

where $\hat{Y}_{t-1}$ are estimated from the first-stage regression.

(a) How does this procedure remove the correlation between Y_{t-1} and v_t in the original model?

(b) What are the advantages of the recommended procedure over the Liviatan approach?

†17.6. (a) Establish (17.4.8).

(b) Evaluate the median lag for $\lambda = 0.2, 0.4, 0.6, 0.8$.

---

*Adapted from G. K. Shaw, op. cit., p. 26.

†Optional.

(c) Is there any systematic relationship between the value of λ and the value of the median lag?

17.7. (a) Prove that for the Koyck model, the mean lag is as shown in (17.4.10).

(b) If λ is relatively large, what are its implications?

17.8. Using the formula for the mean lag given in (17.4.9), verify the mean lag of 10.959 quarters reported in the illustration of Table 17.1.

17.9. Suppose

$$M_t = \alpha + \beta_1 Y_t^* + \beta_2 R_t^* + u_t$$

where M = demand for real cash balances, Y^* = expected real income, and R^* = expected interest rate. Assume that expectations are formulated as follows:

$$Y_t^* = \gamma_1 Y_t + (1 - \gamma_1)Y_{t-1}^*$$
$$R_t^* = \gamma_2 R_t + (1 - \gamma_2)R_{t-1}^*$$

where γ_1 and γ_2 are coefficients of expectation, both lying between 0 and 1.

(a) How would you express M_t in terms of the observable quantities?

(b) What estimation problems do you foresee?

*17.10. If you estimate (17.7.2) by OLS, can you derive estimates of the original parameters? What problems do you foresee? (For details, see Roger N. Waud.†)

17.11. Serial correlation model. Consider the following model:

$$Y_t = \alpha + \beta X_t + u_t$$

Assume that u_t follows the Markov first-order autoregressive scheme given in Chapter 12, namely,

$$u_t = \rho u_{t-1} + \varepsilon_t$$

where ρ is the coefficient of (first-order) autocorrelation and where ε_t satisfies all the assumptions of the classical OLS. Then, as shown in Chapter 12, the model

$$Y_t = \alpha(1 - \rho) + \beta(X_t - \rho X_{t-1}) + \rho Y_{t-1} + \varepsilon_t$$

will have a serially independent error term, making OLS estimation possible. But this model, called the **serial correlation model**, very much resembles the Koyck, adaptive expectation, and partial adjustment models. How would you know in any given situation which of the preceding models is appropriate?**

17.12. Consider the Koyck (or for that matter the adaptive expectation) model given in (17.4.7), namely,

$$Y_t = \alpha(1 - \lambda) + \beta_0 X_t + \lambda Y_{t-1} + (u_t - \lambda u_{t-1})$$

Suppose in the original model u_t follows the first-order autoregressive scheme $u_t - \rho u_{1-t} = \varepsilon_t$, where ρ is the coefficient of autocorrelation and where ε_t satisfies all the classical OLS assumptions.

(a) If $\rho = \lambda$, can the Koyck model be estimated by OLS?

---

*Optional.

†"Misspecification in the 'Partial Adjustment' and 'Adaptive Expectations' Models," *International Economic Review*, vol. 9, no. 2, June 1968, pp. 204–217.

**For a discussion of the serial correlation model, see Zvi Griliches, "Distributed Lags: A Survey," *Econometrica*, vol. 35, no. 1, January 1967, p. 34.

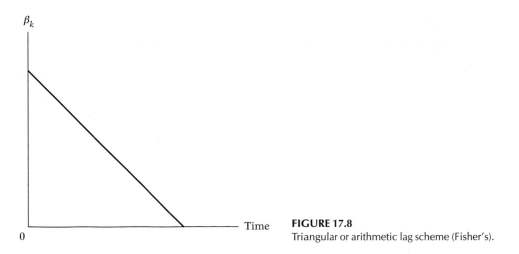

Time FIGURE 17.8
Triangular or arithmetic lag scheme (Fisher's).

(b) Will the estimates thus obtained be unbiased? Consistent? Why or why not?

(c) How reasonable is it to assume that $\rho = \lambda$?

17.13. Triangular, or arithmetic, distributed-lag model.[*] This model assumes that the stimulus (explanatory variable) exerts its greatest impact in the current time period and then declines by equal decrements to zero as one goes into the distant past. Geometrically, it is shown in Fig. 17.8. Following this distribution, suppose we run the following succession of regressions:

$$Y_t = \alpha + \beta\left(\frac{2X_t + X_{t-1}}{3}\right)$$

$$Y_t = \alpha + \beta\left(\frac{3X_t + 2X_{t-1} + X_{t-2}}{6}\right)$$

$$Y_t = \alpha + \beta\left(\frac{4X_t + 3X_{t-1} + 2X_{t-2} + X_{t-1}}{10}\right)$$

etc., and choose the regression that gives the highest R^2 as the "best" regression. Comment on this strategy.

17.14. Based on the quarterly data for the period 1950–1960, F. P. R. Brechling obtained the following demand function for labor for the British economy (the figures in parentheses are standard errors):[†]

$$\dot{E}_t = 14.22 + 0.172Q_t - 0.028t - 0.0007t^2 - 0.297E_{t-1}$$
$$(2.61)\ (0.014)\quad (0.015)\quad (0.0002)\quad (0.033)$$
$$\bar{R}^2 = 0.76 \qquad d = 1.37$$

where $\dot{E}_t = (E_t - E_{t-1})$

Q = output

t = time

[*]This model was proposed by Irving Fisher in "Note on a Short-Cut Method for Calculating Distributed Lags," *International Statistical Bulletin*, 1937, pp. 323–328.

[†]F. P. R. Brechling, "The Relationship between Output and Employment in British Manufacturing Industries," *Review of Economic Studies*, vol. 32, July 1965.

The preceding equation was based on the assumption that the desired level of employment E_t^* is a function of output, time, and time squared and on the hypothesis that $E_t - E_{t-1} = \delta(E_t^* - E_{t-1})$, where δ, the coefficient of adjustment, lies between 0 and 1.

(a) Interpret the preceding regression.

(b) What is the value of δ?

(c) Derive the long-run demand function for labor from the estimated short-run demand function.

(d) How would you test for serial correlation in the preceding model?

17.15. In studying the farm demand for tractors, Griliches used the following model:*

$$T_t^* = \alpha X_{1,t-1}^{\beta_1} X_{2,t-1}^{\beta_2}$$

where T^* = desired stock of tractors

X_1 = relative price of tractors

X_2 = interest rate

Using the stock adjustment model, he obtained the following results for the period 1921–1957:

$$\log T_t = \text{constant} - 0.218 \log X_{1,t-1} - 0.855 \log X_{2,t-1} + 0.864 \log T_{t-1}$$
$$(0.051) \qquad\qquad (0.170) \qquad\qquad (0.035)$$
$$R^2 = 0.987$$

where the figures in the parentheses are the estimated standard errors.

(a) What is the estimated coefficient of adjustment?

(b) What are the short- and long-run price elasticities?

(c) What are the corresponding interest elasticities?

(d) What are the reasons for high or low rate of adjustment in the present model?

17.16. Whenever the lagged dependent variable appears as an explanatory variable, the R^2 is usually much higher than when it is not included. What are the reasons for this observation?

17.17. Consider the lag patterns in Fig. 17.9. What degree polynomials would you fit to the lag structures and why?

17.18. Consider the Eq. (17.13.4)

$$\beta_i = a_0 + a_1 i + a_2 i^2 + \cdots + a_m i^m$$

To obtain the variance of $\hat{\beta}_i$ from the variances of $\hat{a}_i$, we use the following formula:

$$\text{var}(\hat{\beta}_i) = \text{var}(\hat{a}_0 + \hat{a}_1 i + \hat{a}_2 i^2 + \cdots + \hat{a}_m i^m)$$
$$= \sum_{j=0}^{m} i^{2j} \, \text{var}(\hat{a}_j) + 2 \sum_{j<p} i^{(j+p)} \, \text{cov}(\hat{a}_j \hat{a}_p)$$

---

*Zvi Griliches, "The Demand for a Durable Input: Farm Tractors in the United States, 1921–1957," in Arnold C. Harberger, ed., *The Demand for Durable Goods*, University of Chicago Press, Chicago, 1960.

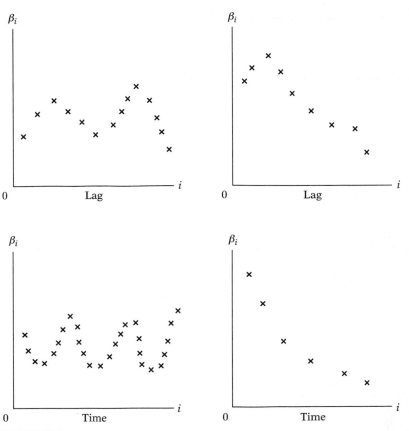

FIGURE 17.9
Hypothetical lag structures.

(a) Using the preceding formula, find the variance of $\hat{\beta}_i$ expressed as

$$\hat{\beta}_i = \hat{a}_0 + \hat{a}_1 i + \hat{a}_2 i^2$$
$$\hat{\beta}_i = \hat{a}_0 + \hat{a}_1 i + \hat{a}_2 i^2 + \hat{a}_3 i^3$$

(b) If the variances of $\hat{a}_i$ are large relative to themselves, will the variance of $\hat{\beta}_i$ be large also? Why or why not?

17.19. Consider the following distributed-lag model:

$$Y_t = \alpha + \beta_0 X_t + \beta_1 X_{t-1} + \beta_2 X_{t-2} + \beta_3 X_{t-3} + \beta_4 X_{t-4} + u_t$$

Assume that β_i can be adequately expressed by the second-degree polynomial as follows:

$$\beta_i = a_0 + a_1 i + a_2 i^2$$

How would you estimate the β's if we want to impose the restriction that $\beta_0 = \beta_4 = 0$?

17.20. The inverted V distributed-lag model. Consider the k-period finite distributed-lag model

$$Y_t = \alpha + \beta_0 X_t + \beta_1 X_{t-1} + \beta_2 X_{t-2} + \cdots + \beta_k X_{t-k} + u_t$$

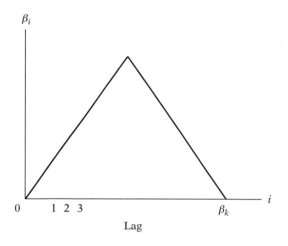

Lag

FIGURE 17.10
Inverted V distributed-lag model.

F. DeLeeuw has proposed the structure for the β's as in Fig. 17.10, where the β's follow the inverted V shape. Assuming for simplicity that k (the maximum length of the lag) is an even number, and further assuming that β_0 and β_k are zero, DeLeeuw suggests the following scheme for the β's:[*]

$$\beta_i = i\beta \qquad 0 \le i \le \frac{k}{2}$$
$$= (k - i)\beta \qquad \frac{k}{2} \le i < k$$

How would you use the DeLeeuw scheme to estimate the parameters of the preceding k-period distributed-lag model?

17.21. Refer to exercise 12.15. Since the d value shown there is of little use in detecting (first-order) autocorrelation (why?), how would you test for autocorrelation in this case?

Problems

17.22. Consider the following model:

$$Y_t^* = \alpha + \beta_0 X_t + u_t$$

where $Y^* =$ desired, or long-run, business expenditure for new plant and equipment, $X_t =$ sales, and $t =$ time. Using the stock adjustment model, estimate the parameters of the long- and short-run demand function for expenditure on new plant and equipment from the data in the table on the next page.

How would you find out if there is serial correlation in the data?

17.23. Use the data of exercise 17.22 but consider the following model:

$$Y_i^* = \beta_0 X_t^{\beta_1} e^{u_t}$$

Using the stock adjustment model (why?), estimate the short- and long-run elasticities of expenditure on new plant and equipment with respect to sales. Com-

---

[*]See his article, "The Demand for Capital Goods by Manufacturers: A Study of Quarterly Time Series," *Econometrica*, vol. 30, no. 3, July 1962, pp. 407–423.

Investment in fixed plant and equipment in manufacturing Y and manufacturing sales X_2 in billions of dollars, seasonally adjusted, United States, 1970–1991

Year	Plant expenditure, Y	Sales, X_2
1970	36.990	52.8050
1971	33.600	55.9060
1972	35.420	63.0270
1973	42.350	72.9310
1974	52.480	84.7900
1975	53.660	86.5890
1976	58.530	98.7970
1977	67.480	113.201
1978	78.130	126.905
1979	95.130	143.936
1980	112.60	154.391
1981	128.68	168.129
1982	123.97	163.351
1983	117.35	172.547
1984	139.61	190.682
1985	152.88	194.538
1986	137.95	194.657
1987	141.06	206.326
1988	163.45	223.541
1989	183.80	232.724
1990	192.61	239.459
1991	182.81	235.142

Source: Economic Report of the President, 1993
Data on Y from Table B-52, p. 407; data on X_2
from Table 8-53, p. 408.

pare your results with those for exercise 17.22. Which model would you choose and why? Is there serial correlation in the data? How do you know?

17.24. Use the data of exercise 17.22 but assume that

$$Y_t = \alpha + \beta X_t^* + u_t$$

where X_t^* are the desired sales. Estimate the parameters of this model and compare the results with those obtained in exercise 17.22. How would you decide which is the appropriate model? Based on the h statistic, would you conclude there is serial correlation in the data?

17.25. Suppose someone convinces you that the relationship between business expenditure for new plant and equipment and sales is as follows:

$$Y_t^* = \alpha + \beta X_t^* + u_t$$

where Y^* is desired expenditure and X^* is desired or expected sales. Use the data given in exercise 17.22 to estimate this model and comment on your results.

17.26. Using the data given in exercise 17.22, determine whether plant expenditure Granger-causes sales or sales Granger-causes plant expenditure. Use up to six lags and comment on your results. What important conclusion do you draw from this exercise?

17.27. Assume that sales in exercise 17.22 has a distributed-lag effect on expenditure on plant and equipment. Use four lags and a second-degree polynomial to estimate the distributed-lag model and comment on your results.

17.28. Schwarz criterion (SC) to determine lag length. To determine the lag length in a distributed-lag model, Schwarz suggests that one minimize the following function:

$$SC = \ln \tilde{\sigma}^2 + m \ln n$$

where $\tilde{\sigma}^2$ is the maximum likelihood estimate of $\sigma^2 (= RSS / n)$, m is the lag length, and n is the number of observations. In essence, one uses a regression model using several lagged values $(= m)$ and chooses that value of m that minimizes the value of SC.

Apply the Schwarz criterion to determine the appropriate lag length for the expenditure on new plant and equipment in relation to sales for the data in exercise 17.22.

17.29. Sims' test of causality.[*] In a twist of Granger causality, Sims exploits the fact that the future cannot cause the present. Suppose we want to find out if X causes Y. Now consider the following model:

$$Y_t = \alpha + \beta_k X_{t-k} + \beta_{k-1} X_{t-k-1} + \cdots + \beta_1 X_{t-1} + \beta_0 X_t +$$
$$\lambda_1 X_{t+1} + \lambda_2 X_{t+2} + \cdots + \lambda_m X_{t+m} + u_t$$

This regression includes the lagged, current, and future, or **lead,** values of the regressor X; terms such as X_{t+1} and X_{t+2} are called **lead terms**. In the preceding regression, there are k lagged and m lead terms. If X is to (Granger) cause Y, the sum of the coefficients of the lead X terms must be statistically equal to zero.[†]

Apply the Sims' test of causality to the data given in exercise 17.22 to determine whether sales (Granger) cause investment expenditure. Decide for yourself the appropriate lead and lag values of the regressor.

---

[*]C. A. Sims, "Money, Income, and Causality," *American Economic Review*, vol. 62, 1972, pp. 540–552.

[†]The choice between Granger and Sims causality tests is not clear. For further discussion of these tests, see G. Chamberlain, "The General Equivalence of Granger and Sims Causality," *Econometrica*, vol. 50, 1982, pp. 569–582.

PART
IV

SIMULTANEOUS-EQUATION MODELS

A casual look at the published empirical work in business and economics will reveal that many economic relationships are of the single-equation type. That is why we devoted the first three parts of this book to the discussion of single-equation regression models. In such models, one variable (the dependent variable Y) is expressed as a linear function of one or more other variables (the explanatory variables, the X's). In such models an implicit assumption is that the cause-and-effect relationship, if any, between Y and the X's is unidirectional: The explanatory variables are the *cause* and the dependent variable is the *effect.*

However, there are situations where there is a two-way flow of influence among economic variables; that is, one economic variable affects another economic variable(s) and is, in turn, affected by it (them). Thus, in the regression of money M on the rate of interest r, the single-equation methodology assumes implicitly that the rate of interest is fixed (say, by the Federal Reserve System) and tries to find out the response of money demanded to the changes in the level of the interest rate. But what happens if the rate of interest depends on the demand for money? In this case, the conditional regression analysis made in this book thus far may not be appropriate because now M depends on r and r depends on M. Thus, we need to consider two equations, one relating M to r and another relating r to M. And this leads us to consider simultaneous-equation models, models in which there is more than one regression equation, one for each interdependent variable.

In Part IV we present a very elementary and often heuristic introduction to the complex subject of **simultaneous-equation models,** the details being left for the references.

In Chapter 18, we provide several examples of simultaneous-equation models and show why the method of ordinary least squares considered previously is generally inapplicable to estimate the parameters of each of the equations in the model.

In Chapter 19, we consider the so-called **identification problem**. If in a system of simultaneous equations containing two or more equations it is not possible to obtain numerical values of each parameter in each equation because the equations are *observationally indistinguishable,* or look too much like one another, then we have the identification problem. Thus, in the regression of quantity Q on price P, is the resulting equation a demand function or a supply function, for Q and P enter into both functions. Therefore, if we have data on Q and P only and no other information, it will be difficult if not impossible to identify the regression as the demand or supply function. It is essential to resolve the identification problem before we proceed to estimation because if we do not know what we are estimating, estimation per se is meaningless. In Chapter 19 we offer various methods of solving the identification problem.

In Chapter 20, we consider several estimation methods that are designed specifically for estimating the simultaneous-equation models and consider their merits and limitations.

CHAPTER 18

SIMULTANEOUS-EQUATION MODELS

In this and the following two chapters we discuss the simultaneous-equation models. In particular, we discuss their special features, their estimation, and some of the statistical problems associated with them.

18.1 THE NATURE OF SIMULTANEOUS-EQUATION MODELS

In Parts I to III of this text we were concerned exclusively with single-equation models, i.e., models in which there was a single dependent variable Y and one or more explanatory variables, the X's. In such models the emphasis was on estimating and/or predicting the average value of Y conditional upon the fixed values of the X variables. The cause-and-effect relationship in such models therefore ran from the X's to the Y.

But in many situations such a one-way or unidirectional cause-and-effect relationship is not meaningful. This occurs if Y is determined by the X's, and some of the X's are, in turn, determined by Y. In short, there is a two-way, or simultaneous, relationship between Y and (some of) the X's, which makes the distinction between *dependent* and *explanatory* variables of dubious value. It is better to lump together a set of variables that can be determined simultaneously by the remaining set of variables—precisely what is done in simultaneous-equation models. In such models there is more than one equation—one for each of the *mutually, or jointly,* dependent or **endogenous variables.**[1] And

---

[1]In the context of the simultaneous-equation models, the jointly dependent variables are called **endogenous variables** and the variables that are truly nonstochastic or can be so regarded are called the **exogenous,** or **predetermined, variables.** (More on this in Chap. 19.)

unlike the single-equation models, in the simultaneous-equation models one may not estimate the parameters of a single equation without taking into account information provided by other equations in the system.

What happens if the parameters of each equation are estimated by applying, say, the method of OLS, disregarding other equations in the system? Recall that one of the crucial assumptions of the method of OLS is that the explanatory X variables are either nonstochastic or if stochastic (random) are distributed independently of the stochastic disturbance term. If neither of these conditions is met, then, as shown later, the least-squares estimators are not only biased but also inconsistent; that is, as the sample size increases indefinitely, the estimators do not converge to their true (population) values. Thus, in the following hypothetical system of equations,[2]

$$Y_{1i} = \beta_{10} + \beta_{12}Y_{2i} + \gamma_{11}X_{1i} + u_{1i} \qquad (18.1.1)$$
$$Y_{2i} = \beta_{20} + \beta_{21}Y_{1i} + \gamma_{21}X_{1i} + u_{2i} \qquad (18.1.2)$$

where Y_1 and Y_2 are mutually dependent, or endogenous, variables and X_1 an exogenous variable and where u_1 and u_2 are the stochastic disturbance terms, the variables Y_1 and Y_2 are both stochastic. Therefore, unless it can be shown that the stochastic explanatory variable Y_2 in (18.1.1) is distributed independently of u_1 and the stochastic explanatory variable Y_1 in (18.1.2) is distributed independently of u_2, application of the classical OLS to these equations individually will lead to inconsistent estimates.

In the remainder of this chapter we give a few examples of simultaneous-equation models and show the bias involved in the direct application of the least-squares method to such models. After discussing the so-called identification problem in Chapter 19, in Chapter 20 we discuss some of the special methods developed to handle the simultaneous-equation models.

18.2 EXAMPLES OF SIMULTANEOUS-EQUATION MODELS

Example 18.1. Demand-and-Supply Model

As is well known, the price P of a commodity and the quantity Q sold are determined by the intersection of the demand-and-supply curves for that commodity. Thus, assuming for simplicity that the demand-and-supply curves are linear and adding the stochastic disturbance terms u_1 and u_2, we may write the empirical demand-and-supply functions as

Demand function:	$Q_t^d = \alpha_0 + \alpha_1 P_t + u_{1t}$	$\alpha_1 < 0$	(18.2.1)
Supply function:	$Q_t^s = \beta_0 + \beta_1 P_t + u_{2t}$	$\beta_1 > 0$	(18.2.2)
Equilibrium condition:	$Q_t^d = Q_t^s$		

---

[2] These economical but self-explanatory notations will be generalized to more than two equations in Chap. 19.

where Q^d = quantity demanded
$\quad\quad Q^s$ = quantity supplied
$\quad\quad t$ = time

and the α's and β's are the parameters. A priori, α_1 is expected to be negative (downward-sloping demand curve), and β_1 is expected to be positive (upward-sloping supply curve).

Now it is not too difficult to see that P and Q are jointly dependent variables. If, for example, u_{1t} in (18.2.1) changes because of changes in other variables affecting Q_t^d (such as income, wealth, and tastes), the demand curve will shift upward if u_{1t} is positive and downward if u_{1t} is negative. These shifts are shown in Fig. 18.1.

As the figure shows, a shift in the demand curve changes both P and Q. Similarly, a change in u_{2t} (because of strikes, weather, import or export restrictions, etc.) will shift the supply curve, again affecting both P and Q. Because of this simultaneous dependence between Q and P, u_{1t} and P_t in (18.2.1) and u_{2t} and P_t in (18.2.2) cannot be independent. Therefore, a regression of Q on P as in (18.2.1)

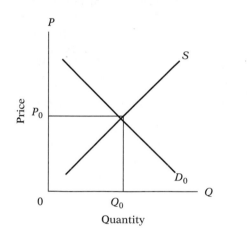

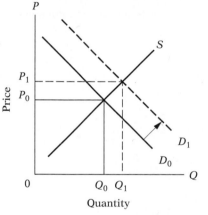

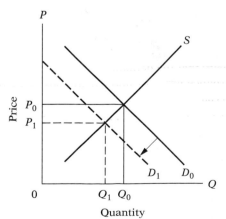

FIGURE 18.1
Interdependence of price and quantity.

would violate an important assumption of the classical linear regression model, namely, the assumption of no correlation between the explanatory variable(s) and the disturbance term.

Example 18.2   Keynesian Model of Income Determination

Consider the simple Keynesian model of income determination:

$$\text{Consumption function:} \qquad C_t = \beta_0 + \beta_1 Y_t + u_t \qquad 0 < \beta_1 < 1 \qquad (18.2.3)$$

$$\text{Income identity:} \qquad Y_t = C_t + I_t(= S_t) \qquad (18.2.4)$$

$$cov\,[u_t,\ Y_t] \neq 0$$

where

C = consumption expenditure

Y = income

I = investment (assumed exogenous)

S = savings

t = time

u = stochastic disturbance term

β_0 and β_1 = parameters

The parameter β_1 is known as the *marginal propensity to consume* (MPC) (the amount of extra consumption expenditure resulting from an extra dollar of income). From economic theory, β_1 is expected to lie between 0 and 1. Equation (18.2.3) is the (stochastic) consumption function; and (18.2.4) is the national income identity, signifying that total income is equal to total consumption expenditure plus total investment expenditure, it being understood that total investment expenditure is equal to total savings. Diagrammatically, we have Fig. 18.2.

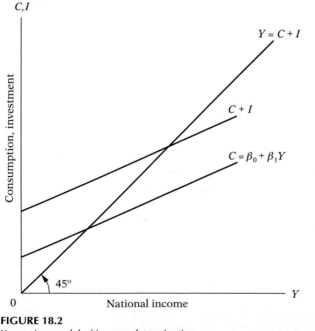

FIGURE 18.2
Keynesian model of income determination.

From the postulated consumption function and Fig. 18.2 it is clear that C and Y are interdependent and that Y_t in (18.2.3) is not expected to be independent of the disturbance term because when u_t shifts (because of a variety of factors subsumed in the error term), then the consumption function also shifts, which, in turn, affects Y_t. Therefore, once again the classical least-squares method is inapplicable to (18.2.3). If applied, the estimators thus obtained will be inconsistent, as we shall show later.

Example 18.3 Wage-Price Models

Consider the following Phillips-type model of money-wage and price determination:

$$\dot{W}_t = \alpha_0 + \alpha_1 \text{UN}_t + \alpha_2 \dot{P}_t + u_{1t} \qquad (18.2.5)$$

$$\dot{P}_t = \beta_0 + \beta_1 \dot{W}_t + \beta_2 \dot{R}_t + \beta_3 \dot{M}_t + u_{2t} \qquad (18.2.6)$$

where $\dot{W}$ = rate of change of money wages

UN = unemployment rate, %

$\dot{P}$ = rate of change of prices

$\dot{R}$ = rate of change of cost of capital

$\dot{M}$ = rate of change of price of imported raw material

t = time

u_1, u_2 = stochastic disturbances.

Since the price variable $\dot{P}$ enters into the wage equation and the wage variable $\dot{W}$ enters into the price equation, the two variables are jointly dependent. Therefore, these stochastic explanatory variables are expected to be correlated with the relevant stochastic disturbances, once again rendering the classical OLS method inapplicable to estimate the parameters of the two equations individually.

Example 18.4 The IS Model of Macroeconomics

The celebrated IS, or goods market equilibrium, model of macroeconomics[3] in its nonstochastic form can be expressed as

Consumption function:	$C_t = \beta_0 + \beta_1 Y_{dt}$	$0 < \beta_1 < 1$	(18.2.7)
Tax function:	$T_t = \alpha_0 + \alpha_1 Y_t$	$0 < \alpha_1 < 1$	(18.2.8)
Investment function:	$I_t = \gamma_0 + \gamma_1 r_t$		(18.2.9)
Definition:	$Y_{dt} = Y_t - T_t$		(18.2.10)
Government expenditure:	$G_t = \bar{G}$		(18.2.11)
National income identity:	$Y_t = C_t + I_t + G_t$		(18.2.12)

---

[3] "The goods market equilibrium schedule, or IS schedule, shows combinations of interest rates and levels of output such that planned spending equals income." See Rudiger Dornbusch and Stanley Fischer, *Macroeconomics*, 3d ed., McGraw-Hill, New York, 1984, p. 102. Note that for simplicity we have assumed away the foreign trade sector.

where Y = national income

C = consumption spending

I = planned or desired net investment

$\bar{G}$ = given level of government expenditure

T = taxes

Y_d = disposable income

r = interest rate

If you substitute (18.2.10) and (18.2.8) into (18.2.7) and substitute the resulting equation for C and Eq. (18.2.9) and (18.2.11) into (18.2.12), you should obtain

IS equation:
$$Y_t = \pi_0 + \pi_1 r_t \tag{18.2.13}$$

where

$$\pi_0 = \frac{\beta_0 - \alpha_0\beta_1 + \gamma_0 + \bar{G}}{1 - \beta_1(1 - \alpha_1)}$$

$$\pi_1 = \frac{1}{1 - \beta_1(1 - \alpha_1)} \tag{18.2.14}$$

Equation (18.2.13) is the equation of the IS, or goods market equilibrium, that is, it gives the combinations of the interest rate and level of income such that the goods market clears or is in equilibrium. Geometrically, the IS curve is shown in Fig. 18.3.

What would happen if we were to estimate, say, the consumption function (18.2.7) in isolation? Could we obtain unbiased and/or consistent estimates of β_0 and β_1? Such a result is unlikely because consumption depends on disposable income, which depends on national income Y, but the latter depends on r and $\bar{G}$ as well as the other parameters entering in π_0. Therefore, unless we take into account all these influences, a simple regression of C on Y_d is bound to give biased and/or inconsistent estimates of β_0 and β_1.

Example 18.5 The LM Model

The other half of the famous IS-LM paradigm is the LM, or money market equilibrium, relation, which gives the combinations of the interest rate and level of income such that the money market is cleared, that is, the demand for money is equal to its supply. Algebraically, the model, in the nonstochastic form, may be expressed as:

Money demand function:	$M_t^d = a + bY_t - cr_t$	(18.2.15)
Money supply function:	$M_t^s = \bar{M}$	(18.2.16)
Equilibrium condition:	$M_t^d = M_t^s$	(18.2.17)

where Y = income, r = interest rate, and $\bar{M}$ = assumed level of money supply, say, determined by the Fed.

Equating the money demand and supply functions and simplifying, we obtain:

LM equation:
$$Y_t = \lambda_0 + \lambda_1\bar{M} + \lambda_2 r_t \tag{18.2.18}$$

where

$$\lambda_0 = -a/b$$
$$\lambda_1 = 1/b \tag{18.2.19}$$
$$\lambda_2 = c/b$$

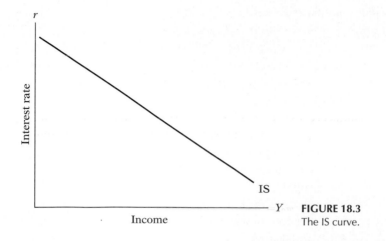

FIGURE 18.3
The IS curve.

For a given $M = \bar{M}$, the LM curve representing the relation (18.2.18) is as shown in Fig. 18.4.

The IS and LM curves show, respectively, that a whole array of interest rates is consistent with goods market equilibrium and a whole array of interest rates is compatible with equilibrium in the money market. Of course, only one interest rate and one level of income will be consistent simultaneously with the two equilibria. To obtain these, all that needs to be done is to equate (18.2.13) and (18.2.18). In exercise 18.4 you are asked to show the level of the interest rate and income that is simultaneously compatible with the goods and money market equilibrium.

Example 18.6 Econometric Models

An extensive use of simultaneous-equation models has been made in the econometric models built by several econometricians. An early pioneer in this field was Professor Lawrence Klein of the Wharton School of the University of Pennsylvania. His initial model, known as **Klein's model I,** is as follows:

Consumption function: $\quad C_t = \beta_0 + \beta_1 P_t + \beta_2 (W + W')_t$
$$+ \beta_3 P_{t-1} + u_{1t}$$

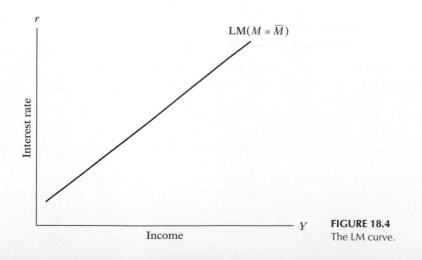

FIGURE 18.4
The LM curve.

Investment function: $\quad I_t = \beta_4 + \beta_5 P_t + \beta_6 P_{t-1} + \beta_7 K_{t-1} + u_{2t}$

Demand for labor: $\quad W_t = \beta_8 + \beta_9(Y + T - W')_t$
$$\qquad\qquad + \beta_{10}(Y + T - W')_{t-1}$$
$$\qquad\qquad + \beta_{11}t + u_{3t}$$

Identity: $\qquad\qquad Y_t + T_t = C_t + I_t + G_t \qquad\qquad\qquad$ (18.2.20)

Identity: $\qquad\qquad Y_t = W_t' + W_t + P_t$

Identity: $\qquad\qquad K_t = K_{t-1} + I_t$

where $\qquad\qquad C$ = consumption expenditure

$\qquad\qquad\qquad I$ = investment expenditure

$\qquad\qquad\qquad G$ = government expenditure

$\qquad\qquad\qquad P$ = profits

$\qquad\qquad\qquad W$ = private wage bill

$\qquad\qquad\qquad W'$ = government wage bill

$\qquad\qquad\qquad K$ = capital stock

$\qquad\qquad\qquad T$ = taxes

$\qquad\qquad\qquad Y$ = income after tax

$\qquad\qquad\qquad t$ = time

$\qquad u_1, u_2,$ and u_3 = stochastic disturbances[4]

In the preceding model the variables $C, I, W, Y, P,$ and K are treated as jointly dependent, or endogenous, variables and the variables $P_{t-1}, K_{t-1},$ and Y_{t-1} are treated as predetermined.[5] In all, there are six equations (including the three identities) to study the interdependence of six endogenous variables.

In Chapter 20 we shall see how such econometric models are estimated. For the time being, note that because of the interdependence among the endogenous variables, in general they are not independent of the stochastic disturbance terms, which therefore makes it inappropriate to apply the method of OLS to an individual equation in the system. As shown in Section 18.3, the estimators thus obtained are inconsistent; they do not converge to their true population values even when the sample size is very large.

18.3 THE SIMULTANEOUS-EQUATION BIAS: INCONSISTENCY OF OLS ESTIMATORS

As stated previously, the method of least squares may not be applied to estimate a single equation embedded in a system of simultaneous equations if one or more of the explanatory variables are correlated with the disturbance term in that equation because the estimators thus obtained are inconsistent. To show

---

[4]L. R. Klein, *Economic Fluctuations in the United States, 1921–1941*, John Wiley & Sons, New York, 1950.

[5]The model builder will have to specify which of the variables in a model are endogenous and which are predetermined. K_{t-1} and Y_{t-1} are predetermined because at time t their values are known. (More on this in Chap. 19.)

this, let us revert to the simple Keynesian model of income determination given in example 18.2. Suppose that we want to estimate the parameters of the consumption function (18.2.3). Assuming that $E(u_t) = 0, E(u_t^2) = \sigma^2, E(u_t u_{t+j}) = 0$ (for $j \neq 0$), and $\text{cov}(I_t, u_t) = 0$, which are the assumptions of the classical linear regression model, we first show that Y_t and u_t in (18.2.3) are correlated and then prove that $\hat{\beta}_1$ is an inconsistent estimator of β_1.

To prove that Y_t and u_t are correlated, we proceed as follows. Substitute (18.2.3) into (18.2.4) to obtain

$$Y_t = \beta_0 + \beta_1 Y_t + u_t + I_t$$

that is,

$$Y_t = \frac{\beta_0}{1 - \beta_1} + \frac{1}{1 - \beta_1} I_t + \frac{1}{1 - \beta_1} u_t \tag{18.3.1}$$

Now

$$E(Y_t) = \frac{\beta_0}{1 - \beta_1} + \frac{1}{1 - \beta_1} I_t \tag{18.3.2}$$

where use is made of the fact that $E(u_t) = 0$ and that I_t being exogenous, or predetermined (because it is fixed in advance), has as its expected value I_t.

Therefore, subtracting (18.3.2) from (18.3.1) results in

$$Y_t - E(Y_t) = \frac{u_t}{1 - \beta_1} \tag{18.3.3}$$

Moreover,

$$u_t - E(u_t) = u_t \qquad \text{(Why?)} \tag{18.3.4}$$

whence

$$\begin{aligned} \text{cov}(Y_t, u_t) &= E[Y_t - E(Y_t)][u_t - E(u_t)] \\ &= \frac{E(u_t^2)}{1 - \beta_1} \qquad \text{using (18.3.3) and (18.3.4)} \\ &= \frac{\sigma^2}{1 - \beta_1} \end{aligned} \tag{18.3.5}$$

Since σ^2 is positive by assumption (why?), the covariance between Y and u given in (18.3.5) is bound to be different from zero.[6] As a result, Y_t and u_t in (18.2.3) are expected to be correlated, which violates the assumption of the classical linear regression model that the disturbances are independent or at least uncorrelated with the explanatory variables. As noted previously, the OLS estimators in this situation are inconsistent.

To show that the OLS estimator $\hat{\beta}_1$ is an inconsistent estimator of β_1 because of correlation between Y_t and u_t, we proceed as follows:

---

[6]It will be greater than zero as long as β_1, the MPC, lies between 0 and 1, and it will be negative if β_1 is greater than unity. Of course, a value of MPC greater than unity would not make much economic sense. In reality therefore the covariance between Y_t and u_t is expected to be positive.

$$\hat{\beta}_1 = \frac{\sum (C_t - \bar{C})(Y_t - \bar{Y})}{\sum (Y_t - \bar{Y})^2}$$

$$= \frac{\sum c_t y_t}{\sum y_t^2}$$

$$= \frac{\sum C_t y_t}{\sum y_t^2} \qquad (18.3.6)$$

where the lowercase letters, as usual, indicate deviations from the (sample) mean values. Substituting for C_t from (18.2.3), we obtain

$$\hat{\beta}_1 = \frac{\sum (\beta_0 + \beta_1 Y_t + u_t) y_t}{\sum y_t^2}$$

$$= \beta_1 + \frac{\sum y_t u_t}{\sum y_t^2} \qquad (18.3.7)$$

where in the last step use is made of the fact that $\sum y_t = 0$ and $(\sum Y_t y_t / \sum y_t^2) = 1$ (why?).

If we take the expectation of (18.3.7) on both sides, we obtain

$$E(\hat{\beta}_1) = \beta_1 + E \left[\frac{\sum y_t u_t}{\sum y_t^2} \right] \qquad (18.3.8)$$

Unfortunately, we cannot evaluate $E(\sum y_t u_t / \sum y_t^2)$ since the expectations operator is a linear operator. [*Note:* $E(A/B) \neq E(A)/E(B)$.] But intuitively it should be clear that unless the term $(\sum y_t u_t / \sum y_t^2)$ is zero, $\hat{\beta}_1$ is a biased estimator of β_1. But have we not shown in (18.3.5) that the covariance between Y and u is nonzero and therefore would $\hat{\beta}_1$ not be biased? The answer is, not quite, since $\text{cov}(Y_t, u_t)$, a population concept, is not quite $\sum y_t u_t$, which is a sample measure, although as the sample size increases indefinitely the latter will tend toward the former. But if the sample size increases indefinitely, then we can resort to the concept of consistent estimator and find out what happens to $\hat{\beta}_1$ as n, the sample size, increases indefinitely. In short, when we cannot explicitly evaluate the expected value of an estimator, as in (18.3.8), we can turn our attention to its behavior in the large sample.

Now an estimator is said to be consistent if its **probability limit**,[7] or **plim** for short, is equal to its true (population) value. Therefore, to show that $\hat{\beta}_1$ of (18.3.7) is inconsistent, we must show that its plim is not equal to the true β_1. Applying the rules of probability limit to (18.3.7), we obtain[8]

$$\text{plim}(\hat{\beta}_1) = \text{plim}(\beta_1) + \text{plim} \left(\frac{\sum y_t u_t}{\sum y_t^2} \right)$$

$$= \text{plim}(\beta_1) + \text{plim} \left(\frac{\sum y_t u_t / n}{\sum y_t^2 / n} \right)$$

---

[7]See App. A for the definition of probability limit.
[8]As stated in App. A, the plim of a constant (for example, β_1) is the same constant and the plim of $(A/B) = \text{plim}(A)/\text{plim}(B)$. Note, however, that $E(A/B) \neq E(A)/E(B)$.

$$= \beta_1 + \frac{\text{plim}(\sum y_t u_t / n)}{\text{plim}(\sum y_t^2 / n)} \tag{18.3.9}$$

where in the second step we have divided $\sum y_t u_t$ and $\sum y_t^2$ by the total number of observations in the sample n so that the quantities in the parentheses are now the sample covariance between Y and u and the sample variance of Y, respectively.

In words, (18.3.9) states that the probability limit of $\hat{\beta}_1$ is equal to true β_1 plus the ratio of the plim of the sample covariance between Y and u to the plim of the sample variance of Y. Now as the sample size n increases indefinitely, one would expect the sample covariance between Y and u to approximate the true population covariance $E[Y_t - E(Y_t)][u_t - E(u_t)]$, which from (18.3.5) is equal to $[\sigma^2/(1 - \beta_1)]$. Similarly, as n tends to infinity, the sample variance of Y will approximate its population variance, say σ_Y^2. Therefore, Eq. (18.3.9) may be written as

$$\text{plim}(\hat{\beta}_1) = \beta_1 + \frac{\sigma^2/(1 - \beta_1)}{\sigma_Y^2}$$

$$= \beta_1 + \frac{1}{1 - \beta_1} \left(\frac{\sigma^2}{\sigma_Y^2} \right) \tag{18.3.10}$$

Given that $0 < \beta_1 < 1$ and that σ^2 and σ_Y^2 are both positive, it is obvious from Eq. (18.3.10) that plim $(\hat{\beta}_1)$ will always be greater than β_1; that is, $\hat{\beta}_1$ will overestimate the true β_1.[9] In other words, $\hat{\beta}_1$ is a biased estimator, and the bias will not disappear no matter how large the sample size.

18.4 THE SIMULTANEOUS-EQUATION BIAS: A NUMERICAL EXAMPLE

To demonstrate some of the points made in the preceding section, let us return to the simple Keynesian model of income determination given in Example 18.2 and carry out the following **Monte Carlo** study.[10] Assume that the values of investment I are as shown in column (3) of Table 18.1. Further assume that

$$E(u_t) = 0$$
$$E(u_t u_{t+j}) = 0 \qquad (j \neq 0)$$
$$\text{var}(u_t) = \sigma^2 = 0.04$$
$$\text{cov}(u_t, I_t) = 0$$

The u_t thus generated are shown in column (4).

---

[9]In general, however, the direction of the bias will depend on the structure of the particular model and the true values of the regression coefficients.

[10]This is borrowed from Kenneth J. White, Nancy G. Horsman, and Justin B. Wyatt, *SHAZAM: Computer Handbook for Econometrics for Use with Basic Econometrics*, McGraw-Hill, New York, pp. 131–134.

For the consumption function (18.2.3) assume that the values of the true parameters are known and are $\beta_0 = 2$ and $\beta_1 = 0.8$.

From the assumed values of β_0 and β_1 and the generated values of u_t we can generate the values of income Y_t from (18.3.1), which are shown in column (1) of Table 18.1. Once Y_t are known, and knowing β_0, β_1, and u_t, one can easily generate the values of consumption C_t from (18.2.3). The C's thus generated are given in column 2.

Since the true β_0 and β_1 are known, and since our sample errors are exactly the same as the "true" errors (because of the way we designed the Monte Carlo study), if we use the data of Table 18.1 to regress C_t on Y_t we should obtain $\beta_0 = 2$ and $\beta_1 = 0.8$, if OLS were unbiased. But from (18.3.7) we know that this will not be the case if the regressor Y_t and the disturbance u_t are correlated. Now it is not too difficult to verify from our data that the (sample) covariance between Y_t and u_t is $\sum y_t u_t = 3.8$ and that $\sum y_t^2 = 184$. Then, as (18.3.7) shows, we should have

$$\hat{\beta}_1 = \beta_1 + \frac{\sum y_t u_t}{\sum y_t^2}$$

$$= 0.8 + \frac{3.8}{184}$$

$$= 0.82065 \qquad (18.4.1)$$

That is, $\hat{\beta}_1$ is upward-biased by 0.02065.

Now let us regress C_t on Y_t, using the data given in Table 18.1. The regression results are

$$\hat{C}_t = 1.4940 + 0.82065 Y_t$$
$$(\text{se})(0.35413)(0.01434) \qquad (18.4.2)$$
$$(t)(4.2188)(57.209) \qquad R^2 = 0.9945$$

As expected, the estimated β_1 is precisely the one predicted by (18.4.1). In passing, note that the estimated β_0 too is biased.

In general the amount of the bias in $\hat{\beta}_1$ depends on β_1, σ^2 and var(Y) and, in particular, on the degree of covariance between Y and u.[11] As Kenneth White et al. note, "This is what simultaneous equation bias is all about. In contrast to single equation models, we can no longer assume that variables on the right hand side of the equation are uncorrelated with the error term."[12] Bear in mind that this bias remains even in large samples.

In view of the potentially serious consequences of applying OLS in simultaneous-equation models, is there a test of simultaneity that can tell us whether in a given instance we have the simultaneity problem? One version of the **Hausman specification test** can be used for this purpose, which we discuss in Chapter 19.

---

[11]See Eq. (18.3.5).
[12]Op. cit., pp. 133–134.

TABLE 18.1

Y_t (1)	C_t (2)	I_t (3)	u_t (4)
18.15697	16.15697	2.0	−0.3686055
19.59980	17.59980	2.0	−0.8004084E-01
21.93468	19.73468	2.2	0.1869357
21.55145	19.35145	2.2	0.1102906
21.88427	19.48427	2.4	−0.2314535E-01
22.42648	20.02648	2.4	0.8529544E-01
25.40940	22.80940	2.6	0.4818807
22.69523	20.09523	2.6	−0.6095481E-01
24.36465	21.56465	2.8	0.7292983E-01
24.39334	21.59334	2.8	0.7866819E-01
24.09215	21.09215	3.0	−0.1815703
24.87450	21.87450	3.0	−0.2509900E-01
25.31580	22.11580	3.2	−0.1368398
26.30465	23.10465	3.2	0.6092946E-01
25.78235	22.38235	3.4	−0.2435298
26.08018	22.68018	3.4	−0.1839638
27.24440	23.64440	3.6	−0.1511200
28.00963	24.40963	3.6	0.1926739E-02
30.89301	27.09301	3.8	0.3786015
28.98706	25.18706	3.8	−0.2588852E-02

Source: Kenneth J. White, Nancy G. Horsman, and Justin B. Wyatt, *SHAZAM Computer Handbook for Econometrics for Use with Damodar Gujarati: Basic Econometrics,* September 1985, p. 132

18.5 SUMMARY AND CONCLUSIONS

1. In contrast to single-equation models, in simultaneous-equation models more than one dependent, or **endogenous,** variable is involved, necessitating as many equations as the number of endogenous variables.

2. A unique feature of simultaneous-equation models is that the endogenous variable (i.e., regressand) in one equation may appear as an explanatory variable (i.e., regressor) in another equation of the system.

3. As a consequence, such an **endogenous explanatory variable** becomes stochastic and is usually correlated with the disturbance term of the equation in which it appears as an explanatory variable.

4. In this situation the classical OLS method may not be applied because the estimators thus obtained are not consistent, that is, they do not converge to their true population values no matter how large the sample size.

5. The Monte Carlo example presented in the text shows the nature of the bias involved in applying OLS to estimate the parameters of a regression equation in which the regressor is correlated with the disturbance term, which is typically the case in simultaneous-equation models.

6. Since simultaneous-equation models are used frequently, especially in econometric models, alternative estimating techniques have been developed

by various authors. These are discussed in Chapter 20, after the topic of the **identification problem** is considered in Chapter 19, a topic logically prior to estimation.

EXERCISES

Questions

18.1. Develop a simultaneous-equation model for the supply of and demand for dentists in the United States. Specify the endogenous and exogenous variables in the model.

18.2. Develop a simple model of the demand for and supply of money in the United States and compare your model with those developed by K. Brunner and A. H. Meltzer* and R. Tiegen.†

18.3. (a) For the demand-and-supply model of Example 18.1, obtain the expression for the probability limit of $\hat{\alpha}_1$.
(b) Under what conditions will this probability limit be equal to the true α_1?

18.4. For the IS-LM model discussed in the text, find the level of interest rate and income that is simultaneously compatible with the goods and money market equilibrium.

18.5. To study the relationship between inflation and yield on common stock, Bruno Oudet** used the following model:

$$R_{bt} = \alpha_1 + \alpha_2 R_{st} + \alpha_3 R_{bt-1} + \alpha_4 L_t + \alpha_5 Y_t + \alpha_6 \text{NIS}_t + \alpha_7 I_t + u_{1t}$$
$$R_{st} = \beta_1 + \beta_2 R_{bt} + \beta_3 R_{bt-1} + \beta_4 L_t + \beta_5 Y_t + \beta_6 \text{NIS}_t + \beta_7 E_t + u_{2t}$$

where L = real per capita monetary base
Y = real per capita income
I = the expected rate of inflation
NIS = a new issue variable
E = expected end-of-period stock returns, proxied by lagged stock price ratios
R_{bt} = bond yield
R_{st} = common stock returns

(a) Offer a theoretical justification for this model and see if your reasoning agrees with that of Oudet.
(b) Which are the endogenous variables in the model? And the exogenous variables?
(c) How would you treat the lagged R_{bt}—endogenous or exogenous?

---

*"Some Further Evidence on Supply and Demand Functions for Money," *Journal of Finance*, vol. 19, May 1964, pp. 240–283.

†"Demand and Supply Functions for Money in the United States," *Econometrica*, vol. 32, no. 4, October 1964, pp. 476–509.

**Bruno A. Oudet, "The Variation of the Return on Stocks in Periods of Inflation," *Journal of Financial and Quantitative Analysis*, vol. 8, no. 2, March 1973, pp. 247–258.

18.6. In their article, "A Model of the Distribution of Branded Personal Products in Jamaica,"* John U. Farley and Harold J. Levitt developed the following model (the personal products considered were shaving cream, skin cream, sanitary napkins, and toothpaste):

$$Y_{1i} = \alpha_1 + \beta_1 Y_{2i} + \beta_2 Y_{3i} + \beta_3 Y_{4i} + u_{1i}$$
$$Y_{2i} = \alpha_2 + \beta_4 Y_{1i} + \beta_5 Y_{5i} + \gamma_1 X_{1i} + \gamma_2 X_{2i} + u_{2i}$$
$$Y_{3i} = \alpha_3 + \beta_6 Y_{2i} + \gamma_3 X_{3i} + u_{3i}$$
$$Y_{4i} = \alpha_4 + \beta_7 Y_{2i} + \gamma_4 X_{4i} + u_{4i}$$
$$Y_{5i} = \alpha_5 + \beta_8 Y_{2i} + \beta_9 Y_{3i} + \beta_{10} Y_{4i} + u_{5i}$$

where Y_1 = percent of stores stocking the product

Y_2 = sales in units per month

Y_3 = index of direct contact with importer and manufacturer for the product

Y_4 = index of wholesale activity in the area

Y_5 = index of depth of brand stocking for the product (i.e., average number of brands of the product stocked by stores carrying the product)

X_1 = target population for the product

X_2 = income per capita in the parish where the area is

X_3 = distance from the population center of gravity to Kingston

X_4 = distance from population center to nearest wholesale town

(a) Can you identify the endogenous and exogenous variables in the preceding model?

(b) Can one or more equations in the model be estimated by the method of least squares? Why or why not?

18.7. To study the relationship between advertising expenditure and sales of cigarettes, Frank Bass used the following model:†

$$Y_{1t} = \alpha_1 + \beta_1 Y_{3t} + \beta_2 Y_{4t} + \gamma_1 X_{1t} + \gamma_2 X_{2t} + u_{1t}$$
$$Y_{2t} = \alpha_2 + \beta_3 Y_{3t} + \beta_4 Y_{4t} + \gamma_3 X_{1t} + \gamma_4 X_{2t} + u_{2t}$$
$$Y_{3t} = \alpha_3 + \beta_5 Y_{1t} + \beta_6 Y_{2t} + u_{3t}$$
$$Y_{4t} = \alpha_4 + \beta_7 Y_{1t} + \beta_8 Y_{2t} + u_{4t}$$

where Y_1 = logarithm of sales of filter cigarettes (number of cigarettes) divided by population over age 20

Y_2 = logarithm of sales of nonfilter cigarettes (number of cigarettes) divided by population over age 20

Y_3 = logarithm of advertising dollars for filter cigarettes divided by population over age 20 divided by advertising price index

Y_4 = logarithm of advertising dollars for nonfilter cigarettes divided by population over age 20 divided by advertising price index

---

Journal of Marketing Research, November 1968, pp. 362–368.

†"A Simultaneous Equation Regression Study of Advertising and Sales of Cigarettes," *Journal of Marketing Research*, vol. 6, August 1969, pp. 291–300.

X_1 = logarithm of disposable personal income divided by population over age 20 divided by consumer price index

X_2 = logarithm of price per package of nonfilter cigarettes divided by consumer price index

(a) In the preceding model the Y's are endogenous and the X's are exogenous. Why does the author assume X_2 to be exogenous?

(b) If X_2 is treated as an endogenous variable, how would you modify the preceding model?

18.8. G. Menges developed the following econometric model for the West German economy:*

$$Y_t = \beta_0 + \beta_1 Y_{t-1} + \beta_2 I_t + u_{1t}$$
$$I_t = \beta_3 + \beta_4 Y_t + \beta_5 Q_t + u_{2t}$$
$$C_t = \beta_6 + \beta_7 Y_t + \beta_8 C_{t-1} + \beta_9 P_t + u_{3t}$$
$$Q_t = \beta_{10} + \beta_{11} Q_{t-1} + \beta_{12} R_t + u_{4t}$$

where Y = national income
    I = net capital formation
    C = personal consumption
    Q = profits
    P = cost of living index
    R = industrial productivity
    t = time
    u = stochastic disturbances

(a) Which of the variables would you regard as endogenous and which as exogenous?

(b) Is there any equation in the system that can be estimated by the single-equation least-squares method?

(c) What is the reason behind including the variable P in the consumption function?

18.9. L. E. Gallaway and P. E. Smith developed a simple model for the United States economy, which is as follows:†

$$Y_t = C_t + I_t + G_t$$
$$C_t = \beta_1 + \beta_2 YD_{t-1} + \beta_3 M_t + u_{1t}$$
$$I_t = \beta_4 + \beta_5 (Y_{t-1} - Y_{t-2}) + \beta_6 Z_{t-1} + u_{2t}$$
$$G_t = \beta_7 + \beta_8 G_{t-1} + u_{3t}$$

where Y = gross national product
      C = personal consumption expenditure

---

*G. Menges, "Ein Ökonometriches Modell der Bundesrepublik Deutschland (Vier Strukturgleichungen)," I.F.O. Studien, vol. 5, 1959, pp. 1–22.

†"A Quarterly Econometric Model of the United States," *Journal of American Statistical Association,* vol. 56, 1961, pp. 379–383.

$$I = \text{gross private domestic investment}$$
$$G = \text{government expenditure plus net foreign investment}$$
$$YD = \text{disposable, or after-tax, income}$$
$$M = \text{money supply at the beginning of the quarter}$$
$$Z = \text{property income before taxes}$$
$$t = \text{time}$$
$$u_1, u_2, \text{ and } u_3 = \text{stochastic disturbances}$$

All variables are measured in the first difference form.

Based on the quarterly data from 1948–1957, the authors applied the least-squares method to each equation individually and obtained the following results:

$$C_t = 0.09 + 0.43YD_{t-1} + 0.23M_t \qquad\qquad R^2 = 0.23$$
$$I_t = 0.08 + 0.43(Y_{t-1} - Y_{t-2}) + 0.48Z_t \qquad R^2 = 0.40$$
$$G_t = 0.13 + 0.67G_{t-1} \qquad\qquad\qquad\qquad R^2 = 0.42$$

(a) How would you justify the use of the single-equation least-squares method in this case?

(b) Why are the R^2 values rather low?

Problems

18.10. You are given the following data on Y (gross domestic product), C (personal consumption expenditure), and I (gross domestic private investment), in billions of 1987 dollars, for the period 1970–1991.

Year	Personal consumption expenditure, C^*	Gross domestic private investment, I^*	Gross domestic product, Y^*
1970	1,813.5	429.7	2,873.9
1971	1,873.7	475.7	2,955.9
1972	1,978.4	532.2	3,107.1
1973	2,066.7	591.7	3,268.6
1974	2,053.8	543.0	3,248.1
1975	2,097.5	437.6	3,221.7
1976	2,207.3	520.6	3,380.8
1977	2,296.6	600.4	3,533.3
1978	2,391.8	664.6	3,703.5
1979	2,448.4	669.7	3,796.8
1980	2,447.1	594.4	3,776.3
1981	2,476.9	631.1	3,843.1
1982	2,503.7	540.5	3,760.3
1983	2,619.4	599.5	3,906.6
1984	2,746.1	757.5	4,148.5
1985	2,865.8	745.9	4,279.8
1986	2,969.1	735.1	4,404.5
1987	3,052.2	749.3	4,539.9
1988	3,162.4	773.4	4,718.6
1989	3,223.3	784.0	4,838.0
1990	3,260.4	739.1	4,877.5
1991	3,240.8	661.1	4,821.0

*Billions of dollars.

Source: Economic Report of the President, 1993, Table B-2, p. 350.

Assume that C is linearly related to Y as in the simple Keynesian model of income determination of Example 18.2. Obtain OLS estimates of the parameters of the consumption function. Save the results for another look at the same data using the methods developed in Chapter 20.

18.11. Using the data given in exercise 18.10, regress gross domestic investment I on GDP and save the results for further examination in a later chapter.

18.12. Consider the macroeconomics identity

$$C + I = Y \quad (= \text{GDP})$$

As before, assume that

$$C_t = \beta_0 + \beta_1 Y_t + u_t$$

and, following the **accelerator model** of macroeconomics, let

$$I_t = \alpha_0 + \alpha_1 (Y_t - Y_{t-1}) + v_t$$

where u and v are error terms. From the data given in exercise 18.10, estimate the accelerator model and save the results for further study.

CHAPTER
19

THE IDENTIFICATION
PROBLEM

In this chapter we consider the nature and significance of the identification problem. The crux of the identification problem is as follows: Recall the demand-and-supply model introduced in Section 18.2. Suppose that we have time series data on Q and P only and no additional information (such as income of the consumer, price prevailing in the previous period, and weather condition). The identification problem then consists in seeking an answer to this question: Given only the data on P and Q, how do we know whether we are estimating the demand function or the supply function? Alternatively, if we *think* we are fitting a demand function, how do we guarantee that it is, in fact, the demand function that we are estimating and not something else?

A moment's reflection will reveal that an answer to the preceding question is necessary before one proceeds to estimate the parameters of our demand function. In this chapter we shall show how the identification problem is resolved. We first introduce a few notations and definitions and then illustrate the identification problem with several examples. This is followed by the rules that may be used to find out whether an equation in a simultaneous-equation model is identified, that is, whether it is the relationship that we are actually estimating, be it the demand or supply function or something else.

19.1 NOTATIONS AND DEFINITIONS

To facilitate our discussion, we introduce the following notations and definitions:

The general M equations model in M endogenous, or jointly dependent, variables may be written as Eq. (19.1.1):

$$Y_{1t} = \beta_{12}Y_{2t} + \beta_{13}Y_{3t} + \cdots + \beta_{1M}Y_{Mt}$$
$$+ \gamma_{11}X_{1t} + \gamma_{12}X_{2t} + \cdots + \gamma_{1K}X_{Kt} + u_{1t}$$

$$Y_{2t} = \beta_{21}Y_{1t} + \beta_{23}Y_{3t} + \cdots + \beta_{2M}Y_{Mt}$$
$$+ \gamma_{21}X_{1t} + \gamma_{22}X_{2t} + \cdots + \gamma_{2K}X_{Kt} + u_{2t}$$

$$Y_{3t} = \beta_{31}Y_{1t} + \beta_{32}Y_{2t} + \cdots + \beta_{3M}Y_{Mt}$$
$$+ \gamma_{31}X_{1t} + \gamma_{32}X_{2t} + \cdots + \gamma_{3K}X_{Kt} + u_{3t}$$

$$\cdots\cdots\cdots\cdots\cdots\cdots\cdots\cdots\cdots\cdots\cdots\cdots\cdots\cdots\cdots\cdots\cdots\cdots\cdots$$

$$Y_{MT} = \beta_{M1}Y_{1t} + \beta_{M2}Y_{2t} + \cdots + \beta_{M,M-1}Y_{M-1,t}$$
$$+ \gamma_{M1}X_{1t} + \gamma_{M2}X_{2t} + \cdots + \gamma_{MK}X_{Kt} + u_{Mt}$$

$$(19.1.1)$$

where $Y_1, Y_2, \ldots, Y_M = M$ endogenous, or jointly dependent, variables

$X_1, X_2, \ldots, X_K = K$ predetermined variables (one of these X variables may take a value of unity to allow for the intercept term in each equation)

$u_1, u_2, \ldots, u_M = M$ stochastic disturbances

$t = 1, 2, \ldots, T =$ total number of observations

$\beta's =$ coefficients of the endogenous variables

$\gamma's =$ coefficients of the predetermined variables

In passing, note that not each and every variable need appear in each equation. As a matter of fact, we see in Section 19.2 that this must not be the case if an equation is to be identified.

As Eq. (19.1.1) shows, the variables entering a simultaneous-equation model are of two types: **endogenous**, that is, those (whose values are) determined within the model; and **predetermined**, that is, those (whose values are) determined outside the model. The endogenous variables are regarded as stochastic, whereas the predetermined variables are treated as nonstochastic.

The predetermined variables are divided into two categories: **exogenous**, current as well as lagged, and **lagged endogenous**. Thus, X_{1t} is a current (present-time) exogenous variable, whereas $X_{1(t-1)}$ is a lagged exogenous variable, with a lag of one time period. $Y_{(t-1)}$ is a lagged endogenous variable with a lag of one time period, but since the value of $Y_{1(t-1)}$ is known at the current time t, it is regarded as nonstochastic, hence, a predetermined variable.[1] In short, current exogenous, lagged exogenous, and lagged endogenous variables are deemed predetermined; their values are not determined by the model in the current time period.

---

[1] It is assumed implicitly here that the stochastic disturbances, the u's, are serially uncorrelated. If this is not the case, Y_{t-1} will be correlated with the current period disturbance term u_t. Hence, we cannot treat it as predetermined.

It is up to the model builder to specify which variables are endogenous and which are predetermined. Although (noneconomic) variables, such as temperature and rainfall, are clearly exogenous or predetermined, the model builder must exercise great care in classifying economic variables as endogenous or predetermined: He or she must defend the classification on a priori or theoretical grounds. However, later in the chapter we provide a statistical test of exogeneity.

The equations appearing in (19.1.1) are known as the **structural**, or **behavioral**, equations because they may portray the structure (of an economic model) of an economy or the behavior of an economic agent (e.g., consumer or producer). The β's and γ's are known as the **structural parameters** or **coefficients**.

From the structural equations one can solve for the M endogenous variables and derive the **reduced-form equations** and the associated **reduced-form coefficients**. A reduced-form equation is one that expresses an endogenous variable solely in terms of the predetermined variables and the stochastic disturbances. To illustrate, consider the Keynesian model of income determination encountered in Chapter 18:

$$\text{Consumption function:} \quad C_t = \beta_0 + \beta_1 Y_t + u_t \quad 0 < \beta_1 < 1 \,(18.2.3)$$

$$\text{Income identity:} \quad Y_t = C_t + I_t \quad\quad\quad\quad (18.2.4)$$

In this model C (consumption) and Y (income) are the endogenous variables and I (investment expenditure) is treated as an exogenous variable. Both these equations are structural equations, (18.2.4) being an identity. As usual, the MPC β_1 is assumed to lie between 0 and 1.

If (18.2.3) is substituted into (18.2.4), we obtain, after simple algebraic manipulation,

$$Y_t = \Pi_0 + \Pi_1 I_t + w_t \quad\quad\quad\quad (19.1.2)$$

where

$$\Pi_0 = \frac{\beta_0}{1 - \beta_1}$$

$$\Pi_1 = \frac{1}{1 - \beta_1} \quad\quad\quad\quad (19.1.3)$$

$$w_t = \frac{u_t}{1 - \beta_1}$$

Equation (19.1.2) is a **reduced-form equation**; it expresses the endogenous variable Y solely as a function of the exogenous (or predetermined) variable I and the stochastic disturbance term u. Π_0 and Π_1 are the associated **reduced-form coefficients**. Notice that these reduced-form coefficients are nonlinear combinations of the structural coefficient(s). why is this imp?

Substituting the value of Y from (19.1.2) into C of (18.2.3), we obtain another reduced-form equation:

$$C_t = \Pi_2 + \Pi_3 I_t + w_t \quad\quad\quad\quad (19.1.4)$$

where

$$\Pi_2 = \frac{\beta_0}{1 - \beta_1} \qquad \Pi_3 = \frac{\beta_1}{1 - \beta_1} \qquad\qquad (19.1.5)$$

$$w_t = \frac{u_t}{1 - \beta_1}$$

The reduced-form coefficients, such as Π_1 and Π_3, are also known as **impact**, or **short-run, multipliers**, because they measure the immediate impact on the endogenous variable of a unit change in the value of the exogenous variable.[2] If in the preceding Keynesian model the investment expenditure is increased by, say, \$1 and if the MPC is assumed to be 0.8, then from (19.1.3) we obtain $\Pi_1 = 5$. This result means that increasing the investment by \$1 will immediately (i.e., in the current time period) lead to an increase in income of \$5, that is, a fivefold increase. Similarly, under the assumed conditions, (19.1.5) shows that $\Pi_3 = 4$, meaning that \$1 increase in investment expenditure will lead immediately to \$4 increase in consumption expenditure.

In the context of econometric models, equations such as (18.2.4) or $Q_t^d = Q_t^s$ (quantity demanded equal to quantity supplied) are known as the *equilibrium conditions*. Identity (18.2.4) states that aggregate income Y must be equal to aggregate consumption (i.e., consumption expenditure plus investment expenditure). When equilibrium is achieved, the endogenous variables assume their equilibrium values.[3]

Notice an interesting feature of the reduced-form equations. Since only the predetermined variables and stochastic disturbances appear on the right sides of these equations, and since the predetermined variables are assumed to be uncorrelated with the disturbance terms, the OLS method can be applied to estimate the coefficients of the reduced-form equations (the Π's). From the estimated reduced-form coefficients one may estimate the structural coefficients (the β's), as shown later. This procedure is known as **indirect least squares** (ILS), and the estimated structural coefficients are called ILS estimates.

We shall study the ILS method in greater detail in Chap. 20. In the meantime, note that since the reduced-form coefficients can be estimated by the OLS method, and since these coefficients are combinations of the structural coefficients, the possibility exists that the structural coefficients can be "retrieved" from the reduced-form coefficients, and it is in the estimation of the structural parameters that we may be ultimately interested. How does one retrieve the structural coefficients from the reduced-form coefficients? The answer is given in Section 19.2, an answer that brings out the crux of the identification problem.

---

[2]In econometric models the exogenous variables play a crucial role. Very often, such variables are under the direct control of the government. Examples are the rate of personal and corporate taxes, subsidies, unemployment compensation, etc.

[3]For details, see Jan Kmenta, *Elements of Econometrics*, 2d ed., Macmillan, New York, 1986, pp. 723–731.

19.2 THE IDENTIFICATION PROBLEM

By the **identification problem** we mean whether numerical est the parameters of a structural equation can be obtained from the est reduced-form coefficients. If this can be done, we say that the particular e tion is *identified*. If this cannot be done, then we say that the equation und consideration is *unidentified*, or *underidentified*.

An identified equation may be either *exactly* (or fully or just) *identified* or *overidentified*. It is said to be exactly identified if unique numerical values of the structural parameters can be obtained. It is said to be overidentified if more than one numerical value can be obtained for some of the parameters of the structural equations. The circumstances under which each of these cases occurs will be shown in the following discussion. *what does this mean?*

The identification problem arises because different sets of structural coefficients may be compatible with the same set of data. To put the matter differently, a given reduced-form equation may be compatible with different structural equations or different hypotheses (models), and it may be difficult to tell which particular hypothesis (model) we are investigating. In the remainder of this section we consider several examples to show the nature of the identification problem.

Underidentification

Consider once again the demand-and-supply model (18.2.1) and (18.2.2), together with the market-clearing, or equilibrium, condition that demand is equal to supply. By the equilibrium condition, we obtain

$$\alpha_0 + \alpha_1 P_t + u_{1t} = \beta_0 + \beta_1 P_t + u_{2t} \tag{19.2.1}$$

Solving (19.2.1), we obtain the equilibrium price

$$P_t = \Pi_0 + v_t \tag{19.2.2}$$

where

$$\Pi_0 = \frac{\beta_0 - \alpha_0}{\alpha_1 - \beta_1} \tag{19.2.3}$$

$$v_t = \frac{u_{2t} - u_{1t}}{\alpha_1 - \beta_1} \tag{19.2.4}$$

Substituting P_t from (19.2.2) into (18.2.1) or (18.2.2), we obtain the following equilibrium quantity:

$$Q_t = \Pi_1 + w_t \tag{19.2.5}$$

where

$$\Pi_1 = \frac{\alpha_1 \beta_0 - \alpha_0 \beta_1}{\alpha_1 - \beta_1} \tag{19.2.6}$$

$$w_t = \frac{\alpha_1 u_{2t} - \beta_1 u_{1t}}{\alpha_1 - \beta_1} \tag{19.2.7}$$

error terms v_t and w_t are linear combinations of the
d u_2.
nd (19.2.5) are reduced-form equations. Now our
l contains four structural coefficients α_0, α_1, β_0, and
e way of estimating them. Why? The answer lies
coefficients given in (19.2.3) and (19.2.6). These
contain all four structural parameters, but there
r structural unknowns can be estimated from only
coefficients. Recall from high school algebra that to estimate
four unknowns we must have four (independent) equations, and, in general,
to estimate k unknowns we must have k (independent) equations. Incidentally,
if we run the reduced form regression (19.2.2) and (19.2.5), we will see that
there are no explanatory variables, only the *constants*, and these *constants* will
simply give the mean values of P and Q (why?).

What all this means is that, given time series data on P (price) and Q
(quantity) and no other information, there is no way the researcher can guarantee whether he or she is estimating the demand function or the supply function. That is, a given P_t and Q_t represent simply the point of intersection of the
appropriate demand-and-supply curves because of the equilibrium condition
that demand is equal to supply. To see this clearly, consider the scattergram
shown in Fig. 19.1.

Figure 19.1a gives a few scatter points relating Q to P. Each scatter point
represents the intersection of a demand and a supply curve, as shown in Fig.
19.1b. Now consider a single point, such as that shown in Fig. 19.1c. There is
no way we can be sure which demand-and-supply curve of a whole family of
curves shown in that panel generated that point. Clearly, some additional information about the nature of the demand-and-supply curves is needed. For example, if the demand curve shifts over time because of change in income, tastes,
etc., but the supply curve remains relatively stable, as in Fig. 19.1d, the scatter
points trace out a supply curve. In this situation, we say that the supply curve
is identified. By the same token, if the supply curve shifts over time because
of changes in weather conditions (in the case of agricultural commodities) or
other extraneous factors but the demand curve remains relatively stable, as in
Fig. 19.1e the scatter points trace out a demand curve. In this case, we say that
the demand curve is identified.

There is an alternative and perhaps more illuminating way of looking at
the identification problem. Suppose we multiply (18.2.1) by λ ($0 \le \lambda \le 1$) and
(18.2.2) by $1 - \lambda$ to obtain the following equations (*note:* we drop the superscripts on Q):

$$\lambda Q_t = \lambda\alpha_0 + \lambda\alpha_1 P_t + \lambda u_{1t} \tag{19.2.8}$$

$$(1 - \lambda)Q_t = (1 - \lambda)\beta_0 + (1 - \lambda)\beta_1 P_t + (1 - \lambda)u_{2t} \tag{19.2.9}$$

Adding these two equations gives the following *linear combination* of the original demand-and-supply equations:

$$Q_t = \gamma_0 + \gamma_1 P_t + w_t \tag{19.2.10}$$

why would our data give only equilibrium pts ?! ??

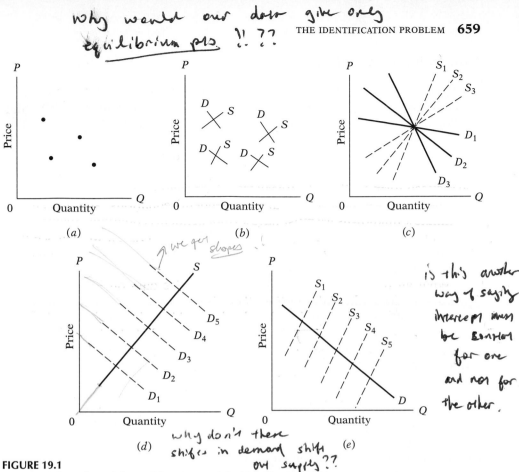

↗ we get slopes !

is this another way of saying intercept must be constant for one and not for the other.

why don't there shifts in demand shift our supply ??

FIGURE 19.1
Hypothetical supply-and-demand functions and the identification problem.

where

$$\gamma_0 = \lambda\alpha_0 + (1 - \lambda)\beta_0$$

$$\gamma_1 = \lambda\alpha_1 + (1 - \lambda)\beta_1 \qquad\qquad (19.2.11)$$

$$w_t = \lambda u_{1t} + (1 - \lambda)u_{2t}$$

The "bogus," or "mongrel," equation (19.2.10) is *observationally indistinguishable* from either (18.2.1) or (18.2.2) because they involve the regression of Q and P. Therefore, if we have time series data on P and Q only, any of (18.2.1), (18.2.2), or (19.2.10) may be compatible with the same data. In other words, the same data may be compatible with the "hypothesis" (18.2.1), (18.2.2), or (19.2.10), and there is no way we can tell which one of these hypotheses we are testing.

For an equation to be identified, that is, for its parameters to be estimated, it must be shown that the given set of data will not produce a structural equation that looks similar in appearance to the one in which we are interested. If we set out to estimate the demand function, we must show that the given data are not consistent with the supply function or some mongrel equation.

Just, or Exact, Identification

The reason we could not identify the preceding demand function or the supply function was that the same variables P and Q are present in both functions and there is no additional information, such as that indicated in Fig. 19.1d or e. But suppose we consider the following demand-and-supply model:

Demand function: $\quad Q_t = \alpha_0 + \alpha_1 P_t + \alpha_2 I_t + u_{1t} \qquad \alpha_1 < 0, \alpha_2 > 0 \quad (19.2.12)$

Supply function: $\quad Q_t = \beta_0 + \beta_1 P_t + u_{2t} \qquad \beta_1 > 0 \qquad\qquad (19.2.13)$

where I = income of the consumer, an exogenous variable, and all other variables are as defined previously.

Notice that the only difference between the preceding model and our original demand-and-supply model is that there is an additional variable in the demand function, namely, income. From economic theory of demand we know that income is usually an important determinant of demand for most goods and services. Therefore, its inclusion in the demand function will give us some additional information about consumer behavior. For most commodities income is expected to have a positive effect on consumption ($\alpha_2 > 0$).

Using the market-clearing mechanism, quantity demanded = quantity supplied, we have

$$\alpha_0 + \alpha_1 P_t + \alpha_2 I_t + u_{1t} = \beta_0 + \beta_1 P_t + u_{2t} \qquad (19.2.14)$$

Solving Eq. (19.2.14) provides the following equilibrium value of P_t:

$$P_t = \Pi_0 + \Pi_1 I_t + v_t \qquad (19.2.15)$$

where the reduced-form coefficients are

$$\Pi_0 = \frac{\beta_0 - \alpha_0}{\alpha_1 - \beta_1}$$

$$\Pi_1 = -\frac{\alpha_2}{\alpha_1 - \beta_1} \qquad (19.2.16)$$

and

$$v_t = \frac{u_{2t} - u_{1t}}{\alpha_1 - \beta_1}$$

Substituting the equilibrium value of P_t into the preceding demand or supply function, we obtain the following equilibrium quantity:

$$Q_t = \Pi_2 + \Pi_3 I_t + w_t \qquad (19.2.17)$$

where

$$\Pi_2 = \frac{\alpha_1 \beta_0 - \alpha_0 \beta_1}{\alpha_1 - \beta_1}$$

$$\Pi_3 = -\frac{\alpha_2 \beta_1}{\alpha_1 - \beta_1} \qquad (19.2.18)$$

and

$$w_t = \frac{\alpha_1 u_{2t} - \beta_1 u_{1t}}{\alpha_1 - \beta_1}$$

Since (19.2.15) and (19.2.17) are both reduced-form equ[...] method can be applied to estimate their parameters. Now t[...] supply model (19.2.12) and (19.2.13) contains five structur[...] α_0, α_1, α_2, β_1, and β_2. But there are only four equations to [...] namely, the four reduced-form coefficients Π_0, Π_1, Π_2, and Π_3 gi[...] and (19.2.18). Hence, unique solution of all the structural coefficients is not possible. But it can be readily shown that the parameters of the supply function can be identified (estimated) because

$$\beta_0 = \Pi_2 - \beta_1\Pi_0$$

$$\beta_1 = \frac{\Pi_3}{\Pi_1}$$

(19.2.19)

But there is no unique way of estimating the parameters of the demand function; therefore, it remains underidentified. Incidentally, note that the structural coefficient β_1 is a nonlinear function of the reduced-form coefficients, which poses some problems when it comes to estimating the standard error of the estimated β_1, as we shall see in Chap. 20.

To verify that the demand function (19.2.12) cannot be identified (estimated), let us multiply it by λ ($0 \le \lambda \le 1$) and (19.2.13) by $1 - \lambda$ and add them up to obtain the following "mongrel" equation:

$$Q_t = \gamma_0 + \gamma_1 P_t + \gamma_2 I_t + w_t$$

(19.2.20)

where

$$\gamma_0 = \lambda\alpha_0 + (1 - \lambda)\beta_0$$
$$\gamma_1 = \lambda\alpha_1 + (1 - \lambda)\beta_1$$
$$\gamma_2 = \lambda\alpha_2$$

(19.2.21)

and

$$w_t = \lambda u_{1t} + (1 - \lambda)u_{2t}$$

Equation (19.2.20) is observationally indistinguishable from the demand function (19.2.12) although it is distinguishable from the supply function (19.2.13), which does not contain the variable I as an explanatory variable. Hence, the demand function remains unidentified.

Notice an interesting fact: It is the presence of an additional variable in the demand function that enables us to identify the supply function! Why? The inclusion of the income variable in the demand equation provides us some additional information about the variability of the function, as indicated in Fig. 19.1d. The figure shows how the intersection of the stable supply curve with the shifting demand curve (on account of changes in income) enables us to trace (identify) the supply curve. As will be shown shortly, very often the identifiability of an equation depends on whether it excludes one or more variables that are included in other equations in the model.

But suppose we consider the following demand-and-supply model:

Demand function: $Q_t = \alpha_0 + \alpha_1 P_t + \alpha_2 I_t + u_{1t}$ $\alpha_1 < 0, \alpha_2 > 0$

(19.2.12)

upply function: $\quad Q_t = \beta_0 + \beta_1 P_t + \beta_2 P_{t-1} + u_{2t} \quad\quad \beta_1 > 0, \beta_2 > 0$

$$(19.2.22)$$

where the demand function remains as before but the supply function includes an additional explanatory variable, price lagged one period. The supply function postulates that the quantity of a commodity supplied depends on its current and previous period's price, a model often used to explain the supply of many agricultural commodities. Note that P_{t-1} is a predetermined variable because its value is known at time t.

By the market-clearing mechanism we have

$$\alpha_0 + \alpha_1 P_t + \alpha_2 I_t + u_{1t} = \beta_0 + \beta_1 P_t + \beta_2 P_{t-1} + u_{2t} \quad\quad (19.2.23)$$

Solving this equation, we obtain the following equilibrium price:

$$P_t = \Pi_0 + \Pi_1 I_t + \Pi_2 P_{t-1} + v_t \quad\quad (19.2.24)$$

where

$$\Pi_0 = \frac{\beta_0 - \alpha_0}{\alpha_1 - \beta_1}$$

$$\Pi_1 = -\frac{\alpha_2}{\alpha_1 - \beta_1} \quad\quad (19.2.25)$$

$$\Pi_2 = \frac{\beta_2}{\alpha_1 - \beta_1}$$

$$v_t = \frac{u_{2t} - u_{1t}}{\alpha_1 - \beta_1}$$

Substituting the equilibrium price into the demand or supply equation, we obtain the corresponding equilibrium quantity:

$$Q_t = \Pi_3 + \Pi_4 I_t + \Pi_5 P_{t-1} + w_t \quad\quad (19.2.26)$$

where the reduced-form coefficients are

$$\Pi_3 = \frac{\alpha_1 \beta_0 - \alpha_0 \beta_1}{\alpha_1 - \beta_1}$$

$$\Pi_4 = -\frac{\alpha_2 \beta_1}{\alpha_1 - \beta_1} \quad\quad (19.2.27)$$

$$\Pi_5 = \frac{\alpha_1 \beta_2}{\alpha_1 - \beta_1}$$

and

$$w_t = \frac{\alpha_1 u_{2t} - \beta_1 u_{1t}}{\alpha_1 - \beta_1}$$

The demand-and-supply model given in equations (19.2.12) and (19.2.22) contain six structural coefficients—α_0, α_1, α_2, β_0, β_1, and β_2—and there are six reduced-form coefficients—Π_0, Π_1, Π_2, Π_3, Π_4, and Π_5—to estimate them. Thus, we have six equations in six unknowns, and normally we should be able to obtain unique estimates. Therefore, the parameters of both the demand-and-supply equations can be identified, and the system as a whole can be identified. (In exercise 19.2 the reader is asked to express the six structural coefficients in terms of the six reduced-form coefficients given previously to show that unique estimation of the model is possible.)

To check that the preceding demand-and-supply functions are identified, we can also resort to the device of multiplying the demand equation (19.2.12) by λ ($0 \leq \lambda \leq 1$) and the supply equation (19.2.22) by $1 - \lambda$ and add them to obtain a mongrel equation. This mongrel equation will contain both the predetermined variables I_t and P_{t-1}; hence, it will be observationally different from the demand as well as the supply equation because the former does not contain P_{t-1} and the latter does not contain I_t.

Overidentification

For certain goods and services, income as well as wealth of the consumer is an important determinant of demand. Therefore, let us modify the demand function (19.2.12) as follows, keeping the supply function as before:

Demand function: $\qquad Q_t = \alpha_0 + \alpha_1 P_t + \alpha_2 I_t + \alpha_3 R_t + u_{1t}$ (19.2.28)

Supply function: $\qquad Q_t = \beta_0 + \beta_1 P_t + \beta_2 P_{t-1} + u_{2t}$ (19.2.22)

where in addition to the variables already defined, R represents wealth; for most goods and services, wealth, like income, is expected to have a positive effect on consumption.

Equating demand to supply, we obtain the following equilibrium price and quantity:

$$P_t = \Pi_0 + \Pi_1 I_t + \Pi_2 R_t + \Pi_3 P_{t-1} + v_t \qquad (19.2.29)$$
$$Q_t = \Pi_4 + \Pi_5 I_t + \Pi_6 R_t + \Pi_7 P_{t-1} + w_t \qquad (19.2.30)$$

where

$$\Pi_0 = \frac{\beta_0 - \alpha_0}{\alpha_1 - \beta_1} \qquad\qquad \Pi_1 = -\frac{\alpha_2}{\alpha_1 - \beta_1}$$

$$\Pi_2 = -\frac{\alpha_3}{\alpha_1 - \beta_1} \qquad\qquad \Pi_3 = \frac{\beta_2}{\alpha_1 - \beta_1}$$

$$\Pi_4 = \frac{\alpha_1 \beta_0 - \alpha_0 \beta_1}{\alpha_1 - \beta_1} \qquad\qquad \Pi_5 = -\frac{\alpha_2 \beta_1}{\alpha_1 - \beta_1} \qquad (19.2.31)$$

$$\Pi_6 = -\frac{\alpha_3 \beta_1}{\alpha_1 - \beta_1} \qquad\qquad \Pi_7 = \frac{\alpha_1 \beta_2}{\alpha_1 - \beta_1}$$

$$w_t = \frac{\alpha_1 u_{2t} - \beta_1 u_{1t}}{\alpha_1 - \beta_1} \qquad\qquad v_t = \frac{u_{2t} - u_{1t}}{\alpha_1 - \beta_1}$$

The preceding demand-and-supply model contains seven structural coefficients, but there are eight equations to estimate them—the eight reduced-form coefficients given in (19.2.31); that is, the number of equations is greater than the number of unknowns. As a result, unique estimation of all the parameters of our model is not possible, which can be shown easily. From the preceding reduced-form coefficients, we can obtain

$$\beta_1 = \frac{\Pi_6}{\Pi_2} \qquad (19.2.32)$$

or

$$\beta_1 = \frac{\Pi_5}{\Pi_1} \tag{19.2.33}$$

that is, there are two estimates of the price coefficient in the supply function, and there is no guarantee that these two values or solutions will be identical.[4] Moreover, since β_1 appears in the denominators of all the reduced-form coefficients, the ambiguity in the estimation of β_1 will be transmitted to other estimates too.

Why was the supply function identified in the system (19.2.12) and (19.2.22) but not in the system (19.2.28) and (19.2.22), although in both cases the supply function remains the same? The answer is that we have "too much," or an **oversufficiency, of information** to identify the supply curve. This situation is the opposite of the case of underidentification, where there is too little information. The oversufficiency of the information results from the fact that in the model (19.2.12) and (19.2.22) the exclusion of the income variable from the supply function was enough to identify it, but in the model (19.2.28) and (19.2.22) the supply function excludes not only the income variable but also the wealth variable. In other words, in the latter model we put "too many" restrictions on the supply function by requiring it to exclude more variables than necessary to identify it. However, this situation does not imply that overidentification is necessarily bad because we shall see in Chap. 20 how we can handle the problem of too much information, or too many restrictions.

We have now exhausted all the cases. As the preceding discussion shows, an equation in a simultaneous-equation model may be underidentified or identified (either over- or just). The model as a whole is identified if each equation in it is identified. To secure identification, we resort to the reduced-form equations. But in Section 19.3, we consider an alternative and perhaps less time-consuming method of determining whether or not an equation in a simultaneous-equation model is identified.

19.3 RULES FOR IDENTIFICATION

As the examples in Section 19.2 show, in principle it is possible to resort to the reduced-form equations to determine the identification of an equation in a system of simultaneous equations. But these examples also show how time-consuming and laborious the process can be. Fortunately, it is not essential to use this procedure. The so-called **order and rank conditions of identification** lighten the task by providing a systematic routine.

To understand the order and rank conditions, we introduce the following notations:

M = number of endogenous variables in the model

m = number of endogenous variables in a given equation

---

[4]Notice the difference between under- and overidentification. In the former case, it is impossible to obtain estimates of the structural parameters, whereas in the latter case, there may be several estimates of one or more structural coefficients.

K = number of predetermined variables in the model
k = number of predetermined variables in a given equation

The Order Condition of Identifiability[5]

A necessary (but not sufficient) condition of identification, known as the **order condition**, may be stated in two different but equivalent ways as follows (the necessary as well as sufficient condition of identification will be presented shortly):

> **Definition 19.1.** In a model of M simultaneous equations in order for an equation to be identified, it must exclude *at least* $M - 1$ variables (endogenous as well as predetermined) appearing in the model. If it excludes exactly $M - 1$ variables, the equation is just identified. If it excludes more than $M - 1$ variables, it is overidentified.

> **Definition 19.2** In a model of M simultaneous equations, in order for an equation to be identified, the number of predetermined variables excluded from the equation must not be less than the number of endogenous variables included in that equation less 1, that is,
>
> $$K - k \geq m - 1 \tag{19.3.1}$$
>
> If $K - k = m - 1$, the equation is just identified, but if $K - k > m - 1$, it is overidentified.

In exercise 19.1 the reader is asked to prove that the preceding two definitions of identification are equivalent.

To illustrate the order condition, let us revert to our previous examples.

Example 19.1

$$\text{Demand function:} \quad Q_t = \alpha_0 + \alpha_1 P_t + u_{1t} \tag{18.2.1}$$
$$\text{Supply function:} \quad Q_t = \beta_0 + \beta_1 P_t + u_{2t} \tag{18.2.2}$$

This model has two endogenous variables P and Q and no predetermined variables. To be identified, each of these equations must exclude at least $M - 1 = 1$ variable. Since this is not the case, neither equation is identified.

Example 19.2

$$\text{Demand function:} \quad Q_t = \alpha_0 + \alpha_1 P_t + \alpha_2 I_t + u_{1t} \tag{19.2.12}$$
$$\text{Supply function:} \quad Q_t = \beta_0 + \beta_1 P_t + u_{2t} \tag{19.2.13}$$

In this model Q and P are endogenous and I is exogenous. Applying the order condition given in (19.3.1), we see that the demand function is unidentified. On the other hand, the supply function is just identified because it excludes exactly $M - 1 = 1$ variable I_t.

---

[5]The term **order** refers to the order of a matrix, that is, the number of rows and columns present in a matrix. See App. B.

land function: $\quad Q_t = \alpha_0 + \alpha_1 P_t + \alpha_2 I_t + u_{1t}$ ⊥ $\quad$ (19.2.12)

ply function: $\quad Q_t = \beta_0 + \beta_1 P_t + \beta_2 P_{t-1} + u_{2t}$ $\quad$ (19.2.22)

Q_t are endogenous and I_t and P_{t-1} are predetermined, Eq. exactly one variable P_{t-1} and Eq. (19.2.22) also excludes exactly ~~one var...~~ nce each equation is identified by the order condition. Therefore, the model as a whole is identified.

Example 19.4

Zero

Demand function: $\quad Q_t = \alpha_0 + \alpha_1 P_t + \alpha_2 I_t + \alpha_3 R_t + u_{1t}$ ⊥ (19.2.28)

Supply function: $\quad Q_t = \beta_0 + \beta_1 P_t + \beta_2 P_{t-1} + u_{2t}$ $\quad$ 2 (19.2.22)

In this model P_t and Q_t are endogenous and I_t, R_t, and P_{t-1} are predetermined. The demand function excludes exactly one variable P_{t-1}, and hence by the order condition it is exactly identified. But the supply function excludes two variables I_t and R_t, and hence it is overidentified. As noted before, in this case there are two ways of estimating β_1, the coefficient of the price variable.

Notice a slight complication here. By the order condition the demand function is identified. But if we try to estimate the parameters of this equation from the reduced-form coefficients given in (19.2.31), the estimates will not be unique because β_1, which enters into the computations, takes two values and we shall have to decide which of these values is appropriate. But this complication can be obviated because it is shown in Chapter 20 that in cases of overidentification the method of indirect least squares is not appropriate and should be discarded in favor of other methods. One such method is **two-stage least squares**, which we shall discuss fully in Chapter 20.

As the previous examples show, identification of an equation in a model of simultaneous equations is possible if that equation excludes one or more variables that are present elsewhere in the model. This situation is known as the *exclusion* (of variables) *criterion*, or *zero restrictions criterion* (the coefficients of variables not appearing in an equation are assumed to have zero values). This criterion is by far the most commonly used method of securing or determining identification of an equation. But notice that the zero restrictions criterion is based on a priori or theoretical expectations that certain variables do not appear in a given equation. It is up to the researcher to spell out clearly why he or she does expect certain variables to appear in some equations and not in others.

The Rank Condition of Identifiability[6]

The order condition discussed previously is *a necessary but not sufficient* condition for identification; that is, even if it is satisfied, it may happen that an equa-

---

[6]The term **rank** refers to the rank of a matrix and is given by the largest-order square matrix (contained in the given matrix) whose determinant is nonzero. Alternatively, the rank of a matrix is the largest number of linearly independent rows or columns of that matrix. See App. B.

tion is not identified. Thus, in Example 19.2, the supply equation was identified by the order condition because it excluded the income variable I_t, which appeared in the demand function. But identification is accomplished only if α_2, the coefficient of I_t in the demand function, is not zero, that is, if the income variable not only probably but actually does enter the demand function.

More generally, even if the order condition $K - k \geq m - 1$ is satisfied by an equation, it may be unidentified because the predetermined variables excluded from this equation but present in the model may not all be independent so that there may not be one-to-one correspondence between the structural coefficients (the β's) and the reduced-form coefficients (the Π's). That is, we may not be able to estimate the structural parameters from the reduced-form coefficients, as we shall show shortly. Therefore, we need both a necessary and sufficient condition for identification. This is provided by the *rank condition* of identification, which may be stated as follows:

> **Rank condition of identification** In a model containing M equations in M endogenous variables, an equation is identified if and only if *at least one nonzero determinant of order* $(M - 1)(M - 1)$ can be constructed from the coefficients of the variables (both endogenous and predetermined) excluded from that particular equation but included in the other equations of the model.

As an illustration of the rank condition of identification, consider the following hypothetical system of simultaneous equations in which the Y variables are endogenous and the X variables are predetermined.[7]

$$Y_{1t} - \beta_{10} \qquad\qquad - \beta_{12}Y_{2t} - \beta_{13}Y_{3t} - \gamma_{11}X_{1t} \qquad\qquad\qquad = u_{1t} \quad (19.3.2)$$

$$Y_{2t} - \beta_{20} \qquad\qquad - \beta_{23}Y_{3t} - \gamma_{21}X_{1t} - \gamma_{22}X_{2t} \qquad\qquad = u_{2t} \quad (19.3.3)$$

$$Y_{3t} - \beta_{30} - \beta_{31}Y_{1t} \qquad\qquad - \gamma_{31}X_{1t} - \gamma_{32}X_{2t} \qquad\qquad = u_{3t} \quad (19.3.4)$$

$$Y_{4t} - \beta_{40} - \beta_{41}Y_{1t} - \beta_{42}Y_{2t} \qquad\qquad\qquad\qquad - \gamma_{43}X_{3t} = u_{4t} \quad (19.3.5)$$

To facilitate identification, let us write the preceding system in Table 19.1, which is self-explanatory.

Let us first apply the order condition of identification, as shown in Table 19.2. By the order condition each equation is identified. Let us recheck with the

TABLE 19.1

Equation no.	Coefficients of the variables							
	1	Y_1	Y_2	Y_3	Y_4	X_1	X_2	X_3
(19.3.2)	$-\beta_{10}$	1	$-\beta_{12}$	$-\beta_{13}$	0	$-\gamma_{11}$	0	0
(19.3.3)	$-\beta_{20}$	0	1	$-\beta_{23}$	0	$-\gamma_{21}$	$-\gamma_{22}$	0
(19.3.4)	$-\beta_{30}$	$-\beta_{31}$	0	1	0	$-\gamma_{31}$	$-\gamma_{32}$	0
(19.3.5)	$-\beta_{40}$	$-\beta_{41}$	$-\beta_{42}$	0	1	0	0	$-\gamma_{43}$

---

[7]The simultaneous-equation system presented in (19.1.1) may be shown in the following alternative form, which may be convenient for matrix manipulations.

TABLE 19.2

Equation no.	No. of predetermined variables excluded, $(K - k)$	No. of endogenous variables included less one, $(m - 1)$	Identified?
(19.3.2)	2	3 - 1 2	Exactly
(19.3.3)	1	2 - 1 1	Exactly
(19.3.4)	1	2 - 1 1	Exactly
(19.3.5)	2	3 - 1 2	Exactly

rank condition. Consider the first equation, which excludes variables Y_4, X_2, and X_3 (this is represented by zeros in the first row of Table 19.1). For this equation to be identified, we must obtain at least one nonzero determinant of order 3×3 from the coefficients of the variables excluded from this equation but included in other equations. To obtain the determinant we first obtain the relevant matrix of coefficients of variables Y_4, X_2, and X_3 included in the other equations. In the present case there is only one such matrix, call it $\mathbf{A}$, defined as follows:

$$\mathbf{A} = \begin{bmatrix} 0 & -\gamma_{22} & 0 \\ 0 & -\gamma_{32} & 0 \\ 1 & 0 & -\gamma_{43} \end{bmatrix} \tag{19.3.6}$$

It can be seen that the determinant of this matrix is zero:

$$\det \mathbf{\Lambda} = \begin{vmatrix} 0 & -\gamma_{22} & 0 \\ 0 & -\gamma_{32} & 0 \\ 1 & 0 & -\gamma_{43} \end{vmatrix} \tag{19.3.7}$$

Since the determinant is zero, the rank of the matrix (19.3.6), denoted by $\rho(\mathbf{A})$, is less than 3. Therefore, Eq. (19.3.2) does not satisfy the rank condition and hence is not identified.

As noted, the rank condition is both a necessary and sufficient condition for identification. Therefore, although the order condition shows that Eq. (19.3.2) is identified, the rank condition shows that it is not. Apparently, the columns or rows of the matrix $\mathbf{A}$ given in (19.3.6) are not (linearly) independent, meaning that there is some relationship between the variables Y_4, X_2, and X_3. As a result, we may not have enough information to estimate the parameters of equation (19.3.2); the reduced-form equations for the preceding model will show that it is not possible to obtain the structural coefficients of that equation from the reduced-form coefficients. The reader should verify that by the rank condition Eq. (19.3.3) and (19.3.4) are also unidentified but Eq. (19.3.5) is identified.

As the preceding discussion shows, *the rank condition tells us whether the equation under consideration is identified or not, whereas the order condition tells us if it is exactly identified or overidentified.*

To apply the rank condition one may proceed as follows:

1. Write down the system in a tabular form, as shown in Table 19.1.
2. Strike out the coefficients of the row in which the equation under consideration appears.

3. Also strike out the columns corresponding to those coefficients in 2 which are nonzero.

4. The entries left in the table will then give only the coefficients of the variables included in the system but not in the equation under consideration. From these entries form all possible matrices, like **A**, of order $M - 1$ and obtain the corresponding determinants. If at least one nonvanishing or nonzero determinant can be found, the equation in question is (just or over) identified. The rank of the matrix, say, **A**, in this case is exactly equal to $M - 1$. If all the possible $(M - 1)(M - 1)$ determinants are zero, the rank of the matrix **A** is less than $M - 1$ and the equation under investigation is not identified.

Our discussion of the order and rank conditions of identification leads to the following general principles of identifiability of a structural equation in a system of M simultaneous equations:

1. If $K - k > m - 1$ and the rank of the **A** matrix is $M - 1$, the equation is overidentified.
2. If $K - k = m - 1$ and the rank of the matrix **A** is $M - 1$, the equation is exactly identified.
3. If $K - k \geq m - 1$ and the rank of the matrix **A** is less than $M - 1$, the equation is underidentified.
4. If $K - k < m - 1$, the structural equation is unidentified. The rank of the **A** matrix in this case is bound to be less than $M - 1$. (Why?)

Henceforth, when we talk about identification we mean exact identification, or overidentification. There is no point in considering unidentified, or underidentified, equations because no matter how extensive the data, the structural parameters cannot be estimated. However, as shown in Chapter 20, parameters of overidentified as well as just identified equations can be estimated.

Which condition should one use in practice: Order or rank? For large simultaneous-equation models, applying the rank condition is a formidable task. Therefore, as Harvey notes,

> Fortunately, the order condition is usually sufficient to ensure identifiability, and although it is important to be aware of the rank condition, a failure to verify it will rarely result in disaster.[8]

*19.4 A TEST OF SIMULTANEITY[9]

If there is no simultaneous equation, or **simultaneity problem**, the OLS estimators produce consistent and efficient estimators. On the other hand, if there

---

[8]Andrew Harvey, *The Econometric Analysis of Time Series*, 2d ed., The MIT Press, Cambridge, Mass., 1990, p. 328.

*Optional.

[9]The following discussion draws from Robert S. Pindyck and Daniel L. Rubinfeld, *Econometric Models and Economic Forecasts*, 3d ed., McGraw-Hill, New York, 1991, pp. 303–305.

is simultaneity, OLS estimators are not even consistent. In the presence of simultaneity, as we will show in Chapter 20, the methods of **two-stage least squares (2SLS)** and **instrumental variables** will give estimators that are consistent and efficient. Oddly, if we apply these alternative methods when there is in fact no simultaneity, these methods yield estimators that are consistent but not efficient (i.e., with smaller variance). All this discussion suggests that we should check for the simultaneity problem before we discard OLS in favor of the alternatives.

As we showed earlier, the simultaneity problem arises because some of the regressors are endogenous and are therefore likely to be correlated with the disturbance, or error, term. Therefore, *a test of simultaneity is essentially a test of whether (an endogenous) regressor is correlated with the error term.* If it is, the simultaneity problem exists, in which case alternatives to OLS must be found; if it is not, we can use OLS. To find out which is the case in a concrete situation, we can use Hausman's specification error test.

Hausman Specification Test

A version of the Hausman specification error test that can be used for testing the simultaneity problem can be explained as follows:[10]

To fix ideas, consider the following two-equation model:

Demand function:	$Q_t = \alpha_0 + \alpha_1 P_t + \alpha_2 I_t + \alpha_3 R_t + u_{1t}$	(19.4.1)
Supply function:	$Q_t = \beta_0 + \beta_1 P_t + u_{2t}$	(19.4.2)

where P = price
  Q = quantity
  I = income
  R = wealth
  $u's$ = error terms

Assume that I and R are exogenous. Of course, P and Q are endogenous.

Now consider the supply function (19.4.2). If there is no simultaneity problem (i.e., P and Q are mutually independent), P_t and u_{2t} should be uncorrelated (why?). On the other hand, if there is simultaneity, P_t and u_{2t} will be correlated. To find out which is the case, the Hausman test proceeds as follows:

First, from (19.4.1) and (19.4.2) we obtain the following reduced-form equations:

$$P_t = \Pi_0 + \Pi_1 I_t + \Pi_2 R_t + v_t \qquad (19.4.3)$$

$$Q_t = \Pi_3 + \Pi_4 I_t + \Pi_3 R_t + w_t \qquad (19.4.4)$$

---

[10] J. A. Hausman, "Specification Tests in Econometrics," *Econometrica*, vol. 46, November 1976, pp. 1251–1271. See also A. Nakamura and M. Nakamura, "On the Relationship among Several Specification Error Tests Presented by Durbin, Wu, and Hausman," *Econometrica*, vol. 49, November 1981, pp. 1583–1588.

where v and w are the reduced form error terms. Estimati
we obtain

$$\hat{P}_t = \hat{\Pi}_0 + \hat{\Pi}_1 I_t + \hat{\Pi}_2 R_t$$

Therefore,

$$P_t = \hat{P}_t + \hat{v}_t$$

where $\hat{P}_t$ are estimated P_t and $\hat{v}_t$ are the estimated residuals. Substitut
(19.4.6) into (19.4.2), we get

$$Q_t = \beta_0 + \beta_1 \hat{P}_t + \beta_1 \hat{v}_t + u_{2t} \qquad (19.4.7)$$

Note: The coefficients of P_t and v_t are the same.

Now under the null hypothesis that there is no simultaneity, the correlation
between $\hat{v}_t$ and u_{2t} should be zero, asymptotically. Thus, if we run the regression
(19.4.7) and find that the coefficient of v_t in (19.4.7) is statistically zero, we can
conclude that there is no simultaneity problem. Of course, this conclusion will
be reversed if we find this coefficient to be statistically significant.

Essentially, then, the Hausman test involves the following steps:

Step 1. Regress P_t on I_t and R_t to obtain $\hat{v}_t$.

Step 2. Regress Q_t on $\hat{P}_t$ and $\hat{v}_t$ and perform a t test on the coefficient of $\hat{v}_t$. If it is significant, do not reject the hypothesis of simultaneity; otherwise, reject it.[11] For efficient estimation, however, Pindyck and Rubinfeld suggest regressing Q_t on P_t and $\hat{v}_t$.[12]

Example 19.5 Pindyck-Rubinfeld Model of Public Spending[13]

To study the behavior of U. S. state and local government expenditure, the
authors developed the following simultaneous equation model:

$$EXP = \beta_1 + \beta_2 AID + \beta_3 INC + \beta_4 POP + u_i \qquad (19.4.8)$$
$$AID = \delta_1 + \delta_2 EXP + \delta_3 PS + v_i \qquad (19.4.9)$$

where EXP = state and local government public expenditures
AID = level of federal grants-in-aid
INC = income of states
POP = state population
PS = population of primary and secondary school children
u and v = error terms

In this model, INC, POP, and PS are regarded exogenous.

---

[11] If more than one endogenous regressor is involved, we will have to use the F test.
[12] Pindyck and Rubinfeld, op. cit., p. 304. *Note:* The regressor is P_t and *not* $\hat{P}_t$.
[13] Pindyck and Rubinfeld, op. cit., pp. 176–177. Notations slightly altered.

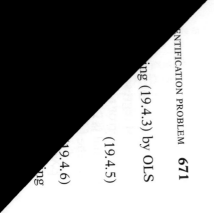

f simultaneity between EXP and AID, the au-
)P, and PS (i.e., the reduced-form regression).
on be w_i. From this regression the calculated
egress EXP on AID, INC, POP, and $\hat{w}_i$, to ob-

0013INC − 0.518POP − 1.39$\hat{w}_i$ (19.4.10)[14]
6)   (−4.63)   (−1.73)

0.99

ie coefficient of $\hat{w}_i$ is not statistically signifi-
cant, and therefore, at this level, there is no simultaneity problem. However, at
the 10% level of significance, it is statistically significant, raising the possibility
that the simultaneity problem is present.

Incidentally, the OLS estimation of (19.4.8) is as follows:

$$\widehat{EXP} = -46.81 + 3.24AID + 0.00019INC - 0.597POP \qquad (19.4.11)$$
$$t = (-0.56)(13.64) \qquad (8.12) \qquad (-5.71)$$
$$R^2 = 0.993$$

Notice an interesting feature of the results given in (19.4.10) and (19.4.11):
When simultaneity is explicitly taken into account, the AID variable is less significant although numerically it is greater in magnitude.

I don't get this!!

*19.5   TESTS FOR EXOGENEITY

We noted earlier that it is the researcher's responsibility to specify which variables are endogenous and which are exogenous. This will depend on the problem at hand and the a priori information the researcher has. But is it possible
to develop a statistical test of exogeneity, in the manner of Granger's causality
test?

The Hausman test discussed in Section 19.4 can be utilized to answer this
question. Suppose we have a three-equation model in three endogenous variables, Y_1, Y_2, and Y_3, and suppose there are three exogenous variables, X_1, X_2,
and X_3. Further, suppose that the first equation of the model is

$$Y_{1i} = \beta_0 + \beta_2 Y_{2i} + \beta_3 Y_{3i} + \alpha_1 X_{1i} + u_{1i} \qquad (19.5.1)$$

If Y_2 and Y_3 are truly endogenous, we cannot estimate (19.5.1) by OLS (why?).
But how do we find that out? We can proceed as follows. We obtain the reduced-
form equations for Y_2 and Y_3 (*Note:* the reduced-form equations will have
only predetermined variables on the right-hand side). From these reduced-
form equations, we obtain $\hat{Y}_{2i}$ and $\hat{Y}_{3i}$, the predicted values of Y_{2i} and Y_{3i},
respectively. Then in the spirit of the Hausman test discussed earlier, we can
estimate the following equation by OLS:

---

[14]As per footnote 12, the authors use AID rather than $\widehat{AID}$ as the regressor.
*Optional.

$$Y_{1i} = \beta_0 + \beta_2 Y_{2i} + \beta_3 Y_{3i} + \alpha_1 X_{1i} + \lambda_2 \hat{Y}_{2i} + \lambda_3 \hat{Y}_{3i} + u_{1i} \qquad (19.5.2)$$

Using the F test, we test the hypothesis that $\lambda_2 = \lambda_3 = 0$. If this hypothesis is rejected, Y_2 and Y_3 can be deemed endogenous, but if it is not rejected, they can be treated as exogenous. For a concrete example, see exercise 19.16.

A Note on Causality and Exogeneity

Is there any connection between causality and exogeneity? For instance, if X Granger-causes Y, does that mean X is exogenous? Unfortunately, the answer is complicated, for there are different degrees of exogeneity, such as weak, strong, and superexogeneity. The discussion of all this is beyond the scope of this book. The interested reader may refer to Maddala for the dimensions of this problem.[15] As he suggests, it is better to keep the concepts of causality and exogeneity separate.

19.6 SUMMARY AND CONCLUSIONS

1. The problem of identification precedes the problem of estimation.
2. The identification problem asks whether one can obtain unique numerical estimates of the structural coefficients from the estimated reduced form coefficients.
3. If this can be done, an equation in a system of simultaneous equations is identified. If this cannot be done, that equation is un- or under-identified.
4. An identified equation can be just identified or overidentified. In the former case, unique values of structural coefficients can be obtained; in the latter, there may be more than one value for one or more structural parameters.
5. The identification problem arises because the same set of data may be compatible with different sets of structural coefficients, that is, different models. Thus, in the regression of price on quantity only, it is difficult to tell whether one is estimating the supply function or the demand function, because price and quantity enter both equations.
6. To assess the identifiability of a structural equation, one may apply the technique of **reduced-form equations**, which expresses an endogenous variable solely as a function of predetermined variables.
7. However, this time-consuming procedure can be avoided by resorting to either the **order condition** or the **rank condition** of identification. Although the order condition is easy to apply, it provides only a necessary condition for identification. On the other hand, the rank condition is both a necessary and sufficient condition for identification. If the rank condition is satisfied, the order condition is satisfied, too, although the converse is not true. In practice, though, the order condition is generally adequate to ensure identifiability.

---

[15]G. S. Maddala, *Introduction to Econometrics*, Macmillan, 2d ed., New York, 1992, pp. 389–395.

8. In the presence of simultaneity, OLS is generally not applicable, as was shown in Chapter 18. But if one wants to use it nonetheless, it is imperative to test for simultaneity explicitly. The **Hausman specification test** can be used for this purpose.

9. Although in practice deciding whether a variable is endogenous or exogenous is a matter of judgment, one can use the Hausman specification test to determine whether a variable or group of variables is endogenous or exogenous.

10. Although they are in the same family, the concepts of causality and exogeneity are different and one may not necessarily imply the other. In practice it is better to keep those concepts separate.

EXERCISES

19.1. Show that the two definitions of the order condition of identification are equivalent.

19.2. Deduce the structural coefficients from the reduced-form coefficients given in (19.2.25) and (19.2.27).

19.3. Obtain the reduced form of the following models and determine in each case whether the structural equations are unidentified, just identified, or overidentified:
(a) Chap. 18, Example 18.2.
(b) Chap. 18, Example 18.3.
(c) Chap. 18, Example 18.6.

19.4. Check the identifiability of the models of exercise 19.3 by applying both the order and rank conditions of identification.

19.5. In the model (19.2.22) and (19.2.28) of the text it was shown that the supply equation was overidentified. What restrictions, if any, on the structural parameters will make this equation just identified? Justify the restrictions you impose.

19.6 From the model

$$Y_{1t} = \beta_{10} + \beta_{12}Y_{2t} + \gamma_{11}X_{1t} + u_{1t}$$
$$Y_{2t} = \beta_{20} + \beta_{21}Y_{1t} + \gamma_{22}X_{2t} + u_{2t}$$

the following reduced-form equations are obtained:

$$Y_{1t} = \Pi_{10} + \Pi_{11}X_{1t} + \Pi_{12}X_{2t} + w_t$$
$$Y_{2t} = \Pi_{20} + \Pi_{21}X_{1t} + \Pi_{22}X_{2t} + v_t$$

(a) Are the structural equations identified?
(b) What happens to identification if it is known a priori that $\gamma_{11} = 0$?

19.7. Refer to exercise 19.6. The estimated reduced-form equation are as follows:

$$Y_{1t} = 4 + 3X_{1t} + 8X_{2t}$$
$$Y_{2t} = 2 + 6X_{1t} + 10X_{2t}$$

(a) Obtain the values of the structural parameters.
(b) How would you test the null hypothesis that $\gamma_{11} = 0$?

19.8. The model

$$Y_{1t} = \beta_{10} + \beta_{12}Y_{2t} + \gamma_{11}X_{1t} + u_{1t}$$
$$Y_{2t} = \beta_{20} + \beta_{21}Y_{1t} + u_{2t}$$

produces the following reduced-form equations:

$$Y_{1t} = 4 + 8X_{1t}$$
$$Y_{2t} = 2 + 12X_{1t}$$

(a) Which structural coefficients, if any, can be estimated from the reduced-form coefficients? Demonstrate your contention.

(b) How does the answer to (a) change if it is known a priori that (1) $\beta_{12} = 0$ and (2) $\beta_{10} = 0$?

19.9. Determine whether the structural equations of the model given in exercise 18.8 are identified?

19.10. Refer to exercise 18.7 and find out which structural equations can be identified.

19.11. The following is a model in five equations with five endogenous variables Y and four exogenous variables X:

	Coefficients of the variables								
Equation no.	Y_1	Y_2	Y_3	Y_4	Y_5	X_1	X_2	X_3	X_4
1	1	β_{12}	0	β_{14}	0	γ_{11}	0	0	γ_{14}
2	0	1	β_{23}	β_{24}	0	0	γ_{22}	γ_{23}	0
3	β_{31}	0	1	β_{34}	β_{35}	0	0	γ_{33}	γ_{34}
4	0	β_{42}	0	1	0	γ_{41}	0	γ_{43}	0
5	β_{51}	0	0	β_{54}	1	0	γ_{52}	γ_{53}	0

Determine the identifiability of each equation with the aid of the order and rank conditions of identifications.

19.12. Consider the following extended Keynesian model of income determination:

Consumption function:	$C_t = \beta_1 + \beta_2 Y_t - \beta_3 T_t + u_{1t}$
Investment function:	$I_t = \alpha_0 + \alpha_1 Y_{t-1} + u_{2t}$
Taxation function:	$T_t = \gamma_0 + \gamma_1 Y_t + u_{3t}$
Income identity:	$Y_t = C_t + I_t + G_t$

where C = consumption expenditure
   Y = income
   I = investment
   T = taxes
   G = government expenditure
   $u's$ = the disturbance terms

In the model the endogenous variables are $C, I, T,$ and Y and the predetermined variables are G and Y_{t-1}.

By applying the order condition, check the identifiability of each of the equations in the system and of the system as a whole. What would happen if r_t, the interest rate, assumed to be exogenous, were to appear on the right-hand side of the investment function?

19.13. Refer to the data given in Table 18.1 of Chap. 18. Using these data, estimate the reduced form regressions (19.1.2) and (19.1.4). Can you estimate β_0 and β_1? Show your calculations. Is the model identified? Why or why not?

19.14. Suppose we propose yet another definition of the order condition of identifiability:

$$K \geq m + k - 1$$

which states that the number of predetermined variables in the system can be no less than the number of unknown coefficients in the equation to be identified. Show that this definition is equivalent to the two other definitions of the order condition given in the text.

19.15. A simplified version of Suits' model of the watermelon market is as follows:*

Demand equation: $\quad P_t = \alpha_0 + \alpha_1(Q_t/N_t) + \alpha_2(Y_t/N_t) + \alpha_3 F_t + u_{1t}$

Crop supply function: $\quad Q_t = \beta_0 + \beta_1(P_t/W_t) + \beta_2 P_{t-1} + \beta_3 C_{t-1} + \beta_4 T_{t-1} + u_{2t}$

where $\quad P =$ price
$(Q/N) =$ per capita quantity demanded
$(Y/N) =$ per capita income
$F_t =$ freight costs
$(P/W) =$ price relative to the farm wage rate
$C =$ price of cotton
$T =$ price of other vegetables
$N =$ population

P and Q are the endogenous variables.
(a) Obtain the reduced form.
(b) Determine whether the demand, the supply, or both functions are identified.

19.16. Consider the following demand-and-supply model for money:

Money demand: $\quad M_t^d = \beta_0 + \beta_1 Y_t + \beta_2 R_t + \beta_3 P_t + u_{1t}$

Money supply: $\quad M_t^s = \alpha_0 + \alpha_1 Y_t + u_{2t}$

where $\quad M =$ money
$Y =$ income
$R =$ rate of interest
$P =$ price
$u's =$ error terms

Assume that R and P are exogenous and M and Y are endogenous. The following table gives data on M (M_2 definition), Y (GDP), R (3-month Treasury bill rate) and P (Consumer Price Index), for the United States for 1970–1991.
(a) Is the demand function identified?
(b) Is the supply function identified?
(c) Obtain the expressions for the reduced-form equations for M and Y.
(d) Apply the test of simultaneity to the supply function.
(e) How would we find out if Y in the money supply function is in fact endogenous?

---

*D. B. Suits, "An Econometric Model of the Watermelon Market," *Journal of Farm Economics*, vol. 37, 1955, pp. 237–251.

Year	M_2, $, billions	Gross domestic product, $, billions	3-Month Treasury bill rate, %	Consumer Price Index, 1982–1984 = 100
1970	628.1	1,017.7	6.458	38.8
1971	712.7	1,097.2	4.348	40.5
1972	805.2	1,207.0	4.071	41.8
1973	861.0	1,349.6	7.041	44.4
1974	908.6	1,458.6	7.886	49.3
1975	1,023.3	1,585.9	5.838	53.8
1976	1,163.7	1,768.4	4.989	56.9
1977	1,286.6	1,974.1	5.265	60.6
1978	1,388.7	2,232.7	7.221	65.2
1979	1,496.7	2,488.6	10.041	72.6
1980	1,629.5	2,708.0	11.506	82.4
1981	1,792.9	3,030.6	14.029	90.9
1982	1,951.9	3,149.6	10.686	96.5
1983	2,186.1	3,405.0	8.6300	99.6
1984	2,374.3	3,772.2	9.5800	103.9
1985	2,569.4	4,038.7	7.4800	107.6
1986	2,811.1	4,268.6	5.9800	109.6
1987	2,910.8	4,539.9	5.8200	113.6
1988	3,071.1	4,900.4	6.6900	118.3
1989	3,227.3	5,250.8	8.1200	124.0
1990	3,339.0	5,522.2	7.5100	130.7
1991	3,439.8	5,677.5	5.4200	136.2

Source: Economic Report of the President, 1993. M2 (Table B65); GDP (Table B1); T-Bill (3-month Treasury Bill rate, Table B69); CPI (All items, Table B56).

CHAPTER
20

SIMULTANEOUS-EQUATION METHODS

Having discussed the nature of the simultaneous-equation models in the previous two chapters, in this chapter we turn to the problem of estimation of the parameters of such models. At the outset it may be noted that the estimation problem is rather complex because there are a variety of estimation techniques with varying statistical properties. In view of the introductory nature of this text, we shall consider only a few of these techniques. Our discussion will be simple and often heuristic, the finer points being left to the references.

20.1 APPROACHES TO ESTIMATION

If we consider the general M equations model in M endogenous variables given in (19.1.1), we may adopt two approaches to estimate the structural equations, namely, single-equation methods, also known as **limited information methods**, and system methods, also known as **full information methods**. In the single-equation methods to be considered shortly, we estimate each equation in the system (of simultaneous equations) individually, taking into account any restrictions placed on that equation (such as exclusion of some variables) without worrying about the restrictions on the other equations in the system,[1] hence the name *limited information methods*. In the system methods, on the other hand, we estimate all the equations in the model simultaneously, taking due

---

[1] For the purpose of identification, however, information provided by other equations will have to be taken into account. But as noted in Chap. 19, estimation is possible only in the case of (fully or over-) identified equations. In this chapter we assume that the identification problem is solved using the techniques of Chap. 19.

678

account of all restrictions on such equations by the omission or absence of some variables (recall that for identification such restrictions are essential), hence the name *full information methods*.

As an example, consider the following four-equations model:

$$
\begin{aligned}
Y_{1t} &= \beta_{10} + && + \beta_{12}Y_{2t} + \beta_{13}Y_{3t} + && + \gamma_{11}X_{1t} + && + u_{1t} \\
Y_{2t} &= \beta_{20} + && + \beta_{23}Y_{3t} && + \gamma_{21}X_{1t} + \gamma_{22}X_{2t} && + u_{2t} \\
Y_{3t} &= \beta_{30} + \beta_{31}Y_{1t} + && && + \beta_{34}Y_{4t} + \gamma_{31}X_{1t} + \gamma_{32}X_{2t} + && + u_{3t} \\
Y_{4t} &= \beta_{40} + && + \beta_{42}Y_{2t} && && + \gamma_{43}X_{3t} + u_{4t}
\end{aligned}
$$

$$(20.1.1)$$

where the Y's are the endogenous variables and the X's are the exogenous variables. If we are interested in estimating, say, the third equation, the single-equation methods will consider this equation only, noting that variables Y_2 and X_3 are excluded from it. In the systems methods, on the other hand, we try to estimate all four equations simultaneously, taking into account all the restrictions imposed on the various equations of the system.

To preserve the spirit of simultaneous-equation models, ideally one should use the systems method, such as the **full information maximum likelihood (FIML) method**.[2] In practice, however, such methods are not commonly used for a variety of reasons. First, the computational burden is enormous. For example, the comparatively small (20 equations) 1955 Klein-Goldberger model of the U.S. economy had 151 nonzero coefficients, of which the authors estimated only 51 coefficients using the time series data. The Brookings-Social Science Research Council (SSRC) econometric model of the U.S. economy published in 1965 initially had 150 equations.[3] Although such elaborate models may furnish finer details of the various sectors of the economy, the computations are a stupendous task even in these days of high-speed computers, not to mention the cost involved. Second, the systems methods, such as FIML, lead to solutions that are highly nonlinear in the parameters and are therefore often difficult to determine. Third, if there is a specification error (say, a wrong functional form or exclusion of relevant variables) in one or more equations of the system, that error is transmitted to the rest of the system. As a result, the systems methods become very sensitive to specification errors.

In practice, therefore, single-equation methods are often used. As Klein puts it,

> Single equation methods, in the context of a simultaneous system, may be less sensitive to specification error in the sense that those parts of the system that are correctly specified may not be affected appreciably by errors in specification in another part.[4]

---

[2] For a simple discussion of this method, see Carl F. Christ, *Econometric Models and Methods*, John Wiley & Sons, New York, 1966, pp. 395–401.

[3] James S. Duesenberry, Gary Fromm, Lawrence R. Klein, and Edwin Kuh, eds., *A Quarterly Model of the United States Economy*, Rand McNally, Chicago, 1965.

[4] Lawrence R. Klein, *A Textbook of Econometrics*, 2d ed., Prentice-Hall, Englewood Cliffs, NJ., 1974, p. 150.

In the rest of the chapter we shall deal with single-equation methods only. Specifically, we shall discuss the following single-equation methods:

1. Ordinary least squares (OLS)
2. Indirect least squares (ILS)
3. Two-stage least squares (2SLS)

20.2 RECURSIVE MODELS AND ORDINARY LEAST SQUARES

We saw in Chapter 18 that because of the interdependence between the stochastic disturbance term and the endogenous explanatory variable(s), the OLS method is inappropriate for the estimation of an equation in a system of simultaneous equations. If applied erroneously, then, as we saw in Section 18.3, the estimators are not only biased (in small samples) but also inconsistent; that is, the bias does not disappear no matter how large the sample size. There is, however, one situation where OLS can be applied appropriately even in the context of simultaneous equations. This is the case of the **recursive, triangular**, or **causal** models. To see the nature of these models, consider the following three-equation system:

$$
\begin{aligned}
Y_{1t} &= \beta_{10} & + \gamma_{11}X_{1t} + \gamma_{12}X_{2t} + u_{1t} \\
Y_{2t} &= \beta_{20} + \beta_{21}Y_{1t} & + \gamma_{21}X_{1t} + \gamma_{22}X_{2t} + u_{2t} \\
Y_{3t} &= \beta_{30} + \beta_{31}Y_{1t} + \beta_{32}Y_{2t} + \gamma_{31}X_{1t} + \gamma_{32}X_{2t} + u_{3t}
\end{aligned}
\qquad (20.2.1)
$$

where, as usual, the Y's and the X's are, respectively, the endogenous and exogenous variables. The disturbances are such that

$$
\operatorname{cov}(u_{1t}, u_{2t}) = \operatorname{cov}(u_{1t}, u_{3t}) = \operatorname{cov}(u_{2t}, u_{3t}) = 0
$$

that is, the same-period disturbances in different equations are uncorrelated (technically, this is the assumption of **zero contemporaneous correlation**).

Now consider the first equation of (20.2.1). Since it contains only the exogenous variables on the right-hand side and since by assumption they are uncorrelated with the disturbance term u_{1t}, this equation satisfies the critical assumption of the classical OLS, namely, uncorrelatedness between the explanatory variables and the stochastic disturbances. Hence, OLS can be applied straightforwardly to this equation. Next consider the second equation of (20.2.1), which contains the endogenous variable Y_1 as an explanatory variable along with the nonstochastic X's. Now OLS can also be applied to this equation, provided Y_{1t} and u_{2t} are uncorrelated. Is this so? The answer is yes because u_1, which affects Y_1, is by assumption uncorrelated with u_2. Therefore, for all practical purposes, Y_1 is a predetermined variable insofar as Y_2 is concerned. Hence, one can proceed with OLS estimation of this equation. Carrying this argument a step further, we can also apply OLS to the third equation in (19.2.1) because both Y_1 and Y_2 are uncorrelated with u_3.

Thus, in the recursive system OLS can be applied to each equation separately. Actually, we do not have a simultaneous-equation problem in this situation. From the structure of such systems, it is clear that there is no interdependence among the endogenous variables. Thus, Y_1 affects Y_2, but Y_2 does not

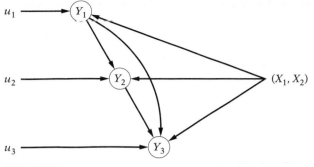

FIGURE 20.1
Recursive model.

affect Y_1. Similarly, Y_1 and Y_2 influence Y_3 without, in turn, being influenced by Y_3. In other words, each equation exhibits a unilateral causal dependence, hence the name causal models.[5] Schematically, we have Fig. 20.1.

As an example of a recursive system, one may postulate the following model of wage and price determination:

Price equation: $\dot{P}_t = \beta_{10} + \beta_{11}\dot{W}_{t-1} + \beta_{12}\dot{R}_t + \beta_{13}\dot{M}_t + \beta_{14}\dot{L}_t + u_{1t}$

Wage equation: $\dot{W}_t = \beta_{20} + \beta_{21}\mathrm{UN}_t + \beta_{32}\dot{P}_t + u_{2t}$

$$(20.2.2)$$

where $\dot{P}$ = rate of change of price per unit of output
$\dot{W}$ = rate of change of wages per employee
$\dot{R}$ = rate of change of price of capital
$\dot{M}$ = rate of change of import prices
$\dot{L}$ = rate of change of labor productivity
UN = unemployment rate, %[6]

The price equation postulates that the rate of change of price in the current period is a function of the rates of change in the prices of capital and of

---

[5]The alternative name *triangular* stems from the fact that if we form the matrix of the coefficients of the endogenous variables given in (20.1.1), we obtain the following triangular matrix:

	Y_1	Y_2	Y_3
Equation 1	1	0	0
Equation 2	β_{21}	1	0
Equation 3	β_{31}	β_{32}	1

Note that the entries above the main diagonal are zeros (why?).
[6]*Note:* The dotted symbol means "time derivative." For example, $\dot{P} = dP/dt$. For discrete time series, dP/dt is sometimes approximated by $\Delta P/\Delta t$, where the symbol Δ is the first difference operator, which was originally introduced in Chap. 12.

raw material, the rate of change in labor productivity, and the rate of change in wages in the previous period. The wage equation shows that the rate of change in wages in the current period is determined by the current period rate of change in price and the unemployment rate. It is clear that the causal chain runs from $\dot{W}_{t-1} \rightarrow \dot{P}_t \rightarrow \dot{W}_t$, and hence OLS may be applied to estimate the parameters of the two equations individually.

Although recursive models have proved to be useful, most simultaneous-equation models do not exhibit such a unilateral cause-and-effect relationship. Therefore, OLS, in general, is inappropriate to estimate a single equation in the context of a simultaneous-equation model.[7]

There are some who argue that, although OLS is generally inapplicable to simultaneous-equation models, one can use it, if only as a standard or norm of comparison. That is, one can estimate a structural equation by OLS, with the resulting properties of biasedness, inconsistency, etc. Then the same equation may be estimated by other methods especially designed to handle the simultaneity problem and the results of the two methods compared, at least qualitatively. In many applications the results of the inappropriately applied OLS may not differ very much from those obtained by more sophisticated methods, as we shall see later. In principle, one should not have much objection to the production of the results based on OLS so long as estimates based on alternative methods devised for simultaneous-equation models are also given. In fact, this approach might give us some idea about how badly OLS does in situations when it is applied inappropriately.[8]

20.3 ESTIMATION OF A JUST IDENTIFIED EQUATION: THE METHOD OF INDIRECT LEAST SQUARES (ILS)

For a just or exactly identified structural equation, the method of obtaining the estimates of the structural coefficients from the OLS estimates of the reduced-form coefficients is known as the **method of indirect least squares (ILS)**, and the estimates thus obtained are known as the **indirect least-squares estimates**. ILS involves the following three steps:

Step 1. We first obtain the reduced-form equations. As noted in Chapter 19, these reduced-form equations are obtained from the structural equations in such a manner that the dependent variable in each equa-

---

[7]It is important to keep in mind that we are assuming that the disturbances across equations are contemporaneously uncorrelated. If this is not the case, we may have to resort to the Zellner SURE (seemingly unrelated regressions) estimation technique to estimate the parameters of the recursive system. See A. Zellner, "An Efficient Method of Estimating Seemingly Unrelated Regressions and Tests for Aggregation Bias," *Journal of the American Statistical Association*, vol. 57, 1962, pp. 348–368.

[8]It may also be noted that in small samples the alternative estimators, like the OLS estimators, are also biased. But the OLS estimator has the "virtue" that it has minimum variance among these alternative estimators. But this is true of small samples only.

tion is the only endogenous variable and is a function solely of the predetermined (exogenous or lagged endogenous) variables and the stochastic error term(s).

Step 2. We apply OLS to the reduced-form equations individually. This operation is permissible since the explanatory variables in these equations are predetermined and hence uncorrelated with the stochastic disturbances. The estimates thus obtained are consistent.[9]

Step 3. We obtain estimates of the original structural coefficients from the estimated reduced-form coefficients obtained in Step 2. As noted in Chapter 19, if an equation is exactly identified, there is a one-to-one correspondence between the structural and reduced-form coefficients; that is, one can derive unique estimates of the former from the latter.

As this three-step procedure indicates, the name ILS derives from the fact that structural coefficients (the object of primary enquiry in most cases) are obtained indirectly from the OLS estimates of the reduced-form coefficients.

An Illustrative Example

Consider the demand-and-supply model introduced in Section 19.2, which for convenience is given below with a slight change in notation:

$$\text{Demand function:} \quad Q_t = \alpha_0 + \alpha_1 P_t + \alpha_2 X_t + u_{1t} \quad (20.3.1)$$
$$\text{Supply function:} \quad Q_t = \beta_0 + \beta_1 P_t + u_{2t} \quad (20.3.2)$$

where Q = quantity
     P = price
     X = income or expenditure

Assume that X is exogenous. As noted previously, the supply function is exactly identified whereas the demand function is not identified.

The reduced-form equations corresponding to the preceding structural equations are

$$P_t = \Pi_0 + \Pi_1 X_t + w_t \quad (20.3.3)$$
$$Q_t = \Pi_2 + \Pi_3 X_t + v_t \quad (20.3.4)$$

where the Π's are the reduced-form coefficients and are (nonlinear) combinations of the structural coefficients, as shown in Eqs. (19.2.16) and (19.2.18), and where w and v are linear combinations of the structural disturbances u_1 and u_2.

---

[9]In addition to being consistent, the estimates "may be best unbiased and/or asymptotically efficient, depending respectively upon whether (*i*) the z's [= X's] are exogenous and not merely predetermined [i.e., do not contain lagged values of endogenous variables] and/or (*ii*) the distribution of the disturbances is normal." (W. C. Hood and Tjalling C. Koopmans, *Studies in Econometric Method*, John Wiley & Sons, New York, 1953, p. 133.)

Notice that each reduced-form equation contains only one endogenous variable, which is the dependent variable and which is a function solely of the exogenous variable X (income) and the stochastic disturbances. Hence, the parameters of the preceding reduced-form equations may be estimated by OLS. These estimates are

$$\hat{\Pi}_1 = \frac{\sum p_t x_t}{\sum x_t^2} \tag{20.3.5}$$

$$\hat{\Pi}_0 = \bar{P} - \hat{\Pi}_1 \bar{X} \tag{20.3.6}$$

$$\hat{\Pi}_3 = \frac{\sum q_t x_t}{\sum x_t^2} \tag{20.3.7}$$

$$\hat{\Pi}_2 = \bar{Q} - \hat{\Pi}_3 \bar{X} \tag{20.3.8}$$

where the lowercase letters, as usual, denote deviations from sample means and where $\bar{Q}$ and $\bar{P}$ are the sample mean values of Q and P. As noted previously, the $\hat{\Pi}_i$'s are consistent estimators and under appropriate assumptions are also minimum variance unbiased or asymptotically efficient (see footnote 9).

Since our primary objective is to determine the structural coefficients, let us see if we can estimate them from the reduced-form coefficients. Now as shown in Section 19.2, the supply function is exactly identified. Therefore, its parameters can be estimated uniquely from the reduced-form coefficients as follows:

$$\beta_0 = \Pi_2 - \beta_1 \Pi_0 \quad \text{and} \quad \beta_1 = \frac{\Pi_3}{\Pi_1}$$

Hence, the estimates of these parameters can be obtained from the estimates of the reduced-form coefficients as

$$\hat{\beta}_0 = \hat{\Pi}_2 - \hat{\beta}_1 \hat{\Pi}_0 \tag{20.3.9}$$

$$\hat{\beta}_1 = \frac{\hat{\Pi}_3}{\hat{\Pi}_1} \tag{20.3.10}$$

which are the ILS estimators. Note that the parameters of the demand function cannot be thus estimated (however, see exercise 20.13).

To give some numerical results, we obtained the data shown in Table 20.1. First we estimate the reduced-form equations, regressing separately price and quantity on per capital real consumption expenditure. The results are as follows:

$$\hat{P}_t = 72.3091 + 0.0043 X_t$$
$$\text{se} = (9.2002) \quad (0.0009)$$
$$t = (7.8595) \quad (4.4104) \quad R^2 = 0.4930 \tag{20.3.11}$$

$$\hat{Q}_t = 84.0702 + 0.0020 X_t$$
$$\text{se} = (4.8960) \quad (0.0005)$$
$$t = (17.1711) \quad (3.7839) \quad R^2 = 0.4172 \tag{20.3.12}$$

Using (20.3.9) and (20.3.10), we obtain these ILS estimates:

$$\hat{\beta}_0 = 51.0562 \tag{20.3.13}$$

$$\hat{\beta}_1 = 0.4566 \tag{20.3.14}$$

TABLE 20.1
Crop production, crop prices, and per capita personal consumption expenditures, 1982 dollars; United States, 1970–1991

Year	Index of crop production (1977 = 100), Q	Index of crop prices received by farmers (1977 = 100), P	Real per capita personal consumption expenditure, X
1970	77	52	3,152
1971	86	56	3,372
1972	87	60	3,658
1973	92	91	4,002
1974	84	117	4,337
1975	93	105	4,745
1976	92	102	5,241
1977	100	100	5,772
1978	102	105	6,384
1979	113	116	7,035
1980	101	125	7,677
1981	117	134	8,375
1982	117	121	8,868
1983	88	128	9,634
1984	111	138	10,408
1985	118	120	11,184
1986	109	107	11,843
1987	108	106	12,568
1988	92	126	13,448
1989	107	134	14,241
1990	114	127	14,996
1991	111	130	15,384

Source: Economic Report of the President, 1993. Data on Q (Table B-94), on P (Table B-96), on X (Table B-5).

Therefore, the estimated ILS regression is[10]

$$\hat{Q}_t = 51.0562 + 0.4566\,P_t \tag{20.3.15}$$

For comparison, we give the results of the (inappropriately applied) OLS regression of Q on P:

$$\hat{Q}_t = 65.1719 + 0.3272\,P_t \tag{20.3.16}$$
$$\text{se} = \quad (9.3294) \quad (0.0835)$$
$$t = \quad (6.9856) \quad (3.9203) \qquad R^2 = 0.4345$$

These results show how OLS can distort the "true" picture when it is applied in inappropriate situations.

---

[10]We have not presented the standard errors of the estimated structural coefficients because, as noted previously, these coefficients are generally nonlinear functions of the reduced-form coefficients and there is no simple method of estimating their standard errors from the standard errors of the reduced-form coefficients. For large-sample size, however, standard errors of the structural coefficients can be obtained approximately. For details, see Jan Kmenta, *Elements of Econometrics,* Macmillan, New York, 1971, p. 444.

Properties of ILS Estimators

We have seen that the estimators of the reduced-form coefficients are consistent and under appropriate assumptions also best unbiased or asymptotically efficient (see footnote 9). Do these properties carry over to the ILS estimators? It can be shown that the ILS estimators inherit all the asymptotic properties of the reduced-form estimators, such as consistency and asymptotic efficiency. But (the small sample) properties such as unbiasedness do not generally hold true. It is shown in Appendix 20A, Section 20A.1, that the ILS estimators $\hat{\beta}_0$ and $\hat{\beta}_1$ of the supply function given previously are biased but the bias disappears as the sample size increases indefinitely (that is, the estimators are consistent).[11]

20.4 ESTIMATION OF AN OVERIDENTIFIED EQUATION: THE METHOD OF TWO-STAGE LEAST SQUARES (2SLS)

Consider the following model:

Income function:
$$Y_{1t} = \beta_{10} + \qquad + \beta_{11}Y_{2t} + \gamma_{11}X_{1t} + \gamma_{12}X_{2t} + u_{1t}$$
$$(20.4.1)$$

Money supply function:
$$Y_{2t} = \beta_{20} + \beta_{21}Y_{1t} \qquad\qquad + u_{2t}$$
$$(20.4.2)$$

where Y_1 = income
Y_2 = stock of money
X_1 = investment expenditure
X_2 = government expenditure on goods and services

The variables X_1 and X_2 are exogenous.

The income equation, a hybrid of quantity-theory–Keynesian approaches to income determination, states that income is determined by money supply, investment expenditure, and government expenditure. The *money supply function* postulates that the stock of money is determined (by the Federal Reserve System) on the basis of the level of income. Obviously, we have a simultaneous-equation problem, which can be checked by the simultaneity test discussed in Chapter 19.

---

[11]Intuitively this can be seen as follows: $E(\hat{\beta}_1) = \beta_1$ if $E(\hat{\Pi}_3/\hat{\Pi}_1) = (\Pi_3/\Pi_1)$. Now even if $E(\hat{\Pi}_3) = \Pi_3$ and $E(\hat{\Pi}_1) = \Pi_3$, it can be shown that $E(\hat{\Pi}_3/\hat{\Pi}_1) \neq E(\hat{\Pi}_3)/E(\hat{\Pi}_1)$; that is, the expectation of the ratio of two variables is not equal to the ratio of the expectations of the two variables. However, as shown in App. 20A.1, $\text{plim}(\hat{\Pi}_3/\hat{\Pi}_1) = \text{plim}(\hat{\Pi}_3)/\text{plim}(\hat{\Pi}_1) = \Pi_3/\Pi_1$ since $\hat{\Pi}_3$ and $\hat{\Pi}_1$ are consistent estimators.

Applying the order condition of identification, it can b
come equation is underidentified whereas the money supply e
identified. There is not much that can be done about the income e
of changing the model specification. The overidentified money suppl
may not be estimated by ILS because there are two estimates of β_{21} (the
should verify this via the reduced-form coefficients).

As a matter of practice, one may apply OLS to the money supply equation, but the estimates thus obtained will be inconsistent in view of the likely
correlation between the stochastic explanatory variable Y_1 and the stochastic
disturbance term u_2. Suppose, however, we find a "proxy" for the stochastic
explanatory variable Y_1 such that, although "resembling" Y_1 (in the sense that
it is highly correlated with Y_1), it is uncorrelated with u_2. Such a proxy is also
known as an **instrumental variable** (see Chapter 17). If one can find such a
proxy, OLS can be used straightforwardly to estimate the money supply function. But how does one obtain such an instrumental variable? One answer is
provided by the **two-stage least squares** (2SLS), developed independently by
Henri Theil[12] and Robert Basmann.[13] As the name indicates, the method involves two successive applications of OLS. The process is as follows:

Stage 1. To get rid of the likely correlation between Y_1 and u_2, regress first
Y_1 on *all* the predetermined variables in the *whole system*, not just
that equation. In the present case, this means regressing Y_1 on X_1
and X_2 as follows:

$$Y_{1t} = \hat{\Pi}_0 + \hat{\Pi}_1 X_{1t} + \hat{\Pi}_2 X_{2t} + \hat{u}_t \qquad (20.4.3)$$

where $\hat{u}_t$ are the usual OLS residuals. From Eq. (20.4.3) we obtain

$$\hat{Y}_{1t} = \hat{\Pi}_0 + \hat{\Pi}_1 X_{1t} + \hat{\Pi}_2 X_{2t} \qquad (20.4.4)$$

where $\hat{Y}_{1t}$ is an estimate of the mean value of Y conditional upon the
fixed X's. Note that (20.4.3) is nothing but a reduced-form regression
because only the exogenous or predetermined variables appear on
the right-hand side.

Equation (20.4.3) can now be expressed as

$$Y_{1t} = \hat{Y}_{1t} + \hat{u}_t \qquad (20.4.5)$$

which shows that the stochastic Y_1 consists of two parts: $\hat{Y}_{1t}$, which
is a linear combination of the nonstochastic X's, and a random com-
ponent $\hat{u}_t$. Following the OLS theory, $\hat{Y}_{1t}$ and $\hat{u}_t$ are uncorrelated.
(Why?)

---

[12]Henri Theil, "Repeated Least-Squares Applied to Complete Equation Systems," The Hague: The Central Planning Bureau, The Netherlands, 1953 (mimeographed).

[13]Robert L. Basmann, "A Generalized Classical Method of Linear Estimation of Coefficients in a Structural Equation," *Econometrica*, vol. 25, 1957, pp. 77–83.

oney supply equation can now be written as

$$= \beta_{20} + \beta_{21}(\hat{Y}_{1t} + \hat{u}_t) + u_{2t}$$

$$= \beta_{20} + \beta_{21}\hat{Y}_{1t} + (u_{2t} + \beta_{21}\hat{u}_t)$$

$$= \beta_{20} + \beta_{21}\hat{Y}_{1t} + u_t^* \qquad (20.4.6)$$

$_1\hat{u}_t.$

.4.6) with (20.4.2), we see that they are very sim-
the only difference being that Y_1 is replaced by
intage of (20.4.6)? It can be shown that although
noney supply equation is correlated or likely to
be correlated with the disturbance term u_2 (hence rendering OLS inappropriate), $\hat{Y}_{1t}$ in (20.4.6) is uncorrelated with u_t^* *asymptotically,*
that is, in the large sample (or more accurately, as the sample size
increases indefinitely). As a result, OLS can be applied to (20.4.6),
which will give consistent estimates of the parameters of the money
supply function.[14]

As this two-stage procedure indicates, the basic idea behind 2SLS is to
"purify" the stochastic explanatory variable Y_1 of the influence of the stochastic disturbance u_2. This goal is accomplished by performing the reduced-form
regression of Y_1 on all the predetermined variables in the system (Stage 1),
obtaining the estimates $\hat{Y}_{1t}$ and replacing Y_{1t} in the original equation by the
estimated $\hat{Y}_{1t}$, and then applying OLS to the equation thus transformed (Stage
2). The estimators thus obtained are consistent; that is, they converge to their
true values as the sample size increases indefinitely.

To illustrate 2SLS further, let us modify the income–money supply model
as follows:

$$Y_{1t} = \beta_{10} + \beta_{12}Y_{2t} + \gamma_{11}X_{1t} + \gamma_{12}X_{2t} \qquad\qquad + u_{1t} \qquad (20.4.7)$$

$$Y_{2t} = \beta_{20} + \beta_{21}Y_{1t} \qquad\qquad + \gamma_{23}X_{3t} + \gamma_{24}X_{4t} + u_{2t} \qquad (20.4.8)$$

where, in addition to the variables already defined, X_3 = income in the previous time period and X_4 = money supply in the previous period. Both X_3 and
X_4 are predetermined.

---

[14]But note that in small samples $\hat{Y}_{1t}$ is likely to be correlated with u_t^*. The reason is as follows:
From (20.4.4) we see that $\hat{Y}_{1t}$ is a weighted linear combination of the predetermined X's, with
$\hat{\Pi}$'s as the weights. Now even if the predetermined variables are truly nonstochastic, the $\hat{\Pi}$'s, being
estimators, are stochastic. Therefore, $\hat{Y}_{1t}$ is stochastic too. Now from our discussion of the reduced-
form equations and indirect least-squares estimation, it is clear that the reduced-coefficients, the
$\hat{\Pi}$'s, are functions of the stochastic disturbances, such as u_2. And since $\hat{Y}_{1t}$ depends on the $\hat{\Pi}$'s, it
is likely to be correlated with u_2, which is a component of u_t^*. As a result, $\hat{Y}_{1t}$ is expected to be
correlated with u_t^*. But as noted previously, this correlation disappears as the sample size tends
to infinity. The upshot of all this is that in small samples the 2SLS procedure may lead to biased
estimation.

It can be readily verified that both Eq. (20.4.7) and (20.4.8
tified. To apply 2SLS, we proceed as follows: In Stage 1 we regre
nous variables on *all* the predetermined variables in the system.

$$Y_{1t} = \hat{\Pi}_{10} + \hat{\Pi}_{11}X_{1t} + \hat{\Pi}_{12}X_{2t} + \hat{\Pi}_{13}X_{3t} + \hat{\Pi}_{14}X_{4t} + \hat{u}$$

$$Y_{2t} = \hat{\Pi}_{20} + \hat{\Pi}_{21}X_{1t} + \hat{\Pi}_{22}X_{2t} + \hat{\Pi}_{23}X_{3t} + \hat{\Pi}_{24}X_{4t} + \hat{u}_{2t} \qquad (20.4.10)$$

In Stage 2 we replace Y_1 and Y_2 in the original (structural) equations by their
estimated values from the preceding two regressions and then run the OLS
regressions as follows:

$$Y_{1t} = \beta_{10} + \beta_{12}\hat{Y}_{2t} + \gamma_{11}X_{1t} + \gamma_{12}X_{2t} + u_{1t}^* \qquad (20.4.11)$$

$$Y_{2t} = \beta_{20} + \beta_{21}\hat{Y}_{1t} + \gamma_{23}X_{3t} + \gamma_{24}X_{4t} + u_{2t}^* \qquad (20.4.12)$$

where $u_{1t}^* = u_{1t} + \beta_{12}\hat{u}_{2t}$ and $\hat{u}_{2t}^* = u_{2t} + \beta_{21}\hat{u}_{1t}$. The estimates thus obtained
will be consistent.

Note the following features of 2SLS.

1. It can be applied to an individual equation in the system without directly
   taking into account any other equation(s) in the system. Hence, for solving
   econometric models involving a large number of equations, 2SLS offers an
   economical method. For this reason the method has been used extensively
   in practice.
2. Unlike ILS, which provides multiple estimates of parameters in the overidentified equations, 2SLS provides only one estimate per parameter.
3. It is easy to apply because all one needs to know is the total number of
   exogenous or predetermined variables in the system without knowing any
   other variables in the system.
4. Although specially designed to handle overidentified equations, the method
   can also be applied to exactly identified equations. But then ILS and 2SLS
   will give identical estimates. (Why?)
5. If the R^2 values in the reduced-form regressions (that is, Stage 1 regressions)
   are very high, say, in excess of 0.8, the classical OLS estimates and 2SLS estimates will be very close. But this result should not be surprising because
   if the R^2 value in the first stage is very high, it means that the estimated
   values of the endogenous variables are very close to their actual values, and
   hence the latter are less likely to be correlated with the stochastic disturbances in the original structural equations. (Why?)[15] If, however, the R^2
   values in the first-stage regressions are very low, the 2SLS estimates will be
   practically meaningless because we shall be replacing the original Y's in the
   second-stage regression by the estimated $\hat{Y}$'s from the first-stage regressions,

---

[15] In the extreme case if $R^2 = 1$ in the first-stage regression, the endogenous explanatory variable
in the original (overidentified) equation will be practically nonstochastic (why?).

we're [handwritten] Ŷ so that it's a proxy of Y is that Ŷ is the part corr... Y but not [illegible] non di...

which will essentially represent the disturbances in the first-stage regressions. In other words, in this case, the $\hat{Y}$'s will be very poor proxies for the original Y's.

6. Notice that in reporting the ILS regression in (20.3.15) we did not state the standard errors of the estimated coefficients (for reasons explained in footnote 10). But we can do this for the 2SLS estimates because the structural coefficients are directly estimated from the second-stage (OLS) regressions. There is, however, a caution to be exercised. The estimated standard errors in the second-stage regressions need to be modified because, as can be seen from Eq. (20.4.6), the error term u_t^* is, in fact, the original error term u_{2t} plus $\beta_{21}\hat{u}_t$. Hence, the variance of u_t^* is not exactly equal to the variance of the original u_{2t}. However, the modification required can be easily effected by the formula given in Appendix 20A, Section 20A.2.

7. In using the 2SLS, bear in mind the following remarks of Henri Theil:

> The statistical justification of the 2SLS is of the large-sample type. When there are no lagged endogenous variables, ... the 2SLS coefficient estimators are consistent if the exogenous variables are constant in repeated samples and if the disturbance[s] [appearing in the various behavioral or structural equations] ... are independently and identically distributed with zero means and finite variances. ... If these two conditions are satisfied, the sampling distribution of 2SLS coefficient estimators becomes approximately normal for large samples. ...
>
> When the equation system contains lagged endogenous variables, the consistency and large-sample normality of the 2SLS coefficient estimators require an additional condition, ... that as the sample increases the mean square of the values taken by each lagged endogenous variable converges in probability to a positive limit. ...
>
> If the [disturbances appearing in the various structural equations are] *not* independently distributed, lagged endogenous variables are not independent of the current operation of the equation system ... , which means these variables are not really predetermined. If these variables are nevertheless treated as predetermined in the 2SLS procedure, the resulting estimators are not consistent.[16]

20.5 2SLS: A NUMERICAL EXAMPLE

To illustrate the 2SLS method, consider the income–money supply model given previously in Eq. (20.4.1) and (20.4.2). As shown, the money supply equation is overidentified. To estimate the parameters of this equation, we resort to the two-stage least-squares method. The data required for analysis are given in Table 20.2; this table also gives some data that are required to answer some of the questions given in the exercises.

Stage 1 regression. We first regress the stochastic explanatory variable income Y_1, represented by GDP, on the predetermined variables private investment X_1 and government expenditure X_2, obtaining the following results:

---

[16]Henri Theil, *Introduction to Econometrics*, Prentice-Hall, Englewood Cliffs, N.J., 1978, pp. 341–342.

TABLE 20.2
Selected macroeconomic data, United States, 1970–1991. All data in billions of dollars, except interest rate

Year	Gross domestic product, Y_1	M_2 money supply, Y_2	Gross private domestic investment, X_1	Federal government expenditure, X_2	Interest rate, %, on 6-month Treasury bills, X_3
1970	1,010.7	628.1	150.3	208.5	6.562
1971	1,097.2	717.2	175.5	224.3	4.511
1972	1,207.0	805.2	205.6	249.3	4.466
1973	1,349.6	861.0	243.1	270.3	7.178
1974	1,458.6	908.6	245.8	305.6	7.926
1975	1,585.9	1,023.3	226.0	364.2	6.122
1976	1,768.4	1,163.7	286.4	392.7	5.266
1977	1,974.1	1,286.6	358.3	426.4	5.510
1978	2,232.7	1,388.7	434.0	469.3	7.572
1979	2,488.6	1,496.7	480.2	520.3	10.017
1980	2,708.0	1,629.5	467.6	613.1	11.374
1981	3,030.6	1,792.9	558.0	697.8	13.776
1982	3,149.6	1,951.9	503.4	770.9	11.084
1983	3,405.0	2,186.1	546.7	840.0	8.750
1984	3,777.2	2,374.3	718.9	892.7	9.800
1985	4,038.7	2,569.4	714.5	969.9	7.660
1986	4,268.6	2,811.1	717.6	1,028.2	6.030
1987	4,539.9	2,910.8	749.3	1,065.6	6.050
1988	4,900.0	3,071.1	793.6	1,109.0	6.920
1989	5,250.8	3,227.3	832.3	1,181.6	8.040
1990	5,522.2	3,339.0	799.5	1,273.6	7.470
1991	5,677.5	3,439.8	721.1	1,332.7	5.490

Source: Economic Report of the President, 1993
X_1 and Y_1 (Table B-1, p. 348)
     Y_2 (Table B-65, p. 423)
     X_2 (Table B-77, p. 439)
     X_3 (Table B-69, p. 428)

$$\hat{Y}_{1t} = 128.0355 + 0.5170 X_{1t} + 3.8126 X_{2t}$$
$$\text{se} = (62.3531) \quad (0.4151) \quad (14.6504) \tag{20.5.1}$$
$$t = (2.0534) \quad (1.2453) \quad (14.6504) \qquad R^2 = 0.9948$$

Stage 2 regression. We now estimate the money supply function (20.4.2), replacing the endogenous Y_1 by $Y_1 (= \hat{Y}_1)$ estimated from (20.5.1). The results are as follows:

$$\hat{Y}_{2t} = 34.5799 + 0.6144 \hat{Y}_{1t}$$
$$\text{se} = (31.5757) \quad (0.0094) \tag{20.5.2}$$
$$t = (1.0951) \quad (65.5730) \qquad R^2 = 0.9954$$

We pointed out previously that the estimated standard errors given in (20.5.2) need to be corrected in the manner suggested in Appendix 20.A, Section 20 A.2. Effecting this correction (most standard econometric packages do it routinely), we obtain the following results:

$$\hat{Y}_{2t} = 34.5799 + 0.6144 \hat{Y}_{1t}$$
$$\text{se} = (30.5416) \quad (0.0091) \tag{20.5.3}$$
$$t = (1.1322) \quad (67.7933) \qquad R^2 = 0.9957$$

As noted in Appendix 20 A, Section 20 A.2, the standard errors given in (20.5.3) do not differ much from those given in (20.5.2) because the R^2 in Stage 1 regression is very high.

OLS regression. For comparison, we give the regression of money stock on income as shown in (20.4.2) without "purging" the stochastic Y_{1t} of the influence of the stochastic disturbance term:

$$\hat{Y}_{2t} = 39.0814 + 0.6129\, Y_{1t}$$
$$\text{se} = (30.4576) \quad (0.0090) \tag{20.5.4}$$
$$t = (1.2831) \quad (67.8498) \qquad R^2 = 0.9957$$

Comparing the "inappropriate" OLS results with the Stage 2 regression, we see that the two regressions are virtually the same. Does this mean that the 2SLS procedure is worthless? Not at all. That in the present situation the two results are practically identical should not be surprising because, as noted previously, the R^2 value in the first stage is very high, thus making the estimated $\hat{Y}_{1t}$ virtually identical with the actual Y_{1t}. Therefore, in this case the OLS and second-stage regressions will be more or less similar. But there is no guarantee that this will happen in every application. An implication, then, is that in overidentified equations one should not accept the classical OLS procedure without checking the second-stage regression(s).

Simultaneity between GDP and money supply. Let us find out if GDP (Y_1) and money supply (Y_2) are mutually dependent. For this purpose we use the Hausman test of simultaneity discussed in Chapter 19.

First we regress GDP on X_1 (investment expenditure) and X_2 (government expenditure), the exogenous variables in the system (i.e., we estimate the reduced-form regression.) From this regression we obtain the estimated GDP and the residuals $\hat{v}_t$, as suggested in Eq. (19.4.7). Then we regress money supply on estimated GDP and v_t to obtain the following results:

$$\hat{Y}_{2t} = 34.5799 + 0.6144\,\hat{Y}_{1t} + 0.3250\,\hat{v}_t$$
$$\text{se} = (26.8831) + (0.0080) \quad (0.1109) \tag{20.5.5}$$
$$t = (1.2863) \quad (77.0193) \quad (2.9312) \qquad R^2 = 0.9968$$

Since the t value of $\hat{v}_t$ is statistically significant (the p value is 0.0086), we cannot reject the hypothesis of simultaneity between money supply and GDP, which should not be surprising. (*Note:* Strictly speaking, this conclusion is valid only in large samples; technically, as the sample size increases indefinitely).

Hypothesis testing. Suppose we want to test the hypothesis that income has no effect on money demand. Can we test this hypothesis with the usual t test from the estimated regression (20.5.2)? Yes, provided the sample is large and provided we correct the standard errors as shown in (20.5.3), we can use the t test to test the significance of an individual coefficient and the F test to test joint significance of two or more coefficients, using formula (8.5.7).[17]

What happens if the error term in a structural equation is autocorrelated and or correlated with the error term in another structural equation in the system? A full answer to this question will take us beyond the scope of the book and is

---

[17]But take this precaution: The restricted and unrestricted RSS in the numerator must be calculated using predicted Y (as in Stage 2 of 2SLS) and the RSS in the denominator is calculated using actual rather than predicted values of the regressors. For an accessible discussion of this point, see T. Dudley Wallace and J. Lew Silver, *Econometrics: An Introduction*, Addison-Wesley, Reading, Mass., 1988, Sec. 8.5.

better left for the references (see the reference given in footnote 7). Nevertheless, estimation techniques (such as Zellner's SURE technique) do exist to handle these complications.

20.6 ILLUSTRATIVE EXAMPLES

In this section we consider some applications of the simultaneous-equation methods.

Example 20.1 Advertising, Concentration and Price Margins

To study the interrelationships among advertising, concentration (as measured by the concentration ratio), and price-cost margins, Allyn D. Strickland and Lenord W. Weiss formulated the following three-equation model.[18]

Advertising intensity function:

$$Ad/S = a_0 + a_1 M + a_2(CD/S) + a_3 C + a_4 C^2 + a_5 Gr + a_6 Dur \quad (20.6.1)$$

Concentration function:

$$C = b_0 + b_1(Ad/S) + b_2(MES/S) \quad (20.6.2)$$

Price-cost margin function:

$$M = c_0 + c_1(K/S) + c_2 Gr + c_3 C + c_4 GD + c_5(Ad/S) + c_6(MES/S) \quad (20.6.3)$$

where   Ad = advertising expense
  S = value of shipments
  C = four-firm concentration ratio
  CD = consumer demand
  MES = minimum efficient scale
  M = price/cost margin
  Gr = annual rate of growth of industrial production
  Dur = dummy variable for durable goods industry
  K = capital stock
  GD = measure of geographic dispersion of output

By the order conditions for identifiability, Eq. (20.6.2) is overidentified, whereas (20.6.1) and (20.6.3) are exactly identified.

The data for the analysis came largely from the 1963 Census of Manufacturers and covered 408 of the 417 four-digit manufacturing industries. The three equations were first estimated by OLS, yielding the results shown in Table 20.3. To correct for the simultaneous-equation bias, the authors reestimated the model using 2SLS. The ensuing results are given in Table 20.4. We leave it to the reader to compare the two results.

---

[18]See their "Advertising, Concentration, and Price-Cost Margins," *Journal of Political Economy*, vol. 84, no. 5, 1976, pp. 1109–1121.

TABLE 20.3
OLS estimates of three equations (*t* ratios in parentheses)

	Dependent variable		
	Ad/S Eq. (20.6.1)	C Eq. (20.6.2)	M Eq. (20.6.3)
Constant	−0.0314 (−7.45)	0.2638 (25.93)	0.1682 (17.15)
C	0.0554 (3.56)	···	0.0629 (2.89)
C_i^2	−0.0568 (−3.38)	···	···
M	0.1123 (9.84)	···	···
CD/S	0.0257 (8.94)	···	···
Gr	0.0387 (1.64)	···	0.2255 (2.61)
Dur	−0.0021 (−1.11)	···	···
Ad/S	···	1.1613 (3.3)	1.6536 (11.00)
MES/S	···	4.1852 (18.99)	0.0686 (0.54)
K/S	···	···	0.1123 (8.03)
GD	···	···	−0.0003 (−2.90)
R^2	0.374	0.485	0.402
df	401	405	401

TABLE 20.4
Two-stage least-squares estimates of three equations (*t* ratios in parentheses)

	Dependent variable		
	Ad/S Eq. (20.6.1)	C Eq. (20.6.2)	M Eq. (20.6.3)
Constant	−0.0245 (−3.86)	0.2591 (21.30)	0.1736 (14.66)
C	0.0737 (2.84)	···	0.0377 (0.93)
C^2	−0.0643 (−2.64)	···	···
M	0.0544 (2.01)	···	···
CD/S	0.0269 (8.96)	···	···
Gr	0.0539 (2.09)	···	0.2336 (2.61)
Dur	−0.0018 (−0.93)	···	···
Ad/S	···	1.5347 (2.42)	1.6256 (5.52)
MES/S	···	4.169 (18.84)	0.1720 (0.92)
K/S	···	···	0.1165 (7.30)
GD	···	···	−0.0003 (−2.79)

Example 20.2 Klein's Model I

In Example 18.6 we discussed briefly the pioneering model of Klein. Initially, the model was estimated for the period 1920–1941. The underlying data are given in Table 20.5; and OLS, reduced-form, and 2SLS estimates are given in Table 20.6. We leave it to the reader to interpret these results.

Example 20.3 The Capital Asset Pricing Model Expressed as a Recursive System

In a rather unusual application of recursive simultaneous-equation modeling, Cheng F. Lee and W. P. Lloyd[19] estimated the following model for the oil industry:

---

[19]"The Capital Asset Pricing Model Expressed as a Recursive System: An Empirical Investigation," *Journal of Financial and Quantitative Analysis*, June 1976, pp. 237–249.

TABLE 20.5
Underlying data for Klein's model I

Year	C^*	P	W	I	K_{-1}	X	W'	G	T
1920	39.8	12.7	28.8	2.7	180.1	44.9	2.2	2.4	3.4
1921	41.9	12.4	25.5	-0.2	182.8	45.6	2.7	3.9	7.7
1922	45.0	16.9	29.3	1.9	182.6	50.1	2.9	3.2	3.9
1923	49.2	18.4	34.1	5.2	184.5	57.2	2.9	2.8	4.7
1924	50.6	19.4	33.9	3.0	189.7	57.1	3.1	3.5	3.8
1925	52.6	20.1	35.4	5.1	192.7	61.0	3.2	3.3	5.5
1926	55.1	19.6	37.4	5.6	197.8	64.0	3.3	3.3	7.0
1927	56.2	19.8	37.9	4.2	203.4	64.4	3.6	4.0	6.7
1928	57.3	21.1	39.2	3.0	207.6	64.5	3.7	4.2	4.2
1929	57.8	21.7	41.3	5.1	210.6	67.0	4.0	4.1	4.0
1930	55.0	15.6	37.9	1.0	215.7	61.2	4.2	5.2	7.7
1931	50.9	11.4	34.5	-3.4	216.7	53.4	4.8	5.9	7.5
1932	45.6	7.0	29.0	-6.2	213.3	44.3	5.3	4.9	8.3
1933	46.5	11.2	28.5	-5.1	207.1	45.1	5.6	3.7	5.4
1934	48.7	12.3	30.6	-3.0	202.0	49.7	6.0	4.0	6.8
1935	51.3	14.0	33.2	-1.3	199.0	54.4	6.1	4.4	7.2
1936	57.7	17.6	36.8	2.1	197.7	62.7	7.4	2.9	8.3
1937	58.7	17.3	41.0	2.0	199.8	65.0	6.7	4.3	6.7
1938	57.5	15.3	38.2	-1.9	201.8	60.9	7.7	5.3	7.4
1939	61.6	19.0	41.6	1.3	199.9	69.5	7.8	6.6	8.9
1940	65.0	21.1	45.0	3.3	201.2	75.7	8.0	7.4	9.6
1941	69.7	23.5	53.3	4.9	204.5	88.4	8.5	13.8	11.6

*Interpretation of column heads is listed in Example 18.6.
Source: These data from G. S. Maddala, *Econometrics*, McGraw-Hill, New York, 1977, p. 238.

$$R_{1t} = \alpha_1 \qquad\qquad\qquad\qquad\qquad\qquad\qquad\qquad\qquad + \gamma_1 M_t + u_{1t}$$
$$R_{2t} = \alpha_2 + \beta_{2t}R_{1t} \qquad\qquad\qquad\qquad\qquad\qquad\qquad + \gamma_2 M_t + u_{2t}$$
$$R_{3t} = \alpha_3 + \beta_{31}R_{1t} + \beta_{32}R_{2t} \qquad\qquad\qquad\qquad\qquad + \gamma_3 M_t + u_{3t}$$
$$R_{4t} = \alpha_4 + \beta_{41}R_{1t} + \beta_{42}R_{2t} + \beta_{43}R_{3t} \qquad\qquad\qquad + \gamma_4 M_t + u_{4t}$$
$$R_{5t} = \alpha_5 + \beta_{51}R_{1t} + \beta_{52}R_{2t} + \beta_{53}R_{3t} + \beta_{54}R_{4t} \qquad\qquad + \gamma_5 M_t + u_{5t}$$
$$R_{6t} = \alpha_6 + \beta_{61}R_{1t} + \beta_{62}R_{2t} + \beta_{63}R_{3t} + \beta_{64}R_{4t} + \beta_{65}R_{5t} \qquad + \gamma_6 M_t + u_{6t}$$
$$R_{7t} = \alpha_7 + \beta_{71}R_{1t} + \beta_{72}R_{2t} + \beta_{73}R_{3t} + \beta_{74}R_{4t} + \beta_{75}R_{5t} + \beta_{76}R_{6t} + \gamma_7 M_t + u_{7t}$$

where R_1 = rate of return on security 1 (= Imperial Oil)

R_2 = rate of return on security 2 (= Sun Oil)

$\vdots$

R_7 = rate of return on security 7 (= Standard of Indiana)

M_t = rate of return on the market index

u_{it} = disturbances ($i = 1, 2, \ldots, 7$)

Before we present the results, the obvious question is: How do we choose which is security 1, which is security 2, and so on? Lee and Lloyd answer this question purely empirically. They regress the rate of return on security i on the rates of return of the remaining six securities and observe the resulting R^2. Thus, there will be seven such regressions. Then they order the estimated R^2 values, from the

TABLE 20.6*
OLS, reduced form and 2SLS estimates of Klein's model I

OLS:

$$C = 16.237 + 0.193P + 0.796(W + W') + 0.089P_{-1} \qquad \bar{R}^2 = 0.978 \qquad DW = 1.367$$
$$(1.203)\ (0.091)\quad (0.040)\quad (0.090)$$

$$I = 10.125 + 0.479P + 0.333P_{-1} - 0.112K_{-1} \qquad \bar{R}^2 = 0.919 \qquad DW = 1.810$$
$$(5.465)\ (0.097)\quad (0.100)\quad\ \ (0.026)$$

$$W = 0.064 + 0.439X + 0.146X_{-1} + 0.130t \qquad \bar{R}^2 = 0.985 \qquad DW = 1.958$$
$$(1.151)\ (0.032)\quad (0.037)\quad\ \ (0.031)$$

Reduced-form:

$$P = 46.383 + 0.813P_{-1} - 0.213K_{-1} + 0.015X_{-1} + 0.297t - 0.926T + 0.443G$$
$$(10.870)\ (0.444)\quad\ \ (0.067)\quad\ \ (0.252)\quad\ \ (0.154)\ (0.385)\ (0.373)$$
$$\bar{R}^2 = 0.753 \qquad DW = 1.854$$

$$W + W' = 40.278 + 0.823P_{-1} - 0.144K_{-1} + 0.115X_{-1} + 0.881t - 0.567T + 0.859G$$
$$(8.787)\ (0.359)\quad\ \ (0.054)\quad\ \ (0.204)\quad\ \ (0.124)\ (0.311)\ (0.302)$$
$$\bar{R}^2 = 0.949 \qquad DW = 2.395$$

$$X = 78.281 + 1.724P_{-1} - 0.319K_{-1} + 0.094X_{-1} + 0.878t - 0.565T + 1.317G$$
$$(18.860)\ (0.771)\quad\ \ (0.110)\quad\ \ (0.438)\quad\ \ (0.267)\ (0.669)\ (0.648)$$
$$\bar{R}^2 = 0.882 \qquad DW = 2.049$$

2SLS:

$$C = 16.543 + 0.019P + 0.810(W + W') + 0.214P_{-1} \qquad \bar{R}^2 = 0.9726$$
$$(1.464)\ (0.130)\quad (0.044)\quad (0.118)$$

$$I = 20.284 + 0.149P + 0.616P_{-1} - 0.157K_{-1} \qquad \bar{R}^2 = 0.8643$$
$$(8.361)\ (0.191)\quad (0.180)\quad\ \ (0.040)$$

$$W = 0.065 + 0.438X + 0.146X_{-1} + 0.130t \qquad \bar{R}^2 = 0.9852$$
$$(1.894)\ (0.065)\quad (0.070)\quad\ \ (0.053)$$

*Interpretation of variables is listed in Example 18.6 (standard errors in parentheses).
Source: G. S. Maddala, *Econometrics*, McGraw-Hill, New York, 1977, p. 242.

lowest to the highest. The security having the lowest R^2 is designated as security 1 and the one having the highest R^2 is designated as 7. The idea behind this is intuitively simple. If the R^2 of the rate of return of, say, Imperial Oil, is lowest with respect to the other six securities, it would suggest that this security is affected least by the movements in the returns of the other securities. Therefore, the causal ordering, if any, runs from this security to the others and there is no feedback from the other securities.

Although one may object to such a purely empirical approach to causal ordering, let us present their empirical results nonetheless, which are given in Table 20.7.

In exercise 5.5 we introduced the *characteristic line* of modern investment theory, which is simply the regression of the rate of return on security i on the market rate of return. The slope coefficient, known as the *Beta coefficient*, is a measure of the volatility of the security's return. What the Lee-Lloyd regression results suggest is that there are significant intra-industry relationships between security returns, apart from the common market influence represented by the market port-

TABLE 20.7
Recursive system estimates for the oil industry

	Linear form dependent variables						
	Standard of Indiana	Shell Oil	Phillips Petroleum	Union Oil	Standard of Ohio	Sun Oil	Imperial Oil
Standard of Indiana							
Shell Oil	0.2100* (2.859)						
Phillips Petroleum	0.2293* (2.176)	0.0791 (1.065)					
Union Oil	0.1754* (2.472)	0.2171* (3.177)	0.2225* (2.337)				
Standard of Ohio	−0.0794 (−1.294)	0.0147 (0.235)	0.4248* (5.501)	0.1468* (1.735)			
Sun Oil	0.1249 (1.343)	0.1710* (1.843)	0.0472 (0.355)	0.1339 (0.908)	0.0499 (0.271)		
Imperial Oil	−0.1077 (−1.412)	0.0526 (0.6804)	0.0354 (0.319)	0.1580 (1.290)	−0.2541* (−1.691)	0.0828 (0.971)	
Constant	0.0868 (0.681)	−0.0384 (1.296)	−0.0127 (−0.068)	−0.2034 (0.986)	0.3009 (1.204)	0.2013 (1.399)	0.3710* (2.161)
Market index	0.3681* (2.165)	0.4997* (3.039)	0.2884 (1.232)	0.7609* (3.069)	0.9089* (3.094)	0.7161* (4.783)	0.6432* (3.774)
R^2	0.5020	0.4658	0.4106	0.2532	0.0985	0.2404	0.1247
Durbin-Watson	2.1083	2.4714	2.2306	2.3468	2.2181	2.3109	1.9592

*Denotes significance at 0.10 level or better for two-tailed test.
Note: The t values appear in parentheses beneath the coefficients.
Source: Cheng F. Lee and W. P. Lloyd, op. cit., Table 3b.

folio. Thus, Standard of Indiana's return depends not only on the market rate of return but also on the rates of return on Shell Oil, Phillips Petroleum, and Union Oil. To put the matter differently, the movement in the rate of return on Standard of Indiana can be better explained if in addition to the market rate of return we also consider the rates of return experienced by Shell Oil, Phillips Petroleum, and Union Oil.

Example 20.4   Revised Form of St. Louis Model[20]

The well-known, and often controversial, St. Louis model originally developed in the late 1960s has been revised from time to time. One such revision is given in

---

[20]*Review*, Federal Reserve Bank of St. Louis, May 1982, p. 14.

TABLE 20.8
The St. Louis model

(1) $$\dot{Y}_1 = C1 + \sum_{i=0}^{4} CM_i(\dot{M}_{t-i}) + \sum_{i=0}^{4} CE(\dot{E}_{t-i}) + \varepsilon 1_t$$

(2) $$\dot{P}_t = C2 + \sum_{i=1}^{4} CPE_i(\dot{PE}_{t-i}) + \sum_{i=0}^{5} CD_i(\dot{X}_{t-i} - \dot{XF}^*_{t-i})$$
$$+ CPA(\dot{PA}_t + CDUM1(DUM1) + CDUM2(DUM2) + \varepsilon 2_t$$

(3) $$\dot{PA}_t = \sum_{i=1}^{21} CPRL_i(\dot{P}_{t-i})$$

(4) $$RL_t = C3 + \sum_{i=0}^{20} CPRL_i(\dot{P}_{t-i}) + \varepsilon 3_t$$

(5) $$U_t - UF_t = CG(GAP_t) + CG1(GAP_{t-1}) + \varepsilon 4_t$$

(6) $$Y_t = (P_t/100)(X_t)$$

(7) $$\dot{Y}_t = [(Y_t/Y_{t-i})^4 - 1]100$$

(8) $$\dot{X}_t = [(X_t/X_{t-i})^4 - 1]100$$

(9) $$\dot{P}_t = [(P_t/P_{t-i})^4 - 1]100$$

(10) $$GAP_t = [(XF_t/X_t)/XF_t]100$$

(11) $$\dot{XF}^*_t = [(XF_t/X_{t-1})^4 - 1]100$$

Y = nominal GNP
M = money stock (M1)
E = high employment expenditures
P = GNP deflator (1972 = 100)
PE = relative price of energy
X = output in 1972 dollars
XF = potential output (Rasche/Tatom)
RL = corporate bond rate
U = unemployment rate
UF = unemployment rate at full employment
DUM1 = control dummy (1971–III to 1973–I = 1; 0 elsewhere)
DUM2 = postcontrol dummy (1973–II to 1975–I = 1; 0 elsewhere)

Source: Federal Reserve Bank of St. Loius, *Review,* May 1982, p. 14.

Table 20.8, and the empirical results based on this revised model are given in Table 20.9. (*Note:* A dot over a variable means the growth rate of that variable.) The model basically consists of Eq. (1), (2), (4), and (5) in Table 20.8, the other equations representing the definitions. Equation (1) was estimated by OLS. Equations (1), (2), and (4) were estimated using the Almon distributed-lag method with (endpoint) constraints on the coefficients. Where relevant, the equations were corrected for first-order (ρ_1) and/or second-order (ρ_2) serial correlation.

Examining the results, we observe that it is the rate of growth in the money supply that primarily determines the rate of growth of (nominal) GNP and not the

TABLE 20.9
In-sample estimation: 1960–I to 1980–IV (absolute value of
t statistic in parentheses)

(1) $\quad \dot{Y}_t = 2.44 + 0.40\dot{M}_t + 0.39\dot{M}_{t-1} + 0.22\dot{M}_{t-2} + 0.06\dot{M}_{t-3}$
$\qquad\quad (2.15)\ (3.38)\qquad (5.06)\qquad\quad (2.18)\qquad\quad (0.82)$

$\qquad\quad - 0.01\dot{M}_{t-4} + 0.06\dot{E}_t + 0.02\dot{E}_{t-1} - 0.02\dot{E}_{t-2}$
$\qquad\qquad (0.11)\qquad\ (1.46)\qquad (0.63)\qquad\quad (0.57)$

$\qquad\quad - 0.02\dot{E}_{t-3} + 0.01\dot{E}_{t-4}$
$\qquad\qquad (0.52)\qquad\ (0.34)$

$\qquad R^2 = 0.39 \qquad se = 3.50 \qquad DW = 2.02$

(2) $\quad \dot{P}_t = 0.96 + 0.01\dot{PE}_{t-1} + 0.04\dot{PE}_{t-2} - 0.01\dot{PE}_{t-3}$
$\qquad\quad (2.53)\ (0.75)\qquad\ (1.96)\qquad\quad (0.73)$

$\qquad\quad + 0.02\dot{PE}_{t-4} - 0.00(\dot{X}_t - \dot{XF}_t^*) + 0.01(\dot{X}_{t-1} - \dot{XF}_{t-1}^*)$
$\qquad\qquad (1.38)\qquad\quad (0.18)\qquad\qquad\quad (1.43)$

$\qquad\quad + 0.02(\dot{X}_{t-2} - \dot{XF}_{t-2}^*) + 0.02(\dot{X}_{t-3} - \dot{XF}_{t-3}^*)$
$\qquad\qquad (4.63)\qquad\qquad\qquad (3.00)$

$\qquad\quad + 0.02(\dot{X}_{t-4} - \dot{XF}_{t-4}^*) + 0.01(\dot{X}_{t-5} - \dot{XF}_{t-5}^*) + 1.03(\dot{PA}_t)$
$\qquad\qquad (2.42)\qquad\qquad\qquad (2.16)\qquad\qquad\qquad (10.49)$

$\qquad\quad - 0.61(DUM1_t) + 1.65(DUM2_t)$
$\qquad\qquad (1.02)\qquad\qquad (2.71)$

$\qquad R^2 = 0.80 \qquad se = 1.28 \qquad DW = 1.97 \qquad \hat{\rho} = 0.12$

(4) $\quad RL_t = 2.97 + 0.96 \sum_{i=0}^{20} \dot{P}_{t-i}$
$\qquad\quad (3.12)\ (5.22)$

$\qquad R^2 = 0.32 \qquad se = 0.33 \qquad DW = 1.76 \qquad \hat{\rho} = 0.94$

(5) $\quad U_t - UF_t = 0.28(GAP_t) + 0.14(GAP_{t-1})$
$\qquad\qquad\quad (11.89)\qquad\quad (6.31)$

$\qquad R^2 = 0.63 \qquad se = 0.17 \qquad DW = 1.95 \qquad \hat{\rho}_1 = 1.43 \qquad \hat{\rho}_2 = 0.52$

Source: Federal Reserve Bank of St. Louis, *Review*, May 1982, p. 14.

rate of growth in high-employment expenditures. The sum of the M coefficients is 1.06, suggesting that a 1 percent (sustained) increase in the money supply on the average leads to about 1.06 percent increase in the nominal GNP. On the other hand, the sum of the E coefficients, about 0.05, suggests that a change in high-employment government expenditure has little impact on the rate of growth of nominal GNP. It is left to the reader to interpret the results of the other regressions reported in Table 20.9.

20.7 SUMMARY AND CONCLUSIONS

1. Assuming that an equation in a simultaneous-equation model is identified (either exactly or over-), we have several methods to estimate it.
2. These methods fall into two broad categories: *Single-equation methods* and *systems methods*.
3. For reasons of economy, specification errors, etc. the single-equation methods are by far the most popular. A unique feature of these methods is that

one can estimate a single equation in a multiequation model without worrying too much about other equations in the system. (*Note:* For identification purposes, however, the other equations in the system count.)

4. Three commonly used single equation methods are **OLS, ILS,** and **2SLS.**

5. Although OLS is, in general, inappropriate in the context of simultaneous-equation models, it can be applied to the so-called **recursive models** where there is a definite but unidirectional cause-and-effect relationship among the endogenous variables.

6. The method of ILS is suited for just or exactly identified equations. In this method OLS is applied to the reduced-form equation, and it is from the reduced-form coefficients that one estimates the original structural coefficients.

7. The method of 2SLS is especially designed for overidentified equations, although it can also be applied to exactly identified equations. But then the results of 2SLS and ILS are identical. The basic idea behind 2SLS is to replace the (stochastic) endogenous explanatory variable by a linear combination of the predetermined variables in the model and use this combination as the explanatory variable in lieu of the original endogenous variable. The 2SLS method thus resembles the **instrumental variable method** of estimation in that the linear combination of the predetermined variables serves as an instrument, or proxy, for the endogenous regressor.

8. A noteworthy feature of both ILS and 2SLS is that the estimates obtained are consistent, that is, as the sample size increases indefinitely, the estimates converge to their true population values. The estimates may not satisfy small-sample properties, such as unbiasedness and minimum variance. Therefore, the results obtained by applying these methods to small samples and the inferences drawn from them should be interpreted with due caution.

EXERCISES

Questions

20.1. State whether each of the following statements is true or false:
  (a) The method of OLS is not applicable to estimate a structural equation in a simultaneous-equation model.
  (b) In case an equation is not identified, 2SLS is not applicable.
  (c) The problem of simultaneity does not arise in a recursive simultaneous-equation model.
  (d) The problems of simultaneity and exogeneity mean the same thing.
  (e) The 2SLS and other methods of estimating structural equations have desirable statistical properties only in large samples.
  (f) There is no such thing as an R^2 for the simultaneous-equation model as a whole.
  *(g) The 2SLS and other methods of estimating structural equations are not

---

*Optional.

applicable if the equation errors are autocorrelated and or are correlated across equations.

(h) If an equation is exactly identified, ILS and 2SLS give identical results.

20.2. Why is it unnecessary to apply the two-stage least-squares method to exactly identified equations?

20.3. Consider the following modified Keynesian model of income determination:

$$C_t = \beta_{10} + \beta_{11}Y_t + u_{1t}$$
$$I_t = \beta_{20} + \beta_{21}Y_t + \beta_{22}Y_{t-1} + u_{2t}$$
$$Y_t = C_t + I_t + G_t$$

where
$$C = \text{consumption expenditure}$$
$$I = \text{investment expenditure}$$
$$Y = \text{income}$$
$$G = \text{government expenditure}$$

G_t and Y_{t-1} are assumed predetermined.

(a) Obtain the reduced-form equations and determine which of the preceding equations are identified (either just or over).

(b) Which method will you use to estimate the parameters of the overidentified equation and of the exactly identified equation? Justify your answer.

20.4. Consider the following results:*

		R^2
OLS :	$\dot{W}_t = 0.276 + 0.258\dot{P}_t + 0.046\dot{P}_{t-1} + 4.959V_t$	$R^2 = 0.924$
OLS :	$\dot{P}_t = 2.693 + 0.232\dot{W}_t - 0.544\dot{X}_t + 0.247\dot{M}_t + 0.064\dot{M}_{t-1}$	$R^2 = 0.982$
2SLS :	$\dot{W}_t = 0.272 + 0.257\dot{P}_t + 0.046\dot{P}_{t-1} + 4.966V_t$	$R^2 = 0.920$
2SLS :	$\dot{P}_t = 2.686 + 0.233\dot{W}_t - 0.544\dot{X}_t + 0.246\dot{M}_t + 0.046\dot{M}_{t-1}$	$R^2 = 0.981$

where $\dot{W}_t$, $\dot{P}_t$, $\dot{M}_t$, and $\dot{X}_t$ are percentage changes in earnings, prices, import prices, and labor productivity (all percentage changes are over the previous year), respectively, and where V_t represents unfilled job vacancies (percentage of total number of employees).

"Since the OLS and 2SLS results are practically identical, 2SLS is meaningless." Comment.

†20.5. Assume that production is characterized by the Cobb-Douglas production function

$$Q_i = AK_i^\alpha L_i^\beta$$

where
$$Q = \text{output}$$
$$K = \text{capital input}$$
$$L = \text{labor input}$$
$$A, \alpha, \text{ and } \beta = \text{parameters}$$
$$i = i\text{th firm}$$

---

*Source: *Prices and Earnings in 1951–1969: An Econometric Assessment*, Department of Employment, United Kingdom, Her Majesty's Stationery Office, London, 1971, p. 30.

†Optional.

Given the price of final output P, the price of labor W, and the price of capital R, and assuming profit maximization, we obtain the following empirical model of production:

Production function:

$$\ln Q_i = \ln A + \alpha \ln K_i + \beta \ln L_i + \ln u_{1i} \tag{1}$$

Marginal product of labor function:

$$\ln Q_i = -\ln \beta + \ln L_i + \ln \frac{W}{P} + \ln u_{2i} \tag{2}$$

Marginal product of capital function:

$$\ln Q_i = -\ln \alpha + \ln K_i + \ln \frac{R}{P} + \ln u_{3i} \tag{3}$$

where u_1, u_2, and u_3 are stochastic disturbances.

In the preceding model there are three equations in three endogenous variables Q, L, and K. P, R, and W are exogenous.

(a) What problems do you encounter in estimating the model if $\alpha + \beta = 1$, that is, when there are constant returns to scale?

(b) Even if $\alpha + \beta \neq 1$, can you estimate the equations? Answer by considering the identifiability of the system.

(c) If the system is not identified, what can be done to make it identifiable?

Note: Equations (2) and (3) are obtained by differentiating Q with respect to labor and capital, respectively, setting them equal to W/P and R/P, transforming the resulting expressions into logarithms, and adding (the logarithm of) the disturbance terms.

20.6. Consider the following demand-and-supply model for money:

Demand for money:	$M_t^d = \beta_0 + \beta_1 Y_1 + \beta_2 R_t + \beta_3 P_t + u_{1t}$
Supply of money:	$M_t^s = \alpha_0 + \alpha_1 Y_t + u_{2t}$

where M = money
   Y = income
   R = rate of interest
   P = price

Assume that R and P are predetermined.

(a) Is the demand function identified?

(b) Is the supply function identified?

(c) Which method would you use to estimate the parameters of the identified equation(s)? Why?

(d) Suppose we modify the supply function by adding the explanatory variables Y_{t-1} and M_{t-1}. What happens to the identification problem? Would you still use the method you used in (c)? Why or why not?

20.7. Refer to exercise 18.10. For the two-equation system there obtain the reduced-form equations and estimate their parameters. Estimate the indirect least-squares regression of consumption on income and compare your results with the OLS regression.

Problems

20.8. Consider the following model:

$$R_t = \beta_0 + \beta_1 M_t + \beta_2 Y_t + u_{1t}$$
$$Y_t = \alpha_0 + \alpha_1 R_t + u_{2t}$$

where M_t (money supply) is exogenous, R_t is the interest rate, and Y_t is GDP.
(a) How would you justify the model?
(b) Are the equations identified?
(c) Using the data given in Table 20.2, estimate the parameters of the identified equations. Justify the method(s) you use.

20.9. Suppose we change the model in exercise 20.8 as follows:

$$R_t = \beta_0 + \beta_1 M_t + \beta_2 Y_t + \beta_3 Y_{t-1} + u_{1t}$$
$$Y_t = \alpha_0 + \alpha_1 R_t + u_{2t}$$

(a) Find out if the system is identified.
(b) Using the data given in Table 20.2, estimate the parameters of the identified equation(s).

20.10. Consider the following model:

$$R_t = \beta_0 + \beta_1 M_t + \beta_2 Y_t + u_{1t}$$
$$Y_t = \alpha_0 + \alpha_1 R_t + \alpha_2 I_t + u_{2t}$$

where the variables are as defined in exercise 20.8. Treating I (domestic investment) and M exogenously, determine the identification of the system. Using the data of Table 20.2, estimate the parameters of the identified equation(s).

20.11. Suppose we change the model of exercise 20.10 as follows:

$$R_t = \beta_0 + \beta_1 M_t + \beta_2 Y_t + u_{1t}$$
$$Y_t = \alpha_0 + \alpha_1 R_t + \alpha_2 I_t + u_{2t}$$
$$I_t = \gamma_0 + \gamma_1 R_t + u_{3t}$$

Assume that M is determined exogenously.
(a) Find out which of the equations are identified.
(b) Estimate the parameters of the identified equation(s) using the data given in Table 20.2. Justify your method(s).

20.12. Verify the standard errors reported in (20.5.3).

20.13. Return to the demand-supply model given in Eqs. (20.3.1) and (20.3.2). Suppose the supply function is altered as follows:

$$Q_t = \beta_0 + \beta_1 P_{t-1} + u_{2t}$$

where P_{t-1} is the price prevailing in the previous period.
(a) If X (expenditure) and P_{t-1} are predetermined, is there a simultaneity problem?
(b) If there is, are the demand and supply functions each identified? If they are, obtain their reduced-form equations and estimate them from the data given in Table 20.1.
(c) From the reduced-form coefficients, can you derive the structural coefficients? Show the necessary computations.

20A.1   BIAS IN THE INDIRECT LEAST-SQUARES ESTIMATORS

To show that the ILS estimators, although consistent, are biased, we use the demand-and-supply model given in Eq. (20.3.1) and (20.3.2). From (20.3.10) we obtain

$$\hat{\beta}_1 = \frac{\hat{\Pi}_3}{\hat{\Pi}_1}$$

Now

$$\hat{\Pi}_3 = \frac{\sum q_t x_t}{\sum x_t^2} \qquad \text{using (20.3.7)}$$

and

$$\hat{\Pi}_1 = \frac{\sum p_t x_t}{\sum x_t^2} \qquad \text{using (20.3.5)}$$

Therefore, on substitution, we obtain

$$\hat{\beta}_1 = \frac{\sum q_t x_t}{\sum p_t x_t} \tag{1}$$

Using (20.3.3) and (20.3.4), we obtain

$$p_t = \Pi_1 x_t + (w_t - \bar{w}) \tag{2}$$
$$q_t = \Pi_3 x_t + (v_t - \bar{v}) \tag{3}$$

where $\bar{w}$ and $\bar{v}$ are the mean values of w_t and v_t, respectively.

Substituting (2) and (3) into (1), we obtain

$$\hat{\beta}_1 = \frac{\Pi_3 \sum x_t^2 + \sum (v_t - \bar{v}) x_t}{\Pi_1 \sum x_t^2 + \sum (w_t - \bar{w}) x_t}$$

$$= \frac{\Pi_3 + \sum (v_t - \bar{v}) x_t / \sum x_t^2}{\Pi_1 + \sum (w_t - \bar{w}) x_t / \sum x_t^2} \tag{4}$$

Since the expectation operator E is a linear operator, we cannot take the expectation of (4), although it is clear that $\hat{\beta}_1 \neq (\Pi_3/\Pi_1)$ generally. (Why?)

But as the sample size tends to infinity, we can obtain

$$\text{plim}\,(\hat{\beta}_1) = \frac{\text{plim}\,\Pi_3 + \text{plim}\,\sum (v_t - \bar{v}) x_t / \sum x_t^2}{\text{plim}\,\Pi_1 + \text{plim}\,\sum (w_t - \bar{w}) x_t / \sum x_t^2} \tag{5}$$

where use is made of the properties of plim, namely, that

$$\text{plim}\,(A + B) = \text{plim}\,A + \text{plim}\,B \text{ and plim}\left(\frac{A}{B}\right) = \frac{\text{plim}\,A}{\text{plim}\,B}$$

Now as the sample size is increased indefinitely, the second term in both the denominator and the numerator of (5) tends to zero (why?), yielding

$$\text{plim} \, (\hat{\beta}_1) = \frac{\Pi_3}{\Pi_1} \tag{6}$$

showing that, although biased, $\hat{\beta}_1$ is a consistent estimator of β_1.

20.A.2 ESTIMATION OF STANDARD ERRORS OF 2SLS ESTIMATORS

The purpose of this appendix is to show that the standard errors of the estimates obtained from the second-page regression of the 2SLS procedure, using the formula applicable in OLS estimation, are not the "proper" estimates of the "true" standard errors. To see this, we use the income–money supply model given in (20.4.1) and (20.4.2). We estimate the parameters of the overidentified money supply function from the second-stage regression as

$$Y_{2t} = \beta_{20} + \beta_{21}\hat{Y}_{1t} + u_t^* \tag{20.4.6}$$

where

$$u_t^* = u_{2t} + \beta_{21}\hat{u}_t \tag{7}$$

Now when we run regression (20.4.6), the standard error of, say, $\hat{\beta}_{21}$ is obtained from the following expression:

$$\text{var}(\hat{\beta}_{21}) = \frac{\hat{\sigma}_{u^*}^2}{\sum \hat{y}_{1t}^2} \tag{8}$$

where

$$\hat{\sigma}_{u^*}^2 = \frac{\sum(\hat{u}_t^*)^2}{n-2} = \frac{\sum(Y_{2t} - \hat{\beta}_{20} - \hat{\beta}_{21}\hat{Y}_{1t})^2}{n-2} \tag{9}$$

But $\sigma_{u^*}^2$ is not the same thing as $\hat{\sigma}_{u_2}^2$, where the latter is an unbiased estimate of the true variance of u_2. This difference can be readily verified from (7). To obtain the true (as defined previously) $\hat{\sigma}_{u_2}^2$, we proceed as follows:

$$\hat{u}_{2t} = Y_{2t} - \hat{\beta}_{20} - \hat{\beta}_{21}Y_{1t}$$

where $\hat{\beta}_{20}$ and $\hat{\beta}_{21}$ are the estimates from the second-stage regression. Hence,

$$\hat{\sigma}_{u_2}^2 = \frac{\sum(Y_{2t} - \hat{\beta}_{20} - \hat{\beta}_{21}Y_{1t})^2}{n-2} \tag{10}$$

Note the difference between (9) and (10): In (10) we use actual Y_1 rather than the estimated Y_1 from the first-stage regression.

Having estimated (10), the easiest way to correct the standard errors of coefficients estimated in the second-stage regression is to multiply each one of them by $\hat{\sigma}_{u_2}/\hat{\sigma}_{u^*}$. Note that if Y_{1t} and $\hat{Y}_{1t}$ are very close, that is, the R^2 in the first-stage regression is very high, the correction factor $\hat{\sigma}_{u_2}/\hat{\sigma}_{u^*}$ will be close to 1, in which case the estimated standard errors in the second-stage regression may be taken as the true estimates. But in other situations, we shall have to use the preceding correction factor.

TIME
SERIES
ECONOMETRICS

Time series data have become so frequently and intensively used in empirical research that econometricians have recently begun to pay very careful attention to such data. In Chapter 1 we remarked that an implicit assumption underlying regression analysis involving time series data is that such data are **stationary.** If this is not the case, the conventional hypothesis-testing procedure based on t, F, chi-square tests, and the like may be suspect. In Chapters 21 and 22 we take a closer look at time series data.

In Chapter 21, we first define a stationary time series and then develop tests to find out whether a time series is stationary. In this connection we introduce some related concepts, such as a **unit root,** a **random walk,** and an **integrated time series.** We then distinguish between a **trend-stationary (TS)** and a **difference-stationary (DS)** time series and point out their practical implications. A common problem in regressions involving time series data is the phenomenon of **spurious regression** and we discuss its practical implications. We then introduce the concept of **cointegration** and point out its importance in empirical research. All these concepts are well illustrated.

In Chapter 22 our primary focus is on forecasting using time series data. Assuming that a time series is stationary or can be made so by appropriate transformation(s), we show how the **ARIMA modeling** made popular by Box and Jenkins can be used for forecasting. We also discuss in this chapter an alternative forecasting method, known as **vector autoregression** *(VAR)*, and consider its advantages over the traditional simultaneous-equation econometric forecasting models. We show with suitable examples how ARIMA and VAR forecasting are actually done.

These two chapters barely scratch the surface of time series econometrics. This is one of the most active areas of econometric research and already several specialized books have been written on this subject. Our objective in these two chapters is merely to introduce the reader to the enticing world of time series econometrics.

CHAPTER

21

TIME SERIES ECONOMETRICS I: STATIONARITY, UNIT ROOTS, AND COINTEGRATION

We noted in Chapter 1 that one of the two important types of data used in empirical analysis is **time series** data. In this and the following chapter we shall take a closer look at such data because they pose several challenges to econometricians and practitioners.

First, empirical work based on time series data assumes that the underlying time series is **stationary.** Although we introduced an intuitive idea of stationarity in Chapter 1, we discuss it more fully in this chapter. More specifically, we will try to find out what **stationarity** means and why one should worry if a time series is not stationary.

Second, in regressing a time series variable on another time series variable, one often obtains a very high R^2 although there is no meaningful relationship between the two. This situation exemplifies the problem of **spurious regression** (see Section 8.2). This problem arises because if both the time series involved exhibit strong **trends** (sustained upward or downward movements), the high R^2 observed is due to the presence of the trend, not to a true relationship between the two. It therefore is very important to find out if the relationship between economic variables is true or spurious. We will see in this chapter how spurious regression can arise if time series are not stationary.

Third, regression models involving time series data are often used for forecasting. In view of the preceding discussion, we would like to know if such forecasting is valid if the underlying time series are not stationary.

In the remainder of this chapter we take a closer look at the stationarity of a time series.

21.1 A LOOK AT SELECTED U.S. ECONOMIC TIME SERIES

To set the stage, let us examine the time series data given in Table 21.1, which presents data on five U.S. economic time series for the quarterly periods of 1970 to 1991, a total of 88 observations for each time series. The series are Gross Domestic Product (GDP), personal disposable income (PDI), personal consumption expenditure (PCE), profits, and dividends.

Figure 21.1 is a plot of the data for GDP, PDI, and PCE from Table 21.1 and Fig. 21.2 presents the other two time series.

A visual plot of the data is usually the first step in the analysis of any time series. The first impression that we get from the time series plotted in Fig. 21.1 and 21.2 is that they all seem to be trending upward, although the trend is not smooth, especially in the profits time series. These time series are in fact examples of **nonstationary time series.** What does that mean? The answer follows.

21.2 STATIONARY STOCHASTIC PROCESS

Any time series data can be thought of as being generated by a **stochastic** or **random process**; and a concrete set of data, such as that shown in Table 21.1, can be regarded as a (particular) **realization** (i.e., a sample) of the underlying stochastic process. The distinction between the stochastic process and its realization is akin to the distinction between population and sample in cross-sectional data. Just as we use sample data to draw inferences about a

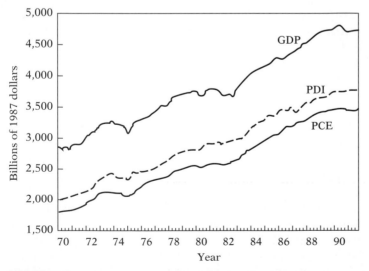

FIGURE 21.1
GDP, PDI, and PCE, United States, 1970–1991 (quarterly).

TABLE 21.1
Macroeconomics data, United States, 1970–I to 1991–IV

Quarter	GDP	PDI	PCE	Profits	Dividend
1970–I	2,872.8	1,990.6	1,800.5	44.7	24.5
1970–II	2,860.3	2,020.1	1,807.5	44.4	23.9
1970–III	2,896.6	2,045.3	1,824.7	44.9	23.3
1970–IV	2,873.7	2,045.2	1,821.2	42.1	23.1
1971–I	2,942.9	2,073.9	1,849.9	48.8	23.8
1971–II	2,947.4	2,098.0	1,863.5	50.7	23.7
1971–III	2,966.0	2,106.6	1,876.9	54.2	23.8
1971–IV	2,980.8	2,121.1	1,904.6	55.7	23.7
1972–I	3,037.3	2,129.7	1,929.3	59.4	25.0
1972–II	3,089.7	2,149.1	1,963.3	60.1	25.5
1972–III	3,125.8	2,193.9	1,989.1	62.8	26.1
1972–IV	3,175.5	2,272.0	2,032.1	68.3	26.5
1973–I	3,253.3	2,300.7	2,063.9	79.1	27.0
1973–II	3,267.6	2,315.2	2,062.0	81.2	27.8
1973–III	3,264.3	2,337.9	2,073.7	81.3	28.3
1973–IV	3,289.1	2,382.7	2,067.4	85.0	29.4
1974–I	3,259.4	2,334.7	2,050.8	89.0	29.8
1974–II	3,267.6	2,304.5	2,059.0	91.2	30.4
1974–III	3,239.1	2,315.0	2,065.5	97.1	30.9
1974–IV	3,226.4	2,313.7	2,039.9	86.8	30.5
1975–I	3,154.0	2,282.5	2,051.8	75.8	30.0
1975–II	3,190.4	2,390.3	2,086.9	81.0	29.7
1975–III	3,249.9	2,354.4	2,114.4	97.8	30.1
1975–IV	3,292.5	2,389.4	2,137.0	103.4	30.6
1976–I	3,356.7	2,424.5	2,179.3	108.4	32.6
1976–II	3,369.2	2,434.9	2,194.7	109.2	35.0
1976–III	3,381.0	2,444.7	2,213.0	110.0	36.6
1976–IV	3,416.3	2,459.5	2,242.0	110.3	38.3
1977–I	3,466.4	2,463.0	2,271.3	121.5	39.2
1977–II	3,525.0	2,490.3	2,280.8	129.7	40.0
1977–III	3,574.4	2,541.0	2,302.6	135.1	41.4
1977–IV	3,567.2	2,556.2	2,331.6	134.8	42.4
1978–I	3,591.8	2,587.3	2,347.1	137.5	43.5
1978–II	3,707.0	2,631.9	2,394.0	154.0	44.5
1978–III	3,735.6	2,653.2	2,404.5	158.0	46.6
1978–IV	3,779.6	2,680.9	2,421.6	167.8	48.9
1979–I	3,780.8	2,699.2	2,437.9	168.2	50.5
1979–II	3,784.3	2,697.6	2,435.4	174.1	51.8
1979–III	3,807.5	2,715.3	2,454.7	178.1	52.7
1979–IV	3,814.6	2,728.1	2,465.4	173.4	54.5
1980–I	3,830.8	2,742.9	2,464.6	174.3	57.6
1980–II	3,732.6	2,692.0	2,414.2	144.5	58.7
1980–III	3,733.5	2,722.5	2,440.3	151.0	59.3
1980–IV	3,808.5	2,777.0	2,469.2	154.6	60.5

TABLE 21.1 (continued)

Quarter	GDP	PDI	PCE	Profits	Dividend
1981–I	3,860.5	2,783.7	2,475.5	159.5	64.0
1981–II	3,844.4	2,776.7	2,476.1	143.7	68.4
1981–III	3,864.5	2,814.1	2,487.4	147.6	71.9
1981–IV	3,803.1	2,808.8	2,468.6	140.3	72.4
1982–I	3,756.1	2,795.0	2,484.0	114.4	70.0
1982–II	3,771.1	2,824.8	2,488.9	114.0	68.4
1982–III	3,754.4	2,829.0	2,502.5	114.6	69.2
1982–IV	3,759.6	2,832.6	2,539.3	109.9	72.5
1983–I	3,783.5	2,843.6	2,556.5	113.6	77.0
1983–II	3,886.5	2,867.0	2,604.0	133.0	80.5
1983–III	3,944.4	2,903.0	2,639.0	145.7	83.1
1983–IV	4,012.1	2,960.6	2,678.2	141.6	84.2
1984–I	4,089.5	3,033.2	2,703.8	155.1	83.3
1984–II	4,144.0	3,065.9	2,741.1	152.6	82.2
1984–III	4,166.4	3,102.7	2,754.6	141.8	81.7
1984–IV	4,194.2	3,118.5	2,784.8	136.3	83.4
1985–I	4,221.8	3,123.6	2,824.9	125.2	87.2
1985–II	4,254.8	3,189.6	2,849.7	124.8	90.8
1985–III	4,309.0	3,156.5	2,893.3	129.8	94.1
1985–IV	4,333.5	3,178.7	2,895.3	134.2	97.4
1986–I	4,390.5	3,227.5	2,922.4	109.2	105.1
1986–II	4,387.7	3,281.4	2,947.9	106.0	110.7
1986–III	4,412.6	3,272.6	2,993.7	111.0	112.3
1986–IV	4,427.1	3,266.2	3,012.5	119.2	111.0
1987–I	4,460.0	3,295.2	3,011.5	140.2	108.0
1987–II	4,515.3	3,241.7	3,046.8	157.9	105.5
1987–III	4,559.3	3,285.7	3,075.8	169.1	105.1
1987–IV	4,625.5	3,335.8	3,074.6	176.0	106.3
1988–I	4,655.3	3,380.1	3,128.2	195.5	109.6
1988–II	4,704.8	3,386.3	3,147.8	207.2	113.3
1988–III	4,734.5	3,407.5	3,170.6	213.4	117.5
1988–IV	4,779.7	3,443.1	3,202.9	226.0	121.0
1989–I	4,809.8	3,473.9	3,200.9	221.3	124.6
1989–II	4,832.4	3,450.9	3,208.6	206.2	127.1
1989–III	4,845.6	3,466.9	3,241.1	195.7	129.1
1989–IV	4,859.7	3,493.0	3,241.6	203.0	130.7
1990–I	4,880.8	3,531.4	3,258.8	199.1	132.3
1990–II	4,900.3	3,545.3	3,258.6	193.7	132.5
1990–III	4,903.3	3,547.0	3,281.2	196.3	133.8
1990–IV	4,855.1	3,529.5	3,251.8	199.0	136.2
1991–I	4,824.0	3,514.8	3,241.1	189.7	137.8
1991–II	4,840.7	3,537.4	3,252.4	182.7	136.7
1991–III	4,862.7	3,539.9	3,271.2	189.6	138.1
1991–IV	4,868.0	3,547.5	3,271.1	190.3	138.5

Notes: GDP (Gross Domestic Product), billions of 1987 dollars, p. A-96.

PDI (Personal disposable income), billions of 1987 dollars, p. A-112.

PCE (Personal consumption expenditure), billions of 1987 dollars, p. A-96.

Profits (corporate profits after tax), billions of dollars, p. A-110.

Dividends (net corporate dividend payments), billions of dollars, p. A-110.

Source: U.S. Department of Commerce, Bureau of Economic Analysis, *Business Statistics, 1963–1991,* June 1992.

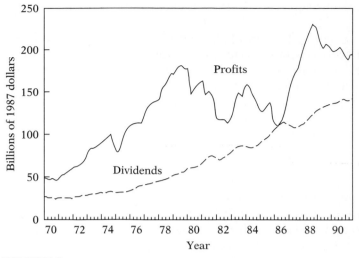

FIGURE 21.2
Profits and dividends, United States, 1970–1991 (quarterly).

population, in time series we use the realization to draw inferences about the underlying stochastic process. A type of stochastic process that has received a great deal of attention and scrutiny by time series analysts is the so-called **stationary stochastic process.**

Broadly speaking, *a stochastic process is said to be stationary if its mean and variance are constant over time and the value of covariance between two time periods depends only on the distance or lag between the two time periods and not on the actual time at which the covariance is computed.*[1]

To explain this statement, let Y_t be a stochastic time series with these properties:

$$\text{Mean}: \qquad E(Y_t) = \mu \qquad\qquad (21.2.1)$$

$$\text{Variance}: \qquad \text{var}(Y_t) = E(Y_t - \mu)^2 = \sigma^2 \qquad\qquad (21.2.2)$$

$$\text{Covariance}: \qquad \gamma_k = E[(Y_t - \mu)(Y_{t+k} - \mu)] \qquad\qquad (21.2.3)$$

where γ_k, the covariance (or autocovariance) at lag k, is the covariance between the values of Y_t and Y_{t+k}, that is, between two Y values k periods apart. If $k = 0$, we obtain γ_0, which is simply the variance of $Y(= \sigma^2)$; if $k = 1$, γ_1 is the covariance between two adjacent values of Y, the type of covariance we encountered in Chapter 12 when we discussed the topic of autocorrelation.

Suppose we shift the origin of Y from Y_t to Y_{t+m}. Now if Y_t is to be stationary, the mean, variance, and autocovariances of Y_{t+m} must be the same as those of Y_t. In short, if a time series is stationary, its mean, variance, and

---

[1]In the time series literature such a stochastic process is known as a **weakly stationary stochastic process.** For the purpose of this chapter, and in most practical situations, this type of stationarity will do.

autocovariance (at various lags) remain the same no matter at what time we measure them.

If a time series is not stationary in the sense just defined, it is called a **nonstationary time series** (keep in mind, we are only talking about weak stationarity); sometimes, nonstationarity could be due to a shift in the mean.

To see all this visually, consider Fig. 21.3. Figure 21.3*a* gives the real rate of return on the S&P 500 stock index for the annual observations from 1872 to 1986, and Fig. 21.3*b* gives the U.K. interest rate spread (difference between long- and short-term interest rates) for the quarterly periods of 1952–1988. The first is an example of a stationary time series and the second of a nonstationary time series.

Looking at the U.S. economic time series in Figs. 21.1 and 21.2, we get the "feeling" that these time series are not stationary because visually, at least, the mean, variance, and autocovariances of the individual series do not seem to be time-invariant. How can we be sure that Fig. 21.3*a* represents a stationary time series and Figs. 21.3*b*, 21.1, and 21.2 represent nonstationary time series? We discuss this question in the next section.

21.3   TEST OF STATIONARITY BASED ON CORRELOGRAM

One simple test of stationarity is based on the so-called **autocorrelation function (ACF).** The ACF at lag k, denoted by ρ_k, is defined as

$$\rho_k = \frac{\gamma_k}{\gamma_0} \tag{21.3.1}$$

$$= \frac{\text{covariance at lag } k}{\text{variance}}$$

Note that if $k = 0$, $\rho_0 = 1$. (Why?)

Since both covariance and variance are measured in the same units of measurement, ρ_k is a unitless, or pure, number. It lies between -1 and $+1$, as any correlation coefficient does. If we plot ρ_k against k, the graph we obtain is known as the **population correlogram.**

Since in practice we only have a realization (i.e., sample) of a stochastic process, we can only compute the **sample autocorrelation function**, $\hat{\rho}_k$. To compute this, we must first compute the **sample covariance** at lag k, $\hat{\gamma}_k$, and the **sample variance,** $\hat{\gamma}_0$, which are defined as[2]

$$\hat{\gamma}_k = \frac{\sum (Y_t - \bar{Y})(Y_{t+k} - \bar{Y})}{n} \tag{21.3.2}$$

$$\hat{\gamma}_0 = \frac{\sum (Y_t - \bar{Y})^2}{n} \tag{21.3.3}$$

where n is sample size and $\bar{Y}$ is the sample mean.

---

[2]Strictly speaking, we should divide the sample covariance at lag k by $(n - k)$ and the sample variance by $(n-1)$ rather than n (why?). But in large samples this should not make much difference.

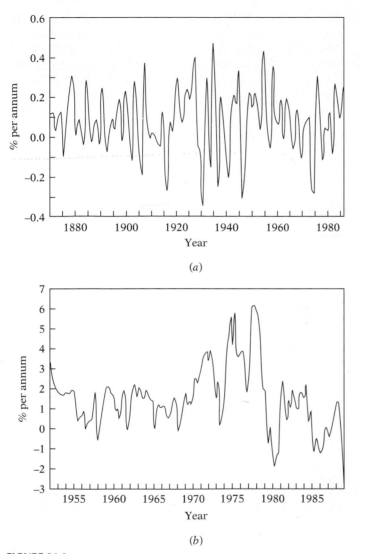

FIGURE 21.3
Examples of stationary and nonstationary time series: (a) S&P 500 index
(real returns 1872–1986): A stationary time series; (b) U.K. interest rate
spread (quarterly 1952–I–1988–IV): A nonstationary time series. (*Source:*
Terence C. Mills. *The Econometric Modelling of Financial Time Series*,
Cambridge, University Press, New York, 1993, pp. 25 and 27.)

Therefore, the sample autocorrelation function at lag k is

$$\hat{\rho}_k = \frac{\hat{\gamma}_k}{\hat{\gamma}_0} \tag{21.3.4}$$

which is simply the ratio of the sample covariance to sample variance. A plot
of $\hat{\rho}_k$ against k is known as the **sample correlogram.**

Figure 21.4 shows the sample correlogram of the GDP time series given in Table 21.1, which was obtained from MICRO TSP 7.0 version. We have shown the correlogram up to 25 lags.[3] How does the sample correlogram in Fig. 21.4 tell us whether the GDP time series is stationary? One striking feature of this sample correlogram is that it starts at a very high value (about 0.97 at lag 1) and tapers off very gradually. Even at lag 14 (i.e., correlation between GDP 14 quarters apart) the autocorrelation coefficient is still a sizable 0.5. This type of pattern is generally an indication that the time series is nonstationary. By contrast, if a stochastic process is purely random its autocorrelation at any lag greater than zero is zero.

FIGURE 21.4
Correlogram, GDP, United States, 1970–I to 1991–IV.

Lag	Sample ACF ($\hat{\rho}_k$)	
1	0.969	| * * * * * * * * * * * * * *
2	0.935	| * * * * * * * * * * * * * *
3	0.901	| * * * * * * * * * * * * *
4	0.866	| * * * * * * * * * * * *
5	0.830	| * * * * * * * * * * * *
6	0.791	| * * * * * * * * * * *
7	0.752	| * * * * * * * * * * *
8	0.713	| * * * * * * * * * *
9	0.675	| * * * * * * * * * *
10	0.638	| * * * * * * * * *
11	0.601	| * * * * * * * * *
12	0.565	| * * * * * * * *
13	0.532	| * * * * * * * *
14	0.500	| * * * * * * *
15	0.468	| * * * * * * *
16	0.437	| * * * * * * *
17	0.405	| * * * * * *
18	0.375	| * * * * * *
19	0.344	| * * * * *
20	0.313	| * * * * *
21	0.279	| * * * * *
22	0.246	| * * *
23	0.214	| * * *
24	0.182	| * *
25	0.153	| * *

95% confidence interval

Note: Box-Pierce Q statistic: 792.98
Ljung-Box (LB) statistic: 891.25

---

[3]Although there are tests about the maximum length of the lag to be used in calculations, in practice lags up to one-third of the sample size are generally used. But this matter is very often subjective.

The statistical significance of any $\hat{\rho}_k$ can be judged by its standard error. Bartlett has shown that if a time series is purely random, that is, it exhibits **white noise** (see Section 21.4), the sample autocorrelation coefficients are *approximately* normally distributed with zero mean and variance $1/n$, where n is the sample size.[4] For our data $n = 88$, implying a variance of $1/88$ or a standard error of $1/\sqrt{88} = 0.1066$. Then, following the properties of the standard normal distribution, the 95% confidence interval for any ρ_k will be $\pm 1.96(0.1066) = 0.2089$ on either side of zero. Thus, if an estimated ρ_k falls inside the interval $(-0.2089, 0.2089)$, we do not reject the hypothesis that the true ρ_k is zero. But if it lies outside this confidence interval, then we can reject the hypothesis that the true ρ_k is zero. The 95% confidence interval is shown as two solid lines in Fig. 21.4.

The reader can see that all the $\hat{\rho}_k$ coefficients up to lag 23 in Fig. 21.4 are individually statistically significant, that is, significantly different from zero.

To test the *joint hypothesis* that all the ρ_k autocorrelation coefficients are simultaneously equal to zero, one can use the **Q statistic** developed by Box and Pierce, which is defined as

$$Q = n \sum_{k=1}^{m} \hat{\rho}_k^2 \qquad (21.3.5)$$

where n = sample size
$\qquad m$ = lag length

The Q statistic is *approximately* (i.e., in large samples) distributed as the chi-square distribution with m df. In an application, if the computed Q exceeds the critical Q value from the chi-square table at the chosen level of significance, one can reject the null hypothesis that all ρ_k are all zero; at least some of them must be nonzero.

A variant of the Box-Pierce Q statistic is the **Ljung-Box (LB) statistic,** which is defined as[5]

$$\text{LB} = n(n+2) \sum_{k=1}^{m} \left(\frac{\hat{\rho}_k^2}{n-k} \right) \sim \chi_m^2 \qquad (21.3.6)$$

Although in large samples both the Q and LB statistic follow the chi-square distribution with m df, the LB statistic has been found to have better (more powerful, in the statistical sense) small-sample properties than the Q statistic.

For our GDP data the Q statistic based on 25 lags is about 793 and the LB statistic is about 891, both being highly significant; the p values of obtaining such chi-square values are practically zero. Therefore, the conclusion is that not all ρ_k of our GDP data are zero.

---

[4]M. S. Bartlett, "On the Theoretical Specification of Sampling Properties of Autocorrelated Time Series," *Journal of the Royal Statistical Society,* Series B, vol. 27, 1946, pp. 27–41.

[5]G. M. Ljung and G. P. E. Box, "On a Measure of Lack of Fit in Time Series Models," *Biometrika,* vol. 66, 1978, pp. 66–72.

Based on the correlogram, then, our overall conclusion is that the GDP time series given in Table 21.1 is not stationary.

21.4 THE UNIT ROOT TEST OF STATIONARITY

An alternative test of stationarity that has recently become popular is known as the **unit root test.** The easiest way to introduce this test is to consider the following model:

$$Y_t = Y_{t-1} + u_t \tag{21.4.1}$$

where u_t is the stochastic error term that follows the classical assumptions, namely, it has zero mean, constant variance σ^2, and is nonautocorrelated. Such an error term is also known as a **white noise error term** in engineering terminology.[6] From Chapter 12 the reader will recognize that Eq. (21.4.1) is a first-order, or AR(1), regression in that we regress the value of Y at time t on its value at time $(t - 1)$. Now if the coefficient of Y_{t-1} is in fact equal to 1, we face what is known as the **unit root problem**, i.e., a nonstationarity situation.[7] Therefore, if we run the regression

$$Y_t = \rho Y_{t-1} + u_t \tag{21.4.2}$$

and actually find that $\rho = 1$, then we say that the stochastic variable Y_t *has a unit root.* In (time series) econometrics, a time series that has a unit root is known as a **random walk** (time series). And a random walk is an example of a nonstationary time series.[8] For example, asset prices, such as stock prices, follow a random walk, that is, they are nonstationary. In the Appendix to this chapter we see that a random walk indeed represents a nonstationary time series.

Equation (21.4.2) is often expressed in an alternative form as

$$\Delta Y_t = (\rho - 1)Y_{t-1} + u_t$$
$$= \delta Y_{t-1} + u_t \tag{21.4.3}$$

where $\delta = (\rho - 1)$ and where Δ, as we know, is the *first-difference* operator introduced in Chapter 12. Note that $\Delta Y_t = (Y_t - Y_{t-1})$. Making use of this definition, the reader can easily see that (21.4.2) and (21.4.3) are the same. However, now the null hypothesis is that $\delta = 0$ (why?).

---

[6]Note that if u_t not only are nonautocorrelated but are also independent, then such an error term is called **strictly white noise.** Also note that if the error term is autocorrelated, as we show below in our discussion of the **augmented Dickey-Fuller (ADF) test**, we can easily allow for this contingency.

[7]A technical point: We can write (21.4.1) as $Y_t - Y_{t-1} = u_t$. Now using the lag operator L so that $LY_t = Y_{t-1}, L^2 Y_t = Y_{t-2}$ and so on, we can write (21.4.1) as $(1 - L)Y_t = u_t$. The term *unit root* refers to the root of the polynomial in the lag operator.

[8]The random walk is often compared with a drunkard's walk. Leaving the bar, the drunkard moves a random distance u_t at time t, and if he or she continues to walk indefinitely, he or she will eventually drift farther and farther away from the bar. The same is said about stock prices. Today's stock price is equal to yesterday's stock price plus a random shock.

If δ is in fact 0, we can write (21.4.3) as

$$\Delta Y_t = (Y_t - Y_{t-1}) = u_t \tag{21.4.4}$$

What (21.4.4) says is that the first differences of a random walk time series ($= u_t$) are a stationary time series because by assumption u_t is purely random.

Now if a time series is differenced once and the differenced series is stationary, we say that the original (random walk) series is **integrated of order 1,** denoted by I(1). Similarly, if the original series has to be differenced twice (i.e., take first difference of the first difference) before it becomes stationary, the original series is **integrated of order 2,** or I(2). In general, if a time series has to be differenced d times, it is integrated of order d or I(d). Thus, any time we have an integrated time series of order 1 or greater, we have a nonstationary time series. By convention, if $d = 0$, the resulting I(0) process represents a stationary time series. We will use the terms *a stationary process* and *an I(0) process* as synonymous.

To find out if a time series Y_t (e.g., GDP) is nonstationary, run the regression (21.4.2) and find out if $\hat{\rho}$ is statistically equal to 1 or, equivalently, estimate (21.4.3) and find out if $\hat{\delta} = 0$ on the basis of, say, the t statistic. Unfortunately, the t value thus obtained does not follow Student's t distribution even in large samples.

Under the null hypothesis that $\rho = 1$, the conventionally computed t statistic is known as the τ **(tau) statistic,** whose critical values have been tabulated by Dickey and Fuller on the basis of Monte Carlo simulations.[9] In the literature the **tau test** is known as the **Dickey-Fuller (DF) test,** in honor of its discoverers. Note that, if the null hypothesis that $\rho = 1$ is rejected (i.e., the time series is stationary), we can use the usual (Student's) t test.

In its simplest form, we estimate a regression like (21.4.2), divide the estimated ρ coefficient by its standard error to compute the Dickey-Fuller τ statistic and refer to the Dickey-Fuller tables to see if the null hypothesis $\rho = 1$ is rejected. However, these tables are not totally adequate, and they have been considerably extended by MacKinnon through Monte Carlo simulations.[10] **ET, MICRO TSP,** and **SHAZAM,** among other statistical packages, give the Dickey-Fuller and MacKinnon critical values of the DF statistic.

If the computed absolute value of the τ *statistic* (i.e., $|\tau|$) exceeds the DF or MacKinnon DF absolute critical τ values, then we do not reject the hypothesis that the given time series is stationary. If, on the other hand, it is less than the critical value, the time series is nonstationary.[11]

---

[9]D. A. Dickey and W. A. Fuller, "Distribution of the Estimators for Autoregressive Time Series with a Unit Root," *Journal of the American Statistical Association,* vol. 74, 1979, pp. 427–431. See also W. A. Fuller, *Introduction to Statistical Time Series,* John Wiley & Sons, New York, 1976.

[10]J. G. MacKinnon, "Critical Values of Cointegration Tests," in R. F. Engle and C. W. J. Granger, eds., *Long-Run Economic Relationships: Readings in Cointegration,* Chapter 13, Oxford University Press, New York, 1991.

[11]If the regression is run in the form of (21.4.3) the estimated τ statistic usually has a negative sign. Therefore, a large negative τ value is generally an indication of stationarity.

For theoretical and practical reasons, the Dickey-Fuller test is applied to regressions run in the following forms:

$$\Delta Y_t = \delta Y_{t-1} + u_t \tag{21.4.3}$$

$$\Delta Y_t = \beta_1 + \delta Y_{t-1} + u_t \tag{21.4.5}$$

$$\Delta Y_t = \beta_1 + \beta_2 t + \delta Y_{t-1} + u_t \tag{21.4.6}$$

where t is the time or trend variable. In each case the null hypothesis is that $\delta = 0$, that is, there is a unit root. The difference between (21.4.3) and the other two regressions lies in the inclusion of the constant (intercept) and the trend term.

If the error term u_t is autocorrelated, one modifies (21.4.6) as follows:

$$\Delta Y_t = \beta_1 + \beta_2 t + \delta Y_{t-1} + \alpha_i \sum_{i=1}^{m} \Delta Y_{t-i} + \varepsilon_t \tag{21.4.7}$$

where, for example, $\Delta Y_{t-1} = (Y_{t-1} - Y_{t-2})$, $\Delta Y_{t-2} = (Y_{t-2} - Y_{t-3})$, etc., that is, one uses lagged difference terms. The number of lagged difference terms to include is often determined empirically, the idea being to include enough terms so that the error term in (21.4.7) is serially independent. The null hypothesis is still that $\delta = 0$ or $\rho = 1$, that is, a unit root exists in Y (i.e., Y is nonstationary). When the DF test is applied to models like (21.4.7), it is called **augmented Dickey-Fuller (ADF) test.** The ADF test statistic has the same asymptotic distribution as the DF statistic, so the same critical values can be used.

Is the U.S. GDP Time Series Stationary?

Let us illustrate the DF test using the GDP data given in Table 21.1. Based on **MICRO TSP 7.0,** regressions corresponding to (21.4.5) and (21.4.6) gave the following results:

$$\begin{aligned} \widehat{\Delta GDP}_t &= 28.2054 - 0.0014\,GDP_{t-1} \\ t &= (1.1576)\,(-0.2192) \\ r^2 &= 0.0018 \quad d = 1.3520 \end{aligned} \tag{21.4.8}$$

$$\begin{aligned} \widehat{\Delta GDP}_t &= 188.9060 + 1.4776t - 0.0603\,GDP_{t-1} \\ t &= (1.8406) \quad (1.6110)\,(-1.6253) \\ R^2 &= 0.0305 \quad d = 1.3147 \end{aligned} \tag{21.4.9}$$

For our purpose the important thing is the t ($=$ tau) statistic of the GDP_{t-1} variable. Note that our null hypothesis is that $\delta = 0$, which is to say that $\rho = 1$, or unit root. Now for model (21.4.8) the 1%, 5%, and 10% critical τ statistics as computed by MacKinnon are -3.5073, -2.8951, and -2.5844, respectively. Since the computed τ value is -0.2192, which in absolute terms is smaller than the 1%, 5%, or 10% critical values, we do not reject the null hypothesis that $\delta = 0$, that is, the GDP series exhibits a unit root, which is another way of saying that the GDP series is nonstationary. On the basis of the correlogram test discussed earlier, we should have anticipated this conclusion.

For model (21.4.9) the 1%, 5%, and 10% critical τ values are -4.0673, -3.4620, and -3.1570, respectively. The computed t ($=$ tau) value of -1.6253

for the GDP_{t-1} is thus not statistically significant, suggesting again that $\delta = 0$ or that there is a unit root in the GNP data. Incidentally, *note that the DF critical values depend on whether there is a constant term and/or trend.*

To allow for the possibility of serial correlation in u_t, we can use a model like (21.4.7) and then apply the **ADF test;** note that the Durbin-Watson d statistic given in (21.4.8) and (21.4.9) suggests such a possibility. Allowing for one lagged value of the first differences of GDP, we obtain the following regression results:[12]

$$\widehat{\Delta GDP}_t = 233.0806 + 1.8922t - 0.0787GDP_{t-1} + 0.3558\Delta GDP_{t-1}$$
$$t = \quad (2.3848) \quad (2.1522) \quad (-2.2153) \quad\quad\quad (3.4647) \quad\quad (21.4.10)$$
$$R^2 = 0.1526 \quad d = 2.0858$$

Since the Durbin-Watson d has increased, perhaps there was serial correlation. But notice that the $\tau = -2.2153$ is still below the ADF critical values of -4.0673 (1%), -3.4620 (5%), and -3.2447 (10%), suggesting that the GDP time series is nonstationary.

To sum up then, the U.S. GDP data for 1970–I to 1991–IV are nonstationary, based on the correlogram and the DF and ADF unit root tests.

Is the First-Differenced GDP Series Stationary?

Let us repeat the preceding exercise, only this time we want to find out whether $\Delta GDP_t = (GDP_t - GDP_{t-1})$ is stationary. For convenience let D_t denote ΔGDP_t. We have the following results:

$$\widehat{\Delta D}_t = 15.5313 - 0.6748 D_{t-1}$$
$$t = (3.4830)(-6.4956) \quad\quad\quad (21.4.11)$$
$$r^2 = 0.3436$$

The 1%, 5%, and 10% critical τ values computed by MacKinnon are -3.5082, -2.8955, and -2.5846, respectively. In absolute terms, the τ value of 6.4956 exceeds any of these critical values, so that we can now reject the hypothesis that δ (the coefficient of D_{t-1}) is zero. That is, the first-differenced GDP data do not exhibit a unit root, which is to say that the data are stationary. That is, they are $I(0)$.[13] Figure 21.5 shows the first-differenced GDP data. Compared with the original GDP series given in Fig. 21.1, the differenced GDP series shown in Fig. 21.5 does not show any trend.

Since ΔGDP_t is stationary, as noted, it is an $I(0)$ stochastic process, which means GDP_t itself is an $I(1)$ time series; essentially, it is a random walk.

Incidentally, since the DF or ADF tells us whether a time series is integrated, it is also known as a test of integration.

---

[12]Adding two lagged values of ΔGDP did not change the results materially.

[13]A technical point: There is some debate about whether we can apply the DF test sequentially, first to the data in level form and then in the first-difference form. On this, see D. A. Dickey and S. S. Pantula, "Determining the Order of Differencing in Autoregressive Processes," *Journal of Business and Statistics*, vol. 5, 1987, pp. 455–461.

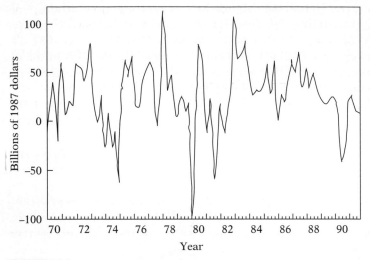

FIGURE 21.5
First differences of GDP, United States, 1970–I to 1991–IV.

21.5 TREND-STATIONARY (TS) AND DIFFERENCE-STATIONARY (DS) STOCHASTIC PROCESS

In regressions involving time series data the time, or trend, variable t is often included as one of the regressors to avoid the problem of spurious correlation (see Chapter 8). Data involving economic time series often tend to move in the same direction because of a trend that is common to all of them. For example, in the regression of PCE on PDI, if we observe a very high R^2, which is typically the case, it may reflect, not the true degree of association between the two variables, but simply the common trend present in them.

To avoid such a spurious association, the common practice is to regress PCE on PDI and t, the trend variable. The coefficient of PDI obtained from this regression now represents the net influence of PDI on PCE, having removed the trend effect. In other words, the explicit introduction of the trend variable in the regression has the effect of detrending (i.e., removing the influence of trend from) both PCE and PDI.

Recently a new breed of time series econometricians has challenged this common practice. According to them, this standard practice may be acceptable only if the trend variable is **deterministic** and not **stochastic.**[14]

Broadly speaking, the trend is deterministic if it is perfectly predictable and not variable. What this means can be seen from Fig. 21.1. If one were

---

[14]See the two interesting and valuable papers: Charles R. Nelson and Charles I. Plosser, "Trends and Random Walks in Macroeconomic Time Series: Some Evidence and Implications," *Journal of Monetary Economics,* vol. 10, 1982, pp. 139–162; James H. Stock and Mark W. Watson, "Variable Trends in Economic Time Series," *Journal of Economic Perspectives,* vol. 2, no. 3, Summer 1988, pp. 147–174.

to sketch a straight trend line through the GDP time series shown there, one would see that a single trend line does not do justice to the data. Maybe there is one trend line for the period 1970–I to 1974–IV, another for 1975–I to 1981–IV, and yet another for 1982–I to 1991–IV. In short, the trend line itself is shifting, that is, it is stochastic. If this is the case, the common practice of detrending the data by a single trend line will be misleading.

How does one find out whether the trend in a series, such as the GDP, is deterministic or variable (i.e., stochastic)? We already have the answer in regression (21.4.6). In estimating this regression if we find that the given time series (e.g., GDP) has a unit root (i.e., is nonstationary), we can conclude that such a time series exhibits a stochastic trend. If it does not have a unit root, the time series exhibits a deterministic trend.

Returning to regressions (21.4.9) and (21.4.10), we have already concluded that the U.S. GDP time series for 1970–I to 1991–IV was nonstationary. Therefore, such a series will exhibit a stochastic trend. As a consequence, if we were to run this regression,

$$\text{GDP}_t = \beta_1 + \beta_2 t + u_t \tag{21.5.1}$$

under the mistaken belief that the trend is deterministic, the detrended GDP obtained as

$$\hat{u}_t = (\text{GDP}_t - \hat{\beta}_1 - \hat{\beta}_2 t) \tag{21.5.2}$$

would not be of much value if in fact the trend is stochastic. Therefore, forecasts based on (21.5.1) would be of dubious value. For this reason we warned in Chapter 5 that one should not use the historically estimated regression line to make forecasts too far out in the future.

Now we introduce two key concepts in time series analysis, namely, a **trend-stationary process (TSP)** and a **difference-stationary process (DSP).** If in the regression

$$Y_t = \beta_1 + \beta_2 t + u_t \tag{21.5.3}$$

u_t is in fact stationary, with, say, mean zero and variance σ^2, then (21.5.3) represents a TSP; if one subtracts the trend (i.e., $\beta_1 + \beta_2 t$) from (21.5.3), the result is a stationary process. However, if Y_t is generated as

$$Y_t - Y_{t-1} = \alpha + u_t \tag{21.5.4}$$

where α is a constant and u_t is stationary, with, say, mean zero and variance σ^2, we call such a process a DSP. Note that $(Y_t - Y_{t-1}) = \Delta Y_t$, that is, the first difference of Y_t.

Returning to our GDP time series, we have already seen that the level of GDP is not a TSP, whereas, as seen in regression (21.4.11), ΔGDP is a DSP.

In brief, a stationary time series can be modeled as a TS process, whereas a nonstationary time series represents a DS process. As Holden, Peel, and Thompson note:

> With a deterministic trend, variables can be made stationary by including a time trend in any regression or by doing a preliminary regression on time and subtract-

ing the estimated trend [as in regression (21.5.2)]. With a stochastic trend, tests for cointegration [discussed later] and nonstationarity are needed.[15]

We conclude by raising this question: What is the practical significance of TSP and DSP? From the point of long-term forecasting, forecasts made from a TSP will be more reliable, whereas those made from a DSP will be unreliable and sometimes very hazardous. As Nathan Balke notes, "The presence of a stochastic trend implies that fluctuations in a time series are the result of shocks not only to the transitory or cyclical component but also to the trend component."[16] That is, disturbances or shocks to such time series will permanently alter their level.

21.6 SPURIOUS REGRESSION

Regressions involving time series data include the possibility of obtaining **spurious** or dubious results in the sense that superficially the results look good but on further probing they look suspect. To see this problem vividly, let us return to the PCE and PDI data for the United States given in Table 21.1. Suppose we regress PCE on PDI to find the relationship between the two. Using the data given in Table 21.1, we obtain the following results:

$$\widehat{PCE}_t = -171.4412 + 0.9672 PDI_t$$
$$t = (-7.4809) \quad (119.8711) \tag{21.6.1}$$
$$R^2 = 0.9940 \quad d = 0.5316$$

These regression results look "fabulous": the R^2 is extremely high, the t ratio of the PDI has an extremely high value, the marginal propensity to consume (MPC) out of PDI is positive and high. The only fly in the ointment is that the Durbin-Watson d is low. As Granger and Newbold[17] have suggested, *an $R^2 > d$ is a good rule of thumb to suspect that the estimated regression suffers from spurious regression.*

If we estimate Eq. (21.4.9) for both PCE and PDI we obtain the following results:

$$\widehat{\Delta PCE}_t = 91.3924 + 0.7987t - 0.0445 PCE_{t-1}$$
$$t = (1.6727) \quad (1.3604) \quad (-1.3761) \tag{21.6.2}$$
$$\widehat{\Delta PDI}_t = 326.6330 + 2.8752t - 0.1569 PDI_{t-1}$$
$$t = (2.7549) \quad (2.5308) \quad (-2.5883) \tag{21.6.3}$$

For the present purpose we are interested in the τ value of the lagged PCE and PDI. The 1%, 5%, and 10% critical τ or DF values as computed by MacKinnon are -4.0673, -3.4620, and -3.2447, respectively. Now in absolute terms, the τ

[15]K. Holden, D. A. Peel, and J. L. Thompson, *Economic Forecasting: An Introduction*, Cambridge University Press, New York, 1990, p. 81.

[16]Nathan S. Balke, "Modelling Trends in Macroeconomic Time Series," *Economic Review*, Federal Reserve Bank of Dallas, May 1991, p. 21. This is a very readable article on the TS and DS processes.

[17]C. W. J. Granger and P. Newbold, "Spurious Regressions in Econometrics," *Journal of Econometrics*, vol. 2, 1974, pp. 111–120.

values of 1.3761 and 2.5883 of the lagged PCE and PDI terms are less than the critical τ value even at the 10% level. Thus, the conclusion is that PCE and PDI each have a unit root, that is, they are nonstationary.

Therefore, when we regressed PCE on PDI in (21.6.1), we may have regressed one nonstationary time series on another nonstationary time series. In such a case the standard t and F testing procedures are not valid.[18] In this sense, regression (21.6.1) is spurious. In passing, note that in (21.6.3) if we take the t value of -2.5883 of PDI_{t-1} on the basis of the conventional t test, it is statistically significant at the 2% level. But on the basis of the τ test this is not significant at even the 10% level, *showing once again why in the case of nonstationary time series one should not rely on the estimated t values.*

We leave it as an exercise for the reader to show that the first-differenced PCE and PDI series, ΔPCE_t and ΔPDI_t, are stationary.

Since ΔPCE and ΔPDI are stationary, why not regress the former on the latter and avoid the problem of nonstationarity, stochastic trend, and related problems? The answer is, solving the nonstationarity problem in this fashion may be like throwing out the baby with the bath water, for, in taking the first (or higher-order) difference we may lose a valuable long-term relationship between PCE and PDI that is given by the levels (as against the first difference) of the two variables. Most economic theory is stated as a long-term relationship between variables in level form and not first-difference form. Thus, Milton Friedman's permanent income hypothesis postulates that the level of permanent consumption is a function of the level of permanent income; the relationship is not stated in terms of the first differences of these variables. Relationships, say, between government expenditure and tax revenues, money supply and prices (recall the Quantity Theory of Money), 3-month and 6-month Treasury bill rates, etc. are also best expressed in level form.

To see this, refer to Fig. 21.1. Although both PCE and PDI are trending upward in a stochastic fashion, they seem to be *trending together.* The movement resembles two dancing partners, each following a random walk, whose random walks seem to be in unison. Synchrony is intuitively the idea behind **cointegrated time series.** As we show in the following section, if PCE and PDI are cointegrated, then the regression results given in (21.6.1) may not be spurious, and the usual t and F tests are valid. As Granger notes, "A test for cointegration can be thought of as a pre-test to avoid 'spurious regression' situations."[19]

21.7 COINTEGRATION

Return to regressions (21.6.1), (21.6.2), and (21.6.3). The latter two show that both PCE and PDI are nonstationary or random walk stochastic processes

---

[18]This problem was noted by Dickey and Fuller, op. cit., and more recently by P. C. B. Phillips in "Time Series Regressions with Unit Roots," *Econometrica,* vol. 55, 1987, pp. 277–302, and "Towards a Unified Asymptotic Theory of Autoregression," *Biometrika,* vol. 74, 1987, pp. 535–547. For an accessible textbook discussion of this and other aspects of time series analysis, see Terence C. Mills, *Time Series Techniques for Economists,* Cambridge University Press, New York, 1990.

[19]C. W. J. Granger, "Developments in the Study of Co-integrated Economic Variables," *Oxford Bulletin of Economics and Statistics,* vol. 48, 1986, p. 226.

[*note:* Each is I(1)]. Despite this, the linear combination of these two variables might be stationary. More specifically, if we write (21.6.1) as

$$u_t = \text{PCE}_t - \beta_1 - \beta_2 \text{PDI}_t \qquad (21.7.1)$$

and find that u_t [i.e., the linear combination $(\text{PCE}_t - \beta_1 - \beta_2 \text{PDI}_t)$] is I(0) or stationary, then we say that the variables PCE and PDI are **cointegrated;** so to speak, they are on the same wavelength. Intuitively, we see that when u_t in (21.7.1) is I(0), the "trends" in PCE and PDI cancel out.[20] And they will be on the same wavelength if they are integrated of the same order. Thus, if a series Y is I(1) and another series X is also I(1), they can be cointegrated. In general, if Y is I(d) and X is also I(d), where d is the same value, these two series can be cointegrated. If that is the case, the regression on the levels of the two variables, as in (21.6.1), is meaningful (i.e., not spurious); and we do not lose any valuable long-term information, which would result if we were to use their first differences instead.

In short, provided we check that the residuals from regressions like (21.6.1) are I(0) or stationary, the traditional regression methodology (including t and F tests) that we have learned so far is applicable to data involving time series. *The valuable contribution of the concepts of unit root, cointegration, etc. is to force us to find out if the regression residuals are stationary.*

In the language of cointegration theory, a regression such as (21.6.1) is known as **cointegrating regression** and the slope parameter β_2 is known as the **cointegrating parameter.**[21]

A number of methods for testing for cointegration have been proposed in journal articles. Two simple methods are (1) the DF or ADF test on u_t estimated from the cointegrating regression and (2) the cointegrating regression Durbin-Watson (CRWD) test.[22]

Engle-Granger (EG) or Augmented Engle-Granger (AEG) Test

We already know how to apply the DF or ADF unit root test. All we have to do is estimate a regression like (21.6.1), obtain the residuals, and use the DF or ADF

---

[20] This intuitive way of looking at cointegration is pointed out in William E. Griffiths, R. Carter Hill, and George G. Judge, *Learning and Practicing Econometrics*, John Wiley & Sons, New York, 1993, pp. 700–702.

[21] The concept of cointegration can be extended to a regression model containing k regressors. In this case we will have k cointegrating parameters. For a general discussion of this, consult the references cited in the various footnotes.

[22] This difference exists between tests for unit roots and tests for cointegration: As David A. Dickey, Dennis W. Jansen, and Daniel I. Thornton observe, "Tests for unit roots are performed on univariate [i.e., single] time series. In contrast, cointegration deals with the relationship among a group of variables, where (unconditionally) each has a unit root." See their article, "A Primer on Cointegration with an Application to Money and Income," *Economic Review*, Federal Reserve Bank of St. Louis, March-April 1991, p. 59. As the name suggests, it is an excellent introduction to cointegration testing.

test.[23] There is one precaution to exercise, however. Since the estimated u is based on the estimated cointegrating parameter β_2, the DF and ADF critical significance values are not quite appropriate. Engle and Granger have calculated these values, which can be found in the references.[24] Therefore, the DF and ADF tests in the present context are known as **Engle-Granger (EG) test** and **augmented Engle-Granger (AEG) test.** However, TSP, SHAZAM, and several other softwares now publish these critical values along with other outputs.[25]

Let us return to the PCE-PDI regression (21.6.1) and subject the residuals estimated from this regression to the DF unit root test.

We obtain the following results:

$$\Delta\hat{u}_t = -0.2753\hat{u}_{t-1}$$
$$t = (-3.7791) \tag{21.7.2}$$
$$r^2 = 0.1422$$

The Engle-Granger 1%, 5%, and 10% critical values of the τ (t statistic in the preceding regression) are, respectively, -2.5899, -1.9439, and -1.6177. Since in absolute terms the estimated τ value of 3.7791 exceeds any of these critical values, the conclusion would be that the estimated u_t is stationary (i.e., it does not have a unit root), and, therefore, PCE and PDI, despite being individually nonstationary, are cointegrated.[26]

Cointegrating Regression Durbin-Watson (CRDW) Test

An alternative, and quicker, method of finding out whether PCE and PDI are cointegrated is the CRWD test, whose critical values were first provided by Sargan and Bhargava.[27] In CRWD we use the Durbin-Watson d value obtained from the cointegrating regression, such as $d = 0.5316$ given in (21.6.1). But now the null hypothesis is that $d = 0$ rather than the standard $d = 2$. Based on

---

[23]If PCE and PDI are not cointegrated, any linear combination of them will be nonstationary and, therefore, the residues u_t will be nonstationary too.

[24]R. F. Engle and C. W. J. Granger, "Co-integration and Error Correction: Representation, Estimation and Testing," *Econometrica*, vol. 55, 1987, pp. 251–276; R. F. Engle and B. Sam Yoo, "Forecasting and Testing in Co-integrated Systems," *Journal of Econometrics*, vol. 35, pp. 143–159; R. F. Engle, "Co-integrated Economic Time Series: An Overview with New Results," in R. F. Engle and C. W. J. Granger, eds., *Long-Run Economic Relationships: Readings in Cointegration*, Oxford University Press, 1991, Chap. 12. This book also contains James MacKinnon's article cited earlier, as well as several seminal articles in this area.

[25]Selected EG and AEG critical values are also reproduced in Russell Davidson and James G. MacKinnon, *Estimation and Inference in Econometrics*, Oxford University Press, New York, 1993, Table 20.2, p. 722. They can also be found in the MICRO-TSP 7.0 and SHAZAM 7.0 versions.

[26]A technical point about the estimated cointegrating regression (21.6.1): Since PCE and PDI are each I(1), one cannot use the estimated standard errors and the associated t values of the estimated coefficients shown in this regression for the purpose of drawing inferences about population parameters.

[27]J. D. Sargan and A. S. Bhargava, "Testing Residuals from Least Squares Regression for Being Generated by the Gaussian Random Walk," *Econometrica*, vol. 51, 1983, pp. 153–174.

10,000 simulations formed from 100 observations each, the 1%, 5%, and 10% critical values to test the hypothesis that the true $d = 0$ are 0.511, 0.386, and 0.322, respectively. Thus, if the computed d value is smaller than, say, 0.511, we reject the hypothesis of cointegration at the 1% level. In our example, the d value of 0.5316 is above this critical level, which would suggest that PCE and PDI are cointegrated, a conclusion similar to the one reached on the basis of the EG test.[28]

To sum up, based on both the EG and CRDW tests, our conclusion is that PCE and PDI are cointegrated.[29] Although they individually exhibit random walks, there seems to be a stable long-run relationship between the two variables; they will not wander away from each other, which is evident from Fig. 21.1.

21.8 COINTEGRATION AND ERROR CORRECTION MECHANISM (ECM)

We just showed that PCE and PDI are cointegrated, that is, there is a long-term equilibrium relationship between the two. Of course, in the short run there may be disequilibrium. Therefore, one can treat the error term in (21.7.1) as the "equilibrium error."[30] And we can use this error term to tie the short-run behavior of PCE to its long-run value. The **error correction mechanism (ECM)** first used by Sargan[31] and later popularized by Engle and Granger corrects for disequilibrium. Without going into theoretical details, we will simply show with our PCE/PDI example how the ECM works; the details can be found in the seminal work of Engle and Granger cited earlier (see footnote number 24).

As a simple example of ECM, consider the following model:

$$\Delta PCE_t = \alpha_0 + \alpha_1 \Delta PDI_t + \alpha_2 \hat{u}_{t-1} + \varepsilon_t \qquad (21.8.1)^{32}$$

where Δ as usual denotes first difference; $\hat{u}_{t-1}$ is the one-period lagged value of the residual from regression (21.6.1), the empirical estimate of the equilibrium error term; and ε is the error term with the usual properties.

---

[28]There is considerable debate about the superiority of CRDW over DF, which can be found in the Engle-Granger–edited book, op. cit. The debate revolves around the power of the two statistics, that is, the probability of not committing a Type II error (i.e., accepting a null hypothesis when it is false).

[29]The EG and CRDW tests are now supplemented by the more powerful tests developed by Johansen. But the discussion of the **Johansen method** is beyond the scope of this book. See S. Johansen and K. Juseliu, "Maximum Likelihood Estimation and Inference on Cointegration—with Applications to the Demand for Money," *Oxford Bulletin of Economics and Statistics*, vol. 52, 1990, pp. 169–210.

[30]This term is due to Griffiths et al., op. cit., p. 701.

[31]J. D. Sargan, "Wages and Prices in the United Kingdom: A Study in Econometric Methodology," originally published in 1964 and reproduced in K. F. Wallis and D. F. Hendry, eds., *Quantitative Economics and Econometric Analysis*, Basil Blackwell, Oxford, 1984.

[32]Additional lagged difference terms of PDI can also be introduced.

Regression (21.8.1) relates the change in PCE to the change in PDI and the "equilibrating" error in the previous period. In this regression ΔPDI captures the short-run disturbances in PDI whereas the error correction term $\hat{u}_{t-1}$ captures the adjustment toward the long-run equilibrium. If α_2 is statistically significant, it tells us what proportion of the disequilibrium in PCE in one period is corrected in the next period. Using the data given in Table 21.1, we obtain the following results:

$$\widehat{\Delta PCE}_t = \underset{(5.3249)}{11.6918} + \underset{(4.1717)}{0.2906\Delta PDI_t} - \underset{(-1.6003)}{0.0867\hat{u}_{t-1}} \tag{21.8.2}$$

$$R^2 = 0.1717 \qquad d = 1.9233$$

These results show that short-run changes in PDI have significant positive effects on PCE and that about 0.09 of the discrepancy between the actual and the long-run, or equilibrium, value of PCE is eliminated or corrected each quarter. But since the p value of the latter coefficient is about 0.11, the statistical significance of this finding is not clear.[33] Looking at the co-integrating regression (21.6.1), we see the long-run MPC is about 0.97, which suggests that there is practically a one-to-one relationship between PCE and PDI and that PCE adjusts to its long-run growth path fairly quickly following a disturbance.

Before we conclude this section, the caution sounded by S. G. Hall is worth remembering:

> While the concept of cointegration is clearly an important theoretical underpinning of the error correction model there are still a number of problems surrounding its practical application; the critical values and small sample performance of many of the tests are unknown for a wide range of models; informed inspection of the correlogram may still be an important tool.[34]

21.9 SUMMARY AND CONCLUSIONS

1. Regression analysis based on time series data implicitly assumes that the underlying time series are stationary. The classical t tests, F tests, etc. are based on this assumption.
2. In practice most economic time series are nonstationary.
3. A stochastic process is said to be **weakly stationary** if its mean, variance, and autocovariances are constant over time (i.e., they are time-invariant).

---

[33] Note that the ECM regression we have used is quite simple. Other variants of this regression can be found in the references. Also note that we have not introduced more dynamics by introducing higher-order lagged differences of PDI as well as PCE.

[34] S. G. Hall, "An Application of the Granger and Engle Two-Step Estimation Procedure to the United Kingdom Aggregate Wage Data," *Oxford Bulletin of Economics and Statistics*, vol. 48, no. 3, August 1986, p. 238. See also John Y. Campbell and Pierre Perron, "Pitfalls and Opportunities: What Macroeconomists Should Know about Unit Roots," *NBER*(National Bureau of Economic Research) *Macroeconomics Annual 1991*, The MIT Press, 1991, pp. 141–219. In my view, this article is a must-read for applied economists.

4. At the informal level, weak stationarity can be tested by the **correlogram** of a time series, which is a graph of autocorrelation at various lags. For stationary time series, the correlogram tapers off quickly, whereas for non-stationary time series it dies off gradually. For a purely random series, the autocorrelations at all lags 1 and greater are zero.

5. At the formal level, stationarity can be checked by finding out if the time series contains a unit root. The **Dickey-Fuller (DF)** and **augmented Dickey-Fuller (ADF)** tests can be used for this purpose.

6. An economic time series can be **trend-stationary (TS)** or **difference-stationary (DS).** A TS time series has a deterministic trend, whereas a DS time series has a variable, or stochastic, trend. The common practice of including the time or trend variable in a regression model to detrend the data is justifiable only for TS time series. The DF and ADF tests can be applied to determine whether a time series is TS or DS.

7. Regression of one time series variable on one or more time series variables often can give nonsensical or spurious results. This phenomenon is known as **spurious regression.** One way to guard against it is to find out if the time series are cointegrated.

8. **Cointegration** means that despite being individually nonstationary, a linear combination of two or more time series can be stationary. The EG, AEG, and CRDW tests can be used to find out if two or more time series are cointegrated.

9. Cointegration of two (or more) time series suggests that there is a long-run, or equilibrium, relationship between them.

10. The **error correction mechanism (ECM)** developed by Engle and Granger is a means of reconciling the short-run behavior of an economic variable with its long-run behavior.

11. The field of time series econometrics is evolving. The established results and tests are in some cases tentative and a lot more work remains. An important question that needs an answer is why some economic time series are stationary and some are nonstationary.

EXERCISES

Questions

21.1. What is meant by weak stationarity?

21.2. What is meant by an integrated time series?

21.3. What is the meaning of a unit root?

21.4. If a time series is I(3), how many times would you have to difference it to make it stationary?

21.5. What are Dickey-Fuller (DF) and augmented DF tests?

21.6. What are Engle-Granger (EG) and augmented EG tests?

21.7. What is the meaning of cointegration?

21.8. What is the difference, if any, between tests of unit roots and tests of cointegration?

21.9. What is spurious regression?

21.10. What is the connection between cointegration and spurious regression?

21.11. What is the difference between a deterministic trend and a stochastic trend?

21.12. What is meant by a trend-stationary process (TSP) and a difference-stationary process (DSP)?

21.13. What is a random walk (model)?

21.14. "For a random walk stochastic process, the variance is infinite." Do you agree? Why?

21.15. What is the error correction mechanism (ECM)? What is its relation with cointegration?

Problems

21.16. Using the data given in Table 21.1, obtain sample correlograms up to 25 lags for the time series PCE, PDI, Profits, and Dividends. What general pattern do you see? Intuitively, which one(s) of these time series seem to be stationary?

21.17. For each of the time series of exercise 21.16, use the DF test to find out if these series contain a unit root. If a unit root exists, how would you characterize such a time series?

21.18. Continue with exercise 21.17. How would you decide if the ADF test is more appropriate than the DF test?

21.19. Consider the Dividends and Profits time series given in Table 21.1. Since dividends depend on profits, consider the following simple model:

$$\text{Dividends}_t = \beta_1 + \beta_2 \text{Profits} + u_t$$

(a) Would you expect this regression to suffer from the spurious regression phenomenon? Why?

(b) Are Dividends and Profits time series cointegrated? How do you test for this explicitly? If, after testing, you find that they are cointegrated, would your answer in (a) change?

(c) Employ the error correction mechanism (ECM) to study the short- and long-run behavior of dividends in relation to profits.

(d) If you examine the Dividends and Profits series individually, do they exhibit stochastic or deterministic trends? What tests do you use?

*(e) Assume Dividends and Profits are cointegrated. Then, instead of regressing dividends on profits, you regress profits on dividends. Is such a regression valid?

21.20. Take the first differences of the time series given in Table 21.1 and plot them. Also obtain a correlogram of each time series up to 25 lags. What strikes you about these correlograms?

21.21. Instead of regressing dividends on profits in level form, suppose you regress the first difference of dividends on the first difference of profits. Would you include the intercept in this regression? Why or why not? Show the calculations.

---

*Optional.

21.22. Continue with the previous exercise. How would you test the first-difference regression for stationarity? In the present example, what would you expect a priori and why? Show all the calculations.

21.23. Based on the U.K. private sector housing starts (X) for the period 1948 to 1984, Terence Mills obtained the following regression results:*

$$\Delta X_t = \quad 31.03 \quad - \quad 0.188X_{t-1}$$
$$\text{se} = \quad (12.50) \quad\quad (0.080)$$
$$(t =) \tau \quad\quad\quad (-2.35)$$

Note: The 5% critical τ value is -2.95 and the 10% critical τ value is -2.60.

(a) On the basis of these results, is the housing starts time series stationary or nonstationary? Alternatively, is there a unit root in this time series? How do you know?

(b) If you were to use the usual t test, is the observed t value statistically significant? On this basis, would you have concluded that this time series is stationary?

(c) Now consider the following regression results:

$$\Delta^2 X_t = \quad 4.76 \quad - \quad 1.39\Delta X_{t-1} + \quad 0.313\Delta^2 X_{t-1}$$
$$\text{se} = \quad (5.06) \quad\quad (0.236) \quad\quad\quad (0.163)$$
$$(t =) \tau \quad\quad\quad (-5.89)$$

where Δ^2 is the second difference operator, that is, the first difference of the first difference. The estimated τ value is now statistically significant. What can you say now about the stationarity of the time series in question?

Note: The purpose of the preceding regression is to find out if there is a **second unit root** in the time series.

APPENDIX 21A

21.A1   A RANDOM WALK MODEL

Suppose $\{u_t\}$ is a random series with mean μ and a (constant) variance σ^2 and it is serially uncorrelated (*note:* $\{\}$ indicates a series). Then the series $\{Y_t\}$ is said to be a random walk if

$$Y_t = Y_{t-1} + u_t \tag{1}$$

In the random walk model, as (1) shows, the value of Y at time t is equal to its value at time $(t-1)$ plus a random shock. Let $Y_0 = 0$ at time $t = 0$, so that

$$Y_1 = u_1$$

---

*Terence C. Mills, op. cit., p. 127. Notation slightly altered.

$$Y_2 = Y_1 + u_2 = u_1 + u_2$$
$$Y_3 = Y_2 + u_3 = u_1 + u_2 + u_3$$

and, in general,

$$Y_t = \sum u_t$$

Therefore,

$$E(Y_t) = E(\sum u_t) = t \cdot \mu \tag{2}$$

In like fashion we can shown that

$$\text{var}(Y_t) = t \cdot \sigma^2 \tag{3}$$

As (2) and (3) show, since both the mean and variance of Y_t change with time t (actually, increase in the present case), the process is nonstationary.

However,

$$Y_t - Y_{t-1} = u_t \tag{4}$$

is a purely random process. That is, the first differences of a random walk time series are stationary.

TIME SERIES ECONOMETRICS II: FORECASTING WITH ARIMA AND VAR MODELS

Having discussed the importance of stationary time series in the previous chapter, here we discuss two practical questions: (1) How does one model a stationary time series, that is, what kind of regression model can one use to describe its behavior? and (2) How does one use the fitted model for the purpose of forecasting? As noted in the **Introduction,** forecasting is an important part of econometric analysis, for some people probably the most important.

A very popular method of modeling stationary time series is the **autoregressive integrated moving average (ARIMA)** method, popularly known as the **Box-Jenkins** methodology.[1] In this chapter we present the rudiments of the Box-Jenkins approach to economic modeling and forecasting. An alternative to the Box-Jenkins method is **vector autoregression (VAR).** We also discuss the essentials of this popular method.

22.1. APPROACHES TO ECONOMIC FORECASTING

Broadly speaking, there are four approaches to economic forecasting based on time series data: (1) Single-equation regression models, (2) simultaneous-equation regression models, (3) autoregressive integrated moving average (ARIMA) models, and (4) vector autoregression (VAR) models.

---

[1]G. P. E. Box and G. M. Jenkins, *Time Series Analysis: Forecasting and Control,* revised ed., Holden Day, San Francisco, 1978.

734

As an example of a single-equation regression model, consider the demand function for automobiles. On the basis of economic theory, we postulate that the demand for automobiles is a function of automobile prices, advertising expenditure, income of the consumer, interest rate (as a measure of the cost of borrowing), and other relevant variables. From time series data, we estimate an appropriate model of auto demand, which can be used for forecasting demand for autos in the future. Of course, as noted in Section 5.10, forecasting errors increase rapidly if we go too far out in the future.

In Chapters 18, 19, and 20 we considered simultaneous-equation models. In their heyday during the 1960s and 1970s, elaborate models of the U.S. economy based on simultaneous equations dominated economic forecasting.[2] But of late, the glamour about such forecasting has subsided owing to the oil price shocks of 1973 and 1979 and the **Lucas critique.**[3] The thrust of this critique is that the parameters estimated from an econometric model are dependent on the policy prevailing at the time the model was estimated and will change if there is a policy change. In short, the estimated parameters are not invariant in the presence of policy changes.

For example, in October 1979 the Fed changed its monetary policy dramatically. Instead of targeting interest rates, it announced that it would henceforth monitor the rate of growth of the money supply. With such a pronounced change, an econometric model estimated from past data will have little forecasting value in the new regime.

The publication by G. P. E. Box and G. M. Jenkins of *Time Series Analysis: Forecasting and Control* (op. cit.) ushered in a new generation of forecasting tools. Popularly known as Box-Jenkins (**BJ**) methodology, but technically known as ARIMA methodology, the emphasis of these new forecasting methods is not on constructing single-equation or simultaneous-equation models but on analyzing the probabilistic, or stochastic, properties of economic time series on their own under the philosophy *"let the data speak for themselves."* Unlike the regression models, in which Y_t is explained by k regressors $X_1, X_2, X_3, \ldots, X_k$, in the BJ-type time series models Y_t may be explained by past, or lagged, values of Y itself and stochastic error terms.[4] For this reason, ARIMA models are sometimes called *a-theoretic* models because they cannot be derived from any economic theory—and economic theories are often the basis of simultaneous-equation models.

VAR methodology superficially resembles simultaneous-equation modeling in that we consider several endogenous variables together. But each endogenous variable is explained by its lagged, or past, values and the lagged values

---

[2] For a textbook treatment of the use of simultaneous-equation models in forecasting, see Robert S. Pindyck and Daniel L. Rubinfeld, *Econometric Models & Economic Forecasts*, McGraw-Hill, 3d ed., New York, 1991, Chaps. 11, 12, and 13.

[3] Robert E. Lucas, "Econometric Policy Evaluation: A Critique," in Carnegie-Rochester Conference Series, *The Phillips Curve*, North-Holland, Amsterdam, 1976, pp. 19–46.

[4] We discuss only the univariate ARIMA models, that is, ARIMA models pertaining to a single time series. But the analysis can be extended to multivariate ARIMA models. For a discussion of such models, consult the references.

of all other endogenous variables in the model; usually, there are no exogenous variables in the model.

In the rest of this chapter we discuss the fundamentals of Box-Jenkins and VAR approaches to economic forecasting. Our discussion is elementary and heuristic. The reader wishing to pursue this subject further is advised to consult the references.[5]

22.2 AR, MA, AND ARIMA MODELING OF TIME SERIES DATA

To introduce several ideas, some old and some new, let us work with the GDP time series data for the United States given in Table 21.1. A plot of this time series is already given in Figs. 21.1 (un-differenced GDP) and 21.5 (first-differenced GDP); recall that GDP in level form is nonstationary but in the (first) differenced form it is stationary.

If a time series is stationary, we can model it in a variety of ways.

An Autoregressive (AR) Process

Let Y_t represent GDP at time t. If we model Y_t as

$$(Y_t - \delta) = \alpha_1(Y_{t-1} - \delta) + u_t \qquad (22.2.1)$$

where δ is the mean of Y and where u_t is an uncorrelated random error term with zero mean and constant variance σ^2 (i.e., it is *white noise*), then we say that Y_t follows a **first-order autoregressive,** or **AR(1)**, stochastic process, which we have already encountered in Chapter 12. Here the value of Y at time t depends on its value in the previous time period and a random term; the Y values are expressed as deviations from their mean value. In other words, this model says that the forecast value of Y at time t is simply some proportion ($= \alpha_1$) of its value at time $(t-1)$ plus a random shock or disturbance at time t; again the Y values are expressed around their mean values.

But if we consider this model,

$$(Y_t - \delta) = \alpha_1(Y_{t-1} - \delta) + \alpha_3(Y_{t-2} - \delta) + u_t \qquad (22.2.2)$$

then we say that Y_t follows a **second-order autoregressive,** or **AR(2)**, process. That is, the value of Y at time t depends on its value in the previous two time periods, the Y values being expressed around their mean value δ.

In general, we can have

$$(Y_t - \delta) = \alpha_1(Y_{t-1} - \delta) + \alpha_2(Y_{t-2} - \delta) + \cdots + \alpha_p(Y_{t-p} - \delta) + u_t \quad (22.2.3)$$

in which case Y_t is a **pth order autoregressive,** or **AR(p)**, process.

---

[5] See Pindyck and Rubinfeld, op. cit., Part 3; Alan Pankratz, *Forecasting with Dynamic Regression Models,* John Wiley & Sons, New York, 1991 (this is an applied book); and Andrew Harvey, *The Econometric Analysis of Time Series,* The MIT Press, 2d ed., Cambridge, Mass., 1990 (this is a rather advanced book). A thorough but accessible discussion can also be found in Terence C. Mills, *Time Series Techniques for Economists,* Cambridge University Press, New York, 1990.

Notice that in all the preceding models only the current and previous Y values are involved; there are no other regressors. In this sense, we say that the "data speak for themselves." They are a kind of *reduced form model* that we encountered in our discussion of the simultaneous-equation models.

A Moving Average (MA) Process

The AR process just discussed is not the only mechanism that may have generated Y. Suppose we model Y as follows:

$$Y_t = \mu + \beta_0 u_t + \beta_1 u_{t-1} \tag{22.2.4}$$

where μ is a constant and u, as before, is the white noise stochastic error term. Here Y at time t is equal to a constant plus a moving average of the current and past error terms. Thus, in the present case, we say that Y follows a **first-order moving average,** or an **MA(1),** process.

But if Y follows the expression

$$Y_t = \mu + \beta_0 u_t + \beta_1 u_{t-1} + \beta_2 u_{t-2} \tag{22.2.5}$$

then it is an **MA(2)** process. More generally,

$$Y_t = \mu + \beta_0 u_t + \beta_1 u_{t-1} + \beta_2 u_{t-2} + \cdots + \beta_q u_{t-q} \tag{22.2.6}$$

is an **MA(q)** process. In short, a moving average process is simply a linear combination of white noise error terms.

An Autoregressive and Moving Average (ARMA) Process

Of course, it is quite likely that Y has characteristics of both AR and MA and is therefore *ARMA*. Thus, Y_t follows an **ARMA (1, 1)** process if it can be written as

$$Y_t = \theta + \alpha_1 Y_{t-1} + \beta_0 u_t + \beta_1 u_{t-1} \tag{22.2.7}$$

because there is one autoregressive and one moving average term. In (22.2.7) θ represents a constant term.

In general, in an **ARMA(p, q)** process, there will be p autoregressive and q moving average terms.

An Autoregressive Integrated Moving Average (ARIMA) Process

The time series models we have already discussed are based on the assumption that the time series involved are (weakly) stationary in the sense defined in Chapter 21. Briefly, the mean and variance for a weakly stationary time series are constant and its covariance is time-invariant. But we know that many economic time series are nonstationary, that is, they are *integrated*; for example, the economic time series in Table 21.1 are integrated.

But we also saw in Chapter 21 that if a time series is integrated of order 1 [i.e., it is I(1)], its first differences are I(0), that is, stationary. Similarly, if a time series is I(2), its second difference is I(0). In general, if a time series is I(d), after differencing it d times we obtain an I(0) series.

Therefore, if we have to difference a time series d times to make it stationary and then apply the $ARMA(p, q)$ model to it, we say that the original time series is **ARIMA(p,d,q)**, that is, it is an **autoregressive integrated moving average** time series, where p denotes the number of autoregressive terms, d the number of times the series has to be differenced before it becomes stationary, and q the number of moving average terms. Thus, an $ARIMA(2, 1, 2)$ time series has to be differenced once ($d = 1$) before it becomes stationary and the (first-differenced) stationary time series can be modeled as an $ARMA(2, 2)$ process, that is, it has two AR and two MA terms. Of course, if $d = 0$ (i.e., a series is stationary to begin with), $ARIMA(p,d = 0,q) = ARMA(p, q)$. Note that an $ARIMA(p,0, 0)$ process means a purely $AR(p)$ stationary process; an $ARIMA(0, 0, q)$ means a purely MA(q) stationary process. Given the values of p, d, and q, one can tell what process is being modeled.

The important point to note is that to use the Box-Jenkins methodology, we must have either a stationary time series or a time series that is stationary after one or more differencings. The reason for assuming stationarity can be explained as follows:

> The objective of B-J [Box-Jenkins] is to identify and estimate a statistical model which can be interpreted as having generated the sample data. If this estimated model is then to be used for forecasting we must assume that the features of this model are constant through time, and particularly over future time periods. Thus the simple reason for requiring stationary data is that any model which is inferred from these data can itself be interpreted as stationary or stable, therefore providing valid basis for forecasting.[6]

22.3 THE BOX-JENKINS (BJ) METHODOLOGY

The million-dollar question obviously is: Looking at a time series, such as the U.S. GDP series in Fig. 21.1, how does one know whether it follows a purely AR process (and if so, what is the value of p) or a purely MA process (and if so, what is the value of q) or an ARMA process (and if so, what are the values of p and q) or an ARIMA process, in which case we must know the values of p, d, and q. The BJ methodology comes in handy in answering the preceding question. The method consists of four steps:

Step 1. **Identification**. That is, find out the appropriate values of p, d, and q. We will show shortly how the **correlogram** and **partial correlogram** aid in this task.

Step 2. **Estimation.** Having identified the appropriate p and q values, the next stage is to estimate the parameters of the autoregressive and moving average terms included in the model. Sometimes this calcula-

---

[6]Michael Pokorny, *An Introduction to Econometrics*, Basil Blackwell, New York, 1987, p. 343.

tion can be done by simple least squares but sometimes we will have to resort to nonlinear (in parameter) estimation methods. Since this task is now routinely handled by several statistical packages, we do not have to worry about the actual mathematics of estimation; the enterprising student may consult the references on that.

Step 3. **Diagnostic checking.** Having chosen a particular ARIMA model, and having estimated its parameters, we next see whether the chosen model fits the data reasonably well, for it is possible that another ARIMA model might do the job as well. This is why Box-Jenkins ARIMA modeling is more an art than a science; considerable skill is required to choose the right ARIMA model. One simple test of the chosen model is to see if the residuals estimated from this model are white noise; if they are, we can accept the particular fit; if not, we must start over. **Thus, the BJ methodology is an iterative process.**

Step 4. **Forecasting.** One of the reasons for the popularity of the ARIMA modeling is its success in forecasting. In many cases, the forecasts obtained by this method are more reliable than those obtained from the traditional econometric modeling, particularly for short-term forecasts. Of course, each case must be checked.

With this general discussion, let us look at these four steps in some detail. Throughout, we will use the GDP data given in Table 21.1 to illustrate the various points.

22.4   IDENTIFICATION

The chief tools in identification are the **autocorrelation function (ACF),** the **partial autocorrelation function (PACF),** and the resulting **correlograms**, which are simply the plots of ACFs and PACFs against the lag length.

In the previous chapter we defined the (population) ACF (ρ_k) and the sample ACF ($\hat{\rho}_k$). The concept of partial autocorrelation is analogous to the concept of partial regression coefficient. In the k-variable multiple regression model, the kth regression coefficient β_k measures the rate of change in the mean value of the regressand for a unit change in the kth regressor X_k, holding the influence of all other regressors constant.

In similar fashion the **partial autocorrelation** ρ_{kk} measures correlation between (time series) observations that are k time periods apart after controlling for correlations at intermediate lags (i.e., lag less than k). In other words, partial autocorrelation is the correlation between Y_t and Y_{t-k} after removing the effect of the intermediate Y's.[7] In Section 7.9 we already introduced the concept of partial correlation in the regression context and showed its relation to

---

[7]In time series data a large proportion of correlation between Y_t and Y_{t-k} may be due to the correlations they have with the intervening lags $Y_{t-1}, Y_{t-2}, \ldots, Y_{t-k+1}$. The partial correlation ρ_{kk} removes the influence of these intervening variables.

simple correlations. Such partial correlations are now routinely computed by most statistical packages.

In Fig. 22.1 we show the correlogram and partial correlogram of the GDP series. From this figure, two facts stand out: First, the ACF declines very slowly; as shown in Fig. 21.4, ACF up to 23 lags are individually statistically significantly different from zero, for they all are outside the 95% confidence bounds. Second, after the first lag, the PACF drops dramatically, and all PACFs after lag 1 are statistically insignificant.

Since the U.S. GDP time series is not stationary, we have to make it stationary before we can apply the Box-Jenkins methodology. In Fig. 21.5 we plotted the first differences of GDP. Unlike Fig. 21.1, we do not observe any trend in this series, perhaps suggesting that the first-differenced GDP time series is stationary.[8] A formal application of the **Dickey-Fuller unit root test** shows that

Lag		Sample ACF ($\hat{\rho}_k$)	Sample PACF ($\hat{\rho}_{kk}$)	
1	* * * * * * * * * * * * *	0.969	0.969	* * * * * * * * * * * * *
2	* * * * * * * * * * * * *	0.935	−0.058	*
3	* * * * * * * * * * * * *	0.901	−0.020	
4	* * * * * * * * * * *	0.866	−0.045	*
5	* * * * * * * * * * *	0.830	−0.024	
6	* * * * * * * * * *	0.791	−0.062	*
7	* * * * * * * * * *	0.752	−0.029	
8	* * * * * * * * *	0.713	−0.024	
9	* * * * * * * * *	0.675	−0.009	
10	* * * * * * * *	0.638	−0.010	
11	* * * * * * * *	0.601	−0.020	
12	* * * * * * *	0.565	−0.012	
13	* * * * * * *	0.532	−0.020	
14	* * * * * *	0.500	−0.012	
15	* * * * * *	0.468	−0.021	
16	* * * * * *	0.437	−0.001	
17	* * * * *	0.405	−0.041	*
18	* * * * *	0.375	−0.005	
19	* * * *	0.344	−0.038	*
20	* * * *	0.313	−0.017	
21	* * * *	0.279	−0.066	*
22	* * *	0.246	−0.019	
23	* * *	0.214	−0.008	
24	* *	0.182	−0.018	
25	* *	0.153	0.017	

95% confidence interval   95% confidence interval

FIGURE 22.1
Correlogram and partial correlogram, GDP, United States, 1970–I to 1991–IV.

[8]It is hard to tell whether the variance of this series is stationary, especially around 1979–1980. The oil embargo of 1979 and a significant change in the Fed's monetary policy in 1979 may have something to do with our difficulty.

that is indeed the case. We can also see this visually from the estimated ACF and PACF correlograms given in Fig. 22.2. Now we have a much different pattern of ACF and PACF. The ACFs at lags 1, 8, and 12 seem statistically different from zero; recall from Chapter 21 that the approximate 95% confidence limits for ρ_k are -0.2089 and $+0.2089$. (*Note:* As discussed in Chapter 21, these confidence limits are asymptotic and so can be considered approximate.) But at all other lags, they are not statistically different from zero. This is also true of the partial autocorrelations, $\hat{\rho}_{kk}$.

Now how do the correlograms given in Fig. 22.2 enable us to find the ARMA pattern of the GDP time series? (*Note:* We will consider only the first-differenced GDP series because it is stationary.) One way of accomplishing this is to consider the ACF and PACF and the associated correlograms of a selected number of ARMA processes, such as AR(1), AR(2), MA(1), MA(2), ARMA(1, 1), ARIMA(2, 2), and so on. Since each of these stochastic processes exhibits typical patterns of ACF and PACF, if the time series under study fits one of these patterns we can identify the time series with that process. Of course, we will have to apply diagnostic tests to find out if the chosen ARMA model is reasonably accurate.

Lag		Sample ACF ($\hat{\rho}_k$)	Sample PACF ($\hat{\rho}_{kk}$)	
1	| * * * *	0.316	0.316	| * * * *
2	| * *	0.186	0.095	| *
3	| *	0.049	-0.038	|
4	| *	0.051	0.033	|
5	|	-0.007	-0.032	|
6	|	-0.019	-0.020	|
7	* |	-0.073	-0.062	* |
8	* * * * |	-0.289	-0.280	* * * * |
9	* |	-0.067	0.128	| * *
10	|	0.019	0.100	| *
11	|	0.037	-0.008	|
12	* * * |	-0.239	-0.311	* * * * |
13	* * |	-0.117	0.011	|
14	* * * |	-0.204	-0.114	* |
15	* * |	-0.128	-0.051	* |
16	|	-0.035	-0.021	|
17	* |	-0.056	-0.019	|
18	|	0.009	0.122	| * *
19	* |	-0.045	-0.071	* |
20	| *	0.066	-0.126	* * |
21	| *	0.084	0.089	| *
22	| *	0.039	-0.060	* |
23	* |	-0.068	-0.121	* * |
24	|	-0.032	-0.041	* |
25	|	0.013	0.092	| *

95% confidence interval   95% confidence interval

FIGURE 22.2
Correlogram and partial correlogram, first differences of GDP, United States, 1970–I to 1991–IV.

TABLE 22.1
Theoretical patterns of ACF and PACF

Type of model	Typical pattern of ACF	Typical pattern of PACF
AR (p)	Decays exponentially or with damped sine wave pattern or both	Significant spikes through lags p
MA(q)	Significant spikes through lags q	Declines exponentially
ARMA (p, q)	Exponential decay	Exponential decay

Note: The terms exponential and geometric decay mean the same things (Recall our discussion of the Koyck distributed lag).

To study the properties of the various standard ARIMA processes would consume a lot of space. What we plan to do is to give general guidelines (see Table 22.1); the references can give the details of the various stochastic processes.

Notice that the ACFs and PACFs of AR(p) and MA(q) processes have opposite patterns; in the AR(p) case the AC declines geometrically or exponentially but the PACF cuts off after a certain number of lags, whereas the opposite happens to an MA(q) process.

Geometrically, these patterns are shown in Fig. 22.3.

A warning. Since in practice we do not observe the theoretical ACFs and PACFs and rely on their sample counterparts, the estimated ACFs and PACFs will not match exactly their theoretical counterparts. What we are looking for is the resemblance between theoretical and sample ACFs and PACFs so that they can point us in the right direction in constructing ARIMA models. And that is why ARIMA modeling requires a great deal of skill, which of course comes from practice.

ARIMA identification of U.S. GDP. Returning to the correlogram and partial correlogram of the stationary (after first-differencing) U.S. GDP for 1970–I to 1991–IV given in Fig. 22.2, what do we see?

Remembering that the ACF and PACF shown there are sample quantities, we do not have a nice pattern as suggested in Table 22.1. The autocorrelations decline up to lag 4, then except at lags 8 and 12, the rest of them are statistically not different from zero (the solid lines shown in this figure give the approximate 95% confidence limits). The partial autocorrelations with spikes at lag 1, 8, and 12 seem statistically significant but the rest are not; if the partial correlation coefficient were significant only at lag 1, we could have identified this as an AR(1) model. Let us therefore assume that the process that generated the (first-differenced) GDP is at the most an AR(12) process. Of course, we do not have to include all the AR terms up to 12, for from the partial correlogram we know that only the AR terms at lag 1, 8, and 12 are significant.

22.5 ESTIMATION OF THE ARIMA MODEL

Let Y_t^* denote the first differences of U.S. GDP. Then our tentatively identified AR model is

$$Y_t^* = \delta + \alpha_1 Y_{t-1}^* + \alpha_8 Y_{t-8}^* + \alpha_{12} Y_{t-12}^* \tag{22.5.1}$$

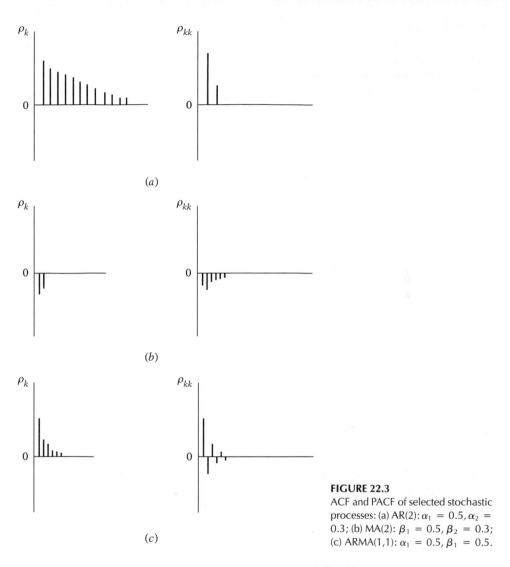

FIGURE 22.3
ACF and PACF of selected stochastic
processes: (a) AR(2): $\alpha_1 = 0.5, \alpha_2 =$
0.3; (b) MA(2): $\beta_1 = 0.5, \beta_2 = 0.3$;
(c) ARMA(1,1): $\alpha_1 = 0.5, \beta_1 = 0.5$.

Using MICRO TSP 7.0 version, we obtained the following estimates:

$$\widehat{Y_t^*} = 23.0894 + 0.3428\,Y_{t-1}^* - 0.2994\,Y_{t-8}^* - 0.2644Y_{t-12}^*$$
$$\text{se} = (2.9774)\ (0.0987) \qquad (0.1016) \qquad (0.0986) \qquad (22.5.2)$$
$$t = (7.7547)\ (3.4695) \qquad (-2.9475) \qquad (-2.6817)$$
$$R^2 = 0.2931 \qquad d = 1.7663$$

We leave it as an exercise for the reader to estimate a model that contains only Y_{t-1}^* and a model that contains both Y_{t-1}^* and Y_{t-8}^* terms and to compare the results with those given in (22.5.2).

22.6   DIAGNOSTIC CHECKING

How do we know that the model in (22.5.2) is a reasonable fit to the data? One simple diagnostic is to obtain residuals from (22.5.2) and obtain the ACF and PACF of these residuals, say, up to lag 25. The estimated AC and PACF are shown in Fig. 22.4. As this figure shows, none of the autocorrelations and partial autocorrelations is individually statistically significant. Nor is the sum of the 25 squared autocorrelations, as shown by the Box-Pierce Q and Ljung-Box LB statistics (see Chapter 21), statistically significant. In other words, the correlograms of both autocorrelation and partial autocorrelation give the impression that the residuals estimated from (22.5.2) are purely random. Hence, there may not be any need to look for another ARIMA model.

22.7 FORECASTING

Remember that the GDP data are for the period 1970–I to 1991–IV. Suppose, on the basis of model (22.5.2), we want to forecast GDP for the first four quarters of 1992. But in (22.5.2) the dependent variable is *change* in the GDP over the previous quarter. Therefore, if we use (22.52.), what we can obtain are the forecasts of GDP changes between the first quarter of 1992 and the fourth quarter of 1991, second quarter of 1992 over the first quarter of 1992, etc.

Autocorrelations	Partial Autocorrelations	Lag	ACF $(\hat{\rho}_k)$	PACF $(\hat{\rho}_{kk})$
		1	0.043	0.043
		2	0.113	0.112
		3	0.020	0.012
		4	−0.100	−0.116
		5	−0.068	−0.065
		6	−0.029	0.001
		7	−0.040	−0.019
		8	−0.112	−0.118
		9	0.065	0.069
		10	0.126	0.151
		11	0.099	0.076
		12	−0.026	−0.106
		13	0.120	0.102
		14	−0.181	−0.150
		15	−0.128	−0.131
		16	−0.073	−0.050
		17	−0.121	−0.038
		18	0.017	0.059
		19	−0.007	−0.027
		20	−0.085	−0.163
		21	0.055	0.059
		22	0.010	−0.016
		23	−0.038	−0.103
		24	−0.053	−0.072
		25	−0.002	0.100

95% confidence interval   95% confidence interval

| Box-Pierce Q-statistic | 14.42 | Probability | 0.9540 | SE of correlations | 0.110 |
| Ljung-Box (LB) Statistic | 17.63 | Probability | 0.8578 | | |

FIGURE 22.4
Correlograms of the residuals obtained from ARIMA model (22.5.2).

To obtain the forecast of GDP level rather than its changes, we can "undo" the first-difference transformation that we had used to obtain the changes. (More technically, we *integrate* the first-differenced series.) Thus, to obtain the forecast value of GDP (not Δ GDP) for 1992–I, we rewrite model (22.5.1) as

$$Y_{1992-I} - Y_{1991-IV} = \delta + \alpha_1[Y_{1991-IV} - Y_{1991-III}]$$
$$+ \quad \alpha_8[Y_{1989-IV} - Y_{1989-III}]$$
$$+ \quad \alpha_{12}[Y_{1988-IV} - Y_{1988-III}] + u_{1992-I} \quad (22.7.1)$$

That is,

$$Y_{1992-I} = \delta + (1 + \alpha_1)Y_{1991-IV} - \alpha_1 Y_{1991-III} + \alpha_8 Y_{1989-IV} - \alpha_8 Y_{1989-III}$$
$$+ \quad \alpha_{12}Y_{1988-IV} - \alpha_{12}Y_{1988-III} + u_{1992-I} \quad (22.7.2)$$

The values of δ, α_1, α_8, and α_{12} are already known from the estimated regression (22.5.1). The value of u_{1992-I} is assumed to be zero (why?). Therefore, we can easily obtain the forecast value of Y_{1992-I}. The numerical estimate of this forecast value is[9]

$$\hat{Y}_{1992-I} = 23.0894 + (1 + 0.3428)\,Y_{1991-IV} - 0.3428\,Y_{1991-III}$$
$$+ (-0.2994)\,Y_{1989-IV} - (-0.2994)\,Y_{1989-III}$$
$$+ (-0.2644)\,Y_{1988-IV} - (-0.2644)\,Y_{1988-III}$$
$$= 23.0894 + 1.3428(4868) - 0.3428(4862.7)$$
$$- 0.2994(4859.7) + 0.2994(4845.6) - 0.2644(4779.7)$$
$$+ 0.2644(4734.5)$$
$$= 4876.7(\text{approx.})$$

Thus the forecast value of GDP for 1992–I is about \$4,877 billion (1987 dollars). Incidentally, the actual value of real GDP for 1992–I was \$4,873.7 billion; the forecast error was an overestimate of \$3 billion.

Note that if you were to use (22.5.2) to compute the forecast change of GDP from 1991–IV to 1992–I, you would obtain this figure as −\$4.25 billion.

22.8 FURTHER ASPECTS OF THE BJ METHODOLOGY

In the preceding paragraphs we have provided but a sketchy introduction to the BJ modeling. There are many aspects of this methodology that we have not considered for lack of space, for example, **seasonality.** Many time series exhibit seasonal behavior. Examples are sales by department stores in conjunction with major holidays, seasonal consumption of ice cream, travels during public holidays, etc. If, for example, we had data on department stores sales by quarters, the sales figures will show spikes in the fourth quarter. In such situations, one can remove the seasonal influence by taking fourth-quarter

---

[9]Although standard computer packages do this computation routinely, we show the detailed calculations to illustrate the mechanics involved.

differences of the sales figures and then decide what kind of ARIMA model to fit.

We have analyzed only a single time series at a time. But nothing prevents the BJ methodology from being extended to the simultaneous study of two or more time series. A foray into that topic would take us far afield. The interested reader may want to consult the references.[10] In the following section, however, we discuss this topic in the context of what is known as vector autoregression.

22.9 VECTOR AUTOREGRESSION (VAR)

In Chapters 18 to 20 we considered simultaneous, or structural, equation models. In such models some variables are treated as endogenous and some as exogenous or predetermined (exogenous plus lagged endogenous). Before we estimate such models, we have to make sure that the equations in the system are identified (either exactly or over-). This identification is often achieved by assuming that some of the predetermined variables are present only in some equations. This decision is often subjective and has been severely criticized by Christopher Sims.[11]

According to Sims, if there is true simultaneity among a set of variables, they should all be treated on an equal footing; there should not be any a priori distinction between endogenous and exogenous variables. It is in this spirit that Sims developed his **VAR** model.

The seeds of this model were already sown in the Granger causality test discussed in Chapter 17. In Eqs. (17.14.1) and (17.14.2), which explain current GNP in terms of lagged money supply and lagged GNP and current money supply in terms of lagged money supply and lagged GNP, we are essentially treating GNP and money supply as a pair of endogenous variables. There are no exogenous variables in this system.

Similarly, in the auto sales (AS) and Treasury bill (TB) model discussed in Example 17.9, AS is explained in terms of its own lagged values as well as the lagged values of TB and TB is explained in terms of its own lagged values and the lagged values of AS.

Both these examples are illustrations of **vector autoregressive models;** the term autoregressive is due to the appearance of the lagged value of the dependent variable on the right-hand side and the term vector is due to the fact that we are dealing with a vector of two (or more) variables.

Estimation of VAR

Returning to the AS/TB example, we saw that when we introduced eight lag terms of each variable as regressors, we could not reject the hypothesis that there is bilateral causality between AS and TB. That is, AS affects TB and TB in

---

[10]For an accessible treatment of this subject, see Terence C. Mills, *Time Series Techniques for Economists*, Cambridge University Press, New York, 1990, Part III.

[11]C. A. Sims, "Macroeconomics and Reality," *Econometrica*, vol. 48, 1980, pp. 1–48.

turn affects AS. These kinds of situations are ideally suited for the application of VAR.

To explain how a VAR model is estimated, we will continue with the AS/TB model. For simplicity, assume that each equation contains four lag values of AS and four lag values of TB as regressors. In this case, one can estimate each of the equations by OLS.[12] Therefore, the actual model we estimate is

$$AS_t = \alpha + \sum_{j=1}^{4} \beta_j \, AS_{t-j} + \sum_{j=1}^{4} \gamma_j \, TB_{t-j} + u_{1t} \qquad (22.9.1)$$

$$TB_t = \alpha' + \sum_{j=1}^{4} \theta_j \, AS_{t-j} + \sum_{j=1}^{4} \lambda_j \, TB_{t-j} + u_{2t} \qquad (22.9.2)$$

where the u's are the stochastic error terms, called **impulses** or **innovations** in the language of VAR.

Using the VAREST command in **MICRO TSP 7.0** version, we obtained the estimates of the parameters of the AS/TB model given in (22.9.1) and (22.9.2), as shown in Table 22.2. Since (22.9.1) and (22.9.2) are OLS regressions, the output of the regressions given in Table 22.2 is to be interpreted in the usual fashion. Of course, with several lags of the same variables, each estimated coefficient will not be statistically significant, possibly due to multicollinearity. But collectively they may be significant on the basis of the standard F test. Thus, in the regression for AS only the AS coefficients at lag 1 and 2 are statistically significant, but none of the rest. On the other hand, in the TB regression all the lagged TB coefficients, as well as the coefficient of AS at lag 1, are statistically significant.

Forecasting with VAR

The estimated VAR model given in Table 22.2 can be used for forecasting the future values of AS and TB. For example, to forecast AS for 1979–I, we need data for AS and TB at lags 1978–IV, 1978–III, 1978–II, and 1978–I. Having forecast AS for 1979–I, we can forecast AS for 1979–II in a similar fashion; now we need data for AS and TB for 1979–I, 1978–IV, 1978–III, and 1978–II. But note that the data for 1979–I will be the forecast value obtained earlier, since the actual data for 1979–I were not available because our sample ended in 1978–IV. As the reader can suspect, in this procedure any error made in forecasting AS in 1979–I will be carried forward in subsequent forecasts.

Some Problems with VAR Modeling

The advocates of VAR emphasize these virtues of the method: (1) The method is simple; one does not have to worry about determining which variables are

---

[12]One can use the **SURE** (seemingly unrelated regression) technique to estimate the two equations together. However, since each regression contains the same number of lagged endogenous variables, the OLS estimation of each equation separately produces identical (and efficient) estimates.

TABLE 22.2
AS/TB VAR Model

VAREST // Dependent Variable is AS
SMPL range: 1959.1–1978.4
Number of observations: 80

Variable	Coefficient	STD. Error	T-Stat.	2-Tail Sig.
AS (-1)	0.5555045	0.1170769	4.7447848	0.0000
AS (-2)	0.3129130	0.1363310	2.2952445	0.0247
AS (-3)	0.0357919	0.1363381	0.2587279	0.7966
AS (-4)	0.0324633	0.1246661	0.2604022	0.7953
TB (-1)	-0.1761464	0.1642311	-1.0725520	0.2871
TB (-2)	0.1498503	0.2559182	0.5855397	0.5600
TB (-3)	-0.2791645	0.2495872	-1.1185050	0.2671
TB (-4)	0.2041068	0.1482409	1.3768588	0.1729
C	1.0779153	0.4998183	2.1566141	0.0344

R-squared	0.738664	Mean of dependent var	7.868741
Adjusted R-squared	0.709218	S.D. of dependent var	1.303142
S.E. of regression	0.702709	Sum of squared resid	35.05978
Log likelihood	-80.51620	F-statistic	25.08514
Durbin-Watson stat	2.075730	Prob(F-statistic)	0.000000

VAREST // Dependent Variable is TB
Date: 5-29-1994 / Time: 8:27
SMPL range: 1959.1–1978.4
Number of observations: 80

Variable	Coefficient	STD. Error	T-Stat.	2-Tail Sig.
AS (-1)	0.1983992	0.0817601	2.4266004	0.0178
AS (-2)	-0.0728026	0.0952062	-0.7646830	0.4470
AS (-3)	-0.0553507	0.0966079	-0.5729423	0.5685
AS (-4)	0.1361520	0.0870601	1.5638857	0.1223
TB (-1)	1.2740809	0.1146901	11.108896	0.0000
TB (-2)	-0.6893779	0.1787194	-3.8573189	0.0002
TB (-3)	0.4829150	0.1742982	2.7706251	0.0071
TB (-4)	-0.2293524	0.1035234	-2.2154630	0.0299
C	-0.7823958	0.3490461	-2.2415258	0.0281

R-squared	0.921100	Mean of dependent var	4.824005
Adjusted R-squared	0.912210	S.D. of dependent var	1.656238
S.E. of regression	0.490734	Sum of squared resid	17.09820
Log likelihood	-51.79294	F-statistic	103.6089
Durbin-Watson stat	2.029895	Prob(F-statistic)	0.000000

endogenous and which ones exogenous. All variables in VAR are endogenous.[13] (2) Estimation is simple, that is, the usual OLS method can be applied to each equation separately. (3) The forecasts obtained by this method are in many cases better than those obtained from the more complex simultaneous-equation models.[14]

But the critics of VAR modeling point out the following problems:

1. Unlike simultaneous-equation models, a VAR model is *a-theoretic* because it uses less prior information. Recall that in simultaneous-equation models exclusion or inclusion of certain variables plays a crucial role in the identification of the model.

2. Because of its emphasis on forecasting, VAR models are less suited for policy analysis.

3. The biggest practical challenge in VAR modeling is to choose the appropriate lag length. Suppose you have a three-variable VAR model and you decide to include eight lags of each variable in each equation. You will have 24 lagged parameters in each equation plus the constant term, for a total of 25 parameters. Unless the sample size is large, estimating that many parameters will consume a lot of degrees of freedom with all the problems associated with that.[15]

4. Strictly speaking, in an m-variable VAR model, all the m variables should be (jointly) stationary. If that is not the case, we will have to transform the data appropriately (e.g., by first-differencing). As Harvey notes, the results from the transformed data may be unsatisfactory. He further notes that "The usual approach adopted by VAR *aficionados* is therefore to work in levels, even if some of these series are non-stationary. In this case, it is important to recognize the effect of unit roots on the distribution of estimators."[16] Worse yet, if the model contains a mix of I(0) and I(1) variables, that is, a mix of stationary and nonstationary variables, transforming the data will not be easy.

5. Since the individual coefficients in the estimated VAR models are often difficult to interpret, the practitioners of this technique often estimate the so-called **impulse response function (IRF).** The IRF traces out the response of the dependent variable in the VAR system to shocks in the error terms, such as u_1 and u_2 in Eqs. (22.9.1) and (22.9.2). Suppose u_1 in the AS equation

---

[13]Sometimes purely exogenous variables are included to allow for trend and seasonal factors.

[14]See, for example, T. Kinal and J. B. Ratner, "Regional Forecasting Models with Vector Autoregression: The Case of New York State," Discussion Paper #155, Department of Economics, State University of New York at Albany, 1982.

[15]If we have an m-equation VAR model with p lagged values of the m variables, in all we have to estimate $(m + pm^2)$ parameters.

[16]Andrew Harvey, *The Econometric Analysis of Time Series*, The MIT Press, 2d ed., Cambridge, Mass., 1990, p. 83.

increases by a value of one standard deviation. Such a shock or change will change AS in the current as well as future periods. But since AS appears in the TB regression, the change in u_1 will also have impact on TB. Similarly, a change of one standard deviation in u_2 of the TB equation will have an impact on AS. The IRF traces out the impact of such shocks for several periods in the future. Although the utility of such IRF analysis has been questioned by researchers, it is the centerpiece of VAR analysis.[17]

For a comparison of the performance of VAR with other forecasting techniques, the reader may consult the references.[18]

An Application of VAR: A VAR Model of the Texas Economy

To test the conventional wisdom, "As the oil patch goes, so goes the Texas economy," Thomas Fomby and Joseph Hirschberg developed a three-variable VAR model of the Texas economy for the period 1974–I to 1988–I.[19] The three variables considered were (1) percentage change in real price of oil, (2) percentage change in Texas nonagricultural employment, and (3) percentage change in nonagricultural employment in the rest of the United States. The authors introduced the constant term and two lagged values of each variable in each equation. Therefore, the number of parameters estimated in each equation was seven. The results of the OLS estimation of the VAR model are given in Table 22.3. The F tests given in this table are to test the hypothesis that collectively the various lagged coefficients are zero. Thus, the F test for the x variable (percentage change in real price of oil) shows that both the lagged terms of x are statistically different from zero; the probability of obtaining an F value of 12.5536 under the null hypothesis that they are both simultaneously equal to zero is very low, about 0.00004. On the other hand, collectively, the two lagged y values (percentage change in Texas nonagricultural employment) are not significantly different from zero to explain x; the F value is only 1.36. All other F statistics are to be interpreted similarly.

On the basis of these and other results presented in their paper, Fomby and Hirschberg conclude that the conventional wisdom about the Texas economy is not quite accurate, for after the initial instability resulting from OPEC oil shocks, the Texas economy is now less dependent on fluctuations in the price of oil.

---

[17]D. E. Runkle, "Vector Autoregression and Reality," *Journal of Business and Economic Statistics,* vol. 5, 1987, pp. 437–454.

[18]S. McNees, "Forecasting Accuracy of Alternative Techniques: A Comparison of U.S. Macroeconomic Forecasts," *Journal of Business and Economic Statistics,* vol. 4, 1986, pp. 5–15; E. Mahmoud, "Accuracy in Forecasting: A Survey," *Journal of Forecasting,* vol. 3, 1984, pp. 139–159.

[19]Thomas B. Fomby and Joseph G. Hirschberg, "Texas in Transition: Dependence on Oil and the National Economy," *Economic Review*, Federal Reserve Bank of Dallas, January 1989, pp. 11–28.

TABLE 22.3
Estimation results for second order* Texas VAR system: 1974–I to 1988–I

Dependent variable: x (percentage change in real price of oil)

Variable	Lag	Coefficient	Standard error	Significance level
x	1	0.7054	0.1409	.8305E−5
x	2	−0.3351	0.1500	.3027E−1
y	1	−1.3525	2.7013	.6189
y	2	3.4371	2.4344	.1645
z	1	3.4566	2.8048	.2239
z	2	−4.8703	2.7500	.8304E−1
Constant	0	−0.9983E−2	0.1696E−1	.5589

$\bar{R}^2 = 0.2982; Q(21) = 8.2618\,(P = .9939)$

Tests for joint significance, dependent variable $= x$

Variable	F-statistic	Significance level
x	12.5536	.4283E−4
y	1.3646	.2654
z	1.5693	.2188

Dependent variable: y (percentage change in Texas nonagricultural employment)

Variable	Lag	Coefficient	Standard error	Significance level
x	1	0.2228E−1	0.8759E−2	.1430E−1
x	2	−0.1883E−2	0.9322E−2	.8407
y	1	0.6462	0.1678	.3554E−3
y	2	0.4234E−1	0.1512	.7807
z	1	0.2655	0.1742	.1342
z	2	−0.1715	0.1708	.3205
Constant	0	−0.1602E−2	0.1053E−1	.1351

$\bar{R}^2 = 0.6316; Q(21) = 21.5900\,(P = .4234)$

Tests for joint significance, dependent variable $= y$

Variable	F-statistic	Significance level
x	3.6283	.3424E−4
y	19.1440	.8287E−6
z	1.1684	.3197

Dependent variable: z (percentage change in nonagricultural employment in rest of United States)

Variable	Lag	Coefficient	Standard error	Significance level
x	1	−0.8330E−2	0.6849E−2	.2299
x	2	0.3635E−2	0.7289E−2	.6202
y	1	0.3849	0.1312	.5170E−2
y	2	−0.4805	0.1182	.1828E−2
z	1	0.7226	0.1362	.3004E−5
z	2	−0.1366E−1	0.1336	.9190
Constant	0	−0.2387E−2	0.8241E−3	.5701E−2

$\bar{R}^2 = 0.6503; Q(21) = 15.6182\,(P = .7907)$

Tests for joint significance, dependent variable $= z$

Variable	F-statistic	Significance level
x	0.7396	.4827
y	8.2714	.8360E−3
z	27.9609	.1000E−7

SOURCE: *Economic Review*, Federal Reserve Bank of Dallas, January 1989, p.21.
*Two-lagged terms of each variable.

22.10 SUMMARY AND CONCLUSIONS

1. Box-Jenkins and VAR approaches to economic forecasting are alternatives to traditional single- and simultaneous-equation models.
2. To forecast the values of a time series, the basic Box-Jenkins strategy is as follows:
   (a) First examine the series for stationarity. This step can be done by computing the autocorrelation function (ACF) and the partial autocorrelation function (PACF) or by a formal unit root analysis. The correlograms associated with ACF and PACF are often good visual diagnostic tools.
   (b) If the time series is not stationary, difference it one or more times to achieve stationarity.
   (c) The ACF and PACF of the stationary time series are then computed to find out if the series is purely autoregressive or purely of the moving average type or a mixture of the two. From broad guidelines given in Table 22.1 one can then determine the values of p and q in the ARMA process to be fitted. At this stage the chosen ARMA(p, q) model is tentative.
   (d) The tentative model is then estimated.
   (e) The residuals from this tentative model are examined to find out if they are white noise. If they are, the tentative model is probably a good approximation to the underlying stochastic process. If they are not, the process is started all over again. Therefore, the Box-Jenkins method is iterative.
   (f) The model finally selected can be used for forecasting.
3. The VAR approach to forecasting considers several time series at a time. The distinguishing features of VAR are as follows:
   (a) It is a truly simultaneous system in that all variables are regarded as endogenous.
   (b) In VAR modeling the value of a variable is expressed as a linear function of the past, or lagged, values of that variable and all other variables included in the model.
   (c) If each equation contains the same number of lagged variables in the system, it can be estimated by OLS without resorting to any systems method, such as two-stage least squares (2SLS) or seemingly unrelated regressions (SURE).
   (d) This simplicity of VAR modeling may be its drawback. In view of the limited number of observations that are generally available in most economic analyses, introduction of several lags of each variable can consume a lot of degrees of freedom.[20]
   (e) If there are several lags in each equation, it is not always easy to interpret each coefficient, especially if the signs of the coefficients alternate. For this reason one examines the impulse response function (IRF) in VAR

---

[20]Followers of Bayesian statistics believe that this problem can be minimized. See R. Litterman, "A Statistical Approach to Economic Forecasting," *Journal of Business and Economic Statistics*, vol. 4, 1986, pp. 1–4.

modeling to find out how the dependent variable responds to a shock administered to one or more equations in the system.

(*f*) There is considerable debate and controversy about the superiority of the various forecasting methods. Single-equation, simultaneous-equation, Box-Jenkins, and VAR methods of forecasting have their admirers as well as detractors. All one can say is that there is no single method that will suit all situations. If that were the case, there would be no need for discussing the various alternatives. One thing is sure: The Box-Jenkins and VAR methodologies have now become an integral part of econometrics.

EXERCISES

Questions

22.1 What are the major methods of economic forecasting?

22.2 What are the major differences between simultaneous-equation and Box-Jenkins approaches to economic forecasting?

22.3 Outline the major steps involved in the application of the Box-Jenkins approach to forecasting.

22.4 What happens if Box-Jenkins techniques are applied to time series that are non-stationary?

22.5 What are the differences between Box-Jenkins and VAR approaches to economic forecasting?

22.6 In what sense is VAR a-theoretic?

22.7 "If the primary object is forecasting, VAR will do the job." Critically evaluate this statement.

22.8 Since the number of lags to be introduced in a VAR model can be a subjective question, how does one decide how many lags to introduce in a concrete application?

22.9 Comment on this statement: "Box-Jenkins and VAR are prime examples of measurement without theory."

22.10 What is the connection, if any, between Granger causality tests and VAR modeling?

Problems

22.11 Consider the data on PDI (personal disposable income) given in Table 21.1. Suppose you want to fit a suitable ARIMA model to these data. Outline the steps involved in carrying out this task.

22.12 Repeat exercise 22.11 for the PCE (personal consumption expenditure) data given in Table 21.1.

22.13 Repeat exercise 22.11 for the Profits data given in Table 21.1.

22.14 Repeat exercise 22.11 for the Dividends data given in Table 21.1.

22.15 In exercise 17.28 you were introduced to the Schwarz Criterion to determine lag length. How would you use this criterion to determine the appropriate lag length in a VAR model?

22.16 Using the data on PCE and PDI given in Table 21.1, develop a bivariate VAR model for the period 1970–I to 1990–IV. Use this model to forecast the values of these variables for the four quarters of 1991 and compare the forecast values with the actual values given in Table 21.1.

22.17 Repeat exercise 22.16, using the data on Dividends and Profits.

*22.18 Refer to MICRO TSP-7.0 or another statistical package and estimate the impulse response function for a period of up to eight lags for the VAR model that you developed in exercise 22.16.

*22.19 Repeat exercise 22.18 for the VAR model that you developed in exercise 22.17.

22.20 Refer to the VAR regression results given in Table 22.3. From the various F tests reported in the three regressions given there, what can you say about the nature of causality in the three variables?

22.21 Continuing with exercise 20.20, can you guess why the authors chose to express the three variables in the model in percentage change form rather than the levels of these variables? (*Hint:* Stationarity.)

---

*Optional.

A REVIEW OF SOME STATISTICAL CONCEPTS

This appendix provides a very sketchy introduction to some of the statistical concepts encountered in the text. The discussion is nonrigorous, and no proofs are given because several excellent books in statistics do that job very well. Some of these books are listed at the end of this appendix.

A.1 SUMMATION AND PRODUCT OPERATORS

The Greek capital letter $\sum$ (sigma) is used to indicate summation. Thus,

$$\sum_{i=1}^{n} x_i = x_1 + x_2 + \cdots + x_n$$

Some of the important properties of the summation operator $\sum$ are

1. $\sum_{i=k}^{n} k = nk$, where k is constant. Thus, $\sum_{i=1}^{4} 3 = 4 \cdot 3 = 12$.
2. $\sum_{i=1}^{n} kx_i = k \sum_{i=1}^{n} x_i$, where k is a constant.
3. $\sum_{i=1}^{n} (a + bx_i) = na + b \sum_{i=1}^{n} x_i$, where a and b are constants and where use is made of properties 1 and 2 above.
4. $\sum_{i=1}^{n} (x_i + y_i) = \sum_{i=1}^{n} x_i + \sum_{i=1}^{n} y_i$.

The summation operator can also be extended to multiple sums. Thus, $\sum\sum$, the double summation operator, is defined as

$$\sum_{i=1}^{n}\sum_{j=1}^{m} x_{ij} = \sum_{i=1}^{n}(x_{i1} + x_{i2} + \cdots + x_{im})$$

$$= (x_{11} + x_{21} + \cdots + x_{n1}) + (x_{12} + x_{22} + \cdots + x_{n2})$$

$$+ \cdots + (x_{1m} + x_{2m} + \cdots + x_{nm})$$

Some of the properties of $\sum\sum$ are

1. $\sum_{i=1}^{n}\sum_{j=1}^{m} x_{ij} = \sum_{j=1}^{m}\sum_{i=1}^{n} x_{ij}$; that is, the order in which the double summation is performed is interchangeable.
2. $\sum_{i=1}^{n}\sum_{j=1}^{m} x_i y_j = \sum_{i=1}^{n} x_i \sum_{j=1}^{m} y_j$.
3. $\sum_{i=1}^{n}\sum_{j=1}^{m}(x_{ij} + y_{ij}) = \sum_{i=1}^{n}\sum_{j=1}^{m} x_{ij} + \sum_{i=1}^{n}\sum_{j=1}^{m} y_{ij}$.
4. $\left[\sum_{i=1}^{n} x_i\right]^2 = \sum_{i=1}^{n} x_i^2 + 2\sum_{i=1}^{n-1}\sum_{j=i+1}^{n} x_i x_j = \sum_{i=1}^{n} x_i^2 + 2\sum_{i<j} x_i x_j$.

The product operator $\prod$ is defined as

$$\prod_{i=1}^{n} x_i = x_1 \cdot x_2 \cdots x_n$$

Thus,

$$\prod_{i=1}^{3} x_i = x_1 \cdot x_2 \cdot x_3$$

A.2 SAMPLE SPACE, SAMPLE POINTS, AND EVENTS

The set of all possible outcomes of a random, or chance, experiment is called the **population**, or **sample space,** and each member of this sample space is called a **sample point**. Thus, in the experiment of tossing two coins, the sample space consists of these four possible outcomes: *HH, HT, TH,* and *TT,* where *HH* means a head on the first toss and also a head on the second toss, *HT* means a head on the first toss and a tail on the second toss, and so on. Each of the preceding occurrences constitutes a sample point.

An **event** is a subset of the sample space. Thus, if we let *A* denote the occurrence of one head and one tail, then, of the preceding possible outcomes, only two belong to *A,* namely *HT* and *TH.* In this case *A* constitutes an event. Similarly, the occurrence of two heads in a toss of two coins is an event. Events are said to be **mutually exclusive** if the occurrence of one event precludes the occurrence of another event. If in the preceding example *HH* occurs, the occurrence of the event *HT* at the same time is not possible. Events are said to be (collectively) **exhaustive** if they exhaust all the possible outcomes of an experiment. Thus, in the example, the events (a) two heads, (b) two tails, and (c) one tail, one head exhaust all the outcomes; hence they are (collectively) exhaustive events.

A.3 PROBABILITY AND RANDOM VARIABLES

Probability

Let A be an event in a sample space. By $P(A)$, the probability of the event A, we mean the proportion of times the event A will occur in repeated trials of an experiment. Alternatively, in a total of n possible equally likely outcomes of an experiment, if m of them are favorable to the occurrence of the event A, we define the ratio m/n as the **relative frequency** of A. For large values of n, this relative frequency will provide a very good approximation of the probability of A.

Properties of probability. $P(A)$ is a real-valued function[1] and has these properties:

1. $0 \leq P(A) \leq 1$ for every A.
2. If $A, B, C, \ldots$ constitute an exhaustive set of events, then $P(A+B+C+\cdots) = 1$, where $A + B + C$ means A or B or C, and so forth.
3. If $A, B, C, \ldots$ are mutually exclusive events, then

$$P(A + B + C + \cdots) = P(A) + P(B) + P(C) + \cdots$$

> **Example 1.** Consider the experiment of throwing a die numbered 1 through 6. The sample space consists of the outcomes 1, 2, 3, 4, 5, and 6. These six events therefore exhaust the entire sample space. The probability of any one of these numbers showing up is 1/6 since there are six equally likely outcomes and any one of them has an equal chance of showing up. Since 1, 2, 3, 4, 5, and 6 form an exhaustive set of events, $P(1 + 2 + 3 + 4 + 5 + 6) = 1$ where 1, 2, 3, ... means the probability of number 1 or number 2 or number 3, etc. And since $1, 2, \ldots, 6$ are mutually exclusive events in that two numbers cannot occur simultaneously, $P(1 + 2 + 3 + 4 + 5 + 6) = P(1) + P(2) + \cdots + P(6) = 1$.

Random Variables

A variable whose value is determined by the outcome of a chance experiment is called a **random variable** (rv). Random variables are usually denoted by the capital letters X, Y, Z, and so on, and the values taken by them are denoted by small letters x, y, z, and so on.

A random variable may be either **discrete** or **continuous.** A discrete rv takes on only a finite (or countably infinite) number of values.[2] For example, in throwing two dice, each numbered 1 to 6, if we define the random variable

---

[1] A function whose domain and range are subsets of real numbers is commonly referred to as a real-valued function. For details, see Alpha C. Chiang, *Fundamental Methods of Mathematical Economics*, 3d ed., McGraw-Hill, 1984, Chap. 2.

[2] For a simple discussion of the notion of countably infinite sets, see R. G. D. Allen, *Basic Mathematics*, Macmillan, London, 1964, p. 104.

X as the sum of the numbers showing on the dice, then X will take one of these values: 2, 3, 4, 5, 6, 7, 8, 9, 10, 11, or 12. Hence it is a discrete random variable. A continuous rv, on the other hand, is one that can take on any value in some interval of values. Thus, the height of an individual is a continuous variable—in the range, say, 60 to 65 inches it can take any value, depending on the precision of measurement.

A.4   PROBABILITY DENSITY FUNCTION (PDF)

Probability Density Function of a Discrete Random Variable

Let X be a discrete rv taking distinct values $x_1, x_2, \ldots, x_n, \ldots$. Then the function

$$f(x) = P(X = x_i) \qquad \text{for } i = 1, 2, \ldots, n, \ldots$$
$$= 0 \qquad \qquad \text{for } x \neq x_i$$

is called the **discrete probability density function** (PDF) of X, where $P(X = x_i)$ means the probability that the discrete rv X takes the value of x_i.

> **Example 2.** In a throw of two dice, the random variable X, the sum of the numbers shown on two dice, can take one of the 11 values shown. The **PDF** of this variable can be shown to be as follows (see also Fig. A.1):
>
> $$x = \quad 2 \quad 3 \quad 4 \quad 5 \quad 6 \quad 7 \quad 8 \quad 9 \quad 10 \quad 11 \quad 12$$
> $$f(x) = (\tfrac{1}{36})(\tfrac{2}{36})(\tfrac{3}{36})(\tfrac{4}{36})(\tfrac{5}{36})(\tfrac{6}{36})(\tfrac{5}{36})(\tfrac{4}{36})(\tfrac{3}{36})(\tfrac{2}{36})(\tfrac{1}{36})$$
>
> These probabilities can be easily verified. In all there are 36 possible outcomes, of which one is favorable to number 2, two are favorable to number 3 (since the sum 3 can occur either as 1 on the first die and 2 on the second die or 2 on the first die and 1 on the second die), and so on.

Probability Density Function of a Continuous Random Variable

Let X be a continuous rv. Then $f(x)$ is said to be the PDF of X if the following conditions are satisfied:

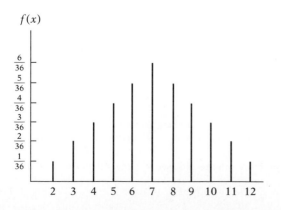

FIGURE A.1
Density function of the discrete random variable of Example 2.

$$f(x) \geq 0$$

$$\int_{-\infty}^{\infty} f(x)\,dx = 1$$

$$\int_{a}^{b} f(x)\,dx = P(a \leq x \leq b)$$

where $f(x)\,dx$ is known as the *probability element* (the probability associated with a small interval of a continuous variable) and where $P(a \leq x \leq b)$ means the probability that X lies in the interval a to b. Geometrically, we have Fig. A.2.

For a continuous rv, in contrast with a discrete rv, the probability that X takes a specific value is zero;[3] probability for such a variable is measurable only over a given range or interval, such as (a, b) shown in Fig. A.2.

Example 3. Consider the following density function:

$$f(x) = \tfrac{1}{9}x^2; \qquad 0 \leq x \leq 3$$

It can be readily verified that $f(x) \geq 0$ for all x in the range 0 to 3 and that $\int_{0}^{3} \tfrac{1}{9}x^2 dx = 1$. (*Note:* The integral is $(\tfrac{1}{27}x^3 \big|_0^3) = 1$.) If we want to evaluate the above PDF between, say, 0 and 1, we obtain $\int_{0}^{1} \tfrac{1}{9}x^2 dx = (\tfrac{1}{27}x^3 \big|_0^1) = \tfrac{1}{27}$; that is, the probability that x lies between 0 and 1 is 1/27.

Joint Probability Density Functions

Discrete joint PDF. Let X and Y be two discrete random variables. Then the function

$$f(x, y) = P(X = x \text{ and } Y = y)$$
$$= 0 \qquad \text{when } X \neq x \text{ and } Y \neq y$$

is known as the **discrete joint probability density function** and gives the (joint) probability that X takes the value of x and Y takes the value of y.

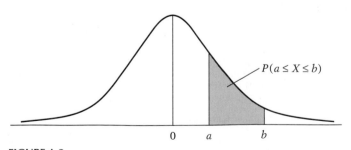

FIGURE A.2
Density function of a continuous random variable.

---

[3]*Note:* $\int_{a}^{a} f(x)\,dx = 0.$

Example 4. The following table gives the joint PDF of the discrete variables X and Y.

		X			
		-2	**0**	**2**	**3**
	3	0.27	0.08	0.16	0
Y					
	6	0	0.04	0.10	0.35

This table tells us that the probability that X takes the value of -2 while Y simultaneously takes the value of 3 is 0.27 and that the probability that X takes the value of 3 while Y takes the value of 6 is 0.35, and so on.

Marginal Probability Density Function

In relation to $f(x, y)$, $f(x)$ and $f(y)$ are called **individual**, or **marginal**, probability density functions. These marginal PDFs are derived as follows:

$$f(x) = \sum_y f(x, y) \qquad \text{marginal PDF of } X$$

$$f(y) = \sum_x f(x, y) \qquad \text{marginal PDF of } Y$$

where, for example, $\sum_y$ means the sum over all values of Y and $\sum_x$ means the sum over all values of X.

Example 5. Consider the data given in Example 4. The marginal PDF of X is obtained as follows:

$$f(x = -2) = \sum_y f(x, y) = 0.27 + 0 = 0.27$$

$$f(x = 0) = \sum_y f(x, y) = 0.08 + 0.04 = 0.12$$

$$f(x = 2) = \sum_y f(x, y) = 0.16 + 0.10 = 0.26$$

$$f(x = 3) = \sum_y f(x, y) = 0 + 0.35 = 0.35$$

Likewise, the marginal PDF of Y is obtained as

$$f(y = 3) = \sum_x f(x, y) = 0.27 + 0.08 + 0.16 + 0 = 0.51$$

$$f(y = 6) = \sum_x f(x, y) = 0 + 0.04 + 0.10 + 0.35 = 0.49$$

As this examples shows, to obtain the marginal PDF of X we we add the column numbers, and to obtain the marginal PDF of Y we add the row numbers. Notice that $\sum_x f(x)$ over all values of X is 1, as is $\sum_y f(y)$ over all values of Y (why?).

Conditional PDF. As noted in Chapter 2, in regression analysis we are often interested in studying the behavior of one variable conditional upon the values of another variable(s). This can be done by considering the conditional PDF.

The function

$$f(x\,|\,y) = P(X = x\,|\,Y = y)$$

is known as the **conditional PDF** of X; it gives the probability that X takes on the value of x given that Y has assumed the value y. Similarly,

$$f(y\,|\,x) = P(Y = y\,|\,X = x)$$

which gives the *conditional PDF of Y*.

The conditional PDFs may be obtained as follows:

$$f(x\,|\,y) = \frac{f(x, y)}{f(y)} \qquad \text{conditional PDF of } X$$

$$f(y\,|\,x) = \frac{f(x, y)}{f(x)} \qquad \text{conditional PDF of } Y$$

As the preceding expressions show, the conditional PDF of one variable can be expressed as the ratio of the joint PDF to the marginal PDF of another variable.

Example 6. Continuing with Examples 4 and 5, let us compute the following conditional probabilities:

$$f(X = -2\,|\,Y = 3) = \frac{f(X = -2, Y = 3)}{f(Y = 3)} = 0.27 / 0.51 = 0.53$$

Notice that the unconditional probability $f(X = -2)$ is 0.27, but if Y has assumed the value of 3, the probability that X takes the value of -2 is 0.53.

$$f(X = 2\,|\,Y = 6) = \frac{f(X = 2, Y = 6)}{f(Y = 6)} = 0.10 / 0.49 = 0.20$$

Again note that the unconditional probability that X takes the value of 2 is 0.26, which is different from 0.20, which is its value if Y assumes the value of 6.

Statistical Independence

Two random variables X and Y are statistically independent if and only if

$$f(x, y) = f(x)f(y)$$

that is, if the joint PDF can be expressed as the product of the marginal PDFs.

Example 7. A bag contains three balls numbered 1, 2, and 3. Two balls are drawn at random, with replacement, from the bag (i.e., the first ball drawn is replaced before the second is drawn). Let X denote the number of the first ball drawn and Y the number of the second ball drawn. The following table gives the joint PDF of X and Y.

		\(X\) 1	2	3
\(Y\)	1	$\frac{1}{9}$	$\frac{1}{9}$	$\frac{1}{9}$
	2	$\frac{1}{9}$	$\frac{1}{9}$	$\frac{1}{9}$
	3	$\frac{1}{9}$	$\frac{1}{9}$	$\frac{1}{9}$

Now $f(X = 1, Y = 1) = \frac{1}{9}, f(X = 1) = \frac{1}{3}$ (obtained by summing the first column), and $f(Y = 1) = \frac{1}{3}$ (obtained by summing the first row). Since $f(X, Y) = f(X)f(Y)$ in this example we can say that the two variables are statistically independent. It can be easily checked that for any other combination of X and Y values given in the above table the joint PDF factors into individual PDFs.

It can be shown that the X and Y variables given in Example 4 are not statistically independent since the product of the two marginal PDFs is not equal to the joint PDF. (*Note:* $f(X, Y) = f(X)f(Y)$ must be true for all combinations of X and Y if the two variables are to be statistically independent.)

Continuous joint PDF. The PDF $f(x, y)$ of two continuous variables X and Y is such that

$$f(x, y) \geq 0$$

$$\int_{-\infty}^{\infty} \int_{-\infty}^{\infty} f(x, y) \, dx \, dy = 1$$

$$\int_{c}^{d} \int_{a}^{b} f(x, y) \, dx \, dy = P(a \leq x \leq b, c \leq y \leq d)$$

Example 8. Consider the following PDF.

$$f(x, y) = 2 - x - y \qquad 0 \leq x \leq 1; 0 \leq y \leq 1$$

It is obvious that $f(x, y) \geq 0$. Moreover[4]

$$\int_{0}^{1} \int_{0}^{1} (2 - x - y) \, dx \, dy = 1$$

The marginal PDF of X and Y can be obtained as

$$f(x) = \int_{-\infty}^{\infty} f(x, y) \, dy \qquad \text{marginal PDF of } X$$

$$f(y) = \int_{-\infty}^{\infty} f(x, y) \, dx \qquad \text{marginal PDF of } Y$$

Example 9. The two marginal PDFs of the joint PDF given in Example 8 are as follows:

---

[4]

$$\int_{0}^{1} \left[\int_{0}^{1} (2 - x - y) \, dx \right] dy = \int_{0}^{1} \left[\left(2x - \frac{x^2}{2} - xy \right) \Big|_{0}^{1} \right] dy$$

$$= \int_{0}^{1} \left(\frac{3}{2} - y \right) dy$$

$$= \left(\frac{3}{2} y - \frac{y^2}{2} \right) \Big|_{0}^{1} = 1$$

Note: The expression $(\frac{3}{2} y - y^2/2) \big|_{0}^{1}$ means the expression in the parentheses is to be evaluated at the upper limit value of 1 and the lower limit value of 0; the latter value is subtracted from the former to obtain the value of the integral. Thus, in the preceding example the limits are $(\frac{3}{2} - \frac{1}{2})$ at $y = 1$ and 0 at $y = 0$, giving the value of the integral as 1.

$$f(x) = \int_0^1 f(x, y)\, dy = \int_0^1 (2 - x - y)\, dy$$

$$\left(2y - xy - \frac{y^2}{2}\right)\Big|_0^1 = \frac{3}{2} - x \qquad 0 \le x \le 1$$

$$f(y) = \int_0^1 (2 - x - y)\, dx$$

$$\left(2x - xy - \frac{x^2}{2}\right)\Big|_0^1 = \frac{3}{2} - y \qquad 0 \le y \le 1$$

To see if the two variables of Example 8 are statistically independent, we need to find out if $f(x, y) = f(x)f(y)$. Since $(2 - x - y) \ne (\frac{3}{2} - x)(\frac{3}{2} - y)$, we can say that the two variables are not statistically independent.

A.5 CHARACTERISTICS OF PROBABILITY DISTRIBUTIONS

A probability distribution can often be summarized in terms of a few of its characteristics, known as the **moments** of the distribution. Two of the most widely used moments are the **mean**, or **expected value**, and the **variance**.

Expected Value

The expected value of a discrete rv X, denoted by $E(X)$, is defined as follows:

$$E(X) = \sum_x x f(x)$$

where $\sum_x$ means the sum over all values of X and where $f(x)$ is the (discrete) PDF of X.

Example 10. Consider the probability distribution of the sum of two numbers in a throw of two dice given in Example 2. (See Fig. A.1.) Multiplying the various X values given there by their probabilities and summing over all the observations, we obtain:

$$E(X) = 2(\tfrac{1}{36}) + 3(\tfrac{2}{26}) + 4(\tfrac{3}{36}) + \cdots + 12(\tfrac{1}{36})$$
$$= 7$$

which is the average value of the sum of numbers observed in a throw of two dice.

Example 11. Estimate $E(X)$ and $E(Y)$ for the data given in Example 4. We have seen that

x	-2	0	2	3
$f(x)$	0.27	0.12	0.26	0.35

Therefore,

$$E(X) = \sum_x x f(x)$$
$$= (-2)(0.27) + (0)(0.12) + (2)(0.26) + (3)(0.35)$$
$$= 1.03$$

Similarly,

y	3	6
$f(y)$	0.51	0.49

$$E(Y) = \sum_y yf(y)$$
$$= (3)(0.51) + (6)(0.49)$$
$$= 4.47$$

The expected value of a continuous rv is defined as

$$E(X) = \int_{-\infty}^{\infty} xf(x)\,dx$$

The only difference between this case and the expected value of a discrete rv is that we replace the summation symbol by the integral symbol.

Example 12. Let us find out the expected value of the continuous PDF given in Example 3.

$$E(X) = \int_0^3 x\left(\frac{x^2}{9}\right)dx$$
$$= \frac{1}{9}\left[\left(\frac{x^4}{4}\right)\right]_0^3$$
$$= \frac{9}{4}$$
$$= 2.25$$

Properties of Expected Values

1. The expected value of a constant is the constant itself. Thus, if b is a constant, $E(b) = b$.
2. If a and b are constants,

$$E(aX + b) = aE(X) + b$$

This can be generalized. If $X_1, X_2, \ldots, X_N$ are N random variables and $a_1, a_2, \ldots, a_N$ and b are constants, then

$$E(a_1X_1 + a_2X_2 + \cdots + a_NX_N + b) = a_1E(X_1) + a_2E(X_2) + \cdots + a_NE(X_N) + b$$

3. If X and Y are *independent* random variables, then

$$E(XY) = E(X)E(Y)$$

That is, the expectation of the product XY is the product of the (individual) expectations of X and Y.

4. If X is a random variable with PDF $f(x)$ and if $g(X)$ is any function of X, then

$$E[g(X)] = \sum_x g(X)f(x) \qquad \text{if } X \text{ is discrete}$$
$$= \int_{-\infty}^{\infty} g(X)f(x)\,dx \qquad \text{if } X \text{ is continuous}$$

Thus, if $g(X) = X^2$,

$$E(X^2) = \sum_x x^2 f(X) \qquad \text{if } X \text{ is discrete}$$

$$= \int_{-\infty}^{\infty} x^2 f(X)\,dx \qquad \text{if } X \text{ is continuous}$$

Example 13. Consider the following PDF:

x	-2	1	2
$f(x)$	$\frac{5}{8}$	$\frac{1}{8}$	$\frac{2}{8}$

Then

$$E(X) = -2(\tfrac{5}{8}) + 1(\tfrac{1}{8}) + 2(\tfrac{2}{8})$$
$$= -\tfrac{5}{8}$$

and

$$E(X^2) = 4(\tfrac{5}{8}) + 1(\tfrac{1}{8}) + 4(\tfrac{2}{8})$$
$$= \tfrac{29}{8}$$

Variance

Let X be a random variable and let $E(X) = \mu$. The distribution, or spread, of the X values around the expected value can be measured by the variance, which is defined as

$$\text{var}(X) = \sigma_X^2 = E(X - \mu)^2$$

The positive square root of σ_X^2, σ_X, is defined as the **standard deviation** of X. The variance or standard deviation gives an indication of how closely or widely the individual X values are spread around their mean value.

The variance defined previously is computed as follows:

$$\text{var}(X) = \sum_x (X - \mu)^2 f(x) \qquad \text{if } X \text{ is a discrete rv}$$

$$= \int_{-\infty}^{\infty} (X - \mu)^2 f(x)\,dx \qquad \text{if } X \text{ is a continuous rv}$$

For computational convenience, the variance formula given above can also be expressed as

$$\text{var}(X) = \sigma_x^2 = E(X - \mu)^2$$
$$= E(X^2) - \mu^2$$
$$= E(X^2) - [E(X)]^2$$

Applying this formula, it can be seen that the variance of the random variable given in Example 13 is $\frac{29}{8} - (-\frac{5}{8})^2 = \frac{207}{64} = 3.23$.

Example 14. Let us find the variance of the random variable given in Example 3.

$$\text{var}(X) = E(X^2) - [E(X)]^2$$

Now

$$E(X^2) = \int_0^3 x^2 \left(\frac{x^2}{9}\right) dx$$

$$= \int_0^3 \frac{x^4}{9} dx$$

$$= \frac{1}{9}\left[\frac{x^5}{5}\right]_0^3$$

$$= 243/45$$

$$= 27/5$$

Since $E(X) = \frac{9}{4}$ (see Example 12), we finally have

$$\text{var}(X) = 243/45 - (\tfrac{9}{4})^2$$

$$= 243/720 = 0.34$$

Properties of Variance

1. $E(X - \mu)^2 = E(X^2) - \mu^2$, as noted before.
2. The variance of a constant is zero.
3. If a and b are constants, then

$$\text{var}(aX + b) = a^2 \, \text{var}(X)$$

4. If X and Y are *independent* random variables, then

$$\text{var}(X + Y) = \text{var}(X) + \text{var}(Y)$$

$$\text{var}(X - Y) = \text{var}(X) + \text{var}(Y)$$

This can be generalized to more than two variables.

5. If X and Y are *independent* rv's and a and b are constants, then

$$\text{var}(aX + bY) = a^2 \, \text{var}(X) + b^2 \, \text{var}(Y)$$

Covariance

Let X and Y be two rv's with means μ_x and μ_y, respectively. Then the **covariance** between the two variables is defined as

$$\text{cov}(X, Y) = E\{(X - \mu_x)(Y - \mu_y)\} = E(XY) - \mu_x\mu_y$$

It can be readily seen that the variance of a variable is the covariance of that variable with itself.

The covariance is computed as follows:

$$\text{cov}(X, Y) = \sum_y \sum_x (X - \mu_x)(Y - \mu_y)f(x, y)$$

$$= \sum_y \sum_x XYf(x, y) - \mu_x\mu_y$$

if X and Y are discrete random variables, and

$$\text{cov}(X, Y) = \int_{-\infty}^{\infty} \int_{-\infty}^{\infty} (X - \mu_x)(Y - \mu_y) f(x, y) \, dx \, dy$$

$$= \int_{-\infty}^{\infty} \int_{-\infty}^{\infty} XYf(x, y) \, dx \, dy - \mu_x \mu_y$$

if X and Y are continuous random variables.

Properties of Covariance

1. If X and Y are independent, their covariance is zero, for

$$\text{cov}(X, Y) = E(XY) - \mu_x \mu_y$$

$$= \mu_x \mu_y - \mu_x \mu_y \qquad \text{since } E(XY) = E(X)E(Y) = \mu_x \mu_y$$
$$\text{when } X \text{ and } Y \text{ are independent}$$

$$= 0$$

2.

$$\text{cov}(a + bX, c + dY) = bd \, \text{cov}(X, Y)$$

where $a, b, c,$ and d are constants.

Example 15. Let us find out the covariance between discrete random variables X and Y whose joint PDF is as shown in Example 4. From Example 11 we already know that $\mu_x = E(X) = 1.03$ and $\mu_y = E(Y) = 4.47$.

$$E(XY) = \sum_y \sum_x XYf(x, y)$$

$$= (-2)(3)(0.27) + (0)(3)(0.08) + (2)(3)(0.16) + (3)(3)(0)$$
$$+ (-2)(6)(0) + (0)(6)(0.04) + (2)(6)(0.10) + (3)(6)(0.35)$$

$$= 6.84$$

Therefore,

$$\text{cov}(X, Y) = E(XY) - \mu_x \mu_y$$
$$= 6.84 - (1.03)(4.47)$$
$$= 2.24$$

Correlation Coefficient

The (population) correlation coefficient ρ (rho) is defined as

$$\rho = \frac{\text{cov}(X, Y)}{\sqrt{\{\text{var}(X) \, \text{var}(Y)\}}} = \frac{\text{cov}(X, Y)}{\sigma_x \sigma_y}$$

Thus defined, ρ is a measure of *linear* association between two variables and lies between -1 and $+1$, -1 indicating perfect negative association and $+1$ indicating perfect positive association.

From the preceding formula, it can be seen that

$$\text{cov}(X, Y) = \rho \sigma_x \sigma_y$$

Example 16. Estimate the coefficient of correlation for the data of Example 4.

From the PDFs given in Example 11 it can be easily shown that $\sigma_x = 2.05$ and $\sigma_y = 1.50$. We have already shown that $\text{cov}(X, Y) = 2.24$. Therefore, applying the preceding formula we estimate ρ as $2.24/(2.05)(1.50) = 0.73$.

Variances of correlated variables. Let X and Y be two rv's. Then

$$\text{var}(X + Y) = \text{var}(X) + \text{var}(Y) + 2\,\text{cov}(X, Y)$$
$$= \text{var}(X) + \text{var}(Y) + 2\rho\sigma_x\sigma_y$$
$$\text{var}(X - Y) = \text{var}(X) + \text{var}(Y) - 2\,\text{cov}(X, Y)$$
$$= \text{var}(X) + \text{var}(Y) - 2\rho\sigma_x\sigma_y$$

If, however, X and Y are independent, $\text{cov}(X, Y)$ is zero, in which case the $\text{var}(X+Y)$ and $\text{var}(X-Y)$ are both equal to $\text{var}(X)+\text{var}(Y)$, as noted previously.

The preceding results can be generalized as follows. Let $\sum_{i=1}^{n} X_i = X_1 + X_2 + \cdots + X_n$, then the variance of the linear combination $\sum X_i$ is

$$\text{var}\left(\sum_{i=1}^{n} x_i\right) = \sum_{i=1}^{n} \text{var}\,X_i + 2\sum\sum_{i<j}\text{cov}(X_i, X_j)$$
$$= \sum_{i=1}^{n} \text{var}\,X_i + 2\sum\sum_{i<j}\rho_{ij}\sigma_i\sigma_j$$

where ρ_{ij} is the correlation coefficient between X_i and X_j and where σ_i and σ_j are the standard deviations of X_i and X_j.

Thus,

$$\text{var}(X_1 + X_2 + X_3) = \text{var}\,X_1 + \text{var}\,X_2 + \text{var}\,X_3 + 2\,\text{cov}(X_1, X_2)$$
$$+ 2\,\text{cov}(X_1, X_3) + 2\,\text{cov}(X_2, X_3)$$
$$= \text{var}\,X_1 + \text{var}\,X_2 + \text{var}\,X_3 + 2\rho_{12}\sigma_1\sigma_2$$
$$+ 2\rho_{13}\sigma_1\sigma_3 + 2\rho_{23}\sigma_2\sigma_3$$

where σ_1, σ_2, and σ_3 are, respectively, the standard deviations of X_1, X_2, and X_3 and where ρ_{12} is the correlation coefficient between X_1 and X_2, ρ_{13} that between X_1 and X_3, and ρ_{23} that between X_2 and X_3.

Conditional Expectation and Conditional Variance

Let $f(x, y)$ be the joint PDF of random variables X and Y. The conditional expectation of X, given $Y = y$, is defined as

$$E(X \mid Y = y) = \sum_x xf(x \mid Y = y) \qquad \text{if } X \text{ is discrete}$$
$$= \int_{-\infty}^{\infty} xf(x \mid Y = y)\,dx \qquad \text{if } X \text{ is continuous}$$

where $E(X \mid Y = y)$ means the conditional expectation of X given $Y = y$ and where $f(x \mid Y = y)$ is the conditional PDF of X. The conditional expectation of Y, $E(Y \mid X = x)$, is defined similarly.

Conditional expectation. Note that $E(X \mid Y)$ is a random variable because it is a function of the conditioning variable Y. However, $E(X \mid Y = y)$, where y is a specific value of Y, is a constant.

Conditional variance. The conditional variance of X given $Y = y$ is defined as

$$\mathrm{var}(X \mid Y = y) = E\{[X - E(X \mid Y = y)]^2 \mid Y = y\}$$

$$= \sum_x [X - E(X \mid Y = y)]^2 f(x \mid Y = y) \qquad \text{if } X \text{ is discrete}$$

$$= \int_{-\infty}^{\infty} [X - E(X \mid Y = y)]^2 f(x \mid Y = y)\, dx \qquad \text{if } X \text{ is continuous}$$

Example 17. Compute $E(Y \mid X = 2)$ and $\mathrm{var}(Y \mid X = 2)$ for the data given in Example 4.

$$E(Y \mid X = 2) = \sum_y yf(Y = y \mid X = 2)$$

$$= 3f(Y = 3 \mid X = 2) + 6f(Y = 6 \mid X = 2)$$

$$= 3(0.16/0.26) + 6(0.10/0.26)$$

$$= 4.15$$

Note: $f(Y = 3 \mid X = 2) = f(Y = 3, X = 2)/f(X = 2) = 0.16/0.26$, and $f(Y = 6 \mid X = 2) = f(Y = 6, X = 2)/f(X = 2) = 0.10/0.26$, so

$$\mathrm{var}(Y \mid X = 2) = \sum_y [Y - E(Y \mid X = 2)]^2 f(Y \mid X = 2)$$

$$= (3 - 4.15)^2 (0.16/0.26) + (6 - 4.15)^2 (0.10/0.26)$$

$$= 2.13$$

Higher Moments of Probability Distributions

Although mean, variance, and covariance are the most frequently used summary measures of univariate and multivariate PDFs, we occasionally need to consider higher moments of the PDFs, such as the third and the fourth moments. The third and fourth moments of a univariate PDF $f(x)$ around its mean value (μ) are defined as

$$\text{Third moment}: E(X - \mu)^3$$
$$\text{Fourth moment}: E(X - \mu)^4$$

In general, the rth moment about the mean is defined as

$$r\text{th moment}: E(X - \mu)^r$$

The third and fourth moments of a distribution are often used in studying the "shape" of a probability distribution, in particular, its **skewness,** S (i.e., lack of symmetry) and **kurtosis,** K (i.e., tallness or flatness), as shown in Fig. A.3.

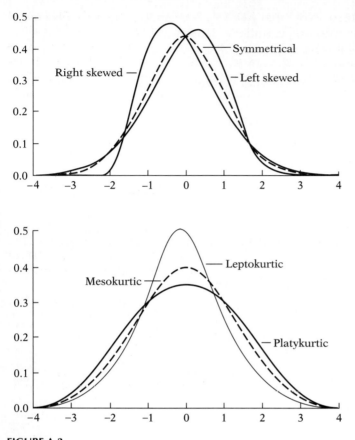

FIGURE A.3
(a) Skewness; (b) kurtosis.

One measure of skewness is defined as

$$S = \frac{[E(X - \mu)^3]^2}{[E(X - \mu)^2]^3}$$

$$= \frac{\text{Square of the third moment about mean}}{\text{Cube of the second moment about mean}}$$

Note: The second moment about the mean is simply the variance.

A commonly used measure of kurtosis is given by

$$K = \frac{E(X - \mu)^4}{[E(X - \mu)^2]^2}$$

$$= \frac{\text{Fourth moment about mean}}{\text{Square of the second moment}}$$

PDFs with values of K less than 3 are called **platykurtic** (fat or short-tailed), and those with values greater than 3 are called **leptokurtic** (slim or long-tailed). See Fig. A.3. A PDF with a kurtosis value of 3 is known as **mesokurtic**, of which the normal distribution is the prime example. (See the discussion of the normal distribution in Section A.6.)

We will show shortly how the measures of skewness and kurtosis can be combined to determine whether a random variable follows a normal distribution. Recall that our hypothesis-testing procedure, as in the t and F tests, is based on the assumption (at least in small or finite samples) that the underlying distribution of the variable (or sample statistic) is normal. It is therefore very important to find out in concrete applications whether this assumption is fulfilled.

A.6 SOME IMPORTANT THEORETICAL PROBABILITY DISTRIBUTIONS

In the text extensive use is made of the following probability distributions.

Normal Distribution

The best known of all the theoretical probability distributions is the normal distribution, whose bell-shaped picture is familiar to anyone with a modicum of statistical knowledge.

A (continuous) random variable X is said to be normally distributed if its PDF has the following form:

$$f(x) = \frac{1}{\sigma \sqrt{2\pi}} \exp\left(-\frac{1}{2} \frac{(x - \mu)^2}{\sigma^2}\right) \qquad -\infty < x < \infty$$

where μ and σ^2, known as the *parameters of the distribution*, are, respectively, the mean and the variance of the distribution. The properties of this distribution are as follows:

1. It is symmetrical around its mean value.
2. Approximately 68 percent of the area under the normal curve lies between the values of $\mu \pm \sigma$, about 95 percent of the area lies between $\mu \pm 2\sigma$, and about 99.7 percent of the area lies between $\mu \pm 3\sigma$, as shown in Fig. A.4.

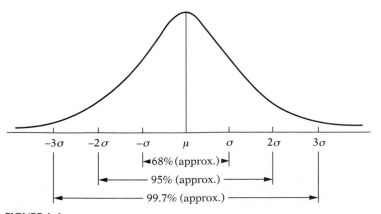

FIGURE A.4
Areas under the normal curve.

3. The normal distribution depends on the two parameters μ and σ^2, so once these are specified, one can find the probability that X will lie within a certain interval by using the PDF of the normal distribution. But this task can be lightened considerably by referring to Table D.1 of Appendix D. To use this table, we convert the given normally distributed variable X with mean μ and σ^2 into a **standardized normal variable** Z by the following transformation:

$$Z = \frac{x - \mu}{\sigma}$$

An important property of any standardized variable is that its mean value is zero and its variance is unity. Thus Z has zero mean and unit variance. Substituting z into the normal PDF given previously, we obtain

$$f(Z) = \frac{1}{\sqrt{2\pi}} \exp\left(-\frac{1}{2}Z^2\right)$$

which is the PDF of the standardized normal variable. The probabilities given in Appendix D, Table D.1, are based on this standardized normal variable.

By convention, we denote a normally distributed variable as

$$X \sim N(\mu, \sigma^2)$$

where $\sim$ means "distributed as," N stands for the normal distribution, and the quantities in the parentheses are the two parameters of the normal distribution, namely, the mean and the variance. Following this convention,

$$X \sim N(0, 1)$$

means X is a normally distributed variable with zero mean and unit variance. In other words, it is a standardized normal variable Z.

Example 18. Assume that $X \sim N(8, 4)$. What is the probability that X will assume a value between $X_1 = 4$ and $X_2 = 12$? To compute the required probability, we compute the Z values as

$$Z_1 = \frac{X_1 - \mu}{\sigma} = \frac{4 - 8}{2} = -2$$

$$Z_2 = \frac{X_2 - \mu}{\sigma} = \frac{12 - 8}{2} = +2$$

Now from Table D.1 we observe that $\Pr(0 \le Z \le 2) = 0.4772$. Then, by symmetry, we have $\Pr(-2 \le Z \le 0) = 0.4772$. Therefore, the required probability is $0.4772 + 0.4772 = 0.9544$. (See Fig. A.4.)

Example 19. What is the probability that in the preceding example X exceeds 12?
The probability that X exceeds 12 is the same as that Z exceeds 2. From Table D.1 it is obvious that this probability is $(0.5 - 0.4772)$ or 0.0228.

4. Let $X_1 \sim N(\mu_1, \sigma_1^2)$ and $X_2 \sim N(\mu_2, \sigma_2^2)$ and assume that they are independent. Now consider the linear combination

$$Y = aX_1 + bX_2$$

where a and b are constants. Then it can be shown that

$$Y \sim N[(a\mu_1 + b\mu_2), (a^2\sigma_1^2 + b^2\sigma_2^2)]$$

This result, which states that *a linear combination of normally distributed variables is itself normally distributed*, can be easily generalized to a linear combination of more than two normally distributed variables.

5. **Central limit theorem.** Let $X_1, X_2, \ldots, X_n$ denote n independent random variables, all of which have the same PDF with mean $= \mu$ and variance $= \sigma^2$. Let $\bar{X} = \sum X_i/n$ (i.e., the sample mean). Then as n increases indefinitely (i.e., $n \to \infty$),

$$\bar{X} \underset{n\to\infty}{\sim} N\left(\mu, \frac{\sigma^2}{n}\right)$$

That is, $\bar{X}$ approaches the normal distribution with mean μ and variance σ^2/n. Notice that this result holds true regardless of the form of the PDF. As a result, it follows that

$$z = \frac{\bar{X} - \mu}{\sigma/\sqrt{n}} = \frac{\sqrt{n}(\bar{X} - u)}{\sigma} \sim N(0, 1)$$

That is, Z is a standardized normal variable.

6. The third and fourth moments of the normal distribution around the mean value are as follows:

$$\text{Third moment}: E(X - \mu)^3 = 0$$
$$\text{Fourth moment}: E(X - \mu)^4 = 3\sigma^4$$

Note: All odd-powered moments about the mean value of a normally distributed variable are zero.

7. As a result, and following the measures of skewness and kurtosis discussed earlier, for a normal PDF skewness $= 0$ and kurtosis $= 3$; that is, a normal distribution is symmetric and mesokurtic. Therefore, a simple test of normality is to find out whether the computed values of skewness and kurtosis depart from the norms of 0 and 3. This is in fact the logic underlying the **Jarque-Bera (JB) test of normality** discussed in the text:

$$JB = n\left[\frac{S^2}{6} + \frac{(K - 3)^2}{24}\right] \qquad (5.13.2)$$

where S stands for skewness and K for kurtosis. Under the null hypothesis of normality, JB is distributed as a **Chi-square** statistic with 2 df.

The χ^2 (Chi-Square) Distribution

Let $Z_1, Z_2, \ldots, Z_k$ be *independent* standardized normal variables (i.e., normal variables with zero mean and unit variance). Then the quantity

$$Z = \sum_{i=1}^{k} Z_i^2$$

is said to possess the χ^2 distribution with k degrees of freedom (df), where the term df means the number of independent quantities in the previous sum. A chi-square-distributed variable is denoted by χ_k^2, where the subscript k indicates the df. Geometrically, the chi-square distribution appears in Fig. A.5.

Properties of the χ^2 distribution are as follows:

1. As Fig. A.5 shows, the χ^2 distribution is a skewed distribution, the degree of the skewness depending on the df. For comparatively few df, the distribution is highly skewed to the right; but as the number of df increases, the distribution becomes increasingly symmetrical. As a matter of fact, for df in excess of 100, the variable

$$\sqrt{2\chi^2} - \sqrt{(2k - 1)}$$

   can be treated as a standardized normal variable, where k is the df.
2. The mean of the chi-square distribution is k, and its variance is $2k$, where k is the df.
3. If Z_1 and Z_2 are two independent chi-square variables with k_1 and k_2 df, then the sum $Z_1 + Z_2$ is also a chi-square variable with df $= k_1 + k_2$.

Example 20. What is the probability of obtaining a χ^2 value of 40 or greater, given the df of 20?

As Table D.4 shows, the probability of obtaining a χ^2 value of 39.9968 (20 df) is 0.005. Therefore, the probability of obtaining a χ^2 value of 40 is less than 0.005, a rather small probability.

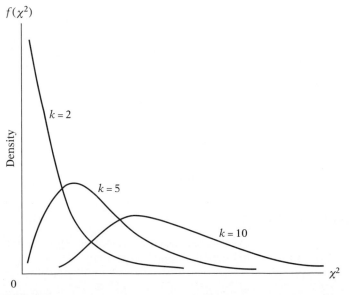

FIGURE A.5
Density function of the χ^2 variable.

Student's t Distribution

If Z_1 is a standardized normal variable [that is, $Z_1 \sim N(0, 1)$] and another variable Z_2 follows the chi-square distribution with k df and is distributed independently of Z_1, then the variable defined as

$$t = \frac{Z_1}{\sqrt{(Z_2/k)}}$$

$$= \frac{Z_1 \sqrt{k}}{\sqrt{Z_2}}$$

follows Student's t distribution with k df. A t-distributed variable is often designated as t_k, where the subscript k denotes the df. Geometrically, the t distribution is shown in Fig. A.6.

Properties of the Student's t distribution are as follows:

1. As Fig. A.6 shows, the t distribution, like the normal distribution, is symmetrical, but it is flatter than the normal distribution. But as the df increase, the t distribution approximates the normal distribution.
2. The mean of the t distribution is zero, and its variance is $k/(k-2)$.

  The t distribution is tabulated in Table D.2.

Example 21. Given df $= 13$, what is the probability of obtaining a t value (a) of about 3 or greater, (b) of about -3 or smaller, and (c) of $|t|$ of about 3 or greater, where $|t|$ means the absolute value (i.e., disregarding the sign) of t?

  From Table D.2, the answers are (a) about 0.005, (b) about 0.005 because of the symmetry of the t distribution, and (c) about $0.01 = 2(0.005)$.

The F Distribution

If Z_1 and Z_2 are independently distributed chi-square variables with k_1 and k_2 df, respectively, the variable

$$F = \frac{Z_1/k_1}{Z_2/k_2}$$

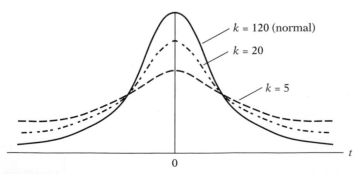

FIGURE A.6
Student's t distribution for selected degrees of freedom.

follows (Fisher's) F distribution with k_1 and k_2 df. An F-distributed variable is denoted by F_{k_1,k_2} where the subscripts indicate the df associated with the two Z variables, k_1 being called the *numerator df* and k_2 the *denominator df.* Geometrically, the F distribution is shown in Fig. A.7.

The F distribution has the following properties:

1. Like the chi-square distribution, the F distribution is skewed to the right. But it can be shown that as k_1 and k_2 become large, the F distribution approaches the normal distribution.

2. The mean value of an F-distributed variable is $k_2/(k_2 - 2)$, which is defined for $k_2 > 2$, and its variance is

$$\frac{2k_2^2(k_1 + k_2 - 2)}{k_1(k_2 - 2)^2(k_2 - 4)}$$

which is defined for $k_2 > 4$.

3. The square of a t-distributed random variable with k df has an F distribution with 1 and k df. Symbolically,

$$t_k^2 = F_{1,k}$$

Example 22. Given $k_1 = 10$ and $k_2 = 8$, what is the probability of obtaining an F value (*a*) of 3.4 or greater and (*b*) of 5.8 or greater?

As Table D.3 shows, these probabilities are (*a*) approximately 0.05 and (*b*) approximately 0.01.

4. If the denominator df, k_2, is fairly large, the following relationship holds between the F and the chi-square distributions:

$$k_1F \sim \chi_{k_1}^2$$

That is, for fairly large denominator df, the numerator df times the F value is approximately the same as a chi-square value with numerator df.

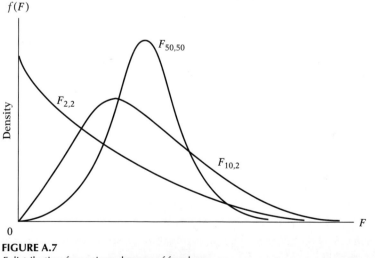

FIGURE A.7
F distribution for various degrees of freedom.

Example 23. Let $k_1 = 20$ and $k_2 = 120$. The 5 percent critical F value for these df is 1.48. Therefore, $k_1 F = (20)(1.48) = 29.6$. From the chi-square distribution for 20 df, the 5 percent critical chi-square value is about 31.41.

In passing, note that since for large df the t, chi-square, and F distributions approach the normal distribution, these three distributions are known as the *distributions related to the normal distribution*.

A.7 STATISTICAL INFERENCE: ESTIMATION

In Section A.6 we considered several theoretical probability distributions. Very often we know or are willing to assume that a random variable X follows a particular probability distribution but do not know the value(s) of the parameter(s) of the distribution. For example, if X follows the normal distribution, we may want to know the value of its two parameters, namely, the mean and the variance. To estimate the unknowns, the usual procedure is to assume that we have a **random sample** of size n from the known probability distribution and use the sample data to estimate the unknown parameters.[5] This is known as the **problem of estimation**. In this section, we take a closer look at this problem. The problem of estimation can be broken down into two categories: point estimation and interval estimation.

Point Estimation

To fix the ideas, let X be a random variable with PDF $f(x; \theta)$, where θ is the parameter of the distribution (for simplicity of discussion only, we are assuming that there is only one unknown parameter; our discussion can be readily generalized). Assume that we know the functional form—that is, we know the theoretical PDF, such as the t distribution—but do not know the value of θ. Therefore, we draw a random sample of size n from this known PDF and then develop a function of the sample values such that

$$\hat{\theta} = f(x_1, x_2, \ldots, x_n)$$

provides us an estimate of the true θ. $\hat{\theta}$ is known as a **statistic**, or an **estimator**, and a particular numerical value taken by the estimator is known as an **estimate**. Note that $\hat{\theta}$ can be treated as a random variable because it is a function of the sample data. $\hat{\theta}$ provides us with a rule, or formula, that tells us how we may estimate the true θ. Thus, if we let

$$\hat{\theta} = \frac{1}{n}(x_1 + x_2 + \cdots + x_n) = \bar{X}$$

---

[5]Let $X_1, X_2, \ldots, X_n$ be n random variables with joint PDF $f(x_1, x_2, \ldots, x_n)$. If we can write

$$f(x_1, x_2, \ldots, x_n) = f(x_1)f(x_2)\cdots f(x_n)$$

where $f(x)$ is the common PDF of each X, then $x_1, x_2, \ldots, x_n$ are said to constitute a random sample of size n from a population with PDF $f(x_n)$.

where $\bar{X}$ is the sample mean, then $\bar{X}$ is an estimator of the true mean value, say, μ. If in a specific case $\bar{X} = 50$, this provides an *estimate of* μ. The estimator $\hat{\theta}$ obtained previously is known as a **point estimator** because it provides only a single (point) estimate of θ.

Interval Estimation

Instead of obtaining only a single estimate of θ, suppose we obtain two estimates of θ by constructing two estimators $\hat{\theta}_1(x_1, x_2, \ldots, x_n)$ and $\hat{\theta}_2(x_1, x_2, \ldots, x_n)$, and say with some confidence (i.e., probability) that the interval between $\hat{\theta}_1$ and $\hat{\theta}_2$ includes the true θ. Thus, in interval estimation, in contrast with point estimation, we provide a range of possible values within which the true θ may lie.

The key concept underlying interval estimation is the notion of the **sampling**, or **probability distribution, of an estimator**. For example, it can be shown that if a variable X is normally distributed, then the sample mean $\bar{X}$ is also normally distributed with mean $= \mu$ (the true mean) and variance $= \sigma^2/n$, where n is the sample size. In other words, the sampling, or probability, distribution of the estimator $\bar{X}$ is $\bar{X} \sim N(\mu, \sigma^2/n)$. As a result, if we construct the interval

$$\bar{X} \pm 2\frac{\sigma}{\sqrt{n}}$$

and say that the probability is approximately 0.95, or 95 percent, that intervals like it will include the true μ, we are in fact constructing an interval estimator for μ. Note that the interval given previously is random since it is based on $\bar{X}$, which will vary from sample to sample.

More generally, in interval estimation we construct two estimators $\hat{\theta}_1$ and $\hat{\theta}_2$, both functions of the sample X values, such that

$$\Pr(\hat{\theta}_1 \leq \theta \leq \hat{\theta}_2) = 1 - \alpha \qquad 0 < \alpha < 1$$

That is, we can state that the probability is $1 - \alpha$ that the interval from $\hat{\theta}_1$ to $\hat{\theta}_2$ contains the true θ. This interval is known as a **confidence interval** of size $1 - \alpha$ for θ, $1 - \alpha$ being known as the **confidence coefficient**. If $\alpha = 0.05$, then $1 - \alpha = 0.95$, meaning that if we construct a confidence interval with a confidence coefficient of 0.95, then in repeated such constructions resulting from repeated sampling we shall be right in 95 out of 100 cases if we maintain that the interval contains the true θ. When the confidence coefficient is 0.95, we often say that we have a 95% confidence interval. In general, if the confidence coefficient is $1 - \alpha$, we say that we have a $100(1 - \alpha)\%$ confidence interval. Note that α is known as the **level of significance**, or the probability of committing a Type I error. This topic is discussed in Section A.8.

Example 23. Suppose that the distribution of height of men in a population is normally distributed with mean $= \mu$ inches and $\sigma = 2.5$ inches. A sample of 100 men drawn randomly from this population had an average height of 67 inches. Establish a 95% confidence interval for the mean height ($= \mu$) in the population as a whole.

As noted, $\bar{X} \sim N(\mu, \sigma^2/n)$, which in this case becomes $\bar{X} \sim N(\mu, 2.5^2/100)$. From Table D.1 one can see that

$$\bar{X} - 1.96\left(\frac{\sigma}{\sqrt{n}}\right) \leq \mu \leq \bar{X} + 1.96\frac{\sigma}{\sqrt{n}}$$

covers 95% of the area under the normal curve. Therefore, the preceding interval provides a 95% confidence interval for μ. Plugging in the given values of $\bar{X}$, σ, and n, we obtain the 95% confidence interval as

$$66.51 \leq \mu \leq 67.49$$

In repeated such measurements, intervals thus established will include the true μ with 95 percent confidence. A technical point may be noted here. Although we can say that the probability that the random interval $[\bar{X} \pm 1.96(\sigma/\sqrt{n})]$ includes μ is 95 percent, we *cannot* say that the probability is 95 percent that the particular interval (66.51, 67.49) includes μ. Once this interval is fixed, the probability that it will include μ is either 0 or 1. What we can say is that if we construct 100 such intervals, 95 out of the 100 intervals will include the true μ; we cannot guarantee that one particular interval will necessarily include μ.

There are several methods of obtaining point estimators, the best known being the **method of least-squares** and the **method of maximum likelihood** (ML). The method of least-squares is discussed fully in Chapter 3, and the method of maximum likelihood is briefly sketched in Chapter 4. Both methods possess several desirable statistical properties, which we consider next.

The desirable statistical properties fall into two categories: small-sample, or finite-sample, properties and large-sample, or asymptotic, properties. Underlying both these sets of properties is the notion that an estimator has a sampling, or probability, distribution.

Small-Sample Properties

Unbiasedness. An estimator $\hat{\theta}$ is said to be an unbiased estimator of θ if the expected value of $\hat{\theta}$ is equal to the true θ; that is,

$$E(\hat{\theta}) = \theta$$

or

$$E(\hat{\theta}) - \theta = 0$$

If this equality does not hold, then the estimator is said to be biased, and the bias is calculated as

$$\text{bias}(\hat{\theta}) = E(\hat{\theta}) - \theta$$

Of course, if $E(\hat{\theta}) = \theta$—that is, $\hat{\theta}$ is an unbiased estimator—the bias is zero.

Geometrically, the situation is as depicted in Fig. A.8. In passing, note that unbiasedness is a property of repeated sampling, not of any given sample: keeping the sample size fixed, we draw several samples, each time obtaining an estimate of the unknown parameter. The average value of these estimates is expected to be equal to the true value if the estimator is to be unbiased.

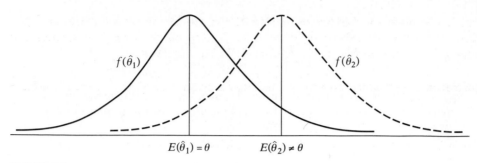

FIGURE A.8
Biased and unbiased estimators.

Minimum variance. $\hat{\theta}_1$ is said to be a minimum-variance estimator of θ if the variance of $\hat{\theta}_1$ is smaller than or at most equal to the variance of $\hat{\theta}_2$, which is any other estimator of θ. Geometrically, we have Fig. A. 9, which shows three estimators of θ, namely $\hat{\theta}_1, \hat{\theta}_2,$ and $\hat{\theta}_3$, and their probability distributions. As shown, the variance of $\hat{\theta}_3$ is smaller than that of either $\hat{\theta}_1$ or $\hat{\theta}_2$. Hence, assuming only the three possible estimators, in this case $\hat{\theta}_3$ is a minimum-variance estimator. But note that $\hat{\theta}_3$ is a biased estimator (why?).

Best unbiased, or efficient, estimator. If $\hat{\theta}_1$ and $\hat{\theta}_2$ are two *unbiased* estimators of θ, and the variance of $\hat{\theta}_1$ is smaller than or at most equal to the variance of $\hat{\theta}_2$, thcn $\hat{\theta}_1$ is a **minimum-variance unbiased**, or **best unbiased**, or **efficient**, estimator. Thus, in Fig. A.9, of the two unbiased estimators $\hat{\theta}_1$ and $\hat{\theta}_2$, $\hat{\theta}_1$ is best unbiased, or efficient.

Linearity. An estimator $\hat{\theta}$ is said to be a linear estimator of θ if it is a linear function of the sample observations. Thus, the sample mean defined as

$$\bar{X} = \frac{1}{n}\sum X_i = \frac{1}{n}(x_1 + x_2 + \cdots + x_n)$$

is a linear estimator because it is a linear function of the X values.

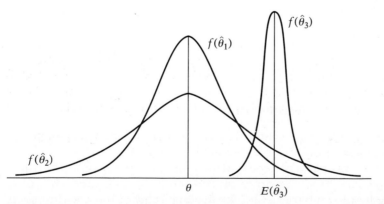

FIGURE A.9
Distribution of three estimators of θ.

Best linear unbiased estimator (BLUE). If $\hat{\theta}$ is linear, is unbiased, and has minimum variance in the class of all linear unbiased estimators of θ, then it is called a *best linear unbiased estimator*, or **BLUE** for short.

Minimum mean-square-error (MSE) estimator. The MSE of an estimator $\hat{\theta}$ is defined as

$$\text{MSE}(\hat{\theta}) = E(\hat{\theta} - \theta)^2$$

This is in contrast with the variance of $\hat{\theta}$, which is defined as

$$\text{var}(\hat{\theta}) = E[\hat{\theta} - E(\hat{\theta})]^2$$

The difference between the two is that $\text{var}(\hat{\theta})$ measures the dispersion of the distribution of $\hat{\theta}$ around its mean or expected value, whereas $\text{MSE}(\hat{\theta})$ measures dispersion around the true value of the parameter. The relationship between the two is as follows:

$$
\begin{aligned}
\text{MSE}(\hat{\theta}) &= E(\hat{\theta} - \theta)^2 \\
&= E[\hat{\theta} - E(\hat{\theta}) + E(\hat{\theta}) - \theta]^2 \\
&= E[\hat{\theta} - E(\hat{\theta})]^2 + E[E(\hat{\theta}) - \theta]^2 + 2E[\hat{\theta} - E(\hat{\theta})][E(\hat{\theta}) - \theta] \\
&= E[\hat{\theta} - E(\hat{\theta})]^2 + E[E(\hat{\theta}) - \theta]^2, \text{ since the last term is zero}^6 \\
&= \text{var}(\hat{\theta}) + \text{bias}(\hat{\theta})^2 \\
&= \text{variance of } \hat{\theta} \text{ } plus \text{ square bias.}
\end{aligned}
$$

Of course, if the bias is zero, $\text{MSE}(\hat{\theta}) = \text{var}(\hat{\theta})$.

The minimum MSE criterion consists in choosing an estimator whose MSE is the least in a competing set of estimators. But notice that even if such an estimator is found, there is a trade-off involved—to obtain minimum variance you may have to accept some bias. Geometrically, the situation is as shown in Fig. A.10. In this figure, $\hat{\theta}_2$ is slightly biased, but its variance is smaller than that of the unbiased estimator $\hat{\theta}_1$. In practice, however, the minimum MSE criterion is used when the best unbiased criterion is incapable of producing estimators with smaller variances.

Large-Sample Properties

It often happens that an estimator does not satisfy one or more of the desirable statistical properties in small samples. But as the sample size increases indefinitely, the estimator possesses several desirable statistical properties. These properties are known as the **large-sample**, or **asymptotic**, **properties**.

Asymptotic unbiasedness. An estimator $\hat{\theta}$ is said to be an asymptotically unbiased estimator of θ if

---

[6]The last term can be written as $2\{[E(\hat{\theta})]^2 - [E(\hat{\theta})]^2 - \theta E(\hat{\theta}) + \theta E(\hat{\theta})\} = 0$. Also note that $E[E(\hat{\theta}) - \theta]^2 = [E(\hat{\theta}) - \theta]^2$, since the expected value of a constant is simply the constant itself.

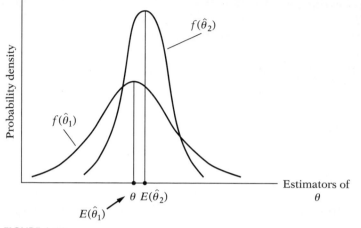

FIGURE A.10
Trade-off between bias and variance.

$$\lim_{n \to \infty} E(\hat{\theta}_n) = \theta$$

where $\hat{\theta}_n$ means that the estimator is based on a sample size of n and where lim means limit and $n \to \infty$ means that n increases indefinitely. In words, $\hat{\theta}$ is an asymptotically unbiased estimator of θ if its expected, or mean, value approaches the true value as the sample size gets larger and larger. As an example, consider the following measure of the sample variance of a random variable X:

$$S^2 = \left(\frac{\sum (X_i - \bar{X})^2}{n} \right)$$

It can be shown that

$$E(S^2) = \sigma^2 \left(1 - \frac{1}{n} \right)$$

where σ^2 is the true variance. It is obvious that in a small sample S^2 is biased, but as n increases indefinitely, $E(S^2)$ approaches true σ^2; hence it is asymptotically unbiased.

Consistency. $\hat{\theta}$ is said to be a consistent estimator if it approaches the true value θ as the sample size gets larger and larger. Figure A.11 illustrates this property.

In this figure we have the distribution of $\hat{\theta}$ based on sample sizes of 25, 50, 80, and 100. As the figure shows, $\hat{\theta}$ based on $n = 25$ is biased since its sampling distribution is not centered on the true θ. But as n increases, the distribution of $\hat{\theta}$ not only tends to be more closely centered on θ (i.e., $\hat{\theta}$ becomes less biased) but its variance also becomes smaller. If in the limit (i.e., when n increases indefinitely) the distribution of $\hat{\theta}$ collapses to the single point θ, that is, if the distribution of $\hat{\theta}$ has zero spread, or variance, we say that $\hat{\theta}$ is a **consistent estimator** of θ.

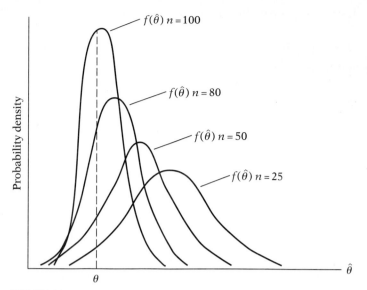

FIGURE A.11
The distribution of $\hat{\theta}$ as sample size increases.

More formally, an estimator $\hat{\theta}$ is said to be a consistent estimator of θ if the probability that the absolute value of the difference between $\hat{\theta}$ and θ is less than δ (an arbitrarily small positive quantity) approaches unity. Symbolically,

$$\lim_{n \to \infty} P\{|\hat{\theta} - \theta| < \delta\} = 1 \qquad \delta > 0$$

where P stands for probability. This is often expressed as

$$\operatorname*{plim}_{n \to \infty} \hat{\theta} = \theta$$

where plim means probability limit.

Note that the properties of unbiasedness and consistency are conceptually very much different. The property of unbiasedness can hold for any sample size, whereas consistency is strictly a large-sample property.

A *sufficient condition* for consistency is that the bias and variance both tend to zero as the sample size increases indefinitely.[7] Alternatively, a sufficient condition for consistency is that the MSE $(\hat{\theta})$ tends to zero as n increases indefinitely. (For MSE$(\hat{\theta})$, see the discussion presented previously.)

Example 24. Let $X_1, X_2, \ldots, X_n$ be a random sample from a distribution with mean μ and variance σ^2. Show that the sample mean $\bar{X}$ is a consistent estimator of μ.

From elementary statistics it is known that $E(\bar{X}) = \mu$ and var$(\bar{X}) = \sigma^2/n$. Since $E(\bar{X}) = \mu$ regardless of the sample size, it is unbiased. Moreover, as n increases indefinitely, var$(\bar{X})$ tends toward zero. Hence, $\bar{X}$ is a consistent estimator of μ.

---

[7]More technically, $\lim_{n \to \infty} E(\hat{\theta}_n) = \theta$ and $\lim_{n \to \infty} \operatorname{var}(\hat{\theta}_n) = 0$.

The following rules about probability limits are noteworthy.

1. *Invariance (Slutsky property).* If $\hat{\theta}$ is a consistent estimator of θ and if $h(\hat{\theta})$ is any continuous function of $\hat{\theta}$, then

$$\plim_{n \to \infty} h(\hat{\theta}) = h(\theta)$$

What this means is that if $\hat{\theta}$ is a consistent estimator of θ, then $1/\hat{\theta}$ is also a consistent estimator of $1/\theta$ and that $\log(\hat{\theta})$ is also a consistent estimator of $\log(\theta)$. Note that this property does not hold true of the expectation operator E; that is, if $\hat{\theta}$ is an unbiased estimator of θ [that is, $E(\hat{\theta}) = \theta$], it is *not true* that $1/\hat{\theta}$ is an unbiased estimator of $1/\theta$; that is, $E(1/\hat{\theta}) \neq 1/E(\hat{\theta}) \neq 1/\theta$.

2. If b is a constant, then

$$\plim_{n \to \infty} b = b$$

That is, the probability limit of a constant is the same constant.

3. If $\hat{\theta}_1$ and $\hat{\theta}_2$ are consistent estimators, then

$$\plim(\hat{\theta}_1 + \hat{\theta}_2) = \plim \hat{\theta}_1 + \plim \hat{\theta}_2$$

$$\plim(\hat{\theta}_1\hat{\theta}_2) = \plim \hat{\theta}_1 \plim \hat{\theta}_2$$

$$\plim\left(\frac{\hat{\theta}_1}{\hat{\theta}_2}\right) = \frac{\plim \hat{\theta}_1}{\plim \hat{\theta}_2}$$

The last two properties, in general, do not hold true of the expectation operator E. Thus, $E(\hat{\theta}_1/\hat{\theta}_2) \neq E(\hat{\theta}_1)/E(\hat{\theta}_2)$. Similarly, $E(\hat{\theta}_1\hat{\theta}_2) \neq E(\hat{\theta}_1)E(\hat{\theta}_2)$. If, however, $\hat{\theta}_1$ and $\hat{\theta}_2$ are independently distributed, $E(\hat{\theta}_1\hat{\theta}_2) = E(\hat{\theta}_1)E(\hat{\theta}_2)$, as noted previously.

Asymptotic efficiency. Let $\hat{\theta}$ be an estimator of θ. The variance of the asymptotic distribution of $\hat{\theta}$ is called the **asymptotic variance** of $\hat{\theta}$. If $\hat{\theta}$ is consistent and its asymptotic variance is smaller than the asymptotic variance of all other consistent estimators of θ, $\hat{\theta}$ is called **asymptotically efficient**.

Asymptotic normality. An estimator $\hat{\theta}$ is said to be asymptotically normally distributed if its sampling distribution tends to approach the normal distribution as the sample size n increases indefinitely. For example, statistical theory shows that if $X_1, X_2, \ldots, X_n$ are independent normally distributed variables with the same mean μ and the same variance σ^2, the sample mean $\bar{X}$ is also normally distributed with mean μ and variance σ^2/n in small as well as large samples. But if the X_i are independent with mean μ and variance σ^2 but are not necessarily from the normal distribution, then the sample mean $\bar{X}$ is asymptotically normally distributed with mean μ and variance σ^2/n; that is, as the sample size n increases indefinitely, the sample mean tends to be normally distributed with mean μ and variance σ^2/n. That is in fact the central limit theorem discussed previously.

A.8 STATISTICAL INFERENCE: HYPOTHESIS TESTING

Estimation and hypothesis testing constitute the twin branches of classical statistical inference. Having examined the problem of estimation, we briefly look at the problem of testing statistical hypotheses.

The problem of hypothesis testing may be stated as follows. Assume that we have an rv X with a known PDF $f(x; \theta)$, where θ is the parameter of the distribution. Having obtained a random sample of size n, we obtain the point estimator $\hat{\theta}$. Since the true θ is rarely known, we raise the question: Is the estimator $\hat{\theta}$ "compatible" with some hypothesized value of θ, say, $\theta = \theta^*$, where θ^* is a specific numerical value of θ? In other words, could our sample have come from the PDF $f(x; \theta = \theta^*)$? In the language of hypothesis testing $\theta = \theta^*$ is called the **null** (or maintained) **hypothesis** and is generally denoted by H_0. The null hypothesis is tested against an **alternative hypothesis**, denoted by H_1, which, for example, may state that $\theta \neq \theta^*$. (*Note:* In some textbooks, H_0 and H_1 are designated by H_1 and H_2, respectively.)

The null hypothesis and the alternative hypothesis can be **simple** or **composite**. A hypothesis is called *simple* if it specifies the value(s) of the parameter(s) of the distribution; otherwise it is called a *composite* hypothesis. Thus, if $X \sim N(\mu, \sigma^2)$ and we state that

$$H_0: \mu = 15 \quad \text{and} \quad \sigma = 2$$

it is a simple hypothesis, whereas

$$H_0: \mu = 15 \quad \text{and} \quad \sigma > 2$$

is a composite hypothesis because here the value of σ is not specified.

To test the null hypothesis (i.e., to test its validity), we use the sample information to obtain what is known as the **test statistic**. Very often this test statistic turns out to be the point estimator of the unknown parameter. Then we try to find out the *sampling*, or *probability, distribution* of the test statistic and use the **confidence interval** or **test of significance** approach to test the null hypothesis. The mechanics are illustrated below.

To fix the ideas, let us revert to Example 23, which was concerned with the height (X) of men in a population. We are told that

$$X_i \sim N(\mu, \sigma^2) = N(\mu, 2.5^2)$$
$$\bar{X} = 67 \quad n = 100$$

Let us assume that

$$H_0 : \mu = \mu^* = 69$$
$$H_1 : \mu \neq 69$$

The question is: Could the sample with $\bar{X} = 67$, the test statistic, have come from the population with the mean value of 69? Intuitively, we may not reject the null hypothesis if $\bar{X}$ is "sufficiently close" to μ^*; otherwise we may reject it in favor of the alternative hypothesis. But how do we decide that $\bar{X}$ is "sufficiently close" to μ^*? We can adopt two approaches, (1) confidence interval and

(2) test of significance, both leading to identical conclusions in any specific application.

The Confidence Interval Approach

Since $X_i \sim N(\mu, \sigma^2)$, we know that the test statistic $\bar{X}$ is distributed as

$$\bar{X} \sim N(\mu, \sigma^2/n)$$

Since we know the probability distribution of $\bar{X}$, why not establish, say, a $100(1-\alpha)$ confidence interval for μ based on $\bar{X}$ and see whether this confidence interval includes $\mu = \mu^*$? If it does, we may not reject the null hypothesis; if it does not, we may reject the null hypothesis. Thus, if $\alpha = 0.05$, we will have a 95 percent confidence interval and if this confidence interval includes μ^*, we may not reject the null hypothesis—95 out of 100 intervals thus established are likely to include μ^*.

The actual mechanics are as follows: since $\bar{X} \sim N(\mu, \sigma^2/n)$, it follows that

$$Z_i = \frac{\bar{X} - \mu}{\sigma/\sqrt{n}} \sim N(0, 1)$$

that is, a standard normal variable. Then from the normal distribution table we know that

$$\Pr(-1.96 \le Z_i \le 1.96) = 0.95$$

That is,

$$\Pr\left(-1.96 \le \frac{\bar{X} - \mu}{\sigma/\sqrt{n}} \le 1.96\right) = 0.95$$

which, on rearrangement, gives

$$\Pr\left[\bar{X} - 1.96\frac{\sigma}{\sqrt{n}} \le \mu \le \bar{X} + 1.96\frac{\sigma}{\sqrt{n}}\right] = 0.95$$

This is a 95% confidence interval for μ. Once this interval has been established, the test of the null hypothesis is simple. All that we have to do is to see whether $\mu = \mu^*$ lies in this interval. If it does, we may not reject the null hypothesis; if it does not, we may reject it.

Turning to our example, we have already established a 95% confidence interval for μ, which is

$$66.51 \le \mu \le 67.49$$

This interval obviously does not include $\mu = 69$. Therefore, we can reject the null hypothesis that the true μ is 69 with a 95% confidence coefficient. Geometrically, the situation is as depicted in Fig. A.12.

In the language of hypothesis testing, the confidence interval that we have established is called the **acceptance region** and the area(s) outside the acceptance region is (are) called the **critical region(s)**, or **region(s) of rejection** of the null hypothesis. The lower and upper limits of the acceptance region (which demarcate it from the rejection regions) are called the **critical values**. In this

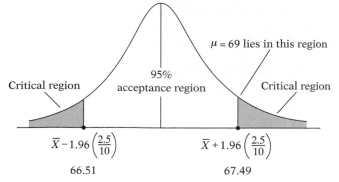

FIGURE A.12
95% confidence interval for μ.

language of hypothesis testing, if the hypothesized value falls inside the acceptance region, one may not reject the null hypothesis; otherwise one may reject it.

It is important to note that in deciding to reject or not reject H_0, we are likely to commit two types of errors: (1) we may reject H_0 when it is, in fact, true; this is called a **type I error** (thus, in the preceding example $\bar{X} = 67$ could have come from the population with a mean value of 69), or (2) we may not reject H_0 when it is, in fact, false; this is called a **type II error**. Therefore, a hypothesis test does not establish the value of true μ. It merely provides a means of deciding whether we may act as if $\mu = \mu^*$.

Type I and type II errors. Schematically, we have

Decision	State of Nature	
	H_0 **is true**	H_0 **is false**
Reject	Type I error	No error
Do not reject	No error	Type II error

Ideally, we would like to minimize both type I and type II errors. But unfortunately, for any given sample size, it is not possible to minimize both the errors simultaneously. The classical approach to this problem, embodied in the work of Neyman and Pearson, is to assume that a type I error is likely to be more serious in practice than a type II error. Therefore, one should try to keep the probability of committing a type I error at a fairly low level, such as 0.01 or 0.05, and then try to minimize the probability of having a type II error as much as possible.

In the literature the probability of type I error is designated as α and is called the **level of significance**, and the probability of type II error is designated as β. The probability of not committing a type II error, $1 - \beta$, is called the **power of the test**. The classical approach to hypothesis testing is to fix α at levels such as 0.01 or 0.05 and then try to maximize the power of the test;

that is, minimize β. How this is actually accomplished is somewhat involved, and we leave the subject for the references. Suffice it to note here that in practice the classical approach simply specifies the value of α without worrying too much about β.

The reader will by now realize that the confidence coefficient $(1 - \alpha)$ discussed earlier is simply one minus the probability of committing a type I error. Thus a 95% confidence coefficient means that we are prepared to accept at the most a 5% probability of committing a type I error—we do not want to reject the true hypothesis by more than 5 out of 100 times.

The p value, or exact level of significance. Instead of preselecting α at arbitrary levels, such as 1, 5, or 10 percent, one can obtain the **p (probability) value**, or **exact level of significance** of a test statistic. The p value is defined as *the lowest significance level at which a null hypothesis can be rejected.*

Suppose that in an application involving 20 df we obtain a t value of 3.552. Now the p value, or the exact probability, of obtaining a t value of 3.552 or greater can be seen from Table D.2 as 0.001 (one-tailed) or 0.002 (two-tailed). We can say that the observed t value of 3.552 is statistically significant at the 0.001 or 0.002 level, depending on whether we are using a one-tail or two-tail test.

Several statistical packages now routinely print out the p value of the estimated test statistics. Therefore, the reader is advised to give the p value wherever possible.

The Test of Significance Approach

Recall that

$$Z_i = \frac{\bar{X} - \mu}{\sigma/\sqrt{n}} \sim N(0, 1)$$

In any given application, $\bar{X}$ and n are known (or can be estimated), but the true μ and σ are not known. But if σ is specified and we assume (under H_0) that $\mu = \mu^*$, a specific numerical value, then Z_i can be directly computed and we can easily look at the normal distribution table to find the probability of obtaining the computed Z value. If this probability is small, say, less than 5 percent or 1 percent, we can reject the null hypothesis—if the hypothesis were true, the chances of obtaining the particular Z value should be very high. This is the general idea behind the test of significance approach to hypothesis testing. The key idea here is the test statistic (here the Z statistic) and its probability distribution under the assumed value $\mu = \mu^*$. Appropriately, in the present case, the test is known as the **Z test**, since we use the Z (standardized normal) value.

Returning to our example, if $\mu = \mu^* = 69$, the Z statistic becomes

$$
\begin{aligned}
Z &= \frac{\bar{X} - \mu^*}{\sigma/\sqrt{n}} \\
&= \frac{67 - 69}{2.5/\sqrt{100}} \\
&= -2/0.25 = -8
\end{aligned}
$$

If we look at the normal distribution table D.1, we see that the probability of obtaining such a Z value is extremely small. (*Note:* The probability of a Z value exceeding 3 or -3 is about 0.001. Therefore, the probability of Z exceeding 8 is even smaller.) Therefore, we can reject the null hypothesis that $\mu = 69$; given this value, our chance of obtaining $\bar{X}$ of 67 is extremely small. We therefore doubt that our sample came from the population with a mean value of 69. Diagrammatically, the situation is depicted in Fig. A.13.

In the language of test of significance, when we say that a test (statistic) is significant, we generally mean that we can reject the null hypothesis. And the test statistic is regarded as significant if the probability of our obtaining it is equal to or less than α, the probability of committing a type I error. Thus if $\alpha = 0.05$, we know that the probability of obtaining a Z value of -1.96 or 1.96 is 5 percent (or 2.5 percent in each tail of the standardized normal distribution). In our illustrative example Z was -8. Hence the probability of obtaining such a Z value is much smaller than 2.5 percent, well below our pre-specified probability of committing a type I error. That is why the computed value of $Z = -8$ is statistically significant; that is, we reject the null hypothesis that the true μ^* is 69. Of course, we reached the same conclusion using the confidence interval approach to hypothesis testing.

We now summarize the steps involved in testing a statistical hypothesis:

Step 1. State the null hypothesis H_0 and the alternative hypothesis H_1 (e.g., $H_0 : \mu = 69$ and $H_1 : \mu \neq 69$).

Step 2. Select the test statistic (e.g., $\bar{X}$).

Step 3. Determine the probability distribution of the test statistic (e.g., $\bar{X} \sim N(\mu, \sigma^2/n)$.

Step 4. Choose the level of significance (i.e., the probability of committing a type I error) α.

Step 5. Using the probability distribution of the test statistic, establish a $100(1 - \alpha)\,\%$ confidence interval. If the value of the parameter under the null hypothesis (e.g., $\mu = \mu^* = 69$) lies in this confidence region, the region of acceptance, do not reject the null hypothesis. But if it falls outside this interval (i.e., it falls into the region of rejection), you may reject the null hypothesis. Keep in mind that in not rejecting or

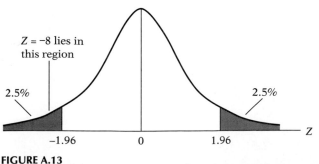

FIGURE A.13
The distribution of the Z statistic.

rejecting a null hypothesis you are taking a chance of being wrong α percent of the time.

REFERENCES

For the details of the material covered in this appendix, the reader may consult the following references:

Hoel, Paul G.: *Introduction to Mathematical Statistics*, 4th ed., John Wiley & Sons, New York, 1974. This book provides a fairly simple introduction to various aspects of mathematical statistics.

Freund, John E., and Ronald E. Walpole: *Mathematical Statistics*, 3rd ed., Prentice Hall, Englewood Cliffs,N.J., 1980. Another introductory textbook in mathematical statistics.

Mood, Alexander M., Franklin A. Graybill,and Duane C. Boes: *Introduction to the Theory of Statistics*, 3d ed. McGraw-Hill, New York, 1974. This is a comprehensive introduction to the theory of statistics but is somewhat more difficult than the preceding two textbooks.

Newbold, Paul: *Statistics for Business and Economics*, Prentice Hall, Englewood Cliffs, N.J., 1984. A comprehensive nonmathematical introduction to statistics with lots of worked-out problems.

This appendix offers the essentials of matrix algebra required to understand Chapter 9 and some of the material in Chapter 18. The discussion is nonrigorous, and no proofs are given. For proofs and further details, the reader may consult the references.

B.1 DEFINITIONS

Matrix

A matrix is a rectangular array of numbers or elements arranged in rows and columns. More precisely, a matrix of **order**, or **dimension**, M by N (written as $M \times N$) is a set of $M \times N$ elements arranged in M rows and N columns. Thus, letting boldface letters denote matrices, an $(M \times N)$ matrix $\mathbf{A}$ may be expressed as

$$\mathbf{A} = [a_{ij}] = \begin{bmatrix} a_{11} & a_{12} & a_{13} & \cdots & a_{1N} \\ a_{21} & a_{22} & a_{23} & \cdots & a_{2N} \\ \cdots\cdots\cdots\cdots\cdots\cdots\cdots\cdots\cdots \\ a_{M1} & a_{M2} & a_{M3} & \cdots & a_{MN} \end{bmatrix}$$

where a_{ij} is the element appearing in the ith row and the jth column of $\mathbf{A}$ and where $[a_{ij}]$ is a shorthand expression for the matrix $\mathbf{A}$ whose typical element is a_{ij}. The order, or dimension, of a matrix—that is, the number of rows and columns—is often written underneath the matrix for easy reference.

$$\mathop{\mathbf{A}}_{2\times 3} = \begin{bmatrix} 2 & 3 & 5 \\ 6 & 1 & 3 \end{bmatrix} \qquad \mathop{\mathbf{B}}_{3\times 3} = \begin{bmatrix} 1 & 5 & 7 \\ -1 & 0 & 4 \\ 8 & 9 & 11 \end{bmatrix}$$

Scalar. A scalar is a single (real) number. Alternatively, a scalar is a 1×1 matrix.

Column Vector

A matrix consisting of M rows and only one column is called a **column vector**. Letting the boldface lowercase letters denote vectors, an example of a column vector is

$$\mathop{\mathbf{x}}_{4\times 1} = \begin{bmatrix} 3 \\ 4 \\ 5 \\ 9 \end{bmatrix}$$

Row Vector

A matrix consisting of only one row and N columns is called a **row vector**.

$$\mathop{\mathbf{x}}_{1\times 4} = \begin{bmatrix} 1 & 2 & 5 & -4 \end{bmatrix} \qquad \mathop{\mathbf{y}}_{1\times 5} = \begin{bmatrix} 0 & 5 & -9 & 6 & 10 \end{bmatrix}$$

Transposition

The transpose of an $M \times N$ matrix $\mathbf{A}$, denoted by $\mathbf{A}'$ (read as $\mathbf{A}$ prime or $\mathbf{A}$ transpose) is an $N\times M$ matrix obtained by interchanging the rows and columns of $\mathbf{A}$; that is, the ith row of $\mathbf{A}$ becomes the ith column of $\mathbf{A}'$. For example,

$$\mathop{\mathbf{A}}_{3\times 2} = \begin{bmatrix} 4 & 5 \\ 3 & 1 \\ 5 & 0 \end{bmatrix} \qquad \mathop{\mathbf{A}'}_{2\times 3} = \begin{bmatrix} 4 & 3 & 5 \\ 5 & 1 & 0 \end{bmatrix}$$

Since a vector is a special type of matrix, the transpose of a row vector is a column vector and the transpose of a column vector is a row vector. Thus

$$\mathbf{x} = \begin{bmatrix} 4 \\ 5 \\ 6 \end{bmatrix} \quad \text{and} \quad \mathbf{x}' = \begin{bmatrix} 4 & 5 & 6 \end{bmatrix}$$

We shall follow the convention of indicating the row vectors by primes.

Submatrix

Given any $M \times N$ matrix $\mathbf{A}$, if all but r rows and s columns of $\mathbf{A}$ are deleted, the resulting matrix of order $r \times s$ is called a **submatrix** of $\mathbf{A}$. Thus, if

$$\mathop{\mathbf{A}}_{3\times 3} = \begin{bmatrix} 3 & 5 & 7 \\ 8 & 2 & 1 \\ 3 & 2 & 1 \end{bmatrix}$$

and we delete the third row and the third column of **A**, we obtain

$$\underset{2\times2}{\mathbf{B}} = \begin{bmatrix} 3 & 5 \\ 8 & 2 \end{bmatrix}$$

which is a submatrix of **A** whose order is 2×2.

B.2 TYPES OF MATRICES

Square Matrix

A matrix that has the same number of rows as columns is called a **square matrix**.

$$\mathbf{A} = \begin{bmatrix} 3 & 4 \\ 5 & 6 \end{bmatrix} \qquad \mathbf{B} = \begin{bmatrix} 3 & 5 & 8 \\ 7 & 3 & 1 \\ 4 & 5 & 0 \end{bmatrix}$$

Diagonal Matrix

A square matrix with at least one nonzero element on the main diagonal (running from the upper-left-hand corner to the lower-right-hand corner) and zeros elsewhere is called a **diagonal matrix**.

$$\underset{2\times2}{\mathbf{A}} = \begin{bmatrix} 2 & 0 \\ 0 & 3 \end{bmatrix} \qquad \underset{3\times3}{\mathbf{B}} = \begin{bmatrix} -2 & 0 & 0 \\ 0 & 5 & 0 \\ 0 & 0 & 1 \end{bmatrix}$$

Scalar Matrix

A diagonal matrix whose diagonal elements are all equal is called a **scalar matrix**. An example is the variance-covariance matrix of the population disturbance of the classical linear regression model given in equation (9.2.3), namely,

$$\text{var-cov}(\mathbf{u}) = \begin{bmatrix} \sigma^2 & 0 & 0 & 0 & 0 \\ 0 & \sigma^2 & 0 & 0 & 0 \\ 0 & 0 & \sigma^2 & 0 & 0 \\ 0 & 0 & 0 & \sigma^2 & 0 \\ 0 & 0 & 0 & 0 & \sigma^2 \end{bmatrix}$$

Identity, or Unit, Matrix

A diagonal matrix whose diagonal elements are all 1 is called an **identity**, or **unit, matrix** and is denoted by **I**. It is a special kind of scalar matrix.

$$\underset{3\times3}{\mathbf{I}} = \begin{bmatrix} 1 & 0 & 0 \\ 0 & 1 & 0 \\ 0 & 0 & 1 \end{bmatrix} \qquad \underset{4\times4}{\mathbf{I}} = \begin{bmatrix} 1 & 0 & 0 & 0 \\ 0 & 1 & 0 & 0 \\ 0 & 0 & 1 & 0 \\ 0 & 0 & 0 & 1 \end{bmatrix}$$

Symmetric Matrix

A square matrix whose elements above the main diagonal are mirror images of the elements below the main diagonal is called a **symmetric matrix**. Alternatively, a symmetric matrix is such that its transpose is equal to itself; that is, $\mathbf{A} = \mathbf{A}'$. That is, the element a_{ij} of $\mathbf{A}$ is equal to the element a_{ji} of $\mathbf{A}'$. An example is the variance-covariance matrix given in equation (9.2.2). Another example is the correlation matrix given in (9.5.1).

Null Matrix

A matrix whose elements are all zero is called a **null matrix** and is denoted by **0**.

Null Vector

A row or column vector whose elements are all zero is called a **null vector** and is also denoted by **0**.

Equal Matrices

Two matrices $\mathbf{A}$ and $\mathbf{B}$ are said to be equal if they are of the same order and their corresponding elements are equal; that is, $a_{ij} = b_{ij}$ for all i and j. For example, the matrices

$$\mathbf{A}_{3\times3} = \begin{bmatrix} 3 & 4 & 5 \\ 0 & -1 & 2 \\ 5 & 1 & 3 \end{bmatrix} \quad \text{and} \quad \mathbf{B}_{3\times3} = \begin{bmatrix} 3 & 4 & 5 \\ 0 & -1 & 2 \\ 5 & 1 & 3 \end{bmatrix}$$

are equal; that is $\mathbf{A} = \mathbf{B}$.

B.3 MATRIX OPERATIONS

Matrix Addition

Let $\mathbf{A} = [a_{ij}]$ and $\mathbf{B} = [b_{ij}]$. If $\mathbf{A}$ and $\mathbf{B}$ are of the same order, we define matrix addition as

$$\mathbf{A} + \mathbf{B} = \mathbf{C}$$

where $\mathbf{C}$ is of the same order as $\mathbf{A}$ and $\mathbf{B}$ and is obtained as $c_{ij} = a_{ij} + b_{ij}$ for all i and j; that is, $\mathbf{C}$ is obtained by adding the corresponding elements of $\mathbf{A}$ and $\mathbf{B}$. If such addition can be effected, $\mathbf{A}$ and $\mathbf{B}$ are said to be *conformable* for addition. For example, if

$$\mathbf{A} = \begin{bmatrix} 2 & 3 & 4 & 5 \\ 6 & 7 & 8 & 9 \end{bmatrix} \quad \text{and} \quad \mathbf{B} = \begin{bmatrix} 1 & 0 & -1 & 3 \\ -2 & 0 & 1 & 5 \end{bmatrix}$$

and $\mathbf{C} = \mathbf{A} + \mathbf{B}$, then

$$\mathbf{C} = \begin{bmatrix} 3 & 3 & 3 & 8 \\ 4 & 7 & 9 & 14 \end{bmatrix}$$

Matrix Subtraction

Matrix subtraction follows the same principle as matrix addition except that $\mathbf{C} = \mathbf{A} - \mathbf{B}$; that is, we subtract the elements of $\mathbf{B}$ from the corresponding elements of $\mathbf{A}$ to obtain $\mathbf{C}$, provided $\mathbf{A}$ and $\mathbf{B}$ are of the same order.

Scalar Multiplication

To multiply a matrix $\mathbf{A}$ by a scalar λ (a real number), we multiply each element of the matrix by λ:

$$\lambda\mathbf{A} = [\lambda a_{ij}]$$

For example, if $\lambda = 2$ and

$$\mathbf{A} = \begin{bmatrix} -3 & 5 \\ 8 & 7 \end{bmatrix}$$

then

$$\lambda\mathbf{A} = \begin{bmatrix} -6 & 10 \\ 16 & 14 \end{bmatrix}$$

Matrix Multiplication

Let $\mathbf{A}$ be $M \times N$ and $\mathbf{B}$ be $N \times P$. Then the product $\mathbf{AB}$ (in that order) is defined to be a new matrix $\mathbf{C}$ of order $M \times P$ such that

$$c_{ij} = \sum_{k=1}^{N} a_{ik}b_{kj} \qquad \begin{aligned} i &= 1, 2, \ldots, M \\ j &= 1, 2, \ldots, P \end{aligned}$$

That is, the element in the ith row and the jth column of $\mathbf{C}$ is obtained by multiplying the elements of the ith row of $\mathbf{A}$ by the corresponding elements of the jth column of $\mathbf{B}$ and summing over all terms; this is known as the *row by column* rule of multiplication. Thus, to obtain c_{11}, the element in the first row and the first column of $\mathbf{C}$, we multiply the elements in the first row of $\mathbf{A}$ by the corresponding elements in the first column of $\mathbf{B}$ and sum over all terms. Similarly, to obtain c_{12}, we multiply the elements in the first row of $\mathbf{A}$ by the corresponding elements in the second column of $\mathbf{B}$ and sum over all terms, and so on.

Note that for multiplication to exist, matrices $\mathbf{A}$ and $\mathbf{B}$ must be conformable with respect to multiplication; that is, the number of columns in $\mathbf{A}$ must be equal to the number of rows in $\mathbf{B}$. If, for example,

$$\mathbf{A}_{2\times3} = \begin{bmatrix} 3 & 4 & 7 \\ 5 & 6 & 1 \end{bmatrix} \quad \text{and} \quad \mathbf{B}_{3\times2} = \begin{bmatrix} 2 & 1 \\ 3 & 5 \\ 6 & 2 \end{bmatrix}$$

$$\mathbf{AB} = \mathbf{C}_{2\times2} = \begin{bmatrix} (3 \times 2) + (4 \times 3) + (7 \times 6) & (3 \times 1) + (4 \times 5) + (7 \times 2) \\ (5 \times 2) + (6 \times 3) + (1 \times 6) & (5 \times 1) + (6 \times 5) + (1 \times 2) \end{bmatrix}$$

$$= \begin{bmatrix} 60 & 37 \\ 34 & 37 \end{bmatrix}$$

But if

$$\mathop{\mathbf{A}}_{2\times3} = \begin{bmatrix} 3 & 4 & 7 \\ 5 & 6 & 1 \end{bmatrix} \quad \text{and} \quad \mathop{\mathbf{B}}_{2\times2} = \begin{bmatrix} 2 & 3 \\ 5 & 6 \end{bmatrix}$$

the product **AB** is not defined since **A** and **B** are not conformable with respect to multiplication.

Properties of Matrix Multiplication

1. Matrix multiplication is not necessarily *commutative*; that is, in general, **AB** $\neq$ **BA**. Therefore, the order in which the matrices are multiplied is very important. **AB** means that **A** is *postmultiplied* by **B** or **B** is *premultiplied* by **A**.
2. Even if **AB** and **BA** exist, the resulting matrices may not be of the same order. Thus, if **A** is $M \times N$ and **B** is $N \times M$, **AB** is $M \times M$ whereas **BA** is $N \times N$, hence of different order.
3. Even if **A** and **B** are both square matrices, so that **AB** and **BA** are both defined, the resulting matrices will not be necessarily equal. For example, if

$$\mathbf{A} = \begin{bmatrix} 4 & 7 \\ 3 & 2 \end{bmatrix} \quad \text{and} \quad \mathbf{B} = \begin{bmatrix} 1 & 5 \\ 6 & 8 \end{bmatrix}$$

then

$$\mathbf{AB} = \begin{bmatrix} 46 & 76 \\ 15 & 31 \end{bmatrix} \quad \text{and} \quad \mathbf{BA} = \begin{bmatrix} 19 & 17 \\ 48 & 58 \end{bmatrix}$$

and **AB** $\neq$ **BA**. An example of **AB** = **BA** is when both **A** and **B** are identity matrices.
4. A row vector postmultiplied by a column vector is a scalar. Thus, consider the ordinary least-squares residuals $\hat{u}_1, \hat{u}_2, \ldots, \hat{u}_n$. Letting **u** be a column vector and **u**′ be a row vector, we have

$$\mathbf{\hat{u}'\hat{u}} = [\hat{u}_1 \hat{u}_2 \hat{u}_3 \cdots \hat{u}_n] \begin{bmatrix} \hat{u}_1 \\ \hat{u}_2 \\ \hat{u}_3 \\ \vdots \\ \hat{u}_n \end{bmatrix}$$

$$= \hat{u}_1^2 + \hat{u}_2^2 + \hat{u}_3^2 + \cdots + \hat{u}_n'^2$$

$$= \sum \hat{u}_i^2 \quad \text{a scalar [see equation (9.3.5)]}$$

5. A column vector postmultiplied by a row vector is a matrix. As an example, consider the population disturbances of the classical linear regression model, namely, $u_1, u_2, \ldots, u_n$. Letting **u** be a column vector and **u**′ a row vector, we obtain

$$\mathbf{uu'} = \begin{bmatrix} u_1 \\ u_2 \\ u_3 \\ \vdots \\ u_n \end{bmatrix} [u_1 u_2 u_3 \cdots u_n]$$

$$
= \begin{bmatrix}
u_1^2 & u_1 u_2 & u_1 u_3 & \cdots & u_1 u_n \\
u_2 u_1 & u_2^2 & u_2 u_3 & \cdots & u_2 u_n \\
\multicolumn{5}{c}{\dotfill} \\
u_n u_1 & u_n u_2 & u_n u_3 & \cdots & u_n^2
\end{bmatrix}
$$

which is a matrix of order $n \times n$. Note that the preceding matrix is symmetrical.

6. A matrix postmultiplied by a column vector is a column vector.
7. A row vector postmultiplied by a matrix is a row vector.
8. Matrix multiplication is *associative*; that is, $(\mathbf{AB})\mathbf{C} = \mathbf{A}(\mathbf{BC})$, where $\mathbf{A}$ is $M \times N$, $\mathbf{B}$ is $N \times P$, and $\mathbf{C}$ is $P \times K$.
9. Matrix multiplication is distributive with respect to addition; that is, $\mathbf{A}(\mathbf{B} + \mathbf{C}) = \mathbf{AB} + \mathbf{AC}$ and $(\mathbf{B} + \mathbf{C})\mathbf{A} = \mathbf{BA} + \mathbf{CA}$.

Matrix Transposition

We have already defined the process of matrix transposition as interchanging the rows and the columns of a matrix (or a vector). We now state some of the properties of transposition.

1. The transpose of a transposed matrix is the original matrix itself. Thus, $(\mathbf{A}')' = \mathbf{A}$.
2. If $\mathbf{A}$ and $\mathbf{B}$ are conformable for addition, then $\mathbf{C} = \mathbf{A} + \mathbf{B}$ and $\mathbf{C}' = (\mathbf{A} + \mathbf{B})' = \mathbf{A}' + \mathbf{B}'$. That is, the transpose of the sum of two matrices is the sum of their transposes.
3. If $\mathbf{AB}$ is defined, then $(\mathbf{AB})' = \mathbf{B}'\mathbf{A}'$. That is, the transpose of the product of two matrices is the product of their transposes in the reverse order. This can be generalized: $(\mathbf{ABCD})' = \mathbf{D}'\mathbf{C}'\mathbf{B}'\mathbf{A}'$.
4. The transpose of an identity matrix $\mathbf{I}$ is the identity matrix itself; that is $\mathbf{I}' = \mathbf{I}$.
5. The transpose of a scalar is the scalar itself. Thus, if λ is a scalar, $\lambda' = \lambda$.
6. The transpose of $(\lambda \mathbf{A})'$ is $\lambda \mathbf{A}'$ where λ is a scalar. [*Note:* $(\lambda \mathbf{A})' = \mathbf{A}'\lambda' = \mathbf{A}'\lambda = \lambda \mathbf{A}'$.]
7. If $\mathbf{A}$ is a square matrix such that $\mathbf{A} = \mathbf{A}'$, then $\mathbf{A}$ is a symmetric matrix. (Cf. the definition of symmetric matrix given previously.)

Matrix Inversion

An inverse of a square matrix $\mathbf{A}$, denoted by $\mathbf{A}^{-1}$ (read $\mathbf{A}$ inverse), if it exists, is a unique square matrix such that

$$
\mathbf{AA}^{-1} = \mathbf{A}^{-1}\mathbf{A} = \mathbf{I}
$$

where $\mathbf{I}$ is an identity matrix whose order is the same as that of $\mathbf{A}$. For example

$$
\mathbf{A} = \begin{bmatrix} 2 & 4 \\ 6 & 8 \end{bmatrix} \qquad
\mathbf{A}^{-1} = \begin{bmatrix} -1 & \frac{1}{2} \\ \frac{6}{8} & -\frac{1}{4} \end{bmatrix} \qquad
\mathbf{AA}^{-1} = \begin{bmatrix} 1 & 0 \\ 0 & 1 \end{bmatrix} = \mathbf{I}
$$

We shall see how $\mathbf{A}^{-1}$ is computed after we study the topic of determinants. In the meantime note these properties of the inverse.

1. $(\mathbf{AB})^{-1} = \mathbf{B}^{-1}\mathbf{A}^{-1}$; that is, the inverse of the product of two matrices is the product of their inverses in the reverse order.
2. $(\mathbf{A}^{-1})' = (\mathbf{A}')^{-1}$; that is, the transpose of $\mathbf{A}$ inverse is the inverse of $\mathbf{A}$ transpose.

B.4   DETERMINANTS

To every square matrix, $\mathbf{A}$, there corresponds a number (scalar) known as the determinant of the matrix, which is denoted by $\det \mathbf{A}$ or by the symbol $|\,\mathbf{A}\,|$, where $|\ \ |$ means "the determinant of." Note that a matrix per se has no numerical value, but the determinant of a matrix is a number.

$$\mathbf{A} = \begin{bmatrix} 1 & 3 & -7 \\ 2 & 5 & 0 \\ 3 & 8 & 6 \end{bmatrix} \qquad |\mathbf{A}| = \begin{vmatrix} 1 & 3 & -7 \\ 2 & 5 & 0 \\ 3 & 8 & 6 \end{vmatrix}$$

The $|\,\mathbf{A}\,|$ in this example is called a determinant of order 3 because it is associated with a matrix of order 3×3.

Evaluation of a Determinant

The process of finding the value of a determinant is known as the *evaluation, expansion,* or *reduction* of the determinant. This is done by manipulating the entries of the matrix in a well-defined manner.

Evaluation of a 2×2 determinant. If

$$\mathbf{A} = \begin{bmatrix} a_{11} & a_{12} \\ a_{21} & a_{22} \end{bmatrix}$$

its determinant is evaluated as follows:

$$|\mathbf{A}| = \begin{vmatrix} a_{11} & a_{12} \\ a_{21} & a_{22} \end{vmatrix} = a_{11}a_{22} - a_{12}a_{21}$$

which is obtained by cross-multiplying the elements on the main diagonal and subtracting from it the cross-multiplication of the elements on the other diagonal of matrix $\mathbf{A}$, as indicated by the arrows.

Evaluation of a 3×3 determinant. If

$$\mathbf{A} = \begin{bmatrix} a_{11} & a_{12} & a_{13} \\ a_{21} & a_{22} & a_{23} \\ a_{31} & a_{32} & a_{33} \end{bmatrix}$$

then

$$|\mathbf{A}| = a_{11}a_{22}a_{33} - a_{11}a_{23}a_{32} + a_{12}a_{23}a_{31} - a_{12}a_{21}a_{33} + a_{13}a_{21}a_{32} - a_{13}a_{22}a_{31}$$

A careful examination of the evaluation of a 3 × 3 determinant shows:

1. Each term in the expansion of the determinant contains one and only one element from each row and each column.
2. The number of elements in each term is the same as the number of rows (or columns) in the matrix. Thus, a 2 × 2 determinant has two elements in each term of its expansion, a 3 × 3 determinant has three elements in each term of its expansion, and so on.
3. The terms in the expansion alternate in sign from + to −.
4. A 2 × 2 determinant has two terms in its expansion, and a 3 × 3 determinant has six terms in its expansion. The general rule is: The determinant of order $N \times N$ has $N! = N(N - 1)(N - 2) \cdots 3 \cdot 2 \cdot 1$ terms in its expansion, where $N!$ is read "N factorial." Following this rule, a determinant of order 5 × 5 will have $5 \cdot 4 \cdot 3 \cdot 2 \cdot 1 = 120$ terms in its expansion.[1]

Properties of Determinants

1. A matrix whose determinantal value is zero is called a **singular matrix**, whereas a matrix with a nonzero determinant is called a **nonsingular matrix**. The inverse of a matrix as defined before does not exist for a singular matrix.
2. If all the elements of any row of **A** are zero, its determinant is zero. Thus,

$$|\mathbf{A}| = \begin{vmatrix} 0 & 0 & 0 \\ 3 & 4 & 5 \\ 6 & 7 & 8 \end{vmatrix} = 0$$

3. $|\mathbf{A}'| = |\mathbf{A}|$; that is, the determinants of **A** and **A** transpose are the same.
4. Interchanging any two rows or any two columns of a matrix **A** changes the sign of $|\mathbf{A}|$.

Example. If

$$\mathbf{A} = \begin{bmatrix} 6 & 9 \\ -1 & 4 \end{bmatrix} \quad \text{and} \quad \mathbf{B} = \begin{bmatrix} -1 & 4 \\ 6 & 9 \end{bmatrix}$$

where **B** is obtained by interchanging the rows of **A**, then

$$|\mathbf{A}| = 24 - (-9) \quad \text{and} \quad |\mathbf{B}| = -9 - (24)$$
$$= 33 \qquad\qquad\qquad\qquad = -33$$

5. If every element of a row or a column of **A** is multiplied by a scalar λ, then $|\mathbf{A}|$ is multiplied by λ.

Example. If

$$\lambda = 5 \quad \text{and} \quad \mathbf{A} = \begin{bmatrix} 5 & -8 \\ 2 & 4 \end{bmatrix}$$

---

[1]To evaluate the determinant of an $N \times N$ matrix, **A**, see the references.

and we multiply the first row of **A** by 5 to obtain

$$\mathbf{B} = \begin{bmatrix} 25 & -40 \\ 2 & 4 \end{bmatrix}$$

it can be seen that $|\mathbf{A}| = 36$ and $|\mathbf{B}| = 180$, which is $5|\mathbf{A}|$.

6. If two rows or columns of a matrix are identical, its determinant is zero.
7. If one row or a column of a matrix is a multiple of another row or column of that matrix, its determinant is zero. Thus, if

$$\mathbf{A} = \begin{bmatrix} 4 & 8 \\ 2 & 4 \end{bmatrix}$$

where the first row of **A** is twice its second row, $|\mathbf{A}| = 0$. More generally, if any row (column) of a matrix is a linear combination of other rows (columns), its determinant is zero.
8. $|\mathbf{AB}| = |\mathbf{A}||\mathbf{B}|$; that is, the determinant of the product of two matrices is the product of their (individual) determinants.

Rank of a Matrix

The rank of a matrix is the order of the largest square submatrix whose determinant is not zero.

Example

$$\mathbf{A} = \begin{bmatrix} 3 & 6 & 6 \\ 0 & 4 & 5 \\ 3 & 2 & 1 \end{bmatrix}$$

It can be seen that $|\mathbf{A}| = 0$. In other words, **A** is a singular matrix. Hence although its order is 3×3, its rank is less than 3. Actually, it is 2, because we can find a 2×2 submatrix whose determinant is not zero. For example, if we delete the first row and the first column of **A**, we obtain

$$\mathbf{B} = \begin{bmatrix} 4 & 5 \\ 2 & 1 \end{bmatrix}$$

whose determinant is -6, which is nonzero. Hence the rank of **A** is 2. As noted previously, the inverse of a singular matrix does not exist. Therefore, for an $N \times N$ matrix **A**, its rank must be N for its inverse to exist; if it is less than N, **A** is singular.

Minor

If the ith row and jth column of an $N \times N$ matrix **A** are deleted, the determinant of the resulting submatrix is called the **minor** of the element a_{ij} (the element at the intersection of the ith row and the jth column) and is denoted by $|\mathbf{M}_{ij}|$.

Example

$$\mathbf{A} = \begin{bmatrix} a_{11} & a_{12} & a_{13} \\ a_{21} & a_{22} & a_{23} \\ a_{31} & a_{32} & a_{33} \end{bmatrix}$$

The minor of a_{11} is

$$| \mathbf{M_{11}} | = \begin{vmatrix} a_{22} & a_{23} \\ a_{32} & a_{33} \end{vmatrix} = a_{22}a_{33} - a_{23}a_{32}$$

Similarly, the minor of a_{21} is

$$| \mathbf{M_{21}} | = \begin{vmatrix} a_{12} & a_{13} \\ a_{32} & a_{33} \end{vmatrix} = a_{12}a_{33} - a_{13}a_{32}$$

The minors of other elements of **A** can be found similarly.

Cofactor

The cofactor of the element a_{ij} of an $N \times N$ matrix **A**, denoted by c_{ij}, is defined as

$$c_{ij} = (-1)^{i+j} | \mathbf{M_{ij}} |$$

In other words, a cofactor is a *signed* minor, the sign being positive if $i + j$ is even and being negative if $i + j$ is odd. Thus, the cofactor of the element a_{11} of the 3×3 matrix **A** given previously is $a_{22}a_{33} - a_{23}a_{32}$, whereas the cofactor of the element a_{21} is $-(a_{12}a_{33} - a_{13}a_{32})$ since the sum of the subscripts 2 and 1 is 3, which is an odd number.

Cofactor matrix. Replacing the elements a_{ij} of a matrix **A** by their cofactors, we obtain a matrix known as the **cofactor matrix** of **A**, denoted by (cof **A**).

Adjoint matrix. The adjoint matrix, written as (adj **A**), is the transpose of the cofactor matrix; that is (adj **A**) = (cof **A**)′.

B.5   FINDING THE INVERSE OF A SQUARE MATRIX

If **A** is square and nonsingular (that is, $| \mathbf{A} | \neq 0$), its inverse $\mathbf{A}^{-1}$ can be found as follows:

$$\mathbf{A}^{-1} = \frac{1}{| \mathbf{A} |}(\text{adj } \mathbf{A})$$

The steps involved in the computation are as follows:

1. Find the determinant of **A**. If it is nonzero, proceed to step 2.
2. Replace each element a_{ij} of **A** by its cofactor to obtain the cofactor matrix.
3. Transpose the cofactor matrix to obtain the adjoint matrix.
4. Divide each element of the adjoint matrix by $| \mathbf{A} |$.

Example. Find the inverse of the matrix

$$\mathbf{A} = \begin{bmatrix} 1 & 2 & 3 \\ 5 & 7 & 4 \\ 2 & 1 & 3 \end{bmatrix}$$

Step 1. We first find the determinant of the matrix. Applying the rules of expanding a 3×3 determinant given previously, we obtain $|\mathbf{A}| = -24$.

Step 2. We now obtain the cofactor matrix, say, $\mathbf{C}$:

$$\mathbf{C} = \begin{bmatrix} \begin{vmatrix} 7 & 4 \\ 1 & 3 \end{vmatrix} & -\begin{vmatrix} 5 & 4 \\ 2 & 3 \end{vmatrix} & \begin{vmatrix} 5 & 7 \\ 2 & 1 \end{vmatrix} \\[2mm] -\begin{vmatrix} 2 & 3 \\ 1 & 3 \end{vmatrix} & \begin{vmatrix} 1 & 3 \\ 2 & 3 \end{vmatrix} & -\begin{vmatrix} 1 & 2 \\ 2 & 1 \end{vmatrix} \\[2mm] \begin{vmatrix} 2 & 3 \\ 7 & 4 \end{vmatrix} & -\begin{vmatrix} 1 & 3 \\ 5 & 4 \end{vmatrix} & \begin{vmatrix} 1 & 2 \\ 5 & 7 \end{vmatrix} \end{bmatrix}$$

$$= \begin{bmatrix} 17 & -7 & -9 \\ -3 & -3 & 3 \\ -13 & 11 & -3 \end{bmatrix}$$

Step 3. Transposing the preceding cofactor matrix, we obtain the following adjoint matrix:

$$(\text{adj } \mathbf{A}) = \begin{bmatrix} 17 & -3 & -13 \\ -7 & -3 & 11 \\ -9 & 3 & -3 \end{bmatrix}$$

Step 4. We now divide the elements of $(\text{adj } \mathbf{A})$ by the determinantal value of -24 to obtain

$$\mathbf{A}^{-1} = -\frac{1}{24} \begin{bmatrix} 17 & -3 & -13 \\ -7 & -3 & 11 \\ -9 & 3 & -3 \end{bmatrix}$$

$$= \begin{bmatrix} -\frac{17}{24} & \frac{3}{24} & \frac{13}{24} \\[2mm] \frac{7}{24} & \frac{3}{24} & -\frac{11}{24} \\[2mm] \frac{9}{24} & -\frac{3}{24} & \frac{3}{24} \end{bmatrix}$$

It can be readily verified that

$$\mathbf{A}\mathbf{A}^{-1} = \begin{bmatrix} 1 & 0 & 0 \\ 0 & 1 & 0 \\ 0 & 0 & 1 \end{bmatrix}$$

which is an identity matrix. The reader should verify that for the illustrative example given in Chapter 9 the inverse of the $\mathbf{X}'\mathbf{X}$ matrix is as shown in equation (9.10.5).

B.6 MATRIX DIFFERENTIATION

To follow the material in Section 9A.2, we need some rules regarding matrix differentiation.

Rule 1. If $\mathbf{a}' = [a_1 \quad a_2 \quad \cdots \quad a_n]$ is a row vector of numbers, and

$$\mathbf{x} = \begin{bmatrix} x_1 \\ x_2 \\ \vdots \\ x_n \end{bmatrix}$$

is a column vector of the variables $x_1, x_2, \ldots, x_n$, then

$$\frac{\partial(\mathbf{a}'\mathbf{x})}{\partial \mathbf{x}} = \mathbf{a} = \begin{bmatrix} a_1 \\ a_2 \\ \vdots \\ a_n \end{bmatrix}$$

Rule 2. Consider the matrix $\mathbf{x}'\mathbf{A}\mathbf{x}$ such that

$$\mathbf{x}'\mathbf{A}\mathbf{x} = \begin{bmatrix} x_1 & x_2 & \cdots & x_n \end{bmatrix} \begin{bmatrix} a_{11} & a_{12} & \cdots & a_{1n} \\ a_{21} & a_{22} & \cdots & a_{2n} \\ \cdots\cdots\cdots\cdots\cdots\cdots \\ a_{n1} & a_{n2} & & a_{nn} \end{bmatrix} \begin{bmatrix} x_1 \\ x_2 \\ \vdots \\ x_n \end{bmatrix}$$

Then

$$\frac{\partial(\mathbf{x}'\mathbf{A}\mathbf{x})}{\partial \mathbf{x}} = 2\mathbf{A}\mathbf{x}$$

which is a column vector of n elements, or

$$\frac{\partial(\mathbf{x}'\mathbf{A}\mathbf{x})}{\partial \mathbf{x}} = 2\mathbf{x}'\mathbf{A}$$

which is a row vector of n elements.

REFERENCES

Chiang, Alpha C.: *Fundamental Methods of Mathematical Economics*, 3d ed., McGraw-Hill, New York, 1984, chaps. 4 and 5. This is an elementary discussion.

Hadley, G.: *Linear Algebra*, Addison-Wesley, Reading, Mass., 1961. This is an advanced discussion.

APPENDIX
C

A LIST OF SELECTED ECONOMETRIC SOFTWARE PACKAGES

Here is a list of some well-known statistical and econometric software packages that can handle most of the econometric techniques discussed in this text. Student versions of some of these packages are available at substantially reduced rates. Some of these packages are also available on mainframe computers. Since these packages are updated regularly, the use is advised to consult the vendor regarding the latest version.

IBM-PC AND COMPATIBLES

BMDP/PC	BMDP Statistical Software Inc., 1440 Sepulveda Blvd., Suite 316, Los Angeles, CA 90025. (213) 479-7799.
DATA-FIT	Oxford Electronic Publishing Company, Oxford University Press, Walton Street, Oxford OX2 6DP, U.K.
ESP	Economic Software Package, 76 Bedford St., Suite 33, Lexington, MA 02173. (617) 861-8852.
ET	William H. Greene, Stern Graduate School of Business, New York University, 100 Trinity Place, New York, NY. (212) 285-6164.
GAUSS	Aptech Systems Inc., 26250 196th Place SE, Kent, WA 98042. (206) 631-6679.
LIMDEP	William H. Greene, Stern Graduate School of Business, New York University, 100 Trinity Place, New York, NY. (212) 285-6164.

MATLAB	Math Works Inc., 20 N. Main St., Sherborn, MA 01770. (617) 653-1415.
MICRO TSP	Quantitative Micro Software, 4521 Campus Drive, Suite 336, Irvine, CA 92715. (714) 856-3368.
MINITAB	Minitab, 3081 Enterprise Drive, State College, PA 16801. (814) 238-3280
PC-GIVE	University of Oxford, Institute of Economics and Statistics, St. Cross Building, Manor Rd., Oxford OX1 3UL. U.K.
PC-TSP	TSP International, P.O. Box 61015, Palo Alto, CA 94306. (415) 326-1927.
RATS	VAR Econometrics, P.O. Box 1818, Evanston, IL 60624-1818. (708) 864-8772.
SAS/STAT	SAS Institute Inc., P.O. Box 8000, SAS Circle, Cary, NC 27511-8000. (919) 467-8000.
SHAZAM	Kenneth J. White, Department of Economics, University of British Columbia, Vancouver, BC V6T 1Y2. Canada. (604) 228-5062.
SORITEC	The Soritec Group Inc., P.O. Box 2939, 8136 Old Keene Mill Road, Springfield, VA 22152. (703) 569-1400.
SPSS/PC+	SPSS Inc., 444 N. Michigan Ave., Chicago, IL 60611. (312) 329-3600.
STATA	Computing Resource Center, 10801 National Blvd., 3rd Floor, Los Angeles, CA 90064. (800) STATAPC.
STATGRAPHICS	STSC Inc., 2115 E. Jefferson St., Rockville, MD 20852. (800) 592-0050.
STATPRO	Penton Software Inc., 420 Lexington Ave., Suite 2846, New York, NY 10017. (800) 211-3414.
SYSTAT	Systat Inc., 1800 Sherman Ave., Evanston, IL 60201. (708) 864-5670.

APPLE MACINTOSH

MATLAB	Math Works Inc., 20 N. Main St., Sherborn, MA 01770. (617) 653-1415.
PC-TSP	TSP International, P.O. Box 61015, Palo Alto, CA 94306. (415) 326-1927.
RATS	VAR Econometrics, P.O. Box 1818, Evanston, IL 60624-1818. (708) 864-8772.
SHAZAM	Kenneth J. White, Department of Economics, University of British Columbia, Vancouver, BC V6T 1Y2. Canada. (602) 228-5062.

APPENDIX
D

STATISTICAL TABLES

TABLE D.1
Areas under the standardized normal distribution

Example

$\Pr(0 \leq Z \leq 1.96) = 0.4750$

$\Pr(Z \geq 1.96) = 0.5 - 0.4750 = 0.025$

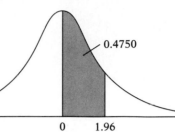

Z	.00	.01	.02	.03	.04	.05	.06	.07	.08	.09
0.0	.0000	.0040	.0080	.0120	.0160	.0199	.0239	.0279	.0319	.0359
0.1	.0398	.0438	.0478	.0517	.0557	.0596	.0636	.0675	.0714	.0753
0.2	.0793	.0832	.0871	.0910	.0948	.0987	.1026	.1064	.1103	.1141
0.3	.1179	.1217	.1255	.1293	.1331	.1368	.1406	.1443	.1480	.1517
0.4	.1554	.1591	.1628	.1664	.1700	.1736	.1772	.1808	.1844	.1879
0.5	.1915	.1950	.1985	.2019	.2054	.2088	.2123	.2157	.2190	.2224
0.6	.2257	.2291	.2324	.2357	.2389	.2422	.2454	.2486	.2517	.2549
0.7	.2580	.2611	.2642	.2673	.2704	.2734	.2764	.2794	.2823	.2852
0.8	.2881	.2910	.2939	.2967	.2995	.3023	.3051	.3078	.3106	.3133
0.9	.3159	.3186	.3212	.3238	.3264	.3289	.3315	.3340	.3365	.3389
1.0	.3413	.3438	.3461	.3485	.3508	.3531	.3554	.3577	.3599	.3621
1.1	.3643	.3665	.3686	.3708	.3729	.3749	.3770	.3790	.3810	.3830
1.2	.3849	.3869	.3888	.3907	.3925	.3944	.3962	.3980	.3997	.4015
1.3	.4032	.4049	.4066	.4082	.4099	.4115	.4131	.4147	.4162	.4177
1.4	.4192	.4207	.4222	.4236	.4251	.4265	.4279	.4292	.4306	.4319
1.5	.4332	.4345	.4357	.4370	.4382	.4394	.4406	.4418	.4429	.4441
1.6	.4452	.4463	.4474	.4484	.4495	.4505	.4515	.4525	.4535	.4545
1.7	.4454	.4564	.4573	.4582	.4591	.4599	.4608	.4616	.4625	.4633
1.8	.4641	.4649	.4656	.4664	.4671	.4678	.4686	.4693	.4699	.4706
1.9	.4713	.4719	.4726	.4732	.4738	.4744	.4750	.4756	.4761	.4767
2.0	.4772	.4778	.4783	.4788	.4793	.4798	.4803	.4808	.4812	.4817
2.1	.4821	.4826	.4830	.4834	.4838	.4842	.4846	.4850	.4854	.4857
2.2	.4861	.4864	.4868	.4871	.4875	.4878	.4881	.4884	.4887	.4890
2.3	.4893	.4896	.4898	.4901	.4904	.4906	.4909	.4911	.4913	.4916
2.4	.4918	.4920	.4922	.4925	.4927	.4929	.4931	.4932	.4934	.4936
2.5	.4938	.4940	.4941	.4943	.4945	.4946	.4948	.4949	.4951	.4952
2.6	.4953	.4955	.4956	.4957	.4959	.4960	.4961	.4962	.4963	.4964
2.7	.4965	.4966	.4967	.4968	.4969	.4970	.4971	.4972	.4973	.4974
2.8	.4974	.4975	.4976	.4977	.4977	.4978	.4979	.4979	.4980	.4981
2.9	.4981	.4982	.4982	.4983	.4984	.4984	.4985	.4985	.4986	.4986
3.0	.4987	.4987	.4987	.4988	.4988	.4989	.4989	.4989	.4990	.4990

Note: This table gives the area in the right-hand tail of the distribution (i.e., $Z \geq 0$). But since the normal distribution is symmetrical about $Z = 0$, the area in the left-hand tail is the same as the area in the corresponding right-hand tail. For example. $P(-1.96 \leq Z \leq 0) = 0.4750$. Therefore, $P(-1.96 \leq Z \leq 1.96) = 2(0.4750) = 0.95$.

TABLE D.2
Percentage points of the *t* distribution

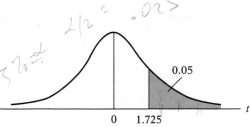

Example

$\Pr(t > 2.086) = 0.025$

$\Pr(t > 1.725) = 0.05$ for df = 20

$\Pr(|t| > 1.725) = 0.10$

Pr df	0.25 0.50	0.10 0.20	0.05 0.10	0.025 0.05	0.01 0.02	0.005 0.010	0.001 0.002
1	1.000	3.078	6.314	12.706	31.821	63.657	318.31
2	0.816	1.886	2.920	4.303	6.965	9.925	22.327
3	0.765	1.638	2.353	3.182	4.541	5.841	10.214
4	0.741	1.533	2.132	2.776	3.747	4.604	7.173
5	0.727	1.476	2.015	2.571	3.365	4.032	5.893
6	0.718	1.440	1.943	2.447	3.143	3.707	5.208
7	0.711	1.415	1.895	2.365	2.998	3.499	4.785
8	0.706	1.397	1.860	2.306	2.896	3.355	4.501
9	0.703	1.383	1.833	2.262	2.821	3.250	4.297
10	0.700	1.372	1.812	2.228	2.764	3.169	4.144
11	0.697	1.363	1.796	2.201	2.718	3.106	4.025
12	0.695	1.356	1.782	2.179	2.681	3.055	3.930
13	0.694	1.350	1.771	2.160	2.650	3.012	3.852
14	0.692	1.345	1.761	2.145	2.624	2.977	3.787
15	0.691	1.341	1.753	2.131	2.602	2.947	3.733
16	0.690	1.337	1.746	2.120	2.583	2.921	3.686
17	0.689	1.333	1.740	2.110	2.567	2.898	3.646
18	0.688	1.330	1.734	2.101	2.552	2.878	3.610
19	0.688	1.328	1.729	2.093	2.539	2.861	3.579
20	0.687	1.325	1.725	2.086	2.528	2.845	3.552
21	0.686	1.323	1.721	2.080	2.518	2.831	3.527
22	0.686	1.321	1.717	2.074	2.508	2.819	3.505
23	0.685	1.319	1.714	2.069	2.500	2.807	3.485
24	0.685	1.318	1.711	2.064	2.492	2.797	3.467
25	0.684	1.316	1.708	2.060	2.485	2.787	3.450
26	0.684	1.315	1.706	2.056	2.479	2.779	3.435
27	0.684	1.314	1.703	2.052	2.473	2.771	3.421
28	0.683	1.313	1.701	2.048	2.467	2.763	3.408
29	0.683	1.311	1.699	2.045	2.462	2.756	3.396
30	0.683	1.310	1.697	2.042	2.457	2.750	3.385
40	0.681	1.303	1.684	2.021	2.423	2.704	3.307
60	0.679	1.296	1.671	2.000	2.390	2.660	3.232
120	0.677	1.289	1.658	1.980	2.358	2.617	3.160
∞	0.674	1.282	1.645	1.960	2.326	2.576	3.090

Note: The smaller probability shown at the head of each column is the area in one tail; the larger probability is the area in both tails.

Source: From E. S. Pearson and H. O. Hartley, eds., *Biometrika Tables for Statisticians*, vol. 1, 3d ed., table 12, Cambridge University Press, New York, 1966. Reproduced by permission of the editors and trustees of *Biometrika*.

TABLE D.3
Upper percentage points of the F distribution

Example

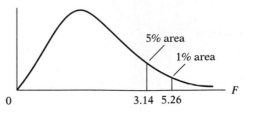

$\Pr(F > 1.59) = 0.25$
$\Pr(F > 2.42) = 0.10$ for df $N_1 = 10$
$\Pr(F > 3.14) = 0.05$ and $N_2 = 9$
$\Pr(F > 5.26) = 0.01$

df for denominator N_2	Pr	df for numerator N_1											
		1	2	3	4	5	6	7	8	9	10	11	12
1	.25	5.83	7.50	8.20	8.58	8.82	8.98	9.10	9.19	9.26	9.32	9.36	9.41
	.10	39.9	49.5	53.6	55.8	57.2	58.2	58.9	59.4	59.9	60.2	60.5	60.7
	.05	161	200	216	225	230	234	237	239	241	242	243	244
2	.25	2.57	3.00	3.15	3.23	3.28	3.31	3.34	3.35	3.37	3.38	3.39	3.39
	.10	8.53	9.00	9.16	9.24	9.29	9.33	9.35	9.37	9.38	9.39	9.40	9.41
	.05	18.5	19.0	19.2	19.2	19.3	19.3	19.4	19.4	19.4	19.4	19.4	19.4
	.01	98.5	99.0	99.2	99.2	99.3	99.3	99.4	99.4	99.4	99.4	99.4	99.4
3	.25	2.02	2.28	2.36	2.39	2.41	2.42	2.43	2.44	2.44	2.44	2.45	2.45
	.10	5.54	5.46	5.39	5.34	5.31	5.28	5.27	5.25	5.24	5.23	5.22	5.22
	.05	10.1	9.55	9.28	9.12	9.01	8.94	8.89	8.85	8.81	8.79	8.76	8.74
	.01	34.1	30.8	29.5	28.7	28.2	27.9	27.7	27.5	27.3	27.2	27.1	27.1
4	.25	1.81	2.00	2.05	2.06	2.07	2.08	2.08	2.08	2.08	2.08	2.08	2.08
	.10	4.54	4.32	4.19	4.11	4.05	4.01	3.98	3.95	3.94	3.92	3.91	3.90
	.05	7.71	6.94	6.59	6.39	6.26	6.16	6.09	6.04	6.00	5.96	5.94	5.91
	.01	21.2	18.0	16.7	16.0	15.5	15.2	15.0	14.8	14.7	14.5	14.4	14.4
5	.25	1.69	1.85	1.88	1.89	1.89	1.89	1.89	1.89	1.89	1.89	1.89	1.89
	.10	4.06	3.78	3.62	3.52	3.45	3.40	3.37	3.34	3.32	3.30	3.28	3.27
	.05	6.61	5.79	5.41	5.19	5.05	4.95	4.88	4.82	4.77	4.74	4.71	4.68
	.01	16.3	13.3	12.1	11.4	11.0	10.7	10.5	10.3	10.2	10.1	9.96	9.89
6	.25	1.62	1.76	1.78	1.79	1.79	1.78	1.78	1.78	1.77	1.77	1.77	1.77
	.10	3.78	3.46	3.29	3.18	3.11	3.05	3.01	2.98	2.96	2.94	2.92	2.90
	.05	5.99	5.14	4.76	4.53	4.39	4.28	4.21	4.15	4.10	4.06	4.03	4.00
	.01	13.7	10.9	9.78	9.15	8.75	8.47	8.26	8.10	7.98	7.87	7.79	7.72
7	.25	1.57	1.70	1.72	1.72	1.71	1.71	1.70	1.70	1.69	1.69	1.69	1.68
	.10	3.59	3.26	3.07	2.96	2.88	2.83	2.78	2.75	2.72	2.70	2.68	2.67
	.05	5.59	4.74	4.35	4.12	3.97	3.87	3.79	3.73	3.68	3.64	3.60	3.57
	.01	12.2	9.55	8.45	7.85	7.46	7.19	6.99	6.84	6.72	6.62	6.54	6.47
8	.25	1.54	1.66	1.67	1.66	1.66	1.65	1.64	1.64	1.63	1.63	1.63	1.62
	.10	3.46	3.11	2.92	2.81	2.73	2.67	2.62	2.59	2.56	2.54	2.52	2.50
	.05	5.32	4.46	4.07	3.84	3.69	3.58	3.50	3.44	3.39	3.35	3.31	3.28
	.01	11.3	8.65	7.59	7.01	6.63	6.37	6.18	6.03	5.91	5.81	5.73	5.67
9	.25	1.51	1.62	1.63	1.63	1.62	1.61	1.60	1.60	1.59	1.59	1.58	1.58
	.10	3.36	3.01	2.81	2.69	2.61	2.55	2.51	2.47	2.44	2.42	2.40	2.38
	.05	5.12	4.26	3.86	3.63	3.48	3.37	3.29	3.23	3.18	3.14	3.10	3.07
	.01	10.6	8.02	6.99	6.42	6.06	5.80	5.61	5.47	5.35	5.26	5.18	5.11

Source: From E. S. Pearson and H. O. Hartley, eds., *Biometrika Tables for Statisticians*, vol. 1, 3d ed., table 18, Cambridge University Press, New York, 1966. Reproduced by permission of the editors and trustees of *Biometrika*.

15	20	24	30	40	50	60	100	120	200	500	∞	Pr	df for denominator N_2
9.49	9.58	9.63	9.67	9.71	9.74	9.76	9.78	9.80	9.82	9.84	9.85	.25	
61.2	61.7	62.0	62.3	62.5	62.7	62.8	63.0	63.1	63.2	63.3	63.3	.10	1
246	248	249	250	251	252	252	253	253	254	254	254	.05	
3.41	3.43	3.43	3.44	3.45	3.45	3.46	3.47	3.47	3.48	3.48	3.48	.25	
9.42	9.44	9.45	9.46	9.47	9.47	9.47	9.48	9.48	9.49	9.49	9.49	.10	2
19.4	19.4	19.5	19.5	19.5	19.5	19.5	19.5	19.5	19.5	19.5	19.5	.05	
99.4	99.4	99.5	99.5	99.5	99.5	99.5	99.5	99.5	99.5	99.5	99.5	.01	
2.46	2.46	2.46	2.47	2.47	2.47	2.47	2.47	2.47	2.47	2.47	2.47	.25	
5.20	5.18	5.18	5.17	5.16	5.15	5.15	5.14	5.14	5.14	5.14	5.13	.10	3
8.70	8.66	8.64	8.62	8.59	8.58	8.57	8.55	8.55	8.54	8.53	8.53	.05	
26.9	26.7	26.6	26.5	26.4	26.4	26.3	26.2	26.2	26.2	26.1	26.1	.01	
2.08	2.08	2.08	2.08	2.08	2.08	2.08	2.08	2.08	2.08	2.08	2.08	.25	
3.87	3.84	3.83	3.82	3.80	3.80	3.79	3.78	3.78	3.77	3.76	3.76	.10	4
5.86	5.80	5.77	5.75	5.72	5.70	5.69	5.66	5.66	5.65	5.64	5.63	.05	
14.2	14.0	13.9	13.8	13.7	13.7	13.7	13.6	13.6	13.5	13.5	13.5	.01	
1.89	1.88	1.88	1.88	1.88	1.88	1.87	1.87	1.87	1.87	1.87	1.87	.25	
3.24	3.21	3.19	3.17	3.16	3.15	3.14	3.13	3.12	3.12	3.11	3.10	.10	5
4.62	4.56	4.53	4.50	4.46	4.44	4.43	4.41	4.40	4.39	4.37	4.36	.05	
9.72	9.55	9.47	9.38	9.29	9.24	9.20	9.13	9.11	9.08	9.04	9.02	.01	
1.76	1.76	1.75	1.75	1.75	1.75	1.74	1.74	1.74	1.74	1.74	1.74	.25	
2.87	2.84	2.82	2.80	2.78	2.77	2.76	2.75	2.74	2.73	2.73	2.72	.10	6
3.94	3.87	3.84	3.81	3.77	3.75	3.74	3.71	3.70	3.69	3.68	3.67	.05	
7.56	7.40	7.31	7.23	7.14	7.09	7.06	6.99	6.97	6.93	6.90	6.88	.01	
1.68	1.67	1.67	1.66	1.66	1.66	1.65	1.65	1.65	1.65	1.65	1.65	.25	
2.63	2.59	2.58	2.56	2.54	2.52	2.51	2.50	2.49	2.48	2.48	2.47	.10	7
3.51	3.44	3.41	3.38	3.34	3.32	3.30	3.27	3.27	3.25	3.24	3.23	.05	
6.31	6.16	6.07	5.99	5.91	5.86	5.82	5.75	5.74	5.70	5.67	5.65	.01	
1.62	1.61	1.60	1.60	1.59	1.59	1.59	1.58	1.58	1.58	1.58	1.58	.25	
2.46	2.42	2.40	2.38	2.36	2.35	2.34	2.32	2.32	2.31	2.30	2.29	.10	8
3.22	3.15	3.12	3.08	3.04	2.02	3.01	2.97	2.97	2.95	2.94	2.93	.05	
5.52	5.36	5.28	5.20	5.12	5.07	5.03	4.96	4.95	4.91	4.88	4.86	.01	
1.57	1.56	1.56	1.55	1.55	1.54	1.54	1.53	1.53	1.53	1.53	1.53	.25	
2.34	2.30	2.28	2.25	2.23	2.22	2.21	2.19	2.18	2.17	2.17	2.16	.10	9
3.01	2.94	2.90	2.86	2.83	2.80	2.79	2.76	2.75	2.73	2.72	2.71	.05	
4.96	4.81	4.73	4.65	4.57	4.52	4.48	4.42	4.40	4.36	4.33	4.31	.01	

df for numerator N_1

TABLE D.3
Upper percentage points of the *F* distribution (*continued*)

df for denominator N_2	Pr	1	2	3	4	5	6	7	8	9	10	11	12
						df for numerator N_1							
10	.25	1.49	1.60	1.60	1.59	1.59	1.58	1.57	1.56	1.56	1.55	1.55	1.54
	.10	3.29	2.92	2.73	2.61	2.52	2.46	2.41	2.38	2.35	2.32	2.30	2.28
	.05	4.96	4.10	3.71	3.48	3.33	3.22	3.14	3.07	3.02	2.98	2.94	2.91
	.01	10.0	7.56	6.55	5.99	5.64	5.39	5.20	5.06	4.94	4.85	4.77	4.71
11	.25	1.47	1.58	1.58	1.57	1.56	1.55	1.54	1.53	1.53	1.52	1.52	1.51
	.10	3.23	2.86	2.66	2.54	2.45	2.39	2.34	2.30	2.27	2.25	2.23	2.21
	.05	4.84	3.98	3.59	3.36	3.20	3.09	3.01	2.95	2.90	2.85	2.82	2.79
	.01	9.65	7.21	6.22	5.67	5.32	5.07	4.89	4.74	4.63	4.54	4.46	4.40
12	.25	1.46	1.56	1.56	1.55	1.54	1.53	1.52	1.51	1.51	1.50	1.50	1.49
	.10	3.18	2.81	2.61	2.48	2.39	2.33	2.28	2.24	2.21	2.19	2.17	2.15
	.05	4.75	3.89	3.49	3.26	3.11	3.00	2.91	2.85	2.80	2.75	2.72	2.69
	.01	9.33	6.93	5.95	5.41	5.06	4.82	4.64	4.50	4.39	4.30	4.22	4.16
13	.25	1.45	1.55	1.55	1.53	1.52	1.51	1.50	1.49	1.49	1.48	1.47	1.47
	.10	3.14	2.76	2.56	2.43	2.35	2.28	2.23	2.20	2.16	2.14	2.12	2.10
	.05	4.67	3.81	3.41	3.18	3.03	2.92	2.83	2.77	2.71	2.67	2.63	2.60
	.01	9.07	6.70	5.74	5.21	4.86	4.62	4.44	4.30	4.19	4.10	4.02	3.96
14	.25	1.44	1.53	1.53	1.52	1.51	1.50	1.49	1.48	1.47	1.46	1.46	1.45
	.10	3.10	2.73	2.52	2.39	2.31	2.24	2.19	2.15	2.12	2.10	2.08	2.05
	.05	4.60	3.74	3.34	3.11	2.96	2.85	2.76	2.70	2.65	2.60	2.57	2.53
	.01	8.86	6.51	5.56	5.04	4.69	4.46	4.28	4.14	4.03	3.94	3.86	3.80
15	.25	1.43	1.52	1.52	1.51	1.49	1.48	1.47	1.46	1.46	1.45	1.44	1.44
	.10	3.07	2.70	2.49	2.36	2.27	2.21	2.16	2.12	2.09	2.06	2.04	2.02
	.05	4.54	3.68	3.29	3.06	2.90	2.79	2.71	2.64	2.59	2.54	2.51	2.48
	.01	8.68	6.36	5.42	4.89	4.56	4.32	4.14	4.00	3.89	3.80	3.73	3.67
16	.25	1.42	1.51	1.51	1.50	1.48	1.47	1.46	1.45	1.44	1.44	1.44	1.43
	.10	3.05	2.67	2.46	2.33	2.24	2.18	2.13	2.09	2.06	2.03	2.01	1.99
	.05	4.49	3.63	3.24	3.01	2.85	2.74	2.66	2.59	2.54	2.49	2.46	2.42
	.01	8.53	6.23	5.29	4.77	4.44	4.20	4.03	3.89	3.78	3.69	3.62	3.55
17	.25	1.42	1.51	1.50	1.49	1.47	1.46	1.45	1.44	1.43	1.43	1.42	1.41
	.10	3.03	2.64	2.44	2.31	2.22	2.15	2.10	2.06	2.03	2.00	1.98	1.96
	.05	4.45	3.59	3.20	2.96	2.81	2.70	2.61	2.55	2.49	2.45	2.41	2.38
	.01	8.40	6.11	5.18	4.67	4.34	4.10	3.93	3.79	3.68	3.59	3.52	3.46
18	.25	1.41	1.50	1.49	1.48	1.46	1.45	1.44	1.43	1.42	1.42	1.41	1.40
	.10	3.01	2.62	2.42	2.29	2.20	2.13	2.08	2.04	2.00	1.98	1.96	1.93
	.05	4.41	3.55	3.16	2.93	2.77	2.66	2.58	2.51	2.46	2.41	2.37	2.34
	.01	8.29	6.01	5.09	4.58	4.25	4.01	3.84	3.71	3.60	3.51	3.43	3.37
19	.25	1.41	1.49	1.49	1.47	1.46	1.44	1.43	1.42	1.41	1.41	1.40	1.40
	.10	2.99	2.61	2.40	2.27	2.18	2.11	2.06	2.02	1.98	1.96	1.94	1.91
	.05	4.38	3.52	3.13	2.90	2.74	2.63	2.54	2.48	2.42	2.38	2.34	2.31
	.01	8.18	5.93	5.01	4.50	4.17	3.94	3.77	3.63	3.52	3.43	3.36	3.30
20	.25	1.40	1.49	1.48	1.46	1.45	1.44	1.43	1.42	1.41	1.40	1.39	1.39
	.10	2.97	2.59	2.38	2.25	2.16	2.09	2.04	2.00	1.96	1.94	1.92	1.89
	.05	4.35	3.49	3.10	2.87	2.71	2.60	2.51	2.45	2.39	2.35	2.31	2.28
	.01	8.10	5.85	4.94	4.43	4.10	3.87	3.70	3.56	3.46	3.37	3.29	3.23

				df for numerator N_1									df for denominator N_2
15	20	24	30	40	50	60	100	120	200	500	∞	Pr	
1.53	1.52	1.52	1.51	1.51	1.50	1.50	1.49	1.49	1.49	1.48	1.48	.25	
2.24	2.20	2.18	2.16	2.13	2.12	2.11	2.09	2.08	2.07	2.06	2.06	.10	10
2.85	2.77	2.74	2.70	2.66	2.64	2.62	2.59	2.58	2.56	2.55	2.54	.05	
4.56	4.41	4.33	4.25	4.17	4.12	4.08	4.01	4.00	3.96	3.93	3.91	.01	
1.50	1.49	1.49	1.48	1.47	1.47	1.47	1.46	1.46	1.46	1.45	1.45	.25	
2.17	2.12	2.10	2.08	2.05	2.04	2.03	2.00	2.00	1.99	1.98	1.97	.10	11
2.72	2.65	2.61	2.57	2.53	2.51	2.49	2.46	2.45	2.43	2.42	2.40	.05	
4.25	4.10	4.02	3.94	3.86	3.81	3.78	3.71	3.69	3.66	3.62	3.60	.01	
1.48	1.47	1.46	1.45	1.45	1.44	1.44	1.43	1.43	1.43	1.42	1.42	.25	
2.10	2.06	2.04	2.01	1.99	1.97	1.96	1.94	1.93	1.92	1.91	1.90	.10	12
2.62	2.54	2.51	2.47	2.43	2.40	2.38	2.35	2.34	2.32	2.31	2.30	.05	
4.01	3.86	3.78	3.70	3.62	3.57	3.54	3.47	3.45	3.41	3.38	3.36	.01	
1.46	1.45	1.44	1.43	1.42	1.42	1.42	1.41	1.41	1.40	1.40	1.40	.25	
2.05	2.01	1.98	1.96	1.93	1.92	1.90	1.88	1.88	1.86	1.85	1.85	.10	13
2.53	2.46	2.42	2.38	2.34	2.31	2.30	2.26	2.25	2.23	2.22	2.21	.05	
3.82	3.66	3.59	3.51	3.43	3.38	3.34	3.27	3.25	3.22	3.19	3.17	.01	
1.44	1.43	1.42	1.41	1.41	1.40	1.40	1.39	1.39	1.39	1.38	1.38	.25	
2.01	1.96	1.94	1.91	1.89	1.87	1.86	1.83	1.83	1.82	1.80	1.80	.10	14
2.46	2.39	2.35	2.31	2.27	2.24	2.22	2.19	2.18	2.16	2.14	2.13	.05	
3.66	3.51	3.43	3.35	3.27	3.22	3.18	3.11	3.09	3.06	3.03	3.00	.01	
1.43	1.41	1.41	1.40	1.39	1.39	1.38	1.38	1.37	1.37	1.36	1.36	.25	
1.97	1.92	1.90	1.87	1.85	1.83	1.82	1.79	1.79	1.77	1.76	1.76	.10	15
2.40	2.33	2.29	2.25	2.20	2.18	2.16	2.12	2.11	2.10	2.08	2.07	.05	
3.52	3.37	3.29	3.21	3.13	3.08	3.05	2.98	2.96	2.92	2.89	2.87	.01	
1.41	1.40	1.39	1.38	1.37	1.37	1.36	1.36	1.35	1.35	1.34	1.34	.25	
1.94	1.89	1.87	1.84	1.81	1.79	1.78	1.76	1.75	1.74	1.73	1.72	.10	16
2.35	2.28	2.24	2.19	2.15	2.12	2.11	2.07	2.06	2.04	2.02	2.01	.05	
3.41	3.26	3.18	3.10	3.02	2.97	2.93	2.86	2.84	2.81	2.78	2.75	.01	
1.40	1.39	1.38	1.37	1.36	1.35	1.35	1.34	1.34	1.34	1.33	1.33	.25	
1.91	1.86	1.84	1.81	1.78	1.76	1.75	1.73	1.72	1.71	1.69	1.69	.10	17
2.31	2.23	2.19	2.15	2.10	2.08	2.06	2.02	2.01	1.99	1.97	1.96	.05	
3.31	3.16	3.08	3.00	2.92	2.87	2.83	2.76	2.75	2.71	2.68	2.65	.01	
1.39	1.38	1.37	1.36	1.35	1.34	1.34	1.33	1.33	1.32	1.32	1.32	.25	
1.89	1.84	1.81	1.78	1.75	1.74	1.72	1.70	1.69	1.68	1.67	1.66	.10	18
2.27	2.19	2.15	2.11	2.06	2.04	2.02	1.98	1.97	1.95	1.93	1.92	.05	
3.23	3.08	3.00	2.92	2.84	2.78	2.75	2.68	2.66	2.62	2.59	2.57	.01	
1.38	1.37	1.36	1.35	1.34	1.33	1.33	1.32	1.32	1.31	1.31	1.30	.25	
1.86	1.81	1.79	1.76	1.73	1.71	1.70	1.67	1.67	1.65	1.64	1.63	.10	19
2.23	2.16	2.11	2.07	2.03	2.00	1.98	1.94	1.93	1.91	1.89	1.88	.05	
3.15	3.00	2.92	2.84	2.76	2.71	2.67	2.60	2.58	2.55	2.51	2.49	.01	
1.37	1.36	1.35	1.34	1.33	1.33	1.32	1.31	1.31	1.30	1.30	1.29	.25	
1.84	1.79	1.77	1.74	1.71	1.69	1.68	1.65	1.64	1.63	1.62	1.61	.10	20
2.20	2.12	2.08	2.04	1.99	1.97	1.95	1.91	1.90	1.88	1.86	1.84	.05	
3.09	2.94	2.86	2.78	2.69	2.64	2.61	2.54	2.52	2.48	2.44	2.42	01	

TABLE D.3
Upper percentage points of the *F* distribution (*continued*)

df for denom- inator N_2	Pr	1	2	3	4	5	6	7	8	9	10	11	12
						df for numerator N_1							
22	.25	1.40	1.48	1.47	1.45	1.44	1.42	1.41	1.40	1.39	1.39	1.38	1.37
	.10	2.95	2.56	2.35	2.22	2.13	2.06	2.01	1.97	1.93	1.90	1.88	1.86
	.05	4.30	3.44	3.05	2.82	2.66	2.55	2.46	2.40	2.34	2.30	2.26	2.23
	.01	7.95	5.72	4.82	4.31	3.99	3.76	3.59	3.45	3.35	3.26	3.18	3.12
24	.25	1.39	1.47	1.46	1.44	1.43	1.41	1.40	1.39	1.38	1.38	1.37	1.36
	.10	2.93	2.54	2.33	2.19	2.10	2.04	1.98	1.94	1.91	1.88	1.85	1.83
	.05	4.26	3.40	3.01	2.78	2.62	2.51	2.42	2.36	2.30	2.25	2.21	2.18
	.01	7.82	5.61	4.72	4.22	3.90	3.67	3.50	3.36	3.26	3.17	3.09	3.03
26	.25	1.38	1.46	1.45	1.44	1.42	1.41	1.39	1.38	1.37	1.37	1.36	1.35
	.10	2.91	2.52	2.31	2.17	2.08	2.01	1.96	1.92	1.88	1.86	1.84	1.81
	.05	4.23	3.37	2.98	2.74	2.59	2.47	2.39	2.32	2.27	2.22	2.18	2.15
	.01	7.72	5.53	4.64	4.14	3.82	3.59	3.42	3.29	3.18	3.09	3.02	2.96
28	.25	1.38	1.46	1.45	1.43	1.41	1.40	1.39	1.38	1.37	1.36	1.35	1.34
	.10	2.89	2.50	2.29	2.16	2.06	2.00	1.94	1.90	1.87	1.84	1.81	1.79
	.05	4.20	3.34	2.95	2.71	2.56	2.45	2.36	2.29	2.24	2.19	2.15	2.12
	.01	7.64	5.45	4.57	4.07	3.75	3.53	3.36	3.23	3.12	3.03	2.96	2.90
30	.25	1.38	1.45	1.44	1.42	1.41	1.39	1.38	1.37	1.36	1.35	1.35	1.34
	.10	2.88	2.49	2.28	2.14	2.05	1.98	1.93	1.88	1.85	1.82	1.79	1.77
	.05	4.17	3.32	2.92	2.69	2.53	2.42	2.33	2.27	2.21	2.16	2.13	2.09
	.01	7.56	5.39	4.51	4.02	3.70	3.47	3.30	3.17	3.07	2.98	2.91	2.84
40	.25	1.36	1.44	1.42	1.40	1.39	1.37	1.36	1.35	1.34	1.33	1.32	1.31
	.10	2.84	2.44	2.23	2.09	2.00	1.93	1.87	1.83	1.79	1.76	1.73	1.71
	.05	4.08	3.23	2.84	2.61	2.45	2.34	2.25	2.18	2.12	2.08	2.04	2.00
	.01	7.31	5.18	4.31	3.83	3.51	3.29	3.12	2.99	2.89	2.80	2.73	2.66
60	.25	1.35	1.42	1.41	1.38	1.37	1.35	1.33	1.32	1.31	1.30	1.29	1.29
	.10	2.79	2.39	2.18	2.04	1.95	1.87	1.82	1.77	1.74	1.71	1.68	1.66
	.05	4.00	3.15	2.76	2.53	2.37	2.25	2.17	2.10	2.04	1.99	1.95	1.92
	.01	7.08	4.98	4.13	3.65	3.34	3.12	2.95	2.82	2.72	2.63	2.56	2.50
120	.25	1.34	1.40	1.39	1.37	1.35	1.33	1.31	1.30	1.29	1.28	1.27	1.26
	.10	2.75	2.35	2.13	1.99	1.90	1.82	1.77	1.72	1.68	1.65	1.62	1.60
	.05	3.92	3.07	2.68	2.45	2.29	2.17	2.09	2.02	1.96	1.91	1.87	1.83
	.01	6.85	4.79	3.95	3.48	3.17	2.96	2.79	2.66	2.56	2.47	2.40	2.34
200	.25	1.33	1.39	1.38	1.36	1.34	1.32	1.31	1.29	1.28	1.27	1.26	1.25
	.10	2.73	2.33	2.11	1.97	1.88	1.80	1.75	1.70	1.66	1.63	1.60	1.57
	.05	3.89	3.04	2.65	2.42	2.26	2.14	2.06	1.98	1.93	1.88	1.84	1.80
	.01	6.76	4.71	3.88	3.41	3.11	2.89	2.73	2.60	2.50	2.41	2.34	2.27
∞	.25	1.32	1.39	1.37	1.35	1.33	1.31	1.29	1.28	1.27	1.25	1.24	1.24
	.10	2.71	2.30	2.08	1.94	1.85	1.77	1.72	1.67	1.63	1.60	1.57	1.55
	.05	3.84	3.00	2.60	2.37	2.21	2.10	2.01	1.94	1.88	1.83	1.79	1.75
	.01	6.63	4.61	3.78	3.32	3.02	2.80	2.64	2.51	2.41	2.32	2.25	2.18

				df for numerator N_1									df for denominator N_2
15	20	24	30	40	50	60	100	120	200	500	∞	Pr	
1.36	1.34	1.33	1.32	1.31	1.31	1.30	1.30	1.30	1.29	1.29	1.28	.25	
1.81	1.76	1.73	1.70	1.67	1.65	1.64	1.61	1.60	1.59	1.58	1.57	.10	22
2.15	2.07	2.03	1.98	1.94	1.91	1.89	1.85	1.84	1.82	1.80	1.78	.05	
2.98	2.83	2.75	2.67	2.58	2.53	2.50	2.42	2.40	2.36	2.33	2.31	.01	
1.35	1.33	1.32	1.31	1.30	1.29	1.29	1.28	1.28	1.27	1.27	1.26	.25	
1.78	1.73	1.70	1.67	1.64	1.62	1.61	1.58	1.57	1.56	1.54	1.53	.10	24
2.11	2.03	1.98	1.94	1.89	1.86	1.84	1.80	1.79	1.77	1.75	1.73	.05	
2.89	2.74	2.66	2.58	2.49	2.44	2.40	2.33	2.31	2.27	2.24	2.21	.01	
1.34	1.32	1.31	1.30	1.29	1.28	1.28	1.26	1.26	1.26	1.25	1.25	.25	
1.76	1.71	1.68	1.65	1.61	1.59	1.58	1.55	1.54	1.53	1.51	1.50	.10	26
2.07	1.99	1.95	1.90	1.85	1.82	1.80	1.76	1.75	1.73	1.71	1.69	.05	
2.81	2.66	2.58	2.50	2.42	2.36	2.33	2.25	2.23	2.19	2.16	2.13	.01	
1.33	1.31	1.30	1.29	1.28	1.27	1.27	1.26	1.25	1.25	1.24	1.24	.25	
1.74	1.69	1.66	1.63	1.59	1.57	1.56	1.53	1.52	1.50	1.49	1.48	.10	28
2.04	1.96	1.91	1.87	1.82	1.79	1.77	1.73	1.71	1.69	1.67	1.65	.05	
2.75	2.60	2.52	2.44	2.35	2.30	2.26	2.19	2.17	2.13	2.09	2.06	.01	
1.32	1.30	1.29	1.28	1.27	1.26	1.26	1.25	1.24	1.24	1.23	1.23	.25	
1.72	1.67	1.64	1.61	1.57	1.55	1.54	1.51	1.50	1.48	1.47	1.46	.10	30
2.01	1.93	1.89	1.84	1.79	1.76	1.74	1.70	1.68	1.66	1.64	1.62	.05	
2.70	2.55	2.47	2.39	2.30	2.25	2.21	2.13	2.11	2.07	2.03	2.01	.01	
1.30	1.28	1.26	1.25	1.24	1.23	1.22	1.21	1.21	1.20	1.19	1.19	.25	
1.66	1.61	1.57	1.54	1.51	1.48	1.47	1.43	1.42	1.41	1.39	1.38	.10	40
1.92	1.84	1.79	1.74	1.69	1.66	1.64	1.59	1.58	1.55	1.53	1.51	.05	
2.52	2.37	2.29	2.20	2.11	2.06	2.02	1.94	1.92	1.87	1.83	1.80	.01	
1.27	1.25	1.24	1.22	1.21	1.20	1.19	1.17	1.17	1.16	1.15	1.15	.25	
1.60	1.54	1.51	1.48	1.44	1.41	1.40	1.36	1.35	1.33	1.31	1.29	.10	60
1.84	1.75	1.70	1.65	1.59	1.56	1.53	1.48	1.47	1.44	1.41	1.39	.05	
2.35	2.20	2.12	2.03	1.94	1.88	1.84	1.75	1.73	1.68	1.63	1.60	.01	
1.24	1.22	1.21	1.19	1.18	1.17	1.16	1.14	1.13	1.12	1.11	1.10	.25	
1.55	1.48	1.45	1.41	1.37	1.34	1.32	1.27	1.26	1.24	1.21	1.19	.10	120
1.75	1.66	1.61	1.55	1.50	1.46	1.43	1.37	1.35	1.32	1.28	1.25	.05	
2.19	2.03	1.95	1.86	1.76	1.70	1.66	1.56	1.53	1.48	1.42	1.38	.01	
1.23	1.21	1.20	1.18	1.16	1.14	1.12	1.11	1.10	1.09	1.08	1.06	.25	
1.52	1.46	1.42	1.38	1.34	1.31	1.28	1.24	1.22	1.20	1.17	1.14	.10	200
1.72	1.62	1.57	1.52	1.46	1.41	1.39	1.32	1.29	1.26	1.22	1.19	.05	
2.13	1.97	1.89	1.79	1.69	1.63	1.58	1.48	1.44	1.39	1.33	1.28	.01	
1.22	1.19	1.18	1.16	1.14	1.13	1.12	1.09	1.08	1.07	1.04	1.00	.25	
1.49	1.42	1.38	1.34	1.30	1.26	1.24	1.18	1.17	1.13	1.08	1.00	.10	∞
1.67	1.57	1.52	1.46	1.39	1.35	1.32	1.24	1.22	1.17	1.11	1.00	.05	
2.04	1.88	1.79	1.70	1.59	1.52	1.47	1.36	1.32	1.25	1.15	1.00	.01	

TABLE D.4
Upper percentage points of the χ^2 distribution

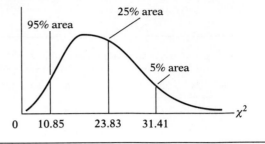

Example

Pr $(\chi^2 > 10.85) = 0.95$

Pr $(\chi^2 > 23.83) = 0.25$ for df $= 20$

Pr $(\chi^2 > 31.41) = 0.05$

Degrees of Freedom \ Pr	.995	.990	.975	.950	.900
1	392704×10^{-10}	157088×10^{-9}	982069×10^{-9}	393214×10^{-8}	.0157908
2	.0100251	.0201007	.0506356	.102587	.210720
3	.0717212	.114832	.215795	.351846	.584375
4	.206990	.297110	.484419	.710721	1.063623
5	.411740	.554300	.831211	1.145476	1.61031
6	.675727	.872085	1.237347	1.63539	2.20413
7	.989265	1.239043	1.68987	2.16735	2.83311
8	1.344419	1.646482	2.17973	2.73264	3.48954
9	1.734926	2.087912	2.70039	3.32511	4.16816
10	2.15585	2.55821	3.24697	3.94030	4.86518
11	2.60321	3.05347	3.81575	4.57481	5.57779
12	3.07382	3.57056	4.40379	5.22603	6.30380
13	3.56503	4.10691	5.00874	5.89186	7.04150
14	4.07468	4.66043	5.62872	6.57063	7.78953
15	4.60094	5.22935	6.26214	7.26094	8.54675
16	5.14224	5.81221	6.90766	7.96164	9.31223
17	5.69724	6.40776	7.56418	8.67176	10.0852
18	6.26481	7.01491	8.23075	9.39046	10.8649
19	6.84398	7.63273	8.90655	10.1170	11.6509
20	7.43386	8.26040	9.59083	10.8508	12.4426
21	8.03366	8.89720	10.28293	11.5913	13.2396
22	8.64272	9.54249	10.9823	12.3380	14.0415
23	9.26042	10.19567	11.6885	13.0905	14.8479
24	9.88623	10.8564	12.4011	13.8484	15.6587
25	10.5197	11.5240	13.1197	14.6114	16.4734
26	11.1603	12.1981	13.8439	15.3791	17.2919
27	11.8076	12.8786	14.5733	16.1513	18.1138
28	12.4613	13.5648	15.3079	16.9279	18.9392
29	13.1211	14.2565	16.0471	17.7083	19.7677
30	13.7867	14.9535	16.7908	18.4926	20.5992
40	20.7065	22.1643	24.4331	26.5093	29.0505
50	27.9907	29.7067	32.3574	34.7642	37.6886
60	35.5346	37.4848	40.4817	43.1879	46.4589
70	43.2752	45.4418	48.7576	51.7393	55.3290
80	51.1720	53.5400	57.1532	60.3915	64.2778
90	59.1963	61.7541	65.6466	69.1260	73.2912
100*	67.3276	70.0648	74.2219	77.9295	82.3581

*For df greater than 100 the expression $\sqrt{2\chi^2} - \sqrt{(2k-1)} = Z$ follows the standardized normal distribution, where k represents the degrees of freedom.

.750	.500	.250	.100	.050	.025	.010	.005
.1015308	.454937	1.32330	2.70554	3.84146	5.02389	6.63490	7.87944
.575364	1.38629	2.77259	4.60517	5.99147	7.37776	9.21034	10.5966
1.212534	2.36597	4.10835	6.25139	7.81473	9.34840	11.3449	12.8381
1.92255	3.35670	5.38527	7.77944	9.48773	11.1433	13.2767	14.8602
2.67460	4.35146	6.62568	9.23635	11.0705	12.8325	15.0863	16.7496
3.45460	5.34812	7.84080	10.6446	12.5916	14.4494	16.8119	18.5476
4.25485	6.34581	9.03715	12.0170	14.0671	16.0128	18.4753	20.2777
5.07064	7.34412	10.2188	13.3616	15.5073	17.5346	20.0902	21.9550
5.89883	8.34283	11.3887	14.6837	16.9190	19.0228	21.6660	23.5893
6.73720	9.34182	12.5489	15.9871	18.3070	20.4831	23.2093	25.1882
7.58412	10.3410	13.7007	17.2750	19.6751	21.9200	24.7250	26.7569
8.43842	11.3403	14.8454	18.5494	21.0261	23.3367	26.2170	28.2995
9.29906	12.3398	15.9839	19.8119	22.3621	24.7356	27.6883	29.8194
10.1653	13.3393	17.1170	21.0642	23.6848	26.1190	29.1413	31.3193
11.0365	14.3389	18.2451	22.3072	24.9958	27.4884	30.5779	32.8013
11.9122	15.3385	19.3688	23.5418	26.2962	28.8454	31.9999	34.2672
12.7919	16.3381	20.4887	24.7690	27.5871	30.1910	33.4087	35.7185
13.6753	17.3379	21.6049	25.9894	28.8693	31.5264	34.8053	37.1564
14.5620	18.3376	22.7178	27.2036	30.1435	32.8523	36.1908	38.5822
15.4518	19.3374	23.8277	28.4120	31.4104	34.1696	37.5662	39.9968
16.3444	20.3372	24.9348	29.6151	32.6705	35.4789	38.9321	41.4010
17.2396	21.3370	26.0393	30.8133	33.9244	36.7807	40.2894	42.7956
18.1373	22.3369	27.1413	32.0069	35.1725	38.0757	41.6384	44.1813
19.0372	23.3367	28.2412	33.1963	36.4151	39.3641	42.9798	45.5585
19.9393	24.3366	29.3389	34.3816	37.6525	40.6465	44.3141	46.9278
20.8434	25.3364	30.4345	35.5631	38.8852	41.9232	45.6417	48.2899
21.7494	26.3363	31.5284	36.7412	40.1133	43.1944	46.9630	49.6449
22.6572	27.3363	32.6205	37.9159	41.3372	44.4607	48.2782	50.9933
23.5666	28.3362	33.7109	39.0875	42.5569	45.7222	49.5879	52.3356
24.4776	29.3360	34.7998	40.2560	43.7729	46.9792	50.8922	53.6720
33.6603	39.3354	45.6160	51.8050	55.7585	59.3417	63.6907	66.7659
42.9421	49.3349	56.3336	63.1671	67.5048	71.4202	76.1539	79.4900
52.2938	59.3347	66.9814	74.3970	79.0819	83.2976	88.3794	91.9517
61.6983	69.3344	77.5766	85.5271	90.5312	95.0231	100.425	104.215
71.1445	79.3343	88.1303	96.5782	101.879	106.629	112.329	116.321
80.6247	89.3342	98.6499	107.565	113.145	118.136	124.116	128.299
90.1332	99.3341	109.141	118.498	124.342	129.561	135.807	140.169

TABLE D.5a
Durbin-Watson d statistic: Significance points of d_L and d_U at 0.05 level of significance

	$k'=1$		$k'=2$		$k'=3$		$k'=4$		$k'=5$		$k'=6$		$k'=7$		$k'=8$		$k'=9$		$k'=10$	
n	d_L	d_U	d_L	d_U	d_L	d_U	d_L	d_U	d_L	d_U	d_L	d_U	d_L	d_U	d_L	d_U	d_L	d_U	d_L	d_U
6	0.610	1.400	—	—	—	—	—	—	—	—	—	—	—	—	—	—	—	—	—	—
7	0.700	1.356	0.467	1.896	—	—	—	—	—	—	—	—	—	—	—	—	—	—	—	—
8	0.763	1.332	0.559	1.777	0.368	2.287	—	—	—	—	—	—	—	—	—	—	—	—	—	—
9	0.824	1.320	0.629	1.699	0.455	2.128	0.296	2.588	—	—	—	—	—	—	—	—	—	—	—	—
10	0.879	1.320	0.697	1.641	0.525	2.016	0.376	2.414	0.243	2.822	—	—	—	—	—	—	—	—	—	—
11	0.927	1.324	0.658	1.604	0.595	1.928	0.444	2.283	0.316	2.645	0.203	3.005	—	—	—	—	—	—	—	—
12	0.971	1.331	0.812	1.579	0.658	1.864	0.512	2.177	0.379	2.506	0.268	2.832	0.171	3.149	—	—	—	—	—	—
13	1.010	1.340	0.861	1.562	0.715	1.816	0.574	2.094	0.445	2.390	0.328	2.692	0.230	2.985	0.147	3.266	—	—	—	—
14	1.045	1.350	0.905	1.551	0.767	1.779	0.632	2.030	0.505	2.296	0.389	2.572	0.286	2.848	0.200	3.111	0.127	3.360	—	—
15	1.077	1.361	0.946	1.543	0.814	1.750	0.685	1.977	0.562	2.220	0.447	2.472	0.343	2.727	0.251	2.979	0.175	3.216	0.111	3.438
16	1.106	1.371	0.982	1.539	0.857	1.728	0.734	1.935	0.615	2.157	0.502	2.388	0.398	2.624	0.304	2.860	0.222	3.090	0.155	3.304
17	1.133	1.381	1.015	1.536	0.897	1.710	0.779	1.900	0.664	2.104	0.554	2.318	0.451	2.537	0.356	2.757	0.272	2.975	0.198	3.184
18	1.158	1.391	1.046	1.535	0.933	1.696	0.820	1.872	0.710	2.060	0.603	2.257	0.502	2.461	0.407	2.667	0.321	2.873	0.244	3.073
19	1.180	1.401	1.074	1.536	0.967	1.685	0.859	1.848	0.752	2.023	0.649	2.206	0.549	2.396	0.456	2.589	0.369	2.783	0.290	2.974
20	1.201	1.411	1.100	1.537	0.998	1.676	0.894	1.828	0.792	1.991	0.692	2.162	0.595	2.339	0.502	2.521	0.416	2.704	0.336	2.885
21	1.221	1.420	1.125	1.538	1.026	1.669	0.927	1.812	0.829	1.964	0.732	2.124	0.637	2.290	0.547	2.460	0.461	2.633	0.380	2.806
22	1.239	1.429	1.147	1.541	1.053	1.664	0.958	1.797	0.863	1.940	0.769	2.090	0.677	2.246	0.588	2.407	0.504	2.571	0.424	2.734
23	1.257	1.437	1.168	1.543	1.078	1.660	0.986	1.785	0.895	1.920	0.804	2.061	0.715	2.208	0.628	2.360	0.545	2.514	0.465	2.670
24	1.273	1.446	1.188	1.546	1.101	1.656	1.013	1.775	0.925	1.902	0.837	2.035	0.751	2.174	0.666	2.318	0.584	2.464	0.506	2.613
25	1.288	1.454	1.206	1.550	1.123	1.654	1.038	1.767	0.953	1.886	0.868	2.012	0.784	2.144	0.702	2.280	0.621	2.419	0.544	2.560
26	1.302	1.461	1.224	1.553	1.143	1.652	1.062	1.759	0.979	1.873	0.897	1.992	0.816	2.117	0.735	2.246	0.657	2.379	0.581	2.513
27	1.316	1.469	1.240	1.556	1.162	1.651	1.084	1.753	1.004	1.861	0.925	1.974	0.845	2.093	0.767	2.216	0.691	2.342	0.616	2.470
28	1.328	1.476	1.255	1.560	1.181	1.650	1.104	1.747	1.028	1.850	0.951	1.958	0.874	2.071	0.798	2.188	0.723	2.309	0.650	2.431
29	1.341	1.483	1.270	1.563	1.198	1.650	1.124	1.743	1.050	1.841	0.975	1.944	0.900	2.052	0.826	2.164	0.753	2.278	0.682	2.396
30	1.352	1.489	1.284	1.567	1.214	1.650	1.143	1.739	1.071	1.833	0.998	1.931	0.926	2.034	0.854	2.141	0.782	2.251	0.712	2.363
31	1.363	1.496	1.297	1.570	1.229	1.650	1.160	1.735	1.090	1.825	1.020	1.920	0.950	2.018	0.879	2.120	0.810	2.226	0.741	2.333
32	1.373	1.502	1.309	1.574	1.244	1.650	1.177	1.732	1.109	1.819	1.041	1.909	0.972	2.004	0.904	2.102	0.836	2.203	0.769	2.306
33	1.383	1.508	1.321	1.577	1.258	1.651	1.193	1.730	1.127	1.813	1.061	1.900	0.994	1.991	0.927	2.085	0.861	2.181	0.795	2.281
34	1.393	1.514	1.333	1.580	1.271	1.652	1.208	1.728	1.144	1.808	1.080	1.891	1.015	1.979	0.950	2.069	0.885	2.162	0.821	2.257
35	1.402	1.519	1.343	1.584	1.283	1.653	1.222	1.726	1.160	1.803	1.097	1.884	1.034	1.967	0.971	2.054	0.908	2.144	0.845	2.236
36	1.411	1.525	1.354	1.587	1.295	1.654	1.236	1.724	1.175	1.799	1.114	1.877	1.053	1.957	0.991	2.041	0.930	2.127	0.868	2.216
37	1.419	1.530	1.364	1.590	1.307	1.655	1.249	1.723	1.190	1.795	1.131	1.870	1.071	1.948	1.011	2.029	0.951	2.112	0.891	2.198
38	1.427	1.535	1.373	1.594	1.318	1.656	1.261	1.722	1.204	1.792	1.146	1.864	1.088	1.939	1.029	2.017	0.970	2.098	0.912	2.180
39	1.435	1.540	1.382	1.597	1.328	1.658	1.273	1.722	1.218	1.789	1.161	1.859	1.104	1.932	1.047	2.007	0.990	2.085	0.932	2.164
40	1.442	1.544	1.391	1.600	1.338	1.659	1.285	1.721	1.230	1.786	1.175	1.854	1.120	1.924	1.064	1.997	1.008	2.072	0.952	2.149
45	1.475	1.566	1.430	1.615	1.383	1.666	1.336	1.720	1.287	1.776	1.238	1.835	1.189	1.895	1.139	1.958	1.089	2.022	1.038	2.088
50	1.503	1.585	1.462	1.628	1.421	1.674	1.378	1.721	1.335	1.771	1.291	1.822	1.246	1.875	1.201	1.930	1.156	1.986	1.110	2.044
55	1.528	1.601	1.490	1.641	1.452	1.681	1.414	1.724	1.374	1.768	1.334	1.814	1.294	1.861	1.253	1.909	1.212	1.959	1.170	2.010
60	1.549	1.616	1.514	1.652	1.480	1.689	1.444	1.727	1.408	1.767	1.372	1.808	1.335	1.850	1.298	1.894	1.260	1.939	1.222	1.984
65	1.567	1.629	1.536	1.662	1.503	1.696	1.471	1.731	1.438	1.767	1.404	1.805	1.370	1.843	1.336	1.882	1.301	1.923	1.266	1.964
70	1.583	1.641	1.554	1.672	1.525	1.703	1.494	1.735	1.464	1.768	1.433	1.802	1.401	1.837	1.369	1.873	1.337	1.910	1.305	1.948
75	1.598	1.652	1.571	1.680	1.543	1.709	1.515	1.739	1.487	1.770	1.458	1.801	1.428	1.834	1.399	1.867	1.369	1.901	1.339	1.935
80	1.611	1.662	1.586	1.688	1.560	1.715	1.534	1.743	1.507	1.772	1.480	1.801	1.453	1.831	1.425	1.861	1.397	1.893	1.369	1.925
85	1.624	1.671	1.600	1.696	1.575	1.721	1.550	1.747	1.525	1.774	1.500	1.801	1.474	1.829	1.448	1.857	1.422	1.886	1.396	1.916
90	1.635	1.679	1.612	1.703	1.589	1.726	1.566	1.751	1.542	1.776	1.518	1.801	1.494	1.827	1.469	1.854	1.445	1.881	1.420	1.909
95	1.645	1.687	1.623	1.709	1.602	1.732	1.579	1.755	1.557	1.778	1.535	1.802	1.512	1.827	1.489	1.852	1.465	1.877	1.442	1.903
100	1.654	1.694	1.634	1.715	1.613	1.736	1.592	1.758	1.571	1.780	1.550	1.803	1.528	1.826	1.506	1.850	1.484	1.874	1.462	1.898
150	1.720	1.746	1.706	1.760	1.693	1.774	1.679	1.788	1.665	1.802	1.651	1.817	1.637	1.832	1.622	1.847	1.608	1.862	1.594	1.877
200	1.758	1.778	1.748	1.789	1.738	1.799	1.728	1.810	1.718	1.820	1.707	1.831	1.697	1.841	1.686	1.852	1.675	1.863	1.665	1.874

	k' = 11		k' = 12		k' = 13		k' = 14		k' = 15		k' = 16		k' = 17		k' = 18		k' = 19		k' = 20	
n	d_L	d_U	d_L	d_U	d_L	d_U	d_L	d_U	d_L	d_U	d_L	d_U	d_L	d_U	d_L	d_U	d_L	d_U	d_L	d_U
16	0.098	3.503	—		—		—		—		—		—		—		—		—	
17	0.138	3.378	0.087	3.557	—		—		—		—		—		—		—		—	
18	0.177	3.265	0.123	3.441	0.078	3.603	—		—		—		—		—		—		—	
19	0.220	3.159	0.160	3.335	0.111	3.496	0.070	3.642	—		—		—		—		—		—	
20	0.263	3.063	0.200	3.234	0.145	3.395	0.100	3.542	0.063	3.676	—		—		—		—		—	
21	0.307	2.976	0.240	3.141	0.182	3.300	0.132	3.448	0.091	3.583	0.058	3.705	—		—		—		—	
22	0.349	2.897	0.281	3.057	0.220	3.211	0.166	3.358	0.120	3.495	0.083	3.619	0.052	3.731	—		—		—	
23	0.391	2.826	0.322	2.979	0.259	3.128	0.202	3.272	0.153	3.409	0.110	3.535	0.076	3.650	0.048	3.753	—		—	
24	0.431	2.761	0.362	2.908	0.297	3.053	0.239	3.193	0.186	3.327	0.141	3.454	0.101	3.572	0.070	3.678	0.044	3.773	—	
25	0.470	2.702	0.400	2.844	0.335	2.983	0.275	3.119	0.221	3.251	0.172	3.376	0.130	3.494	0.094	3.604	0.065	3.702	0.041	3.790
26	0.508	2.649	0.438	2.784	0.373	2.919	0.312	3.051	0.256	3.179	0.205	3.303	0.160	3.420	0.120	3.531	0.087	3.632	0.060	3.724
27	0.544	2.600	0.475	2.730	0.409	2.859	0.348	2.987	0.291	3.112	0.238	3.233	0.191	3.349	0.149	3.460	0.112	3.563	0.081	3.658
28	0.578	2.555	0.510	2.680	0.445	2.805	0.383	2.928	0.325	3.050	0.271	3.168	0.222	3.283	0.178	3.392	0.138	3.495	0.104	3.592
29	0.612	2.515	0.544	2.634	0.479	2.755	0.418	2.874	0.359	2.992	0.305	3.107	0.254	3.219	0.208	3.327	0.166	3.431	0.129	3.528
30	0.643	2.477	0.577	2.592	0.512	2.708	0.451	2.823	0.392	2.937	0.337	3.050	0.286	3.160	0.238	3.266	0.195	3.368	0.156	3.465
31	0.674	2.443	0.608	2.553	0.545	2.665	0.484	2.776	0.425	2.887	0.370	2.996	0.317	3.103	0.269	3.208	0.224	3.309	0.183	3.406
32	0.703	2.411	0.638	2.517	0.576	2.625	0.515	2.733	0.457	2.840	0.401	2.946	0.349	3.050	0.299	3.153	0.253	3.252	0.211	3.348
33	0.731	2.382	0.668	2.484	0.606	2.588	0.546	2.692	0.488	2.796	0.432	2.899	0.379	3.000	0.329	3.100	0.283	3.198	0.239	3.293
34	0.758	2.355	0.695	2.454	0.634	2.554	0.575	2.654	0.518	2.754	0.462	2.854	0.409	2.954	0.359	3.051	0.312	3.147	0.267	3.240
35	0.783	2.330	0.722	2.425	0.662	2.521	0.604	2.619	0.547	2.716	0.492	2.813	0.439	2.910	0.388	3.005	0.340	3.099	0.295	3.190
36	0.808	2.306	0.748	2.398	0.689	2.492	0.631	2.586	0.575	2.680	0.520	2.774	0.467	2.868	0.417	2.961	0.369	3.053	0.323	3.142
37	0.831	2.285	0.772	2.374	0.714	2.464	0.657	2.555	0.602	2.646	0.548	2.738	0.495	2.829	0.445	2.920	0.397	3.009	0.351	3.097
38	0.854	2.265	0.796	2.351	0.739	2.438	0.683	2.526	0.628	2.614	0.575	2.703	0.522	2.792	0.472	2.880	0.424	2.968	0.378	3.054
39	0.875	2.246	0.819	2.329	0.763	2.413	0.707	2.499	0.653	2.585	0.600	2.671	0.549	2.757	0.499	2.843	0.451	2.929	0.404	3.013
40	0.896	2.228	0.840	2.309	0.785	2.391	0.731	2.473	0.678	2.557	0.626	2.641	0.575	2.724	0.525	2.808	0.477	2.892	0.430	2.974
45	0.988	2.156	0.938	2.225	0.887	2.296	0.838	2.367	0.788	2.439	0.740	2.512	0.692	2.586	0.644	2.659	0.598	2.733	0.553	2.807
50	1.064	2.103	1.019	2.163	0.973	2.225	0.927	2.287	0.882	2.350	0.836	2.414	0.792	2.479	0.747	2.544	0.703	2.610	0.660	2.675
55	1.129	2.062	1.087	2.116	1.045	2.170	1.003	2.225	0.961	2.281	0.919	2.338	0.877	2.396	0.836	2.454	0.795	2.512	0.754	2.571
60	1.184	2.031	1.145	2.079	1.106	2.127	1.068	2.177	1.029	2.227	0.990	2.278	0.951	2.330	0.913	2.382	0.874	2.434	0.836	2.487
65	1.231	2.006	1.195	2.049	1.160	2.093	1.124	2.138	1.088	2.183	1.052	2.229	1.016	2.276	0.980	2.323	0.944	2.371	0.908	2.419
70	1.272	1.986	1.239	2.026	1.206	2.066	1.172	2.106	1.139	2.148	1.105	2.189	1.072	2.232	1.038	2.275	1.005	2.318	0.971	2.362
75	1.308	1.970	1.277	2.006	1.247	2.043	1.215	2.080	1.184	2.118	1.153	2.156	1.121	2.195	1.090	2.235	1.058	2.275	1.027	2.315
80	1.340	1.957	1.311	1.991	1.283	2.024	1.253	2.059	1.224	2.093	1.195	2.129	1.165	2.165	1.136	2.201	1.106	2.238	1.076	2.275
85	1.369	1.946	1.342	1.977	1.315	2.009	1.287	2.040	1.260	2.073	1.232	2.105	1.205	2.139	1.177	2.172	1.149	2.206	1.121	2.241
90	1.395	1.937	1.369	1.966	1.344	1.995	1.318	2.025	1.292	2.055	1.266	2.085	1.240	2.116	1.213	2.148	1.187	2.179	1.160	2.211
95	1.418	1.929	1.394	1.956	1.370	1.984	1.345	2.012	1.321	2.040	1.296	2.068	1.271	2.097	1.247	2.126	1.222	2.156	1.197	2.186
100	1.439	1.923	1.416	1.948	1.393	1.974	1.371	2.000	1.347	2.026	1.324	2.053	1.301	2.080	1.277	2.108	1.253	2.135	1.229	2.164
150	1.579	1.892	1.564	1.908	1.550	1.924	1.535	1.940	1.519	1.956	1.504	1.972	1.489	1.989	1.474	2.006	1.458	2.023	1.443	2.040
200	1.654	1.885	1.643	1.896	1.632	1.908	1.621	1.919	1.610	1.931	1.599	1.943	1.588	1.955	1.576	1.967	1.565	1.979	1.554	1.991

Source: This table is an extension of the original Durbin-Watson table and is reproduced from N. E. Savin and K. J. White, "The Durbin-Watson Test for Serial Correlation with Extreme Small Samples or Many Regressors," *Econometrica*, vol. 45, November 1977, pp. 1989–96 and as corrected by R. W. Farebrother, *Econometrica*, vol. 48, September 1980, p. 1554. Reprinted by permission of the Econometric Society.

Note: n = number of observations, k' = number of explanatory variables excluding the constant term.

Example. If $n = 40$ and $k' = 4$, $d_L = 1.285$ and $d_U = 1.721$. If a computed d value is less than 1.285, there is evidence of positive first-order serial correlation; if it is greater than 1.721, there is no evidence of positive first-order serial correlation; but if d lies between the lower and the upper limit, there is inconclusive evidence regarding the presence or absence of positive first-order serial correlation.

TABLE D.5*b*
Durbin-Watson *d* statistic: Significance points of d_L and d_U at 0.01 level of significance

	$k'=1$		$k'=2$		$k'=3$		$k'=4$		$k'=5$		$k'=6$		$k'=7$		$k'=8$		$k'=9$		$k'=10$	
n	d_L	d_U	d_L	d_U	d_L	d_U	d_L	d_U	d_L	d_U	d_L	d_U	d_L	d_U	d_L	d_U	d_L	d_U	d_L	d_U
6	0.390	1.142	—	—	—	—	—	—	—	—	—	—	—	—	—	—	—	—	—	—
7	0.435	1.036	0.294	1.676	—	—	—	—	—	—	—	—	—	—	—	—	—	—	—	—
8	0.497	1.003	0.345	1.489	0.229	2.102	—	—	—	—	—	—	—	—	—	—	—	—	—	—
9	0.554	0.998	0.408	1.389	0.279	1.875	0.183	2.433	—	—	—	—	—	—	—	—	—	—	—	—
10	0.604	1.001	0.466	1.333	0.340	1.733	0.230	2.193	0.150	2.690	—	—	—	—	—	—	—	—	—	—
11	0.653	1.010	0.519	1.297	0.396	1.640	0.286	2.030	0.193	2.453	0.124	2.892	—	—	—	—	—	—	—	—
12	0.697	1.023	0.569	1.274	0.449	1.575	0.339	1.913	0.244	2.280	0.164	2.665	0.105	3.053	—	—	—	—	—	—
13	0.738	1.038	0.616	1.261	0.499	1.526	0.391	1.826	0.294	2.150	0.211	2.490	0.140	2.838	0.090	3.182	—	—	—	—
14	0.776	1.054	0.660	1.254	0.547	1.490	0.441	1.757	0.343	2.049	0.257	2.354	0.183	2.667	0.122	2.981	0.078	3.287	—	—
15	0.811	1.070	0.700	1.252	0.591	1.464	0.488	1.704	0.391	1.967	0.303	2.244	0.226	2.530	0.161	2.817	0.107	3.101	0.068	3.374
16	0.844	1.086	0.737	1.252	0.633	1.446	0.532	1.663	0.437	1.900	0.349	2.153	0.269	2.416	0.200	2.681	0.142	2.944	0.094	3.201
17	0.874	1.102	0.772	1.255	0.672	1.432	0.574	1.630	0.480	1.847	0.393	2.078	0.313	2.319	0.241	2.566	0.179	2.811	0.127	3.053
18	0.902	1.118	0.805	1.259	0.708	1.422	0.613	1.604	0.522	1.803	0.435	2.015	0.355	2.238	0.282	2.467	0.216	2.697	0.160	2.925
19	0.928	1.132	0.835	1.265	0.742	1.415	0.650	1.584	0.561	1.767	0.476	1.963	0.396	2.169	0.322	2.381	0.255	2.597	0.196	2.813
20	0.952	1.147	0.863	1.271	0.773	1.411	0.685	1.567	0.598	1.737	0.515	1.918	0.436	2.110	0.362	2.308	0.294	2.510	0.232	2.714
21	0.975	1.161	0.890	1.277	0.803	1.408	0.718	1.554	0.633	1.712	0.552	1.881	0.474	2.059	0.400	2.244	0.331	2.434	0.268	2.625
22	0.997	1.174	0.914	1.284	0.831	1.407	0.748	1.543	0.667	1.691	0.587	1.849	0.510	2.015	0.437	2.188	0.368	2.367	0.304	2.548
23	1.018	1.187	0.938	1.291	0.858	1.407	0.777	1.534	0.698	1.673	0.620	1.821	0.545	1.977	0.473	2.140	0.404	2.308	0.340	2.479
24	1.037	1.199	0.960	1.298	0.882	1.407	0.805	1.528	0.728	1.658	0.652	1.797	0.578	1.944	0.507	2.097	0.439	2.255	0.375	2.417
25	1.055	1.211	0.981	1.305	0.906	1.409	0.831	1.523	0.756	1.645	0.682	1.776	0.610	1.915	0.540	2.059	0.473	2.209	0.409	2.362
26	1.072	1.222	1.001	1.312	0.928	1.411	0.855	1.518	0.783	1.635	0.711	1.759	0.640	1.889	0.572	2.026	0.505	2.168	0.441	2.313
27	1.089	1.233	1.019	1.319	0.949	1.413	0.878	1.515	0.808	1.626	0.738	1.743	0.669	1.867	0.602	1.997	0.536	2.131	0.473	2.269
28	1.104	1.244	1.037	1.325	0.969	1.415	0.900	1.513	0.832	1.618	0.764	1.729	0.696	1.847	0.630	1.970	0.566	2.098	0.504	2.229
29	1.119	1.254	1.054	1.332	0.988	1.418	0.921	1.512	0.855	1.611	0.788	1.718	0.723	1.830	0.658	1.947	0.595	2.068	0.533	2.193
30	1.133	1.263	1.070	1.339	1.006	1.421	0.941	1.511	0.877	1.606	0.812	1.707	0.748	1.814	0.684	1.925	0.622	2.041	0.562	2.160
31	1.147	1.273	1.085	1.345	1.023	1.425	0.960	1.510	0.897	1.601	0.834	1.698	0.772	1.800	0.710	1.906	0.649	2.017	0.589	2.131
32	1.160	1.282	1.100	1.352	1.040	1.428	0.979	1.510	0.917	1.597	0.856	1.690	0.794	1.788	0.734	1.889	0.674	1.995	0.615	2.104
33	1.172	1.291	1.114	1.358	1.055	1.432	0.996	1.510	0.936	1.594	0.876	1.683	0.816	1.776	0.757	1.874	0.698	1.975	0.641	2.080
34	1.184	1.299	1.128	1.364	1.070	1.435	1.012	1.511	0.954	1.591	0.896	1.677	0.837	1.766	0.779	1.860	0.722	1.957	0.665	2.057
35	1.195	1.307	1.140	1.370	1.085	1.439	1.028	1.512	0.971	1.589	0.914	1.671	0.857	1.757	0.800	1.847	0.744	1.940	0.689	2.037
36	1.206	1.315	1.153	1.376	1.098	1.442	1.043	1.513	0.988	1.588	0.932	1.666	0.877	1.749	0.821	1.836	0.766	1.925	0.711	2.018
37	1.217	1.323	1.165	1.382	1.112	1.446	1.058	1.514	1.004	1.586	0.950	1.662	0.895	1.742	0.841	1.825	0.787	1.911	0.733	2.001
38	1.227	1.330	1.176	1.388	1.124	1.449	1.072	1.515	1.019	1.585	0.966	1.658	0.913	1.735	0.860	1.816	0.807	1.899	0.754	1.985
39	1.237	1.337	1.187	1.393	1.137	1.453	1.085	1.517	1.034	1.584	0.982	1.655	0.930	1.729	0.878	1.807	0.826	1.887	0.774	1.970
40	1.246	1.344	1.198	1.398	1.148	1.457	1.098	1.518	1.048	1.584	0.997	1.652	0.946	1.724	0.895	1.799	0.844	1.876	0.749	1.956
45	1.288	1.376	1.245	1.423	1.201	1.474	1.156	1.528	1.111	1.584	1.065	1.643	1.019	1.704	0.974	1.768	0.927	1.834	0.881	1.902
50	1.324	1.403	1.285	1.446	1.245	1.491	1.205	1.538	1.164	1.587	1.123	1.639	1.081	1.692	1.039	1.748	0.997	1.805	0.955	1.864
55	1.356	1.427	1.320	1.466	1.284	1.506	1.247	1.548	1.209	1.592	1.172	1.638	1.134	1.685	1.095	1.734	1.057	1.785	1.018	1.837
60	1.383	1.449	1.350	1.484	1.317	1.520	1.283	1.558	1.249	1.598	1.214	1.639	1.179	1.682	1.144	1.726	1.108	1.771	1.072	1.817
65	1.407	1.468	1.377	1.500	1.346	1.534	1.315	1.568	1.283	1.604	1.251	1.642	1.218	1.680	1.186	1.720	1.153	1.761	1.120	1.802
70	1.429	1.485	1.400	1.515	1.372	1.546	1.343	1.578	1.313	1.611	1.283	1.645	1.253	1.680	1.223	1.716	1.192	1.754	1.162	1.792
75	1.448	1.501	1.422	1.529	1.395	1.557	1.368	1.587	1.340	1.617	1.313	1.649	1.284	1.682	1.256	1.714	1.227	1.748	1.199	1.783
80	1.466	1.515	1.441	1.541	1.416	1.568	1.390	1.595	1.364	1.624	1.338	1.653	1.312	1.683	1.285	1.714	1.259	1.745	1.232	1.777
85	1.482	1.528	1.458	1.553	1.435	1.578	1.411	1.603	1.386	1.630	1.362	1.657	1.337	1.685	1.312	1.714	1.287	1.743	1.262	1.773
90	1.496	1.540	1.474	1.563	1.452	1.587	1.429	1.611	1.406	1.636	1.383	1.661	1.360	1.687	1.336	1.714	1.312	1.741	1.288	1.769
95	1.510	1.552	1.489	1.573	1.468	1.596	1.446	1.618	1.425	1.642	1.403	1.666	1.381	1.690	1.358	1.715	1.336	1.741	1.313	1.767
100	1.522	1.562	1.503	1.583	1.482	1.604	1.462	1.625	1.441	1.647	1.421	1.670	1.400	1.693	1.378	1.717	1.357	1.741	1.335	1.765
150	1.611	1.637	1.598	1.651	1.584	1.665	1.571	1.679	1.557	1.693	1.543	1.708	1.530	1.722	1.515	1.737	1.501	1.752	1.486	1.767
200	1.664	1.684	1.653	1.693	1.643	1.704	1.633	1.715	1.623	1.725	1.613	1.735	1.603	1.746	1.592	1.757	1.582	1.768	1.571	1.779

	k' = 11		k' = 12		k' = 13		k' = 14		k' = 15		k' = 16		k' = 17		k' = 18		k' = 19		k' = 20	
n	d_L	d_U	d_L	d_U	d_L	d_U	d_L	d_U	d_L	d_U	d_L	d_U	d_L	d_U	d_L	d_U	d_L	d_U	d_L	d_U
16	0.060	3.446	—	—																
17	0.084	3.286	0.053	3.506	—	—														
18	0.113	3.146	0.075	3.358	0.047	3.357	—	—												
19	0.145	3.023	0.102	3.227	0.067	3.420	0.043	3.601	—	—										
20	0.178	2.914	0.131	3.109	0.092	3.297	0.061	3.474	0.038	3.639	—	—								
21	0.212	2.817	0.162	3.004	0.119	3.185	0.084	3.358	0.055	3.521	0.035	3.671	—	—						
22	0.246	2.729	0.194	2.909	0.148	3.084	0.109	3.252	0.077	3.412	0.050	3.562	0.032	3.700	—	—				
23	0.281	2.651	0.227	2.822	0.178	2.991	0.136	3.155	0.100	3.311	0.070	3.459	0.046	3.597	0.029	3.725	—	—		
24	0.315	2.580	0.260	2.744	0.209	2.906	0.165	3.065	0.125	3.218	0.092	3.363	0.065	3.501	0.043	3.629	0.027	3.747	—	—
25	0.348	2.517	0.292	2.674	0.240	2.829	0.194	2.982	0.152	3.131	0.116	3.274	0.085	3.410	0.060	3.538	0.039	3.657	0.025	3.766
26	0.381	2.460	0.324	2.610	0.272	2.758	0.224	2.906	0.180	3.050	0.141	3.191	0.107	3.325	0.079	3.452	0.055	3.572	0.036	3.682
27	0.413	2.409	0.356	2.552	0.303	2.694	0.253	2.836	0.208	2.976	0.167	3.113	0.131	3.245	0.100	3.371	0.073	3.490	0.051	3.602
28	0.444	2.363	0.387	2.499	0.333	2.635	0.283	2.772	0.237	2.907	0.194	3.040	0.156	3.169	0.122	3.294	0.093	3.412	0.068	3.524
29	0.474	2.321	0.417	2.451	0.363	2.582	0.313	2.713	0.266	2.843	0.222	2.972	0.182	3.098	0.146	3.220	0.114	3.338	0.087	3.450
30	0.503	2.283	0.447	2.407	0.393	2.533	0.342	2.659	0.294	2.785	0.249	2.909	0.208	3.032	0.171	3.152	0.137	3.267	0.107	3.379
31	0.531	2.248	0.475	2.367	0.422	2.487	0.371	2.609	0.322	2.730	0.277	2.851	0.234	2.970	0.196	3.087	0.160	3.201	0.128	3.311
32	0.558	2.216	0.503	2.330	0.450	2.446	0.399	2.563	0.350	2.680	0.304	2.797	0.261	2.912	0.221	3.026	0.184	3.137	0.151	3.246
33	0.585	2.187	0.530	2.296	0.477	2.408	0.426	2.520	0.377	2.633	0.331	2.746	0.287	2.858	0.246	2.969	0.209	3.078	0.174	3.184
34	0.610	2.160	0.556	2.266	0.503	2.373	0.452	2.481	0.404	2.590	0.357	2.699	0.313	2.808	0.272	2.915	0.233	3.022	0.197	3.126
35	0.634	2.136	0.581	2.237	0.529	2.340	0.478	2.444	0.430	2.550	0.383	2.655	0.339	2.761	0.297	2.865	0.257	2.969	0.221	3.071
36	0.658	2.113	0.605	2.210	0.554	2.310	0.504	2.410	0.455	2.512	0.409	2.614	0.364	2.717	0.322	2.818	0.282	2.919	0.244	3.019
37	0.680	2.092	0.628	2.186	0.578	2.282	0.528	2.379	0.480	2.477	0.434	2.576	0.389	2.675	0.347	2.774	0.306	2.872	0.268	2.969
38	0.702	2.073	0.651	2.164	0.601	2.256	0.552	2.350	0.504	2.445	0.458	2.540	0.414	2.637	0.371	2.733	0.330	2.828	0.291	2.923
39	0.723	2.055	0.673	2.143	0.623	2.232	0.575	2.323	0.528	2.414	0.482	2.507	0.438	2.600	0.395	2.694	0.354	2.787	0.315	2.879
40	0.744	2.039	0.694	2.123	0.645	2.210	0.597	2.297	0.551	2.386	0.505	2.476	0.461	2.566	0.418	2.657	0.377	2.748	0.338	2.838
45	0.835	1.972	0.790	2.044	0.744	2.118	0.700	2.193	0.655	2.269	0.612	2.346	0.570	2.424	0.528	2.503	0.488	2.582	0.448	2.661
50	0.913	1.925	0.871	1.987	0.829	2.051	0.787	2.116	0.746	2.182	0.705	2.250	0.665	2.318	0.625	2.387	0.586	2.456	0.548	2.526
55	0.979	1.891	0.940	1.945	0.902	2.002	0.863	2.059	0.825	2.117	0.786	2.176	0.748	2.237	0.711	2.298	0.674	2.359	0.637	2.421
60	1.037	1.865	1.001	1.914	0.965	1.964	0.929	2.015	0.893	2.067	0.857	2.120	0.822	2.173	0.786	2.227	0.751	2.283	0.716	2.338
65	1.087	1.845	1.053	1.889	1.020	1.934	0.986	1.980	0.953	2.027	0.919	2.075	0.886	2.123	0.852	2.172	0.819	2.221	0.786	2.272
70	1.131	1.831	1.099	1.870	1.068	1.911	1.037	1.953	1.005	1.995	0.974	2.038	0.943	2.082	0.911	2.127	0.880	2.172	0.849	2.217
75	1.170	1.819	1.141	1.856	1.111	1.893	1.082	1.931	1.052	1.970	1.023	2.009	0.993	2.049	0.964	2.090	0.934	2.131	0.905	2.172
80	1.205	1.810	1.177	1.844	1.150	1.878	1.122	1.913	1.094	1.949	1.066	1.984	1.039	2.022	1.011	2.059	0.983	2.097	0.955	2.135
85	1.236	1.803	1.210	1.834	1.184	1.866	1.158	1.898	1.132	1.931	1.106	1.965	1.080	1.999	1.053	2.033	1.027	2.068	1.000	2.104
90	1.264	1.798	1.240	1.827	1.215	1.856	1.191	1.886	1.166	1.917	1.141	1.948	1.116	1.979	1.091	2.012	1.066	2.044	1.041	2.077
95	1.290	1.793	1.267	1.821	1.244	1.848	1.221	1.876	1.197	1.905	1.174	1.934	1.150	1.963	1.126	1.993	1.102	2.023	1.079	2.054
100	1.314	1.790	1.292	1.816	1.270	1.841	1.248	1.868	1.225	1.895	1.203	1.922	1.181	1.949	1.158	1.977	1.136	2.006	1.113	2.034
150	1.473	1.783	1.458	1.799	1.444	1.814	1.429	1.830	1.414	1.847	1.400	1.863	1.385	1.880	1.370	1.897	1.355	1.913	1.340	1.931
200	1.561	1.791	1.550	1.801	1.539	1.813	1.528	1.824	1.518	1.836	1.507	1.847	1.495	1.860	1.484	1.871	1.474	1.883	1.462	1.896

Source: Savin and White, op. cit., by permission of the Econometric Society.

Note: n = number of observations

k' = number of explanatory variables excluding the constant term.

TABLE D.6a
Critical values of runs in the runs test

									N_2										
N_1	2	3	4	5	6	7	8	9	10	11	12	13	14	15	16	17	18	19	20
2											2	2	2	2	2	2	2	2	2
3				2	2	2	2	2	2	2	2	2	2	3	3	3	3	3	3
4			2	2	2	3	3	3	3	3	3	3	3	3	4	4	4	4	4
5			2	2	3	3	3	3	3	4	4	4	4	4	4	4	5	5	5
6		2	2	3	3	3	3	4	4	4	4	5	5	5	5	5	5	6	6
7		2	2	3	3	3	4	4	5	5	5	5	5	6	6	6	6	6	6
8		2	3	3	3	4	4	5	5	5	6	6	6	6	6	7	7	7	7
9		2	3	3	4	4	5	5	5	6	6	6	7	7	7	7	8	8	8
10		2	3	3	4	5	5	5	6	6	7	7	7	7	8	8	8	8	9
11		2	3	4	4	5	5	5	6	6	7	7	7	8	8	8	9	9	9
12	2	2	3	4	4	5	6	6	7	7	7	8	8	8	9	9	9	10	10
13	2	2	3	4	5	5	6	6	7	7	8	8	9	9	9	10	10	10	10
14	2	2	3	4	5	5	6	7	7	8	8	9	9	9	10	10	10	11	11
15	2	3	3	4	5	6	6	7	7	8	8	9	9	10	10	11	11	11	12
16	2	3	4	4	5	6	6	7	8	8	9	9	10	10	11	11	11	12	12
17	2	3	4	4	5	6	7	7	8	9	9	10	10	11	11	11	12	12	13
18	2	3	4	5	5	6	7	8	8	9	9	10	10	11	11	12	12	13	13
19	2	3	4	5	6	6	7	8	8	9	10	10	11	11	12	12	13	13	13
20	2	3	4	5	6	6	7	8	9	9	10	10	11	12	12	13	13	13	14

Note: Tables D.6a and D.6b give the critical values of runs n for various values of N_1 (+ symbol) and N_2 (− symbol). For the one-sample runs test, any value of n that is equal to or smaller than that shown in Table D.6a or equal to or larger than that shown in Table D.6b is significant at the 0.05 level.

Source: Sidney Siegel, *Nonparametric Statistics for the Behavioral Sciences*, McGraw-Hill Book Company, New York, 1956, table F, pp. 252–253. The tables have been adapted by Siegel from the original source: Frieda S. Swed and C. Eisenhart, "Tables for Testing Randomness of Grouping in a Sequence of Alternatives," *Annals of Mathematical Statistics*, vol. 14, 1943. Used by permission of McGraw-Hill Book Company and *Annals of Mathematical Statistics*.

TABLE D.6*b*
Critical values of runs in the runs test

N_1	2	3	4	5	6	7	8	9	10	11	12	13	14	15	16	17	18	19	20
																		N_2	
2																			
3																			
4				9	9														
5			9	10	10	11	11												
6			9	10	11	12	12	13	13	13	13								
7				11	12	13	13	14	14	14	14	15	15	15					
8				11	12	13	14	14	15	15	16	16	16	16	17	17	17	17	17
9					13	14	14	15	16	16	16	17	17	18	18	18	18	18	18
10					13	14	15	16	16	17	17	18	18	18	19	19	19	20	20
11					13	14	15	16	17	17	18	19	19	19	20	20	20	21	21
12					13	14	16	16	17	18	19	19	20	20	21	21	21	22	22
13						15	16	17	18	19	19	20	20	21	21	22	22	23	23
14						15	16	17	18	19	20	20	21	22	22	23	23	23	24
15						15	16	18	18	19	20	21	22	22	23	23	24	24	25
16							17	18	19	20	21	21	22	23	23	24	25	25	25
17							17	18	19	20	21	22	23	23	24	25	25	26	26
18							17	18	19	20	21	22	23	24	25	25	26	26	27
19							17	18	20	21	22	23	23	24	25	26	26	27	27
20							17	18	20	21	22	23	24	25	25	26	27	27	28

Example. In a sequence of 30 observations consisting of 20 + signs ($= N_1$) and 10 − signs ($= N_2$), the critical values of runs at the 0.05 level of significance are 9 and 20, as shown by Tables D.6*a* and D.6*b*, respectively. Therefore, if in an application it is found that the number of runs is equal to or less than 9 or equal to or greater than 20, one can reject (at the 0.05 level of significance) the hypothesis that the observed sequence is random.

SELECTED
BIBLIOGRAPHY

Introductory

Frank, C. R., Jr.: *Statistics and Econometrics*, Holt, Rinehart and Winston, New York, 1971.
Gujarati, Damodar N.: *Essentials of Econometrics*, McGraw-Hill, New York, 1992.
Hu, Teh-Wei: *Econometrics: An Introductory Analysis*, University Park Press, Baltimore, 1973.
Katz, David A.: *Econometric Theory and Applications*, Prentice Hall, Englewood Cliffs, N.J., 1982.
Klein, Lawrence R.: *An Introduction to Econometrics*, Prentice Hall, Englewood Cliffs, N.J., 1962.
Walters, A. A.: *An Introduction to Econometrics*, Macmillan, London, 1968.

Intermediate

Aigner, D. J.: *Basic Econometrics*, Prentice Hall, Englewood Cliffs, N.J., 1971.
Dhrymes, Phoebus J.: *Introductory Econometrics*, Springer-Verlag, New York, 1978.
Dielman, Terry E.: *Applied Regression Analysis for Business and Economics*, PWS-Kent, Boston, 1991.
Draper, N. R., and H. Smith: *Applied Regression Analysis*, 2d ed., John Wiley & Sons, New York, 1981.
Dutta, M.: *Econometric Methods*, South-Western Publishing Company, Cincinnati, 1975.
Goldberger, A. S.: *Topics in Regression Analysis*, Macmillan, New York, 1968.
Griffiths, William E., R. Carter Hill and George G. Judge: *Learning and Practicing Econometrics*, John Wiley & Sons, New York, 1993.
Huang, D. S.: *Regression and Econometric Methods*, John Wiley & Sons, New York, 1970.
Judge, George G., Carter R. Hill, William E. Griffiths, Helmut Lütkepohl, and Tsoung-Chao Lee: *Introduction to the Theory and Practice of Econometrics*, John Wiley & Sons, New York, 1982.
Kelejian, H. A., and W. E. Oates: *Introduction to Econometrics: Principles and Applications*, 2d ed., Harper & Row, New York, 1981.
Koutsoyiannis, A.: *Theory of Econometrics*, Harper & Row, New York, 1973.
Maddala, G. S.: *Introduction to Econometrics*, Macmillan, 2d ed., New York, 1992.
Mark, Stewart B., and Kenneth F. Wallis: *Introductory Econometrics*, 2d ed., John Wiley & Sons, New York, 1981. A Halsted Press Book.

824

Murphy, James L.: *Introductory Econometrics,* Richard D. Irwin, Homewood, Ill., 1973.
Netter, J., and W. Wasserman: *Applied Linear Statistical Models,* Richard D. Irwin, Homewood, Ill., 1974.
Pindyck, R. S., and D. L. Rubinfeld: *Econometric Models and Econometric Forecasts,* 3d ed., McGraw-Hill, New York, 1990.
Sprent, Peter: *Models in Regression and Related Topics,* Methuen, London, 1969.
Tintner, Gerhard: *Econometrics,* John Wiley & Sons (science ed.), New York, 1965.
Valavanis, Stefan: *Econometrics: An Introduction to Maximum-Likelihood Methods,* McGraw-Hill, New York, 1959.
Wonnacott, R. J., and T. H. Wonnacott: *Econometrics,* 2d ed., John Wiley & Sons, New York, 1979.

Advanced

Chow, Gregory C.: *Econometric Methods,* McGraw-Hill, New York, 1983.
Christ, C. F.: *Econometric Models and Methods,* John Wiley & Sons, New York, 1966.
Dhrymes, P. J.: *Econometrics: Statistical Foundations and Applications,* Harper & Row, New York, 1970.
Fomby, Thomas B., Carter R. Hill, and Stanley R. Johnson: *Advanced Econometric Methods,* Springer-Verlag, New York, 1984.
Goldberger, A. S.: *A Course in Econometrics,* Harvard University Press, Cambridge, Mass., 1991.
Goldberger, A. S.: *Econometric Theory,* John Wiley & Sons, New York, 1964.
Greene, William H.: *Econometric Analysis,* 2d ed., Macmillan, New York, 1993.
Harvey, A. C.: *The Econometric Analysis of Time Series,* 2d ed., MIT Press, Cambridge, Mass., 1990.
Johnston, J.: *Econometric Methods,* 3d ed., McGraw-Hill, New York, 1984.
Judge, George G., Carter R. Hill, William E. Griffiths, Helmut Lütkepohl, and Tsoung-Chao Lee, *Theory and Practice of Econometrics,* John Wiley & Sons, New York, 1980.
Klein, Lawrence R.: *A Textbook of Econometrics,* 2d ed., Prentice Hall, Englewood Cliffs, N.J., 1974.
Kmenta, Jan: *Elements of Econometrics,* 2d ed., Macmillan, New York, 1986.
Madansky, A.: *Foundations of Econometrics,* North-Holland, Amsterdam, 1976.
Maddala, G. S.: *Econometrics,* McGraw-Hill, New York, 1977.
Malinvaud, E.: *Statistical Methods of Econometrics,* 2d ed., North-Holland, Amsterdam, 1976.
Theil, Henry: *Principles of Econometrics,* John Wiley & Sons, New York, 1971.

Specialized

Belsley, David A., Edwin Kuh, and Roy E. Welsh: *Regression Diagnostics: Identifying Influential Data and Sources of Collinearity,* John Wiley & Sons, New York, 1980.
Dhrymes, P. J.: *Distributed Lags: Problems of Estimation and Formulation,* Holden-Day, San Francisco, 1971.
Goldfeld, S. M., and R. E. Quandt: *Nonlinear Methods of Econometrics,* North-Holland, Amsterdam, 1972.
Graybill, F. A.: *An Introduction to Linear Statistical Models, vol. 1,* McGraw-Hill, New York, 1961.
Hamilton, James D.: *Time Series Analysis,* Princeton University Press, Princeton, 1994.
Mills, T. C.: *Time Series Techniques for Economists,* Cambridge University Press, 1990.
Rao, C. R.: *Linear Statistical Inference and Its Applications,* 2d ed., John Wiley & Sons, New York, 1975.
Zellner, A.: *An Introduction to Bayesian Inference in Econometrics,* John Wiley & Sons, New York, 1971.

Applied

Berndt, Ernst R.: *The Practice of Econometrics: Classic and Contemporary,* Addison-Wesley, 1991.
Bridge, J. I.: *Applied Econometrics,* North-Holland, Amsterdam, 1971.

Cramer, J. S.: *Empirical Econometrics*, North-Holland, Amsterdam, 1969.

Desai, Meghnad: *Applied Econometrics*, McGraw-Hill, New York, 1976.

Kennedy, Peter: *A Guide to Econometrics*, 2d ed., MIT Press, Cambridge, Mass., 1985.

Leser, C. E. V.: *Econometric Techniques and Problems*, 2d ed., Hafner, London, 1974.

Mills, T. C.: *The Econometric Modelling of Financial Time Series*, Cambridge University Press, 1993.

Rao, Potluri, and Roger LeRoy Miller: *Applied Econometrics*, Wadsworth, Belmont, Calif., 1971.

Note: For a list of the seminal articles on the various topics discussed in this book, please refer to the extensive bibliography given at the end of each chapter in Fomby et al., cited above.

NAME INDEX

SUBJECT INDEX

ACF (*see* Autocorrelation function)
ADF test (*see* Dickey–Fuller test, augmented)
Adjoint matrix, 801
ADL models (*see* Autoregressive distributed lag model)
AEG test (*see* Engle–Granger test, augmented)
AER (*see* Average economic regression)
Akaike's Information criterion, 209
Almon (or polynomial) distributed lag (PDL) models, 612–619
Alternative hypothesis, 121
Amemiya's Prediction criterion, 209
Analogy principle, 88
Analysis, regression (*see* Regression analysis)
Analysis of variance (ANOVA), 245
  in matrix notation, 294–295
  and regression analysis, 134–144
Analysis-of-covariance (ANCOVA) models, 502–509
ANOVA (*see* Analysis of variance)
AR process (*see* Autoregressive process)
ARCH model (*see* Autoregressive conditional heteroscedasticity model)
ARIMA:
  methodology, 735
  model, estimation of, 742–743
  process, 737–746
  (*See also* Autoregressive integrated moving average process)
ARMA process, 737
  (*See also* Autoregressive and moving average process)
ARMA(1,1) scheme, 408
Asymptote, 174
Autocorrelation, 63–64, 400–440
  BLUE estimator, under, 409–410
  defined, 400–406
  detecting, 415–426
    in autoregressive models, 605–609
    Breusch–Godfrey test, 425–426
    Durbin–Watson d Test, 420–425
    runs (or Geary) test for, 419–420
  example, 433–436
  with heteroscedasticity, 436–439
  OLS estimation in the presence of, 406–415
  using OLS in the presence of, 410–415
  remedial measures for, 426–433
  spatial, 405
Autocorrelation function (ACF), 739–742
Autocovariance, coefficient of, 407

Autoregression, 405
  vector (*see* Vector autoregression)
Autoregressive conditional heteroscedasticity (ARCH) model, 436–439
Autoregressive distributed lag (ADL) model, 485
Autoregressive integrated moving average (ARIMA) process, 737–746
Autoregressive moving average, first-order, 408
Autoregressive and moving average (ARMA) process, 737
Autoregressive (AR) process, 736
Autoregressive scheme, (Markov) first-order, 407
Average, moving, first-order, 407
Average economic regression (AER), 452–454

Ballentine, 74–75
Bayesian tradition, 9
Berenblutt–Webb test, 429–430
Best linear unbiased estimator (BLUE), 291, 781
  in the presence of autocorrelation, 409–410
Best unbiased estimators (BUE), 105, 780
$\hat{\beta}$, variance-covariance matrix of, 290–291
Beta (β) coefficient, 159
Bias:
  selectivity, 26
  simultaneous-equation, 642–647
  specification, 204–207
Bivariate normal probability density function, 113–114
BJ methodology (*see* Box–Jenkins methodology)
BLUE (*see* Best linear unbiased estimator)
Box–Jenkins (BJ) methodology, 735, 738–739
Box–Pierce Q statistic, 717
Breusch–Godfrey test, 425–426
Breusch–Pagan–Godfrey test, 377–378
BUE (*see* Estimator(s), best unbiased)

Capital asset pricing model (CAPM), 156, 475
  expressed as a recursive system, 694–697
Causal models, 680
Causality:
  and exogeneity, 673
  the Granger test, 620–623
  the Sim's test, 632
Causation versus regression, 20

831